COUNTERTERRORISM LAW

CASES AND MATERIALS

by

CHARLES A. SHANOR
Professor of Law
Emory University

with

AMANDA W. SHANOR

FOUNDATION PRESS
2011

THOMSON REUTERS

This publication was created to provide you with accurate and authoritative information concerning the subject matter covered; however, this publication was not necessarily prepared by persons licensed to practice law in a particular jurisdiction. The publisher is not engaged in rendering legal or other professional advice and this publication is not a substitute for the advice of an attorney. If you require legal or other expert advice, you should seek the services of a competent attorney or other professional.

Nothing contained herein is intended or written to be used for the purposes of 1) avoiding penalties imposed under the federal Internal Revenue Code, or 2) promoting, marketing or recommending to another party any transaction or matter addressed herein.

© 2011 By THOMSON REUTERS/FOUNDATION PRESS
   1 New York Plaza, 34th Floor
   New York, NY 10004
   Phone Toll Free 1–877–888–1330
   Fax 646–424–5201
   foundation–press.com

Printed in the United States of America

ISBN 978–1–60930–016–6

Mat #41158109

In Memory of

Elbert Parr Tuttle

Judge, General, and Mentor

PREFACE

COUNTERTERRORISM LAW: CASES AND MATERIALS

In the aftermath of 9/11, 2001, I taught a seminar on legal issues related to terrorism with voluminous and sometimes disjointed photocopied materials. Students liked the seminar and I learned a great deal from it. Demand, however, exceeded the availability of seminar spaces, so I agreed to teach a Counterterrorism Law course, for which I prepared increasingly edited and coherent materials and eventually this casebook.

A decade after the 9/11 attacks, there is now a relatively stable framework for this eclectic and rapidly-changing field. While rooted in traditional national security law, counterterrorism law addresses recent structural shifts in criminal law, civil liberties, victim compensation, judicial review, and distribution of governmental powers. Nearly 80% of the principle cases in this book postdate 9/11, a fraction no doubt consistent with dates of the statutory and administrative materials. Counterterrorism law will continue to evolve, though perhaps at a slower pace than in this past decade, as lower court decisions are reconsidered by higher courts and as legislation, regulations, and executive practices, here and abroad, shift in response to terrorist threats, public opinion, technological change, and international dialogue.

Emory Law School has been generous in funding research assistance and administrative support. This book would not have been possible without the research contributions of Laurie Blank, Joe Hicks, Alex Whitman, Eric Fredrickson, and others who made useful but less extensive contributions. The introductory chapter owes a debt of gratitude to Jeffrey Holzgrefe, who teaches at Agnes Scott College and Emory Law, and the military commission chapter was enhanced by Captain Edward White, whose experience in this venue was invaluable. I owe my daughter Amanda an enormous debt for converting her experience at the Yale Law 9/11 clinic with Harold Koh and her work as a Fellow at Georgetown Law with David Cole into many improvements to this book. Without her enthusiasm, the final chapter would have been reserved for a later edition.

In the final months of preparing the manuscript for publication, I was incredibly fortunate to have the tireless and upbeat assistance of Marianne D'Souza and the multi-talented aid of Jay Burhan Haider (Emory Law 2010). All mistakes, of course, are mine alone.

Finally, I could not have completed this project without the love and support of my wife, Susan, who is the cornerstone of my life.

Charles A. Shanor
Atlanta, GA.
March 31, 2011

Summary of Contents

Table of Contents

Table of Cases

The Principal cases are in bold type. Cases cited or discussed in the text are normal type.

UNITED STATES CASES

INTERNATIONAL CASES

COUNTERTERRORISM LAW

CASES AND MATERIALS

I

TERRORISM: A BRIEF INTRODUCTION

War is a challenge to law, and the law must adjust. It must recognize that the old wineskins of international law, domestic criminal procedure, or other prior frameworks are ill-suited to the bitter wine of this new warfare. This war *** demands new rules be written. Falling back on the comfort of prior practices supplies only illusory comfort.

Al-Bihani v. Obama, 590 F. 3d 866 (C.A.D.C.2010)
(Judge Brown, concurring)

Terrorism and Counterterrorism, a college course, and Counterterrorism Law, a law school course, are both recent developments. A great cataclysm, the terrorist attacks of September 11, 2001, installed each course in higher education institutions in the United States. When these attacks occurred, I remember asking myself how terrorism (or the particular brand of terrorism that produced the 9/11 attacks) had eluded my notice. After all, I had taught and written on military law and constitutional law, had taught criminal law, had interests in world religions, and kept abreast of historical, political, social, and religious trends, developments, and movements. In short, my bubble was broken, much as the post-Cold War bubble of "superpower" invulnerability burst for the American people.

Teaching and writing in the counterterrorism field is my personal response to 9/11, an effort to better comprehend the effects of "the new terrorism"[1] on the law and to explore the law's reactions to it. I have titled this book "Counterterrorism Law" because it is more about society's reactions to terrorism than about terrorism itself. Antiterrorism Law would be too narrow a term for this book's scope, for the book covers a wide range of ways in which nations, including the United States, have modified legal structures to deal with this new global threat.

This chapter, Terrorism: A Brief Introduction, though short and generally non-legal, is an essential backdrop to the remainder of this book. It provides a common definitional and historical framework concerning terrorism and counterterrorism for students who have lived in the post-9/11 world for much of their lives and thus accept it as normal, perhaps inevitable. The chapter is organized into six parts: (A) What is Terrorism?; B) Terrorism as a Legal

---

[1] The media typically refer to the new terrorism as "Islamic terrorism." The phenomenon is part of "radical neofundamentalism." See David Westbrook, DEPLOYING OURSELVES: ISLAMIST VIOLENCE AND THE RESPONSIBLE PROJECTION OF U.S. FORCE (Paradigm Publishers, 2011). "Takfiri terrorism," though not yet in the legal or popular lexicon, is a useful descriptive term discussed later in this chapter.

Term; (C) A Brief History of Terrorism; (D) The Challenge of Takfiri Terrorism; (E) A Briefer History of Counterterrorism; and (F) A Roadmap to this Book.

My thesis, though a casebook may not be the place for a thesis, is that the new terrorism poses unique challenges to the law in ways that differ from earlier national security challenges. These challenges include boundary-blurring between criminal and military law, reconsideration of traditional detention and interrogation practices, mingling of investigation and intelligence-gathering, growing but cabined exceptions to constitutional protections of individual rights, recasting of immigration law, new fault lines between courts, the executive, and Congress, and so on. The law's accommodation to the challenge of terrorism, and especially radical Islamic terrorism or takfiri terrorism, is a new twist on old tensions between civil liberties and national security that have arisen throughout history, not only in the United States, but around the world.

A. WHAT IS TERRORISM?

The basic dictionary definition of terrorism – "the use of violence and threats to intimidate or coerce, especially for political purposes" – seems straightforward. However, defining terrorism for political and philosophical purposes has proven difficult, if not impossible. Thousands of pages have been devoted to nuances of who should or should not be considered a terrorist.[2] There is a rich literature concerning what draws individuals to adopt terrorist tactics, sometimes in pursuit of noble and sometimes less noble goals. And of course there are historical studies of terrorism, about which one might with some accuracy say that one whose cause is unsuccessful is more likely to be deemed a terrorist than one whose cause is successful. Few today would view the African National Congress as a terrorist organization, though it was once so perceived.

Generally, terrorism differs from garden-variety violent crime both in motivation and scope. Its motivation is seldom financial, and is often political. It's scope is generally not limited to the immediate victim. The terrorist uses violence to instill fear in a population; his violence, unlike that of the murderer or mugger, requires an audience. But not all politically motivated violence is terrorism. States use violence, including war, to protect their populations or interests. Political opposition groups may use violence in response to violence, injustice, or oppression, as a tool for political change. The adage "one man's terrorist is another man's freedom fighter" captures

---

[2] See, e.g. Bruce Hoffman, "Defining Terrorism," INSIDE TERRORISM (2006), reprinted in Howard, Sawyer, and Bajema, TERRORISM AND COUNTERTERRORISM: UNDERSTANDING THE NEW SECURITY ENVIRONMENT, pp. 4-33 (Third Ed., McGraw-Hill, 2009) (Hoffman notes at p. 28 that Alex Schmid in POLITICAL TERRORISM: A RESEARCH GUIDE devoted more than a hundred pages to examining many definitions of terrorism only to conclude in a second edition of the book that the "search for an adequate definition is still on." Hoffman points out that another noted terrorism scholar, Walter Laqueur, "despaired of defining terrorism, *** maintaining that it is neither possible to do so nor worthwhile to make the attempt.")

the difficulties inherent in the concept of "terrorist."[3] If causes are relevant, the range of who is a terrorist narrows; if causes are irrelevant, and only actions count, the range widens.

Since the label "terrorist" is pejorative, those accused of being terrorists generally deny the charge.[4] Likewise, others seek to take advantage politically of the label by slinging it at opponents. Contrast the word "jihadist." This word, pejorative in the United States and other western countries, is a rallying cry among some Middle Eastern Islamic populations.[5] Likewise, calling a member of al Qaeda an "enemy combatant" or "unlawful enemy combatant," terms we will encounter later in this book, is not pejorative to those so labeled. As Ghassan Abdallah Ghazi Al Shiribi, an Al Qaeda operative known as "the electronic builder" and "Abu Zubaydah's right hand man," told a military panel at Guantanamo Bay, "If they come up with the classification enemy combatant, it is my honor to have this classification in this world until the end, until eternity, God be my witness."

There is frequent interplay between the words "terrorism" and "insurgency" and the words "terrorist" and "freedom fighter" or "revolutionary." But terrorism is neither war nor rebellion. Terrorism differs from traditional war or armed conflict: armed conflict generally involves the military forces or militias of one or more nations or non-state entities using violence against other similar entities, while terrorism generally involves individuals, alone or in concert within an organization, using violence against civilians and other noncombatants (including military forces not engaged in an armed conflict and therefore not combatants at the moment of the terrorist attack). Terrorism is likewise not rebellion, which tends to be directed at political change within a nation-state; though terrorism may be used as a tactic in rebellion, terrorism is directed at spreading fear in a population, whether or not in search of specific regime change.[6]

---

[3] Robert Kennedy, "Is One Person's Terrorist Another's Freedom Fighter?" in *Terrorism & Political Violence*, Vol. 11, No. 1, (Spring, 1999), pp. 1-21.

[4] An exception is the leader of the first attack on the World Trade Center, Ramzi Ahmed Yousef, who at his 1998 trial said: "Yes, I am a terrorist and I am proud of it. And I support terrorism *** against the United States Government and against Israel."

[5] This reaction is not based solely upon ambiguity of the term "jihad," which may refer both to internal struggle for self-betterment and outwardly-directed warfare in defense of religious beliefs but rather on broader perspectives. See Eqbal Ahmad, "Terrorism: Theirs and Ours" (1998), in Howard, et.al, supra n. 2 at pp. 34-41.

[6] Jeffrey Holzgrefe, who teaches a terrorism and counterterrorism class at Agnes Scott College, stresses the importance of using a consistent definition of terrorism. His suggestion is as follows:

"Terrorists are members of, or inspired by, non-state groups who clandestinely use, or threaten to use, extra-judicial violence against non-combatants to terrorize a particular target group into acceding to their demands for political change. They therefore differ from: states whose military personnel engage in acts of war when they openly or clandestinely use violence against the military personnel of another state; states whose military personnel engage in war crimes when they openly or clandestinely use violence against the civilian members of another state; guerrillas who engage in guerrilla warfare when they openly use extrajudicial violence against the military personnel of a local or foreign state; unlawful combatants who engage in unlawful combat when they clandestinely use, or threaten to use, extrajudicial violence against military personnel of a foreign state."

This useful definition tracks in substantial part what the reader will find throughout this book. However, this is a law book, and the ultimate source for legal definitions of terrorism, as Chapter

Notes

1. Motivations. Is a person less of a "terrorist" if his or her cause is just? For example, violent action to draw attention to slavery or apartheid might be viewed as morally justifiable. Does the person who blows up the home of a particularly repressive plantation owner in the 1830s or a police station of a repressive enforcer of apartheid laws in 1950 a "terrorist"?

2. Labeling Terrorists. Who determines who is a terrorist? If it is the state, does that mean Stalin was not a "terrorist" or that Hitler was not a "terrorist"? Does a liberal democracy have special purchase to label actions "terrorist"?

3. Psychology of Terrorists. There is a rich literature on psychological motivations of terrorists. Eric Hoffer's THE TRUE BELIEVER (1951) is a classic on fanaticism which talks about similarities between true believer communists, fascists, and Christians (among others). Recently, various psychologists have spilled ink profiling suicide bombers. Should the law take account of suicide bombers who try (unsuccessfully) to blow up innocents because they perceive their actions to be those of a soldier? What if the bomber is motivated by self-loathing and lack of worldly success, believing suicide is honorable for self and family? Societal strategies and interventions for dealing with such individuals might be quite different.

4. Global Incidence of Terrorism. Obviously, with ambiguity concerning what terrorism is, it would be difficult to get exact counts of incidents of terrorism or deaths from terrorism. Numerous global counts have been attempted. One type of terrorism, suicide bombing, has been a real growth industry over the past decades. One study shows the incidence of global suicide bombings per year growing from 4.7/year from 1981-1990 to 16/year from 1991-2000 to 180/year from 2001-2005. Even more recent study, shows that terrorism incidents vary dramatically by country. Of 65,788 attacks from September 12, 2001 to December 31, 2009, the countries in order of frequency of attacks are: Iraq (22,820), Afghanistan (6,080), Pakistan (5,602), India (5,161), Nepal (3,899), Thailand (3,783), Israel (3,259), Congo (2,669), Russia (1,727), Somalia (1,414), and the Philippines (1,344).

5. Terrorism in the United States Since 9/11. The second study above shows 24 terrorist attacks in which 16 people died in the United States. 13 of these deaths were from one attack (Nidal Hasan's shootings at Fort Hood). Another study, from December 2001 (shoe bomber Richard Reid) through December 25, 2009 (underwear bomber Umar Farouk Abdulmuttallab), lists 32 terrorist plots or efforts, 29 of which were prevented and 3 of which were carried out. All but one is listed as "Muslim Extremist" ideology; Nidal Hasan, is listed simply as "Muslim" with a footnote saying "mental health issues may have heavily influenced Hasan's motive." What conclusions do you draw from the pieces of data in Notes 4 and 5?

II demonstrates, lies with the words chosen by legislative bodies, administrative actors, and judicial interpreters. These words are sometimes more and sometimes less inclusive than Holgrefe's core definition.

B. TERRORISM AS A LEGAL TERM

The law has not been immune to problems concerning the definition of terrorism.   In 2005, decade-long negotiations for a Comprehensive Convention on International Terrorism failed because of the diversity of political perspectives in the international community. Eventually, unable to agree on the statement "The targeted and deliberate killing of civilians and non-combatants cannot be justified or legitimized by any cause or grievance," The United Nations proceeded *without definition* to declare that member states "consistently, unequivocally and strongly condemn terrorism in all its forms and manifestations, committed by whomever, wherever and for whatever purposes, as it constitutes one of the most serious threats to international peace and security."

Even within a nation-state, terrorism as a legal category is sometimes easier to describe and illustrate by examples than it is to define. This should come as no surprise to an experienced law student. What is "law" is a tough jurisprudential question, yet most students have little difficulty identifying laws. "Contract" may be generally defined, but that doesn't answer the question whether a particular apparent agreement will be enforced as a contract by a court in a particular jurisdiction. For a lawyer, statutes and judicial decisions are no less critical to defining "terrorism" than they are in other contexts.

We will look at specific statutes dealing with terrorism in Chapter II, but it is useful to realize that different institutional contexts may lead to different definitions of terrorism more generally. Bruce Hoffman notes[7] the following definitions of terrorism used, respectively, by the Federal Bureau of Investigation (FBI), the Department of Homeland Security (DHS), and the Department of Defense (DoD):

(FBI) the unlawful use of force or violence against persons or property to intimidate or coerce a Government, the civilian population, or any segment thereof, in furtherance of political or social objectives.

(DHS) any activity that involves an act that:

Is dangerous to human life or potentially destructive of critical infrastructure or key resources; and ...must also be intended

(i) to intimidate or coerce a civilian population; (ii) to influence the policy of a government by intimidation or coercion; or (iii) to affect the conduct of a government by mass destruction, assassination, or kidnapping.

(DoD) the calculated use of unlawful violence or threat of unlawful violence to inculcate fear; intended to coerce or to intimidate governments or societies in the pursuit of goals that are generally political, religious, or ideological objectives.

Consider the different priorities of these institutions. As Hoffman notes, the FBI's mission is "investigating and solving crimes;" its definition broadly

---

[7] Supra n. 2, at p. 26.

covers not only terror threats to governments and the citizenry, but also politically or socially motivated acts against private property. DHS, with a mandate to protect the U.S. from terrorism and to minimize the damage from terrorist acts that may occur, defines terrorism more narrowly. Some acts considered terrorism under the FBI definition (e.g. radical environmentalists vandalizing a private car dealership) would not be considered terrorism under the DHS definition. The DoD definition, consistent with the DoD's stated mission to "provide the military forces needed to deter war and to protect" the United States, hones in on threats as well as overt acts, and focuses on terrorism targeting societies and governments. Hoffman, at 27; mission statements of DHS, Homeland Security Act of 2002, §101(b), and DoD, http://www.defense.gov/about/#mission.

Notes

1.   **Absence of Definition.**   As noted above, the United Nations proceeded *without definition* to declare that member states "consistently, unequivocally and strongly condemn terrorism in all its forms and manifestations, committed by whomever, wherever and for whatever purposes, as it constitutes one of the most serious threats to international peace and security." Is there any possible usefulness to such a statement by the U.N.? By member states of the U.N.? Could a court such as the International Court of Justice use this statement to label a particular action customary as a violation of international law? The answer would turn on whether there is sufficient consensus among states, commentators, etc.

2.   **Institutional Priorities.**   Try using some specific examples of "terrorism" to see if they fit within the differing definitions of terrorism used by the FBI, DHS, and DoD. In these definitions, is it "terrorism" for the military regime in Myanmar to condemn pro-democracy leader Aung San Suu Kyi to house arrest, for China to imprison rights activist Liu Xiaobo, or for the Nazis to refuse to allow journalist and pacifist Carl von Ossietzky to leave Germany in 1936? What makes the use of violence "unlawful" under the FBI and DoD definitions? Is the concept to be defined under domestic Myanmar, Chinese, or German law, United States law, or international law? Would the fact that the three individuals listed above were Nobel Peace Prize winners make any difference in these definitions? Is confinement of these individuals "dangerous to human life or potentially destructive of critical infrastructure or key resources" under the DHS definition? Do these agency definitions apply at all to state actors?

C. A BRIEF HISTORY OF TERRORISM

Historical perspective on terrorism and the rise of various terrorist groups and modes of operating is useful for stimulating thoughts about whether all acts of terrorism should be treated the same by the law, what the law should do to respond to various types of terrorism, and how historical terrorism and contemporary terrorism compare. It thus provides an important foundation for looking at specific counterterrorism policies and antiterrorism laws.

Origins. The earliest documented use of tactics similar to the methods of modern terrorists was by a Jewish faction known as the Sicarii. The Sicarii campaign included guerilla attacks on and assassination of Roman occupational authorities, soldiers, and Jews whom the Sicarii regarded as collaborators during the Roman occupation of Palestine. Centuries later, (11th-13th centuries) a Shiite Muslim sect, the Nizaris, produced a group known as the "Assassins." The Assassins struck fear into Muslim communities they perceived as not subscribing to pure Islam, assassinating and threatening prominent figures across the Muslim world, including religious leaders, sultans, and caliphs. The Assassins seized and governed their own territories at times, but were often oppressed, opposed, or overthrown by rival Muslim leaders or even the outraged populations of the territories they controlled.

States have used tactics to terrorize civilian populations for centuries. In the ninth to seventh centuries B.C.E., the Assyrians used fear-inducing tactics including torturing, mutilating, and murdering enemies and rebels. They publicized these tactics as a warning to enemies in perhaps the first use of psychological warfare. The Mongols also used terror tactics as their empire spread across Asia in the 11th through 14th centuries, butchering entire villages and populations, leaving only enough survivors to spread the word of their brutal methods.

Ironically, the term "terrorism" was coined not to describe a group resisting a government but to describe the actions of a government itself. The agents of the Jacobin French Revolutionary government and the Committee of Public Safety who enforced the "Reign of Terror" were labeled "terrorists." Their methods included both legal and extra-legal killings of enemies of the new government. These tactics had immediate effects upon the victims, but, like modern acts of terrorism, sought to influence a much broader population.

Terrorism in the 19th and 20th Centuries.[8] Modern non-state terrorism began to emerge in the 19th century. Anarchists and those resisting autocratic governments began to use violence to inspire the population to revolution or expose state oppression. Assassination was a key tool of these terrorists, whose victims included a number of heads of state including Czar

---

[8] State crimes against humanity by totalitarian governments in the 20th century are sometimes colloquially called terrorism because the leaders of such states created terror in their populations to retain and expand their control. The Soviet Union under Josef Stalin imprisoned or killed millions of its own citizens from the 1930s onward, conducting show trials of Stalin's rivals and keeping the population in a near-perpetual state of fear. Ironically, the victims of this campaign of state terror were accused of conspiracy to commit terrorism against the Soviet Union. The German Nazi Party, which had risen to power amid a campaign of terrorism and street battles against political opponents such as the Communists and other parties of the left, terrorized Jews and other groups in Germany and the territories it occupied, engaging in systematic genocide. At the Nuremberg Trials, Nazi Germany's actions were frequently labeled as terrorism. Many right-wing dictatorships in Latin America notoriously utilized "death squads" to assassinate and intimidate their political enemies, and regimes in Cambodia and Yugoslavia resorted to terrorizing their own populations or conducting genocide against minority groups. Jeff Holzgrefe's definition, supra note 6, excludes such state actions, and they are not the focus of this book.

Alexander II of Russia, who was killed by a bomb in 1881, and American President William McKinley, who was shot by an anarchist in 1901. Some of these attacks were conducted by solo terrorists or assassins acting alone, while others were parts of larger networks, some of which used cell-based structures.

Terrorism became a key tool of nationalist groups beginning in the late 19th and early 20th centuries. The 1914 assassination of Archduke Franz Ferdinand of Austria-Hungary, arguably a terrorist attack by a group of Serbian nationalists,[9] was the spark that ignited the First World War. In addition to provoking a war between states, this event was also one of the earliest examples of state-sponsored terrorism, as Serbian intelligence had ties to the assassin and his group, the Black Hand.[10]

In the political upheaval that surrounded the First World War and its aftermath, terrorism became a more common tactic among nationalist groups. For example, the Irish Republican Army used a widespread campaign of terrorism against British occupation in the late 1910s and early 1920s, including assassinations and ambushes. This campaign of terrorism proved at least partially successful, as it led to independence for the southern portion of Ireland in 1922.

In the 1960s and 1970s, numerous leftist and nationalist groups conducted bombings, shootings, kidnappings, hijackings, and assassinations of government and military officials and civilians throughout Europe and elsewhere. These groups, including the Baader-Meinhof Gang in Germany, the Red Brigades in Italy, the Japanese Red Army, and various Palestinian groups, sometimes cooperated to provide resources, safehouses, and training. Groups resisting colonial and racist regimes in Africa, such as the Algerian resistance against the French and the African National Congress's campaign against the South African apartheid government, used terrorist tactics that included suicide bombings and attacks against civilians. South American rebel groups, such as Shining Path in Peru and the Revolutionary Armed Forces of Columbia (FARC), utilized terrorism to fight their nations' governments; in Uruguay, a group known as the Tupamaros pioneered the tactics of urban guerilla warfare. In 1968, members of the Popular Front for the Liberation of Palestine hijacked an Israeli El Al airplane departing from Rome, beginning a long campaign of terrorist attacks by Palestinian nationals against Israeli targets. In 1972, members of the "Black September" organization, a Palestinian terrorist group, conducted one of the most infamous and well-known terrorist attacks in history when it kidnapped and later murdered 11 members of the Israeli national team at the Summer Olympics in Munich. This attack at such a prominent venue attracted international media coverage, and showed how terrorist attacks could capture the world's attention to the actions and cause of the terrorists.

---

[9] To the extent that anarchists limited their attacks to assassinating heads of state, their actions, however unlawful, failed to involve generating fear to obtain political change.

[10] Chapter 13 contains materials showing how United States law has altered otherwise applicable rules of sovereign immunity for such states.

As the Cold War wound down and the Soviet Union collapsed, the dominant force behind international terrorism shifted from leftist and nationalist groups to a widespread radical Islamic movement, ushering in a new age of terrorism. After the 1979 Islamic Revolution in Iran, many Islamic terrorist groups found backing by the Islamic Republic of Iran and other Middle Eastern states. The Soviet invasion of Afghanistan trained "mujahedeen" from throughout the Muslim world, including a young Osama bin Laden. Islamic fundamentalists, many trained alongside bin Laden, subsequently conducted attacks in Israel and conducted high profile operations such as the attacks that killed hundreds of American embassy personnel and Marines stationed in Lebanon in 1983, leading to American troop withdrawal from that nation.[11] In 1981, Islamic radicals assassinated President Anwar al-Sadat of Egypt, the first Arab leader to negotiate with Israel. Other attacks by Islamic fundamentalist terrorists, often backed by Iran and Libya, continued throughout the 1980s, including terrorist attacks on a discotheque in Berlin in 1986 that killed three American servicemen and Libya-supported bombing of a Pan American flight over Lockerbie, Scotland in 1988.

In the latter part of the 20th century, new terrorist tactics and tools emerged that made terrorism both more dangerous and harder to combat, including the use of weapons of mass destruction. Members of a fanatical Japanese religious cult conducted two terrorist attacks in 1994 and 1995 using sarin gas, marking the first successful terrorist attacks using chemical weapons. In 2001, five people were killed in the United States by letters laced with infectious anthrax, a spore. [12] In the 1990s and 2000s, the use of a new and devastating terrorist tactic, the suicide bombing, became widespread. Suicide bombings, first used by the Tamil Tigers of Sri Lanka, were used by Islamic radicals against civilian, political, and military targets in Israel, Iraq, Afghanistan, Pakistan, England, and elsewhere. Former Pakistani Prime Minister Benazir Bhutto was assassinated by a suicide bomber in 2007 during a major political crisis in Pakistan.

In the first decade of the 21st Century, suicide bombings have became increasingly common throughout the Middle East, used by groups such as the Taliban and al Qaeda in Afghanistan and Pakistan, various insurgent groups in Iraq, and by Hamas and Palestinian Islamic Jihad in Israel and the Palestinian territories. Chechen separatists conducted terrorist attacks on schools, theaters, and apartment buildings throughout Russia in the 2000s. In 2008, a group of terrorists linked to a violent Pakistani separatist group captured the world's attention when it simultaneously attacked various targets with massive shooting and bombing attacks in Mumbai, India that killed 164 people.

Terrorism and the United States. Early domestic terrorism in the United States included the Haymarket Square bombing in 1886 that killed a number

---

[11] See infra, Chapter II, as to whether attacks on military operations would be considered terrorism under various statutes.

[12]   The anthrax attacks were often mislabeled "bioterrorism" in popular and even technical literature, but such spores, unlike viruses and bacteria, are not contagious.

of Chicago police officers and a series of bombings by leftist radicals after the
First World War (including bombings on Wall Street and of Attorney General
A. Mitchell Palmer's home). These latter bombings led to a severe crackdown
on and deportation of alleged leftist radicals. Variations on terrorist tactics,
including assassinations, beatings, bombings, and lynchings, were used to
intimidate the black population of the South by groups such as the Ku Klux
Klan from the 1860s onward. Modern terrorist tactics in the 1960s and 1970s
included the bombing of an African-American church during the civil rights
movement by Ku Klux Klan members in 1963 and the bombing of the
Pentagon and various other sites by the anti-war Weather Underground in
the early 1970s.

The first attack by Islamic terrorists on American soil took place in 1993
when Islamic fundamentalists bombed one of the World Trade Center towers
with a truck bomb. These terrorists were apprehended, tried, and convicted
in New York City. In 1995, the largest terrorist attack in American history to
that point took place when Timothy McVeigh, a right-wing fanatic with ties
to the "militia" movement, detonated a large bomb at a federal building in
Oklahoma City, killing 168. Theodore Kaczynski, known as the
"Unabomber," sent out over a dozen letter bombs from the late 1970s until
1995 in support of a radical anti-technology ideology. Another homegrown
extremist, Eric Robert Rudolph, killed two people during the Summer
Olympics in Atlanta in 1996 with a bomb placed in Atlanta's Centennial
Olympic Park. Rudolph continued bombing abortion clinics and other sites
until his capture in 1998.

In the late 1990s and early 2000s, international Islamic terrorist groups,
particularly a group centered in Afghanistan known as al Qaeda, began to
attack American targets throughout the world, eventually culminating in the
largest and most devastating terrorist attack in American history. The
American embassies in Kenya and Tanzania were simultaneously bombed in
1998, and the *U.S.S. Cole* was attacked off the coast of Yemen in late 2000.[13]
On September 11, 2001, four American airplanes were hijacked by al Qaeda
operatives and were crashed into targets on the American east coast. Two of
the planes hit the World Trade Center towers in New York City, while a third
crashed into the Pentagon in Washington, D.C. The fourth plane crashed in
rural Pennsylvania. Nearly 3,000 people were killed in the attacks.

The American-led "War on Terror" marked the first concerted
international effort against a multinational network of terrorists. Terrorist
attacks by Islamic fundamentalists, however, continued. Al Qaeda and
similar groups bombed civilian targets in Bali in 2002, Istanbul in 2003,
Madrid in 2004, and London and Amman in 2005. Even so, a number of
terrorist plots have been uncovered and prevented throughout the world,
including the arrests of numerous cells in the United States and Europe and
the thwarting of a plot to bomb a number of trans-Atlantic airliners in 2006.
At the time of this writing, Islamic terrorists continue to have strong

---

[13] Though al Qaeda was responsible for all three of these attacks and the 9/11 attacks referred to
later in this paragraph, the *U.S.S. Cole* and Pentagon attacks may not fit some definitions of
terrorism because the targets were military rather than civilian.

followings in Southeast Asia and the Middle East. Indeed, most analysts believe that al Qaeda has moved from being an operational force to being an inspirational enterprise. From a central organization, it has morphed into an international terrorism franchise with local groups and causes drawing upon its central message of attacking the forces of modernity, pluralism, capitalism, and democracy.

Notes

1. Historical Perspective. Has anything changed about terrorism over the centuries? Is it all just blood and gore? Should different concepts be used if states use terrorist tactics rather than opponents of states using terrorism?

2. Changing Causes? Have there been causes that recur in the history of terrorism? Consider the following: response to repressive regimes, racial and religious divides, ideological commitments.

3. National and Temporal Experiences. Perceptions of terrorism may differ between citizens of different countries or different social groups within a country. Consider how nonwhites and whites viewed violence used for racial social agendas in the Jim Crow era and toward the end of South African apartheid.

D. THE CHALLENGE OF TAKFIRI TERRORISM

Takfiris believe in Islam strictly according to the understanding of Muhammad and his companions, and do not accept any deviation from their path; ***. Those who change their religion from Islam to any other way of life, or *** they worship, follow or obey anything other than [fundamental] Islam, the takfiris declare *** apostates from Islam and so no longer Muslim. *** This belief allows Takfiris to justify the use of violence against fellow Muslims [and non-Muslims]. Takfiris *** consider all political authority that does not abide by their interpretation of Islam as illegitimate and apostate [and] violence against such regimes is considered legitimate. *** Takfiris believe that one who deliberately kills [himself] attempting to kill enemies is a martyr [for whom] all sin is absolved ***, allowing carte blanche for the indiscriminate killing of non-combatants, for example. Some Takfiris are not bound by the usual religious constraints regarding wearing a beard, drinking alcohol, or eating pork when such restrictions would interfere with waging effective jihad. To Takfiris, strict adherence to those laws precludes necessary covert action in defense of Islam. Because Takfiris "blend in," they can organize, plan, and take action *** with less risk of identification, interference, or interception.[14]

---

[14] This description from Wikipedia, the most-used reference work of our time, is accurate even though the source is agreed by all scholars to be non-authoritative. A more acceptable scholarly source is David Kilcullen, THE ACCIDENTAL GUERRILLA (Oxford University Press, 2009).

Most readers, including those who have read some or all the Report of the 9/11 Commission, will recognize in this definition both the ideology and the operations of the nineteen men who perpetrated the 9/11 terrorism. What remains elusive is why takfiri terrorism is a growth industry in the 21st Century. Some stock answers to this question include: a strong and wealthy patron of the movement (Osama bin Laden), a training ground for takfiri "mujadeen" opposing the Soviet occupation of Afghanistan, authoritarian and undemocratic regimes in various Arab states, presence of American military force in the Middle East, opposition to Israel and American support for Israel, poverty in the nations that have produced most of the takfiri terrorists, and so on. This list is inadequate, for it fails to explain (for example) why most impoverished Muslims reject takfiri terrorism and why the Arab world has no desire for governance by Osama bin Laden and his allies. It also confuses opportunities for training with reasons why takfiri recruitment continues to expand. It also only scratches the surface, omitting some ramifications of takfiri ideology and missing some special contextual components of the movement that help answer the question "Why now, rather than decades or centuries ago?

Here are a few of the most important components of modern takfiri terrorism that, I believe, make it different from earlier terrorist threats. First, this brand of terrorism is not susceptible to compromise with secular concerns that have defused earlier terrorist campaigns. A group that uses terrorism to accomplish political or social change may be given a place at the table through negotiations or electoral processes. The person with a central tenet that heaven awaits martyrdom does not want a place at the table, but wants to blow up the table and everyone sitting at it. Second, takfiri terrorists no longer need (or even want) territory for their operations. The attackable training grounds in Afghanistan have been replaced by operational manuals distributed over the internet from which an individual or small cell of true believers can build and deliver a bomb or organize a small weapons killing spree. Third, the central figure for making the new terrorism work is no longer a chief or operational leader. It is the publicist who spreads the message of jihad over the internet, often with glossy photos and half-truths, who inspires volunteers to march toward martyrdom. Fourth, takfiris understand that they can't beat the modern nation-state and capitalistic mechanisms with a better polis or better way of satisfying material wants and needs. Their genius lies in suckering nations and people with more material concerns into beating themselves, spending trillions of dollars on wars in unwinnable places while recruiting and expanding in other places, including the nation-states that could be doing far more productive things with their resources. Fifth, takfiris need not invent anything, including modern weapons of mass destruction. They simply need to convert such items created by others to their own uses in ways comparable to their ingenious conversion of passenger jets into missiles of mass destruction, bringing down tall buildings and ending thousands of lives. Finally, takfiris thrive in the global village connected by mass media and autonomous internet users. Every success or even unsuccessful attempt brings a small but important number within their viewing audience to their side while magnifying every effort in the minds of potential victims.

Notes

1. War? Osama bin Laden issued a lengthy fatwa (religious statement) in 1996 declaring "war" on the Israelis, Americans, and those who would support them:

> Terrorizing you, while you are carrying arms on our land, is legitimate, reasonable and morally demanded duty. It is also a rightful act well known to all humans and all creatures. Your example and our example are like a snake that entered into a house of a man and got killed by him. The coward is the one who lets you roam freely and safely while carrying arms in his country. Those youths are different from your soldiers; your problem is how to convince your soldiers to be daring and fight. While our problem will be how to restrain our youths from waiting for their turn to fight. *** My Muslim Brothers of the world: Your brothers in land of the two holiest sites and Palestine are calling upon you for help and asking you to take part in fighting against the enemy, your enemy; the Israelis and Americans.

When a private citizen, the leader of a group but not a country, declares war, how should those on whom war is declared respond? The United States to a large extent ignored this fatwa, but President Clinton authorized cruise missile strikes at bin Laden's training camps in Afghanistan. After the 9/11 attacks organized and sanctioned by bin Laden, President Bush declared the "War on Terrorism." Was this a good move tactically?

2. Ideology. How would you counter the ideology of takfiri terrorism? Who can take on this role? What support do those who do so need? If only a tiny portion of Muslims respond to bin Laden's call to arms, how likely is it that countervailing arguments will prevail among that small minority?

3. Recruitment. If takfiris are drawn together by jihadist web sites, should those web sites be closed down? Who could effectively close them down? Would they stay down or be replaced by others? Would it be a better strategy to leave the web sites active and trace those who visit the sites?

4. Success for al Qaeda. What would that entail? Removal of U.S. troops from the Middle East? The collapse of the state of Israel? Overthrow of progressive or western-oriented regimes in the Middle East? Creation of a world-wide community ruled by sharii'a law? Death of all infidels?

5. Tactical Objectives, WMD, and Lesser Attacks. What is the point of a major strike such as 9/11? Did bin Laden not foresee that the U.S. would respond with massive military force? Does the lack of any comparable attack since 9/11 show that al Qaeda is being contained? If you think so, here is an excerpt from *Inspire*, a glossy English-language magazine put out by al Qaeda in the Arabian Peninsula (AQAP), largely with the help of two American converts who have substantial language and web design skills. It deals with what the authors refer to as Operation Hemorrhage:

The strategy of al Qaeda was to strike big while the enemy was off guard. The blessed operations of Washington and New York represent the greatest special operations in the history of man. Nineteen men ended the lives of almost three thousand Americans, cost the U.S. treasury trillions of dollars, and embroiled America in a War on Terror that it would definitely eventually lose *** However, to bring down America we do not need to strike big. In such an environment of security phobia that is sweeping America, it is more feasible to stage smaller attacks that involve less players and less time to launch and thus we may circumvent the security barriers America worked so hard to erect. This strategy of attacking the enemy with smaller, but more frequent operations is what some might refer to as the strategy of a thousand cuts. The aim is to bleed the enemy to death.

http://info.publicintelligence.net/InspireNovember2010.pdf. Do you believe this version of what has happened since 9/11? Regardless of your answer to this question, what would be appropriate responses to Operation Hemorrhage?

6. Endless Terrorism? Is modern Islamic terrorism (sometimes called takfiri terrorism) susceptible of reaching an endpoint? Consider as you answer this question several characteristics of takfiri terrorism: (1) God, not humanistic values, is the source of its ideology; (2) it is not confined to a single nation-state; (3) it seeks to establish a caliphate governed by sharia law in historic Muslim lands from Spain to Indonesia; (4) it has no operational leader and has an increasingly flat and diffused organizational structure; and (5) it has a recruiting and indoctrination tool not available to previous generations of terrorists (the internet).

E. A BRIEFER HISTORY OF COUNTERTERRORISM

Intertwined with the history of terrorism are the responses of states to such tactics, often called counterterrorism. Great Britain faced terrorism across its far-flung territories as its empire waned, and met varying degrees of success in its many strategies. In Malaysia, for example, the British countered a campaign of terrorism and revolutionary activity by Communist guerillas with a strategy known as the "Briggs Plan," which combined with small detachments of specially-trained troops, included the first campaign to win over the "hearts and minds" of an occupied population to counter terrorism. After a 12-year campaign, the British suppressed the terrorist threat and paved the way for Malaysian independence from the British Empire. In Kenya, however, the British responded to the Mau Mau Rebellion with heavy-handed tactics against the population at large, including the use of massive prison camps. Although the rebellion was defeated, it paved the way to a British withdrawal and the grooming of an indigenous government to replace the colonial administration. The British responded harshly and at times indiscriminately against civilian populations (even with acts of terror of their own) in combating terrorist campaigns in Cyprus, Palestine, and Ireland; these campaigns ended with the British position becoming politically and militarily untenable and eventual independence for all three former colonies.

France conducted a counterterrorism campaign against rebels in Algeria in the 1950s. The French effort was actually successful, as the terrorist network in Algiers was brutally crushed, but it involved tactics that ultimately turned public opinion in France and Algeria against the French campaign. While the French forces used some legitimate tactics such as networks of spies, military checkpoints, and an effective intelligence operation, it also turned the Arab section of Algiers into a virtual concentration camp and utilized torture and even murder. Although the French won the "Battle of Algiers," (memorialized in a movie of that is the best single cinematic exploration of terrorist tactics and counterterrorism excesses), they lost the war. Algeria won its independence several years later.

In response to international terrorism in the 1960s and 1970s, many states began to implement military counterterrorism strategies that stretched beyond their own borders. Israel, which had faced terrorist attacks and cross-border raids by Palestinian groups since its founding, launched retaliatory cross-border raids against towns and refugee camps that harbored terrorist groups. As terrorism began to target Israeli interests internationally, the Israeli response became international as well. In the aftermath of the Munich Massacre, Israel launched air strikes on Palestinian militant targets in Lebanon and commenced Operation Wrath of God, which reportedly killed many Palestinian militants and terrorists linked to Black September and the terrorist attack in Munich. Israel also successfully sent a commando team to extract hostages from an airliner hijacked by German and Palestinian terrorists held in Entebbe, Uganda in 1976. German commandos similarly freed dozens of hostages from Palestinian terrorists acting in concert with German Red Army Faction members in a raid on the Mogadishu airport in 1977. Israel was also the first country to use targeted killing of terrorists, a tactic since adopted by the United States, which uses air strikes by unmanned drones. In the 1990s and 2000s, as terrorist attacks and suicide bombings became increasingly common, Israel constructed a wall around the Gaza Strip and parts of the West Bank in an effort to prevent Palestinian terrorists from reaching targets in Israel. The construction of the wall was heavily criticized by the international community, but terrorist attacks in Israel steadily dropped in the years after completion of the barrier.

The United States also used military force to respond to terrorism. President Carter, for example, ordered a rescue attempt into Iran to retrieve hostages being held at the American Embassy in 1979, which ended in catastrophe when two American helicopters collided and a number of American servicemen were killed. President Reagan ordered the bombing of sites around Tripoli after Libyan-backed terrorists killed American servicemen in Germany in 1986. President Clinton also ordered cruise missile strikes in Iraq, Sudan, and Afghanistan in retaliation for terrorist attacks throughout the 1990s. President George W. Bush responded to the 9/11 attacks by declaring a "War on Terror," attacking al Qaeda and its protectors, the Taliban government of Afghanistan. One of the justifications given for the subsequent invasion of Iraq was that Saddam Hussein was amassing weapons of mass destruction which could be delivered to American soil, perhaps by terrorists. The response to the 9/11 attacks has also resulted in unprecedented international cooperation in combating terrorism. Intelligence agencies have worked together to undermine terrorist cells, track leaders of al Qaeda and other groups, and cut off the funding of terrorist groups.

Counterterrorism responses to 9/11 in the United States also have included two major pieces of legislation, the USA PATRIOT Act and the Homeland Security Act. Provisions of both will be addressed later in this book, but it is worth mentioning here that in addition to providing new tools for dealing with terrorists and a reorganization of the executive branch's agencies for addressing terrorism, both pieces of legislation have had collateral consequences. The PATRIOT Act forced Congress and later the courts to examine closely the balance between civil liberties and national security; the Homeland Security Act reordered priorities of many components of the federal government, especially those relating to immigration and border security.

Counterterrorism laws differ substantially among countries, even among the world's democracies. National counterterrorism laws reflect state experiences in dealing with localized and international terrorism as well as varied constitutional systems and cultural priorities. Israel, for example, has antiterrorism legislation dating back to the pre-nation British Mandate supplemented by newer laws following the first (1987-94) and second (2000) intifadas. The independent Israeli judiciary has wide-ranging powers of judicial review, as revealed in several cases covered by this book. Great Britain has lengthy experience with terrorism, including anticolonial, Irish paramilitary, and takfiri terrorism (e.g. 2005 London transit system attacks). Britain responded to the 2001 al Qaeda attacks on United States targets with the Antiterrorism, Crime, and Security Act of 2001 (ATCSA) and to the transit attacks with the Prevention of Terrorism Act 2005 and the Terrorism Act of 2006. These statutory responses took place within the context of a country with no written constitution, a system premised on the supremacy of Parliament, and a European framework that includes the European Convention on Human Rights (ECHR). British statutory provisions and ECHR limitations on counterterrorism efforts distinctive from those of American law are provided at various points in this book. Finally, there are occasional references to the counterterrorism laws of other countries including India, the world's largest democracy and the most frequent target of terrorism attacks. In this casebook edition, there are only infrequent references to civil tradition democracies such as France, Germany, and Spain, all of which have counterterrorism laws and practices reflective of that tradition as well as their own experiences.

The United States' experience is unique for many reasons. First, our experience base with terrorism is quite limited compared to that of other countries. The primary laws specifically directed at terrorism are the USA PATRIOT Act, the Homeland Security Act, and the Military Commissions Acts, all enacted in the wake of the 9/11 attacks. Other laws designed for different purposes, such as the Foreign Intelligence Surveillance Act and the

Classified Information Procedures Act, have played important roles in dealing with takfiri terrorism.   Second, the United States has dealt with little domestic terrorism; its greatest threats have come from sources halfway around the world.   Cabining or countering such attacks has involved the projection of military force and intelligence operations to remote locales often not amenable to normal police investigative work. Third, the United States has a written constitution containing robust protections of free speech and privacy as well as protections from self-incrimination, cruel and unusual punishment, and unreasonable search and seizure.   The right to habeas corpus, a procedural mechanism for raising civil liberties concerns by those detained or incarcerated, is a distinctive Anglo-American mechanism. These civil liberties have been augmented through legislation such as the Freedom of Information Act and the Privacy Act.   Fourth, United States criminal law provides more onerous penalties for terrorism offenses and more generous causes of action for tort claims against both terrorists and counterterrorism operations than most nations. Its civil law, while generally robust in providing remedies for victims, has specific components in the counterterrorism area that make it less so (e.g. the state secrets doctrine and the terrorism exception to the Foreign Sovereign Immunity Act). Finally, the United States, as a nation of immigrants more distinctive for its ideals than specific cultural characteristics, has been especially conflicted on border security and immigration matters.

Notes

1. Context and Counterterrorism. Does the British experience in dealing with terrorism differently in different colonies provide any insight into better and less useful tools for countering terrorism?

2. The End of Terrorism. What ends a period of terrorism? Is it resolution of an underlying tension, such as apartheid in South Africa? Inclusion of an excluded political or social group into the political process? Has terrorism ever ended with the elimination of all terrorists by a state that was the target of their attacks?

3. Criminal Law as Counterterrorism. Is there any precedent historically for successfully using criminal prosecution to eliminate terrorism?   If so, what preconditions would need to exist for this tool to be successful?   How would perpetrators of terrorism be located and brought to trial?   Would you anticipate any problems with their trial compared to trials of ordinary criminals?

4. Military Power and Counterterrorism. How useful is military power against terrorism? Can you categorize circumstances where it would be more and circumstances where it would be less useful?

5. Other Counterterrorism Tools. What would you do to counter the ideological appeal of terrorism?   Is economic development a deterrent to terrorism? Education?   Political reform? Would the tools for stopping terrorists be the same as those for deterring people who might support terrorism, either financially or otherwise?

6. The Problem of Suicide Bombing. It is impossible to mete out criminal punishment to a successful suicide bomber. How might society and the law approach dealing with suicide bombing if normal punishment is unavailing?

F. A ROAD MAP TO THIS BOOK

How can societies best respond to the threat of terrorism and, in particular, to takfiri terrorism? The answer is not clear. There are tools for finding takfiris, from traditional intelligence to internet surveillance and data-mining, but these extract civil liberties prices. There are defensive moves such as airport and cargo inspections, though these extract high monetary costs. Information may be extracted from captured members of a terrorist cell, but some extraction techniques are morally repulsive to liberal democracies. One can isolate, perhaps for a lifetime, committed terrorists not susceptible of rehabilitation, but the questions are: after what kinds of processes and at what price to our notions of fairness? Finally, we can use military power, from troop operations "surges" to drone strikes. But are such military operations lawful under domestic and international law? This book explores the law concerning these questions, organizing the decisions of Congress, the President, and the courts around various counterterrorism strategies and processes.

Chapter II explores antiterrorism criminal laws, while Chapter III examines legal issues in finding terrorists. Chapter IV considers the interface between counterterrorism and technology, foreign intelligence surveillance. Chapters V-VII explore legal battles over civilian and military detentions and interrogations of alleged terrorists, including those detained in facilities at Guantanamo Bay, Cuba, at Bagram Airfield in Afghanistan, and elsewhere. Trial processes concerning terrorist defendants are treated in the context of both civilian trials (Chapter VIII) and military commission proceedings (Chapter IX).. Chapter X focuses on various aspects of international humanitarian law concerning the use of military force as a counterterrorism tool. Chapters XI and XII consider, respectively, the immigration system as a counterterrorism tool and civil liability as a mechanism for holding terrorists, their supporters, and counterrerrorism officials responsible for their actions. Finally, Chapter XIII looks at the allocation of authority in the United States to deal with terrorism

II

TERRORISM: CRIME AND PUNISHMENT

Everyone agrees that the Government's interest in combating terrorism is an urgent objective of the highest order.

Holder v. Humanitarian Law Project, 130 S.Ct. 2705 (2010)

The lack of consensus in defining terrorism, discussed in Chapter I, has not prevented states and the international community from criminalizing terrorism in many specific contexts. *Domestically*, states have formulated numerous antiterrorism laws. A lawyer prosecuting or defending a terrorism charge must look carefully at the specific statute and the facts of the case to determine whether a prohibited act of "terrorism" occurred. Because this book is prepared primarily for use in United States law school classes, United States antiterrorism criminal law will be the focus of section A of this chapter. However, for comparative purposes, differing approaches other nations have taken to criminalizing terrorism will also be referenced. *Internationally*, even without a generic definition of terrorism, agreements among nations have been reached to deal with specific components of terrorism such as airline hijacking, genocide, and tracing terrorist finances. Moreover, some domestic statutes have facilitated claims that terrorists have violated the "law of nations" and international tribunals have dealt with cases alleging terrorism. Section B of this chapter considers cases in which terrorism as a violation of international law is at issue. Finally, Section C presents concerns in terrorism cases about sentencing. Should there be enhanced penalties for terrorism beyond the penalties for others who commit the same acts (e.g. killing, torture, or arson) for other reasons? May victim testimony prejudice the Defendant's ability to receive a fair trial? Under what circumstances, if any, should the death penalty be used? How are plea bargaining issues handled in terrorism cases?

Questions of jurisdiction, evidence, and other conduct of civilian trials are reserved for Chapter VIII. Comparable concerns in military commission trials are the subject of Chapter IX.

A. DOMESTIC ANTITERRORISM CRIMES

1. AN OVERVIEW OF ANTITERRORISM STATUTES

The United States Code contains hundreds of statutes and regulations that address terrorism in various ways. Most are criminal provisions in Title 18 of the United States Code, though others are used for isolating terrorists and terrorist organizations from access to funds and expanding tort liability for support of terrorism. Here are four federal statutes which define terrorism. As you know from your criminal law course, each element of the offense must be met for inculpation under a criminal statute.

The first (and most straightforward) is 22 U.S.C. 2656(f)(d)(2), from the Foreign Relations Act for Fiscal Years 1988 and 1989. It defines terrorism as "premeditated, politically motivated violence perpetrated against noncombatant targets by subnational groups or clandestine agents."

A second, 18 U.S.C. §2331(1), defines "international terrorism" to:

(A) Involve violent acts of acts dangerous to human life that are a violation of the criminal laws of the United States or of any State, or that would be a criminal violation if committed within the jurisdiction of the United States or of any State;

(B) Appear to be intended-

(i) to intimidate or coerce a civilian population;

(ii) to influence the policy of a government by intimidation or coercion; or to affect the conduct of a government by mass destruction, assassination or kidnapping; and

(C) Occur primarily outside the territorial jurisdiction of the United States, or transcend national boundaries in terms of the means by which they are accomplished, the persons they appear intended to intimidate or coerce, or the locale in which their perpetrators operate or seek asylum.

A provision in the USA Patriot Act, 18 U.S.C. §2331(5), borrows from the foregoing definition to define "domestic terrorism" as the foregoing acts occurring "primarily within the jurisdiction of the United States."

Under a third statute, the Secretary of State may designate an organization as a "terrorist organization" if it engages in "terrorist activity" threatening "the security of United States nationals or the national security of the United States." 8 U.S.C. §1189 (a)(1). A following provision, 8 U.S.C. §1189(a)(3), defines the "terrorist activity" which may preclude admission of an alien into the United States as:

(I) The hijacking or sabotage of any conveyance....

(II) The seizing or detaining, and threatening to kill, injure, or continue to detain, another individual in order to compel a third person including a governmental organization) to do or abstain from doing any act as an explicit or implicit condition for the release of the individual seized or detained.

(III) A violent attack upon an internationally protected person.

(IV) The use of any—

(a) biological agent, chemical agent, or nuclear weapon or device, or

(b) explosive, firearm, or other weapons or dangerous device (other than for mere personal monetary gain), with intent to endanger, directly or indirectly, the safety of one or more individuals or to cause substantial damage to property. ...

(VI) A threat, attempt, or conspiracy to do any of the foregoing.

A fourth statute, the Military Commissions Act of 2006, contains the following definition of "terrorism":

(24) TERRORISM.—Any person subject to this chapter who intentionally kills or inflicts great bodily harm on one or more protected persons, or intentionally engages in an act that evinces a wanton disregard for human life, in a manner calculated to influence or affect the conduct of government or civilian population by intimidation or coercion, or to retaliate against government conduct, shall be punished, if death results to one or more of the victims, by death or such other punishment as a military commission under this chapter may direct, and, if death does not result *** by such punishment, other than death, as a military commission *** may direct.

Notes and Problems

1. **Applications.** Under the above definitions, which of the following would be "terrorism" or "terrorist activity"?

a. Al Qaeda, to cause United States withdrawal of personnel from Muslim countries, attacked the *USS Cole* at port in Yemen.

b. Ted Kaczynski, a hermetic neo-luddite, promised to stop sending mail bombs if newspapers would print his manifesto on the decline of human freedom caused by modern technologies.

c. Washington, D.C. sniper John Allen Muhammad wanted to cover his tracks as a cover for killing his ex-wife. His accomplice, John Lee Malvo, wanted to help create a multiracial utopia. Both together sought $10,000,000 "ransom" to stop their attacks.

d. Gangs of narcotics traffickers murdered local officials, competing gang members, and innocent citizens on the streets in Tijuana, Mexico.

e. Suicide bombers with ethnic grievances and al Qaeda support killed Iraqi officials, US personnel, and innocent bystanders in Iraq.

2.   **Procedures.** Procedures differ considerably among these definitional frameworks. Criminal prosecutions involve trial and pretrial processes with the full range of constitutional protections including the right to counsel, the presumption of innocence, jury trial, *Miranda* warnings, proof beyond a reasonable doubt, *Brady* disclosure of the prosecution's evidence, etc. The Secretary of State exclusion of aliens requires far less process and proof, and there is considerable discretion in her designations of organizations as terrorist organizations. The Military Commissions Act of 2006 operates under procedures and presumptions that differ in some respects from those in federal criminal trials. For example, evidentiary rules are relaxed, there is no jury trial, coerced evidence may be admissible, and the defense may be denied access to certain evidence for national security reasons. Later portions of this book will explore these differences in greater detail.

3. Criminal Law and Prevention of Terrorism. Critics argue that criminal law focuses on punishment of "ordinary crime" rather than prevention of terrorism. Although the definitions above concern completed acts of violence, several traditional components of the criminal law focus on prevention. Consider the following crimes as they relate to terrorism:

- *Attempt.* Four individuals discuss plans to explode gas lines leading to Kennedy Airport, causing a major conflagration. They seek to locate the gas lines and obtain some materials they believe would explode if combined. The plotters are very stupid. They discuss their plans in a restaurant where a waiter overhears them and calls in the FBI, which arrests the four. Evidence later shows (1) that the materials, if combined, would not explode and (2) that, even if the materials exploded, the gas lines would not because of self-sealing devices in the lines preventing large amounts of gas being exposed to oxygen (a necessary element for a conflagration).

- *Conspiracy.* Jose Padilla joins al Qaeda, filling out a form and attending a training camp in Afghanistan where he is instructed on various techniques for killing and maiming as well as how to disguise his communications with other members of al Qaeda by speaking in code. There is no evidence showing that he conspires to participate in the September 11 attacks nor that he uses his al Qaeda connections and training to kill or maim United States citizens.

- *Incitement.* An Imam at a mosque in Rome, Georgia urges those who attend services to engage in "jihad" against the United States in opposition for US support for Israel and occupation of Iraq. He talks extensively of the rewards in heaven (many virgins and other treats) for those who "martyr" themselves in the course of jihad.

4. A Problem with Inchoate Crimes and Terrorism. What if a particular terrorist talks about violent acts but does not take substantial steps to operationalize attack plans? This issue arose in the prosecution of the Liberty City Seven, in which the defendants planned to bomb the Sears Tower and other buildings for al Qaeda. John Pistole, the deputy director of the FBI, said the defendants were "more aspirational than operational" with their plans. Two hung juries resulted from prosecuting the Liberty City Seven, and one defendant was acquitted. Finally, the government obtained convictions in a third trial.

5. Spitting on the Sidewalk. The FBI suspects that someone is preparing to engage in terrorist activity, but knows that it cannot prove its suspicions in civilian court, even using attempt, support, conspiracy, and incitement tools. Can the FBI selectively use minor infractions of the law to incapacitate terrorism suspects? In earlier times, the FBI successfully prosecuted mobster Al Capone on tax evasion charges, which were much easier to prove than charges for murder or conspiracy to murder, or other crimes. Former Attorney General John Ashcroft famously said he would arrest terrorist suspects for "spitting on the sidewalk" to put them out of commission before harm could be done to the American people. If a terrorist raises money through drug dealing, violates currency restrictions, immigration rules, or otherwise runs afoul of lesser laws, why not use the Capone approach today? What legal objections might a defendant have to being prosecuted for such non-terrorism offenses?

6. State Law. As you know, much criminal law is state law, and some states have enacted criminal antiterrorism statutes. For example, Virginia in 2002 provided the death penalty for killings committed with "the intent to intimidate or coerce a civilian population or influence the policy, conduct or activities of the government *** through intimidation or coercion." Going back to problem 1c above, who might be found guilty under this statute? Would every serial killer be a terrorist under the Virginia statute?

7. Murder, Terrorism, Both? In 1998, Mir Amal Kasi killed two CIA employees and wounded three others with a rifle while they were waiting in their cars to enter CIA headquarters in Langley, Virginia. Kasi managed to flee the scene, escaping to Pakistan and Afghanistan, where he evaded arrest for two years. The FBI found him in Pakistan and forcibly brought him back to the United States, where he was tried for murder and related crimes. A jury convicted Kasi and the judge sentenced him to death. On appeal, Kasi argued that the jury, which heard evidence of his opposition to US involvement in Muslim lands, prejudicially viewed him as a "terrorist." The Virginia Supreme Court in *Kasi v. Virginia*, 508 S.E. 2d 57 (Va. 1998). refused to allow Kasi to inquire into the jury deliberations. Here is another argument he made and the Virginia Supreme Court's response:

> The defendant says that because his crimes were "political," he somehow is entitled to First Amendment protection, and that his death sentence should be commuted to avoid possible violent acts of reprisal. As the [Virginia] Attorney General observes, defendant received the death sentence, not because he had a political motive, but because he murdered two innocent men, and maimed three others, in an extremely brutal and premeditated manner. *** There is nothing "arbitrary" about a death sentence imposed under the circumstances of this case and, thus, there is no basis for commutation.

Why was Kasi not prosecuted for "terrorism" under either federal or Virginia law? What is gained and what is lost? Incidentally, were Kasi's arguments consistent?

8. Political Use of the Label "Terrorist". On August 14, 2007, THE NEW YORK TIMES ran a front-page story with this lead line: "The Bush administration is preparing to declare that Iran's Revolutionary Guard Corps is a foreign terrorist organization." The Revolutionary Guard comprises the bulk of Iran's armed forces and is the base of Iran President Mahmoud Ahmadinejad's support. The usual reason for the designation is to make it unlawful for anyone subject to United States jurisdiction to provide material support to such an organization. However, it is not clear that the Revolutionary Guard receives any such support. What reasons might the administration have for making this designation?

2. PROVIDING MATERIAL SUPPORT

Most acts of terrorism can be and are prosecuted under ordinary criminal laws. A terrorist who kills someone is prosecuted for murder; one who blows up an empty building is prosecuted for arson or destruction of property. The problem with such statutes is that law enforcers do not want to wait for terrorists to strike. Prevention, rather than after-the-fact punishment, is highly desirable.

Some have criticized criminal law as oriented toward punishment rather than prevention, but that is not an entirely accurate criticism. One who prepares a murder or arson may be apprehended in advance of the act and charged with attempted murder or attempted arson. Agreements to engage in terrorism may be punished as conspiracies, and trying to get others to commit murder or arson can be punished as solicitation of those crimes.

It may be fairly argued, however, that terrorists seek to inflict more widespread damage on society than ordinary criminals and are more resistant to incentives provided by punishment compared to ordinary criminals. The law could account for these factors by pushing criminal punishment closer to the point at which an individual *considers* acts of terrorism even without acts that would satisfy attempt, solicitation, or conspiracy actus reus requirements. The law could also expand liability by punishing *association* rather than specific acts combined with certain mental states. How far has the law moved in these directions? Has it moved far enough to meet contemporary terrorism threats? Has it gone too far, perhaps intruding on free speech, freedom of association, and other values highly prized in the United States and other democracies?

A good starting point to search out answers to these questions is with two statutes that criminalize the provision of material support to terrorist activities and terrorist organizations. 18 USC §2339A (providing material support to aid terrorist offenses) and 18 U.S.C. § 2339B (providing material support to a foreign terrorist organization) have been more frequently used after 9/11 for prosecutions than other terrorist offenses. Unlike the statutes considered in the previous subsection of this chapter, these offenses do not themselves involve the use of violence as preparation for use of violence.

The material support statutes may also be used in the following situations:

- An American religious zealot makes himself available for service in an army that is fighting the United States.

- Six individuals participate in a terrorist group's training camp in Afghanistan.

- Another individual tries to set up a terrorist training camp within the United States.

- Individuals and a charitable entity are charged with transferring funds to a terrorist organization.

- An attorney representing a convicted terrorist serving a life sentence *** allegedly facilitates the passing of information and instructions to terrorist confederates of her client outside of the prison.

Norman Abrams, "The Material Support Terrorism Offenses: Perspectives Derived from the (Early) Model Penal Code," 1 J. NAT. SEC. L. & POLICY 5, at 9 (2005) (providing footnotes to cases). These provisions are innovative, as Professor Abrams Notes, because "Normally, ***[liability for preparation for crime] is derivative from a substantive offense and is not itself defined as a separate substantive crime, though it is, of course, a basis for making a person liable for the substantive offense."

Here are the provisions:

18 U.S.C. 2339A. Providing Material Support to Terrorists.

(a) Offense.--Whoever provides material support or resources or conceals or disguises the nature, location, source, or ownership of material support or resources, knowing or intending that they are to be used in preparation for, or in carrying out, a violation of or [various offenses] or in preparation for, or in carrying out, the concealment of an escape from the commission of any such violation, or attempts or conspires to do such an act, shall be fined under this title, imprisoned not more than 15 years, or both, and, if the death of any person results, shall be imprisoned for any term of years or for life. ***

(b) Definitions.--As used in this section--

(1) the term "material support or resources" means *any property, tangible or intangible, or service, including* currency or monetary instruments or financial securities, financial services, lodging, training, expert advice or assistance, safehouses, false documentation or identification, communications equipment, facilities, weapons, lethal substances, explosives, personnel *(1 or more individuals who may be or include oneself)*, and transportation, except medicine or religious materials;

(2) *the term "training" means instruction or teaching designed to impart a specific skill, as opposed to general knowledge; and*

(3) *the term "expert advice or assistance" means advice or assistance derived from scientific, technical or other specialized knowledge.*

18 U.S.C. §2339 B. Providing Material Support or Resources to Designated Foreign Terrorist Organizations.

(a) Prohibited activities.–

(1) Unlawful conduct.--Whoever knowingly provides material support or resources to a foreign terrorist organization, or attempts or conspires to do so, shall be fined under this title or imprisoned not more than 15 years, or both, and, if the death of any person results, shall be imprisoned for any term of years or for life. *To violate this paragraph, a person must have knowledge that the organization is a designated terrorist organization (as defined in subsection (g)(6)), that the organization has engaged or engages in terrorist activity (as defined in section 212(a)(3)(B) of the Immigration and Nationality Act), or that the organization has engaged or engages in terrorism (as defined in section 140(d) (2) of the Foreign Relations Authorization Act, Fiscal Years 1988 and 1989).* ***

(g) Definitions.--As used in this section-- ***

(4) the term "material support or resources" has the same meaning given that term in section 2339A (including the definitions of "training" and "expert advice or assistance" in that section); ***

(h) Provision of personnel.--*No person may be prosecuted under this section in connection with the term "personnel" unless that person has knowingly provided, attempted to provide, or conspired to provide a* *foreign terrorist organization with 1 or more individuals (who may be or include himself) to work under that terrorist organization's direction or control or to organize, manage, supervise, or otherwise direct the operation of that organization. Individuals who act entirely independently of the foreign terrorist organization to advance its goals or objectives shall not be considered to be working under the foreign terrorist organization's direction and control.*

(i) Rule of construction.--Nothing in this section shall be construed or applied so as to abridge the exercise of rights guaranteed under the First Amendment to the Constitution of the United States.

(j) Exception.--No person may be prosecuted under this section in connection with the term "personnel", "training", or "expert advice or assistance" if the provision of that material support or resources to a foreign terrorist organization was approved by the Secretary of State with the concurrence of the Attorney General. ***

What differences do you see between the focus of these two statutes? What are the elements of each offense? Which statute is broader?

Two cases concerning material support follow. The first provides an overview of some ways in which material support statutes work in conjunction with other national security laws. The second explores the constitutionality of criminalizing material support for terrorism.

UNITED STATES v. ABU-JIHAAD
600 F. Supp. 2d 362 (D. Conn. 2009)

MARK R. KRAVITZ, District Judge.

Following a six-day trial in March 2008, a jury convicted Defendant Hassan Abu-Jihaad on two charges: (1) disclosing national defense information to those not entitled to receive it in violation of 18 U.S.C. § 793(d); and (2) providing material support to terrorists in violation of 18 U.S.C. § 2339A ***. The Government alleged that in 2001, while Mr. Abu-Jihaad was serving as a U.S. Navy Signalman aboard the destroyer, the *U.S.S. Benfold,* he disclosed classified information regarding the movement of the Fifth Fleet Battle Group, which included the aircraft carrier, the *U.S.S. Constellation,* to individuals in London associated with Azzam Publications, an organization that the Government alleged supported violent Islamic jihad. According to the Government, Mr. Abu-Jihaad knew or intended that the information he disclosed would be used to kill United States nationals. By its verdict, the jury agreed with the Government's assertions. *** [T[he central issue *** is whether the evidence *** would permit a rational jury to find Mr. Abu-Jihaad guilty of both charges beyond a reasonable doubt *** [T]he Court believes that the evidence was sufficient to support a jury verdict beyond a reasonable doubt that Mr. Abu-Jihaad disclosed classified information. However, *** the Court concludes that Mr. Abu-Jihaad's conviction on the material support charge should be set aside. ***

[National defense information] *** [T]o be found guilty of disclosing

national defense information to those not entitled to receive it in violation of 18 U.S.C. § 793(d), the Government was required to prove the following essential elements:

(1) *First,* that Mr. Abu-Jihaad lawfully had possession of, access to, control over, or was entrusted with information relating to the national defense.

(2) *Second,* that Mr. Abu-Jihaad had reason to believe that such information could be used to the injury of the United States or to the advantage of any foreign nation.

(3) *Third,* that Mr. Abu-Jihaad willfully communicated, delivered, transmitted or caused to be communicated, delivered, or transmitted such information.

(4) *Fourth,* that Mr. Abu-Jihaad did so to a person not entitled to receive it.

*** Mr. Abu-Jihaad mounts essentially two main challenges to the jury's verdict on 18 U.S.C. § 793(d). First, he contends that while he may have had access to the confidential information in the *Constellation* battlegroup's Transit Plan, the information in the Battlegroup Document itself does not relate to the national defense and was not "closely held," as that term is used in relevant case law and this Court's instructions to the jury. Second, he argues that the evidence was insufficient to permit a rational juror to conclude beyond a reasonable doubt that he communicated national defense information to a person not entitled to receive it.

1. Closely Held National Defense Information. Mr. Abu-Jihaad's argument regarding the "national defense" element of this offense is that much of the information in the Battlegroup Document is flat wrong and/or was commonly known and therefore the information in the Battlegroup Document could not possibly relate to our national defense. The Government rejoins that there are three specific pieces of information in the Battlegroup Document that the Government contends do relate to national defense and were closely held as of the date the Battlegroup Document was apparently created:

* The fact that vessels would stop in Hawaii on March 20, 2001 to load ammunition;

* The fact that the battlegroup would deploy from San Diego on March 15 and the *Constellation* would be in Sydney, Australia on April 6, 2001; and

* The fact that the battlegroup would transit the Strait of Hormuz at night on April 29, 2001.

The Court agrees with the Government that a rational jury was entitled to conclude beyond a reasonable doubt that each of these pieces of information constituted closely held national defense information at the time the Battlegroup Document was created.

The phrase "information relating to the national defense" is not defined in 18 U.S.C. § 793(d). Nonetheless, courts have uniformly held-and this Court instructed the jury-that "national defense" is a "generic concept of broad connotations, referring to the military and naval establishments and the related activities of national preparedness." *** Given the breadth of the phrase "information relating to the national defense," a rational jury could conclude beyond a reasonable doubt that the particular information noted above qualifies as national defense information. *** To be sure, completely inaccurate information regarding the battlegroup may well not relate to the national defense. However, the date on which the *Benfold* would arrive in Hawaii to load ammunition was accurate, as was the date the battlegroup would deploy from San Diego and the date on which the *Constellation* would be in Sydney. The Battlegroup Document was wrong about the date for transiting the Strait of Hormuz-it was not the evening of April 29 but rather was the evening of May 2 (with a transit of additional vessels in the battlegroup on May 3). Nonetheless, given the proximity of the dates, Admiral Hart testified that he would still have been concerned if enemies of the United States knew that information. As described, the Strait of Hormuz is a choke point where U.S. Navy vessels are particularly vulnerable to attack. ***

Though the phrase "information relating to the national defense" is quite broad, it is cabined by two limitations, one judge-made and the other statutory. First, the information must be "closely held." *** Mr. Abu-Jihaad argues based on Ms. Raskin's testimony that there was so much information about the battlegroup-its schedule and its itinerary-that was publicly available that the information in the Battlegroup Document was not closely held. However, viewing the evidence in the light most favorable to the Government, the Court believes that a rational jury could conclude beyond a reasonable doubt that the above-noted three pieces of information were closely held by the Government. *** A second limitation [is that]the statute requires that the individual who discloses national defense information have "reason to believe [the information] could be used to the injury of the United States or to the advantage of any foreign nation...." *** The structure and text of the Battlegroup Document, which focuses on vulnerabilities and weaknesses, only confirm that the information in the document is intended to injure the United States. Furthermore, the evidence presented permitted the jury to conclude beyond a reasonable doubt that Azzam was a conduit of information to violent Islamic jihadi groups. In view of what happened to the *Cole,* it is abundantly clear that advance knowledge of key battlegroup dates by Islamic jihadi groups would be injurious to U.S. interests.

2. Disclosure by Mr. Abu-Jihaad. This brings us to the core issue in the case, both before the jury and now with this Court-was there evidence presented that would permit a rational jury to conclude beyond a reasonable doubt that Mr. Abu-Jihaad was the source of the national defense information contained in the Battlegroup Document. This is not an easy issue because, very frankly, there is evidence pointing in both directions. *** The Court concludes that when all of the reasonable inferences are accumulated in the light most favorable to the Government and the evidence is viewed in its totality, there was sufficient evidence to support the jury's finding that Mr. Abu-Jihaad supplied the key national defense information in the Battlegroup Document ***

[Providing material support to terrorists] Mr. Abu-Jihaad was also convicted of providing material support to terrorists in violation of 18 U.S.C. § 2339A and § 2. Section 2339A makes it a crime to provide "material support or resources ... knowing or intending that they are to be used in preparation for, or in carrying out, a violation" of certain enumerated statutes. "Material support or resources" are defined as follows: "currency or other financial securities, financial services, lodging, training, safehouses, false documentation or identification, communications equipment, facilities, weapons, lethal substances, explosives, *personnel,* transportation, *and other physical assets,* except medicine or religious materials." Mr. Abu-Jihaad was charged with providing "personnel" and "physical assets," knowing or intending that such support would be used in preparation for, or in carrying out, a violation of 18 U.S.C. § 2332(b)-that is, a plan to kill United States nationals.

The jury was asked to answer a special interrogatory regarding the material support element of the charge. Specifically, the jury was asked whether it found unanimously that the Government had proved beyond a reasonable doubt that Mr. Abu-Jihaad provided material support in the form of: (a) personnel, or (b) physical assets. The jury answered each interrogatory in the affirmative. Therefore, the Court will assess the evidence offered on each ground.

1. Physical Assets. The Government did not at trial, and does not claim here, that Mr. Abu-Jihaad's provision of national defense information to Azzam was a "physical asset" within the meaning of 18 U.S.C. § 2339A, or that Mr. Abu-Jihaad created the diskette containing the Battlegroup Document. Instead, the Government argued that "by providing ... the information that [would end up] in the Microsoft Word document on that floppy disk, [Mr. Abu-Jihaad] essentially set in motion the steps that caused that floppy disk to be created by Ahsan and given to Ahmad." *** According to the Government, it was "reasonably foreseeable" to Mr. Abu-Jihaad that whomever he provided information to would commit it to a physical asset such as a floppy disk.

Taking the evidence in the light most favorable to the Government and fully cognizant of the deference owed to the jury, the Court does not believe that a rational juror could conclude beyond a reasonable doubt that Mr. Abu-Jihaad provided material support to Azzam in the form of a physical asset. The Court says this for two principal reasons.

First and foremost, there was no evidence whatsoever regarding how Mr. Abu-Jihaad transmitted national defense information to Azzam, what was said when the information was provided, or how he expected Azzam would distribute or transmit the information he provided. Consequently, there was no evidence that would suggest that Mr. Abu-Jihaad knew the information he provided would be transcribed into a Microsoft Word document and copied onto a floppy disk, let alone that he "caused" the information to be placed on a floppy disk. What we do know from the evidence is that the Battlegroup Document ended with these words: "**Please destroy message.**" Those words are hardly consistent with someone who intends to cause the information to be put into a computer file that would be copied onto a floppy disk and then distributed. Indeed, Mr. Ahsan did precisely the opposite of what he had been told to do. He was told to destroy the message and instead he typed it out and then copied it onto a diskette to deliver it to Mr. Ahmad. ***

Second, the Government's emphasis on what was supposedly "reasonably foreseeable" to Mr. Abu-Jihaad does not comport with the requirements of 18 U.S.C. § 2(b). *** Therefore, "to establish a conviction through the use of section 2(b), the government must prove that the defendant had the mental state necessary to violate the underlying criminal statute and that the defendant '*wilfully caused*' another to commit the necessary act." Here, there was no evidence from which a rational jury could conclude beyond a reasonable doubt that Mr. Abu-Jihaad *willfully caused* Mr. Ahsan to violate § 2339A by copying the Battlegroup Document onto a floppy disk. Indeed, there is no evidence that Mr. Abu-Jihaad even knew that Mr. Ahsan would place the information Mr. Abu-Jihaad provided Azzam into a Microsoft Word document or copy that document on to a floppy disk. In sum, knowing that Azzam was a conduit of information to violent Islamic groups (a conclusion the jury was entirely justified in drawing) is quite a different thing from concluding that Mr. Abu-Jihaad willfully caused Mr. Ahsan to create a Microsoft Word document and then copy it onto a diskette. Accordingly, the Court grants Mr. Abu-Jihaad's motion for a judgment of acquittal insofar as he was convicted of providing physical assets to terrorists in violation of 18 U.S.C. § 2339A and § 2(b).

2. Personnel. As to "personnel," the Government argued to the jury-and the jury accepted-that by providing national defense information to Azzam, Mr. Abu-Jihaad had provided himself as "personnel." Mr. Abu-Jihaad's conviction for providing personnel presents a much closer question than the conviction for providing physical assets. ***

Section 2339A was enacted in 1994 as part of the Violent Crime Control and Law Enforcement Act. In 1996, Congress added § 2339B as a part of the Antiterrorism and Effective Death Penalty Act. As amended, § 2339B makes it unlawful to "provide[ ] material support or resources to a foreign terrorist organization, or attempt[ ] or conspire[ ] to do so...." 18 U.S.C. § 2339B(a)(1). Congress applied the § 2339A definition of "material support and resources" to § 2339B. *** [12] The term "personnel" remained undefined for the purposes of both sections.

---

[12] The term "material support or resources" was originally defined as constituting:

> currency or other financial securities, financial services, lodging, training, safehouses, false documentation or identification, communications equipment, facilities, weapons, lethal substances, explosives, personnel, transportation, and other physical assets, but does not include humanitarian assistance to persons not directly involved in such violations.

In 1996, Congress amended the definition of "material support or resources" to replace the phrase "but does not include humanitarian assistance to persons not directly involved in such violations" with the phrase "except medicine or religious materials."

The definition of "material support and resources" was amended in 2001 pursuant to the USA PATRIOT Act, [13] and again in December 2004, pursuant to the Intelligence Reform and Terrorism Prevention Act ("IRTPA"). The IRTPA defined "expert advice or assistance" to mean "advice or assistance derived from scientific, technical, or other specified knowledge." It also defined "training" as "instruction or teaching designed to impart a specific skill, as opposed to general knowledge." These definitions were added to § 2339A and, accordingly, applied to both §§ 2339A and 2339B.

In addition, the IRTPA made several changes to the term "personnel." First, the IRTPA changed "personnel" in § 2339A to "personnel (1 or more individuals who may be or include oneself)." This change was added to clarify that a person can provide himself as personnel. Second, the IRTPA added a definition of "personnel" to § 2339B:

> No person may be prosecuted under this section in connection with the term "personnel" unless that person has knowingly provided, attempted to provide, or conspired to provide a foreign terrorist organization with 1 or more individuals (who may be or include himself) to work under that terrorist organization's direction or control or to organize, manage, supervise, or otherwise direct the operation of that organization. Individuals who act entirely independently of the foreign terrorist organization to advance its goals or objectives shall not be considered to be working under the foreign terrorist organization's direction and control.

*** [14] Unlike the other changes made by IRTPA to the definition of "material support and resources," this detailed definition of "personnel" was added to § 2339B and not to § 2339A.

Notably, all of the legislative history states that the new language added to § 2339B in 2004 was only a *clarification* of the definition of personnel and not a substantive change.

These changes to § 2339B were enacted against a backdrop of numerous legal challenges to that provision on the ground of vagueness. Central among those legal challenges was a case brought by the Humanitarian Law Project in the Ninth Circuit [which] found that this overly-broad definition violated the First Amendment in the context of § 2339B because it encompassed pure speech, including conduct as benign as handing out pamphlets.[16]

Other courts, however, interpreted the pre-2004 definition of "personnel" differently. For instance, in *United States v. Lindh,* 212 F.Supp.2d 541 (E.D.Va.2002), the district court concluded that:

---

[13] The definition of "material support or resources" was amended to include "monetary instruments" and "expert advice or assistance."

[14] The IRTPA also clarified the degree of knowledge required to violate § 2339B as follows: "To violate [§ 2339B(a)(1)], a person must have knowledge that the organization is a designated terrorist organization ... that the organization has engaged or engages in terrorist activity ... or that the organization has engaged or engages in terrorism."

[16] Following the amendments to § 2339B in the IRTPA, most courts have rejected overbreadth and vagueness challenges to that provision. ***.

providing "personnel" to HUM or al Qaeda necessarily means that the persons provided to the foreign terrorist organization work under the direction and control of that organization. One who is merely present with other members of the organization, but is not under the organization's direction and control, is not part of the organization's "personnel." ... Simply put, the term "personnel" does not extend to independent actors. Rather, it describes employees or employee-like operatives who serve the designated group and work at its command or ... who provide themselves to serve the organization.

In *United States v. Sattar,* 314 F.Supp.2d 279 (S.D.N.Y.2004), Judge John G. Koeltl of the Southern District of New York attempted to find a middle ground between the expansive definition of "personnel" in the *Humanitarian Law Project* cases and the narrow definition in *Lindh.* *** [T]he court concluded that a lawyer who had acted in concert with others to make a coconspirator available was guilty of providing "personnel," regardless of the fact that she was not acting as an employee or quasi-employee of the terrorist organization.

All of these cases were decided before Congress added the more detailed definition of "personnel" to § 2339B. Thus, as an initial matter, the Court must decide whether the amended definition of "personnel" in § 2339B applies to § 2339A as well, for even the Government concedes that if the amended definition in § 2339B applies to § 2339A, the evidence is wanting. Though the legislative history describes the definition of "personnel" in § 2339B as a mere clarification, the fact that Congress chose not to apply the more detailed definition to § 2339A causes the Court to believe that the definition Congress provided for § 2339B should not apply to § 2339A. The Court must presume that Congress was aware that the definition of "personnel" was relevant to both sections, but chose to include the more detailed definition in one section and not the other. This presumption is even stronger because Congress changed the definition of "personnel" in § 2339A by adding "1 or more individuals who may be or include oneself" at the same time it added the more detailed definition of "personnel" to § 2339B. Nor is there any indication in the legislative history that Congress intended the § 2339B definition to apply to § 2339A.

Therefore, the Court is left with the language of § 2339A, which does not define either the word "provide" or "personnel." *** Ordinarily, the term "provide" means to make available, to furnish, and to arrange for, supply, or transfer, *see* Random House Webster's Unabridged Dictionary (2001), and that is what the Court told the jury (without objection). ***

Likewise, the term "personnel" is also not defined in § 2339A. The plain meaning of that term includes "a body of persons *employed by or active* in an organization, service or place of work." In the context of § 2339A, it seems apparent that the term refers to those individuals who are provided or made available to prepare for or carry out the crimes prohibited by the statute. The individual need not be an "employee" or "quasi-employee," but there must be some form of coordination, joint action, or understanding. Entirely independent action is not sufficient to qualify as being at least "active in" an organization as required by the definition of personnel. Therefore, one who makes resources in the form of individuals (including himself) available, or furnishes individuals (including himself), for the purpose of actively preparing for or carrying out the crimes prohibited by the statute through some form of coordinated action is guilty of violating § 2339A. *See, e.g., United States v. Marzook,* 383 F.Supp.2d 1056, 1064 (N.D.Ill.2005) (holding that the term "personnel" includes recruiting others to join Hamas).

In sum, the Court is inclined to agree with the definition of "personnel" embraced by Judge Koeltl in *Sattar* and to reject the more narrow definition of "personnel" adopted in *Lindh.* The Court in *Lindh* did not provide a clear standard for determining who should be considered "employees" or "quasi-employees," except to say that Lindh's conduct clearly fell within the statute. Furthermore, this Court's interpretation of the plain meaning of the term "personnel" does not support such a limited definition.[17] And although the Court is cognizant of the fact that Congress amended § 2339B in part because of the Ninth Circuit's expansive definition of "personnel" ***, the Court does not believe that the *** expansive definition is consistent with the plain meaning of phrase "providing ... personnel."

*** The difficulty of applying that definition to the facts of this case arises from the Government's theory of guilt, which was that by disclosing national defense information to Azzam, Mr. Abu-Jihaad was, in effect, making himself available to terrorists for the purpose of killing U.S. nationals. That is, by providing information alone to Azzam-an act that was not directly prohibited by § 2339A-Mr. Abu-Jihaad provided personnel-that is, Mr. Abu-Jihaad himself-to Azzam, knowing that he or his assistance would be used to prepare for, or carry out, the killing of U.S. nationals.

That theory of guilt puts a strain on the language of the statute. For if the Government's argument were accepted, an individual who provided a terrorist organization with, say, weapons-perhaps by selling them at market price-would also be deemed to have provided the organization with personnel-namely, the gun dealer himself. Of course, one can imagine situations where an individual makes both himself and others available to terrorist organizations and also provides the organizations with weapons, money, or other tangible resources. But that is not invariably the case. That is, merely providing an organization with a resource, even a prohibited resource, is not necessarily the same thing as providing personnel to prepare for or carry out the prohibited purposes of the statute through some form of coordinated or joint action. For if that were the case, then much of the definition of "material support or resources" would be entirely redundant; providing weapons, explosives, or anything else on the list would also automatically constitute the provision of personnel as well.

To be sure, context and facts matter. Yet, it is context and facts that are entirely missing in this case. For we do not know how Mr. Abu-Jihaad conveyed the defense information to Azzam or what arrangements, if any, they had with each other. It could well be that Mr. Abu-Jihaad asked Azzam how he could help in supporting jihad, they told him to send defense information about the movements of the battlegroup so terrorists could attack the battlegroup, and Mr. Abu-Jihaad did as requested. In those circumstances, the Court would have little difficulty concluding that Mr. Abu-Jihaad had volunteered himself as personnel, acting in coordination with Azzam to kill U.S. nationals. On the other hand, perhaps Mr. Abu-Jihaad on a whim simply sent defense information to Azzam on one occasion, not knowing if Azzam wanted it and without any pre-disclosure or post-disclosure communication with Azzam about the information. In those circumstances, he surely provided defense information to someone not entitled to receive it, as the Court has previously found, but it would be linguistically odd to describe that lone, voluntary act as making personnel available to Azzam. *** [T]his theory of the evidence is at least equally plausible as the Government's theory of guilt.

The Government recognizes this gap in the evidence and seeks to get around it by pointing to a general request by Azzam to its readership in November 2000, in which it sought aid for the Taliban by requesting money, gas masks, or battlefield medical services. Of course, Azzam also exhorted its readers to assist in violent jihad. But to build a *quid pro quo* or understanding from these generalized requests for assistance is more than the evidence will bear, even taking all reasonable inferences in the light most favorable to the Government. In short, the evidence showed beyond a reasonable doubt that Mr. Abu-Jihaad provided classified defense information to Azzam. He may also have made himself available to assist Azzam in violent jihad. However, we simply do not know that from the evidence presented, even viewing the evidence in the light most favorable to the Government. Therefore, the Court will grant the Motion for Judgment of Acquittal on the material support charge under 18 U.S.C. § 2339A. ***

Notes

1. Antiterrorism and National Security. *Abu-Jihaad* puts antiterrorism law in the context of the broader national security concern of keeping sensitive information out of the hands of those not authorized to possess that information. What is the mens rea of the crime of disclosing national defense information? The actus reus? Could Julian Assange, the Australian responsible for posting vast troves of confidential government documents on his Wikileaks website in late 2010, be prosecuted under the statute that ensnared Abu-Jihaad? Would this be a good statute to use in prosecuting Pfc. Bradley Manning, the member of the U.S. armed forces who allegedly provided the documents to Assange on a disk labeled "Lady Gaga"?

2. Standard for conviction. Was Abu-Jihaad convicted by the jury under the traditional "guilty beyond a reasonable doubt" standard? Is this standard consistent with the Court's discussion of evidence concerning both guilt and innocence? With the witnesses against Abu-Jihaad, is the jury more or less likely to convict than in an ordinary criminal case?

3. Irony in Abu-Jihaad? The "material support" statutes have been criticized as being too broad, but this case seems to show that in some ways these statutes are narrower than other national security statutes (or at least the Espionage Statute).

4. Other National Security Crimes.

a. Treason, the original national security crime and the only specific crime mentioned in the Constitution, carries the death penalty but is difficult to prove. In addition, noncitizens cannot commit treason for they have not broken faith with their homeland. Is terrorism committed by a citizen necessarily treason? What terrorist acts would be treasonous and which not?

b. The War Crimes Act, 18 U.S.C. §2441, allows for the death penalty when the actions of US nationals or members of the US armed forces are involved. This statute does not apply to non-citizens. Should terrorism ever be a "war crime"?

5. Loophole in the Material Support Statutes? The foregoing statutes focus on *providing* material support including military-style training. What should the law do about one who *receives* such training rather than helping provide it? In 2004, a new section, 2339D, was added to the material support statutes. 2339D makes it a crime to "knowingly receive military-type training from or on behalf of" any designated foreign terrorist organization. If one receives such training other than from a designated organization, cannot be linked with terrorist co-conspirators, and cannot be linked to any violent act, yet the FBI believes the person shows a "credible threat of committing a terrorist act in the future," there is no criminal statute that applies to him. Should the law be revised in light of this "loophole?" See Robert M. Chesney, "Optimizing Criminal Prosecution as a Counterterrorism Tool," in Benjamin Wittes, LEGISLATING THE WAR ON TERROR (Brookings Institution Press, 2009), pp. 110-114. Professor Chesney describes the case of Hamid Hayat, who confessed to receiving such training and planning attacks on various civilian buildings, including stores. Because the confession showed clear intent to engage in terrorism, the government ultimately prevailed by arguing under the earlier statutes that Hayat had provided himself as "personnel" for terrorist acts. If an individual confesses to being a "member" of al Qaeda but to nothing more, can that membership alone be similarly prosecuted?

6. Ex Post Facto and Material Support. The material support statutes would seem on their face to apply to Guantanamo Bay detainees who were trained by al Qaeda and materially supported al Qaeda and the Taliban against coalition forces. Sections 2339 A and B, however, applied until late 2001 only to conduct "in the United States," thus leaving out those whose support preceded the effective date of that change in the law.

7. Comparative Approaches to Early Apprehension and Threat Management. Compare the following statute, the UK Terrorism Act of 2006, to the approach of United States law in §§ 2339 A and 2339B. Would this statute meet US constitutional standards? Would it be a useful tool for law enforcement if constitutional?

1. Encouragement of terrorism

(1) This section applies to a statement that is likely to be understood by some or all of the members of the public to whom it is published as a direct or indirect encouragement or other inducement to them to the commission, preparation or instigation of acts of terrorism *** .

(2) A person commits an offence if—

(a) he publishes a statement to which this section applies or causes anotherto publish such a statement; and

(b) at the time he publishes it or causes it to be published, he—

(i) intends members of the public to be directly or indirectly encouraged or otherwise induced by the statement to commit, prepare or instigate acts of terrorism ***; or

(ii) is reckless as to whether members of the public will be directly or indirectly encouraged or otherwise induced by the statement to commit, prepare or instigate such acts or offences.

(3) For the purposes of this section, the statements that are likely to be understood by members of the public as indirectly encouraging the commission or preparation of acts of terrorism *** include every statement which—

(a) glorifies the commission or preparation (whether in the past, in the future or generally) of such acts or offences; and

(b) is a statement from which those members of the public could reasonably be expected to infer that what is being glorified is being glorified as conduct that should be emulated by them in existing circumstances.

(4) For the purposes of this section the questions how a statement is likely to be understood and what members of the public could reasonably be expected to infer from it must be determined having regard both—

(a) to the contents of the statement as a whole; and

(b) to the circumstances and manner of its publication.

(5) It is irrelevant for the purposes of subsections (1) to (3)—

(a) whether anything mentioned in those subsections relates to the commission, preparation or instigation of one or more particular acts of terrorism or Convention offences, of acts of terrorism *** of a particular description or of acts of terrorism *** generally; and,

(b) whether any person is in fact encouraged or induced by the statement to commit, prepare or instigate any such act or offence.

(6) In proceedings for an offence under this section against a person in whose case it is not proved that he intended the statement directly or indirectly to encourage or otherwise induce the commission, preparation or instigation of acts of terrorism *** , it is a defence for him to show—

(a) that the statement neither expressed his views nor had his endorsement ***; and

(b) that it was clear, in all the circumstances of the statement's publication, that it did not express his views and (apart from the possibility of his having been given and failed to comply with a notice under subsection (3) of that section) did not have his endorsement. ***

HOLDER v. HUMANITARIAN LAW PROJECT
130 S.Ct. 2705 (2010)

CHIEF JUSTICE ROBERTS delivered the opinion of the Court.

Congress has prohibited the provision of "material support or resources" to certain foreign organizations that engage in terrorist activity. That prohibition is based on a finding that the specified organizations "are so tainted by their criminal conduct that any contribution to such an organization facilitates that conduct." The plaintiffs in this litigation seek to provide support to two such organizations. Plaintiffs claim that they seek to facilitate only the lawful, nonviolent purposes of those groups, and that *** the statute is too vague, in violation of the Fifth Amendment, and that it infringes their rights to freedom of speech and association, in violation of the First Amendment. We conclude that the material-support statute is constitutional as applied to the particular activities plaintiffs have told us they wish to pursue. We do not, however, address the resolution of more difficult cases that may arise under the statute in the future.

This litigation concerns 18 U.S.C. § 2339B, which makes it a federal crime to "knowingly provid[e] material support or resources to a foreign terrorist organization." Congress has amended the definition of "material support or resources" periodically, but at present it is defined as follows:

> "[T]he term 'material support or resources' means any property, tangible or intangible, or service, including currency or monetary instruments or financial securities, financial services, lodging, training, expert advice or assistance, safehouses, false documentation or identification, communications equipment, facilities, weapons, lethal substances, explosives, personnel (1 or more individuals who may be or include oneself), and transportation, except medicine or religious materials." § 2339A(b)(1).

The authority to designate an entity a "foreign terrorist organization" rests with the Secretary of State. She may, in consultation with the Secretary of the Treasury and the Attorney General, so designate an organization upon finding that it is foreign, engages in "terrorist activity" or "terrorism," and thereby "threatens the security of United States nationals or the national security of the United States." *** An entity designated a foreign terrorist organization may seek review of that designation before the D.C. Circuit within 30 days of that designation. *** In 1997, the Secretary of State designated 30 groups as foreign terrorist organizations. Two of those groups are the Kurdistan Workers' Party (also known as the Partiya Karkeran Kurdistan, or PKK) and the Liberation Tigers of Tamil Eelam (LTTE). The PKK is an organization founded in 1974 with the aim of establishing an independent Kurdish state in southeastern Turkey. The LTTE is an organization founded in 1976 for the purpose of creating an independent Tamil state in Sri Lanka. The District Court in this action found that the PKK and the LTTE engage in political and humanitarian activities. The Government has presented evidence that both groups have also committed numerous terrorist attacks, some of which have harmed American citizens. ***

In [the Intelligence Reform and Terrorism Prevention Act of 2004] IRTPA, Congress clarified the mental state necessary to violate § 2339B, requiring knowledge of the foreign group's designation as a terrorist organization or the group's commission of terrorist acts. Congress also added the term "service" to the definition of "material support or resources," and defined "training" to mean "instruction or teaching designed to impart a specific skill, as opposed to general knowledge," It also defined "expert advice or assistance" to mean "advice or assistance derived from scientific, technical or other specialized knowledge." Finally, IRTPA clarified the scope of the term "personnel" by providing:

> "No person may be prosecuted under [§ 2339B] in connection with the term 'personnel' unless that person has knowingly provided, attempted to provide, or conspired to provide a foreign terrorist organization with 1 or more individuals (who may be or include himself) to work under that terrorist organization's direction or control or to organize, manage, supervise, or otherwise direct the operation of that organization. Individuals who act entirely independently of the foreign terrorist organization to advance its goals or objectives shall not be considered to be working under the foreign terrorist organization's direction and control." ***

*** [Plaintiffs] raise three constitutional claims. First, plaintiffs claim that § 2339B violates the Due Process Clause of the Fifth Amendment because these *** statutory terms are impermissibly vague. Second, plaintiffs claim that § 2339B violates their freedom of speech under the First Amendment. Third, plaintiffs claim that § 2339B violates their First Amendment freedom of association.

Plaintiffs *** claim that § 2339B is invalid to the extent it prohibits them from engaging in certain specified activities. *** [T]hose activities are: (1) "train[ing] members of [the] PKK on how to use humanitarian and international law to peacefully resolve disputes"; (2) "engag[ing] in political advocacy on behalf of Kurds who live in Turkey"; and (3) "teach[ing] PKK members how to petition various representative bodies such as the United Nations for relief." ***[4] "train[ing] members of [the] LTTE to present claims for tsunami-related aid to mediators and international bodies"; *** [5] "offer[ing] their legal expertise in negotiating peace agreements between the LTTE and the Sri Lankan government"; and *** [6] "engag[ing] in political advocacy on behalf of Tamils who live in Sri Lanka." *** Plaintiffs seek preenforcement review of a criminal statute [and have standing because they] face "a credible threat of prosecution" and "should not be required to await and undergo a criminal prosecution ***." ***

Plaintiffs claim *** that we should interpret the material-support statute, when applied to speech, to require proof that a defendant intended to further a foreign terrorist organization's illegal activities. That interpretation, they say, would end the litigation because plaintiffs' proposed activities consist of speech, but plaintiffs do not intend to further unlawful conduct by the PKK or the LTTE. *** We reject plaintiffs' interpretation of § 2339B because it is inconsistent with the text of the statute. Section 2339B(a)(1) prohibits "knowingly" providing material support. It then specifically describes the type of knowledge that is required: "To violate this paragraph, a person must have knowledge that the organization is a designated terrorist organization ..., that the organization has engaged or engages in terrorist activity ..., or that the organization has engaged or engages in terrorism...." Congress plainly *** chose knowledge about the organization's connection to terrorism, not specific intent to further the organization's terrorist activities. Plaintiffs' interpretation is also untenable in light of the sections immediately surrounding § 2339B, both of which do refer to intent to further terrorist activity. *** [P]laintiffs *** argue that a specific intent requirement should apply only when the material-support statute applies to speech. There is no basis whatever *** to read the same provisions in that statute as requiring intent in some circumstances but not others. It is therefore clear that plaintiffs are asking us not to interpret § 2339B, but to revise it. ***

We turn to the question whether the material-support statute, as applied to plaintiffs, is impermissibly vague under the Due Process Clause of the Fifth Amendment. "A conviction fails to comport with due process if the statute under which it is obtained fails to provide a person of ordinary intelligence fair notice of what is prohibited, or is so standardless that it authorizes or encourages seriously discriminatory enforcement." We consider whether a statute is vague as applied to the particular facts at issue, for "[a] plaintiff who engages in some conduct that is clearly proscribed cannot complain of the vagueness of the law as applied to the conduct of others." We have said that when a statute "interferes with the right of free speech or of association, a more stringent vagueness test should apply." "But 'perfect clarity and precise guidance have never been required even of regulations that restrict expressive activity.' " *** Plaintiffs do not argue that the material-support statute grants too much enforcement discretion to the Government. We therefore address only whether the statute "provide[s] a person of ordinary intelligence fair notice of what is prohibited."

As a general matter, the statutory terms at issue here are quite different from the sorts of terms that we have previously declared to be vague. We have in the past "struck down statutes that tied criminal culpability to whether the Defendant's conduct was 'annoying' or 'indecent'-wholly subjective judgments without statutory definitions, narrowing context, or settled legal meanings." *** Applying the statutory terms in this action- "training," "expert advice or assistance," "service," and "personnel"-does not require similarly untethered, subjective judgments.

Congress also took care to add narrowing definitions to the material-support statute over time. These definitions increased the clarity of the statute's terms. *** And the knowledge requirement of the statute further reduces any potential for vagueness ***. Of course, the scope of the material-support statute may not be clear in every application. But the dispositive point here is that the statutory terms are clear in their application to plaintiffs' proposed conduct, which means that plaintiffs' vagueness challenge must fail. Even assuming that a heightened standard applies because the material-support statute potentially implicates speech, the statutory terms are not vague as applied to plaintiffs. ***

Most of the activities in which plaintiffs seek to engage readily fall within the scope of the terms "training" and "expert advice or assistance." Plaintiffs want to "train members of [the] PKK on how to use humanitarian and international law to peacefully resolve disputes," and "teach PKK members how to petition various representative bodies such as the United Nations for relief." A person of ordinary intelligence would understand that instruction on resolving disputes through international law falls within the statute's definition of "training" because it imparts a "specific skill," not "general knowledge."

Plaintiffs' activities also fall comfortably within the scope of "expert advice or assistance": A reasonable person would recognize that teaching the PKK how to petition for humanitarian relief before the United Nations involves advice derived from, as the statute puts it, "specialized knowledge." In fact, plaintiffs themselves have repeatedly used the terms "training" and "expert advice" throughout this litigation to describe their own proposed activities, demonstrating that these common terms readily and naturally cover plaintiffs' conduct. ***

Plaintiffs also contend that they want to engage in "political advocacy" on behalf of Kurds living in Turkey and Tamils living in Sri Lanka. They are concerned that such advocacy might be regarded as "material support" in the form of providing "personnel" or "service[s]," and assert that the statute is unconstitutionally vague because they cannot tell.

As for "personnel," Congress enacted a limiting definition in IRTPA that answers plaintiffs' vagueness concerns. Providing material support that constitutes "personnel" is defined as knowingly providing a person "to work under that terrorist organization's direction or control or to organize, manage, supervise, or otherwise direct the operation of that organization." The statute makes clear that "personnel" does not cover *independent* advocacy: "Individuals who act entirely independently of the foreign terrorist organization to advance its goals or objectives shall not be considered to be working under the foreign terrorist organization's direction and control."

"[S]ervice" similarly refers to concerted activity, not independent advocacy. Context confirms that ordinary meaning here. The statute prohibits providing a service "*to* a foreign terrorist organization." *** The use of the word "to" indicates a connection between the service and the foreign group. We think a person of ordinary intelligence would understand that independently advocating for a cause is different from providing a service to a group that is advocating for that cause. *** On the other hand, a person of ordinary intelligence would understand the term "service" to cover advocacy performed in coordination with, or at the direction of, a foreign terrorist organization.

Plaintiffs argue that this construction of the statute poses difficult questions of exactly how much direction or coordination is necessary for an activity to constitute a "service." *** "Would any communication with any member be sufficient? With a leader? Must the 'relationship' have any formal elements, such as an employment or contractual relationship? What about a relationship through an intermediary?" The problem with these questions is that they are entirely hypothetical. Plaintiffs have not provided any specific articulation of the degree to which *they* seek to coordinate their advocacy with the PKK and the LTTE. They have instead described the form of their intended advocacy only in the most general terms. *** Deciding whether activities described at such a level of generality would constitute prohibited "service[s]" under the statute would require "sheer speculation"-which means that plaintiffs cannot prevail in their preenforcement challenge. It is apparent with respect to these claims that "gradations of fact or charge would make a difference as to criminal liability," and so "adjudication of the reach and constitutionality of [the statute] must await a concrete fact situation."

*** Plaintiffs claim that Congress has banned their "pure political speech." *** It has not. Under the material-support statute, plaintiffs may say anything they wish on any topic. They may speak and write freely about the PKK and LTTE, the governments of Turkey and Sri Lanka, human rights, and international law. They may advocate before the United Nations. As the Government states: "The statute does not prohibit independent advocacy or expression of any kind." Section 2339B also "does not prevent [plaintiffs] from becoming members of the PKK and LTTE or impose any sanction on them for doing so." Congress has not, therefore, sought to suppress ideas or opinions in the form of "pure political speech." Rather, Congress has prohibited "material support," which most often does not take the form of speech at all. And when it does, the statute is carefully drawn to cover only a narrow category of speech to, under the direction of, or in coordination with foreign groups that the speaker knows to be terrorist organizations.

For its part, the Government takes the foregoing too far, claiming that the only thing truly at issue in this litigation is conduct, not speech. Section 2339B is directed at the fact of plaintiffs' interaction with the PKK and LTTE, the Government contends, and only incidentally burdens their expression. The Government argues that the proper standard of review is therefore the one set out in *United States v. O'Brien*, 391 U.S. 367 (1968). In that case, *** we applied what we have since called "intermediate scrutiny," under which a "content-neutral regulation will be sustained under the First Amendment if it advances important governmental interests unrelated to the suppression of free speech and does not burden substantially more speech than necessary to further those interests." *** *O'Brien* does not provide the applicable standard for reviewing a content-based regulation of speech, and §

2339B regulates speech on the basis of its content. Plaintiffs want to speak to the PKK and the LTTE, and whether they may do so under § 2339B depends on what they say. If plaintiffs' speech to those groups imparts a "specific skill" or communicates advice derived from "specialized knowledge"-for example, training on the use of international law or advice on petitioning the United Nations-then it is barred. *** On the other hand, plaintiffs' speech is not barred if it imparts only general or unspecialized knowledge.

The Government argues that § 2339B should nonetheless receive intermediate scrutiny because it *generally* functions as a regulation of conduct. That argument runs headlong into a number of our precedents ***. The law here may be described as directed at conduct *** but as applied to plaintiffs the conduct triggering coverage under the statute consists of communicating a message. *** [W]e are outside of *O'Brien* 's test, and we must [apply] a more demanding standard."

The First Amendment issue before us is more refined than either plaintiffs or the Government would have it. It is not whether the Government may prohibit pure political speech, or may prohibit material support in the form of conduct. It is instead whether the Government may prohibit what plaintiffs want to do-provide material support to the PKK and LTTE in the form of speech.

Everyone agrees that the Government's interest in combating terrorism is an urgent objective of the highest order. *** The objective of combating terrorism does not justify prohibiting their speech, plaintiffs argue, because their support will advance only the legitimate activities of the designated terrorist organizations, not their terrorism.

Whether foreign terrorist organizations meaningfully segregate support of their legitimate activities from support of terrorism is an empirical question. When it enacted § 2339B in 1996, Congress made specific findings regarding the serious threat posed by international terrorism. *** One of those findings explicitly rejects plaintiffs' contention that their support would not further the terrorist activities of the PKK and LTTE: "[F]oreign organizations that engage in terrorist activity are so tainted by their criminal conduct that *any contribution to such an organization* facilitates that conduct."

Plaintiffs argue that the reference to "any contribution" in this finding meant only monetary support. There is no reason to read the finding to be so limited, particularly because Congress expressly prohibited so much more than monetary support in § 2339B. Congress's use of the term "contribution" is best read to reflect a determination that any form of material support furnished "to" a foreign terrorist organization should be barred, which is precisely what the material-support statute does. Indeed, when Congress enacted § 2339B, Congress simultaneously removed an exception that *** for the provision of material support in the form of "humanitarian assistance to persons not directly involved in" terrorist activity. *** That repeal demonstrates that Congress considered and rejected the view that ostensibly peaceful aid would have no harmful effects.

We are convinced that Congress was justified in rejecting that view. The PKK and the LTTE are deadly groups. *** Material support meant to "promot[e] peaceable, lawful conduct" *** can further terrorism by foreign groups in multiple ways. "Material support" is a valuable resource by definition. Such support frees up other resources within the organization that may be put to violent ends. It also importantly helps lend legitimacy to foreign terrorist groups-legitimacy that makes it easier for those groups to persist, to recruit members, and to raise funds-all of which facilitate more terrorist attacks. "Terrorist organizations do not maintain *organizational* 'firewalls' that would prevent or deter ... sharing and commingling of support and benefits." *** "Indeed, some designated foreign terrorist organizations use social and political components to recruit personnel to carry out terrorist operations, and to provide support to criminal terrorists and their families in aid of such operations." *** Money is fungible, and "[w]hen foreign terrorist organizations that have a dual structure raise funds, they highlight the civilian and humanitarian ends to which such moneys could be put." *** But "there is reason to believe that foreign terrorist organizations do not maintain legitimate *financial* firewalls between those funds raised for civil, nonviolent activities, and those ultimately used to support violent, terrorist operations." ***

The dissent argues that there is "no natural stopping place" for the proposition that aiding a foreign terrorist organization's lawful activity promotes the terrorist organization as a whole. But Congress has settled on just such a natural stopping place: The statute reaches only material support coordinated with or under the direction of a designated foreign terrorist organization. Independent advocacy that might be viewed as promoting the group's legitimacy is not covered.

Providing foreign terrorist groups with material support in any form also furthers terrorism by straining the United States' relationships with its allies and undermining cooperative efforts between nations to prevent terrorist attacks. We see no reason to question Congress's finding that "international cooperation is required for an effective response to terrorism, as demonstrated by the numerous multilateral conventions in force providing universal prosecutive jurisdiction over persons involved in a variety of terrorist acts, including hostage taking, murder of an internationally protected person, and aircraft piracy and sabotage." *** The material-support statute furthers this international effort by prohibiting aid for foreign terrorist groups that harm the United States' partners abroad: "A number of designated foreign terrorist organizations have attacked moderate governments with which the United States has vigorously endeavored to maintain close and friendly relations," and those attacks "threaten [the] social, economic and political stability" of such governments. ***

We also find it significant that Congress has been conscious of its own responsibility to consider how its actions may implicate constitutional concerns. First, § 2339B only applies to *** a limited number of [foreign terrorist] organizations designated by the Executive Branch, *** and any groups so designated may seek judicial review of the designation. Second, in response to the lower courts' holdings in this litigation, Congress added clarity to the statute by providing narrowing definitions of the terms "training," "personnel," and "expert advice or assistance," as well as an explanation of the knowledge required to violate § 2339B. Third, in effectuating its stated intent not to abridge First Amendment rights, Congress has also displayed a careful balancing of interests in creating limited exceptions to the ban on material support. The definition of material support, for example, excludes medicine and religious materials. *** Finally, and most importantly, Congress has avoided any restriction on independent advocacy, or indeed any activities not directed to, coordinated with, or controlled by foreign terrorist groups.

***[P]laintiffs simply disagree with the considered judgment of Congress and the Executive that providing material support to a designated foreign terrorist organization-even seemingly benign support-bolsters the terrorist activities of that organization. That judgment, however, is entitled to significant weight, and we have persuasive evidence before us to sustain it. Given the sensitive interests in national security and foreign affairs at stake, the political branches have adequately substantiated their determination that, to serve the Government's interest in preventing terrorism, it was necessary to prohibit providing material support in the form of training, expert advice, personnel, and services to foreign terrorist groups, even if the supporters meant to promote only the groups' nonviolent ends.

We turn to the particular speech plaintiffs propose to undertake. First, plaintiffs propose to "train members of [the] PKK on how to use humanitarian and international law to peacefully resolve disputes." Congress can, consistent with the First Amendment, prohibit this direct training. It is wholly foreseeable that the PKK could use the "specific skill[s]" that plaintiffs propose to impart as part of a broader strategy to promote terrorism. *** Second, plaintiffs propose to "teach PKK members how to petition various representative bodies such as the United Nations for relief." The Government acts within First Amendment strictures in banning this proposed speech because it teaches the organization how to acquire "relief," which plaintiffs never define with any specificity, and which could readily include monetary aid. *** Money is fungible *** and Congress logically concluded that money a terrorist group such as the PKK obtains using the techniques plaintiffs propose to teach could be redirected to funding the group's violent activities.

Finally, plaintiffs propose to "engage in political advocacy on behalf of Kurds who live in Turkey," and "engage in political advocacy on behalf of Tamils who live in Sri Lanka." *** [P]laintiffs do not specify their expected level of coordination with the PKK or LTTE or suggest what exactly their "advocacy" would consist of. Plaintiffs' proposals are phrased at such a high level of generality that they cannot prevail in this preenforcement challenge.

***[T]he dissent fails to address the real dangers at stake [by providing training on how to use humanitarian and international law to peacefully resolve disputes, and how to petition various representative bodies such as the United Nations for relief]. It instead considers only the possible benefits of plaintiffs' proposed activities in the abstract. The dissent seems unwilling to entertain the prospect that training and advising a designated foreign terrorist organization on how to take advantage of international entities might benefit that organization in a way that facilitates its terrorist activities. In the dissent's world, such training is all to the good. Congress and the Executive, however, have concluded that we live in a different world: one in which the designated foreign terrorist organizations "are so tainted by their criminal conduct that any contribution to such an organization facilitates that conduct." ***

All this is not to say that any future applications of the material-support statute to speech or advocacy will survive First Amendment scrutiny. It is also not to say that any other statute relating to speech and terrorism would satisfy the First Amendment. In particular, we in no way suggest that a regulation of independent speech would pass constitutional muster, even if the Government were to show that such speech benefits foreign terrorist organizations. We also do not suggest that Congress could extend the same prohibition on material support at issue here to domestic organizations. We simply hold that, in prohibiting the particular forms of support that plaintiffs seek to provide to foreign terrorist groups, § 2339B does not violate the freedom of speech.

Plaintiffs' final claim is that the material-support statute *** criminalizes the mere fact of their associating with the PKK and the LTTE *** [and they] also argue that the material-support statute burdens their freedom of association because it prevents them from providing support to designated foreign terrorist organizations, but not to other groups. *** Any burden on plaintiffs' freedom of association in this regard is justified for the same reasons that we have denied plaintiffs' free speech challenge. [The Court summarily rejects these claims.]. ***

JUSTICE BREYER, with whom JUSTICES GINSBURG and SOTOMAYOR join, dissenting.

***I do not think this statute is unconstitutionally vague. But I cannot agree with the Court's conclusion that the Constitution permits the Government to prosecute the plaintiffs criminally for engaging in coordinated teaching and advocacy furthering the designated organizations' lawful political objectives. In my view, the Government has not met its burden of showing that an interpretation of the statute that would prohibit this speech- and association-related activity serves the Government's compelling interest in combating terrorism. And I would interpret the statute as normally placing activity of this kind outside its scope. *** All the activities involve the communication and advocacy of political ideas and lawful means of achieving political ends. Even the subjects the plaintiffs wish to teach-using international law to resolve disputes peacefully or petitioning the United Nations, for instance-concern political speech. We cannot avoid the constitutional significance of these facts on the basis that some of this speech takes place outside the United States and is directed at foreign governments, for the activities also involve advocacy in *this* country directed to *our* government and *its* policies. The plaintiffs, for example, wish to write and distribute publications and to speak before the United States Congress. ***

[T]his speech and association for political purposes is the *kind* of activity to which the First Amendment ordinarily offers its strongest protection is elementary. *** Not even the "serious and deadly problem" of international terrorism can require *automatic* forfeiture of First Amendment rights. ***

*** [W]e must at the very least "measure the validity of the means adopted by Congress against both the goal it has sought to achieve and the specific prohibitions of the First Amendment." *** [P]recisely how does application of the statute to the protected activities before us *help achieve* that important security-related end? *** The Government makes two efforts to answer this question. *First,* the Government says that the plaintiffs' support for these organizations is "fungible" in the same sense as other forms of banned support. Being fungible, the plaintiffs' support could, for example, free up other resources, which the organization might put to terrorist ends. *** The proposition that the two very different kinds of "support" [money and speech] are "fungible," however, is not *obviously* true. *** It is far from obvious that these advocacy activities can themselves be redirected, or will free other resources that can be directed, towards terrorist ends. *** The Government has provided us with no empirical information that might convincingly support this claim. *** The most one can say in the Government's favor about these statements is that they *might* be read as offering highly general support for its argument. The statements do not, however, explain in any detail how the plaintiffs' political-advocacy-related activities might actually be "fungible" and therefore capable of being diverted to terrorist use. Nor do they indicate that Congress itself was concerned with "support" of this kind.

[Additionally,] ***the Government says that the plaintiffs' proposed activities will "bolste[r] a terrorist organization's efficacy and strength in a community" and "undermin[e] this nation's efforts to *delegitimize and weaken* those groups." *** In the Court's view, too, the Constitution permits application of the statute to activities of the kind at issue in part because those activities could provide a group that engages in terrorism with "legitimacy." The Court suggests that, armed with this greater "legitimacy," these organizations will more readily be able to obtain material support of the kinds Congress plainly intended to ban-money, arms, lodging, and the like.

Yet the Government does not claim that the statute forbids *any* speech "legitimating" a terrorist group. Rather, it reads the statute as permitting (1) membership in terrorist organizations, (2) "peaceably assembling with members of the PKK and LTTE for lawful discussion," or (3) "independent advocacy" on behalf of these organizations. The Court, too, emphasizes that activities not *"coordinated with"* the terrorist groups are not banned. *** And it argues that speaking, writing, and teaching aimed at furthering a terrorist organization's peaceful political ends could "mak[e] it easier for those groups to persist, to recruit members, and to raise funds."

But this "legitimacy" justification cannot by itself warrant suppression of political speech, advocacy, and association. Speech, association, and related activities on behalf of a group will often, perhaps always, help to legitimate that group. Thus, were the law to accept a "legitimating" effect, in and of itself and without qualification, as providing sufficient grounds for imposing such a ban, the First Amendment battle would be lost in untold instances where it should be won. Once one accepts this argument, there is no natural stopping place. The argument applies as strongly to "independent" as to "coordinated" advocacy. That fact is reflected in part in the Government's claim that the ban here, so supported, prohibits a lawyer hired by a designated group from filing on behalf of that group an *amicus* brief before the United Nations or even before this Court. ***

Moreover, the risk that those who are taught will put otherwise innocent speech or knowledge to bad use is omnipresent, at least where that risk rests on little more than (even informed) speculation. Hence to accept this kind of argument without more and to apply it to the teaching of a subject such as international human rights law is to adopt a rule of law that, contrary to the Constitution's text and First Amendment precedent, would automatically forbid the teaching of any subject in a case where national security interests conflict with the First Amendment. The Constitution does not allow all such conflicts to be decided in the Government's favor.

The majority, as I have said, cannot limit the scope of its arguments through its claim that the plaintiffs remain free to engage in the protected activity *as long as it is not "coordinated."* That is because there is no practical way to organize classes for a group (say, wishing to learn about human rights law) without *"coordination."* *** Second, the majority discusses the plaintiffs' proposal to "'teach PKK members how to petition various representative bodies such as the United Nations *for relief.'* " *** In *this* context, as the record makes clear, the word "relief" does not refer to "money." It refers to recognition under the Geneva Conventions. *** Throughout, the majority emphasizes that it would defer strongly to Congress' "informed judgment." *** But here, there is no evidence that Congress has made such a judgment regarding the specific activities at issue in these cases. ***

Notes

1. Hypotheticals. The Court alludes early on to "more difficult cases that may arise under the statute." What might some such cases be?

2. Vagueness. The vagueness argument is dismissed by the Court. Is this a dismissal based on (a) the facts of this case, (b) judicial perceptions about the limits of language, or (c) congressional efforts to revise the language to be more precise or (d) all of the above?

3. Mens Rea. The Court Notes that the mens rea requirements of 2239A and 2239B differ. This may explain why there are fewer prosecutions under A than B; for the former, the mens rea is "knowing or intending" use for terrorism, while for the latter it suffices that one has knowledge that the organization has been designated a foreign terrorist organization or has engaged in terrorist activity. Do you think these two classes of supporters should be viewed as equally culpable?

4. Independence. The Court Notes that "independent advocacy" on behalf of goals advocated by a terrorist organization is not prohibited. How would you prove that your advocacy was independent? Is the Court's ruling likely to deter individuals from meeting with terrorist organization leaders to resolve conflicts in which their organizations participate? If a State Department official after such a meeting announces that there is merit to certain claims of a terrorist organization, should she fear prosecution under the statute? If the NEW YORK TIMES edited and published an op-ed by a Hamas member (as it has done on occasion), could it face prosecution under the statute? What if a lawyer filed an amicus brief on behalf of a designated group?

5. Timing. Why did the plaintiffs challenge the statute rather than awaiting prosecution? Did this adversely affect their chances of prevailing?

6. Level of Scrutiny. Why does the Court reject using the more lenient *O'Brien* test for conduct to assess this case? When the Court uses strict scrutiny, why do the plaintiffs nevertheless lose on their free speech challenge to 2339B?

7. Foreign and Domestic. Chief Justice Roberts says in dictum at the end of his opinion that the prohibitions of 2339B might not be constitutional if applied to material support of "domestic organizations." Should this distinction matter? Does speech with a domestic group raise the same "freeing up" concerns as with a foreign group?

8. Coordinated Advocacy. The Court only ruled on the issues of trainings and advice regarding international law and conflict resolution but did not reach HLP's coordinated advocacy claim, stating that the group had not sufficiently detailed what it proposed to do. Under the Court's reasoning, do you think meeting with a member of Congress together with the representative of a designated group could be constitutionally proscribed? Why or why not?

9. Citizenship and Material Support. In May 2010, Senator Joseph Liebermann introduced the Terrorist Expatriation Act, a bill to strip U.S. citizenship from persons the Secretary of State determined had "engag[ed] in . . . hostilities against the United States" or "provid[ed] material support or resources to a foreign terrorist organization." Is this bill constitutional? In *Afroyim v. Rusk,* 387 U.S. 253, and *Vance v. Terrazas,* 444 U.S. 252, the Supreme Court held that Congress cannot revoke American citizenship unless the person knowingly, voluntarily, and intentionally renounces it. In both cases, the Court reasoned that citizenship is a constitutional right which cannot be taken away by an act of Congress. Would or should the Court make a similar ruling today—or would it hold that the Constitution permits materially supporting a designated organization to be dispositive evidence that a citizen intentionally renounced American citizenship?

10. Religious Speech. Several material support or incitement cases in the United States have involved religious speech. For example, a visa was denied to a religious scholar whose sermons implicitly condoned antidemocratic violence and an imam in a Virginia mosque was convicted on conspiracy and incitement charges when two listeners went to Afghanistan to fight United States forces. Such prosecution of religious speech may be constitutional, expecially after HLP, but arguably "government is ill-equipped to make judgments about the meaning of religious speech." See Huq, "The Signaling Function of Religious Speech in Domestic Counterterrorism," Chicago Public Law and Legal Theory Working Paper No. 338, February 2011, arguing that association with "insular groups that break off from the cultural or subcultural mainstream to form their own discrete ethical and normative subcultures" would better identify likely terrorists. Would this be constitutionally preferable? Do you see any difficulties with this approach?

11. Continuum of Support for Terrorism. Is speaking out in support of a terrorist group the same thing as giving it money? Is giving money the same as giving bombs? Not all terrorist financers share the same objectives or interests: some seek to aid specific violent conduct, some the general social or political objective that the group shares, others provide support to terrorist groups simply in the course of seeking a profit. Terrorist financing can perhaps best be understood as a continuum—where one end of the spectrum is support that constitutes a form of waging war and other represents support to the social and political movements, communities, and goals associated with a given terrorist group. Some forms of support may incentivize a terrorist group toward specific violent acts, while others may constrain the violent activities of the group. For example, Hamas is arguably more constrained, because it is currently the government of Palestine, by its constituents, while al Qaeda is not similarly constrained. *See* Timothy Wittig, UNDERSTANDING TERRORIST FINANCING (MacMillan Palsgrave, 2011). In your view, is the speech *HLP* sought to engage in more likely to encourage a group to violence, dissuade it, or have little effect?

B. INTERNATIONAL ANTITERRORISM LAW

1. IN UNITED STATES COURTS

Generally, United States courts, including the federal district courts, interpret domestic antiterrorism laws in light of statutory language and consistency with the Constitution of the United States. The same would be true of judicial interpretations of treaty provisions to which the United States is bound. In recent years, however, the federal courts have looked at whether terrorism violates "the law of nations," albeit in the context of tort claims rather than criminal prosecutions. The following two cases vividly present this issue. The second case also provides some examples of antiterrorism treaty provisions.

SAPERSTEIN v. The PALESTINIAN AUTHORITY
2006 WL 3804718 (SD Fla. 2006)

PATRICIA A. SEITZ, *United States District Court.*

*** The allegations *** accepted as true for purposes of this motion to dismiss, are as follows. Defendant PA is in de jure and de facto control of territories in the Gaza Strip and in the Judea and Samaria regions of the West Bank. Defendant PLO is in de jure and de facto control of Defendant PA. *** The PA and PLO advocated, encouraged, solicited, facilitated, incited, sponsored, organized, planned and executed acts of violence and terrorism against Jewish civilians in Israel, Gaza and the Judea and Samaria regions of the West Bank. The United States and Israel repeatedly demanded that the PA and PLO take effective measures to prevent further terrorist attacks. In violation of their undertakings and obligations under the Oslo Accords and under international customary law and local law, the PA and PLO refused and ignored American and Israeli demands to take effective measures to prevent further terrorist attacks. *** Defendants PA and PLO, through their respective agents continuously advocated, encouraged, solicited, facilitated and incited the use of violence and terrorism against Jewish civilians in Israel, Gaza and the Judea and Samaria regions of the West Bank. ***

The ATS provides: "the district courts shall have original jurisdiction of any civil action by an alien for a tort only, committed in violation of the law of nations or a treaty of the United States." The Eleventh Circuit has recognized that the ATS "establishes a federal forum where courts may fashion domestic common law remedies to give effect to violations of customary international law." Thus, the ATS "creates both subject matter jurisdiction and a private right of action." Federal subject matter jurisdiction exists when: (1) an alien sues (2) for a tort (3) committed in violation of the law of nations.

Under the ATS, the "law of nations" refers to a body of law known as customary international law. Conduct violates the "law of the nations" if it contravenes "well-established, universally recognized norms of international law."

The Congress first enacted the ATS as part of the Judiciary Act of 1789. The only "violation[s] of the law of nations" known at that time were "violation of safe conducts, infringement of the rights of ambassadors, and piracy." *Sosa v. Alvarez-Machain*, 542 U.S. 692 (2004). Since 1789, new claims may be recognized under common law principles, but they must "rest on a norm of international character accepted by the civilized world and defined with a specificity comparable to the features of the 18th Century paradigms we have recognized."

In *Sosa,* the Supreme Court admonished the lower federal courts to be extremely cautious about discovering new offenses among the law of nations. The Court then discussed the five reasons underlying this cautionary restraint: 1) common law judges in the past were seen as "discovering law, but they are now seen as making or creating law; 2) since *Erie v. Tompkins,* the role of federal common law has been dramatically reduced, and courts have generally looked for legislative guidance before taking innovative measures; 3) creating private rights of action is generally best left to the legislature; 4) decisions involving international law may have collateral consequences that impinge on the discretion of the legislative and executive branches in managing foreign affairs; and 5) there is no mandate from Congress encouraging judicial creativity in this area, and, in fact, there is legislative hints in the opposite direction.

In *Tel Oren v. Libyan Arab Republic,* 726 F.2d 774 (D.C.Cir.1984), cert. denied, 470 U.S. 1003 (1985), victims of a 1978 terrorist attack in Israel sued a number of parties, including several private organizations, for violations of the law of nations under the ATS. The terrorists seized a civilian bus, a taxi, a passing car, and subsequently a second civilian bus and took the passengers hostage. The terrorists tortured, shot, wounded and murdered many of the hostages. A three-judge panel unanimously dismissed the case with three separate opinions. Judge Edwards gave the ATS the broadest reach, generally agreeing *** that acts of official torture violate the law of nations. Judge Edwards, however, found no consensus that private actors are bound by the law of nations with regard to torture.[8] Only a year later, the court of appeals addressed the issue again in *Sanchez-Espinoza v. Reagan,* 770 F.2d 202 (D.C.Cir.1985), a case involving allegations of "execution, murder, abduction, torture, rape, [and] wounding" by the Nicaraguan Contras. In *Sanchez-Espinoza,* the appellate court stated quite clearly that the law of nations "does not reach private, non-state conduct of this sort" for the reasons stated by Judge Edwards and Judge Bork in *Tel-Oren.*

In *Tel Oren,* Judge Edwards undertook an in-depth analysis of whether to stretch *Filartiga's* reasoning to incorporate torture perpetuated by a party other than a recognized state or one of its officials. Judge Edwards observed that the extension would necessarily require the court to venture out of the realm of established international law in which states are the actors and would mandate an assessment of the extent to which international law imposes not only rights but also obligations on individuals. He concluded his analysis saying that he "was not prepared to extend the definition of the 'law of nations' absent direction from the Supreme Court."

Judge Edwards also examined the question of whether terrorism in and of itself was a law of nations violation, regardless of whether it is conducted by a state or private actor. In finding that condemnation of terrorism was not universal, he stated that "the nations of the world are so divisively split on the legitimacy of such aggression as to make it impossible to pinpoint an area of harmony or consensus." Thus, he concluded that the law of nations, defined as the principles and rules that states feel themselves bound to observe, did not outlaw politically motivated terrorism.

The 1995 *Kadic v. Karadzic* decision, 70 F.3d 232 (C.A.2 1995), is the most recent circuit court opinion thoroughly analyzing those actions for which international law imposes individual liability. In *Kadic,* the plaintiffs, Croat and Muslim citizens of Bosnia-Herzegovina, sued the president of the

---

[8] Judge Edwards acknowledged that piracy and slave trading were areas in which individual liability was imposed.

self-proclaimed Bosnian-Serb republic within Bosnia Herzegovina. Plaintiffs asserted causes of action for various atrocities at the hands of the Bosnian-Serb republic including, genocide, rape, forced prostitution and impregnation, torture, and other cruel, inhuman and degrading treatment such as assault and battery, sex and ethnic inequality, summary execution and wrongful death. The district court dismissed the case finding that defendant was not a state actor for purposes of the ATS but the court of appeals reversed. In so doing, the Second Circuit found that the law of nations, as understood in the modern era, did not confine its reach to state action. The court of appeals held that "certain forms of conduct violate the laws of nations whether undertaken by those acting under the auspices of a state or only as private individuals, such as piracy, slave-trading, aircraft hijacking, genocide, and war crimes." The Second Circuit, however, held that torture and summary execution, when not perpetrated in the course of genocide or war crimes, are proscribed by international law only when committed by state officials under color of law.

These cases reflect the trend toward finding that certain conduct violates the law of nations whether committed by a state or a private actor. However, which conduct falls into this realm has not been completely defined. Plaintiffs contend that a violation of the "law of war" now called "international humanitarian law" is recognized as a breach of the law of nations and the actions alleged in the TAC constitute such violations. *** With this legal landscape in mind and noting the Supreme Court's cautionary advice regarding the creation of new offenses in the law of nations in *Sosa,* the Court turns to the Plaintiffs' allegations. ***

To resolve Defendants' motion, it is necessary to determine if the Plaintiffs' *** allegations fit the categories of conduct that prior courts have found constitute a violation of the law of nations, even when carried out by a private actor. The conduct in *Tel Oren* is substantially similar to the conduct in the present case. Judge Edwards, in *Tel Oren,* made it abundantly clear that politically motivated terrorism has not reached the status of a violation of the law of nations. In their own words, Plaintiffs describe Defendants' conduct as terrorism. Beginning with their introduction, Plaintiffs state that they bring this action for damages caused by Defendants' "acts of terrorism as defined in federal law, and by reason of related tortious terrorist behavior." Further, Plaintiffs specifically allege that the PA and PLO failed to "denounce and condemn acts of terror, apprehend, prosecute and imprison persons involved directly, and/or indirectly in acts of terrorism and outlaw and dismantle the infrastructure of terrorist organizations." Thus, if the conduct of the Defendants is construed as terrorism, then Plaintiffs have not alleged a violation of the law of nations.

Plaintiffs attempt to get around such facts in their response to Defendants' motion to dismiss by characterizing the allegations in the TAC as a "murder of [a] civilian[ ] in the course of an armed conflict," or a war crime. In doing this, Plaintiffs are grasping at the *Kadic* decision and attempting to bring the alleged conduct within the language of Common Article 3. Plaintiffs' strategy in this regard is certainly obvious, as the Second

Circuit in *Kadic* based much of its analysis of the definition of "war crimes" on Common Article 3. However, Plaintiffs then make the overreaching leap by stating that if the conduct falls within Common Article 3 and is prohibited thereby, then they have sufficiently alleged a violation of the law of nations for purposes of the ATS. Essentially, Plaintiffs are saying that if they allege a murder of an innocent person during an armed conflict, then they have alleged a per se violation of the law of nations and federal courts have subject matter jurisdiction over the dispute under the ATS. No court has so held. In fact, as discussed above, international customary law is not taken from one source but rather is "discerned from [a] myriad of decisions made in numerous and varied international and domestic arenas."

Further, while Plaintiffs' reliance on the *Kadic* decision's references to Common Article 3 is understandable, the severe and horrendous conduct alleged in that case, including "brutal acts of rape, forced prostitution, forced impregnation, torture and summary execution" against an entire class of citizens, differentiate it from this case. Unlike the conduct alleged here, the abominate actions the Croat and Muslim plaintiffs asserted in *Kadic* did not require the same extent of canvassing of international law to determine if the prohibition of such conduct was "universally recognized." Thus, the Second Circuit's reliance on Common Article 3 was sufficient to ascertain a consensus in customary international law. In fact, the appellate court specifically directed their decision to the particular horrendous allegations by stating that the "offenses alleged by the [plaintiffs], if proved, would violate the most fundamental norms of the law of war embodied in common article 3." The court of appeals did not make a blanket holding that any alleged violation of Common Article 3 would be sufficient for the purposes of the ATS.

Further, two practical considerations highlight the flaws in Plaintiffs' desired expansion of the law of nations. First, if it were accepted that any alleged violation of Common Article 3 was sufficient for subject matter jurisdiction under the ATS, then a violation of any provision in the Article would yield the same result. This includes such unspecific conduct as "violence to life," "cruel treatment" and "outrages upon personal dignity." For federal courts to interpret such ambiguous standards to assess its own subject matter jurisdiction would pose problems for federal courts and would not meet the defined standards of specificity that *Sosa* requires. Second, if Plaintiffs' specific allegation, i.e., the murder of an innocent civilian during an armed conflict, was sufficient for the purposes of the AT S, then whenever an innocent person was murdered during an "armed conflict" anywhere in the world, whether it be Bosnia, the Middle East or Darfur, Sudan, the federal courts would have subject matter jurisdiction over the dispute. Clearly, such an interpretation would not only make district courts international courts of civil justice, it would be in direct contravention of the Supreme Court's specific prudential guidance admonishing lower courts to be cautious in creating new offenses under the law of nations. For the foregoing reasons, Plaintiffs do not sufficiently allege a violation of the law of nations and, thus, this Court lacks subject matter jurisdiction. ***

ALMOG v. ARAB BANK, PLC
471 F. Supp 257 (E.D.N.Y 2007)

GERSHON, *District Judge.*

More than 1,600 plaintiffs, consisting of United States and foreign nationals, bring claims for damages against Defendant Arab Bank, PLC, for knowingly providing banking and administrative services to various organizations identified by the U.S. government as terrorist organizations that sponsored suicide bombings and other murderous attacks on innocent civilians in Israel. *** [P]laintiffs allege that Arab Bank materially supported the efforts and goals of the terrorist organizations in two ways. First, Arab Bank provided banking services, including maintaining accounts, for HAMAS and other terrorist organizations. *** Plaintiffs also allege that Arab Bank maintained accounts and solicited and collected funds for the various charitable organizations, including the Popular Committee, organizations that are part of the Coalition, the HRA, the Al-Ansar Society and the Tulkarem Charitable Committee, all of which it knew are affiliated with the various terrorist organizations. In addition, plaintiffs allege that Arab Bank maintained accounts for individual supporters of terrorist organizations, such as HAMAS and al Qaeda. Arab Bank knew that the accounts of these various organizations and individuals were being used to fund the suicide bombings and other attacks sponsored by the terrorist organizations. Finally, Arab Bank laundered funds for the terrorist and front organizations, including the Holy Land Foundation for Relief and Development ("HLF"), which raised funds for HAMAS in the United States.

Plaintiffs' second factual theory is that Arab Bank administered the financial infrastructure by which the Saudi Committee distributed a comprehensive benefit of $5,316.06 to designated families of Palestinian "martyrs" and those wounded or imprisoned in perpetrating terrorist attacks. Despite its knowledge that the Saudi Committee was distributing this benefit to families of "martyrs," Arab Bank essentially served as a "paymaster" through its branch offices within the West Bank and the Gaza Strip. *** Each plaintiff alleges that he or she is a victim, or family member of a victim, of the actions of suicide bombers and murderers who were supported, encouraged, and enticed by funds collected and disbursed by Arab Bank. ***

The ATS provides that "[t]he district courts shall have original jurisdiction of any civil action by an alien for a tort only, committed in violation of the law of nations or a treaty of the United States." On its face, the statute requires that plaintiffs must 1) be aliens, 2) claiming damages for a tort only, 3) resulting from a violation of the law of nations or a treaty of the United States. *** The essential issues in contention are therefore whether plaintiffs have pled a violation of the law of nations that should be recognized by this court under the ATS, and whether Arab Bank can be liable for aiding and abetting those violations.[15]

---

[15] In the context of the ATS, the phrase "law of nations" is consistently used interchangeably with the phrases "norm of international law" and "international law. *** In addition, the law of nations can encompass customary international law, and, to the

Any discussion of the ATS must begin with the Supreme Court's recent decision in *Sosa v. Alvarez-Machain,* 542 U.S. 692, (2004).   Humberto Alvarez-Machain, the plaintiff in *Sosa,* was a Mexican national who had been indicted for the torture and murder of an agent of the United States Drug Enforcement Agency (the "DEA").   The DEA authorized a plan whereby a group of Mexican nationals, including Jose Francisco Sosa, seized Alvarez-Machain and brought him back to the United States for trial.   Alvarez-Machain brought a civil action against Sosa, among others, seeking damages under the ATS for a violation of the law of nations, namely, arbitrary arrest and detention.   The defendant argued that the ATS provides courts only with subject matter jurisdiction and neither creates nor authorizes a court to recognize a cause of action for an alleged violation of the law of nations.

The Supreme Court, in *Sosa,* stated that, "although the ATS is a jurisdictional statute creating no new causes of action .... [t]he jurisdictional grant is best read as having been enacted on the understanding that the common law would provide a cause of action for the modest number of international law violations with a potential for personal liability at the time" the ATS was enacted. *** Having held that, under the ATS's jurisdictional grant, federal courts can recognize a cause of action that arose after enactment of the ATS, the *Sosa* Court set out the standard for doing so: "federal courts should not recognize private claims under federal common law for violations of any international law norm with less definite content and acceptance among civilized nations than the historical paradigms familiar when § 1350 was enacted." [16] The norm of international law may not be merely aspirational; rather, it must be specific and well-defined. The Court rejected Alvarez-Machain's contention that there was an international norm against arbitrary detention on the ground that it was not specific enough to create a federal remedy. *** *Sosa* instructs that courts consider the *current* state of the law of nations in deciding whether to recognize a claim under the ATS. *** The current law of nations "is composed only of those rules that States universally abide by, or accede to, out of a sense of legal obligation and mutual concern."   First, then, in order for a rule to become a norm of international law, States must universally abide by or accede to it.   The question is not one of whether the rule is often violated, but whether virtually all States recognize its validity.   Thus, that a norm of international law is honored in the breach does not diminish its binding effect *** Second, States must abide by or accede to the rule from a sense of *legal obligation* and not for moral or political reasons.   Whether States abide by or accede to a rule out of a sense of legal obligation is shown by, among other things, state practice.

Third, "[i]t is only where the nations of the world have demonstrated that the wrong is of *mutual,* and not merely *several,* concern, by means of express international accords, that a wrong generally recognized becomes an international law violation within the meaning of the statute." Matters of

---

extent that it does, the phrase "customary international law" is also used interchangeably with the phrase "the law of nations."

[16] These include the violation of safe conducts, infringement of the rights of ambassadors, and piracy.

"mutual" concern are those involving States' actions performed with regard to each other. Matters of "several" concern are "matters in which States are separately and independently interested." "[O]ffenses that may be purely intra-national in their execution, such as official torture, extrajudicial killings, and genocide, do violate customary international law because the nations of the world have demonstrated that such wrongs are of mutual concern and capable of impairing international peace and security." ***

[T]reaties, also referred to as conventions or covenants, *** constitute primary evidence of the law of nations. *** The more States that have ratified a treaty, especially those States with greater relative influence in international affairs, the greater the treaty's evidentiary value. Likewise, a treaty's evidentiary value is increased if the State parties actually implement and abide by the principles set forth in the treaty either internationally or within their own borders. In addition to treaties, United Nations Security Council resolutions, which are binding on all Member States, are evidence of the law of nations.

Finally, under *Sosa,* in deciding whether to recognize a claim under the ATS, a court must consider the practical consequences of making the claim available to litigants in the federal courts. For instance, there may be collateral consequences, such as implications on foreign relations, that advise against recognizing a claim. The Court in *Sosa* also cautioned courts to tread lightly in exercising their discretion because courts generally have to look for "legislative guidance before exercising innovative authority over substantive law" and because the "decision to create a private right of action is one better left to legislative judgment in the great majority of cases." *** The first issue I address is whether plaintiffs have pled a violation of the law of nations. Later, I address whether the allegations against Arab Bank are sufficient for it to be held liable for those violations. ***

Acts of genocide and crimes against humanity violate the law of nations and these norms are of sufficient specificity and definiteness to be recognized under the ATS. *** The Convention on the Prevention and Punishment of the Crime of Genocide ("Genocide Convention") defines genocide as: "any of the following acts committed with intent to destroy, in whole or in part, a national, ethnical, racial or religious group" *** To be a crime against humanity, the emphasis must not be on the individual but rather on the collective-the individual is victimized not because of his or her individual attributes but because of membership in a targeted civilian population. Although the requirement of widespread or systematic action ensures that a plaintiff must allege not just one act but, instead, a course of conduct, "a single act by a perpetrator, taken within the context of a widespread or systematic attack against a civilian population entails individual criminal responsibility and an individual perpetrator need not commit numerous offences to be held liable."

Applying the standards provided in the Genocide Convention and the Rome Statute to the facts alleged here, plaintiffs have successfully stated claims for genocide and crimes against humanity. The amended complaints allege that HAMAS, the PIJ, the AAMB, and the PFLP act with the united purpose and shared mission to eradicate the State of Israel, murder or throw out the Jews, and liberate the area by replacing it with an Islamic or Palestinian State through the use of suicide bombings and other shockingly egregious violent acts. These goals reflect an intent to target people based on criteria prohibited by both the Genocide Convention and the Rome Statute.

Plaintiffs allege that the terrorist organizations seek to accomplish their shared goal by cooperating in the planning and commission of suicide bombings and other murderous attacks using explosives, incendiary weapons, and lethal devices in public places, which has resulted in the systematic and continuous killing and injury of thousands of unarmed innocent civilians in Israel, the West Bank, and the Gaza Strip. These are precisely the sorts of acts proscribed in both the Genocide Convention and the Rome statute.

Plaintiffs also allege that the terrorist organizations have developed and implemented a sophisticated financial structure through which they seek to accomplish their goals. The amended complaints describe dozens upon dozens of instances in which hundreds of innocent civilians were killed, and countless others injured, in attacks caused by individuals sponsored by the terrorist organizations. The acts as alleged constitute the "widespread" and "systematic" action necessary for claims of genocide and crimes against humanity. Even the acts other than suicide bombings, specifically those that defendant contends are nothing more than street crimes, may be sufficient for liability if plaintiffs can prove they were committed as part of a genocidal scheme or crimes against humanity. ***

The third international norm which plaintiffs allege Arab Bank has violated is the financing of suicide bombings and other murderous attacks on innocent civilians which are intended to intimidate or coerce a civilian population. The underlying norm thus differs from the genocide norm with respect to the purpose of the perpetrators, and it differs from the more general crimes against humanity norm in that it specifically condemns bombings and other attacks intended to coerce or intimidate a civilian population. This particular claim for liability under the ATS is similar to the U.S. nationals' claims under the ATA, but the alien plaintiffs do not rely on domestic law; rather, they rely on the body of international law *** . In 1997, the United Nations General Assembly adopted the International Convention for the Suppression of Terrorist Bombings ("Bombing Convention").

The Bombing Convention states in pertinent part:

Article 2

1. Any person commits an offence within the meaning of this Convention if that person unlawfully and intentionally delivers, places, discharges or detonates an explosive or other lethal device in, into or against a place of public use, a State or government facility, a public transportation system or an infrastructure facility:

(a) With the intent to cause death or serious bodily injury ***

This Convention focuses on the principal method of attacking civilians alleged in the amended complaints in that it specifically makes it an offense to bomb public places or public transportation systems with the intent to cause death or serious bodily harm. The Bombing Convention particularly condemns such acts when they are, as alleged here, intended to provoke a state of terror in the general public or a group of persons. It specifies that such acts are not justifiable by any racial, ethnic, religious, political, or other similar considerations. In terms of its evidentiary weight, the Bombing Convention is significant. It has been ratified by over 120 United Nations Member States, including the United States (June 26, 2002). ***

Two years after the Bombing Convention was adopted by the General Assembly, the International Convention for the Suppression of the Financing of Terrorism ("Financing Convention") was also adopted by the General Assembly of the United Nations. It has been ratified by over 130 countries, including the United States (June 26, 2002). The United States implemented the Financing Convention via the Suppression of the Financing of Terrorism Convention Implementation Act of 2002. The Convention makes it an offense to finance certain acts, including those proscribed in the Bombing Convention. ***

Thus, the Financing Convention, along with the Bombing Convention, specifically condemns suicide bombings and other murderous attacks against innocent civilians intended to intimidate or coerce a population. Once again, this Convention provides that such acts "are under no circumstances justifiable by considerations of a political, philosophical, ideological, racial, ethnic, religious or other similar nature."

The prohibition against attacks on innocent civilians that is reflected in both of these Conventions is not a new one. The three-century-old "principle of distinction," which requires parties to a conflict to at all times distinguish between civilians and combatants, forbids the deliberate attacking of civilians. State practice establishes the principle of distinction as a long-established norm of the customary law of armed conflict. ***

Under the customary law of armed conflict, as reflected in the Geneva Conventions, all "parties" to a conflict, including insurgent military groups, must adhere to these most fundamental requirements. While the principle of distinction and the Geneva Conventions apply expressly only in situations of armed conflict, their long-standing existence supports the conclusion, made explicit in the Bombing and Financing Conventions, that attacks against innocent civilians of the type alleged here are condemned by international law. ***

In the face of all these sources evidencing universal condemnation of the types of acts alleged here, Arab Bank does not address the actual conduct condemned by these sources. Rather, it argues that the underlying suicide bombings and other murderous acts alleged in Count Three, which it says are "commonly referred to as terrorism," cannot be a violation of the law of nations because there is no consensus on the meaning of "terrorism." *** [T]here is no need to resolve any definitional disputes as to the scope of the word "terrorism," for the Conventions expressing the international norm provide their own specific descriptions of the conduct condemned. Although the Conventions refer to such acts as "terrorism," the pertinent issue here is only whether the acts as alleged by plaintiffs violate a norm of international law, however labeled. *** [T]he specific conduct alleged-organized, systematic suicide bombings and other murderous attacks on innocent civilians intended to intimidate or coerce a civilian population-are universally condemned. ***

In a similar way, the *Yousef* court, after holding that there was no jurisdiction under the universality principle, held that there was jurisdiction in the district court to try the defendant for bombing a Philippines Airlines flight under the Montreal Convention, which expressly addresses offenses against aircraft. It did so because it found that the conduct charged, "whether it is termed 'terrorist'-constitutes the core conduct proscribed by the Montreal Convention and its implementing legislation." *cf. Filartiga,* 630 F.2d at 882 ("For although there is no universal agreement as to the precise extent of the 'human rights and fundamental freedoms' guaranteed to all by the Charter, there is at present no dissent from the view that the guaranties include, at a bare minimum, the right to be free from torture."); *but see Saperstein v. Palestinian Authority,* No. 04-CV-20225, 2006 WL 3804718, at *7 (S.D.Fla. Dec.22, 2006) (stating that, because politically motivated terrorism has not reached the status of a violation of the law of nations, "if the conduct of the Defendants is construed as terrorism, then Plaintiffs have not alleged a violation of the law of nations"). In sum, regardless of whether there is universal agreement as to the precise scope of the word "terrorism," the conduct involved here is specifically condemned in the Conventions upon which this court relies.

Arab Bank attempts to undermine the weight of the international sources discussed above by arguing that state practice does not support the existence of a universal norm. The basis for this argument is that "some 80 nations in Africa, in the Arab world and elsewhere expressly exempt from the definition of terrorism conduct that they believe furthers the rights of self-determination of a people." To begin with, Arab Bank ignores that the international sources relied upon here themselves evidence state practice. *** [T]reaties evidence the "customs and practices" of the States that ratify them. This is so because ratification of a treaty that embodies specific norms of conduct evidences a State's acceptance of the norms as legal obligations. Here, the international sources specifically articulate a universal standard that condemns the conduct alleged.

In addition, Arab Bank's state practice argument is based upon a flawed premise and is devoid of factual support. As for the premise, Arab Bank's argument is that the acts alleged here-organized, systematic suicide bombings and other murderous acts intended to intimidate a civilian population-are viewed by some States as acceptable acts in furtherance of the right to self-determination. However, Arab Bank offers no authority for the proposition that the right to self-determination can be effectuated in violation of the law of nations. *** Indeed, the Bombing Convention, the Financing Convention and Resolution 1566 all expressly acknowledge that violation of the principles embodied in those documents are under no circumstances justifiable by political, philosophical, ideological, racial, ethnic, or religious considerations.   Moreover, there have been no formal reservations to either of the Conventions purporting to assert that a right to self-determination justifies committing otherwise condemned acts. On the contrary, even the statements relied upon, which are made by officials of varying official stature, never expressly state that the type of conduct alleged here is a legitimate means of asserting the right to self-determination.

Turning to the lack of factual support for Defendant's state practice argument, it is significant that the United States prohibits the specific conduct alleged in the cases at hand.   Arab Bank has offered no evidence that it is lawful in any State to engage in organized, systematic murderous attacks on civilians for the purpose of coercing or intimidating the civilian population. Both sides to this litigation note that the Palestinian Authority has explicitly condemned suicide bombings and that it "arrests, convicts, and sentences to imprisonment terrorists who kill Israeli citizens in the occupied territories." ***

The next issue to be addressed is whether the international norm is of mutual, and not merely several, concern.   Suicide bombings and other murderous attacks to intimidate or coerce a civilian population are indisputably of mutual concern.   The Bombing Convention states that the occurrence of terrorist attacks by means of explosives or other lethal devices is a matter of grave concern to the international community as a whole. The Financing Convention states that "the financing of terrorism is a matter of grave concern to the international community as a whole."   In addition, Congress has found that "international terrorism affects the interstate and foreign commerce of the United States by harming international trade and market stability, and limiting international travel by United States citizens as well as foreign visitors to the United States." Indeed, the scope of the nationalities represented by plaintiffs in this very case illustrates one type of impact on the international community that arises when innocent civilians are targeted to be attacked.

In sum, in light of the universal condemnation of organized and systematic suicide bombings and other murderous acts intended to intimidate or coerce a civilian population, this court finds that such conduct violates an established norm of international law.   The court further finds that the conduct alleged by plaintiffs is sufficiently specific and well-defined to be recognized as a claim under the ATS. This becomes evident when the conduct alleged here and condemned by the law of nations is viewed in contrast to the conduct alleged in cases where it was found not to be sufficiently specific or well-defined. *** This Court's consideration of whether to exercise its discretion to recognize a claim under the ATS is informed by the legislative guidance provided by Congress.   Although Congress has not created a cause of action under the ATS, it has created criminal penalties and, with respect to U.S. nationals, civil liability for the acts alleged by plaintiffs.

Finally, the collateral consequences about which the *Sosa* Court expressed concern seem limited here.   The Court in *Sosa* specifically noted the potential consequences on U.S. foreign policy that could accompany recognition of new claims under the ATS. *** Based upon all of the factors set forth above, organized, systematic suicide bombings and other murderous attacks against innocent civilians for the purpose of intimidating a civilian population are a violation of the law of nations for which this court can and does recognize a cause of action under the ATS. ***

Whether Arab Bank is liable for its alleged conduct under the ATS, like the question of whether the suicide bombings and attacks alleged by plaintiffs violate the law of nations, is a question of international law. In a variety of ATS cases, courts have concluded that international law provides for the imposition of liability on a party that does not directly perform the underlying act. There is nothing novel or unusual under international law about imposing such liability. And the Genocide, Bombing, and Financing Conventions explicitly condemn acts of complicity or aiding and abetting by non-primary actors. Indeed, under the Financing Convention, the acts of Arab Bank alleged by plaintiffs amount to primary violations, as the entire focus of that Convention is on stopping the financing of terrorists and terrorist organizations which support offenses against civilians as defined in the Convention. ***

In sum, the amended complaints adequately allege Arab Bank's knowledge that its assistance would facilitate the terrorist organizations in accomplishing the underlying violations of the law of nations and that its provision of banking and administrative services substantially assisted the perpetration of those violations. Arab Bank provided practical assistance to the organizations sponsoring the suicide bombings and helped them further their goal of encouraging bombers to serve as "martyrs." Indeed, as already noted, the allegations state a primary violation of the Financing Convention, under which it is sufficient that Arab Bank is alleged to have provided or collected funds with the knowledge that they were to be used in any way to contribute to acts that include using an explosive with the intent to cause death or serious bodily injury or to attack innocent civilians with the purpose of intimidating or coercing a civilian population.

Finally, that defendant is a private entity not acting under color of state law does not affect its liability. The rule against genocide and crimes against humanity is enforceable against non-state actors. The third international norm alleged to have been violated here, the prohibition of suicide bombings and other murderous attacks on civilians designed to intimidate or coerce a civilian population, also creates responsibility without regard to whether the actions are taken under color of state law. As with plaintiffs' genocide and crimes against humanity allegations, plaintiffs here allege widespread, organized and systematic attacks on civilians. *** Neither the Bombing Convention, the Financing Convention nor the other sources of international law which give rise to this norm require state action. ***

In addition to these findings, Congress expressed that it was enacting its prohibition on material support to foreign terrorist organizations pursuant to its power under Article I, Section 8, Clause 10, of the U.S. Constitution, to "define and punish ... Offenses against the Law of Nations" and thus appears to have recognized that providing material support to a foreign terrorist organization is a violation of the law of nations.   This provides further support that Arab Bank's conduct renders it liable under the ATS and alleviates *Sosa's* concern that there has been "no congressional mandate to seek out and define new and debatable violations of the law of nations...." ***

Notes

1. Outcomes. What explains the difference in the outcomes of these two cases? Is it a difference in how the plaintiffs pled their cases, a difference in the factual allegations of violations of "the law of nations," or simply divergence of judicial opinions in an area open to many interpretations?

2. Substance of the "Law of Nations." Customary "law of nations" prohibits such outrageous conduct that it might well be criminalized domestically.   The "law of nations" may also come together through treaties through which nations agree collectively to eliminate antisocial behavior. *Almog* and *Saperstein* serve as windows to this wider vista. Should the "Law of Nations" be fixed at a given point in time? For example, should it be fixed in 1789 when the Art. I, Section 8, Clause 10 power to punish the "Law of Nations" became operative?   Or would a date when the ATS was passed (or amended) be better?   Or should both the constitutional power and the statutory grant of jurisdiction be viewed as changing (and expanding?) over time?   Is that consistent with due process (including prior publication of what conduct is unlawful) to criminal defendants?

3. Crime and Tort. Modern domestic law tends to distinguish sharply between criminal and tort law. Public prosecutors initiate criminal prosecutions; injured individuals initiate tort suits. Procedures differ, sometimes dramatically. Criminal procedures often serve to protect civil liberties, sometimes to the point that the guilty may go free because the state bumbled. Tort procedures are generally designed to be more evenhanded, a search for whether the plaintiff's injury should be compensated by the defendant. And of course the basic remedies differ significantly: incarceration for criminal miscreants, monetary payment for tortfeasors. These differences obscure common origins of crime and tort, origins which came together in the Alien Tort Statute in 1789 and which underlie its application today.

4. Domesticating International Law. *Almog* and *Saperstein* focus, because of the ATS language and history, on a precise issue: is terrorism a violation of the law of nations? The courts, looking at the cases before them, do not elaborate upon the broader issue of when international law is enforceable as a part of domestic law.   That is a complex question on which there is vigorous disagreement among scholars and judges. For example, *Roper v. Simmons*, 543 U.S. 551 (2005) involved whether the death penalty for a juvenile offender violated the Eighth Amendment prohibition of "cruel and unusual punishment." Some justices thought this question should be decided wholly through an assessment of whether domestic views of the punishment made it "cruel and unusual" while other justices thought the views of other western democracies (unanimously opposed to this criminal penalty) should be considered. *Medellin v. Texas*, 554 U.S. 491 (2008), a death penalty case involving aliens rather than minors, deeply divided the Court over whether the Vienna Convention, a treaty ratified by the United States, was a part of domestic law or whether specific domestic authorizing legislation was required to make it applicable in state courts.

5. Domestic Counterterrorism Tools and International Law. Nations differ widely on how they handle terrorism. They cooperate, as we saw in *Almog*, through treaties. They also coordinate counterterrorism investigations and share information to find terrorists, as we shall see in later chapters. What if certain tools are viewed by most but not all nations as off limits? Sometimes, as with using torture to obtain information about terrorist activities, there is a consensus that takes the form of a treaty (The Convention Against Torture). Other times, as with detention practices, most nations, without a convention or treaty, repudiate a particular tool, such as military detention or military commission trial of terrorist suspects. A particularly strong view against international law being imported into United States law was expressed by Judge Brown of the D.C. Circuit: "The idea that international norms hang over domestic law as a corrective force to be implemented by courts is not only alien to our caselaw, but an aggrandizement of the judicial role beyond the Constitution's conception of the separation of powers." *Al-Bihani v. Obama*, 619 F.3d 1 (CADC, 2010) (denial of rehearing en banc). Her view was repudiated by other members of the court.

6. Non-State Violations of the "Law of Nations." Neither the Almog nor the Saperstein court addresses whether private companies may violate the "law of nations" absent a treaty providing for individual actor liability. This is in fact a vexing question. Traditionally, and certainly at the time the ATS was passed, the law of nations viewed states rather than individuals as its primary objects. Piracy was an exception, and terrorism might over time become another. For the moment, however, most lower courts facing the question have held that private companies may not be subjected to liability under the ATS.

7. Federal Court Jurisdiction. Does the assertion of jurisdiction by the federal courts in these cases square with your notions from Civil Procedure of the reach of federal court jurisdiction? Is the hook citizenship, diversity, or territory? Should some crimes be deemed so horrendous that they should be punishable in the courts of all nations? This topic will be explored further in Chapter IX.

2. IN INTERNATIONAL COURTS

International Courts that deal with criminal offenses do not have free-ranging jurisdiction. Examples historically of such courts were the Nuremberg and Tokyo tribunals following World War II, which tried and punished war crimes committed by the Germans and Japanese. More recently, the International Criminal Tribunal for Yugoslavia (ICTY) and similar tribunals for Rwanda (ICTR), Sierra Leone (Special Court for Sierra Leone) and Cambodia (Khmer Rouge Tribunal) have served as forums in which to prosecute alleged crimes under international law, including crimes against humanity, war crimes, and genocide. Finally, the permanent International Criminal Court (ICC), which the United States was instrumental in shaping but whose treaty the United States has not signed or ratified, began operating in 2002 with 106 member states. The ICC currently has four active cases stemming from conflicts in the Democratic Republic of the Congo, Uganda, the Central African Republic, and Darfur.

What states, persons, and crimes are subject to the jurisdiction of these tribunals? Many details of the answers to this question are beyond the scope of this book, which focuses on antiterrorism law rather than a broader swath of international crimes, crimes against humanity, or other violations of the laws of war. For us, the issue is simply whether these courts, if they otherwise have jurisdiction over states or persons, have jurisdiction over "terrorism" as an international crime. Terrorism as an international crime could conceivably be defined under treaties or could be a matter of customary international law.

As you saw in *Almog*, here are treaties which make certain acts of terrorism criminal (e.g. airline hijacking, terrorist financing, and terrorist bombings). These treaties have not been signed by all states, and states that have not signed a treaty do not consent to jurisdiction over their citizens concerning such matters. Additionally, in the case of an armed conflict, international humanitarian law prohibits "[a]cts or threats of violence the primary purpose of which is to spread terror among the civilian population," Finally, the United Nations has declared that "acts, methods, and practices of terrorism are contrary to the purposes and principles of the United Nations and that knowingly financing, planning and inciting terrorist acts are also contrary to the purposes and principles of the United Nations." S.C. Res. 1373 (2001) of 28 September 2001. The breadth of this resolution is somewhat questionable, however, in light of an earlier declaration by the General Assembly noting "the legitimacy of the struggle, in particular of national liberation movements, against colonial and racist regimes." G.A. Res 40/61 of 9 Dec. 1985.

The following decision considers whether customary international law prohibits terrorism and, if so, whether it may be punished by the ICTY.

PROSECUTOR v. STANISLAV GALIC
ICTY Appeals Chamber
30 November 2006

[The trial court opinion noted that General Galic, "conducted a protracted campaign of shelling and sniping upon civilian areas of Sarajevo and upon the civilian population thereby inflicting terror and mental suffering upon its civilian population." The trial court set forth the prosecutor's position as having two separate components. As to the first, "the Prosecution explained its position that the character of the armed conflict in Sarajevo as international or non-international was "irrelevant" to the charges against the Accused. As to the second, "The Prosecution further maintained that the prohibition against terrorizing the civilian population amounts to a rule of *customary* international law applicable to all armed conflicts. In support of this the Prosecution cited certain rules on aerial warfare prepared in the 1920s but not finalized, two UN resolutions from 1994 condemning atrocities in the former Yugoslavia, and the Spanish penal code from 1995." The trial court panel of three judges, with one judge dissenting, found jurisdiction to convict of a violation of Protocol I and did not reach the second question (whether terrorism violated customary international law). The language which follows comprised a significant limitation on the reach of its opinion: "the Majority is not required to decide whether an offence of terror in a *general* sense falls within the jurisdiction of the Tribunal, but only whether a *specific* offence of killing and wounding civilians in time of armed conflict with the intention to inflict terror on the civilian population, as alleged in the Indictment, is an offence over which it has jurisdiction. While the Tribunal may have jurisdiction over other conceivable varieties of the crime of terror, it will be for Trial Chambers faced with charges correspondingly different from Count 1 of the present Indictment to decide that question."

The dissenting trial judge said: "an offence will fall within the jurisdiction of the Tribunal only if it existed as a form of liability under international customary law. When considering an offence, a Trial Chamber must verify that the provisions upon which a charge is based reflect customary law. Furthermore, it must establish that individual criminal liability attaches to a breach of such provisions under international customary law at the time relevant to an indictment in order to satisfy the *ratione personae* requirement. Once it is satisfied that a certain act or set of acts is indeed criminal under customary international law, a Trial Chamber must finally confirm that this offence was defined with sufficient clarity under international customary law for its general nature, its criminal character and its approximate gravity to have been sufficiently foreseeable and accessible."

The following paragraphs are from the opinion of the five judge appeals panel. They are followed by a dissenting opinion by Judge Shomberg. Both opinions focus on interpretation of Art. 3 of the ICTY Statute, which states: "The International Tribunal shall have the power to prosecute persons for violation of the laws or customs of war."]

79.   Galić argues *** that the Trial Chamber violated the principle of *nullum crimen sine lege* in convicting him under Count 1. He argues that the International Tribunal has no jurisdiction over the crime of acts or threats of violence the primary purpose of which is to spread terror among the civilian population as "there exists no international crime of terror".   *** [H]e submits that the Trial Chamber erred in finding that the 22 May 1992 Agreement was binding upon the parties to the conflict.   Further, he challenges the Trial Chamber's finding with regard to the elements of the crime. Finally, he argues that the Prosecution has not proved that the acts of "sniping" and "shelling" were carried out with the primary purpose of spreading terror among the civilian population.

80.   The Prosecution *** asserts that Galić "fails to address the Appeals Chamber's jurisprudence that a clearly applicable treaty-based provision is sufficient to satisfy the requirements of *nullum crimen sine lege* and that the principle does not prevent a court from developing, within reasonable limits, the elements of an offence." With regard to the 22 May Agreement, the Prosecution submits that Galić had the relevant information at trial and that as a result he has now waived his right to appeal on this point. With regard to Galić's arguments that he did not act with the required intent, the Prosecution argues that this claim is "vague and unsupported" and fails to address the detailed reasoning of the Trial Chamber. The Prosecution claims that Galić "must do significantly more than make unsubstantiated claims in

order to justify the intervention of the Appeals Chamber"; it submits that his argument should be dismissed on that basis alone.

81.   Pursuant to Article 1 of the Statute, the International Tribunal has jurisdiction over "serious violations of international humanitarian law". What is encompassed by "international humanitarian law" is however not specified in the Statute. *** This body of law exists in the form of both conventional law and customary law. While there is international customary law which is not laid down in conventions, some of the major conventional humanitarian law has become part of customary international law. ***

82.   When first seized of the issue of the scope of its jurisdiction *ratione materiae,* the International Tribunal interpreted its mandate as applying not only to breaches of international humanitarian law based on customary international law but also to those based on international instruments entered into by the conflicting parties – including agreements concluded by conflicting parties under the auspices of the ICRC to bring into force rules pertaining to armed conflicts – provided that the instrument in question is:

(i) [...] unquestionably binding on the parties at the time of the alleged offence; and (ii) [...] not in conflict with or derogat[ing] from peremptory norms of international law, as are most customary rules of international humanitarian law.

83.   However, while conventional law can form the basis for the International Tribunal's jurisdiction, provided that the above conditions are met, an analysis of the jurisprudence of the International Tribunal demonstrates that the Judges have consistently endeavoured to satisfy themselves that the crimes charged in the indictments before them were crimes under customary international law at the time of their commission and were sufficiently defined under that body of law. This is because in most cases, treaty provisions will only provide for the prohibition of a certain conduct, not for its criminalisation, or the treaty provision itself will not sufficiently define the elements of the prohibition they criminalise and customary international law must be looked at for the definition of those elements. ***

84.   In recent judgments, the Appeals Chamber also had recourse to customary international law because the elements of the crimes or the modes of liability were not defined or not defined sufficiently in conventional law. ***

85.   The Appeals Chamber rejects Galić's argument that the International Tribunal's jurisdiction for crimes under Article 3 of the Statute can only be based on customary international law. However, while binding conventional law that prohibits conduct and provides for individual criminal responsibility could provide the basis for the International Tribunal's jurisdiction, in practice the International Tribunal always ascertains that the treaty provision in question is also declaratory of custom.

86.   On appeal, Galić argued that the 22 May 1992 Agreement was not binding on the parties and even if binding did not give rise to individual criminal responsibility on the part of the parties. The Appeals Chamber does

not consider it necessary to address this argument on the ground that, as will be demonstrated below, it is satisfied that the prohibition of terror against the civilian population as enshrined in Article 51(2) of Additional Protocol I and Article 13(2) of Additional Protocol II, was a part of customary international law from the time of its inclusion in those treaties. The Appeals Chamber, by majority, Judge Schomburg dissenting, is further satisfied that a breach of the prohibition of terror against the civilian population gave rise to individual criminal responsibility pursuant to customary international law at the time of the commission of the offences for which Galić was convicted.

87.   In the present case, the crime of acts or threats of violence the primary purpose of which is to spread terror among the civilian population was charged under Article 3 of the Statute, on the basis of Article 51(2) of Additional Protocol I and Article 13(2) of Additional Protocol II, both of which state:

The civilian population as such, as well as individual civilians, shall not be the object of attack. Acts or threats of violence the primary purpose of which is to spread terror among the civilian population are prohibited. ***

The purposes of Additional Protocols I and II, as expressly stated by the High Contracting Parties in the preambles to those treaties, were to "reaffirm and develop the provisions protecting the victims of armed conflicts" and "to ensure a better protection for the victims" of armed conflicts. Additional Protocol II, further, is considered to embody the "fundamental principles on protection for the civilian population". Articles 51(2) of Additional Protocol I and 13(2) of Additional Protocol II, in essence, contribute to the purpose of those treaties. They do not contain new principles but rather codify in a unified manner the prohibition of attacks on the civilian population. The principles underlying the prohibition of attacks on civilians, namely the principles of distinction and protection, have a long-standing history in international humanitarian law. These principles incontrovertibly form the basic foundation of international humanitarian law and constitute "intransgressible principles of international customary law". *** The Appeals Chamber therefore affirms the finding of the Trial Chamber that the prohibition of terror, as contained in the second sentences of both Article 51(2) of Additional Protocol I and Article 13(2) of Additional Protocol II, amounts to "a specific prohibition within the general (customary) prohibition of attack on civilians".

88.   The Appeals Chamber found further evidence that the prohibition of terror among the civilian population was part of customary international law from at least its inclusion in the second sentences of both Article 51(2) of Additional Protocol I and Article 13(2) of Additional Protocol II. The 1923 Hague Rules on Warfare prohibited "[a]ny air bombardment for the purpose of terrorizing the civil population or destroying or damaging private property without military character or injuring non-combatants". Similarly, the 1938 Draft Convention for the Protection of Civilian Populations against New Engines of War expressly prohibited "[a]erial bombardment for the purpose of terrorising the civilian population". Even more importantly, Article 33 of

Geneva Convention IV, an expression of customary international law, prohibits in clear terms "measures of intimidation or of terrorism" as a form of collective punishment, as they are "opposed to all principles based on humanity and justice". Further, Article 6 of the 1956 New Delhi Draft Rules for protection of civilians states that "[a]ttacks directed against the civilian population, as such, whether with the object of terrorizing it or for any other reason, are prohibited." More recently, Article 6 of the 1990 Turku Declaration of Minimum Humanitarian Standards envisaged that "[a]cts or threats of violence the primary purpose or foreseeable effect of which is to spread terror among the population are prohibited."

89.   Another indication of the customary international law nature of the prohibition of terror at the time of the events alleged in this case can be found in the number of States parties to Additional Protocols I and II by 1992. Also, references to official pronouncements of States and their military manuals further confirm the customary international nature of the prohibition. ***

90.   In light of the foregoing, the Appeals Chamber finds that the prohibition of terror against the civilian population as enshrined in Article 51(2) of Additional Protocol I and Article 13(2) of Additional Protocol II clearly belonged to customary international law from at least the time of its inclusion in those treaties.

91.   The crime of acts or threats of violence the primary purpose of which is to spread terror among the civilian population was charged under Article 3 of the Statute. The conditions that must be fulfilled for a violation of international humanitarian law to be subject to Article 3 of the Statute are ("*Tadić* conditions"):

i)   the violation must constitute an infringement of a rule of international humanitarian law;

ii)   the rule must be customary in nature or, if it belongs to treaty law, the required conditions must be met [...];

iii)   the violation must be "serious", that is to say, it must constitute a breach of a rule protecting important values, and the breach must involve grave consequences for the victim. ***;

iv)   the violation of the rule must entail, under customary or conventional law, the individual criminal responsibility of the person breaching the rule.

92.   Individual criminal responsibility *** can be inferred from, *inter alia*, state practice indicating an intention to criminalize the prohibition, including statements by government officials and international organizations, as well as punishment of violations by national courts and military tribunals.

93.   The first reference to terror against the civilian population as a war crime, as correctly noted by the Trial Chamber, is found in the 1919 Report of the Commission on Responsibilities, created by the Peace Conference of Paris to inquire into breaches of the laws and customs of war committed by Germany and its allies in World War I. The Commission found evidence of

the existence of "a system of terrorism carefully planned and carried out to the end", stated that the belligerents employed "systematic terrorism", and listed among the list of war crimes "systematic terrorism". Although the few trials organized on that basis in Leipzig did not elaborate on the concept of "systematic terrorism", this is nonetheless an indication that, in 1919, there was an intention to criminalize the deliberate infliction of terror upon the civilian population. Further, in 1945, Australia's War Crimes Act referred to the work of the 1919 Commission on Responsibilities and included "systematic terrorism" in its list of war crimes.

94.   With respect to national legislation, the Appeals Chamber Notes that numerous States criminalize violations of international humanitarian law — encompassing the crime of acts or threats of violence the primary purpose of which is to spread terror among the civilian population— within their jurisdiction. ***

96.   *** [N]umerous States have incorporated provisions as to the criminalization of terror against the civilian population as a method of warfare in a language similar to the prohibition set out in the Additional Protocols. The Criminal Codes of the Czech Republic and the Slovak Republic, for example, criminalize "terroris[ing] defenseless civilians with violence or the threat of violence". Further, numerous States have incorporated provisions that criminalize terrorization of civilians in time of war. ***

97.   The Appeals Chamber also Notes the references by the Trial Chamber to the laws in force in the former Yugoslavia at the time of the commission of the offences charged *** Those provisions not only amount to further evidence of the customary nature of terror against the civilian population as a crime, but are also relevant to the assessment of the foreseeability and accessibility of that law to Galić.

98.   In addition to national legislation, the Appeals Chamber Notes the conviction in 1997 by the Split County Court in Croatia for acts that occurred between March 1991 and January 1993, under, *inter alia,* Article 51 of Additional Protocol I and Article 13 of Additional Protocol II, including "a plan of terrorising and mistreating the civilians", "open[ing] fire from infantry arms [...] with only one goal to terrorise and expel the remaining civilians", "open[ing] fire from howitzers, machine guns, automatic rifles, anti-aircraft missiles only to create the atmosphere of fear among the remaining farmers", and "carrying out the orders of their commanders with the goal to terrorise and threaten with the demolishing of the Peruča dam".

In light of the foregoing, the Appeals Chamber finds *** that customary international law imposed individual criminal liability for violations of the prohibition of terror against the civilian population as enshrined in Article 51(2) of Additional Protocol I and Article 13(2) of Additional Protocol II, from at least the period relevant to the Indictment. ***

JUDGE SCHOMBURG [partial dissent]

    *** I cannot agree with the majority of the bench which affirmed Galic's conviction under Count 1 for the crime of "acts and threats of violence the primary purpose of which is to spread terror among the civilian population" ("terrorization against a civilian population"). In my view, there is no basis to find that this prohibited conduct as such was penalized beyond any doubt under customary international criminal law at the time relevant to the Indictment. Rather, I would have overturned Galic's conviction under Count 1 and convicted him under Counts 4 and 7 for the same underlying criminal conduct, taking into account the acts of terrorization against a civilian population as an aggravating factor in sentencing, thus arriving at the same adjusted sentence. ***

4.   The Indictment in this case charged the Appellant under Count 1 (violations of the laws or customs of war: unlawfully inflicting terror upon civilians) with having "conducted a protracted campaign of sniping and shelling upon the civilian population." This same criminal conduct also served as a basis for Counts 4 and 7 of the Indictment (violations of the laws or customs of war: attack on civilians). The Trial Chamber found that the "series of military attacks on civilians in ABiH-held areas of Sarajevo and during the Indictment period were carried out from SRK-controlled territories with the aim to spread terror among the civilian population" and "constituted a campaign of sniping and shelling against civilians." It established Galic's individual criminal responsibility for these acts and convicted him under Count 1 for what it called "the crime of terror". The majority of the Appeals Chamber affirms this conviction, subject to two changes: first, it renames the crime; second, it holds without sufficient reasoning that the crime was founded in customary international law during the Indictment period. *** I respectfully submit that it is not possible to assert beyond any doubt that the crime was indeed part of customary international law at the time of Galic's criminal conduct.

5.   It is the settled jurisprudence of the Appeals Chamber since *Tadic* that the International Tribunal has jurisdiction for a violation of international humanitarian law under Article 3 of the Statute only when four conditions are met: [1] the violation must constitute an infringement of a rule of international humanitarian law; [2] the rule must be customary in nature or, if it belongs to treaty law, the required conditions must be met [...]; [3] the violation must be serious, that is to say, it must constitute a breach of a rule protecting important values, and the breach must involve grave consequences for the victim. [...]; [4] the violation of the rule must entail, under customary or conventional law, the individual criminal responsibility of the person breaching the rule.

6.   Furthermore, when taking recourse to customary international law, the International Tribunal must be very careful in assessing what undeniably belongs to this body of law. Indeed, it was the Secretary-General's view that "the application of the principle *nullum crimen sine lege* requires that the international tribunal should apply rules of international humanitarian law which are beyond any doubt part of customary law [...]."

7.   It is generally accepted that the existence of customary law has primarily to be deducted from the practice and *opinio juris* of states. There can be no doubt – as explained in the Judgement – that the *prohibition* of acts

and threats of violence the primary purpose of which is to spread terror among the civilian population, as set out in Article 51(2), 2nd Sentence of Additional Protocol I and Article 13(2), 2nd Sentence of Additional Protocol II, was part of customary international law. The violation of this prohibition by Galic clearly fulfilled the first three *Tadic* conditions. However, the core question of this case is whether the fourth *Tadic* condition was met as well, that is, whether the aforementioned prohibition was penalized, thus attaching individual criminal responsibility to Galic.

The Judgement comes to the conclusion that the fourth *Tadic* condition was satisfied, stating "that *numerous* states criminalise violations of international humanitarian law — encompassing the crime of acts or threats of violence the primary purpose of which is to spread terror among the civilian population — within their jurisdiction" and "that *numerous* States have incorporated provisions as to the criminalisation of terror against the civilian population as a method of warfare in a language similar to the prohibition set out in the Additional Protocols." Upon further analysis, it is questionable whether these claims are accurate. Indeed, the temporal point of departure when determining whether there was state practice must be the time period relevant to the Indictment, which charged Galic for acts committed between 1992 and 1994. ***

The Appeals Chamber was thus only able to establish with certainty that just an extraordinarily limited number of states at the time relevant to the Indictment had penalized terrorization against a civilian population in a manner corresponding to the prohibition of the Additional Protocols, these being Cote D'Ivoire, the then Czechoslovakia, Ethiopia, the Netherlands, Norway and Switzerland. It is doubtful whether this can be viewed as evidence of "extensive and virtually uniform" state practice on this matter. Moreover, one must consider that Norway's Penal Code only generally refers to breaches of the Additional Protocols, thus raising the question of *nullum crimen sine lege certa*. The same concern applies to Switzerland's Military Penal Code. The Netherlands later even repealed the relevant provision when implementing the ICC Statute in national law, *i.e.* after the relevant time period *(lex mitior)*.

Furthermore, it must be considered that many states did *not* choose to pass legislation in this respect, even though they had legislation penalizing attacks on civilians. Examples are the United States,[27] the United Kingdom,[28] Australia,[29] Germany,[30] Italy[31] and Belgium.[32] *** [I]t is not sufficient to

---

[27] U.S. Code, Title 18, Chapter 118, Section 2441 (c) (1) defines as a war crime "a grave breach in any of the international conventions signed at Geneva 12 August 1949, or any protocol to such convention to which the United States is a party". The United States has not even ratified either Additional Protocol I or Additional Protocol II.

[28] Section 1 of the Geneva Conventions Act of 1957, as amended in 1995, punishes grave breaches of the Additional Protocol I, referring specifically to Art. 85 of the Additional Protocol. There is no mention of "terrorization against a civilian population."

[29] The War Crimes Act of 1945, *** was substantially modified in 1989 and did not contain the phrase "murder and massacres — systematic terrorism" thereafter.

[30] *** [O]ne of the most recent documents implementing the Rome Statute of an International Criminal Court, the 2002 German Code of Crimes Against International Law

simply refer to a "continuing trend of nations criminalising terror as a method of warfare" when this trend *** is of no relevance to the time period in which Galic's criminal conduct falls.***

14.   Furthermore, it is doubtful whether the arguments relating to the 1919 Report of the Commission on Responsibilities presented in paragraph 93 of the Judgement withstand careful scrutiny. The citations (which were also employed in the Trial Judgement) are taken out of context: When reading the original text in the 1948 work by the U.N. War Crimes Commission, one could ask whether the 1919 Commission was not just making a broader statement without actually coining legal definitions:

In particular, the Commission established the fact that multiple violations of the rights of combatants, of the rights of civilians, and of the rights of both had been committed, which were the outcome of the "most cruel practices which primitive barbarism, aided by all the resources of modern science, could devise for the execution of a system of terrorism carefully planned and carried out to the end. Not even prisoners, or wounded, or women, or children have been respected by belligerents who deliberately sought to strike terror into every heart for the purpose of repressing all resistance."

It is true that the Commission mentioned "systematic terrorism" on its list of recommended war crimes. However, it is uncertain what the Commission actually meant by "systematic terrorism" and whether their idea of the concept corresponds to Art. 51(2), 2nd Sentence of Additional Protocol I and Article 13(2), 2nd Sentence of Additional Protocol II. Moreover, the Judgement correctly states that "the few trials [...] in Leipzig did not elaborate on the concept of 'systematic terrorism'" In this context, it has to be recalled that there was no penalization of terrorization against a civilian population in either Nuremberg or the Tokyo Charters. The same applies to Control Council Law No. 10.

The Judgement refers in paragraph 97 to a judgement rendered in 1997 by the County Court of Split, Croatia. It is questionable whether a single judgement can be considered an example of state practice. On the contrary, one could argue that the existence of just *one* judgement rendered in a region where there was much comparable criminal conduct actually militates against the proposition that there was relevant state practice.

Finally, it must be considered that the Trial Chamber made no finding as to the nature of the conflict being international or non-international at that time. However, an additional finding would have been required by the Appeals Chamber even though the relevant provisions of Additional Protocol I (applying

---

(*Völkerstrafgesetzbuch*) does not encompass this crime or a similar criminal conduct as a crime *sui generis*. *** Moreover, there was and there is no provision in the German Penal Code penalizing terrorization against the civilian population.

[31] Book III, Title IV, Section 2, Art. 185 of the Criminal Military Code of War penalizes to "utilise la violence contre des personnes privees ennemies qui ne prennent pas part aux operations militaires". There is no mention of "terror".

[32] The Law of 16 June 1993 penalized in its Art. *lter* (11) "le fait de soumettre ä une attaque delibdree la population civile ou des personnes civiles qui ne prennent pas directement part aux hostilities". There is no mention of terror. ***

to international armed conflicts) and Additional Protocol II (applying to non-international armed conflicts) are identical. At least, pursuant to the view of the majority which is based primarily on an interpretation of the Additional Protocols, the Appeals Chamber should have made a much more detailed determination of why according to the opinion of the majority *both* the relevant provisions of Additional Protocol I and Additional Protocol II would amount to international customary law.

Moreover, with all due respect, I cannot agree *** that "the conclusion [that criminal responsibility attaches to the prohibition of terrorization against a civilian population] also follows logically from the ban [...] on 'declaring that no quarter will be given.' For me, the argument that "if threats that no quarter will be given are crimes, then surely threats that a party will not respect other foundational principles of international law – such as the prohibition against targeting civilians – are also crimes" appears to be incorrect since it could be made *in* any context *in* relation to any and every violation of international humanitarian law. While the act of declaring that no quarter will be given is undoubtedly penalized under international customary law (and was so during the Indictment period) it is nevertheless distinct from terrorization against a civilian population. In particular, the placement of Article 40 of Additional Protocol I in the part on methods and means of warfare, combatant and prisoner-of-war status, under the subsection dealing with methods and means of warfare, as well as its origin in Article 23(d) of the Hague Regulations, makes clear that the prohibition of declaring that no quarter will be given refers to enemy combatants. Having said this, I agree *** that the prohibitions *are similar* in nature in that they both aim at protecting those who are either hors-de-combat or civilians. However, as an international criminal court, we are under the obligation to define what is a crime under our Statute *with precision* in order to avoid any violation of the fundamental principle of *nullum crimen sine lege certa.*

What then is supposed to be the foundation of state practice, apart from the few states mentioned above? Moreover, while noting that *de jure* all member States of the United Nations are on an equal footing, I nevertheless observe that none of the permanent members of the Security Council or any other prominent state have penalized terrorization against a civilian population.

*** [A]s the recent Study on Customary International Humanitarian Law carried out by the International Committee of the Red Cross recognizes:

> [I]n the area of international humanitarian law, where many rules require abstention from certain conduct, omissions pose a particular problem in the assessment of *opinio juris* because it has to be proved that the abstention is not a coincidence but based on a legitimate expectation.

In addition, and even though I am fully aware of Article 10 of the Statute of the International Criminal Court, it must be pointed out that the Rome Statute does not have a provision referring to terrorization against a civilian population. If indeed this crime was beyond doubt part of customary international law, in 1998 (!) states would undoubtedly have included it in the relevant provisions of the Statute or in their domestic legislation implementing the Statute.

To be abundantly clear: The conduct prohibited *** should be penalized as a crime *sui generis*. However, this Tribunal is not acting as a legislator; it is under the obligation to apply only customary international law applicable at the time of the criminal conduct, in this case the time between 1992 and 1994. It is not necessary to dwell on the question of whether *today* the crime of terrorization against a civilian population is part of customary international law. In fact, there might be some indicators that this is indeed the case. However, one cannot conscientiously base a conviction in criminal matters on a "continuing trend of nations criminalising terror as a method of warfare" or on a "trend in prohibiting terror [...] continued after 1992" The use of the term "trend" clearly indicates that at the time of the commission of the crimes in question, this development had not yet amounted to undisputed state practice. The case in question is about a conduct that happened fourteen years ago, which must be assessed accordingly. The International Tribunal is required to adhere strictly to the principle of *nullum crimen sine lege praevia* and must ascertain that a crime was "beyond any doubt part of customary law." It would be detrimental *** if our jurisprudence gave the appearance of inventing crimes – thus highly politicizing its function – where the conduct in question was not without any doubt penalized at the time when it took place.

It is even less understandable in the present case why the majority chose this wrong approach when it would have been possible to arrive at the same result in an undisputable way: *i.e.* overturn Gallic's conviction under Count I and convict him under Counts 4 and 7 for the *same* underlying criminal conduct, namely the campaign of shelling and sniping, constituting the crime of attacks on civilians, this offence being without any doubt part of customary international law. In light of the finding of the Trial Chamber, which held that Galic "intended to conduct that campaign with the primary purpose of spreading terror within the civilian population of Sarajevo", it would have been furthermore possible to consider this an aggravating circumstance in sentencing, which would also necessitate the [upwardly] adjusted sentence as handed down by the Appeals Chamber. *** However, the Appeals Chamber erroneously upheld Galic's conviction under Count 1 of the Indictment for the crime of acts and threats of violence the primary purpose of which is to spread terror.

Notes

1. ICTY Jurisdiction. Why does the appellate court focus on custom rather than treaty? Who has the better of the argument, the majority or the dissent? How does the dissent view punishment the defendant like the majority, given that the majority finds criminalization of terrorism under customary international law is proper and the dissent rejects that view (at least as of 1992)?

2. Sentencing. Did you notice that the appeals court <u>increased</u> Galic's sentence? Could that happen in an appeal following conviction in the United States? The answer to this question will be obvious after you have read the cases in the next section of this chapter.

3. Special Court for Sierra Leone. In its *AFRC* case, concluded in February 2008, the Special Court for Sierra Leone found that the criminalization of acts of terror against the civilian population in times of armed conflict under international law was "well settled" at the time of the Indictment, referring several times to the judgment in *Galic*. The crimes addressed occurred in 1998 and 1999, and the Indictment was presented in 2005. Is it significant that the Sierra Leone Court appeared to examine the state of the law at the time of the Indictment rather than at the time of the crimes (the relevant time to the *Galic* court)? Would Judge Schomberg be willing to accept the criminalization of terrorism at this time, either six or thirteen years after the crimes in *Galic*?

4. ICTY and ICC. Terrorism was deliberately excluded from the jurisdiction of the International Criminal Court, though it can be an added component of crimes that do fall within the ICC jurisdiction, and particular terroristic acts committed in the course of an international or non-international armed conflict may be covered (e.g. taking hostages with intent to compel acts by others on threat of injuring or killing the hostage; Art. 8(2)(a)(viii), par. 3 and Art. 8(2)(c)(iii)). The omission of terrorism (and drug trafficking) from ICC jurisdiction was an accommodation to the United States, whose position was: "[T]he United States is properly concerned that the work of the ICC not compromise important, complex, and costly investigations carried out by its criminal justice or military authorities.***[Terrorism and drug trafficking] are the acts of criminal organizations as part of ongoing patterns of criminal activity.***The object is not only to prosecute crimes but also prevent them. ***A great deal of sensitive and confidential information is gathered and used in a variety of ways to track criminal activity and target suspects. *** [T]he Prosecutor of the ICC in this national and bilateral investigative work could jeopardize bringing criminals to justice." U.S. Position Paper dated March 30, 1995.

C. SENTENCING

This short section provides insights into sentencing in terrorism cases in the United States federal courts. Other countries' practices vary, both methodologically and practically. It is not unusual in European cases, for example, to see shorter sentences than in the United States for terrorism offenses. Moreover, the death penalty is not an option in Europe. The cases presented below raise fundamental issues concerning terrorism sentencing. How do the Federal Sentencing Guidelines apply in terrorism cases? What is the range of judicial discretion in sentencing convicted terrorists? Should victim impact statements be limited in terrorism cases involving multiple victims and varying types of impacts?

UNITED STATES V. ABU ALI
528 F. 3d 210 (C.A.4, 2008)

Joint opinion of JUDGES WILKINSON, MOTZ, AND TRAXLER:

*** Finally, we address the *** reasonableness of Abu Ali's sentence and its variation from the applicable guidelines range of life imprisonment. *** First, the district court ascertained the applicable guidelines range [and] accepted as accurate the presentence report's findings and guidelines calculation, namely an adjusted offense level of forty-nine and a criminal history category of VI. As a result, the recommended sentence for Abu Ali under the Sentencing Guidelines was life imprisonment. Neither party challenges the correctness of the guidelines calculation here. [It] also recognized that Abu Ali's conviction on Count Eight, conspiracy to commit aircraft piracy, carried a mandatory minimum of twenty years imprisonment. Thus, any sentence imposed could not fall below this statutory floor.

Having established these guideposts, the court then considered what sentence would be "sufficient, but not greater than necessary, to comply with" the other factors articulated in 18 U.S.C. § 3553(a). The court discussed the relevant factors seriatim and made the following observations.

First, *** the court emphasized that "Abu Ali never planted any bombs, shot any weapons, or injured any people, and there is no evidence that he took any steps in the United States with others to further the conspiracy" [and] commented on the Defendant's lack of a prior criminal history and his good behavior ***.

Next, though cognizant of the seriousness of Abu Ali's crimes, the court held that a sentence which "forced [Abu Ali] to spend his most productive years in prison" and "consume[d] the *majority* of the remainder of [his] natural life" would constitute sufficient punishment, promote respect for the law, and afford adequate deterrence to criminal conduct. In addition, the court pointed to the low recidivism rates for criminals after the age of fifty and noted that "the decisions that a 21-year old man may make are not necessarily the same decisions that would be made by a man of substantially advanced age who has had great time to reflect and mature." Thus, the court predicted that Abu Ali would not present a danger to public safety if eventually released at a more-advanced age.

Finally, in order to avoid imposing disparate sentences amongst similarly situated defendants, the court considered two other cases-those of John Walker Lindh, *see United States v. Lindh,* 227 F.Supp.2d 565 (E.D.Va.2002) (sentencing Lindh to twenty years imprisonment), and of Timothy McVeigh and Terry Nichols, *see United States v. McVeigh,* 153 F.3d 1166 (10th Cir.1998) (upholding death sentence for McVeigh); *United States v. Nichols,* 169 F.3d 1255 (10th Cir.1999) (affirming sentence of life imprisonment for Nichols). Using these cases as poles on a potential sentencing spectrum, the district court found that a sentence of less than life imprisonment was warranted.

Because Abu Ali took fewer steps in furtherance of his conspiracies than McVeigh and Nichols, and because his actions resulted in less material harm, the court deemed a sentence similar to those received by McVeigh and Nichols as excessive. Instead, it held Abu Ali's crimes to be more akin to those of Lindh. As a result, the court was "persuaded that, in light of the similarities to [Lindh's] case, a sentence of less than life imprisonment is necessary to prevent an unwarranted disparity in Mr. Abu Ali's case." *** [T]he district court found that a non-guidelines sentence was appropriate and imposed a sentence of thirty years imprisonment, followed by thirty years of supervised release. Based on the Defendant's life expectancy, this represented a significant downward deviation from the applicable guidelines range. ***

In *United States v. Booker,* 543 U.S. 220, 245 (2005), the Supreme Court rendered the Sentencing Guidelines "effectively advisory." Nevertheless, district courts in the post- *Booker* landscape must follow specific steps to arrive at an appropriate sentence.

First, the district court must correctly calculate a Defendant's sentence under the now-advisory guidelines. *** Next, the district court must allow "both parties an opportunity to argue for whatever sentence they deem appropriate" [and] "consider all of the § 3553(a) factors," keeping in mind the "overarching provision instructing district courts to 'impose a sentence sufficient, but not greater than necessary' to accomplish the goals of sentencing." In so doing, the court "must make an individualized assessment based on the facts presented" and cannot "presume that the Guidelines range is reasonable." If the sentencing court believes "an outside-Guidelines sentence is warranted, [it] must consider the extent of the deviation and ensure that the justification is sufficiently compelling to support the degree of the variance."

Finally, the district court "must adequately explain the chosen sentence." This "allow[s] for meaningful appellate review" and "promote[s] the perception of fair sentencing." Notably, if the court imposes "an unusually lenient or an unusually harsh sentence," it must provide "sufficient justifications" for its selection.

Under *Booker,* we review a sentence for reasonableness *** Reasonableness review includes both procedural and substantive components. *** [W]hen determining whether the district Court's proffered justification for imposing a non-guidelines sentence "is sufficiently compelling to support the degree of the variance," common sense dictates that "a major departure should be supported by a more significant justification than a minor one." *** [W]e must affirm a variance sentence unless we find the district court abused its discretion.

The dispute in this case centers on the district Court's decision to impose a variance sentence that significantly deviated from the applicable guidelines range. While the deviation happened to be forty percent (based on Abu Ali's life expectancy), we recognize that relying on a particular percentage "suffers from infirmities of application," and we thus simply take note that the variance was "major" and, as a result, "should be supported by a more significant justification than a minor one." *** [We] must engage in "meaningful appellate review" and the district Court's "justification[s] [must be] sufficiently compelling to support the degree of the variance."

In reaching its decision, the district court examined each of the § 3553(a) sentencing factors. However, it was the Court's consideration of § 3553(a)(6), which instructs courts to consider "the need to avoid unwarranted sentence disparities among defendants with similar records who have been found guilty of similar conduct," that served as the driving force behind its ultimate determination. Though it recognized that "there are very few cases to which to compare Mr. Abu Ali's case[,]" the district court devoted most of its attention in explaining the significant downward deviation to a discussion of § 3553(a)(6), focusing on comparisons of Abu Ali's case to those of Lindh and McVeigh/Nichols, respectively. Moreover, the court relied on the sentences imposed in those cases to quantitatively locate the sentence it deemed appropriate for Abu Ali. Given the emphasis the district court placed on this factor, and because the comparisons, as discussed below, were inapposite, we hold that the court abused its discretion when imposing the sentence. As a result, resentencing is required.

First, the court erred when it significantly relied on the need to avoid an unwarranted sentence disparity between the defendant and John Walker Lindh. Lindh pled guilty to two charges in connection with his fighting for the Taliban in Afghanistan and, pursuant to the terms of his plea agreement, was sentenced to twenty years imprisonment. With very little discussion of exactly why Lindh's case was similar to that of Abu Ali's, the district court simply observed that "while it does not rest its judgment solely on a comparison to the Walker Lindh case, the Court is persuaded that, in light of the similarities to [Lindh's] case, a sentence of less than life imprisonment is *necessary* to prevent an unwarranted disparity in Mr. Abu Ali's case."

Using Lindh's case as a comparative benchmark for the sentencing of Abu Ali was problematic to say the least. To begin, it is highly questionable that Lindh's conduct is at all similar to that of the defendant. In May 2001, and thus before September 11, Lindh traveled to Pakistan with the hopes of fighting for the Taliban "on the front line in Afghanistan." "[I]nterested only in fighting with the Taliban against the Northern Alliance in Afghanistan," Lindh declined an offer to "tak[e] part in operations against the United States, Israel or Europe" when approached by an al Farooq camp administrator in the summer of 2001. Instead, he only "wished to fight on the front line against the Northern Alliance." In November 2001, after the September 11 terrorist attacks, Lindh and his fighting unit "surrendered themselves and their weapons to Northern Alliance troops." According to the sentencing court, Lindh claimed that he was not aware of the September 11 attacks until after they had occurred. Based on his fighting with the Taliban, Lindh eventually pled guilty to two charges: supplying services to the Taliban and carrying an explosive during the commission of a felony.

While unquestionably serious, the crimes for which Lindh was convicted are different than Abu Ali's in terms of both their substance and scope. When Lindh was apprehended, he was a foot soldier on a foreign battlefield fighting the Northern Alliance in Afghanistan. Although he had spent time in al-Qaeda-linked military training camps, Lindh was focused on fighting for the Taliban on the front lines. In fact, he declined an opportunity to participate in terrorist attacks against the United States, and claimed he had no prior knowledge of the specific attacks that did take place on September 11, 2001. In his capacity as a Taliban front-line soldier, the magnitude of the threat personally posed by Lindh was limited to those American, and American-allied, soldiers who were within his line of sight on the battlefield.

Lindh and Abu Ali are not comparable. The degree of harm contemplated by Abu Ali was broader in scope and more devastating in terms of its potential impact. *** Abu Ali joined an al-Qaeda cell intent on inflicting massive civilian casualties on American soil. He pledged to engage in jihad against the United States and, as a member of the cell, participated in the planning of several plots, including: assassinating the President of the United States, destroying airliners destined for the United States, and returning to the United States as part of a sleeper cell that, if successful, would engage in terrorist operations within the United States, particularly targeting public gathering places. Abu Ali's designs were not limited to a foreign battlefield or directed at a foreign enemy, but rather aimed at civilian targets in the American homeland. Put simply, his conduct was markedly different than that of Lindh, completely undermining the usefulness of any comparison between the two.

In addition to their dissimilar conduct, Abu Ali and Lindh are not similarly situated defendants *** Lindh, unlike Abu Ali, was sentenced pursuant to a plea agreement with the government [after he] pled guilty to two charges. Pursuant to the deal, Lindh agreed to fully cooperate with the prosecution *** assign any profits or proceeds arising from publicity to the United States government [and] he accepted responsibility and showed remorse for his conduct. As the district court noted in Lindh's sentencing order, Lindh had stated emphatically that he "condemn[ed] terrorism on every level" and openly realized he "made a mistake by joining the Taliban."

In exchange for Lindh's pleading guilty, the government agreed to dismiss the remaining nine counts from the original indictment. This included a charge of carrying a destructive device during a crime of violence, which has a statutory mandatory minimum of thirty years imprisonment. After accepting the plea, the district court sentenced Lindh to the maximum possible sentence pursuant to the agreement, twenty years imprisonment.

By comparison, Abu Ali refused to cooperate with the government, expressed no responsibility or remorse for any of his offenses, and stands convicted of a crime that carries a mandatory minimum (not maximum) of twenty years imprisonment. Although Abu Ali had every right to go to trial and claim innocence until proven guilty, he has now been proven guilty and thus cannot avail himself of the benefits typically afforded those who reach plea agreements with the government and accept responsibility for their illegal conduct before going to trial. *** [A]ny comparison to Lindh's case *** was misplaced.

The district court also erred in its application of § 3553(a)(6) when it relied on a comparison to the case of Timothy McVeigh and Terry Nichols. In making the comparison, the court noted "two very significant distinctions between that case and the case of Mr. Abu Ali." First, "Abu Ali took far fewer and much less significant steps in accomplishing the conspiracies for which he was convicted." Second, "the magnitude and enormity of the impact of the criminal actions of McVeigh and Nichols stand in stark contrast to that which exists in the case of Mr. Abu Ali." Thus, it found that imposing a sentence of life imprisonment on Abu Ali would have led to an unwarranted disparity under § 3553(a)(6). Because this application overlooks several critical points, it likewise was mistaken.

First, though the district court accurately noted that Abu Ali never "injured any people" and "no victim was injured in the United States[,]" this should not trivialize the severity of his offenses. Plotting terrorist attacks on the civilian population and conspiring to assassinate the President of the United States are offenses of the utmost gravity, and the Guidelines and for that matter any other measure of severity manifestly treat them as such. Had Abu Ali's plans come to fruition, they would, according to his own words, have led to massive civilian casualties and the assassination of senior U.S. officials. As the district court properly recognized, but failed to adequately appreciate, we cannot "wait until there are victims of terrorist attacks to fully enforce the nation's criminal laws against terrorism."

To deviate on the basis of unrealized harm is to require an act of completion for an offense that clearly contemplates incomplete conduct. By definition, conspiracy offenses do not require that all objects of the conspiracy be accomplished. The Guidelines appropriately recognize this fact: while they normally afford a three-level decrease for non-specific offense conspiracies that were not on the verge of completion, they specifically exclude from this decrease any conspiracies that involve or promote "a federal crime of terrorism."

Furthermore, the lack of completion in this case should not be taken to indicate any change of heart by the defendant. Instead, he continued conspiring until he was arrested *** on suspicion of membership in an al-Qaeda-linked terrorist cell. It was only because of his arrest that he was forced to desist from further execution of his plans. Thus, the defendant should not benefit simply because his plans were disrupted by Saudi officials before he could see them through.

Second, while Abu Ali may not have "planted any bombs, shot any weapons, or ... took any steps in the United States with others to further the conspiracy," the steps he did take were significant. Indeed, he joined the al-Faq'asi terrorist cell in Saudi Arabia with the hopes of facilitating terrorist attacks in the United States. He researched international flights that might be suitable for hijacking and investigated the locations of nuclear power plants that could serve as potential targets for attack. He also participated in a course on explosives and plotted various ways and methods of assassinating the President of the United States. These were serious and significant steps in their own right.

Finally, while the Oklahoma City bombing was undoubtedly one of the most heinous and devastating acts in our nation's history, to require a similar infliction of harm before imposing a similar sentence would effectively raise the bar too high. We should not require that a defendant do what McVeigh and Nichols did in order to receive a life sentence.

For these reasons, the district court abused its discretion when it compared Abu Ali's case to those of Lindh and of McVeigh and Nichols, respectively, and used those comparisons as a basis for its sentence.

A word finally in response to the dissent. *** [W]e have followed [the Supreme Court's] directive that "all sentences" be reviewed "under a deferential abuse-of-discretion standard." *** [O]ur difference with the sentencing court here is based on the fact that the specific justifications offered were not "sufficiently compelling to support the degree of the variance." ***

Next, the dissent raises several issues with respect to the sentence itself. First, there is obviously disagreement over the *** comparison of Abu Ali to John Walker Lindh and Timothy McVeigh, to the district Court's ultimate decision. *** [T]his factor not only received most of the district Court's attention during sentencing, but it was also the driving force behind the decision and served to quantitatively locate the specific sentence selected. *** We also reject the view that the gravity of Abu Ali's conduct should be so deeply discounted because his efforts to commit a horrific crime were thwarted. Although it is true that Abu Ali's dream of inflicting devastating harm on America did not become a reality, it bears repeating that he was stopped *only* because he was apprehended before his plots could be put into action, and not because he had changed his mind or abandoned his plans. *** Likewise, any comparison to McVeigh and Nichols should be rejected where it is distinguished on the basis that Abu Ali's conduct "resulted in no loss of life or economic destruction." ***

Finally, we have not failed to "view the justifications provided by the district court as a whole." *** [T]he sentencing Court's other considerations cannot overcome its misapplication of § 3553(a)(6), the factor which led to the location of its sentence. A brief examination of some of these ancillary factors demonstrates that the substantial variance at issue here cannot be sustained in light of the district Court's erroneous comparisons to Lindh and McVeigh.

To begin, the district court, as well as the dissent, Notes the Defendant's relative youth at the time he committed these heinous crimes. *** However, it is clear that Abu Ali has not demonstrated any [remorse as he has matured]. Moreover, if we were to permit some sort of sweeping "youth exception" for terrorism offenses, or any offense for that matter, we would be disregarding [the] basic tenet that deviations must be made on an individualized rather than wholesale basis.

We are similarly unmoved by the district Court's (and dissent's) references to letters describing Abu Ali's "general decent reputation as a young man" and his overall "good character." What person of "decent reputation" seeks to assassinate leaders of countries? What person of "good character" aims to destroy thousands of fellow human beings who are innocent of any transgressions against him? This is not good character as we understand it, and to allow letters of this sort to provide the basis for such a substantial variance would be to deprive "good character" of all its content.

A final example is the district Court's observation that its variance sentence alleviates the need for taxpayers to provide Abu Ali with geriatric care at an advanced age. It seems uncontroversial to note that, in addition to its speculative nature, the concern over who pays for the Defendant's incarceration can only go so far in supporting a variance.

To be clear, the purpose of this discussion is not to quibble with the various points made by the district court in support of its sentence. Rather, we simply want to make plain that, having given each rationale its "due deference" and viewing the entire decision as "a whole," we believe the additional reasons provided by the district court do not sufficiently "justify the extent of the variance" in light of the district Court's misplaced Lindh and McVeigh comparisons. ***

Finally, the assertion is made that we have invoked some sort of "terrorism exception" to [sentencing deference to district courts.] This is not the case. Our decision creates no blanket exception, but rather rests on the specific nature of these circumstances. *** Abu Ali was no idle planner. *** [H]is goals were of the most serious and heinous sort.

Given the gravity of Abu Ali's offense, and the district Court's erroneous application of § 3553(a)(6), we have seen nothing to justify a variance of the degree imposed here. It bears reminding that this is not some mere doctrinal dispute of surpassing abstraction. At some point, the debate risks becoming wholly divorced from the broader reality: that the defendant sought to destabilize our government and to shake it to its core. To this day, he wishes he had succeeded. Not only that, but the defendant gave no discernable thought to the personal loss and heartache that would have been suffered by untold hundreds or thousands of victims, spouses, children, parents, and friends had his plans come to fruition. This is a fact that *any* sentencing system, not just the United States Sentencing Guidelines, would take into account. It is not too much to ask that a sentencing proceeding not lose sight of the immensity and scale of wanton harm that was and remains Abu Ali's plain and clear intention. *** [W]e find the district Court's significant downward deviation not to be justified. Thus, the sentence imposed must be vacated. While we of course leave the sentencing function to the able offices of the trial court on remand, we trust that any sentence imposed will reflect the full gravity of the situation before us. ***

DIANA GRIBBON MOTZ, Circuit Judge, dissenting:

With respect, I dissent from the majority's decision to reverse, as unreasonably lenient, Abu Ali's sentence of thirty years' imprisonment followed by thirty years' supervised release. In sentencing Abu Ali, the district court correctly calculated the Guidelines range and carefully considered the applicable statutory factors. The court then explained its several, entirely reasonable justifications for finding this sentence-a sentence less than the Guidelines recommendation of life imprisonment, but substantially more than the twenty-year statutory minimum-"sufficient, but not greater than necessary," to achieve the statutory sentencing goals. *** This is not to say that the district court imposed the only possible reasonable sentence. But it certainly fashioned *a* reasonable sentence *** The majority seems to believe that the particular context of the sentence in this case, involving as it does terrorist crimes, renders appropriate some form of special-and less deferential-review. Even if Congress could constitutionally institute such a rule, to date it has not. *** In stark contrast to our sister circuits, the majority has chosen to ignore the Supreme Court's mandate that appellate courts *must*, without exception, review sentencing decisions under a highly deferential standard. *** Given that the district court committed no procedural error, appropriate appellate review of the justifications offered by the district court here involves only consideration of the "substantive reasonableness" of the sentence. *** Section 3553(a) instructs district courts to impose a sentence "sufficient, but not greater than necessary," to further the following purposes: "reflect the seriousness" of the crime; "promote respect for the law"; deliver "just punishment"; "deter[ ] ... criminal conduct"; "protect the public"; and provide the defendant with needed training, medical care, or treatment. *** The district court carefully considered each of the applicable factors and concluded that they justified a sentence of thirty years' imprisonment followed by thirty years' supervised release.

First, *** Abu Ali's participation in [the offenses] was relatively attenuated and resulted in *no* injury to any person or property. *** Second, the district court considered whether the proposed sentence would "reflect the seriousness of the offense, ... promote respect for the law, and ... provide just punishment." *** The court concluded that a sentence that would consume the majority of Abu Ali's natural life, forcing him "to spend most of his productive years in prison" and to lose the chance to have a family or career, would "adequately and reasonably" reflect the seriousness of his crimes, promote respect for the law, and still provide just punishment for the offenses. The court further noted that the "substantial term of supervised release" it imposed to follow the term of imprisonment would "run for the remainder of Mr. Abu Ali's life expectancy." *** Third, the district court considered whether its proposed sentence would "afford adequate deterrence to criminal conduct." The court concluded that it would, explaining that *** imposition of a thirty-year term of supervised release after thirty years of imprisonment would provide "additional deterrence" because "court and probation and law enforcement" would monitor Abu Ali's conduct for the remainder of his life, and he would "immediately face [yet another] lengthy term of imprisonment if he violates any law, terms of release[,] or orders of this Court during the term of supervised release." *** Fourth, the district court considered whether its sentence would "protect the public from further crimes of the defendant." The court concluded that it would. *** [T]he court relied on the fact that, when released from a thirty-year term of imprisonment, Abu Ali would be "of substantially greater age" and so unlikely to commit further crimes. *** Fifth, the district court considered whether its sentence provided Abu Ali "with needed educational ... training, medical care" or other treatment "in the most effective manner." Again, the court found that it would. The court reasoned that thirty years of imprisonment would permit Abu Ali, who had excelled in his studies, some opportunity to pursue his education while incarcerated but would remove the burden on the public of paying for the geriatric medical care that he would likely require if given a term of life imprisonment. Finally, after weighing all of these statutory factors, the court considered the need to avoid imposing disparate sentences upon similarly situated defendants. *** [T]he court concluded that Abu Ali engaged in conduct more similar to that of John Walker Lindh, who received a sentence of twenty years' imprisonment, than that of Timothy McVeigh or Terry Nichols, who received a death sentence and life imprisonment, respectively.

The majority explicitly acknowledges that "the district court examined each of the § 3553(a) sentencing factors." *** Notwithstanding the majority's arguments, Lindh's criminal conduct is similar-not identical, but similar-to Abu Ali's. *** Nor, contrary to the majority's suggestion, did the district court err in relying on a comparison to Timothy McVeigh and Terry Nichols and then holding that Abu Ali's conduct differed sufficiently from McVeigh's and Nichols' that a less severe sentence for Abu Ali would be consistent with § 3553(a)(6). *** [T]he majority fails to appreciate and weigh the gravity of the *actual* harms and devastating losses of life inflicted by McVeigh and Nichols. *** Given the similarity of their overall objectives, the district court did not abuse its discretion in determining that a comparison between Abu Ali and McVeigh and Nichols was appropriate. ***

Any decision to deviate from the Guidelines range necessarily creates sentencing disparities between the person being sentenced-here Abu Ali-and other, hypothetical, defendants convicted of the same crimes and assigned identical initial Guidelines ranges. Perhaps it is the disparities with these hypothetical defendants that concerns the majority and causes it to focus its fire on the district Court's analysis of the § 3553(a)(6) sentencing factor. *** The majority today pays lip service to the standard of review to which it is bound and then *** affords no deference to the district Court's considered judgment that the § 3553(a) factors as "a whole" support the chosen sentence and instead parses the district Court's opinion to note disagreement with the Court's application of a single statutory factor. *** Proper application of this deferential abuse-of-discretion standard requires affirmance. ***

Notes

1. Majority and Dissent. Who has the better of the disagreement about sentencing? What would you do if you were the district court judge receiving this case for resentencing?

2. Terrorism and Sentencing. How do the Sentencing Guidelines treat terrorism? Does the Fourth Circuit add to the Guidelines in terrorism cases?

3. Sentencing Takfiri Terrorists. Times Square attempted car bomber Faisal Shahzad defiantly pled guilty to 10 terrorism and weapons counts, some requiring life sentences, on June 21, 2010. In open court, Shahzad, a Pakistani-born United States citizen, called himself a Muslim soldier and a "proud terrorist," "the first droplet of the flood that will follow." He said he wanted to "plead guilty and 100 times more" and that, if the United States did not get out of Iraq and Afghanistan, and "stop meddling in Muslim lands," attacks on the United States would continue. When asked by the judge at the sentencing hearing whether the Koran wanted him to kill people, Shahzad responded: The Koran gives us the right to defend, and that's what I am doing." His life sentence, he said, was "only for the limit God has given me life in this world. I'm happy with the deal that God has given me." Not surprisingly, Shahzad was sentenced to life imprisonment on October 5, 2010. Reconsider whether Shahzad might have been considered an enemy soldier and what consequences would flow from this as you read Chapters V and X.

4. Resentencing Other Terrorists. The Ninth Circuit on Feb. 2, 2010 threw out the 22-year prison sentence of Millennium Bomber Ahmed Ressam, who planned to set off bombs at the Los Angeles airport on New Year's Eve in 1999. The court said the sentence was too light, that he did not deserve the substantial reduction from the Guidelines minimum of 65 years because he backed out of his cooperation agreement after three years, recanting his earlier testimony. It also ordered a new judge to be assigned to resentencing since the first resentencing by the district judge had repeated the original 22 year sentence. *United States v. Ressam*, 593 F.3d 1095 (9th Cir.2010). Of special note is that this pre-AUMF case could not have been heard by a military tribunal. See Chapter IX.

5. Stacking Sentence Enhancements. The court explained in *In re Terrorist Bombings of U.S. Embassies in East Africa*, 552 F. 3d 93 (2d Cir. 2008) that:

> El-Hage's base offense level was 66, his criminal history category was VI, and his corresponding sentence under the Guidelines was life imprisonment. The offense level of 66 comprised a base offense level of 43 *** in cases where a conspiracy to murder results in the death of a victim-and 23 additional points arising from five enhancements. Those enhancements are as follows: (1) a three-level enhancement *** because El-Hage targeted his victims on the basis of their national origin (the "hate crime enhancement"); (2) a three-level enhancement *** because the intended victims included government officers and employees whose status as such motivated the offenses (the "official victim enhancement"); (3) a three-level enhancement *** because El-Hage was a manager or supervisor of the conspiracy (the "role-in-the-offense enhancement"); (4) a two-level enhancement *** for obstruction of the administration of justice; and (5) a twelve-level enhancement *** because the felonies involved were intended to promote a federal crime of terrorism (the "terrorism enhancement"). Section 3A1.4 further mandated that El-Hage's criminal history category should be set at VI.

El-Hage argued that the "hate crime" and "government victim enhancements" permit "duplicative punishment" for the same underlying "terrorism" offense. The court rejected his argument, opining:

> Each of these enhancements addresses a "discrete harm," arising from El-Hage's underlying conduct: The hate crime enhancement covers the selection of victims based on their national origin, while the government victim enhancement deals with the selection of victims based on their status as government employees. The terrorism enhancement, as its name indicates, addresses acts of terrorism. While it may be that some offenses, such as those

committed by El-Hage, trigger all three enhancements because they constitute (1) acts of terrorism that targeted victims based on (2) their perceived national origin and (3) their status as government employees, it is equally plain that a terrorist act need not necessarily target government victims or select its victims on the basis of national origin; nor do all offenses that target victims based on their (a) national origin or (b) status as government employees constitute acts of terrorism; and, almost needless to say, crimes targeting victims on the basis of national origin need not entail any animus whatsoever toward government employees and vice versa. Accordingly, we see no "double counting," much less impermissible double counting, arising from the application of these enhancements.

The Court also rejected El-Hage's argument that his actions were the result of political beliefs rather than hate, that he targeted victims based on U.S. citizenship rather than national origin, and that military personnel should be excluded from the "government personnel" enhancement. Since the victims were targeted for their "actual or perceived race, color, religion, national origin, ethnicity, gender, disability, or sexual orientation," the court found the Defendant's motivation irrelevant. It found no evidence that the defendant considered citizenship to differ from national origin. Finally, it said that El-Hage was not engaged in combat (where combatant exemptions would apply in wartime); his actions were those of a cold-blooded murderer, not a soldier. El-Hage's only victory is that the court sent the case back for resentencing after *Booker* held that the Sentencing Guidelines were advisory rather than mandatory. What likelihood do you forsee that El-Hage would do better on resentencing?

6. Lindh and McVeigh. Is Abu Ali somewhere between these two comparators? How does his sentence compare to each? Why is this not the end of the argument?

7. Other Comparators. How would you, as a district court judge after this decision, go about finding other comparators than the two used here? Would you cease to seek comparators? Do the guidelines require comparators? How do you think El-Hage should fare upon remand for resentencing?

8. The Death Penalty. Should El-Hage have received the death penalty, as did Timothy McVeigh in the following case? Are there any reasons not to sentence an alien "takfiri" terrorist to death as compared to a domestic terrorist not part of the takfiri movement? Is the site of the terrorism (in the United States or overseas) relevant?

UNITED STATES v. McVEIGH
153 F. 3d 1166 (C.A. 10, 1998)

EBEL, Circuit Judge.

Defendant-appellant Timothy J. McVeigh ("McVeigh") was tried, convicted, and sentenced to death on eleven counts stemming from the bombing of the Alfred P. Murrah Federal Building ("Murrah Building") in Oklahoma City, Oklahoma, that resulted in the deaths of 168 people. McVeigh appeals his conviction and sentence on the grounds that *** (E) the district court erred by admitting victim impact testimony during the guilt phase of trial, *** (H) the district court erred by excluding mitigating evidence during the penalty phase showing the reasonableness of McVeigh's beliefs with regard to events at the Branch Davidian compound in Waco, Texas, and (I) the victim impact testimony admitted during the penalty phase produced a sentence based on emotion rather than reason. We affirm. ***

McVeigh complains that even if the district court did not err by admitting the testimony of each of the eighteen witnesses individually, the overall effect of so many witnesses describing the impact of the bombing allowed passion to overwhelm reason, rendering the guilt determination constitutionally unreliable. McVeigh characterizes his argument as an Eighth Amendment issue. However, a claim that admitted evidence injected an intolerably high degree of emotion into the guilt phase of trial more properly involves an alleged violation of the Due Process Clause. Thus, we address McVeigh's charge of error as a due process claim.

The testimony of the eighteen witnesses totals only 456 pages out of more than six thousand pages of trial transcript. More importantly, it is to be expected that such a large-scale crime will produce more powerful evidence than a smaller-scale crime. The emotional impact of the testimony stemmed directly from the enormity of the crime itself. We also note that the government in this case exercised considerable restraint in avoiding overly emotional testimony. The government did not introduce any post-mortem pictures of victims nor did it dwell excessively on the heart-wrenching devastation caused by the blast. On several occasions, the prosecution engaged in self-control by skipping over testimony it thought would cross the line or repeat testimony already delivered by another witness. Here, the overwhelming nature of the crime necessarily allowed the government to introduce testimony reflecting the magnitude of the act. Thus, we find no constitutional error. ***

During the penalty phase, McVeigh presented, and the district court allowed, evidence relevant to the opinion he held at the time of the Oklahoma City bombing pertaining to the events that occurred during the standoff between the federal government and the Branch Davidians at Waco, Texas, from February 28, 1993, to April 19, 1993. This evidence consisted mainly of the testimony of experts familiar with materials, such as video tapes, magazine articles, and pamphlets, that McVeigh had likely seen prior to the bombing which were critical of the Government's actions at Waco. However, McVeigh also sought to present evidence to which he had not been exposed prior to the bombing that he claims tended to show that the actions of the federal government during Waco were objectively wrongful and outrageous. In particular, McVeigh sought to introduce expert testimony, documentary films, and government reports critical of the Government's actions at Waco. Much of this material was not even generated until after the Oklahoma City bombing had occurred. McVeigh argues that this evaluative Waco evidence was necessary for the jury to understand that his opinions regarding the events at Waco were objectively reasonable. It is this second category of Waco evidence that the district court refused to allow into the record.

There is no hint in the appellate record that the district court limited McVeigh's ability to present evidence regarding what he actually knew or thought of the events at Waco, up to the time of the Oklahoma City bombing, or that the district court denied him the opportunity to present to the jury his views regarding Waco. McVeigh's attorneys were allowed to argue that the events at Waco were both a motivating factor for the commission of the crime and a mitigating factor with regards to punishment. ***

During the penalty phase of the trial, the government presented the testimony of thirty-eight witnesses who described the impact of the bombing. These witnesses consisted of twenty-six relatives of deceased victims, three injured survivors, one employee of the Murrah Building day care center, and eight rescue and medical workers. Although significant in number, these witnesses comprised an extremely small percentage of the number of potential witnesses the government might have called to testify about the 168 victims who died in the blast and the impact of the explosion on the numerous injured victims. McVeigh challenges the testimony of twenty-seven of these witnesses, arguing that their testimony injected a constitutionally intolerable level of emotion into the proceeding and resulted in the imposition of a capital sentence based on passion rather than reason in violation of *Payne v. Tennessee,* 501 U.S. 808 (1991). ***

Victim impact evidence is simply another form or method of informing the sentencing authority about the specific harm caused by the crime in question *** [E]vidence about the victim and about the impact of the murder on the victim's family is relevant to the jury's decision as to whether or not the death penalty should be imposed. There is no reason to treat such evidence differently than other relevant evidence is treated. ***

Payne allows the introduction of victim impact testimony to aid the jury in making a "reasoned moral response" when imposing sentence upon a defendant convicted of a capital offense. First, the sentence must be the result of a reasoned decision. The evidence must not be so unduly prejudicial that its admission allows emotion to overwhelm reason. Second, the sentence must be based on moral considerations. Because the consequences of the crime are an important ingredient in the moral equation, the government can present testimony demonstrating the harm caused by the Defendant's actions. Third, the sentence must reflect the jury's judgment. The jury must balance all of the relevant mitigating and aggravating factors in determining an appropriate sentence.

On appeal, McVeigh challenges the introduction of the following six categories of victim impact testimony: (a) last contacts with a deceased victim; (b) efforts to learn the fate of a victim; (c) thoughts on learning of a victim's death; (d) life history of a victim; (e) pure love and innocence of children killed by the explosion; and (f) efforts to cope with loss by the family and relatives of a deceased victim. McVeigh also contends that the cumulative impact of the challenged testimony inevitably influenced the jury to render a sentence based on passion rather than reason in violation of *Payne.* *** We find no constitutional error in the admission of the challenged victim impact testimony. The devastating effects that the deaths of the victims had on their families and loved ones is "certainly part and parcel of the circumstances" of the crime properly presented to the jury at the penalty phase of trial.

McVeigh criticizes the introduction of testimony about witnesses' last contacts with deceased family members, including Whicher's pre-continuing objection description of her last contacts with her husband and her children's feelings of regret at not hugging their father good-bye that morning, Treanor's pre-continuing objection account of her now deceased daughter's giving " me a real hard kiss on the lips and hugg[ing] me again and ... rubb[ing] noses," and Gary Campbell's pride in watching his daughter who died in the blast show him her office and talking about her desires to succeed in her career. All of this testimony was properly admitted under *Payne* as relevant to understanding the uniqueness of the life lost and the impact of the death on each victim's family.

McVeigh challenges the admission of testimony describing witnesses' often agonizing efforts to find out what happened to their loved ones. For example, McVeigh highlights the following pre-continuing objection testimony: Leonard's searches of various hospitals looking for her husband; Florence's week-long wait to learn the fate of his wife; and Treanor's realization that her in-laws and her young daughter were at the Murrah Building for an appointment at the Social Security office the morning of the explosion. This type of testimony is well within the limits set by *Payne,* as even McVeigh's counsel admitted during the penalty phase.

McVeigh contests***: Westberry's description of her grandson's uncontrollable crying on hearing of her husband's death; Whicher's recollection of " screaming out that I wanted to die" and frightening her children; and Treanor's recounting of the recovery and return of her deceased daughter's hand six months after the explosion. McVeigh also takes exception to Gregory Sohn's testimony about breaking down upon learning of his wife's death and Sharon McCullough's account of her son's cries of " I don't want my dad to be dead" as he saw pictures of the remains of the Murrah Building on television and the prayer he offered later when he calmed down. *Payne* explicitly allows for the introduction of this kind of evidence describing the impact of a victim's death on a witness and his or her family.

Numerous witnesses, both pre- and post-continuing objection, testified about the professional and personal histories of victims who perished in the bombing, including reflections on the admirable qualities of the deceased. McVeigh argues that this testimony impermissibly allowed witnesses to eulogize their loved ones. We disagree. Although victim histories arguably were covered by McVeigh's continuing objection, the unique qualities of a murdered individual and his or her life accomplishments constitute the core impact evidence describing a victim's "uniqueness as an individual human being" allowed by [*Payne*].

In discussing the suffering of children affected by the bombing, McVeigh contends that the Government's witnesses prejudicially described the innocence and unconditional love manifested by children. For example, Don Browning related the story of a little girl from the day care center who had been outside the building when the bomb exploded. The girl approached a police officer and his dog, hugged the dog, and said, "Mr. Police Dog, will you find my friends?" Also, Glenn Seidl recalled his son Clint's counselor telling him that Clint was concerned because "Clint has never seen you cry. He's never seen you scared. He thinks the people that have done this are after you and him ... and this very professional lady gets a tear in her eye and says that ... [Clint] wants to pay" the counselor the $180 he has saved in his bank account to help his father. Even though covered by McVeigh's continuing objection, we do not see how the admission of this testimony violated *Payne*. If love and innocence are particular qualities of the affected children, then informing the jury of that fact is not improper. ***

Discussions of the impact of the blast on the families of the victims represents the bulk of the testimony challenged by McVeigh. A few examples of this evidence include: Leonard's adult son, who was married some time after the bombing, came to her at 3:00 a.m. one morning "crying very hard. And he said: 'I want my dad back. I want him to see me graduate from college. I want him to meet my wife and be at my wedding. I want him to see my first child.' " *** Todd McCarthy testified, "I am now charged with teaching my son love and compassion when all he sees is hate. And that's a job I don't think anybody would want to have." Michael Lenz, whose wife and unborn child were killed, nearly committed suicide:[T]here was a point where I actually stuck a pistol in my mouth. I couldn't pull the trigger, thank God.... [W]hen I reached that low point in my life, there is nothing, nothing more dangerous than a man who has no reason to live. I've been there. *** *Payne* specifically allows witnesses to describe the effects of the crime on their families. All of the evidence challenged by McVeigh served that purpose. Thus, we find no error. ***

Taken as a whole, this evidence is poignant and emotional. The question before us, then, is whether allowing such a substantial amount of victim impact testimony reflecting the magnitude of such a large-scale crime violates the limits on such testimony set forth in *Payne*. We conclude that it does not. *** The bombing of the Murrah Building was the deadliest act of domestic terrorism in the history of the United States. The magnitude of the crime cannot be ignored. It would be fundamentally unfair to shield a defendant from testimony describing the full effects of his deeds simply because he committed such an outrageous crime. The sheer number of actual victims and the horrific things done to them necessarily allows for the introduction of a greater amount of victim impact testimony in order for the government to show the "harm" caused by the crime. In addition, the jury could not have been shocked to learn that some victims had exemplary backgrounds and poignant family relationships, nor that they left behind grief-stricken loved ones. As Justice Souter eloquently wrote:

> Murder has foreseeable consequences. When it happens, it is always to distinct individuals, and, after it happens, other victims are left behind. Every defendant knows, if endowed with the mental competence for criminal responsibility, that the life he will take by his homicidal behavior is that of a

unique person, like himself, and that the person to be killed probably has close associates, "survivors," who will suffer harms and deprivations from the victim's death. Just as defendants know that they are not faceless human ciphers, they know that their victims are not valueless fungibles.... The fact that the defendant may not know the details of a victim's life and characteristics, or the exact identities and needs of those who may survive, should not in any way obscure the further facts that ... harm to some group of survivors is a consequence of a successful homicidal act so foreseeable as to be virtually inevitable.

We also observe that in this case the government deliberately limited the victim impact testimony it chose to present, saying nothing about the vast majority of the 168 people who died in the blast. Nor did the government attempt to introduce any gruesome post-mortem photographs of the deceased. The testimony of the Government's witnesses occupied only about two days during the penalty phase of trial. In addition to the Government's self-restraint, the district court took a number of steps that significantly minimized the overall impact of the testimony. First, the district court issued a number of rulings prior to the commencement of the penalty phase on various motions in limine to restrict evidence by the government such as photographs and exhibits, a significant portion of which the district court excluded. Second, at the conclusion of those rulings, the district court stated that it would allow " objective" evidence describing the " fact" of " the loss of ... people to an agency and ... the loss of a family member ... the empty chair, but not the emotional aspect of that, the grieving process, the mourning process." The government followed this instruction, and we have found few instances where the type of non-objective emotional testimony described by the district court was admitted. Third, at the close of the penalty phase, the judge instructed the jury not to be swayed by emotion, and we presume that the jury honored those instructions. Finally, the jury deliberated for two days and made specific findings in McVeigh's favor on a number of mitigating factors. We consider all of these factors persuasive evidence that the jury made a reasoned, moral judgment.

Notes

1. **McVeigh and Bin Laden.** How close are the issues in *McVeigh* to issues that might occur in a trial of bin Laden for the 9/11 attacks?

2. **Death penalty.** Were bin Laden convicted, should he be sentenced to death?

3. **Victim Impact Statements.** According to the court, what are the limitations for allowing victim impact statements in sentencing? Does the legal rule allow too much input from family members, unfairly prejudicing the sentencing process? Do you agree with the Court's decision in this case? Up to this point, there is not a case that illustrates the outer limits of victim impact statements. Based on the information from this case, what might those facts look like? How does the type of crime influence the Court's decision and your answer?

4. Impact Statement Policy. How important is the cathartic effect of allowing the victims and their loved ones to testify? Are there other ways to provide the cathartic outlet that are less likely to prejudice the defendant?

5. Plea Agreements Generally. Most criminal cases in the United States are not resolved by a trial. Rather, most cases are disposed of through the system of plea bargaining, whereby the accused and prosecutor work out a mutually satisfactory disposition of the case subject to court approval. It usually involves the Defendant's pleading guilty to a lesser offense or to only one or some of the counts of a multi-count indictment in return for a lighter sentence than possible for the graver charge." Plea bargaining works benefits both the accused and the State. The suspect avoids the risk of a longer sentence following conviction. The State saves the expense of a full criminal trial, and provides a tool to obtain additional information that could lead to the arrest and conviction of more suspects when the State's evidence against them is weak.

6. Expatriation Pleas with Aliens. Plea Agreements concerning those about to be tried for terrorism offenses pose some peculiar issues. Since most of those indicted in the United States so far are aliens, what should be considered in a plea that would return the individual to his or her home country? One important factor is the likelihood that those sent overseas will return to the battlefield. For a listing of those who have returned to fight against the United States following release from Guantanamo, see: http://en.wikipedia.org/wiki/ Lists_of_former_ Guantanamo_captives_alleged_to_have_returned_to_terrorism.

7. Hamdi's Plea. Yaser Esam Hamdi, who was born in Louisiana, grew up in Saudi Arabia, and was captured in Afghanistan fighting for the Taliban (though he denied fighting against the United States or having any involvement with al Qaeda). In 2004, following Hamdi's victory in the United States Supreme Court, discussed infra in Chapter V, he entered into a plea agreement under which the United States agreed to transport him to Saudi Arabia by a day certain. Hamdi renounced his American citizenship, terrorism, and violent jihad. He promised to 'remain and reside' for at least 5 years in Saudi Arabia, never to travel to Afghanistan, Iraq, Israel, Palestine, Syria, the West Bank, or the Gaza Strip, and not to travel to the United States for at least 10 years. Failing to fulfill any part of the agreement was to lead to immediate detention by the United States as an enemy combatant. Hamdi also renounced all claims against the United States. How effective do you think the restrictions and conditions placed in this agreement are? How might the United States monitor adherence to the terms of the agreement?

8. Lindh and Hamdi. The 2002 plea agreement in which John Walker Lindh received a twenty year sentence is discussed at length in *Abu Ali*. Compare the plea agreement for Hamdi above. Are you surprised to learn that, after announcement of the Hamdi plea agreement, Lindh and his lawyer sought to reduce his sentence? See Dean E. Murphy, "American Taliban Soldier Seeks Less Prison Time," NEW YORK TIMES 9/29/2004. When the Lindh agreement was announced, the Department of Justice called it "an important victory for the people of the United States in the battle against terrorism." Lindh was incarcerated at a medium-security federal prison in California, where his parents visited him monthly. How would you have received this petition were you the federal judge who had approved the Lindh plea? Are there factors that Lindh's argument does not take into account? If you were Lindh's lawyer, would you be worried about malpractice or loss of clients?

9. Transnational Sentencing Issues. Omar Khadr, whose case is discussed in Chapter IX, entered into a plea agreement that called for an eight year sentence with eligibility to transfer to a Canadian prison after one year. When transferred to Canada, Canadian officials will determine how much time he will serve, with the norm being "full parole" after a third of the sentence is served. Could Khadr, rather than serving about 20 months after repatriation, actually serve even less than that by receiving credit for the time served at Guantanamo? No, because Canadian law only credits pretrial time served where there is a murder conviction resulting in a life sentence. There might be ways for Khadr to receive less if treated as a juvenile, but that route is closed because the plea agreement specifies that he receive an "adult sentence" of eight years.

III

FINDING TERRORISTS

The good news is that there aren't many terrorists....The bad news is the scarcity of terrorists makes them hard to find.

> Steven D. Levitt & Stephen J. Dubner,
> SUPERFREAKONOMICS (HarperCollins 2009), p. 88.

[T]he "war on terror" has accelerated the development of a new criminal process [that] has increasingly displaced traditional methods of investigating, prosecuting, and punishing people who have engaged in conduct that is subject to criminal penalties-whether or not that conduct is considered "terrorism." *** [T]his new process is largely consistent with constitutional norms that are changing under the same pressures that drive the development of the new criminal process. Those pressures, in turn, derive not just from specific events but also from the perception of emergency and rapid change that characterizes modern society and political life. *** [N]ot only [has war] changed in its functions, to become more like policing, but *** policing too has changed, to become more like war.

> John T. Parry, "Terrorism and the New Criminal Process," 15 WILLIAM & MARY BILL OF RIGHTS JOURNAL 765 (2007)

Finding terrorists after an attack is generally a law enforcement task. Collecting evidence from the scene, gathering information from witnesses, following up on leads from various sources, identifying and questioning suspects – all are standard fare in criminal investigatory work. Done thoroughly and carefully, criminal investigations often lead to successful prosecutions. In the United States, such care includes attention to preserving evidence, maintaining chain of custody, obtaining search warrants, providing Miranda warnings, and ultimately convincing a jury of guilt beyond a reasonable doubt.

An excellent description of an FBI investigation of a terrorist incident overseas, the USS Cole bombing, may be found in an article in THE NEW YORKER at: http://www.lawrencewright.com/WrightSoufan.pdf.

Read the article and make a list of the problems that arose in the investigation. These problems will give you a sense of why such investigations are more difficult than normal criminal investigations in the investigating country (here the United States).

Either at home or abroad, investigating destructive acts like the Cole bombing has led countries to attempt to provide additional security to their populations by discovering and disrupting terrorists' plans prior to massive damage and loss of life. This chapter therefore focuses upon the law governing several prophylactic tools used to discover terrorists' plans in advance of attacks. Part A examines physical searches, Part B ethnic profiling, Part C national security letters, Part D data mining and Part E financing tools. Part F discusses some broad policy issues raised by the chapter. Electronic surveillance, which has a unique statutory framework and a special role in bridging between criminal investigations and military interdiction of terrorists, is reserved for Chapter IV.

A. PHYSICAL SEARCHES

In the absence of definitive Supreme Court case law, two Second Circuit cases frame the issues surrounding physical searches where counterterrorism operations are the justification for warrantless searches. The first of the two searches took place in New York City, the second in Nairobi, Kenya. The outcomes are the same (the prosecution is permitted to use the evidence) but nuances of analysis make the cases worth comparing.

MACWADE v. KELLY
460 F. 3d 260 (2d Cir. 2006)

STRAUB, Circuit Judge.

We consider whether the government may employ random, suspicionless container searches in order to safeguard mass transportation facilities from terrorist attack. The precise issue before us is whether one such search regime, implemented on the New York City subway system, satisfies the special needs exception to the Fourth Amendment's usual requirement of individualized suspicion. *** Plaintiffs [raise] three claims: (1) the special needs doctrine applies only in scenarios where the subject of a search possesses a diminished expectation of privacy, and because subway riders enjoy a full expectation of privacy in their bags, the District Court erred in applying the special needs exception here; (2) the District Court erred in finding that the search program serves a " special need" in the first instance; and (3) even if the search program serves a special need, the District Court erred in balancing the relevant factors because (a) the searches are intrusive; (b) there is no immediate terrorist threat; and (c) the City's evidence fails as a matter of law to establish that the Program is effective. ***

The New York City subway system is a singular component of America's urban infrastructure. The subway is an icon of the City's culture and history, an engine of its colossal economy, a subterranean repository of its art and music, and, most often, the place where millions of diverse New Yorkers and visitors stand elbow to elbow as they traverse the metropolis. Quantified, the subway system is staggering. It comprises 26 interconnected train lines and 468 far-flung passenger stations. It operates every hour of every day. On an average weekday, it carries more than 4.7 million passengers and, over the course of a year, it transports approximately 1.4 billion riders. By any measure, the New York City subway system is America's largest and busiest.

Given the subway's enclosed spaces, extraordinary passenger volume, and cultural and economic importance, it is unsurprising-and undisputed-that terrorists view it as a prime target. *** In 2004, terrorists killed over 240 people by using concealed explosives to bomb commuter trains in Madrid and Moscow. On July 7, 2005, terrorists-again using concealed explosives-killed more than 56 people and wounded another 700 individuals by launching a coordinated series of attacks on the London subway and bus systems. Two weeks later, on July 21, 2005, terrorists launched a second but unsuccessful wave of concealed explosive attacks on the London subway system.

That same day, the New York City Police Department ("NYPD") announced the Container Inspection Program (the " Program") that is the subject of this litigation. The NYPD designed the Program chiefly to deter terrorists from carrying concealed explosives onto the subway system and, to a lesser extent, to uncover any such attempt. Pursuant to the Program, the NYPD establishes daily inspection checkpoints at selected subway facilities. A "checkpoint" consists of a group of uniformed police officers standing at a folding table near the row of turnstiles disgorging onto the train platform. At the table, officers search the bags of a portion of subway riders entering the station. *** [T]o enhance the Program's deterrent effect, the NYPD selects the checkpoint locations "in a deliberative manner that may appear random, undefined, and unpredictable." In addition to switching checkpoint locations, the NYPD also varies their number, staffing, and scheduling so that the "deployment patterns ... are constantly shifting." While striving to maintain the veneer of random deployment, the NYPD bases its decisions on a sophisticated host of criteria, such as fluctuations in passenger volume and threat level, overlapping coverage provided by its other counter-terrorism initiatives, and available manpower.

The officers assigned to each checkpoint give notice of the searches and make clear that they are voluntary. Close to their table they display a large poster notifying passengers that "backpacks and other containers [are] subject to inspection." The Metropolitan Transportation Authority, which operates the subway system, makes similar audio announcements in subway stations and on trains. A supervising sergeant at the checkpoint announces through a bullhorn that all persons wishing to enter the station are subject to a container search and those wishing to avoid the search must leave the station. Although declining the search is not by itself a basis for arrest, the police may arrest anyone who refuses to be searched and later attempts to reenter the subway system with the uninspected container.

Officers exercise virtually no discretion in determining whom to search. The supervising sergeant establishes a selection rate, such as every fifth or tenth person, based upon considerations such as the number of officers and the passenger volume at that particular checkpoint. The officers then search individuals in accordance with the established rate only.

Once the officers select a person to search, they limit their search as to scope, method, and duration. As to scope, officers search only those containers large enough to carry an explosive device, which means, for example, that they may not inspect wallets and small purses. Further, once they identify a container of eligible size, they must limit their inspection "to what is minimally necessary to ensure that the ... item does not contain an explosive device," which they have been trained to recognize in various forms. They may not intentionally look for other contraband, although if officers incidentally discover such contraband, they may arrest the individual carrying it. Officers may not attempt to read any written or printed material. Nor may they request or record a passenger's personal information, such as his name, address, or demographic data.

The preferred inspection method is to ask the passenger to open his bag and manipulate his possessions himself so that the officer may determine, on a purely visual basis, if the bag contains an explosive device. If necessary, the officer may open the container and manipulate its contents himself. Finally, because officers must conduct the inspection for no "longer than necessary to ensure that the individual is not carrying an explosive device," a typical inspection lasts for a matter of seconds.

*** [M]ost relevant to this appeal is the testimony of three defense expert witnesses: *** The expert testimony established that terrorists "place a premium" on success. Accordingly, they seek out targets that are predictable and vulnerable-traits they ascertain through surveillance and a careful assessment of existing security measures. They also plan their operations carefully: they "rehearse [the attack], they train it, they do dry runs." In light of these priorities, the Al Qaeda Manual advises that terrorists "traveling on a mission" should avoid security "check points along the way."

The witnesses also testified that the Program's flexible and shifting deployment of checkpoints deters a terrorist attack because it introduces the variable of an unplanned checkpoint inspection and thus "throws uncertainty into every aspect of terrorist operations-from planning to implementation." Terrorists "don't want to be in a situation where one of their bombs doesn't go off, because on the day that they chose to go in subway station X, there were police doing searches." That unpredictability deters both a single-bomb attack and an attack consisting of multiple synchronized bombings, such as those in London and Madrid.

Because the Program deters a terrorist from planning to attack the subway in the first place, the witnesses testified, the fact that a terrorist could decline a search and leave the subway system makes little difference in assessing the Program's efficacy. Similarly, the precise number of checkpoints employed on any given day is relatively unimportant because the critical aspects of the Program are that it is "random" and "routine," the combination of which "creates an incentive for terrorists to choose ... an easier target." Finally, the testimony established that each of the City's counter-terrorism programs incrementally increases security and that taken together, the programs "address the broad range of concerns related to terrorist activity" and "have created an environment in New York City that has made it more difficult for terrorists to operate." ***

The Fourth Amendment to the Constitution provides that, " The right of the people to be secure in their persons, houses, papers, and effects, against unreasonable searches and seizures, shall not be violated, and no Warrants shall issue, but upon probable cause...." *** [T]he concept of reasonableness is the "touchstone of the constitutionality of a governmental search." *** [W]e upheld a program employing metal detectors and hand searches of carry-on baggage at airports. We determined that the "purpose" of the search program was not to serve "as a general means for enforcing the criminal laws" but rather to "prevent airplane hijacking" by "terrorists[.]" We then dispensed with the traditional warrant and probable cause requirements and instead balanced "the need for a search against the offensiveness of the intrusion." *** When the risk is the jeopardy to hundreds of human lives and millions of dollars of property inherent in the pirating or blowing up of a large airplane, the danger alone meets the test of reasonableness, so long as the search is conducted in good faith for the purpose of preventing hijacking or like damage and with reasonable scope and the passenger has been given advance notice of his liability to such a search so that he can avoid it by choosing not to travel by air. *** [O]ur reasoning came to be known as the "special needs exception" roughly one decade later. Both before and after the doctrine's formal denomination, courts have applied it in a variety of contexts relevant here, including random airport searches, and highway sobriety checkpoints.

The doctrine's central aspects are as follows. First, as a threshold matter, the search must "serve as [its] immediate purpose an objective distinct from the ordinary evidence gathering associated with crime investigation." Second, once the government satisfies that threshold requirement, the court determines whether the search is reasonable by balancing several competing considerations. These balancing factors include (1) the weight and immediacy of the government interest, (2) "the nature of the privacy interest allegedly compromised by" the search, (3) "the character of the intrusion imposed" by the search, and (4) the efficacy of the search in advancing the government interest. ***

Plaintiffs first raise the purely legal contention that, as a threshold matter, the special needs doctrine applies only where the subject of the search possesses a reduced privacy interest. *** [T]he Supreme Court never has implied-much less actually held-that a reduced privacy expectation is a *sine qua non* of special needs analysis.*** [T]he nature of the relevant privacy interest must not be treated in isolation or accorded dispositive weight, but rather must be balanced against other fact-specific considerations. *** [W]e expressly hold that the special needs doctrine does not require *** that the subject of the search possess a reduced privacy interest. Instead, once the government establishes a special need, the nature of the privacy interest is a factor to be weighed in the balance.

Plaintiffs next maintain that *** the Program serves the special need of preventing a terrorist attack on the subway. Plaintiffs contend that the Program's immediate objective is merely to gather evidence for the purpose of enforcing the criminal law. *** [We find] the Program aims to prevent a terrorist attack on the subway. Defendants implemented the Program in response to a string of bombings on commuter trains and subway systems abroad, which indicates that its purpose is to prevent similar occurrences in New York City. In its particulars, the Program seeks out explosives only: officers are trained to recognize different explosives, they search only those containers capable of carrying explosive devices, and they may not intentionally search for other contraband, read written or printed material, or request personal information. Additionally, the Program's voluntary nature illuminates its purpose: that an individual may refuse the search *provided* he leaves the subway establishes that the Program seeks to prevent a terrorist, laden with concealed explosives, from boarding a subway train in the first place.

As a legal matter, courts traditionally have considered special the Government's need to "prevent" and "discover ... latent or hidden" hazards, in order to ensure the safety of mass transportation mediums, such as trains, airplanes, and highways. We have no doubt that concealed explosives are a hidden hazard, that the Program's purpose is prophylactic, and that the nation's busiest subway system implicates the public's safety. Accordingly, preventing a terrorist from bombing the subways constitutes a special need that is distinct from ordinary post hoc criminal investigation. Further, the fact that an officer incidentally may discover a different kind of contraband and arrest its possessor does not alter the Program's intended purpose. ***

Having concluded that the Program serves a special need, we next balance the factors set forth above to determine whether the search is reasonable and thus constitutional. ***

Given the "enormous dangers to life and property from terrorists" bombing the subway, "we need not labor the point with respect to need...." As they must, plaintiffs concede that the interest in preventing such an attack is "paramount" but contend that the lack of "any specific threat to the subway system" weakens that interest by depriving it of immediacy. Plaintiffs again overstate the relevance of a specific, extant threat. *** [T]he threat in this case is sufficiently immediate. In light of the thwarted plots to bomb New York City's subway system, its continued desirability as a target, and the recent bombings of public transportation systems in Madrid, Moscow, and London, the risk to public safety is substantial and real. ***

*** [T]he nature of the privacy interest compromised by the search remains an important balancing factor. Whether an expectation of privacy exists for Fourth Amendment purposes depends upon two questions. "First, we ask whether the individual, by his conduct, has exhibited an actual expectation of privacy...." Second, we inquire whether the individual's expectation of privacy is one that society is prepared to recognize as reasonable." *** [A] person carrying items in a closed, opaque bag has manifested his subjective expectation of privacy by keeping his belongings from plain view and indicating "that, for whatever reason, [he] prefer[s] to keep [them] close at hand." *** Accordingly, a subway rider who keeps his bags on his person possesses an undiminished expectation of privacy therein. We therefore weigh this factor in favor of plaintiffs. ***

Although a subway rider enjoys a full privacy expectation in the contents of his baggage, the kind of search at issue here minimally intrudes upon that interest. Several uncontested facts establish that the Program is narrowly tailored to achieve its purpose: (1) passengers receive notice of the searches and may decline to be searched so long as they leave the subway (2) police search only those containers capable of concealing explosives, inspect eligible containers only to determine whether they contain explosives, inspect the containers visually unless it is necessary to manipulate their contents, and do not read printed or written material or request personal information, (3) a typical search lasts only for a matter of seconds, (4) uniformed personnel conduct the searches out in the open, which reduces the fear and stigma that removal to a hidden area can cause, and (5) police exercise no discretion in selecting whom to search, but rather employ a formula that ensures they do not arbitrarily exercise their authority. Although defendants need not employ "the least intrusive means," to serve the state interest, it appears they have approximated that model. ***

In considering the "degree to which the seizure advances the public interest," we must remember not to wrest "from politically accountable officials ... the decision as to which among reasonable alternative law enforcement techniques should be employed to deal with a serious public danger." *** The District Court credited the expert testimony of Sheehan, Cohen, and Clarke concerning the Program's deterrent effect. *** [P]laintiffs claim that the Program can have no meaningful deterrent effect because the NYPD employs too few checkpoints. *** We will not-and *may not*-second-guess the minutiae of their considered decisions. *** [T]he expert testimony established that terrorists seek predictable and vulnerable targets, and the Program generates uncertainty that frustrates that goal, which, in turn, deters an attack. *** [T]he absence of a formal study of the Program's deterrent effect does not concern us.

Plaintiffs further claim that the Program is ineffective because police notify passengers of the searches, and passengers are free to walk away and attempt to reenter the subway at another point or time. Yet we always have viewed notice and the opportunity to decline as beneficial aspects of a suspicionless search regime because those features minimize intrusiveness. Striking a search program as ineffective on account of its narrow tailoring would create a most perverse result: those programs "more pervasive and more invasive of privacy" more likely would satisfy the Fourth Amendment.

Importantly, if a would-be bomber declines a search, he must leave the subway or be arrested-an outcome that, for the purpose of preventing subway bombings, we consider reasonably effective***, An unexpected change of plans might well stymie the attack, disrupt the synchronicity of multiple bombings, or at least reduce casualties by forcing the terrorist to detonate in a less populated location.

Finally, plaintiffs claim that since no other city yet has employed a similar search program, New York's must be ineffective. In the first place, plaintiffs' inference is flawed: other cities must design programs according to their own resources and needs, which, quite apart from the question of efficacy, may not warrant or make possible such an initiative. Further, the upshot of plaintiffs' argument-that a program must be duplicated *before* it may be constitutional-strikes us as unsustainable.*** In sum, we hold that the Program is reasonable, and therefore constitutional, because (1) preventing a terrorist attack on the subway is a special need; (2) that need is weighty; (3) the Program is a reasonably effective deterrent; and (4) even though the searches intrude on a full privacy interest, they do so to a minimal degree. ***

Notes

1. Specificity of Threat. Was there any specific threat that led to the subway search program in New York City?   Should the court have required more specificity?

2. Ending the Program. Now that the court has approved the search process, how long may New York continue it? Indefinitely?

3. Skepticism. Academic commentators have been skeptical of expansion of the "special needs" doctrine in this case, saying we are trading civil liberties for apparent, not actual, security. Does the court address this concern?

4. Sting Operations. To catch domestic terrorists before they kill or injure, law enforcement authorities have increasingly relied on sting operations in which FBI agents pretend to be fellow terrorists.   For example, FBI agents, after intercepting a series of emails from nineteen-year-old Mohamed Osman Mohamud to undisclosed contacts in Pakistan from August to December 2009, pretended to be eager jihadists. They discussed possible targets for an attack, assembled and detonated test explosives for Mohamud, and helped him prepare a video taking responsibility for the planned attack. Mohamud was arrested on November 26, 2010, when he attempted to detonate a realistic but harmless "bomb" at a Christmas tree lighting ceremony in a crowded public square in Portland, Oregon. Mohamud, who faces a maximum punishment of life in prison for attempting to use a weapon of mass destruction, has pled not guilty. His lawyer says his client was entrapped, the victim of a plot "instigated by government agents" and "directed by government agents" who provided the money, transportation, training, and explosives to Mohamud. Attorney General Holder says that those who call FBI sting operations entrapment "simply do not have their facts straight or do not have a full understanding of the law." What do you think? See Kevin Johnson, "The FBI says it foiled ***Terror Plot. But how far would the plan have gone without the FBI's help?" in USA TODAY, Dec. 16, 2010, p. A1.

5. Airport Searches. After the 9/11 attacks, Congress passed the Aviation and Transportation Security Act (ATSA) and created a federally-operated airport agency (the Transportation Security Agency or TSA) and a three-step security checkpoint process: X-Ray of all carry-on baggage and shoes; walk-through metal detector or alternative "pat-down" screening; and additional screening for passengers who set off the metal detector or are selected randomly to undergo this step. If at any stage of the screening process, a passenger refuses screening, the passenger is denied and the passenger will not be permitted to fly. In 2010, TSA began employing a more advanced form of body imaging known as Advanced Imaging Technology (AIT) to screen a passenger's entire body (see below). This image is viewed remotely by an agent who does not see the passenger but who is in remote communication with the agent at the gate. Passengers may decline the AIT screen provided that they undergo a pat-down which includes a genital area pat-down by a same-sex TSA employee. AIT screening has raised 4th Amendment privacy considerations. Some passengers feel that this screening permits TSA agents to see them as if they were naked and consider it an unreasonable search. How do you think this screening method fits into the balancing test from *MacWade*? Is the government interest immediate and substantial? Do airline passengers have a reasonable expectation of privacy here? How compelling are the governmental interests involved? Would you feel differently if (a) the whole body image is not stored and cannot be printed, transmitted or saved, (b) the image is automatically deleted once the passenger is cleared, (c) hat officers may not take cameras or cell phones into the room where the whole body image is sent, and (4) TSA uses millimeter wave technology to blur all facial features and a backscatter technology has an algorithm applied to the entire image, rendering individual identification of the passenger impossible? What do you conclude about our notions of privacy as you answer these questions? Should individuals who have religiously-based privacy norms that allow neither full-body imaging nor genital pat-down s be provided with an exemption by TSA?

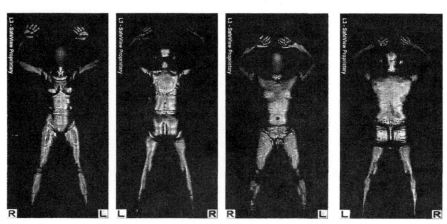

6. Another View of Airport Searches. Here is the take on airport security provided by economists Steven D. Levitt & Stephen J. Dubner, in **SUPERFREAKONOMICS** (HarperCollins 2009), p.65:

> The beauty of terrorism—if you're a terrorist—is that you can succeed even by failing. We perform [removal of shoes at airport security] thanks to a bumbling British national named Richard

Reid, who, even though he couldn't ignite his shoe bomb, exacted a huge price. Let's say it takes an average of one minute to remove and replace your shoes in the airport security line. In the United States alone, this procedure happens roughly 560 million times per year, Five hundred and sixty million minutes equals more than 1,065 years—which, divided by 77.8 years (the average life expectancy at birth) yields a total of nearly 14 person-lives. So even if Richard Reid failed to kill a single person, he levied a tax that is the time equivalent of 14 lives per year.

7. Foreign Investigations. You saw from the report of the Cole investigation that there are many challenges to an overseas investigation beyond those of domestic efforts to foil and arrest terrorists in the United States. The next case raises issues of differences in applicable law when such investigations are conducted overseas.

In re TERRORIST BOMBINGS OF U.S. EMBASSIES IN EAST AFRICA
552 F. 3d 157 (2d Cir. 2008)

JOSÉ A. CARANES, Circuit Judge:

Defendant-appellant Wadih El-Hage, a citizen of the United States, challenges his conviction *** on numerous charges arising from his involvement in the August 7, 1998 bombings of the American Embassies in Nairobi, Kenya and Dar es Salaam, Tanzania (the "August 7 bombings"). *** Because we hold that the Fourth Amendment's requirement of reasonableness-and not the Warrant Clause-governs extraterritorial searches of U.S. citizens and that the searches challenged on this appeal were reasonable, we find no error in the District Court's denial of El-Hage's suppression motion. In addition, the District Court's *ex parte, in camera* evaluation of evidence submitted by the government in opposition to El-Hage's suppression motion was appropriate in light of national security considerations that argued in favor of maintaining the confidentiality of that evidence. ***

American intelligence became aware of al Qaeda's presence in Kenya by mid-1996 and identified five telephone numbers used by suspected al Qaeda associates. From August 1996 through August 1997, American intelligence officials monitored these telephone lines, including two El-Hage used: a phone line in the building where El-Hage lived and his cell phone. The Attorney General of the United States then authorized intelligence operatives to target El-Hage in particular. This authorization, first issued on April 4, 1997, was renewed in July 1997. Working with Kenyan authorities, U.S. officials searched El-Hage's home in Nairobi on August 21, 1997, pursuant to a document shown to El-Hage's wife that was "identified as a Kenyan warrant authorizing a search for 'stolen property.' " At the completion of the search, one of the Kenyan officers gave El-Hage's wife an inventory listing the items seized during the search. El-Hage was not present during the search of his home. It is uncontested that the agents did not apply for or obtain a warrant from a U.S. court.

El-Hage filed a pretrial motion pursuant to the Fourth Amendment for the suppression of (1) evidence seized during the August 1997 search of his home in Nairobi and the fruits thereof; (2) evidence obtained through electronic surveillance of four telephone lines, including the telephone for his Nairobi residence and his Kenyan cellular phone, conducted between August 1996 and August 1997; and (3) tape recordings or summaries of telephone conversations resulting from electronic surveillance of El-Hage's home in Arlington, Texas, conducted in August and September 1998 pursuant to the Foreign Intelligence Surveillance Act of 1978 ("FISA"). El-Hage urged the suppression of the evidence resulting from the search of his Nairobi home and surveillance of his Kenyan telephone lines (collectively, the "Kenyan searches") on the grounds that neither search was authorized by a valid warrant and, in the alternative, that the searches were unreasonable. With respect to the electronic surveillance of his home in Texas, El-Hage maintained that the government failed to comply with certain safeguards set forth in FISA. ***

In order to determine whether El-Hage's suppression motion was properly denied ***, we must first determine whether and to what extent the Fourth Amendment's safeguards apply to overseas searches involving U.S. citizens. In *United States v. Toscanino*, a case involving a Fourth Amendment challenge to overseas wiretapping of a non-U.S. citizen, we observed that it was "well settled" that "the Bill of Rights has extraterritorial application to the conduct abroad of federal agents directed against United States citizens." Nevertheless, we have not yet determined the specific question of the applicability of the Fourth Amendment's Warrant Clause to overseas searches.[5] Faced with that question now, we hold that the Fourth Amendment's warrant requirement does not govern searches conducted abroad by U.S. agents; such searches of U.S. citizens need only satisfy the Fourth Amendment's requirement of reasonableness. ***

[W]hether a warrant is required for overseas searches of U.S. citizens has not been decided by the Supreme Court, by our Court, or, as far as we are able to determine, by any of our sister circuits. While never addressing the question directly, the Supreme Court provided some guidance on the issue in *United States v. Verdugo-Urquidez*, 494 U.S. 259, where the Court examined whether an alien with "no voluntary attachment to the United States" could invoke the protections of the Fourth Amendment to suppress evidence obtained through a warrantless search conducted in Mexico. Relying on "the

---

[5] We interpret the statement in *Toscanino* that "[i]t is no answer to argue that the foreign country which is the situs of the search does not afford a procedure for issuance of a warrant," 500 F.2d at 280, as nothing more than a rejection of the argument that the Fourth Amendment does not apply in foreign countries where U.S. agents cannot obtain local search warrants. In addition, we observe that one of *Toscanino's* holdings-that aliens may invoke the Fourth Amendment against searches conducted abroad by the U.S. government-is no longer valid in light of *Verdugo-Urquidez*, 494 U.S. 259 which we discuss below.

text of the Fourth Amendment, its history, and [the Court's] cases discussing the application of the Constitution to aliens and extraterritorially," the Supreme Court held that the Fourth Amendment affords no protection to aliens searched by U.S. officials outside of our borders. With respect to the applicability of the Warrant Clause abroad, the Court expressed doubt that the clause governed any overseas searches conducted by U.S. agents, explaining that warrants issued to conduct overseas searches "would be a dead letter outside the United States." Elaborating on this observation in a concurring opinion, Justice Kennedy concluded:

> The absence of local judges or magistrates available to issue warrants, the differing and perhaps unascertainable conceptions of reasonableness and privacy that prevail abroad, and the need to cooperate with foreign officials all indicate that the Fourth Amendment's warrant requirement should not apply in Mexico as it does in this country.

Both Justice Stevens, in a concurring opinion, and Justice Blackmun, in dissent, also took a dim view of applying the Warrant Clause to searches conducted abroad, noting that U.S. judicial officers have no power to issue such warrants. Accordingly, in *Verdugo-Urquidez,* seven justices of the Supreme Court endorsed the view that U.S. courts are not empowered to issue warrants for foreign searches

These observations and the following reasons weigh against imposing a warrant requirement on overseas searches.

First, there is nothing in our history or our precedents suggesting that U.S. officials must first obtain a warrant before conducting an overseas search. *** This dearth of authority is not surprising in light of the history of the Fourth Amendment and its Warrant Clause as well as the history of international affairs. As the Verdugo-Urquidez Court explained, "[w]hat we know of the history of the drafting of the Fourth Amendment ... suggests that its purpose was to restrict searches and seizures which might be conducted by the United States in domestic matters." *** Accordingly, we agree with the Ninth Circuit's observation that "foreign searches have neither been historically subject to the warrant procedure, nor could they be as a practical matter."[7]

Second, nothing in the history of the foreign relations of the United States would require that U.S. officials obtain warrants from foreign magistrates before conducting searches overseas or, indeed, to suppose that all other states have search and investigation rules akin to our own. As the Supreme Court explained in *Verdugo-Urquidez:*

> For better or for worse, we live in a world of nation-states in which our Government must be able to function effectively in

---

[7] A U.S. citizen who is a target of a search by our government executed in a foreign country is not without constitutional protection-namely, the Fourth Amendment's guarantee of reasonableness which protects a citizen from unwarranted government intrusions. Indeed, in many instances, as appears to have been the case here, searches targeting U.S. citizens on foreign soil will be supported by probable cause.

the company of sovereign nations. Some who violate our laws may live outside our borders under a regime quite different from that which obtains in this country. Situations threatening to important American interests may arise halfway around the globe, situations which in the view of the political branches of our Government require an American response with armed force. If there are to be restrictions on searches and seizures which occur incident to such American action, they must be imposed by the political branches through diplomatic understanding, treaty, or legislation.

The American procedure of issuing search warrants on a showing of probable cause simply does not extend throughout the globe and, pursuant to the Supreme Court's instructions, the Constitution does not condition our Government's investigative powers on the practices of foreign legal regimes "quite different from that which obtains in this country."

Third, if U.S. judicial officers were to issue search warrants intended to have extraterritorial effect, such warrants would have dubious legal significance, if any, in a foreign nation. *** A warrant issued by a U.S. court would neither empower a U.S. agent to conduct a search nor would it necessarily compel the intended target to comply. It would be a nullity, or in the words of the Supreme Court, "a dead letter."

Fourth and finally, it is by no means clear that U.S. judicial officers could be authorized to issue warrants for overseas searches, although we need not resolve that issue here.

For these reasons, we hold that the Fourth Amendment's Warrant Clause has no extraterritorial application and that foreign searches of U.S. citizens conducted by U.S. agents are subject only to the Fourth Amendment's requirement of reasonableness.[9] ***

In addition, the purpose of the search has no bearing on the factors making a warrant requirement inapplicable to foreign searches-namely, (1) the complete absence of any precedent in our history for doing so, (2) the inadvisability of conditioning our Government's surveillance on the practices of foreign states, (3) a U.S. warrant's lack of authority overseas, and (4) the absence of a mechanism for obtaining a U.S. warrant. Accordingly, we cannot endorse the view that the normal course is to obtain a warrant for overseas searches involving U.S. citizens unless the search is "primarily" targeting foreign powers.

Turning to the question of whether the searches at issue in this appeal-the search of El-Hage's Nairobi home and the surveillance of his Kenyan telephone lines-were reasonable *** We conclude that [they were], for at least

---

[9] Because we conclude that the Warrant Clause has no extraterritorial application, we need not reach the questions of whether the searches at issue meet the good faith exception to the exclusionary rule.

the following four reasons.

First, complex, wide-ranging, and decentralized organizations, such as al Qaeda, warrant sustained and intense monitoring in order to understand their features and identify their members. ***Second, foreign intelligence gathering of the sort considered here must delve into the superficially mundane because it is not always readily apparent what information is relevant. ***Third, members of covert terrorist organizations, as with other sophisticated criminal enterprises, often communicate in code, or at least through ambiguous language. Hence, more extensive and careful monitoring of these communications may be necessary. Fourth, because the monitored conversations were conducted in foreign languages, the task of determining relevance and identifying coded language was further complicated.

Because the surveillance of suspected al Qaeda operatives must be sustained and thorough in order to be effective, we cannot conclude that the scope of the Government's electronic surveillance was overbroad. While the intrusion on El-Hage's privacy was great, the need for the government to so intrude was even greater. Accordingly, the electronic surveillance, like the search of El-Hage's Nairobi residence, was reasonable under the Fourth Amendment. ***

Notes

1. Fourth Amendment Abroad. The court rejects the warrant requirement abroad as a constitutional requirement. Could Congress mandate some warrant process for United States authorities abroad? Should it? Does the court also relax what is "reasonable" to take account of the foreign location? What facts in a search for terrorism-related information in Kenya might make the search unreasonable?

2. Foreign Law Enforcement Effects. What if the Kenyan officials used blatantly unreasonable processes in searching El-Hage's Nairobi home? Would the court find the search "unreasonable" if United States authorities were apprised of incriminating search results after the fact? What foreknowledge or involvement of the United States would suffice to lead the court to attribute the Kenyan officials' unreasonable acts to United States officials?

3. Miranda Warnings at Home and Abroad. If warrants are not required in connection with foreign arrests, would *Miranda* warnings likewise be unnecessary? Ahmed Ghailani, captured abroad in 2004, was not moved into the criminal prosecution system until June 2009. He was prosecuted and convicted even though he was not Mirandized upon capture. Conversely, Christmas Day bomber Umar Farouk Abdulmutallab was Mirandized less than an hour after the plane he intended to destroy landed in Detroit in 2009. The location of the captivity or arrest appears to have been critical in the different handling of these cases.

4. Terrorist Exception to Domestic *Miranda* Warnings? A more serious looming issue is whether terrorist suspects in the United States should qualify for a "terrorist exception" to *Miranda* warnings. In early May, 2010, Attorney General Eric Holder said "We need to give serious consideration to at least modifying the public safety exception" to the Miranda warning requirement to give the FBI "the necessary flexibility" to question terrorism suspects. Do you agree? What parameters might be constructed to assure that this exception does not swallow the rule? Could you base an argument from *MacWade* for such an exception or is it limited to the search and seizure context? Assistant Attorney General for National Security David Kris has suggested that legislation might solve this problem even though *Miranda* is a constitutional rule if there is a national security exception to the *Miranda* rule. In *New York v. Quarles*, 467 U.S. 469 (1984), Kris noted, the Court said that questioning of an ordinary criminal prompted by concerns about public safety need not be preceded by *Miranda* warnings. Maybe, he suggested, the "public-safety exception" might apply in the context of modern international terrorism when questioning is "designed to mitigate that threat." The FBI issued guidance in late 2010 telling agents that, in light of the "magnitude and complexity" of terrorist threats," they should conduct "significantly more extensive public safety interrogation without Miranda warnings than would be permissible in an ordinary criminal case." http://topics.nytimes.com/top/reference/timestopics/ organizations/f/federal_bureau_of_investigation/index.html?inline=nyt-org

B. ETHNIC PROFILING

Racial and ethnic profiling has been resoundingly criticized in the context of domestic law enforcement efforts. Shortly prior to the 9/11 attacks, in the wake of a scandal concerning racial profiling by the New Jersey state police, Congress was on the verge of passing, with virtually no opposition, a federal anti-profiling statute that would have imposed obligations on law enforcement officers in state and local governments to keep records concerning stops and arrests by race and, if the disparities in rates of stops and arrests differed significantly, take steps to eliminate or justify the differences as nonracial at the risk of losing federal law enforcement funding. This legislation was quietly taken off the congressional agenda after 9/11, no doubt to rethink profiling after 19 men fitting a number of ethnic profiling characteristics caused widespread concern over possible future terrorist attacks by individuals sharing such characteristics. The fact that would-be shoe bomber Richard Reid did not fit that profile was not sufficient to reinstate anti-profiling sentiment.

In June 2003, the Department of Justice issued the following guidance concerning the use of race by federal law enforcement agencies.

GUIDANCE REGARDING THE USE OF RACE BY FEDERAL LAW ENFORCEMENT AGENCIES
www.justice.gov/crt/about/documents/guidance.on.race.pdf

In his February 27, 2001, Address to a Joint Session of Congress, President George W. Bush declared that racial profiling is "wrong and we will end it in America." *** "Racial profiling" at its core concerns the invidious use of race or ethnicity as a criterion in conducting stops, searches and other law enforcement investigative procedures. It is premised on the erroneous assumption that any particular individual of one race or ethnicity is more likely to engage in misconduct than any particular individual of another race or ethnicity.

Racial profiling in law enforcement is not merely wrong, but also ineffective. ***This guidance prohibits racial profiling in law enforcement practices without hindering the important work of our Nation's public safety officials, particularly the intensified anti-terrorism efforts precipitated by the events of September 11, 2001.

I. Traditional Law Enforcement Activities. Two standards in combination should guide use by Federal law enforcement authorities of race or ethnicity in law enforcement activities:

- In making routine or spontaneous law enforcement decisions, such as ordinary traffic stops, Federal law enforcement officers may not use race or ethnicity to any degree, except that officers may rely on race and ethnicity in a specific suspect description. This prohibition applies even where the use of race or ethnicity might otherwise be lawful.

- In conducting activities in connection with a specific investigation, Federal law enforcement officers may consider race and ethnicity only to the extent that there is trustworthy information, relevant to the locality or time frame, that links persons of a particular race or ethnicity to an identified criminal incident, scheme, or organization. This standard applies even where the use of race or ethnicity might otherwise be lawful.

II. National Security and Border Integrity. The above standards do not affect current Federal policy with respect to law enforcement activities and other efforts to defend and safeguard against threats to national security or the integrity of the Nation's borders, to which the following applies:

- In investigating or preventing threats to national security or other catastrophic events (including the performance of duties related to air transportation security), or in enforcing laws protecting the integrity of the Nation's borders, Federal law enforcement officers may not consider race or ethnicity except to the extent permitted by the Constitution and laws of the United States. ***

"[T]he Constitution prohibits selective enforcement of the law based on considerations such as race." *Whren v. United States*, 517 U.S. 806, 813 (1996). *** Put simply, "to the extent that race is used as a proxy" for criminality, "a racial stereotype requiring strict scrutiny is in operation." *Cf. Bush v. Vera*, 517 U.S. at 968 (plurality). ***

Since the terrorist attacks on September 11, 2001, the President has emphasized that federal law enforcement personnel must use every legitimate tool to prevent future attacks, protect our Nation's borders, and deter those who would cause devastating harm to our Nation and its people through the use of biological or chemical weapons, other weapons of mass destruction, suicide hijackings, or any other means. *** The Constitution prohibits consideration of race or ethnicity in law enforcement decisions in all but the most exceptional instances. Given the incalculably high stakes involved in such investigations, however, Federal law enforcement officers who are protecting national security or preventing catastrophic events (as well as airport security screeners) may consider race, ethnicity, and other relevant factors to the extent permitted by our laws and the Constitution. Similarly, because enforcement of the laws protecting the Nation's borders may necessarily involve a consideration of a person's alienage in certain circumstances, the use of race or ethnicity in such circumstances is properly governed by existing statutory and constitutional standards. *** [T]he legality of particular, race-sensitive actions taken by Federal law enforcement officials in the context of national security and border integrity will depend to a large extent on the circumstances at hand. In absolutely no event, however, may Federal officials assert a national security or border integrity rationale as a mere pretext for invidious discrimination. *** [L]aw enforcement strategies not actually premised on *bona fide* national security or border integrity interests therefore will not stand. *** [A]s illustrated below, when addressing matters of national security, border integrity, or the possible catastrophic loss of life, existing legal and constitutional standards are an appropriate guide for Federal law enforcement officers.

- *Example*: The FBI receives reliable information that persons affiliated with a foreign ethnic insurgent group intend to use suicide bombers to assassinate that country's president and his entire entourage during an official visit to the United States. Federal law enforcement may appropriately focus investigative attention on identifying members of that ethnic insurgent group who may be present and active in the United States and who, based on other available information, might conceivably be involved in planning some such attack during the state visit.

- *Example*: U.S. intelligence sources report that terrorists from a particular ethnic group are planning to use commercial jetliners as weapons by hijacking them at an airport in California during the next week. Before allowing men of that ethnic group to board commercial airplanes in California airports during the next week, Transportation Security Administration personnel, and other federal and state authorities, may subject them to heightened scrutiny.

Because terrorist organizations might aim to engage in unexpected acts of catastrophic violence in any available part of the country (indeed, in multiple places simultaneously, if possible), there can be no expectation that the information must be specific to a particular locale or even to a particular identified scheme. [A]s in the example below, reliance solely upon generalized stereotypes is forbidden.

- *Example*: At the security entrance to a Federal courthouse, a man who appears to be of a particular ethnicity properly submits his briefcase for x-ray screening and passes through the metal detector. The inspection of the briefcase reveals nothing amiss, the man does not activate the metal detector, and there is nothing suspicious about his activities or appearance. In the absence of any threat warning, the federal security screener may not order the man to undergo a further inspection solely because he appears to be of a particular ethnicity.

Notes

1. Easy Cases? Are the examples used in the guidance too easy? Aren't there likely to be situations in which the FBI information is not completely "reliable" but the other factors are present in the first example? What is meant by "other available information" at the end of the first example? In the second example, what if the profiling occurs one month or one year after the information from "intelligence sources?" What if a tip comes from a tip to a local law enforcement official? What if, instead of an assassination tip or a 9/11 plot, there is simply a lot of internet buzz that focuses on "a big truck" with "a bomb" in a "major city" driven by "an African man"?

2. Changes to the Guidance. In early June, 2008, Attorney General Michael Mukasey acknowledged that the guidelines above were being reexamined, but would not provide any details. Leaked information indicates that the FBI agents would be allowed to "ask open-ended questions about activities of Muslim- or Arab-Americans, or investigate them if their jobs and backgrounds match trends that analysts deem suspect." Rumor has it that the guidelines "are about 40 pages long," in contrast to the current guidance having only three examples of profiling in the national security context. A DoJ spokesman says the new guidelines "will not give the FBI any more authority than it already has." "Threat assessments" have been used since 2003 to open investigations, according to DoJ.

3. Concerns with Changes. The ACLU objected to the proposed changes, saying the FBI would begin investigations "by assuming that everyone's a suspect, and then you weed out the innocent." It noted that two white Americans—Unabomber Ted Kaczynski and Oklahoma City bomber Timothy McVeigh—would not have appeared in any ethnic profile. House members rejected an $11 million request by the FBI for a security assessment center because they were uncertain how suspect profiles would be compiled without "needless intrusions into the privacy of innocent citizens" and "chasing false leads." Finally, Senators Leahy and Specter asked that guidelines be postponed until after a September 17, 2008 meeting of the Senate Judiciary Committee hearing to provide more time for Congress and "other interested parties" to consult on the changes. Despite "a laudatory effort to ensure that front-line agents are given clear rules to follow in pursuit of their investigations," the letter expressed concern with the "broader latitude" to consider race and ethnicity in national security matters." See http://leahy.senate.gov/press/200808/081808a.html.

4. A Picture Worth 1000 Words? A photo of the 23 "most wanted terrorists" is at http://www.fbi.gov/wanted/terrorists/fugitives.htm. Does the picture raise profiling issues? In a column supporting ethnic profiling, Fareed Zakaria commented, "[a]s a swarthy young man with an exotic name, trust me, we're being checked *** I've taken more than 50 flights all over the country since September 11, and I've been searched about 60 percent of the time. Either they are checking me out or I'm the unluckiest man alive." "Freedom vs. Security," NEWSWEEK (July 8, 2002), available at http://www.newsweek.com/2002/07/07/freedom-vs-security.html.

5. Equal Protection. Federal racial or ethnic profiling is subject to "strict scrutiny," though there may be "overriding national interests which justify federal legislation *** unacceptable for an individual state." *Hampton v. Mow Sun Wong*, 426 U.S. 88 (1976). Strict scrutiny requires the federal government to have a "compelling interest" in race-based action and a "narrowly tailored" solution. Could more aggressive profiling, meet this standard? In *Korematsu v. U.S.*, 323 U.S. 214 (1944), the Court allowed internment of people of Japanese ancestry in the United States, including American citizens. It found a compelling interest in preventing espionage and sabotage. Is the solution today with al-Qaeda and other takfiri terrorists similar? If so, could enchanced racial profiling meet racial profiling standards?

C. NATIONAL SECURITY LETTERS

One tool for locating terrorists is the National Security Letter (NSL), authorized in Foreign Intelligence Security Act (FISA) § 215. This is a letter, typically from the FBI, to an individual or organization that may possess information relevant to the FBI's efforts to locate terrorists. The letter directs the recipient to turn over described records in that person's possession (such as phone records, bank records, internet transmission records, or library records) to the FBI. The purpose of the NSL is thus similar to that of a subpoena directed at a non-party to a criminal or civil matter. The differences between the NSL and subpoena are, however, substantial. A subpoena is issued over the signature of a judge and may be challenged through a motion to the court to quash the subpoena on grounds that it violates statutory or constitutional provisions. FISA, as amended by the USA PATRIOT Act in 2001, provided no such processes with respect to NSLs. This and other rather components to NSLs led two district courts to find some of them invalid under the Fourth and First Amendments. Here is the description of one such court:

> The crux of the problem is that the form NSL, like the one issued in this case, which is preceded by a personal call from an FBI agent, is framed in imposing language on FBI letterhead and which, citing the authorizing statute, orders a combination of disclosure *in person* and in complete secrecy, essentially coerces the reasonable recipient into immediate compliance. Objectively viewed, it is improbable that an FBI summons invoking the authority of a certified "investigation to protect against international terrorism or clandestine intelligence activities," and phrased in tones sounding virtually as biblical commandment, would not be perceived with some apprehension by an ordinary person and therefore elicit passive obedience from a reasonable NSL recipient. The full weight of this ominous writ is especially felt when the NSL's plain language, in a measure that enhances its aura as an expression of public will, prohibits disclosing the issuance of the NSL to "any person." Reading such strictures, it is also highly unlikely that an NSL recipient reasonably would know that he may have a right to contest the NSL, and that a process to do so may exist through a judicial proceeding.

Because neither the statute, nor an NSL, nor the FBI agents dealing with the recipient say as much, all but the most mettlesome and undaunted NSL recipients would consider themselves effectively barred from consulting an attorney or anyone else who might advise them otherwise, as well as bound to absolute silence about the very existence of the NSL. Furthermore, it is doubtful that an NSL recipient, not necessarily a lawyer, would be willing to undertake any creative exercises in statutory construction to somehow reach the Government's proposed reading of [the statute], especially because that construction is not apparent from the plain language of the statute, the NSL itself, or accompanying government communications, and any penalties for non-compliance or disclosure are also unspecified in the NSL or in the statute. For the reasonable NSL recipient confronted with the NSL's mandatory language and the FBI's conduct related to the NSL, resistance is not a viable option. *** *Doe v. Ashcroft (Doe I)*, 334 F. Supp. 2d 471 (SDNY 2004).

The USA Patriot Improvement and Reauthorization Act of 2005 made several changes to the NSL process. First, the standard for issuing an NSL was raised from one of simple "relevancy" to a counterterrorism or national security investigation to a requirement that the government provide the recipient of the letter with a "statement of facts" demonstrating "reasonable grounds" to believe the order is relevant to such an investigation. Second, the request must now provide a particularized description of the records sought. Third, the amendments allowed the recipient to petition a federal court to modify or set aside the letter "if compliance would be unreasonable, oppressive, or otherwise unlawful" or "there is no reason to believe that disclosure may endanger the national security of the United States, interfere with a criminal, counterterrorism, or counterintelligence investigation***." Fourth, the NSL was modified to allow a recipient to seek legal advice regarding her options and assistance in seeking the judicial review discussed above. Finally, in 2006, Congress raised the bar for NSLs concerning library records, "book sale records, book customer lists, firearms sales records, tax return records, educational records, or medical records containing information that would identify a person." 18 U.S.C. §2709(f). This legislation also excluded libraries from the definition of "wire or electronic communication service provider" with respect to NSLs seeking subscriber information and billing records.

Even after these changes, NSL's letters have remained controversial. An Inspector General report issued in 2006 revealed that an estimated 150,000 NSLs were issued between 2003 and 2005. More recent reports indicate that in 2007 the FBI made 16,804 NSL requests pertaining to 4,327 U.S. persons, a figure that grew in 2008 to 24,744 requests concerning 7,225 United States persons. In congressional testimony, FBI General Counsel Valerie Caproni (House Judiciary Committee, March 20, 2007) provided this assessment of the NSL process: "we got an F report card when we're just not used to that. *** [T]he agents my age in the FBI, all grew up as criminal agents in a system which is transparent *** [T]hey're going to have a federal district judge yelling at them. The national security side occurs largely without that level of transparency." The Inspector General Report noted that "[W]hen Congress lowered the evidentiary standard for issuing National Security Letters . . . it authorized the FBI to collect information *** on persons who are not subjects of FBI investigations. This means that the FBI—and other law enforcement or Intelligence Community agencies with access to FBI databases—is able to review and store information about American citizens and others in the United States who are not subjects of FBI foreign counterintelligence investigations and about whom the FBI has no individualized suspicion of illegal activity."

A watchdog organization, the Center for National Security Studies, argues that there are still two main administrative problems with NSLs: "First, the rules for gathering Americans' sensitive records are too loose. Second, the financial, Internet and phone records obtained are kept for too long, even if there is no reasonable basis to believe an individual is doing anything wrong." Testimony of Lisa Graves (House Permanent Select Committee on Intelligence, March 28, 2007). Finally, the Center for National Securities study testimony concludes that the changes in the NSL legal framework were not all in favor of citizen privacy: "Compliance can now be compelled, as with a subpoena, and violating the gag can be severely punished *** Of course, giving the businesses that receive NSLs the right to challenge them was the right thing to do, but it is nowhere close to a sufficient check on these intrusive powers. Indeed, it is probably more cost-effective for some businesses to turn over information that they will never have to account to their customers about rather than pay lawyers to fight an overly broad request***."

The Bill or Rights Defense Committee says these are the seven things that all citizens need to know about NSLs:

1. National Security Letters can be used by the FBI to obtain information about your banking, sites you visit on the Internet and your phone calls.

2. You do not need to be suspected of terrorism for the FBI to demand your records.

3. You will NOT be told if the FBI has used an NSL to obtain your records.

4. Even if an investigation clears you of any wrongdoing, the FBI retains your records indefinitely.

5. An Inspector General Report delivered to Congress found that there were 143,074 NSLs requested from 2003-2005.

6. Each NSL may demand hundreds or thousands of records of private information on Americans.

7. From the 143,074 NSLs requested, there was only 1 confirmed terrorism-related conviction.

http://www.bordc.org/nsl/nsl-seventhings.pdf

Now that you have a general background in NSLs, consider this decision concerning NSL letters issued following the amendments:

JOHN DOE, INC. v. MUKASEY
549 F. 3d 861 (2d Cir. 2008)

JON O. NEWMAN, Circuit Judge:

This appeal concerns challenges to the constitutionality of statutes regulating the issuance by the Federal Bureau of Investigation ("FBI") of a type of administrative subpoena generally known as a National Security Letter ("NSL") to electronic communication service providers ("ECSPs"). ECSPs are typically telephone companies or Internet service providers. An NSL, in the context of this appeal, is a request for information about specified persons or entities who are subscribers to an ECSP and about their telephone or Internet activity. Primarily at issue on this appeal are challenges to the provisions (1) prohibiting the recipient from disclosing the fact that an NSL has been received, and (2) structuring judicial review of the nondisclosure requirement. ***

The NSL. In February 2004, the FBI delivered the NSL at issue in this litigation to John Doe, Inc. The letter directed John Doe, Inc., "to provide the [FBI] the names, addresses, lengths of service and electronic communication transactional records, to include [other information] (not to include message content and/or subject fields) for [a specific] email address." The letter certified that the information sought was relevant to an investigation against international terrorism or clandestine intelligence activities and advised John Doe, Inc., that the law "prohibit[ed] any officer, employee or agent" of the company from "disclosing to any person that the FBI has sought or obtained access to information or records" pursuant to the NSL provisions. The letter also asked that John Doe provide the relevant information personally to a designated FBI office. *** *** Subsection 2709(c), as it existed in 2004, imposed a blanket nondisclosure requirement prohibiting an ECSP from disclosing receipt of an NSL ***. The Plaintiffs *** contended that section 2709 violated the First and Fourth Amendments by authorizing the FBI to compel the disclosure of private records relating to constitutionally protected speech and association; they also contended that the nondisclosure requirement of subsection 2709(c) violated the First Amendment by permanently barring NSL recipients from disclosing that the FBI had sought or obtained information from them. ***

Amendments to the NSL statutes. While appeals *** were pending, Congress amended the NSL statutes in two respects. First, although leaving intact subsections 2709(a) and (b), requiring compliance with NSLs, Congress amended the nondisclosure prohibition of subsection 2709(c) to require nondisclosure only upon certification by senior FBI officials that "otherwise there may result a danger to the national security of the United States, interference with a criminal, counterterrorism, or counterintelligence investigation, interference with diplomatic relations, or danger to the life or physical safety of any person." ("the enumerated harms"). The

Reauthorization Act amended subsection 2709(c) by replacing the single paragraph of former subsection 2709(c) with four subdivisions, the fourth of which was amended by the Additional Reauthorization Act. *** Second, in the Reauthorization Act, Congress added provisions for judicial review *** to permit the recipient of an NSL to petition a United States district court for an order modifying or setting aside the NSL, and the nondisclosure requirement. The NSL may be modified if "compliance would be unreasonable, oppressive, or otherwise unlawful." The nondisclosure requirement, which prohibits disclosure by the NSL recipient of the fact that the FBI has sought or obtained access to the requested information, may be modified or set aside, upon a petition filed by the NSL recipient, if the district court "finds that there is no reason to believe that disclosure may endanger the national security of the United States" or cause other of the enumerated harms (worded slightly differently from subsection 2709(c)(1)), (3). The nondisclosure requirement further provides that if the Attorney General or senior governmental officials certify that disclosure may endanger the national security or interfere with diplomatic relations, such certification shall be treated as "conclusive" unless the court finds that the certification was made "in bad faith." ***

The validity of the NSL issued to John Doe, Inc., is no longer at issue because the Government has withdrawn it, but the prohibition on disclosing receipt of the NSL remains. We therefore consider only the Government's challenges to the District Court's rulings with respect to the nondisclosure requirement, although to the extent that the nondisclosure requirement encounters valid constitutional objections, we will consider the provisions authorizing the issuance of NSLs in connection with the issue of severance.***

A judicial order "forbidding certain communications when issued in advance of the time that such communications are to occur" is generally regarded as a "prior restraint," and is "the most serious and the least tolerable infringement on First Amendment rights." ***Where expression is conditioned on governmental permission, *** the First Amendment generally requires procedural protections to guard against impermissible censorship.***: (1) any restraint imposed prior to judicial review must be limited to "a specified brief period"; (2) any further restraint prior to a final judicial determination must be limited to "the shortest fixed period compatible with sound judicial resolution"; and (3) the burden of going to court to suppress speech and the burden of proof in court must be placed on the government. *** [However,]the national security context in which NSLs are authorized imposes on courts a significant obligation to defer to judgments of Executive Branch officials. "[C]ourts traditionally have been reluctant to intrude upon the authority of the Executive in ... national security affairs," and the Supreme Court has acknowledged that terrorism might provide the basis for arguments "for heightened deference to the judgments of the political branches with respect to matters of national security," *Zadvydas v. Davis*, 533 U.S. 678 (2001).*** [Moreover,] courts should resolve ambiguities in statutes in a manner that avoids substantial constitutional issues.

Less clear is the authority of courts to revise a statute to overcome a constitutional defect. *** [I]n limited circumstances the Supreme Court has undertaken to fill in a statutory gap arising from the invalidation of a portion of a statute. *** Closely related to the issue of whether a court should revise a statute to avoid or overcome a constitutional defect is the issue of whether to sever the unconstitutional portion of a statute or invalidate an entire statute or even an entire statutory scheme. In general, the choice, as stated by the Supreme Court, depends on whether "the legislature [would] have preferred what is left of its statute to no statute at all." ***

From the Plaintiffs' standpoint, the nondisclosure requirement of subsection 2709(c) is a straightforward content-based prior restraint that must be tested against all the substantive and procedural limitations applicable to such an impairment of expression. In their view, the nondisclosure requirement is content-based because it proscribes disclosure of the entire category of speech concerning the fact and details of the issuance of an NSL, and it is a prior restraint in the literal sense that it is imposed before an NSL recipient has an opportunity to speak. From these premises, the Plaintiffs conclude that subsection 2709(c) is unconstitutional under strict scrutiny review because it prohibits disclosure in circumstances not narrowly tailored to a compelling governmental interest and operates as a licensing scheme without the procedural requirement of placing on the Government the burden of initiating judicial review and sustaining a burden of proof. The Plaintiffs also challenge subsection 3511(b) on the grounds that (1) the judicial review provisions do not require the Government to initiate judicial review and to sustain a burden of proof and (2) certification of certain risks by senior governmental officials is entitled to a conclusive presumption (absent bad faith). These aspects of subsection 3511(b) are alleged to violate First Amendment procedural standards and the separation of powers.

The Government responds that, to whatever extent the nondisclosure requirement can be considered a content-based prior restraint, it is subject to less rigorous scrutiny than that imposed on more typical First Amendment claimants who wish to speak or parade in public places, distribute literature, or exhibit movies. The Government points out that the nondisclosure requirement arises not to suppress a pre-existing desire to speak, but only as a result of governmental interaction with an NSL recipient. In the Government's view, the nondisclosure requirement survives a First Amendment challenge on the same rationale that has permitted secrecy requirements to be imposed on witnesses before grand juries, and judicial misconduct proceedings, and on a person or entity that acquired sensitive material through pretrial discovery. ***

In assessing these contentions, we need to interpret the nondisclosure requirements before ruling on their constitutionality. *** [S]ubsection 2709(c) specifies what senior FBI officials must certify to trigger the nondisclosure requirement, and subsection 3511(b) specifies, in similar but not identical language, what a district court must find in order to modify or set aside such a requirement. Senior FBI officials must certify that in the absence of a nondisclosure requirement "there may result a danger to the national security of the United States, interference with a criminal, counterterrorism, or counterintelligence investigation, interference with diplomatic relations, or danger to the life or physical safety of any person." Upon challenge by an NSL recipient, a district court may modify or set aside a nondisclosure requirement "if it finds that there is no reason to believe that disclosure may endanger the national security of the United States, interfere with a criminal, counterterrorism, or counterintelligence investigation, interfere with diplomatic relations, or endanger the life or physical safety of any person."

These provisions present three issues for interpretation: (1) what is the scope of the enumerated harms? (2) what justifies a nondisclosure requirement? and (3) which side has the burden of proof?

The enumerated harms. *** These harms are "danger to the national security of the United States, interference with a criminal, counterterrorism, or counterintelligence investigation, interference with diplomatic relations, or danger to the life or physical safety of any person." The last phrase is particularly troublesome. It could extend the Government's power to impose secrecy to a broad range of information relevant to such matters as ordinary tortious conduct, based on the risk of "danger to the physical safety of any person." A secrecy requirement of such broad scope would present highly problematic First Amendment issues. However, this potential reach of the nondisclosure requirement can be reined in if all the enumerated harms are keyed to the same standard that governs information sought by an NSL, *i.e.,*"relevant to an authorized investigation to protect against international terrorism or clandestine intelligence activities." *** [We construe] this requirement to apply only when senior FBI officials certify that disclosure may result in an enumerated harm that is related to "an authorized investigation to protect against international terrorism or clandestine intelligence activities."

The required showing. *** A district court, considering a challenge filed within one year of the issuance of an NSL, is authorized to modify or set aside a nondisclosure requirement "if it finds that there is no reason to believe that disclosure may" risk one of the enumerated harms. At oral argument, the Government took the position that "reason" in the quoted phrase means "good reason." We accept this common-sense understanding of subsection 3511(b)(2). *** Moreover, a reason will not qualify as "good" if it surmounts only a standard of frivolousness. *** The upholding of nondisclosure does not require the certainty, or even the imminence of, an enumerated harm, but some reasonable likelihood must be shown. The Government acknowledges that "while the 'reason to believe' standard in subsection 3511(b) unquestionably contemplates a deferential standard of review, in no way does it foreclose a court from evaluating the reasonableness of the FBI's judgments."

The burden of proof. *** As the Government acknowledged at oral argument, subsection 3511(b) is silent as to the burden of proof. The Government also acknowledged at oral argument that these provisions should be understood to place on the Government the burden to persuade a district court that there is a good reason to believe that disclosure may risk one of the enumerated harms, and that a district court, in order to maintain a nondisclosure order, must find that such a good reason exists. This avoids requiring a district court, in order to modify or set aside a nondisclosure order, to find a negative, *i.e.*, that no good reason exists to believe that disclosure may risk one of the enumerated harms.

*** We will therefore construe subsection 2709(c)(1) to mean that the enumerated harms must be related to "an authorized investigation to protect against international terrorism or clandestine intelligence activities," (2) and construe subsections 3511(b)(2) and (3) to place on the Government the burden to persuade a district court that there is a good reason to believe that disclosure may result in one of the enumerated harms, and to mean that a district court, in order to maintain a nondisclosure order, must find that such a good reason exists.

IV. Constitutionality of the NSL Statutes

(a) *Basic approach.* Turning to the First Amendment issues with respect to the NSL statutes as thus construed, we believe that the proper path to decision lies between the broad positions asserted by the parties. Although the nondisclosure requirement is in some sense a prior restraint, as urged by the Plaintiffs, it is not a typical example of such a restriction for it is not a restraint imposed on those who customarily wish to exercise rights of free expression, such as speakers in public fora, distributors of literature, or exhibitors of movies. And although the nondisclosure requirement is triggered by the content of a category of information, that category, consisting of the fact of receipt of an NSL and some related details, is far more limited than the broad categories of information that have been at issue with respect to typical content-based restrictions.

On the other hand, we do not accept the Government's contentions that the nondisclosure requirement can be considered to satisfy First Amendment standards based on analogies to secrecy rules applicable to grand juries, judicial misconduct proceedings, and certain interactions between individuals and governmental entities. The justification for grand jury secrecy inheres in the nature of the proceeding. As the Supreme Court has noted, such secrecy serves several interests common to most such proceedings, including enhancing the willingness of witnesses to come forward, promoting truthful testimony, lessening the risk of flight or attempts to influence grand jurors by those about to be indicted, and avoiding public ridicule of those whom the grand jury declines to indict. *** Unlike the grand jury proceeding, as to which interests in secrecy arise from the nature of the proceeding, the nondisclosure requirement of subsection 2709(c) is imposed at the demand of the Executive Branch under circumstances where secrecy might or might not be warranted, depending on the circumstances alleged to justify such secrecy.

The Government's analogy to permissible limitations on disclosures in connection with judicial misconduct proceedings also fails to justify the nondisclosure requirement of subsection 2709(c). *** These interests *** inhere in the nature of judicial misconduct proceedings. *** The

Government's analogy to certain interactions between an individual and governmental entities is also unavailing. The Government seeks to enlist cases involving classification of former CIA employees' information as top secret, and a prohibition on disclosure of information obtained by a litigant through court-ordered discovery. We fail to appreciate the analogy between the individuals or the entity seeking disclosure in those cases and John Doe, Inc., who had no interaction with the Government until the Government imposed its nondisclosure requirement upon it.

The nondisclosure requirement of subsection 2709(c) is not a typical prior restraint or a typical content-based restriction warranting the most rigorous First Amendment scrutiny. On the other hand, the Government's analogies to nondisclosure prohibitions in other contexts do not persuade us to use a significantly diminished standard of review. In any event, John Doe, Inc., has been restrained from publicly expressing a category of information, albeit a narrow one, and that information is relevant to intended criticism of a governmental activity.

The panel is not in agreement as to whether, in this context, we should examine subsection 2709(c) under a standard of traditional strict scrutiny or under a standard that, in view of the context, is not quite as "exacting" a form of strict scrutiny. Ultimately, this disagreement has no bearing on our disposition because, as we discuss below, the only two limitations on NSL procedures required by First Amendment procedural standards would be required under either degree of scrutiny. We note that, for purposes of the litigation in this Court, the Government has conceded that strict scrutiny is the applicable standard.

(b) *Strict scrutiny.* Under strict scrutiny review, the Government must demonstrate that the nondisclosure requirement is "narrowly tailored to promote a compelling Government interest," and that there are no "less restrictive alternatives [that] would be at least as effective in achieving the legitimate purpose that the statute was enacted to serve." Since "[i]t is obvious and unarguable that no governmental interest is more compelling than the security of the Nation," the principal strict scrutiny issue turns on whether the narrow tailoring requirement is met, and this issue, as the District Court observed, essentially concerns the process by which the nondisclosure requirement is imposed and tested.

With subsections 2709(c) and 3511(b) interpreted as set forth above, two aspects of that process remain principally at issue: the absence of a requirement that the Government initiate judicial review of the lawfulness of a nondisclosure requirement and the degree of deference a district court is obliged to accord to the certification of senior governmental officials in ordering nondisclosure.

(i) *Absence of requirement that the Government initiate judicial review.* *** The Government could inform each NSL recipient that it should give the Government prompt notice, perhaps within ten days, in the event that the recipient wishes to contest the nondisclosure requirement. Upon receipt of such notice, the Government could be accorded a limited time, perhaps 30 days, to initiate a judicial review proceeding to maintain the nondisclosure requirement, and the proceeding would have to be concluded within a prescribed time, perhaps 60 days. *** [T]he NSL could inform the recipient that the nondisclosure requirement would remain in effect during the entire interval of the recipient's decision whether to contest the nondisclosure requirement, the Government's prompt application to a court, and the Court's prompt adjudication on the merits. The NSL could also inform the recipient that the nondisclosure requirement would remain in effect if the recipient declines to give the Government notice of an intent to challenge the requirement or, upon a challenge, if the Government prevails in court. If the Government is correct that very few NSL recipients have any interest in challenging the nondisclosure requirement (perhaps no more than three have done so thus far), this "reciprocal notice procedure" would nearly eliminate the Government's burden to initiate litigation (with a corresponding minimal burden on NSL recipients to defend numerous lawsuits). Thus, the Government's litigating burden can be substantially minimized, and the resulting slight burden is not a reason for precluding application of [this requirement]. *** The availability of a minimally burdensome reciprocal notice procedure for governmental initiation of judicial review and the inadequacy of the Government's attempts to avoid [this requirement] persuade us that this safeguard, normally required where strict scrutiny applies, must be observed. Therefore, in the absence of Government-initiated judicial review, subsection 3511(b) is not narrowly tailored to conform to First Amendment procedural standards. We conclude, as did the District Court, that subsection 3511(b) does not survive either traditional strict scrutiny or a slightly less exacting measure of such scrutiny.

(ii) *Deference to administrative discretion.* The Plaintiffs contended, and the District Court agreed, that the judicial review contemplated by subsection 3511(b) authorizes a degree of deference to the Executive Branch that is inconsistent with First Amendment standards. Although acknowledging that "national security is a compelling interest justifying nondisclosure in certain situations," the District Court faulted the review provision in several respects. First, the Court stated that the statute "requires the court to blindly credit a finding that there 'may' be a reason-potentially any conceivable and not patently frivolous reason-for it to believe disclosure will result in a certain harm." Our construction of the statute, however, avoids that concern. As indicated above, we interpret subsection 3511(b) to place on the Government the burden to show a "good" reason to believe that disclosure may result in an enumerated harm, *i.e.*, a harm related to "an authorized investigation to protect against international terrorism or clandestine intelligence activities." and to place on a district court an obligation to make the "may result" finding only after consideration, albeit deferential, of the Government's explanation concerning the risk of an enumerated harm.

Assessing the Government's showing of a good reason to believe that an enumerated harm may result will present a district court with a delicate task. While the court will normally defer to the Government's considered assessment of *why* disclosure in a particular case may result in an enumerated harm related to such grave matters as international terrorism or clandestine intelligence activities, it cannot, consistent with strict scrutiny standards, uphold a nondisclosure requirement on a conclusory assurance that such a likelihood exists. In this case, the director of the FBI certified that "the disclosure of the NSL itself or its contents may endanger the national security of the United States." To accept that conclusion without requiring some elaboration would "cast Article III judges in the role of petty functionaries, persons required to enter as a court judgment an executive officer's decision, but stripped of capacity to evaluate independently whether the Executive's decision is correct."

In showing why disclosure would risk an enumerated harm, the Government must at least indicate the nature of the apprehended harm and provide a court with some basis to assure itself (based on *in camera* presentations where appropriate) that the link between disclosure and risk of harm is substantial. As the Government acknowledges, "Nothing in [subs]ection 3511(b) would require a district court to confine judicial review to the FBI's necessarily unelaborated public statement about the need for nondisclosure. The provisions in [subs]ections 3511(d) and (e) for *ex parte* and *in camera* review provide a ready mechanism for the FBI to provide a more complete explanation of its reasoning, and the court is free to elicit such an explanation as part of the review process."

We have every confidence that district judges can discharge their review responsibility with faithfulness to First Amendment considerations and without intruding on the prerogative of the Executive Branch to exercise its judgment on matters of national security. Such a judgment is not to be second-guessed, but a court must receive some indication that the judgment has been soundly reached. As the Supreme Court has noted in matters of similar gravity, the Constitution "envisions a role for all three branches when individual liberties are at stake."

The District Court's second reason for considering the judicial review procedure of subsection 3511(b) deficient was a perceived preclusion of a Court's authority, when presented with a "plausible, reasonable, and specific" enumerated harm, to balance "the potential harm against the particular First Amendment interest raised by a particular challenge." We see no deficiency in this regard. *** That is why we have interpreted the statutory standard to permit a nondisclosure requirement only upon an adequate demonstration that a good reason exists reasonably to apprehend a risk of an enumerated harm, and have expressly read the enumerated harms as being linked to international terrorism or clandestine intelligence activities. *** A demonstration of a reasonable likelihood of potential harm, related to international terrorism or clandestine intelligence activities, will virtually always outweigh the First Amendment interest in speaking about such a limited and particularized occurrence as the receipt of an NSL and will suffice to maintain the secrecy of the fact of such receipt.

The District Court's third objection to the judicial review procedure is far more substantial. The Court deemed inconsistent with strict scrutiny standards the provision of subsections 3511(b)(2) and (b)(3) specifying that a certification by senior governmental officials that disclosure may "endanger the national security of the United States or interfere with diplomatic relations ... shall be treated as conclusive unless the court finds that the certification was made in bad faith." We agree. *** To accept deference to that extraordinary degree would be to reduce strict scrutiny to no scrutiny, save only in the rarest of situations where bad faith could be shown. Under either traditional strict scrutiny or a less exacting application of that standard, some demonstration from the Executive Branch of the need for secrecy is required in order to conform the nondisclosure requirement to First Amendment standards. The fiat of a governmental official, though senior in rank and doubtless honorable in the execution of official duties, cannot displace the judicial obligation to enforce constitutional requirements. "Under no circumstances should the Judiciary become the handmaiden of the Executive."

V. Remedy

To recapitulate our conclusions, we (1) construe subsection 2709(c) to permit a nondisclosure requirement only when senior FBI officials certify that disclosure may result in an enumerated harm that is related to "an authorized investigation to protect against international terrorism or clandestine intelligence activities," (2) construe subsections 3511(b)(2) and (b)(3) to place on the Government the burden to show that a good reason exists to expect that disclosure of receipt of an NSL will risk an enumerated harm, (3) construe subsections 3511(b)(2) and (b)(3) to mean that the Government satisfies its burden when it makes an adequate demonstration as to why disclosure in a particular case may result in an enumerated harm, (4) rule that subsections 2709(c) and 3511(b) are unconstitutional to the extent that they impose a nondisclosure requirement without placing on the Government the burden of initiating judicial review of that requirement, and (5) rule that subsections 3511(b)(2) and (b)(3) are unconstitutional to the extent that, upon such review, a governmental official's certification that disclosure may endanger the national security of the United States or interfere with diplomatic relations is treated as conclusive.

Implementing these conclusions requires us to apply the principles of judicial interpretation and limited revision of statutes and consider the related issue of severance***. We are satisfied that conclusions (1), (2), and (3) fall within our judicial authority to interpret statutes to avoid constitutional objections or conform to constitutional requirements. Conclusions (4) and (5) require further consideration.

We deem it beyond the authority of a court to "interpret" or "revise" the NSL statutes to create the constitutionally required obligation of the Government to initiate judicial review of a nondisclosure requirement. However, the Government might be able to assume such an obligation without additional legislation. *** [T]there appears to be no impediment to the Government's including notice of a recipient's opportunity to contest the nondisclosure requirement in an NSL. If such notice is given, time limits on the nondisclosure requirement pending judicial review *** would have to be applied to make the review procedure constitutional. We would deem it to be within our judicial authority to conform subsection 2709(c) to First

Amendment requirements, by limiting the duration of the nondisclosure requirement, absent a ruling favorable to the Government upon judicial review, to the 10-day period in which the NSL recipient decides whether to contest the nondisclosure requirement, the 30-day period in which the Government considers whether to seek judicial review, and a further period of 60 days in which a court must adjudicate the merits, unless special circumstances warrant additional time. If the NSL recipient declines timely to precipitate Government-initiated judicial review, the nondisclosure requirement would continue, subject to the recipient's existing opportunities for annual challenges to the nondisclosure requirement provided by subsection 3511(b). If such an annual challenge is made, the standards and burden of proof that we have specified for an initial challenge would apply, although the Government would not be obliged to initiate judicial review.

In those instances where an NSL recipient gives notice of an intent to challenge the disclosure requirement, the Government would have several options for completing the reciprocal notice procedure by commencing such review. First, it is arguable that the Government can adapt the authority now set forth in subsection 3511(c) for the purpose of initiating judicial review. That provision authorizes the Attorney General to "invoke the aid of any [relevant] district court" in the event of "a failure to comply with a request for ... information made to any person or entity under section 2709(b)" or other provisions authorizing NSLs. Since an NSL includes both a request for information and a direction not to disclose that the FBI has sought or obtained information, an NSL recipient's timely notice of intent to disclose, furnished in response to notice in an NSL of an opportunity to contest the nondisclosure requirement, can perhaps be considered the functional equivalent of the "failure to comply" contemplated by subsection 3511(c). Second, the Government might be able to identify some other statutory authority to invoke the equitable power of a district court to prevent a disclosure that the Government can demonstrate would risk harm to national security. Third, and as a last resort, the Government could seek explicit congressional authorization to initiate judicial review of a nondisclosure requirement that a recipient wishes to challenge. We leave it to the Government to consider how to discharge its obligation to initiate judicial review.

In view of these possibilities, we need not invalidate the entirety of the nondisclosure requirement of subsection 2709(c) or the judicial review provisions of subsection 3511(b). Although the conclusive presumption clause of subsections 3511(b)(2) and (b)(3) must be stricken, we invalidate subsection 2709(c) and the remainder of subsection 3511(b) only to the extent that they fail to provide for Government-initiated judicial review. The Government can respond to this partial invalidation ruling by using the suggested reciprocal notice procedure. With this procedure in place, subsections 2709(c) and 3511(b) would survive First Amendment challenge.

These partial invalidations of subsections 2709(c) and 3511(b) oblige us to consider the issue of severance. *** We have no doubt that if Congress had understood that First Amendment considerations required *** it would have wanted the remainder of the NSL statutes to remain in force. *** We therefore sever the conclusive presumption language of subsection 3511(b) and leave intact the remainder of subsection 3511(b) and the entirety of section 2709 (with Government-initiated judicial review required). ***

Notes

1. Balance. Does the court strike the right balance between national security and First Amendment considerations? Is this balance consistent with the Supreme Court's subsequent decision in *Holder v. Humanitarian Law Project*?

2. Government Responses. Other than by appealing this order, how might the government respond in the legislative arena to address the problems identified by the court without giving up this "essential tool" for national security? If you were the Attorney General, would you institute the "reciprocal notice" requirement nationwide or only in circuits which, like this one, require it?

3. FOIA and NSLs. In *Cattledge v. Mueller*, 323 Fed.Appx. 464 (C.A. 7, 2009) (unpublished), the plaintiff asked the FBI to produce NSLs issued during a particular time period. The FBI did so, but redacted all information relating the the individual investigated and the institution from whom information was sought. In other words, the FBI provided copies of its standard NSL form. Cattledge persisted, then requesting the particular NSLs relevant to him. The FBI refused, citing FOIA exemption 7(E), which government agencies to refuse to release "records or information compiled for law enforcement purposes, but only to the extent that the production of such law enforcement records or information ... would disclose techniques and procedures for law enforcement investigations or prosecutions ... if such disclosure could reasonably be expected to risk circumvention of the law." The Court held the exemption applicable, saying "Even if the existence of a law-enforcement technique is generally known, the exemption still protects the circumstances under which it is used, if they are not known. Furthermore, we previously recognized that a government agency may properly refuse to confirm or deny whether it has any records responsive to a person's request for records about himself." The court referenced Section Chief of the Record/Information Dissemination Section of the FBI David Hardy's explanation that "disclosing the subjects of NSLs would enable terrorist groups to vet their members and circumvent the law by shifting operations to those free of government suspicion. He further noted that if the information was disclosed, these groups could analyze which of their members were investigated to learn when and how NSLs are issued and thus avoid raising suspicion in the future."

4. Discovery of NSLs by Criminal Defendants. Suppose the government prosecutes an individual and the individual suspects that NSLs were issued which led to evidence used against him. In order to defend himself, arguing perhaps that the government has violated his constitutional rights, should he be able to discover those NSLs? The courts have uniformly said no. See *U. S. v. Amawi*, 531 F. Supp. 2d 823 (N.D. Ohio, 2008) in which the court said "production of NSLs and/or information and documents obtained in response to service of NSLs is not discoverable under Rule 16 or otherwise. To the extent that the defendants seek discovery under the *Jencks* Act, the government has already agreed to a timetable for *Jencks* materials. Assuming that information or documents obtained *via* an NSL came within the *Jencks* Act, that agreement moots the instant request. It would appear likely, or at least possible, that the defendants could obtain the information that they seek directly from the entities on whom NSLs may have been served regarding their records and transactions with such entities. Presumably they know who their financial institutions, phone companies and internet service providers, credit card companies, and travel providers were during the pertinent period. Contacting those entities directly may well enable them to get as much or more information than the government may have obtained through service of any NSLs. having received the NSLs. To the extent that the defendants assert a constitutional basis for their motion, it finds its basis in the Fourth Amendment, rather than the First Amendment. The decision in *Doe* has no applicability to the Defendants' motion." The Court, in closing, did note that the Defendants' motion did not seek "to suppress any NSL-derived information or documents." Would such a motion be more likely to succeed?

D. DATA MINING

Data mining is "the non-trivial extraction of implicit, previously unknown, and potentially useful information from data." William J. Frawley et al., *Knowledge Discovery in Databases: An Overview*, 13 AI Mag. 57, 70 (1992). In the counterterrorism context, data mining is the computerized sifting of digital data to identify suspect individuals and behaviors for further investigation using traditional law enforcement techniques. Far from being one concrete process, data mining consists of a collection of computer-driven programs with different aims and methods used by the Government and private companies to track, investigate, pinpoint, and even predict the actions of individuals.

Steven D. Levitt & Stephen J. Dubner in SUPERFREAKONOMICS (HarperCollins 2009), pp 90-95, tell a story about a British bank employee named Ian Horsley who wondered if algorithms that he worked with to detect fraud could "sift through an endless stream of retail banking data and successfully detect ***would-be terrorists." Levitt and Dubner describe the problem as follows:

> Let's say you *could* develop a banking algorithm that was 99 percent accurate. We'll assume the United Kingdom has 500 terrorists. The algorithm would correctly identify 495 of them, or 99 percent. But there are roughly 50 million adults in the United Kingdom who have nothing to do with terrorism, and the algorithm would also wrongly identify 1 percent of *them*, or 500,000 people. At the end of the day, this wonderful, 99-prcent-accurate algorithm spits out too many false positives—half a million people who would be rightly indignant if they were hauled in by the authorities on suspicion of terrorism....[I]f you want to hunt terrorists, 99 percent is not even close to good enough." *** Horsley, using

the data for the 7/7/2005 Islamic suicide bombers in London and a bunch of folks arrested who "resembled a terrorist closely enough to get arrested" created an algorithm to identify those whose data resembled the known cohort of terrorists and those who resembled them enough to be arrested. Horsley "was able to generate a list of about 30 highly suspicious individuals" from customers of a large British bank. Horsley's estimate was that "at least 5 of these 30 are almost certainly involved in terrorist activities." The authors note that "Five out of 30 isn't perfect—the algorithm misses many terrorists and still falsely identifies some innocents—but it sure beats 495 out of 55,495.

By the way, for his efforts in hunting down would-be terrorists through data mining, Horsley was knighted.

In the United States before 9/11, government use of data mining was curtailed by both private groups and individual lawmakers due to concerns about privacy and other civil liberties. However, after 9/11, Government data mining as a counterterrorism tool increased substantially, as lawmakers and individuals became more willing to trade a measure of privacy for the promise of increased security. Today, the Government develops and applies computer programs to search databases of raw information to generate leads, culminating in arrests and/or prevention of terrorist attacks. However, there is intense debate concerning whether such programs are legal statutorily and under the Constitution, which has led to oversight hearings and several of the programs being terminated after Congress pulled their funding. See Peter P. Swire, *Privacy and Information Sharing in the War on Terrorism*, 51 Vill. L. Rev. 951 (2006).

Data mining has both tangible benefits and potential costs. It can help apprehend and build cases against criminals, keep potentially dangerous individuals off airplanes, and deter others from attempting to fly, prevent terrorists from entering the country, hiding their identities, and discourage funding of terrorist activities. Costs include arrests based on inaccurate data, innocent people being kept off airplanes, and innocent individuals being investigated.

Several data mining programs have been used by the United States government to identify terrorist suspects. For example, the National Security Agency (NSA) collected phone call data consisting of numbers called but not the content of the phone conversations, from "tens of millions of Americans" to create "a database of every call ever made" within the United States. This program is discussed in Chapter IV. Domestically, the FBI reported having databases with more than 659 million records, about a quarter of which come from FBI records and criminal case files and the rest from suspicious financial activity reports, no-fly lists, airline passenger records, and lost and stolen passport data. An FBI agent can now run 1,000 names through the database in 30 minutes or less, a search that would have taken 32,333 hours prior to 2002.

Some data mining programs have been discontinued. The Total (later Terrorist) Information Awareness Program (TIA) was a research project of the Defense Advanced Research Projects Agency (DARPA) in 2002 to develop technology programs to "counter asymmetric threats by achieving total information awareness useful for preemption, national security warning, and national security decision making." Serious public relations mistakes such as adopting the logo below, contributed to Congress's decision to cut off funding for TIA in its original form.

Similar fates befell two other Programs. The first was The Computer-Assisted Passenger Prescreening System (CAPPS), an airline passenger prescreening program that used computer-generated profiles to select passengers for additional security screening. Litigation made airlines wary of voluntarily sharing such data, the European Union objected, and Congress become concerned about false positives and a lack of procedures for correcting errors. In 2005, Congress prohibited the use of appropriated funds for CAPPS II or its successor, Secure Flight, until the Government Accountability Office certified that the system met certain privacy requirements. The second, MATRIX, was a search system that used a private database of over 3.9 billion public records collected from thousands of sources, including FAA pilot licenses and aircraft ownership records, property ownership records, state sexual offender lists, corporation filings, criminal history information, drivers license information and photo images, motor vehicle registration information, bankruptcy filings, and information from commercial sources that "are generally available to the public or legally permissible under federal law." Although initially a number of considered participation in MATRIX, concerns about law enforcement action being taken on the basis of data mining performed privately without public or legislative input led to MATRIX being terminated.

***

The Fourth Amendment protects individuals from "unreasonable searches and seizures" and requires that "no warrants shall issue" without probable cause and a sworn statement concerning "the place to be searched and the person or things to be seized." The Supreme Court has held that the Amendment does not shield individuals from all warrantless searches but prevents "unreasonable" searches. *Smith v. Maryland* lays out the Court's view of privacy rights for warrantless access of certain electronic information, but does not address the relatively new technology of data mining. Consider, as you read the case, how the Court's analysis might apply to data mining and retention.

SMITH v. MARYLAND
442 U.S. 735 (1979)

JUSTICE BLACKMUN delivered the opinion of the Court.

This case presents the question whether the installation and use of a pen register constitutes a "search" within the meaning of the Fourth Amendment, made applicable to the States through the Fourteenth Amendment.

On March 5, 1976, in Baltimore, Md., Patricia McDonough was robbed. She gave the police a description of the robber and of a 1975 Monte Carlo automobile she had observed near the scene of the crime. After the robbery, McDonough began receiving threatening and obscene phone calls from a man identifying himself as the robber. On one occasion, the caller asked that she step out on her front porch; she did so, and saw the 1975 Monte Carlo she had earlier described to police moving slowly past her home. On March 16, police spotted a man who met McDonough's description driving a 1975 Monte Carlo in her neighborhood. By tracing the license plate number, police learned that the car was registered in the name of petitioner, Michael Lee Smith.

The next day, the telephone company, at police request, installed a pen register at its central offices to record the numbers dialed from the telephone at petitioner's home. The police did not get a warrant or court order before having the pen register installed. The register revealed that on March 17 a call was placed from petitioner's home to McDonough's phone. *** Petitioner was indicted in the Criminal Court of Baltimore for robbery. By pretrial motion, he sought to suppress "all fruits derived from the pen register" on the ground that the police had failed to secure a warrant prior to its installation. ***

The Fourth Amendment guarantees "[t]he right of the people to be secure in their persons, houses, papers, and effects, against unreasonable searches and seizures." In determining whether a particular form of government-initiated electronic surveillance is a "search" within the meaning of the Fourth Amendment, our lodestar is *Katz v. United States,* 389 U.S. 347 (1967). In *Katz,* Government agents had intercepted the contents of a telephone conversation by attaching an electronic listening device to the outside of a public phone booth. The Court rejected the argument that a "search" can occur only when there has been a "physical intrusion" into a "constitutionally protected area," noting that the Fourth Amendment "protects people, not places." Because the Government's monitoring of Katz' conversation "violated the privacy upon which he justifiably relied while using the telephone booth," the Court held that it "constituted a 'search and seizure' within the meaning of the Fourth Amendment."

Consistently with *Katz,* this Court uniformly has held that the application of the Fourth Amendment depends on whether the person invoking its protection can claim a "justifiable," a "reasonable," or a "legitimate expectation of privacy" that has been invaded by government action. *** This inquiry, as Mr. Justice Harlan aptly noted in his *Katz* concurrence, normally embraces two discrete questions. The first is whether the individual, by his conduct, has "exhibited an actual (subjective) expectation of privacy - whether, in the words of the *Katz* majority, the individual has shown that "he seeks to preserve [something] as private." The second question is whether the individual's subjective expectation of privacy is "one that society is prepared to recognize as 'reasonable,'" - whether, in the words of the *Katz* majority, the individual's expectation, viewed objectively, is "justifiable" under the circumstances.

In applying the *Katz* analysis to this case, it is important to begin by specifying precisely the nature of the state activity that is challenged. The activity here took the form of installing and using a pen register. Since the pen register was installed on telephone company property at the telephone company's central offices, petitioner obviously cannot claim that his "property" was invaded or that police intruded into a "constitutionally protected area." Petitioner's claim, rather, is that, notwithstanding the absence of a trespass, the State, as did the Government in *Katz,* infringed a "legitimate expectation of privacy" that petitioner held. Yet a pen register differs significantly from the listening device employed in *Katz,* for pen registers do not acquire the *contents* of communications. *** Given a pen register's limited capabilities, therefore, petitioner's argument that its installation and use constituted a "search" necessarily rests upon a claim that he had a "legitimate expectation of privacy" regarding the numbers he dialed on his phone.

This claim must be rejected. First, we doubt that people in general entertain any actual expectation of privacy in the numbers they dial. All telephone users realize that they must "convey" phone numbers to the telephone company, since it is through telephone company switching equipment that their calls are completed. All subscribers realize, moreover, that the phone company has facilities for making permanent records of the numbers they dial, for they see a list of their long-distance (toll) calls on their monthly bills. In fact, pen registers and similar devices are routinely used by telephone companies "for the purposes of checking billing operations, detecting fraud and preventing violations of law." Electronic equipment is used not only to keep billing records of toll calls, but also "to keep a record of all calls dialed from a telephone which is subject to a special rate structure."

Pen registers are regularly employed "to determine whether a home phone is being used to conduct a business, to check for a defective dial, or to check for overbilling." *** Telephone users, in sum, typically know that they must convey numerical information to the phone company; that the phone company has facilities for recording this information; and that the phone company does in fact record this information for a variety of legitimate business purposes. Although subjective expectations cannot be scientifically gauged, it is too much to believe that telephone subscribers, under these circumstances, harbor any general expectation that the numbers they dial will remain secret.

Petitioner argues, however, that, whatever the expectations of telephone users in general, he demonstrated an expectation of privacy by his own conduct here, since he "us[ed] the telephone *in his house* to the exclusion of all others." But the site of the call is immaterial for purposes of analysis in this case. Although petitioner's conduct may have been calculated to keep the *contents* of his conversation private, his conduct was not and could not have been calculated to preserve the privacy of the number he dialed. Regardless of his location, petitioner had to convey that number to the telephone company in precisely the same way if he wished to complete his call. The fact that he dialed the number on his home phone rather than on some other phone could make no conceivable difference, nor could any subscriber rationally think that it would.

Second, even if petitioner did harbor some subjective expectation that the phone numbers he dialed would remain private, this expectation is not "one that society is prepared to recognize as 'reasonable.'" *Katz,* 389 U.S., at 361. This Court consistently has held that a person has no legitimate expectation of privacy in information he voluntarily turns over to third parties. *E. g., United States v. Miller,* 425 U.S., at 442-444. In *Miller,* for example, the Court held that a bank depositor has no "legitimate 'expectation of privacy' " in financial information "voluntarily conveyed to . . . banks and exposed to their employees in the ordinary course of business." *** Because the depositor "assumed the risk" of disclosure, the Court held that it would be unreasonable for him to expect his financial records to remain private. ***

We therefore conclude that petitioner in all probability entertained no actual expectation of privacy in the phone numbers he dialed, and that, even if he did, his expectation was not "legitimate." The installation and use of a pen register, consequently, was not a "search," and no warrant was required. ***

JUSTICE STEWART, dissenting.

In *Katz v. United States,* the Court acknowledged the "vital role that the public telephone has come to play in private communication[s]." The role played by a private telephone is even more vital, and since *Katz* it has been abundantly clear that telephone conversations carried on by people in their homes or offices are fully protected by the Fourth and Fourteenth Amendments. *** Nevertheless, the Court today says that those safeguards do not extend to the numbers dialed from a private telephone, apparently because when a caller dials a number the digits may be recorded by the telephone company for billing purposes. But that observation no more than describes the basic nature of telephone calls. A telephone call simply cannot be made without the use of telephone company property and without payment to the company for the service. The telephone conversation itself must be electronically transmitted by telephone company equipment, and may be recorded or overheard by the use of other company equipment. Yet we have squarely held that the user of even a public telephone is entitled "to assume that the words he utters into the mouthpiece will not be broadcast to the world." *Katz*, 389 U.S. at 352.

The central question in this case is whether a person who makes telephone calls from his home is entitled to make a similar assumption about the numbers he dials. What the telephone company does or might do with those numbers is no more relevant to this inquiry than it would be in a case involving the conversation itself. It is simply not enough to say, after *Katz*, that there is no legitimate expectation of privacy in the numbers dialed because the caller assumes the risk that the telephone company will disclose them to the police. *** The numbers dialed from a private telephone - although certainly more prosaic than the conversation itself - are not without "content." Most private telephone subscribers may have their own numbers listed in a publicly distributed directory, but I doubt there are any who would be happy to have broadcast to the world a list of the local or long distance numbers they have called. This is not because such a list might in some sense be incriminating, but because it easily could reveal the identities of the persons and the places called, and thus reveal the most intimate details of a person's life.

JUSTICE MARSHALL, dissenting.

Implicit in the concept of assumption of risk is some notion of choice. At least in the third-party consensual surveillance cases, which first incorporated risk analysis into Fourth Amendment doctrine, the defendant presumably had exercised some discretion in deciding who should enjoy his confidential communications. By contrast here, unless a person is prepared to forgo use of what for many has become a personal or professional necessity, he cannot help but accept the risk of surveillance. It is idle to speak of "assuming" risks in contexts where, as a practical matter, individuals have no realistic alternative. *** The use of pen registers, I believe, constitutes...an extensive intrusion. To hold otherwise ignores the vital role telephonic communication plays in our personal and professional relationships as well as the First and Fourth Amendment interests implicated by unfettered official surveillance. Privacy in placing calls is of value not only to those engaged in criminal activity. The prospect of unregulated governmental monitoring will undoubtedly prove disturbing even to those with nothing illicit to hide. Many individuals, including members of unpopular political organizations or journalists with confidential sources, may legitimately wish to avoid disclosure of their personal contacts. Permitting governmental access to telephone records on less than probable cause may thus impede certain forms of political affiliation and journalistic endeavor that are the hallmark of a truly free society. Particularly given the Government's previous reliance on warrantless telephonic surveillance to trace reporters' sources and monitor protected political activity, I am unwilling to insulate use of pen registers from independent judicial review.

Notes

1. Breadth of the Decision. *Smith v. Maryland* makes it clear a privacy interest in information transmitted to third parties is not "an expectation that society is prepared to recognize as reasonable" under the Fourth Amendment. However, modern data mining raises several issues not addressed in the opinion. The NSA Call Records Program has complied millions of phone records and plans to retain them indefinitely. Does the scale of the NSA program have any bearing on the constitutional argument? Do call records begin to count as "content" when the data is collected over an extended period of time with the purpose of detailing the calling habits of the individuals under surveillance? Does *Smith* allow the Government to collect data on banking transactions, charitable donations, and even library records? Where is the line between "descriptive" data and "content?"

2. Constitutional v. Statutory Law. While *Smith* seems to give broad constitutional authority to law enforcement to collect and mine data on individuals, some statutory measures are aimed at curbing abuses. The Privacy Act, 5 U.S.C. §552a (2000 & Supp. IV 2004), states that a Government agency may "retain in its records only such information about an individual as is relevant and necessary to accomplish a purpose of the agency required to be accomplished by statute or by executive order of the President" and "maintain no record describing how any individual exercises rights guaranteed by the First Amendment unless expressly authorized by statute or by executive order of the President." In addition, the Stored Communications Act of 1986, 18 U.S.C. §2701, provides that "a governmental entity may require the disclosure by a provider of electronic communication service of the contents of a wire or electronic communication...if such provider...has been provided with certification in writing by...the Attorney General of the United States that no warrant or court order is required by law." Both provisions include measures to allow the Executive Branch to opt out of regulations through either an order or a certification. Do these statutes offer citizens enough privacy protection? In the case of the NSA Call Records Program, is the government requesting the "contents of a wire or electronic communication?" The telecom companies asserting the defense that their disclosures of call records were based upon a good faith request by the Attorney General. Should this shield them from liability? Based on your reading of *Smith* and the Court's discussion of "content," were the Government or the telecoms in violation of The Stored Communications Act?

3. Privacy and the First Amendment. An article reported that "an antiterrorism database used by the Defense Department in an effort to prevent attacks against military instillations included intelligence tips about antiwar planning meetings held at churches, libraries, college campuses and other locations." Eric Lichtblau & Mark Mazzetti, *Military Data Reveal Tips on Antiwar Activities*, NEW YORK TIMES, November 21, 2006, at A17. As explained above, storing such information violates The Privacy Act. In response to the article, Defense Department officials stressed that they were tightening procedures to prevent inclusion of protected First Amendment activities in the database. Are Justice Marshall's fears of the application of data collection techniques well-founded in the counterterrorism context?

4. International Issues with Data Privacy. Differences in data privacy laws between the United States and Europe have led to concerns that U.S. Government actions have run afoul of European law, though this issue is complicated by the fact that much European privacy law is national, making data more easily transferable from some countries than others. Two contexts of international data sharing after 9/11 have proven difficult.

(a) The U.S. Bureau of Customs and Border Protection ("CBP") began demanding access to European airline passenger data before planes took off from Europe to the United States to prevent suspected terrorists from entering the United States and allow U.S. authorities to determine which passengers required surveillance while in the country. To enforce its request for information, the CBP threatened to prevent airline passengers from entering the country and impose fines on the airlines that did not comply with the request. This placed the European airlines in the untenable position of acquiescing to U.S. demands and possibly violating European privacy laws or facing the fines and business consequences of non-compliance. This issue was eventually resolved through an agreement that allowed U.S. authorities access to most of the flight information in exchange for assurances that the information would not be retained after a certain period of time. This agreement was held illegal under European law, not based upon privacy concerns, but rather because the European Commission exceeded its jurisdiction by concluding an agreement used to investigate crime under its trade authority. Joined Cases C-317/04 and C-318/04, Eur. Parliament v. Council, ¶¶ 55-59 (May 30, 2006). Europe and the United States have since concluded a new accord detailing the type of information to be shared and setting rules for the retention and destruction of collected data.

(b) The United States Treasury Department requested and received information on international bank transfers from the Society for Worldwide International Financial Communication (SWIFT). The information was obtained through Treasury Department administrative subpoenas for the data held in SWIFT's U.S. operations center. While the actual amount of data is secret for national security reasons, the number of recorded transfers could number in the billions. Francesca Bignami, *European v. American Liberty: A Comparative Privacy Analysis of Antiterrorism Data Mining*, 48 B.C. L. REV. 609, 671 (2007). While such information is arguably not protected by the U.S. Constitution, the data was linked to European individuals and businesses which led to a concern that the program violated European privacy laws. As discussed in Section E below, this controversial program led to a comprehensive US-EU agreement to impose restrictions on data collection consistent with EU privacy concerns.

5. False Positives. Counterterrorism data mining sometimes produces "false positives" in which innocent people are blacklisted from aircraft or erroneously targeted investigation. The reasons for false positives are three-fold: (1) a flawed or overly-broad algorithm, (2) mistakes in the database to which the algorithm is applied, and (3) the basic nature of antiterrorism investigations. Developing algorithms to apply to databases involves constructing a profile of the thing or person to be searched. It is nearly impossible to account for every contingency, so even the most comprehensive algorithms return incorrect results sometimes. Mistakes in the database may occur either because the information was entered wrong initially or because two or more databases were merged, producing distortions in the character of the data. Finally, searching for terrorist activity amidst a sea of legitimate information leads to a high incidence of false positives. When the occurrence of a particular activity is low (identifying suspected terrorists) and the volume of the information is very high (airline passenger or phone record database) the incidents of false positives will increase. See Christopher Slobogin, *Government Data Mining and The Fourth Amendment*, 75 U. Chi. L. Rev. 317, 324-28 (2008).

6. Profiling. Another danger in data mining is improper racial or religious profiling as part of algorithms designed to pinpoint possible terrorist suspects. While profiling is used in traditional investigations as well, the automated nature of data mining greatly facilitates the application of such profiles. Problems with this kind of system already stalled the development of Secure Flight (formerly CAPPS II) after several innocent people, including Yousef Islam (formerly Cat Stevens), were prevented from boarding flights due to a computer's determination that their characteristics too closely resembled that of a pre-programmed profile. Is using a computer profile any more legitimate than profiling in traditional law enforcement?

7. Mission Creep. Data mining programs may be expanded from counterterrorism activities to other law enforcement activities or governmental functions. Databases and algorithms used to track terrorists could be adapted to track down people delinquent on their taxes, in arrears on child support, or with outstanding traffic tickets. While such an adaptations may seem of little consequence, the use of data mining requires a balancing between individual privacy interests and the necessity to protect national security. Should personal data be stored and used for law enforcement outside of an counterterrorism context? It is sobering to note that a primitive system of data mining, involving data stored on IBM punch cards, was used by the Nazis to organize the shipment of Jews and other "undesirables" to concentration camps during the Holocaust. See Edwin Black, *IBM and the Holocaust* 8-10 (2002). Preventing data mining from "creeping" into illegitimate uses is a policy issue raised by data mining.

8. Data Mining and Traditional Link Analysis. Is the data-mining discussed above different from connecting the dots in ordinary criminal investigations? Data-mining is often done in advance of commission of a terrorist attack. Computers are used in data-mining. Data-mining is generally not subject-specific, but seeks general patterns. Does that matter? Are expectations of privacy different in data-mining situations? See *U.S. DoJ v. Reporters Comm. For Freedom of the Press*, 489 U.S. 749 (1989) ("[T]here is a vast difference between the public records" found through diligent searching in various locations and "a computerized summary located in a single clearinghouse of information.")

9. Privacy. What expectations do we have in our bank records, credit card records, health data, travel or proposed travel records, book and magazine purchases, etc. being data-mined? Some of these records are regularly data-mined by retailers and advertisers. Is it different because government is doing the data mining for security rather than commercial purposes? The Privacy Act, 5 U.S.C. § 552a, limits federal agency collection, retention, and use of personally identifiable data. There is no broad NSA or counterterrorism exclusion in this statute, though there is a limited exception for computer matching and interagency data sharing for national security and law enforcement. Not surprisingly, litigation is underway seeking to use the Privacy Act to block data mining.

10.   Congressional Regulation?   In 2006, when it passed the Patriot Improvement Act, Congress deferred data mining regulation pending a report by the Attorney General on data mining. There is a definition in that act of data mining, incidentally, which includes only "electronic databases" collected by departments "for purposes other than intelligence or law enforcement" and does not use "personal identifiers." § 126(b)(1). There is a lot of counterterrorism data-mining which falls outside this definition. What, if any, protections against data mining would you like to see Congress provide?

11. Data Mining, Data Bases, and Data Search Tools. The fear of Big Brother that animates so many critiques of data mining may not be as serious as other more mundane problems revealed in the following article, "Flaws Found In Watch List For Terrorists," by Siobhan Gorman, THE WALL STREET JOURNAL (August 22, 2008)

> The government's main terrorist-watch-list system is hobbled by technology challenges, and the $500 million program designed to upgrade it is on the verge of collapse, according to a preliminary congressional investigation. The database, which includes an estimated 400,000 people and as many as 1 million names, has been criticized for flagging ordinary Americans. Now, the congressional report finds that the system has problems identifying true potential terrorists, as well. Among the flaws in the database, which was quickly built by Lockheed Martin Corp. in the wake of the Sept. 11, 2001, terrorist attacks, is its inability to do key-word searches. Instead, an analyst needs to rely on an indexing system *** Meanwhile, tens of thousands of "potentially vital" messages from the Central Intelligence Agency have not been included in the database*** [L]awmakers called on the inspector general who oversees the office of Director of National Intelligence Mike McConnell to investigate the problems. The database "may have left us less able to connect the dots than we were before," Rep. Brad Miller (D., N.C.) said in an interview. "Now, we seem to have lost the dots." The database's search engine, he added, "is blindfolded." *** When tested, the new system failed to find matches for terrorist-suspect names that were spelled slightly different from the name entered into the system, a common challenge when translating names from Arabic to English. It also could not perform basic searches of multiple words connected with terms such as "and" and "or." Because the format of the data in the current database is "omplex, undocumented, and brittle," some significant data will be lost when the system is replaced***. For example, scraps of information such as phone and credit-card numbers found when law-enforcement and intelligence officials empty a suspect's pocket, often called "pocket litter," will not be moved to the new system. ***

12. The Future of Internet Data Mining. The United States carried over 70% of the world's internet traffic a decade ago. Today it carries about 25%. Traffic that previously went from Country A through an ISP in the United States and then to Country A is now likely to remain on national (e.g. Chinese or Japanese) or regional (European or Asian and Pacific) networks. This has significant security remifications for the United States; data mining would be either impossible or more difficult if no United States ISP is involved. Because of this change and the lack of investment in internet intelligence collection, John Arquilla, a professor at the Naval Postgraduate School in Monterrey says "We've given terrorists a free ride in cyberspace." One reason for bypassing the United States may be the desire of internet users not to have their privacy breached by clandestine data mining by the United States. Can you think of other reasons? See Markoff, "Internet Traffic Begins to Bypass the U.S.," NEW YORK TIMES, 8/30/2008, p. B1.

13. Update on TSA Data Matching. The TSA in late November 2009 took over the task of matching the names on airline passenger lists against the terror watch list, allowing TSA to track passengers from the moment of ticket purchase to or within the United States. With this program, Secure Flight, according to a TSA administrator, TSA can note when people on the watch lists book tickets to fly on the same day or to the same city. The program seeks to avoid false matches because passengers must provide date of birth, sex, and full legal name, which must match information provided at the airport. The system still won't work if the individual is not on the watch list (e.g. the December 2009 bomber).

E. TERRORISM FINANCING

Al Qaeda's 9/11 terrorist attacks cost well uner $500,000, but the al Qaeda's terrorist network costs many millions of dollars a year. Tracking terrorist financing poses significant practical and legal challenges. Prior to 9/11, domestic and international anti-money laundering efforts were primarily focused on combating drug trafficking and large-scale financial fraud. In the years following 9/11, the United States instituted the Terrorist Finance Tracking Program, which faced international backlash but resulted in a landmark agreement between the United States and European Union. Section 314 of the USA PATRIOT Act created a system that uses the Financial Crimes Enforcement Network (FCEN) to coordinate requests for information by law enforcement agencies with financial institutions. Lastly, the U.N. created the Consolidated List to provide for international cooperation in freezing the assets of certain terrorists. Executive Order 13,224 authorized the Treasury Department to freeze the assets of entities in the United States reasonably believed to be providing support to terrorists.

Subsection 1 provides a brief overview of the three main international and U.S. efforts to address terrorist financing. Subsection 2 addresses the Executive's power and authority to freeze the assets of U.S. entities.

1. INTERNATIONAL AND DOMESTIC FRAMEWORKS

The Society for Worldwide Interbank Financial telecommunication (SWIFT) is a global network for transmitting instructions for international money transfers between banks. SWIFT provides nearly 13 million transfer instructions to over 8,000 financial institutions every day. SWIFT messages generally include the identities of the sender and recipient of the funds, their bank account numbers, and the amount of the transfer. It has two operations centers, one at its headquarters in Belgium, and one in the United States. Shortly after 9/11, President Bush invoked the International Emergency Economic Powers Act and issued Executive Order 13224, which granted the Treasury Department's Office of Foreign Asset Control (OFAC) authority to issue administrative subpoenas to obtain financial records related to terrorism. OFAC then launched the Terrorist Finance Tracking Program (TFTP), and shortly afterward, began to access SWIFT data. Because SWIFT keeps one set of records in the United States, it is subject to federal jurisdiction, and complied with the subpoenas. SWIFT became the primary source of data for the TFTP. In 2006, the New York Times revealed the TFTP's use of SWIFT data, and described the program in some detail. A firestorm of controversy erupted with both U.S. and European officials criticizing the program. The U.S. maintained that the subpoenas were legal, and SWIFT was required to abide by them. In the U.S. SWIFT does not come within the definition of "financial institution" to which the Right to Financial Privacy Act of 1978 requirements apply. SWIFT never challenged the legality of OFAC's administrative subpoenas in U.S. court. The E.U. maintained that SWIFT's doing so violated European law. In the European Union, SWIFT was determined to be a "data controller" which must provide notice to individuals whose information is sought.

In 2009, under pressure from the E.U., SWIFT announced plans to relocate its U.S. servers to Europe by the end of 2009, which would have cut off OFAC's ability to access SWIFT's database. In 2009, however, the U.S. and E.U. reached a temporary agreement to allow the Treasury Department to continue to access SWIFT's data and on July 7, 2010, the U.S. and E.U. reached a five-year agreement. Article 4 of this agreement provides the process for obtaining data, and Article 5 imposes significant limitations on the U.S. Here are excerpts from both articles:

ARTICLE 4

1. For the purposes of this Agreement, the U.S. Treasury Department shall serve production orders ("Requests"), under authority of U.S. law, upon a Designated Provider present in the territory of the United States in order to obtain data necessary for the purpose of the prevention, investigation, detection, or prosecution of terrorism or terrorist financing that are stored in the territory of the European Union.

2. The Request (together with any supplemental documents) shall: ***

(b) clearly substantiate the necessity of the data;

(c) be tailored as narrowly as possible in order to minimize the amount of data requested ***; and

(d) not seek any data relating to the Single Euro Payments Area. ***

5. For the purposes of this Agreement,*** the Request shall have binding legal effect as provided under U.S. law, within the European Union as well as the United States. The Designated Provider is thereby authorized and required to provide the data to the U.S. Treasury Department. ***

ARTICLE 5

*** 2. Provided Data shall be processed exclusively for the prevention, investigation, detection, or prosecution of terrorism or its financing.

3. The TFTP does not and shall not involve data mining or any other type of algorithmic or automated profiling or Security and Integrity.

***6. Each individual TFTP search of Provided Data shall be narrowly tailored, shall demonstrate a reason to believe that the subject of the search has a nexus to terrorism or its financing, and shall be logged, including such nexus to terrorism or its financing required to initiate the search.

7. Provided Data may include identifying information about the originator and/or recipient of a transaction, including name, account number, address, and national identification number. The Parties recognize the special sensitivity of personal data revealing racial or ethnic origin, political opinions, or religious or other beliefs, trade union membership, or health and sexual life ("sensitive data"). ***

Article 6 of the agreement requires the U.S. Treasury Department to conduct an annual review and permanently delete any data that "are no longer necessary to combat terrorism or its financing." The agreement also ensures some level of redress for individuals who believe their information is acquired in violation of the agreement. Article 16 provides, "Any person has the right to seek the rectification, erasure, or blocking of his or her personal data processed by the U.S. Treasury Department pursuant to this Agreement where the data are inaccurate or the processing contravenes this Agreement." Article 18 provides further:

> Any person who considers his or her personal data to have been processed in breach of this Agreement is entitled to seek effective administrative and judicial redress in accordance with the laws of the European Union, its Member States, and the United States, respectively. *** All persons, regardless of nationality or country of residence, shall have available under U.S. law a process for seeking judicial redress from an adverse administrative action.

Adopted on October 15, 1999, Security Council Resolution 1267 demanded that the Taliban cease its support of international terrorism and turn over Usama bin Laden. The resolution established a Sanctions Committee to designate financial resources of the Taliban, and to order the freezing of the organization's funds. On December 19, 2000, the United Nations Security Council enacted Resolution 1333 expanding the financial embargo imposed on the Taliban by Resolution 1267 to include freezing the funds of Osama bin Laden and his associates. It required the Sanctions

Committee–known as the 1267 Committee–to maintain a list of individuals suspected of "associating with" Osama bin Laden. Security Council Resolution 1617 defines "associated with" as:

> Participating in the financing, planning, facilitating, preparing, or perpetrating of acts or activities by, in conjunction with, under the name of, on behalf of, or in support of; supplying, selling or transferring arms and related materiel to; recruiting for; or otherwise supporting acts or activities of Al-Qaida, Usama bin Laden or the Taliban, or any cell, affiliate, splinter group or a derivative thereof.

The 1267 Committee, comprised of the same membership as the Security Council, distributes the list to all 191 U.N. member states. At the end of 2009, the list included 396 individuals and 107 entities. Each state is then bound by the U.N. Charter to

> Freeze without delay the funds and other financial assets or economic resources, including funds derived from property owned or controlled directly or indirectly; prevent the entry into or the transit through their territories; prevent the direct or indirect supply, sale, or transfer of arms and related material, including military and paramilitary equipment, technical advice, assistance or training related to military activities, with regard to the individuals, groups, undertakings and entities placed on the Consolidated List.

In addition, each state is obliged to disseminate the list as widely as possible, including to financial institutions, businesses, and professionals. Any country can propose a name to be included on the consolidated list. However, the fifteen committee members must unanimously agree before a name is added to those "associated with" the Taliban or Al Qaida.

Resolution 1455 requires all U.N. members to submit reports to the U.N. regarding measures taken to comply with requirements as to the Consolidated List. As of mid-2010, 154 states had submitted reports claiming to have incorporated the list and its sanctions requirements into their domestic legal and administrative regimes.

The Financial Action Task Force (FATF) is an inter-governmental body that examines anti-money laundering efforts and promote international cooperation to counter such activity. In 1990, The FATF developed an international framework for combating money laundering known as the Forty Recommendations. These recommended, among other things, that every nation establish a central agency to receive, analyze and disseminate financial information to combat money laundering, and assist other countries in their anti-money laundering efforts. These central agencies are known as financial intelligence units (FIUs).

The FAFTs primary enforcement mechanism is the Non-Cooperative Countries and Territories (NCCT) Initiative. If a country is listed as an NCCT, FATF issues a statement to financial institutions warning them to give special attention to relations and transactions with person and institutions in the non-compliant country. The FATF may suspend the non-complying country's membership, but this has never been done. While the FATF recommendations have no truly binding effect, through its relative success it has come to be known as the "crown jewel of soft law."

The United States' FIU is the Financial Crimes Enforcement Network (FinCEN). In addition to making and fielding requests from foreign FIUs, FinCEN serves two primary functions in tracking terrorist financing domestically. First, pursuant to section 314 of the USA PATRIOT Act, FinCEN acts as an intermediary between regulatory and law enforcement authorities and financial institutions. Law enforcement agencies submit requests for information to FinCEN. FinCEN then sends a request to financial institutions believed to have the desired information. From September 26, 2002 to July 13, 2010, FinCEN had processed 1216 requests, 343 of which were related to terrorism. Those requests included 11,822 subjects of interest. Financial institutions responded with 79,161 subject matches. According to feedback that FinCEN solicits from law enforcement agencies, one 314(a) Request on average yields 7.7 new accounts identified, 12.5 new transactions identified, and 6.9 follow up initiatives taken by law enforcement with financial institutions. Second, FinCEN collects Suspicious Activity Reports (SAR's) from money services businesses (MSB's). MSB's must report suspicious activity involving any transaction or pattern of transactions at or above $2,000 to FinCEN. From July 2003 through 2009, MSB's filed 4,914 SAR's indicating possible terrorist financing.

Notes

1. Geography. The U.S. – E.U. agreement prevents the U.S. from seeking information concerning any transaction that occurred within the E.U. How significant is this limitation?

2. Data Mining. To what extent does this agreement undermine the use of data mining discussed above in section D of this chapter?

3. The 9/11 Attacks as a Case Study. About $300,000 of the 9/11 attack funds was deposited in U.S. banks. The attackers received wire transfers totaling $130,000 from facilitators in the United Arab Emirates and Germany. They physically carried large amounts of cash and traveler's checks into the country with them which they deposited in banks. The remainder was left in overseas accounts and accessed by credit or debit card. The terrorists conducted their finances in largely the same was as many average banking customers do. They deposited larger amounts of money in bank accounts, and then regularly withdrew small amounts through ATM's. The 9/11 Commission's Terrorist Financing Staff Monograph found, "No financial institution filed a suspicious activity report and, even with the benefit of hindsight, none of them should have." To what extent do you think the efforts described above aid in tracking terrorist activity, and in preventing terrorist attacks on the U.S.?

4. Do Terrorists use Banks? A common view is that "cutting off money" to terrorist groups will starve them of resources and cripple their ability to finance themselves and engage in terrorist violence. In the words of David Cohen, Assistant Secretary of Treasury for Terrorist Financing,

> "The key idea underlying [Treasury's] work is this: If we can deter those who would donate money to violent extremist groups, disrupt the means and mechanisms through which they transmit money, and degrade their financial support networks, we can make an extraordinarily valuable contribution to our national security." Remarks before the Council on Foreign Relations (Jan. 28, 2010).

Economic and sociological research suggests this view may not reflect reality, for many terrorist groups minimally interact with Western financial institutions or regulated currencies. Instead, they use other ways to exchange value, common in the parts of the world in which they operate. These include systems of barter or trade in commodities (e.g. trading vehicles, electronics, or construction supplies for opium), micro-trading in goods (e.g. trading animal skins or fava beans for tractor parts), exploitation of non-monetary things of value (e.g. control of an electric plant or opium production that in turn can be used to trade for both monetary and non-monetary things of value), and hawala (an informal system of value transfer common in the Middle East and South Asia that works through international networks of brokers). Hawala operates like this: an individual goes to a local hawala broker in Egypt and gives him a sum of money to be picked up by his brother in Pakistan; the broker in Egypt calls a broker in Pakistan, often someone he is related to; the brother picks up an equivalent sum from the broker in Pakistan (minus a commission); at some point later, the brokers settle debts (not necessarily in monetary terms) on a purely honorary system, with no promissory notes or legal enforcement involved. Indeed, in over 70% of foreign terrorist organizations operate where non-formal economies such as the foregoing are the norm and the majority of individuals do not have access to formal banking institutions, for example only 5% of Afgans use banks. *See* Timothy Wittig, UNDERSTANDING TERRORIST FINANCING (MacMillan Palsgrave 2011).

5. Are our Enemies Laughing? If many of the ways that terrorists finance themselves are not monetary or through the formal financial sector, this may render Western attempts to curb terrorist financing that focus on banks and monetary transactions relatively marginal. John Cassara, former special agent in Treasury's Office of Terrorism Finance and Financial Intelligence, has relayed that a businessman with ties to the South Asian finance underworld expressed the point: "Don't you know that the terrorists are moving money and value right under your nose? But the West doesn't see it. Your enemies are laughing at you."

2. BLOCKING THE ASSETS OF UNITED STATES ENTITIES

While the U.S. and the international community have dramatically increased efforts to track terrorist finances, the legal battles in U.S. courts have concerned the power and authority of the executive to block assets it suspects may support "Specially Designated Global Terrorists" (SDGTs). Executive Order 13224 authorized OFAC to freeze the assets of individuals or entities indefinitely pending investigation to determine whether it will designate the entity as a "Specially Designated Global Terrorist" (SDGT). In addition to individuals suspected of engaging in terrorism, OFAC has frozen the assets of several charity organizations based wholly or partly in the United States. The legality of such asset freezes by an executive agency has been and continues to be challenged. However, courts have granted OFAC a high degree of deference.

KINDHEARTS v. GEITHNER [KINDHEARTS I]
647 F. Supp. 2d 857 (N.D. Ohio, 2009)

JAMES G. CARR, District Judge.

Plaintiff KindHearts for Charitable Humanitarian Development, Inc. (KindHearts), an Ohio corporation, challenges a provisional determination by the Office of Foreign Assets Control (OFAC) of the United States Treasury Department that plaintiff is a Specially Designated Global Terrorist (SDGT). KindHearts also challenges the block OFAC placed on plaintiff's assets [approximately $1,000,000] pending a full investigation. OFAC alleges that KindHearts provides material support to Hamas, which is also an SDGT. OFAC's authority to designate SDGTs and block the assets of entities under investigation for supporting terrorism stems from the International Emergency Economic Powers Act (IEEPA), and Executive Order 13224 (E.O. 13224).

KindHearts alleges that OFAC's actions are unconstitutional because: 1) OFAC's block is an unreasonable seizure in violation of the Fourth Amendment; 2) provisions authorizing OFAC to designate SDGT and block assets pending investigation are void for vagueness under the Fifth Amendment; 3) OFAC denied KindHearts procedural due process before provisionally determining it to be an SDGT and blocking its assets; and 4) OFAC has unconstitutionally restricted plaintiff's access to the resources it needs to mount a defense. ***

The IEEPA requires the President to declare a national emergency to "deal with any unusual and extraordinary threat, which has its source in whole or substantial part outside the United States, to the national security, foreign policy or economy of the United States." *** On September 24, 2001, President Bush issued E.O. 13224, declaring a national emergency with respect to "grave acts and threats of terrorism." He invoked his authority under the IEEPA, authorizing the Secretary of Treasury, in consultation with the Secretary of State and Attorney General, to designate "persons" (defined as individuals or entities) whose property or interests in property should be blocked because they "act for or on behalf of" or are "owned or controlled by" designated terrorists, or because they "assist in, sponsor, or provide financial, material or technological support for, or financial or other services to or in support of" or are "otherwise associated" with them.[1]

---

[1] In *Humanitarian Law Project v. U.S. Department of Treasury*, 463 F. Supp. 2d 1049, 1070-71 (C.D. Cal. 2006), the court declared unconstitutional the "otherwise associated" criterion. The Treasury Department subsequently issued a regulation that defined that provision as "(a) To

Individuals or entities designated under E.O. 13224 are labeled "Specially Designated Global Terrorists." In § 10 of the Executive Order, the President states that under the Order no prior notice of a listing or designation needs to be provided to those with a presence in the United States because of the targeted organization's ability to transfer funds or assets instantaneously, which would render the blocking measures ineffectual.

In October, 2001, the Patriot Act amended the IEEPA. *** The amendment permitted the Treasury Secretary to impose all the blocking effects of a designation, including freezing an organization's assets indefinitely and criminalizing all its transactions, without designating the organization a SDGT. The Treasury only needs to assert that it is investigating whether the entity should be designated. The amendment also provided that an agency record containing classified information could be "submitted to the reviewing court *ex parte* and *in camera*." ***

1. Fourth Amendment

[The court first concluded that OFAC blocks are seizures triggering Fourth Amendment scrutiny, rejecting a holding to the contrary of the D.C. Circuit in *Holy Land Foundation v. Ashcroft*, 333 F.3d 156 (D.C. Cir. 2003).]

Defendants argue that this court should jettison the probable cause and warrant requirements in favor of an open-ending balancing of interests. Defendants contend that courts are free to apply an indeterminate "reasonableness" inquiry in light of the doctrine that "the Fourth Amendment does not proscribe all searches and seizures, but only those that are unreasonable." ***

Reasonableness is the ultimate standard under the Fourth Amendment. This does not, however, mean that courts always are free to conduct open-ended balancing of interests whenever the government has seized property. On the contrary, searches and seizures are usually "reasonable" only when conducted with a judicial warrant supported by probable cause. The reasonableness clause under the Fourth Amendment "derives content and meaning through reference to the warrant clause." *** Under most circumstances searches and seizures conducted without a warrant are "*per se* unreasonable under the Fourth Amendment—subject only to a few specifically established and well-delineated exceptions." ***

First, "special needs" warrantless searches and seizures need only be reasonable under all the circumstances; no warrant or probable cause is required. Special needs searches and seizures share at least three basic characteristics. First, they must serve a purpose above and beyond normal criminal law enforcement. Second, circumstances must make "the warrant and probable cause requirement impracticable." Third, the method of search or seizure must have built-in limits, such as a confined geographic scope or regular, suspicionless application, that restrict executive discretion and

---

own or control; or (b) To attempt, or conspire with one or more persons, to act for or on behalf of or to provide financial, material, or technological support, or financial or other services to."

ensure that all citizens know the circumstances under which they are subject to a special needs search or seizure.

OFAC's exercise of its blocking power lacks the characteristics that excuse the warrant and probable cause requirements as to administrative, roadblocks, and border searches and seizures. Most importantly, OFAC's blocking power entails no built-in limitations curtailing executive discretion and putting individuals on notice that they are subject to blocking.

Traffic checkpoints and border searches are focused geographically, as they occur only at he checkpoint or near the national border. In cases of administrative searches, the government may only search discrete categories of individuals—such as closely-regulated businesses—and even then the regulatory regime must be "carefully limited in time, place and scope."

Second, in method, OFAC's blocking power has more in common with ordinary law enforcement activity than with any of the activities considered in the special needs cases. OFAC does not block pending investigation every entity sending money overseas: it only blocks those it suspects have violated the law. In this case, OFAC targeted KindHearts as a potential violator and conducted a preliminary investigation before imposing the block. It necessarily had gathered information in advance that it considered sufficient to justify seizure of KindHearts' assets. No such prior determination occurs with a border crossing or checkpoint. Everyone passing through is stopped, detained and examined. Thus, unlike traditional law enforcement investigatory activities, special needs searches expose everyone within their scope or zone of their operation to a cursory search or brief seizure in the interest of public safety and welfare or border integrity.

OFAC's blocking power, which focuses on single entities, and does so on the basis of some suspicion, more closely resembles *** traditional law enforcement investigative activity than warrantless searches allowed under the special needs exception. This is true, even though, at this point, OFAC's actions may be deemed "civil," but actions violating E.O. 13224 may also become the basis for criminal sanctions. Investigations with the potential for criminal prosecution have historically triggered the warrant and probable cause requirements.

Finally, for the special needs exception to apply, both the probable cause and warrant requirements must categorically be impracticable in light of the Government's purpose. The government provides no explanation as to why the probable cause warrant requirements were impracticable in this case. *** In conclusion, OFAC blocking actions do not fit within the special needs exception to the warrant and probable cause requirements.

[The court also concluded that the OFAC block did not fall under the "exigent circumstances" exception.]

4. Procedural Due Process

KindHearts asserts a due process challenge to OFAC's provisional designation of it as a SDGT. KindHearts claims that the statute on its face does not accommodate, and in any event, OFAC failed to provide constitutionally mandated due process. ***

KindHearts contends that IEEPA § 1702(a)(1)(B) is unconstitutional on its face because it fails to include procedural safeguards. The law does not require notice, an opportunity to be heard or pre- or post-deprivation process. *** OFAC can thus freeze an American corporation's assets just by announcing that the corporation is under investigation—under the statute it does not need to provide any process to that corporation. ***

KindHearts correctly contends that the IEEPA contains no procedural protections. *** Under [*U.S. v. Salerno*, 481 U.S. 739 (1987)], "a plaintiff can only succeed in a facial challenge by establishing that no set of circumstances exist under which the Act would be valid, *i.e.*, that the law is unconstitutional in all of its applications." *** OFAC does not contend that due process requirements do not apply at all. Indeed, it contends that it has met those requirements. Thus, it implicitly acknowledges the mandate of due process: it only disputes the claim of noncompliance. Although OFAC, as discussed in the next subsection, failed to afford adequate post-deprivation due process, the statute under which it acted can, if properly administered, be implemented consonant with due process requirements. It is, therefore, not unconstitutional on its face. ***

To determine whether KindHearts received constitutionally required process [See *Mathews v. Eldridge*, 424 U.S. 319 (1976)] in conjunction with OFAC's block pending investigation, I must weigh 1) "the private interest affected by the official action;" 2) "the risk of an erroneous deprivation of such interest through the procedures used;" and 3) "the Government's interest, including the function involved and the fiscal and administrative burdens that additional or substitute procedural requirement would entail."

To the extent that the government has provided notice of the basis for its blocking notice, it has done so in a piecemeal and partial manner. *** In sum, the "notice" KindHearts has received to date, since the Government's provisional determination to designate it an SDGT, is the letter KindHearts received informing it of the Government's decision, the thirty-five unclassified, non-privileged exhibits, and a redacted version of the provisional determination evidentiary memo. OFAC claims it relied on the thirty-five exhibits in making its blocking decision, in addition to seven other exhibits that it did not rely on in making its provisional determination decision. Those seven exhibits and the redacted block evidentiary memorandum have been handed over to KindHearts. KindHearts remains largely uninformed about the basis for the Government's actions. To the extent that it has become usefully informed, that information came only after long, unexplained and inexplicable delay and following multiple requests for information. ***

Applying the first factor from the *Mathews* balancing test—the private interest affected by OFAC's action—it is clear that the private interest is substantial. An American corporation has had all its assets seized and been put out of business without being told, in any meaningful or useful way why, or on what basis the government took that action.

Applying the second *Mathews* factor—the risk of erroneous deprivation—I conclude that the failure to provide adequate and timely notice creates a substantial risk of wrongful deprivation. This is especially so in view of the fact that the government does not contend that KindHearts was donating its funds exclusively to Hamas. But the government has not provided its estimate of the approximate amounts of such donations, or what portion of KindHearts' funds went to Hamas or individuals or entities related to Hamas. Nor, as importantly, has the government stated which recipients, to the extent that it knows of specific recipients, were Hamas fronts or Hamas affiliated. Without this sort of information, KindHearts cannot meaningfully challenge the Government's actions. Not knowing to whom, in the Government's view, its funds should not have gone, it cannot rebut the Government's claim that recipients were Hamas connected. An inability to rebut necessarily enhances, if it does not entirely ensure, the likelihood of erroneous deprivation.[26] ***

Applying the third *Mathews* factor—the governmental interest and burden of providing additional procedural protection—I note that OFAC has not explained, either to KindHearts or this court, why it failed to provide timely notice of the basis and reasons for its blocking order, or why it took so long for it to provide the scanty information it ultimately has produced. OFAC apparently assumes that no explanation is needed. If so, it necessarily concedes that the third *Mathews* factor indisputably favors KindHearts. Absent an explanation for its conduct and dismissive treatment of KindHearts' oft-repeated requests, it cannot claim that to have done otherwise would have been unacceptably or unduly burdensome.

In sum, consideration of the *Mathews* factors leads inescapably to the conclusion that OFAC violated KindHearts' fundamental right to be told on what basis and for what reasons the government deprived it of all access to all its assets and shut down its operations. *** OFAC did not meet its obligation to provide meaningful notice regarding its deprivation of KindHearts' property. *** Despite the due process requirement of prompt post-deprivation hearing, KindHearts received no response to its administrative challenge for over one year. When OFAC finally responded, it merely stated it had received KindHearts' challenge and had provisionally determined to designate it an SDGT. It provided no reasons for its decision. It merely enclosed a copy of the unclassified record on which it relied in making its provisional determination and invited KindHearts to send another response. ***

On balancing the pertinent factors, I conclude that OFAC has failed to provide a meaningful hearing, and to do so with sufficient promptness to moderate or avoid the consequences of delay. OFAC did not provide timely or sufficient notice to enable KindHearts to prepare an effective challenge. OFAC ignored KindHearts' initial response. What reply OFAC made to

---

[26] *** OFAC's refusal to let KindHearts pay its lawyers to bring its challenges to the government's actions amplifies the risks of erroneous deprivation. This is so, even though KindHearts has counsel in this lawsuit, which involves the prospect, but no guarantee of fee-shifting under the Equal Access to Justice Act.

KindHearts' responses and requests was delayed and did not cure the deficiencies of its earlier notice. Even if OFAC may ultimately show it had an adequate basis for the blocking order, that does not justify the length of the Government's delay in giving KindHearts an opportunity to be heard. ***

KindHearts argues that OFAC also severely restricted its due process right to meaningfully respond to allegations against it by: 1) denying it access to its own documents for over two years; 2) placing unreasonable restrictions on its ability to review and use the documents; and 3) requiring counsel to give the government results of any independent investigation taken as part of KindHearts' defense. ***

Denying access by KindHearts' counsel to its client's records deprived them of an important, if not the principal means for challenging the blocking order and defending against final designation of their client as a SDGT. This action, coupled with OFAC's delay in providing any significant information from its own files about its basis and reasons for the blocking order, left KindHearts' attorneys almost entirely unequipped to marshal and present evidence. This, in turn, would have lessened significantly the benefits from having an opportunity to be heard, had a due process hearing been afforded to KindHearts. ***

OFAC prohibits use of blocked funds to pay attorney fees. *** In June, 2008, after OFAC's attorney fees restrictions were challenged as unconstitutional in a separate lawsuit, *Al Haramain,* OFAC implemented its new policy. The policy permits expenditure of blocked funds at rates based on the attorney compensation provisions of the Equal Access to Justice Act, and Criminal Justice Act. *** After formally announcing the policy in June, 2008, OFAC applied the policy to KindHearts' counsel. Though it released some blocked funds [$27,040], the amount released was far less than the $46,000 counsel sought. ***

I find *** that OFAC's application of its policy to KindHearts in this case has been arbitrary and capricious. This is so because: 1) OFAC has provided no sufficient statement of reasons for authorizing payment of $27,040, rather than the full and still rather modest, amount requested, or some amount in between; 2) OFAC has not addressed the effect on the generation of attorneys' fees of certain special circumstances in this case, such as its delay in responding to communications on behalf of KindHearts, and its general unresponsiveness, in any event, to the requests in those communications, and the complexity of nearly all the manifold issues; and 3) there is a disconnect between the facts underlying the request for access to blocked funds for attorneys' fees and the purposes, as described by OFAC, underlying its June, 2008, attorney fee policy. *** The court reserved ruling on remedies for the Constitutional violations so that the parties could submit briefs on the issue, given the unique circumstances.

******

The court ordered further briefing on what remedy if any was appropriate, given its decision on the constitutional issues. Below is the Court's remedial decision:

KINDHEARTS v. GEITHNER [KINDHEARTS II]
710 F. Supp. 2d 637 (N.D. Ohio, 2010)

JAMES G. CARR, District Judge.

Analogizing to exigent circumstances and forfeiture cases, the government argues that a post-hoc probable cause determination can cure the Fourth Amendment violation. KindHearts argues such review is inappropriate because: 1) I do not have authority to issue a warrant; 2) a warrant cannot issue after a seizure; 3) post-seizure review in the Fourth Amendment context is limited to situations where an exception to the warrant requirement applies; and 4) neither I nor Congress have formulated an appropriate probable cause standard for BPIs. I agree with the government that, under the unique circumstances of this case, I can and should implement post-hoc probable cause review. ***

As the parties point out, my August 18 Order did not delineate the level of probable cause that must be shown in the context of a BPI carried out under IEEPA. *** As the Supreme Court recognized in *Camara* [387 U.S. 523 (1967)] and *U.S. District Court (Keith)* [407 U.S. 297 (1972)], probable cause standards *** may vary depending on the context. This is not a conventional criminal case, and thus the typical Fourth Amendment probable cause standard is inapplicable. I therefore find that, given the unique circumstances of this case, the content of the probable cause showing differs from the formulation applicable to a search warrant sought in conjunction with a criminal investigation. I conclude that the government need not show probable cause to believe that evidence of a crime will be found. The government must instead show that, at the time of the original seizure, it had probable cause—that is, a reasonable ground—to believe that KindHearts, specifically, was subject to designation under E.O. 13224 § 1.

I further find that if the government can show probable cause for the original seizure, even at this very late date, the post-hoc judicial finding of such cause remedies the Fourth Amendment violation. *** While it would have been easier for all involved if OFAC had obtained independent judicial review and a warrant prior to seizing KindHearts' assets, or if it had provided KindHearts with a prompt and meaningful way to challenge the seizure, I find that this post-hoc probable cause determination, though not typical, provides a necessary check on otherwise unrestrained executive discretion. This is particularly so in these specific circumstances, where that discretion has been used in a way that violates the Constitution.

KindHearts argues that the 5 U.S.C. § 706(2)(B) requires that I invalidate the BPI. The APA states that a reviewing court "shall . . . hold unlawful and set aside agency action, findings, and conclusions found to be . . . contrary to a constitutional right." The APA also instructs reviewing courts to take "due account . . . of the rule of prejudicial error." Thus, harmless errors in agency action need not be set aside. *** If the government shows probable cause for the seizure, even at this very late date, then the *Fourth Amendment* violation will be remedied and thus harmless, and the government can retain the plaintiff's assets pending completion of the administrative SDGT process.

In my August 18 Order, I held that the Government's "blocking order failed to provide [KindHearts with] the two fundamental requirements of due process: meaningful notice and [an] opportunity to be heard." I do not here revisit that determination, but I must decide what remedy flows from these violations of the Fifth Amendment's Due Process Clause. *** I must now determine whether those violations are harmless. *** The government therefore must persuade me that its Fifth Amendment violations are harmless beyond a reasonable doubt.

The government argues: 1) "[t]he most logical way to conduct harmless error analysis is to allow the current proceeding [presumably designation] to progress to a final conclusion"; 2) "[p]laintiff has now received all notice to which it is due and has been invited to respond to that notice"; and 3) "[n]o amount of additional notice would have changed the[] facts" justifying the BPI.

KindHearts responds: 1) permitting OFAC "to proceed with designation before it has cured the [due process] defects in its BPI process would be to deny KindHearts the constitutional BPI process to which it is entitled[,]" and "would risk irreparable injury and undermine the Court's ability to provide a meaningful remedy for the BPI violations"; 2) I already held OFAC's notice to be constitutionally inadequate so far; and 3) "had OFAC provided KindHearts adquate notice and a meaningful opportunity to defend itself, KindHearts would have responded to the actual bases for the freeze, not to vague and general assertions," and "OFAC has made no . . . showing" to the contrary.

As to the Government's first argument, the government concedes that the BPI constitutes final agency action. Each final agency action merits its own review, including determination of what remedy should issue for OFAC's constitutional violations; I held as much in my October 26 Order, and I decline to short-circuit that process now.

As to the Government's second argument, the government continues to emphasize that "KindHearts possesses ample notice of the allegations supporting a BPI." I have, however, *** found the notice OFAC provided KindHearts constitutionally inadequate, and I decline to revisit that holding now.

As to the Government's third argument, the government fails to show that KindHearts could submit nothing that would adequately address the agency's concerns. Harmless errors are those "small errors or defects that have little, if any, likelihood of having changed the result of the trial." Here, KindHearts still does not know what facts to rebut, or what other grounds the government has for its action. As KindHearts points out, "OFAC has yet to afford KindHearts constitutionally adequate notice of the charges against it that would allow KindHearts to know what to look for" in its documents. Demonstrating that OFAC's error is harmless thus requires the government to prove *beyond a reasonable doubt* that KindHearts could marshal no evidence to rebut still unknown factual and legal reasons for the

Government's action. The government has not met its burden, instead focusing its argument on the adequacy of the "notice" provided thus far. The Government's failure to provide KindHearts with adequate notice and a meaningful opportunity to respond was, therefore, not harmless.

Having found OFAC's error not harmless, I must now determine what remedy is appropriate. KindHearts states: "Putting aside the Court's other constitutional holdings, KindHearts agrees with OFAC that the typical remedy for an unconstitutional agency process includes 'remand . . . with instructions as to what additional process is due.'" KindHearts then continues, however: "OFAC resists the necessary accompaniment to remand: setting aside the extant, unconstitutional order." The government responds that solely remand is appropriate.

I *** agree with the government that, notwithstanding the APA's dictate that we set aside unconstitutional agency action, the proper remedy for a notice violation in the context of designation proceedings is to remand to OFAC, without vacatur of the BPI, with instructions as to what additional notice is required.

This leaves me with the difficult question of precisely *what* the government must disclose to KindHearts to provide KindHearts with adequate notice. *** I appreciate the Government's interest in national security and foreign policy implicated here. Courts have found that their duty to protect individual rights extends to requiring disclosure of classified information to give a party an ability to respond to allegations made against it. ***

The rationale for requiring such disclosure is that, otherwise, an individual or entity accused of terrorist connections, "like Joseph K. in *The Trial*[,] . . . [can prevail only if he can] prove that he is not a terrorist regardless of what might be implied by the Government's confidential information. It is difficult to imagine how even someone innocent of all wrongdoing can meet such a burden." ***

I propose, subject to giving the parties an opportunity to comment and be heard, that:

1. I convene, under 8 U.S.C. ß 1189(b)(2), an *ex parte, in camera* meeting with the government to determine what classified evidence will give KindHearts adequate notice, and whether that evidence is capable of further declassification or adequate summarization;

2. If so, the government will expeditiously declassify and/or summarize whatever classified information I find will give KindHearts constitutionally adequate notice;

3. If declassification or summarization of classified information is insufficient or impossible, then KindHearts' counsel will obtain an adequate security clearance to view the necessary documents, and will then view these documents *in camera*, under protective order, and without disclosing the contents to KindHearts; and

4. The government will then provide KindHearts' counsel with an opportunity to respond to these documents (through a closed, classified hearing if KindHearts' counsel views classified information).

***

The following case follows a proceeding in which the court determined that OFAC had violated the plaintiff's procedural due process rights with reasoning similar to *Kindhearts*. Here, the court considers whether that violation was harmless error.

AL HARAMAIN ISLAMIC FOUNDATION, INC. v. TREASURY
585 F. Supp.2d 1233 (D. Or., 2008)

KING, District Judge.

OFAC froze AHIF-Oregon's assets and property on February 19, 2004, pending investigation. It was not until February 6, 2008, when OFAC "redesignated" AHIF-Oregon as an SDGT, thereby finalizing the blocking order, that AHIF-Oregon received a comprehensive explanation for the blocking order. OFAC redesignated AHIF-Oregon because it believed AHIF-Oregon is "owned or controlled" by Soliman H.S. Al-Buthe and Aqeel Al-Aqil, or acted on behalf of them. In addition, OFAC reported that, "As a branch of the Saudi charity Al-Haramain Islamic Foundation, [AHIF-Oregon] had acted for or on behalf of, or has assisted in, sponsored, or provided financial, material, or technological support for, or financial or other services to or in support of Al Qaida and other SDGTs." ***

Just after freezing AHIF-Oregon's assets in February of 2004, OFAC issued a press release explaining it had blocked AHIF-Oregon's assets "to ensure the preservation of its assets pending further OFAC investigation." It described AHIF-Oregon's "parent" as being headquartered in Saudi Arabia, and described OFAC's other blocking actions against the AHIF branches in Bosnia, Somalia, Indonesia, Tanzania, Kenya, and Pakistan. OFAC provided unclassified documents to AHIF-Oregon in April 2004, asserting that it was considering designating AHIF-Oregon as an SDGT on the basis of that information as well as classified documents it did not disclose. *** AHIF-Oregon responded to the documents OFAC provided, believing that, on the basis of these records, OFAC was targeting it for distributing the Koran to prisoners and others, and for raising funds for Chechen refugees.

OFAC mailed a supplemental record on July 23, 2004, which included documents about AHIF-SA and its branches, newspaper articles about jihad in Chechnya and Saudi financial support for Chechen fighters, as well as newspaper articles about terrorism in Africa, Asia and Europe. AHIF-Oregon objected to inclusion of documents related to AHIF-SA because it asserted it had no control over it and had no relationship with its branches. AHIF-Oregon also submitted documentation to show that Russia supported its efforts in Chechnya. OFAC provided additional documents on August 20, 2004.

On September 9, 2004, OFAC designated AHIF-Oregon and its director Al-Buthe as SDGTs[.] *** It issued a press release which reported "[t]he investigation shows direct links between the U.S. branch and Usama bin Laden," mentioned allegations of criminal violations of tax laws, and mentioned Al-Aqil and the fact that he had been previously designated, but did not state that Al-Aqil owns or controls AHIF-Oregon. The press release also noted suspected financing of Chechen mujahideen and the designations of other branches of AHIF. In November 2007, approximately three months after plaintiffs commenced this lawsuit, OFAC notified AHIF-Oregon and Al-Buthe that it was considering redesignating them. It provided unclassified documents, including translations of Russian and Arabic newspapers from 2000 to 2004, that it had not provided earlier. It was not until February 2008 that OFAC finally gave AHIF-Oregon a comprehensive explanation for the designation and blocking order. OFAC redesignated AHIF-Oregon because it believed AHIF-Oregon is "owned or controlled" by Soliman H.S. Al-Buthe and Aqeel Al-Aqil, or acted on behalf of them. OFAC also concluded that because AHIF-Oregon was a branch of the AHIF-SA, "it had acted for or on behalf of, or has assisted in, sponsored, or provided financial, material, or technological support for, or financial or other services to or in support of Al Qaida and other SDGTs." ***

[In a previous proceeding] I concluded that AHIF-Oregon was entitled to post-deprivation notice, after the February 2004 blocking order, without "unreasonable delay," and certainly before the September 9, 2004 designation finalizing the blocking order.

Additionally, even if the September 9, 2004 designation letter and press release could serve as notice, for purposes of the redesignation process, it did not give AHIF-Oregon the reasons for the designation in the kind of detail required by the Due Process Clause. ***

The government bears the burden of proving that the due process error is harmless beyond a reasonable doubt. The purpose of the "harmless error standard" is to "avoid 'setting aside convictions for small errors or defects that have *little, if any, likelihood of having changed the result of the trial,*' because reversal would entail substantial social costs."

AHIF-Oregon asserts that it would have changed its strategy with regard to its investigation of the facts, the information it presented to OFAC, and how it and its board members behaved. AHIF-Oregon contends specifically that if it had known Al-Buthe's ownership and control were at issue, it would have challenged his designation and he would have resigned from the board. It also argues it would have provided evidence demonstrating it had never had any interactions with al Qaeda or other SDGTs, that its money never went to an SDGT, and that it had no control or involvement over AHIF-SA's activities. AHIF-Oregon argues that, because it had no knowledge of what was at issue, my decision to uphold the redesignation was based on an incomplete administrative record.

The government responds by suggesting that the redesignation corrected any due process violation. In AHIF, I described the redesignation notice as a "lengthy explanation" and questioned why OF AC could not have issued such an explanation as a proposed decision just after the blocking order. Such a comprehensive notice would have provided AHIF-Oregon with the facts and law and would have given it the opportunity to respond to OFAC's concerns in a knowing and intelligent way. I disagree with the government, however, that the redesignation cured the earlier deficient notice. The redesignation itself came too late to provide the requisite notice to AHIF-Oregon; the administrative record was closed upon issuance of the redesignation. Furthermore, the redesignation *process*, culminating in the redesignation determination, might have been a cure for the earlier lack of notice had OFAC provided sufficient notice of what issues were of concern. For example, had the initial designation itself provided AHIF-Oregon with all the reasons for the designation, the redesignation *process* would have been more meaningful. As I explained in some detail in AHIF, however, the press release issued with the initial designation contained comments not supported by the administrative record, contained improper grounds for designation, and did not expressly connect Al-Aqil and AHIF-Oregon, or AHIF-Oregon and the other branches. Thus, while the designation contained some of the rationale that in the end makes the due process violation harmless, as I explain below, the redesignation by no means cures the due process violation.

As for whether the due process violation was harmless, the government maintains its earlier position that the documents it provided AHIF-Oregon gave the organization the necessary notice. It contends it highlighted the provisions of the executive order that it was most concerned about. It also suggests that AHIF-Oregon's participation in the administrative and district court proceedings demonstrates that any error was harmless.

The question for me is whether AHIF-Oregon would have presented something different that would have changed OFAC's decision or would have made me find the redesignation to be arbitrary and capricious. After careful review of the record and AHIF-Oregon's briefing, the answer is no. I find that any due process violation was harmless. As a result of the records OF AC provided to AHIF-Oregon, as well as the initial designation, the organization was aware that its provision of funds to Chechnya was of concern to the agency. It submitted a lengthy explanation for that conduct. Similarly, it knew that its relationship to the larger organization was at issue and in its responses to the agency it attempted to minimize that relationship.

AHIF-Oregon contends that had it known Al-Buthe's membership on the board was problematic, he would have resigned. Al-Buthe's resignation would not have changed the outcome, however. *** Not only was Al-Buthe one of the founders, but he was its treasurer and was one of only two people with access to its bank account. He raised funds from Saudi Arabian sources and disbursed those funds to AHIF-Oregon and he was the individual who delivered the money to AHIF-SA for use in Chechnya. Additionally, he continues to be heavily involved with the organization. In fact, even now, he is the source, or the fundraiser, of much of the money the organization has used to pay its attorneys. Al-Aqil, in contrast, resigned from the board in March of 2003 and from AHIF-SA's board in January of 2004. The administrative record contains no evidence Al-Aqil was involved with AHIF-

Oregon after his resignation or at the time of AHIF-Oregon's designation. Furthermore, now that AHIF-Oregon knows Al-Buthe's involvement is one of the agency's concerns, as it has known since the September 2004 designation, it is not clear to me why he has not yet resigned.

Given my acceptance of the Government's argument that money is fungible, that even money used for charitable purposes frees up other money for violent activities, and that the law prohibits giving *any* financial support to or in support of terrorist acts, I am persuaded beyond a reasonable doubt that nothing AHIF-Oregon could have done would have changed the agency's decision, or would have changed my evaluation of the agency's decision. Based on the above, I conclude that the due process violation was harmless.

Although the blocking is a seizure, such an action [does not violate the Fourth Amendment] if it is reasonable. Searches and seizures, however, are usually only "reasonable" when supported by probable cause and a warrant, except for "specifically established and well-delineated exceptions." "Over and over again this Court has emphasized that the mandate of the Fourth Amendment requires adherence to judicial processes, and that searches conducted outside the judicial process, without approval by judge or magistrate, are per se unreasonable under the Fourth Amendment[.]"

Aside from its argument that the blocking action is per se reasonable, which I am unwilling to accept, the government relies on the special needs exception. *** [T]he two factors that must be present for the special needs exception to apply are: (1) the primary purpose of the seizure must be beyond criminal law enforcement; and (2) a warrant and probable cause must be impracticable.

I find the first factor met. When analyzing the Government's actions under this factor, courts undertake a "close review" to find whether the "purpose actually served . . . is ultimately indistinguishable from the general interest in crime control." Courts consider the "programmatic purpose" and "distinguish[] general crime control programs and those that have another particular purpose, such as protection of citizens against special hazards or protection of our borders. . . . The nature of the 'emergency,' which is simply another word for threat, takes the matter out of the realm of ordinary crime control."[8]

*** [T]he primary focus of the asset seizure scheme used to freeze AHIF-Oregon's assets is not for criminal law enforcement purposes. Rather, the President declared a national emergency due to the terrorist attacks in New York, Pennsylvania and the Pentagon, and directed that assets and property in the hands of specified governments, entities and individuals be frozen to stop future attacks. The purpose of the asset seizure scheme is not to obtain information about whether the asset owner has committed an act of

---

[8] *** I respectfully disagree with *KindHearts for Charitable Humanitarian Development, Inc. v. Geithner.* In that case, the court considered the "method" and "modus operandi" of the asset seizure program, rather than the purpose behind the program, and concluded the blocking actions had "more in common with ordinary law enforcement activity." *** [T]he focus of the inquiry is on the programmatic purpose of the activity not the method by which the activity is carried out.

terrorism, but rather is to withhold assets to ensure future terrorist acts are not committed. As OFAC Director Szubin explained in his first declaration, the purpose of the freezing order is to "depriv[e] the designated person of the benefit of the property. . . that might otherwise be used to further ends that conflict with U.S. interests. Blocking assets of designated terrorists and their supporters prevents their possible use in the orchestration, assistance or support of unlawful and dangerous global terrorist plots." ***

As for the second factor, the government has persuasively explained why it is impracticable to obtain a warrant. First, the government must act quickly to prevent asset flight. I agree with plaintiffs that this reason alone would be insufficient to satisfy the impracticability requirement since the government could seize first and obtain a warrant later. The government has also explained, however, how impossible it would be to meet the specificity requirements in an application for a warrant, and how difficult it would be to track down assets belonging to the designated individual and apply for a warrant in each jurisdiction in which the asset is located. ***

Szubin explains that OFAC and the President often rely on the holder of the property to freeze the asset and report to OFAC about the existence of the asset. As a result, it would be difficult to apply for a warrant for every asset in each jurisdiction in which the asset might be located. Such a requirement would interfere with the President's and OFAC's ability to act fast in blocking assets that are often very liquid and transferrable. OFAC provides notice of blocking actions through press releases and by updating its website, as well as by publishing a notice in the Federal Register. Once they have obtained notice, OFAC relies on holders of blocked property "to comply with their obligations to identify and take appropriate steps to freeze the property", including placing blocked funds into an interest-bearing blocked account in accordance with OFAC regulations. ***

Since I have determined that both the first and second factors apply in this special needs analysis, I must now "assess the constitutionality of the search by balancing the need to search against the intrusiveness of the search." As I noted in AHIF, the effect of the seizure of assets on AHIF-Oregon is "substantial. The effect of the Government's blocking and designation orders is effectively to close AHIF-Oregon's doors." AHIF-Oregon's assets have now been frozen for more than five years. Nevertheless, a designated entity may seek a license from OFAC to engage in any transaction involving blocked property.

On the other side of the scale, the Government's interest in seizing the assets of organizations with links to international terrorist organizations are substantial, as I have indicated above. I believe the Government's interest in stopping the financing of terrorism outweighs AHIF-Oregon's privacy interests.

Finally, plaintiffs contend I must consider whether there are safeguards in place that act as "constitutionally adequate substitute[s] for a warrant." This factor is explicitly called for in the category of "closely regulated" businesses where administrative searches take place to ensure compliance with a regulatory scheme. Where "some quantum of individualized suspicion" is missing, the "safeguards are generally relied upon to assure that the individual's reasonable expectation of privacy is not 'subject to the discretion of the official in the field.'" Here, however, OFAC froze AHIF-Oregon's assets due to its "reason to believe" that AHIF "may be engaged in activities that violate" the IEEPA. *** [B]ecause individualized suspicion is required before OFAC undertakes an asset seizure, no additional safeguards are necessary to act as a substitute for a warrant.

In sum, I find OFAC's seizure of AHIF-Oregon's assets was reasonable within the meaning of the Fourth Amendment because it was supported by the special needs of the government.

Notes

1. Harmless Error. How likely is the remedy proposed by the *Kindhearts* court to practically benefit Kindhearts? If it turns out not to change Kindhearts' position, would that mean the *Al Haramain* court was right?

2. Special Needs. In finding that a post hoc showing of reasonable ground to believe Kindhearts was subject to designation would remedy the Fourth Amendment violation, is the conclusion in *Kindhearts* any different than that in *Al Haramain*? If not, what are the potential legal ramifications of the different approaches the courts used to get there?

3. Ninth Circuit Appeal. Following the district court's opinion, AHIF-Oregon appealed to the Ninth Circuit. Oral argument there focused on (1) whether the Constitution required the government to provide AHIF-Oregon with notice of the charges against it; (2) whether an organization may be designated for a relationship to a *non*-designated group; (3) whether due process permits a group to be designated based on undisclosed classified evidence; (4) even if AHIF-Oregon's rights had been violated, whether that error was harmless; and (5) whether the Multicultural Association's First Amendment claim presented the same or different issues as those in *Humanitarian Law Project*. The government argued that AHIF-Oregon had "guessed exactly right" about the charges against it, and so the error if any was harmless. It further contended that if OFAC was required to provide notice of charges to organizations it designates, "the program would grind to a halt." One member of the appellate panel inquired how that consideration figures into the constitutional analysis, since, if you live in a district with a lot of bank robberies, you still must provide notice to the people you charge with bank robbery.

4. Speech with Domestic Designated Groups. The Multicultural Association of South Oregon joined AHIF-Oregon's suit, arguing that its First Amendment rights were violated because it could not speak out in coordination with AHIF-Oregon, organize events such as press conferences with it, or write op-eds criticizing the government's treatment of the organization without fear of itself being frozen. On appeal, the lawyer for AHIF-Oregon and the Multicultural Association argued that speech coordinated with a *domestic* designated terrorist group is different from the speech proscribable under *Humanitarian Law Project*, which explicitly did not reach the issue of coordinated advocacy and did "not suggest that Congress could extend the same prohibition on material support at issue here to domestic organizations." Unlike the listed groups in *HLP*, AHIF-

Oregon's assets are frozen, so there are no funds that the Multicultural Association's speech could "free up." Do you think that the government's interest in delegitimizing a domestic designated terrorist group might alone be sufficient under strict scrutiny to save the Government's case?

5. Ninth Circuit Appeal. Following the district Court's opinion, AHIF-Oregon appealed to the Ninth Circuit. Oral argument there focused on (1) whether the Constitution required the government to provide AHIF-Oregon with notice of the charges against it; (2) whether an organization may be designated for a relationship to a *non*-designated group; (3) whether due process permits a group to be designated based on undisclosed classified evidence; (4) even if AHIF-Oregon's rights had been violated, whether that error was harmless; and (5) whether the Multicultural Association's First Amendment claim presented the same or different issues as those in *Humanitarian Law Project.* The government argued that AHIF-Oregon had "guessed exactly right" about the charges against it, and so the error if any was harmless. It further contended that if OFAC was required to provide notice of charges to organizations it designates, "the program would grind to a halt." One member of the appellate panel inquired how that consideration figures into the constitutional analysis, since, if you live in a district with a lot of bank robberies, you still must provide notice to the people you charge with bank robbery. On the First Amendment issue, AHIF-Oregon argued that speech coordinated with a *domestic* designated terrorist group is different; unlike the listed groups in *HLP*, AHIF-Oregon's assets are frozen, so there are no funds that the Multicultural Association's speech could "free up." Do you think that the Government's interest in delegitimizing a domestic designated terrorist group might alone be sufficient under strict scrutiny to save the Government's case?

6. Effect of SDGT Designations. At the end of 2009, OFAC was blocking assets other than those relating to state sponsors of terrorism valued at a total of $19,886,207. At the same time, blocked assets relating state sponsors of terrorism totaled $280,000,000. In addition there was at least another $287,000,000 relating to state sponsors of terrorism in the United States that was not blocked.

7. Comparative Law on Blocking Assets. Foreign courts have also recognized the fundamental need to afford the affected party sufficient notice to permit a meaningful response. For example, In *A and Others v. United Kingdom*, App. no. 3455/05, Eur. Ct. H.R. (2009), the European Court of Human Rights ruled that use of classified evidence to justify preventive detention of suspected terrorists violated the European Convention on Human Right's guarantee of a fair hearing unless the government provided the detainee "with sufficient information about the allegations against him to enable him to give effective instructions to the special advocate." *Id.* at ¶ 220. Merely providing "cleared counsel" with access to secret information, the Court held, was insufficient, because the detainee himself must be apprised of enough detail to allow him to instruct his attorney regarding a response. *See also Sec'y of State for the Home Dep't v. AF* [2009] UKHL 28 (UK Law Lords' decision applying same principles to imposition of "control orders," a form of curfew or house arrest on suspected terrorists, The Canadian Supreme Court has ruled that use of secret evidence to deport a foreign national violates due process where less restrictive alternatives, such as providing access to "cleared counsel," are not pursued *Charkaoui v. Canada (Citizenship and Immigration),* [2007] 1 S.C.R. 350, at ¶¶ 76-87.

In *Kadi and Al Barakaat Int'l Found. v. Council and Comm'n*, 2008 E.C.R I-6351, the European Court of Justice, Europe's highest court, held that the United Nations Security Council's listing of an individual as a designated terrorist, triggering laws freezing his assets in Europe, violated his European constitutional rights of defense and judicial review because the Security Council did not communicate to Kadi the evidence used against him or afford him an opportunity to respond. *See also HM Treasury v. Ahmed* [2010] UKSC 2 (UK Supreme Court applying same principle to UK law freezing assets of designated terrorists).

Most recently, the General Court of the European Community ruled that a statement of reasons that the Security Council provided to Mr. Kadi after the ECJ decision was also constitutionally deficient, because it "did not grant him even the most minimal access to the evidence against him," *Kadi v. Council and Comm'n*, Case No. T-85/09, 2010 EUR-Lex LEXIS 825, at ¶ 173, and the "few pieces of information and the imprecise allegations in the summary of reasons appear clearly insufficient to enable the applicant to launch an effective challenge to the allegations against him." *Id.* at ¶ 174.

8. Principles. Two core principles are reflected in these decisions: (1) where the government relies on classified evidence affirmatively, it must provide the affected party with sufficient details regarding the facts and charges to allow it a meaningful response; and (2) where means are available that would increase fairness without undermining confidentiality, there is no justification for failing to pursue them.

IV

ELECTRONIC SURVEILLANCE

———————

"Beginning in the 1960s ***Congress devoted significant energy to designing surveillance regimes to authorize collection of evidence and intelligence *** It crafted *** a series of rules that has served this country well for a generation—rules under which nearly all domestic wiretaps required warrants, national security investigations became subject to limited judicial oversight, and the Justice Department kept a close eye on the spooks. Congress today needs to engage in a similar process of thinking through surveillance law for a new generation of technology, threat, and human cultural engagement with electronic communications. *** [I]t is hard to discern what this body of law will look like. It will, however, both deeply challenge contemporary civil libertarian sensibilities and require an unprecedented level of oversight—internal and external, executive and congressional and judicial—of the intelligence and law enforcement worlds."

> Benjamin Wittes, LAW AND THE LONG WAR: THE
> FUTURE OF JUSTICE IN THE AGE OF TERROR
> (Penguin Books, 2008), pp. 223-24.

Congress revised the legislation to which Wittes refers, the Foreign Intellegence Surveillance Act (FISA) in 2008, to deal with internet and cell phone technology, but legislation has yet to deal with even newer technology challenges such as social networking communications.

I have organized this chapter into four parts: (A) an overview of FISA and its constitutionality, (B) an introduction to surveillance outside FISA beginning after the 9/11 attacks in 2001, (C) current issues under FISA as amended by the Foreign Intelligence Surveillance Act Amendment Act of 2008 (FISAAA), which created new surveillance rules frequently used in dealing with potential terrorism and (D) comparative and policy materials concerning surveillance.

A. OVERVIEW OF THE FOREIGN INTELLIGENCE SURVEILLANCE ACT (FISA)

Surveillance and searches are both subject to the Fourth Amendment: The right of the people to be secure in their persons, houses, papers, and effects, against unreasonable searches and seizures shall not be violated, and no Warrants shall issue, but upon probable cause, supported by Oath or affirmation, and particularly describing the place to be searched, and the persons or things to be seized.

National security searches and surveillances involve standards and processes different from those applicable in ordinary domestic police work. In ordinary police work, the police must generally obtain a warrant unless a specific judicially-crafted "exception" to the Fourth Amendment applies. *Katz v. United States* 389 U.S. 347 (1967). Exceptions recognized to date include searches incident to arrest, auto, boat, and airplane searches, "stop and frisk" searches, and searches of people and things at the United States' borders. ***

Is there a "national security" exception to the Fourth Amendment warrant requirement *** when the target of surveillance is within the United States? In *United States v. United States District Court (Keith)* (407 U.S. 297 1972), the Supreme Court implied that a warrant should not be required if it would "unduly frustrate" the President's exercise of foreign affairs responsibilities. *United States v. Truong Dinh Hung* F. 2d (4ᵗʰ Cir. 1980), interpreting *Keith*, held that executive competence as well as a need for "stealth, speed, and secrecy" justified a limited exception to the Fourth Amendment. *Truong* opined that searches should only be allowed without warrants when foreign intelligence surveillance was the "primary purpose" of the surveillance.

Meanwhile, to provide a more detailed framework for regulating national security wiretaps and other surveillance, Congress passed a statute, the Foreign Intelligence Surveillance Act of 1978 (FISA), 50 U.S.C. §1801 et seq. This section will examine how FISA works, compare FISA to federal law enforcement searches under Title III of the Omnibus Crime Control and Safe Streets Act of 1986, 18 U.S.C. §§ 2510-2522, and explore the constitutionality of the FISA process.

How FISA works. FISA regulates collection of "foreign intelligence" (counterintelligence) information within the U.S., whether or not there has been a probable violation of any law. Foreign intelligence information "relates to" protection against possible hostile acts, sabotage or terrorism, or clandestine intelligence activities by a "foreign power" or its "agents." §1801(e)(1). The "agent" may be an alien or a US citizen, and "foreign power" is broad enough to include factions of nations (e.g. the Irish Republican Army or the African National Congress) as well as "any group engaged in international terrorism" (e.g. al Qaeda). With an amendment passed in 2005, "lone wolf" terrorists not affiliated with a terrorist organization are also subject to FISA searches. FISA restrictions exist concerning United States citizens and permanent residents: the person must be about to violate U.S.

law, cannot be targeted "solely on the basis of activities" that are protected speech under the First Amendment, and the information must be "necessary to" U.S. national security, national defense, or foreign affairs.

The scope of FISA has grown substantially over the years. Originally, FISA was limited to electronic surveillance. A 1994 amendment expanded the statute to permit covert physical entries, a 1998 amendment added authority to obtain pen/trap orders and certain business records, and a 2001 amendment allowed "roving wiretaps" of any phone the surveillance target may use. 2008 amendments extended the reach of FISA overseas, with less stringent controls on government surveillance than for domestic surveillance. The number of surveillance orders grew rapidly after the 9/11 attacks, from 199 in 1979 to 1228 in 2002. FISA applications peaked in 2007 at 2370; by 2009, DoJ sent only 1376 applications to the FISC. This is a reflection, according to DoJ, of the changed framework put in place in 2008, discussed infra, rather than a decline in overall surveillance.

FISA authorized creation of two secret courts, the Foreign Intelligence Surveillance Court (FISC) and the Foreign Intelligence Surveillance Court of Review (FISCR). FISC is comprised of eleven federal judges appointed by the Chief Justice; FISCR has three members similarly appointed. Both courts meet in secret, and both involve ex parte proceedings; the Attorney General requests a surveillance order about which the target of the request is ignorant and is unrepresented.

A journalist's description of the FISA Court's secretive haunts gives a feel for how unusual this court and its processes are in the American judicial syatem:

> Pass through a set of double-glass doors marked "Restricted Area" on the sixth floor of the Justice Department, and walk down the hall. Stride past a row of chairs where agents of the Federal Bureau of Investigation and the National Security Agency wait to testify.

> Step through a heavy door snaked with wires, then through another, and press a button on the wall. The doors will slowly swing shut, then audibly secure themselves totheir frames. If you are carrying a radio, it will go dead.

> You are now sealed inside a conference room with an oddly textured ceiling, no windows, and a single table running down the middle. You have entered the Foreign Intelligence Surveillance Court, the most secretive institution in the American judiciary.

Benjamin Wittes, "Inside America's Most Secretive Court," LEGAL TIMES, Feb. 19, 1996.

FISC judges have only once denied surveillance in over 13,000 requests, and they generally do not write or publish opinions granting surveillance. Challenges to surveillance orders generally occur only when the government later prosecutes a surveillance target. See e.g. *United States v. Duggan*, 743

F. 2d 59(2d Cir. 1984). The appropriate relationship between national security surveillance and the use of information obtained through such surveillance to prosecute crime has been a matter of substantial concern over many years. One of the two instances in which the FISC and the FISCR have published written opinions dealt with this issue. *In re All Matters Submitted to the Foreign Intelligence Surveillance Court* (FISC 2002), rev'd by *In re Sealed Case No. 02-001* 310 F. 3d 717 (FISCR 2003). A second public FISCR ruling, which generally upheld a 2007 piece of legislation superseded by the 2008 amendments, is excerpted in section B, infra.

The background for these opinions requires an understanding of the "minimization procedures" which FISA required the Attorney General to adopt and the FISA judges to follow in order to "minimize the acquisition and retention, and prohibit the dissemination" of nonpublic information concerning U.S. persons. Beginning in 1995, the Attorney General's procedures called for erection of a "wall" between the FBI and the Criminal Division of the DOJ in FISA surveillance cases. This "wall" avoided a potential constitutional problem: if the standards for national security surveillance do not meet Fourth Amendment minimums, may a defendant exclude evidence at trial obtained in the course of FISA surveillance?

Three matters brought this issue to a head. First, the Department of Justice disclosed to the FISC in September 2000 that in over 75 cases, the "wall" had been breached; prosecutors had been provided access to raw national security intercepts. Second, the USA PATRIOT Act, passed October 26, 2001, changed the FISA framework to enhance national security after September 11. Congress abandoned *Truong's* "primary purpose" test to allow surveillance whenever national security information was "a significant purpose" of the surveillance. It also permitted intelligence officers to "consult" with federal law enforcement officers to "coordinate efforts to investigate or protect against" threats to national security. Third, the Attorney General issued a memorandum to the Director of the FBI on March 6, 2002 requiring, *inter alia*, that all FISA-obtained information concerning "any crime which has been, is being, or is about to be committed" must be turned over to the DOJ for potential prosecution.

On May 17, 2002, the FISC, sitting *en banc*, disapproved this last portion of the Attorney General's new minimization procedures on the ground that they were "designed to amend the law and substitute the FISA for Title III electronic surveillances and Rule 41 searches." The court imposed a variety of requirements designed to restore much of the "wall" between FISA activities and criminal prosecutions. When the FISC thereafter required modification of surveillance in a specific case, the Attorney General appealed to the FISCR. Reversing, the FISCR held 1) that the minimization procedures did not require a "wall" between intelligence and criminal prosecutions, 2) that the FISC had impermissibly intruded into the executive branch operations, 3) that the USA PATRIOT Act was intended in part to break down the wall, and 4) that FISA intelligence used in criminal prosecutions was constitutionally permissible so long as the surveillance was not primarily conducted to enhance ordinary criminal prosecutions. *In re Sealed Case No. 02-001*

(FISCR 2003). The FISCR was impressed that, when the provisions of FISA and Title III were compared, a FISA order "comes close to meeting Title III, [which] bears on its reasonableness under the Fourth Amendment." ***

The bottom line to the FISCR was that these differences are based on different purposes behind national security surveillances and criminal prosecutions. The purpose of the former is to prevent acts of terror, sabotage, and the like; the purpose of the latter is to punish the wrongdoer and deter others from engaging in criminal acts. As the FISCR noted, punishment of the September 11 hijackers "is a moot point." In other words, FISA surveillance and searches are special needs cases for Fourth Amendment warrant purposes. Therefore, no warrant based on probable cause is required as a prerequisite to surveillance. If this decision is upheld by courts in which the targets of FISA surveillance are tried for violations of federal law, the Fourth Amendment will provide no defense to the use of FISA-obtained information at trial. ***

Adapted and updated from Shanor & Hogue, NATIONAL SECURITY AND MILITARY LAW IN A NUTSHELL (WEST 2003), pp 50-58.

*****

Five years after the 2002 FISCR decision, dealing with facts that received international notoriety, one court reached a different conclusion concerning the requirements of the Fourth Amendment. Though its order was vacated on appeal following a monetary settlement paid to the plaintiff by the United States government, the following opinion is still a useful exploration of why FISA and the Fourth Amendment are in some tension.

MAYFIELD v. UNITED STATES
504 F. Supp. 2d 1023 (D.Or. 2007), vacated 599 F. 3d 964 (C.A.9 2010)

AIKEN, District Judge.

On March 11, 2004, in Madrid, Spain, terrorists' bombs exploded on commuter trains, murdering 191 persons, and injuring another 1600 persons, including three United States citizens. Shortly after the bombings, the Spanish National Police ("SNP") recovered fingerprints from a plastic bag containing explosive detonators. The bag was found in a Renault van located near the bombing site. The FBI technicians programmed the computer to return 20 candidates whose known prints had features in common with what was identified as Latent Finger Print # 17 ("LFP # 17"). *** Mayfield's AFIS "score" ranked # 4 on the list of 20 candidates. Mayfield is an American citizen *** and a practicing Oregon lawyer. Prior to his arrest, he had not traveled outside the United States since 1994, and he had never been arrested for a crime. Plaintiffs allege that FBI examiners were aware of Mayfield's Muslim faith and that this knowledge influenced their examination of Mayfield's fingerprints. *** On March 20, 2004, the FBI issued a formal report matching Mayfield's print to LFP # 17. On March 21, 2004, FBI surveillance agents began to watch Mayfield and to follow Mayfield and members of his family when they traveled to and from the Bilal Mosque, the family's place of worship; to and from Mayfield's law office, his place of employment; to and from the children's school; and to and from family activities.

Plaintiffs allege that at some point after the wrongful fingerprint identification, the FBI applied to the Foreign Intelligence Security Court ("FISC") for an order authorizing the FBI to place electronic listening devices ("bugs") in the "shared and intimate" rooms of the Mayfield family home; executed repeated "sneak and peek" searches of the Mayfield family home, occurring when the family was away from the home and performed "so incompetently that the FBI left traces of their searches behind, causing the Mayfield family to be frightened and believe that they had been burglarized;" obtained private and protected information about the Mayfields from third parties; executed "sneak and peek" searches of the law office of Brandon Mayfield; and placed wiretaps on Mayfield's office and home phones. *** Plaintiffs allege that DOJ and FBI employees "concocted false and misleading affidavits" in order to justify even more intrusive searches and ultimately to justify Mayfield's arrest as a "material witness." *** [N]o mention was made of Spain's April 13, 2004, report to the FBI that stated the SNP did not agree with the FBI's fingerprint match of LFP # 17 and Mayfield. *** [A] court-appointed expert witness *** selected by Mayfield and his defense attorneys *** "compared the latent prints that were submitted on Brandon Mayfield, and [he] concluded that the latent print is the left index finger of Mr. Mayfield."

Based on these affidavits, broad search warrants were sought and issued. Mayfield's family home and law office were searched. Computer and paper files from his family home, including his children's homework, were seized. Mayfield was ultimately arrested and initially held in the lock down unit at the Multnomah County Detention Center. His family was not told where he was being held. He and his family were told, however, that he was being held as a primary suspect on offenses punishable by death, and that the FBI had made a 100% match of his fingerprint with the Madrid train bombing fingerprint. Plaintiffs allege that leaks to the media by the FBI and DOJ led to local, national, and international headlines that Brandon Mayfield's fingerprints linked him to the Madrid bombings.

Mayfield was ultimately arrested and imprisoned from May 6, 2004, through May 20, 2004. On May 19, 2004, the SNP advised the FBI, and on May 20, 2004, news reports revealed, that Spain had matched the Madrid fingerprint with an Algerian, Ouhane Daoud. Mayfield was released from prison the following day. ***

Plaintiffs challenge the Patriot Act amendments to FISA that allow federal agents to circumvent Fourth Amendment probable cause requirements when investigating persons suspected of crimes. *** Plaintiffs request a declaration from this court that FISA, as amended by the Patriot Act, violates the Fourth Amendment because it:

a. permit[s] the federal government to perform covert physical searches and electronic surveillance and wiretaps of the home, office and vehicles of a person without first requiring the government to demonstrate to a court the existence of probable cause that the person has committed a crime;

b. permit[s] the federal government to perform covert physical searches and electronic surveillance and wiretaps of a person without first requiring the government to demonstrate to a court that the primary purpose of the searches and surveillance is to obtain foreign intelligence information; and

c. permit[s] the federal government to covertly collect, disseminate and retain information collected through covert physical searches and electronic surveillance without first requiring the government to demonstrate to a court the existence of probable cause that the person who is the target of physical searches and electronic surveillance has committed a crime, or, alternatively, that the primary purpose of the searches and surveillance [is] to obtain foreign intelligence information.

Prior to the Patriot Act, the government was required to certify that the *primary purpose* of its surveillance was to obtain foreign intelligence information. The Patriot Act now authorizes FISA surveillance and searches as long as a *significant purpose* of the surveillance and searches is the gathering of foreign intelligence. This amendment allows the government to obtain surveillance orders under FISA even if the Government's primary purpose is to gather evidence of domestic criminal activity.   The practical result of this amendment, objected to by plaintiffs, is that in criminal investigations, the government can now avoid the Fourth Amendment's probable cause requirement when conducting surveillance or searches of a criminal suspect's home or office merely by asserting a desire to also gather foreign intelligence information from the person whom the government intends to criminally prosecute. The government is now authorized to conduct physical searches and electronic surveillance upon criminal suspects without first proving to an objective and neutral magistrate that probable cause exists to believe that a crime has been committed. The government need only represent that the targeted individual was an agent of a foreign power (a representation that must be accepted unless "clearly erroneous") and that "a significant purpose" of the surveillance and search is to collect foreign intelligence.

Here, the government chose to go to the FISC, despite the following evidence: Mayfield did not have a current passport; he had not been out of the country since completing his military duty as a U.S. Army lieutenant in Germany during the early 1990s; the fingerprint identification had been determined to be "negative" by the SNP; the SNP believed the bombings were conducted by persons from northern Africa; and there was no evidence linking Mayfield with Spain or North Africa. The government nevertheless made the requisite showing to the FISC that Mayfield was an "agent of a foreign power." That representation, which by law the FISC could not ignore unless clearly erroneous, provided the government with sufficient justification to compel the FISC to authorize covert searches and electronic surveillance in support of a criminal investigation. ***

*** At issue here are two fundamental concerns: the safety of our nation and the constitutional rights of citizens. *** Prior to passage of the Patriot

Act, the government would have been required to follow the traditional process and demonstrate probable cause to a "detached and neutral magistrate" that Mayfield had committed a crime. *** Instead, FISA contains a "foreign intelligence standard" of probable cause which requires a showing that the target may be an agent of a foreign government and the place or facility to be searched is being used in furtherance of espionage or terrorist activities.

Significantly, a seemingly minor change in wording has a dramatic and significant impact on the application of FISA. A warrant under FISA now issues if "a significant purpose" of the surveillance is foreign intelligence. Now, for the first time in our Nation's history, the government can conduct surveillance to gather evidence for use in a criminal case without a traditional warrant, as long as it presents a non-reviewable assertion that it also has a significant interest in the targeted person for foreign intelligence purposes. *** The hard won legislative compromise previously embodied in FISA reduced the probable cause requirement only for national security intelligence gathering. The Patriot Act effectively eliminates that compromise by allowing the Executive Branch to bypass the Fourth Amendment in gathering evidence for a criminal prosecution.

*** [The Supreme Court's] decisions in *Katz* and *Keith* drew a line between surveillance conducted by law enforcement officials to investigate crime-which requires a traditional warrant based on probable cause-and surveillance conducted by intelligence officials to obtain foreign intelligence information. Notably, the primary purpose of the electronic surveillance and physical searching of Mayfield's home was to gather evidence to prosecute him for crimes. Mayfield was ultimately arrested to compel his testimony before a Grand Jury investigating his alleged involvement in the crimes of bombing places of public use, providing national support to terrorists and conspiracy to kill, kidnap, maim or injure persons or damage property in a foreign county. The government stipulated that it did not demonstrate to the FISC that its primary purpose in wiretapping, electronically eavesdropping, or physically searching Mayfield's home or law office was to gather foreign intelligence. "*** Thus, FISA now permits the Executive Branch to conduct surveillance and searches of American citizens without satisfying the probable cause requirements of the Fourth Amendment. As plaintiffs allege, when proceeding pursuant to FISA, "there is no [need for] showing or finding that a crime has been or is being committed, as in the case of a search or seizure for law enforcement purposes." "Additionally, and with respect to the nexus to criminality required by the definitions of an 'agent of a foreign power,' the government need not show probable cause as to each and every element of the crime involved or about to be involved." When the FISC reviews a FISA search application, the government satisfies most FISA requirements simply by certifying that the requirements are met. The statute directs that the FISC is not to scrutinize such statements, but is to defer to the Government's certification unless it is "clearly erroneous."

This procedure allows the government to avoid traditional Fourth Amendment judicial oversight used to obtain a surveillance order. The government must provide the court with "a full and complete statement of the facts and circumstances relied upon by the applicant to justify his belief that an order should be issued." The court may "require the applicant to furnish additional testimony or documentary evidence in support of the application." Finally, as to most substantive requirements, the court must find probable cause to believe they are satisfied.

The FISA also allows the government to retain information collected, and use the collected information in criminal prosecutions without providing any meaningful opportunity for the target of the surveillance to challenge its legality. Nor does FISA require notice. The Fourth Amendment ordinarily requires that the subject of a search be notified that the search has occurred. Although in some circumstances the government is permitted to delay the provision of notice, the Supreme Court has never upheld a statute that, like FISA, authorizes the government to search a person's home or intercept his communications without ever informing the person that his or her privacy has been violated. Except for the investigations that result in criminal prosecutions, FISA targets never learn that their homes or offices have been searched or that their communications have been intercepted. Therefore, most FISA targets have no way of challenging the legality of the surveillance or obtaining any remedy for violations of their constitutional rights.

FISA also does not require particularity. The Fourth Amendment prohibits the government from conducting intrusive surveillance unless it first obtains a warrant describing with particularity the things to be seized as well as the place to be searched. *** Finally, FISA authorizes surveillance terms up to 120-days. Title III limits the term of surveillance to 30 days. *** FISA's provisions relating to the duration of surveillance orders violates the Fourth Amendment requirements for criminal investigations.

The government does not refute plaintiffs' historical recitation of law leading up to the enactment of FISA. Similarly, the parties agree that when surveying the case law prior to *In re Sealed Case,* 310 F.3d 717 (Foreign Int.Surv.Ct.Rev.2003), every Article III court that had considered the issue directly concluded that to justify non-probable cause searches and electronic surveillance, the Government's purpose, or at least its primary purpose, must have been the collection of foreign intelligence. Specifically, as originally drafted and implemented over its 24-year history, FISA applications were properly granted only when "the purpose" of the surveillance was foreign intelligence gathering.

In the history underlying *In re Sealed Case,* the government sought to conduct surveillance of an "agent of a foreign power." *** The FISCR *** held the 2002 Procedures consistent with the Patriot Act, found the 2002 Procedures constitutionally reasonable, and held that they met Fourth Amendment standards. While the court permitted *amicus* briefs, only the government was allowed to appear and participate at oral argument. Moreover, only the government is allowed under FISA to seek Supreme Court review of a FISCR decision, which it declined to do. Even without the benefit of full adversarial proceedings, the FISCR conceded that "the constitutional question presented by this case-whether Congress' disapproval of the primary purpose test is consistent with the Fourth Amendment-has no definitive jurisprudential answer."

The government cites *In re Sealed Case* as "highly persuasive" authority for this court. *** In this case, the court declines to adopt the analysis and conclusion reached by the FISCR in *In re Sealed Case*. Notably, the FISCR's two fundamental premises underlying its ruling are contradictory. FISCR determined both that FISA never contained a purpose requirement, and that in altering the purpose requirement, Congress did not undermine the validity of searches conducted pursuant to FISA. Regarding FISCR's second premise, FISCR found that the primary purpose test "generates dangerous confusion and creates perverse organizational incentives arising from the purported need to distinguish between intelligence gathering and criminal investigation." However, a provision of the Patriot Act, unchallenged by plaintiffs here, eliminates the DOJ "wall" and with it the "dangerous confusion" and "perverse organizational incentives" referred to and relied on by the FISCR. Moreover, to the extent the "primary purpose" test imposes any restraint on the sharing of FISA surveillance with criminal investigators, investigators are, of course, free to seek orders authorizing surveillance under Title III, and traditional search warrants that satisfy Fourth Amendment requirements. Finally, Title III includes predicate offenses for which surveillance is justified for virtually all terrorism and espionage-related offenses. As such, Title III provides a satisfactory alternative when criminal investigators cannot have access to FISA surveillance.

The FISCR also attempts, without merit, to distinguish the Supreme Court's "special needs" cases. "Special needs" cases are those where the Supreme Court has found it appropriate to carve out an exception to the Fourth Amendment's requirement of probable cause based upon an individualized suspicion of wrongdoing. In these cases, the Court found that special needs, beyond the normal need of law enforcement, might justify an otherwise unconstitutional search. Prior to the Patriot Act, FISA may have had as its "general programmatic purpose ... to protect the nation against terrorism and espionage threats directed by foreign powers." After the Patriot Act, however, FISA surveillance, including the surveillance at bar, may have as its "programmatic purpose" the generation of evidence for law enforcement purposes-which is forbidden without criminal probable cause and a warrant.

Finally and perhaps most significantly, *In re Sealed Case* ignores congressional concern with the appropriate balance between intelligence gathering and criminal law enforcement. It is notable that our Founding Fathers anticipated this very conflict as evidenced by the discussion in the Federalist Papers. Their concern regarding unrestrained government resulted in the separation of powers, checks and balances, and ultimately, the Bill of Rights. Where these important objectives merge, it is critical that we, as a democratic Nation, pay close attention to traditional Fourth Amendment principles. The Fourth Amendment has served this Nation well for 220 years, through many other perils. Title III *** recognizes that wiretaps are searches requiring fidelity to the Fourth Amendment.

Moreover, the constitutionally required interplay between Executive action, Judicial decision, and Congressional enactment, has been eliminated by the FISA amendments. Prior to the amendments, the three branches of government operated with thoughtful and deliberate checks and balances-a principle upon which our Nation was founded. These constitutional checks and balances effectively curtail overzealous executive, legislative, or judicial activity regardless of the catalyst for overzealousness. The Constitution contains bedrock principles that the framers believed essential. Those principles should not be easily altered by the expediencies of the moment.

Despite this, the FISCR holds that the Constitution need not control the conduct of criminal surveillance in the United States. In place of the Fourth Amendment, the people are expected to defer to the Executive Branch and its representation that it will authorize such surveillance only when appropriate. *** I conclude that 50 U.S.C. §§ 1804 and 1823, as amended by the Patriot Act, are unconstitutional because they violate the Fourth Amendment of the United States Constitution. ***

Notes

1. Appeal. If you were the government, would you appeal? What aspects of this case were particularly unattractive to the government as a vehicle for litigating the Fourth Amendment issue? What factors would you as a government attorney would you have taken into account in making a settlement offer to the plaintiff?

2. Changed Purpose. Does the change made by the USA PATRIOT Act from "primary purpose" to "significant purpose" carry the weight that the Court's analysis gives it? The court stresses that the sole or at least dominant purpose of this surveillance was to collect evidence of criminal activity. Is this matter as clear as the court indicates?

3. Process Concerns. The court is skeptical of the *Sealed Case* decision because it was decided ex parte. Is this concern justified? Does the *Sealed Case* decision, discussed by both the *Mayfield* court and in the introductory materials to this section, have about it an air of abstraction, a lack of factual detail?

4. Conflict. Who has the better argument over the Fourth Amendment issue, the *Sealed Case* court or the *Mayfield* court? Consider the different contexts of the two cases and the effect that may have had on resolution of the Fourth Amendment issue. Note that the FISCR has no appellate jurisdiction over the *Mayfield* Court's decision. Did Congress not fully appreciate national security interests when it designed FISA this way?

5. *Mayfield* as Authority. As noted in my introduction to this case, Mayfield was vacated and has no precedential value. Why would a casebook editor include such a case in these materials?

6. Timing of Judicial Involvement in Surveillance. On the theory that the FISCR is correct that no warrant meeting normal probable cause standards is required *prior to* a FISA search, the remainder of these materials will explore surveillance that goes even farther than that under FISA. In the following materials, the surveillance involves *no prior* FISA warrant.

B. SURVEILLANCE OUTSIDE FISA AND AMENDMENT OF FISA

FISA, with its procedure for ex parte receipt of warrants from a federal judge, was not the sole vehicle the United States used to obtain information concerning the operations and communications of alleged terrorists. In December, 2005, the NEW YORK TIMES reported that President Bush had authorized the NSA to monitor calls between persons in the USA and individuals overseas thought to be affiliated with terrorists. This program was called the Terrorist Surveillance Program (TSP). This monitoring was not done under FISA processes; no FISA warrant was sought from a FISC judge. Here is a brief explanation given by the Department of Justice in a letter to congressional oversight committees concerning the rationale for not seeking FISA warrants:

> "As you know, in response to unauthorized disclosures in the media, the President has described certain activities of the National Security Agency ("NSA") that he has authorized since shortly after September 11, 2001. As described by the President, the NSA intercepts certain international communications into and out of the United States of people linked to al Qaeda or an affiliated terrorist organization. The purpose of these intercepts is to establish an early warning system to detect and prevent another catastrophic terrorist attack on the United States. The President has made clear that he will use his constitutional and statutory authorities to protect the American people from further terrorist attacks, and the NSA activities the President described are part of that effort. Leaders of the Congress were briefed on these activities more than a dozen times."

A firestorm of political commentary followed. Some argued that the President was unlawfully interfering with the civil liberties of Americans while others argued the President could engage in such surveillance to safeguard national security. Memos by the Congressional Research Service (CRS) and DoJ consider the arguments thoroughly.

See   http://mypetjawa.mu.nu/archives/Justice_Department_wiretap_defense_domestic_eavesdropping.pdf; and http://www.fas.org/sgp/crs/intel/m010506.pdf.

The Bush Administration vigorously defended its surveillance outside the FISA framework, both in the media and in litigation. The administration argued that (1) FISA was not preclusive of the TSP and (2) even if it was, the President had inherent authority to engage in this surveillance. A dissenting judge assessed the Government's arguments in ACLU v. NSA, 493 F. 3d 644 (C.A. 6, 2007), in which the majority did not reach the merits, as follows:

> *1. The TSP violated FISA and Title III* *** In enacting FISA, Congress directed that electronic surveillance conducted inside the United States for foreign intelligence purposes was to be undertaken only as authorized by specific federal statutory authority. *** The statute clearly states that ***

FISA "shall be the *exclusive means* by which electronic surveillance ... and the interception of domestic wire, oral, and electronic communications may be conducted." *** [T]he legislative history of FISA clearly reinforces the conclusion that FISA and Title III constitute the sole means by which electronic surveillance may lawfully be conducted. During a conference session on the FISA legislation, members of Congress rejected language that would have described FISA and Title III as the "exclusive *statutory* means" by which electronic surveillance was permitted, preferring instead the broader construction, "exclusive means." *** The government, however, contends that Congress authorized the TSP in the aftermath of the September 11, 2001 attacks by enacting the Authorization for Use of Military Force (AUMF), (Sept. 18, 2001). In addition, the government Notes that "foreign intelligence gathering is ... vital to the successful prosecution of war."

But FISA itself expressly and specifically restricts the President's authority even in times of war. *** FISA thus limits warrantless electronic surveillance to the first 15 days following a declaration of war, a more formal action than even the enactment of an authorization for the use of force. This 15-day period of warrantless surveillance was enacted to permit "consideration of any amendment to this Act that may be appropriate during a wartime emergency." *** Congress has in fact amended FISA multiple times since September 11, 2001, increasing the President's authority by permitting "roving" wiretaps and expanding the permissible use of pen-register devices. But Congress has never suspended FISA's application nor altered the 15-day limit on warrantless electronic surveillance. *** No reference to surveillance, is found in the AUMF. *** [T]his interpretation of the AUMF directly conflicts with the specific statutory language of both FISA and Title III. *** The TSP plainly violated FISA and Title III and, unless there exists some authority for the President to supersede this statutory authority, was therefore unlawful.

2. Inherent authority. A contrary position would, according to the government, "present a grave constitutional question of the highest order." *** [Under the three zones of power analysis in *Youngstown*], [w]e must thus determine into which zone the TSP fits. From that determination, the program will stand or fall. The government argues that the TSP fits into Zone 1, where the President's authority is at its zenith. But this argument ignores Congress's clear directive that FISA and Title III constitute the exclusive means for undertaking electronic surveillance within the United States for foreign intelligence purposes. The result might not be

> what the President would prefer, but that does not give him
> license to "disregard limitations" that Congress has "placed on
> his powers." In light of FISA and Title III, I have no doubt
> that the TSP falls into Zone 3, where the President's
> authority is at its lowest ebb. *** Congress has unequivocally
> acted within its constitutional power to limit the President's
> authority over warrantless electronic surveillance within this
> country. ***

Eventually, however, the administration agreed to subject this surveillance to after-the-fact oversight by the FISC on a voluntary basis. Congress then held hearings and in 2007 passed temporary legislation (the Protecting America Act or PAA) to allow continuation of warrantless wiretaps of foreign nationals outside the United States while further study was given to the matter. Permanent legislation was passed in 2008 which protected companies that had secretly provided surveillance data at the request of the Bush Administration. The legislation, The Foreign Intelligence Surveillance Act of 1978 Amendments Act of 2008 (FISAAA) or the FISA Amendments Act of 2008 (FAA), created a new framework for foreign intelligence surveillance outside the United States.

Section 702 carves out of the FISA warrant process certain surveillance for persons outside the United States. Reading this section is useful. Congress delineated different rules concerning surveillance of persons in the United States from those for persons outside the United States as follows:

> (a) Authorization- Notwithstanding any other provision of law,
> *** the Attorney General and the Director of National
> Intelligence may authorize jointly, for a period of up to 1 year
> from the effective date of the authorization, the targeting of
> persons reasonably believed to be located outside the United
> States to acquire foreign intelligence information.

> (b) Limitations- *** -

> (1) may not intentionally target any person known at the time of
> acquisition to be located in the United States;

> (2) may not intentionally target a person reasonably believed to
> be located outside the United States if the purpose of such
> acquisition is to target a particular, known person reasonably
> believed to be in the United States;

> (3) may not intentionally target a United States person
> reasonably believed to be located outside the United States;

> (4) may not intentionally acquire any communication as to which
> the sender and all intended recipients are known at the time of
> the acquisition to be located in the United States; and

> (5) shall be conducted in a manner consistent with the fourth
> amendment to the Constitution of the United States.

Section 702 applies only when the target of surveillance is "outside the

United States." Moreover, the surveillance must be "consistent with the fourth amendment." That, as we will see, is a leading statement, since the Fourth Amendment rules for national security surveillance are not clear. Where applicable, FISAAA surveillance authorized by the AG and the DNI *does not need to be done pursuant to a previously issued warrant overseen by the FISC as under FISA*, though Section 702(c) requires that the FISA minimization procedures and certification procedures be followed. Minimization protects the privacy of the target; certification by the AG and DNI certifies "under oath and under seal" that "exigent circumstances exist because, without immediate implementation *** intelligence important to the national security of the United States may be lost or not timely acquired and time does not permit the issuance of an order" by a FISC judge. Such certification does not have to precede the surveillance, but must follow it by not more than 7 days. The FISAAA requires that the AG and the DNI establish targeting procedures and minimization procedures, both of which are presumably classified, but which will be reviewed by the FISC. The certification procedures must be "reasonably designed to *** ensure that [surveillance] is limited to targeting persons reasonably believed to be located outside the United States; and [to] prevent the intentional acquisition of any communication as to which the sender and all intended recipients are known at the time of the acquisition to be located in the United States." The procedures must be "consistent with the requirements of the fourth amendment," have "a significant purpose *** to obtain foreign intelligence information" and "involve[] obtaining foreign intelligence information from or with the assistance of an electronic communication service provider." These certifications are "not required to identify the specific facilities, places, premises, or property at which an acquisition authorized under subsection (a) will be directed or conducted." Judicial review is provided for, but only for 30 days following the AG/DNI communication of a proposed procedure to the FISC (a time period in which it is not likely any target will even know he or she is subject to surveillance).

The most controversial provisions of the FISAAA were those dealing with eliminating potential liability of the service providers who carried out surveillance at the request of the Bush Administration before the FISAAA:

> No cause of action shall lie in any court against any electronic communication service provider for providing any information, facilities, or assistance in accordance with a directive issued [by the Bush administration] ***.

Congress also specifically protected service providers prospectively from liability under state law as follows:

SEC. 803. PREEMPTION.

(a) In General- No State shall have authority to--

(1) conduct an investigation into an electronic communication service provider's alleged assistance to an element of the intelligence community;

(2) require through regulation or any other means the disclosure

of information about an electronic communication service provider's alleged assistance to an element of the intelligence community;

(3) impose any administrative sanction on an electronic communication service provider for assistance to an element of the intelligence community; or

(4) commence or maintain a civil action or other proceeding to enforce a requirement that an electronic communication service provider disclose information concerning alleged assistance to an element of the intelligence community.

(b) Suits by the United States- The United States may bring suit to enforce the provisions of this section.

(c) Jurisdiction- The district courts of the United States shall have jurisdiction over any civil action brought by the United States to enforce the provisions of this section.

(d) Application- This section shall apply to any investigation, action, or proceeding that is pending on or commenced after the date of the enactment of the FISA Amendments Act of 2008. ***

Because of the special sensitivity of Congress towards surveillance of persons within the United States, the following provision was enacted:

SEC. 703. CERTAIN ACQUISITIONS INSIDE THE UNITED STATES TARGETING UNITED STATES PERSONS OUTSIDE THE UNITED STATES.

(a) Jurisdiction of the Foreign Intelligence Surveillance Court-

(1) IN GENERAL- The Foreign Intelligence Surveillance Court shall have jurisdiction to review an application and to enter an order approving the targeting of a United States person reasonably believed to be located outside the United States to acquire foreign intelligence information *** and such acquisition is conducted within the United States. ***

(b) Application-

(1) IN GENERAL- *** Each application *** shall include--

(A) the identity of the Federal officer making the application;

(B) the identity, *** or a description of the United States person who is the target ***;

(C) a statement of the facts and circumstances relied upon *** [that]the target *** is--

(i) a person reasonably believed to be located outside the United States; and

(ii) a foreign power, an agent of a foreign power, or an officer or employee of a foreign power;

(D) a statement of proposed minimization procedures ***;

(E) a description of the nature of the information sought and the type of communications or activities to be subjected to acquisition;

(F) a certification made by the Attorney General *** that--

(i) the certifying official deems the information sought to be foreign intelligence information;

(ii) a significant purpose of the acquisition is to obtain foreign intelligence information;

(iii) such information cannot reasonably be obtained by normal investigative techniques;

(iv) designates the type of foreign intelligence information being sought according to the categories described in section 101(e); and

(v) includes a statement of the basis for the certification that--

(I) the information sought is the type of foreign intelligence information designated; and

(II) such information cannot reasonably be obtained by normal investigative techniques;

(G) a summary statement of the means by which the acquisition will be conducted and whether physical entry is required to effect the acquisition;

(H) the identity of any electronic communication service provider necessary to effect the acquisition, provided that the application is not required to identify the specific facilities, places, premises, or property at which the acquisition authorized under this section will be directed or conducted;

(I) a statement of the facts concerning any previous applications that have been made to any judge of the Foreign Intelligence Surveillance Court involving the United States person specified in the application and the action taken on each previous application; and

(J) a statement of the period of time for which the acquisition is required to be maintained, provided that such period of time shall not exceed 90 days per application. ***

Section 704 (a)(2) provides for discontinuance of surveillance if a person outside the United states "is reasonably believed to be in the United States" but that the surveillance may recommence when the person leaves the United States. Section 705 provides for joint applications when one target is inside and one outside the United States.

These new provisions, combined with the FISA provisions that apply to other electronic communications (e.g. of citizens within the United States), are said by the FISAAA to be "the exclusive means by which electronic surveillance and the interception of domestic wire, oral, or electronic communications may be conducted."

Finally, some definitions were expanded to deal with terrorist organizations. For example, the FISA definition of Foreign Power was expanded in section 110 (a)(1) to include "an entity not substantially composed of United States persons that is engaged in the international proliferation of weapons of mass destruction" and the definition of Agent of a Foreign Power was expanded in 110(a)(2)(C) to include one who "engages in the international proliferation of weapons of mass destruction, or activities in preparation therefore; or engages in the international proliferation of weapons of mass destruction, or activities in preparation therefore for or on behalf of a foreign power." More generally, the statute was expanded by striking `sabotage or international terrorism' and inserting `sabotage, international terrorism, or the international proliferation of weapons of mass destruction'.

Notes

1. **Telecommunications Carriers.** The immunity of telecommunications carriers was a major stumbling block to passage of the Amendments. Who won, the Bush Administration or Congressional Democrats (who wanted to grant no immunity)? Why would this issue be such a problem to either the administration or Congressional Democrats? Is there any constitutional issue about the retroactive immunity granted to the carriers?

2. **Changes.** Note any provisions that you think are less protective of the privacy of the person whose communications are intercepted than existed under FISA or the privacy available when a search is conducted in accordance with the Fourth Amendment for ordinary law enforcement purposes.

3. **ACLU Participation.** The ACLU sought permission of the FISA Court to present its views on the FISA Amendments amicus curiae in connection with pending requests for intercept authorization, arguing that, unless it is allowed to participate, the court will not hear an important perspective on the Amendments. If you were on the FISA Court, would you allow the ACLU to present its views? Explain. The ACLU takes the position on the merits that the Amendments violate the Fourth Amendment. What do you think is the proper resolution of this issue?

4. **Federalism.** Does the preemption provision of Section 803 withstand a Tenth Amendment attack? One court found the Tenth Amendment argument unpersuasive:

> The court agrees with the United States: section 803 does not violate the Tenth Amendment because it does not "commandeer" state officials; rather, it prohibits them from investigating certain activities initiated by federal agencies that are "element[s] of the intelligence community." Because intelligence activities in furtherance of national security goals are primarily the province of the federal government, Congressional action preempting state activities in this context is especially uncontroversial from the standpoint of federalism.

In re NATIONAL SECURITY AGENCY TELECOMMUNICATIONS RECORDS LITIGATION, 633 F. Supp 2d 949 (N.D. Cal., June 3, 2009)

5. The FISCR's view of the Constitutionality of the FISAA. The court which decided the *Mayfield* case would a *fortiori* consider the FISAA unconstitutional. Do you see why? But the FISCR, which decided *In re Sealed Case*, might well reach a contrary conclusion. Does this mean that the prospects for implementation of the FISAAA are dependent on the forum? Which forum is the more important, the forum that authorizes surveillance or the forum that deals with criminal prosecutions based on evidence acquired from surveillance?

6. The Future of FISA? Assistant Attorney General David S. Kris, in Chapter VII, "Modernizing FISA: Progress to Date and Work Still to Come," in INSTITUTIONALIZING COUNTERTERRORISM: A REVIEW OF LEGISLATING THE WAR ON TERROR: AN AGENDA FOR REFORM, Edited by Benjamin Wittes (2009) argues that the 2008 FISA amendments, designed to deal with new technologies, do not end the need for more Congressional changes. Here is a concise summary of Kris' argument:

> Kris believes that the F[IS]AA does not represent the endgame for amendments to foreign intelligence surveillance authorities. *** [I]t is possible in the long run "to imagine" a framework of only two major national security-oriented collection statutes: one to replace the varying laws gocverning national security letters, FISA pen registers and trap-and-trace devices, mail cover regulations, and Patriot Act business records and authorities; and one governing the "acquisition of information for which a warrant would be required if undertaken for law enforcement purposes in the United States," which would treat physical and electronic [intelligence] searches similarly.

Adam R. Perlman, review of INSTITUTIONALIZING COUNTERTERRORISM: A REVIEW OF LEGISLATING THE WAR ON TERROR: AN AGENDA FOR REFORM, Edited by Benjamin Wittes (2009), *Engage*: Volume 11, Issue 3, p. 112, available at http://ssrn.com/abstract=1719650. Do you agree with Kris?

C. FOREIGN INTELLIGENCE LAW TODAY

1. CONSTITUTIONALITY OF SURVEILLANCE OUTSIDE FISA

Despite the notoriety of the Bush Administration's TSP surveillance, no cases resolved its constitutionality. In *ACLU v. NSA*, 438 F. Supp. 2d 754 (E.D. Mich, 2006), a district judge held this program unlawful under the Fourth and First Amendments, did not fit within the realm of exclusive executive power, and was in violation of the exclusive provisions of FISA. The Sixth Circuit reversed, ducking the substantive question. The second case in this section considers the constitutionality of the interim legislation preceding the FISAA.

ACLU v. NSA
493 F.3d 644 (C.A.6 2007)

ALICE M. BATCHELDER, Circuit Judge.

***The plaintiffs in this action include journalists, academics, and lawyers who regularly communicate with individuals located overseas, who the plaintiffs believe are the types of people the NSA suspects of being al Qaeda terrorists, affiliates, or supporters, and are therefore likely to be monitored under the TSP. From this suspicion, and the limited factual foundation in this case, the plaintiffs allege that they have a "well founded belief" that their communications are being tapped. According to the plaintiffs, the NSA's operation of the TSP-and the possibility of warrantless surveillance-subjects them to conditions that constitute an irreparable harm. ***

The NSA had invoked the State Secrets Doctrine to bar the discovery or admission of evidence that would "expose [confidential] matters which, in the interest of national security, should not be divulged." *See United States v. Reynolds,* 345 U.S. 1 (1953). The NSA argued that, without the privileged information, none of the named plaintiffs could establish standing. The district court applied the state secrets privilege, but rejected the NSA's argument, holding instead that three publicly acknowledged facts about the TSP-(1) it eavesdrops, (2) without warrants, (3) on international telephone and email communications in which at least one of the parties is a suspected al Qaeda affiliate-were sufficient to establish standing. Moreover, the district court found these three facts sufficient to grant summary judgment to the plaintiffs on the merits of their claims, resulting in a declaratory judgment and the imposition of an injunction. These three facts constitute all the evidence in the record relating to the NSA's conduct under the TSP. *** [T]he district court construed the Fourth Amendment as an absolute rule that " requires prior warrants for any reasonable search," and announced that " searches conducted without prior approval by a judge or magistrate were per se unreasonable." ***

Notably, the plaintiffs do *not* allege as injury that they personally, either as individuals or associations, anticipate or fear any form of direct reprisal by the government (e.g., the NSA, the Justice Department, the Department of Homeland Security, etc.), such as criminal prosecution, deportation, administrative inquiry, civil litigation, or even public exposure. *** The plaintiffs' primary alleged injury *** is their inability to communicate with their overseas contacts by telephone or email due to their self-governing ethical obligations. Under this claim, the *immediate* injury results directly from the plaintiffs' own actions and decisions, based on (1) their subjective belief that the NSA might be intercepting their communications, and (2) the ethical requirements governing such circumstances, as dictated by their respective professional organizations or affiliations. *** The plaintiffs explain that they have an ethical duty to keep their communications confidential, which, under the circumstances, requires that they refrain from communicating with the overseas contacts by telephone or email, lest they violate that duty. *** The injury manifests itself in both a quantifiable way (as the added time and expense of traveling overseas) and a non-quantifiable way (as the incomplete or substandard performance of their professional responsibilities and obligations). *** The second alleged injury *** is the "chilling effect" on the overseas contacts' willingness to communicate with the plaintiffs by telephone or email. *** The plaintiffs' third alleged injury is the NSA's violation of their legitimate expectation of privacy in their overseas telephone and email communications. ***

***Because there is no evidence that any plaintiff's communications have ever been intercepted, and the state secrets privilege prevents discovery of such evidence, there is no proof that interception would be detrimental to the plaintiffs' contacts, and the anticipated harm is neither imminent nor concrete-it is hypothetical, conjectural, or speculative. Therefore, this harm cannot satisfy the "injury in fact" requirement of standing. Because the plaintiffs cannot avoid this shortcoming, they do not propose this harm-the harm that *causes* their refusal to communicate-as an "injury" that warrants redress. Instead, they propose the injuries that *result* from their refusal to communicate and those injuries do appear imminent and concrete. *** But, by proposing only injuries that *result* from this refusal to engage in communications (e.g., the inability to conduct their professions without added burden and expense), they attempt to supplant an insufficient, speculative injury with an injury that appears sufficiently imminent and concrete, but is only incidental to the alleged wrong (i.e., the NSA's conduct)-this is atypical and, as will be discussed, impermissible. ***

The plaintiffs allege that the NSA has, by conducting the warrantless wiretaps, violated the "plaintiffs' privacy rights guaranteed by the Fourth Amendment." *** The plaintiffs do not, and cannot, assert that any of their own communications have ever been intercepted. *** [I]t would be unprecedented for this court to find standing for plaintiffs to litigate a Fourth Amendment cause of action without any evidence that the plaintiffs themselves have been subjected to an illegal search or seizure. *** It is also unclear from the record whether the plaintiffs' or their contacts' refusal to communicate can fairly be traced to the President's authorization of an ambiguous warrantless wiretapping program, or if that same refusal would exist regardless of the authorization of the TSP. And any wiretap would be merely one component of counter-terrorist or military intelligence surveillance. ***

[FISA Claims] The Foreign Intelligence Surveillance Act of 1978 ("FISA"),-as the separate and distinct counterpart to Title III-governs the interception of electronic communications involving foreign intelligence information. FISA is fraught with detailed statutory definitions and is expressly limited, by its own terms, to situations in which the President has authorized "electronic surveillance," for the purposes of acquiring "foreign intelligence information." .

First, the surveillance in question must acquire "foreign intelligence information," which includes "information that relates to ... the ability of the United States to protect against ... international terrorism." In the present case, the NSA intercepts communications in which it has a *"reasonable basis* to conclude that one party to the communication is a member of al Qaeda, affiliated with al Qaeda, or a member of an organization affiliated with al Qaeda, or working in support of al Qaeda." The proclaimed purpose is to prevent future terrorist attacks, and thus the NSA's conduct satisfies this statutory requirement.

Next, the interception must occur by "electronic surveillance." *** "[E]lectronic surveillance" has a very particular, detailed meaning under FISA-a legal definition that requires careful consideration of numerous factors such as the types of communications acquired, the location of the parties to the acquired communications, the location where the acquisition occurred, the location of any surveillance, device, and the reasonableness of the parties' expectation of privacy. The plaintiffs have not shown, and cannot show, that the NSA's surveillance activities include the sort of conduct that would satisfy FISA's definition of "electronic surveillance," and the present record does not demonstrate that the NSA's conduct falls within FISA's definitions.

Finally, even assuming, *arguendo*, that FISA applies to the NSA's warrantless wiretapping, the plaintiffs cannot sustain a claim under FISA. FISA's civil suit provision permits an "aggrieved person" to bring a cause of action for a violation of that statute:

An *aggrieved person*, other than a foreign power or an agent of a foreign power, *** who has been subjected to an *electronic surveillance* or about whom information obtained by *electronic surveillance* of such person has been disclosed or used in violation of [50 U.S.C. § 1809] shall have a cause of action against any person who committed such violation ***.

There are at least three reasons why the plaintiffs cannot maintain their claims under FISA's statutory authorization. First, the plaintiffs have not alleged, and the record does not contain sufficient facts from which to conclude, that they are "aggrieved persons." FISA defines an "aggrieved person" as "a person who is the target of an electronic surveillance or any other person whose communications or activities were subject to electronic surveillance." *** The plaintiffs have not shown that they were actually the target of, or subject to, the NSA's surveillance; thus-for the same reason they could not maintain their Fourth Amendment claim-they cannot establish that they are "aggrieved persons" under FISA's statutory scheme. Second, as previously discussed, the plaintiffs have not demonstrated that the NSA's wiretapping satisfies the statutory definition of "electronic surveillance," which is also required by FISA's liability provision. Third, FISA does not authorize the declaratory or injunctive relief sought by the plaintiffs, but allows only for the recovery of money damages. No matter how these claims are characterized, the plaintiffs have not asserted a viable FISA cause of action. ***

JULIA SMITH GIBBONS, Circuit Judge, concurring.

The disposition of all of the plaintiffs' claims depends upon the single fact that the plaintiffs have failed to provide evidence that they are personally subject to the TSP. Without this evidence, on a motion for summary judgment, the plaintiffs cannot establish standing for any of their claims, constitutional or statutory. ***

RONALD LEE GILMAN, Circuit Judge, dissenting.

***I am persuaded that the TSP as originally implemented violated the Foreign Intelligence Surveillance Act of 1978 (FISA). *** [Judge Gilman first finds that the Plaintiffs have standing to pursue their FISA claim.] *** Mootness became an issue in this case in January of 2007, when the government publicly announced that a judge of the Foreign Intelligence Surveillance Court had issued orders authorizing the government to conduct electronic surveillance of "international communications into or out of the United States where there is probable cause to believe" that one party to the communication is "a member or agent of al Qaeda or an associated terrorist organization."

As a result of these orders, electronic surveillance that had been occurring under the TSP "will now be conducted subject to the approval" of the FISC, and "the President has determined not to reauthorize" the TSP. The government, in short, decided to voluntarily cease electronic surveillance of international communications in this country outside of FISA. *** The government urges us to find that there is "no longer any live genuine controversy to adjudicate" because the TSP ceased to exist when the President's last authorization for it expired, thus resolving and mooting the plaintiffs' claims. But the government continues to assert that the TSP did not violate the Constitution or any federal statute prior to the January 2007 FISC orders. *** I conclude that this case is not moot and that this court may properly continue to exercise jurisdiction over it. [Judge Gilman proceeds to the merits, an excerpt of which is presented supra at pp. 171-72.]

Notes

1. A Better Case?   An article by Adam Liptak, "Spying Program May Be Tested by Terror Case," NEW YORK TIMES 8/26/2007, discusses a pending case which might allow further scrutiny of the TSP program.

> After a bloody raid by American military forces on an enemy camp in Rawah, Iraq, on June 11, 2003, a Defense Department report took inventory. Eighty suspected terrorists killed. An enormous weapons cache recovered. And, in what the report called "pocket litter," a notebook with the name and phone number of the imam [Yassim M Aref] of a mosque halfway around the world, here in the state capital [Albany, NY]. *** [T]he Federal Bureau of Investigation quickly began a sting operation aimed at Mr. Aref. Federal agents used an informant with a long history of fraud who spun tales to Mr. Aref about a fictitious plot involving shoulder-launched missiles and the assassination of a Pakistani diplomat in New York. Mr. Aref and a friend who owned a pizzeria were convicted of supporting terrorism *** Lawyers for Mr. Aref say they have proof that he was subjected to illegal surveillance by the National Security Agency, pointing to a classified order from the trial judge,

unusual testimony from an F.B.I. agent and court documents concerning the calls to Syria. *** Unlike earlier and pending appeals disputing the program, *** Mr. Aref's challenge can draw on the constitutional protections available to criminal defendants. *** Before the trial, Mr. Aref's lawyers asked the government for information about the N.S.A. surveillance reported in The Times. In March 2006, the government responded to one request with a classified filing that the defense lawyers, who had security clearances, were not allowed to see. That same day, Judge Thomas J. McAvoy denied the defense request in a classified order. ***

2. Judicial Review by Service Providers. The NSA surveillance program operated through an intermediary, the service provider (e.g. the telephone or cable company providing the service for the person subject to surveillance). Suppose such a service provider, rather than intercepting communications at the request of the Bush Administration, took the position that such interceptions violated the Fourth Amendment. Would the Fourth Amendment be implicated if the private companies did the interceptions? Wouldn't the fact that the administration pressured such companies to engage in the surveillance trigger the Fourth Amendment? The following excerpt concerning a challenge to amendments to FISA enacted in 2008 to establish new procedures in place of the TSP program, indicates that such companies might have standing. *In re Directives Pursuant to Section 105B of the Foreign Intelligence Surveillance Act,* 551 F. 3d 1004 (FISCR 2008).

> The FISC determined that the petitioner had standing to mount a challenge to the legality of the directives based on the Fourth Amendment rights of third-party customers. At first blush, this has a counter-intuitive ring: it is common ground that litigants ordinarily cannot bring suit to vindicate the rights of third parties. But that prudential limitation may in particular cases be relaxed by congressional action. *** Here, the petitioner easily exceeds the constitutional threshold for standing. It faces an injury in the nature of the burden that it must shoulder to facilitate the Government's surveillances of its customers; that injury is obviously and indisputably caused by the government through the directives; and this court is capable of redressing the injury. *** The PAA [amending FISA] expressly declares that a service provider that has received a directive "may challenge the legality of that directive," and "may file a petition with the Court of Review" for relief from an adverse FISC decision, There are a variety of ways in which a directive could be unlawful, and the PAA does nothing to circumscribe the types of claims of illegality that can be brought. We think that the language is broad enough to permit a service provider to bring a constitutional challenge to the legality of a directive regardless of whether the provider or one of its customers suffers the infringement that makes the directive unlawful. The short of it is that the PAA grants an aggrieved service provider a right of action and extends that right to encompass claims brought by it on the basis of customers' rights. *** Thus, the petitioner's Fourth Amendment

claim on behalf of its customers falls within the ambit of the statutory provision. It follows inexorably that the petitioner has standing to maintain this litigation.

3. **Kenyan Surveillance.** *In re TERRORIST BOMBINGS OF U.S. EMBASSIES IN EAST AFRICA,* supra Chapter III. The Second Circuit, mentions that there was not only a physical search in Kenya but also electronic surveillance. Does this mean that the Second Circuit would have no trouble finding TSP, PAA, and FISAAA electronic surveillance to be constitutional?

In re DIRECTIVES [redacted text] * PURSUANT TO SECTION 105B FISA
551 F. 3d 1004 (FISCR 2008)

SELYA, Chief Judge.

This petition for review stems from directives issued to the petitioner [redacted text] pursuant to a now-expired set of amendments to the Foreign Intelligence Surveillance Act of 1978 (FISA). Among other things, those amendments, known as the Protect America Act of 2007 (PAA), authorized the United States to direct communications service providers to assist it in acquiring foreign intelligence when those acquisitions targeted third persons (such as the service provider's customers) reasonably believed to be located outside the United States. Having received [redacted text] such directives, the petitioner challenged their legality before the Foreign Intelligence Surveillance Court (FISC). When that court found the directives lawful and compelled obedience to them, the petitioner brought this petition for review. ***

On August 5, 2007, Congress enacted the PAA as a measured expansion of FISA's scope. Subject to certain conditions, the PAA allowed the government to conduct warrantless foreign intelligence surveillance on targets (including United States persons) "reasonably believed" to be located outside the United States. This proviso is of critical importance here.

Under the new statute, the Director of National Intelligence (DNI) and the Attorney General (AG) were permitted to authorize, for periods of up to one year, "the acquisition of foreign intelligence information concerning persons reasonably believed to be outside the United States" if they determined that the acquisition met five specified criteria. These criteria included (i) that reasonable procedures were in place to ensure that the targeted person was reasonably believed to be located outside the United States; (ii) that the acquisitions did not constitute electronic surveillance;[2] (iii) that the surveillance would involve the assistance of a communications service provider; (iv) that a significant purpose of the surveillance was to obtain foreign intelligence information; and (v) that minimization procedures in place met the requirements ***. Except in limited circumstances (not

---

[*] The text and footnotes *** redacted from this opinion contain classified information.

[2] The PAA specifically stated, however, that "[n]othing in the definition of electronic surveillance *** shall be construed to encompass surveillance directed at a person reasonably believed to be located outside of the United States."

relevant here), this multi-part determination was required to be made in the form of a written certification "supported as appropriate by affidavit of appropriate officials in the national security field." Pursuant to this authorization, the DNI and the AG were allowed to issue directives to "person[s]"-a term that includes agents of communications service providers-delineating the assistance needed to acquire the information.

The PAA was a stopgap measure. By its terms, it sunset on February 16, 2008. Following a lengthy interregnum, the lapsed provisions were repealed on July 10, 2008, through the instrumentality of the FISA Amendments Act of 2008. But because the certifications and directives involved in the instant case were issued during the short shelf life of the PAA, they remained in effect. We therefore assess the validity of the actions at issue here through the prism of the PAA. [redacted text]

Beginning in [redacted text] 2007, the government issued directives to the petitioner commanding it to assist in warrantless surveillance of certain customers [redacted text and footnote]. These directives were issued pursuant to certifications that purported to contain all the information required by the PAA. *** [T]he certifications permit surveillances conducted to obtain foreign intelligence for national security purposes when those surveillances are directed against foreign powers or agents of foreign powers reasonably believed to be located outside the United States. ***

B. *The Fourth Amendment Challenge.*

***First, [petitioner] asserts that the government, in issuing the directives, had to abide by the requirements attendant to the Warrant Clause of the Fourth Amendment. Second, it argues that even if a foreign intelligence exception to the warrant requirements exists and excuses compliance with the Warrant Clause, the surveillances mandated by the directives are unreasonable and, therefore, violate the Fourth Amendment. ***

1. *The Nature of the Challenge.* As a threshold matter, the petitioner asserts that its Fourth Amendment arguments add up to a facial challenge to the PAA. *** We *** deem the petitioner's challenge an as-applied challenge and limit our analysis accordingly. This means that, to succeed, the petitioner must prove more than a theoretical risk that the PAA could on certain facts yield unconstitutional applications. Instead, it must persuade us that the PAA is unconstitutional as implemented here.

2. *The Foreign Intelligence Exception.* The recurrent theme permeating the petitioner's arguments is the notion that there is no foreign intelligence exception to the Fourth Amendment's Warrant Clause. *** While the *Sealed Case* court avoided an express holding that a foreign intelligence exception exists by assuming arguendo that whether or not the warrant requirements were met, the statute could survive on reasonableness grounds, we believe that [this] reading of that decision is plausible.

The petitioner argues correctly that the Supreme Court has not explicitly recognized such an exception; indeed, the Court reserved that question in *United States v. United States District Court (Keith)*, 407 U.S. 297 (1972). But the Court has recognized a comparable exception, outside the foreign intelligence context, in so-called "special needs" cases. In those cases, the Court excused compliance with the Warrant Clause when the purpose behind the governmental action went beyond routine law enforcement and insisting upon a warrant would materially interfere with the accomplishment of that purpose.

The question, then, is whether the reasoning of the special needs cases applies by analogy to justify a foreign intelligence exception to the warrant requirement for surveillance undertaken for national security purposes and directed at a foreign power or an agent of a foreign power reasonably believed to be located outside the United States. Applying principles derived from the special needs cases, we conclude that this type of foreign intelligence surveillance possesses characteristics that qualify it for such an exception.

For one thing, the purpose behind the surveillances ordered pursuant to the directives goes well beyond any garden-variety law enforcement objective. It involves the acquisition from overseas foreign agents of foreign intelligence to help protect national security. Moreover, this is the sort of situation in which the Government's interest is particularly intense.

The petitioner has a fallback position. Even if there is a narrow foreign intelligence exception, it asseverates, a definition of that exception should require the foreign intelligence purpose to be the primary purpose of the surveillance. For that proposition, it cites the Fourth Circuit's decision in *United States v. Truong Dinh Hung,* 629 F.2d 908, 915 (4th Cir.1980). That dog will not hunt.

This court previously has upheld as reasonable under the Fourth Amendment the Patriot Act's substitution of "a significant purpose" for the talismanic phrase "primary purpose." As we explained there, the Fourth Circuit's "primary purpose" language-from which the pre-Patriot Act interpretation of "purpose" derived-drew an "unstable, unrealistic, and confusing" line between foreign intelligence purposes and criminal investigation purposes. A surveillance with a foreign intelligence purpose often will have some ancillary criminal-law purpose. The prevention or apprehension of terrorism suspects, for instance, is inextricably intertwined with the national security concerns that are at the core of foreign intelligence collection. In our view the more appropriate consideration is the programmatic purpose of the surveillances and whether-as in the special needs cases-that programmatic purpose involves some legitimate objective beyond ordinary crime control.

Under this analysis, the surveillances authorized by the directives easily pass muster. Their stated purpose centers on garnering foreign intelligence. There is no indication that the collections of information are primarily related to ordinary criminal-law enforcement purposes. Without something more than a purely speculative set of imaginings, we cannot infer that the purpose of the directives (and, thus, of the surveillances) is other than their stated purpose.

We add, moreover, that there is a high degree of probability that requiring a warrant would hinder the Government's ability to collect time-sensitive information and, thus, would impede the vital national security interests that are at stake. *See, e.g., Truong Dinh Hung* (explaining that when the object of a surveillance is a foreign power or its collaborators, "the government has the greatest need for speed, stealth, and secrecy"). [redacted text] Compulsory compliance with the warrant requirement would introduce an element of delay, thus frustrating the Government's ability to collect information in a timely manner. [redacted text]

For these reasons, we hold that a foreign intelligence exception to the Fourth Amendment's warrant requirement exists when surveillance is conducted to obtain foreign intelligence for national security purposes and is directed against foreign powers or agents of foreign powers reasonably believed to be located outside the United States.

3. *Reasonableness.* This holding does not grant the government carte blanche: even though the foreign intelligence exception applies in a given case, governmental action intruding on individual privacy interests must comport with the Fourth Amendment's reasonableness requirement. Thus, the question here reduces to whether the PAA, as applied through the directives, constitutes a sufficiently reasonable exercise of governmental power to satisfy the Fourth Amendment.

We begin with bedrock. The Fourth Amendment protects the right "to be secure ... against unreasonable searches and seizures." To determine the reasonableness of a particular governmental action, an inquiring court must consider the totality of the circumstances. *** The more important the Government's interest, the greater the intrusion that may be constitutionally tolerated. *** At the outset, we dispose of two straw men-arguments based on a misreading of our prior decision in *Sealed Case*. First, the petitioner Notes that we found relevant six factors contributing to the protection of individual privacy in the face of a governmental intrusion for national security purposes. *See In re Sealed Case,* 310 F.3d at 737-41 (contemplating prior judicial review, presence or absence of probable cause, particularity, necessity, duration, and minimization). *** In *Sealed Case,* we did not formulate a rigid six-factor test for reasonableness. That would be at odds with the totality of the circumstances test that must guide an analysis in the precincts patrolled by the Fourth Amendment. We merely indicated that the six enumerated factors were relevant under the circumstances of that case.

Second, the petitioner asserts that our *Sealed Case* decision stands for the proposition that, in order to gain constitutional approval, the PAA procedures must contain protections equivalent to the three principal warrant requirements: prior judicial review, probable cause, and particularity. That is incorrect. What we said there-and reiterate today-is that the more a set of procedures resembles those associated with the traditional warrant requirements, the more easily it can be determined that those procedures are within constitutional bounds. We therefore decline the petitioner's invitation to reincorporate into the foreign intelligence exception the same warrant requirements that we already have held inapplicable.

***[W]e turn to the petitioner's contention that the totality of the circumstances demands a finding of unreasonableness here. That contention boils down to *** the PAA lacks (i) a particularity requirement, (ii) a prior judicial review requirement for determining probable cause that a target is a foreign power or an agent of a foreign power, and (iii) any plausible proxies for the omitted protections. For good measure, the petitioner suggests that the PAA's lack of either a necessity requirement or a reasonable durational limit diminishes the overall reasonableness of surveillances conducted pursuant thereto.

The government rejoins that the PAA, as applied here, constitutes reasonable governmental action. It emphasizes both the protections spelled out in the PAA itself and those mandated under the certifications and directives. This matrix of safeguards comprises at least five components: targeting procedures, minimization procedures, a procedure to ensure that a significant purpose of a surveillance is to obtain foreign intelligence information, procedures incorporated through Executive Order 12333 § 2.5, and [redacted text] procedures [redacted text] outlined in an affidavit supporting the certifications.

The record supports the government. Notwithstanding the parade of horribles trotted out by the petitioner, it has presented no evidence of any actual harm, any egregious risk of error, or any broad potential for abuse in the circumstances of the instant case. Thus, assessing the intrusions at issue in light of the governmental interest at stake and the panoply of protections that are in place, we discern no principled basis for invalidating the PAA as applied here. ***

The petitioner's arguments about particularity and prior judicial review are defeated by the way in which the statute has been applied. When combined with the PAA's other protections, the [redacted text] procedures and the procedures incorporated through the Executive Order are constitutionally sufficient compensation for any encroachments.

The [redacted text] procedures [redacted text] are delineated in an ex parte appendix filed by the government. They also are described, albeit with greater generality, in the Government's brief. [redacted text] Although the PAA itself does not mandate a showing of particularity, this pre-surveillance procedure strikes us as analogous to and in conformity with the particularity showing contemplated by *Sealed Case*. [redacted text]

The procedures incorporated through section 2.5 of Executive Order 12333, made applicable to the surveillances through the certifications and directives, serve to allay the probable cause concern. That section states in relevant part:

> The Attorney General hereby is delegated the power to approve the use for intelligence purposes, within the United States or against a United States person abroad, of any technique for which a warrant would be required if undertaken for law enforcement purposes, provided that such techniques shall not be undertaken unless the Attorney General has determined in each case that there is *probable*

cause to believe that the technique is directed against *a foreign power or an agent of a foreign power.*

Thus, in order for the government to act upon the certifications, the AG first had to make a determination that probable cause existed to believe that the targeted person is a foreign power or an agent of a foreign power. Moreover, this determination was not made in a vacuum. The AG's decision was informed by the contents of an application made pursuant to Department of Defense (DOD) regulations. Those regulations required that the application include a statement of facts demonstrating both probable cause and necessity. They also required a statement of the period-not to exceed 90 days-during which the surveillance was thought to be required. [redacted text and footnote]

The petitioner's additional criticisms about the surveillances can be grouped into concerns about potential abuse of executive discretion and concerns about the risk of government error (including inadvertent or incidental collection of information from non-targeted United States persons). We address these groups of criticisms sequentially.

The petitioner suggests that, by placing discretion entirely in the hands of the Executive Branch without prior judicial involvement, the procedures cede to that Branch overly broad power that invites abuse. But this is little more than a lament about the risk that government officials will not operate in good faith. That sort of risk exists even when a warrant is required. In the absence of a showing of fraud or other misconduct by the affiant, the prosecutor, or the judge, a presumption of regularity traditionally attaches to the obtaining of a warrant.

Here-where an exception affords relief from the warrant requirement-common sense suggests that we import the same presumption. Once we have determined that protections sufficient to meet the Fourth Amendment's reasonableness requirement are in place, there is no justification for assuming, in the absence of evidence to that effect, that those prophylactic procedures have been implemented in bad faith.

Similarly, the fact that there is some potential for error is not a sufficient reason to invalidate the surveillances. [redacted text] Equally as important, some risk of error exists under the original FISA procedures-procedures that received our imprimatur in *Sealed Case,_* A prior judicial review process does not ensure that the types of errors complained of here [redacted text] would have been prevented.

It is also significant that effective minimization procedures are in place. These procedures serve as an additional backstop against identification errors as well as a means of reducing the impact of incidental intrusions into the privacy of non-targeted United States persons. The minimization procedures implemented here are almost identical to those used under FISA to ensure the curtailment of both mistaken and incidental acquisitions. These minimization procedures were upheld by the FISC in this case, and the petitioner stated at oral argument that it is not quarreling about minimization but, rather, about particularity. Thus, we see no reason to question the adequacy of the minimization protocol.

The petitioner's concern with incidental collections is overblown. It is settled beyond peradventure that incidental collections occurring as a result of constitutionally permissible acquisitions do not render those acquisitions unlawful.[9] The government assures us that it does not maintain a database of incidentally collected information from non-targeted United States persons, and there is no evidence to the contrary. On these facts, incidentally collected communications of non-targeted United States persons do not violate the Fourth Amendment. To the extent that the petitioner may be concerned about the adequacy of the targeting procedures, *** those procedures include provisions designed to prevent errors. [redacted text] Furthermore, a PAA provision *** requires the AG and the DNI to assess compliance with those procedures and to report to Congress semi-annually.

4. *A Parting Shot.* The petitioner fires a parting shot. It presented for the first time at oral argument a specific privacy concern that could possibly arise under the directives. *** [T]he petitioner is firing blanks: no issue falling within this description has arisen to date. Were such an issue to arise, there are safeguards in place that may meet the reasonableness standard. We do, however, direct the government promptly to notify the petitioner if this issue arises under the directives. *** We discuss with greater specificity the petitioner's argument, the Government's safeguards, and our order in the classified version of this opinion.

5. *Recapitulation.* After assessing the prophylactic procedures applicable here, including the provisions of the PAA, the affidavits supporting the certifications, section 2.5 of Executive Order 12333, and the declaration mentioned above, we conclude that they are very much in tune with the considerations discussed in *Sealed Case.* Collectively, these procedures require a showing of particularity, a meaningful probable cause determination, and a showing of necessity. They also require a durational limit not to exceed 90 days-an interval that we previously found reasonable. Finally, the risks of error and abuse are within acceptable limits and effective minimization procedures are in place.

Balancing these findings against the vital nature of the Government's national security interest and the manner of the intrusion, we hold that the surveillances at issue satisfy the Fourth Amendment's reasonableness requirement. *** Our government is tasked with protecting an interest of utmost significance to the nation-the safety and security of its people. But the Constitution is the cornerstone of our freedoms, and government cannot unilaterally sacrifice constitutional rights on the altar of national security. Thus, in carrying out its national security mission, the government must simultaneously fulfill its constitutional responsibility to provide reasonable

---

[9] The petitioner has not charged that the Executive Branch is surveilling overseas persons in order *intentionally* to surveil persons in the United States. Because the issue is not before us, we do not pass on the legitimacy vel non of such a practice.

protections for the privacy of United States persons. The judiciary's duty is to hold that delicate balance steady and true. *** [O]ur decision does not constitute an endorsement of broad-based, indiscriminate executive power. Rather, our decision recognizes that where the government has instituted several layers of serviceable safeguards to protect individuals against unwarranted harms and to minimize incidental intrusions, its efforts to protect national security should not be frustrated by the courts. This is such a case. ***

Notes

1. **Redactions.** Is the case readable with the redactions? What, if anything, is lost as a result of redactions?

2. **Balance.** Do you think the balance between national security and individual liberty is properly drawn? Argue both sides of this question.

3. **Notice Requirement.** The court Notes that FISA does not contain a provision requiring notification of affected parties when the search is electronic rather than physical. Why did Congress intentionally choose to omit this requirement? What's so different between electronic and physical searches that one requires notice and the other does not?

4. **Recording Retention.** FISA does not share Article III's requirement that recorded information be retained and stored for a fixed period. Indeed, FISA requires all recordings made in the course of surveillance to promptly be destroyed because, as the court Notes, Congress believed this to be the best safeguard of individual privacy. Why is there a difference between the two statutes? If destruction serves privacy, what's the point of the recording retention requirement in Article III?

5. **Amicus Briefs.** Throughout the opinion, the court mentions arguments made by *amicus curiae* arguing on behalf of the two parties. Do you have any sense of who the parties are who wrote these amicus briefs? Which interest groups would have a stake in the plaintiff's victory? Who would want the U.S. government to win?

6. **Publication of the Opinion**. The opinion was not published until after the FISAA replaced the PAA. Why would the court delay publication until Congress had passed the permanent statute? Now that the FISC says the PAA was constitutional, what chance is there of any litigant challenging the FISAAA on similar grounds?

2. LITIGATION OF SURVEILLANCE CHALLENGES

Assuming that the FISA. PAA, and FISAAA are constitutional, the challenges to litigating electronic surveillance cases are substantial. The issue of standing to challenge surveillance is significant, as *ACLU v. NSA* proves. If your client thinks it has been the target of surveillance, could it seek documents showing surveillance through a Freedom of Information Act (FOIA) request? If your client was indicted by a grand jury based in part on electronic surveillance, could you obtain the relevant grand jury records concerning such surveillance? Assuming your client could somehow show that electronic surveillance led to his prosecution, an even more powerful barrier to litigation against the government would be the state secrets doctrine, pursuant to which cases may be dismissed for their potential to interfere with national security concerns. Here, in brief, is a presentation of surveillance litigation issues concerning (a) FOIA, and grand jury records, (b) standing, and (c) the relation between the electronic surveillance statutory framework and the common law state secrets doctrine.

******

FOIA and Grand Jury Records. FOIA is generally not of assistance to individuals who desire to find out whether they have been the targets of surveillance. This is because FOIA broadly exempts from disclosure records concerning (1) intra-agency communications, (2) law enforcement records, and (3) national security information. In *Electronic Frontier Foundation v. Office of the Dir. of Nat'l Intelligence,* 542 F.Supp.2d 1181, 1184 (N.D.Cal.2008) ("*EFF*") rev'd 595 F.3d 949 (C.A.9 2010), the District Court ordered disclosure under FOIA of a wide range of documents concerning meetings of telecommunications carriers with the NSA director's office personnel prior to passage of FISAAA. EFF was seeking, ultimately, to show that nefarious bargains were made between the Bush Administration and telecommunications carriers to exempt the carriers from liability for spying under the NSA program discussed in Section 2, *supra*. The Ninth Circuit reversed, noting that if any FOIA exemption applied, NSA was entitled to withhold the records. The Ninth Circuit remanded the case, instructing the district Court to consider further three exemptions. Here are the most significant parts of the opinion:

> FOIA Exemption 3 allows a responding agency to withhold information "specifically exempted from disclosure by statute." 5 U.S.C. § 552(b)(3). The government argues two statutes justify its withholdings: First, Section 103(c)(7) of the National Security Act of 1947, obligating the Director of National Intelligence to "protect intelligence sources and methods from unauthorized disclosure,"; and second, Section 6 of the National Security Agency Act of 1959, which prevents "disclosure of the organization or any function of the National Security Agency, or any information with respect to the activities thereof, or of the names, titles, salaries, or number of persons employed by such agency."

> Under these statutes and Exemption 3, the Government's summary judgment brief argued, "ODNI and DOJ withheld information that could reveal whether any particular telecommunications carrier has assisted, or may in the future assist, the government with intelligence activities." The government claimed disclosure "could deter telecommunications companies from assisting the government in the future," and disclosure "provides our adversaries with valuable information about our intelligence sources, methods, and capabilities."

The Government's argument was predicated on the following inference: Revealing the identity of carriers and their agents working for a carrier liability shield would allow foreign intelligence agents to determine contours of NSA intelligence operations, sources, and methods. In other words, knowledge of which firms were and were not lobbying for liability protection could lead to inferences regarding the firms that participate in the surveillance program. EFF disputes the propriety of this inference. However, because the district court did not address Exemption 3 due to confusion in the parties' summary judgment briefing, we remand for the district court to address these claims in the first instance. ***

If your client is being prosecuted for a federal crime, wiretap information on which the government intends to rely in a Grand Jury proceeding may be subject to a motin to suppress on the grounds that the wiretap was illegal under statute or unconstitutional under the Fourth Amendment. Supposing that the information was from electronic surveillance under FISA and the FISAAA, however, you are not entitled to such access, as the Fourth Circuit explained in *In re Grand Jury Subpoena (T-112)*, 597F.3d189 (C.A.4,2010):

*** FISA contains both a notice clause as well as an exclusionary procedure for illegally seized electronic surveillance. The notice clause requires the government to notify the subject of a wiretap before the government introduces "any information obtained or derived from an electronic surveillance." Similarly, FISA's exclusionary procedure allows a party aggrieved by allegedly unlawful "evidence obtained or derived from an electronic surveillance" to "move to suppress the evidence."

The list of legal proceedings at which those FISA sections apply is phrased very similarly to the domestic surveillance regulations of Title III of the Omnibus Crime Control and Safe Streets Act of 1968, but with one significant exception: FISA omits any reference to grand juries and legislative committees, while they are included in Title III. Thus FISA allows motions to suppress illegal wiretaps or the fruits thereof "before any court, department, officer, agency, regulatory body, or other authority," and FISA's notice provision contains an identically worded clause. In striking contrast, Section 2515 of Title III prohibits use of illegal wiretaps "before any court, *grand jury,* department, officer, agency, regulatory body, *legislative committee,* or other authority." *** The omission of grand juries from FISA's exclusionary and notice mandates is too pointed to be inadvertent, and too clear a recognition that, at least in the most critical area of foreign and national security surveillance, Congress did not seek to displace the historic grand jury investigatory norms [recognized in earlier case law]. *** Congress plainly wished to provide some limits on litigating foreign intelligence matters. The telling absence of grand juries *** allows the government to introduce FISA evidence at the grand jury stage without triggering notice procedures. *** There may be other places to litigate FISA surveillance, but Congress has made plain that grand juries are not among them. *** Nor is this result surprising. Congress has long recognized that a separate set of guidelines and rules are needed in the foreign intelligence context. *** Congress obviously desired in foreign intelligence to "[s]trik[e] a sound balance between the need for such surveillance and the protection of civil liberties." In light of the fact that Congress intended FISA to strike this balance, it is significant that grand juries were omitted from the legislation. ***

******

Standing. As you know from *ACLU v. NSA*, standing has generally been problematic for FISA claims. There is, however, one case in which limited standing has been granted under FISA and a more significant standing decision under the FISAAA (the FAA in that court's terminology). These cases follow.

In re: NSA TELECOMMUNICATIONS RECORDS LITIGATION

This order pertains to:
Al-Haramain Islamic Foundation v.Bush
595 F. Supp 2d 1077 (N.D. Calif 2009)

VAUGHN R. WALKER, Chief Judge.

***This court *** on July 2, 2008, issued a ruling that: (2) FISA did not appear to provide plaintiffs with a viable remedy unless they could show that they were "aggrieved persons" within the meaning of FISA. *** At issue on these cross-motions is the adequacy of the first amended complaint [FAC] to enable plaintiffs to proceed with their suit. ***[2] As with the original complaint, plaintiffs are the Al-Haramain Islamic Foundation, Inc, an Oregon non-profit corporation ("Al-Haramain Oregon"), and two of its individual attorneys, Wendell Belew and Asim Ghafoor, both United States citizens ("plaintiffs"). *** [P]laintiffs have greatly expanded their factual recitation, which now runs to ten pages, up from a little over one page detail[ing] a number of public pronouncements of government officials about the Terrorist Surveillance Project ("TSP") and its surveillance activities as well as events publicly known about the TSP including a much-publicized hospital room confrontation between former Attorney General John Ashcroft and then-

---

[2] These motions do not implicate the recent amendments to FISA enacted after the July 2 order (FISA Amendments Act of 2008 (FISAAA), enacted July 10, 2008).

White House counsel (later Attorney General) Alberto Gonzales.

Of more specific relevance to plaintiffs' effort to allege sufficient facts to establish their "aggrieved person" status, the FAC also recites a sequence of events pertaining directly to the Government's investigations of Al-Haramain Oregon. *** In addition to numerous documents drawn from United States government websites and the websites of news organizations, plaintiffs submit the sworn declarations of plaintiffs Wendell Belew and Asim Ghafoor attesting to the specifics and contents of the telephone conversations described in *** the FAC. *** To proceed with their FISA claim, plaintiffs must present to the court enough specifics based on non-classified evidence to establish their "aggrieved person" status under FISA. *** Defendants advance one apparently new argument in this regard: that the adjudication of "aggrieved person" status for any or all plaintiffs cannot be accomplished without revealing information protected by the state secrets privilege ("SSP"). This argument rests on the unsupported assertion that "[t]he Court cannot exercise jurisdiction based on anything less than the actual facts", presumably in contrast to *inferences* from other facts (on which defendants contend the FAC exclusively relies). Defendants' position boils down to this: only affirmative confirmation by the government or equally probative evidence will meet the "aggrieved person" test; the government is not required to confirm surveillance and the information is not otherwise available without invading the SSP. In Defendants' view, therefore, plaintiffs simply cannot proceed on their claim without the Government's active cooperation-and the government has evinced no intention of cooperating here.

Defendants' stance does not acknowledge the Court's ruling in the July 2, 2008 order that FISA "preempts" or displaces the SSP for matters within its purview and that, while obstacles abound, canons of construction require that the court avoid interpreting and applying FISA in a way that renders FISA *** superfluous. ***

Plaintiffs also point to the DC Circuit's recent decision in *In Re Sealed Case,* 494 F.3d 139 (D.C.Cir.2007), which reversed the district Court's dismissal of a *Bivens* action by a Drug Enforcement Agency employee based on the Government's assertion of the SSP. The district court had concluded that the plaintiff's unclassified allegations of electronic eavesdropping in violation of the Fourth Amendment were insufficient to establish a prima facie case. The DC Circuit upheld the dismissal as to a defendant called "Defendant II" of whom the court wrote "nothing about this person would be admissible in evidence at trial," but reversed the dismissal as to defendant Huddle, noting that although plaintiff's case "is premised on circumstantial evidence 'as in any lawsuit, the plaintiff may prove his case by direct or circumstantial evidence.'" Plaintiffs accordingly argue that circumstantial evidence of electronic surveillance should be sufficient to establish a prima facie case. The court agrees with plaintiffs that this approach comports with the intent of Congress in enacting FISA as well as concepts of due process which are especially challenging-but nonetheless especially important-to uphold in cases with national security implications and classified evidence.

Plaintiffs articulate their proposed standard, in summary, as follows:

"plaintiffs' burden of proving their 'aggrieved person' status is to produce unclassified prima facie evidence, direct and/or circumstantial, sufficient to raise a reasonable inference on a preponderance of the evidence that they were subjected to electronic surveillance." ***

Defendants summarize plaintiffs' allegations thusly, asserting that they are "obviously" insufficient "under any standard":

> the sum and substance of plaintiffs' factual allegations are that: (i) the [TSP] targeted communications with individuals reasonably believed to be associated with al Qaeda; (ii) in February 2004, the Government blocked the assets of AHIF-Oregon based on its association with terrorist organizations; (iii) in March and April of 2004, plaintiffs Belew and Ghafoor talked on the phone with an officer of AHIF-Oregon in Saudi Arabia (Mr. al-Buthe [sic]) about, inter alia, persons linked to bin-Laden; (iv) in the September 2004 designation of AHIF-Oregon, [OFAC] cited the organization's direct links to bin-Laden as a basis for the designation; (v) the OFAC designation was based in part on classified evidence; and (vi) the FBI stated it had used surveillance in an investigation of the Al-Haramain Islamic Foundation. Plaintiffs specifically allege that interception of their conversations in March and April 2004 formed the basis of the September 2004 designation, and that any such interception was electronic surveillance as defined by the FISA conducted without a warrant under the TSP.

The court does not find fault with Defendants' summary but disagrees with Defendants' sense of the applicable legal standard. Defendants seem to agree that legislative history and precedents defining "aggrieved person" from the Title III context may be relevant to the FISA context, but argue that "Congress incorporated Article III standing requirements in any determination as to whether a party is an 'aggrieved person' under the FISA" and assert that "the relevant case law makes clear that Congress intended that 'aggrieved persons' would be solely those litigants that meet Article III standing requirements to pursue Fourth Amendment claims." Tellingly, defendants in their reply brief consistently refer to their motion as a "summary judgment motion" and argue that plaintiffs cannot sustain their burden on "summary judgment" based on the allegations of the FAC. Defendants are getting ahead of themselves.

Defendants attack plaintiffs' FAC by asserting that plaintiffs seek to proceed with the lawsuit based on "reasonable inferences" and "logical probabilities" but that they cannot avoid summary judgment because "their evidence does not actually establish that they were subject to the alleged warrantless surveillance that they challenge in this case." At oral argument, moreover, counsel for defendants contended that the only way a litigant can sufficiently establish aggrieved person status at the pleading stage is for the government to have admitted the unlawful surveillance. *** While the court is presented with a legal problem almost totally without directly relevant precedents, to find plaintiffs' showing inadequate would effectively render those provisions of FISA without effect, an outcome the court is required to attempt to avoid. ***

In their opposition, defendants do not fully engage with plaintiffs' motion, but rather seem to hold themselves aloof from it *** Defendants have not lodged classified declarations with their opposition as seems to be called for *** upon the filing of a motion or request by an aggrieved person. Defendants, rather, assert that

The discretion *** belongs to the Attorney General, and under the present circumstances-where there has been no final determination that those procedures apply in this case to overcome the Government's successful assertion of privilege and where serious harm to national security is at stake-the Attorney General has not done so. Section 1806(f) does not grant the Court jurisdiction to invoke those procedures on its own to decide a claim or grant a moving party access to classified information, and any such proceedings would raise would raise serious constitutional concerns.

***It appears from Defendants' response to plaintiffs' motion that defendants believe they can prevent the court from taking any action under 1806(f) by simply declining to act.

But the statute is more logically susceptible to another, plainer reading: the occurrence of the action by the Attorney General described in the clause beginning with "if" makes mandatory on the district court (as signaled by the verb "shall") the in camera/ex parte review provided for in the rest of the sentence. The non-occurrence of the Attorney General's action does not necessarily stop the process in its tracks as defendants seem to contend. Rather, a more plausible reading is that it leaves the court free to order discovery of the materials or information sought by the "aggrieved person" in whatever manner it deems consistent with section 1806(f)'s text and purpose. Nothing in the statute prohibits the court from exercising its discretion to conduct an in camera/ex parte review following the plaintiff's motion and entering other orders appropriate to advance the litigation if the Attorney General declines to act. ***

To be more specific, the court will review the Sealed Document ex parte and in camera. The court will then issue an order regarding whether plaintiffs may proceed-that is, whether the Sealed Document establishes that plaintiffs were subject to electronic surveillance not authorized by FISA. As the court understands its obligation with regard to classified materials, only by placing and maintaining some or all of its future orders in this case under seal may the court avoid indirectly disclosing some aspect of the Sealed Document's contents. Unless counsel for plaintiffs are granted access to the Court's rulings and, possibly, to at least some of Defendants' classified filings, however, the entire remaining course of this litigation will be *ex parte*. This outcome would deprive plaintiffs of due process to an extent inconsistent with Congress's purpose in enacting FISA ***. Accordingly, this order provides for members of plaintiffs' litigation team to obtain the security clearances necessary to be able to litigate the case, including, but not limited to, reading and responding to the Court's future orders. ***

Notes

1. Appeal. If you were the government, would you appeal? How far? "All the way to the Supreme Court"? Assess your chances of prevailing in light of the language and history of FISA challenges, including *ACLU v. NSA* and the various decisions of the FISCR.

2. *Ex Parte* and *In Camera* Review. The court in this case retains the right to review evidence from the government with only the government present and without any recording of the nature of evidence. Is this an acceptable compromise between the plaintiff's right to sue and the Government's national security interest? What are the problems with holding evidentiary hearings ex parte?

3. Attorney General's Discretion. The U.S. argues that the statute is worded such that any failure to act by the Attorney General will limit the ability for a court to examine evidence in the case. The court rejects this view and holds that the statute allows judicial discretion in holding *ex parte* and *in camera* proceedings. Based on what you know about constitutional law, would it ever be permissible to limit the Court's discretion in this way? What does Article III imply about Congress' ability to limit federal Court's jurisdiction?

4. Security Clearance. The court requires lawyers for the plaintiffs to obtain security clearance high enough to give them access to the secret government information that comprises the evidence in this case. What if the lawyer can't obtain such clearance?

AMNESTY INTERNATIONAL USA v. CLAPPER
__ F. 3d __, 2011 WL 941524 (C.A. 2, March 21, 2011)

GERARD E. LYNCH, Circuit Judge:

Attorneys, journalists, and labor, legal, media, and human rights organizations brought this action facially challenging the constitutionality of Section 702 of the Foreign Intelligence Surveillance Act of 1978 ("FISA"), which was added to FISA by Section 101(a)(2) of the FISA Amendments Act of 2008 (the "FAA") ***. Section 702 creates new procedures for authorizing government electronic surveillance targeting non-United States persons outside the United States for purposes of collecting foreign intelligence. The plaintiffs complain that the procedures violate the Fourth Amendment, the First Amendment, Article III of the Constitution, and the principle of separation of powers because they "allow[] the executive branch sweeping and virtually unregulated authority to monitor the international communications . . . of law-abiding U.S. citizens and residents." *** The *only* issue presented by this appeal is whether the plaintiffs are legally in a position to assert these claims in a federal court, not whether the claims are to any degree valid. *** The 2008 FAA amends FISA. It leaves much of the preexisting surveillance authorization procedure intact, but it creates new procedures for the authorization of foreign intelligence electronic surveillance targeting non-United States persons located outside the United States. The plaintiffs complain that the new procedures unlawfully permit broader collection of intelligence with less judicial oversight. ***

In practice, these new authorization procedures mean that surveillance orders can be significantly broader under the FAA than they previously could have been. Prior to the FAA, surveillance orders could only authorize the government to monitor specific individuals or facilities. Under the FAA, by contrast, the plaintiffs allege that an acquisition order could seek, for example, "[a]ll telephone and e-mail communications to and from countries of foreign policy interest -- for example, Russia, Venezuela, or Israel -- including communications made to and from U.S. citizens and residents." Moreover, the specific showing of probable cause previously required, and the requirement of judicial review of that showing, have been eliminated. *** An additional distinction concerns who monitors compliance with statutory limitations on the surveillance procedures. The preexisting FISA scheme allowed ongoing judicial review by the FISC. But under the FAA, the judiciary may not monitor compliance on an ongoing basis; the FISC may review the minimization procedures only prospectively, when the government seeks its initial surveillance authorization. Rather, the executive -- namely the AG and DNI -- bears the responsibility of monitoring ongoing compliance, and although the FISC receives the executive's reports, it cannot rely on them to alter or revoke its previous surveillance authorizations. ***

The plaintiffs sought a declaration that the FAA is unconstitutional. The government, in addition to defending the FAA's constitutionality on the merits, argued that the plaintiffs lacked standing to challenge the facial validity of the statute, contending that the Act could be challenged only by persons who had been electronically surveilled in accordance with its terms and the plaintiffs could not show that they had been so surveilled. The plaintiffs advanced what they characterized as two independent bases for standing to challenge the FAA's constitutionality: first, that they have an actual and well-founded fear that their communications will be monitored in the future; and, second, that in light of that fear they have taken costly and burdensome measures to protect the confidentiality of certain communications. *** The plaintiffs' evidence tended to show that their work "requires them to engage in sensitive and sometimes privileged telephone and e-mail communications with colleagues, clients, journalistic sources, witnesses, experts, foreign governmental officials, and victims of human rights abuses located outside the United States." The individuals with whom the plaintiffs communicate include "people the U.S. Government believes or believed to be associated with terrorist organizations," "political and human rights activists who oppose governments that are supported economically or militarily by the U.S. government," and "people located in geographic areas that are a special focus of the U.S. government's counterterrorism or diplomatic efforts."[11] *** The plaintiffs believe that, because of the nature of

---

[11] The plaintiffs submitted a number of declarations providing examples of such individuals: Attorney Scott McKay, for instance,communicates with his client Sami Omar Al-Hussayen, a Saudi Arabian resident who has faced criminal charges in connection with the September 11

their communications with these individuals, the communications will likely be "acquired, retained, analyzed, and disseminated" under the FAA.

Their fear of future surveillance, according to the plaintiffs, inflicts present injuries. For instance, in order to protect the confidentiality of sensitive and privileged communications the plaintiffs have "ceased engaging in certain conversations on the telephone and by e-mail," which, in turn, "compromises [their] ability to locate witnesses, cultivate sources, gather information, communicate confidential information to their clients, and to engage in other legitimate and constitutionally protected communications." In addition, the FAA has "force[d] plaintiffs to take costly and burdensome measures," such as traveling long distances to meet personally with individuals.

The attorney plaintiffs assert that they are obligated to take these measures in order to comply with their "ethical obligation to avoid communicating confidential information about client matters over telephone, fax, or e-mail if they have reason to believe that it is likely to be intercepted by others." *** The government did not submit any evidence of its own either in opposition to the plaintiffs' submissions, or in support of its own summary judgment motion. Additionally, at oral argument on the summary judgment motions, the government said it accepted the factual submissions of the plaintiffs as true for purposes of those motions. ***

Article III of the United States Constitution empowers federal courts to hear only "cases" and "controversies." *** The Supreme Court has said that "the irreducible constitutional minimum of standing contains three elements":

> First, the plaintiff must have suffered an injury in fact -- an invasion of a legally protected interest which is (a) concrete and particularized, and (b) actual or imminent, not conjectural or hypothetical. Second, there must be a causal connection between the injury and the conduct complained of -- the injury has to be fairly traceable to the challenged action of the defendant, and not the result of the independent action of some third party not before the court. Third, it must be likely, as opposed to merely speculative, that the injury will be redressed by a favorable decision.

---

terrorist attacks and is now a defendant in several related civil cases. McKay also helps represent Khalid Sheik Mohammed, who is being held at Guantanamo Bay for alleged acts of terrorism, and in the course of this representation McKay regularly communicates with Mohammed's family members, experts, and investigators around the world. Attorney Sylvia Royce represents Mohammedou Ould Salahi, a Mauritanian national and Guantanamo Bay prisoner, who allegedly acted as a liaison between al Qaeda and German Islamic radicals. Royce communicates information about Salahi's case with his brother in Germany, and with her Mauritanian and French co-counsel.

Lujan v. Defenders of Wildlife, 504 U.S. 555, 560-61 (1992). "The party invoking federal jurisdiction bears the burden of establishing these elements." ***

*** [T]he parties have focused on whether the plaintiffs' asserted injuries satisfy the injury-in-fact component of the standing inquiry. Although they are correct that the plaintiffs' *** possibility of being monitored in the future -- raises a question of injury in fact, because probabilistic injuries constitute injuries in fact only when they reach a certain threshold of likelihood, the plaintiffs' second asserted injury alleges the most mundane of injuries in fact: the expenditure of funds. The plaintiffs' declarations *** establish that they have already incurred professional and economic costs to avoid interception. *** Thus, we have little doubt that the plaintiffs have satisfied the injury-in-fact requirement. *** The plaintiffs must also prove that the injuries are caused by the challenged statute and that a favorable judgment would redress them. *** If the plaintiffs can show that it was not unreasonable for them to incur costs out of fear that the government will intercept their communications under the FAA, then the measures they took to avoid interception can support standing. If the possibility of interception is remote or fanciful, however, their present-injury theory fails because the plaintiffs would have no reasonable basis for fearing interception under the FAA, and they cannot bootstrap their way into standing by unreasonably incurring costs to avoid a merely speculative or highly unlikely potential harm. Any such costs would be gratuitous, and any ethical concerns about not taking those measures would be unfounded. *** Here, the plaintiffs' actions were "fairly traceable" to the FAA. *** [T]he professional and economic harms the plaintiffs suffered here were fairly traceable to the FAA, and were not the result of an "unreasonable decision" on their part "to bring about a harm that [they] knew to be avoidable."

In addition to their present-injury theory, the plaintiffs advance a future-injury theory of standing. A future injury or threat of injury does not confer standing if it is "conjectural or hypothetical" and not "real and immediate." To determine whether the plaintiffs have standing under their future-injury theory, we would need to determine whether the FAA creates an objectively reasonable likelihood that the plaintiffs' communications are being or will be monitored under the FAA. As noted above, we conclude that the future injuries alleged by the plaintiffs are indeed sufficiently likely to confer standing under the test established in the case law for basing standing on the risk of future harm.

The government's first argument against the plaintiffs' standing -- on both theories -- is that the FAA does not create a sufficiently high likelihood that those communications will be monitored. In our judgment, however, *** the plaintiffs have established that they reasonably fear being monitored under the allegedly unconstitutional FAA, and that they have undertaken costly measures to avoid it. Those present injuries -- fairly traceable to the FAA and likely to be redressable by a favorable judgment -- support the plaintiffs' standing to challenge the statute.

The government next argues that the plaintiffs lack standing because any injury they suffer is indirect. That is, the government contends that because the FAA does not directly target the plaintiffs, any injury the plaintiffs suffer is a result of their reaction to the government's potential monitoring of third parties. The government essentially argues that this indirectness defeats the plaintiffs' standing because it attenuates the causal chain linking the plaintiffs' injuries to the FAA. *** [W]e disagree.*** The plaintiffs need not show that they have been or certainly will be monitored. *** When a plaintiff asserts a *present* injury based on conduct taken in anticipation of *future* government action, we evaluate the likelihood that the future action will in fact come to pass. ***

Assessing whether a threatened injury, by itself, is sufficiently probable to support standing is a "qualitative, not quantitative" inquiry that is "highly case-specific." *** One factor that bolsters a plaintiff's argument that the injury is likely to come to pass *** is the existence of a policy that authorizes the potentially harmful conduct. However, the cases do not establish any talismanic, dispositive facts a plaintiff must plead in order to establish a certain threshold of probability. Some cases suggest that the risk of that harm need not be particularly high. See *Massachusetts v. EPA,* 549 U.S. 497, 525 n.23 (2007). The probability required "logically varies with the severity of the probable harm." Ultimately, courts consider the totality of the circumstances, and where a "plaintiff's interpretation of a statute is 'reasonable enough' and under that interpretation the plaintiff 'may legitimately fear that it will face enforcement of the statute,' then the plaintiff has standing to challenge the statute." ***

The plaintiffs *** have asserted that the FAA permits broad monitoring through mass surveillance orders that authorize the government to collect thousands or millions of communications, including communications between the plaintiffs and their overseas contacts. The FAA is susceptible to such an interpretation, and the government has not controverted this interpretation or offered a more compelling one. *** Here, the fact that the government has authorized the potentially harmful conduct means that the plaintiffs can reasonably assume that government officials will actually engage in that conduct by carrying out the authorized surveillance. It is fanciful, moreover, to question whether the government will ever undertake broad-based surveillance of the type authorized by the statute. The FAA was passed specifically to permit surveillance that was not permitted by FISA but that was believed necessary to protect the national security. That both the Executive and the Legislative branches of government believe that the FAA authorizes new types of surveillance, and have justified that new authorization as necessary to protecting the nation against attack, makes it extremely likely that such surveillance will occur.

Furthermore, the plaintiffs have good reason to believe that their communications, in particular, will fall within the scope of the broad surveillance that they can assume the government will conduct. *** Conferring standing on these plaintiffs is not tantamount to conferring standing on "any or all citizens who no more than assert that certain practices of law enforcement offices are unconstitutional." Most law abiding citizens have no occasion to communicate with suspected terrorists; relatively few Americans have occasion to engage in international communications relevant to "foreign intelligence." These plaintiffs however, have successfully demonstrated that their legitimate professions make it quite likely that their communications will be intercepted if the government -- as seems inevitable -- exercises the authority granted by the FAA.

The government argues the plaintiffs have failed to establish standing because the FAA does not itself authorize surveillance, but only authorizes the FISC to authorize surveillance. As a result, the government says the plaintiffs must speculate about at least two intervening steps between the FAA and any harm they might suffer as a result of the government conducting surveillance: first, that the government will apply for surveillance authorization under the FAA, and, second, that the FISC will grant authorization.

But this argument fails. *** With respect to the first step *** it is more than reasonable to expect that the government will seek surveillance authorization under the FAA. We therefore cannot say that uncertainty about this step significantly attenuates the link between the FAA and the plaintiffs' harms.

Nor does the second intervening step add significant uncertainty. As discussed above, under the FAA the FISC must enter an order authorizing surveillance if the government submits a certification that conforms to the statutory requirements. The FAA does not require or even permit the FISC to make an independent determination of the necessity or justification for the surveillance. It verges on the fanciful to suggest that the government will more than rarely fail to comply with the formal requirements of the FAA once it has decided that the surveillance is warranted.

Empirical evidence supports this expectation: in 2008, the government sought 2,082 surveillance orders, and the FISC approved 2,081 of them. We do not know how many of these applications, if any, came after the FAA was enacted on July 10, 2008. At the very least, though, the evidence does not show that the FISC actually rejects a significant number of applications for FAA surveillance orders.[23] Without a stronger showing that the FISC interposes a significant intervening step, we cannot find that the mere existence of this intervening step prevents the plaintiffs from obtaining standing to challenge the FAA.

---

[23] Moreover, under the FAA the government can often conduct surveillance without FISC authorization. In exigent circumstances, for example, the government may start wiretapping before applying for FISC authorization, so long as the government applies for authorization within 7 days. In addition, if the FISC denies any application for a surveillance order, the government may conduct the applied-for surveillance while it appeals the FISC denial.

Because the plaintiffs' undisputed testimony clearly establishes that they are suffering injuries in fact, and because we find those injuries are causally connected to the FAA -- because they are taken in anticipation of future government action that is reasonably likely to occur -- and are redressable by a favorable judgment,[24] we find the plaintiffs have standing.

The plaintiffs' asserted economic and professional costs incurred to protect the confidentiality of their communications can be characterized as indirect injuries, because the FAA does not target the plaintiffs themselves and the plaintiffs incur injuries due to their responses, and the responses of the third-party individuals with whom they communicate, to the anticipated FAA-authorized surveillance of those individuals. The government argues that the indirectness of these injuries defeats the plaintiffs' standing. We disagree. *** [Though it is] "ordinarily substantially more difficult" to establish standing based on indirect injuries than on direct injuries *** plaintiffs have satisfied these requirements through their uncontroverted testimony that they have altered their conduct and thereby incurred specific costs in response to the FAA. *** The heart of the government's challenge to the plaintiffs' standing based on the indirectness of their injury -- much like the government's challenge to the plaintiffs' standing based on the likelihood of future injury -- goes to whether the plaintiffs' injuries are causally connected to the challenged legislation. The causal chain linking the plaintiffs' indirect injuries to the challenged legislation is similar to that discussed above: it turns on the likelihood that the plaintiffs' communications with the regulated third parties will be monitored. ***

The Supreme Court and this Court have frequently found standing on the part of plaintiffs who were not directly subject to a statute, and asserted only indirect injuries. *** [I]n *Friends of the Earth v. Laidlaw*, the Supreme Court recognized plaintiffs' standing to challenge a corporation's alleged Clean Water Act violation. The plaintiffs did not claim that the defendant took direct actions against them. Instead, they showed that because they feared exposure to the defendant's pollution they had ceased to engage in certain recreational activities in the area, such as swimming, camping, and birdwatching. *Friends of the Earth*, 528 U.S. at 181-82. The Court found that the plaintiffs' decision to curtail those activities was "enough for injury in fact," and found that the plaintiffs' reactions were reasonable responses to the threat of exposure to pollution. ***

Since it is reasonable for the plaintiffs to seek to avoid being monitored, we must consider whether the particular measures they took were reasonable. They were. In some instances the plaintiffs did not communicate

---

[24] Neither the district court nor the parties discuss the third constitutional standing requirement -- redressability -- in any depth. *** The plaintiffs have established that the relief they seek would redress their asserted injuries in fact, because their injuries stem from their reasonable fear of being monitored by FAA-authorized government surveillance, and if a court grants their requested relief -- an injunction prohibiting the government from conducting surveillance under the FAA -- the feared surveillance would no longer be permitted and therefore would, presumably, no longer be carried out.

certain information they otherwise would have communicated by e-mail or telephone; and in other instances they incurred the costly burdens of traveling to communicate or to obtain that information in person rather than electronically. These are not overreactions to the FAA; they are appropriate measures that a reasonably prudent person who plausibly anticipates that his conversations are likely to be monitored, and who finds it important to avoid such monitoring, would take to avoid being overheard. The plaintiffs have therefore established that those injuries are linked to the statute they challenge.

In sum, the FAA has put the plaintiffs in a lose-lose situation: either they can continue to communicate sensitive information electronically and bear a substantial risk of being monitored under a statute they allege to be unconstitutional, or they can incur financial and professional costs to avoid being monitored. Either way, the FAA directly affects them. ***

The government's principal arguments against the above analysis rest on a single case, *Laird v. Tatum,* 408 U.S. 1 (1972). *Laird* is unquestionably relevant to this case, as it is the only case in which the Supreme Court specifically addressed standing to challenge a government surveillance program. Because *Laird* significantly differs from the present case, however, we disagree with the government's contention that *Laird* controls the instant case, and that *Laird* created different and stricter standing requirements for surveillance cases than for other types of cases.

In *Laird*, the plaintiffs challenged a surveillance program that authorized the Army to collect, analyze, and disseminate information about public activities that had potential to create civil disorder. The Army collected its data from a number of sources, but most of it came from "the news media and publications in general circulation" or from "agents who attended meetings that were open to the public and who wrote field reports describing the meetings." The Court noted that the court of appeals had characterized the information gathered as "nothing more than a good newspaper reporter would be able to gather by attendance at public meetings and the clipping of articles from publications available on any newsstand." Roughly sixty government agents around the country participated in the surveillance program. *** The Court denied plaintiffs standing. It held that the plaintiffs' complaints about "the very existence of the Army's data-gathering system" and their "[a]llegations of a subjective 'chill' are not an adequate substitute for a claim of specific present objective harm or a threat of specific future harm." *** The government argues that "[t]his case is directly governed by *Laird*," because the only specific present harms the plaintiffs allege flow from a subjective chill. *Laird*, however, differs dramatically from this case.

In *Laird*, the plaintiffs did not clearly allege any injuries whatsoever. They did not claim that the government surveillance they sought to challenge, which relied principally on monitoring through publicly available sources activities conducted entirely in public, harmed them. They did not claim that they, or anyone with whom they regularly interacted, would be subject to any illegal or unconstitutional intrusion if the program they challenged was allowed to continue. Rather, they claimed only that they *might* be injured *if* the information lawfully collected by the military were misused in some unspecified way at some unspecified point in the future, and they alleged that the surveillance scheme had a chilling effect, while essentially admitting that they themselves had not been chilled, and that the program had not altered their behavior in any way.

By contrast, the instant plaintiffs clearly have alleged specific and concrete injuries. Unlike the *Laird* plaintiffs, they do not challenge a program of information gathering that they concede is lawful, on the theory that the information gathered may be misused in the future by government agents acting illegally and without authorization; rather, they challenge a specific statute that expressly authorizes surveillance that they contend is in itself unconstitutional. *** And far from alleging an undefined "chill" that has not affected their own behavior in any way, they detail specific, reasonable actions that they have taken to their own tangible, economic cost, in order to carry out their legitimate professional activities in an ethical and effective manner, which can be done only by taking every precaution to avoid being overheard in the way that the challenged statute makes reasonably likely. ***

The government next argues, however, that even if *Laird* does not directly govern this case, it created special standing rules for surveillance cases that are stricter than those that apply to other types of cases, and that those special rules preclude standing in this case. We disagree. *** First, the *Laird* plaintiffs so obviously lacked standing that the Court did not need to create stricter standing rules in the surveillance context in order to deny plaintiffs standing. *** Second, *Laird* in fact contains no such purported special rules for surveillance cases. *** To the contrary, *Laird*'s final sentence makes clear that the result in that case was dictated by the well-established general principles of standing:

> [T]here is nothing in our Nation's history or in this Court's decided cases, including our holding today, that can properly be seen as giving any indication that actual or threatened injury by reason of unlawful activities of the military would go unnoticed or unremedied.

*** Third, while the government relies heavily on *ACLU v. NSA* and *United Presbyterian* to support its interpretation of *Laird*, those cases do not bind us, and they are factually distinguishable from the instant case.[32] Moreover, we

---

[32] In *ACLU v. NSA*, the plaintiffs challenged a narrow surveillance program that monitored particular individuals the government suspected were associated with al Qaeda. The FAA, by contrast, authorizes a considerably broader surveillance program. This fact increases the likelihood that the instant plaintiffs will be harmed in the future, which is a key consideration in determining whether the plaintiffs should have standing to challenge the underlying statute. In *United Presbyterian*, the plaintiffs challenged an executive order that, inter alia, established procedures for the FBI and other intelligence agencies to divide their overlapping surveillance duties. The D.C. Circuit said the plaintiffs essentially challenged the "constitutionality of the entire national intelligence-gathering system." 738 F.2d at 1381. But, unlike the instant

do not find their interpretations of *Laird* to be persuasive. *** We do not see any reason why the law of standing should be stricter or different in the surveillance context, and those cases do not offer any such reasons.

Under the traditional, well-established rules of standing, the plaintiffs here have alleged that they reasonably anticipate direct injury from the enactment of the FAA because, unlike most Americans, they engage in legitimate professional activities that make it reasonably likely that their privacy will be invaded and their conversations overheard -- unconstitutionally, or so they argue -- as a result of the surveillance newly authorized by the FAA, and that they have already suffered tangible, indirect injury due to the reasonable steps they have undertaken to avoid such overhearing, which would impair their ability to carry out those activities. Nothing more is required for standing under well-established principles. And nothing in *Laird*, where the plaintiffs alleged no comparable injury, purports to change those principles. *** We therefore find that plaintiffs have standing to challenge the constitutionality of the FAA in federal court.

Notes

1. **Standing Basics.** Make sure you know the three requirements of standing and why the Court says each is met, as well as how the present and future injury components work and why indirect injury suffices.

2. **FISA v. FAA.** The court early on distinguishes FISA standing (and *ACLU v. NSA*) from FAA standing. Does it follow through on why these differences matter? Where does "broader surveillance" under the FAA and the lack of advance judicial oversight for particular warrants surface in connection with the three requirements of standing?

3. **Distinguishing *Laird*.** Review the two distinctions of *Laird v. Tatum* that the court makes. Do you find these distinctions convincing? Do the same distinctions exist when we compare *Laird* to the facts of *ACLU v. NSA*?

4. **Government Response.** Why do you think the government did not factually controvert the claims of the plaintiffs? What would have been the result of doing so?

5. **On to the Merits?** Are there any other hurdles for the plaintiffs (assuming this decision sticks with the court en banc and the Supreme Court)? The next case discusses one potential hurdle—the state secrets doctrine. If the merits are reached, are there any differences between this case and the FISCR decision in *In re Directives*, supra?

******

---

plaintiffs, the United Presbyterian plaintiffs failed to establish any particular risk that they would be surveilled under the executive order they challenged.

State Secrets. The state secrets doctrine is important to much litigation concerning national security and antiterrorism matters. This doctrine will be explored in depth in Chapter VI, where it has been a powerful impediment to those claiming to have been taken by the United States to countries where they allegedly were tortured. The question for FISA purposes, reserved by Judge Walker in the preceding opinion at pg. 194 for subsequent consideration, is much narrower. In short, the question is whether FISA preempts operation of a common law privilege that would preclude any litigant from finding out the details of the surveillance. If you feel lost in the following opinion because you are unfamiliar with the basics of the state secrets doctrine or privilege, read the introduction to the Chapter VI materials on this topic. The following two cases concern application of the doctrine in the surveillance context. The first involves the Ninth Circuit taking a skeptical look at another decision by District Judge Walker.. The second case shows how Judge Walker responded to this decision.

AL-HARAMAIN ISLAMIC FOUNDATION v. BUSH
507 F. 3d 1190 (C.A. 9 2007)

McKEOWN, Circuit Judge:

Following the terrorist attacks on September 11, 2001, President George W. Bush authorized the National Security Agency ("NSA") to conduct a warrantless communications surveillance program. The program intercepted international communications into and out of the United States of persons alleged to have ties to Al Qaeda and other terrorist networks. *** Al-Haramain Islamic Foundation, a designated terrorist organization *** brought suit against President Bush and other executive branch agencies and officials. They claimed that they were subject to warrantless electronic surveillance in 2004 in violation of the Foreign Intelligence Surveillance Act ("FISA"), various provisions of the United States Constitution, and international law. The government countered that the suit is foreclosed by the state secrets privilege, an evidentiary privilege that protects national security and military information in appropriate circumstances. Essential to substantiating Al-Haramain's allegations against the government is a classified "Top Secret" document (the "Sealed Document") that the government inadvertently gave to Al-Haramain in 2004 during a proceeding to freeze the organization's assets. ***

In light of extensive government disclosures about the TSP [Terrorist Surveillance Program], the government is hard-pressed to sustain its claim that the very subject matter of the litigation is a state secret. Unlike a truly secret or "black box" program that remains in the shadows of public knowledge, the government has moved affirmatively to engage in public discourse about the TSP. *** After *in camera* review and consideration of the Government's documentation of its national security claim, we also agree that the Sealed Document is protected by the state secrets privilege. *** Nonetheless, our resolution of the state secrets issue as applied to the Sealed Document does not conclude the litigation. Al-Haramain also claims that

FISA preempts the common law state secrets privilege. We remand for determination of this claim, a question the district court did not reach in its denial of the Government's motion to dismiss.

The state secrets privilege is a common law evidentiary privilege that permits the government to bar the disclosure of information if "there is a reasonable danger" that disclosure will "expose military matters which, in the interest of national security, should not be divulged." *United States v. Reynolds,* 345 U.S. 1 (1953). The privilege is not to be lightly invoked. *** [O]n appeal the government argues that the state secrets privilege mandates the dismissal of Al-Haramain's claims for three reasons: (1) the very subject matter of the litigation is a state secret; (2) Al-Haramain cannot establish standing to bring suit, absent the Sealed Document; and (3) Al-Haramain cannot establish a prima facie case, and the government cannot defend against Al-Haramain's assertions, without resorting to state secrets.

***We agree with the district Court's conclusion that the very subject matter of the litigation-the Government's alleged warrantless surveillance program under the TSP-is not protected by the state secrets privilege. Two discrete sets of unclassified facts support this determination. First, President Bush and others in the administration publicly acknowledged that in the months following the September 11, 2001, terrorist attacks, the President authorized a communications surveillance program that intercepted the communications of persons with suspected links to Al Qaeda and related terrorist organizations. Second, in 2004, Al-Haramain was officially declared by the government to be a "Specially Designated Global Terrorist" due to its purported ties to Al Qaeda. The subject matter of the litigation-the TSP and the Government's warrantless surveillance of persons or entities who, like Al-Haramain, were suspected by the NSA to have connections to terrorists-is simply not a state secret. At this early stage in the litigation, enough is known about the TSP, and Al-Haramain's classification as a "Specially Designated Global Terrorist," that the subject matter of Al-Haramain's lawsuit can be discussed, as it has been extensively in publicly-filed pleadings, televised arguments in open court in this appeal, and in the media and the blogosphere, without disturbing the dark waters of privileged information. *** The public now knows the following additional facts about the program, beyond the general contours outlined by other officials: (1) at least one participant for each surveilled call was located outside the United States; (2) the surveillance was conducted without FISA warrants; (3) inadvertent calls involving purely domestic callers were destroyed and not reported; (4) the inadvertent collection was recorded and reported; and (5) U.S. identities are expunged from NSA records of surveilled calls if deemed non-essential to an understanding of the intelligence value of a particular report. These facts alone, disclosed by General Hayden in a public address, provide a fairly complete picture of the scope of the TSP. *** [A DoJ] white paper disclosed other, as yet, non-public information about the TSP, such as the NSA's "use of signals intelligence to identify and pinpoint the enemy." The "NSA activities are directed at the enemy, and not at domestic activity that might incidentally aid the war effort," and were "designed to enable the Government to act quickly and flexibly (and with secrecy) to find agents of al

Qaeda and its affiliates." The TSP, intended to "'connect the dots' between potential terrorists," was "carefully reviewed approximately every 45 days" by the Department of Justice, and Congressional leaders were briefed more than a dozen times on the agency's activities.

To be sure, there are details about the program that the government has not yet disclosed, but because of the voluntary disclosures *** the nature and purpose of the TSP, the "type" of persons it targeted, and even some of its procedures are not state secrets. In other words, the Government's many attempts to assuage citizens' fears that *they* have not been surveilled now doom the Government's assertion that the very subject matter of this litigation, the existence of a warrantless surveillance program, is barred by the state secrets privilege. ***

Al-Haramain's case does involve privileged information, but that fact alone does not render the very subject matter of the action a state secret. *** [W]e must still address the Government's invocation of the state secrets privilege as to the Sealed Document and its assertion that Al-Haramain cannot establish either standing or a prima facie case without the use of state secrets. Our analysis of the state secrets privilege involves three steps. First, we must "ascertain that the procedural requirements for invoking the state secrets privilege have been satisfied." Second, we must make an independent determination whether the information is privileged. In deciding whether the privilege attaches, we may consider a party's need for access to the allegedly privileged information. Finally, "the ultimate question to be resolved is how the matter should proceed in light of the successful privilege claim."

With respect to the first step, *Reynolds* requires the government to make a "formal claim of privilege, lodged by the head of the department which has control over the matter, after actual personal consideration by that officer." The parties do not dispute that the procedural requirements for invoking the state secrets privilege have been met. *** Next, we must determine whether the circumstances before us counsel that the state secrets privilege is applicable, without forcing a disclosure of the very thing that the privilege is designed to protect. Two claims of privilege are at issue, although they are intertwined and we refer generally to both under the rubric of the Sealed Document: (1) whether Al-Haramain was subject to surveillance and (2) the Sealed Document. This case presents a most unusual posture because Al-Haramain has seen the Sealed Document and believes that its members were subject to surveillance. The district court held, however, that "because the government has not officially confirmed or denied whether plaintiffs were subject to surveillance, even if plaintiffs know they were, this information remains secret. Furthermore, while plaintiffs know the contents of the [Sealed] Document, it too remains secret."

The district court also concluded that the government did not waive its privilege by inadvertent disclosure of the Sealed Document. Because Al-Haramain unwittingly knows the contents of the Sealed Document, its allegations and pleadings are founded on information that it believes is derived from the document without revealing the content of the document.

This convoluted sentence and explication underscore the practical difficulty for us in writing about a privileged document, while being cautious not to disclose any national security information. Unlike the alleged spies in *Totten* and *Tenet,* who were knowing parties to a secret contract with the government, Al-Haramain is privy to knowledge that the government fully intended to maintain as a national security secret. Unlike the contract for secret services in *Totten,* which was "itself a fact not to be disclosed," the fact of the previously-secret surveillance program is "itself a fact [that has been] disclosed."

Despite this wrinkle, we read *Reynolds* as requiring an *in camera* review of the Sealed Document in these circumstances. "[T]he showing of necessity which is made will determine how far the court should probe in satisfying itself that the occasion for invoking the privilege is appropriate." We reviewed the Sealed Document *in camera* because of Al-Haramain's admittedly substantial need for the document to establish its case.

Having reviewed it *in camera,* we conclude that the Sealed Document is protected by the state secrets privilege, along with the information as to whether the government surveilled Al-Haramain. We take very seriously our obligation to review the documents with a very careful, indeed a skeptical, eye, and not to accept at face value the Government's claim or justification of privilege. Simply saying "military secret," "national security" or "terrorist threat" or invoking an ethereal fear that disclosure will threaten our nation is insufficient to support the privilege. Sufficient detail must be-and has been-provided for us to make a meaningful examination. The process of *in camera* review ineluctably places the court in a role that runs contrary to our fundamental principle of a transparent judicial system. It also places on the court a special burden to assure itself that an appropriate balance is struck between protecting national security matters and preserving an open court system. That said, we acknowledge the need to defer to the Executive on matters of foreign policy and national security and surely cannot legitimately find ourselves second guessing the Executive in this arena.

For example, at some level, the question whether Al-Haramain has been subject to NSA surveillance may seem, without more, somewhat innocuous. The organization posits that the very existence of the TSP, and Al-Haramain's status as a "Specially Designated Global Terrorist," suggest that the government is in fact intercepting Al-Haramain's communications. But our judicial intuition about this proposition is no substitute for documented risks and threats posed by the potential disclosure of national security information. Thus, we look to the Government's filings, along with publicly available materials and relevant case law, to review the district Court's privilege determination.

It is no secret that the Sealed Document has something to do with intelligence activities. Beyond that, we go no further in disclosure. The filings involving classified information, including the Sealed Document, declarations and portions of briefs, are referred to in the pleadings as *In Camera or Ex Parte* documents. Each member of the panel has had unlimited access to these documents.

We have spent considerable time examining the Government's declarations (both publicly filed and those filed under seal). We are satisfied that the basis for the privilege is exceptionally well documented. Detailed statements underscore that disclosure of information concerning the Sealed Document and the means, sources and methods of intelligence gathering in the context of this case would undermine the Government's intelligence capabilities and compromise national security. Thus, we reach the same conclusion as the district court: the government has sustained its burden as to the state secrets privilege.

We must next resolve how the litigation should proceed in light of the Government's successful privilege claim. The privilege, once found to exist, "cannot be compromised by any showing of need on the part of the party seeking the information." The effect of the Government's successful invocation of privilege "is simply that the evidence is unavailable, as though a witness had died, and the case will proceed accordingly, with no consequences save those resulting from the loss of evidence."

After correctly determining that the Sealed Document was protected by the state secrets privilege, the district court then erred in forging an unusual path forward in this litigation. Though it granted the Government's motion to deny Al-Haramain access to the Sealed Document based on the state secrets privilege, the court permitted the Al-Haramain plaintiffs to file *in camera* affidavits attesting to the contents of the document from their memories.

The district Court's approach-a commendable effort to thread the needle-is contrary to established Supreme Court precedent. If information is found to be a privileged state secret, there are only two ways that litigation can proceed: (1) if the plaintiffs can prove "the essential facts" of their claims "without resort to material touching upon military secrets," or (2) in accord with the procedure outlined in FISA. By allowing *in camera* review of affidavits attesting to individuals' memories of the Sealed Document, the district court sanctioned "material touching" upon privileged information ***. Although FISA permits district court judges to conduct an *in camera* review of information relating to electronic surveillance, there are detailed procedural safeguards that must be satisfied before such review can be conducted. The district court did not address this issue nor do we here.

Moreover, the district Court's solution is flawed: if the Sealed Document is privileged because it contains very sensitive information regarding national security, permitting the same information to be revealed through reconstructed memories circumvents the document's absolute privilege. That approach also suffers from a worst of both world's deficiency: either the memory is wholly accurate, in which case the approach is tantamount to release of the document itself, or the memory is inaccurate, in which case the court is not well-served and the disclosure may be even more problematic from a security standpoint. The state secrets privilege, because of its unique national security considerations, does not lend itself to a compromise solution in this case. The Sealed Document, its contents, and any individuals' memories of its contents, even well-reasoned speculation as to its contents, are completely barred from further disclosure in this litigation by the common law state secrets privilege.

***Al-Haramain cannot establish that it suffered injury in fact, a "concrete and particularized" injury, because the Sealed Document, which Al-Haramain alleges proves that its members were unlawfully surveilled, is protected by the state secrets privilege. *** Because we affirm the district Court's conclusion that the Sealed Document, along with data concerning surveillance, are privileged, and conclude that no testimony attesting to individuals' memories of the document may be admitted to establish the contents of the document, Al-Haramain cannot establish that it has standing, and its claims must be dismissed, unless FISA preempts the state secrets privilege.

Under FISA, if an "aggrieved person" requests discovery of materials relating to electronic surveillance, and the Attorney General files an affidavit stating that the disclosure of such information would harm the national security of the United States, a district court may review *in camera* and ex parte the materials "as may be necessary to determine whether the surveillance of the aggrieved person was lawfully authorized and conducted." The statute further provides that the court may disclose to the aggrieved person, using protective orders, portions of the materials "where such disclosure is necessary to make an accurate determination of the legality of the surveillance." The statute, unlike the common law state secrets privilege, provides a detailed regime to determine whether surveillance "was lawfully authorized and conducted." *** Al-Haramain posits that FISA preempts the state secrets privilege. The district court chose not to rule on this issue. *** Rather than consider the issue for the first time on appeal, we remand to the district court to consider whether FISA preempts the state secrets privilege and for any proceedings collateral to that determination.

Notes

1. **Basics.** How broad is the state secrets doctrine in the Ninth Circuit? How does the government invoke it? What judicial oversight is there when it is invoked? Why is the doctrine so powerful in civil cases like Al-Haramain's? Do you think that the Fourth Circuit, in the context of these facts, would take the broad or narrow view of the state secrets doctrine? The Obama administration, incidentally, has supported the broader (Fourth Circuit) view in its briefs on the subject.

2. **Preemption.** Consider how you would argue the preemption on remand, both for the government and for Al-Haramain. Remember (from constitutional law or elsewhere) that preemption is very much a function of the federal statutory framework and congressional intention. You might review any relevant parts of FISA and its amendments to see if there are any provisions that you think are relevant. Moreover, you might recall that Supreme Court preemption cases are far less predictable in terms of orientations of individual justices than cases in many other fields. The district Court's decision on remand follows.

In re NATIONAL SECURITY AGENCY
TELECOMMUNICATIONS RECORDS LITIGATION
Al-Haramain Islamic Foundation v. Bush
564 F. Supp. 2d 1109 (N.D. Calif. 2008)

VAUGHN R. WALKER, Chief Judge.

The court of appeals has remanded the above case for this court "to consider whether FISA preempts the state secrets privilege and for any proceedings collateral to that determination." *** Plaintiffs' complaint alleges six causes of action of which the first is under the Foreign Intelligence Surveillance Act, ("FISA"). [That they were surveilled without FISA warrants.] *** For the reasons stated herein, the court has determined that: (1) FISA preempts the state secrets privilege in connection with electronic surveillance for intelligence purposes and would appear to displace the state secrets privilege for purposes of plaintiffs' claims; and (2) FISA nonetheless does not appear to provide plaintiffs a viable remedy unless they can show that they are "aggrieved persons" within the meaning of FISA. ***

Along with their complaint, plaintiffs filed under seal a copy of a classified document that had inadvertently been disclosed by defendant Office of Foreign Assets Control ("OFAC") to counsel for Al-Haramain as part of a production of unclassified documents relating to Al-Haramain's potential status as a "specially designated global terrorist." This document, which has proven central to all phases of this litigation including the issues now before this court, will be referred to herein as the "Sealed Document." *** Plaintiffs argue *** that FISA preempts the state secrets privilege. Specifically, plaintiffs argue that FISA vests the courts with control over materials relating to electronic surveillance, subject to "appropriate security procedures and protective orders." As a result, plaintiffs contend that *** the state secrets privilege [is] superfluous in FISA litigation. ***

Both the plain text and the legislative history make clear that Congress intended FISA to "occupy the field through the establishment of a comprehensive regulatory program supervised by an expert administrative agency." Congress through FISA established a comprehensive, detailed program to regulate foreign intelligence surveillance in the domestic context. *** The court is charged with determining whether FISA preempts or displaces not a common-law set of rules for conducting foreign intelligence surveillance, but rather a privilege asserted by the government to avoid public and judicial scrutiny of its activities related to national security. In this case, those activities include foreign intelligence surveillance, the subject matter that Congress through FISA sought comprehensively to regulate. This imperfect overlap between the preempting statute and the common-law rule being preempted does not, however, create serious problems with finding the state secrets privilege preempted or displaced by FISA in the context of matters within FISA's purview. FISA does not preempt the state secrets privilege as to matters that are not within FISA's purview; for such matters, the lack of comprehensive federal legislation leaves an appropriate role for this judge-made federal common law privilege. ***

Plaintiffs argue that the in camera procedure described in FISA's section 1806(f) applies to preempt the protocol described in *Reynolds* in this case. [FISA] provides that in cases in federal courts in which "aggrieved persons" seek to discover materials relating to, or information derived from, electronic surveillance, the United States attorney general may file "an affidavit under oath that disclosure or an adversary hearing would harm the national security of the United States." In that event, the court "shall" conduct an in camera, ex parte review of such materials relating to the surveillance "as may be necessary to determine whether the surveillance *** was lawfully authorized and conducted." The procedure described in section 1806(f), while not identical to the procedure described in *Reynolds,* has important characteristics in common with it-enough, certainly, to establish that it preempts the state secrets privilege as to matters to which it relates. Section 1806(f) is Congress's specific and detailed prescription for how courts should handle claims by the government that the disclosure of material relating to or derived from electronic surveillance would harm national security; it leaves no room in a case to which section 1806(f) applies for a *Reynolds*-type process. Moreover, its similarities are striking enough to suggest that section 1806(f), which addresses a range of circumstances in which information derived from electronic surveillance might become relevant to judicial proceedings, is in effect a codification of the state secrets privilege for purposes of relevant cases under FISA, as modified to reflect Congress's precise directive to the federal courts for the handling of materials and information with purported national security implications. In either event, the *Reynolds* protocol has no role where section 1806(f) applies. ***

The legislative history, moreover, buttresses the Court's reading of the statutory text as intending that FISA replace judge-made federal common law rules:

> [T]he development of the law regulating electronic surveillance for national security purposes has been uneven and inconclusive. This is to be expected where the development is left to the judicial branch in an area where cases do not regularly come before it. Moreover, the development of standards and restrictions by the judiciary with respect to electronic surveillance for foreign intelligence purposes accomplished through case law threatens both civil liberties and the national security because that development occurs generally in ignorance of the facts, circumstances, and techniques of foreign intelligence electronic surveillance not present in the particular case before the court. *** [T]he tiny window to this area which a particular case affords provides inadequate light by which judges may be relied upon to develop case law which adequately balances the rights of privacy and national security.

Foreign Intelligence Surveillance Act of 1978, HR Rep No 95-1283 Part I at 21. This legislative history is evidence of Congressional intent that FISA should displace federal common law rules such as the state secrets privilege with regard to matters within FISA's purview.

Defendants advance essentially three points in support of their contention that "nothing in FISA indicates any intention by Congress *** to abrogate the state secrets privilege" in the case of intelligence-driven electronic surveillance. First, defendants argue that the privilege derives, not only from the common law, but also from the President's Article II powers, so that a "clear expression" of congressional intent is required to abrogate that privilege; furthermore, abrogation would raise fundamental constitutional problems which should be avoided. Second, defendants note the common law origins of the state secrets privilege and advert to the principle that abrogation of common law requires a "clear and direct" legislative expression of intent, which they contend is absent. Finally, defendants contend that section 1806(f) serves a fundamentally different purpose from the state secrets privilege and that the former cannot therefore "preempt" the latter because section 1806(f) governs disclosure by the government of intelligence derived from electronic surveillance whereas the state secrets privilege is fundamentally a rule of non-disclosure. The court disagrees with all three of these contentions, the second and third of which have been fully addressed in the paragraphs above.

The weakness of Defendants' first argument-that the Constitution grants the executive branch the power to control the state secrets privilege-is evident in the authorities they marshal for it. *** When Congress acts to contravene the President's authority, federal courts must give effect to what Congress has required. *** It is not entirely clear whether defendants acknowledge Congress's authority to enact FISA as the exclusive means by which the executive branch may undertake foreign intelligence surveillance in the domestic context. *** [The court finds that] Congress appears clearly to have intended to-and did-establish the exclusive means for foreign intelligence surveillance activities to be conducted. Whatever power the executive may otherwise have had in this regard, FISA limits the power of the executive branch to conduct such activities and it limits the executive branch's authority to assert the state secrets privilege in response to challenges to the legality of its foreign intelligence surveillance activities. *** As part of their argument that the state secrets privilege has a constitutional basis in Article II, defendants contend that a "clear statement of congressional intent" to abrogate the privilege is required. ***

The determination that FISA preempts the state secrets privilege does not necessarily clear the way for plaintiffs to pursue their claim for relief against these defendants under FISA's section 1810. *** In summary, FISA makes little provision for notice to surveilled individuals except when the government chooses to disclose surveillance materials and the provisions that exist are easy for the government to avoid. This must be presumed to be part of Congress's design for FISA because the notification procedure in Title III-which, moreover, contemplated special handling of cases involving national security concerns-predated FISA by a decade. Congress could have modeled FISA on Title III in this regard, but did not do so. In consequence, the cases are few and far between in which an individual ever learns of having been subject to electronic surveillance within FISA's purview and therefore possibly having standing as an aggrieved party for FISA section 1810 purposes.

One of the few cases in which an individual surveilled under a FISA warrant became aware of his status as an "aggrieved party" is that of Brendan Mayfield, *** Ironically, the Mayfield case seems an ideal one for the government to provide notification under section 1825(b), discussed above, which directs the attorney general to notify United States persons whose residences have been subjected to physical search after the attorney general "determines there is no national security interest in continuing to maintain the secrecy of the search." Yet the government leaned toward secrecy rather than candor. Only after Mayfield had filed litigation and moved to compel notification did the government notify him of the physical search and, in doing so, contended that both the fact and the extent of notification were entirely within the attorney general's discretion. *** The Mayfield case illustrates the limited effectiveness of FISA's narrowly-defined notice provision relating to physical searches. Limited and imperfect as FISA's notification provision for physical searches may be, FISA contains no comparable provision for United States persons who have been subjected to electronic surveillance as opposed to physical search.

In the Al-Haramain case, notification to plaintiffs of their potential status as "aggrieved parties" came in the form of an accident: the inadvertent disclosure of the Sealed Document during discovery proceedings, a disclosure that the various United States entities involved took immediate and largely successful steps to undo. To speak metaphorically, the inadvertent disclosure by OFAC of the Sealed Document amounted to a small tear in the thick veil of secrecy behind which the government had been conducting its electronic surveillance activities. *** By refusing to allow the use of the Sealed Document in any form for the adjudication of plaintiffs' claims in this matter, the court of appeals required that the small tear be stitched closed, leaving plaintiffs with actual but not useful notice and without the sole item of evidence they had offered in support of their claims.

***The next major obstacle to seeking civil remedies under FISA is the lack of a practical vehicle for obtaining and/or using admissible evidence in support of such claims. An aggrieved party must be able to produce evidence sufficient to establish standing to proceed as an "aggrieved party" and, later, to withstand motions for dismissal and/or summary judgment. This effort is encumbered with legal and practical obstacles. *** FISA does not provide for the preservation of recordings and other information obtained pursuant to a FISA warrant. Rather, Congress intended to allow such material to be destroyed, the idea being that to allow destruction would better protect the privacy of individuals surveilled than to require preservation. By contrast, Title III expressly requires intercepted communications to be recorded and expressly prohibits destruction of the recordings except upon an order of the issuing or denying judge. Also, "in any event [they] shall be kept for ten years." *** By failing to impose parallel obligations on the government agencies and officials who are the putative defendants in an action alleging

FISA violations, FISA provides little help to "aggrieved persons" who might seek to become civil plaintiffs.

Plaintiffs and plaintiff amici contend that FISA provides the means for them to overcome this evidentiary hurdle. *** As relevant here, section 1806(f) provides:

> whenever any motion or request is made by an aggrieved person pursuant to any other statute or rule of the United States *** before any court *** of the United States *** to discover or obtain applications or orders or other materials relating to electronic surveillance or to discover, obtain, or suppress evidence or information obtained or derived from electronic surveillance under this chapter, the United States district court *** shall, notwithstanding any other law, if the Attorney General files an affidavit under oath that disclosure or an adversary hearing would harm the national security of the United States, review in camera and ex parte the application, order, and such other materials relating to the surveillance as may be necessary to determine whether the surveillance of the aggrieved person was lawfully authorized and conducted. In making this determination, the court may disclose to the aggrieved person, under appropriate security procedures and protective orders, portions of the application, order, or other materials relating to the surveillance only where such disclosure is necessary to make an accurate determination of the legality of the surveillance.

The parties have argued at length in their papers and in court about the meaning and application of this convoluted pair of sentences. ***

Defendants contend that section 1806(f) does not come into play unless and until the government has acknowledged that it surveilled the "aggrieved person" *** it is not available as a means for an individual to discover having been surveilled absent such governmental acknowledgment. Defendants further assert that, assuming *arguendo* that FISA "preempts" the state secrets privilege, *** plaintiffs would still be unable to establish their standing as "aggrieved persons" for section 1810 purposes without "inherently risk[ing] or requir[ing] the disclosure of state secrets to the plaintiffs and the public at large." *** Defendant amici also contrast FISA's section 1806(f) with 18 USC section 3504(a)(1), enacted in 1970 as part of the Organized Crime Control Act. The latter establishes a procedure by which "a party aggrieved" seeking to exclude evidence based on a claim that it was obtained illegally may obligate "the opponent of the claim" (i.e., the government) "to affirm or deny the occurrence of the alleged unlawful act." Defendant amici argue that "[t]he existence of the carefully circumscribed discovery right in § 3504 negates any suggestion that § 1806(f) implicitly covers the same ground." *** Defendant amici argue that Congress could have incorporated into FISA a procedure like that provided for in section 3504(a)(1) by which an individual could require the executive branch to confirm or deny the existence of electronic surveillance and, since Congress did not do so, it must be presumed not to have intended such a procedure to be available under FISA.

Plaintiff amici counter *** that section 1806(f)'s scope is expansive enough to provide for in camera review in *any* civil or criminal case-not merely cases arising under FISA-in which a claim of unlawful surveillance is raised. They point out that the text of section 1806(f) referring to "any motion or request *** pursuant to any other statute or rule of the United States" does not suggest a limitation to criminal statutes. They also point to language in the conference report on the final version of FISA stating "[t]he conferees agree that an in camera and ex parte proceeding is appropriate for determining the lawfulness of electronic surveillance in both criminal and civil cases." And plaintiff amici find support in the District of Columbia Circuit's opinion in *ACLU Foundation of Southern California v. Barr,* 952 F.2d 457, 465 n. 7 (D.C.Cir.1991), which cited FISA's legislative history for the proposition that Congress had intended a Court's in camera, ex parte review under section 1806(f) to "determine whether the surveillance was authorized and conducted in a manner that did not violate any constitutional or statutory right." Thus, plaintiff amici contend, section 1810 is one such "other statute" referred to in section 1806(f) under which in camera review is available.

Next, plaintiff amici characterize Defendants' contention that section 1806(f) is only available in cases in which the government has acknowledged having surveilled a party as "look[ing] at section 1806(f) through the wrong end of the telescope." Plaintiff amici correctly observe that section 1806(f) only comes into play when the attorney general notifies the court that "disclosure or an adversary hearing would harm the national security"-for example, in opposing a discovery request. A "motion or request *** by an aggrieved person" alone is not sufficient to trigger in camera review. Therefore, they argue, Defendants' position that the government must have acknowledged surveillance sets the bar higher than FISA prescribes.

Third, plaintiff amici address what they believe the bar should be-that is, what an individual must show to establish being "aggrieved" for section 1806(f) purposes. They assert that a person need only have a "colorable basis for believing he or she had been surveilled." *** The court agrees with plaintiffs that section 1806(f) is not limited to criminal proceedings, but may also be invoked in civil actions, including actions brought under section 1810. The court disagrees with Defendants' proposed limitation of section 1806(f) to cases in which the government has acknowledged the surveillance at issue. The plain language of the statute, which the court must use as its primary compass, does not support Defendants' purported limitations.

The court parts company with plaintiffs, however, with regard to what an individual must show to establish being "aggrieved" for section 1806(f) purposes and, consequently, the availability of section 1806(f) to plaintiffs in this case in its current posture. As the court reads section 1806(f), a litigant must first establish himself as an "aggrieved person" before seeking to make a "motion or request *** to discover or obtain applications or orders or other materials relating to electronic surveillance [etc]." If reports are to be believed, plaintiffs herein would have had little difficulty establishing their "aggrieved person" status if they were able to support their request with the Sealed Document. But the court of appeals, applying the state secrets privilege, has unequivocally ruled that plaintiffs in the current posture of the case may not use "the Sealed Document, its contents, and any individuals' memories of its contents, even well-reasoned speculation as to its contents." 507 F.3d at 1204. Plaintiffs must first establish "aggrieved person" status without the use of the Sealed Document and may then bring a "motion or request" under § 1806(f) in response to which the attorney general may file an affidavit opposing disclosure. At that point, in camera review of materials responsive to the motion or request, including the Sealed Document, might well be appropriate. *** While attempting a precise definition of such a standard is beyond the scope of this order, it is certain that plaintiffs' showing thus far with the Sealed Document excluded falls short of the mark. Plaintiff amici hint at the proper showing when they refer to "independent evidence disclosing that plaintiffs have been surveilled" and a "rich lode of disclosure to support their claims" in various of the MDL cases. To proceed with their FISA claim, plaintiffs must present to the court enough specifics based on non-classified evidence to establish their "aggrieved person" status under FISA.

It is a testament to the obstacles to seeking civil remedies for alleged violations of FISA that section 1810 has lain "dormant for nearly thirty years." Dormant indeed. The print version of the United States Code Annotated contains no case Notes under section 1810. The parties have cited no other case in which a plaintiff has actually brought suit under section 1810, let alone secured a civil judgment under it. By contrast, the civil liability provisions of Title III, have been used successfully by "aggrieved persons" with regularity since they were enacted in 1968. *** [T]he court must be wary of unwarranted interpretations of FISA that would make section 1810 a more robust remedy than Congress intended it to be. As noted, Title III predated FISA by a full decade. If Congress had so intended, it could have written FISA to offer a more fulsome and accessible remedy patterned on Title III. Congress may therefore be presumed to have intended *not* to provide such a remedy and the court should not strain to construe FISA in a manner designed to give section 1810 greater effect than Congress intended.

*** This is not to say that it is impossible to obtain relief under section 1810, but the fact that no one has ever done so reinforces the Court's reading of the plain terms of the statute: section 1810 is not user-friendly and the impediments to using it may yet prove insurmountable. ***

The lack of precedents under section 1810 complicates the task of charting a path forward. The court of appeals reversed the Oregon district Court's plan for allowing plaintiffs to proceed with their suit, but did not suggest a way for plaintiffs to proceed without using the Sealed Document. Nonetheless, the court believes that dismissal with prejudice is not appropriate. Accordingly, plaintiffs' FISA claim will be dismissed with leave to amend. Plaintiffs should have the opportunity to amend their claim to establish that they are "aggrieved persons" within the meaning of 50 USC §

1801(k). In the event plaintiffs meet this hurdle, the court will have occasion to consider the treatment of the Sealed Document under section 1806(f) and the significant practical challenges of adjudicating plaintiffs' claim under section 1810.

For the reasons stated herein, plaintiffs' claim under FISA is DISMISSED with leave to amend. Plaintiffs shall have thirty (30) days to amend their complaint in accordance with this order. Should plaintiffs seek to amend their non-FISA claims, they shall do so by means of a noticed motion before this court in accordance with the local rules. ***

Notes

1. Appeal. If you were the government, would you appeal? How far? "All the way to the Supreme Court"? How broad an incursion into the state secrets doctrine is this decision?

2. Who Has Information? If you were part of a terrorist organization, would you see any difference between your ability to obtain information from the FBI or CIA versus a federal judge who had reviewed information in camera? If the judge has some vulnerability to terrorist reprisals compared to the FBI or CIA, should such matters come before secret FISC judges rather than a named federal district judge?

D. SURVEILLANCE: COMPARATIVE AND POLICY PERSPECTIVES

1. COMPARATIVE ELECTRONIC SURVEILLANCE

Rapid developments in communications technologies and terrorist attacks on the U.S. and elsewhere have caused every modern democracy to struggle with balancing security and privacy. Because terrorist attacks in other parts of the world preceded the 9/11 attacks on the United States, various nations instituted surveillance regimes that were more flexible and less Cold War-focused than the original FISA regime in the United States. Over the past decade, many of these states have updated those regimes, often expanding the use of electronic surveillance.

Europe. Chapter III discussed Europe's reaction to United States efforts to trace terrorist finances through SWIFT. The concern for privacy shown there applies equally to electronic surveillance. Article 8 of the European Convention on Human Rights (ECHR) provides that (1) "everyone has the right to respect for his private and family life, his home and his correspondence" and that (2) "there shall be no interference by a public authority with the exercise of this right except such as in accordance with the law and is necessary in a democratic society in the interests of national security, public safety or the economic well-being of the country, for the prevention of disorder or crime, for the protection of health or morals, or for protection of the rights and freedoms of others." The European Court of

Human Rights has held that "private life" and "correspondence" includes communication by telephone, fax, or email, whether of a personal, business or professional nature. Surveillance is in "accordance with the law" if a domestic law authorizes it and is "necessary in a democratic society" if it addresses national security concerns proportionately. Decisions by the European Court of Human Rights are only binding on the states that are party to a particular suit. However, to avoid future penalties each country in Europe generally tries to comply with all of its decisions. Nonetheless, the laws concerning electronic surveillance vary widely across Europe, particularly with regard to who authorizes and oversees surveillance, and what type of redress is available to those who believe their rights have been violated.

In the U.K. electronic surveillance in governed by the Regulation of Investigatory Powers Act (RIPA). RIPA requires all surveillance, except in rare cases of emergency, to be authorized by a warrant issued by the Home Secretary. Unlike the FISA courts, the Home Secretary is appointed by the Prime Minister. The substance of the law parrots the terms of Article 8. Ex post oversight is robust, for RIPA created two official posts which the Prime Minister appoints, to conduct oversight. First, the Intelligence Services Commissioner reviews warrants issued by the Home Secretary for intrusive surveillance (i.e., "bugging"). Second, the Interception of Communications Commissioner reviews warrants for intercepting communications. Both are allowed complete access to all information held by any agency in the U.K. and each submits a published annual report detailing the Government's surveillance activities. Moreover, individuals can file complaints with the Investigatory Powers Tribunal (IPT). The IPT's private proceedings avoid many of the state secrets and standing issues plaintiffs face in the U.S. The IPT has the authority to award compensation, and to cancel any warrant or authorization for electronic surveillance. The U.K. has no warrantless program similar to the U.S. Terrorist Surveillance Program.

In Germany, the "G-10" law governing most surveillance requires the executive to submit an application to a judge demonstrating that the surveillance is "necessary" for an investigation of a statutorily specified offense, which includes membership in a terrorist organization. The judge must also find that "determinate facts" indicate that the suspect is involved in one of the listed offenses. The executive officials must further consult with the G-10 Commission (nine members of parliament) prior to surveillance, or in cases of emergencies, as soon as possible thereafter. However, the Constitutional Court has held that automated wiretaps of international communications by the Intelligence Service for the purposes of preventing terrorism or trafficking in drugs or weapons, does not require a warrant because it is authorized by statute and is legal if "the interests of the Federal Republic of Germany are directly affected." Complaints and reports of abuse are also heard by the G-10 Commission, which has the authority to suspend surveillance that it finds to be illegal. Exclusion of the illegally obtained material and civil damages are available. Like the IPT in the U.K., the G-10 Commission operates mostly in secret. General supervision of electronic surveillance is also conducted by the G-10 Board, which meets every six months to review the Executive's surveillance activities.

Swedish law requires law enforcement and intelligence agencies to obtain a court order for conventional electronic surveillance. However, in 2008, Sweden enacted a law that allows the National Defense Radio Establishment (Forsvarets Radioanstalt, or FRA) to conduct automated surveillance, without a warrant, of all phone and internet traffic that crosses its border. Like the Terrorist Surveillance Program in the U.S., Sweden's warrantless surveillance is ostensibly aimed only at international communication. However, critics point out that internet communications between two people in Sweden are often transmitted by servers located outside the country. This, it is argued, results in regular warrantless surveillance of entirely domestic communication. Unlike the U.S. Terrorist Surveillance Program, Swedish (and German) surveillance is primarily conducted by computers, which monitor communications for specified terms. Humans review a communication only if any of those specified terms are detected. Such programs do not target specific individuals for surveillance.

Canada. Canada's criminal code requires judicial authorization for domestic electronic surveillance; authorities must demonstrate that other investigatory procedures have been tried and failed, or are unlikely to succeed. Following 9/11, Canada's Anti-terrorism Act waived these requirements where the judge is satisfied that the surveillance is in relation to terrorism. Moreover, when electronic surveillance is directed at foreign entities and the information could not reasonably be obtained through other means, the Communications Security Establishment only needs authorization by the Minister of National Defense to conduct electronic surveillance. The Anti-terrorism Act, by its own terms, requires review by special Parliamentary committees, and certain portions sunset if not extended. Several portions were allowed to expire in 2007, but the provisions relating to electronic surveillance are still in force.

Australia. Electronic Surveillance in Australia is governed by the Telecommunications Interception Act of 1979 (TIA) which, like FISA allows the Australian Security Intelligence Organization to intercept communications for the purpose of collecting "intelligence relating to the capabilities, intentions or activities of a foreign power." However, the Attorney General rather than a court approves warrants for such surveillance if he or she is satisfied that the surveillance is "important in relation to the defense of the Commonwealth or to the conduct of the Commonwealth's international affairs." It is not clear in Australia that "foreign power" includes terrorists acting without state support. Legislation has been proposed to clarify this matter.

India. Electronic surveillance in India is governed by the Information Technology Act of 2000 ("IT Act, 2000"). A 2008 amendment to the IT Act specifically allows both the national government and individual state governments to engage in electronic surveillance for reasons including national security and "preventing incitement to the commission of any cognizable offence". IT Act § 69(1). The Act requires the government to list the reasons for surveillance in writing to the Certifier of Controlling Authorities, a technical agency, but there is no vetting process for those requests. India also set up a special court system to handle surveillance issues as well as other electronic issues, the "Cyber Appellate Tribunal." Civil courts do not have jurisdiction. IT Act § 61. Decisions of the Cyber Appellate Tribunal can be appealed to the High Courts. Recently, the Indian government proposed legislation modeled on United States law to amend their surveillance laws. India has also pushed for greater access to encrypted data transmitted on smart phones and other devices, such as demanding BlackBerry maker R.I.M. set up a server in India from which the government can monitor messages sent over their "BBM" service. Vikas Bajaj and Ian Austen, "Privacy vs. National Security: India's Demands for Surveillance Seen as Roadblock." NEW YORK TIMES, Sept. 28, 2010, Pg. B1.

Japan. Japan is noteworthy because it is likely more protective of privacy than any other modern democracy. Prior to 1999 any electronic surveillance was considered to be a violation of Japan's Constitution. While wiretapping was reportedly conducted a few times, there was no authorization procedure to allow for any legitimate electronic surveillance by the government. In 1999 Japan enacted the Communications Interception Law. This law provided for the first time that law enforcement officials could obtain a warrant from a court to conduct electronic surveillance. The warrants can only be granted for investigation of cases involving drug trafficking, weapons trafficking, organized murder, and smuggling of illegal immigrants. The warrants only authorize surveillance for 10 days, and can be extended to a total of no more than 30 days.

2. SURVEILLANCE POLICY

Jack M. Balkin, "The Constitution in the National Surveillance State," 93 MINN. L. REV. 1 (2008), writes:

During the last part of the twentieth century the United States began developing a new form of governance that features the collection, collation, and analysis of information about populations both in the United States and around the world. This new form of governance is the National Surveillance State. *** In the National Surveillance State, the government uses surveillance, data collection, collation and analysis to identify problems, to head off potential threats, to govern populations, and to deliver valuable social services. *** The War on Terror may be the most familiar justification for the rise of the National Surveillance State, but it is hardly the sole or even the most important cause.

Government's increasing use of surveillance and data mining is a predictable result of accelerating developments in information technology. *** The question is not whether we will have a surveillance state in the years to come, but what sort of state we will have. Will we have a government without sufficient controls over public and private surveillance, or will we have a government that protects individual dignity and conforms both public and private surveillance to the rule of law? *** Governments will use surveillance, data collection and data mining technologies not only to keep Americans safe from terrorist attacks but also to prevent ordinary crime and deliver social services. *** Moreover, much of the surveillance in the national surveillance state will be conducted and analyzed by private parties. ***

The National Surveillance State grows naturally out of the Welfare State and the National Security State; it is their logical successor. The Welfare State governs domestic affairs by spending and transferring money and by creating government entitlements, licenses and public works. The National Security State promotes foreign policy through investments in defense industries and defense related technologies, through creating and expanding national intelligence agencies like the CIA and the NSA, and through the placement of American military forces and weapons systems around the globe to counter military threats and project national power world-wide.

The Welfare State created a huge demand for data processing technologies to identify individuals-- think about all the uses for your Social Security Number - - and deliver social services like licenses, benefits and pensions. The National Security State created the need for effective intelligence collection and data analysis. It funded the development of increasingly powerful technologies for surveillance, data collection and data mining, not to mention increasingly powerful computer and telecommunications technologies. American investments in defense technologies spurred the electronics industry, the computer industry, and eventually, the birth of the Internet itself. *** In the National Surveillance State the line between public and private modes of surveillance and security has blurred if not vanished. *** The NSA program would be impossible without the assistance of telecommunications companies; government now requires new communications technologies designed with back ends that facilitate government surveillance. ***

Older models of law enforcement have focused on apprehension and prosecution of wrongdoers after the fact and the threat of criminal or civil sanctions to deter future bad behavior. The National Surveillance State supplements this model of prosecution and deterrence with technologies of prediction and prevention. Computer security tries to identify potential weaknesses and block entry by suspicious persons before they have a chance to strike. Private companies and government agencies use databases to develop profiles of individuals who are likely to violate laws, drive up costs or cause problems, and then deflect them, block them, or deny them benefits, access or opportunities. The Government's No Fly and Selectee watch lists and its still planned Secure Flight Screening program collect information on passengers and create profiles that seek to block dangerous people from boarding planes. ***

We leave traces of ourselves continually, including our location, our communications contacts, our consumption choices, even our DNA. Data mining allows inferences not only about the direct subjects of surveillance, but about *other people* with whom they live, work and communicate. Instead of spying on a particular person, data about other persons combined with public facts about a person can allow governments and private businesses to draw increasingly powerful inferences about that person's motives, desires and behaviors.***

Individuals can no longer protect themselves simply by preventing the government from watching them, for the government may no longer need to watch *them* in particular to gain knowledge that can be used against them.

Equally important, the rise of the National Surveillance State portends the death of amnesia. ***

The National Surveillance State poses three major dangers for our freedom. The National Surveillance State emphasizes ex ante prevention rather than ex post apprehension and prosecution. Thus the first danger is that government will create a parallel track of preventative law enforcement that routes around the traditional guarantees of the Bill of Rights. *** The second danger is that traditional law enforcement and social services will increasingly resemble the parallel track. *** If data mining can help us locate terrorists, why not use it to find deadbeat dads, or even people who haven't paid their parking tickets? If surveillance technologies signal that certain people are likely threats to public order, why not create a system of preventive detention outside the ordinary criminal justice system? Why not impose sanctions outside the criminal law, like denying people the right to board airplanes or use public facilities and transportation systems? *** Private power and public-private cooperation pose a third danger. Because the Constitution does not reach private parties, government has increasing incentives to rely on private enterprise to collect and generate information for it. ***

If something like the National Surveillance State is inevitable, how do we continue to protect individual rights and constitutional government? *** The more power the state amasses, the more Americans need constitutional guarantees to keep governments honest and devoted to the public good.*** We might begin by distinguishing between an authoritarian information state and a democratic information state. Authoritarian information states are *information gluttons* and *information misers*. *** By contrast, democratic informational states are *information gourmets* and *information philanthropists*.*** [C]ourts have largely debilitated the Fourth Amendment to meet the demands of the regulatory and welfare state, the National Security State, and the war on drugs. Much government collection and use of personal data now falls outside the Fourth Amendment's protection-- at least as the courts currently construe it. Courts have held that there is no expectation of privacy in business records and information that people give to third parties like banks and other businesses; in the digital age this accounts for a vast amount of personal information. Most e-mail messages are copied onto privately held servers, making their protection limited if not non-existent. Courts have also held that the Fourth Amendment poses few limits on foreign intelligence surveillance; the latter is largely regulated by FISA; as a result, the Executive branch has increasingly justified domestic surveillance by asserting that it is a permissible byproduct of foreign intelligence gathering***

Congress must pass new superstatutes to regulate the collection, collation, purchase and analysis of data. These new superstatutes would have three basic features. First, they would restrict the kinds of data governments may collect, collate and use against people. They would strengthen the very limited protections of e-mail and digital business records, and rein in how the government purchases and uses data collected by private parties. They would institutionalize government "amnesia" by requiring that some kinds of data be regularly destroyed after a certain amount of time unless there were good reasons for retaining them. Second, the new superstatutes would create a code of proper conduct for private companies who collect, analyze, and sell personal information. Third, the new superstatutes would create a series of oversight mechanisms for executive bureaucracies that collect, purchase, process, and use information. ***

Judicial oversight need not require a traditional system of warrants—it could be a system of prior disclosure and explanation and subsequent regular reporting and minimization. This is especially important as surveillance practices shift from operations targeted at individual suspected persons to surveillance programs that do not begin with identified individuals and focus on matching and discovering patterns based on the analysis of large amounts of data and contact information. We need a set of procedures that translate the values of the Fourth Amendment (with its warrant requirement) and the Fifth Amendment's Due Process Clause into a new technological context. Currently, however, we exclude more and more executive action from judicial review on the twin grounds of secrecy and efficiency. The Bush Administration's secret NSA program is one example; the explosion in the use of administrative warrants that require no judicial oversight is another. ***

Finally, technological oversight will probably be an indispensable supplement to legal procedures. The best way to control the watchers is to watch them as well. We should construct surveillance architectures so that government surveillance is regularly recorded and available for audit by ombudsmen and executive branch inspectors. Records of surveillance can, in turn, be subjected to data analysis and pattern matching to discover any unusual behavior that suggests abuse of procedures. These technological audits can automate part of the process of oversight; they can assist ombudsmen, executive officials, Congress, and the courts in ensuring that surveillance practices stay within legal bounds. We can prevent some kinds of abuse by technological design; at the very least technology can force disclosure of information that executive officials would otherwise keep hidden. *** We mastered at least some of the problems caused by the rise of the Administrative and Welfare state; we must hope that we can do so the same for the National Surveillance State, which is already here.

V

DETENTION OF SUSPECTED TERRORISTS

The United States does not have a statute authorizing preventive detention of suspected terrorists without charge. Some consider that irresponsible, as *** the government might want to detain a suspected al Qaeda operative, but not be prepared to file charges in open court as required for a criminal prosecution. *** Others hail the absence of such a preventive-detention law as a testament to the United States' commitment to individual liberty. *** Preventive-detention laws in other countries have often been abused [and in the United States (Palmer Raids of 1919-20, WWII internment of Japanese Americans, and post-9/11 detention of Arab and Muslim foreign nationals)] not one person detained was identified as posing the threat that was said to justify the sweeps in the first place. *** [M]any existing laws and authorities can be and have been invoked in an emergency to effectuate preventive detention [and] *** there are numerous laws on the books that can be and have been employed for those purposes. *** The proper question, *** [is whether] there a case for preventive detention of persons suspected of terrorism beyond the preventive-detention authorities that already exist? *** Should different rules apply in light of the potentially catastrophic harms posed by twenty-first century terrorists? Should special rules apply to al Qaeda, a terrorist organization that has declared war on the United States and attacked us here and abroad, against whom Congress has authorized a military response, and with whom the United States is in an ongoing military conflict in Afghanistan? If preventive detention is permissible under some circumstances, what are the appropriate substantive and procedural safeguards that should accompany it? These are some of the most difficult and controversial legal questions of the day. ***

> Professor David Cole,"Out of the Shadows: Preventive Detention, Suspected Terrorists, and War," 97 Cal. L. Rev. 693 (2009)

Arrest by law enforcement officials of a terrorist suspect generally follows the criminal procedure rules of the country in which the suspect is captured. In the United States, arrest without probable cause (or in some cases reasonable suspicion) and without a *Miranda* warning can lead to release of the person arrested or to exclusion of evidence when the person is tried. Criminal arrest will not be examined in this book, as it is treated in law school criminal procedure courses. Rather, this chapter considers the detention processes used to hold suspected terrorists while further evidence is sought concerning their activities and to detention of terrorist suspects believed by the government to be subject to military detention.

In this chapter, Section A covers two civilian detention situations specific to government efforts to deal with potential terrorist threats after 9/11: "high interest detainees" and "material witnesses." It also contains Notes about two processes used to bring back persons captured elsewhere: (1) the diplomatic process of extradition and (2) the self-help process called rendition. Section B concerns military detention and its limits in the "war on terror," where conflicts involve a non-state party, battlefields are ephemeral, and conflict is potentially endless. Section C contains comparative detention materials, mainly from Israel and the United Kingdom.

This chapter is followed by Chapter VI, which addresses interrogation of terrorist suspects, including the process of "extraordinary rendition" and Chapter VII, which covers habeas corpus and other aspects of release from military detention.

A. CIVIL DETENTION AFTER 9/11

After September 11, to pursue leads on suspected terrorists in the United States, federal civilian officials detained a number of people. A few "high interest detainees" were thought to have engaged in terrorist activities related to 9/11. They were held under restrictive conditions designed to prevent them from communicating with the general prison population or the outside world. A second group of detainees were held on "material witness" warrants for varying periods and often suffered indignities while detained. The following two cases describe both types of detentions after 9/11 and explore high-level federal officials' liability toward civilian detainees. Broader consideration of civil liability for terrorism and counterterrorism is contained in Chapter XII.

ASHCROFT v. IQBAL
129 S.Ct. 1937 (2009)

Justice KENNEDY delivered the opinion of the Court.

Respondent Javaid Iqbal is a citizen of Pakistan and a Muslim. In the wake of the September 11, 2001, terrorist attacks he was arrested in the United States on criminal charges and detained by federal officials. Respondent claims he was deprived of various constitutional protections while in federal custody. To redress the alleged deprivations, respondent filed a complaint against numerous federal officials, including John Ashcroft, the former Attorney General of the United States, and Robert Mueller, the

Director of the Federal Bureau of Investigation (FBI). *** As to these two petitioners, the complaint alleges that they adopted an unconstitutional policy that subjected respondent to harsh conditions of confinement on account of his race, religion, or national origin. *** Respondent's account of his prison ordeal could, if proved, demonstrate unconstitutional misconduct by some governmental actors. But the allegations and pleadings with respect to these actors are not before us here. This case instead turns on a narrower question: Did respondent, as the plaintiff in the District Court, plead factual matter that, if taken as true, states a claim that petitioners deprived him of his clearly established constitutional rights. We hold respondent's pleadings are insufficient.

Following the 2001 attacks, the FBI and other entities within the Department of Justice began an investigation of vast reach to identify the assailants and prevent them from attacking anew. The FBI dedicated more than 4,000 special agents and 3,000 support personnel to the endeavor. By September 18 "the FBI had received more than 96,000 tips or potential leads from the public." *** In the ensuing months the FBI questioned more than 1,000 people with suspected links to the attacks in particular or to terrorism in general. Of those individuals, some 762 were held on immigration charges; and a 184-member subset of that group was deemed to be "of 'high interest' " to the investigation. The high-interest detainees were held under restrictive conditions designed to prevent them from communicating with the general prison population or the outside world.

Respondent was one of the detainees. According to his complaint, in November 2001 agents of the FBI and Immigration and Naturalization Service arrested him on charges of fraud in relation to identification documents and conspiracy to defraud the United States. Pending trial for those crimes, respondent was housed at the Metropolitan Detention Center (MDC) in Brooklyn, New York. Respondent was designated a person "of high interest" to the September 11 investigation and in January 2002 was placed in a section of the MDC known as the Administrative Maximum Special Housing Unit (ADMAX SHU). As the facility's name indicates, the ADMAX SHU incorporates the maximum security conditions allowable under Federal Bureau of Prison regulations. ADMAX SHU detainees were kept in lockdown 23 hours a day, spending the remaining hour outside their cells in handcuffs and leg irons accompanied by a four-officer escort.

Respondent pleaded guilty to the criminal charges, served a term of imprisonment, and was removed to his native Pakistan. He then filed [suit] against 34 current and former federal officials and 19 "John Doe" federal corrections officers. See *Bivens v. Six Unknown Fed. Narcotics Agents,* 403 U.S. 388 (1971). The defendants range from the correctional officers who had day-to-day contact with respondent during the term of his confinement, to the wardens of the MDC facility, all the way to petitioners-officials who were at the highest level of the federal law enforcement hierarchy

The 21-cause-of-action complaint does not challenge respondent's arrest or his confinement in the MDC's general prison population. Rather, it concentrates on his treatment while confined to the ADMAX SHU. The complaint sets forth various claims against defendants who are not before us. For instance, the complaint alleges that respondent's jailors "kicked him in the stomach, punched him in the face, and dragged him across" his cell without justification, subjected him to serial strip and body-cavity searches when he posed no safety risk to himself or others, and refused to let him and other Muslims pray because there would be "[n]o prayers for terrorists."

The allegations against petitioners are the only ones relevant here. The complaint contends that petitioners designated respondent a person of high interest on account of his race, religion, or national origin, in contravention of the First and Fifth Amendments to the Constitution. *** It further alleges that "[t]he policy of holding post-September-11th detainees in highly restrictive conditions of confinement until they were 'cleared' by the FBI was approved by Defendants Ashcroft and Mueller in discussions in the weeks after September 11, 2001." Lastly, the complaint posits that petitioners "each knew of, condoned, and willfully and maliciously agreed to subject" respondent to harsh conditions of confinement "as a matter of policy, solely on account of [his] religion, race, and/or national origin and for no legitimate penological interest." The pleading names Ashcroft as the "principal architect" of the policy, and identifies Mueller as "instrumental in [its] adoption, promulgation, and implementation." ***

In *Bivens*-proceeding on the theory that a right suggests a remedy-this Court "recognized for the first time an implied private action for damages against federal officers alleged to have violated a citizen's constitutional rights." Because implied causes of action are disfavored, the Court has been reluctant to extend *Bivens* liability "to any new context or new category of defendants." *** Based on the rules our precedents establish, respondent correctly concedes that Government officials may not be held liable for the unconstitutional conduct of their subordinates under a theory of *respondeat superior*. *** [A] plaintiff must plead that each Government-official defendant, through the official's own individual actions, has violated the Constitution.

The factors necessary to establish a *Bivens* violation will vary with the constitutional provision at issue. *** [T]o state a claim based on a violation of a clearly established right, respondent must plead sufficient factual matter to show that petitioners adopted and implemented the detention policies at issue not for a neutral, investigative reason but for the purpose of discriminating on account of race, religion, or national origin.*** Where a complaint pleads facts that are "merely consistent with" a Defendant's liability, it "stops short of the line between possibility and plausibility of 'entitlement to relief.' " *** [W]here the well-pleaded facts do not permit the court to infer more than the mere possibility of misconduct, the complaint has alleged-but it has not "show[n]"-"that the pleader is entitled to relief." ***

We begin our analysis by identifying the allegations in the complaint that are not entitled to the assumption of truth. Respondent pleads that petitioners "knew of, condoned, and willfully and maliciously agreed to subject [him]" to harsh conditions of confinement "as a matter of policy, solely on account of [his] religion, race, and/or national origin and for no legitimate penological interest." The complaint alleges that Ashcroft was the "principal architect" of this invidious policy, and that Mueller was "instrumental" in adopting and executing it. These bare assertions *** amount to nothing more than a "formulaic recitation of the elements" of a constitutional discrimination claim, namely, that petitioners adopted a policy "'because of,' not merely 'in spite of,' its adverse effects upon an identifiable group." As such, the allegations are conclusory and not entitled to be assumed true. To be clear, we do not reject these bald allegations on the ground that they are unrealistic or nonsensical. *** It is the conclusory nature of respondent's allegations, rather than their extravagantly fanciful nature, that disentitles them to the presumption of truth.

We next consider the factual allegations in respondent's complaint to determine if they plausibly suggest an entitlement to relief. The complaint alleges that "the [FBI], under the direction of Defendant Mueller, arrested and detained thousands of Arab Muslim men ... as part of its investigation of the events of September 11." It further claims that "[t]he policy of holding post-September-11th detainees in highly restrictive conditions of confinement until they were 'cleared' by the FBI was approved by Defendants Ashcroft and Mueller in discussions in the weeks after September 11, 2001.". Taken as true, these allegations are consistent with petitioners' purposefully designating detainees "of high interest" because of their race, religion, or national origin. But given more likely explanations, they do not plausibly establish this purpose.

The September 11 attacks were perpetrated by 19 Arab Muslim hijackers who counted themselves members in good standing of al Qaeda, an Islamic fundamentalist group. Al Qaeda was headed by another Arab Muslim-Osama bin Laden-and composed in large part of his Arab Muslim disciples. It should come as no surprise that a legitimate policy directing law enforcement to arrest and detain individuals because of their suspected link to the attacks would produce a disparate, incidental impact on Arab Muslims, even though the purpose of the policy was to target neither Arabs nor Muslims. On the facts respondent alleges the arrests Mueller oversaw were likely lawful and justified by his nondiscriminatory intent to detain aliens who were illegally present in the United States and who had potential connections to those who committed terrorist acts. As between that "obvious alternative explanation" for the arrests, and the purposeful, invidious discrimination respondent asks us to infer, discrimination is not a plausible conclusion.

*** Respondent's constitutional claims against petitioners rest solely on their ostensible "policy of holding post-September-11th detainees" in the ADMAX SHU once they were categorized as "of high interest." To prevail on that theory, the complaint must contain facts plausibly showing that petitioners purposefully adopted a policy of classifying post-September-11 detainees as "of high interest" because of their race, religion, or national origin.

This the complaint fails to do. Though respondent alleges that various other defendants, who are not before us, may have labeled him a person of "of high interest" for impermissible reasons, his only factual allegation against petitioners accuses them of adopting a policy approving "restrictive conditions of confinement" for post-September-11 detainees until they were " 'cleared' by the FBI." Accepting the truth of that allegation, the complaint does not show, or even intimate, that petitioners purposefully housed detainees in the ADMAX SHU due to their race, religion, or national origin. All it plausibly suggests is that the Nation's top law enforcement officers, in the aftermath of a devastating terrorist attack, sought to keep suspected terrorists in the most secure conditions available until the suspects could be cleared of terrorist activity. Respondent does not argue, nor can he, that such a motive would violate petitioners' constitutional obligations. He would need to allege more by way of factual content to "nudg[e]" his claim of purposeful discrimination "across the line from conceivable to plausible." *** [W]e express no opinion concerning the sufficiency of respondent's complaint against the defendants who are not before us. Respondent's account of his prison ordeal alleges serious official misconduct that we need not address here. Our decision is limited to the determination that respondent's complaint does not entitle him to relief from petitioners. ***

***Litigation, though necessary to ensure that officials comply with the law, exacts heavy costs in terms of efficiency and expenditure of valuable time and resources that might otherwise be directed to the proper execution of the work of the Government. The costs of diversion are only magnified when Government officials are charged with responding to *** "a national and international security emergency unprecedented in the history of the American Republic."

It is no answer to these concerns to say that discovery for petitioners can be deferred while pretrial proceedings continue for other defendants. ***Even if petitioners are not yet themselves subject to discovery orders, then, they would not be free from the burdens of discovery. ***

Justice SOUTER, with whom Justice STEVENS, Justice GINSBURG, and Justice BREYER join, dissenting.

*** *Bivens* allows personal liability based on a federal officer's violation of an individual's rights under the First and Fifth Amendments, and it comes to us with the explicit concession of petitioners Ashcroft and Mueller that an officer may be subject to *Bivens* liability as a supervisor on grounds other than *respondeat superior*. The Court apparently rejects this concession and, although it has no bearing on the majority's resolution of this case, does away with supervisory liability under *Bivens*. The majority then misapplies *** pleading standard[s] *** to conclude that the complaint fails to state a claim. ***

[Justice BREYER filed an additional separate dissent]

Notes

1. The Impact of Pleading Standards. What impact will this decision will have on the ability of other defendants to vindicate their rights? How pivotal do you think the national security backdrop was to this decision?

2. Lower-level Actors. The Court says it leaves open the possibility of liability for actors having more personal involvement in individual cases of allegedly unconstitutional conduct.   Is this accountability enough to ensure the Constitution is upheld?   What accountability does the Court leave for unconstitutional programs of potentially very broad scope—political accountability? Put another way, must a legal right have a *legal* remedy?

3. Distraction of Discovery. Should high-level government officials be spared the distraction of discover? To what degree does your answer depend on your view of whether the nation has "a national and international security emergency unprecedented in the history of the American Republic"?

4. Vicarious Liability Under *Bivens*. The dissent focuses in large part on the majority's rejection of Ashcroft and Muller's concession regarding vicarious liability under *Bivens*. To what degree is supervisory liability under *Bivens* important to enforcing constitutional rights? Is monetary liability, recoverable under *Bivens*, a different kind of enforcement or incentive scheme for constitutional rights than a suit in equity? What impact might this decision have on cases alleging torture?

As this book went to press, the Supreme Court had just heard oral argument in the appeal of the Ninth Circuit case excerpted below. From the questions, it appeared the Court was skeptical of the circuit court's decision. By the time this book reaches you, the decision of the Supreme Court should be available.

AL-KIDD v. ASHCROFT
580 F.3d 949 (2009), en banc pet den 598 F. 3d. 1129 (9th Cir. 2010),
cert granted 131 S.Ct. 415 (Mem.)(2010)

MILAN D. SMITH, JR., Circuit Judge:

According to the allegations *** Abdullah al-Kidd (al-Kidd), a United States citizen and a married man with two children, was arrested at a Dulles International Airport ticket counter. He was handcuffed, taken to the airport's police substation, and interrogated. Over the next sixteen days, he was confined in high security cells lit twenty-four hours a day in Virginia, Oklahoma, and then Idaho, during which he was strip searched on multiple occasions. Each time he was transferred to a different facility, al-Kidd was handcuffed and shackled about his wrists, legs, and waist. He was eventually released from custody by court order, on the conditions that he live with his wife and in-laws in Nevada, limit his travel to Nevada and three other states, surrender his travel documents, regularly report to a probation officer, and consent to home visits throughout the period of supervision. By the time al-Kidd's confinement and supervision ended, fifteen months after his arrest, al-Kidd had been fired from his job as an employee of a government contractor because he was denied a security clearance due to his arrest, and had separated from his wife. He has been unable to obtain steady employment since his arrest.

Al-Kidd was not arrested and detained because he had allegedly committed a crime. He alleges that he was arrested and confined because former United States Attorney General John Ashcroft (Ashcroft), subordinates operating under policies promulgated by Ashcroft, and others within the United States Department of Justice (DOJ), unlawfully used the federal material witness statute, 18 U.S.C. § 3144, to investigate or preemptively detain him.[15][*] Ashcroft asserts that he is entitled to absolute and qualified immunity against al-Kidd's claims. *** [Al-Kidd] and his then-wife were the target of a Federal Bureau of Investigation (FBI) surveillance as part of a broad anti-terrorism investigation allegedly aimed at Arab and Muslim men.[1]

No evidence of criminal activity by al-Kidd was ever discovered. Al-Kidd planned to fly to Saudi Arabia in the spring of 2003 to study Arabic and Islamic law on a scholarship at a Saudi university.

On February 13, 2003, a federal grand jury in Idaho indicted Sami Omar Al-Hussayen for visa fraud and making false statements to U.S. officials. On March 14, the Idaho U.S. Attorney's Office submitted an application to a magistrate judge of the District of Idaho, seeking al-Kidd's arrest as a material witness in the Al-Hussayen trial. Appended to the application was an affidavit by Scott Mace, a Special Agent of the FBI in Boise (the Mace Affidavit). The Mace Affidavit described two contacts al-Kidd had with Al-Hussayen: al-Kidd had received "in excess of $20,000" from Al-Hussayen (though the Mace Affidavit does not indicate what this payment was for), and al-Kidd had "met with Al-Hussayen's associates" after returning from a trip to Yemen. It also contained evidence of al-Kidd's contacts with officials of the Islamic Assembly of North America (IANA, an organization with which Al-Hussayen was affiliated),-including one official "who was recently arrested in New York." It ended with the statement, "[d]ue to Al-Kidd's demonstrated involvement with the defendant ... he is believed to be in possession of information germane to this matter which will be crucial to the prosecution." The Mace Affidavit did not elaborate on what "information" al-Kidd might have had, nor how his testimony might be "germane"-let alone "crucial"-to the prosecution of Al-Hussayen.

The affidavit further stated:

Kidd is scheduled to take a one-way, first class flight (costing

---

[*] The text of this statute is as follows: If it appears from an affidavit filed by a party that the testimony of a person is material in a criminal proceeding, and if it is shown that it may become impracticable to secure the presence of the person by subpoena, a judicial officer may order the arrest of the person and treat the person in accordance with the provisions of section 3142 of this title. No material witness may be detained because of inability to comply with any condition of release if the testimony of such witness can adequately be secured by deposition, and if further detention is not necessary to prevent a failure of justice. Release of a material witness may be delayed for a reasonable period of time until the deposition of the witness can be taken pursuant to the Federal Rules of Criminal Procedure.

[1] Al-Kidd is Muslim, but is African-American and not of Arab descent.

approximately $5,000) to Saudi Arabia on Sunday, March 16, 2003, at approximately 6:00 EST. ***It is believed that if Al-Kidd travels to Saudi Arabia, the United States Government will be unable to secure his presence at trial via subpoena.

In fact, al-Kidd had a round-trip, coach class ticket, costing approximately $1700. The Mace Affidavit omitted the facts that al-Kidd was a U.S. resident and citizen; that his parents, wife, and two children were likewise U.S. residents and citizens; and that he had previously cooperated with the FBI on several occasions when FBI agents asked to interview him. The magistrate judge issued the warrant the same day. [He was arrested two days later and treated as discussed above.] [Kidd was] released at the end of Al-Hussayen's trial, more than fifteen months after being arrested.[16] In July 2004, al-Kidd was fired from his job. He alleges he was terminated when he was denied a security clearance because of his arrest. He is now separated from his wife, and has been unable to find steady employment. He was also deprived of his chance to study in Saudi Arabia on scholarship.

Al-Kidd was never called as a witness in the Al-Hussayen trial or in any other criminal proceeding.

Defendant-Appellant Ashcroft was Attorney General of the United States during the relevant time period. According to al-Kidd's complaint, following the September 11, 2001 terrorist attacks, Ashcroft developed and promulgated a policy by which the FBI and DOJ would use the federal material witness statute as a pretext "to arrest and detain terrorism *suspects* about whom they did not have sufficient evidence to arrest on criminal charges but wished to hold preventatively or to investigate further." (Cited in, and emphasis added, in al-Kidd's complaint.)

To support this allegation, the complaint first quotes Ashcroft's own statement at a press briefing:

> Today, I am announcing several steps that we are taking to enhance our ability to protect the United States from the threat of terrorist aliens. These measures form one part of the department's strategy to prevent terrorist attacks by taking *suspected terrorists* off the street ... Aggressive *detention* of lawbreakers and *material witnesses* is vital to preventing, disrupting or delaying new attacks.

***The complaint also cites internal DOJ memoranda quoted in a report by the DOJ's Office of the Inspector General (OIG Report), which describe the use of "aggressive arrest and detention tactics in the war on terror," including the use of material witness warrants to confine aliens suspected of terrorist involvement. The complaint also quotes the public statements of a number of DOJ and White House officials implying or stating outright that suspects

---

[16] Al-Hussayen was not convicted of any of the charges brought against him. His trial ended in acquittal on the most serious charges, including conspiracy to provide material support to terrorists. After the jury failed to reach a verdict on the remaining lesser charges, the district court declared a mistrial. The government agreed not to retry Al-Hussayen and deported him to Saudi Arabia for visa violations.

were being held under material witness warrants as an alternative means of investigative arrest or preventative detention. In addition to this direct evidence, the complaint cites a number of press reports describing the detention of numerous Muslim individuals under material witness warrants. The complaint further alleges that the policies designed and promulgated by Ashcroft have caused individuals to be "impermissibly arrested and detained as material witnesses even though there was no reason to believe it would have been impracticable to secure their testimony voluntarily or by subpoena," in violation of the terms of § 3144.

In his complaint, al-Kidd links his personal detention to these broader policies not only through inference, but also through the statements of Robert Mueller, the Director of the FBI. On March 27, while al-Kidd was jailed in Idaho, Mueller testified before Congress, listing five "major successes" in the FBI's efforts toward "identifying and dismantling terrorist networks." The first was the capture of Khalid Shaikh Mohammed, identified as "a key planner and the mastermind of the September 11th attack." The second was al-Kidd, identified as having been "arrested ... en route to Saudi Arabia." The other three "successes" all involved individuals "indicted" or "charged" with some crime connected to terrorism. *** Finally, the complaint *** alleges "a general policy" of extensive mistreatment of material witnesses at the New York City Metropolitan Correctional Center (MCC). *** The complaint avers that Ashcroft "knew or reasonably should have known of the unlawful, excessive, and punitive manner in which the federal material witness statute was being used," and that such manner "would also foreseeably subject" detainees "to unreasonable and unlawful use of force, to unconstitutional conditions of confinement, and to punishment without due process."

In March 2005, al-Kidd filed this lawsuit [seeking] damages ***for violations of al-Kidd's rights under the Fourth and Fifth Amendments to the Constitution, and for a direct violation of § 3144. Ashcroft moved to dismiss *** Ashcroft argues that he is entitled to absolute prosecutorial immunity as to the § 3144 and Fourth Amendment Claims. *** He also argues that he is entitled to qualified immunity from liability for all three claims.

Absolute Immunity. In *Bivens* actions and those taken under 42 U.S.C. § 1983, "[m]ost public officials are entitled only to qualified immunity." Prosecutors are entitled to *absolute* immunity, however, when they engage in activities "intimately associated with the judicial phase of the criminal process," and done "in the course of [their] role as an advocate for the State," They are entitled only to qualified immunity, however, when they perform investigatory or administrative functions, or are essentially functioning as police officers or detectives. In addition, the United States Attorney General is not entitled to absolute immunity in the performance of his or her "national security functions." ***

To determine whether an action is "prosecutorial," and so entitled to absolute immunity, the Supreme Court has adopted a "'functional approach,' which looks to 'the nature of the function performed, not the identity of the actor who performed it.'" *** As the Supreme Court has acknowledged, the distinction between the roles of "prosecutor" and "investigator" is not always clear. *** Ashcroft contends that the decision to seek a material witness warrant is always a prosecutorial function. He has presented us with no historical evidence that a common-law tradition of absolute immunity from suit for prosecutors in seeking material witness arrests exists, and our own research has uncovered none, even though the practice of detaining witnesses who are not criminal suspects dates back to at least the 1840s. *** Other circuits, however, have held that the decision to seek a material witness warrant to secure a witness's testimony at trial is sufficiently related to judicial proceedings to be protected by absolute prosecutorial immunity. *** Al-Kidd *** contends *** that in his case, the decision to arrest was an act in furtherance of an investigative or national security function, for which the Attorney General may claim only qualified immunity. That is, al-Kidd claims he was arrested not in order to secure his testimony at Al-Hussayen's trial, but in order to detain, interrogate, and gather evidence against *him,* in particular. *** Ashcroft responds that any investigation into the purpose or motive behind the decision to arrest al-Kidd is inconsistent with the "functional" approach the Supreme Court has outlined. *** Because the application for the arrest warrant had the words "Material Witness" in the caption, Ashcroft seems to contend, our inquiry must stop there. *** al-Kidd has averred ample facts to render plausible the allegation of an investigatory function:

- Al-Kidd's arrest was sought a month *after* Al-Hussayen was indicted, and more than a year *before* trial began, temporally distant from the time any testimony would have been needed. ***

- The FBI had previously investigated and interviewed al-Kidd, but had never suggested, let alone demanded, that he appear as a witness. ***

- The FBI conducted lengthy interrogations with al-Kidd while in custody, including about matters apparently unrelated to Al-Hussayen's alleged visa violations. ***

- Al-Kidd *never actually testified* for the prosecution in Al-Hussayen's or any other case, despite his assurances that he would be willing to do so. ***

All of these are objective indicia *** that al-Kidd's arrest functioned as an investigatory arrest or national security-related preemptive detention, rather than as one to secure a witness's testimony for trial. Finally:

- Ashcroft's immediate subordinate, FBI Director Mueller, testified before Congress that al-Kidd's *arrest* (rather than, say, the obtaining of the evidence he was supposedly going to provide against Al-Hussayen) constituted a "major success[ ]" in "identifying and dismantling terrorist networks." ***

We conclude that the practice of detaining a material witness in order to investigate him, on the facts alleged by al-Kidd, fulfills an investigative function.

Qualified Immunity. The Attorney General may still be entitled to qualified immunity for acts taken in furtherance of an investigatory or national security function. *** Determining whether officials are owed qualified immunity involves two inquiries: (1) whether, taken in the light most favorable to the party asserting the injury, the facts alleged show the officer's conduct violated a constitutional right; and (2) if so, whether the right was clearly established in light of the specific context of the case. *** Al-Kidd's complaint does not allege that Ashcroft was directly involved in the decision to detain al-Kidd. But "direct, personal participation is not necessary to establish liability for a constitutional violation." Supervisors can be held liable for the actions of their subordinates (1) for setting in motion a series of acts by others, or knowingly refusing to terminate a series of acts by others, which they knew or reasonably should have known would cause others to inflict constitutional injury; (2) for culpable action or inaction in training, supervision, or control of subordinates; (3) for acquiescence in the constitutional deprivation by subordinates; or (4) for conduct that shows a "reckless or callous indifference to the rights of others." Any one of these bases will suffice to establish the personal involvement of the defendant in the constitutional violation.

The Fourth Amendment Claim. Al-Kidd's complaint principally alleges that Ashcroft "developed, implemented and set into motion a policy and/or practice under which the FBI and DOJ would use the material witness statute to arrest and detain terrorism *suspects* about whom they did not have sufficient evidence to arrest on criminal charges but wished to hold preventively or to investigate further." *** [M]aterial witness arrests are "seizures" within the meaning of the Fourth Amendment and are therefore subject to its reasonableness requirement. *** Al-Kidd does not contend that § 3144 is facially unconstitutional. Rather, *** Al-Kidd alleges that he was arrested without probable cause pursuant to a general policy, designed and implemented by Ashcroft, whose programmatic purpose was not to secure testimony, but to investigate those detained. Assuming that allegation to be true, he has alleged a constitutional violation. *** Our holding does nothing to curb the use of the material witness statute for its stated purpose. *What we do hold is that probable cause-including individualized suspicion of criminal wrongdoing-is required when 18 U.S.C. § 3144 is not being used for its stated purpose, but instead for the purpose of criminal investigation.* We thus do not render the material witness statute "entirely superfluous"; it is only the *misuse* of the statute, resulting in the detention of a person without probable cause for purposes of criminal investigation, that is repugnant to the Fourth Amendment. ***

Ashcroft alternatively contends that if we conclude that the use of material witness orders for investigatory purposes violates the Constitution, we should still grant him qualified immunity because that constitutional right was not "clearly established" in March 2003, when al-Kidd was arrested. We disagree.

In March 2003, no case had squarely confronted the question of whether misuse of the material witness statute to investigate suspects violates the Constitution. *** However, this alone is not enough to give Ashcroft immunity: "'while there may be no published cases holding similar policies [un]constitutional, this may be due more to the obviousness of the illegality than the novelty of the legal issue.' " *** What *was* clearly established in March 2003? *** The definition of probable cause *** was certainly clearly established. While the Supreme Court's decision *permitting* suspicionless seizures in some circumstances *** had not yet been decided, [the Supreme Court had held] that an investigatory programmatic purpose renders a program of seizures without probable cause unconstitutional *** Ashcroft [was] on notice that the material witness detentions-involving a far more severe seizure than a mere traffic stop-would be similarly subject to an inquiry into programmatic purpose.

Moreover, the history and purposes of the Fourth Amendment were known well before 2003. *** Finally, months before al-Kidd's arrest, one district court in a high-profile case had already indicated, in the spring of 2002, that *§ 3144 itself* should not be abused as an investigatory anti-terrorism tool, calling out Ashcroft by name:

> Other reasons may motivate prosecutors and law enforcement officers to rely upon the material witness statute. Attorney General John Ashcroft has been reported as saying: "Aggressive detention of lawbreakers and material witnesses is vital to preventing, disrupting or delaying new attacks." *Relying on the material witness statute to detain people who are presumed innocent under our Constitution in order to prevent potential crimes is an illegitimate use of the statute.* ***

Awadallah I, 202 F.Supp.2d at 77 n. 28. *** We therefore hold that al-Kidd's right not to be arrested as a material witness in order to be investigated or preemptively detained was clearly established in 2003. ***

The § 3144 Claim. In addition to alleging that Ashcroft misused § 3144 for unconstitutional purposes the statute did not intend, al-Kidd alleges that his arrest violated the terms of § 3144 itself. Section 3144 authorizes the arrest of material witnesses only if (1) "the testimony of a person is material in a criminal proceeding," and (2) "it may become impracticable to secure the presence of the person by subpoena." *** Al-Kidd claims that, in his case, the Mace Affidavit fails to demonstrate probable cause for either the materiality of his testimony or the reasons it would be impracticable to secure that testimony by subpoena. *** Although the arrest was conducted pursuant to a warrant issued by a magistrate judge, we allow challenges to the validity of searches and seizures conducted pursuant to a warrant if the affidavit in support of the warrant included false statements or material omissions that were made intentionally or recklessly. *** Ashcroft does not contest that such an inquiry would be appropriate ***. Rather, he argues that al-Kidd has not pled sufficient acts or omissions to establish supervisory liability for the § 3144 Claim. ***

Since the argument and initial briefing in this case, the Supreme Court, in *Ashcroft v. Iqbal,* 129 S.Ct. 1937 (2009), has clarified [the law in] cases such as these. *** The Court held that a pleading "that offers 'labels and conclusions' or 'a formulaic recitation of the elements of a cause of action' " is insufficient to state a claim under Rule 8 of the Federal Rules of Civil Procedure. *** Here, unlike Iqbal's allegations, al-Kidd's complaint "plausibly suggest[s]" unlawful conduct, and does more than contain bare allegations of an impermissible policy. While the complaint similarly alleges that Ashcroft is the "principal architect" of the policy, the complaint in this case contains specific statements that Ashcroft himself made regarding the post-September 11th use of the material witness statute. Ashcroft stated that enhanced tactics, such as the use of the material witness statute, "form one part of the department's concentrated strategy to prevent terrorist attacks by taking suspected terrorists off the street," and that "[a]ggressive detention of lawbreakers and material witnesses is vital to preventing, disrupting or delaying new attacks." Other top DOJ officials candidly admitted that the material witness statute was viewed as an important "investigative tool" where they could obtain "evidence" about the witness. The complaint also contains reference to congressional testimony from FBI Director Mueller, stating that al-Kidd's arrest was one of the Government's anti-terrorism successes-without any caveat that al-Kidd was arrested only as a witness. *** Al-Kidd need not show that Ashcroft "actually instruct[ed] his subordinates to bypass the plain text of the statute," as Ashcroft contends. The complaint clearly alleges facts which might support liability on the basis of Ashcroft's *knowing failure* to act in the light of even unauthorized abuses, but also alleges facts which may support liability on the basis that Ashcroft purposely used the material witness statute to preventatively detain suspects and that al-Kidd was subjected to this policy. ***[T]he complaint contains allegations that plausibly suggest that Ashcroft purposely instructed his subordinates to bypass the plain reading of the statute. ***

Further, the complaint notes that the "abuses occurring under the material witness statute after September 11, 2001, were highly publicized in the media, congressional testimony and correspondence, and in various reports by governmental and non-governmental entities," which could have given Ashcroft sufficient notice to require affirmative acts to supervise and correct the actions of his subordinates. The complaint also avers that "the Justice Department has issued apologies to 10-12 individuals who were improperly arrested as material witnesses." Given that the government maintains that it does nothing wrong in the pretextual use of the material witness statute to investigate and preemptively detain, it is reasonable to infer that its apologies were for violations of the terms of the statute itself, of which the DOJ, and presumably its leader, were aware. *** Drawing on our "judicial experience and common sense," as the Supreme Court urges us to do, we find that al-Kidd has met his burden of pleading a claim for relief that is plausible, and that his suit on the § 3144 claim should be allowed to proceed. *** In the district court, moving forward, al-Kidd will bear a significant burden to show that the Attorney General himself was personally involved in a policy or practice of alleged violations of § 3144. ***

[BEA, Circuit Judge, concurred in part and dissented in part; in the denial of rehearing en banc, the following dissent argues that the majority of the panel erred:]

O'SCANNLAIN, Circuit Judge, joined by KOZINSKI, Chief Judge, and KLEINFELD, GOULD, TALLMAN, CALLAHAN, BEA and IKUTA, Circuit Judges, dissenting from the denial of rehearing en banc:

The majority holds that a former Attorney General of the United States may be *personally liable* for promulgating a policy under which his subordinates took actions expressly authorized by law. Judge Bea's dissent from the panel decision clearly and ably describes the several legal errors the panel makes in reaching this startling conclusion. For my part, I write to express my concern at the scope of this decision. First, the majority holds that al-Kidd's detention under a *valid* material witness warrant violated his clearly established constitutional rights-a conclusion that effectively declares the material witness statute unconstitutional as applied to al-Kidd. Second, the majority holds that a cabinet-level official may be personally liable for actions taken by his subordinates alone. Because of the gratuitous damage this decision inflicts upon orderly federal law enforcement, I must respectfully dissent from our refusal to rehear this case en banc. ***

By permitting al-Kidd's suit to proceed, the majority commits two distinct but equally troubling legal errors, each of which will have far-reaching implications for how government officials perform their duties. First, the majority strips Ashcroft of his official immunity, holding that it was clearly established at the time of al-Kidd's arrest that prosecutors violate the Fourth Amendment when they obtain and execute a material witness warrant as a pretext for other law-enforcement objectives. Second, by holding that Ashcroft may be personally liable if his *subordinates* swore false affidavits to obtain the warrant authorizing al-Kidd's arrest, the majority stretches beyond recognition the rule that a government official is liable only when he personally violates the constitution.

The majority begins by effectively declaring the material witness statute unconstitutional, at least as applied to al-Kidd. But al-Kidd does not appear to contest that he met the statutory requirements for arrest as a material witness. Nor does he contend that the material witness statute is *facially* unconstitutional. The majority nevertheless holds that because prosecutors used a material witness warrant to arrest al-Kidd as a *pretext* to a criminal investigation, his detention violated the Fourth Amendment. This conclusion-that the material witness statute authorized al-Kidd's arrest while the Fourth Amendment forbade it-can only mean that the material witness statute itself is unconstitutional in this circumstance.[4] ***

The majority does not stop at declaring a 200-year-old statute unconstitutional, however. It also distorts the bedrock Fourth Amendment principle that an official's subjective reasons for making an arrest are

---

[4] I acknowledge that the majority does not *say* that it is declaring the material witness statute unconstitutional. *** By concluding that the Constitution invalidates arrests authorized by the statute, the majority must conclude that the statute is unconstitutional to the extent it authorizes arrests such as the one in this case-put another way, that the statute is unconstitutional as applied to al-Kidd.

constitutionally irrelevant. The majority holds that if prosecutors used the material witness warrant as a *pretext* to arrest al-Kidd "with the *ulterior* and ... unconstitutional *purpose* of investigating or preemptively detaining" him, they violated his Fourth Amendment rights. This holding is impossible to square with Supreme Court precedent, which has "flatly dismissed the idea that an *ulterior motive* might serve to strip the agents of their legal justification." Given that al-Kidd has conceded that he met the facial requirements for arrest under the material witness statute, the prosecutor's purpose for arresting him is immaterial to the Fourth Amendment analysis because "[s]ubjective intent alone ... does not make otherwise lawful conduct illegal or unconstitutional."

The majority, unfortunately, disagrees. Although it acknowledges that an officer's subjective intentions are irrelevant to "ordinary, probable-cause Fourth Amendment analysis," it holds that because al-Kidd's arrest was not supported by probable cause *that al-Kidd had committed a crime,* his detention was constitutionally infirm. To reach this novel result, the majority relies on the Supreme Court's "programmatic purpose" test. Contrary to the majority's analysis, that test is totally inapplicable here. The Supreme Court uses the programmatic purpose test to evaluate the constitutionality of *warrantless* searches. Because al-Kidd was arrested under a valid warrant, however, the programmatic purpose test, and its concern for the purpose of an arrest, is entirely inapplicable here. Thus, the majority concludes that the material witness warrant authorizing al-Kidd's arrest is unconstitutional only after examining the subjective reasons prosecutors sought the warrant, something the Supreme Court has repeatedly forbidden us to do. This error alone warranted en banc review.

The majority then compounds its error by holding that the right to be free from a detention under a pretextual material witness warrant was clearly established at the time of al-Kidd's arrest. The majority claims this result is compelled by three sources: the clearly established definition of probable cause, "the history and purposes of the Fourth Amendment," and a footnote in a district court opinion.

The majority's reliance on the first two sources proves too much, of course. All government officials are presumed to be aware of the definition of probable cause and the history and purposes of the Fourth Amendment. If this is sufficient clearly to establish how the Fourth Amendment applies in a particular setting, then how can *any* Fourth Amendment rule ever *not* be "clearly established"?

The majority's reliance on *Awadallah* is possibly even more troubling. The majority's assertion that three sentences of dicta in a footnote to a subsequently reversed district court opinion clearly establish a right that the majority expended nearly three-thousand words describing is truly astonishing. Under the majority's reasoning, our Government's officials may find themselves subject to suits for decisions that they did not-and, even if they spent their time doing nothing but reading reports of federal judicial decisions, could not-know contravened the Constitution. *** One shudders at the thought that this decision might deter the incumbent and future Attorneys General from exercising the full range of their lawful authority to protect the security of the United States.

The majority goes further still, however, by holding that Ashcroft may be held personally liable to al-Kidd if his *subordinates* provided false testimony in support of their application for a material witness warrant. *** In light of *Iqbal*'s holding that "each Government official, his or her title notwithstanding, is only liable for his or her own misconduct," al-Kidd" complaint fails to allege facts sufficient to establish a cause of action against Ashcroft. *** [T]he majority permits al-Kidd to seek damages from Ashcroft for his subordinates' alleged misconduct, a result indisputably at odds with *Iqbal*.

After this decision, *** any cabinet-level official must worry that he might be personally liable if his *subordinates* take an action perfectly *consistent* with then-existing federal law.[6] ***

GOULD, Circuit Judge, with whom KOZINSKI, Chief Judge, and O'SCANNLAIN, KLEINFELD, CALLAHAN, BEA, and IKUTA, Circuit Judges, join, dissenting from the denial of rehearing en banc:

*** If an Attorney General of the United States can be held liable and subject to monetary damages primarily because of actions of law enforcement subordinates, who allegedly gained and executed a material witness warrant for contrived purposes, I fear that it will become more difficult to persuade a person of great talent and integrity to leave his or her current occupation in order to hold the nation's highest law office. The panel majority's decision in effect says "good bye" to many talented persons who would otherwise be willing to serve as Attorney General with great distinction and attendant benefit to our country.

Notes

1. Probable Cause in the War on Terror. The court in *al-Kidd* presupposed that the Fourth Amendment's requirements apply to the detention of material witnesses in a counterterrorism context in the same manner as they would to those in a criminal context. Are there reasons to question the assumption that the criminal justice paradigm and doctrine from criminal cases is the correct approach? What facts would be necessary to distinguish a "criminal law detention" from a "national security" one? Should the national security context change the probable cause inquiry for preventive detentions under material witness warrants? Would "aggressive arrest and detention tactics in the war on terror," including detention of material witnesses for the purposes al-Kidd alleges, be prudent regardless of its constitutionality?

2. Congressional Fix? The material witness statute, § 3144, authorizes arrest

---

[6] The *possibility* the federal government might reimburse Ashcroft for any judgment against him hardly removes the likelihood that this decision might deter the current or future Attorneys General from carrying out their duties. Claims for reimbursement have been denied on occasion. Moreover, the decision to provide or to deny such reimbursement is entirely within the discretion of the current Attorney General, and is not subject to judicial review.

of material witnesses if affidavits establish probable cause to believe (1) "the testimony of a person is material in a criminal proceeding," and (2) "it may become impracticable to secure the presence of the person by subpoena." Senator Patrick Leahy introduced *A Bill to Amend the Material Witness Statute to Strengthen Procedural Safeguards, and for Other Purposes*, to permit the detention of material witnesses "for a period not to exceed 5 days, or until the testimony of the witness can adequately be secured by deposition or by appearance before the court or grand jury, whichever is earlier." If Congress authorized it, would detention without probable cause for interrogation or preventative detention violate the Fourth Amendment? Would the five day period in the proposed statute be sufficient to accomplish the Bush Administration's purposes?

3. Use of Material Witness Statute. According to a 2005 Human Rights Watch/A.C.L.U. report, at least seventy more individuals were improperly arrested and detained under the material witness statute since September 11th. *Witness to Abuse: Human Rights Abuses under the Material Witness Law since September 11*, 17 HUMAN RIGHTS WATCH 1-3 (June 2005), http://www.hrw.org/en/reports/2005/06/26/witness-abuse. All but one of these (al-Kidd) were Muslim men and sixty-four of the seventy were of Middle Eastern or South Asian descent, raising critics' concerns about religious and racial profiling. Does this information change your Fourth Amendment analysis or policy judgment? Does it raise other constitutional concerns?

4. The Panel Dissent. Judge Bea's dissent in the three-judge panel decision in *al-Kidd* argues that "Reading the minds of government officials is notoriously expensive, uncertain, and fraught with error. *** If official immunity were to depend upon proof of the officials' good intentions, the value of that immunity would be lost. *** The sole reason the majority provides for stripping former Attorney General John Ashcroft of his official immunity is that *** they acted with a forbidden state of mind: they *really* arrested him not to testify against the indicted terror suspect, but to investigate al-Kidd himself." What is the line between "reading the minds of government officials" and the "pragmatic purpose of a government program" that the majority refers to? Should officials benefit from qualified or absolute immunity for policy choices such as the use of the material witness statute or is personal liability appropriate? Is a policy decision regarding the use of the material witness statute "prosecutorial" in your view?

5. Supreme Court Briefing and Argument. The Reply Brief for the United States in the Supreme Court commences with this observation: "[R]espondent's arguments rest on his claim that the prosecutors who sought a material witness warrant had an improper subjective motive. Accepting his position would require this Court to adopt some test for identifying a prescribed motivation or purpose." Do you agree that this would be a difficult inquiry for a court to make? Is this inquiry consistent with the text of the material witness statute (see footnote 1 of the Ninth Circuit opinion)? Does the requirement that a magistrate issue the warrant provide sufficient protection against abusive use of material witness warrants? Late in the brief, the Government argues further that the logic of the Ninth Circuit's decision is not limited to material witness warrants because "Prosecutors often bring charges against lower-level offenders in circumstances where defendants could allege that their "immediate purpose" is not to proceed with a prosecution but to obtain information about more important suspects." Do you agree that upholding the decision woul have such consequences? Incidentally, at oral argument, the Court explored whether, should it reverse, absolute or qualified immunity would be the more appropriate approach to take.

6. Bringing a Suspect to the U.S. by Extradition. Extradition occurs when a person suspected of criminal activity in one country (the requesting country) who is found in another country (the host country) is surrendered through diplomatic channels for trial and punishment in the requesting country. Several components of extradition treaties are noteworthy. First, these treaties operate on the basis of reciprocity: the extraditable offense must be a criminal offense in both countries. Second, some countries, including Israel, Mexico, and many European countries, refuse to extradite their own citizens. Third, some countries, including Canada and Mexico, refuse to extradite fugitives who could receive the death penalty for their crimes in the requesting country. Mexico even applies this principle where the penalty could be a life penalty without parole. Fourth, there is a "political offense exception" to most extradition treaties that sometimes frustrates United States efforts to extradite individuals who argue their crimes were political. See *Quinn v. Robinson* 783 F.2d 776 (9ᵗʰ Cir. 1986), in which an IRA terrorist claimed his extradition on murder charges fell within the political offense loophole. Fifth, the "doctrine of specialty," demands that the extradited person be tried only on the charges set forth in the documentation provided in support of the extradition, but this doctrine of specialty may be "waived" by the host country. U.S Department of Justice, U.S. Attorney's Manual 9-15.500.

7. Extradition Treaties. Should the United States seek modification of extradition treaties to deal with extradition of terrorists? What changes do you think would be appropriate? What are the chances of obtaining cooperation from other countries?

8. Bringing a Suspect to the U.S. by Rendition. Self-help may occur in the absence of a treaty, because the host country lacks the will to extradite a fugitive, or because extradition would be too time-consuming (perhaps leading to the escape of the fugitive). Such self-help, euphemistically, is called irregular rendition. Techniques of rendition include (from the least to the most controversial) informal surrender by the host nation, luring the suspect by subterfuge or deception, forcible kidnapping, and military rendition. Examples of these various techniques are fascinating and notorious. *Informal surrender* occurred when Pakistanis turned Ramzi Ahmed Yousef, the mastermind of the 1993 World Trade Center bombing, over to United States agents, who transported him to the United States the next day without extradition processes or protest. As a *lure*, the FBI and CIA in 1987 enticed suspected terrorist Fawaz Yunis onto a ship in international waters off the coast of Cyprus on the pretext of engaging in a drug deal, arrested him on the spot, and returned him to the United States. His challenge to the Court's jurisdiction based on trickery was rejected. *United States v. Yunis* 859 F.2d 953 (DC Cir. 1988). One example of United States *forcible abduction* is the retrieval of John Surratt, accused in the Lincoln assignation conspiracy, from Alexandria, Egypt. Another was the 1960 kidnapping by Israeli agents of Adolph Eichmann, a notorious participant in Hitler's extermination of Jews in Europe. Though Argentina protested vigorously to this "violation of its sovereignty" and the United Nations passed a resolution condemning such tactics, Eichmann was tried, convicted, and executed in Israel. Finally, *military rendition*, sometimes called "gunboat diplomacy," has been increasingly used in recent years by the United States in cases involving terrorism and narcotics. Two examples are the 1985 diversion by military fighter jets to Italy of an Egyptian plane carrying the Achillo Lauro highjackers away from the crime scene and the 1989 dispatch of troops to Panama to extract General Manuel Antonio Noriega after they took control of Panama City.

9.   Effects of Forceful Rendition on Trial.   Can a defendant prosecuted in the United States object to trial here on the ground that he or she was forcibly abducted without the permission of the host country? The Supreme Court in two cases, *Ker v. Illinois* 119 U.S. 436 (S.Ct. 1886) and *Frisbee v. Collins* 342 U.S. 519 (S.Ct. 1952) held that the legality of the abduction was not a defense to federal court jurisdiction. This proposition, known as the Ker-Frisbee doctrine, was found subject to an exception for "shocking governmental misconduct" (torture during prolonged interrogation) in *US v. Toscanino* 500 F.2d 267 (2d Cir. 1974), but this exception was rejected by another circuit court in *Matta-Ballesteros v. Henman* 896 F.2d (7th Cir. 1990). Most recently, the Supreme Court held that the US-Mexico Extradition Treaty provided only one of several means for obtaining jurisdiction over a fugitive, even if the kidnapping was "shocking" to the host country.   In doing so, it allowed the repatriation by force of an individual implicated in the kidnapping, torture, and murder of a DEA special agent in Mexico. As for the defense that the kidnapping violated international law, the Court said that even if it did, the Ker-Frisbee doctrine permitted trial of the defendant. *United States v. Alvarez-Machain* 504 U.S. 655 (S.Ct. 1992).

10. Rendition Policy. What are the benefits and disadvantages of the United States engaging in rendition? Think about this question in terms of effects on relations with the country from which rendition occurs and the reaction of other countries when the fact of rendition becomes known. Should the United States change its policies concerning rendition?

11. Institutional Responsibilities. The Senate ratifies treaties, so extradition treaties are for Congress.   Rendition, on the other hand, has been left to the executive branch. Should Congress pass legislation concerning rendition? What powers might Congress rely upon to do so? Would this violate separation of powers principles? What leverage other than legislation does Congress have in this area? The Ker-Frisbee doctrine keeps the courts largely out of the rendition area. Should the courts revisit this doctrine?

12. Extraordinary Rendition.   When a person wanted by one country is captured by it or in a second country and thereafter taken to yet another country, this is called "extraordinary rendition."   Because this process is used for interrogation purposes, it will be covered in Chapter VI.

B. MILITARY DETENTION

Detention of those suspected of crimes in the United States is promptly followed by a bail hearing, which may lead to release of the person. Longer-term or permanent detention of a criminal suspect is permissible only upon conviction. Conversely, detention of an enemy in war is not viewed as punitive, but designed to incapacitate the person from returning to the field of battle until the end of hostilities. Because the gulf between permissible detention in civilian and military contexts is great, it is particularly important to determine when the latter is legally permissible. The following cases explore the dividing line between those who may be subjected to military detention rather than criminal arrest and the role of courts in overseeing that dividing line. Subsection 1 explores the extent of detention authority through the lens of an early post-9/11 Supreme Court decision and lower court applications of Bush Administration assertions of authority to detain "enemy combatants." Subsection two looks at the problem of military detention slightly differently, reflecting the Obama Administration's abandonment of the "enemy combatant" label. Finally, the case in subsection 3 examines limitations to direct judicial review of military detention determinations.

1. ENEMY COMBATANT OR NOT?

HAMDI v. RUMSFELD
542 U.S. 507 (2004)

JUSTICE O'CONNOR announced the judgment of the Court and delivered an opinion, in which THE CHIEF JUSTICE, JUSTICE KENNEDY, and JUSTICE BREYER join.

At this difficult time in our Nation's history, we are called upon to consider the legality of the Government's detention of a United States citizen on United States soil as an "enemy combatant" and to address the process that is constitutionally owed to one who seeks to challenge his classification as such. *** We hold that although Congress authorized the detention of combatants in the narrow circumstances alleged here, due process demands that a citizen held in the United States as an enemy combatant be given a meaningful opportunity to contest the factual basis for that detention before a neutral decisionmaker.

On September 11, 2001, the al Qaeda terrorist network used hijacked commercial airliners to attack prominent targets in the United States. *** This case arises out of the detention of a man whom the Government alleges took up arms with the Taliban during this conflict. His name is Yaser Esam Hamdi. Born an American citizen in Louisiana in 1980, Hamdi moved with his family to Saudi Arabia as a child. By 2001, the parties agree, he resided in Afghanistan. At some point that year, he was seized by members of the Northern Alliance, a coalition of military groups opposed to the Taliban government, and eventually was turned over to the United States military. The Government asserts that it initially detained and interrogated Hamdi in

Afghanistan before transferring him to the United States Naval Base in Guantanamo Bay in January 2002. In April 2002, upon learning that Hamdi is an American citizen, authorities transferred him to a naval brig in Norfolk, Virginia, where he remained until a recent transfer to a brig in Charleston, South Carolina. The Government contends that Hamdi is an "enemy combatant," and that this status justifies holding him in the United States indefinitely—without formal charges or proceedings—unless and until it makes the determination that access to counsel or further process is warranted. ***

[A] declaration from one Michael Mobbs (hereinafter "Mobbs Declaration"), who identified himself as Special Advisor to the Under Secretary of Defense for Policy *** set[s] forth what remains the sole evidentiary support that the Government has provided to the courts for Hamdi's detention. The declaration states that Hamdi "traveled to Afghanistan" in July or August 2001, and that he thereafter "affiliated with a Taliban military unit and received weapons training." It asserts that Hamdi "remained with his Taliban unit following the attacks of September 11" and that, during the time when Northern Alliance forces were "engaged in battle with the Taliban," "Hamdi's Taliban unit surrendered" to those forces, after which he "surrender[ed] his Kalishnikov assault rifle" to them. The Mobbs Declaration also states that, because al Qaeda and the Taliban "were and are hostile forces engaged in armed conflict with the armed forces of the United States," "individuals associated with" those groups "were and continue to be enemy combatants." Mobbs states that Hamdi was labeled an enemy combatant "[b]ased upon his interviews and in light of his association with the Taliban." According to the declaration, a series of "U.S. military screening team[s]" determined that Hamdi met "the criteria for enemy combatants," and "a subsequent interview of Hamdi has confirmed that he surrendered and gave his firearm to Northern Alliance forces, which supports his classification as an enemy combatant." ***

The threshold question before us is whether the Executive has the authority to detain citizens who qualify as "enemy combatants." *** The Government maintains that no explicit congressional authorization is required, because the Executive possesses plenary authority to detain pursuant to Article II of the Constitution. We do not reach the question whether Article II provides such authority, however, because we agree with the Government's alternative position, that Congress has in fact authorized Hamdi's detention, through the AUMF [Authorization for Use of Military Force]. *** Hamdi objects, nevertheless, that Congress has not authorized the *indefinite* detention to which he is now subject. *** We take Hamdi's objection to be not to the lack of certainty regarding the date on which the conflict will end, but to the substantial prospect of perpetual detention. *** It is a clearly established principle of the [international] law of war [including the Geneva Conventions] that detention may last no longer than active hostilities. *** Certainly, we agree that indefinite detention for the purpose of interrogation is not authorized. *** [But] [i]f the record establishes that United States troops are still involved in active combat in Afghanistan, those detentions are part of the exercise of "necessary and appropriate force," and therefore are authorized by the AUMF. ***

Even in cases in which the detention of enemy combatants is legally authorized, there remains the question of what process is constitutionally due to a citizen who disputes his enemy-combatant status. Hamdi argues that he is owed a meaningful and timely hearing and that "extra-judicial detention [that] begins and ends with the submission of an affidavit based on third-hand hearsay" does not comport with the Fifth and Fourteenth Amendments. The Government counters that any more process than was provided below would be both unworkable and "constitutionally intolerable." Our resolution of this dispute requires a careful examination both of the writ of habeas corpus, which Hamdi now seeks to employ as a mechanism of judicial review, and of the Due Process Clause, which informs the procedural contours of that mechanism in this instance.

*** Congress envisioned that habeas petitioners would have some opportunity to present and rebut facts and that courts in cases like this retain some ability to vary the ways in which they do so as mandated by due process. The Government *** asks us to hold that *** the presentation of the Mobbs Declaration to the habeas court completed the required factual development. *** Under the Government's most extreme rendition of this argument, "[r]espect for separation of powers and the limited institutional capabilities of courts in matters of military decision-making in connection with an ongoing conflict" ought to eliminate entirely any individual process, restricting the courts to investigating only whether legal authorization exists for the broader detention scheme. At most, the Government argues, courts should review its determination that a citizen is an enemy combatant under a very deferential "some evidence" standard. Under this review, a court would assume the accuracy of the Government's articulated basis for Hamdi's detention, as set forth in the Mobbs Declaration, and assess only whether that articulated basis was a legitimate one.

In response, Hamdi emphasizes that this Court consistently has recognized that an individual challenging his detention may not be held at the will of the Executive without recourse to some proceeding before a neutral tribunal to determine whether the Executive's asserted justifications for that detention have basis in fact and warrant in law. *** The ordinary mechanism that we use for balancing such serious competing interests, and for determining the procedures that are necessary to ensure that a citizen is not "deprived of life, liberty, or property, without due process of law," is the test that we articulated in *Mathews v. Eldridge,* 424 U.S. 319 (1976). *Mathews* dictates that the process due in any given instance is determined by weighing "he private interest that will be affected by the official action" against the Government's asserted interest, "including the function involved" and the burdens the Government would face in providing greater process. The *Mathews* calculus then contemplates a judicious balancing of these concerns, through an analysis of "the risk of an erroneous deprivation" of the private interest if the process were reduced and the "probable value, if any, of additional or substitute safeguards." ***

[S]ubstantial interests lie on both sides of the scale in this case. Hamdi's "private interest ... affected by the official action," is the most elemental of liberty interests—the interest in being free from physical detention by one's own government. *** Nor is the weight on this side of the *Mathews* scale offset by the circumstances of war or the accusation of treasonous behavior, for "[i]t is clear that commitment for *any* purpose constitutes a significant deprivation of liberty that requires due process protection," and at this stage in the *Mathews* calculus, we consider the interest of the *erroneously* detained individual. *** [T]he risk of erroneous deprivation of a citizen's liberty in the absence of sufficient process here is very real. Moreover, as critical as the Government's interest may be in detaining those who actually pose an immediate threat to the national security of the United States during ongoing international conflict, history and common sense teach us that an unchecked system of detention carries the potential to become a means for oppression and abuse of others who do not present that sort of threat. Because we live in a society in which "[m]ere public intolerance or animosity cannot constitutionally justify the deprivation of a person's physical liberty," our starting point for the *Mathews v. Eldridge* analysis is unaltered by the allegations surrounding the particular detainee or the organizations with which he is alleged to have associated. We reaffirm today the fundamental nature of a citizen's right to be free from involuntary confinement by his own government without due process of law, and we weigh the opposing governmental interests against the curtailment of liberty that such confinement entails.

On the other side of the scale are the weighty and sensitive governmental interests in ensuring that those who have in fact fought with the enemy during a war do not return to battle against the United States. As discussed above, the law of war and the realities of combat may render such detentions both necessary and appropriate, and our due process analysis need not blink at those realities. Without doubt, our Constitution recognizes that core strategic matters of warmaking belong in the hands of those who are best positioned and most politically accountable for making them.

The Government also argues [that] *** military officers who are engaged in the serious work of waging battle would be unnecessarily and dangerously distracted by litigation half a world away, and discovery into military operations would both intrude on the sensitive secrets of national defense and result in a futile search for evidence buried under the rubble of war. To the extent that these burdens are triggered by heightened procedures, they are properly taken into account in our due process analysis.

Striking the proper constitutional balance here is of great importance to the Nation during this period of ongoing combat. But it is equally vital that our calculus not give short shrift to the values that this country holds dear or to the privilege that is American citizenship. *** We therefore hold that a citizen-detainee seeking to challenge his classification as an enemy combatant must receive notice of the factual basis for his classification, and a fair opportunity to rebut the Government's factual assertions before a neutral decisionmaker. *** At the same time, the exigencies of the circumstances may demand that, aside from these core elements, enemy combatant proceedings may be tailored to alleviate their uncommon potential to burden the Executive at a time of ongoing military conflict. Hearsay, for example, may need to be accepted as the most reliable available evidence from the Government in such a proceeding. Likewise, the Constitution would not be offended by a presumption in favor of the Government's evidence, so long as that presumption remained a rebuttable one and fair opportunity for rebuttal were provided. Thus, once the Government puts forth credible evidence that the habeas petitioner meets the enemy-combatant criteria, the onus could shift to the petitioner to rebut that evidence with more persuasive evidence that he falls outside the criteria. A burden-shifting scheme of this sort would meet the goal of ensuring that the errant tourist, embedded journalist, or local aid worker has a chance to prove military error while giving due regard to the Executive once it has put forth meaningful support for its conclusion that the detainee is in fact an enemy combatant. In the words of *Mathews*, process of this sort would sufficiently address the "risk of erroneous deprivation" of a detainee's liberty interest while eliminating certain procedures that have questionable additional value in light of the burden on the Government. [2]

We think it unlikely that this basic process will have the dire impact on the central functions of warmaking that the Government forecasts. The parties agree that initial captures on the battlefield need not receive the process we have discussed here; that process is due only when the determination is made to *continue* to hold those who have been seized. The Government has made clear in its briefing that documentation regarding battlefield detainees already is kept in the ordinary course of military affairs. Any factfinding imposition created by requiring a knowledgeable affiant to summarize these records to an independent tribunal is a minimal one. Likewise, arguments that military officers ought not have to wage war under the threat of litigation lose much of their steam when factual disputes at enemy-combatant hearings are limited to the alleged combatant's acts. This focus meddles little, if at all, in the strategy or conduct of war, inquiring only into the appropriateness of continuing to detain an individual claimed to have taken up arms against the United States. ***

[T]he proposed "some evidence" standard is inadequate. Any process in which the Executive' factual assertions go wholly unchallenged or are simply presumed correct without any opportunity for the alleged combatant to demonstrate otherwise falls constitutionally short. *** This standard therefore is ill suited to the situation in which a habeas petitioner has received no prior proceedings before any tribunal and had no prior opportunity to rebut the Executive's factual assertions before a neutral decisionmaker.

Today we are faced only with such a case. Aside from unspecified

---

[2] Because we hold that Hamdi is constitutionally entitled to the process described above, we need not address at this time whether any treaty guarantees him similar access to a tribunal for a determination of his status.

"screening" processes, and military interrogations in which the Government suggests Hamdi could have contested his classification, Hamdi has received no process. An interrogation by one's captor, however effective an intelligence-gathering tool, hardly constitutes a constitutionally adequate factfinding before a neutral decisionmaker. That even purportedly fair adjudicators "are disqualified by their interest in the controversy to be decided is, of course, the general rule." Plainly, the "process" Hamdi has received is not that to which he is entitled under the Due Process Clause.

There remains the possibility that the standards we have articulated could be met by an appropriately authorized and properly constituted military tribunal. Indeed, it is notable that military regulations already provide for such process in related instances, dictating that tribunals be made available to determine the status of enemy detainees who assert prisoner-of-war status under the Geneva Convention. In the absence of such process, however, a court that receives a petition for a writ of habeas corpus from an alleged enemy combatant must itself ensure that the minimum requirements of due process are achieved. Both courts below recognized as much, focusing their energies on the question of whether Hamdi was due an opportunity to rebut the Government's case against him. The Government, too, proceeded on this assumption, presenting its affidavit and then seeking that it be evaluated under a deferential standard of review based on burdens that it alleged would accompany any greater process. As we have discussed, a habeas court in a case such as this may accept affidavit evidence like that contained in the Mobbs Declaration, so long as it also permits the alleged combatant to present his own factual case to rebut the Government's return. *** He unquestionably has the right to access to counsel in connection with the proceedings on remand.

JUSTICE SOUTER, with whom JUSTICE GINSBURG joins, concurring in part, dissenting in part, and concurring in the judgment.

*** [I]n a moment of genuine emergency, when the Government must act with no time for deliberation, the Executive may be able to detain a citizen if there is reason to fear he is an imminent threat to the safety of the Nation and its people (though I doubt there is any want of statutory authority). This case, however, does not present that question ***; Hamdi has been locked up for over two years. *** I would not reach any questions of what process he may be due in litigating disputed issues in a proceeding under the habeas statute or prior to the habeas enquiry itself. *** Although I think litigation of Hamdi's status as an enemy combatant is unnecessary, the terms of the plurality's remand will allow Hamdi to offer evidence that he is not an enemy combatant, and he should at least have the benefit of that opportunity. *** I do not mean to imply agreement that the Government could claim an evidentiary presumption casting the burden of rebuttal on Hamdi, or that an opportunity to litigate before a military tribunal might obviate or truncate enquiry by a court on habeas. ***

JUSTICE SCALIA, with whom JUSTICE STEVENS joins, dissenting.

*** Where the Government accuses a citizen of waging war against it, our constitutional tradition has been to prosecute him in federal court for treason or some other crime. *** The relevant question, then, is whether there is a different, special procedure for imprisonment of a citizen accused of wrongdoing *by aiding the enemy in wartime.* ***Citizens aiding the enemy have been treated as traitors subject to the criminal process. ***

There are times when military exigency renders resort to the traditional criminal process impracticable. *** Our Federal Constitution contains a provision explicitly permitting suspension, but limiting the situations in which it may be invoked *** The proposition that the Executive lacks indefinite wartime detention authority over citizens is consistent with the Founders' general mistrust of military power permanently at the Executive's disposal. In the Founders' view, the "blessings of liberty" were threatened by "those military establishments which must gradually poison its very fountain." *** Except for the actual command of military forces, all authorization for their maintenance and all explicit authorization for their use is placed in the control of Congress under Article I, rather than the President under Article II. *** A view of the Constitution that gives the Executive authority to use military force rather than the force of law against citizens on American soil flies in the face of the mistrust that engendered these provisions.*** It follows from what I have said that Hamdi is entitled to a habeas decree requiring his release unless (1) criminal proceedings are promptly brought, or (2) Congress has suspended the writ of habeas corpus. ***

The plurality finds justification for Hamdi's imprisonment in the Authorization for Use of Military Force *** This is not remotely a congressional suspension of the writ, and no one claims that it is. ***

It should not be thought, however, that the plurality's evisceration of the Suspension Clause augments, principally, the power of Congress. As usual, the major effect of its constitutional improvisation is to increase the power of the Court. Having found a congressional authorization for detention of citizens where none clearly exists; and having discarded the categorical procedural protection of the Suspension Clause; the plurality then proceeds, under the guise of the Due Process Clause, to prescribe what procedural protections *it* thinks appropriate. It "weigh[s] the private interest ... against the Government's asserted interest," and—just as though writing a new Constitution—comes up with an unheard-of system in which the citizen rather than the Government bears the burden of proof, testimony is by hearsay rather than live witnesses, and the presiding officer may well be a "neutral" military officer rather than judge and jury. It claims authority to engage in this sort of "udicious balancing" from *Mathews v. Eldridge,* 424 U.S. 319 (1976), a case involving ... *the withdrawal of disability benefits!* Whatever the merits of this technique when newly recognized property rights are at issue (and even there they are questionable), it has no place where the Constitution and the common law already supply an answer.

*** If Hamdi is being imprisoned in violation of the Constitution (because without due process of law), then his habeas petition should be granted; the Executive may then hand him over to the criminal authorities, whose detention for the purpose of prosecution will be lawful, or else must release him.

There is a certain harmony of approach in the plurality's making up for Congress's failure to invoke the Suspension Clause and its making up for the Executive's failure to apply what it says are needed procedures—an approach that reflects what might be called a Mr. Fix-it Mentality. The plurality seems to view it as its mission to Make Everything Come Out Right, rather than merely to decree the consequences, as far as individual rights are concerned, of the other two branches' actions and omissions. Has the Legislature failed to suspend the writ in the current dire emergency? Well, we will remedy that failure by prescribing the reasonable conditions that a suspension should have included. And has the Executive failed to live up to those reasonable conditions? Well, we will ourselves make that failure good, so that this dangerous fellow (if he is dangerous) need not be set free. The problem with this approach is not only that it steps out of the courts' modest and limited role in a democratic society; but that by repeatedly doing what it thinks the political branches ought to do it encourages their lassitude and saps the vitality of government by the people. *** If civil rights are to be curtailed during wartime, it must be done openly and democratically, as the Constitution requires, rather than by silent erosion through an opinion of this Court.*** Because the Court has proceeded to meet the current emergency in a manner the Constitution does not envision, I respectfully dissent.

JUSTICE THOMAS, dissenting.

The Executive Branch, acting pursuant to the powers vested in the President by the Constitution and with explicit congressional approval, has determined that Yaser Hamdi is an enemy combatant and should be detained. This detention falls squarely within the Federal Government's war powers, and we lack the expertise and capacity to second-guess that decision. As such, petitioners' habeas challenge should fail, and there is no reason to remand the case. *** I acknowledge that the question whether Hamdi's executive detention is lawful is a question properly resolved by the Judicial Branch, though the question comes to the Court with the strongest presumptions in favor of the Government. *** [T]he question whether Hamdi is actually an enemy combatant is "of a kind for which the Judiciary has neither aptitude, facilities nor responsibility and which has long been held to belong in the domain of political power not subject to judicial intrusion or inquiry." *** In this context, due process requires nothing more than a good-faith executive determination. *** The Government's asserted authority to detain an individual that the President has determined to be an enemy combatant, at least while hostilities continue, comports with the Due Process Clause. *** Accordingly, I conclude that the Government's detention of Hamdi as an enemy combatant does not violate the Constitution. By detaining Hamdi, the President, in the prosecution of a war and authorized by Congress, has acted well within his authority. Hamdi thereby received all the process to which he was due under the circumstances. I therefore believe that this is no occasion to balance the competing interests, as the plurality unconvincingly attempts to do.

Although I do not agree with the plurality that the balancing approach of *Mathews v. Eldridge,* 424 U.S. 319 (1976), is the appropriate analytical tool with which to analyze this case,[5] I cannot help but explain that the plurality misapplies its chosen framework, one that if applied correctly would probably lead to the result I have reached. The plurality devotes two paragraphs to its discussion of the Government's interest, though much of those two paragraphs explain why the Government's concerns are misplaced. *** At issue here is the far more significant interest of the security of the Nation. The Government seeks to further that interest by detaining an enemy soldier not only to prevent him from rejoining the ongoing fight. Rather, as the Government explains, detention can serve to gather critical intelligence regarding the intentions and capabilities of our adversaries, a function that the Government avers has become all the more important in the war on terrorism.

Additional process, the Government explains, will destroy the intelligence gathering function. It also does seem quite likely that, under the process envisioned by the plurality, various military officials will have to take time to litigate this matter. And though the plurality does not say so, a meaningful ability to challenge the Government's factual allegations will probably require the Government to divulge highly classified information to the purported enemy combatant, who might then upon release return to the fight armed with our most closely held secrets.

The plurality manages to avoid these problems by discounting or entirely ignoring them. *** [It] simply assures the Government that the alleged burdens "are properly taken into account in our due process analysis." *** Ultimately, the plurality's dismissive treatment of the Government's asserted interests arises from its apparent belief that enemy-combatant determinations are not part of "the actual prosecution of a war," or one of the "central functions of war making." This seems wrong: Taking *and holding* enemy combatants is a quintessential aspect of the prosecution of war. Moreover, this highlights serious difficulties in applying the plurality's balancing approach here. First, in the war context, we know neither the strength of the Government's interests nor the costs of imposing additional process.

Second, it is at least difficult to explain why the result should be different for other military operations that the plurality would ostensibly recognize as "central functions of war making." *** Because a decision to bomb a particular target might extinguish *life* interests, the plurality's analysis seems to require notice to potential targets. To take one more example, in November 2002, a Central Intelligence Agency (CIA) Predator drone fired a

---

[5] Evidently, neither do the parties, who do not cite *Mathews* even once.

Hellfire missile at a vehicle in Yemen carrying an al Qaeda leader, a citizen of the United States, and four others. It is not clear whether the CIA knew that an American was in the vehicle. But the plurality's due process would seem to require notice and opportunity to respond here as well. I offer these examples not because I think the plurality would demand additional process in these situations but because it clearly would not. The result here should be the same.

*** Though common sense suffices, the Government thoroughly explains that counsel would often destroy the intelligence gathering function. Equally obvious is the Government's interest in not fighting the war in its own courts, and protecting classified information. ***

Notes

1. *Mathews* **Balancing.** The plurality applies the procedural due process framework of *Mathews v. Eldridge* to frame what process Hamdi is entitled to for determining whether he is an enemy combatant. It thus does not require either criminal process or civil procedures. Hamdi is entitled only to an administrative process that meets minimum and flexible standards. Justices SOUTER and GINSBURG do not concede that this is the right framework, but are content to allow the hearing process to proceed to provide Hamdi an opportunity to show he is not an enemy combatant. Justice THOMAS believes not even this process is necessary. Only two justices, the somewhat odd pairing of SCALIA and STEVENS, would require criminal process for individuals held in the United States.

2. **Citizen, Noncitizen.** Do the due process rights granted Hamdi apply to aliens held in the United States? What of aliens held outside the United States, including those held in Guantanamo Bay? Issues concerning judicial habeas corpus review of military detentions outside the United States are generally reserved for Chapter VII.

3. **Access to Counsel.** Traditionally, access to counsel in criminal cases includes unmonitored conversations between the accused and his or her lawyer. Department of Justice rules require monitoring of such conversations between War on Terrorism detainees and their lawyers. Does *Hamdi* indicate whether such limitations are constitutionally permissible?

4. **DoD Response to** *Hamdi.* Immediately following the Supreme Court decision in *Hamdi*, the Department of Defense instituted an administrative review process modeled on the plurality opinion. Padilla and al-Marri, discussed in the next two cases, were provided with such administrative review but argued, as you will see, that they were entitled to more as they should have not been treated as enemy combatants at all.

5. **Detention of Citizen on U.S. Soil.** In a companion case, *Rumsfeld v. Padilla*, 542 U.S. 426 (2004), the Court held that an American citizen held in a naval brig in Charleston, S.C. was required to file his habeas petition in the district court there, since that was the location of his immediate custodian. The Court in *Rumsfeld v. Padilla* did not decide whether "the President has authority to detain Padilla militarily pursuant to the Commander in Chief Clause of the

Constitution, the congressional AUMF, and this Court's decision in *Ex parte Quirin,* 317 U.S. 1 (1942)." On the merits, *Padilla* is harder than *Hamdi.* Hamdi was in Afghanistan, allegedly with a rifle and aligned with Taliban forces; Padilla was arrested deplaning at O'Hare airport in Chicago. At oral argument, the Solicitor General was asked whether military authorities could shoot Padilla, alleged to have been dispatched by al Qaeda to explode a "dirty bomb" in the U.S., as he got off the plane. Is military detention of Padilla an alternative to his arrest on a federal warrant charging federal crimes? The Fourth Circuit decision concerning Padilla which was issued following a new habeas petition in the correct venue (South Carolina) follows.

PADILLA v. HANFT
423 F. 3d 386 (4th Cir. 2005)

LUTTIG, Circuit Judge.

Appellee Jose Padilla, a United States citizen, associated with forces hostile to the United States in Afghanistan and took up arms against United States forces in that country in our war against al Qaeda. Upon his escape to Pakistan from the battlefield in Afghanistan, Padilla was recruited, trained, funded, and equipped by al Qaeda leaders to continue prosecution of the war in the United States by blowing up apartment buildings in this country. Padilla flew to the United States on May 8, 2002, to begin carrying out his assignment, but was arrested by civilian law enforcement authorities upon his arrival at O'Hare International Airport in Chicago.

Thereafter, in a letter to the Secretary of Defense, the President of the United States personally designated Padilla an "enemy combatant" against this country, stating that the United States is "at war" with al Qaeda, that "Mr. Padilla engaged in conduct that constituted hostile and war-like acts, including conduct in preparation for acts of international terrorism that had the aim to cause injury to or adverse effects on the United States," and that "Mr. Padilla represents a continuing, present and grave danger to the national security of the United States." *** [T]he President directed the Secretary of Defense to take Padilla into military custody, in which custody Padilla has remained ever since. ***

The exceedingly important question before us is whether the President of the United States possesses the authority to detain militarily a citizen of this country who is closely associated with al Qaeda, an entity with which the United States is at war; who took up arms on behalf of that enemy and against our country in a foreign combat zone of that war; *and* who thereafter traveled to the United States for the avowed purpose of further prosecuting that war on American soil, against American citizens and targets.***

The Authorization for Use of Military Force Joint Resolution (AUMF), upon which the President explicitly relied *** to detain Padilla, was enacted by Congress in the immediate aftermath of the September 11, 2001, terrorist attacks on the United States. It provides as follows:

> [T]he President is authorized to use all necessary and appropriate force against those nations, organizations, or persons he determines

planned, authorized, committed, or aided the terrorist attacks that occurred on September 11, 2001, or harbored such organizations or persons, in order to prevent any future acts of international terrorism against the United States by such nations, organizations or persons.

*** In *Hamdi v. Rumsfeld* (2004), the Supreme Court held *** that the AUMF authorized the military detention of Yaser Esam Hamdi, an American citizen who fought alongside Taliban forces in Afghanistan, was captured by United States allies on a battlefield there, and was detained in the United States by the military. *** [The Court concluded] based upon "longstanding law-of-war principles," that Hamdi's detention was "necessary and appropriate" within the meaning of the AUMF because "[t]he capture and detention of lawful combatants and the capture, detention, and trial of unlawful combatants, by 'universal agreement and practice,' are 'important incident[s] of war,'" (quoting *Ex parte Quirin*, 317 U.S. 1, 28 (1942)). The rationale for this law-of-war principle, Justice O'Connor explained for the plurality, is that "detention to prevent a combatant's return to the battlefield is a fundamental incident of waging war."

As the AUMF authorized Hamdi's detention by the President, so also does it authorize Padilla's detention. *** Like Hamdi, Padilla associated with forces hostile to the United States in Afghanistan. And, like Hamdi, Padilla took up arms against United States forces in that country in the same way and to the same extent as did Hamdi. Because, like Hamdi, Padilla is an enemy combatant, and because his detention is no less necessary than was Hamdi's in order to prevent his return to the battlefield, the President is authorized by the AUMF to detain Padilla as a fundamental incident to the conduct of war. *** [Moreover,] in *Ex parte Quirin,* 317 U.S. 1 (1942), on which the plurality in *Hamdi* itself heavily relied, *** the Court held that Congress had authorized the military trial of Haupt, a United States citizen who entered the country with orders from the Nazis to blow up domestic war facilities but was captured before he could execute those orders. *** Haupt's citizenship was no bar to his military trial as an unlawful enemy belligerent ***

Like Haupt, Padilla associated with the military arm of the enemy, and with its aid, guidance, and direction entered this country bent on committing hostile acts on American soil. Padilla thus falls within *Quirin* 's definition of enemy belligerent, as well as within the definition of the equivalent term accepted by the plurality in *Hamdi*. *** We understand the plurality's *reasoning* in *Hamdi* to be that the AUMF authorizes the President to detain all those who qualify as "enemy combatants" within the meaning of the laws of war, such power being universally accepted under the laws of war as necessary in order to prevent the return of combatants to the battlefield during conflict. Given that Padilla qualifies as an enemy combatant under both the definition adopted by the Court in *Quirin* and the definition accepted by the controlling opinion in *Hamdi,* his military detention as an enemy combatant by the President is unquestionably authorized by the

AUMF as a fundamental incident to the President's prosecution of the war against al Qaeda in Afghanistan.[3]

Padilla marshals essentially four arguments for the conclusion that his detention is unlawful. *** Padilla principally argues that ***, although he too stood alongside Taliban forces in Afghanistan, he was seized on American soil, whereas Hamdi was captured on a foreign battlefield. *** [Hamdi's] reasoning was that Hamdi's detention was an exercise of "necessary and appropriate force" within the meaning of the AUMF because "detention to prevent a combatant's return to the battlefield is a fundamental incident of waging war." This reasoning simply does not admit of a distinction between an enemy combatant captured abroad and detained in the United States, such as Hamdi, and an enemy combatant who escaped capture abroad but was ultimately captured domestically and detained in the United States, such as Padilla. As *** Padilla poses the same threat of returning to the battlefield as Hamdi posed at the time of the Supreme Court's adjudication of Hamdi's petition. Padilla's detention is thus "necessary and appropriate" to the same extent as was Hamdi's.*** Although at issue in *Quirin* was the authority of the President to subject a United States citizen who was also an enemy combatant to military trial, the plurality in *Hamdi* went to lengths to observe that Haupt, *who had been captured domestically,* could instead have been permissibly *detained* for the duration of hostilities.*** [4]

Padilla also argues, and the district court held, that Padilla's military detention is "neither necessary nor appropriate" because he is amenable to criminal prosecution. *** [T]he availability of criminal process does not distinguish him from Hamdi [because Hamdi also] was detained in the United States and amenable to criminal prosecution. *** [C]riminal prosecution may well not achieve the very purpose for which detention is authorized in the first place--the prevention of return to the field of battle. Equally important, in many instances criminal prosecution would impede the Executive in its efforts to gather intelligence from the detainee and to restrict the detainee's communication with confederates so as to ensure that the detainee does not pose a continuing threat to national security even as he is confined--impediments that would render military detention not only an appropriate, but also the necessary, course of action to be taken in the interest of national security. *** To subject to such exacting scrutiny the President's determination that criminal prosecution would not adequately protect the Nation's security at a very minimum fails to accord the President

---

[3] Under *Hamdi*, the power to detain that is authorized under the AUMF is not a power to detain indefinitely. Detention is limited to the duration of the hostilities as to which the detention is authorized. Because the United States remains engaged in the conflict with al Qaeda in Afghanistan, Padilla's detention has not exceeded in duration that authorized by the AUMF.

[4] Padilla also argues that the locus of capture should be legally relevant to the scope of the AUMF's authorization because there is a higher probability of an erroneous determination that one is an enemy combatant when the seizure occurs on American soil. It is far from clear that this is actually the case. In any event, Padilla's argument confuses the scope of the President's *power* to detain enemy combatants under the AUMF with the *process* for establishing that a detainee is in fact an enemy combatant. *Hamdi* itself provides process to guard against the erroneous detention of non-enemy combatants.

the deference that is his when he acts pursuant to a broad delegation of authority from Congress, such as the AUMF.

As for Padilla's attempted distinction of *Quirin* on the grounds that, unlike Haupt, he has never been charged and tried by the military, the plurality in *Hamdi* rejected as immaterial the distinction between detention and trial (apparently regarding the former as a lesser imposition than the latter), noting that "nothing in *Quirin* suggests that [Haupt's United States] citizenship would have precluded his *mere detention* for the duration of the relevant hostilities."

Padilla, citing *Ex parte Endo,* 323 U.S. 283 (1944), and relying upon *Quirin,* next argues that only a clear statement from Congress can authorize his detention, and that the AUMF is not itself, and does not contain, such a clear statement. *** [T]he AUMF constitutes such a clear statement according to the Supreme Court. In *Hamdi,* stating that "it [was] of no moment that the AUMF does not use specific language of detention," the plurality held that the AUMF "clearly and unmistakably authorized" Hamdi's detention, ***

Finally, Padilla argues that, even if his detention is authorized by the AUMF, it is unlawful under *Ex parte Milligan,* 71 U.S. (4 Wall.) 2 (1866). In *Milligan,* the Supreme Court held that a United States citizen associated with an anti-Union secret society but unaffiliated with the Confederate army could not be tried by a military tribunal while access to civilian courts was open and unobstructed. *Milligan* purported to restrict the power of Congress as well as the power of the President. *Quirin,* however, confirmed that *Milligan* does not extend to enemy combatants. As the Court in *Quirin* explained, the *Milligan* Court's reasoning had "particular reference to the facts before it," namely, that Milligan was not "a part of or associated with the armed forces of the enemy." The *Hamdi* plurality in turn reaffirmed this limitation on the reach of *Milligan,* emphasizing that *Quirin,* a unanimous opinion, "both postdates and clarifies *Milligan.*" Thus confined, *Milligan* is inapposite here because Padilla, unlike Milligan, associated with, and has taken up arms against the forces of the United States on behalf of, an enemy of the United States. ***

Notes

1. *Hamdi.* The Supreme Court's decision in *Hamdi* was made easier because of Hamdi's capture on a battlefield. In other ways its decision may not seem so easy. Congress had not officially "declared war" as it has the power to do under Article 1 of the Constitution. Is this significant? The Court says that the authority to make war includes the authority to detain those captured. Would it also include authority to interrogate those captured? To try those captured before military commissions? Going back to Chapter IV, did the AUMF authorize electronic surveillance not authorized by FISA? Later chapters in this book will address interrogation and military commission trials.

2. **Padilla Distinctions.** The Fourth Circuit has no problem finding that Padilla is similarly situated to Hamdi in terms of his military involvement in

Afghanistan against the United States. The more difficult issue conceptually is why criminal process is not used since Padilla was captured upon returning to the United States. *Quirin,* which you will read in Chapter IX since it primarily deals with military commission trials, is the central authority on which the court relies. As for the four distinctions Padilla argues from Hamdi, the Fourth Circuit finds the purposes behind military detention and the discretion owed by courts to executive determinations strongly supportive of military detention. Do you agree with the Fourth Circuit's reasoning? Was there any reason not to use criminal law, including inchoate crimes (preparation and conspiracy) and material support, to try Padilla?

3. AUMF Basics. Does the AUMF limit its reach to traditional battlefields? Does it permit the use of American military force anywhere in the world? Even in countries friendly to the United States when such use would violate their sovereignty? Is the AUMF limited by time or is the authorization forever? How broadly does the language reaching those who "planned, authorized, committed, or aided the terrorist attacks" of September 11, 2001 reach? Since that time, new terrorist organizations, like Al Qaeda in the Arabian Peninsula (AQAP) have attempted terrorist operations such as by sending explosive parcels on airlines bound for the United States. Is military force and detention authorized against AQAP? Those who "harbor" those involved in the September 11 attacks are also subject to military action. Does that mean military force, such as that exercised in Afghanistan against the Taliban, which refused to turn over Osama bin Laden and others, now apply to allow military force against Pakistan, where he is allegedly hiding now? Chapter X will explore this issue in more detail.

AL-MARRI v. PUCCIARELLI
534 F.3d 213 (4th Cir. 2008) (en banc)

PER CURIAM:

Ali Saleh Kahlah al-Marri filed a petition for a writ of habeas corpus challenging his military detention as an enemy combatant. *** The parties present two principal issues for our consideration: (1) assuming the Government's allegations about al-Marri are true, whether Congress has empowered the President to detain al-Marri as an enemy combatant; and (2) assuming Congress has empowered the President to detain al-Marri as an enemy combatant provided the Government's allegations against him are true, whether al-Marri has been afforded sufficient process to challenge his designation as an enemy combatant. *** [T]he *en banc* court now holds: (1) by a 5 to 4 vote *** that, if the Government's allegations about al-Marri are true, Congress has empowered the President to detain him as an enemy combatant; and (2) by a 5 to 4 vote that, assuming Congress has empowered the President to detain al-Marri as an enemy combatant provided the Government's allegations against him are true, al-Marri has not been afforded sufficient process to challenge his designation as an enemy combatant. *** [Judge Traxler was the deciding judge on both points. His opinion on whether al-Marri was a proper subject for military detention is excerpted below after that of Judge Motz. Excerpts of his opinion dealing with the due process issue may be found infra in Chapter VII.]

DIANA GRIBBON MOTZ, Circuit Judge, concurring in the judgment:

*** Even assuming the truth of the Government's allegations, they provide no basis for treating al-Marri as an enemy combatant or as anything other than a civilian. *** With regret, we recognize that this view does not command a majority of the court. Our colleagues hold that the President can order the military to seize from his home and indefinitely detain anyone in this country -- including an American citizen -- even though he has never affiliated with an enemy nation, fought alongside any nation's armed forces, or borne arms against the United States anywhere in the world. We cannot agree that in a broad and general statute, Congress silently authorized a detention power that so vastly exceeds all traditional bounds. *** Although our preferred disposition does not command a majority of the court *** the evidentiary proceedings envisioned by Judge Traxler will at least place the burden on the Government to make an initial showing that "the normal due process protections available to all within this country" are impractical or unduly burdensome in al-Marri's case and that the hearsay declaration that constitutes the Government's only evidence against al-Marri is "the most reliable available evidence" supporting the Government's allegations. ***

Al-Marri, a citizen of Qatar, lawfully entered the United States with his wife and children on September 10, 2001, to pursue a master's degree at Bradley University in Peoria, Illinois, where he had obtained a bachelor's degree in 1991. The following day, terrorists hijacked four commercial airliners and used them to kill and inflict grievous injury on thousands of Americans. Three months later, on December 12, 2001, FBI agents arrested al-Marri at his home in Peoria as a material witness in the Government's investigation of the September 11th attacks. Al-Marri was imprisoned in civilian jails in Peoria and then New York City. [In 2002 and 2003, al-Marri was charged with various counts of fraud.] On Friday, June 20, 2003, the court scheduled a hearing on pre-trial motions, including a motion to suppress evidence against al-Marri assertedly obtained by torture. On the following Monday, June 23, before that hearing could be held, the Government moved *ex parte* to dismiss the indictment based on an order signed that morning by the President.

In the order, President George W. Bush stated that he "DETERMINE[D] for the United States of America that" al-Marri: (1) is an enemy combatant; (2) is closely associated with al Qaeda; (3) "engaged in conduct that constituted hostile and war-like acts, including conduct in preparation for acts of international terrorism"; (4) "possesses intelligence . . . that . . . would aid U.S. efforts to prevent attacks by al Qaeda"; and (5) "represents a continuing, present, and grave danger to the national security of the United States." The President determined that al-Marri's detention by the military was "necessary to prevent him from aiding al Qaeda" and thus ordered the Attorney General to surrender al-Marri to the Secretary of Defense and further directed the Secretary of Defense to "detain him as an enemy combatant." *** [A]l-Marri was then transferred to military custody and brought to the Naval Consolidated Brig in South Carolina.

Since that time (that is, for five years) the military has held al-Marri as an enemy combatant, without charge and without any indication when this confinement will end. For the first sixteen months of his military confinement, the Government did not permit al-Marri any communication with the outside world, including his attorneys, his wife, and his children. He alleges that he was denied basic necessities, interrogated through measures creating extreme sensory deprivation, and threatened with violence. *** [T]he Government answered al-Marri's petition, citing the Declaration of Jeffrey N. Rapp, Director of the Joint Intelligence Task Force for Combating Terrorism, as support for the President's order to detain al-Marri as an enemy combatant.

The Rapp Declaration asserts that al-Marri: (1) is "closely associated with al Qaeda, an international terrorist organization with which the United States is at war"; (2) trained at an al Qaeda terrorist training camp in Afghanistan sometime between 1996 and 1998; (3) in the summer of 2001, was introduced to Osama Bin Laden by Khalid Shaykh Muhammed; (4) at that time, volunteered for a "martyr mission" on behalf of al Qaeda; (5) was ordered to enter the United States sometime before September 11, 2001, to serve as a "sleeper agent" to facilitate terrorist activities and explore disrupting this country's financial system through computer hacking; (6) in the summer of 2001, met with terrorist financier Mustafa Ahmed al-Hawsawi, who gave al-Marri money, including funds to buy a laptop; (7) gathered technical information about poisonous chemicals on his laptop; (8) undertook efforts to obtain false identification, credit cards, and banking information, including stolen credit card numbers; (9) communicated with known terrorists, including Khalid Shaykh Muhammed and al-Hawsawi, by phone and e-mail; and (10) saved information about jihad, the September 11th attacks, and Bin Laden on his laptop computer.

The Rapp Declaration does *not* assert that al-Marri: (1) is a citizen, or affiliate of the armed forces, of any nation at war with the United States; (2) was seized on, near, or having escaped from a battlefield on which the armed forces of the United States or its allies were engaged in combat; (3) was ever in Afghanistan during the armed conflict between the United States and the Taliban there; or (4) directly participated in any hostilities against United States or allied armed forces.

*** Both parties recognize that it does not violate the Due Process Clause for the President to order the military to seize and detain individuals who "qualify" as enemy combatants for the duration of a war. They disagree, however, as to whether the evidence the Government has proffered, even assuming its accuracy, establishes that al-Marri fits within the "legal category of enemy combatant." The Government principally contends that its evidence establishes this, and therefore the AUMF grants the President *statutory* authority to detain al-Marri as an enemy combatant. Alternatively, the Government asserts that the President has inherent *constitutional* authority to order al-Marri's indefinite military detention. *** The precedent interpreting the AUMF on which the Government relies for this argument consists of two cases: the Supreme Court's opinion in *Hamdi,* 542 U.S. 507

and our opinion in *Padilla v. Hanft,* 423 F.3d 386 (4th Cir. 2005). The "legal background" for the AUMF, which the Government cites, consists of two cases from earlier conflicts, *Ex Parte Quirin,* 317 U.S. 1 (1942) (World War II), and *Ex Parte Milligan,* 71 U.S. (4 Wall.) 2 (1866) (U.S. Civil War), as well as constitutional and law-of-war principles

With respect to the latter, we note that American courts have often been reluctant to follow international law in resolving domestic disputes. In the present context, however, they, like the Government here, have relied on the law of war -- treaty obligations including the Hague and Geneva Conventions and customary principles developed alongside them. The law of war provides clear rules for determining an individual's status during an international armed conflict, distinguishing between "combatants" (members of a nation's military, militia, or other armed forces, and those who fight alongside them) and "civilians" (all other persons).[17] American courts have repeatedly looked to these careful distinctions made in the law of war in identifying which individuals fit within the "legal category" of "enemy combatant" under our Constitution. *** Hamdi's detention was upheld because, in fighting against the United States on the battlefield in Afghanistan with the Taliban, the *de facto* government of Afghanistan at the time, Hamdi bore arms with the army of an enemy nation and so, under the law of war, was an enemy combatant. *** In *Padilla,* a panel of this court similarly held that the AUMF authorized the President to detain as an enemy combatant an American citizen who "was armed and present in a combat zone" in Afghanistan as part of Taliban forces during the conflict there with the United States. *** *Hamdi* and *Padilla* ground their holdings on [the] central teaching from *Quirin,* i.e., enemy combatant status rests on an individual's affiliation during wartime with the "military arm of the enemy government." In *Quirin,* that enemy government was the German Reich; in *Hamdi* and *Padilla,* it was the Taliban government of Afghanistan.

Hamdi and *Padilla* also rely on this principle from *Quirin* to distinguish (but not disavow) *Milligan.* In *Milligan,* the Court *** recognized that Milligan had committed "an enormous crime" during "a period of war" and at a place "within . . . the theatre of military operations, and which had been and was constantly threatened to be invaded by the enemy." But it found no support in the "laws and usages of war" for subjecting Milligan to military

---

[17] [relocated note] Thus, "civilian" is a term of art in the law of war, not signifying an innocent person, but rather someone in a certain legal category who is not subject to military seizure or detention. So, too, a "combatant" is by no means always a wrongdoer, but rather a member of a different "legal category" who is subject to military seizure and detention. For example, our brave soldiers fighting in Germany during World War II were "combatants" under the law of war, and viewed from Germany's perspective they were "enemy combatants." While civilians are subject to trial and punishment in civilian courts for all crimes committed during wartime in the country in which they are captured and held, combatant status protects an individual from trial and punishment by the capturing nation, unless the combatant has violated the law of war. Nations in international conflicts can summarily remove the adversary's "combatants," i.e., the "enemy combatants," from the battlefield and detain them for the duration of such conflicts, but no such provision is made for "civilians."

jurisdiction as a combatant, for although he was a "dangerous enem[y]" of the nation, he was a civilian and had to be treated as such.

Quirin, Hamdi, and *Padilla* all emphasize that *Milligan's* teaching -- that our Constitution does not permit the Government to subject *civilians* within the United States to military jurisdiction -- remains good law. *** Thus, although *Hamdi, Quirin,* and *Padilla* distinguish *Milligan,* they recognize that its core holding remains the law of the land. That is, civilians within this country (even "dangerous enemies" like Milligan who perpetrate "enormous crime[s]" on behalf of "secret" enemy organizations bent on "overthrowing the Government" of this country) may not be subjected to military control and deprived of constitutional rights.

In sum, the holdings of *Hamdi* and *Padilla* share two characteristics: (1) they look to law-of-war principles to determine who fits within the "legal category" of enemy combatant; and (2) following the law of war, they rest enemy combatant status on affiliation with the military arm of an enemy nation. *** [U]nlike Hamdi and Padilla, al-Marri is not alleged to have been part of a Taliban unit, not alleged to have stood alongside the Taliban or the armed forces of any other enemy nation, not alleged to have been on the battlefield during the war in Afghanistan, not alleged to have even been in Afghanistan during the armed conflict there, and not alleged to have engaged in combat with United States forces anywhere in the world. *** Our dissenting colleagues *** contend that the definition of enemy combatant has somehow expanded to permit a person to be so classified because of his criminal conduct on behalf of a terrorist organization. We have searched extensively for authority that would support the dissents' position; we have found none.

First, the Supreme Court's most recent terrorism cases -- *Hamdan* and *Boumediene* -- provide no support for the dissenters' position. In *Hamdan,* the Court held that because the conflict between the United States and al Qaeda in Afghanistan is not "between nations," it is a "'conflict not of an international character'" -- and so is governed by Common Article 3 of the Geneva Conventions.

Common Article 3 and other Geneva Convention provisions applying to non-international conflicts (in contrast to those applying to international conflicts) simply do *not* recognize the "legal category" of enemy combatant. As the International Committee of the Red Cross -- the official codifier of the Geneva Conventions -- explains, "an 'enemy combatant' is a person who, either lawfully or unlawfully, engages in hostilities for the opposing side in an *international* armed conflict"; in contrast, "[i]n non-international armed conflict combatant status *does not exist."* *** [O]ur dissenting colleagues and the Government ignore *Hamdan's* holding that the conflict with al Qaeda in Afghanistan is a non-international conflict and ignore the fact that, in such conflicts, the legal category of enemy combatant does not exist. *** Moreover, even were the Supreme Court ultimately to approve the detention of Boumediene, Hamdan, and those like them, that would not bolster the view that the Government can militarily detain al-Marri as an enemy combatant. Because the legal status of enemy combatant does not exist in non-international conflicts, the law of war leaves the detention of persons in such conflicts to the applicable law of the detaining country. In al-Marri's case, the applicable law is our Constitution. Under our Constitution, even if the Supreme Court should hold that the Government may detain indefinitely Boumediene, Hamdan, and others like them, who were captured *outside* the United States and lack substantial and voluntary connections to this country, that holding would provide no support for approving al-Marri's military detention. For not only was al-Marri seized and detained *within* the United States, he also has substantial connections to the United States and so plainly is protected by the Due Process Clause. ***

We recognize the understandable instincts of those who wish to treat domestic terrorists as "combatants" in a "global war on terror." Allegations of criminal activity in association with a terrorist organization, however, do not permit the Government to transform a civilian into an enemy combatant subject to indefinite military detention, just as allegations of murder in association with others while in military service do not permit the Government to transform a civilian into a soldier subject to trial by court martial.

To be sure, enemy combatants may commit crimes just as civilians may. When an enemy combatant violates the law of war, that conduct will render the person an "unlawful" enemy combatant, subject not only to detention but also to military trial and punishment. But merely engaging in unlawful behavior does not make one an enemy combatant. *** Had the *Quirin* petitioners never "secretly and without uniform" passed our "military lines," they still would have been enemy combatants, subject to military detention, but would not have been *unlawful* enemy combatants subject to military trial and punishment.

Neither *Quirin* nor any other precedent even suggests *** that individuals with constitutional rights, unaffiliated with the military arm of any enemy government, can be subjected to military jurisdiction and deprived of those rights solely on the basis of their conduct on behalf of a terrorist organization. In fact, *Milligan* rejected the Government's attempt to do just this. ***

Finally, we do not find our dissenting colleagues' respective new definitions of enemy combatant at all compelling. The dissents do not contend that, under *traditional* law-of-war principles, enemy combatant status would extend to al-Marri. (Williams, C.J., concurring in part and dissenting in part) ("The plurality opinion may very well be correct that, under the traditional 'law of war,' persons not affiliated with the military of a *nation-state* may not be considered enemy combatants."); (Wilkinson, J., concurring in part and dissenting in part) ("Traditionally, the definition of 'enemy' has been state-based . . . ."). Instead, to justify al-Marri's indefinite military detention, the dissents resort to inventing novel definitions of enemy combatant, drawing on their own beliefs as to when detention is appropriate. That these judicially-created definitions differ so markedly from one another follows from the fact that each is simply the product of judicial conjecture;

any limits on whom the Executive may detain as an enemy combatant are thus left to an individual judge. ***

In sum, neither the Government nor our dissenting colleagues have offered, and although we have exhaustively searched, we have not found, any authority that permits us to hold that the AUMF empowers the President to detain al-Marri as an enemy combatant. If the Government's allegations are true, and we assume they are for present purposes, al-Marri, like Milligan, is a dangerous enemy of this nation who has committed serious crimes and associated with a secret terrorist organization that has engaged in hostilities against us. But, like Milligan, al-Marri is still a civilian: he does not fit within the "permissible bounds of "[t]he legal category of enemy combatant." Therefore, we believe the AUMF provides the President no statutory authority to order the military to seize and indefinitely detain al-Marri. ***

TRAXLER, Circuit Judge, concurring in the judgment:

*** I agree *** that the Authorization for Use of Military Force ("AUMF") *** grants the President the power to detain enemy combatants in the war against al Qaeda, including belligerents who enter our country for the purpose of committing hostile and war-like acts such as those carried out by the al Qaeda operatives on 9/11. And, I agree that the allegations made by the government against al-Marri, if true, would place him within this category and permit the President to militarily detain him.

However, I depart from my dissenting colleagues on the issue of whether al-Marri has been afforded a fair opportunity to challenge the factual basis for his designation as an enemy combatant. Because the process afforded al-Marri by the district court to challenge the factual basis for his designation as an enemy combatant did not meet the minimal requirements of due process guaranteed by the Fifth Amendment, I *** remand for further evidentiary proceedings on the issue of whether al-Marri is, in fact, an enemy combatant subject to military detention. ***

*** [T]he AUMF *** grants the President the authority to detain enemy combatants who associate themselves "with al Qaeda, an entity with which the United States is at war," and "travel[ ] to the United States for the avowed purpose of further prosecuting that war on American soil, against American citizens and targets," even though the government cannot establish that the combatant also "took up arms on behalf of that enemy and against our country in a *foreign* combat zone of that war." *** [T]he alleged enemy combatants in *Hamdi* and *Padilla* were affiliated with the military arm of an enemy government, specifically the Taliban government of Afghanistan. *** [N]either court was required to decide whether their affiliation with al Qaeda and, in the case of Padilla, the mission to carry out additional terrorist acts within this country, would also have supported their detention as enemy combatants.

In my opinion, however, there is no doubt that individuals who are dispatched here by al Qaeda, the organization known to have carried out the 9/11 attacks upon our country, as sleeper agents and terrorist operatives charged with the task of committing additional attacks upon our homeland

"are [also] individuals Congress sought to target in passing the AUMF."
Hamdi. Citing the right of the United States "to protect United States
citizens *both at home and abroad,"* the AUMF authorized the President's use
of "all necessary and appropriate force against"the nations *and organizations*
that "planned, authorized, committed, or aided" the 9/11 attacks, "or
harbored such organizations or persons, in order to prevent any future acts of
international terrorism against the United States." Clearly, Congress was
not merely authorizing military retaliation against a reigning foreign
government known to have *supported* the enemy force that attacked us in our
homeland, but was also authorizing military action against al Qaeda
operatives who, like the 9/11 hijackers, were sent by the al Qaeda
organization to the United States to conduct additional terror operations
here.

As persuasively pointed out by the government, it was the 9/11 attacks
which triggered the passage of the AUMF. *** The hijackers never engaged
in combat operations against our forces on a foreign battlefield. Yet al-Marri
would have us rule that when Congress authorized the President to deal
militarily with those responsible for the 9/11 attacks upon our country, it did
not intend to authorize the President to deal militarily with al Qaeda
operatives identically situated to the 9/11 hijackers. *** I am also
unpersuaded by the claim that because al Qaeda itself is an international
terrorist organization instead of a "nation state" or "enemy government," the
AUMF cannot apply, consistent with the laws of war and our constitutional
guarantees, to such persons. The premise of that claim seems to be that
because al Qaeda is not technically in control of an enemy nation or its
government, it cannot be considered as anything other than a criminal
organization whose members are entitled to all the protections and
procedures granted by our constitution. *** In my view, al Qaeda is much
more and much worse than a criminal organization. And while it may be an
unconventional enemy force in a historical context, it is an enemy force
nonetheless. The fact that it allied itself with an enemy government of a
foreign nation only underscores this point, rendering attempts to distinguish
its soldiers or operatives as something meaningfully different from military
soldiers in service to the Taliban government (or al Qaeda operatives such as
Hamdi and Padilla, who fought beside them) equally strained. The President
attacked the Taliban in Afghanistan as *retaliation* for al Qaeda's strike upon
our nation *because* al Qaeda was centralized there and allied with the
Taliban, and it also strains credulity to assert that while we are legitimately
at war with the Taliban government, we cannot be at war with al Qaeda.

In sum, the war that al Qaeda wages here and abroad against American
interests may be viewed as unconventional, but it is a war nonetheless and
one initially declared by our enemy. The members of this enemy force come
from different countries and they are positioned globally. They fight us with
conventional weapons in Afghanistan and Iraq, but they have also infiltrated
our borders and those of our allies, bent on committing, at a minimum,
sabotage and other war-like acts targeting both military and civilian
installations and citizens. *** And when they cross our borders with the
intent to attack our country from within on behalf of those forces, they are

not appreciably different from the soldiers in *Quirin,* who infiltrated our borders to commit acts of sabotage against our military installations here -- although as history and intelligence inform us, al Qaeda soldiers target not only our military installations, but also the citizens of this country. *** When they enter this country "with hostile purpose," they are enemy belligerents subject to detention.

In my view, limiting the President's authority to militarily detain soldiers or saboteurs as enemy combatants to those who are part of a formal military arm of a foreign nation or enemy government is not compelled by the laws of war, and the AUMF plainly authorizes the President to use all necessary and appropriate force against al Qaeda. *** I find it unnecessary to reach the question of whether the President possesses inherent authority to detain al-Marri.

If the allegations of the Rapp Declaration are true, I am also of the view that al-Marri would fall within the category of persons who may be lawfully detained pursuant to the authority granted by the AUMF.

According to Rapp, al-Marri was *not* simply a civilian who lawfully entered the United States and was residing peacefully here while pursuing a higher educational goal. Nor, for that matter, was he a civilian who became sympathetic to al-Qaeda's mission and sought to support it in indirect ways. And he was certainly not a common criminal bent on committing criminal acts for personal reasons or gain. On the contrary, the allegations are that al-Marri directly allied himself with al Qaeda abroad, volunteered for assignments (including a martyr mission), received training and funding from al Qaeda abroad, was dispatched by al Qaeda to the United States as an al Qaeda operative with orders to serve as a sleeper agent, and was tasked with facilitating and ultimately committing terrorist attacks against the United States within this country. *** [H]e would not be appreciably different from either the German soldier dispatched here to attack military installations in *Quirin* or the al Qaeda operatives dispatched here to attack this country on 9/11. ***

Notes

1. Enemy Combatants. There seems to be agreement that traditionally, enemy combatants were fighting for nation-states in armed conflicts and that al-Qaeda is not a nation-state. There also seems to be agreement that the traditional definition does not well fit the facts of the "war on terror." Should the definition be changed? Who should do this?

2. Sources of Law. Judge Motz refers extensively to international law while Judge Traxler refers exclusively to domestic law. Which approach is correct?

3. Following Supreme Court Precedent. How do the two opinions read the Supreme Court authorities differently? You have not yet read all the cases discussed, but try to articulate which view seems the better view of these precedents.

4. The Disappearing Al-Marri Decision. In December of 2008, the Supreme Court granted certiorari in *Al-Marri v. Spagone* (formerly *Al-Marri v. Pucciarelli*) to consider whether the Authorization for Use of Military Force authorized or the Constitution allowed the military detention of al-Marri. Following the grant of certiorari, President Obama issued an executive memorandum to review the status of al-Marri's detention. The Government subsequently moved to dismiss the case and to criminally prosecute al-Marri—rendering his habeas action based on military detention moot. When it dismissed the case, the Supreme Court also vacated the Fourth Circuit's *en banc* decision, leaving no circuit precedent on the scope of statutory or constitutional authority to militarily detain U.S. residents. Why might the Court do this? Since *al-Marri* was vacated, why would your casebook editor include this "non-case"?

2. DETENTION AUTHORITY (DELETE ENEMY COMBATANT)

The following cases demonstrate a shift away from the "enemy combatant" analysis which animated *al-Marri*, its predecessors, and the approach of the Department of Justice during the Bush Administration. The first case is a district court decision that was viewed as the correct approach to post-"enemy combatant" detention decisions for a few months, when the D.C. Circuit decided the other two cases in this subsection.

HAMLILY v. OBAMA
616 F. Supp. 2d 63 (D.D.C. 2009)

JOHN D. BATES, District Judge.

Petitioners are detainees at the United States Naval Base at Guantanamo Bay who have challenged the legality of their detentions by seeking writs of habeas corpus. *** In *Hamdi v. Rumsfeld,* 542 U.S. 507 (2004), the Supreme Court acknowledged that the district courts would have to address this issue in a piecemeal fashion by delimiting "[t]he permissible bounds" of the Government's detention authority "as subsequent cases are presented to them." [2] ***

On March 13, 2009, in response to a prior order of this Court, the government submitted a refinement of its position with respect to its authority to detain those individuals being held at Guantanamo. The government proposed the following "definitional framework":

> The President has the authority to detain persons that the President determines planned, authorized, committed, or aided the terrorist attacks that occurred on September 11,

---

[2] In *Hamdi*, the Supreme Court spoke of the lower courts defining the permissible bounds of the "legal category of enemy combatant." In attempting to define the scope of its authority to detain a class of individuals held at Guantanamo, the new Administration has ceased using the term "enemy combatant." Irrespective of nomenclature, however, this Court's inquiry into the scope of the government's detention authority is essentially the same as that envisioned by the Supreme Court in *Hamdi*.

2001, and persons who harbored those responsible for those attacks.] The President also has the authority to detain persons who were part of, or substantially supported, Taliban or al Qaida forces or associated forces that are engaged in hostilities against the United States or its coalition partners, including any person who has committed a belligerent act, or has directly supported hostilities, in aid of such enemy armed forces.

The government contends that its proposed framework is based principally upon the AUMF *** Acknowledging the Supreme Court's decision in *Hamdi*, the government also asserts that "[t]he detention authority conferred by the AUMF is necessarily informed by principles of the laws of war." According to the government, then, because the law of war has evolved primarily in the context of international armed conflicts between nations, the President has the authority to detain "those persons whose relationship to al-Qaida or the Taliban would, in appropriately analogous circumstances in a traditional international armed conflict, render them detainable." *** [Petitioners] assert that the Government's claimed detention authority far exceeds that which is permitted by the AUMF and the Constitution and does considerable violence to fundamental principles of the law of war. Specifically, petitioners contend that the government has developed "new detention standards by 'analogy to' the law of war" in "an attempt to create a new legal standard to deal with what [it] contend[s] are new and different circumstances." Such an attempt is, in petitioners' view, contrary to both domestic and international law because neither body of law permits the government "to detain individuals based merely on some unspecified degree of association with persons or entities targeted by the AUMF." Petitioners assert, then, that "[t]he Court should follow *Hamdi* 's lead, and rule that the scope of the Executive's detention power in these cases is that authorized by the traditional law of war." That, according to petitioners, encompasses only "individuals who were lawful combatants under Article 4 of the Geneva Conventions (members of an armed force of a State or other militia as described in Article 4), and civilians who become unlawful combatants by reason of their direct participation in hostilities as that standard is understood in international law." ***

[The Court rejects the concept of "substantial support" as an independent basis for detention. Likewise, the Court finds that "directly support[ing] hostilities" is not a proper basis for detention. In short, the Court can find no authority in domestic law or the law of war, nor can the government point to any, to justify the concept of "support" as a valid ground for detention. The Court does not accept the Government's position in full, then, even given the deference accorded to the Executive in this realm, because it is ultimately the province of the courts to say "what the law is," and in this context that means identifying the "permissible bounds" of the Executive's detention authority. Detention based on substantial or direct support of the Taliban, al Qaeda or associated forces, without more, is simply not warranted by domestic law or the law of war.

With the exception of these two "support"-based elements, however, the Court will adopt the Government's proposed framework ***. The AUMF and the law of war do authorize the government to detain those who are "part of" the "Taliban or al Qaida forces." Because the AUMF permits the President "to use all necessary and appropriate force" against "organizations" involved in the September 11 attacks, it naturally follows that force is also authorized against the members of those organizations. In light of *Hamdi* and subsequent cases, such force includes the power to detain. That is consistent with the law of war principles governing non-international conflicts. The authority also reaches those who were members of "associated forces," which the Court interprets to mean "co-belligerents" as that term is understood under the law of war. Lastly, the Government's detention authority covers "any person who has committed a belligerent act," which the Court interprets to mean any person who has directly participated in hostilities. But while the Court concludes that the concepts of "substantial support" and "direct support" are not, under the law of war, independent bases for detention, evidence tending to demonstrate that a petitioner provided significant "support" is relevant in assessing whether he was "part of" a covered organization (through membership or otherwise) or "committed a belligerent act" (through direct participation in hostilities).

*** Before addressing the parties' arguments regarding the law of war, and any restrictions they place upon the scope of the Government's detention authority, one must first assess the source of this authority under domestic law-the AUMF. The AUMF authorizes the President "to use all necessary and appropriate force against those ... organizations ... he determines planned, authorized, committed, or aided" the September 11 attacks "to prevent any future acts of international terrorism against the United States by such ... organizations...." By authorizing the use of force against the "organizations" responsible for the September 11 attacks, Congress also, necessarily, authorized the use of force (including detention) against their members. Further, given that the AUMF was passed in response to the September 11 attacks "to prevent any future acts of international terrorism against the United States by ... [the] organizations" responsible for those attacks, it would contravene Congress's clear purpose to conclude that the AUMF failed to authorize the use of force, including detention, against members of those organizations.

Of course, the AUMF's broad authorization does not resolve the scope of the Government's detention authority-it only establishes that it reaches members of "organizations" covered by the statute. The question, then, is whether this authority is consistent with the law of war. *** Petitioners argue *** that because they cannot be classified as "combatants" under Article 4(A) of the Third Geneva Convention or Article 43 of Additional Protocol I, they must be "civilians"-a classification that means they are not subject to military force (*i.e.,* detention) "unless and for such time as they take a direct part in hostilities." Putting aside for the moment the restrictive definition of "direct participation."[14] advanced by petitioners, their advocacy of a detention authority based upon the dichotomy between combatants and civilians in traditional international armed conflicts is flawed. To begin with, the U.S. conflict with al Qaeda is a non-international armed conflict; hence, Article 4 and Additional Protocol I do not apply. Moreover, the government no longer seeks to detain petitioners on the basis that they are "enemy combatants." Indeed, the Government's abandonment of this term is an implicit acknowledgment that "[i]n non-international armed conflict combatant status does not exist." ***

This Court agrees that the lack of combatant status in non-international armed conflicts does not, by default, result in civilian status for all, even those who are members of enemy "organizations" like al Qaeda. Moreover, the Government's claimed authority to detain those who were "part of" those organizations is entirely consistent with the law of war principles that govern non-international armed conflicts. Common Article 3, by its very terms, contemplates the "detention" of "[p]ersons taking no active part in the hostilities, including members of armed forces who have laid down their weapons and those placed hors de combat," and commands that they be treated "humanely." At a minimum, this restriction establishes that States engaged in non-international armed conflict can detain those who are "part of" enemy armed groups. Similarly, Part IV of Additional Protocol II, in particular Article 13, sets forth protections for the "civilian population" in non-international armed conflicts. Such protections for "civilians" would be superfluous "if every member of the enemy in a non-international armed conflict is a civilian." The clear implication of Part IV, then, is that Additional Protocol II recognizes a class of individuals who are separate and apart from the "civilian population"-*i.e.,* members of enemy armed groups. Indeed, it makes clear that "[t]hose who belong to armed forces or armed groups may be attacked at any time." As for the practical application of these principles, historical examples are few and far between. There are, however, several decisions of the International Criminal Tribunal for the former Yugoslavia ("ICTY") that have recognized that, in a non-international armed conflict, membership in an armed group makes one liable to attack and incapacitation independent of direct participation in hostilities.

In sum, then, the Court *** rejects petitioners' argument "that the laws of war permit a state to detain only individuals who 'directly participate' in hostilities in non-international armed conflicts." The Court also concludes that the authority claimed by the government to detain those who were "part of ... Taliban or al Qaida forces" is consistent with the law of war. Even

---

[14] Although petitioners' counsel retreated from the position that the government could only detain civilians captured "for such time as" they were directly participating in hostilities, petitioners still maintain that active and direct participation in hostilities against the United States is required for detention. In petitioners' view, "direct participation" should be defined as "immediate and actual action on the battlefield likely to cause harm to the enemy because there is a direct causal relationship between the activity engaged in and the harm done to the enemy." The definition of "direct participation in hostilities" is, at present, unsettled, and petitioners' own expert, Professor Gary D. Solis, advocates a definition of "direct participation" that is substantially broader than the one urged by petitioners in their brief.

though this portion of the Government's framework is consistent with the law of war, however, the Government's position cannot be said to reflect customary international law because, candidly, none exists on this issue. ***

In addition to members of al Qaeda and the Taliban, the Government's detention authority also reaches those who were members of "associated forces." For purposes of these habeas proceedings, the Court interprets the term "associated forces" to mean "co-belligerents" as that term is understood under the law of war.[16] The government itself advocates this reading of the language. A "co-belligerent" in an international armed conflict context is a state that has become a "'fully fledged belligerent fighting in association with one or more belligerent powers.'" One only attains co-belligerent status by violating the law of neutrality-*i.e.*, the duty of non-participation and impartiality. If those duties are violated, then the adversely affected belligerent is permitted to take reprisals against the ostensibly neutral party. This is also consistent with historical practice in the United States. Accordingly, the government has the authority to detain members of "associated forces" as long as those forces would be considered co-belligerents under the law of war.[17]

With respect to the criteria to be used in determining whether someone was "part of" the "Taliban or al Qaida or associated forces," the Court will not attempt to set forth an exhaustive list because such determinations must be made on an individualized basis. But this Court will, by necessity, employ an approach that is more functional than formal, as there are no settled criteria for determining who is a "part of" an organization such as al Qaeda. "[M]ere sympathy for or association with an enemy organization does not render an individual a member" of that enemy organization. The key inquiry, then, is not necessarily whether one self-identifies as a member of the organization (although this could be relevant in some cases), but whether the individual functions or participates within or under the command structure of the organization-*i.e.*, whether he receives and executes orders or directions. Thus, as *Gherebi* observed, this could include an individual "tasked with housing, feeding, or transporting al-Qaeda fighters ... but an al-Qaeda doctor or cleric, or the father of an al-Qaeda fighter who shelters his son out of familial loyalty, [is likely not detainable] assuming such individuals had no independent role in al-Qaeda's chain of command." Moreover, as the government conceded at oral argument, its framework does not encompass those individuals who unwittingly become part of the al Qaeda apparatus-some level of knowledge or intent is required. These are, of course, non-exclusive factors and the Court's determinations will be made on a case-by-case basis in light of all the facts presented.

---

[16] Like many other elements of the law of war, co-belligerency is a concept that has developed almost exclusively in the context of international armed conflicts. However, there is no reason why this principle is not equally applicable to non-state actors involved in non-international conflicts.

[17] "Associated forces" do not include terrorist organizations who merely share an abstract philosophy or even a common purpose with al Qaeda-there must be an actual association in the current conflict with al Qaeda or the Taliban.

As proposed by the government, the detention authority reaches not only those who were "part of" the Taliban, al Qaeda or associated forces, but also individuals who "substantially supported" any of those organizations. Petitioners argue that "the law of war provides no authority for detention based on 'support' of opposing enemy forces, and respondents cite none." Consequently, they assert that a "support"-based approach "represents a marked departure from the law of war." *** The government initially asserted that the concept of "support" is anchored in the principle of co-belligerency. *** After repeated attempts by the Court to elicit a more definitive justification for the "substantial support" concept in the law of war, it became clear that the government has none. Nevertheless, the government asserted that "substantial support" is intended to cover those individuals "who are not technically part of al-Qaeda," but who have some meaningful connection to the organization by, for example, providing financing. Regardless of the reasonableness of this approach from a policy perspective, a detention authority that sweeps so broadly is simply beyond what the law of war will support. *** The law of war permits detention of individuals who were "part of" one of the organizations targeted by the AUMF. That is the outer limit of the Executive's detention authority as stated in the AUMF and consistent with the law of war. Detaining an individual who "substantially supports" such an organization, but is not part of it, is simply not authorized by the AUMF itself or by the law of war. Hence, the Government's reliance on "substantial support" as a basis for detention independent of membership in the Taliban, al Qaeda or an associated force is rejected. ***

For essentially the same reasons, the Court also finds that the Government's detention authority does not extend to those individuals who have only "directly supported hostilities." *** The government does, however, have the authority to detain "any person who has committed a belligerent act." And just as the Court will consider evidence relating to "substantial support" of covered organizations in assessing whether an individual was functionally "part of" the organization, so, too, will it consider evidence of "direct support" for hostilities in assessing whether an individual "committed a belligerent act."

For purposes of these habeas proceedings, the Court interprets the phrase "committed a belligerent act" to cover any person who has directly participated in hostilities. That conclusion is consistent with the law of war. As the Court has noted above, the precise scope of the phrase "direct participation in hostilities" remains unsettled and the International Committee of the Red Cross is coordinating an effort among experts "to clarify the precise meaning of the notion of 'direct participation in hostilities', which has never been defined in treaty law." In these proceedings, the Court will rely on the settled aspects of the standard. "[L]ittle doubt exists that a civilian carrying out an attack would be directly participating in hostilities. In the same vein, legal experts seem to agree that civilians preparing or returning from combat operations are still considered to be directly participating in hostilities, although precise indication as to when preparation begins and return ends remains controversial." But any further refinement of the concept of "direct participation" will await examination of particular cases. *** Therefore, the Court concludes that under the AUMF the President has the authority to detain persons that the President determines planned, authorized, committed, or aided the terrorist attacks that occurred on September 11, 2001, and persons who harbored those responsible for those attacks. The President also has the authority to detain persons who are or were part of Taliban or al Qaeda forces or associated forces that are engaged in hostilities against the United States or its coalition partners, including any person who has committed (*i.e.,* directly participated in) a belligerent act in aid of such enemy armed forces.

Notes

1. Executive Acquiescence. The Obama Administration, in early October 2009, indicated that it would accept the detention authority parameters in *Hamlily* and *Gherebi* (not clearly delineating between them). Does this mean that there will be no appellate decisions on this issue?

2. Administration v. *Hamlily*. Here is the language of the Obama Administration, followed by the *Hamlily* bottom line. Look carefully at the two to focus precisely on the differences, which are italicized in the Administration position. Think of examples of individuals who would be subject to military detention under the former but not under the latter.

> (a) The President has the authority to detain persons that the President determines planned, authorized, committed, or aided the terrorist attacks that occurred on September 11, 2001, and persons who harbored those responsible for those attacks. The President also has the authority to detain persons who were part of, *or substantially supported,* Taliban or al-Qaida forces or associated forces that are engaged in hostilities against the United States or its coalition partners, including any person who has committed a belligerent act, *or has directly supported hostilities,* in aid of such enemy armed forces.

> (b) The President has the authority to detain persons that the President determines planned, authorized, committed, or aided the terrorist attacks that occurred on September 11, 2001, and persons who harbored those responsible for those attacks. The President also has the authority to detain persons who were part of Taliban or al-Qaida forces or associated forces that are engaged in hostilities against the United States or its coalition partners, including any person who has committed a belligerent act in aid of such enemy armed forces.

3. *Al-Marri* and *Padilla* Re-considered. What would happen to al-Marri under the *Hamlily* framework? What would happen to Padilla?

AL-BIHANI v. OBAMA
590 F. 3d 866, reh'g en banc denied 619 F. 3d 1 (C.A.D.C. 2010),
Cert. pet. filed 11/29/10

BROWN, Circuit Judge:

Ghaleb Nassar Al-Bihani *** claims his detention is unauthorized by statute and the procedures of his habeas proceeding were constitutionally infirm *** Al-Bihani, a Yemeni citizen, has been held at the U.S. naval base detention facility in Guantanamo Bay, Cuba since 2002. *** [He] accompanied and served a paramilitary group allied with the Taliban, known as the 55th Arab Brigade, which included Al Qaeda members within its command structure and which fought on the front lines against the Northern Alliance. He worked as the brigade's cook and carried a brigade-issued weapon, but never fired it in combat. Combat, however-in the form of bombing by the U.S.-led Coalition that invaded Afghanistan in response to the attacks of September 11, 2001-forced the 55th to retreat from the front lines in October 2001. At the end of this protracted retreat, Al-Bihani and the rest of the brigade surrendered, under orders, to Northern Alliance forces, and they kept him in custody until his handover to U.S. Coalition forces in early 2002. The U.S. military sent Al-Bihani to Guantanamo for detention and interrogation. *** Al-Bihani's many arguments present this court with two overarching questions regarding the detainees at the Guantanamo Bay naval base. The first concerns whom the President can lawfully detain pursuant to statutes passed by Congress. The second asks what procedure is due to detainees challenging their detention in habeas corpus proceedings. [This part of the opinion in in Chapter VII.] *** In this decision, we aim to narrow the legal uncertainty that clouds military detention.

Al-Bihani challenges the statutory legitimacy of his detention by advancing a number of arguments based upon the international laws of war. He first argues that relying on "support," or even "substantial support" of Al Qaeda or the Taliban as an independent basis for detention violates international law. As a result, such a standard should not be read into the ambiguous provisions of the Authorization for Use of Military Force (AUMF) ***. Al-Bihani interprets international law to mean anyone not belonging to an official state military is a civilian, and civilians, he says, must commit a direct hostile act, such as firing a weapon in combat, before they can be lawfully detained. Because Al-Bihani did not commit such an act, he reasons his detention is unlawful. Next, he argues the members of the 55th Arab Brigade were not subject to attack or detention by U.S. Coalition forces under the laws of co-belligerency because the 55th, although allied with the Taliban against the Northern Alliance, did not have the required opportunity to declare its neutrality in the fight against the United States. His third argument is that the conflict in which he was detained, an international war between the United States and Taliban-controlled Afghanistan, officially ended when the Taliban lost control of the Afghan government. Thus, absent a determination of future dangerousness, he must be released. Lastly, Al-Bihani posits a type of "clean hands" theory by which any authority the government has to detain him is undermined by its failure to accord him the prisoner-of-war status to which he believes he is entitled by international law.

Before considering these arguments in detail, we note that all of them rely heavily on the premise that the war powers granted by the AUMF and other statutes are limited by the international laws of war. This premise is mistaken. There is no indication in the AUMF, the Detainee Treatment Act of 2005, or the MCA of 2006 or 2009, that Congress intended the international laws of war to act as extra-textual limiting principles for the President's war powers under the AUMF. The international laws of war as a whole have not been implemented domestically by Congress and are therefore not a source of authority for U.S. courts. Even assuming Congress had at some earlier point implemented the laws of war as domestic law through appropriate legislation, Congress had the power to authorize the President in the AUMF and other later statutes to exceed those bounds. Further weakening their relevance to this case, the international laws of war are not a fixed code. Their dictates and application to actual events are by nature contestable and fluid. Therefore, while the international laws of war are helpful to courts when identifying the general set of war powers to which the AUMF speaks, their lack of controlling legal force and firm definition render their use both inapposite and inadvisable when courts seek to determine the limits of the President's war powers. Therefore, putting aside that we find Al-Bihani's reading of international law to be unpersuasive, we have no occasion here to quibble over the intricate application of vague treaty provisions and amorphous customary principles. The sources we look to for resolution of Al-Bihani's case are the sources courts always look to: the text of relevant statutes and controlling domestic caselaw.

Under those sources, Al-Bihani is lawfully detained whether the definition of a detainable person is *** "an individual who was part of or supporting Taliban or al Qaeda forces, or associated forces that are engaged in hostilities against the United States or its coalition partners," or the modified definition offered by the government that requires that an individual "substantially support" enemy forces. The statutes authorizing the use of force and detention not only grant the government the power to craft a workable legal standard to identify individuals it can detain, but also cabin the application of these definitions. The AUMF authorizes the President to "use all necessary and appropriate force against those nations, organizations, or persons he determines planned, authorized, committed, or aided the terrorist attacks that occurred on September 11, 2001, or harbored such organizations or persons." *** The 2006 MCA authorized the trial of an individual who "engaged in hostilities or who has purposefully and materially supported hostilities against the United States or its co-belligerents who is not a lawful enemy combatant (including a person who is part of the Taliban, al Qaeda, or associated forces)." In 2009, Congress enacted a new version of the MCA with a new definition that authorized the trial of "unprivileged enemy belligerents," a class of persons that includes those who "purposefully and materially supported hostilities against the United States or its coalition partners." The provisions of the 2006 and 2009 MCAs are illuminating in this case because the Government's detention authority logically covers a category of persons no narrower than is covered by its military commission authority. Detention authority in fact sweeps wider, also extending at least to traditional P.O.W.s, and arguably to other categories of persons. But for this case, it is enough to recognize that any person subject to a military commission trial is also subject to detention, and that category of persons includes those who are part of forces associated with Al Qaeda or the Taliban or those who purposefully and materially support such forces in hostilities against U.S. Coalition partners.

In light of these provisions of the 2006 and 2009 MCAs, the facts that were both found by the district court and offered by Al-Bihani *** place Al-Bihani within the "part of" and "support" prongs of the relevant statutory definition. The district court found Al Qaeda members participated in the command structure of the 55th Arab Brigade, making the brigade an Al Qaeda-affiliated outfit, and it is unquestioned that the 55th fought alongside the Taliban while the Taliban was harboring Al Qaeda. Al-Bihani's evidence confirmed these points, establishing that the 55th "supported the Taliban against the Northern Alliance," a Coalition partner, and that the 55th was "aided, or even, at times, commanded, by al-Qaeda members." Al-Bihani's connections with the 55th therefore render him detainable. His acknowledged actions-accompanying the brigade on the battlefield, carrying a brigade-issued weapon, cooking for the unit, and retreating and surrendering under brigade orders-strongly suggest, in the absence of an official membership card, that he was part of the 55th. Even assuming, as he argues, that he was a civilian "contractor" rendering services, those services render Al-Bihani detainable under the "purposefully and materially supported" language of both versions of the MCA. That language constitutes a standard whose outer bounds are not readily identifiable. But wherever the outer bounds may lie, they clearly include traditional food operations essential to a fighting force and the carrying of arms. Viewed in full, the facts show Al-Bihani was part of and supported a group-prior to and after September 11-that was affiliated with Al Qaeda and Taliban forces and engaged in hostilities against a U.S. Coalition partner. Al-Bihani, therefore, falls squarely within the scope of the President's statutory detention powers.[2]

The government can also draw statutory authority to detain Al-Bihani directly from the language of the AUMF. The AUMF authorizes force against those who "harbored ... organizations or persons" the President determines "planned, authorized, committed, or aided the terrorist attacks of September 11, 2001." It is not in dispute that Al Qaeda is the organization responsible for September 11 or that it was harbored by the Taliban in Afghanistan. It is also not in dispute that the 55th Arab Brigade defended the Taliban against the Northern Alliance's efforts to oust the regime from power. Drawing from these facts, it cannot be disputed that the actual and foreseeable result of the 55th's defense of the Taliban was the maintenance of Al Qaeda's safe haven

---

[2] In reaching this conclusion, we need not rely on the evidence suggesting that Al-Bihani attended Al Qaeda training camps in Afghanistan and visited Al Qaeda guesthouses. We do note, however, that evidence supporting the military's reasonable belief of either of those two facts with respect to a non-citizen seized abroad during the ongoing war on terror would seem to overwhelmingly, if not definitively, justify the government's detention of such a non-citizen.

in Afghanistan. This result places the 55th within the AUMF's wide ambit as an organization that harbored Al Qaeda, making it subject to U.S. military force and its members and supporters-including Al-Bihani-eligible for detention.

Al-Bihani disagrees with this conclusion, arguing that the 55th Arab Brigade was not lawfully subject to attack and detention. He points to the international laws of co-belligerency to demonstrate that the brigade should have been allowed the opportunity to remain neutral upon notice of a conflict between the United States and the Taliban. We reiterate that international law, including the customary rules of co-belligerency, do not limit the President's detention power in this instance. But even if Al-Bihani's argument were relevant to his detention and putting aside all the questions that applying such elaborate rules to this situation would raise, the laws of co-belligerency affording notice of war and the choice to remain neutral have only applied to nation states. The 55th clearly was not a state, but rather an irregular fighting force present within the borders of Afghanistan at the sanction of the Taliban. Any attempt to apply the rules of co-belligerency to such a force would be folly, akin to this court ascribing powers of national sovereignty to a local chapter of the Freemasons.

While we think the facts of this case show Al-Bihani was both part of and substantially supported enemy forces, we realize the picture may be less clear in other cases where facts may indicate only support, only membership, or neither. We have no occasion here to explore the outer bounds of what constitutes sufficient support or indicia of membership to meet the detention standard. We merely recognize that both prongs are valid criteria that are independently sufficient to satisfy the standard.

With the Government's detention authority established as an initial matter, we turn to the argument that Al-Bihani must now be released according to longstanding law of war principles because the conflict with the Taliban has allegedly ended. Al-Bihani offers the court a choice of numerous event dates-the day Afghans established a post-Taliban interim authority, the day the United States recognized that authority, the day Hamid Karzai was elected President-to mark the official end of the conflict. No matter which is chosen, each would dictate the release of Al-Bihani if we follow his reasoning. His argument fails on factual and practical grounds. First, it is not clear if Al-Bihani was captured in the conflict with the Taliban or with Al Qaeda; he does not argue that the conflict with Al Qaeda is over. Second, there are currently 34,800 U.S. troops and a total of 71,030 Coalition troops in Afghanistan, with tens of thousands more to be added soon. The principle Al-Bihani espouses-were it accurate-would make each successful campaign of a long war but a Pyrrhic prelude to defeat. The initial success of the United States and its Coalition partners in ousting the Taliban from the seat of government and establishing a young democracy would trigger an obligation to release Taliban fighters captured in earlier clashes. Thus, the victors would be commanded to constantly refresh the ranks of the fledgling democracy's most likely saboteurs.

In response to this commonsense observation, Al-Bihani contends the current hostilities are a different conflict, one against the Taliban reconstituted in a non-governmental form, and the government must prove that Al-Bihani would join this insurgency in order to continue to hold him. But even the laws of war upon which he relies do not draw such fine distinctions. The Geneva Conventions require release and repatriation only at the "cessation of active hostilities." Third Geneva Convention art. 118. That the Conventions use the term "active hostilities" instead of the terms "conflict" or "state of war" found elsewhere in the document is significant. It serves to distinguish the physical violence of war from the official beginning and end of a conflict, because fighting does not necessarily track formal timelines. The Conventions, in short, codify what common sense tells us must be true: release is only required when the fighting stops.

Even so, we do not rest our resolution of this issue on international law or mere common sense. The determination of when hostilities have ceased is a political decision, and we defer to the Executive's opinion on the matter, at least in the absence of an authoritative congressional declaration purporting to terminate the war. *** In the absence of a determination by the political branches that hostilities in Afghanistan have ceased, Al-Bihani's continued detention is justified.

Al-Bihani also argues he should be released because the Government's failure to accord him P.O.W. status violated international law and undermined its otherwise lawful authority to detain him. Even assuming Al-Bihani is entitled to P.O.W. status, we find no controlling authority for this "clean hands" theory in statute or in caselaw. The AUMF, DTA, and MCA of 2006 and 2009 do not hinge the Government's detention authority on proper identification of P.O.W.s or compliance with international law in general. In fact, the MCA of 2006, in a provision not altered by the MCA of 2009, explicitly precludes detainees from claiming the Geneva conventions-which include criteria to determine who is entitled to P.O.W. status-as a source of rights. ***

WILLIAMS, Senior Circuit Judge, concurring in part and concurring in the judgment:

I agree with the majority's decision to affirm the district Court's denial of Al Bihani's petition for a writ of habeas corpus. I take a slightly different view of the central substantive issue in this case, and a significantly different view as to the necessity of reaching any of Al Bihani's procedural arguments. ***

He argues that he cannot be detained on the basis of his relationship with the 55th Brigade, for two reasons. First, Al Bihani says, the Authorization for the Use of Military Force (2001) ("AUMF")-properly interpreted in light of applicable law-of-war principles-cannot be read to have authorized the U.S. government to conduct hostilities against the 55th Brigade. Second, even if the 55th Brigade were the kind of organization targeted by the AUMF, he himself was not a part of the 55th Brigade, nor was his involvement with the unit enough to subject him to the lawful exercise of U.S. force. Neither argument is persuasive. *** Al Bihani acknowledges that both before and after 9/11, the 55th Brigade fought alongside the Taliban in Afghanistan in its fight against the Northern Alliance, Petitioner-Appellant's and he cannot reasonably dispute that the Taliban "harbored" al Qaeda, which committed the 9/11 attacks. *** [T]he AUMF clearly authorized the President to attack the 55th Brigade. By its terms, the AUMF allows force against "organizations" that "harbored" those who were responsible for the 9/11 attacks. The 55th Brigade fought to preserve the Taliban regime in Afghanistan even as the Taliban was harboring al Qaeda in Afghanistan. This makes the 55th Brigade, itself, an organization that "harbored" al Qaeda within the meaning of the AUMF.

No contrary interpretation of the AUMF is plausible. If the AUMF did *not* authorize U.S. force against an organization fighting in Afghanistan to stabilize and protect the Taliban's power after 9/11, then the American military campaign that started on October 7, 2001, was illegal-under *domestic* law-to the extent that it targeted not just Taliban forces fighting the Northern Alliance, but also 55th Brigade forces fighting with the Taliban against the Northern Alliance. Whatever the appropriate role of the laws of war in determining what powers the President derived from the AUMF, it cannot be to render unlawful the President's use of force in Afghanistan in the fall of 2001-which the Supreme Court has repeatedly acknowledged was permitted under the AUMF. Under the best reading of the AUMF, then, Congress authorized that military campaign, aimed at removing the Taliban from the seat of government and minimizing its ongoing influence in Afghanistan, including the attacks on ancillary forces aiding the Taliban.

Because the 55th Brigade was properly the target of U.S. force in Afghanistan pursuant to the AUMF, it follows that members of the 55th Brigade taken into custody on the battlefield in Afghanistan in the fall of 2001 may be detained "for the duration of the particular conflict in which they were captured." In addition to detention based on a person's having been "part of" an AUMF-targeted organization, the government asserts that Congress authorized force against, and therefore detention of, someone who provided "substantial support" to such a group.

Al Bihani argues, by contrast, that he was not a *part of* the 55th Brigade at all, but merely "a cook's assistant ... near the front lines." To be sure, the people he was cooking for were the members of the 55th Brigade, as his counsel acknowledged at oral argument. Al Bihani maintains, though, that notwithstanding his cooking, and his having been provided a weapon, he was effectively a "civilian contractor" rather than a bona fide member of the brigade. In support of this contention, he cites principally a document produced by the International Committee of the Red Cross (ICRC), entitled *Interpretive Guidance on the Notion of Direct Participation in Hostilities Under International Humanitarian Law.* That work, in his view, says that "individuals who accompany ... armed forces and provide food" are properly viewed as civilians. As a result, such food-providers can't permissibly be detained unless they themselves take hostile acts directly against their would-be detainers.

The question whether a person was a "part of" an informal, non-state military organization like the 55th Brigade overlaps significantly with the question whether that person "supported" or indeed "substantially" or "materially" supported the organization. Both these terms are highly elastic, ranging from core membership and support to vague affiliation and cheerleading. But whatever their range, it seems hard to imagine how someone could be shown to be a member of such a group (for purposes of detention under the AUMF) without evidence that he also significantly supported it (for those purposes).

Regardless, however, of whether the operative inquiry probes membership in the unit, or support of the unit, or substantial or material support of the unit, or some combination of these considerations, Al Bihani's involvement with the 55th Brigade-cooking for and carrying arms provided by the 55th Brigade, and doing so near the front lines of hostilities between the Taliban and the Northern Alliance-was ample to make him properly subject to U.S. force directed at the 55th Brigade pursuant to the AUMF. Purely on the basis of these activities, he was sufficiently enmeshed with the brigade to fall into the category of persons whom the AUMF allowed the U.S. military to target. The alternative conclusion-which would have it that the President was authorized to use force against the fighting members of the 55th Brigade on the front lines in northern Afghanistan, but not against the armed people who enabled them to fight-is senseless. Because Al Bihani was effectively part of the 55th Brigade, and a sufficient supporter of same, his detention for the duration of the hostilities in which he was captured is lawful.

The ICRC document does not alter this analysis. The work itself explicitly disclaims that it should be read to have the force of law. "[W]hile reflecting the ICRC's views," the authors write, "the Interpretive Guidance is not and cannot be a text of a legally binding nature." ***

Within the portion of the opinion addressing the petitioner's substantive argument that his activities in Afghanistan do not put him in the class of people whom the President may detain pursuant to the AUMF, the majority unnecessarily addresses a number of other points. Most notable is the paragraph that begins "Before considering these arguments in detail," and that reaches the conclusion that "the premise that the war powers granted by the AUMF and other statutes are limited by the international laws of war ... is mistaken." The paragraph appears hard to square with the approach that the Supreme Court took in *Hamdi*. In any event, there is no need for the Court's pronouncements, divorced from application to any particular argument. Curiously, the majority's dictum goes well beyond what even the *government* has argued in this case. *** Because the petitioner's detention is lawful by virtue of facts that he has conceded-a conclusion that the majority seems not to dispute-the majority's analysis of the constitutionality of the *procedures* the district court used is unnecessary. *** [T]he facts that Al Bihani says are correct readily yield a ruling that his detention is legally permissible. ***

Notes

1. A Mistaken Premise? Judge Brown says the premise that the United States must abide by international law concerning detention of opponents in the "war on terror" is mistaken. Judge Williams, citing the Supreme Court's *Hamdi* decision, says Judge Brown is mistaken. Who is correct? Review *Hamdi* if necessary. Consider how Al-Bihani's circumstances are similar to and different from those of Hamdi. Why does Judge Williams agree with Judge Brown that military detention is lawful notwithstanding Al-Bihani's argument that he is not properly subject to military detention under the Geneva Conventions? At the end of her opinion, Judge Brown specifically notes that the Military Commission Act of 2009 provisions "preclude" detainee claims based on international law. Judge Williams, at the end of his concurrence, says the International Committee of the Red Cross position cited by al-Bihani concerning his detention does not have the "force of law." What are the grounds for these positions? Do you find them persuasive?

2. Military Detention of Material Supporters. Al-Bihani argues he is not properly detainable because he was only a cook, his unit was neither a Taliban nor an al-Qaeda unit, that the military conflict with the Taliban ended when that government was displaced in Afghanistan, and that independent contractors cannot be militarily detained. Why does al-Bihani lose each of these arguments? Does the court's holding mean that anyone who meets the "material support" criteria of the statutes you studied in Chapter II can be militarily detained? If Ralph Fertig and the Humanitarian Law Project provided the support to the Taliban that they gave the Tamil Tigers, could he and the leaders of HLP be militarily detained? Why or why not?

3. Support and Membership. The court says the detention decision concerning al-Bihani has two prongs: support and membership. It also notes that the two overlap in this case, that al-Bihani is not a borderline case, and that "the picture [could be] less clear in other cases." What might some such cases be? Does the discussion of membership in the Communist Party versus al Qaeda in *HLP* help answer this question?

4. Uncertainty. Judge Brown says that the government's detention decisions "do not hinge on proper identification of POWs." Why not? Isn't this a problem that differs from WWII military detentions? Is Judge Williams' concurrence forthcoming because he views this as a situation where "the 55th Brigade was properly a target of U.S. force in Afghanistan" so "it follows that members of the 55th Brigade taken into custody on the battlefield of Afghanistan in the fall of 2001" may be detained until the end of the conflict? What if the brigade did not wear uniforms and al-Bihani said he was not a member of the brigade? What if he spoke a language not the primary language of most of the brigade members captured? What if a brigade roster was found and Al-Bihani's name was not on it?

5. Basic Interpretive Lens. The court notes the "wide ambit" of the AUMF (the basic domestic statute supporting detention of al-Bihani) and the "laws of co-belligerency" (the basic international law framework for his inclusion as a military detainee). Do these starting points minimize the judicial role in reviewing detention decisions? You will have more evidence with which to answer this question after you read Chapter VII. Incidentally, you will see other parts of *al-Bihani* in Chapter VII concerning habeas corpus procedural issues not covered here.

6. End of the Conflict. In note 3 above you were asked to think about why the conflict in Afghanistan was not over, contrary to Al-Bihani's argument. Who should make the determination that a conflict has ended? Is this issue always, as the majority says, a "political decision?" Would this mean a case posing such a question should be avoided by the judiciary as a "political question" under the *Baker v. Carr* factors you studied in constitutional law (textual commitment to another branch of government, lack of judicially discoverable and manageable standards, etc.)?

SALAHI v. OBAMA

625 F. 3d 745 (C.A.D.C. 2010)

TATEL, Circuit Judge:

*** The United States seeks to detain Mohammedou Ould Salahi on the grounds that he was "part of" al-Qaida not because he fought with al-Qaida or its allies against the United States, but rather because he swore an oath of allegiance to the organization, associated with its members, and helped it in various ways, including hosting its leaders and referring aspiring jihadists to a known al-Qaida operative. After an evidentiary hearing at which Salahi testified, the district court found that although Salahi "was an al-Qaida sympathizer" who "was in touch with al-Qaida members" and provided them with "sporadic support," the government had failed to show that he was in fact "part of" al-Qaida at the time of his capture. The district court thus granted the writ and ordered Salahi released. Since then, however, this Court has issued three opinions that cast serious doubt on the district Court's approach to determining whether an individual is "part of" al-Qaida. We agree with the government that we must therefore vacate the district Court's judgment, but because that court, lacking the benefit of these recent cases, left unresolved key factual questions necessary for us to determine as a matter of law whether Salahi was "part of" al-Qaida when captured, we remand for further proceedings consistent with this opinion. *** Although the government previously claimed authority to detain Salahi on other grounds as well-because he allegedly aided the September 11 attacks and because he "purposefully and materially support[ed]" forces associated with al-Qaida "in hostilities against U.S. Coalition partners," *Al- Bihani v. Obama,* 590 F.3d 866, 872 (D.C.Cir.2010)-it has since dropped those claims and now relies solely on the allegation that Salahi was "part of" al-Qaida at the time of his capture. ***

Mohammedou Ould Salahi was born in 1970 in Mauritania. In December 1990, he traveled from Germany, where he was attending college, to Afghanistan "to support the mujahideen"-Islamic rebels seeking to overthrow Afghanistan's Soviet-supported Communist government. *** In March 1991, shortly after finishing his training, Salahi swore *bayat,* an oath of loyalty, to al-Qaida. He left Afghanistan soon after taking this oath but returned in January 1992. Having "heard rumors that the mujahideen had invaded Kabul and started fighting among themselves," Salahi decided to travel back to Germany in March 1992. At this point, he alleges, he "severed all ties with ... al Qaida."

According to the government, however, the record contains significant evidence that Salahi recruited for al-Qaida and provided it with other support after his alleged withdrawal in 1992. For example, the district court found that Salahi sent a fax to al-Qaida operative Christopher Paul in January 1997, asking for his help in finding "a true Group and Place" for "some Brothers" interested in fighting jihad. Salahi admitted to interrogators that he knew Paul to be a "man of great respect in Al-Qaida" and that he sent the fax to "facilitate getting the [aspiring jihadists] to fight."

As the district court recognized, "[t]he most damaging allegation against Salahi is that, in October 1999, he encouraged Ramzi bin al-Shibh, Marwan al-Shehhi, and Ziad Jarrah to join al-Qaida." Bin al-Shibh helped coordinate the September 11 attacks, and al-Shehhi and Jarrah were two of the September 11 pilots. The government contends that while bin al-Shibh, al-Shehhi, and Jarrah had originally intended to travel to Chechnya to wage jihad against Russian forces, Salahi convinced them to travel instead to Afghanistan to receive military training. According to the government, the three men followed Salahi's advice and with his assistance traveled to Afghanistan, where they were recruited by al-Qaida into the September 11 plot. But the district court, having discounted portions of the Government's evidence as unreliable and inconsistent, found only that "Salahi provided lodging for three men for one night at his home in Germany, that one of them was Ramzi bin al-Shibh, and that there was discussion of jihad and Afghanistan."

In addition to Salahi' connection to bin al-Shibh, the district court found that Salahi "had an ongoing and relatively close relationship" with Abu Hafs al-Mauritania, who "is believed to be one of [Usama] bin Laden's spiritual advisors and a high-ranking leader of al-Qaida." Abu Hafs is Salahi's cousin and is married to the sister of Salahi's ex-wife. In August 1993, Salahi accompanied Abu Hafs to an al-Qaida safe house in Mauritania. Several years later, Abu Hafs asked Salahi to meet with Abu Hajar al-Iraqi, allegedly al-Qaida's telecommunications chief, when al-Iraqi visited Germany in late 1995 and early 1996 to explore purchasing telecommunications equipment for al-Qaida operations in Sudan. *** The record contains evidence of additional contacts with Abu Hafs. ***

The government also alleges that Salahi interacted with members of an al-Qaida cell during a brief stay in Montreal, Canada, from November 1999 to January 2000. Although this Montreal al-Qaida cell has been linked to the unsuccessful Millennium Plot to bomb Los Angeles International Airport, the government does not allege that Salahi participated in that effort. Much about Salahi's connections to the Montreal cell remains hazy and disputed, and for its part, the district court concluded that the Government's evidence of Salahi's activities in Canada did not "add [anything] of significance to the proof that Salahi was 'part of' al-Qaida," although the evidence might be sufficient "to support a criminal charge of providing material support" to the organization.

After leaving Canada, Salahi returned to Mauritania, where according to the government he "performed computer activities with a goal of helping al-Qaida." For example, Salahi considered creating an Internet discussion group about fighting jihad but dropped the plan after a German al-Qaida operative, Christian Ganczarski, suggested that the discussion group would attract attention from authorities.. Salahi may also have subscribed to electronic mailing lists through which he received emails discussing cyber-attacks. Two such emails were found on a computer Salahi used at his workplace in Mauritania. The computer also contained a third document with instructions on implementing cyber-attacks. The district court concluded that although these three documents are "not evidence that Salahi engaged in ... cyber-attacks," they nonetheless corroborate Salahi's statements to interrogators that "he knew about and had some involvement in planning for denial of service computer attacks."

Salahi was captured in Mauritania in November 2001 and has been held at the United States Naval Station at Guantanamo Bay, Cuba, since 2002. In December 2004, Salahi appeared before a Combatant Status Review Tribunal, which concluded that he was lawfully detained. He then filed the habeas petition that is the subject of this appeal.

In its opinion granting Salahi's petition, the district court began by rejecting the Government's argument that because Salahi had once sworn *bayat* to al-Qaida, the burden should shift to him to prove that he later withdrew from the organization. After reviewing all the evidence, the district court then concluded that Salahi "was an al-Qaida sympathizer" and "perhaps a 'fellow traveler.' "It also found that Salahi "was in touch with al-Qaida members" and provided them with "sporadic support." Nonetheless, the court concluded, Salahi was not "part of" al-Qaeda at the time of his capture because the government had failed to prove that after leaving Afghanistan in 1992, he continued receiving and executing orders within al-Qaida's "command structure."

The government appeals. We review the district Court's factual findings for clear error. Legal questions, including the ultimate determination of whether the facts found by the district court establish that Salahi was "part of" al-Qaida, are reviewed *de novo*.

Before considering the Government's arguments, we think it important to emphasize the precise nature of the Government's case against Salahi. The government has not criminally indicted Salahi for providing material support to terrorists or the "foreign terrorist organization" al-Qaida. Nor does the government seek to detain Salahi under the AUMF on the grounds that he aided the September 11 attacks or "purposefully and materially support[ed]" forces associated with al-Qaida "in hostilities against U.S. Coalition partners." *Al-Bihani,* 590 F.3d at 872. Instead, the government claims that Salahi is detainable under the AUMF because he was "part of" al-Qaeda when captured.

Reiterating the argument it made in the district court, the government contends that Salahi should bear the burden of proving that he disassociated from al-Qaeda after swearing *bayat* to the organization in 1991. In support, the government cites the plurality's statement in *Hamdi v. Rumsfeld* that "once the Government puts forth credible evidence that [a] habeas petitioner meets the [AUMF's detention] criteria, the onus [may] shift to the petitioner to rebut that evidence with more persuasive evidence that he falls outside the criteria."

Here, as noted, the relevant inquiry is whether Salahi was "part of" al-Qaida when captured. Therefore, in order to shift the burden of proof to Salahi, we would have to presume that having once sworn *bayat* to al-Qaida, Salahi remained a member of the organization until seized in November 2001. Although such a presumption may be warranted in some cases, such as where an individual swore allegiance to al-Qaida on September 12, 2001, and was captured soon thereafter, the unique circumstances of Salahi's case make the Government's proposed presumption inappropriate here.

When Salahi took his oath of allegiance in March 1991, al-Qaida and the United States shared a common objective: they both sought to topple Afghanistan's Communist government. Not until later did al-Qaida begin publicly calling for attacks against the United States. To be sure, the roots of the conflict between al-Qaida and the United States stretch back at least as far as Iraq's August 1990 invasion of Kuwait, following which Saudi Arabian leaders allowed U.S. forces to deploy to their country. Usama bin Laden was immediately critical of this arrangement, "paint[ing] the U.S. forces as occupiers of sacred Islamic ground," and after leaving Saudi Arabia in April 1991, he relocated to Sudan and began "buying property there which he used to host and train Al Qaeda militants ... for use against the United States and its interests, as well as for *jihad* operations in the Balkans, Chechnya, Kashmir, and the Philippines." Bin Laden, however, did not issue his first *fatwa* against U.S. forces until 1992-the very year in which, according to Salahi's sworn declaration, Salahi severed all ties with al-Qaida. In light of all this, Salahi's March 1991 oath of *bayat* is insufficiently probative of his relationship with al-Qaida at the time of his capture in November 2001 to justify shifting the burden to him to prove that he disassociated from the organization. In so concluding, we have no doubt about the relevance of Salahi's oath to the ultimate question of whether he was "part of" al-Qaida at the time of his capture. We conclude only that given the facts of this particular case, Salahi's oath does not warrant shifting the burden of proof.

The government next challenges the district Court's use of the "command structure" test-a standard that district judges in this circuit, operating without any meaningful guidance from Congress, developed to determine whether a Guantanamo habeas petitioner was "part of" al-Qaida. *See Hamlily v. Obama,* 616 F.Supp.2d 63, 75 (D.D.C.2009); *Gherebi v. Obama,* 609 F.Supp.2d 43, 68-69 (D.D.C.2009). As applied by the district court in this case, the command-structure test required the government to prove that Salahi "'receive[d] and execute[d] orders or directions' from al-Qaida operatives after 1992 when, according to Salahi, he severed ties with the organization. Having found no such evidence, the court concluded that Salahi was not "part of" al-Qaida at the time of his capture.

As the government points out, the district Court's approach is inconsistent with our recent decisions in *Awad* and *Bensayah,* which were issued after the district court granted Salahi's habeas petition. These decisions make clear that the determination of whether an individual is "part of" al-Qaida "must be made on a case-by-case basis by using a functional rather than a formal approach and by focusing upon the actions of the individual in relation to the organization." Evidence that an individual operated within al-Qaida's command structure is "sufficient but is not necessary to show he is 'part of' the organization." "[T]here may be other indicia that a particular individual [was] sufficiently involved with the organization to be deemed part of it." *Bensayah,* 610 F.3d at 725. For example, since petitioner in *Awad* joined and was accepted by al-Qaida fighters who were engaged in hostilities against Afghan and allied forces, he could properly be considered "part of" al-Qaida even if he never formally received or executed any orders. *See Awad,* 608 F.3d at 3-4, 11.

As we explained in *Bensayah,* however, "the purely independent conduct of a freelancer is not enough" to establish that an individual is "part of" al-Qaida. Thus, as government counsel conceded at oral argument, the Government's failure to prove that an individual was acting under orders from al-Qaida may be *relevant* to the question of whether the individual was "part of" the organization when captured. Consider this very case. Unlike petitioner in *Awad,* who affiliated with al-Qaida fighters engaged in active hostilities against U.S. allies in Afghanistan, Salahi is not accused of participating in military action against the United States. Instead, the government claims that Salahi was "part of" al-Qaida because he swore *bayat* and thereafter provided various services to the organization, including recruiting, hosting leaders, transferring money, etc. Under these circumstances, whether Salahi performed such services pursuant to al-Qaida orders may well be relevant to determining if he was "part of" al-Qaida or was instead engaged in the "purely independent conduct of a freelancer." The problem with the district Court's decision is that it treats the absence of evidence that Salahi received and executed orders as dispositive. The decision therefore cannot survive *Awad* and *Bensayah.*

The government urges us to reverse and direct the district court to deny Salahi's habeas petition. Although we agree that *Awad* and *Bensayah* require that we vacate the district Court's judgment, we think the better course is to remand for further proceedings consistent with those opinions. Because the district court, lacking the guidance of these later decisions, looked primarily for evidence that Salahi participated in al-Qaida's command structure, it did not make definitive findings regarding certain key facts necessary for us to determine as a matter of law whether Salahi was in fact "part of" al-Qaida when captured. *See Barhoumi,* 609 F.3d at 423 (noting that whether the facts found by the district court are sufficient to establish that an individual was "part of" al-Qaida is a legal question that we review *de novo*). For example, does the Government's evidence support the inference that even if

Salahi was not acting under express orders, he nonetheless had a tacit understanding with al-Qaida operatives that he would refer prospective jihadists to the organization? Has the government presented sufficient evidence for the court to make findings regarding what Salahi said to bin al-Shibh during their "discussion of jihad and Afghanistan"? Did al-Qaida operatives ask Salahi to assist the organization with telecommunications projects in Sudan, Afghanistan, or Pakistan? Did Salahi provide any assistance to al-Qaida in planning denial-of-service computer attacks, even if those attacks never came to fruition? May the court infer from Salahi's numerous ties to known al-Qaida operatives that he remained a trusted member of the organization? *See id.* at 16 ("Salahi ... associated with at least a half-dozen known al-Qaida members and terrorists[ ] and somehow found and lived among or with al-Qaida cell members in Montreal."); *cf. Awad,* 608 F.3d at 3 (noting that the al-Qaida fighters Awad joined "treated [him] as one of their own"). With answers to questions like these, which may require additional testimony, the district court will be able to determine in the first instance whether Salahi was or was not "sufficiently involved with [al-Qaida] to be deemed part of it."

A final note: since we are remanding for further factual findings, we think it appropriate to reiterate this Court's admonition in *Al-Adahi,* also decided after the district court issued its decision in this case, that a court considering a Guantanamo detainee's habeas petition must view the evidence collectively rather than in isolation. Merely because a particular piece of evidence is insufficient, standing alone, to prove a particular point does not mean that the evidence "may be tossed aside and the next [piece of evidence] may be evaluated as if the first did not exist." The evidence must be considered in its entirety in determining whether the government has satisfied its burden of proof.

Although the district court generally followed this approach, its consideration of certain pieces of evidence may have been unduly atomized. For example, the court found that Salahi's "limited relationships" with certain al-Qaida operatives were "too brief and shallow to serve as an *independent* basis for detention." Even if Salahi's connections to these individuals fail independently to prove that he was "part of" al-Qaida, those connections make it more likely that Salahi was a member of the organization when captured and thus remain relevant to the question of whether he is detainable. *Cf. Al- Adahi,* 613 F.3d at 1107 (noting that petitioner's "close association [with Usama bin Laden] made it far more likely that [he] was or became part of" al-Qaida).

The district court may also have evaluated Salahi's oath of *bayat* in isolation. In its conclusion, the district court stated, "[T]he government wants to hold Salahi indefinitely, because of its concern that he might *renew* his oath to al-Qaida and become a terrorist upon his release." This suggests that the district court may have failed to consider the possibility that the "sporadic support" Salahi "undoubtedly ... provide[d]" al-Qaida demonstrates that he remained a member of the organization, thus having no need to renew his oath because he continued to abide by his original vow of allegiance.

The President seeks to detain Salahi on the grounds that he was "part of" al-Qaida at the time he was captured. Because additional fact-finding is required to resolve that issue under this Circuit's evolving case law, we vacate and remand for further proceedings consistent with this opinion.

Notes

1. *Salahi* **rejects** *Hamlily*. What does the D.C. Circuit find wrong with the *Hamlily* Court's formulation of who may be detained? Does the Circuit Court find that the lower court was too rigid in its conception of membership in al Qaeda? What was the source of that rigidity? Do you think the Circuit Court accepted the Government's position?

2. **Dropped Theory.** The court noted that the government had dropped its theory, prominent in *al-Bihani*, that Salahi provided material support to forces associated with al-Qaida and "now relies solely on the allegation that Salahi was part of al-Qaida at the time of his capture." Why would the government drop that argument?

3. *Bayat.* Salami undisputedly swore *bayat*, an oath of loyalty, to al-Qaida, something al-Bihani never did. Yet the court finds this is "insufficiently probative of his relationship with al-Qaida at the time of his capture" to shift the burden to Salami to show he was not "part of" al-Qaida. Why not, assuming the burden can sometimes shift? We will explore evidence and processes in habeas proceedings further in Chapter VII.

4. **Command Structure.** Two D.C. Circuit decisions referenced here, *Awad* and *Bensayah*, conclude that whether an individual was "part of" al-Qaida should be made "using a functional rather than a formal approach." What is the difference between these approaches and how do they relate to "command structure"? To the "purely independent conduct of a freelancer"? Does this mean that lone wolf terrorists may not be militarily detained? What should be done with individuals who, inspired by al-Qaida's attacks on the United States, make plans to slip into this country to blow up buildings and people?

5. **Factual Application.** Salahi swore loyalty to al Qaeda, had many ties with leading al Qaeda figures, and encouraged others, including bin al Shibh, to wage war on the United States. Why was this not enough to make him a proper subject of military detention? On remand, what do you think the district court is likely to decide?

6. Implementing and Reviewing the Application of Detainee Decisions. Whatever the standards for determining who is detained militarily, there remain the questions of what evidence suffices to show judges reviewing military decisions, often in the field of battle, that correct decisions were made. The following case explores this interplay between military decisions and judicial review.

3. DIRECT JUDICIAL REVIEW?

PARHAT v. GATES
532 F.3d 834 (C.A.D.C. 2008)

GARLAND, Circuit Judge.

A Combatant Status Review Tribunal has decided that petitioner Huzaifa Parhat, a detainee at the United States Naval Base at Guantanamo Bay, Cuba, is an "enemy combatant." This is the first case in which this court has considered the merits of a petition to review such a decision under the Detainee Treatment Act of 2005. The Act grants this court jurisdiction to "determine the validity of any final decision of a Combatant Status Review Tribunal that an alien is properly detained as an enemy combatant." We conclude that the Tribunal's decision in Parhat's case was not valid.

Parhat is an ethnic Uighur, who fled his home in the People's Republic of China in opposition to the policies of the Chinese government. It is undisputed that he is not a member of al Qaida or the Taliban, and that he has never participated in any hostile action against the United States or its allies. The Tribunal's determination that Parhat is an enemy combatant is based on its finding that he is "affiliated" with a Uighur independence group, and the further finding that the group was "associated" with al Qaida and the Taliban. The Tribunal's findings regarding the Uighur group rest, in key respects, on statements in classified State and Defense Department documents that provide no information regarding the sources of the reporting upon which the statements are based, and otherwise lack sufficient indicia of the statements' reliability. Parhat contends, with support of his own, that the Chinese government is the source of several of the key statements

Parhat's principal argument on this appeal is that the record before his Combatant Status Review Tribunal is insufficient to support the conclusion that he is an enemy combatant, even under the Defense Department's own definition of that term. We agree. To survive review under the Detainee Treatment Act, a Tribunal's determination of a detainee's status must be based on evidence that both the Tribunal and the court can assess for reliability. Because the evidence the government submitted to Parhat's Tribunal did not permit the Tribunal to make the necessary assessment, and because the record on review does not permit this court to do so, we cannot find that the Government's designation of Parhat as an enemy combatant is supported by a "preponderance of the evidence" and "was consistent with the standards and procedures" established by the Secretary of Defense, as required by the Act.

To affirm the Tribunal's determination under such circumstances would be to place a judicial imprimatur on an act of essentially unreviewable executive discretion. That is not what Congress directed us to do when it authorized judicial review of enemy combatant determinations under the Act. Accordingly, we direct the government to release Parhat, to transfer him, or to expeditiously convene a new Combatant Status Review Tribunal to consider evidence submitted in a manner consistent with this opinion. As discussed in Part V, this disposition is without prejudice to Parhat's right to seek release immediately through a writ of habeas corpus in the district court, pursuant to the Supreme Court's recent decision in *Boumediene v. Bush* .

We also deny, without prejudice, the Government's motion to protect from public disclosure all nonclassified record information that it has labeled "law enforcement sensitive," as well as the names and "identifying information" of all U.S. government personnel mentioned in the record. Although we do not doubt that there is information in these categories that warrants protection, the government has proffered only a generic explanation of the need for protection, providing no rationale specific to the information actually at issue in this case.

By resting its motion on generic claims, equally applicable to all of the more than one hundred other detainee cases now pending in this court, the government effectively "proposes unilaterally to determine whether information is 'protected.'" *Bismullah v. Gates*, 501 F.3d 178, 188 (D.C. Cir. 2007). *** [A]s we held in *Bismullah*, "[i]t is the court, not the Government, that has discretion to seal a judicial record, which the public ordinarily has the right to inspect and copy." ***

Parhat is a Chinese citizen of Uighur heritage. The Uighurs are from the far-western Chinese province of Xinjiang, which the Uighurs call East Turkistan. According to Parhat, he fled China in May 2001 because of "oppression and torture imposed on [Ui]gh[u]r people by the Chinese Government." *** Parhat arrived at a Uighur camp in Afghanistan in June 2001. ***

A CSRT was held for Parhat on December 6, 2004. The proceedings consisted of an unclassified session, at which Parhat was present and answered questions under oath, followed by a classified session, at which Parhat was not present and in which the Tribunal considered classified documents not made available to him. The only evidence regarding the circumstances of Parhat's background and capture was his own interviews and testimony. Parhat denied association with al Qaida or the Taliban, stated that he had gone to Afghanistan solely to join the resistance against China, and said that he regarded China alone -- and not the United States -- as his enemy. The Tribunal did not find to the contrary.

Nonetheless, the Tribunal determined that Parhat was an enemy combatant. It did so on the theory that he was "affiliated" with a Uighur independence group known as the East Turkistan Islamic Movement (ETIM), that ETIM was "associated" with al Qaida and the Taliban, and that ETIM is engaged in hostilities against the United States and its coalition partners. The basis for the charge of Parhat's "affiliation" with ETIM was that the Uighur camp at which he lived and received training on a rifle and pistol was run by an ETIM leader. The Tribunal acknowledged, however, that "no source document evidence was introduced to indicate . . . that the Detainee had actually joined ETIM, or that he himself had personally committed any hostile acts against the United States or its coalition partners." The grounds for the charges that ETIM was "associated" with al Qaida and the Taliban, and that it is engaged in hostilities against the United States or its coalition partners, were statements in classified documents that do not state (or, in most instances, even describe) the sources or rationales for those statements. Parhat denied knowing anything about an al Qaida or Taliban association with Uighur camps.

Notwithstanding its determination that Parhat was an enemy combatant, the Tribunal stated that "this Detainee does present an attractive candidate for release." It "urge[d] favorable consideration for release . . . and also urge[d] that he not be forcibly returned to the People's Republic of China" because he "will almost certainly be treated harshly if he is returned to Chinese custody." The Defense Department did not release him. ***

The DTA grants this court jurisdiction to "determine the validity of any final decision of a Combatant Status Review Tribunal that an alien is properly detained as an enemy combatant." DTA § 1005(e)(2)(A). The scope of our review is "limited to the consideration of":

> (i) whether the status determination of the [CSRT] was consistent with the standards and procedures specified by the Secretary of Defense for [CSRTs] (including the requirement that the conclusion of the Tribunal be supported by a preponderance of the evidence and allowing a rebuttable presumption in favor of the Government's evidence); and (ii) to the extent the Constitution and laws of the United States are applicable, whether the use of such standards and procedures to make the determination is consistent with the Constitution and laws of the United States. ***

Each CSRT is composed of "three neutral commissioned officers." The Recorder, also a commissioned officer, is charged with gathering the "Government Information," which is defined as "reasonably available information in the possession of the U.S. Government bearing on the issue of whether the detainee" meets the enemy combatant criteria. *** The Recorder must also make the Government Information available to the detainee's assigned Personal Representative, a military officer who is "neither a lawyer [n]or an advocate," but who must explain the CSRT process to the detainee and may assist the detainee in preparing for it. *** The CSRT must "determine whether the preponderance of the evidence supports the conclusion that [the] detainee meets the criteria to be designated as an enemy combatant." There is a rebuttable presumption that the Government Evidence is "genuine and accurate." The Tribunal "may consider hearsay evidence, taking into account the reliability of such evidence in the circumstances." *** [T]he DOD Order and the Navy Memorandum both define an "enemy combatant" as: "an individual who was part of or supporting Taliban or al Qaida forces, or associated forces that are engaged in hostilities against the United States or its coalition partners. This includes any person who has committed a belligerent act or has directly supported hostilities in aid of enemy armed forces."

Parhat contends that the record before his CSRT does not support its finding that he is an enemy combatant, even under the Government's own definition, and hence that the Tribunal's determination is not "consistent with the standards and procedures specified by the Secretary of Defense for Combatant Status Review Tribunals." ***

*** The parties agree that, for a detainee who is not a member of al Qaida or the Taliban, DOD's definition establishes three elements that the government must prove by a preponderance of the evidence to designate an individual as an enemy combatant:

> (1) the petitioner was part of or supporting "forces"; (2) those forces were associated with al Qaida or the Taliban; and (3) those forces are engaged in hostilities against the United States or its coalition partners. In Parhat's case, this means that the government must show that: (1) Parhat was part of or supporting ETIM; (2) ETIM was associated with al Qaida or the Taliban; and (3) ETIM is engaged in hostilities against the United States or its coalition partners.

The first element of the DOD definition of enemy combatant requires proof that Parhat was "part of or supporting" ETIM. Neither Parhat nor any other detainee stated that Parhat was a *member* of ETIM. And as the CSRT noted, "no source document evidence was introduced to indicate . . . that the Detainee had actually joined ETIM." *** As we discuss below, the evidence on the second and third elements of DOD's definition of enemy combatant, unlike the evidence on the first, does not disclose from whence it came. It is therefore insufficient to support the Tribunal's determination because it does not permit the Tribunal or this court to assess its reliability. *** If, in order to support the proposition that ETIM is associated with the Taliban (a necessary element of the Government's definition of "enemy combatant"), the government is going to rely on [certain] statement[s] *** then it must also give the Tribunal an opportunity to consider contrary evidence. Because the Tribunal was not afforded that opportunity, we cannot conclude that reliance on the interview report "was consistent with the standards and procedures specified by the Secretary of Defense." *** Proving the third element of DOD's definition of enemy combatant requires evidence that ETIM engaged in hostilities against the United States or its coalition partners. As with the second element, the principal evidence supporting this element comes from the four government intelligence documents ***. Because the documents are classified, much of the following discussion is redacted from the public version of this opinion. *** [T]here is no allegation or evidence that Parhat personally engaged in any such hostilities.[Classified material redacted.] ***

[T]he principal evidence against Parhat regarding the second and third elements of DOD's definition of enemy combatant *** do not say who "reported" or "aid" or "suspected" those things. Nor do they provide any of the underlying reporting upon which the documents' bottom-line assertions are founded, nor any assessment of the reliability of that reporting. Because of those omissions, the Tribunal could not and this court cannot assess the reliability of the assertions in the documents. And because of this deficiency, those bare assertions cannot sustain the determination that Parhat is an enemy combatant.

The CSRT's obligation to assess the reliability of evidence is expressly stated in the Navy Memorandum's provision on "Admissibility of Evidence." This provision states that the Tribunal may consider hearsay evidence -- which the intelligence reports plainly are -- but in so doing it must "tak[e] into account the reliability of such evidence in the circumstances." *** [T]he Memorandum *** establish[es] a "*rebuttable* presumption that the Government Evidence is 'genuine and accurate.'" If a Tribunal cannot assess the reliability of the Government's evidence, then the "rebuttable" presumption becomes effectively irrebuttable.

This court, in turn, has two responsibilities with respect to the reliability of the evidence presented to the CSRT. First, in order to judge "whether the [CSRT's determination] was consistent with the standards and procedures specified by the Secretary of Defense for Combatant Status Review Tribunals," we must assure ourselves that the CSRT had the opportunity to -- and did -- evaluate the reliability of the evidence it considered. Second, in order to ensure, as the DTA requires, that "the conclusion of the Tribunal [is] supported by a preponderance of the evidence," allowing only a "rebuttable" presumption in favor of the Government" evidence, we must be able to assess the reliability of that evidence ourselves

Insistence that the Tribunal and court have an opportunity to assess the reliability of the record evidence is not simply a theoretical exercise. Parhat contends that the ultimate source of key assertions in the four intelligence documents is the government of the People's Republic of China, and he offers substantial support for that contention. *** The CSRT's own written decision makes clear both its inability to assess the reliability of most of the evidence presented to it and the importance of its being able to do so. *** [T]he underlying decision *** states: "The Tribunal found the Detainee to be an enemy combatant because of his *apparent* ETIM affiliation . . . [classified material redacted], but despite the fact that the ETIM *is said to be* making plans for future terrorist activities against U.S. interests, no source document evidence was introduced to indicate how this group has actually done so . . . ." It further states that the "Detainee is considered to be an enemy combatant because he is *said to be* affiliated with the ETIM," and that "[t]he camp at which he trained was an ETIM camp *apparently* funded in part by Usama bin Laden and the Taliban."

Moreover, in the two instances in which the CSRT did have exogenous information with which to assess the reliability of statements made in the intelligence documents, it found sufficient discrepancies to question one statement and to "doubt the veracity" of the other. *** [T]hat is precisely the kind of assessment that the Tribunal could not make with respect to the bulk of the evidence ***

Second, the government insists that the statements made in the documents are reliable because the State and Defense Departments would not have put them in intelligence documents were that not the case. This comes perilously close to suggesting that whatever the government says must be treated as true, thus rendering superfluous both the role of the Tribunal and the role that Congress assigned to this court. ***

To be clear, we do *not* suggest that hearsay evidence is never reliable -- only that it must be presented in a form, or with sufficient additional information, that permits the Tribunal and court to assess its reliability. Nor do we suggest that the government must always submit the underlying basis for its factual assertions in order to make such an assessment possible. In many cases, such submissions will be advisable and reasonably available: the detainees' counsel are cleared for classified information, and, where its source is highly sensitive, *Bismullah* held that it can be shown to the court (and CSRT) alone. *** But there may well be other forms in which the government can submit information that will permit an appropriate assessment of the information's reliability while protecting the anonymity of a highly sensitive source. Courts have frequently relied on such methods in the Fourth Amendment context, and have permitted the use of appropriate nonclassified substitutions under the Classified Information Procedures Act (CIPA). ***

Congress has directed this court "to determine the validity of any final decision of a Combatant Status Review Tribunal that an alien is properly detained as an enemy combatant." In so doing, we are to "determine," inter alia, whether the CSRT's decision "was consistent with the standards and procedures specified by the Secretary of Defense for Combatant Status Review Tribunals[,] including the requirement that the conclusion of the Tribunal be supported by a preponderance of the evidence." A CSRT's decision regarding enemy combatant status was not consistent with those standards and procedures unless the Tribunal had -- and took -- the opportunity to assess the reliability of the evidence that the government presented to it. Nor can this court conclude that such a decision was consistent with those standards and procedures unless we, too, are able to assess the reliability of the Government's evidence. Because the evidence that the government submitted to Parhat's CSRT did not permit the Tribunal to make the necessary assessment, and because the record on review does not permit the court to do so, we cannot find that the Government's designation of Parhat as an enemy combatant was consistent with the specified standards and procedures and is supported by a preponderance of the evidence.***

Notes

1. **Comparing *Padilla*, *al-Marri*, and *Parhat*.** Make a chart comparing these cases by:

- Where was each captured?
- What was the alleged tie to terrorism of each?
- How threatening was each to the United States?
- What was the evidence against each?
- Who had what burdens of proof to show "enemy combatant" status?
- Who was a citizen or what other ties did each have to the United States?

- What process was used to determine the "enemy combatant" status of each?

- What was the appellate route for each?

- What happens to each after these decisions?

- To what extent is international law relevant in each case?

- Do the courts in all three cases see the same balance of responsibility between the courts and the executive branch in dealing with terrorists?

2. Different Forums? If the government believes Padilla, al-Marri, and Parhat engaged in unlawful preparation for acts of terrorism but only Padilla was an "enemy combatant," where could each be tried? Civilian court? Military commission? The choices of forum and differences in these forums are the subject of the next two chapters.

3. Preventive Detention? Even if the government was not able to criminally prosecute Pedilla, al-Marri, or Parhat — might they be able to preventatively detain them? Several human rights organizations have argued that the United States must either "try or release" detainees held at the Guantanamo Bay detention facility. Others have insisted that the same is true of detainees held in other U.S. run facilities, such as the Bagram Air Force Base. The U.S. and other countries have long used preventive detention as a means to prevent enemies from returning to the battlefield during an armed conflict—as well as in a variety of other contexts, for example, the civil commitment of mentally disabled individuals who cannot be criminally tried. Would a federal statute, beyond the AUMF, be necessary to authorize preventive detention? What process would be needed to ensure that the correct individuals were detained? The questions of release from detention will be discussed more fully in Chapter 4.

4. National Security Courts. Some scholars, most notably Jack Goldsmith and Neal Katyal (Acting Solicitor General as this book goes to press), have called on Congress to enact a preventative detention statue that would empower the Executive to preventively detain individuals who are suspected terrorists. Upon what constitutional authority would such a plan rely? What constitutional challenges might advocates raise against such a statute?

C. COMPARATIVE PERSPECTIVES ON DETENTION

1. Israel. The Israeli-Palestinian conflict has involved a high level of violence for many years. Against the backdrop of fighting by organized armies, paramilitary groups, terrorist organizations, and private individuals, Israel passed the following statute regarding the detention of unlawful combatants. The case following the statute looks at the legality of the statute under international law. Compare and contrast the Israeli approach with that of the United States.

Incarceration of Unlawful Combatants Law 5762-2002

1. This Law is intended to regulate the incarceration of unlawful combatants not entitled to prisoner-of-war status, in a manner conforming with the obligations of the State of Israel under the provisions of international humanitarian law.

Definitions

2. *** "unlawful combatant" means a person who has participated either directly or indirectly in hostile acts against the State of Israel or is a member of a force perpetrating hostile acts   against the State of Israel, where the conditions prescribed in Article 4 of the Third Geneva   Convention *** with respect to prisoners-of-war and granting prisoner-of-war status in international humanitarian law, do not apply to him; "prisoner" means a person incarcerated by virtue of an order issued by the Chief of General Staff pursuant to the provisions of this Law.

3. (a) Where the Chief of General Staff has reasonable cause to believethat a person being held by the State authorities is an unlawful combatant and that his release will harm State   security, he may issue an order under his hand, directing that such person be incarcerated at   a   place   to   be determined (hereinafter referred to as "an incarceration order"); an incarceration order shall include the grounds for incarceration, without prejudicing State security requirements.

(b) An incarceration order may be granted in the absence of the person held by the State authorities.

(c) An incarceration order shall be brought to the attention of the prisoner at the earliest possible date and he shall be given the opportunity to put his submissions in respect of the   order before an officer of at least the rank of lieutenant-colonel to be appointed by the Chief of General Staff; the submissions of the prisoner shall be recorded by the officer and shall be brought before the Chief of General Staff; where the Chief of General Staff finds, after reviewing the submissions of the prisoner, that the conditions prescribed in subsection (a) have not been fulfilled, he shall quash the incarceration order. ***

4. (a) A prisoner shall be brought before a judge of the District Court no later than fourteen   days after the date of granting the incarceration order; where the judge of the District Court   finds   that   the   conditions prescribed in section 3(a) have not been fulfilled he shall quash the incarceration order.

(b) Where the prisoner is not brought before the District Court and where a hearing has not commenced before it within fourteen days of the date of granting the incarceration order, the   prisoner   shall   be   released,   unless there exists another ground for his detention under the provisions of any law.

(c)   Once every six months from the date of issue of an order *** the prisoner shall be   brought before a judge of the District Court; where the Court finds that his release will not harm State security or that there are special grounds justifying his release, it shall quash the incarceration order. [Appeals are provided in (d).] ***

(e) It shall be permissible to depart from the laws of evidence in proceedings under this Law, for reasons to be recorded; the court may admit evidence, even in the absence of the prisoner or his legal representative, or not disclose such evidence to the aforesaid if, after having reviewed the evidence or heard the submissions, even in the absence of the prisoner or his legal representative, it is convinced that disclosure of the evidence to the prisoner or his legal representative is likely to harm State security or public security; ***

(f) The hearing in proceedings under this Law shall be conducted in camera, unless the court   has provided otherwise in this matter.

6. (a) The prisoner may meet with a lawyer at the earliest possible date on which such a   meeting may be held without harming State security requirements, but no later than seven days prior to his being brought before a judge of the District Court. ***

7. For the purposes of this Law, a person who is a member of a force perpetrating hostile acts   against the State of Israel or who has participated in hostile acts of such a force, either   directly or indirectly, shall be deemed to be a person whose release would harm State   security as long as the hostile acts of such force against the State of Israel have not yet   ceased, unless proved otherwise.

8. A determination of the Minister of Defense, by a certificate under his hand, that a particular   force is perpetrating hostile acts against the State of Israel or that hostile acts of such force   against the State of Israel have ceased or have not yet ceased, shall serve as proof in any   legal   proceedings, unless proved otherwise. ***

9. (a) A prisoner shall be held under proper conditions which shall not impair his health or dignity. ***

ANONYMOUS v. STATE OF ISRAEL

Supreme Court of Israel, sitting as the Ct. of Criminal Appeals

June 11, 2008

PRESIDENT D. BEINISCH:

*** [T]he appeals raise fundamental questions concerning the interpretation of the provisions of the Internment of Unlawful Combatants Law, whether the arrangements provided in the law are constitutional and to what extent the law is consistent with international humanitarian law.

1. [Appellants, inhabitants of the Gaza Strip, were] placed under administrative detention [in 2002 and 2003] pursuant to the Administrative Detentions (Temporary Provision) (Territory of Gaza Strip) Order. The detention of the [appellants] was extended from time to time by the military commander and upheld on judicial review by the Gaza Military Court. *** On

12 September 2005 a statement was published by the Southern District Commander with regard to the end of military rule in the territory of the Gaza Strip. On the same day, in view of the change in circumstances and also the change in the relevant legal position, internment orders were issued against the appellants; these were signed by the chief of staff under section 3 of the Internment of Unlawful Combatants Law, which is the law that is the focus of the case before us. ***

2. [The Israeli judiciary] held that *** the appellants were clearly associated with the Hezbollah organization and that they participated in combat activities against the citizens of Israel before they were detained. The court emphasized *** the individual threat presented by the two appellants and the risk that they would return to their activities if they were released*** . *** [E]ach of the two appellants was closely associated with the Hezbollah organization, both of them were intensively active in that organization, the existing evidence with regard to them showed that their return to the territory was likely to act as an impetus for terror attacks and the long period during which both of them had been imprisoned had not reduced the threat that they present. ***

4. *** The appellants *** claimed that the law is inconsistent with the rules of international humanitarian law that it purports to realize. Finally the appellants argued that the end of Israel's military rule in the Gaza Strip prevents it, under the laws of war, from detaining the appellants. ***

6. The Internment of Unlawful Combatants Law *** allows the internment of *foreign* persons who belong to a terrorist organization or who participate in hostilities against the security of the state, and it was intended to prevent these persons returning to the cycle of hostilities against Israel. *** The simple language of the law and its legislative history indicate that the law was intended to prevent a person who represents a threat to the security of the state because of his activity or his belonging to a terrorist organization from returning to the cycle of hostilities. ***

9. With regard to the presumption of conformity to international humanitarian law, *** section 1 of the law expressly declares that its purpose is to regulate the internment of unlawful combatants '... in a manner that is consistent with the commitments of the State of Israel under the provisions of international humanitarian law.' The premise in this context is that an international armed conflict prevails between the State of Israel and the terrorist organizations that operate outside Israel.

The international law that governs an international armed conflict is enshrined mainly in the Hague Convention (IV) Respecting the Laws and Customs of War on Land (1907) (hereafter: 'the Hague Convention') and the regulations appended to it, whose provisions have the status of customary international law ***; the Geneva Convention (IV) relative to the Protection of Civilian Persons in Time of War, 1949 (hereafter: 'the Fourth Geneva Convention'), whose customary provisions constitute a part of the law of the State of Israel and some of which have been considered in the past by this court ***; and the Protocol Additional to the Geneva Convention of 12 August 1949 Relating to the Protection of Victims of International Armed Conflicts

(Protocol I), 1977 (hereafter: 'the First Protocol'), to which Israel is not a party, but whose customary provisions also constitute a part of the law of the State of Israel. ***

11. *** [The] statutory definition of 'unlawful combatant' relates to those persons who take part in hostilities against the State of Israel or who are members of a force that carries out such hostilities, and who are not prisoners of war under international humanitarian law. *** [In short] an 'unlawful combatant' under section 2 of the law is a *foreign* party who belongs to a terrorist organization that operates against the security of the State of Israel. This definition may include residents of a foreign country that maintains a state of hostilities against the State of Israel, who belong to a terrorist organization that operates against the security of the state and who satisfy the other conditions of the statutory definition of 'unlawful combatant.' This definition may also include inhabitants of the Gaza Strip which today is no longer held under belligerent occupation. *** In our case, in view of the fact that the Gaza Strip is no longer under the effective control of the State of Israel, we are drawn to the conclusion that the inhabitants of the Gaza Strip constitute foreign parties who may be subject to the Internment of Unlawful Combatants Law in view of the nature and purpose of this law. ***

12. The appellants argued before us that the definition of 'unlawful combatant' in section 2 of the law is contrary to the provisions of international humanitarian law, since international law does not recognize the existence of an independent and separate category of 'unlawful combatants.' In their view there are only two categories in international law, 'combatants' and 'civilians,' who are subject to the provisions and protections enshrined in the Third and Fourth Geneva Conventions respectively. In their view international law does not have an intermediate category that includes persons who are not protected by either of these conventions. *** [W]e should point out that the question of the conformity of the term 'unlawful combatant' to the categories recognized by international law has already been addressed in our case law in *Public Committee against Torture in Israel v. Government of Israel*, in which it was held that the term 'unlawful combatants' does not constitute a separate category but is a sub-category of 'civilians' recognized by international law. This conclusion is based on the approach of customary international law, according to which the category of 'civilians' includes everyone who is not a 'combatant.' *** In this context, two additional points should be made: *first*, the finding that 'unlawful combatants' belong to the category of 'civilians' in international law is consistent with the official interpretation of the Geneva Conventions, according to which in an armed conflict or a state of occupation, every person who finds himself in the hands of the opposing party is entitled to a certain status under international humanitarian law — a prisoner of war status which is governed by the Third Geneva Convention or a protected civilian status which is governed by the Fourth Geneva Convention ***. *Second*, it should be emphasized that *prima facie* the statutory definition of 'unlawful combatant' under section 2 of the law applies to a broader group of people than the group of 'unlawful combatants' discussed in *Public Committee against Torture in Israel v. Government of Israel*, in view of the difference in the measures under

discussion: the judgment in *Public Committee against Torture in Israel v. Government of Israel* considered the legality of the measure of a military operation intended to cause the death of an 'unlawful combatant.' According to international law, it is permitted to attack an 'unlawful combatant' only during the period of time when he is taking a direct part in the hostilities. By contrast, the Internment of Unlawful Combatants Law addresses the measure of internment. For the purposes of detention under the law, it is not necessary that the 'unlawful combatant' will take a *direct* part in the hostilities, nor is it essential that his detention will take place during the period of time when he is taking part in hostilities; all that is required is that the conditions of the definition of 'unlawful combatant' in section 2 of the law are proved. This statutory definition does not conflict with the provisions of international humanitarian law since, *** the Fourth Geneva Convention also permits the detention of a protected 'civilian' who endangers the security of the detaining state. ***

13. Further to our finding that 'unlawful combatants' are members of the category of 'civilians' from the viewpoint of international law, it should be noted that this court has held in the past that international humanitarian law does not grant 'unlawful combatants' the same degree of protection to which innocent civilians are entitled, and that in this respect there is a difference from the viewpoint of the rules of international law between 'civilians' who are not 'unlawful combatants' and 'civilians' who are 'unlawful combatants.' *** [S]omeone who is an 'unlawful combatant' is subject to the Fourth Geneva Convention, but according to the provisions of the aforesaid convention it is possible to apply various restrictions to them and *inter alia* to detain them when they represent a threat to the security of the state.***

15. Now that we have determined that the definition of 'unlawful combatant' in the law does not conflict with the two-category classification of 'civilians' and 'combatants' in international law and the case law of this court, let us turn to examine the provisions of the law that regulate the detention of unlawful combatants. Section 3(a) of the law provides [see above].

Section 7 of the law adds in this context a probative presumption, which provides the following:

> "With regard to this law, a person who is a member of a force that carries out hostilities against the State of Israel or who took part in the hostilities of such a force, whether directly or indirectly, shall be regarded as someone whose release will harm state security as long as the hostilities of that force against the State of Israel have not ended, as long as the contrary has not been proved."

The appellants argued before us that the detention provisions provided in the law *de facto* create a third category of detention, which is neither criminal arrest nor administrative detention, and which is not recognized at all by Israeli law or international law. We cannot accept this argument. The mechanism provided in the law is a mechanism of administrative detention in every respect, which is carried out in accordance with an order of the chief of staff, who is an officer of the highest security authority. *** [W]e are dealing with an administrative detention whose purpose is to protect state security by removing from the cycle of hostilities anyone who is a member of a terrorist organization or who is taking part in the organization's operations against the State of Israel, in view of the threat that he represents to the security of the state and the lives of its inhabitants.

16. *** [T]he actual power provided in the law for the administrative detention of a 'civilian' who is an 'unlawful combatant' on account of the threat that he represents to the security of the state is not contrary to the provisions of international humanitarian law. Thus article 27 of the Fourth Geneva Convention, which lists a variety of rights to which protected civilians are entitled, recognizes the possibility of a party to a dispute adopting 'control and security' measures that are justified on security grounds. The wording of the aforesaid article 27 is as follows:

> '... the Parties to the conflict may take such measures of control and security in regard to protected persons as may be necessary as a result of the war.'

With regard to the types of control measures that are required for protecting state security, article 41 of the convention prohibits the adoption of control measures that are more severe that assigned residence or internment in accordance with the provisions of articles 42-43 of the convention. Article 42 enshrines the rule that a 'civilian' should not be interned unless it is 'absolutely necessary' for the security of the detaining power. Article 43 goes on to oblige the detaining power to approve the detention in a judicial or administrative review, and to hold periodic reviews of the continuing need for internment at least twice a year. Article 78 of the convention concerns the internment of protected civilians that are inhabitants of a territory that is held by an occupying power, and it provides that it is possible to employ various security measures against them for essential security reasons, including assigned residence and internment. *** [T]he Fourth Geneva Convention allows the internment of protected 'civilians' in administrative detention, when this is necessary for reasons concerning the essential security needs of the detaining power. ***

18. It is one of the first principles of our legal system that administrative detention is conditional upon the existence of a ground for detention that derives from the individual threat of the detainee to the security of the state. *** The requirement of an individual threat for the purposes of placing someone in administrative detention is an essential part of the protection of the constitutional right to dignity and personal liberty. *** It is this risk that justifies the use of the unusual measure of administrative detention that violates human liberty.

19. It should be noted that the individual threat to the security of the state represented by the detainee is also required by the principles of international humanitarian law. *** [T]he state should make use of the measure of detention only when it has serious and legitimate reasons to believe that the person concerned endangers its security. *** [T]he membership of organizations whose goal is to harm the security of the state [i]s a ground for

recognizing a threat, but *** the supreme principle [is] that the threat is determined in accordance with the individual activity of that person. ***

20. *** The dispute between the parties before us *** concerns the level of the individual threat that the state is liable to prove for the purpose of administrative detention under the law. This dispute arises because of the combination of two main provisions of the law: *one* is the provision of section 2 of the law that according to a simple reading states that an 'unlawful combatant' is not only someone who takes a direct or indirect part in hostilities against the State of Israel, but also someone who is a 'member of a force carrying out hostilities.' The *other* is the probative presumption provided in section 7 of the law, according to which a person who is a member of a force that carries out hostilities against the State of Israel shall be regarded as someone whose release will harm the security of the state unless the contrary is proved. Relying on the combination of these two provisions of the law taken together, the state argued that it is sufficient to prove that a person is a member of a terrorist organization in order to prove his individual threat to the security of the state in such a manner that gives rise to a ground for detention under the law. By contrast, the appellants' approach was that relying upon a vague 'membership' in an organization that carries out hostilities against the State of Israel as a basis for administrative detention under the law makes the requirement of proving an individual threat meaningless, which is contrary to constitutional principles and international humanitarian law.

21. Deciding the aforesaid dispute is affected to a large degree by the interpretation of the definition of 'unlawful combatant' in section 2 of the law. As we have said, the statutory definition of 'unlawful combatant' contains two limbs: one, 'a person who took part in hostilities against the State of Israel, whether directly or indirectly,' and the other, a person who is 'a member of a force carrying out hostilities against the State of Israel,' when the person concerned does not satisfy the conditions granting [] prisoner of war status under international humanitarian law. *** [I]n order to detain a person it is not sufficient for him to have made a remote, negligible or marginal contribution to the hostilities against the State of Israel. *** [T]he state needs to prove that the detainee made a contribution to the waging of hostilities against the state, whether directly or indirectly, in a manner that can indicate his individual threat. *** [I]n order to establish a ground for detention with regard to someone who is a member of an active terrorist organization whose self-declared goal is to fight unceasingly against the State of Israel, it is not necessary for that person to take a direct or indirect part in the hostilities themselves, and it is possible that his connection and contribution to the organization will be expressed in other ways that are sufficient to include him in the cycle of hostilities in its broad sense, in such a way that his detention will be justified under the law. *** [S]ince administrative detention is an unusual and extreme measure, and in view of its violation of the constitutional right to personal liberty, clear and convincing evidence is required in order to prove a security threat that establishes a basis for administrative detention ***. [T]he provisions of the Internment of Unlawful Combatants Law should be interpreted similarly. ***

[T]he provisions of sections 2 and 3 of the law should be interpreted in such a way that the state is liable to prove, with clear and convincing administrative evidence, that even if the detainee did not take a direct or indirect part in the hostilities against the State of Israel, he belonged to a terrorist organization and made a significant contribution to the cycle of hostilities in its broad sense, in such a way that his administrative detention is justified in order to prevent his returning to the aforesaid cycle of hostilities. ***

46. From the provisions of sections 3, 7 and 8 of the Internment of Unlawful Combatants Law it can be seen that a detention order under the law need not include a defined date for the end of the detention. The law itself does not provide a maximum period of time for the detention imposed thereunder, apart from the determination that the detention should not continue after the hostilities of the force to which the detainee belongs against the State of Israel 'have ended' (see sections 7 and 8 of the law). According to the appellants, this is an improper detention without any time limit, which disproportionately violates the constitutional right to personal liberty. In reply, the state argues that the length of the detention is not 'unlimited,' but depends on the duration of the hostilities being carried out against the security of the State of Israel by the force to which the detainee belongs. *** [M]aking a detention order that does not include a specific time limit for its termination does indeed raise a significant difficulty, especially in the circumstances that we are addressing, where the 'hostilities' of the various terrorist organizations, including the Hezbollah organization which is relevant to the appellants' cases, have continued for many years, and naturally it is impossible to know when they will end. In this reality, detainees under the Internment of Unlawful Combatants Law may remain in detention for prolonged periods of time. Notwithstanding, *** the fundamental arrangement that allows detention orders to be made without a defined date for their termination does not depart from the margin of proportionality, especially in view of the judicial review arrangements that are provided in the law.

As we have said, the purpose of the Internment of Unlawful Combatants Law is to prevent 'unlawful combatants' as defined in section 2 of the law from returning to the cycle of hostilities, as long as the hostilities are continuing and threatening the security of the citizens and residents of the State of Israel. For similar reasons the Third Geneva Convention allows prisoners of war to be interned until the hostilities have ended, in order to prevent them returning to the cycle of hostilities as long as the fighting continues. Even where we are concerned with civilians who are detained during an armed conflict, international humanitarian law provides that the rule is that they should be released from detention immediately after the specific ground for the detention has elapsed and no later than the date when the hostilities end. *** [T]he appeals should be denied.

2. The United Kingdom. The United Kingdom and Irish revolutionary forces have a long and violent history spanning over two centuries. Following the September 11th attacks, the British parliament passed the Anti-terrorism, Crime and Security Act of 2001. In 2004, the House of Lords struck down the act as violative of the UK's Human Rights Act 1998, which gave domestic effect to the central obligations of the European Convention on Human Rights. After you read the Act and the Court's decision, consider how the UK and Israeli courts differ in their approach to the nature of the conflict they address. Do they differ in how they categorize unlawful combatants/enemy combatants under international humanitarian law? What legal framework does the House of Lords use? How does this impact each Court's views of the authority to detain and required procedures?

Anti-terrorism, Crime and Security Act of 2001

Part 4, Immigration and Asylum

21. Suspected international terrorist: certification

(1) The Secretary of State may issue a certificate under this section in respect of a person if the Secretary of State reasonably—

(a) believes that the person's presence in the United Kingdom is a risk to national security, and

(b) suspects that the person is a terrorist.

(2) In subsection (1)(b) "terrorist" means a person who—

(a) is or has been concerned in the commission, preparation or instigation of acts of international terrorism,

(b) is a member of or belongs to an international terrorist group, or

(c) has links with an international terrorist group.

(3) A group is an international terrorist *** if—

(a) it is subject to the control or influence of persons outside the United Kingdom, and

(b) the Secretary of State suspects that it is concerned in the commission, preparation or instigation of acts of international terrorism.

(4) For the purposes of subsection (2)(c) a person has links with an international terrorist group only if he supports or assists it. ***

(6) Where the Secretary of State issues a certificate under subsection (1) he shall as soon as is reasonably practicable—

(a) take reasonable steps to notify the person certified, and

(b) send a copy of the certificate to the Special Immigration Appeals Commission.***

23. Detention

(1) A suspected international terrorist may be detained under a provision specified in subsection (2) despite the fact that his removal or departure from the United Kingdom is prevented (whether temporarily or indefinitely) by—

(a) a point of law which wholly or partly relates to an international agreement, or

(b) a practical consideration.

(2) The provisions mentioned in subsection (1) are—

    (a) *** (detention of persons liable to examination or removal), and

    (b) *** (detention pending deportation).

A and OTHERS v. UNITED KINGDOM
House of Lords
[2004] UKHL 56

LORD BINGHAM OF CORNHILL

2. *** [T]he appellants were certified by the Home Secretary under section 21 of the Anti-terrorism, Crime and Security Act 2001 *** and were detained under section 23 of that Act ***

3. The appellants share certain common characteristics which are central to their appeals. All are foreign (non-UK) nationals. None has been the subject of any criminal charge. In none of their cases is a criminal trial in prospect. All challenge the lawfulness of their detention. *** First, it was provided by *** the Immigration Act 1971 that the Secretary of State might detain a non-British national pending the making of a deportation order against him. *** [T]he same schedule authorised the Secretary of State to detain a person against whom a deportation order had been made "pending his removal or departure from the United Kingdom". In *R v Governor of Durham Prison* *** it was held, *** that such detention was permissible only for such time as was reasonably necessary for the process of deportation to be carried out. Thus there was no warrant for the long-term or indefinite detention of a non-UK national whom the Home Secretary wished to remove. This ruling was wholly consistent with the obligations undertaken by the United Kingdom in the European Convention on Human Rights, the core articles of which were given domestic effect by the Human Rights Act 1998. Among these articles is article 5(1) which guarantees the fundamental human right of personal freedom: "Everyone has the right to liberty and security of person". This must be read in the context of article 1, by which contracting states undertake to secure the Convention rights and freedoms to "everyone within their jurisdiction". But the right of personal freedom, fundamental though it is, cannot be absolute and article 5(1) of the Convention goes on to prescribe certain exceptions. One exception is crucial to these appeals: "(1) Everyone has the right to liberty and security of person. No one shall be deprived of his liberty save in the following cases and in accordance with a procedure prescribed by law: f) the lawful arrest or detention of ..... a person against whom action is being taken with a view to deportation ....." *** [T]here is, again, no warrant for the long-term or indefinite detention of a non-UK national whom the Home Secretary wishes to remove. Such a person may be detained only during the process of deportation. Otherwise, the Convention is breached and the Convention rights of the detainee are violated. ***

11. The derogation related to article 5(1), in reality article 5(1)(f), of the Convention. *** It was stated in the Schedule:

"There exists a terrorist threat to the United Kingdom from persons suspected of involvement in international terrorism. In particular, there are foreign nationals present in the United Kingdom who are suspected of being concerned in the commission, preparation or instigation of acts of international terrorism, of being members of organisations or groups which are so concerned or of having links with members of such organisations or groups, and who are a threat to the national security of the United Kingdom." *** [It was recognised that the extended power in the new legislation to detain a person against whom no action was being taken with a view to deportation might be inconsistent with article 5(1)(f). Hence the need for derogation. *** [Lord Bingham found that although the derogation was lawful in light of earlier UK and ECHR jurisprudence, the fact that the certification and detention was limited to foreign nationals was disproportionate and discriminatory.]

LORD NICHOLLS OF BIRKENHEAD

Indefinite imprisonment without charge or trial is anathema in any country which observes the rule of law. It deprives the detained person of the protection a criminal trial is intended to afford. Wholly exceptional circumstances must exist before this extreme step can be justified. The government contends that these post-9/11 days are wholly exceptional. The circumstances require and justify the indefinite detention of non-nationals suspected of being international terrorists. ***

In the present case *** Parliament must be regarded as having attached insufficient weight to the human rights of non-nationals. The subject matter of the legislation is the needs of national security. This subject matter dictates that, in the ordinary course, substantial latitude should be accorded to the legislature. But the human right in question, the right to individual liberty, is one of the most fundamental of human rights. Indefinite detention without trial wholly negates that right for an indefinite period. With one exception all the individuals currently detained have been imprisoned now for three years and there is no prospect of imminent release. It is true that those detained may at any time walk away from their place of detention if they leave this country. Their prison, it is said, has only three walls. But this freedom is more theoretical than real. This is demonstrated by the continuing presence in Belmarsh of most of those detained. They prefer to stay in prison rather than face the prospect of ill treatment in any country willing to admit them. ***

The difficulty with according to Parliament the substantial latitude normally to be given to decisions on national security is the weakness already mentioned: security considerations have not prompted a similar negation of the right to personal liberty in the case of nationals who pose a similar security risk. The government, indeed, has expressed the view that a 'draconian' power to detain British citizens who may be involved in international terrorism 'would be difficult to justify' ***. But, in practical terms, power to detain indefinitely is no more draconian in the case of a British citizen than in the case of a non-national. *** Part of the explanation for the difference in treatment may be that the government has misconceived the human rights of non-nationals in this situation. *** Unwanted aliens who cannot be deported, as much as nationals, are not to be detained indefinitely without charge or trial save in wholly exceptional circumstances. ***

LORD HOFFMANN

*** [The detention power] requires that the Home Secretary should reasonably suspect the foreigners of a variety of activities or attitudes in connection with terrorism, including supporting a group influenced from abroad whom the Home Secretary suspects of being concerned in terrorism. If the finger of suspicion has pointed and the suspect is detained, his detention must be reviewed by the Special Immigration Appeals Commission. They can decide that there were no reasonable grounds for the Home Secretary's suspicion. But the suspect is not entitled to be told the grounds upon which he has been suspected. So he may not find it easy to explain that the suspicion is groundless. In any case, suspicion of being a supporter is one thing and proof of wrongdoing is another. Someone who has never committed any offence and has no intention of doing anything wrong may be reasonably suspected of being a supporter on the basis of some heated remarks overheard in a pub. The question in this case is whether the United Kingdom should be a country in which the police can come to such a person's house and take him away to be detained indefinitely without trial. ***

The Home Secretary has adduced evidence, both open and secret, to show the existence of a threat of serious terrorist outrages. ***I am willing to accept that credible evidence of such plots exist. *** But the question is whether such a threat is a threat to the life of the nation. The Attorney General's submissions and the judgment of the Special Immigration Appeals Commission treated a threat of serious physical damage and loss of life as necessarily involving a threat to the life of the nation. But in my opinion this shows a misunderstanding of what is meant by "threatening the life of the nation". *** This is a nation which has been tested in adversity, which has survived physical destruction and catastrophic loss of life. I do not underestimate the ability of fanatical groups of terrorists to kill and destroy, but they do not threaten the life of the nation. Whether we would survive Hitler hung in the balance, but there is no doubt that we shall survive Al-Qaeda. *** Terrorist violence, serious as it is, does not threaten our institutions of government or our existence as a civil community. *** For these reasons I think that the Special Immigration Appeals Commission made an error of law and that the appeal ought to be allowed. *** The real threat to the life of the nation, in the sense of a people living in accordance with its traditional laws and political values, comes not from terrorism but from laws such as these. That is the true measure of what terrorism may achieve. It is for Parliament to decide whether to give the terrorists such a victory.

LORD SCOTT OF FOSCOTE

***Section 23 constitutes, in my opinion, a derogation from article 5(1) at the extreme end of the severity spectrum. An individual who is detained under section 23 will be a person accused of no crime but a person whom the Secretary of State has certified that he "reasonably ... suspects ... is a terrorist". The individual may then be detained in prison indefinitely. True it is that he can leave the United Kingdom if he elects to do so but the reality in many cases will be that the only country to which he is entitled to go will be a country where he is likely to undergo torture if he does go there. *** Indefinite imprisonment in consequence of a denunciation on grounds that are not disclosed and made by a person whose identity cannot be disclosed is the stuff of nightmares, associated whether accurately or inaccurately with France before and during the Revolution, with Soviet Russia in the Stalinist era and now associated, as a result of section 23 of the 2001 Act, with the United Kingdom. *** I am unable to accept that the Secretary of State has established that section 23 is "strictly required" by the public emergency. He should, at the least, in my opinion, have to show that monitoring arrangements or movement restrictions less severe that incarceration in prison would not suffice.

Notes

1.   **Comparative Detention Practices.** Approaches to detention of suspected terrorists vary greatly across the globe.   Some countries, such as Ireland, Germany, Brazil, and Colombia, apply the same pre-trial detention procedures to all detainees, whether suspected of terrorism or not; terrorist suspects are dealt with entirely within the existing criminal justice system and must be criminally tried or released.   Other countries, such as Canada, South Africa, and New Zealand, largely detain terrorist suspects through their immigration detention systems; in these nations, the criminal justice framework is applied to nationals suspected of terrorism while non-national suspects may be detained without trial for extended periods via the immigration system with judicial review of that detention, prompt notification of charges, and access to counsel.   Finally, countries such as Pakistan, India, the Russian Federation, and Nigeria utilize a national security paradigm in which terrorist suspects may be detained potentially indefinitely by executive or administrative officials due to a national security emergency without the right to a judicial hearing.   See generally Stella Burch Elias, "Rethinking "Preventive Detention" from a Comparative Perspective: Three Frameworks for Detaining Terrorist Suspects," 41 COLUM. HUM. RTS. L. REV. 99 (2009).

2.   **Comparative Detention Procedures.** The procedures used to detain suspected terrorists also run the gamut.   Some countries such as France, the United Kingdom, and Turkey require that suspects be given immediate or near immediate notice of the charges they face. Italy permits 24 months of pre-trial detention during the investigation of a terrorist attack.   In Indonesia, lawmakers are considering the adoption of amendments to its anti-terrorism law that would permit the detention of people believed to be involved in terrorism for at least 30 days without declaring them suspects and 120 days without a hearing on their detention.   Some nations, such as Greece, Germany, and Ireland, afford suspected terrorists a right to counsel or more robustly state funded counsel—while others

afford none at all. In France, Spain, and Turkey, access to counsel may be restricted or altered, subject to an incommunicado period in which a detainee may not speak with counsel or the condition that a police officer be present in detainee-counsel meetings.

3. Experience and Rights. Is it a fair statement that many countries that afford more considerable rights to terrorism suspects have long histories combating terrorism, such as the UK and Ireland (with the Irish Republican Army) and France (during the Algerian War for Independence) and Israel? Should the United States follow the lead of Israel or the UK?

4. Detention for Bargaining Purposes. In 2000, the Israeli Supreme Court considered whether a person, who did not himself pose a danger to national security, could be held in administrative detention to serve as a 'bargaining chip' in negotiations to release prisoners or missing persons from among the Israeli security forces. *John Does v. Ministry of Defense*, Crim FH 7048/97 (2000). Noting that no western nation detains individuals who do not themselves pose national security risks and that holding people as bargaining chips is prohibited by international law, the majority declared such a tactic unlawful. The Court recognized that its decision "does not make it easier for the State in its struggles against those that rise up against it," but stated that "not every efficient means is lawful."

> "I am aware of the suffering of the families of prisoners and missing persons from the [Israeli security forces]. It is heavy as a stone. The passage of years and the uncertainty wound the human spirit. *** I am not oblivious to this pain, together with the prime interest of the State of Israel in returning its sons to its borders. *** However, as important as the purpose is of the release of prisoners and missing persons, it is not sufficient *** to legitimize all means. It is not possible *** to right a wrong with a wrong. *** [T]he State of Israel will not be still and will not rest until it finds a way to solve this painful problem. As a state and a society, our comfort is in the fact that the way to the solution will suit our foundational values."

Justice M. Cheshin's minority opinion took a different view:

> "In the north of Israel battles are taking place – land battles and battles from the air. These are not couch-battles. These are not battles of words. These are real battles, battles in which fighters are killed and wounded. *** In war ***members of one camp fall in the hands of the other camp. And when the war or the battles are over (without a definitive victory) – or possibly by agreement in the course of the war or the battles – the battling sides exchange those that fell in their hands from the other camp. And sons return to their homeland. *** If the State is obligated to release the petitioners from detention how shall we fight our enemies? They will hold our people and we shall not be permitted to hold their people?"

How do the two opinions diverge in their understanding of the armed conflict? Is detention for negotiation morally permissible? Consider what sort of conflict must be ongoing to justify detention for hostage trade or other negotiation purposes. Is bargaining chip detention constitutional within the American framework?

5.   India Preventive Detention.   Generally, under the Indian Constitution authorities must present a case to a magistrate within 24 hours of arrest. India Const. art.22, cl. 2.   The arrestee must be informed of the grounds for arrest and given the right to obtain counsel.   Art.22, cl. 1.   However, unlike many constitutional democracies, India explicitly provides for "preventative detention" in its Constitution. Art.22, cl. 3. *See* Andrew Hardin and John Hatchard, Preventative Detention and Security Law: A Comparative Survey (Springer, 1993), at 59.   The Constitution generally limits preventative detention to three months, but gives Parliament a wide exception to make laws providing for longer periods of preventative detention.   Art.22, cl. 4(b).   The detainee does not need to be told the grounds for her detention if doing so would be "against the public interest." Art.22, cl. 6. India regularly uses preventative detention in response to ordinary criminal matters as well as terrorist threats.   *See* U.S. State Dept., Country   Reports   on   Human   Rights   Practices   2009, *available   at:* http://www.state.gov/g/drl/rls/hrrpt/2009/sca/136087.htm.

Three Indian statutes provide for preventative detention: the Conservation of Foreign Exchange and Prevention of Smuggling Activities Act ("COFEPOSA") of 1974, the National Security Act ("NSA") of 1980, and the Unlawful Activities (Prevention) Act (UAPA) of 2008. Under COFEPOSA, the national government or a state government may detain a person in order to prevent her from "acting in a manner prejudicial to the conservation or augmentation of foreign exchange," but must inform the detainee of the grounds for detention within 15 days. Additionally, the government must inform a three-member Advisory Board within five weeks of the date of detention, and the Board must determine if there is cause for continued detention within eleven weeks of the date of detention. The India Supreme Court limited the scope of preventative detention under COFEPOSA by holding that a person cannot be held in preventative detention without "adequate evidence" and that authorities must examine whether there was any "organized act or activities" to give rise to the detention.   Batra v. Union of   India   (Supreme   Court,   2009)   *available   at:* http://www.aboutcorporateindia.com/aci/Legal_2009/orders_mar/poojabatra.pdf.

Under the 1980 National Security Act, the government may preventatively detain an individual if the government is "satisfied" that the individual is a threat to national security, public order, or the maintenance of essential supplies and services.   The government may withhold the evidence supporting an individual's detention, though not the grounds for it. Detainees may not question their accusers, nor challenge the evidence and are not entitled to counsel.   A detainee may be held for up to three months without any review, and up to a year if a three-judge Advisory Board approves the extension.   The judiciary gives the executive broad deference on preventative detention under the NSA.

Unlike the other two acts providing for preventative detention, the UAPA, as amended after the Mumbai terrorist attacks of 2008, directly addresses preventative detention of suspected terrorists.   It defines an "act of terrorism" broadly, as an act "likely to threaten" or "likely to strike terror in the people" committed by "any *** means of whatever nature."   UAPA § 4.   Authorities are allowed to use evidence from intercepted communications to detain and the standard of evidence required is low: the arresting officer's "personal knowledge" suffices. UAPA § 12. Likewise, there is no judicial review of detentions. Rather, review is entrusted to a "such authority appointed by the Central Government or, as the case may be, the State Government which shall make an independent review of the evidence gathered in the course of investigation." UAPA § 13.

VI

INTERROGATION AND TREATMENT OF DETAINEES

Let me make very clear the position of my government and our country. We do not condone torture. I have never ordered torture. I will never order torture. The values of this country are such that torture is not a part of our soul and our being.

—President George W. Bush
June 22, 2004

Coercive interrogation of criminal suspects in the United States is counterproductive. If the police interrogate suspects in violation of long-established standards arising from constitutional norms emanating from the due process clauses of the Fifth and Fourteenth Amendments, evidence from such interrogations cannot be used against the suspect in a criminal proceeding. A fortiori, interrogation that is not only coercive but also amounts to torture is barred. Such treatment of suspects may, of course, also lead to civil or criminal liability, as well as loss of employment, for those who engage in such practices.

In the traditional military context, interrogation of captured enemy combatants is not unusual. Soldiers are advised, for example, upon being interrogated, to provide only "name, rank, and serial number." Mistreatment and abuse of captured enemy combatants is largely addressed by the Geneva Conventions, which provide most basically that combatants must be treated in accord with the standards used by a nation to deal with its own soldiers' criminal behavior. Civilians are also provided protection under the Geneva Conventions: unless they are involved in hostilities, they should not be subjected to detention at all, much less interrogation. To deal with terrorism, the United States and other nations have adopted interrogation techniques different from and harsher than the treatment accorded criminal suspects, traditional captured combatants, or civilian noncombatants. It is this treatment of alleged terrorists that provides the backbone for this chapter.

Section A opens with two important non-legal questions: (1) Is harsh interrogation or torture an effective means of obtaining information? and (2) Is harsh interrogation or torture ever morally justified as a means of obtaining information? Section B looks at the practices of United States military and CIA, interrogators in the war on terror. Section C examines the legal limits on interrogation under international and national law. Section D explores the legal liability of contract interrogators, while Section E focuses on a process known as "extraordinary rendition," in which a terrorist suspect is captured by one country and sent to another country for interrogation. Section F provides perspective on United States interrogations by comparing Israeli interrogation practices. Finally, Section G briefly explores non-interrogation issues concerning treatment of detainees.

A. TWO PRELIMINARY QUESTIONS

1. IS HARSH INTERROGATION EFFECTIVE?

Empirical evidence answering this question could take two forms, anecdotal evidence and statistical or systematic evidence. The problem with the former is that it can only answer the question whether a particular interrogation yielded useful information. The problem with the latter is that, to the best of my knowledge, there has been no broad study of human subjects subjected to such interrogation, and I would hope there won't be.

The reason for skepticism concerning answers produced by harsh interrogation was well stated by Cesare Beccaria in the 18th century: "[Pain] may increase to such a degree, that, occupying the mind entirely, it will compel the sufferer to use the shortest method of freeing himself from torment. [The victim of torture] will accuse himself of crimes of which he is innocent *** [Innocent people] have confessed themselves guilty: innumerable instances may be found in all nations, and in every age." While Beccaria focuses on self-incrimination rather than divulging information, it is not a long leap to the conclusion that one tortured who knows nothing might manufacture knowledge or incriminate others to free himself of pain.

Examples exist of correct information being divulged under duress. Here are some from Benjamin Wittes and Stuart Taylor, Jr. "Looking Forward, Not Backward: Refining American Interrogation Law" in LEGISLATING THE WAR ON TERROR: AN AGENDA FOR REFORM 318-319 (Brookings, 2009):

- In 1946, British forces found and detained the wife of Rudolph Hoess, the former commandant of Auschwitz. Through several days of interrogation, she claimed that Hoess was dead. Then the British told her that unless she wrote down her husband's whereabouts quickly, they would put her three sons on a train to the Soviet Union, where it was understood that the KGB would kill them. She gave the British the information they wanted. They caught Hoess that evening, disguised as a farm worker.

- In 1978, in a decision finding coercive British interrogations of suspected Irish Republican Army terrorists to be unlawful but not severe enough to constitute torture, the European Court of Human Rights nonetheless found that they had been effective in obtaining "a considerable amount of intelligence information, including the identification of 700 members of both IRA factions and the discovery of individual responsibility for about 85 previously unexplained criminal incidents."

- A 1984 federal appeals court decision recited the following findings of fact: Two kidnappers seized a taxi driver and held him for ransom. One was caught while collecting the ransom. He refused to tell police where the cabbie was held. Several officers "threatened him and physically abused him by twisting his arm and choking him until he revealed where [the cab driver] was being held." The court found that the officers had acted "in a reasonable manner to obtain information they needed in order to protect another individual from bodily harm or death."

- A Sri Lankan army officer told terrorism scholar Bruce Hoffman a personal story, apparently from sometime in the 1990s but impossible to verify, as an example of the need for ruthlessness to defeat terrorists such as the Tamil Tigers. The officer's unit caught three hardened Tamil Tigers suspected of having recently planted in the city of Colombo "a bomb that was then ticking away, the minutes counting down to catastrophe." The officer asked the three where the bomb was. They were silent. He asked again, adding that if they did not answer, he would kill them. They remained silent. He pulled his pistol from his gun belt, pointed it at one man's forehead and shot him dead. The other two talked immediately. The bomb, hidden in a crowded railway station and set to explode during evening rush hour, was found and defused.

- In 1995, Philippine intelligence agents caught an al-Qaeda member named Abdul Hakim Murad in a Manila bomb factory. Murad was defiant through 67 days of savage torture, including beatings that broke his ribs and lighted cigarettes crushed into his genitals. He finally broke when agents disguised as Mossad agents threatened to take him to Israel. He then revealed a plot to assassinate Pope John Paul II, crash eleven U.S. airliners carrying some 4,000 people into the Pacific Ocean, and fly a private Cessna loaded with explosives into the CIA's headquarters. Philippine authorities finally turned him over to the United States.

- Israel's secret services have broken up terrorist cells while planned bombings were in the operational stage, as Israel's High Court of Justice detailed in the very same 1999 decision in whichit declared unlawful, absent legislativwe authorization, the coercive methods that the security services called "a moderate degree of physical pressure." Indeed it said that such coercion "has led to the thwarting of murderous attacks" and citedseveral cases in which interrogators had obtained lifesaving intelligence. For example, an applicant who complained of Israeli torture had admitted under interrogation "that he was involved in numerous terrorist activities in the course of which many Israeli citizens were killed," including "the bombing of the café 'Appropo' in Tel Aviv, in which three women were murdered and 30 people were injured...A powerful [identical] explosive device *** was found in the applicant's village (Tzurif) subsequent to the dismantling and interrogation of the terrorist cell to which he belonged. Uncovering this explosive device thwarted [a similar] attack."

- An Al Qaeda terrorist named Jamal Beghal was arrested in the Dubai airport in October 2001. His lawyer later charged that he had been "tossed into a darkened cell, handcuffed to a chair, blindfolded and beaten and that his family was threatened." After some weeks, he suddenly decided to cooperate and revealed secrets that thwarted a planned bombing of the U.S. embassy in Paris and that could possibly—had he been caught and interrogated sooner—have prevented the September 11 attacks.

Though incomplete, some anecdotal evidence indicates that harsh interrogations have produced information in the war on terror, though how reliable, how much, and whether less intrusive techniques would have been equally effective by themselves, cannot be accurately assessed. For example, Khalid Sheik Mohammed (KSM) refused to talk until he had been subjected to the harshest interrogation technique allowed for his interrogators. After being waterboarded 183 times in March of 2003, according to a later released Department of Justice memo, KSM allegedly provided information used to capture and deter other al Qaeda leaders. More generally, the former head of field interrogations for the U.S. Army argues that coercive tactics work: "Our experience in Afghanistan showed that the harsher the methods we used— though they never contravened the [Geneva] Conventions, let alone crossed over into torture—the better the information we got and the sooner we got it.... If a prisoner will say anything to stop the pain, my guess is he will start with the truth." Benjamin Wittes, LAW AND THE LONG WAR 193 (2008). In 2003, "Army Lt. Col. Allen B. West, a battalion commander in Iraq, threatened an unresponsive detainee with death by twice firing his pistol during an interrogation while demanding to know the whereabouts of his accomplices. The detainee, an Iraqi policeman who was allegedly part of a plot to kill West and his soldiers, revealed his cohorts' names and plans for a sniper attack the next day. This may well have saved the lives of U.S. soldiers." Wittes and Taylor, "Looking Forward, not Backward," p. 19.

Former Vice President Dick Cheney repeatedly called for the release of top secret reports that he urged would demonstrate the effectiveness of the enhanced interrogation program used in the War on Terror. However, reports released thus far are less than conclusive. The Bush administration publicly claimed that coercive interrogation was successfully used to extract valuable information from Mohammed al-Qahtani, a Guantanamo detainee. A 2005 report stated only that al-Qahtani "provided extremely valuable intelligence" including insights into Al Qaeda's planning for 9/11 and "important and time-urgent information." Yet the only specifics we know are that al-Qahtani had been en route to meet Mohammed Atta when he was captured, and the he identified 30 of Osama bin-Laden's bodyguards among his fellow Guantanamo detainees. A 2009 Office of Inspector General report, http://thelede.blogs.nytimes.com/2009/08/24/reading-the-cia-interrogation-report/?hp, did not make such a clear-cut assessment:

> The [CIA] detention and interrogation of terrorists has provided intelligence that has enabled the identification and apprehension of other terrorists and warned of terrorist plots planned for the United States and around the world. The CTC Detention and Interrogation Program has resulted in the issuance of thousands of individual intelligence reports and analytic products supporting the counterterrorism efforts of U.S. policymakers and military commanders. The effectiveness of particular interrogation techniques in eliciting information that might not otherwise have been obtained cannot be so easily measured, however.

The former Director of National Intelligence, Mike McConnell, contends that "We have people walking around in this country that are alive today because this process happened." John L. Helgerson, the former CIA inspector general who investigated the agency's detention and interrogation program, said his work did not put him in "a position to reach definitive conclusions about the effectiveness of particular interrogation methods." "Certain of the techniques seemed to have little effect, whereas waterboarding and sleep deprivation were the two most powerful techniques and elicited a lot of information," he said in an interview. "But we didn't have the time or resources to do a careful, systematic analysis of the use of particular techniques with particular individuals and independently confirm the quality of the information that came out." Walter Pincus, "How a Detainee Became and Asset," WASHINGTON POST (Aug 29. 2009).

But see these comments of Admiral Lee Gunn:

> Senior Bush administration officials, including former Vice President Dick Cheney, continue to insist that the use of "enhanced" interrogation techniques such as waterboarding saved American lives. But those assertions are never accompanied by hard evidence or actual facts. By contrast, many experienced interrogators have shown that abusive interrogation practices actually impede efforts to elicit actionable intelligence, and that non-coercive, rapport-building techniques have yielded some of the most accurate and complete information.

http://judiciary.senate.gov/hearings/testimony.cfm?id=3686&wit_id=7651.
One experienced interrogator discusses these issues as follows:

> [O]btaining reliable information from jihadist foot soldiers in Afghanistan and Iraq is vital to protect our troops, who are in harm's way. But even on the battlefield and under exigent circumstances, rapport building is more effective in gaining information for force protection in my opinion. Enhanced and coercive interrogation techniques are ineffective even under extreme circumstances. I've spoken to a number of FBI agent's who were seconded to Gitmo as interrogator's. In confidence, they told me the vast majority of detainees questioned under these stressful conditions were of little or no

value as sources of useful intelligence. *** Without compromising delicate investigations, I can tell you that the FBI has amassed a considerable amount of reliable information on al Qaeda using rapport building. *** I am convinced of the efficacy of rapport building interrogation techniques by these and other experiences. *** [M]y heart tells me that torture and all forms of excessive coercion are inhumane and un-American, and my experience tells me that they just don't work.

These anecdotes, while valuable, unleash a barrage of further questions. How does one know which individuals being interrogated will have information? With which suspects should such techniques be used? If information is not forthcoming, how soon and how much should the techniques be ratcheted up? And what are the collateral consequences, both on those using such interrogation techniques, and the nation or entity that authorizes their use? ***

There are 3 questions I would like this committee to ponder. Has the use of coercive interrogation techniques lessened Al Qaeda's thirst for revenge against the US? Have these methods helped to recruit a new generation of jihadist martyrs? Has the use of coercive interrogation produced the reliable information its proponents claim for it? I would suggest that the answers are "no", "yes" and "no". Based on my experience in talking to al Qaeda members, I am persuaded that revenge, in the form of a catastrophic attack on the homeland, is coming, that a new generation of jihadist martyrs, motivated in part by the images from Abu Ghraib, is, as we speak, planning to kill American and that nothing gleaned from the use of coercive interrogation techniques will be of any significant use in the forestalling this calamitous eventuality. *** If I were the director of marketing for al Qaeda and intent on replenishing the ranks of jihadists. I know what my first piece of marketing collateral would be. It would be a blast e-mail with an attachment. The attachment would contain a picture of Private England (sp) pointing at the stacked, naked bodies of the detainees at Abu Ghraib. The picture screams out for revenge and the day of reckoning will come.

Retired FBI agent John Cloonan Senate Judiciary Committee testimony: http://judiciary.senate.gov/hearings/testimony.cfm?id=3399&wit_id=7228.

2. IS HARSH INTERROGATION EVER JUSTIFIED?

Even if effective, at least sometimes, is harsh interrogation morally permissible? From a human rights perspective, the clear philosophical answer is "no". Philosophers tend to place the individual human being, whatever he may have done or might know, at the center of the discourse. It is morally wrong to treat persons as a means to the end, to brutalize a person to obtain information that person may have. As Jacob Timerman is quoted by Benjamin Wittes, "You cannot start down that road. That is what I believe about torture." Wittes, supra, p. 182.

Most philosophical responses to the Timerman position begin with the "ticking time bomb" scenario: a terrorist in custody admits that his bomb is about to explode in a heavily-populated city, but he refuses to divulge its location. Is it morally permissible to torture him to make him divulge the location? Many thoughtful analysts answer this question affirmatively. As Benjamin Wittes concludes in a passage that cites Anthony Lewis, John McCain, and the executive director of an Israeli human rights group, "[D]ig deep enough—and it often does not take much digging—and the most categorical opposition to coercive interrogation gives way to consequentialism. *** Categorical opposition to coercive interrogation is not a tenable position for anyone with actual responsibility fo protecting a country." Wittes, pp. 184-185.

If the consequences of not obtaining information are severe enough, pragmatic weighing of innocent deaths versus torture of someone who can save those lives leads inexorably to torture. In the television series "24," Jack Bauer regularly interrogates terrorists using various forms of agonizing torture. When Jack saves Los Angeles from nuclear annihilation or averts chemical or biological disasters elsewhere, the viewer cheers Jack's success even while finding his methods abhorrent.

Ticking time bomb torture is of course quite problematical. Can an interrogator ever know with certainty that the subject of interrogation has the information? How does the interrogator know traditional methods of interrogation will not work? And how often does a suspect have information that can only be obtained through that individual? These are real world difficulties not found on "24".

B. POST 9/11 INTERROGATIONS

Thousands of individuals detained by the United States since 9/11 in Afghanistan or Iraq were interrogated by military authorities. Those interrogations, at least for the most part, occurred according to the published rules of the Department of Defense. Such interrogations took place in the field during military operations or after an individual was moved to a field detention facility. Some percentage of these thousands were moved to more serious prison facilities, such as at Baghdad's Abu Ghraib Prison or to the Bagram Air Force Base prison in Afghanistan. A total of about 800 individuals were moved to the Guantanamo Bay detention facility where many were questioned. Approximately 100 alleged "high-value" terrorists were admittedly transferred by military authorities to the CIA and taken to "black sites" outside the United States for interrogation. A handful of detainees have been held in military prison facilities in the United States while awaiting trial and many thousands of immigrants detained shortly after 9/11 were held in local jails. Talking about post 9/11interrogations requires attention to what the detaining authority was, when interrogation occurred, and where the interrogation occurred. The following materials are organized by who the interrogators were (or are) since the rules differ for the military and the CIA.

1. MILITARY INTERROGATIONS

I will start with military standards for interrogation, because military authorities conducted the bulk of interrogations in Iraq and Afghanistan after 9/11. UCMJ Article 93 is very direct concerning treatment of detainees: – "Any person subject to this chapter who is guilty of cruelty toward, or oppression or maltreatment of, any person subject to his orders shall be punished as a court-martial may direct." This prohibition applies to interrogation while in custody as well as general conditions of custody.

According to General John Kelly, who served as commanding general for Anbar Province, Iraq until April 2009, the number one rule was to get the insurgent (alleged terrorist) out of the hands of the men fighting in the field and into the hands of cooler, more detached, and more experienced military personnel for interrogation. According to General John Kelly, this was to avoid abuses that might occur if buddies of soldiers who had been killed or wounded in combat were responsible for interrogating those who were or might have been involved in the killing or wounding. According to General Kelly, most insurgents detained in Anbar Province were treated well and were eager to talk volubly with their captors. Others (a total of about 8000 over an indeterminate period of time) were sent to Bucca Prison, where they were interrogated by trained military interrogators.

The U.S. Army Field Manual 34-52, Intelligence Interrogation, contains the following broad prohibition against the use of force:

> The use of force, mental torture, threats, insults, or exposure to unpleasant and inhumane treatment of any kind is prohibited by law and is neither authorized nor condoned by the US Government. Experience indicates that the use of force is not necessary to gain the cooperation of sources for interrogation. Therefore, the use of force is a poor technique, as it yields unreliable results, may damage subsequent collection efforts, and can induce the source to say whatever he thinks the interrogator wants to hear. However, the use of force is not to be confused with psychological ploys, verbal trickery, or other nonviolent and noncoercive ruses used by the interrogator in questioning hesitant or uncooperative sources.

> The psychological techniques and principles outlined should neither be confused with, nor construed to be synonymous with, unauthorized techniques such as brainwashing, mental torture, or any other form of mental coercion to include drugs. These techniques and principles are intended to serve as guides in obtaining the willing cooperation of a source. The absence of threats in interrogation is intentional, as their enforcement and use normally constitute violations of international law and may result in prosecution under the UCMJ.

> Additionally, the inability to carry out a threat of violence or force renders an interrogator ineffective should the source challenge the

threat. Consequently, from both legal and moral viewpoints, the restrictions established by international law, agreements, and customs render threats of force, violence, and deprivation useless as interrogation techniques.

The Department of Defense September 2006 Army Field Manual 2 22.3 or FM 2-22.3 Human Intelligence Collector Operations [HUMINT] guides military interrogators in such situations as follows:

5-75. If used in conjunction with intelligence interrogations, actions prohibited include, but are not limited to—

- Forcing the detainee to be naked, perform sexual acts, or pose in a sexual manner.

- Placing hoods or sacks over the head of a detainee; using duct tape over the eyes.

- Applying beatings, electric shock, burns, or other forms of physical pain.

- "Waterboarding."

- Using military working dogs.

- Inducing hypothermia or heat injury.

- Conducting mock executions.

- Depriving the detainee of necessary food, water, or medical care.

5-76. *** In attempting to determine if a contemplated approach or technique should be considered prohibited, and therefore should not be included in an interrogation plan, consider these two tests before submitting the plan for approval:

- If the proposed approach technique were used by the enemy against one of your fellow soldiers, would you believe the soldier had been abused?

- Could your conduct in carrying out the proposed technique violate a law or regulation? Keep in mind that even if you personally would not consider your actions to constitute abuse, the law may be more restrictive.

5-77. If you answer yes to either of these tests, the contemplated action should not be conducted. *** Where there is doubt *** consult your supervisor or servicing judge advocate.

5-78. Security internees are detainees who are not combatants but who pose a security threat, may be under investigation, or who pose a threat to US forces if released. HUMINT collectors are required to treat all detainees humanely. EPWs are entitled to additional protections guaranteed by the GPW that security internees may not be eligible for. For example, allowing a security internee to communicate with a family member (a right that an EPW has under the Geneva Conventions) could allow him to pass information that would compromise a sensitive investigation and endanger the lives of soldiers and civilians. HUMINT collectors should consult with their SJA for clarification of detainees' status and rights. *** The potential for abuse of the detainee is greatest at initial capture and tactical questioning phase. With the excitement and stress of the battlefield, unskilled personnel may exercise poor judgment or be careless and thus resort to illegal techniques to elicit critical information. ***

Notes

1. Saying and Doing. The DoD rules for interrogation seem fairly progressive, but Human Rights Watch is critical of DoD for not implementingthe rules. What might you suggest would be needed to make rules like these effective?

2. DoD and CIA. The DoD rules were not applied to the CIA for several years. Should the rules differ for the two organizations? CIA was charged with interrogating "high-value" detainees at secret locations. Is this reason enough to have different rules?

3. DoD and Contractors. If contractors are hired to guard military detainees overseas, do the Geneva Conventions apply to them? Do the DoD rules apply to contractors hired by DoD? If DoD turns prisoners over to another country (Afghanistan, Iraq, Saudi Arabia, Egypt, etc.) do the above rules apply? Can the DoD simply delegate interrogations to others not obligated under international law and domestic laws and regulations?

2. CIA INTERROGATIONS

Some high value terrorist suspects, such as al Qaeda leaders, were moved from military authorities to the CIA for interrogation. According to the head of the CIA, those subjected to serious CIA interrogation numbered about 100. According to a heavily redacted "Background Paper on CIA's Combined Use of Interrogation Techniques," written in December of 2004 and released by the Department of Justice in 2009, "once a [high-value detainee or HVD] is turned over to CIA a predictable set of events occur:

1) *Rendition.*

   a. The HVD is flown to a Black Site***During the flight, the detainee is securely shackled and is deprived of sight and sound through the use of blindfolds, earmuffs, and hoods. ***

2) *Reception at Black Site.* The HVD is subjected to administrative procedures*** [and] finds himself in the complete control of Americans.*** Reception procedures include:

   a. The HVD's head and face are shaved

   b. A series of photographs are taken of the HVD while nude to document the physical condition of the HVD upon arrival.

   c. A Medical Officer interviews the HVD and a medial evaluation is conducted to assess the physical condition of the HVD. ***

   d. A Psychologist interviews the HVD to assess his mental state [and determine] if there are any contraindications to the use of interrogation techniques. ***

Transitioning to Interrogation—the Initial Interview.

Interrogators use the initial interview to assess the initial resistence posture of the HVD and to determine—in a relatively benign environment—if the HVD intends to willingly participate with CIA interrogators. ***

C. Interrogation.***

For descriptive purposes, these techniques can be separated into three categories: Conditioning Techniques; Corrective techniques; and Coercive Techniques. To more completely describe the three categories of techniques and their effects, we begin with a summary of the detention conditions that are used in all CIA HVD facilities and that may be a factor in interrogations.

1) Existing detention conditions. *** Specifically, the HVD will be exposed to white noise/loud sounds (not to exceed 79 decibels) and constant light during portions of the interrogation process. These conditions *** deny the HVD any auditory clues about his surroundings and deter and disrupt the HVD's potential efforts to communicate with other detainees. Constant light provides an improved environment *** to monitor the HVD.

2) Conditioning Techniques. The HVD is typically reduced to a baseline, dependent state using the three interrogation techniques discussed below in combination. Establishing this baseline state is important to demonstrate to the HVD that he has no control over basic human needs, The baseline state also creates in the detainee a mindset, in which he learns to perceive and value his personal welfare, comport, and immediate needs more than the information he is protecting. The use of these conditioning techniques do not generally bring immediate results; rather, it is the cumulative effect of these techniques, used over time and in combination with other interrogation techniques and intelligence exploitation methods, which achieve interrogation objectives. These conditioning techniques require little to no physical interaction between the detainee and the interrogator. The specific conditioning interrogation techniques are:

 a. *Nudity.****

 b. *Sleep Deprivation.* The HVD is placed in the vertical shackling position to begin sleep deprivation. Other shackling procedures may be used during interrogations. The detainee is diapered for sanitary purposes, although the diaper is not used at all times.

 c. *Dietary manipulation.* The HVD is fed Ensure Plus or other food at regular intervals. The HVD receives a target of 1500 calories per day OMS guidelines.

3) *Corrective Techniques.* Techniques that require physical interaction between the interrogator and detainee are used principally to correct, startle or to achieve another enabling objective with the detainee. These techniques—the *insult slap, abdominal slap, facial hold,* and *attention grasp*—are not used simultaneously but are often used interchangeably

during an individual interrogation session. These techniques generally are used while the detainee is subjected to the conditioning techniques outlined above *(nudity, sleep deprivation,* and *dietary manipulation)*. Examples of application include:

   a. *Insult Slap.* The insult slap *** is used sparingly but periodically throughout the interrogation process when the interrogator needs to immediately correct the detainee or provide a consequence to a detainee's response non-response. The interrogator will continually assess the effectiveness of the insult slap and continue to employ it sc long as it has the desired effect on the detainee. Because of the physical dynamics of the various techniques, the insult slap can be used in combination with water dousing or kneeling stress positions. Other combinations are possible but may not be practical.

   b. *Abdominal Slap.* The abdominal slap *** provides the variation necessary to keep a high level of unpredictability in the interrogation process. The abdominal slap will he used sparingly and periodically throughout the interrogation process when the interrogator wants to immediately correct the detainee***

   c. *Facial hold.* The facial hold *** is not painful and is used to correct the detainee in a way that demonstrates the interrogator's control over the HVD.***

   d. *Attention Grasp.**** It may be used several tines in the same interrogation. ***grasp the HVD and pull him into close proximity of the interrogator (face to face).

4) ***Coercive Techniques.*** Certain interrogation techniques place the detainee in more physical and psychological stress and, therefore, are considered more effective tools in persuading a resistant HVD to participate with CIA interrogators. These techniques—*walling, water dousing, stress positions, wall standing,* and *cramped confinement*—are typically not used in combination, although some combined use is possible. For example, an HVD in stress positions or wall standing can be water doused at the same time. Other combinations of these techniques may be used while the detainee is being subjected to the conditioning techniques discussed above (nudity, sleep deprivation, and dietary manipulation). Examples of coercive techniques include:

   a. ***Walling***. Walling *** wears down the HVD physically, heightens uncertainty in the detainee about what the interrogator may do to him, and creates a sense of dread when the HVD knows he is about to be walled again.***An HVD may be walled one time (one impact with the wall) to make a point or twenty to thirty times consecutively when the interrogator requires a more significant response to a question. During an interrogation session that is designed to be intense, an HVD will be walled multiple times in the session. ***

   b. ***Water Dousing***. The frequency and duration of water dousing applications are based on water temperature and other safety considerations as established by OMS guidelines. It is an effective interrogation technique and may he used frequently within those guidelines.***

   c. ***Stress Positions.*** The frequency and duration of use of the stress positions are based on the interrogator's assessment of their continued effectiveness during interrogation. These techniques are usually self-limiting in that temporary muscle fatigue usually leads to the HVD being unable to maintain the stress position after period of time. ***

   d. ***Wall Standing.*** The frequency and duration of wall standing are based on the interrogator's assessment of its continued effectiveness during interrogation. Wall standing is usually self-limiting in that temporary muscle fatigue usually leads to the HVD being unable to maintain the position after a period of time. ***

   e. ***Cramped Confinement.*** Current OMS guidance on the duration of cramped confinement limits confinement in the large box to no more than 8 hours at a time for no more than 18 hours a day, and confinement in the small box to 2 hours.***

D. Interrogation – A day-to-day look. This section provides a look at a prototypical interrogation with an emphasis on the application of interrogations techniques, in combination and separately. ***[Large segments of this section are redacted.] ***

5) Continuing Sessions.***

Interrogation techniques assessed as being the most effective will be emphasized while techniques will (sic) little assessed effectiveness will be minimized.

   a. ***

   b. The use of *cramped confinement* may be introduced if interrogators assess that it will have the appropriate effect on the HVD. ***

   c. ***

   d. Sleep deprivation may continue to the 70 to 120 hour range, or possibly beyond for the hardest resistors, but in no case exceed the 180-hour time limit. Sleep deprivation will end sooner if the medical or psychologist observer finds contraindications to continued sleep deprivation. ***

   e. ***

   f. ***

   g. The interrogators' objective is to transition the HVD to a point where he is participating in a predictable, reliable, and sustainable manner. Interrogation techniques may still be applied as required, but become less frequent. ***

   h. The entire interrogation process *** may last for thirty days. *** On average, the actual use of interrogation technique *** can vary upwards to fifteen days based on the resilience of the HVD.

*** If the interrogation team anticipates the potential need to use interrogation techniques beyond the 30-day approval period, it will submit a new interrogation plan to HQS for evaluation and approval.

2. *Summary.*

- Since the start of this program, interrogation techniques have been used in combination and separately to achieve critical intelligence collection objectives.

- The use of interrogation techniques in combination is essential to the creation of an interrogation environment conductive to intelligence collection. HVDs are well-trained, often battle-hardened terrorist operatives, and highly committed to jihad. They are intelligent and resourceful leaders and able to resist standard interrogation approaches. ***

- However, there is no template or script that states with certainty how these techniques will be used in combination during interrogation. ***

- All CIA interrogations are conducted on the basis of the "least coercive measure" principle. Interrogators employ interrogation techniques in an escalating manner consistent with the HVD's responses and actions. Intelligence production is more sustainable over the long term if the actual use of interrogation techniques diminishes steadily and the interrogation environment improve in accordance with the HVD's demonstrated consistent participation with the interrogators.

In addition to the above techniques, the 2004 CIA Inspector General's Report details that Enhanced Interrogation Techniques include:

- "In the context of cramped confinement, "Insects placed in a confinement box involve placing a harmless insect in the box with the detainee.

- The application of stress positions may include having the detainee sit on the floor with his legs extended straight out in front of him with his arms raised above his head or kneeling on the floor while leaning back at a 45 degree angle.

- Sleep deprivation will not exceed 11 days at a time.

The application of the waterboard technique involves binding the detainee to a bench with his feed elevated above his head. The detainee's head is immobilized and an interrogator places a cloth over the detainee's mouth and nose while pouring water onto the cloth in a controlled manner. Airflow is restricted for 20 to 40 seconds and the technique produces the sensation of drowning and suffocation.

The 2004 Report also details interrogation aberrations from approved techniques, including the use of mock executions to the threat of execution with a gun and assault by a power drill.

Notes

1. Interrogation and Prosecution. Why does the criminal justice system treat evidence obtained through duress with skepticism? Should we consider concerns around the effectiveness of coercive interrogation differently in the criminal and national security contexts?

2. What role for the law? As Jessica Montell, executive director of the Israeli human rights group, B'Tselem put it "If I as an interrogator feel that the person in front of me has information that can prevent a catastrophe from happening, I imagine that I would do what I would have to do in order to prevent that catastrphe from happening. The state's obligation is then to put me on trial, for breaking the law...and then the Court decides whether or not it's reasonable that I broke the law in order to avert this catastrphe." See Benjamin Wittes, LAW AND THE LONG WAR 184 (2008). Some critics have argued that the public expects intelligence operatives to do "everything necessary" but does not want to face up to the realities that must include placing intelligence operatives, and perhaps also higher ranking officials, in a Catch-22. Take as an example Jack Bauer, the star of the TV series "24," who has achieved notoriety for his use of torture to save Los Angeles from a nuclear attack and avert other catastrophes. Should he be tried for his actions (not merely hauled before a congressional panel). Justice Scalia does not think Jack Bauer need worry. As he noted in a public speech, "Who's going to convict Jack Bauer?"

3. Torture Warrants? Some (led by Harvard Law Professor Alan Dershowitz) have argued that Congress should enact a system that would issue torture warrants—either with review by a federal court or through presidential authorization by written finding to the House and Senate Intelligence Committees. What is your view? Should torture be recognized by the law? How does the legal status of law effect the use of coercive techniques by intelligence officials? If coercive techniques are flatly prohibited, will they be covertly used (e.g. in "black sites") or avoided by intelligence officers?

C. LEGAL LIMITS ON INTERROGATION TECHNIQUES

The Geneva Conventions, other treaties including the Convention Against Torture, and customary international law establish rules concerning the treatment and interrogation of prisoners of war and others detained in international armed conflicts. Common Article III of the Geneva Conventions sets minimum standards for the treatment of detainees held during non-international (not nation state against nation state) conflicts: detainees "shall in all circumstances be treated humanely, without any adverse distinction based on race, color, religion or faith, sex, birth or wealth, or any other similar criteria." It also directs that the following categories of acts "are and shall remain prohibited at any time and in any place whatsoever."

(a) Violence to life and person, in particular murder of all kinds, mutilation, cruel treatment and torture;

(b) Taking of hostages;

(c) Outrages upon personal dignity, in particular humiliating and degrading treatment;

(d) The passing of sentences and the carrying out of executions without previous judgment pronounced by a regularly constituted court affording all the judicial guarantees which are recognized as indispensable by civilized peoples.

To the extent that Geneva III applies to a given conflict, these restrictions are binding as a matter of domestic criminal law through the War Crimes Act, 18 U.S.C. § 2441. In 2006, the Supreme Court in *Hamdan v. Rumsfeld*, 126 S.Ct. 2749, 2795 (2006): http://www.aclu.org/torturefoia/released/082409/olcremand/2004olc97.pdf concluded that Geneva III applies to the armed conflict between the United States and al Qaeda.

After September 11 and the invasion of Afghanistan, the Bush Administration faced the problem of whether (or to what extent) these international law rules applied to Taliban and al Qaeda prisoners captured in the "War on Terror" in Afghanistan. A memo dated January 9, 2002 from the Office of Legal Counsel in the Department of Justice to The General Counsel of the Department of Defense took the following position: "[Y]ou have asked whether the laws of armed conflict apply to the conditions of detention and the procedures for trial of members of the al Qaeda organization, which as a non-state actor cannot be a party to the international agreements governing war. We further conclude that these treaties do not apply to the Taliban militia."

President Bush announced that Taliban and al Qaeda detainees would not be treated as Prisoners of War under Geneva Convention III. Secretary of State Colin Powell requested reconsideration of this decision. A January 25, 2002 memo from Counsel to the President Alberto Gonzales advised the President to stick with his decision. The Legal Advisor to the State Department then countered in a memo to the Counsel to the President that "the structure of the Conventions" demanded that the provisions apply to "all persons involved in the conflict" if they apply to the conflict at all and that, on practical grounds, "the risk of prosecution [of U.S. personnel] for violation of the [War Crimes Act, which incorporates the Geneva Conventions obligations] is negligible."

Defense Secretary Rumsfeld ordered an examination of the legality of interrogation practices in the war on terrorism. The Working Group on Detainee Interrogations in the Global War on Terrorism issued a report on April 4, 2003 which concluded that "The United States' primary obligation concerning torture and related practices stems from the Convention Against Torture***" [the "torture convention" or "CAT"]. The memo argued that the United States ratified the convention on the understanding that:

> "***[torture] must be specifically intended to inflict severe physical or mental pain or suffering and that mental pain or suffering refers to prolonged mental harm caused by or resulting from (1) the intentional infliction or threatened infliction of severe physical pain or suffering; (2) the administration or application, or threatened administration or application, of mind altering substances or other procedures calculated to disrupt profoundly the senses or the

personality; (3) the threat of imminent death; or (4) the threat that another person will eminently be subjected to death, severe physical pain or suffering, or the administration or application of mind altering substances or other procedures calculated to disrupt profoundly the senses or personality.

It noted the obligation of the United States to keep "law enforcement and military personnel" informed regarding the prohibition on torture and to review "interrogation rules, methods, and practices." The DoD Working Group also concluded that the CAT prohibition on "cruel, inhuman and degrading treatment or punishment" was "vague and ambiguous" and noted that a reservation to this prohibition "means the cruel, unusual and inhuman treatment or punishment prohibited by the 5th, 8th, and 14th Amendments to the U.S. Constitution ***" An additional treaty, the International Covenant on Civil and Political Rights (ICCPR) was found "not to apply outside the United States." Various federal statutes, concluded the memo, were inapplicable overseas or would, if applied, "violate the Constitution's sole vesting of the Commander-in-Chief authority in the President."

The Secretary, on April 16, 2003, issued a detailed memorandum on Counter-Resistance Techniques in the War on Terrorism that authorized a number of techniques with certain safeguards, limited the application of the techniques to "interrogations of unlawful combatants held at Guantanamo Bay" and "reiterate[d] that US Armed Forces shall continue to treat detainees humanely and *** consistent with the Geneva Conventions."

Meanwhile, a memo drafted by the Department of Justice took this restrictive view of the meaning of torture: pain 'equivalent in intensity to the pain accompanying serious physical injury, such as organ failure, impairment of bodily function or even death." This memorandum was later withdrawn by the Department of Justice and a more traditional definition of "torture" was adopted.

A 2004 report by the CIA Inspector General's Office (released by the Department of Justice in 2009) detailed that as a result of close consultation between the CIA Office of General Counsel and the Department of Justice, a document titled "Legal Principles Applicable to CIA Detention and Interrogation of Captured Al-Qa'ida Personnel" was produced. The document reaffirmed the inapplicability of the federal torture statute, concluded that the federal War Crimes statute does not apply to Al-Qaeda, and stated that the Convention Against Torture "permits the use of [cruel, inhuman, or degrading treament] in exigent circumstances, such as a national emergency or war." The CIA Inspector General noted further that "the interrogation of Al-Qa'ida members does not violate the Fifth and Fourteen Amendments because those provisions do not apply extraterritorially, nor does it violate the Eight Amendment because it only applies to persons upon whom criminal sanction have been imposed." The analysis further stated that even were the Fifth, Eighth, or Fourteenth Amendments to apply, every one of the enhanced interrogation techniques described above, including the water board, are permissible "where the CIA interrogators do not specifically intend to cause the detainee to undergo severe physical or mental pain or suffering."

In 2005, Congress passed the Detainee Treatment Act (DTA), §1403(a) of which states that "No individual in the custody or under the physical control of the United States Government, regardless of nationality or physical location, shall be subject to cruel, inhuman, or degrading treatment or punishment." The DTA explicitly limited the Department of Defense (though not the intelligence community) from utilizing harsher treatments on detainees in their custody than those detailed in the Army Field Manual. § 1402(a). At the same time, the DTA defined prohibited treatment in relation to U.S. Constitutional rights as "treatment or punishment prohibited by the Fifth, Eight, and Fourteenth Amendments to the Constitution of the United States, as defined in the United States Reservations, Declarations and Understandings to the United Nations Convention Against Torture and Other Forms of Cruel, Inhuman or Degrading Treatment or Punishment."

President Bush issued the following signing statement when approving the bill:

> The executive branch shall construe [the provisions] relating to detainees, in a manner consistent with the constitutional authority of the President to supervise the unitary executive branch and as Commander in Chief and consistent with the constitutional limitations on the judicial power, which will assist in achieving the shared objective of the Congress and the President *** of protecting the American people from further terrorist attacks. Further, *** the executive branch shall construe Title X not to create a private right of action. Finally, *** the executive branch shall construe section 1005 to preclude the Federal courts from exercising subject matter jurisdiction over any existing or future action, including applications for writs of habeas corpus, described in section 1005.

As will be addressed further in Chapter VII, both the DTA (as later amended by the Graham-Levin Amendment) and the later Military Commissions Act of 2006 stripped the federal judiciary of ability to enforce the ban on cruel, inhuman, or degrading treatment. Human rights organizations argued that by stripping the courts of jurisdiction "Congress has effectively permitted the use of evidence obtained through torture." Human Rights Watch, Landmark Torture Ban Undercut: Congress would allow evidence obtained by torture (Dec. 15, 2005).

The Military Commissions Act of 2006 (MCA), in addition to authorizing trials by military commission, contains the following provisions:

SEC. 5. TREATY OBLIGATIONS NOT ESTABLISHING GROUNDS FOR CERTAIN CLAIMS. *** No person may invoke the Geneva Conventions or any protocols thereto in any habeas corpus or other civil action or proceeding to which the United States, or a current or former officer, employee, member of the Armed Forces, or other agent of the United States is a party as a source of rights in any court of the United States or its States or territories. ***

SEC. 6. IMPLEMENTATION OF TREATY OBLIGATIONS

(a) IMPLEMENTATION OF TREATY OBLIGATIONS.— ***

(2) PROHIBITION ON GRAVE BREACHES.—The provisions of section 2441 of title 18, United States Code, as amended by this section, fully satisfy the obligation under Article 129 of the Third Geneva Convention for the United States to provide effective penal sanctions for grave breaches which are encompassed in common Article 3 in the context of an armed conflict not of an international character. No foreign or international source of law shall supply a basis for a rule of decision in the courts of the United States in interpreting the prohibitions enumerated in subsection (d) of such section 2441.

(3) INTERPRETATION BY THE PRESIDENT.—

(A) As provided by the Constitution and by this section, the President has the authority for the United States to interpret the meaning and application of the Geneva Conventions and to promulgate higher standards and administrative regulations for violations of treaty obligations which are not grave breaches of the Geneva Conventions. ***

(D) Nothing in this section shall be construed to affect the constitutional functions and responsibilities of Congress and the judicial branch of the United States. ***

(b) REVISION TO WAR CRIMES OFFENSE UNDER FEDERAL CRIMINAL CODE.—

[Section 2441 of title 18, United States Code, is amended as follows]

"(1) PROHIBITED CONDUCT.—In subsection (c)(3), the term 'grave breach of common Article 3' means ***:

"(A) TORTURE.—The act of a person who commits, or conspires or attempts to commit, an act specifically intended to inflict severe physical or mental pain or suffering (other than pain or suffering incidental to lawful sanctions) upon another person within his custody or physical control for the purpose of obtaining information or a confession, punishment, intimidation, coercion, or any reason based on discrimination of any kind.

"(B) CRUEL OR INHUMAN TREATMENT.—

The act of a person who commits, or conspires or attempts to commit, an act intended to inflict severe or serious physical or mental pain or suffering (other than pain or suffering incidental to lawful sanctions), including serious physical abuse, upon another within his custody or control.

"(C) PERFORMING BIOLOGICAL EXPERIMENTS.— ***

"(D) MURDER.— ***

"(E) MUTILATION OR MAIMING.— ***

"(F) INTENTIONALLY CAUSING SERIOUS BODILY INJURY.— ***

"(G) RAPE.— ***

"(H) SEXUAL ASSAULT OR ABUSE.— ***

"(I) TAKING HOSTAGES.— ***

"(2) DEFINITIONS.—In the case of an offense under subsection (a) by reason of subsection (c)(3)— ***

"(D) the term 'serious physical pain or suffering' shall be applied for purposes of paragraph (1)(B) as meaning bodily injury that involves—

"(i) a substantial risk of death;

"(ii) extreme physical pain;

"(iii) a burn or physical disfigurement of a serious nature (other than cuts, abrasions, or bruises); or

"(iv) significant loss or impairment of the function of a bodily member, organ, or mental faculty; and

"(E) the term 'serious mental pain or suffering' shall be applied for purposes of paragraph (1)(B) in accordance with the meaning given the term 'severe mental pain or suffering' (as defined in section 2340(2) of this title), except that—

"(i) the term 'serious' shall replace the term 'severe' where it appears; and

"(ii) as to conduct occurring after the date of the enactment of the Military Commissions Act of 2006, the term 'serious and non-transitory mental harm (which need not be prolonged)' shall replace the term 'prolonged mental harm' where it appears. ***

"(5) DEFINITION OF GRAVE BREACHES.—The definitions in this subsection are intended only to define the grave breaches of common Article 3 and not the full scope of United States obligations under that Article." ***

(c) ADDITIONAL PROHIBITION ON CRUEL, INHUMAN, OR DEGRADING TREATMENT OR PUNISHMENT.—

(1) IN GENERAL.—No individual in the custody or under the physical control of the United States Government, regardless of nationality or physical location, shall be subject to cruel, inhuman, or degrading treatment or punishment.

(2) CRUEL, INHUMAN, OR DEGRADING TREATMENT OR PUNISHMENT DEFINED.—In this sub section, the term "cruel, inhuman, or degrading treatment or punishment" means cruel, unusual and inhumane treatment or punishment prohibited by the Fifth, Eighth, and Fourteenth Amendments to the Constitution of the United States, as defined in the United States Reservations, Declarations and Understandings to the United Nations Convention Against Torture and Other Forms of Cruel, Inhuman or Degrading Treatment or Punishment done at New York, December 10, 1984.

(3) COMPLIANCE.—The President shall take action to ensure compliance with this subsection, including through the establishment of administrative rules and procedures.

"§ 948r. Compulsory self-incrimination prohibited; treatment of statements obtained by torture and other statements

"(a) IN GENERAL.—No person shall be required to testify against himself at a proceeding of a military commission under this chapter.

"(b) EXCLUSION OF STATEMENTS OBTAINED BY TORTURE.—A statement obtained by use of torture shall not be admissible in a military commission under this chapter, except against a person accused of torture as evidence that the statement was made.

"(c) STATEMENTS OBTAINED BEFORE ENACTMENT OF DETAINEE TREATMENT ACT OF 2005.—A statement obtained before December 30, 2005 (the date of the enactment of the Defense Treatment Act of 2005) in which the degree of coercion is disputed may be admitted only if the military judge finds that—

    "(1) the totality of the circumstances renders the statement reliable and possessing sufficient probative value; and

    "(2) the interests of justice would best be served by admission of the statement into evidence.

"(d) STATEMENTS OBTAINED AFTER ENACTMENT OF DETAINEE TREATMENT ACT OF 2005.—A statement obtained on or after December 30, 2005 *** in which the degree of coercion is disputed may be admitted only if the military judge finds that—

    "(1) the totality of the circumstances renders the statement reliable and possessing sufficient probative value;

    "(2) the interests of justice would best be served by admission of the statement into evidence; and

    "(3) the interrogation methods used to obtain the statement do not amount to cruel, inhuman, or degrading treatment prohibited by section 1003 of the Detainee Treatment Act of 2005.

In 2008, Congress moved to limit the rest of the intelligence community, including the CIA, to the Army Field Manual techniques. The bill passed both houses of Congress but failed to garner the votes necessary to defeat President George W. Bush's veto. That same year, President Bush issued Executive Order 13440. The order states that:

> "Pursuant to the authority of the President under the Constitution and the laws of the United States, including the Military Commissions Act of 2006, this order interprets the meaning and application of the text of Common Article 3 with respect to certain detentions and interrogations [by the CIA], and shall be treated as authoritative for all purposes as a matter of United States law, including satisfaction of the international obligations of the United States."

The order detailed that "the interrogation practices are determined by the Director of the Central Intelligence Agency, based upon professional advice, to be safe for use with each detainee with whom they are used; and detainees in the program receive the basic necessities of life, including adequate food and water, shelter from the elements, necessary clothing, protection from extremes of heat and cold, and essential medical care."

On January 22, 2009, President Obama revoked Executive Order 13440 and signed another, 13491, banning the use of harsh interrogation methods by the CIA and limiting the CIA to the nineteen techniques permitted by the Army Field Manual. The banned procedures are often referred to as "enhanced interrogation techniques" including waterboarding and wall slamming. At the time, Dennis Blair, who would later become Obama's Director of National Intelligence, submitted a written statement to the Senate endorsing this position, saying: "Any program of detention and interrogation must comply with the Geneva Conventions, the Conventions on Torture, and the Constitution. There must be clear standards for humane treatment that apply to all agencies of U.S. Government, including the Intelligence Community."

Executive Order 13491 also created a Special Interagency Task Force to review interrogation and transfer policies. In 2009, this taskforce proposed and President Obama approved the establishment of a multiagency interrogation unit, termed the High Value Interrogation Group, within the Federal Bureau of Investigation and operating under policies set by the National Security Council that would oversee the questioning of high-value detainees. This order strips the CIA of its primary role in interrogating top terrorism suspects. These interrogators are limited to techniques permitted by the Army Field Manual, which does not permit tactics such as water boarding or sleep deprivation. The Task Force also advised the new interrogation unit to develop a "scientific research program for interrogation" to assess current techniques and develop new ones. The new interrogation unit will be authorized to travel abroad to interrogate high value terrorist suspects and would Mirandize detainees of their rights on a case-by-case basis.

Notes

1. Torture or Not? What actions constitute "torture" and what presumably less serious actions constitute "cruel, inhumane, or degrading" treatment? What is the difference (a) under international law and (b) under U.S. law? Is "torture" a term that can be defined up (to include fewer situations) or defined down (to include more situations)?

2. Is Motivation Relevant? Is torture (or cruel, inhumane, and degrading punishment) justified when the victim may have information that, if learned, could save numerous lives from an imminent terrorist attack? In a novel by a Yale law professor, the daughter of a former CIA director and professional psychologist who worked on interrogations as a CIA contractor, offers this analysis: "I won't say extreme measures are never necessary. I will say, well—

once you admit they are necessary in certain rare cases?—you wind up deciding that all the cases are rare ones." Stephen Carter, JERICHO'S FALL (Knopf 2009).

3. Who decides? As seen in the back and forth between the White House and agencies, both the definition of torture and whether the Geneva Conventions apply to detainees are matters of hot debate. Who is or should be the final interpreter of the U.S. obligations under international law—The President? Congress? The Courts?

4. Changing Standards. Why would the MCA distinguish between actions before and after December 30, 2005? Do you agree with Congress that this was an appropriate line to draw?

5. Interrogation Evidence. What evidence can be admitted from interrogations? How do the standards differ in civilian trials and military commission trials?

6. The View of the Interrogated. If you were a terrorist facing interrogation, what would you know about your interrogation by United States authorities? How would this knowledge affect your responses to interrogation? What if you were innocent? What process do you believe is necessary to ensure both effective and ethical detention and interrogation policies? Under the War Crimes Act of 1996, any violation of Common Article 3 of the Geneva Conventions constitutes a war crime and can be criminally prosecuted.

7. Who is responsible? The NEW YORK TIMES reported that "the strong impression that emerges from the [released] documents, many with long passages blacked out for secrecy, is by no means one of gung-ho operatives running wild. It is a portrait of overwhelming control exercised from C.I.A. headquarters and the Department of Justice." Scott Shane and Mark Mazzetti, "Report Shows Tight CIA Control on Interrogations," NEW YORK TIMES (Aug. 25, 2009). Who (if anyone) should be liable for the treatment of suspected terrorists in U.S. custody? CIA officers who went beyond the scope of the legal advice they received? Lawyers who gave this legal advice? Authorizing political officials? No one? Why?

8. Prosecution for Abusive Interrogation. President Obama in January 2009 announced that he intended to "look forward and not back" in dealing with detainee abuse. However, in August 2009, Attorney General Eric H. Holder Jr. appointed a federal prosecutor to investigate abuses enumerated in the 2004 CIA Inspector General Report, including several cases involving the deaths of detainees in CIA custody. The NATIONAL JOURNAL'S Stuart Taylor speculated that political calculations drove the announcement of the inquiry: "I doubt that Holder or Obama has any intention of prosecuting such underlings as the CIA agent who strayed beyond Justice Department legal guidance by threatening terrorist mastermind Khalid Shaikh Mohammed with the murder of his children...I also see no reason to disbelieve Holder's and Obama's promises not to go after interrogators who acted 'in good faith and within the scope of legal guidance,' or to suspect them of targeting the high-level Bush administration officials who approved brutal methods such as waterboarding." Taylor, "Why Holder May Enrage the Left," NATIONAL JOURNAL, September 5, 2009. What role should politics play in determining liability for detainee abuse?

9. Other Countries' Prosecutions. Some countries have been more willing to use judicial actions to punish alleged United States torturers. Germany and

Italy, for example, have issued arrest warrants and allowed civil suits in pending cases that include CIA agents as defendants. Judge Baltasar Garzon of Spain announced in August, 2009 that he would move forward with a suit brought by Spanish human rights organizations against six senior Bush Administration lawyers, including former Attorney General Alberto Gonzales and former Office of Legal Counsel attorneys John Yoo and Jay Bybee for facilitating torture of detainees at Guantanamo Bay. These countries have generally dropped these prosecutions shortly after their initiation.

D. LIABILITY OF INTERROGATORS

The Detainee Treatment Act (DTA) created certain protections for U.S. agents. Below is an excerpt of the relevant DTA provisions.

Sec. 1404. PROTECTION OF UNITED STATES GOVERNMENT PERSONNEL ENGAGED IN AUTHORIZED INTERROGATIONS.

(a) Protection of United States Government Personnel- In any civil action or criminal prosecution against an officer, employee, member of the Armed Forces, or other agent of the United States Government who is a United States person, arising out of the officer, employee, member of the Armed Forces, or other agent's engaging in specific operational practices, that involve detention and interrogation of aliens who the President or his designees have determined are believed to be engaged in or associated with international terrorist activity that poses a serious, continuing threat to the United States, its interests, or its allies, and that were officially authorized and determined to be lawful at the time that they were conducted, it shall be a defense that such officer, employee, member of the Armed Forces, or other agent did not know that the practices were unlawful and a person of ordinary sense and understanding would not know the practices were unlawful. Good faith reliance on advice of counsel As explained above, the Military Commissions Act (MCA) amended the War Crimes Act so only "grave breaches" of Common Article 3 of the Geneva Conventions could be the basis for a prosecution, a change made retroactive to November 26, 1997. The MCA further amended Section 1404 of the DTA to guarantee the United States would provide defense counsel and pay counsel fees, court costs, bail, and other expenses incident to the representation of an officer prosecuted.

The CIA and the military also utilized contract interrogators. In the following opinion, the D.C. Circuit considered the potential liability of contractors for detainee abuse. As you read the decision, remember the *Iqbal* and *al Kidd* decisions in Chapter IV concerning liability of U.S. government officials. Should contractors receive the same level of immunity as government interrogators, whether military or CIA?

SALEH v. TITAN CORPORATION

580 F.3d 1 (C.A.D.C. 2009), cert pet filed 78 USLW 3652 (Apr. 26, 2010)

SILBERMAN, Senior Circuit Judge:

Plaintiff Iraqi nationals brought separate suits against two private military contractors that provided services to the U.S. government at the Abu Ghraib military prison during the war in Iraq. *** Defendants CACI and Titan contracted to provide in Iraq interrogation and interpretation services, respectively, to the U.S. military, which lacked sufficient numbers of trained personnel to undertake these critical wartime tasks. The contractors' employees were combined with military personnel for the purpose of performing the interrogations, and the military retained control over the tactical and strategic parameters of the mission. Two separate groups of plaintiffs *** brought suit alleging that they or their relatives had been abused by employees of the two contractors during their detention and interrogation by the U.S. military at the Abu Ghraib prison complex. While the allegations in the two cases are similar, the Saleh plaintiffs also allege a broad conspiracy between and among CACI, Titan, various civilian officials (including the Secretary and two Undersecretaries of Defense), and a number of military personnel, whereas the Ibrahim plaintiffs allege only that CACI and Titan conspired in the abuse.

As we were told, a number of American servicemen have already been subjected to criminal court-martial proceedings in relation to the events at Abu Ghraib and have been convicted for their respective roles. While the federal government has jurisdiction to pursue criminal charges against the contractors should it deem such action appropriate, and although extensive investigations were pursued by the Department of Justice upon referral from the military investigator, no criminal charges eventuated against the contract employees. (Iraqi contract employees are also subject to criminal suit in Iraqi court.) Nor did the government pursue any contractual remedies against either contractor. The U.S. Army Claims Service has confirmed that it will compensate detainees who establish legitimate claims for relief under the Foreign Claims Act, 10 U.S.C. § 2734. Saleh pursued such a route, succeeding in obtaining $5,000 in compensation, despite the fact that the Army's investigation indicated that Saleh was never actually interrogated or abused.

While the terms "torture" and "war crimes" are mentioned throughout plaintiffs' appellate briefs and were used sporadically at oral argument, the factual allegations in the plaintiffs' briefs are in virtually all instances limited to claims of "abuse" or "harm." *** And only one specified instance of activity that would arguably fit the definition of torture (or possibly war crimes) is alleged with respect to the actions of a CACI employee.[18]

---

[18] The Torture Victim Protection Act, § 3(b)(1), 28 U.S.C. § 1350, defines "torture" as "any act, directed against an individual in the offender's custody or physical control, by which severe pain or suffering (other than pain or suffering arising only from or inherent in, or incidental to, lawful sanctions), whether physical or mental, is intentionally inflicted on that individual *for such purposes* as obtaining from that individual or a third person information or a confession, punishing that individual for an act that individual or a third person has committed or is

Plaintiffs brought a panoply of claims, including under the Alien Tort Statute ("ATS"), the Racketeer Influenced and Corrupt Organizations Act, government contracting laws, various international laws and agreements, and common law tort. In a thoughtful opinion, District Judge Robertson dismissed all of the Ibrahim plaintiffs' claims except those for assault and battery, wrongful death and survival, intentional infliction of emotional distress, and negligence. Following our decisions in *Tel-Oren v. Libyan Arab Republic*, 726 F.2d 774 (D.C.Cir.1984) (Edwards, J., concurring), and *Sanchez-Espinoza v. Reagan*, 770 F.2d 202 (D.C.Cir.1985), the district court held that because there is no consensus that *private* acts of torture violate the law of nations, such acts are not actionable under the ATS's grant of jurisdiction.[19]

As for the remaining claims, the district court found that there was, as yet, insufficient factual support to sustain the application of the preemption defense, which the defendants had asserted. The judge ordered limited discovery regarding the military's supervision of the contract employees as well as the degree to which such employees were integrated into the military chain of command. A year later, the district court dismissed the federal claims of the Saleh plaintiffs. The two sets of cases were consolidated for discovery purposes.

Following discovery, the contractors filed for summary judgment, again asserting that all remaining claims against them should be preempted as claims against civilian contractors providing services to the military in a combat context. In the absence of controlling authority, the district judge fashioned a test of first impression, according to which this preemption defense attaches only where contract employees are "under the direct command and *exclusive* operational control of the military chain of command." He concluded that Titan's employees were "fully integrated into [their] military units," essentially functioning "as soldiers in all but name." Although CACI employees were also integrated with military personnel and were within the chain of command, they were nevertheless found to be subject to a "dual chain of command" because the company retained the power to give "advice and feedback" to its employees and because interrogators were instructed to report abuses up both the company and military chains of command. The CACI site manager, moreover, said that he had authority to prohibit interrogations inconsistent with the company ethics policy, which the district court deemed to be evidence of "dual oversight." Thus, the remaining tort claims were held preempted as to Titan but not as to CACI. ***

---

suspected of having committed, intimidating or coercing that individual or a third person, or for any reason based on discrimination of any kind." (emphasis added) *See Price v. Socialist People's Libyan Arab Jamalhiriya*, 294 F.3d 82, 91-94 (D.C.Cir.2002). There is an allegation that one of *CACI's* employees observed and encouraged the beating of a detainee's soles with a rubber hose, which could well constitute torture or a war crime.

[19] The ATS reads, in its entirety, "The district courts shall have original jurisdiction of any civil action by an alien for a tort only, committed in violation of the law of nations or a treaty of the United States." 28 U.S.C. § 1350.

We think the district judge properly focused on the chain of command and the degree of integration that, in fact, existed between the military and both contractors' employees rather than the contract terms-and affirm his findings in that regard. We disagree, however, somewhat with the district Court's legal test: "exclusive" operational control. That CACI's employees were expected to report to their civilian supervisors, as well as the military chain of command, any abuses they observed and that the company retained the power to give advice and feedback to its employees, does not, in our view, detract meaningfully from the military's operational control, nor the degree of integration with which CACI's employees were melded into a military mission. We also agree with the district Court's disposition of the ATS claim against Titan.

We conclude that plaintiffs' D.C. tort law claims are preempted for either of two alternative reasons: (a) the Supreme Court's decision in *Boyle;* and (b) the Court's other preemption precedents in the national security and foreign policy field. ***

Although both defendants assert that they meet the district Court's "direct command and exclusive operational control" test for application of the preemption defense, CACI disputes the appropriateness of that test, arguing that it does not adequately protect the federal interest implicated by combatant activities. In CACI's view, the wartime interests of the federal government are as frustrated when a contractor within the chain of command exercises *some* level of operational control over combatant activities as would be true if all possible operational influence is exclusively in the hands of the military. For their part, the Iraqi plaintiffs agree with the district Court's finding that CACI exerted sufficient operational control over its employees as to have been able to prevent the alleged prisoner abuse and thus that the company should be subject to suit. As to Titan, plaintiffs argue that the district court overlooked critical material facts, including allegations that Titan breached its contract and that the military lacked the authority to discipline Titan employees.

As noted, both defendants asserted a defense based on sovereign immunity, which the district court has reserved. Presumably, they would argue that, notwithstanding the exclusion of "contractors with the United States" from the definition of "Federal agency" in the Federal Tort Claims Act ("FTCA")-which, of course, waives sovereign immunity-when a contractor's individual employees under a service contract are integrated into a military operational mission, the contractor should be regarded as an extension of the military for immunity purposes. The Supreme Court in *Boyle v. United Technologies Corp.,* 487 U.S. 500 (1992), the primary case on which defendants rely for their preemption claim, reserved the question whether sovereign immunity could be extended to nongovernmental employees, even in a case where the contractor provided a discrete product to the military.*** In *Boyle,* the court observed that the contractor could not satisfy both the Government's procurement design and the state's prescribed duty of care. ***Since the selection of the appropriate design of military equipment was obviously a governmental discretionary function and a lawsuit against a contractor that conformed to that design would impose the same costs on the government indirectly that the governmental immunity would avoid, the conflict is created.

The crucial point is that the court looked to the FTCA exceptions to the waiver of sovereign immunity to determine that the conflict was significant and to measure the boundaries of the conflict. ***[T]he relevant exception to the FTCA's waiver of sovereign immunity is the provision excepting "any claim arising out of the combatant activities of the military or armed forces, or the Coast Guard, during time of war." We note that this exception is *** more like a field preemption, *** because it casts an immunity net over any claim that *arises* out of combat activities. ***

The parties do not seriously dispute the proposition that uniquely federal interests are implicated in these cases, nor do the plaintiffs contend that the detention of enemy combatants is not included within the phrase "combat activities." Moreover, although the parties dispute the degree to which the contract employees were integrated into the military's operational activities, there is no dispute that they were in fact integrated and performing a common mission with the military under ultimate military command. They were subject to military direction, even if not subject to normal military discipline. Instead, the plaintiffs argue that there is not a significant conflict in applying state or Iraqi tort law to the behavior of both contractors' employees because the U.S. government itself openly condemned the behavior of those responsible for abusing detainees at Abu Ghraib-at least the Army personnel involved.

In order to determine whether a significant conflict exists between the federal interests and D.C. tort law, it is necessary to consider the reasons for the combat activities exception. ***[T]he combatant activities exception was designed "to recognize that during wartime encounters[,] no duty of reasonable care is owed to those against whom force is directed as a result of authorized military action." *** To be sure, to say that tort duties of reasonable care do not apply on the battlefield is not to say that soldiers are not under any legal restraint. Warmaking is subject to numerous proscriptions under federal law and the laws of war. Yet, it is clear that all of the traditional rationales for *tort* law-deterrence of risk-taking behavior, compensation of victims, and punishment of tortfeasors-are singularly out of place in combat situations, where risk-taking is the rule. *** In short, the policy embodied by the combatant activities exception is simply the elimination of tort from the battlefield, both to preempt state or foreign regulation of federal wartime conduct and to free military commanders from the doubts and uncertainty inherent in potential subjection to civil suit. And the policies of the combatant activities exception are equally implicated whether the alleged tortfeasor is a soldier or a contractor engaging in combatant activities at the behest of the military and under the military's control. Indeed, these cases are really indirect challenges to the actions of the U.S. military (direct challenges obviously are precluded by sovereign immunity).

The nature of the conflict in this case is somewhat different from that in

Boyle ***. [I]t is the imposition *per se* of the state or foreign tort law that conflicts with the FTCA's policy of eliminating tort concepts from the battlefield. The very purposes of tort law are in conflict with the pursuit of warfare. Thus, the instant case presents us with a more general conflict preemption, to coin a term, "battle-field preemption": the federal government occupies the field when it comes to warfare, and its interest in combat is always "precisely contrary" to the imposition of a non-federal tort duty. *** Just as in *Boyle,* however, the "scope of displacement" of the preempted non-federal substantive law must be carefully tailored so as to coincide with the bounds of the federal interest being protected. *** Here, the district court concluded that the federal interest in shielding the military from battlefield damage suits is sufficiently protected if claims against contract employees "under the direct command and exclusive operational control of the military chain of command such that they are functionally serving as soldiers" are preempted.

We agree with CACI that this "exclusive operational control" test does not protect the full measure of the federal interest embodied in the combatant activities exception. Surely, unique and significant federal interests are implicated in situations where operational control falls short of exclusive. As CACI argues, that a contractor has exerted *some* limited influence over an operation does not undermine the federal interest in immunizing the operation from suit. *** The district Court's test as applied to CACI and Titan, moreover, creates a powerful (and perverse) economic incentive for contractors, who would obviously be deterred from reporting abuse to military authorities if such reporting alone is taken to be evidence of retained operational control. That would be quite anomalous since even uniformed military personnel are obliged to refuse manifestly unlawful orders, *see United States v. Calley,* 22 U.S.C.M.A. 534, 544 (1973), and, moreover, are encouraged to report such outside of the chain of command to inspector generals. ***

We think that the following formulation better secures the federal interests concerned: During wartime, where a private service contractor is integrated into combatant activities over which the military retains command authority, a tort claim arising out of the contractor's engagement in such activities shall be preempted. We recognize that a service contractor might be supplying services in such a discrete manner-perhaps even in a battlefield context-that those services could be judged separate and apart from combat activities of the U.S. military. *** [T]he executive branch has broadly condemned the shameful behavior at Abu Ghraib documented in the now infamous photographs of detainee abuse. This disavowal does not, however, bear upon the issue presented in this tort suit against these defendants.***

Our holding is also consistent with the Supreme Court's recent decision in *Wyeth v. Levine,* 555 U.S. ---- (2009). *** The Court cited two "cornerstones" of preemption jurisprudence***. The first is congressional intent, which *** is much clearer in the case of the statutory text of the combatant activities exception. *** And the second is the strong presumption against preemption in fields that the states have traditionally occupied but where Congress has legislated nonetheless. *** [T]he Constitution specifically commits the Nation's war powers to the federal government, and as a result, the states have traditionally played no role in warfare.*** The federal Government's interest in preventing military policy from being subjected to fifty-one separate sovereigns (and that is only counting the *American* sovereigns) is not only broad-it is also obvious. *** Arguments for preemption of state prerogatives are particularly compelling in times of war. *** On the other side of the balance, the interests of any U.S. state (including the District of Columbia) are *de minimis* in this dispute-all alleged abuse occurred in Iraq against Iraqi citizens. The scope of displacement under our "ultimate military authority" test is thus appropriately broader than either *Boyle's* discretionary functions test or the rule proposed by the district court. *** We therefore reverse the district Court's holding as to CACI and affirm its Titan holding on a broader rationale.

It will be recalled that our jurisdiction to entertain the ATS issue extends only to the plaintiffs' appeals against Titan and *not* to CACI's appeals from the district Court's denial of its summary judgment motion on preemption grounds. The statute is a simple, if mysterious, one. It states, "the district court shall have original jurisdiction of any civil action by an alien for a tort only, committed in violation of the law of nations or a treaty of the United States." The Supreme Court recently has wrestled with its meaning and its scope. *Sosa v. Alvarez-Machain,* 542 U.S. 692 (2004). Appellants argue that the district court erred in dismissing their claims against Titan under this statute based on their reading of *Sosa.* Titan argues that the district court correctly followed our precedents in *Tel-Oren,* 726 F.2d 774 (D.C.Cir.1984) (Edwards, J., concurring), and *Sanchez-Espinoza v. Reagan,* 770 F.2d 202 (D.C.Cir.1985), which conclude that the ATS provides a cause of action against states but not private persons and which survive the Supreme Court's analysis in *Sosa.*

The latter case involved a tort claim brought, *inter alia,* against a Mexican national, Sosa, who purportedly acted on the DEA's behalf to abduct a Mexican physician accused of torture and murder and bring him from Mexico to stand trial in the United States. *** The court noted, but declined to decide, the issue which divides us from the Second Circuit, whether a private actor, as opposed to a state, could be liable under the ATS. *** Plaintiffs rely heavily on the Second Circuit's opinion in *Kadiã v. Karãdzíc,* 70 F.3d 232, 239 (2d Cir.1995), which held that for certain categories of action, including genocide, the scope of the law of nations is not confined solely to state action but reaches conduct "whether undertaken by those acting under the auspices of a state or only as private individuals." Despite the apparent breadth of this formulation, it must be remembered that in *Kadi,* the defendant was the self-proclaimed President of the Serbian Republic of Bosnia-Herzegovina, *** rendering *** a quasi-state entity such as Radovan Karãdzíc's militia *** easily distinguishable from a private actor such as Titan. *** [W]e have little difficulty in affirming the district judge's dismissal of the ATS claim against Titan. As we have noted, appellants' claim-as it appeared in their briefs and oral argument before us-is stunningly broad. They claim that any "abuse" inflicted or supported by Titan's translator employees on plaintiff detainees is condemned by a settled consensus of international law. *** We think that is an untenable, even absurd, articulation of a supposed consensus of international law. (Indeed, it is doubtful that we can discern a U.S. national standard of treatment of prisoners-short of the Eighth Amendment.) ***

Assuming, *arguendo,* that appellants had adequately alleged torture (or war crimes), there still remains the question whether they would run afoul of *Sosa's* comments. Although torture committed by a state is recognized as a violation of a settled international norm, that cannot be said of private actors. ***

Alternatively, it is asserted that defendants, while private parties, acted under the color of law. Although we have not held either way on this variation, in *Tel-Oren,* Judge Edwards' concurring opinion, while not a court holding, suggests that the ATS extends that far. And the Supreme Court in *Sosa* implied that it might be significant for Sosa to establish that Alvarez was acting "on behalf of a government." (although which government-the U.S. or Mexico-is unclear). Of course, plaintiffs are unwilling to assert that the contractors are state actors. [I]it would virtually concede that the contractors have sovereign immunity. [T]hey cannot artfully allege that the contractors acted under color of law for jurisdictional purposes while maintaining that their action was private when the issue is sovereign immunity. *** In light of the Supreme Court's recognition of Congress' superior legitimacy in creating causes of action, we note that it is not as though Congress has been silent on the question of torture or war crimes. *** The judicial restraint required by *Sosa* is particularly appropriate where, as here, a Court's reliance on supposed international law would impinge on the foreign policy prerogatives of our legislative and executive branches. *See, e.g., Garamendi,* 539 U.S. at 413-15; *Zschernig,* 389 U.S. at 440-41.***

Finally, appellants' ATS claim runs athwart of our preemption analysis which is, after all, drawn from congressional stated policy, the FTCA. If we are correct in concluding that state tort law is preempted on the battlefield because it runs counter to federal interests, the application of international law to support a tort action on the battlefield must be equally barred. To be sure, ATS would be drawing on federal common law that, in turn, depends on international law, so the normal state preemption terms do not apply. But *** an elaboration of international law in a tort suit applied to a battlefield is preempted by the same considerations that led us to reject the D.C. tort suit. *** Thus, plaintiffs' remaining claims are dismissed.

GARLAND, Circuit Judge, dissenting:

The plaintiffs in these cases allege that they were beaten, electrocuted, raped, subjected to attacks by dogs, and otherwise abused by private contractors working as interpreters and interrogators at Abu Ghraib prison. At the current stage of the litigation, we must accept these allegations as true. The plaintiffs do not contend that the United States military authorized or instructed the contractors to engage in such acts. No Executive Branch official has defended this conduct or suggested that it was employed to further any military purpose. To the contrary, both the current and previous Administrations have repeatedly and vociferously condemned the conduct at Abu Ghraib as contrary to the values and interests of the United States. So, too, has the Congress.

No act of Congress and no judicial precedent bars the plaintiffs from suing the private contractors-who were neither soldiers nor civilian government employees. Indeed, the only statute to which the defendants point expressly excludes private contractors from the immunity it preserves for the government. Neither President Obama nor President Bush nor any other Executive Branch official has suggested that subjecting the contractors to tort liability for the conduct at issue here would interfere with the nation's foreign policy or the Executive's ability to wage war. To the contrary, the Department of Defense has repeatedly stated that employees of private contractors accompanying the Armed Forces in the field are *not* within the military's chain of command, and that such contractors *are* subject to civil liability.

Under the circumstances of these cases, there is no warrant for displacing the ordinary operation of state law and dismissing the plaintiffs' complaints solely on preemption grounds.

Notes

1. *Sosa*. The majority states that while international law recognizes claims for torture by governments, it may not recognize such claims for torture by individuals, and suggests that *Sosa* is therefore inapplicable. Is that view in tension with the Court's holding that the contractors here were "integrated into combatant activities"?

2. Exemption. The FTCA expressly excludes contractors from its protections, yet the court found that the FTCA preempts the tort claims here. Were you persuaded that preemption, furthers federal interests where contractors are not acting pursuant to a duty imposed by the government, and where federal law also outlaws torture and war crimes? Would the Court's blanket bar on liability for military contractors extend to a similar case where the plaintiff was a U.S. citizen?

3. Contract Employees v. Soldiers. Neither tort liability nor military discipline attach to contractors for the actions alleged in *Saleh*. Are there any other consequences contractor employees might face? Soldiers are subject to military discipline under the Uniform Code of Military Justice for similar acts. In addition, to qualify for immunity from tort claims, the Attorney General must certify under the Westfall Act that soldiers were acting in the scope of their employment.

4. Contractor v. Armed Forces. What happens when military personnel engage in activities that are publicly controversial, such as the abuses at Abu Ghraib? The commandant in charge of Abu Ghraib was removed from her command, and the military leadership, up through the Secretary of Defense and President, received public excoriation in the media and on Capitol Hill. Both forms of punishment may accompany contractor misbehavior, but they are not running for office, nor are they sworn to uphold United States law. However, the contractor may lose future government contracts and be subject to penalties under the contracts under which the misbehavior occurred. Consider how these differing situations affect the government in using contractors. Does *Sale* incentivize contractors to take on "dirty work" that runs afoul of state or federal law and the Government to continue farming out such work?

E. EXTRAORDINARY RENDITION OF TERRORIST SUSPECTS

The United States, Britain, and perhaps other countries have engaged in "extraordinary "or "irregular" rendition. This consists of removing "high value" terrorist suspects from various countries and taking them to third-party nations. Why would a nation do this? As one CIA agent allegedly said: "If you want a serious interrogation, you send a prisoner to Jordan. If you want them to be tortured, you send them to Syria. If you want someone to disappear—never to be seen again—you send them to Egypt." Critics term this "torture by proxy" or "outsourcing torture." Allegedly, the United States has: (1) held individuals in U.S.-controlled secret detention facilities ("black sites") or in foreign facilities run with U.S. involvement, (2) held individualsin foreign facilities at the direction of the United States and (3) transferred individuals into the full custody of other nations. More than one of these strategies may be used with a given terrorist suspect. See Center for Human Rights & Global Justice, *Fate and Whereabouts Unknown: Detainees in the "War on Terror"* (2005). See generally Jane Mayer, *The Black Sites: A Rare Look Inside the C.I.A.'s Secret Interrogation Program,* NEW YORKER, Aug. 13, 2007.

Extraordinary rendition was regularly used during President Bill Clinton's administration and its use expanded under President George W. Bush following the terrorist attacks of September 11, 2001. In fall of 2006, President Bush acknowledged that the United States operated a secret detention, interrogation, and rendition program authorized under a classified September 17, 2001 presidential finding. Then National Security Advisor Condoleezza Rice reported to the Senate Committee on Armed Services in November 2008 that "in the spring of 2002, CIA sought policy approval from the National Security Council to begin an interrogation program for high-level al Qaida terrorists." In establishing the CIA program, the United States negotiated agreements with foreign governments to set up U.S.-run detention facilities, often referred to as "black sites". In January of 2009, President Obama ordered the secret prisons run by the CIA in at least eight countries (including possibly Thailand. Romania, Poland, and Afghanistan) to be shut down. Later that year, the Obama administration announced it would continue to send terrorist suspects to third countries for interrogation and detention, but would (1) seek more robust diplomatic assurances from those countries that they would not torture those rendered and (2) institute a more vigorous monitoring program of prisoners who have been sent to other countries to ensure they are not tortured there.

Extraordinary rendition may violate domestic and international law. In 1998 Congress passed a statute declaring it "the policy of the United States not to expel, extradite, or otherwise effect the involuntary return of any person to a country in which there are substantial grounds for believing the person would be in danger of being subjected to torture, regardless of whether the person is physically present in the United States." Foreign Affairs Reform and Restructuring Act of 1998 (FARRA), 8 U.S.C. §1231 (1998). Torture also is unlawful under the Convention Against Torture (CAT), which FARRA implements. The effectiveness of FARRA and CAT in deterring extraordinary rendition is questionable: the former applies only to aliens who come to the United States, and the latter is not self-executing.

The United States' use of extraordinary rendition has also been criticized internationally. In 2006, the United Nations' Committee Against Torture formally called for the United States to publicly condemn any policy of secret detention as well as to "rescind any interrogation technique, including methods involving sexual humiliation, 'water boarding', 'ham shackling' and using dogs to induce fear, that constitute torture or cruel, inhuman or degrading treatment or punishment, in all places of detention under its *de facto* effective control, in order to comply with its obligations under the Convention [Against Torture]." The Council of Europe described the system of "targeting, apprehending and detaining terrorist suspects" as a "global spider's web" of which the United States is the "chief architect." Dick Marty, Comm. on Legal Affairs and Human Rights, Council of Europe. On February 14, 2007, the European Parliament passed a resolution condemning CIA practices, "recall[ing] that imposing or executing or allowing directly or indirectly secret and illegal detentions, which are instruments resulting in people's ·disappearance', constitute serious violations of human rights per se and that the active or passive involvement in such secret and illegal detentions by a European country renders that county responsible under the [European Convention on Human Rights]" and requiring that European countries "take active steps to prevent any other authority from operating detention centres that are not subject to political and judicial oversight or where *incommunicado* detention is permitted." European Parliament, *Resolution on the Alleged Use of European Countries by the CIA for the Transportation and Illegal Detention of Prisoners, 2006/2200(INI)* (Feb. 14, 2007).

When media stories revealed that "ghost detainees" were being harshly interrogated by CIA personnel at "black sites" or sent to countries to be tortured by others, the United States issued vigorous denials. Secretary of State Condoleeza Rice promptly responded that "rendition is a vital tool in combating transnational terrorism...[but] the United States does not permit, tolerate or condone torture under any circumstances." Letter to UK Foreign Secretary Jack Straw dated December 5, 2005. See also press conference of President Bush, April 28, 2005 ("We operate within the law and we send people to countries where they say they're not going to torture people.").

Individuals rendered in the extraordinary rendition program have sought damages from the U.S. government, U.S. officials, and private contractors that implement aspects of the program. Procedural hurdles to damages suits against U.S. officials and even government contractors are imposing even if rendition and torture of an innocent person occurs. Subsection 1 below considers generally procedural bars to liability for extraordinary rendition. Subsection 2 examines in greater detail the bar that has proven most effective, that of the state secrets doctrine.

1. GENERAL BARS TO EXTRAORDINARY RENDITION LIABILITY

ARAR v. ASHCROFT
585 F. 3d 559 (2d Cir 2009), cert. denied 130 S. Ct. 3409 (2010)

DENNIS JACOBS, Chief Judge:

Maher Arar appeals from a judgment *** dismissing his complaint ***. Arar alleges that he was detained while changing planes at Kennedy Airport in New York (based on a warning from Canadian authorities that he was a member of Al Qaeda), mistreated for twelve days while in United States custody, and then removed to Syria via Jordan pursuant to an inter-governmental understanding that he would be detained and interrogated under torture by Syrian officials. The complaint alleges a violation of the Torture Victim Protection Act ("TVPA") and of his Fifth Amendment substantive due process rights arising from the conditions of his detention in the United States, the denial of his access to counsel and to the courts while in the United States, and his detention and torture in Syria. *** We have no trouble affirming the district Court's conclusions that Arar sufficiently alleged personal jurisdiction over the defendants who challenged it, and that Arar lacks standing to seek declaratory relief. We do not reach issues of qualified immunity or the state secrets privilege. As to the TVPA, we agree with the unanimous position of the panel that Arar insufficiently pleaded that the alleged conduct of United States officials was done under color of foreign law. We agree with the district court that Arar insufficiently pleaded his claim regarding detention in the United States ***. Our attention is therefore focused on whether Arar's claims for detention and torture in Syria can be asserted under *Bivens v. Six Unknown Named Agents of Federal Bureau of Narcotics*, 403 U.S. 388 (1971) (" *Bivens* ").

To decide the *Bivens* issue, we must determine whether Arar's claims invoke *Bivens* in a new context; and, if so, whether an alternative remedial scheme was available to Arar, or whether (in the absence of affirmative action by Congress) "'special factors counsel[ ] hesitation.' " This opinion holds that "extraordinary rendition" is a context new to *Bivens* claims, but avoids any categorical ruling on alternative remedies-because the dominant holding of this opinion is that, in the context of extraordinary rendition, hesitation is warranted by special factors. *** [I]f a civil remedy in damages is to be created for harms suffered in the context of extraordinary rendition, it must be created by Congress, which alone has the institutional competence to set parameters, delineate safe harbors, and specify relief. *** Administrations past and present have reserved the right to employ rendition, and notwithstanding prolonged public debate, Congress has not prohibited the practice, imposed limits on its use, or created a cause of action for those who allege they have suffered constitutional injury as a consequence.

[Arar, a dual citizen of Canada and of Syria, was detained at Kennedy airport, fingerprinted, asked about terrorist ties, and detained. INS "(1) ordered his removal to Syria, (2) made a (required) finding that such removal would be consistent with Article 3 of the Convention Against Torture ("CAT"), and (3) barred him from re-entering the United States for five years." He was then flown to Amman, Jordan and then delivered to Syrian officials, who "detained him at a Syrian Military Intelligence facility. Arar was in Syria for a year, the first ten months in an underground cell six feet by three, and seven feet high. He was interrogated for twelve days on his arrival in Syria, and in that period was beaten on his palms, hips, and lower back with a two-inch-thick electric cable and with bare hands. Arar alleges that United States officials conspired to send him to Syria for the purpose of interrogation under torture, and directed the interrogations from abroad by providing Syria with Arar's dossier, dictating questions for the Syrians to ask him, and receiving intelligence learned from the interviews." Interrogation ceased after Canadian Embassy officials inquired of Syria about Arar. Eventually, Arar was "released to the custody of a Canadian embassy official in Damascus, and was flown to Ottawa the next day." He sought "damages from federal officials for harms suffered as a result of his detention and confinement in the United States and his detention and interrogation in Syria."]

The TVPA creates a cause of action for damages against any "individual who, under actual or apparent authority, or color of law, of any foreign nation ... subjects an individual to torture." *** Accordingly, to state a claim under the TVPA, Arar must adequately allege that the defendants possessed power under Syrian law, and that the offending actions (*i.e.,* Arar's removal to Syria and subsequent torture) derived from an exercise of that power, or that defendants could not have undertaken their culpable actions absent such power. The complaint contains no such allegation. *** At most, it is alleged that the defendants encouraged or solicited certain conduct by foreign officials. Such conduct is insufficient to establish that the defendants were in some way clothed with the authority of Syrian law or that their conduct may otherwise be fairly attributable to Syria. ***

Count Four of the complaint alleges that the conditions of confinement in the United States (prior to Arar's removal to Syria), and the denial of access to courts during that detention, violated Arar's substantive due process rights under the Fifth Amendment. *** Arar alleges that "Defendants"-undifferentiated-"denied Mr. Arar effective access to consular assistance, the courts, his lawyers, and family members" in order to effectuate his removal to Syria. But he fails to specify any culpable action taken by any single defendant, and does not allege the "meeting of the minds" that a plausible conspiracy claim requires. He alleges (in passive voice) that his requests to make phone calls "were ignored," and that "he was told" that he was not entitled to a lawyer, but he fails to link these denials to any defendant, named or unnamed. Given this omission, and in view of Arar's rejection of an opportunity to re-plead, *** this Count of the complaint must be dismissed.

*** Arar's remaining claims seek relief on the basis of torture and detention in Syria, and are cast as violations of substantive due process. At the outset, Defendants argue that the jurisdictional bar of the INA deprived the District Court of subject-matter jurisdiction over these counts because Arar's removal was conducted pursuant to a decision that was "at the discretion" of the Attorney General. *** However, the application of the INA's jurisdictional bar is problematic in this case because the proceedings under the INA are alleged to have been irregular *** In short, it is not clear that the INA's judicial review provisions govern circumstances of involuntary rendition such as those alleged here. *** In any event, we need not decide the vexed question of whether the INA bar defeats jurisdiction of Arar's substantive due process claims, because we conclude below that the case must be dismissed at the threshold for other reasons.

In *Bivens*, the Supreme Court "recognized for the first time an implied private action for damages against federal officers alleged to have violated a citizen's constitutional rights." *** [However,] the Supreme Court has warned that the *Bivens* remedy is an extraordinary thing that should rarely if ever be applied in "new contexts." *** This case requires us to examine whether allowing this *Bivens* action to proceed would extend *Bivens* to a new "context," and if so, whether such an extension is advisable. *** The context of this case is international rendition, specifically, "extraordinary rendition." Extraordinary rendition is treated as a distinct phenomenon in international law. *** [T]he context of extraordinary rendition in Arar's case is the complicity or cooperation of United States government officials in the delivery of a non-citizen to a foreign country for torture (or with the expectation that torture will take place). This is a "new context": no court has previously afforded a *Bivens* remedy for extraordinary rendition. *** The Supreme Court tells us that *** [i]n order to determine whether to recognize a *Bivens* remedy in a new context, we must consider: whether there is an alternative remedial scheme available to the plaintiff; and whether " 'special factors counsel[ ] hesitation' " in creating a *Bivens* remedy. *** Among the "special factors" that have "counsel[ed] hesitation" and thereby foreclosed a *Bivens* remedy are: military concerns, separation of powers, the comprehensiveness of available statutory schemes, national security concerns, and foreign policy considerations. ***

Although this action is cast in terms of a claim for money damages against the defendants in their individual capacities, it operates as a constitutional challenge to policies promulgated by the executive. *** Here, we need not decide categorically whether a *Bivens* action can lie against policymakers because in the context of extraordinary rendition, such an action would have the natural tendency to affect diplomacy, foreign policy, and the security of the nation, and that fact counsels hesitation. ***

A. Security and Foreign Policy. The Executive has practiced rendition since at least 1995. A suit seeking a damages remedy against senior officials who implement such a policy is in critical respects a suit against the government as to which the government has not waived sovereign immunity. Such a suit unavoidably influences government policy, probes government secrets, invades government interests, enmeshes government lawyers, and thereby elicits government funds for settlement. *** A suit seeking a damages remedy against senior officials who implement an extraordinary rendition policy would enmesh the courts ineluctably in an assessment of the validity and rationale of that policy and its implementation in this particular case, matters that directly affect significant diplomatic and national security concerns. It is clear from the face of the complaint that Arar explicitly targets the "policy" of extraordinary rendition; he cites the policy twice in his complaint, and submits documents and media reports concerning the practice. His claim cannot proceed without inquiry into the perceived need for the policy, the threats to which it responds, the substance and sources of the intelligence used to formulate it, and the propriety of adopting specific responses to particular threats in light of apparent geopolitical circumstances and our relations with foreign countries.*** True, courts can-with difficulty and resourcefulness-consider state secrets and even reexamine judgments made in the foreign affairs context *when they must,* that is, when there is an unflagging duty to exercise our jurisdiction. *** Absent clear congressional authorization, the judicial review of extraordinary rendition would offend the separation of powers and inhibit this country's foreign policy. *** These concerns must counsel hesitation in creating a new damages remedy that Congress has not seen fit to authorize.

B. Classified Information. The extraordinary rendition context involves exchanges among the ministries and agencies of foreign countries on diplomatic, security, and intelligence issues. The sensitivities of such classified material are "too obvious to call for enlarged discussion." Even the probing of these matters entails the risk that other countries will become less willing to cooperate with the United States in sharing intelligence resources to counter terrorism. "At its core, *** this suit arises from the Executive Branch's alleged determination that (a) Arar was affiliated with Al Qaeda, and therefore a threat to national security, and (b) his removal to Syria was appropriate in light of U.S. diplomatic and national security interests." To determine the basis for Arar's alleged designation as an Al Qaeda member and his subsequent removal to Syria, the district court would have to consider what was done by the national security apparatus of at least three foreign countries, as well as that of the United States. Indeed, the Canadian government-which appears to have provided the intelligence that United States officials were acting upon when they detained Arar-paid Arar compensation for its role in the events surrounding this lawsuit, but has *also* asserted the need for Canada itself to maintain the confidentiality of certain classified materials related to Arar's claims.

C. Open Courts. Allegations of conspiracy among government agencies that must often work in secret inevitably implicate a lot of classified material that cannot be introduced into the public record. Allowing Arar's claims to proceed would very likely mean that some documents or information sought by Arar would be redacted, reviewed *in camera,* and otherwise concealed from the public. Concealment does not bespeak wrongdoing: in such matters, it is just as important to conceal what has *not* been done. Nevertheless, these measures would excite suspicion and speculation as to the true nature and depth of the supposed conspiracy, and as to the scope and depth of judicial oversight. Indeed, after an inquiry at oral argument as to whether classified materials relating to Arar's claims could be made available for review *in camera,* Arar objected to the supplementation of the record with material he could not see. *** The Court's reliance on information that cannot be introduced into the public record is likely to be a common feature of any *Bivens* actions arising in the context of alleged extraordinary rendition. This should provoke hesitation, given the strong preference in the Anglo-American legal tradition for open court proceedings, a value incorporated into modern First and Sixth Amendment law. The risk of limiting access, of course, is that where a proceeding "has been concealed from public view an unexpected outcome can cause a reaction that the system at best has failed and at worst has been corrupted." *** Granted, there are circumstances in which a court may close proceedings to which a public right of access presumptively attaches. And the problems posed by the need to consider classified material are unavoidable in some criminal prosecutions and in other cases where we have a duty, imposed by Congress, to exercise jurisdiction. But this is not such a circumstance or such a case. ***

A government report states that this case involves assurances received from other governments in connection with the determination that Arar's removal to Syria would be consistent with Article 3 of the CAT. This case is not unique in that respect. Cases in the context of extraordinary rendition are very likely to present serious questions relating to private diplomatic assurances from foreign countries received by federal officials, and this feature of such claims opens the door to graymail.

The regulations promulgated pursuant to the FARRA explicitly authorize the removal of an alien to a foreign country following receipt from that country of sufficiently reliable assurances that the alien will not be tortured. Should we decide to extend *Bivens* into the extraordinary rendition context, resolution of these actions will require us to determine whether any such assurances were received from the country of rendition and whether the relevant defendants relied upon them in good faith in removing the alien at issue. Any analysis of these questions would necessarily involve us in an inquiry into the work of foreign governments and several federal agencies, the nature of certain classified information, and the extent of secret diplomatic relationships. An investigation into the existence and content of such assurances would potentially embarrass our government through inadvertent or deliberate disclosure of information harmful to our own and other states. *** These considerations strongly counsel hesitation in acknowledging a *Bivens* remedy in this context. ***

Arar invokes *Bivens* to challenge policies promulgated and pursued by the executive branch, not simply isolated actions of individual federal employees. Such an extension of *Bivens* is without precedent and implicates questions of separation of powers as well as sovereign immunity. *** [T]here is further reason to hesitate where, as in this case, the challenged government policies are the subject of classified communications: a possibility that such suits will make the government "vulnerable to 'graymail,' *i.e.,* individual lawsuits brought to induce the [government] to settle a case (or prevent its filing) out of fear that any effort to litigate the action would reveal classified information that may undermine ongoing covert operations," or otherwise compromise foreign policy efforts. *Tenet v. Doe,* 544 U.S. 1, 11 (2005). We cast no aspersions on Arar, or his lawyers; this dynamic inheres in any case where there is a risk that a defendant might "disclose classified information in the course of a trial." This is an endemic risk in cases (however few) which involve a claim like Arar's.

The risk of graymail is itself a special factor which counsels hesitation in creating a *Bivens* remedy. There would be hesitation enough in an ordinary graymail case, *i.e.,* where the tactic is employed against the *government,* which can trade settlement cash (or the dismissal of criminal charges) for secrecy. But the graymail risk in a *Bivens* rendition case is uniquely troublesome. The interest in protecting military, diplomatic, and intelligence secrets is located (as always) in the *government*; yet a *Bivens* claim, by definition, is never pleaded against the government. So in a *Bivens* case, there is a dissociation between the holder of the non-disclosure interest (the government, which cannot be sued directly under *Bivens*) and the person with the incentive to disclose (the defendant, who cannot waive, but will be liable for any damages assessed). In a rendition case, the *Bivens* plaintiff could in effect pressure the individual defendants until the *government* cries uncle. Thus any *Bivens* action involving extraordinary rendition would inevitably suck the government into the case to protect its considerable interests, and-if disclosure is ordered-to appeal, or to suffer the disclosure, or to pay.

This pressure on the government to pay a settlement has (at least) two further perverse effects. First, a payment from the Treasury tends to obviate any payment or contribution by the individual defendants. Yet, "[*Bivens*] is concerned solely with deterring the unconstitutional acts of individual officers" by extracting payment from individual wrongdoers. *** Second, the individual defendant in such a case has no incentive to resist discovery that imperils government interests; rather, discovery induces the government to settle. *** In the end, a *Bivens* action based on rendition is-in all but name-a claim against the government. It is not for nothing that Canada (the government, not an individual officer of it) paid Arar $10 million dollars.

In the small number of contexts in which courts have implied a *Bivens* remedy, it has often been easy to identify both the line between constitutional and unconstitutional conduct, and the alternative course which officers should have pursued. The guard who beat a prisoner should not have beaten him; the agent who searched without a warrant should have gotten one; and the immigration officer who subjected an alien to multiple strip searches without cause should have left the alien in his clothes. This distinction may or may not amount to a special factor counseling hesitation in the implication of a *Bivens* remedy. But it is surely remarkable that the context of extraordinary rendition is so different, involving as it does a complex and rapidly changing legal framework beset with critical legal judgments that have not yet been made, as well as policy choices that are by no means easily reached.

Consider: should the officers here have let Arar go on his way and board his flight to Montreal? Canada was evidently unwilling to receive him; it was, after all, Canadian authorities who identified Arar as a terrorist (or did something that led their government to apologize publicly to Arar and pay him $10 million). Should a person identified as a terrorist by his own country be allowed to board his plane and go on to his destination? Surely, that would raise questions as to what duty is owed to the other passengers and the crew. Or should a suspected terrorist en route to Canada have been released on the Canadian border-over which he could re-enter the United States virtually at will? Or should he have been sent back whence his plane came, or to some third country? Should those governments be told that Canada thinks he is a terrorist? If so, what country would take him? Or should the suspected terrorist have been sent to Guantanamo Bay or-if no other country would take him-kept in the United States with the prospect of release into the general population?

None of this is to say that extraordinary rendition is or should be a favored policy choice. At the same time, the officials required to decide these vexed issues are "subject to the pull of competing obligations." *** Congress is the appropriate branch of government to decide under what circumstances (if any) these kinds of policy decisions-which are directly related to the security of the population and the foreign affairs of the country-should be subjected to the influence of litigation brought by aliens.

All of these special factors notwithstanding, we cannot ignore that, as the panel dissent put it, "there is a long history of judicial review of Executive and Legislative decisions related to the conduct of foreign relations and national security." Where does that leave us? We recognize our limited competence, authority, and jurisdiction to make rules or set parameters to govern the practice called rendition. By the same token, we can easily locate that competence, expertise, and responsibility elsewhere: in Congress. Congress may be content for the Executive Branch to exercise these powers without judicial check. But if Congress wishes to create a remedy for individuals like Arar, it can enact legislation that includes enumerated eligibility parameters, delineated safe harbors, defined review processes, and specific relief to be afforded. Once Congress has performed this task, *then* the courts in a proper case will be able to review the statute and provide judicial oversight ***. [14] ***

---

[14] Dissents by their nature express views that are not the law. *** A brief survey will suffice. Judge SACK'S dissent deems "artificial" our characterization of the new *** context in this case as "entirely one of 'international rendition, specifically extraordinary rendition.' " *** Judge SACK *** reconceives the context, at some points characterizing the constitutional tort as encompassing only those events that occurred within the United States while at other points requiring that the entire narrative be considered as a seamless whole, JFK to Syria. But this case is emphatically and obviously about extraordinary rendition (and its alleged abuse), as is elsewhere acknowledged in the opinions of Judge CALABRESI and Judge PARKER. As to the extraordinary rendition context [the dissenters concede: "It is difficult to deny the existence of 'special factors counseling hesitation' in this case[,]" *** Judge CALABRESI's dissent urges that we

CALABRESI, Circuit Judge, joined by Judges POOLER, SACK, and PARKER, dissenting.

*** In its utter subservience to the executive branch, its distortion of *Bivens* doctrine, its unrealistic pleading standards, its misunderstanding of the TVPA and of § 1983, as well as in its persistent choice of broad dicta where narrow analysis would have sufficed, the majority opinion goes seriously astray. It does so, moreover, with the result that a person—whom we must assume (a) was totally innocent and (b) was made to suffer excruciatingly (c) through the misguided deeds of individuals acting under color of federal law—is effectively left without a U.S. remedy.

All this, as the other dissenters have powerfully demonstrated, is surely bad enough. I write to discuss one last failing, an unsoundness that, although it may not be the most significant to Maher Arar himself, is of signal importance to us as federal judges: the majority's unwavering willfulness. *** When a court concludes that a *Bivens* action is appropriate, it is holding that, on the then-present state of the law, the Constitution requires the court to create a remedy. As even the staunchest critics of *Bivens* recognize, a holding that a particular constitutional right implies a remedy "can presumably not even be repudiated by Congress." While Congress can vitiate the need for a judicially created *Bivens* remedy by providing an "alternative ... process for protecting the [constitutional] interest," *Wilkie v. Robbins*, 551 U.S. 537, 550 (2007), it cannot overturn a holding that *some* remedy is necessary. *** So, how might the *Bivens* issue have been avoided? *** [T]his might be done through first examining the significance of the state secrets privilege to this case. That privilege has long required dismissal in those rare cases where national security interests so drastically limit the evidence that can be introduced as to deprive either a plaintiff or a defendant of an opportunity to make its case. In a case such as this, where the Government asserts that the plaintiff's claim implicates vital national secrets, we must, before we move to the merits, examine the consequences of our duty to guard against any potentially harmful disclosures.

The majority obviously shares our concerns about the protection of state secrets, as virtually every "special factor" identified in the majority opinion concerns classified material. But, as Judge Sack says, this amounts to double-counting of the Government's interest in preserving state secrets. We *already* possess a well-established method for protecting secrets, one that is more than adequate to meet the majority's concern. *** Even more mystifying is the majority's insistence that it is respecting "[t]he preference for open rather

---

forgo considering whether specific factors counsel hesitation under *Bivens* so that we could instead remand to see whether the case might eventually be dismissed as unmanageable under the state secrets privilege-which Judge CALABRESI seems equally to disapprove. *** Judge CALABRESI fails to consider that application of the state secrets privilege is often performed witness-by-witness; question-by-question; page-by-page; paragraph-by-paragraph-and can take years. It is not judicial activism to hesitate before requiring such an exercise in circumstances in which a *Bivens* claim may not lie. In any event, the state secrets doctrine has roots in separation of powers principles, and is not itself devoid of constitutional implications. *See* *** *El-Masri v. United States*, 479 F.3d 296, 303 (4th Cir.2007).

than clandestine court proceedings." How, exactly, does the majority promote openness***? *** When a court properly applies the state secrets doctrine, the case at bar will proceed only if the alleged state secrets are not vital to a claim or defense, so there should be little fear that a substantive holding will ultimately turn on secret material. By contrast, consider the harm done to the openness of the court system by what the majority does here. It bars any action in the face of what we are required to assume are outrageous constitutional violations, and it does so simply because state secrets *might possibly* be involved, without having a court look into that very question. As a result, even if the Government's claimed need for secrecy turned out to be wholly illusory, there would be no recourse! Indeed, even if the Government declassified every document relating to this case, even if all four countries involved announced that they had nothing to hide and that Arar's claim should proceed so that they could be exonerated, there would be no open judicial testing of Arar's allegations. Which approach should give us more cause to hesitate? ***

The state secrets doctrine has recently come in for significant criticism, much of it warranted. *** There is much to these concerns. But I would note three reasons that a threshold dismissal for want of evidence due to the existence of state secrets (if that were eventually determined necessary) would be preferable to the constitutional holding made today. And this would be so, I suggest, quite apart from the importance of adhering to the canon of constitutional avoidance.

First, a dismissal because a party simply cannot (for reasons of state secrets) proffer necessary evidence says nothing about the merits of the underlying claim. *** Second, a routine practice of first considering state secrets avoids the risk of a certain type of Government gamesmanship. If the Government has the option of seeking a state secrets dismissal both before *and* after a decision on some open question, then it has the ability to moot unfavorable rulings. Consider the strategy in this case. The Government's initial filing before the District Court sought a state secrets dismissal. In its brief for this *en banc* hearing, however, *after* it had won a favorable substantive ruling from the District Court and the panel, the Government did not mention any interest in a remand for a state secrets dismissal. It seems more than likely that, had the District Court or the panel found *against* the Government on the *Bivens* question, the Government would be arguing to us that the opinion below should be vacated pending a state secrets determination. *** Third, and most important, a holding that Arar, *even if all of his allegations are true,* has suffered no remediable constitutional harm *legitimates* the Government's actions in a way that a state secrets dismissal would not. The conduct that Arar alleges is repugnant, but the majority signals—whether it intends to or not—that it is not *constitutionally* repugnant. *** While a state secrets dismissal would similarly move the locus of redress to the political branches, it would do so not by holding that the harm done to Arar is of no concern to the judiciary or to the Constitution. It would do so, instead, by acknowledging an institutional limitation—due to the presence of state secrets—that is independent of the merits of Arar's claim and would, thereby, invite other branches to look into those possible merits.

This leads to my final point. Whether extraordinary rendition is constitutionally permissible is a question that seems to divide our country. It seems to me obvious, however, that regardless of the propriety of such renditions, an issue on which I won't hide my strong feelings, mistakes *will* be made in its operation. And *more* obvious still is that a civilized polity, when it errs, admits it and seeks to give redress. In some countries, this occurs through a royal commission. In the United States, for better or worse, courts are, almost universally, involved. This being so, and regardless of whether the Constitution itself requires that there be such redress, the object must be to create and use judicial structures that *facilitate* the giving of compensation, at least to innocent victims, while protecting from disclosure those facts that cannot be revealed without endangering national security. That might well occur here through the application of a sophisticated state secrets doctrine. It does not occur when, at the outset, Arar's claims—though assumed true and constitutionally significant—are treated as lacking any remedy. And this is just what today's unfortunate holding does. It hampers an admission of error, if error occurred; it decides constitutional questions that should be avoided; it is, I submit, on all counts, utterly wrong. I therefore must regretfully, but emphatically, dissent.

[Three additional dissents omitted]

Notes

1. Legal Complexities. It might be useful, given the complexity of this case, to make a list of Arar's claims and the reasons for the Court's dismissal of his claims.

2. Need for Reform? Do you think these reasons suggest any need for Congress to change the law? Argue both sides of this issue.

3. Congressional Remedies, Executive Action. There is no *Bivens* remedy where Congress has created an alternative statutory scheme for relief. *Wilkie* v. *Robbins*, 551 U.S. 537, 550, 554 (2007). Arar's question within this framework is nuanced. Where Congress had created a scheme (immigration laws and Torture Victim Protection Act) but government actors denied Arar the statutory remedies Congress provided, should a *Bivens* remedy exist?

4. Pause to Consider. The majority holds that "whenever thoughtful discretion would pause even to consider" whether to grant a *Bivens* remedy, the courts should dismiss the claim at the threshold. Is this a test that can only be struck one way? Will reasonable minds (and thoughtful judges) always find some reason to "pause even to consider"? If so, is *Bivens* chimerical after this case?

5. State secrets and gray mail. Much of the majority's analysis centers on state secrets. Would dismissing this case by way of the state secrets privilege, discussed in the next two cases in this chapter, be preferable, as Judge Calabresi suggests? Or does the risk of gray mail (a threat to reveal state secrets during litigation) make it appropriate to consider state secrets as a special factor?

6. Institutional incentives and the risk of mistake. What institutional effects would a Second Circuit decision finding a *Bivens* remedy for Arar have upon the broader rendition program? On Congress to provide a remedy to Arar and others like him? Contrast this opinion's likely effect on extraordinary rendition and on Congress. What role should the courts play, particularly where such an arguably important—and controversial—counter terrorism program is at stake? Mistakes happen in any program, such as extraordinary rendition. Who should bear the burden of mistake in the context of sensitive national security programs and why? How does the type of harm from mistake (e.g. surveillance of the wrong person vs. rendering the wrong person) affect your calculus?

2. STATE SECRETS AND EXTRAORDINARY RENDITION LIABILITY

The two cases in this section concern suits by or on behalf of individuals who alleged they were subjected to the CIA's secret extraordinary rendition program. In both cases, the United States intervened, invoking the state secrets privilege, and sought dismissal on the basis that the subject matter of the suit—the rendition program—is a state secret. Before turning to these cases, a brief historical overview of the history of this doctrine or privilege is in order.

In 1807, in the famous trial of Aaron Burr, Burr tried to force President Jefferson to produce letters exchanged between Jefferson and General Wilkinson. The government responded that the letters contained information which should not be made public. Chief Justice Marshall, who presided over the trial, wrote "That there may be matter, the production of which the court would not require, is certain . . . What ought to be done under such circumstances presents a delicate question, the discussion of which, it is hoped, will never be rendered necessary in this country."

In the 1876 case *Totten v. United States,* 92 U.S. 105 (1876), the Supreme Court first precluded disclosure of government-held information for security reasons. During the Civil War Totten had entered a secret contract with President Lincoln to gather military intelligence in the South. The administrator of Totten's estate sought to recover money allegedly owed Totten for his service as a spy. The Court held not merely that certain information could not be introduced into evidence, but that the suit itself was barred. Justice Field noted: "Our objection is not to the contract, but to the action upon it in the Court of Claims. *** Both employer and agent must have understood that the lips of the other were to be for ever sealed respecting the relation of either to the matter. This condition of the engagement was implied from the nature of the employment, and is implied in all secret employments of the government in time of war, or upon matters affecting our foreign relations[.]"

Shortly after Word War II, the Supreme Court formally recognized the state secrets privilege in *United States v. Reynolds,* 345 U.S. 1, 11, (1953). In 1948 three civilians were killed when a military aircraft crashed near Waycross, Georgia. The widows of the three civilians sued the United States under the Tort Claims Act. The plaintiffs sought to discover the Air Force's official accident investigation report. The Air Force objected to production of the documents asserting that they contained military secrets. The district court judge held that the plaintiffs had shown good cause, and ordered that the Air Force to produce the documents to the court, so that they could be reviewed in camera. The Air Force continued to refuse production "for the reason that the aircraft in question, together with the personnel on board, were engaged in a highly secret mission of the Air Force." And because "the demanded material could not be furnished without seriously hampering national security, flying safety and the development of highly technical and secret military equipment." Consequently the district court entered an order that the facts on the issue of negligence would be taken as established in plaintiffs' favor. The Third Circuit affirmed, but the Supreme Court reversed and provided the analytical framework for the modern state secrets privilege. That is,

> The privilege belongs to the Government and must be asserted by it; it can neither be claimed nor waived by a private party. It is not to be lightly invoked. There must be a formal claim of privilege, lodged by the head of the department which has control over the matter, after actual personal consideration by that officer. The court itself must determine whether the circumstances are appropriate for the claim of privilege, and yet do so without forcing a disclosure of the very thing the privilege is designed to protect.

The Court recognized that this later requirement would be the most difficult. It explained that the circumstances are appropriate for the privilege if there is "a reasonable danger that compulsion of the evidence will expose military matters which, in the interest of national security, should not be divulged." But how is a court to make that determination "without forcing a disclosure of the very thing the privilege is designed to protect"? The Court developed a deferential balancing test:

> [W]e will not go so far as to say that the court may automatically require a complete disclosure to the judge before the claim of privilege will be accepted in any case. It may be possible to satisfy the court, from all the circumstances of the case, that there is a reasonable danger that compulsion of the evidence will expose military matters which, in the interest of national security, should not be divulged. When this is the case, the occasion for the privilege is appropriate, and the court should not jeopardize the security which the privilege is meant to protect by insisting upon an examination of the evidence, even by the judge alone, in chambers. *** In each case, the showing of necessity which is made will determine how far the court should probe in satisfying itself that the occasion for invoking the privilege is appropriate.

Prior to *Reynolds*, courts occasionally refused to hear cases potentially involving state secrets at their discretion, on a case-by-case basis. With World War II and the advent of advanced military technologies and dedicated intelligence gathering agencies, *Reynolds* developed a formal state secrets privilege that protected the government from even confirming or denying that it engaged in certain activities at all. A major irony surrounds *Reynolds*. In

2000, the investigation report that the plaintiffs in *Reynolds* sought to discover was declassified. The report contained a detailed account of a failure of the Air Force's routine maintenance procedures, and an ordinary mechanical failure in the aircraft's engine which caused a fire on board. The fire was likely exacerbated by a mistake made by the pilot as the fire broke out. The Air Force had further neglected to brief the civilians on emergency procedures before the flight as was required by Air Force regulation. The report made no mention of any military secrets.

During the Vietnam War, the NSA developed two broad foreign surveillance programs. "Operation Minaret" targeted electronic communications. "Operation Shamrock" targeted telegraphic communications. At the same time the CIA developed a program called "Operation Chaos," which sought to determine the extent of foreign government involvement in the American anti-war movement. As part of Operation Chaos the CIA submitted "watchlists" containing names of individuals to the NSA. Allegedly, the NSA, under operations Shamrock and Minaret, then conducted surveillance of the individuals named on the watchlists.

In 1978, in *Halkin v. Helmes*, Vietnam protesters and civil rights organizations sued the CIA, NSA, and several telecommunications companies asserting constitutional and statutory violations in connection with Operations Minaret and Shamrock. Some information concerning Operation Shamrock had been made public during a congressional investigation, but Operation Minaret was not a subject of the investigation. Consequently the district court ruled that litigation could proceed as to Operation Shamrock, but the Government's invocation of the state secrets privilege would stand as to Operation Minaret. The District of Columbia Circuit Court broadened the state secrets bar because, although the existence of Operation Shamrock was known, there was a reasonable danger that "confirmation or denial that a particular plaintiff's communications have been acquired would disclose NSA capabilities and other valuable intelligence information to a sophisticated intelligence analyst."

In 1985, the District of Columbia Circuit addressed another case of alleged warrantless electronic surveillance in *Ellsberg v. Mitchell* 807 F.2d 204 (1986). *Ellsberg* involved the Pentagon Papers prosecution. The court again upheld the Government's invocation of the state secrets privilege and reiterated that it must be assumed any information disclosed during litigation would be obtained by a "sophisticated foreign intelligence analyst." The court did require the government to justify its claim of privilege in as much detail as possible before in camera review, with the trial judge insisting (1) that the formal claim of privilege be made on the public record and (2) that the government either (a) publicly explain in detail the kinds of injury to national security it seeks to avoid and the reason those harms would result from revelation of the requested information or (b) indicate why such an explanation would itself endanger national security. The *Ellsberg* court also explained the practical implications of the Government's invocation of the privilege: "the evidence is unavailable, as though a witness had died, and the case will proceed accordingly." When the government is a defendant in a civil suit "the effect is the same *** as if the government were not involved in the controversy."

EL-MASRI v. UNITED STATES
479 F. 3d 296 (4th Cir. 2007)

KING, Circuit Judge.

***El-Masri alleged that the defendants were involved in a CIA operation in which he was detained and interrogated in violation of his rights under the Constitution and international law. The United States *** assert[s] that El-Masri's civil action could not proceed because it posed an unreasonable risk that privileged state secrets would be disclosed. *** The heart of El-Masri's appeal is his assertion that the facts essential to his Complaint have largely been made public, either in statements by United States officials or in reports by media outlets and foreign governmental entities. He maintains that the subject of this action is simply "a rendition and its consequences," and that its critical facts-the CIA's operation of a rendition program targeted at terrorism suspects, plus the tactics employed therein-have been so widely discussed that litigation concerning them could do no harm to national security. *** El-Masri's contention *** misapprehends the nature of our assessment of a dismissal on state secrets grounds. The controlling inquiry is not whether the general subject matter of an action can be described without resort to state secrets. Rather, we must ascertain whether an action can be *litigated* without threatening the disclosure of such state secrets. Thus, for purposes of the state secrets analysis, the "central facts" and "very subject matter" of an action are those facts that are essential to prosecuting the action or defending against it.

El-Masri is therefore incorrect in contending that the central facts of this proceeding are his allegations that he was detained and interrogated under abusive conditions, or that the CIA conducted the rendition program that has been acknowledged by United States officials. Facts such as those furnish the general terms in which El-Masri has related his story to the press, but advancing a case in the court of public opinion, against the United States at large, is an undertaking quite different from prevailing against specific defendants in a court of law. If El-Masri's civil action were to proceed, the facts central to its resolution would be the roles, if any, that the defendants played in the events he alleges. To establish a prima facie case, he would be obliged to produce admissible evidence not only that he was detained and interrogated, but that the defendants were involved in his detention and interrogation in a manner that renders them personally liable to him. Such a showing could be made only with evidence that exposes how the CIA organizes, staffs, and supervises its most sensitive intelligence operations. With regard to Director Tenet, for example, El-Masri would be obliged to show in detail how the head of the CIA participates in such operations, and how information concerning their progress is relayed to him. With respect to the defendant corporations and their unnamed employees, El-Masri would have to demonstrate the existence and details of CIA espionage contracts, an endeavor practically indistinguishable from that categorically barred by *Totten* and *Tenet v. Doe*. Even marshalling the evidence necessary to make the requisite showings would implicate privileged state secrets, because El-Masri would need to rely on witnesses whose identities, and evidence the very existence of which, must remain confidential in the interest of national security.

Furthermore, *** the defendants could not properly defend themselves without using privileged evidence. The main avenues of defense available in this matter are to show that El-Masri was not subject to the treatment that he alleges; that, if he was subject to such treatment, the defendants were not involved in it; or that, if they were involved, the nature of their involvement does not give rise to liability. Any of those three showings would require disclosure of information regarding the means and methods by which the CIA gathers intelligence. If, for example, the truth is that El-Masri was detained by the CIA but his description of his treatment is inaccurate, that fact could be established only by disclosure of the actual circumstances of his detention, and its proof would require testimony by the personnel involved. Or, if El-Masri was in fact detained as he describes, but the operation was conducted by some governmental entity other than the CIA, or another government entirely, that information would be privileged. Alternatively, if the CIA detained El-Masri, but did so without Director Tenet's active involvement, effective proof thereof would require a detailed explanation of how CIA operations are supervised. Similarly, although an individual CIA officer might demonstrate his lack of involvement in a given operation by disclosing that he was actually performing some other function at the time in question, establishing his alibi would likely require him to reveal privileged information.

Moreover, proof of the involvement-or lack thereof-of particular CIA officers in a given operation would provide significant information on how the CIA makes its personnel assignments. Similar concerns would attach to evidence produced in defense of the corporate defendants and their unnamed employees. And, like El-Masri's prima facie case, any of the possible defenses suggested above would require the production of witnesses whose identities are confidential and evidence the very existence of which is a state secret. *** [V]irtually any conceivable response to El-Masri's allegations would disclose privileged information.

***Even if we assume, arguendo, that the state secrets privilege does not apply to the information that media outlets have published concerning those topics, dismissal of his Complaint would nonetheless be proper because the public information does not include the facts that are central to litigating his action. Rather, those central facts-the CIA means and methods that form the subject matter of El-Masri's claim-remain state secrets. ***

El-Masri also contends that, instead of dismissing his Complaint, the district court should have employed some procedure under which state secrets would have been revealed to him, his counsel, and the court, but withheld from the public. *** We need not dwell long on El-Masri's proposal in this regard, for it is expressly foreclosed by *Reynolds,* the Supreme Court decision that controls this entire field of inquiry. *Reynolds* plainly held that when "the occasion for the privilege is appropriate, ... the court should not jeopardize the security which the privilege is meant to protect by insisting upon an examination of the evidence, even by the judge alone, in chambers." ***

Contrary to El-Masri's assertion, the state secrets doctrine does not represent a surrender of judicial control over access to the courts. *** [I]t is the court, not the Executive, that determines whether the state secrets privilege has been properly invoked. In order to successfully claim the state secrets privilege, the Executive must satisfy the court that disclosure of the information sought to be protected would expose matters that, in the interest of national security, ought to remain secret. Similarly, in order to win dismissal of an action on state secrets grounds, the Executive must persuade the court that state secrets are so central to the action that it cannot be fairly litigated without threatening their disclosure. ***

In this matter, the reasons for the United States' claim of the state secrets privilege and its motion to dismiss were explained largely in the Classified Declaration, which sets forth in detail the nature of the information that the Executive seeks to protect and explains why its disclosure would be detrimental to national security. *** It is no doubt frustrating to El-Masri that many of the specific reasons for the dismissal of his Complaint are classified. *** That El-Masri is unfamiliar with the Classified Declaration's explanation for the privilege claim does not imply, as he would have it, that no such explanation was required. ***

As we have observed in the past, the successful interposition of the state secrets privilege imposes a heavy burden on the party against whom the privilege is asserted. That party loses access to evidence that he needs to prosecute his action and, if privileged state secrets are sufficiently central to the matter, may lose his cause of action altogether. Moreover, a plaintiff suffers this reversal not through any fault of his own, but because his personal interest in pursuing his civil claim is subordinated to the collective interest in national security. In view of these considerations, we recognize the gravity of our conclusion that El-Masri must be denied a judicial forum for his Complaint, and reiterate our past observations that dismissal on state secrets grounds is appropriate only in a narrow category of disputes.

Notes

1. Justice? Is it just that the Government can beat up on *El-Masri* and not have to face the music? What, if anything, does this formulation of the issue leave out?

2. Criminal v. Civil. How do criminal and civil uses of state secrets differ?

3. Applications. Does the *El-Masri* formulation of the state secrets doctrine apply across the board to all contexts in which state secrets might become involved in litigation, or is it fact-bound to the context of the secrets that would be involved in this litigation? See the next case if you think context does not matter (and forum also, for that matter).

4. Introduction to the Next Case. As with many aspects of modern military and intelligence operations, the United States relied on private contractors to support the rendition program. The following, from Jane Mayer, "Outsourcing: The C.I.A.'s Travel Agent," THE NEW YORKER, October 30, 2006, provides a glimpse of the possible role of private companies in the extraordinary rendition program. It also provides a follow-up on the fate of el-Masri.

On the official Web site of Boeing, the world's largest aerospace company, there is a section devoted to a subsidiary called Jeppesen International Trip Planning *** [A]mong the international trips that the company plans for the [CIA] are secret "extraordinary rendition" flights for terrorism suspects. Most of the planes used in rendition flights are owned and operated by tiny charter airlines that function as C.I.A. front companies, but it is not widely known that the agency has turned to a division of Boeing, the publicly traded blue-chip behemoth, to handle many of the logistical and navigational details for these trips, including flight plans, clearance to fly over other countries, hotel reservations, and ground-crew arrangements. *** A former Jeppesen employee, who asked not to be identified, said recently that he had been startled to learn, during an internal corporate meeting, about the company's involvement with the rendition flights. At the meeting, he recalled, Bob Overby, the managing director of Jeppesen International Trip Planning, said, "We do all of the extraordinary rendition flights—you know, the torture flights. Let's face it, some of these flights end up that way." The former employee said that another executive told him, "We do the spook flights." He was told that two of the company's trip planners were specially designated to handle renditions. He was deeply troubled by the rendition program, he said, and eventually quit his job. He recalled Overby saying, "It certainly pays well. They"—the C.I.A.—"spare no expense. They have absolutely no worry about costs. What they have to get done, they get done." *** The British journalist Stephen Grey, in his book Ghost Plane, refers to documents obtained by Spanish law-enforcement officials, along with flight logs, which indicate that international flight planners provided essential logistical support for many of the C.I.A.'s renditions, including that of Khaled el-Masri, a German car salesman who was apparently mistaken for an Al Qaeda suspect with a similar name, in January of 2004. *** Masri, who is a Muslim, was arrested at the border while crossing from Serbia into Macedonia by bus. He has alleged in court papers that Macedonian authorities turned him over to a C.I.A. rendition team. Then, he said, masked figures stripped him naked, shackled him, and led him onto a Boeing 737 business jet. Flight plans prepared by Jeppesen show that from Skopje, Macedonia, the 737 flew to Baghdad, where it had military clearance to land, and then on to Kabul. On board, Masri has said, he was chained to the floor and injected with sedatives. After landing, he was put in the trunk of a car and driven to a building where he was placed in a dank cell. He spent the next four months there, under interrogation. Masri was released in May, 2004, on the orders of Condoleezza Rice, then the national-security adviser, after she learned that he had mistakenly been identified as a terrorism suspect. ***

MOHAMED v. JEPPESEN DATAPLAN, INC.
614 F. 3d 1070 (CA9, 2010), cert.pet.filed 79 USLW 3370 (Dec. 7, 2010)

FISHER, Circuit Judge.

This case requires us to address the difficult balance the state secrets doctrine strikes between fundamental principles of our liberty, including justice, transparency, accountability and national security. Although as judges we strive to honor *all* of these principles, there are times when exceptional circumstances create an irreconcilable conflict between them. On those rare occasions, we are bound to follow the Supreme Court's admonition that "even the most compelling necessity cannot overcome the claim of privilege if the court is ultimately satisfied that [state] secrets are at stake." *United States v. Reynolds,* 345 U.S. 1, 11, (1953). ***

Plaintiffs allege that the Central Intelligence Agency ("CIA"), working in concert with other government agencies and officials of foreign governments, operated an extraordinary rendition program to gather intelligence by apprehending foreign nationals suspected of involvement in terrorist activities and transferring them in secret to foreign countries for detention and interrogation by United States or foreign officials. According to plaintiffs, this program has allowed agents of the U.S. government "to employ interrogation methods that would [otherwise have been] prohibited under federal or international law." Relying on documents in the public domain, plaintiffs, all foreign nationals, claim they were each processed through the extraordinary rendition program. They also make the following individual allegations.

Plaintiff Ahmed Agiza, an Egyptian national who had been seeking asylum in Sweden, was captured by Swedish authorities, allegedly transferred to American custody and flown to Egypt. In Egypt, he claims he was held for five weeks "in a squalid, windowless, and frigid cell," where he was "severely and repeatedly beaten" and subjected to electric shock through electrodes attached to his ear lobes, nipples and genitals. Agiza was held in detention for two and a half years, after which he was given a six-hour trial before a military court, convicted and sentenced to 15 years in Egyptian prison. According to plaintiffs, "[v]irtually every aspect of Agiza's rendition, including his torture in Egypt, has been publicly acknowledged by the Swedish government." ***

Plaintiff Binyam Mohamed, a 28-year-old Ethiopian citizen and legal resident of the United Kingdom, was arrested in Pakistan on immigration charges. Mohamed was allegedly flown to Morocco under conditions similar to those described above, where he claims he was transferred to the custody of Moroccan security agents. These Moroccan authorities allegedly subjected Mohamed to "severe physical and psychological torture," including routinely beating him and breaking his bones. He says they cut him with a scalpel all over his body, including on his penis, and poured "hot stinging liquid" into the open wounds. He was blindfolded and handcuffed while being made "to listen to extremely loud music day and night." After 18 months in Moroccan custody, Mohamed was allegedly transferred back to American custody and flown to Afghanistan. He claims he was detained there in a CIA "dark prison" where he was kept in "near permanent darkness" and subjected to loud noise, such as the recorded screams of women and children, 24 hours a day. Mohamed was fed spar- ingly and irregularly and in four months he lost between 40 and 60 pounds. Eventually, Mohamed was transferred to the U.S. military prison at Guantanamo Bay, Cuba, where he remained for nearly five years. He was released and returned to the United Kingdom during the pendency of this appeal. ***

Plaintiffs contend that publicly available information establishes that defendant Jeppesen Dataplan, Inc., a U.S. corporation, provided flight planning and logistical support services to the aircraft and crew on all of the flights transporting each of the five plaintiffs among the various locations where they were detained and allegedly subjected to torture. The complaint asserts "Jeppesen played an integral role in the forced" abductions and detentions and "provided direct and substantial services to the United States for its so-called 'extraordinary rendition' program," thereby "enabling the clandestine and forcible transportation of terrorism suspects to secret overseas detention facilities." It also alleges that Jeppesen provided this assistance with actual or constructive "knowledge of the objectives of the rendition program," including knowledge that the plaintiffs "would be subjected to forced disappearance, detention, and torture" by U.S. and foreign government officials.

Plaintiffs brought suit against Jeppesen under the Alien Tort Statute, alleging seven theories of liability marshaled under two claims, one for "forced disappearance" and another for "torture and other cruel, inhuman or degrading treatment."   *** Regarding Jeppesen's alleged actual or constructive knowledge that its services were being used to facilitate "forced disappearance," plaintiffs allege that Jeppesen "knew or reasonably should have known that the flights involved the transportation of terror suspects pursuant to the extraordinary rendition program," that their "knowledge of the objectives of the rendition program" may be inferred from the fact that they allegedly "falsified flight plans submitted to European air traffic control authorities to avoid public scrutiny of CIA flights" and that a Jeppesen employee admitted actual knowledge that the company was performing extraordinary rendition flights for the U.S. government. Similarly, plaintiffs allege that Jeppesen knew or should have known that that torture would result because it should have known it was carrying terror suspects for the CIA and that "the governments of the destination countries routinely subject detainees to torture and other forms of cruel, inhuman, or degrading treatment." They also rely on U.S. State Department country reports describing torture as "routine" in some of the countries to which plaintiffs were allegedly rendered, and note that Jeppesen claims on its website that it "monitors 13527 political and security situations" as part of its trip planning services. ***

Before Jeppesen answered the complaint, the United States moved to intervene and to dismiss plaintiffs' complaint under the state secrets doctrine. The then-Director of the CIA, General Michael Hayden, filed two declarations in support of the motion to dismiss, one classified, the other redacted and unclassified. The public declaration states that "[d]isclosure of the information covered by this privilege assertion reasonably could be expected to cause serious-and in some instances, exceptionally grave-damage to the national security of the United States and, therefore, the information should be excluded from any use in this case." It further asserts that "because highly classified information is central to the allegations and issues in this case, the risk is great that further litigation will lead to disclosures harmful to U.S. national security and, accordingly, this case should be dismissed." *** On September 23, 2009, the Obama administration announced new policies for invoking the state secrets privilege, effective October 1, 2009, in a memorandum from the Attorney General. The government certified both in its briefs and at oral argument before the en banc court that officials at the "highest levels of the Department of Justice" of the new administration had reviewed the assertion of privilege in this case and determined that it was appropriate under the newly announced policies. ***

The Supreme Court has long recognized that in exceptional circumstances courts must act in the interest of the country's national security to prevent disclosure of state secrets, even to the point of dismissing a case entirely. *See Totten v. United States,* 92 U.S. 105 (1876). The contemporary state secrets doctrine encompasses two applications of this principle. One completely bars adjudication of claims premised on state secrets (the "*Totten* bar"); the other is an evidentiary privilege ("the *Reynolds* privilege") that excludes privileged evidence from the case and *may* result in dismissal of the claims.[3] *See United States v. Reynolds,* 345 U.S. 1 (1953). We first address the nature of these applications and then apply them to the facts of this case.

A. The Totten Bar. In 1876 the Supreme Court stated "as a *general principle* [ ] that public policy forbids the maintenance of any suit in a court of justice, the trial of which would inevitably lead to the disclosure of matters which the law itself regards as confidential." The Court again invoked the principle in 1953, citing *Totten* for the proposition that "where the very subject matter of the action" is "a matter of state secret," an action may be "dismissed on the pleadings without ever reaching the question of evidence" because it is "so obvious that the action should never prevail over the privilege." This application of *Totten* 's general principle-which we refer to as the *Totten* bar-is "designed not merely to defeat the asserted claims, but to preclude judicial inquiry" entirely. *Tenet v. Doe,* 544 U.S. 1 (2005).

The Court first applied this bar in *Totten* itself, where the estate of a Civil War spy sued the United States for breaching an alleged agreement to compensate the spy for his wartime espionage services. Setting forth the "general principle" quoted above, the Court held that the action was barred

---

[3] Were this a *criminal* case, the state secrets doctrine would apply more narrowly. *See El-Masri v. United States,* 479 F.3d 296, 313 n. 7 (4th Cir.2007) ("[T]he Executive's authority to protect [state secrets] is much broader in civil matters than in criminal prosecutions."); *see also Reynolds,* 345 U.S. at 12.

because it was premised on the existence of a "contract for secret services with the government," which was "a fact not to be disclosed."

A century later, the Court applied the *Totten* bar in *Weinberger v. Catholic Action of Hawaii/Peace Education Project,* 454 U.S. 139 (1981). There, the plaintiffs sued under the National Environmental Policy Act of 1969, to compel the Navy to prepare an environmental impact statement regarding a military facility where the Navy allegedly proposed to store nuclear weapons. The Court held that the allegations were "beyond judicial scrutiny" because, "[d]ue to national security reasons, ... the Navy can neither admit nor deny that it proposes to store nuclear weapons at [the facility]." ***

Plaintiffs contend that the *Totten* bar applies *only* to a narrow category of cases they say are not implicated here, namely claims premised on a plaintiff's espionage relationship with the government. We disagree. We read the Court's discussion of *Totten* in *Reynolds* to mean that the *Totten* bar applies to cases in which "the very subject matter of the action" is "a matter of state secret." "[A] contract to perform espionage" is only an example. This conclusion is confirmed by *Weinberger,* which relied on the *Totten* bar to hold that a case involving nuclear weapons secrets, and having nothing to do with espionage contracts, was "beyond judicial scrutiny." *** We therefore reject plaintiffs' unduly narrow view of the *Totten* bar and reaffirm our holding in *Al-Haramain* that the bar "has evolved into the principle that where the very subject matter of a lawsuit is a matter of state secret, the action must be dismissed without reaching the question of evidence." ***

We also disagree with plaintiffs' related contention that the *Totten* bar cannot apply unless the *plaintiff* is a party to a secret agreement with the government. The environmental groups and individuals who were the plaintiffs in *Weinberger* were not parties to agreements with the United States, secret or otherwise. The purpose of the bar, moreover, is to prevent the revelation of state secrets harmful to national security, a concern no less pressing when the plaintiffs are strangers to the espionage agreement that their litigation threatens to reveal. ***

B. The Reynolds Privilege. In addition to the *Totten* bar, the state secrets doctrine encompasses a "privilege against revealing military [or state] secrets, a privilege which is well established in the law of evidence." A successful assertion of privilege under *Reynolds* will remove the privileged evidence from the litigation. Unlike the *Totten* bar, a valid claim of privilege under *Reynolds* does not automatically require dismissal of the case. In some instances, however, the assertion of privilege will require dismissal because it will become apparent during the *Reynolds* analysis that the case cannot proceed without privileged evidence, or that litigating the case to a judgment on the merits would present an unacceptable risk of disclosing state secrets.

Reynolds involved a military aircraft carrying secret electronic equipment. After the plane crashed, the estates of three civilian observers killed in the accident brought tort claims against the government. In discovery, plaintiffs sought production of the Air Force's official accident investigation report and the statements of three surviving crew members.

The Air Force refused to produce the materials, citing the need to protect national security and military secrets. ***   The Supreme Court *** *** provided guidance on how claims of privilege should be analyzed and held that, under the circumstances, the district court should have sustained the privilege without even requiring the government to produce the report for in camera review. The Court did not, however, dismiss the case outright. Rather, given that the secret electronic equipment was unrelated to the cause of the accident, it remanded to the district court, affording plaintiffs the opportunity to try to establish their claims without the privileged accident report and witness statements.

Analyzing claims under the *Reynolds* privilege involves three steps:

First, we must "ascertain that the procedural requirements for invoking the state secrets privilege have been satisfied." Second, we must make an independent determination whether the information is privileged.... Finally, "the ultimate question to be resolved is how the matter should proceed in light of the successful privilege claim." ***

1. Procedural Requirements. *** "The privilege belongs to the Government and must be asserted by it*** " *** To ensure that the privilege is invoked no more often or extensively than necessary, *Reynolds* held that "[t]here must be a formal claim of privilege, lodged by the head of the department which has control over the matter, after actual personal consideration by that officer." *** In the present case, General Michael Hayden, then-Director of the CIA, asserted the initial, formal claim of privilege and submitted detailed public and classified declarations. *** [T]he current Attorney General, Eric Holder, has also reviewed and approved the ongoing claim of privilege. Although *Reynolds* does not require review and approval by the Attorney General when a different agency head has control of the matter, such additional review by the executive branch's chief lawyer is appropriate and to be encouraged.***

Plaintiffs contend that the Government's assertion of privilege was premature, urging that the *Reynolds* privilege cannot be raised before an obligation to produce specific evidence subject to a claim of privilege has actually arisen. We disagree. The privilege may be asserted at any time, even at the pleading stage *** rather than waiting for an evidentiary dispute to arise during discovery or trial. ***

2. The Court's Independent Evaluation of the Claim of Privilege. When the privilege has been properly invoked, "we must make an independent determination whether the information is privileged." The court must sustain a claim of privilege when it is satisfied, "from all the circumstances of the case, that there is a reasonable danger that compulsion of the evidence will expose ... matters which, in the interest of national security, should not be divulged." If this standard is met, the evidence is absolutely privileged, irrespective of the plaintiffs' countervailing need for it. *** We do not offer a detailed definition of what constitutes a state secret. *** We do note, however, that an executive decision to *classify* information is insufficient to establish that the information is privileged. *** [T]reating it as conclusive would trivialize the Court's role, which the Supreme Court has clearly admonished "cannot be abdicated to the caprice of executive officers."

3. How Should the Matter Proceed?   When a court sustains a claim of privilege, it must then resolve "'how the matter should proceed in light of the successful privilege claim.'"   The court must assess whether it is feasible for the litigation to proceed without the protected evidence and, if so, how. *** Ordinarily, simply excluding or otherwise walling off the privileged information may suffice to protect the state secrets and "'the case will proceed accordingly, with no consequences save those resulting from the loss of evidence.'"   *Al- Haramain,* 507 F.3d at 1204.

In some instances, however, application of the privilege may require dismissal of the action. When this point is reached, the *Reynolds* privilege converges with the *Totten* bar, because both require dismissal. There are three circumstances when the *Reynolds* privilege would justify terminating a case.

First, if "the plaintiff cannot prove the *prima facie* elements of her claim with nonprivileged evidence, then the court may dismiss her claim as it would with any plaintiff who cannot prove her case." Second, "'if the privilege deprives the defendant of information that would otherwise give the defendant a valid defense to the claim, then the court may grant summary judgment to the defendant.'"   Third, and relevant here, even if the claims and defenses might theoretically be established without relying on privileged evidence, it may be impossible to proceed with the litigation because-privileged evidence being inseparable from nonprivileged information that will be necessary to the claims or defenses-litigating the case to a judgment on the merits would present an unacceptable risk of disclosing state secrets. As we shall explain, this circumstance exists here and requires dismissal. ***

We therefore turn to the application of the state secrets doctrine in this case. *** [W]e conclude that *** dismissal is warranted even under *Reynolds*. Recognizing the serious consequences to plaintiffs of dismissal, we explain our ruling so far as possible within the considerable constraints imposed on us by the state secrets doctrine itself.

The categorical, "absolute protection [the Court] found necessary in enunciating the *Totten* rule" is appropriate only in narrow circumstances. *** The Court has applied the *Totten* bar on just three occasions, involving two different kinds of state secrets: In *Tenet* and *Totten* the Court applied the *Totten* bar to "the distinct class of cases that depend upon clandestine spy relationships," and in *Weinberger* the Court applied the *Totten* bar to a case that depended on whether the Navy proposed to store nuclear weapons at a particular facility. *** Because the *Totten* bar is rarely applied and not clearly defined, because it is a judge-made doctrine with extremely harsh consequences and because conducting a more detailed analysis will tend to improve the accuracy, transparency and legitimacy of the proceedings, district courts presented with disputes about state secrets should ordinarily undertake a detailed *Reynolds* analysis before deciding whether dismissal on the pleadings is justified.

Here, some of plaintiffs' claims *might well fall within the Totten* bar. In particular, their allegations that Jeppesen conspired with agents of the

United States in plaintiffs' forced disappearance, torture and degrading treatment are premised on the existence of an alleged covert relationship between Jeppesen and the government ***. On the other hand, allegations based on plaintiffs' theory that Jeppesen should be liable simply for what it "should have known" about the alleged unlawful extraordinary rendition program while participating in it are not so obviously tied to proof of a secret agreement between Jeppesen and the government.

We do not resolve the difficult question of precisely which claims may be barred under *Totten* because application of the *Reynolds* privilege leads us to conclude that this litigation cannot proceed further. *** [R]esolving this case under *Reynolds* avoids difficult questions about the precise scope of the *Totten* bar and permits us to conduct a searching judicial review, fulfilling our obligation under *Reynolds* "to review the [Government's claim] with a very careful, indeed a skeptical, eye, and not to accept at face value the Government's claim or justification of privilege."

There is no dispute that the government has complied with *Reynolds'* procedural requirements for invoking the state secrets privilege by filing General Hayden's formal claim of privilege in his public declaration. We therefore focus on *** *First*, whether and to what extent the matters the government contends must be kept secret are in fact matters of state secret; and *second*, if they are, whether the action can be litigated without relying on evidence that would necessarily reveal those secrets or press so closely upon them as to create an unjustifiable risk that they would be revealed. ***

1. Whether and to What Extent the Evidence Is Privileged. The government asserts the state secrets privilege over four categories of evidence. In particular, the government contends that neither it nor Jeppesen should be compelled, through a responsive pleading, discovery responses or otherwise, to disclose: "[1] information that would tend to confirm or deny whether Jeppesen or any other private entity assisted the CIA with clandestine intelligence activities; [2] information about whether any foreign government cooperated with the CIA in clandestine intelligence activities; [3] information about the scope or operation of the CIA terrorist detention and interrogation program; [or 4] any other information concerning CIA clandestine intelligence operations that would tend to reveal intelligence activities, sources, or methods." ***

We have thoroughly and critically reviewed the Government's public and classified declarations and are convinced that at least some of the matters it seeks to protect from disclosure in this litigation are valid state secrets, "which, in the interest of national security, should not be divulged." The Government's classified disclosures to the court are persuasive that compelled or inadvertent disclosure of such information in the course of litigation would seriously harm legitimate national security interests. In fact, every judge who has reviewed the Government's formal, classified claim of privilege in this case agrees that in this sense the claim of privilege is proper, although we have different views as to the scope of the privilege and its impact on plaintiffs' case. *** We are precluded from explaining precisely which matters the privilege covers lest we jeopardize the secrets we are bound to protect. We can say, however, that the secrets fall within one or more of the four categories identified by the government and that we have independently and critically confirmed that their disclosure could be expected to cause significant harm to national security.

2. *Effect on the Proceedings.* Having determined that the privilege applies, we next determine whether the case must be dismissed under the *Reynolds* privilege.[10] *** [W]e do not rely on the first two circumstances in which the *Reynolds* privilege requires dismissal-that is, whether plaintiffs could prove a prima facie case without privileged evidence, or whether the privilege deprives Jeppesen of evidence that would otherwise give it a valid defense to plaintiffs' claims.[11] Instead, we assume without deciding that plaintiffs' prima facie case and Jeppesen's defenses may not inevitably depend on privileged evidence. Proceeding on that assumption, we hold that dismissal is nonetheless required under *Reynolds* because there is no feasible way to litigate Jeppesen's alleged liability without creating an unjustifiable risk of divulging state secrets.

We reach this conclusion because all seven of plaintiffs' claims, even if taken as true, describe Jeppesen as providing logistical support in a broad, complex process, certain aspects of which, the government has persuaded us, are absolutely protected by the state secrets privilege. Notwithstanding that some information about that process has become public, Jeppesen's alleged role and its attendant liability cannot be isolated from aspects that are secret and protected. Because the facts underlying plaintiffs' claims are so infused with these secrets, *any* plausible effort by Jeppesen to defend against them would create an unjustifiable risk of revealing state secrets, even if plaintiffs

---

[10] As noted earlier, the district court did not conduct a detailed analysis of plaintiffs' several claims because it concluded that the subject matter of the entire case is a state secret and therefore dismissed under the *Totten* bar. One option, vigorously urged by the dissent, would be to remand to the district court for that court to conduct a more detailed analysis in the first instance. As the case has developed during these en banc proceedings, however, we find remand unnecessary because our own *Reynolds* analysis persuades us that the litigation cannot proceed. Although it would have been preferable for the district court to conduct this analysis first, we now have had to do it ourselves and it makes no sense to suspend our own judgment that-given the record before us and the nature of plaintiffs' claims-this case realistically cannot be litigated against Jeppesen without compromising state secrets. There is thus no point, and much risk, in remanding to the district court to go through the *Reynolds* analysis as the dissent would prefer. We accept and respect the principles that motivate the dissent, but those principles do not justify prolonging the process here.

[11] ***[A]t least some of plaintiffs' claims would require proof of an agreement or covert relationship between the government and Jeppesen. These claims might well be barred under *Totten* and certainly would fall even under a *Reynolds* analysis. The dissent, however, suggests that plaintiffs could establish a prima facie case for at least two of their claims without relying on privileged evidence and perhaps without any discovery at all-namely, that Jeppesen recklessly provided flight and logistical support for rendition flights while it knew or should have known its support was being used for forced disappearance and torture. Although our holding does not require us to resolve this question, we are not so sure. Plaintiffs' reliance on information set forth in the dissent's Appendix would have to overcome evidentiary and other obstacles, such as hearsay problems and the fact that the vast majority of the media reports cited as putting Jeppesen on notice were published *after* Jeppesen's services were alleged to have occurred. In any event, our own analysis under the third aspect of *Reynolds* persuades us these "knew or should have known" claims must be dismissed as well.

could make a prima facie case on one or more claims with nonprivileged evidence.

Here, further litigation presents an unacceptable risk of disclosure of state secrets no matter what legal or factual theories Jeppesen would choose to advance during a defense. Whether or not Jeppesen provided logistical support in connection with the extraordinary rendition and interrogation programs, there is precious little Jeppesen could say about its relevant conduct and knowledge without revealing information about how the United States government does *or does not* conduct covert operations. *** Although district courts are well equipped to wall off isolated secrets from disclosure, the challenge is exponentially greater in exceptional cases like this one, where the relevant secrets are difficult or impossible to isolate and even efforts to define a boundary between privileged and unprivileged evidence would risk disclosure by implication. In these rare circumstances, the risk of disclosure that further proceedings would create cannot be averted through the use of devices such as protective orders or restrictions on testimony.

Dismissal at the pleading stage under *Reynolds* is a drastic result and should not be readily granted. We are not persuaded, however, by the dissent's views that the state secrets privilege can never be "asserted during the pleading stage to excise entire allegations," or that the government must be required "to make its claims of state secrets with regard to specific items of evidence or groups of such items as their use is sought in the lawsuit."

A case may fall outside the *Totten* bar and yet it may become clear during the *Reynolds* analysis that dismissal is required at the outset. Here, our detailed *Reynolds* analysis reveals that the claims and possible defenses are so infused with state secrets that the risk of disclosing them is both apparent and inevitable. Dismissal under these circumstances, like dismissal under the *Totten* bar, reflects the general principle that "public policy forbids the maintenance of any suit in a court of justice, the trial of which would inevitably lead to the disclosure of matters which the law itself regards as confidential, and respecting which it will not allow the confidence to be violated."

* * *

Although we are necessarily precluded from explaining precisely why this case cannot be litigated without risking disclosure of state secrets, or the nature of the harm to national security that we are convinced would result from further litigation, we are able to offer a few observations.

First, we recognize that plaintiffs have proffered hundreds of pages of publicly available documents, many catalogued in the dissent's Appendix, that they say corroborate some of their allegations concerning Jeppesen's alleged participation in aspects of the extraordinary rendition program. As the government has acknowledged, its claim of privilege does not extend to public documents. Accordingly, we do not hold that any of the documents plaintiffs have submitted are subject to the privilege; rather, we conclude that even assuming plaintiffs could establish their entire case *solely* through nonprivileged evidence-unlikely as that may be-any effort by Jeppesen to defend would unjustifiably risk disclosure of state secrets. *Second,* we do not hold that the existence of the extraordinary rendition program is itself a state secret. The program has been publicly acknowledged by numerous government officials including the President of the United States. *** *Third,* we acknowledge the Government's certification at oral argument that its assertion of the state secrets privilege comports with the revised standards set forth in the current administration's September 23, 2009 memorandum, adopted several years after the government first invoked the privilege in this case. Those standards require the responsible agency to show that "assertion of the privilege is necessary to protect information the unauthorized disclosure of which reasonably could be expected to cause significant harm to the national defense or foreign relations." They also mandate that the Department of Justice "will not defend an invocation of the privilege in order to: (i) conceal violations of the law, inefficiency, or administrative error; (ii) prevent embarrassment to a person, organization, or agency of the United States government; (iii) restrain competition; or (iv) prevent or delay the release of information the release of which would not reasonably be expected to cause significant harm to national security." That certification here is consistent with our independent conclusion, having reviewed the Government's public and classified declarations, that the government is not invoking the privilege to avoid embarrassment or to escape scrutiny of its recent controversial transfer and interrogation policies, rather than to protect legitimate national security concerns.***

Our holding today is not intended to foreclose-or to pre-judge-possible *nonjudicial* relief, should it be warranted for any of the plaintiffs. Denial of a judicial forum based on the state secrets doctrine poses concerns at both individual and structural levels. *** Other remedies may partially mitigate these concerns, however, although we recognize each of these options brings with it its own set of concerns and uncertainties.

First, that the judicial branch may have deferred to the executive branch's claim of privilege in the interest of national security does not preclude the government from honoring the fundamental principles of justice. The government*** may be able to find ways to remedy such alleged harms while still maintaining the secrecy national security demands. For instance, the government made reparations to Japanese Latin Americans abducted from Latin America for internment in the United States during World War II. Second, Congress has the authority to investigate alleged wrongdoing and restrain excesses by the executive branch. *** Third, Congress also has the power to enact private bills. *** When national security interests deny alleged victims of wrongful governmental action meaningful access to a judicial forum, private bills may be an appropriate alternative remedy. Fourth, Congress has the authority to enact remedial legislation authorizing appropriate causes of action and procedures to address claims like those presented here. ***

For all the reasons the dissent articulates-including the impact on human rights, the importance of constitutional protections and the constraints of a judge-made doctrine-we do not reach our decision lightly or without close and skeptical scrutiny of the record and the Government's case for secrecy and dismissal. We expect our decision today to inform district courts that *Totten* has its limits, that every effort should be made to parse claims to salvage a case like this using the *Reynolds* approach, that the standards for peremptory dismissal are very high and it is the district Court's role to use its fact-finding and other tools to full advantage before it concludes that the rare step of dismissal is justified. We also acknowledge that this case presents a painful conflict between human rights and national security. As judges, we have tried our best to evaluate the competing claims of plaintiffs and the government and resolve that conflict according to the principles governing the state secrets doctrine set forth by the United States Supreme Court. ***

BEA, Circuit Judge, concurring:

*** I write separately only because I would decide this case under *Totten v. United States,* The *Totten* bar requires our courts to dismiss cases "where the very subject matter of the action" is "a matter of state secret." In this case, every claim in the Plaintiffs' complaint is based on the allegation that officials of the United States government arrested and detained Plaintiffs and subjected them to specific interrogation techniques. Those alleged facts, not merely Jeppesen's role in such activities, are a matter of state secret.

HAWKINS, Circuit Judge, with whom Judges SCHROEDER, CANBY, THOMAS, and PAEZ, Circuit Judges, join, dissenting:

*** The majority dismisses the case in its entirety before Jeppesen has even filed an answer to Plaintiffs' complaint. Outside of the narrow *Totten* context, the state secrets privilege has never applied to prevent parties from litigating the truth or falsity of allegations, or facts, or information simply because the government regards the truth or falsity of the allegations to be secret. Within the *Reynolds* framework, dismissal is justified if and only if specific privileged evidence is itself indispensable to establishing either the truth of the plaintiffs' allegations or a valid defense that would otherwise be available to the defendant.

This is important, because an approach that focuses on specific evidence after issues are joined has the benefit of confining the operation of the state secrets doctrine so that it will sweep no more broadly than clearly necessary. The state secrets doctrine is a judicial construct without foundation in the Constitution, yet its application often trumps what we ordinarily consider to be due process of law. This case now presents a classic illustration. Plaintiffs have alleged facts, which must be taken as true for purposes of a motion to dismiss, that any reasonable person would agree to be gross violations of the norms of international law, remediable under the Alien Tort Statute. They have alleged in detail Jeppesen's complicity or recklessness in participating in these violations. The government intervened, and asserted that the suit would endanger state secrets. The majority opinion here accepts that threshold objection by the government, so Plaintiffs' attempt to prove their case in court is simply cut off. They are not even allowed to attempt to prove their case by the use of nonsecret evidence in their own hands or in the hands of third parties.

It is true that, judicial construct though it is, the state secrets doctrine has become embedded in our controlling decisional law. *** But the doctrine is so dangerous as a means of hiding governmental misbehavior under the guise of national security, and so violative of common rights to due process, that courts should confine its application to the narrowest circumstances that still protect the Government's essential secrets.[1] When, as here, the doctrine is successfully invoked at the threshold of litigation, the claims of secret are necessarily broad and hypothetical. The result is a maximum interference with the due processes of the courts, on the most general claims of state secret privilege. It is far better to require the government to make its claims of state secrets with regard to specific items of evidence or groups of such items as their use is sought in the lawsuit. An official certification that evidence is truly a state secret will be more focused if the head of a department must certify that specific evidence sought in the course of litigation is truly a secret and cannot be revealed without danger to overriding, essential government interests. And when responsive pleading is complete and discovery under way, judgments as to whether secret material is essential to Plaintiffs' case or Jeppesen's defense can be made more accurately.

By refusing to examine the voluminous public record materials submitted by Plaintiffs in support of their claims,[2] and by failing to undertake an analysis of Jeppesen's ability to defend against those claims, the district court forced every judge of the court of appeals to undertake that effort. This was no small undertaking. Materials the government considers top secret had to be moved securely back and forth across the country and made available in a "cone of silence" environment to first the three-judge panel assigned the case and then the twenty-seven active judges of this court to evaluate whether the case merited en banc consideration. This quite literally put the cart before the horse, depriving a reviewing court of a record upon which its traditional review function could be carried out. This is more than a matter of convenience. Making factual determinations is the particular province of trial courts and for sound reason: they are good at it. *** Finding remand "unnecessary," as the majority does here not only rewards district courts for failing to do their job, but ensures that future appeals courts will have to do that job for them. *** Jeppesen has yet to answer or even to otherwise plead, so we have no idea what those defenses or assertions might be. Making assumptions about the contours of future litigation involves mere speculation, and doing so flies straight in the face of long standing principles of Rule 12 law by extending the inquiry to what *might* be divulged in future

---

[1] Abuse of the Nation's information classification system is not unheard of. Former U.S. Solicitor General Erwin Griswold, who argued the government's case in the Pentagon Papers matter, later explained in a *Washington Post* editorial that "[i]t quickly becomes apparent to any person who has considerable experience with classified material that there is massive overclassification, and that the principal concern of the classifiers is not with national security, but rather with governmental embarrassment of one sort or another." *** Even in *Reynolds,* avoidance of embarrassment-not preservation of state secrets-appears to have motivated the Executive's invocation of the privilege. *** Courts should be concerned to prevent a concentration of unchecked power that would permit such abuses.

[2] A summary of the some 1,800 pages of that information appears as an Appendix to this dissent.

litigation. *** Because of this fundamental defect in the posture of this matter, the remainder of the dissent focuses on the scope of the state secrets privilege rather than its application to speculative facts.

*** Courts have applied the *Totten* bar in one of two scenarios: (1) The plaintiff is party to a secret agreement with the government; or (2) The plaintiff sues to solicit information from the government on a "state secret" matter. More generally, the *Totten* bar has been applied to suits against the government, and never to a plaintiff's suit against a third-party/non-governmental entity.

Here, the "very subject matter" of this lawsuit is Jeppesen's involvement in an overseas detention program. Plaintiffs are neither parties to a secret agreement with the government, nor are they attempting, as the result of this lawsuit, to solicit information from the government on a "state secret" matter. Rather, they are attempting to remedy "widespread violations of individual constitutional rights" occurring in a program whose existence has been made public.

Totten's logic simply cannot be stretched to encompass the claims here, as they are brought by third-party plaintiffs against non-government defendant actors for their involvement in tortious activities. *** Instead of "avoid[ing] difficult questions about the precise scope of the *Totten* bar" the majority ought to have found the *Totten* bar inapplicable, and rejected the district Court's analysis. *Totten* cannot and does not apply to Plaintiffs' claims.

*** *Reynolds* cannot, as the majority contends, be asserted during the pleading stage to excise entire allegations. The majority argues that because pleadings can serve as evidence, the state secrets privilege "may be asserted at any time, even at the pleading stage." Thus, the majority argues, this court would be incorrect to conclude that neither the Federal Rules nor *Reynolds* would permit us to dismiss this case at the *pleadings stage* on the basis of an evidentiary privilege that must be invoked *during discovery* or *at trial*. In the majority's view, the privilege applies at the pleadings stage in such a manner that permits it to remove from a complaint any allegations where "secret and nonsecret information cannot be separated."

Whatever validity there may be to the idea that evidentiary privileges can apply at the pleadings stage, it is wrong to suggest that such an application would permit the removal of *entire allegations* resulting in out-and-out dismissal of the entire suit. *** Because the *Reynolds* privilege, like any other evidentiary privilege, " 'extends only to [evidence] and not to facts,' " it cannot be invoked to prevent a litigant from persuading a jury of the truth or falsity of an allegation by reference to non-privileged evidence, regardless whether privileged evidence might also be probative of the truth or falsity of the allegation.[13]

---

[13] Contrary to the majority's assertion, the *Reynolds* privilege cannot be asserted prospectively, without an examination of the evidence on an item-by-item basis. To conclude that *Reynolds*, like *Totten*, applies to prevent the litigation of allegations, rather than simply discovery of evidence, would be to erode the distinction between the two versions of the doctrine. ***

The majority claims there is "no feasible way to litigate Jeppesen's alleged liability *without creating an unjustifiable risk of divulging state secrets*,"[14] ignoring well-established principles of civil procedure which, at this stage of the litigation, do not permit the prospective evaluation of hypothetical claims of privilege that the government has yet to raise and the district court has yet to consider. *** The majority's analysis here is premature. This court should not determine that there is no feasible way to litigate Jeppesen's liability without disclosing state secrets; such a determination is the district Court's to make once a responsive pleading has been filed, or discovery requests made. We should remand for the government to assert the privilege with respect to secret evidence, and for the district court to determine what evidence is privileged and whether any such evidence is indispensable either to Plaintiffs' prima facie case or to a valid defense otherwise available to Jeppesen. Only if privileged evidence is indispensable to either party should it dismiss the complaint.

The majority concludes its opinion with a recommendation of alternative remedies. Not only are these remedies insufficient, but their suggestion understates the severity of the consequences to Plaintiffs from the denial of judicial relief. Suggesting, for example, that the Executive could "honor [ ] the fundamental principles of justice" by determining "whether plaintiffs' claims have merit," disregards the concept of checks and balances. Permitting the executive to police its own errors and determine the remedy dispensed would not only deprive the judiciary of its role, but also deprive Plaintiffs of a fair assessment of their claims by a neutral arbiter. The majority's suggestion of payment of reparations to the victims of extraordinary rendition, such as those paid to Japanese Latin Americans for the injustices suffered under Internment during World War II, over fifty years after those injustices were suffered elevates the impractical to the point of absurdity. Similarly, a congressional investigation, private bill, or enacting of "remedial legislation," leaves to the legislative branch claims which the federal courts are better equipped to handle.

Arbitrary imprisonment and torture under any circumstance is a "'gross and notorious ... act of despotism.' " But " 'confinement [and abuse] of the person, by secretly hurrying him to [prison], where his sufferings are unknown or forgotten; is a less public, a less striking, and therefore a more dangerous engine of arbitrary government.' " I would remand to the district court to determine whether Plaintiffs can establish the prima facie elements of their claims or whether Jeppesen could defend against those claims without resort to state secrets evidence. ***

---

[14] The majority cites *El-Masri v. United States,* 479 F.3d 296, 308-13 (4th Cir.2007), as a comparable case wherein the court found further litigation risked disclosure of state secrets and threatened grave harm to American national security. However, noting that the Fourth Circuit appears to have "merged the concept of 'subject matter' with the notion of proof of a prima facie case," this court in *Al-Haramain* expressly rejected *El-Masri*'s logic. In the Ninth Circuit, "the 'subject matter' of a lawsuit [is not necessarily] one and the same [as] the facts necessary to litigate the case." Accordingly, "[b]ecause the Fourth Circuit has accorded an expansive meaning to the 'subject matter' of an action, one that we have not adopted, *El-Masri* does not support dismissal based on the subject matter of the suit."

Notes

1. Certiorari? The ACLU announced immediately after this decision that it would be seeking reversal in the Supreme Court. Do you think the Court should review the case? If it reviews it, should it reverse or change the theory in any way?

2. Law of the Circuit. Explain how the ninth and fourth circuits differ in their views of state secrets doctrine. Which court has the better view?

3. Doctrinal Issues. Is *Totten* confined to agreements? Between the parties? Was *Reynolds* so different from *Totten* in application of the privilege? Is the decision a recipe for extensive involvement of the judiciary in the executive branch's rendition program? Is it a recipe for limiting the privilege in other contexts?

4. Facts and Law. Do the horrific allegations of the complaint matter? Is it relevant that the United States is asserting the privilege, not Jeppesen? Is it important that other countries, not the United States (at least not directly), were responsible for mistreatment of the plaintiffs?

3. DIPLOMATIC ASSURANCES

Many governments, including the United States, seek assurances from foreign governments that transferred individuals will be treated humanely and not face torture by the receiving government. These diplomatic assurances may relate to a specific individual or be part of a broader agreement between two governments. Diplomatic assurances may be embodied in a variety of media: a memorandum of understanding between the relevant governments, an exchange of letters, or another less formal written or oral agreement. Assurances may or may not include provisions for the subsequent monitoring transferred individuals. Moreover, the existence or terms of the assurances may or may not be disclosed to the transferred individuals, to judicial or administrative oversight bodies, or to the public more generally. As the case below illustrates, there continue to be outstanding questions regarding the legality of diplomatic assurances and what process the government must provide to individuals transferred following diplomatic assurances.

KHOUZAM v. CHERTOFF
549 F.3d 235 (3rd Cir. 2008)

RENDELL, Circuit Judge.

Sameh Sami S. Khouzam, a citizen of Egypt and a Coptic Christian, challenges the legality of his detention and imminent removal based on diplomatic assurances by Egypt that he would not be tortured if he was returned. In 1998, Khouzam was denied admission to the United States and taken into custody upon arriving without proper documentation. After years of proceedings, Khouzam was granted relief from removal because it was more likely than not that he would be tortured if returned to Egypt. His removal was deferred, rather than withheld, because there were serious reasons to believe that he committed a murder prior to departing Egypt. Khouzam was released from custody in 2006. In 2007, without notice or a hearing, the Department of Homeland Security ("DHS") again detained Khouzam, and prepared to remove him based on diplomatic assurances by Egypt that he would not be tortured. *** Khouzam argues that (1) the Government violated certain statutes and the Due Process Clause by failing to provide him a hearing to test the reliability of the diplomatic assurances; (2) diplomatic assurances from Egypt are categorically unreliable; and (3) the Government failed to comply with relevant regulations. The Government argues, in the alternative, that (1) federal courts lack jurisdiction to consider Khouzam's claims; (2) Khouzam's claims are non-justiciable; (3) Khouzam received all of the process to which he was entitled; and (4) the Government complied with all relevant regulations. ***

This matter comes to us after proceedings that spanned a decade. *** Khouzam was denied asylum and withholding of removal based on a determination that there were "serious reasons" to believe that Khouzam had committed a homicide before leaving Egypt.[20] *** Khouzam was eligible for relief under CAT based on a finding by the Immigration Judge ("IJ") that there was "overwhelming" evidence that Khouzam would be subjected to torture in Egypt *** [A]fter Khouzam had been in custody for eight years, the Court granted the petition after concluding that "there was no significant likelihood of [Khouzam's] removal in the reasonably foreseeable future." As a condition of release, Khouzam was required to report regularly to a Bureau of Immigration and Customs Enforcement ("ICE") facility in York, Pennsylvania, the city where Khouzam intended to reside.

When Khouzam reported to the ICE facility on May 29, 2007, he was retaken into custody and informed that he was subject to imminent deportation. Khouzam's counsel received the following explanation in a letter of the same date from Julie L. Myers, the DHS Assistant Secretary for the ICE:

> *** I have credited as sufficiently reliable the diplomatic assurances received by the Department of State from the Government of Egypt that your client, Mr. Khouzam, would not be tortured if removed there. The Secretary of Homeland Security has, therefore, *** terminated Mr. Khouzam's deferral of removal to Egypt *** . The Department of Homeland Security will not remove Mr. Khouzam to Egypt prior to June 1, 2007.

The Government provided no prior notice to Khouzam regarding the diplomatic assurances. Nor did the Government provide Khouzam any opportunity to review the assurances, or to present evidence or arguments challenging the assurances before an IJ, the BIA, or any other body. ***

---

[20] Neither asylum nor withholding of removal may be granted if "there are serious reasons to believe that the alien committed a serious nonpolitical crime outside the United States before the alien arrived in the United States." Only deferral of removal may be awarded to such an alien if there is a likelihood of torture.

At the heart of this case lie certain statutory and regulatory provisions implementing CAT in the United States, a treaty which was ratified by the Senate in 1990. *** Article 3 of CAT provides, without exception, that "[n]o State Party shall expel, return ('refouler') or extradite a person to another State where there are substantial grounds for believing that he would be in danger of being subjected to torture." *** On October 21, 1998, President Clinton signed into law the Foreign Affairs Reform and Restructuring Act of 1998 ("FARRA"), which was enacted by Congress to give Article 3 of CAT "wholesale effect" domestically. *See Medellin v. Texas*, 128 S. Ct. 1346, 1365 (2008).

FARRA establishes that,

> It shall be the policy of the United States not to expel, extradite, or otherwise effect the involuntary return of any person to a country in which there are substantial grounds for believing the person would be in danger of being subjected to torture, regardless of whether the person is physically present in the United States. Congress accordingly required "the heads of the appropriate agencies" to prescribe implementing regulations.

FARRA further provides that "[n]otwithstanding any other provision of law, and except as provided" in the implementing regulations themselves, "no court shall have jurisdiction to review the regulations adopted to implement" the provisions of section 2242. Congress also directed that "nothing in [§ 2242] shall be construed as providing any court jurisdiction to consider or review claims raised under the [CAT or § 2242], or any other determination made with respect to the application of the policy [stated in § 2242(a)], except as part of the review of a final order of removal pursuant to section 242 of the [INA]."

The Department of Justice ("DOJ") accordingly promulgated regulations that established procedures for raising a CAT claim. Under these regulations an alien is entitled to protection from removal if the alien can prove "that it is more likely than not that he or she would be tortured if removed to the proposed country of removal." Section 1208.18(c) establishes procedures for the use of diplomatic assurances, and reads in full:

> Diplomatic assurances against torture obtained by the Secretary of State.
>
> (1) The Secretary of State may forward to the Attorney General assurances that the Secretary has obtained from the government of a specific country that an alien would not be tortured there if the alien were removed to that country.
>
> (2) If the Secretary of State forwards assurances described in paragraph (c)(1) of this section to the Attorney General for consideration by the Attorney General or her delegates under this paragraph, the Attorney General shall determine, in consultation with the Secretary of State, whether the assurances are sufficiently reliable to allow the alien's removal to that country consistent with Article 3 of the Convention Against Torture. The Attorney General's

authority under this paragraph may be exercised by the Deputy Attorney General or by the Commissioner, Immigration and Naturalization Service, but may not be further delegated.

(3) Once assurances are provided under paragraph (c)(2) of this section, the alien's claim for protection under the Convention Against Torture shall not be considered further by an immigration judge, the Board of Immigration Appeals, or an asylum officer.

Section 1208.18 provides no limitations on when diplomatic assurances may be invoked, either in terms of particular categories of aliens, or the status of an alien's CAT claims in the adjudicatory process. It stands apart as a separate process that may be followed by the Government with respect to aliens with either ongoing or completed CAT proceedings.*** Of particular importance here, section 1208.17(f) provides for termination on the basis of diplomatic assurances, and reads in full:

At any time while deferral of removal is in effect, the Attorney General may determine whether deferral should be terminated based on diplomatic assurances forwarded by the Secretary of State pursuant to the procedures in § 1208.18(c).

Neither this paragraph, nor any provision in FARRA or the implementing CAT regulations, sets forth any procedures to be afforded the alien once the Attorney General makes a determination that a deferral should be terminated based on diplomatic assurances.***

Legality of the DHS's Termination of Khouzam's Deferral of Removal. Khouzam argues that no diplomatic assurance from Egypt could ever be sufficient to allow the Government to return him there under FARRA. *** We construe Khouzam's argument as an argument that the regulations must be interpreted under FARRA to preclude individualized determinations in his fact pattern. This argument must fail. Congress left it to responsible agencies to implement the obligations of the United States under CAT. *** We do not find it unreasonable for the DOJ to create a procedure for making an individualized determination, in every case, as to whether particular diplomatic assurances are sufficient to permit removal under FARRA. *** Thus, we reject Khouzam's argument that the diplomatic assurances from Egypt are categorically insufficient under FARRA and its implementing regulations.

Khouzam contends that we must interpret FARRA as requiring notice and a hearing prior to his removal in order to avoid serious constitutional questions that would otherwise arise. *** FARRA does not contain a provision for removal based on diplomatic assurances, and does not address what level of process is due to someone in Khouzam's position. ***Rather, Congress left the specific issue of CAT procedures to the Executive Branch by way of the authority to regulate. *** [T]the regulations adopted to implement FARRA set forth elaborate notice and hearing procedures for termination of deferral of removal in general cases. However, the terse portion of the regulation addressing termination on the basis of diplomatic assurances is silent with regard to what process, if any, is to be afforded the alien. There is nothing in the diplomatic assurance regulations themselves that we could fairly construe as providing an alien with any process whatsoever, let alone the right to a hearing.

While the statute and regulations do not *require* a specific procedure whereby Khouzam could challenge the diplomatic assurances, through notice and an opportunity to test their reliability at a hearing, neither do they specifically *preclude* such a procedure. *** By its terms, section 1208.18(c)(3) precludes an IJ, the BIA, or an asylum officer from "*further*" considering "the *alien's* claim for protection under [CAT]" once diplomatic assurances are proffered by the Government. We read this language only as requiring that any proceedings then underway must cease when the Government offers diplomatic assurances before an alien's substantive CAT claim has been resolved. Here, Khouzam's claim for protection under CAT was resolved by the Second Circuit before the Government proffered diplomatic assurances. The regulation does not refer to proceedings to test diplomatic assurances because such proceedings would not involve the "*alien's* claim for protection." Such proceedings would instead involve the *Government's* claim that diplomatic assurances are sufficiently reliable to justify removal, notwithstanding any likelihood of torture previously proven by the alien. Here, Khouzam seeks to challenge the use of a removal tool by the Government. Accordingly, neither the Government's assertion of diplomatic assurances, nor Khouzam's challenge to those assurances, fall within the purview of section 1208.18(c)(3).

Finding no statutory or regulatory provision that either affords or prohibits procedures to challenge diplomatic assurances, we next consider whether Khouzam was entitled to process. The Government, citing *Shaughnessy v. United States ex rel. Mezei*, 345 U.S. 206 (1953), and *United States ex rel. Knauff v. Shaughnessy*, 338 U.S. 537 (1950), argues that Khouzam is entitled to no process because he was intercepted prior to entry. *Mezei* established the "entry fiction" whereby an alien intercepted "on the threshold of initial entry," though physically present in the United States, stands on a "different footing" for due process purposes than an alien who has "passed through our gates." *Knauff* upheld regulations affording the Attorney General special powers to exclude aliens only during war or the existence of a specific national emergency proclaimed in May of 1941.

Neither case is applicable here. One dispositive difference is that Khouzam, unlike the aliens in *Mezei* and *Knauff*, has already been granted statutory relief from removal. Moreover, we have repeatedly held that aliens detained immediately upon arrival without proper documentation are entitled to due process of law during deportation proceedings implicating statutory relief from removal. *** In fact, the basic dictates of due process must be met whether an alien facing removal overstayed a visa, ***; entered the country undetected, ***; or became a legal resident but then committed an enumerated crime, ***. Further, we have recognized this right to due process not only where, as here, mandatory statutory relief from removal was at issue but also where the alien was seeking discretionary statutory relief. *** Khouzam was entitled to due process before he could be removed on the basis of the termination of his deferral of removal. Next, we determine whether the Government met this constitutional obligation.

In *Mathews v. Eldridge*, 424 U.S. 319 (1976), the Supreme Court explained that "[t]he fundamental requirement of due process is the opportunity to be heard at a meaningful time and in a meaningful manner." *** It is obvious that Khouzam was not afforded notice and a full and fair hearing prior to his imminent removal on the basis of diplomatic assurances. In fact, Khouzam was afforded no notice and no hearing whatsoever. *** The Government merely provided Khouzam with a cursory three-line letter dated three months after the termination decision had been made. Khouzam had no opportunity to develop a record with his own evidence. *** Second, Khouzam had no opportunity to make arguments on his own behalf. The Government argues that Khouzam, after receiving notice of the termination, could have sent the DHS a letter explaining why he thought the decision was wrong. We refuse to regard the general ability of an alien to correspond with an agency as sufficient to satisfy due process, particularly after the agency has decided the pertinent issue. In addition to whatever other flaws may exist in this purported opportunity to argue, we note that Khouzam would not have had the benefit of a neutral and impartial decisionmaker.*** [W]e conclude that the Government terminated Khouzam's deferral of removal without constitutionally sufficient process.

After establishing a due process violation, an alien facing removal must normally also demonstrate "substantial prejudice."***. Yet this case presents a special problem. The Government did not conduct a hearing or provide any meaningful record justification for the termination decision. Khouzam accordingly has no record upon which to base an argument, and we have no record upon which we may assess prejudice. Such a complete lack of process is inherently prejudicial. ***

We do not attribute the lack of due process to either FARRA or its implementing regulations, for neither expressly directed the Executive to act in a manner that offends the Fifth Amendment. *** The process of arriving at diplomatic assurances as outlined in the regulations is not problematic. It is the ability to test those assurances prior to removal, an issue not covered in the regulations, that gives us pause from the standpoint of due process. Both FARRA and its implementing regulations are silent as to the process to be afforded to an alien subject to removal on the basis of diplomatic assurances. Therefore, neither can be said to offend the Constitution facially, nor can any particular provision be identified that "reaches too far" under Khouzam's circumstances. Instead, the Executive, without relying on any statutory or regulatory provision, reached too far by failing to provide Khouzam constitutionally adequate process.

Because the Government violated the Due Process Clause by terminating Khouzam's deferral of removal without affording him an opportunity to test the reliability of Egypt's diplomatic assurances, the termination order was invalid. Since Khouzam was taken into custody on the basis of this invalid order, he must be restored to the pre-existing terms of release granted by the District Court of the District of New Jersey on February 6, 2006.

We will remand the matter to the BIA in order to ensure that Khouzam is afforded due process before he may be removed on the basis of diplomatic assurances. While it is not our role to define the procedures to be used, we follow the example of the Supreme Court and outline the basic requirements of due process in this context. *** Prior to removal on the basis of diplomatic assurances, Khouzam must be afforded notice and an opportunity to test the reliability of those assurances in a hearing ***. The alien must have an opportunity to present, before a neutral and impartial decisionmaker, evidence and arguments challenging the reliability of diplomatic assurances proffered by the Government, and the Government's compliance with the relevant regulations. The alien must also be afforded an individualized determination of the matter based on a record disclosed to the alien. We *** have no doubt that the Government can readily adapt such processes to removal based on diplomatic assurances.***

Notes

1. Reliability of Diplomatic Assurances. From what countries would a transferring government most likely seek diplomatic assurances—one more likely or less likely to engage in abusive practices? Does your answer make the need for diplomatic assurances more necessary? Less reliable? Under international law, countries are under an absolute duty not to expel, return or extradite any person to a country if there is risk torture or other ill-treatment. This principle, nonrefoulement, applies to transfers of individuals regardless of whether the grounds for transfer are immigration, criminal, or national security. No treaty currently addresses the use of diplomatic assurances. Does the use of diplomatic assurances demonstrate a disregard for international standards? Or can diplomatic assurances bridge the gap between the absolutes of international law and domestic security needs?

2. Disclosure of Diplomatic Assurances. Much of the debate over diplomatic assurances regards not whether or when they should be used—but who may be privy to their terms. The European Court on Human Rights recently held that diplomatic assurances do not absolve a court from the obligation to examine whether such assurances "provided, in their practical application, a sufficient guarantee that the applicant would be protected against the risk of treatment prohibited by the Convention." *Saadi v. Italy*, (ECHR) (2008)¶148. Would the disclosure of diplomatic assurances—to courts, to transferred individuals, or the public—reduce the willingness of countries to engage in assurances? What standards should a court utilize in assessing the reliability of diplomatic assurances? Is such an assessment the obligation of federal courts—or an inappropriate role for the courts, better left solely to the political branches?

3. Killing in Lieu of Rendition. While the United States has pursued capture, interrogation, and rendition of some terrorist suspects, it has explored at least two programs that aim to kill potential terrorists abroad without capture, interrogation or rendition. First, in 2009, CIA Director Leon Panetta briefed Congress that in 2001 the CIA had launched a program to utilize paramilitary teams to kill al Qaeda leaders. He also revealed that in 2004, the CIA contracted Blackwater, a North-Carolina based private security company, to undertake operational responsibility for the targeting of suspected terrorist commanders, training, and weaponry—but no missions were conducted before the program was canceled. The paramilitary program was devised as an alternative to the CIA's use of missile strikes using drone aircraft against al Qaeda operatives (used by the Clinton, Bush, and Obama Administrations). Panetta told lawmakers that Congress had not been earlier briefed on the paramilitary program because former Vice President Dick Cheney had instructed the CIA not to do so because the agency already had authority to kill al Qaeda leaders. Second, the Bush Administration argued that killing al Qaeda leaders was no different from killing a soldier in battle—and so not prohibited by executive order ban on assassinations signed by President Gerald Ford in 1976. What do you think of this argument? What diplomatic or practical issues might such a program face?

F. ISRAEL'S APPROACH TO ABUSIVE INTERROGATION

PUBLIC COMMITTEE AGAINST TORTURE IN ISRAEL v. STATE OF ISRAEL

Supreme Court of Israel sitting as High Court of Justice
H.C.J. 5100/94 (1999)

PRESIDENT A. BARAK

The General Security Service [hereinafter the "GSS"] investigates individuals suspected of committing crimes against Israel's security. Authorization for these interrogations is granted by directives that regulate interrogation methods. These directives authorize investigators to apply physical means against those undergoing interrogation, including shaking the suspect and placing him in the "Shabach" position. *** Are these interrogation practices legal? 1. Ever since it was established, the State of Israel has been engaged in an unceasing struggle for its security—indeed, its very existence. Terrorist organizations have set Israel's annihilation as their goal. Terrorist acts and the general disruption of order are their means of choice. In employing such methods, these groups do not distinguish between civilian and military targets. They carry out terrorist attacks in which scores are murdered in public areas—in areas of public transportation, city squares and centers, theaters and coffee shops. They do not distinguish between men, women and children. They act out of cruelty and without mercy. *** The GSS ***investigates those suspected of hostile terrorist activities. The purpose of these interrogations includes the gathering of information regarding terrorists in order to prevent them from carrying out terrorist attacks. In the context of these interrogations, GSS investigators also make use of physical means.

9. [*Shaking*] *** Among the investigation methods outlined in the GSS interrogation regulations, shaking is considered the harshest. The method is defined as the forceful and repeated shaking of the suspect's upper torso, in a manner which causes the neck and head to swing rapidly. According to an expert opinion *** the shaking method is likely to cause serious brain damage, harm the spinal cord, cause the suspect to lose consciousness, vomit and urinate uncontrollably and suffer serious headaches. ***[T]he state

argues that the shaking method is only resorted to in very specific cases, and only as a last resort. The directives define the appropriate circumstances for its use, and the rank responsible for authorizing its use. The investigators were instructed that, in every case where they consider the use of shaking, they must examine the severity of the danger that the interrogation is intending to prevent, consider the urgency of uncovering the information presumably possessed by the suspect in question, and seek an alternative means of preventing the danger. Finally, the directives state that, in cases where this method is to be used, the investigator must first provide an evaluation of the suspect's health and ensure that no harm comes to him. According to the respondent, shaking is indispensable to fighting and winning the war on terrorism. It is not possible to prohibit its use without seriously harming the ability of the GSS to effectively thwart deadly terrorist attacks. Its use in the past has lead to the prevention of murderous attacks.

10. ["Shabach" Position] *** [A] suspect investigated under the "Shabach" position has his hands tied behind his back. He is seated on a small and low chair, whose seat is tilted forward, towards the ground. One hand is tied behind the suspect, and placed inside the gap between the chair's seat and back support. His second hand is tied behind the chair, against its back support. The suspect's head is covered by a sack that falls down to his shoulders. Loud music is played in the room. According to the briefs submitted, suspects are detained in this position for a long period of time, awaiting interrogation. Petitioners claim that prolonged sitting in this position causes serious muscle pain in the arms, the neck and headaches. The state did not deny the use of this method. It submits that both crucial security considerations and the safety of the investigators require the tying of the suspect's hands as he is being interrogated. The head covering is intended to prevent contact with other suspects. Loud music is played for the same reason.

11. [The "Frog Crouch"] *** According to the petition, the suspect was interrogated in a "frog crouch" position. This refers to consecutive, periodical crouches on the tips of one's toes, each lasting for five minute intervals. ***

12. [Excessively Tight Handcuffs] *** [S]everal petitioners complained of excessively tight hand or leg cuffs. They contended that this practice results in serious injuries to the suspect's hands, arms and feet, due to the length of the interrogations. The petitioners contend that particularly small cuffs were used. The state, for its part, denies the use of unusually small cuffs, arguing that those used were of standard issue and were properly applied. Even so, the state is prepared to admit that prolonged hand or foot cuffing is likely to cause injuries to the suspect's hands and feet. The state contends, however, that injuries of this nature are inherent to any lengthy interrogation.

13. [Sleep Deprivation] In a number of petitions petitioners complained of being deprived of sleep as a result of being tied in the "Shabach" position, while subject to the playing of loud music, or of being subjected to intense non-stop interrogations without sufficient rest breaks. They claim that the purpose of depriving them of sleep is to cause them to break from exhaustion. While the state agrees that suspects are at times deprived of

regular sleep hours, it argues that this does not constitute an interrogation method aimed at causing exhaustion, but rather results from the long amount of time necessary for conducting the interrogation.

14. Before us are a number of petitions. *** All the petitions raise two essential arguments. First, they submit that the GSS is never authorized to conduct interrogations. Second, they argue that the physical means employed by GSS investigators not only infringe the human dignity of the suspect undergoing interrogation, but also constitute criminal offences. These methods, argue the petitioners, are in violation of international law as they constitute "torture." ***

15. According to the state, GSS investigators are authorized to interrogate those suspected of committing crimes against the security of Israel. *** With respect to the physical means employed by the GSS, the state argues that these methods do not violate international law. Indeed, it is submitted that these methods cannot be described as "torture," as "cruel and inhuman treatment," or as "degrading treatment," which are all strictly prohibited under international law. The state further contends that the practices of the GSS do not cause pain and suffering. Moreover, the state argues that these means are legal under domestic Israeli law. This is due to the "necessity defense" of article 34(11) of the Penal Law-1977. In the specific cases where the "necessity defense" would apply, GSS investigators are entitled to use "moderate physical pressure" as a last resort in order to prevent real injury to human life and well-being. Such "moderate physical pressure" may include shaking. Resort to such means is legal, and does not constitute a criminal offence. ***

22. An interrogation, by its very nature, places the suspect in a difficult position. "The criminal's interrogation," wrote Justice Vitkon over twenty years ago, "is not a negotiation process between two open and honest merchants, conducting their affairs in mutual trust."　*** Indeed, the authority to conduct interrogations, like any administrative power, is designed for a specific purpose, and must be exercised in conformity with the basic principles of the democratic regime. In setting out the rules of interrogation, two values clash. On the one hand lies the desire to uncover the truth, in accord with the public interest in exposing crime and preventing it. On the other hand is the need to protect the dignity and liberty of the individual being interrogated. This having been said, these values are not absolute. A democratic, freedom-loving society does not accept that investigators may use any means for the purpose of uncovering the truth. *** At times, the price of truth is so high that a democratic society is not prepared to pay. To the same extent, however, a democratic society, desirous of liberty, seeks to fight crime and, to that end, is prepared to accept that an interrogation may infringe the human dignity and liberty of a suspect—provided that it is done for a proper purpose and that the harm does not exceed that which is necessary. Concerning the collision of values, with respect to the use of evidence obtained in a violent police interrogation, ***

23. *** First, a reasonable investigation is necessarily one free of torture, free of cruel, inhuman treatment, and free of any degrading conduct whatsoever.

There is a prohibition on the use of "brutal or inhuman means" in the course of an investigation. Human dignity also includes the dignity of the suspect being interrogated. This conclusion is in accord with international treaties, to which Israel is a signatory, which prohibit the use of torture, "cruel, inhuman treatment" and "degrading treatment." These prohibitions are "absolute." There are no exceptions to them and there is no room for balancing. Indeed, violence directed at a suspect's body or spirit does not constitute a reasonable investigation practice. The use of violence during investigations can lead to the investigator being held criminally liable.

Second, a reasonable investigation is likely to cause discomfort. It may result in insufficient sleep. The conditions under which it is conducted risk being unpleasant. Of course, it is possible to conduct an effective investigation without resorting to violence. Within the confines of the law, it is permitted to resort to various sophisticated techniques. Such techniques—accepted in the most progressive of societies—can be effective in achieving their goals. In the end result, the legality of an investigation is deduced from the propriety of its purpose and from its methods. Thus, for instance, sleep deprivation for a prolonged period, or sleep deprivation at night when this is not necessary to the investigation time-wise, may be deemed disproportionate.

24. We shall now turn from the general to the particular. Clearly, shaking is a prohibited investigation method. It harms the suspect's body. It violates his dignity. It is a violent method which cannot form part of a legal investigation. It surpasses that which is necessary. Even the state did not argue that shaking is an "ordinary" investigatory method which every investigator, whether in the GSS or the police, is permitted to employ. The argument before us was that the justification for shaking is found in the "necessity defense." That argument shall be dealt with below. In any event, there is no doubt that shaking is not to be resorted to in cases outside the bounds of "necessity" or as part of an "ordinary" investigation.

25. It was argued before the Court that one of the employed investigation methods consists of compelling the suspect to crouch on the tips of his toes for periods of five minutes. The state did not deny this practice. This is a prohibited investigation method. It does not serve any purpose inherent to an investigation. It is degrading and infringes an individual's human dignity.

26. The "Shabach" method is composed of several components: the cuffing of the suspect, seating him on a low chair, covering his head with a sack, and playing loud music in the area. Does the general power to investigate authorize any of the above acts? Our point of departure is that there are actions which are inherent to the investigatory power. Therefore, we accept that the suspect's cuffing, for the purpose of preserving the investigators' safety, is included in the general power to investigate. Provided the suspect is cuffed for this purpose, it is within the investigator's authority to cuff him. The state's position is that the suspects are indeed cuffed with the intention of ensuring the investigators' safety or to prevent the suspect from fleeing from legal custody. Even petitioners agree that it is permissible to cuff a suspect in such circumstances and that cuffing constitutes an integral part of an interrogation. The cuffing associated with the "Shabach" position,

however, is unlike routine cuffing. The suspect is cuffed with his hands tied behind his back. One hand is placed inside the gap between the chair's seat and back support, while the other is tied behind him, against the chair's back support. This is a distorted and unnatural position. The investigators' safety does not require it. Similarly, there is no justification for handcuffing the suspect's hands with especially small handcuffs, if this is in fact the practice. The use of these methods is prohibited. As has been noted, "cuffing that causes pain is prohibited." Moreover, there are other ways of preventing the suspect from fleeing which do not involve causing pain and suffering.

27. The same applies to seating the suspect in question in the "Shabach" position. We accept that seating a man is inherent to the investigation. This is not the case, however, when the chair upon which he is seated is a very low one, tilted forward facing the ground, and when he is seated in this position for long hours. This sort of seating is not authorized by the general power to interrogate. Even if we suppose that the seating of the suspect on a chair lower than that of his investigator can potentially serve a legitimate investigation objective—for instance, to establish the "rules of the game" in the contest of wills between the parties, or to emphasize the investigator's superiority over the suspect—there is no inherent investigative need to seat the suspect on a chair so low and tilted forward towards the ground, in a manner that causes him real pain and suffering. Clearly, the general power to conduct interrogations does not authorize seating a suspect on a tilted chair, in a manner that applies pressure and causes pain to his back, all the more so when his hands are tied behind the chair, in the manner described. All these methods do not fall within the sphere of a "fair" interrogation. They are not reasonable. They infringe the suspect's dignity, his bodily integrity and his basic rights in an excessive manner. They are not to be deemed as included within the general power to conduct interrogations.

28. We accept that there are interrogation related concerns regarding preventing contact between the suspect under interrogation and other suspects, and perhaps even between the suspect and the interrogator. These concerns require means to prevent the said contact. The need to prevent contact may, for instance, flow from the need to safeguard the investigators' security, or the security of the suspects and witnesses. It can also be part of the "mind game" which pits the information possessed by the suspect, against that found in the hands of his investigators. For this purpose, the power to interrogate—in principle and according to the circumstances of each particular case—may include the need to prevent eye contact with a given person or place. In the case at bar, this was the explanation provided by the state for covering the suspect's head with a sack, while he is seated in the "Shabach" position. From what was stated in the declarations before us, the suspect's head is covered with a sack throughout his "wait" in the "Shabach" position. It was argued that the head covering causes the suspect to suffocate. The sack is large, reaching the shoulders of the suspect. All these methods are not inherent to an interrogation. They are not necessary to prevent eye contact between the suspect being interrogated and other suspects. Indeed, even if such contact is prevented, what is the purpose of causing the suspect to suffocate? Employing this method is not related to the

purpose of preventing the said contact and is consequently forbidden. Moreover, the statements clearly reveal that the suspect's head remains covered for several hours, throughout his wait. For these purposes, less harmful means must be employed, such as letting the suspect wait in a detention cell. Doing so will eliminate any need to cover the suspect's eyes. In the alternative, the suspect's eyes may be covered in a manner that does not cause him physical suffering. For it appears that, at present, the suspect's head covering—which covers his entire head, rather than eyes alone—for a prolonged period of time, with no essential link to the goal of preventing contact between the suspects under investigation, is not part of a fair interrogation. It harms the suspect and his dignity. It degrades him. It causes him to lose his sense of time and place. It suffocates him. All these things are not included in the general authority to investigate. In the cases before us, the State declared that it will make an effort to find a "ventilated" sack. This is not sufficient. The covering of the head in the circumstances described, as distinguished from the covering of the eyes, is outside the scope of authority and is prohibited.

29. Cutting off the suspect from his surroundings can also include preventing him from listening to what is going on around him. We are prepared to assume that the authority to investigate an individual may include preventing him from hearing other suspects under investigation or voices and sounds that, if heard by the suspect, risk impeding the interrogation's success. At the same time, however, we must examine whether the means employed to accomplish this fall within the scope of a fair and reasonable interrogation. In the case at bar, the detainee is placed in the "Shabach" position while very loud music is played. Do these methods fall within the scope or the general authority to conduct interrogations? Here too, the answer is in the negative. Being exposed to very loud music for a long period of time causes the suspect suffering. Furthermore, the entire time, the suspect is tied in an uncomfortable position with his head covered. This is prohibited. It does not fall within the scope of the authority to conduct a fair and effective interrogation. In the circumstances of the cases before us, the playing of loud music is a prohibited.

30. To the above, we must add that the "Shabach" position employs all the above methods simultaneously. This combination gives rise to pain and suffering. This is a harmful method, particularly when it is employed for a prolonged period of time. For these reasons, this method is not authorized by the powers of interrogation. It is an unacceptable method. "The duty to safeguard the detainee's dignity includes his right not to be degraded and not to be submitted to sub-human conditions in the course of his detention, of the sort likely to harm his health and potentially his dignity." ***

31. The interrogation of a person is likely to be lengthy, due to the suspect's failure to cooperate, the complexity of the information sought, or in light of the need to obtain information urgently and immediately. Indeed, a person undergoing interrogation cannot sleep like one who is not being interrogated. The suspect, subject to the investigators' questions for a prolonged period of time, is at times exhausted. This is often the inevitable result of an

interrogation. This is part of the "discomfort" inherent to an interrogation. This being the case, depriving the suspect of sleep is, in our opinion, included in the general authority of the investigator. *** The above described situation is different from one in which sleep deprivation shifts from being a "side effect" of the interrogation to an end in itself. If the suspect is intentionally deprived of sleep for a prolonged period of time, for the purpose of tiring him out or "breaking" him, it is not part of the scope of a fair and reasonable investigation. Such means harm the rights and dignity of the suspect in a manner beyond what is necessary.

32. All these limitations on an interrogation, which flow from the requirement that an interrogation be fair and reasonable, is the law with respect to a regular police interrogation. The power to interrogate granted to the GSS investigator is the same power the law bestows upon the ordinary police investigator. The restrictions upon the police investigations are equally applicable to GSS investigations. There is no statute that grants GSS investigators special interrogating powers that are different or more significant than those granted the police investigator. From this we conclude that a GSS investigator, whose duty it is to conduct the interrogation according to the law, is subject to the same restrictions applicable to police interrogators. ***

35. Indeed, we are prepared to accept that, in the appropriate circumstances, GSS investigators may avail themselves of the "necessity defense" if criminally indicted. This, however, is not the issue before this Court. We are not dealing with the criminal liability of a GSS investigator who employed physical interrogation methods under circumstances of "necessity." Nor are we addressing the issue of the admissibility or probative value of evidence obtained as a result of a GSS investigator's application of physical means against a suspect. We are dealing with a different question. The question before us is whether it is possible, *ex ante*, to establish permanent directives setting out the physical interrogation means that may be used under conditions of "necessity." Moreover, we must decide whether the "necessity defense" can constitute a basis for the authority of a GSS investigator to investigate, in the performance of his duty. According to the state, it is possible to imply from the "necessity defense"—available *post factum* to an investigator indicted of a criminal offence—the *ex ante* legal authorization to allow the investigator to use physical interrogation methods. Is this position correct?

36. In the Court's opinion, the authority to establish directives respecting the use of physical means during the course of a GSS interrogation cannot be implied from the "necessity defense." The "necessity defense" does not constitute a source of authority, which would allow GSS investigators to make use physical means during the course of interrogations. The reasoning underlying our position is anchored in the nature of the "necessity defense." The defense deals with cases involving an individual reacting to a given set of facts. It is an improvised reaction to an unpredictable event. *See* Feller, *supra* at 209. Thus, the very nature of the defense does not allow it to serve as the source of authorization. ***

The "necessity defense" has the effect of allowing one who acts under the circumstances of "necessity" to escape criminal liability. The "necessity defense" does not possess any additional normative value. It cannot authorize the use of physical means to allow investigators to execute their duties in circumstances of necessity. The very fact that a particular act does not constitute a criminal act—due to the "necessity defense"—does not in itself authorize the act and the concomitant infringement of human rights. *** Granting GSS investigators the authority to apply physical force during the interrogation of suspects suspected of involvement in hostile terrorist activities, thereby harming the suspect's dignity and liberty, raises basic questions of law and society, of ethics and policy, and of the rule of law and security. These questions and the corresponding answers must be determined by the legislative branch. This is required by the principle of the separation of powers and the rule of law, under our understanding of democracy.

38. We conclude, therefore, that, according to the existing state of the law, neither the government nor the heads of the security services have the authority to establish directives regarding the use of physical means during the interrogation of suspects suspected of hostile terrorist activities, beyond the general rules which can be inferred from the very concept of an interrogation itself. Similarly, the individual GSS investigator—like any police officer—does not possess the authority to employ physical means that infringe a suspect's liberty during the interrogation, unless these means are inherent to the very essence of an interrogation and are both fair and reasonable.***

39. This decision opened with a description of the difficult reality in which Israel finds herself. We conclude this judgment by revisiting that harsh reality. We are aware that this decision does not make it easier to deal with that reality. This is the destiny of a democracy—it does not see all means as acceptable, and the ways of its enemies are not always open before it. A democracy must sometimes fight with one hand tied behind its back. Even so, a democracy has the upper hand. The rule of law and the liberty of an individual constitute important components in its understanding of security. At the end of the day, they strengthen its spirit and this strength allows it to overcome its difficulties. This having been said, there are those who argue that Israel's security problems are too numerous, and require the authorization of physical means. Whether it is appropriate for Israel, in light of its security difficulties, to sanction physical means is an issue that must be decided by the legislative branch, which represents the people. We do not take any stand on this matter at this time. It is there that various considerations must be weighed. The debate must occur there. It is there that the required legislation may be passed, provided, of course, that the law "befit[s] the values of the State of Israel, is enacted for a proper purpose, and [infringes the suspect's liberty] to an extent no greater than required."

40. Deciding these petitions weighed heavily on this Court. True, from the legal perspective, the road before us is smooth. We are, however, part of Israeli society. Its problems are known to us and we live its history. We are not isolated in an ivory tower. We live the life of this country. We are aware

of the harsh reality of terrorism in which we are, at times, immersed. The possibility that this decision will hamper the ability to properly deal with terrorists and terrorism disturbs us. We are, however, judges. We must decide according to the law. This is the standard that we set for ourselves. When we sit to judge, we ourselves are judged. Therefore, in deciding the law, we must act according to our purest conscience. ***

Notes

1. **What is Prohibited?** Compare the U.S. Army and CIA interrogation standards with those in Israel. Would shaking, frog crouch, excessively tight handcuffs, or sleep deprivation be allowed under United States interrogation standards? Would waterboarding be allowed under Israeli standards?

2. **Educating the Enemy.** Has the Supreme Court of Israel supplied a template to terrorists who are captured, in essence letting them know exactly how far their interrogators can go and therefore letting them know that they will not have to endure more severe efforts to obtain information about other terrorists or future plans for attacks? Do you think the Israeli military would follow these guidelines if there was an imminent threat of death or injury to Israelis that the captured terrorist surely knew but would not voluntarily divulge? Would the necessity defense work in such a case?

3. **International Law.** Does the Supreme Court of Israel take international law more seriously than the United States Supreme Court? What factors might account for differences in treatment of international law other than judicial predispositions towards "narrow nationalistic" or "utopian one-world" views?

4. **Dignity.** The Supreme Court of Israel adopts a "harms the body" and "violates the dignity" approach. It then applies that approach to specific interrogation tactics. Do you agree with each application?

5. **It's About Us.** President Barak's famous Paragraph 39, which includes his famous quote on democracies fighting "with one hand tied," argues that democracies must avoid harsh interrogation so our values will not be undermined. Do you agree? Would you make any exceptions?

G. NON-INTERROGATION TREATMENT OF DETAINEES

There is a very thorough (1249 page) collection of documents "written by U.S. government officials to prepare the way for and to legitimize coercive interrogation and torture in Afghanistan, Guantanamo, and Abu Ghraib" entitled THE TORTURE PAPERS: THE ROAD TO ABU GHRAIB., edited by Karen J Greenberg and Joshua L. Dratel, (Cambridge University Press 2005). For a torture at Guantanamo, see http://slate.com/id/2119122/. Below is a short description of non-interrogation abuses.

By the Numbers:
Findings of the Detainee Abuse and Accountability Project
Human Rights Watch, April 2006

The DAA Project has to date documented at least 330 cases in which U.S. military and civilian personnel are alleged to have abused detainees, ranging from beatings and assaults, to torture, sexual abuse, and homicide. Among the cases:

- At least 600 U.S. personnel are implicated (numerous cases involve more than one perpetrator). Military personnel comprise over 95 percent of those implicated (at least 570 people), and at least ten CIA or other intelligence personnel are implicated, and approximately twenty civilian contractors working for either the military or the CIA.

- At least 460 detainees have been subjected to abuse, including people held in Iraq, Afghanistan, and at Guantánamo Bay.

- The majority of the approximately 330 cases took place in Iraq (at least 220 cases), followed by Afghanistan (at least sixty cases), and Guantánamo Bay (at least fifty cases).

- DAA Project researchers found that authorities opened investigations into approximately 210 out of the 330 cases (about 65 percent).

- In the remaining 35 percent of cases—approximately 120 cases— either no investigation was opened or the authorities have not publicly disclosed whether one took place. Over 70 percent of these 120 unresolved cases involve incidents that took place more than two years ago.

- The 210 cases in which there is evidence of an investigation involve at least 410 personnel (in many cases, more than one perpetrator is alleged to be involved in a case).

- Almost all of the military personnel who have been investigated are enlisted soldiers (approximately 95 percent of the total), not officers.

- Of the approximately 410 personnel implicated in cases that the military and civilian authorities have investigated, only about a third have faced any kind of disciplinary or criminal action. As of April 10, 2006, the DAA Project identified seventy-nine military personnel who were ordered by commanders for court-martial. (This number includes summary courts-martial conducted abroad, for which thirty days' confinement is the maximum sentence.) Only one person, a civilian contractor, has been indicted in federal court.

- Of the seventy-nine courts-martial ordered by commanders, fifty-four resulted in conviction or a guilty plea. Another fifty-seven people have faced non-judicial proceedings in which punishments include no or minimal prison time. (See box below on "Parallel Disciplinary Mechanisms: Criminal and Non-judicial Proceedings.")

- 75 percent of the cases in which investigations were conducted do not appear to have resulted in any kind of punishment (approximately 160 of the 210 investigated cases, involving approximately 260 accused personnel). The DAA Project found approximately 110 cases (involving approximately 190 accused personnel) were closed without punishment. And in at least fifty cases (involving at least seventy other people), the Project could not find any evidence that investigations had resulted in punishment and could not determine whether the case was still open. Researchers identified more than 1,000 individual criminal acts of abuse.

- The most common alleged types of abuse were assault (found in at least 220 cases), use of physical or non-physical humiliation (at least ninety cases), sexual assault or abuse (at least sixty cases), and use of "stress" techniques (at least forty cases). *******

Criminal Punishments: Verdicts and Sentencing

Even though approximately 600 U.S. personnel are implicated in the cases of detainee abuse documented by the DAA Project, as of April 10, 2006, only seventy-nine military personnel are known to have been recommended for court-martial, and only sixty-four appear to have actually been court-martialed. (This number includes eleven summary courts-martial, in which the maximum sentence is thirty days of confinement, and thirteen special courts-martial, in which the maximum sentence is one year). Ten courts-martial are still pending, and charges were dropped in the five other cases.

With respect to the sixty-four concluded courts-martial, the DAA Project found that:

- Approximately 85 percent—fifty-four of the sixty-four concluded courts-martial—resulted in guilty verdicts on at least one charge. (In at least five instances, the accused pled guilty before the verdict.) Ten defendants were acquitted of all charges or had verdicts overturned.

- Of the fifty-four guilty verdicts, forty resulted in sentences involving prison time (74 percent). In the other fourteen verdicts, defendants were sentenced to punishments not involving prison time, such as extra duty, discharge, or reduction in rank.

- In close to 75 percent of the sentences resulting in confinement (thirty out of forty instances), the punishment imposed was less than a year of prison time; the average sentence was about four months. The remaining ten personnel were sentenced to imprisonment for periods ranging from one year to one instance of life imprisonment; the average for the nine people sentenced to less than life was approximately four years. While those cases actually brought to court-martial produced a relatively high rate of conviction, punishments that included prison time were not consistent. Substantial prison sentences were given in a few high profile cases covered by the media, but a number of other equally serious cases resulted in punishments far less severe. Examples of people sentenced to significant prison time include Charles Graner and Ivan Frederick, both convicted for assaults and other misconduct in the notorious photographed abuses at Abu Ghraib prison in late 2003, who were sentenced to ten and eight years respectively. Two other soldiers have received heavy sentences: Sgt. Michael P. Williams and Spec. Brent May were convicted of murder for the killings of two men they detained near Baghdad in August 2004. Williams was sentenced to life in prison; May was given five years.

However, other serious cases resulted in light punishments. Examples include:

- In April 2003, a Marine in the 3rd Battalion, 5th Marine Regiment in Iraq was alleged to have "mock executed" four Iraqi juveniles by forcing them to kneel next to a ditch while the Marine fired his weapon to simulate an execution. He was found guilty of cruelty and maltreatment and sentenced to thirty days of hard labor without confinement, and a fine of $1,056.

- In April 2004, three Marines in the 2nd Battalion, 2nd Marine Regiment in Iraq were alleged to have shocked a detainee "with an electric transformer" during an interrogation. According to investigation documents, a Marine witness stated that one of the three Marines "held the wires against the shoulder area of the detainee and that the detainee 'danced' as he was shocked," a second Marine operated the transformer, and a third guarded the detainee. After court-martial, the first Marine was given one year of confinement and a dishonorable discharge; the second received eight months of confinement and a dishonorable discharge. The third Marine, the detainee's guard escort, was given sixty days of confinement.

- In June 2003, two soldiers were charged in summary courts-martial with assault for beating an Iraqi detainee. The investigation determined that one of the soldiers punched the detainee in the face several times and fractured his jaw, and that the other soldier also hit the detainee. Both soldiers were convicted of assault and were reduced in rank, ordered to forfeit pay, and were sentenced to sixty and forty-five days imprisonment, respectively. (Two other soldiers and a lieutenant were found guilty of assault in a non-judicial hearing and given punishments not involving prison time.)

- Two homicide cases from December 2002, in Afghanistan, have resulted in only minor punishments for the personnel prosecuted.

Notes

1. The Role of the Freedom of Information Act (FOIA). A significant amount of the information that the public knows regarding U.S. detention and interrogation programs has come through ACLU suits under the FOIA. Well before detainee treatment at Abu Ghraib became a national scandal, lawyers from the American Civil Liberties Union filed a request for information regarding the treatment of detainees in U.S. custody. Over a six-year period, this litigation produced over 100,000 pages of previously secret documents. The New York Times described that case as having "produced revelation after revelation: battles between the Federal Bureau of Investigation and the military over the treatment of detainees at the Guantánamo Bay prison camp; autopsy reports on prisoners who died in custody in Afghanistan and Iraq; the Justice Department's long-secret memorandums justifying harsh interrogation methods; and day-by-day descriptions of what happened inside the Central Intelligence Agency's overseas prisons." Scott Shane, "ACLU Lawyers Mine Documents for Interrogation Facts," NEW YORK TIMES (Aug. 29 2009).

The possible release of the documents (including Justice Department memos authorizing interrogation methods, the presidential order authorizing CIA black sites, and documents pertaining to internal CIA investigations of abuse of detainees), photographs, and interrogation videos that these suits seek has been hotly contested. The CIA court admits that it resists the release of documents, including the original authorization of the CIA black site program, because releasing CIA interrogation procedures "is reasonably likely to degrade the [U.S. Government's] ability to effectively question terrorist detainees and elicit information necessary to protect the American people."

Beginning in 2007, it came to light that the CIA, following considerable debate and ultimately authorization by internal legal counsel, had destroyed videotapes made during interrogation of top terrorism suspects. The tapes allegedly included footage of the water boarding of detainees. Both Congress and the Department of Justice launched probes into the legality of the destruction of the tapes. In 2009, the Obama Administration confirmed that the CIA had destroyed ninety-two tapes, constituting hundreds of hours, of interrogations.

What do you think is gained or lost by the disclosure of these documents, tapes, and photographs? For detainees? For the nation's security? For the ability of the people to control their government?

2. Twenty-One Photographs. The Department of Defense refused to release 21 photographs of prisoner abuse to the ACLU. DoD took the position before the District Court and the Second Circuit that exemptions in FOIA concerning law enforcement records that could endanger "any individual" (7(F) and a provision which shelters from release documents infringing the personal privacy of individuals (7C). Both courts rejected these arguments. See *ACLU v. DoD*, 543 F. 3d 59 (2d Cir. 2008). President Obama indicated he would abide by these orders. Before this occurred, however, the President changed his mind, apparently convinced that the disclosure might endanger American service members in Afghanistan, Iraq, and elsewhere. An appeal to the Supreme Court was authorized. The problem with this appeal was that the FOIA exemptions were not designed to deal with indirect national security problems that might arise from disclosures concerning abusive practices. Documents compiled for "law enforcement purposes" which might "endanger the life of any individual" stumbled on both prongs: an Army internal investigation was not "for law enforcement purposes" but rather for national security purposes and the unidentified possible servicemembers were not "any individual." With redactions, the photos did not infringe on the privacy of the victims of abuse. Finally, the Second Circuit rejected the Government's argument that the Geneva Conventions prohibited disclosure because the photos would subject the detainees to "insults and public curiosity." Do you see any ironies to the government positions on these issues?

3. Congress to the Rescue. While the case was pending in the Supreme Court, Congress passed Sec. 565 of the Homeland Security Appropriations Act, 2010, the "Protected National Security Documents Act of 2010." This legislation stated that certain documents which the Secretary of Defense certifies "would endanger citizens of the United States, members of the United States Armed Forces, or employees of the United States" should not be disclosed. These documents were defined as photographs taken between September 11, 2001 and January 22, 2009 "relating to treatment of individuals detained by the armed forces outside the United States." The provision was effective on the date of enactment and the Secretary immediately provided the required notice. Immediately thereafter, the Court issued a brief order granting certiorari, vacating the judgment of the Second Circuit, and remanding the case for reconsideration in light of the new law. *DoD v. ACLU*, 130 S. Ct. 777 (Nov. 30, 2009).

4. Suits by or on Behalf of Abused Detainees. The following case considers whether an individual abused while in detention can obtain monetary relief for this abuse. This case could be placed in Chapter XII, but because its content is so intimately bound up with issues of detention and a special problem of judicial review of detainee claims, we will consider it here.

AL-ADAHI v. OBAMA
596 F. Supp. 2d 111 (D.D.C. 2009)

GLADYS KESSLER, District Judge.

Petitioners Mohammad Ali Abdullah Bawazir and Zahir Omar Khamis Bin Hamdoon have been detained at the United States Naval Base at Guantanamo Bay, Cuba, since shortly after the terrorist attacks of September 11, 2001. They both have habeas corpus petitions pending before the Court. Petitioners bring this action against Respondents in order to enjoin certain treatment that they are undergoing as a result of the voluntary hunger strikes they have undertaken to protest their lengthy detentions without judicial scrutiny of the legality of such detentions. *** Parties do not dispute that Respondents' method for forced-feeding is to strap a hunger-striking detainee into a restraint-chair, with straps tightly restraining his arms, legs, chest, and forehead, and to administer a nutritional formula via a feeding tube inserted through one nostril. The process of administering the formula usually takes approximately one hour. ***

The Court wishes to emphasize, at the very beginning of its analysis, how seriously it has weighed the allegations made by Petitioners. The detainees at Guantanamo Bay have waited many long years (some have waited more than seven years) to have their cases heard by a judge so that the legality of their detention could be adjudicated in a court of law. During that time they, like all prisoners, have remained at the mercy of their captors. From all accounts-those presented in classified information the Court has had access to, in affidavits of counsel, and in reports from journalists and human rights groups-their living conditions at Guantanamo Bay have been harsh. There have been several episodes of widespread protests by the detainees, and many of them have engaged in hunger strikes of both short-term and very long-term (5 years and more) duration. Many detainees have complained of brutal treatment, lack of medical care, and long placements in solitary confinement. To this Court's knowledge, none of these allegations, or the Government's denials, have been fully tested and subjected to the rigors of cross-examination in open court. They may never be.

Despite being painfully aware of this situation *** this Court lacks jurisdiction and therefore does not have the authority to grant the relief they request. ***

Section 7 of the Military Commissions Act of 2006 ("MCA"), amends 28 U.S.C.A. § 2241. This section of the MCA deals with the right of enemy combatants to bring habeas corpus petitions, and to ask for relief related to their conditions of confinement; § 2241(e)(1), its first sub-section, was the provision under review in *Boumediene*. The amendment to its second sub-section, § 2241(e)(2), strips federal courts of jurisdiction as to "any other action against the United States ... relating to any aspect of the detention, transfer, treatment, trial, or conditions of confinement." Petitioners seek an injunction to alter the conditions under which they are force-fed and provided medical treatment. The relief they seek clearly falls under § 2241(e)(2). *See In re Guantanamo Bay Detainee Litigation*, 577 F.Supp.2d 312, 314 (D.D.C.2008) (Hogan, J.) (finding that request for blanket and pillow in cell "directly 'relat[es]' to Petitioner's 'detention, ... treatment, ... or conditions of confinement,' " under § 2241(e)(2)). If this section of the MCA remains valid after the decision in *Boumediene*, the Court has no jurisdiction to decide this Motion.

Petitioners challenge the validity of § 2241(e)(2) by arguing that the Supreme Court ruled all of Section 7 of the MCA unconstitutional in *Boumediene*. Their challenge must fail. Although the Court, resolves the question of jurisdiction by reference to the explicit language of *Boumediene*, case law, and canons of statutory interpretation, the issue is not absolutely clear-cut. However, any difficulty resolving the jurisdictional issue only argues in favor of denying Petitioners' request. *See Munaf,* 128 S.Ct. at 2219 (noting that difficult jurisdictional issues make "success more *unlikely* due to potential impediments to even reaching the merits") (emphasis in original). *Boumediene* struck down as unconstitutional § 2241(e)(1), which denied detainees the right to habeas corpus review in federal court. In doing so, the Supreme Court, in clear and direct language, refused to address "the reach of the writ with respect to claims of unlawful conditions of treatment or confinement." Those are precisely the claims which Petitioners raise in the pending Motion.

In addition to the Supreme Court's own language, there is a presumption that when a court invalidates a statute as unconstitutional, it does soon grounds drawn as narrowly as possible. ***

Finally, the Court finds persuasive the analysis of other judges in this District who have also considered the issue. Three judges have now ruled that *Boumediene* did not invalidate § 2241(e)(2). *** Here *** the two provisions of § 2241(e) do not flow from a common Congressional intent, i.e., limiting judicial review of detention. Rather, § 2241(e)(1) dealt with challenges to the legal justification for detention, whereas § 2241(e)(2) deals with challenges to "aspect[s]" of that detention, namely the conditions of such detention. The two subsections address separate and distinct topics *** [T]here is reason to believe that the "legislature [would] have preferred what is left of [this] statute to no statute at all [.]" ***

The Supreme Court has held that "[a] prison official's 'deliberate indifference' to a substantial risk of serious harm to an inmate violates the Eighth Amendment." *Farmer v. Brennan,* 511 U.S. 825 (1994). To determine whether an official acted with such indifference, courts look to the official's subjective awareness of the risk. Additionally, courts facing these issues must be mindful of the limits of their expertise in evaluating prison policies. A regulation that "impinges on inmates' constitutional rights" may still be valid if "it is reasonably related to legitimate penological interests."

At oral argument, the parties agreed that for a court to intervene in conditions of confinement decisions, the actions of the prison staff must demonstrate "deliberate indifference" to the detainee's well-being. *** Courts considering similar cases have found that force-feeding hunger-strikers, or the use of a restraint-chair, does not in and of itself sink to the level of deliberate indifference. *** Respondents' treatment of these Petitioners does not approach "deliberate indifference." Respondents are acting out of a need to preserve the life of the Petitioners rather than letting them die from their hunger strikes. The use of the restraint-chair has been determined to be necessary to achieve that end. It is standard policy to use the restraints on all hunger-striking detainees, with less restraint used for those who, like Petitioner Bawazir, are compliant. Use of the chair has been vetted by officials from the Bureau of Prisons, is overseen by professional medical staff, and was initiated by Respondents only after using less restrictive measures that were met with resistance from detainees.

Although there is evidence that Petitioners were kept in the restraint-chair for a longer period than Respondents admit to, such extended periods of force-feeding and restraint do not in and of themselves reflect deliberate indifference. *** [T]he restraint-chair is used as a matter of policy to protect staff and detainees; restraints are lessened for compliant detainees like Bawazir. Petitioners insist that the use of the chair on a compliant detainee amounts to such an unnecessary and painful restriction that it is tantamount to torture.[12] Resolution of this issue requires the exercise of penal and medical discretion by staff with the appropriate expertise, and is precisely the type of question that federal courts, lacking that expertise, leave to the discretion of those who do possess such expertise. *** Petitioners do not allege that use of the restraint-chair poses a risk of death or grave danger or

---

[12] Curiously, neither party devotes any serious attention in their pleadings to the definition of "torture" and whether the conduct in question meets that definition. Given the parties' avoidance of the issue, as well as the conclusion that the Court lacks jurisdiction, it is not necessary to reach the issue.

permanent injury to Petitioners. *** [T]he treatment of these two Petitioners-namely, the use of a restraint-chair for forced-feeding-does not in and of itself demonstrate that irreparable injury is likely. Short of establishing this, Petitioners cannot prevail on this factor.[13]

Additionally, Respondents have demonstrated that they are delivering the regular medical care that the declarations attest to. *** Respondents have demonstrated, based on prior experience, that significant harm could befall medical and security staff at Guantanamo Bay if the injunction is granted. *** An injunction that interferes with the restraint-chair protocols for these Petitioners-however compliant they may be at the moment-could endanger medical staff in the future if Petitioners become combative or assaultive.

In addition, the possibility that granting the injunction could provide other detainees with a roadmap of how to evade the restraint-chair policy. *** Any order to prohibit its use could upset the balance of security that Respondents have worked-and, unlike the Court, have been trained-to achieve. *** Petitioners have failed to demonstrate that barring the use of a restraint-chair for them would further the public interest. ***

Notes

1. Jurisdiction and Merits. The bulk of the case excerpt deals with the Court's lack of jurisdiction. Why then would the court proceed to discuss the lack of merit to the claim?

2. FOIA and Abuse Cases. Suppose a detainee alleging abuse sought unredacted pictures of detainees being abused to help prove he was abused. If you were a district judge hearing such a request, how would you rule?

3. General Credibility. Why didn't the district court rule on al-Adahi's general credibility?

---

[13] The Court does not minimize what Petitioners are suffering. It is impossible to fully assess the extent of any such suffering they may be experiencing without exposing them to the searchlight of in-person testimony and cross-examination. However, they have chosen to express their protest by engaging in a hunger strike. It is the obligation of the Government to keep them alive.

VII

RELEASE FROM MILITARY DETENTION

The extent of the showing required of the Government in these cases is a matter to be determined. We need not explore it further at this stage. We do hold that when the judicial power to issue habeas corpus properly is invoked the judicial officer must have adequate authority to make a determination in light of the relevant law and facts and to formulate and issue appropriate orders for relief, including, if necessary, an order directing the prisoner's release.

Rasul v. Bush, 542 U.S. 466 (2004)

We make no attempt to anticipate all of the evidentiary and access-to-counsel issues that will arise during the course of the detainees' habeas corpus proceedings. *** [O]ur opinion does not address the content of the law that governs petitioners' detention. That is a matter yet to be determined.

Boumedienne v. Bush, 553 U.S. 723 (2008)

Release from military detention can come through judicial decision, administrative action, or escape. The first avenue, judicial decision, is the most interesting legally and will occupy the bulk of this chapter. However, administrative action is by far the most common route for release. There will be no coverage of escape, an extralegal event that is very uncommon in the context of terrorist suspects, at least when the United States is the custodian of the detainees.

Habeas corpus is covered in this chapter in three parts. Section A explores the fundamentals of habeas corpus jurisdiction through the interaction between Congress and the Supreme Court over whether habeas corpus extends to detainees at Guantanamo Bay. Section B considers habeas jurisdiction and its exercise in Afghanistan and Iraq, other U.S. fronts in the "war on terror." Section C turns back to Guantanamo, this time to look at implementation of habeas process and substance by the district and circuit courts in the District of Columbia following resolution of the jurisdictional issues treated in Section A.

Sections D and E, respectively, deal briefly with administrative release from military custody and detention options used by other countries.

A. HABEAS CORPUS JURISDICTION: GUANTANAMO

The writ of habeas corpus is the primary way prisoners held by the United States have challenged the legality of detention and obtained orders for release. Habeas, sometimes called "The Great Writ," has long been the fundamental safeguard of liberty, for it is a critical mechanism by which substantive liberties are implemented by the courts.

Habeas corpus means "Thou (shalt) have the body." The writ has ancient English roots in the Magna Carta of 1215, was developed at common law in England in the sixteenth century to challenge both criminal and non-criminal confinement, and was written into British statue in the Habeas Corpus Act of 1679. At common law, the writ was aimed at ensuring that officials who had been delegated the power of the Crown, especially jailers, were not abusing that power. *See* Sir Matthew Hale's THE PREROGATIVE OF THE KING 228-29 (D.E.C., ed., London: Bernard Quaritch, 1975).

In the United States, the Framers included the writ as one of the few individual rights protected in the Constitution prior to adoption of the Bill of Rights. The Suspension Clause (Art. I, Sec. 9, Cl. 2) provides: "The privilege of the Writ of Habeas Corpus shall not be suspended, unless when in Cases of Rebellion or Invasion the public Safety may require it." Congress granted federal courts jurisdiction over habeas petitions in the statute that firstestablished the federal courts, the Judiciary Act of 1789. The current version of this statute, 28 USC § 2241, is discussed in the following cases. There are, therefore, both statutory and constitutional bases for habeas corpus.

1. STATUTORY HABEAS AVAILABILITY

After the September 11 attacks, President Bush issued a Military Order dated November 13, 2001. 66 FR 57833. Section 7(b)(2) of this order stated that, with respect to non-U.S. citizens detained "the individual shall not be privileged to seek any remedy or maintain any proceeding, directly or indirectly *** in (i) any court of the United States, or any State thereof, (ii) any court of any foreign nation, or (iii) any international tribunal."

The Supreme Court, in *Rasul v. Bush*, 542 U.S. 466 (2004), held that the federal habeas corpus statute gave federal courts jurisdiction over the claims of prisoners detained in a DoD facility at Guantanamo Bay, Cuba to challenge their detention, despite the President's order. The Court distinguished a World War II case *Johnson v. Eisentrager*, 339 U.S. 763, (1950) which held that constitutional habeas corpus did not reach an alien detained in Germany by United States military authorities. Here are some excerpts from *Rasul* which discuss and distinguish *Eisentrager*:

RASUL v. BUSH
542 U.S. 466 (2004)

JUSTICE STEVENS delivered the opinion of the Court.

These two cases present the narrow but important question whether United States courts lack jurisdiction to consider challenges to the legality of the detention of foreign nationals captured abroad in connection with hostilities and incarcerated at the Guantanamo Bay Naval Base, Cuba. *** Petitioners in these cases are 2 Australian citizens and 12 Kuwaiti citizens who were captured abroad during hostilities between the United States and the Taliban. Since early 2002, the U.S. military has held them—long with, according to the Government's estimate, approximately 640 other non-Americans captured abroad—at the Naval Base at Guantanamo Bay. The United States occupies the Base, which comprises 45 square miles of land and water along the southeast coast of Cuba, pursuant to a 1903 Lease Agreement executed with the newly independent Republic of Cuba in the aftermath of the Spanish-American War. Under the Agreement, "the United States recognizes the continuance of the ultimate sovereignty of the Republic of Cuba over the [leased areas]," while "the Republic of Cuba consents that during the period of the occupation by the United States ... the United States shall exercise complete jurisdiction and control over and within said areas." In 1934, the parties entered into a treaty providing that, absent an agreement to modify or abrogate the lease, the lease would remain in effect "[s]o long as the United States of America shall not abandon the ... naval station of Guantanamo." ***

Congress has granted federal district courts, "within their respective jurisdictions," the authority to hear applications for habeas corpus by any person who claims to be held "in custody in violation of the Constitution or laws or treaties of the United States." 28 U.S.C. § 2241(a), (c)(3). The statute traces its ancestry to the first grant of federal court jurisdiction: Section 14 of the Judiciary Act of 1789 authorized federal courts to issue the writ of habeas corpus to prisoners "in custody, under or by colour of the authority of the United States, or committed for trial before some court of the same." Act of Sept. 24, 1789, ch. 20, §14, 1 Stat. 82. In 1867, Congress extended the protections of the writ to "all cases where any person may be restrained of his or her liberty in violation of the constitution, or of any treaty or law of the United States." Act of Feb. 5, 1867, ch. 28, 14 Stat. 385.

Habeas corpus is, however, "a writ antecedent to statute, ... throwing its root deep into the genius of our common law." The writ appeared in English law several centuries ago, became "an integral part of our common-law heritage" by the time the Colonies achieved independence, and received explicit recognition in the Constitution, which forbids suspension of "[t]he Privilege of the Writ of Habeas Corpus ... unless when in Cases of Rebellion or Invasion the public Safety may require it," Art. I, §9, cl. 2.

As it has evolved over the past two centuries, the habeas statute clearly has expanded habeas corpus "beyond the limits that obtained during the 17th and 18th centuries." But "[a]t its historical core, the writ of habeas corpus has served as a means of reviewing the legality of Executive detention, and it is in that context that its protections have been strongest." *INS v. St. Cyr,* 533 U.S. 289 (2001). *** The question now before us is whether the habeas statute confers a right to judicial review of the legality of Executive detention of aliens in a territory over which the United States exercises plenary and exclusive jurisdiction, but not "ultimate sovereignty."

Respondents' primary submission is that the answer to the jurisdictional question is controlled by our decision in [*Johnson v.*]*Eisentrager,* 339 U.S. 763 (1950). In that case, we held that a Federal District Court lacked authority to issue a writ of habeas corpus to 21 German citizens who had been captured by U.S. forces in China, tried and convicted of war crimes by an American military commission headquartered in Nanking, and incarcerated in the Landsberg Prison in occupied Germany. *** [T]his Court summarized the six critical facts in the case:

> We are here confronted with a decision whose basic premise is that these prisoners are entitled, as a constitutional right, to sue in some court of the United States for a writ of *habeas corpus*. To support that assumption we must hold that a prisoner of our military authorities is constitutionally entitled to the writ, even though he (a) is an enemy alien; (b) has never been or resided in the United States; (c) was captured outside of our territory and there held in military custody as a prisoner of war; (d) was tried and convicted by a Military Commission sitting outside the United States; (e) for offenses against laws of war committed outside the United States; (f) and is at all times imprisoned outside the United States.

On this set of facts, the Court concluded, "no right to the writ of *habeas corpus* appears."

Petitioners in these cases differ from the *Eisentrager* detainees in important respects: They are not nationals of countries at war with the United States, and they deny that they have engaged in or plotted acts of aggression against the United States; they have never been afforded access to any tribunal, much less charged with and convicted of wrongdoing; and for more than two years they have been imprisoned in territory over which the United States exercises exclusive jurisdiction and control. [Moreover,] the Court in *Eisentrager* made quite clear that all six of the facts critical to its disposition were relevant only to the question of the prisoners' *constitutional* entitlement to habeas corpus. The Court had far less to say on the question of the petitioners' *statutory* entitlement to habeas review. ***

Putting *Eisentrager* *** to one side, Respondents contend that we can discern a limit on [the federal habeas statute] through application of the "longstanding principle of American law" that congressional legislation is presumed not to have extraterritorial application unless such intent is clearly manifested. *EEOC v. Arabian American Oil Co.,* 499 U.S. 244 (1991). Whatever traction the presumption against extraterritoriality might have in other contexts, it certainly has no application to the operation of the habeas statute with respect to persons detained within "the territorial jurisdiction" of the United States. By the express terms of its agreements with Cuba, the United States exercises "complete jurisdiction and control" over the Guantanamo Bay Naval Base, and may continue to exercise such control permanently if it so chooses. Respondents themselves concede that the habeas statute would create federal-court jurisdiction over the claims of an American citizen held at the base. Considering that the statute draws no distinction between Americans and aliens held in federal custody, there is little reason to think that Congress intended the geographical coverage of the statute to vary depending on the detainee's citizenship. Aliens held at the base, no less than American citizens, are entitled to invoke the federal courts' authority under § 2241.

Application of the habeas statute to persons detained at the base is consistent with the historical reach of the writ of habeas corpus. At common law, courts exercised habeas jurisdiction over the claims of aliens detained within sovereign territory of the realm, as well as the claims of persons detained in the so-called "exempt jurisdictions," where ordinary writs did not run, and all other dominions under the sovereign's control. ***

In the end, the answer to the question presented is clear. Petitioners contend that they are being held in federal custody in violation of the laws of the United States.[15] No party questions the District Court's jurisdiction over petitioners' custodians. Section 2241, by its terms, requires nothing more. We therefore hold that §2241 confers on the District Court jurisdiction to hear petitioners' habeas corpus challenges to the legality of their detention at the Guantanamo Bay Naval Base. *** [T]he federal courts have jurisdiction to determine the legality of the Executive's potentially indefinite detention of individuals who claim to be wholly innocent of wrongdoing. ***

JUSTICE KENNEDY, concurring in the judgment.

*** In my view, the correct course is to follow the framework of *Eisentrager*. *** *Eisentrager* indicates there is a realm of political authority over military affairs where the judicial power may not enter. The existence of this realm acknowledges the power of the President as Commander in Chief, and the joint role of the President and the Congress, in the conduct of military affairs. A faithful application of *Eisentrager,* then, requires an initial inquiry into the general circumstances of the detention to determine whether the Court has the authority to entertain the petition and to grant relief after considering all of the facts presented. A necessary corollary of *Eisentrager* is that there are circumstances in which the courts maintain the power and the responsibility to protect persons from unlawful detention even where military affairs are implicated.

The facts here are distinguishable from those in *Eisentrager* in two critical ways, leading to the conclusion that a federal court may entertain the petitions. First, Guantanamo Bay is in every practical respect a United States territory, and it is one far removed from any hostilities. *** The second critical set of facts is that the detainees at Guantanamo Bay are being held indefinitely, and without benefit of any legal proceeding to determine their status. *** Perhaps, where detainees are taken from a zone of hostilities, detention without proceedings or trial would be justified by military necessity for a matter of weeks; but as the period of detention stretches from months to

---

[15] Petitioners' allegations—that, although they have engaged neither in combat nor in acts of terrorism against the United States, they have been held in Executive detention for more than two years in territory subject to the long-term, exclusive jurisdiction and control of the United States, without access to counsel and without being charged with any wrongdoing—unquestionably describe "custody in violation of the Constitution or laws or treaties of the United States."

years, the case for continued detention to meet military exigencies becomes weaker. *** I would hold that federal-court jurisdiction is permitted in these cases. This approach would avoid creating automatic statutory authority to adjudicate the claims of persons located outside the United States, and remains true to the reasoning of *Eisentrager.* ***

JUSTICE SCALIA, with whom THE CHIEF JUSTICE and JUSTICE THOMAS join, dissenting.

The Court today holds that the habeas statute extends to aliens detained by the United States military overseas, outside the sovereign borders of the United States and beyond the territorial jurisdictions of all its courts. This is not only a novel holding; it contradicts a half-century old precedent on which the military undoubtedly relied, *Johnson v. Eisentrager.* *** I would leave it to Congress to change § 2241, and dissent from the Court's unprecedented holding. *** Even a cursory reading of the habeas statute shows that it presupposes a federal district court with territorial jurisdiction over the detainee. *** Here, as the Court allows, the Guantanamo Bay detainees are not located within the territorial jurisdiction of any federal district court. One would think that is the end of this case. *** [T]he [*Eisentrager*] opinion *had* to pass judgment on whether the statute granted jurisdiction, since that was the basis for the judgments of both lower courts. A conclusion of no constitutionally conferred right would obviously not support reversal of a judgment that rested upon a statutorily conferred right. And absence of a right to the writ under the clear wording of the habeas statute is what the *Eisentrager* opinion held: "Nothing in the text of the Constitution extends such a right, *nor does anything in our statutes.*" "[T]hese prisoners at no relevant time were within any territory over which the United States is sovereign, and the scenes of their offense, their capture, their trial and their punishment *were all beyond the territorial jurisdiction of any court of the United States.*" *** *Eisentrager*'s directly-on-point statutory holding makes it exceedingly difficult for the Court to reach the result it desires today. *** Today, the Court springs a trap on the Executive, subjecting Guantanamo Bay to the oversight of the federal courts even though it has never before been thought to be within their jurisdiction—and thus making it a foolish place to have housed alien wartime detainees.

In abandoning the venerable statutory line drawn in *Eisentrager,* the Court boldly extends the scope of the habeas statute to the four corners of the earth *** The consequence of this holding, as applied to aliens outside the country, is breathtaking. It permits an alien captured in a foreign theater of active combat to bring a § 2241 petition against the Secretary of Defense. Over the course of the last century, the United States has held millions of alien prisoners abroad. A great many of these prisoners would no doubt have complained about the circumstances of their capture and the terms of their confinement. The military is currently detaining over 600 prisoners at Guantanamo Bay alone; each detainee undoubtedly has complaints—real or contrived—about those terms and circumstances. The Court's unheralded expansion of federal-court jurisdiction is not even mitigated by a comforting assurance that the legion of ensuing claims will be easily resolved on the merits. To the contrary, the Court says that the "[p]etitioners' allegations ... unquestionably describe 'custody in violation of the Constitution or laws or treaties of the United States.' " From this point forward, federal courts will entertain petitions from these prisoners, and others like them around the world, challenging actions and events far away, and forcing the courts to oversee one aspect of the Executive's conduct of a foreign war. ***

The Commander in Chief and his subordinates had every reason to expect that the internment of combatants at Guantanamo Bay would not have the consequence of bringing the cumbersome machinery of our domestic courts into military affairs. Congress is in session. If it wished to change federal judges' habeas jurisdiction from what this Court had previously held that to be, it could have done so. And it could have done so by intelligent revision of the statute, instead of by today's clumsy, countertextual reinterpretation that confers upon wartime prisoners greater habeas rights than domestic detainees. The latter must challenge their present physical confinement in the district of their confinement, whereas under today's strange holding Guantanamo Bay detainees can petition in any of the 94 federal judicial districts. The fact that extraterritorially located detainees lack the district of detention that the statute requires has been converted from a factor that precludes their ability to bring a petition at all into a factor that frees them to petition wherever they wish—and, as a result, to forum shop. For this Court to create such a monstrous scheme in time of war, and in frustration of our military commanders' reliance upon clearly stated prior law, is judicial adventurism of the worst sort. I dissent.

Notes

1. Custodian, Detainee, Location. The Court holds that, if the custodian can be reached by the habeas statute, "Section 2241, by its terms, requires nothing more." It is therefore irrelevant whether a detainee is or is not a citizen. How much did the location of imprisonment—Guananamo—and the U.S.'s control of that location figure in the Court's decision? Under *Rasul*, can individuals captured and detained by US forces in Afghanistan, Iraq, or elsewhere gain access to federal courts to assert that they are wrongly detained?

2. The Next Move. Contemporaneously with *Rasul*, the Supreme Court held in *Hamdi v. Rumsfeld*, 542 U.S. 507 (2004), that a U.S. citizen detained as an "unlawful enemy combatant" was entitled to a hearing before a neutral decisionmaker. The Court did not provide details concerning how such a hearing should be conducted and also noted that an administrative alternative to habeas which was sufficiently fair to challengers to detention could provide an acceptable substitute for habeas. In response to both decisions, the Secretary of Defense then issued, within days after *Rasul* and *Hamdi*, an Order Establishing Combatant Status Review Tribunal dated July 7, 2004. The intent was to provide a military hearing process to review whether a detainee was properly held at Guantanamo in lieu of habeas hearings before federal judges.

3. Habeas Writ, Habeas Statute. *Rasul* was a statutory decision, so Congress could amend the habeas statute to preclude or expand statutory habeas. In 2005, Congress passed the Detainee Treatment Act (DTA), Section 1005 of which provided:

(e) Judicial Review of Detention of Enemy Combatants

(1) IN GENERAL- Section 2241 of title 28, United States Code [the general habeas statute], is amended by adding at the end the following:

"(e) Except as provided in section 1005 of the Detainee Treatment Act of 2005, no court, justice, or judge shall have jurisdiction to hear or consider:

> (1) an application for a writ of habeas corpus filed by or on behalf of an alien detained by the Department of Defense at Guantanamo Bay, Cuba." ***

> (2) REVIEW OF DECISIONS OF COMBATANT STATUS REVIEW TRIBUNALS OF PROPRIETY OF DETENTION *** [only by the D.C. Circuit]

> (3) REVIEW OF FINAL DECISIONS OF MILITARY COMMISSIONS ***[only by the D.C. Circuit] ***

This amendment overturned the Supreme Court's interpretation of 28 U.S.C. §2241, precluding statutory habeas review. The DTA also provided for direct review of CRST and military commission decisions in one court, the D.C. Circuit.

4. Supreme Court Response. The following year, the Supreme Court decided *Hamdan v. Rumsfeld*, 548 U.S. 557 (2006), in which the petitioner challenged whether he could be tried by military commission. To reach the merits of this petition, the Court first had to consider whether the DTA precluded its review of the case. Here is an excerpt from the portion of Justice Stevens' opinion answering that question:

> The Government's motion to dismiss, based on the Detainee Treatment Act of 2005 (DTA), is denied. DTA §1005(e)(1) provides that "no court ... shall have jurisdiction to hear or consider ... an application for ... habeas corpus filed by ... an alien detained ... at Guantanamo Bay." Section 1005(h)(2) provides that §§1005(e)(2) and (3)—which give the D. C. Circuit "exclusive" jurisdiction to review the final decisions of, respectively, combatant status review tribunals and military commissions—"shall apply with respect to any claim whose review is ... pending on" the DTA's effective date, as was Hamdan's case. The Government's argument that §§1005(e)(1) and (h) repeal this Court's jurisdiction to review the decision below is rebutted by ordinary principles of statutory construction. A negative inference may be drawn from Congress' failure to include §1005(e)(1) within the scope of §1005(h)(2). "If ... Congress was reasonably concerned to ensure that [§§1005(e)(2) and (3)] be applied to pending cases, it should have been just as concerned about [§1005(e)(1)], unless it had the different intent that the latter [section] not be applied to the general run of pending cases." *** The legislative history shows that Congress not only considered the respective temporal reaches of §§1005(e)(1), (2), and (3) together at every stage, but omitted paragraph (1) from its directive only after having *rejected* earlier proposed versions of the statute that would have included what is now paragraph (1) within that directive's scope. Congress' rejection of the very language that would have achieved the

result the Government urges weighs heavily against the Government's interpretation.

Do you find this justification for judicial review convincing?

5. Venue for Guantanamo Habeas Cases. Following *Hamdan*, Guantanamo detainees could in theory file petitions in any district court. These were soon centralized by the federal judiciary into the district courts for the District of Columbia. This meant, of course, that all habeas decisions by district judges would occur before the DC Circuit.

6 Congress' Move Again. Congress soon considered stripping statutory habeas from Guantanamo detainees. Here are arguments made on the Senate floor. Who (in your view) won?

Sen. Gordon Smith (R-Ore.): At the heart of the habeas issue is whether the president should have the sole authority to indefinitely detain unlawful enemy combatants without any judicial restraints. ***Permanent detention of foreigners without reason damages our moral integrity regarding international rule of law issues. *** Habeas corpus is a cornerstone of our constitutional order, and a suspension of that right, whether for U.S. citizens or foreigners under U.S. control, ought to trouble us all. It certainly gives me pause. *** One of the most controversial decisions of [President Abraham Lincoln's] administration was the suspension of habeas corpus for all military-related cases, ignoring the ruling of a U.S. circuit court against this order. He *** imprisoned the entire Maryland Legislature because of their attempts to secede from the Union.

Sen. Jeff Sessions (R-Ala): [S]ection 7 [[will]] get the lawyers out of Guantanamo Bay. *** [T]hese lawyers have even bragged about the fact that their presence and activities at Guantanamo have made it harder for the military to do its job. *** The litigation is brutal for [the United States]. It's huge. We have over 100 lawyers now from big and small firms working to represent the detainees. Every time an attorney goes down there, it makes it that much harder [for the U.S. military] to do what they're doing. You can't run an interrogation ... with attorneys. What are they going to do now that we're getting court orders to get more lawyers down there?'" *** [T]he new law applies globally, rather than just to Guantanamo detainees. We are legislating through this law for future generations, creating a system that will operate not only throughout this war, but for future wars in which our nation fights.

Sen. Arlen Specter (R-Pa.), Senate Judiciary Committee Chairman: What we are doing is defending the jurisdiction of the federal courts to maintain the rule of law. If the federal courts are not open, if the federal courts do not have jurisdiction to determine constitutionality, then how are we to determine what is constitutional? *** [This bill] would take our civilized society back some 900 years to King John at Runnymede which led to the adoption of the Magna Carta in 1215, which is the antecedent for habeas corpus and was the basis for including in the Constitution of the United States the principle that habeas corpus may not be suspended.

Sen. Lindsay Graham (R-S.C.): I don't believe judges should be making military decisions in a time of war. There is a reason the Germans and the Japanese and every other prisoner held by America have never gone to federal court and asked the judge to determine their status. This is not a role the judiciary should be playing. *** Why am I worried about having federal judges turning every enemy combatant decision into a trial? In 1950 the Supreme Court, denying habeas rights to German and Japanese prisoners, said: 'Such trials would hamper the war effort and bring aid and comfort to the enemy.' I agree with that. *** 'It would be very difficult to devise a more effective fettering of a field commander than to allow the very enemies he has ordered to reduce to submission to call him to account in his own civil courts and divert his efforts and attention from the military offensive abroad to the legal defensive at home.' I agree with that.

Sen. Patrick Leahy (D-Vt.):   Habeas corpus provides a remedy against arbitrary detentions and constitutional violations. *** We are about to put the darkest blot possible on this nation's conscience. It would not be limited to enemy combatants in the traditional sense of foreign fights captured in the battlefield, but it would apply to any alien picked up anywhere in the world and suspected of possibly supporting enemies of the United States. We do not need this bill for those truly captured on the battlefield *** This bill *** would not even require an administrative determination that the Government's suspicions have a reasonable basis in fact. *** And we wonder why some of our closest allies ask us, what in heaven's name has happened to the conscience and moral compass of this great nation? Are we so terrified of some terrorists around this country that we will run scared and hide?

Sen. Jon Kyl (R-Ariz.): During World War II, the United States held millions of axis enemy combatants. *** By the end of the war, over 425,000 enemy war prisoners were detained in prison camps inside the United States. Overall, the United States detained over 2 million enemy combatants during World War II. Prisoner camps for these combatants existed in all but three of the then-48 states. If the Specter amendment had been law during World War II, all of these 2 million enemy combatants would have been allowed to file habeas corpus lawsuits. *** We cannot allow enemy war prisoners to sue us in our own courts.

7. **Congress Replies to *Hamdan*.** The Military Commissions Act of 2006 (MCA), passed approximately four months after the *Hamdan* decision, provided as follows:

> SEC. 7. HABEAS CORPUS MATTERS
>
> (a) IN GENERAL.—[The general habeas statute, 28 U.S.C. 2241] is amended by striking . . . subsection (e) added by section 1005(e)(1) of [the DTA] and inserting the following new subsection (e): ***
>
> "(e)(1) No court, justice, or judge shall have jurisdiction to hear or consider an application for a writ of habeas corpus by or on behalf of an alien detained by the United States who has been determined by the United States to have been properly detained as an enemy combatant or is awaiting such determination.
>
> (e)(2) Except as provided in paragraphs (2) and (3) of section 1005(e) of the Detainee Treatment Act of 2005, no court, justice, or judge shall have jurisdiction to hear or consider any other action against the United States or its agents relating to any aspect of the detention, transfer, treatment, trial, or conditions of confinement of an alien who is or was detained by the United States and has been determined by the United States to have been properly detained as an enemy combatant or is awaiting such determination."

Effective Date.--The amendment made by subsection (a) shall take effect on the date of the enactment of this Act, and shall apply to all cases, without exception, pending on or after the date of the enactment of this Act which relate to any aspect of the detention, transfer, treatment, trial, or conditions of detention of an alien detained by the United States since September 11, 2001.

Compare the breadth of MCA § 7 with that of the DTA. If MCA § 7 precludes statutory habeas, does § 7 violate the Suspension Clause? Read on.

2. CONSTITUTIONAL HABEAS AND GUANTANAMO

BOUMEDIENE v. BUSH
553 U.S. 723 (2008)

JUSTICE KENNEDY delivered the opinion of the Court.

Petitioners are aliens designated as enemy combatants and detained at the United States Naval Station at Guantanamo Bay, Cuba. *** Petitioners present a question not resolved by our earlier cases relating to the detention of aliens at Guantanamo: whether they have the constitutional privilege of habeas corpus, a privilege not to be withdrawn except in conformance with the Suspension Clause, Art. I, § 9, cl. 2. We hold these petitioners do have the habeas corpus privilege. Congress has enacted a statute, the Detainee Treatment Act of 2005 (DTA), that provides certain procedures for review of the detainees' status. We hold that those procedures are not an adequate and effective substitute for habeas corpus. Therefore § 7 of the Military Commissions Act of 2006 (MCA), operates as an unconstitutional suspension of the writ. We do not address whether the President has authority to detain these petitioners nor do we hold that the writ must issue. These and other questions regarding the legality of the detention are to be resolved in the first instance by the District Court.

Under the Authorization for Use of Military Force (AUMF), the President is authorized "to use all necessary and appropriate force against those nations, organizations, or persons he determines planned, authorized, committed, or aided the terrorist attacks that occurred on September 11, 2001, or harbored such organizations or persons, in order to prevent any future acts of international terrorism against the United States by such nations, organizations or persons."

In *Hamdi v. Rumsfeld*, 542 U.S. 507 (2004), five Members of the Court recognized that detention of individuals who fought against the United States in Afghanistan "for the duration of the particular conflict in which they were captured, is so fundamental and accepted an incident to war as to be an exercise of the 'necessary and appropriate force' Congress has authorized the President to use." After *Hamdi*, the Deputy Secretary of Defense established Combatant Status Review Tribunals (CSRTs) to determine whether individuals detained at Guantanamo were "enemy combatants," as the Department defines that term. *** The Government maintains these procedures were designed to comply with the due process requirements identified by the plurality in *Hamdi*.

Interpreting the AUMF, the Department of Defense ordered the detention of these petitioners, and they were transferred to Guantanamo. *** All are foreign nationals, but none is a citizen of a nation now at war with the United States. Each denies he is a member of the al Qaeda terrorist network that carried out the September 11 attacks or of the Taliban regime that provided sanctuary for al Qaeda. Each petitioner appeared before a separate CSRT; was determined to be an enemy combatant; and has sought a writ of habeas corpus in the United States District Court for the District of Columbia.***

As a threshold matter, we must decide whether MCA § 7 denies the federal courts jurisdiction to hear habeas corpus actions pending at the time of its enactment. We hold the statute does deny that jurisdiction, so that, if the statute is valid, petitioners' cases must be dismissed. ***

III

In deciding the constitutional questions now presented we must determine whether petitioners are barred from seeking the writ or invoking the protections of the Suspension Clause either because of their status, *i.e.,* petitioners' designation by the Executive Branch as enemy combatants, or their physical location, *i.e.,* their presence at Guantanamo Bay. The Government contends that noncitizens designated as enemy combatants and detained in territory located outside our Nation's borders have no constitutional rights and no privilege of habeas corpus. ***

The Framers viewed freedom from unlawful restraint as a fundamental precept of liberty, and they understood the writ of habeas corpus as a vital instrument to secure that freedom. Experience taught, however, that the common-law writ all too often had been insufficient to guard against the abuse of monarchial power. That history counseled the necessity for specific language in the Constitution to secure the writ and ensure its place in our legal system. *** The Court has been careful not to foreclose the possibility that the protections of the Suspension Clause have expanded along with post-1789 developments that define the present scope of the writ. See *INS v. St. Cyr,* 533 U.S. 289, 300-301 (2001). But the analysis may begin with precedents as of 1789, for the Court has said that "at the absolute minimum" the Clause protects the writ as it existed when the Constitution was drafted and ratified.

We know that at common law a petitioner's status as an alien was not a categorical bar to habeas corpus relief. See, *e.g., Sommersett's Case,* 20 How. St. Tr. 1, 80-82 (1772). *** We know as well that common-law courts entertained habeas petitions brought by enemy aliens detained in England-"entertained" at least in the sense that the courts held hearings to determine the threshold question of entitlement to the writ. See *Case of Three Spanish Sailors,* 2 Black. W. 1324 (C.P. 1779). *** As the Court noted in *Rasul,* 542 U.S., at 481-482, common-law courts granted habeas corpus relief to prisoners detained in the exempt jurisdictions. But these areas, while not in theory part of the realm of England, were nonetheless under the Crown's control. ***

Each side in the present matter argues that the very lack of a precedent on point supports its position. *** Both arguments are premised, however, upon the assumption that the historical record is complete and that the common law, if properly understood, yields a definite answer to the questions before us. There are reasons to doubt both assumptions. Recent scholarship points to the inherent shortcomings in the historical record. And given the unique status of Guantanamo Bay and the particular dangers of terrorism in the modern age, the common-law courts simply may not have confronted cases with close parallels to this one. We decline, therefore, to infer too much, one way or the other, from the lack of historical evidence on point.

IV

Drawing from its position that at common law the writ ran only to territories over which the Crown was sovereign, the Government says the Suspension Clause affords petitioners no rights because the United States does not claim sovereignty over the place of detention.

Guantanamo Bay is not formally part of the United States. And under the terms of the lease between the United States and Cuba, Cuba retains "ultimate sovereignty" over the territory while the United States exercises "complete jurisdiction and control." Under the terms of the 1934 Treaty, however, Cuba effectively has no rights as a sovereign until the parties agree to modification of the 1903 Lease Agreement or the United States abandons the base. *** [W]e take notice of the obvious and uncontested fact that the United States, by virtue of its complete jurisdiction and control over the base, maintains *de facto* sovereignty over this territory.

The Court has discussed the issue of the Constitution's extraterritorial application on many occasions. These decisions undermine the Government's argument that, at least as applied to noncitizens, the Constitution necessarily stops where *de jure* sovereignty ends. *** [T]he Constitution applies in full in incorporated Territories surely destined for statehood but only in part in unincorporated Territories. ***

Practical considerations weighed heavily as well in *Johnson v. Eisentrager,* 339 U.S. 763 (1950), where the Court addressed whether habeas corpus jurisdiction extended to enemy aliens who had been convicted of violating the laws of war. The prisoners were detained at Landsberg Prison in Germany during the Allied Powers' postwar occupation. The Court stressed the difficulties of ordering the Government to produce the prisoners in a habeas corpus proceeding. It "would require allocation of shipping space, guarding personnel, billeting and rations" and would damage the prestige of military commanders at a sensitive time. In considering these factors the Court sought to balance the constraints of military occupation with constitutional necessities.

True, the Court in *Eisentrager* denied access to the writ, and it noted the prisoners "at no relevant time were within any territory over which the United States is sovereign, and [that] the scenes of their offense, their capture, their trial and their punishment were all beyond the territorial jurisdiction of any court of the United States." The Government seizes upon this language as proof positive that the *Eisentrager* Court adopted a formalistic, sovereignty-based test for determining the reach of the Suspension Clause. We reject this reading. *** The Government's formal sovereignty-based test raises troubling separation-of-powers concerns as well. The political history of Guantanamo illustrates the deficiencies of this approach. The United States has maintained complete and uninterrupted control of the bay for over 100 years. *** Yet the Government's view is that the Constitution had no effect there, at least as to noncitizens, because the United States disclaimed sovereignty in the formal sense of the term. The necessary implication of the argument is that by surrendering formal sovereignty over any unincorporated territory to a third party, while at the same time entering into a lease that grants total control over the territory back to the United States, it would be possible for the political branches to govern without legal constraint.

Our basic charter cannot be contracted away like this. The Constitution grants Congress and the President the power to acquire, dispose of, and govern territory, not the power to decide when and where its terms apply. Even when the United States acts outside its borders, its powers are not "absolute and unlimited" but are subject "to such restrictions as are expressed in the Constitution." Abstaining from questions involving formal sovereignty and territorial governance is one thing. To hold the political branches have the power to switch the Constitution on or off at will is quite another. The former position reflects this Court's recognition that certain matters requiring political judgments are best left to the political branches. The latter would permit a striking anomaly in our tripartite system of government, leading to a regime in which Congress and the President, not this Court, say "what the law is." *Marbury v. Madison.*

*** In comparison the procedural protections afforded to the detainees in the CSRT hearings are far more limited, and, we conclude, fall well short of the procedures and adversarial mechanisms that would eliminate the need for habeas corpus review. Although the detainee is assigned a "Personal Representative" to assist him during CSRT proceedings, the Secretary of the Navy's memorandum makes clear that person is not the detainee's lawyer or even his "advocate." The Government's evidence is accorded a presumption of validity. The detainee is allowed to present "reasonably available" evidence, but his ability to rebut the Government's evidence against him is limited by the circumstances of his confinement and his lack of counsel at this stage. And although the detainee can seek review of his status determination in the Court of Appeals, that review process cannot cure all defects in the earlier proceedings.

*** [T]he detainees here are similarly situated to the *Eisentrager* petitioners in that the sites of their apprehension and detention are technically outside the sovereign territory of the United States. As noted earlier, this is a factor that weighs against finding they have rights under the Suspension Clause. But there are critical differences between Landsberg

Prison, circa 1950, and the United States Naval Station at Guantanamo Bay in 2008. Unlike its present control over the naval station, the United States' control over the prison in Germany was neither absolute nor indefinite. *** Guantanamo Bay, on the other hand, is no transient possession. In every practical sense Guantanamo is not abroad; it is within the constant jurisdiction of the United States. See *Rasul.*

*** [W]e recognize, as the Court did in *Eisentrager,* that there are costs to holding the Suspension Clause applicable in a case of military detention abroad. Habeas corpus proceedings may require expenditure of funds by the Government and may divert the attention of military personnel from other pressing tasks. While we are sensitive to these concerns, we do not find them dispositive. Compliance with any judicial process requires some incremental expenditure of resources. Yet civilian courts and the Armed Forces have functioned along side each other at various points in our history. The Government presents no credible arguments that the military mission at Guantanamo would be compromised if habeas corpus courts had jurisdiction to hear the detainees' claims. And in light of the plenary control the United States asserts over the base, none are apparent to us. *** [T]he cases before us lack any precise historical parallel. They involve individuals detained by executive order for the duration of a conflict that, if measured from September 11, 2001, to the present, is already among the longest wars in American history. The detainees, moreover, are held in a territory that, while technically not part of the United States, is under the complete and total control of our Government. Under these circumstances the lack of a precedent on point is no barrier to our holding.

We hold that Art. I, § 9, cl. 2, of the Constitution has full effect at Guantanamo Bay. If the privilege of habeas corpus is to be denied to the detainees now before us, Congress must act in accordance with the requirements of the Suspension Clause. *** The MCA does not purport to be a formal suspension of the writ; and the Government, in its submissions to us, has not argued that it is. Petitioners, therefore, are entitled to the privilege of habeas corpus to challenge the legality of their detention.

V

In light of this holding the question becomes whether the statute stripping jurisdiction to issue the writ avoids the Suspension Clause mandate because Congress has provided adequate substitute procedures for habeas corpus. The Government submits there has been compliance with the Suspension Clause because the DTA review process in the Court of Appeals provides an adequate substitute. ***

Our case law does not contain extensive discussion of standards defining suspension of the writ or of circumstances under which suspension has occurred. This simply confirms the care Congress has taken throughout our Nation's history to preserve the writ and its function. ***

The two leading cases addressing habeas substitutes *** provide little guidance here. The statutes at issue were attempts to streamline habeas corpus relief, not to cut it back. *** [H]ere we confront statutes, the DTA and the MCA, that were intended to circumscribe habeas review. Congress' purpose is evident not only from the unequivocal nature of MCA § 7's jurisdiction-stripping language, ("No court, justice, or judge shall have jurisdiction to hear or consider an application for a writ of habeas corpus ..."), but also from a comparison of the DTA to the statutes at issue in [earlier cases] *** When Congress has intended to replace traditional habeas corpus with habeas-like substitutes,*** it has granted to the courts broad remedial powers to secure the historic office of the writ.

In contrast the DTA's jurisdictional grant is quite limited. The Court of Appeals has jurisdiction not to inquire into the legality of the detention generally but only to assess whether the CSRT complied with the "standards and procedures specified by the Secretary of Defense" and whether those standards and procedures are lawful. If Congress had envisioned DTA review as coextensive with traditional habeas corpus, it would not have drafted the statute in this manner. *** [T]here has been no effort to preserve habeas corpus review as an avenue of last resort. No saving clause exists in either the MCA or the DTA. And MCA § 7 eliminates habeas review for these petitioners.

To the extent any doubt remains about Congress' intent, the legislative history confirms what the plain text strongly suggests: In passing the DTA Congress did not intend to create a process that differs from traditional habeas corpus process in name only. It intended to create a more limited procedure. *** The present cases thus test the limits of the Suspension Clause in[new] ways***.

We do not endeavor to offer a comprehensive summary of the requisites for an adequate substitute for habeas corpus. We do consider it uncontroversial, however, that the privilege of habeas corpus entitles the prisoner to a meaningful opportunity to demonstrate that he is being held pursuant to "the erroneous application or interpretation" of relevant law. St. Cyr, 533 U.S., at 302. And the habeas court must have the power to order the conditional release of an individual unlawfully detained-though release need not be the exclusive remedy and is not the appropriate one in every case in which the writ is granted. *** These are the easily identified attributes of any constitutionally adequate habeas corpus proceeding. But, depending on the circumstances, more may be required.

Indeed, common-law habeas corpus was, above all, an adaptable remedy. *** Habeas corpus proceedings need not resemble a criminal trial, even when the detention is by executive order. But the writ must be effective. The habeas court must have sufficient authority to conduct a meaningful review of both the cause for detention and the Executive's power to detain.

To determine the necessary scope of habeas corpus review, therefore, we must assess the CSRT process, the mechanism through which petitioners' designation as enemy combatants became final. *** What matters is the sum total of procedural protections afforded to the detainee at all stages, direct and collateral. *** Although we make no judgment as to whether the CSRTs, as currently constituted, satisfy due process standards, we agree with petitioners that, even when all the parties involved in this process act with diligence and in good faith, there is considerable risk of error in the tribunal's findings of fact. This is a risk inherent in any process that, in the words of the former Chief Judge of the Court of Appeals, is "closed and accusatorial." See *Bismullah III*, 514 F.3d, at 1296 (Ginsburg, C. J., concurring in denial of rehearing en banc). And given that the consequence of error may be detention of persons for the duration of hostilities that may last a generation or more, this is a risk too significant to ignore.

For the writ of habeas corpus, or its substitute, to function as an effective and proper remedy in this context, the court that conducts the habeas proceeding must have the means to correct errors that occurred during the CSRT proceedings. This includes some authority to assess the sufficiency of the Government's evidence against the detainee. It also must have the authority to admit and consider relevant exculpatory evidence that was not introduced during the earlier proceeding. Federal habeas petitioners long have had the means to supplement the record on review, even in the post-conviction habeas setting.

The extent of the showing required of the Government in these cases is a matter to be determined. We need not explore it further at this stage. We do hold that when the judicial power to issue habeas corpus properly is invoked the judicial officer must have adequate authority to make a determination in light of the relevant law and facts and to formulate and issue appropriate orders for relief, including, if necessary, an order directing the prisoner's release.

We now consider whether the DTA allows the Court of Appeals to conduct a proceeding meeting these standards. *** The DTA does not explicitly empower the Court of Appeals to order the applicant in a DTA review proceeding released should the court find that the standards and procedures used at his CSRT hearing were insufficient to justify detention. This is troubling. Yet, for present purposes, we can assume congressional silence permits a constitutionally required remedy. In that case it would be possible to hold that a remedy of release is impliedly provided for. The DTA might be read, furthermore, to allow the petitioners to assert most, if not all, of the legal claims they seek to advance, including their most basic claim: that the President has no authority under the AUMF to detain them indefinitely. *** At oral argument, the Solicitor General urged us to adopt both these constructions, if doing so would allow MCA § 7 to remain intact.

*** The more difficult question is whether the DTA permits the Court of Appeals to make requisite findings of fact. *** Assuming the DTA can be construed to allow the Court of Appeals to review or correct the CSRT's factual determinations, as opposed to merely certifying that the tribunal applied the correct standard of proof, we see no way to construe the statute to allow what is also constitutionally required in this context: an opportunity for the detainee to present relevant exculpatory evidence that was not made part of the record in the earlier proceedings. *** There is no language in the DTA that can be construed to allow the Court of Appeals to admit and consider newly discovered evidence that could not have been made part of the CSRT record because it was unavailable to either the Government or the detainee when the CSRT made its findings. This evidence, however, may be critical to the detainee's argument that he is not an enemy combatant and there is no cause to detain him.

By foreclosing consideration of evidence not presented or reasonably available to the detainee at the CSRT proceedings, the DTA disadvantages the detainee by limiting the scope of collateral review to a record that may not be accurate or complete. ***

We do not imply DTA review would be a constitutionally sufficient replacement for habeas corpus but for these limitations on the detainee's ability to present exculpatory evidence. For even if it were possible, as a textual matter, to read into the statute each of the necessary procedures we have identified, we could not overlook the cumulative effect of our doing so. To hold that the detainees at Guantanamo may, under the DTA, challenge the President's legal authority to detain them, contest the CSRT's findings of fact, supplement the record on review with exculpatory evidence, and request an order of release would come close to reinstating the § 2241 habeas corpus process Congress sought to deny them. The language of the statute, read in light of Congress' reasons for enacting it, cannot bear this interpretation. Petitioners have met their burden of establishing that the DTA review process is, on its face, an inadequate substitute for habeas corpus.

Although we do not hold that an adequate substitute must duplicate § 2241 in all respects, it suffices that the Government has not established that the detainees' access to the statutory review provisions at issue is an adequate substitute for the writ of habeas corpus. MCA § 7 thus effects an unconstitutional suspension of the writ. In view of our holding we need not discuss the reach of the writ with respect to claims of unlawful conditions of treatment or confinement.

VI

In light of our conclusion that there is no jurisdictional bar to the District Court's entertaining petitioners' claims the question remains whether there are prudential barriers to habeas corpus review under these circumstances. *** The real risks, the real threats, of terrorist attacks are constant and not likely soon to abate. The ways to disrupt our life and laws are so many and unforeseen that the Court should not attempt even some general catalogue of crises that might occur. Certain principles are apparent, however. Practical considerations and exigent circumstances inform the definition and reach of the law's writs, including habeas corpus. The cases and our tradition reflect this precept. *** Here, as is true with detainees apprehended abroad, a relevant consideration in determining the courts' role is whether there are suitable alternative processes in place to protect against the arbitrary exercise of governmental power.

The cases before us, however, do not involve detainees who have been held for a short period of time while awaiting their CSRT determinations. Were that the case, or were it probable that the Court of Appeals could complete a prompt review of their applications, the case for requiring temporary abstention or exhaustion of alternative remedies would be much stronger. These qualifications no longer pertain here. In some of these cases six years have elapsed without the judicial oversight that habeas corpus or an adequate substitute demands. And there has been no showing that the Executive faces such onerous burdens that it cannot respond to habeas corpus actions. To require these detainees to complete DTA review before proceeding with their habeas corpus actions would be to require additional months, if not years, of delay. The first DTA review applications were filed over a year ago, but no decisions on the merits have been issued. While some delay in fashioning new procedures is unavoidable, the costs of delay can no longer be borne by those who are held in custody. The detainees in these cases are entitled to a prompt habeas corpus hearing.

Our decision today holds only that the petitioners before us are entitled to seek the writ; that the DTA review procedures are an inadequate substitute for habeas corpus; and that the petitioners in these cases need not exhaust the review procedures in the Court of Appeals before proceeding with their habeas actions in the District Court. The only law we identify as unconstitutional is MCA § 7, 28 U.S.C.A. § 2241(e) (Supp.2007). *** The Executive is entitled to a reasonable period of time to determine a detainee's status before a court entertains that detainee's habeas corpus petition. *** Except in cases of undue delay, federal courts should refrain from entertaining an enemy combatant's habeas corpus petition at least until after the Department, acting via the CSRT, has had a chance to review his status.

Although we hold that the DTA is not an adequate and effective substitute for habeas corpus, it does not follow that a habeas corpus court may disregard the dangers the detention in these cases was intended to prevent. *** Certain accommodations can be made to reduce the burden habeas corpus proceedings will place on the military without impermissibly diluting the protections of the writ. *** Channeling future cases to one district court would no doubt reduce administrative burdens on the Government. This is a legitimate objective that might be advanced even without an amendment to § 2241.

Another of Congress' reasons for vesting exclusive jurisdiction in the Court of Appeals, perhaps, was to avoid the widespread dissemination of classified information. *** We make no attempt to anticipate all of the evidentiary and access-to-counsel issues that will arise during the course of the detainees' habeas corpus proceedings. We recognize, however, that the Government has a legitimate interest in protecting sources and methods of intelligence gathering; and we expect that the District Court will use its discretion to accommodate this interest to the greatest extent possible. * * *

*** Within the Constitution's separation-of-powers structure, few exercises of judicial power are as legitimate or as necessary as the responsibility to hear challenges to the authority of the Executive to imprison a person. Some of these petitioners have been in custody for six years with no definitive judicial determination as to the legality of their detention. Their access to the writ is a necessity to determine the lawfulness of their status, even if, in the end, they do not obtain the relief they seek.

Because our Nation's past military conflicts have been of limited duration, it has been possible to leave the outer boundaries of war powers undefined. If, as some fear, terrorism continues to pose dangerous threats to us for years to come, the Court might not have this luxury. This result is not inevitable, however. The political branches, consistent with their independent obligations to interpret and uphold the Constitution, can engage in a genuine debate about how best to preserve constitutional values while protecting the Nation from terrorism.

It bears repeating that our opinion does not address the content of the law that governs petitioners' detention. That is a matter yet to be determined. We hold that petitioners may invoke the fundamental procedural protections of habeas corpus. The laws and Constitution are designed to survive, and remain in force, in extraordinary times. Liberty and security can be reconciled; and in our system they are reconciled within the framework of the law. The Framers decided that habeas corpus, a right of first importance, must be a part of that framework, a part of that law. ***

CHIEF JUSTICE ROBERTS, dissenting.

Today the Court strikes down as inadequate the most generous set of procedural protections ever afforded aliens detained by this country as enemy combatants. The political branches crafted these procedures amidst an ongoing military conflict, after much careful investigation and thorough debate. The Court rejects them today out of hand, without bothering to say what due process rights the detainees possess, without explaining how the statute fails to vindicate those rights, and before a single petitioner has even attempted to avail himself of the law's operation. And to what effect? The majority merely replaces a review system designed by the people's representatives with a set of shapeless procedures to be defined by federal courts at some future date. One cannot help but think, after surveying the modest practical results of the majority's ambitious opinion, that this decision is not really about the detainees at all, but about control of federal policy regarding enemy combatants.

***The important point for me, however, is that the Court should have resolved these cases on other grounds. Habeas is most fundamentally a procedural right, a mechanism for contesting the legality of executive detention. The critical threshold question in these cases, prior to any inquiry about the writ's scope, is whether the system the political branches designed protects whatever rights the detainees may possess. If so, there is no need for any additional process, whether called "habeas" or something else.

Congress entrusted that threshold question in the first instance to the Court of Appeals for the District of Columbia Circuit, as the Constitution surely allows Congress to do. But before the D.C. Circuit has addressed the issue, the Court cashiers the statute, and without answering this critical threshold question itself. The Court does eventually get around to asking whether review under the DTA is, as the Court frames it, an "adequate substitute" for habeas, but even then its opinion fails to determine what rights the detainees possess and whether the DTA system satisfies them. The majority instead compares the undefined DTA process to an equally undefined habeas right-one that is to be given shape only in the future by district courts on a case-by-case basis. This whole approach is misguided. *** How the detainees' claims will be decided now that the DTA is gone is anybody's guess. But the habeas process the Court mandates will most likely end up looking a lot like the DTA system it replaces, as the district court judges shaping it will have to reconcile review of the prisoners' detention with the undoubted need to protect the American people from the terrorist threat-precisely the challenge Congress undertook in drafting the DTA. All that today's opinion has done is shift responsibility for those sensitive foreign policy and national security decisions from the elected branches to the Federal Judiciary. ***

*** It is grossly premature to pronounce on the detainees' right to habeas without first assessing whether the remedies the DTA system provides vindicate whatever rights petitioners may claim.*** If the CSRT procedures meet the minimal due process requirements outlined in *Hamdi*, and if an Article III court is available to ensure that these procedures are followed in future cases, there is no need to reach the Suspension Clause question. ***

The majority's overreaching is particularly egregious given the weakness of its objections to the DTA. Simply put, the Court's opinion fails on its own terms. The majority strikes down the statute because it is not an "adequate substitute" for habeas review, but fails to show what rights the detainees have that cannot be vindicated by the DTA system.

Because the central purpose of habeas corpus is to test the legality of executive detention, the writ requires most fundamentally an Article III court able to hear the prisoner's claims and, when necessary, order release. Beyond that, the process a given prisoner is entitled to receive depends on the circumstances and the rights of the prisoner. ***

*** *Hamdi* merits scant attention from the Court-a remarkable omission, as *Hamdi* bears directly on the issues before us. *** After "a careful examination both of the writ ... and of the Due Process Clause," this Court enunciated the "basic process" the Constitution entitled Hamdi to expect from a habeas court under § 2241. That process consisted of the right to "receive notice of the factual basis for his classification, and a fair opportunity to rebut the Government's factual assertions before a neutral decision maker." In light of the Government's national security responsibilities, the plurality found the process could be "tailored to alleviate [the] uncommon potential to burden the Executive at a time of ongoing military conflict." For example, the Government could rely on hearsay and could claim a presumption in favor of its own evidence.

Hamdi further suggested that this "basic process" on collateral review could be provided by a military tribunal. It pointed to prisoner-of-war tribunals as a model that would satisfy the Constitution's requirements. Only "[i]n the *absence* of such process" before a military tribunal, the Court held, would Article III courts need to conduct full-dress habeas proceedings to "ensure that the minimum requirements of due process are achieved." *Ibid.*. And even then, the petitioner would be entitled to no more process than he would have received from a properly constituted military review panel, given his limited due process rights and the Government's weighty interests.

***For my part, I will assume that any due process rights petitioners may possess are no greater than those of American citizens detained as enemy combatants. It is worth noting again that the *Hamdi* controlling opinion said the Constitution guarantees citizen detainees only "basic" procedural rights, and that the process for securing those rights can "be tailored to alleviate [the] uncommon potential to burden the Executive at a time of ongoing military conflict." ***Contrary to the repeated suggestions of the majority, DTA review need not parallel the habeas privileges enjoyed by noncombatant American citizens. It need only provide process adequate for noncitizens detained as alleged combatants. ***Today's Court opines that the Suspension Clause guarantees prisoners such as the detainees "a meaningful opportunity to demonstrate that [they are] being held pursuant to the erroneous application or interpretation of relevant law." Further, the Court holds that to be an adequate substitute, any tribunal reviewing the detainees' cases "must have the power to order the conditional release of an individual unlawfully detained." The DTA system-CSRT review of the Executive's determination followed by D.C. Circuit review for sufficiency of the evidence and the constitutionality of the CSRT process-meets these criteria.

For all its eloquence about the detainees' right to the writ, the Court makes no effort to elaborate how exactly the remedy it prescribes will differ from the procedural protections detainees enjoy under the DTA. The Court objects to the detainees' limited access to witnesses and classified material, but proposes no alternatives of its own. Indeed, it simply ignores the many difficult questions its holding presents. *** What it does say leaves open the distinct possibility that its "habeas" remedy will, when all is said and done, end up looking a great deal like the DTA review it rejects. *** So who has won? Not the detainees. The Court's analysis leaves them with only the prospect of further litigation to determine the content of their new habeas right, followed by further litigation to resolve their particular cases, followed by further litigation before the D.C. Circuit-where they could have started had they invoked the DTA procedure. ***And certainly not the American people, who today lose a bit more control over the conduct of this Nation's foreign policy to unelected, politically unaccountable judges.

JUSTICE SCALIA, dissenting.

Today, for the first time in our Nation's history, the Court confers a constitutional right to habeas corpus on alien enemies detained abroad by our military forces in the course of an ongoing war. *** My problem with today's opinion is more fundamental still: The writ of habeas corpus does not, and never has, run in favor of aliens abroad; the Suspension Clause thus has no application. ***

America is at war with radical Islamists. *** On September 11, 2001, the enemy brought the battle to American soil, killing 2,749 at the Twin Towers in New York City, 184 at the Pentagon in Washington, D. C., and 40 in Pennsylvania. It has threatened further attacks against our homeland; one need only walk about buttressed and barricaded Washington, or board a plane anywhere in the country, to know that the threat is a serious one. Our Armed Forces are now in the field against the enemy, in Afghanistan and Iraq. Last week, 13 of our countrymen in arms were killed.

The game of bait-and-switch that today's opinion plays upon the Nation's Commander in Chief will make the war harder on us. It will almost certainly cause more Americans to be killed. That consequence would be tolerable if necessary to preserve a time-honored legal principle vital to our constitutional Republic. But it is this Court's blatant *abandonment* of such a principle that produces the decision today. The President relied on our settled precedent in *Johnson v. Eisentrager,* 339 U.S. 763 (1950), when he established the prison at Guantanamo Bay for enemy aliens. ***Had the law been otherwise, the military surely would not have transported prisoners there, but would have kept them in Afghanistan, transferred them to another of our foreign military bases, or turned them over to allies for detention. Those other facilities might well have been worse for the detainees themselves.

In the long term, then, the Court's decision today accomplishes little, except perhaps to reduce the well-being of enemy combatants that the Court ostensibly seeks to protect. In the short term, however, the decision is devastating. At least 30 of those prisoners hitherto released from Guantanamo Bay have returned to the battlefield. Some have been captured or killed. But others have succeeded in carrying on their atrocities against innocent civilians. In one case, a detainee released from Guantanamo Bay masterminded the kidnapping of two Chinese dam workers, one of whom was later shot to death when used as a human shield against Pakistani commandoes. Another former detainee promptly resumed his post as a senior Taliban commander and murdered a United Nations engineer and three Afghan soldiers. Still another murdered an Afghan judge. It was reported only last month that a released detainee carried out a suicide bombing against Iraqi soldiers in Mosul, Iraq.

These, mind you, were detainees whom *the military* had concluded were not enemy combatants. Their return to the kill illustrates the incredible difficulty of assessing who is and who is not an enemy combatant in a foreign theater of operations where the environment does not lend itself to rigorous evidence collection. *** But even when the military has evidence that it can bring forward, it is often foolhardy to release that evidence to the attorneys representing our enemies. *** Henceforth, as today's opinion makes unnervingly clear, how to handle enemy prisoners in this war will ultimately lie with the branch that knows least about the national security concerns that the subject entails. ***

The Court tries to reconcile *Eisentrager* with its holding today by pointing out that in postwar Germany, the United States was "answerable to its

Allies" and did not "pla[n] a long-term occupation." Those factors were not mentioned in *Eisentrager*. Worse still, it is impossible to see how they relate to the Court's asserted purpose in creating this "functional" test-namely, to ensure a judicial inquiry into detention and prevent the political branches from acting with impunity. Can it possibly be that the Court trusts the political branches more when they are beholden to foreign powers than when they act alone? *** What drives today's decision is neither the meaning of the Suspension Clause, nor the principles of our precedents, but rather an inflated notion of judicial supremacy. ***Our power "to say what the law is" is circumscribed by the limits of our statutorily and constitutionally conferred jurisdiction. And that is precisely the question in these cases: whether the Constitution confers habeas jurisdiction on federal courts to decide petitioners' claims. It is both irrational and arrogant to say that the answer must be yes, because otherwise we would not be supreme. *** Today the Court warps our Constitution in a way that goes beyond the narrow issue of the reach of the Suspension Clause, invoking judicially brainstormed separation-of-powers principles to establish a manipulable "functional" test for the extraterritorial reach of habeas corpus (and, no doubt, for the extraterritorial reach of other constitutional protections as well). ***And, most tragically, it sets our military commanders the impossible task of proving to a civilian court, under whatever standards this Court devises in the future, that evidence supports the confinement of each and every enemy prisoner.

The Nation will live to regret what the Court has done today. I dissent.

Notes

1. What is the Holding? The Court explains: "Based on this language from *Eisentrager,* and the reasoning in our other extraterritoriality opinions, we conclude that at least three factors are relevant in determining the reach of the Suspension Clause: (1) the citizenship and status of the detainee and the adequacy of the process through which that status determination was made; (2) the nature of the sites where apprehension and then detention took place; and (3) the practical obstacles inherent in resolving the prisoner's entitlement to the writ." What parts of this test were most important to the Court's decision? Which are likely to be given the most significance in future cases testing the scope of this decision?

2. Was this a Facial Strike? When a court invalidates a statute as unconstitutional, it can do so facially (that is, invalidate it in all respects) or only as to the specific petitioners before it. The Supreme Court has long favored as applied challenges and looked to save any aspects of a statute that do not pose a constitutionally problem. Interestingly, *Boumediene* is not explicit as to whether it facially invalidated MCA § 7 or only struck it down as applied to the *Boumediene* petitioners, which is to say as to anyone held in Guantanamo. While the Court speaks broadly, deciding that "§ 7 of the Military Commissions Act of 2006 (MCA), operates as an unconstitutional suspension of the writ," its analysis goes deeply into the history, US relationship with, and practical challenges of habeas review at Guantanamo Bay, Cuba. What is the better interpretation of

Boumediene in your view—as an as applied holding or a facial strike? Why would the Court not explicitly attempt to save any part of MCA § 7 that it could, in deference to the political branches and democratic process? To what degree can the breadth of the Court's decision, if not how it will later be interpreted and applied, be attributed to the political and social mood of the nation (tired of war and concerned with Executive overreach) at the time of the holding?

3. How Much of the MCA Was Invalidated? As you saw above, MCA § 7 contains two parts. One deals with habeas actions seeking release, the other with other challenges, such as conditions of confinement challenges. Did *Boumediene* strike them both down, or only 2241(e)(1)? Does *Boumediene* only invalidate 2241(e)(1) and so 2241(e)(2) survives to bar conditions claims by detainees at Guantanamo, and presumably elsewhere? Is that the best reading of the Court's decision?

4. Safety, Justice, and Practical Concerns While the Justices split on their interpretation of the law, they also disagreed about the practical implications of the decision. The majority stresses the importance of not permitting the Executive to turn the Constitution on and off at will as well as many years of detention as evidence that judicial review would not be impracticable or anomalous. In contrast, Justice Scalia's dissent argues that permitting habeas corpus jurisdiction will lead to the inevitable release of detainees as well as greater danger to the U.S. and its citizens. Whose argument is more convincing? What practical considerations are most important—and which do you think are most likely to come to fruition, regardless of their theoretical import?

5. The Double Importance of Prior Process. The logic of *Boumediene* is odd. The majority asks what process the detainees had already been given in addressing not only if an adequate alternative to habeas had been provided but also in the threshold question of whether the suspension clause extends to Guantanamo. Can the Executive Branch, in deciding what prior process detainees receive, alter the Constitution's reach to (and so prevent federal court review of) detention of those prisoners? Is this approach more deferential to the political branches than a more cursory reading of *Boumediene* would indicate? The petitioners in *Eisentragger*, to whom habeas review was denied, had earlier received complete adversarial military commissions. Together, do the decisions in *Boumediene* and *Eisentragger* suggest that prior process is the litmus test for later habeas review? What of the other factors in the Court's multi-factored balancing test? In tying habeas review to prior process, and deeming the CSRT process wanting, was the majority engaging in a back door due process inquiry? If so, why would the Court not do so openly, analyzing its recent decision in *Hamdi*, as Justice Roberts suggests?

6. The History of the Great Writ. In both *Rasul* and *Boumediene*, the Court delves deep into the history of the writ over many centuries. How important was history of the writ to the outcome of these cases? How important should it be in decisions, such as these, that regard arguably uniquely modern global threats?

7. Swift Review or a Litigation Machine? There is strong disagreement among the Justices over what the decision will mean for detainee trials. While the majority argues that the decision should lead to immediate and swift review of detentions, there is also a strong argument that it will simply lead to more litigation as the procedures of the new habeas proceedings are determined and challenged through adversarial processes. Did the majority truly help the detainees in a practical sense or, as the dissent suggests, did abolishing the DTA process merely complicate their bid for swift review of their detention? These matters will be considered in more detail in Section C.

8. The Never-ending War? Is the War on Terror different from other wars in U.S. history because it has no discernable end? Victory over a stateless enemy will be elusive and legal measures used to combat terrorism could last decades. This raises the specter of potentially indefinite detention, even if detainees are held only for the duration of hostilities. What impact did this aspect of the war have on the majority's decision? Was it considered by the dissent?

9. Remnants of DTA Process. The majority goes to great pains to state that it is only holding MCA § 7 unconstitutional and that the other parts of the DTA are still good law. Many commentators have argued that *Boumediene* "gutted" the DTA, and that the Court may as well have found it unconstitutional. Does the DTA remain in force? If so, what purpose does it serve after *Boumediene*? Should Congress pass new legislation replacing the DTA and the MCA? In order to be constitutional under this case, what would that new legislation entail?

B. HABEAS IN NON-GUANTANAMO VENUES

The location of detention, Guantanamo Bay, played some role in *Boumediene*. What if the detainee had been held at the Bagram Theater Internment Facility at Bagram Air Force Base, the largest U.S. military base in Afghanistan? Or in Iraq at one of several penal facilities there. Would the federal courts have habeas jurisdiction over Bagram? If President Obama closes the Guantanamo Bay detention facility, could the U.S. move some or of all the Guantanamo detainees to Bagram? Think about both these questions as you read the next decision, which interprets the reach of *Boumediene*.

AL MAQALEH v. GATES
605 F. 3d 84 (C.A.D.C., 2010)

SENTELLE, Chief Judge:

Three detainees at Bagram Air Force Base in Afghanistan petitioned the district court for habeas corpus relief from their confinement by the United States military. Appellants (collectively "the United States" or "the government") moved to dismiss for lack of jurisdiction based on § 7(a) of the Military Commissions Act of 2006, ("MCA"). The district court greed with the United States that § 7(a) of the MCA purported to deprive the court of jurisdiction, but held that this section could not constitutionally be applied to deprive the court of jurisdiction under the Supreme Court's test articulated in *Boumediene v. Bush*, 553 U.S. 723 (2008). ***

All three petitioners are being held as unlawful enemy combatants at the Bagram Theater Internment Facility on the Bagram Airfield Military Base in Afghanistan. Petitioner Fadi Al-Maqaleh is a Yemeni citizen who alleges he was taken into custody in 2003. While Al-Maqaleh's petition asserts "on information and belief" that he was captured beyond Afghan borders, a sworn declaration from Colonel James W. Gray, Commander of Detention Operations, states that Al-Maqaleh was captured in Zabul, Afghanistan. Redha Al-Najar is a Tunisian citizen who alleges he was captured in Pakistan in 2002. Amin Al-Bakri is a Yemeni citizen who alleges he was captured in Thailand in 2002. Both Al-Najar and Al-Bakri allege they were first held in some other unknown location before being moved to Bagram.

Bagram Airfield Military Base is the largest military facility in Afghanistan occupied by United States and coalition forces. The United States entered into an "Accommodation Consignment Agreement for Lands and Facilities at Bagram Airfield" with the Islamic Republic of Afghanistan in 2006, which "consigns all facilities and land located at Bagram Airfield ... owned by [Afghanistan,] or Parwan Province, or private individuals, or others, for use by the United States and coalition forces for military purposes." (Accommodation and Consignment Agreement for Lands and Facilities at Bagram Airfield Between the Islamic Republic of Afghanistan and the United States of America) (internal capitalization altered). The Agreement refers to Afghanistan as the "host nation" and the United States "as the lessee." The leasehold created by the agreement is to continue "until the United States or its successors determine that the premises are no longer required for its use."

Afghanistan remains a theater of active military combat. *** While the United States provides overall security to Bagram, numerous other nations have compounds on the base. Some of the other nations control access to their respective compounds. The troops of the other nations are present at Bagram both as part of the American-led military coalition in Afghanistan and as members of the International Security Assistance Force (ISAF) of the North Atlantic Treaty Organization. The mission of the ISAF is to support the Afghan government in the maintenance of security in Afghanistan. According to the United States, as of February 1, 2010, approximately 38,000 non-United States troops were serving in Afghanistan as part of the ISAF, representing 42 other countries.

*** After the change in presidential administrations on January 22, 2009, the court invited the government to express any change in its position on the jurisdictional question. The government informed the district court that it "adheres to its previously articulated position."

While we will discuss specific points of law in more detail below, for a full understanding, we must first set forth some of the legal history underlying the controversy over the availability of the writ of habeas corpus and the constitutional protections it effectuates to noncitizens of the United States held beyond the sovereign territory of the United States. [The court surveys the law –*Eisentrager*, *Rasul*, DTA 2005, *Hamdan*, MCA 2006, and *Boumedienne*. It then discussed the last of these in part as follows:]

*** [T]he Court stated that "nothing in *Eisentrager* says that *de jure* sovereignty is or has ever been the only relevant consideration in determining the geographic reach of the Constitution or of habeas corpus." *** [Addressing] the question of the jurisdiction of United States courts to consider habeas petitions from detainees in Guantanamo, the Court concluded that "at least three factors are relevant in determining the reach of the Suspension Clause." Those three factors, which we must apply today in answering the same question as to detainees at Bagram, are:

> (1) the citizenship and status of the detainee and the adequacy of the process through which that status determination was made; (2) the nature of the sites where apprehension and then detention took place; and (3) the practical obstacles inherent in resolving the prisoner's entitlement to the writ.

Applying these factors to the detainees at Guantanamo, the Court held that the petitioners had the protection of the Suspension Clause.

Our duty, as explained above, is to determine the reach of the right to habeas corpus and therefore of the Suspension Clause to the factual context underlying the petitions we consider in the present appeal. *** At the outset, we note that each of the parties has asserted both an extreme understanding of the law after *Boumediene* and a more nuanced set of arguments upon which each relies in anticipation of the possible rejection of the bright-line arguments. The United States would like us to hold that the *Boumediene* analysis has no application beyond territories that are, like Guantanamo, outside the *de jure* sovereignty of the United States but are subject to its *de facto* sovereignty. As the government puts it in its reply brief, "[t]he real question before this Court, therefore, is whether Bagram may be considered effectively part of the United States in light of the nature and history of the U.S. presence there." We disagree.

Relying upon three independent reasons, the Court in *Boumediene* expressly repudiated the argument of the United States in that case to the effect "that the *Eisentrager* Court adopted a formalistic, sovereignty-based test for determining the reach of the Suspension Clause." *** We note that the very fact that the *Boumediene* Court set forth the three-factor test outlined above parallels the *Eisentrager* Court's further reasoning addressed by the *Boumediene* Court in its rejection of the bright-line *de jure* sovereignty argument before it. That is, had the *Boumediene* Court intended to limit its understanding of the reach of the Suspension Clause to territories over which the United States exercised *de facto* sovereignty, it would have had no need to outline the factors to be considered either generally or in the detail which it in fact adopted. We therefore reject the proposition that *Boumediene* adopted a bright-line test with the effect of substituting *de facto* for *de jure* in the otherwise rejected interpretation of *Eisentrager*.

For similar reasons, we reject the most extreme position offered by the petitioners. At various points, the petitioners seem to be arguing that the fact of United States control of Bagram under the lease of the military base is sufficient to trigger the extraterritorial application of the Suspension Clause, or at least satisfy the second factor of the three set forth in *Boumediene*. Again, we reject this extreme understanding. Such an interpretation would seem to create the potential for the extraterritorial extension of the Suspension Clause to noncitizens held in any United States military facility in the world, and perhaps to an undeterminable number of other United States-leased facilities as well. *** If it were the Supreme Court's intention to declare such a sweeping application, it would surely have said so. Just as we reject the extreme argument of the United States that would render most of the decision in *Boumediene* dicta, we reject the first line of argument offered by petitioners. Having rejected the bright-line arguments of both parties, we must proceed to their more nuanced arguments, and reach a conclusion based on the application of the Supreme Court's enumerated factors to the case before us.

The first of the enumerated factors is "the citizenship and status of the detainee and the adequacy of the process through which that status determination was made." Citizenship is, of course, an important factor in determining the constitutional rights of persons before the court. It is well established that there are "constitutional decisions of [the Supreme] Court expressly according differing protection to aliens than to citizens." *United States v. Verdugo-Urquidez,* 494 U.S. at 273, 110 S.Ct. 1056. However, clearly the alien citizenship of the petitioners in this case does not weigh against their claim to protection of the right of habeas corpus under the Suspension Clause. So far as citizenship is concerned, they differ in no material respect from the petitioners at Guantanamo who prevailed in *Boumediene.* As to status, the petitioners before us are held as enemy aliens. But so were the *Boumediene* petitioners. While the *Eisentrager* petitioners were in a weaker position by having the status of war criminals, that is immaterial to the question before us. This question is governed by *Boumediene* and the status of the petitioners before us again is the same as the Guantanamo detainees, so this factor supports their argument for the extension of the availability of the writ.

So far as the adequacy of the process through which that status determination was made, the petitioners are in a stronger position for the availability of the writ than were either the *Eisentrager* or *Boumediene* petitioners. As the Supreme Court noted, the *Boumediene* petitioners were in a very different posture than those in *Eisentrager* in that "there ha[d] been no trial by military commission for violations of the laws of war." Unlike the *Boumediene* petitioners or those before us, "[t]he *Eisentrager* petitioners were charged by a bill of particulars that made detailed factual allegations against them." The *Eisentrager* detainees were "entitled to representation by counsel, allowed to introduce evidence on their own behalf, and permitted to cross-examine the prosecution's witnesses" in an adversarial proceeding. The status of the *Boumediene* petitioners was determined by Combatant Status Review Tribunals (CSRTs) affording far less protection. Under the CSRT proceeding, the detainee, rather than being represented by an attorney, was advised by a "Personal Representative" who was "not the detainee's lawyer or even his 'advocate.' " The CSRT proceeding was less protective than the military tribunal procedures in *Eisentrager* in other particulars as well, and the Supreme Court clearly stated that "[t]he difference is not trivial."

The status of the Bagram detainees is determined not by a Combatant Status Review Tribunal but by an "Unlawful Enemy Combatant Review

Board" (UECRB). As the district court correctly noted, proceedings before the UECRB afford even less protection to the rights of detainees in the determination of status than was the case with the CSRT.[4] Therefore, as the district court noted, "while the important adequacy of process factor strongly supported the extension of the Suspension Clause and habeas rights in *Boumediene,* it even more strongly favors petitioners here." Therefore, examining only the first of the Supreme Court's three enumerated factors, petitioners have made a strong argument that the right to habeas relief and the Suspension Clause apply in Bagram as in Guantanamo. However, we do not stop with the first factor.

The second factor, "the nature of the sites where apprehension and then detention took place," weighs heavily in favor of the United States. Like all petitioners in both *Eisentrager* and *Boumediene,* the petitioners here were apprehended abroad. While this in itself would appear to weigh against the extension of the writ, it obviously would not be sufficient, otherwise *Boumediene* would not have been decided as it was. However, the nature of the place where the detention takes place weighs more strongly in favor of the position argued by the United States and against the extension of habeas jurisdiction than was the case in either *Boumediene* or *Eisentrager.* In the first place, while *de facto* sovereignty is not determinative, for the reasons discussed above, the very fact that it was the subject of much discussion in *Boumediene* makes it obvious that it is not without relevance. As the Supreme Court set forth, Guantanamo Bay is "a territory that, while technically not part of the United States, is under the complete and total control of our Government." While it is true that the United States holds a leasehold interest in Bagram, and held a leasehold interest in Guantanamo, the surrounding circumstances are hardly the same. The United States has maintained its total control of Guantanamo Bay for over a century, even in the face of a hostile government maintaining *de jure* sovereignty over the property. In Bagram, while the United States has options as to duration of the lease agreement, there is no indication of any intent to occupy the base with permanence, nor is there hostility on the part of the "host" country. Therefore, the notion that *de facto* sovereignty extends to Bagram is no more real than would have been the same claim with respect to Landsberg in the *Eisentrager* case. While it is certainly realistic to assert that the United States has *de facto* sovereignty over Guantanamo, the same simply is not true with respect to Bagram. Though the site of detention analysis weighs in favor of the United States and against the petitioners, it is not determinative.

But we hold that the third factor, that is "the practical obstacles inherent in resolving the prisoner's entitlement to the writ," particularly when considered along with the second factor, weighs overwhelmingly in favor of the position of the United States. It is undisputed that Bagram, indeed the

---

[4] The Government argues that in our analysis of this first factor, we should consider new procedures that it has put into place at Bagram in the past few months for evaluating the continued detention of individuals. But we will decide this case based on the procedures that have been in place, not on the new procedures that are being implemented only now when the case is before the Court of Appeals.

entire nation of Afghanistan, remains a theater of war. Not only does this suggest that the detention at Bagram is more like the detention at Landsberg than Guantanamo, the position of the United States is even stronger in this case than it was in *Eisentrager*. As the Supreme Court recognized in *Boumediene*, even though the active hostilities in the European theater had "c[o]me to an end," at the time of the *Eisentrager* decision, many of the problems of a theater of war remained:

> In addition to supervising massive reconstruction and aid efforts the American forces stationed in Germany faced potential security threats from a defeated enemy. In retrospect the post-War occupation may seem uneventful. But at the time *Eisentrager* was decided, the Court was right to be concerned about judicial interference with the military's efforts to contain "enemy elements, guerilla fighters, and 'were-wolves.'"

In ruling for the extension of the writ to Guantanamo, the Supreme Court expressly noted that "[s]imilar threats are not apparent here." In the case before us, similar, if not greater, threats are indeed apparent. The United States asserts, and petitioners cannot credibly dispute, that all of the attributes of a facility exposed to the vagaries of war are present in Bagram. *** We therefore conclude that under both *Eisentrager* and *Boumediene*, the writ does not extend to the Bagram confinement in an active theater of war in a territory under neither the *de facto* nor *de jure* sovereignty of the United States and within the territory of another *de jure* sovereign.

We are supported in this conclusion by the rationale of *Eisentrager*, which was not only not overruled, but reinforced by the language and reasoning just referenced from *Boumediene*. As we referenced in the background discussion of this opinion, we set forth more fully now concerns expressed by the Supreme Court in reaching its decision in *Eisentrager*:

> Such trials would hamper the war effort and bring aid and comfort to the enemy. They would diminish the prestige of our commanders, not only with enemies but with wavering neutrals. It would be difficult to devise more effective fettering of a field commander than to allow the very enemies he is ordered to reduce to submission to call him to account in his own civil courts and divert his efforts and attention from the military offensive abroad to the legal defensive at home. Nor is it unlikely that the result of such enemy litigiousness would be a conflict between judicial and military opinion highly comforting to enemies of the United States.

Those factors are more relevant to the situation at Bagram than they were at Landsberg. While it is true, as the Supreme Court noted in *Boumediene*, that the United States forces in Germany in 1950 faced the possibility of unrest and guerilla warfare, operations in the European theater had ended with the surrender of Germany and Italy years earlier. Bagram remains in a theater of war. We cannot, consistent with *Eisentrager* as elucidated by *Boumediene*, hold that the right to the writ of habeas corpus and the constitutional protections of the Suspension Clause extend to

Bagram detention facility in Afghanistan, and we therefore must reverse the decision of the district court denying the motion of the United States to dismiss the petitions.

We do not ignore the arguments of the detainees that the United States chose the place of detention and might be able "to evade judicial review of Executive detention decisions by transferring detainees into active conflict zones, thereby granting the Executive the power to switch the Constitution on or off at will." However, that is not what happened here. Indeed, without dismissing the legitimacy or sincerity of appellees' concerns, we doubt that this fact goes to either the second or third of the Supreme Court's enumerated factors. We need make no determination on the importance of this possibility, given that it remains only a possibility; its resolution can await a case in which the claim is a reality rather than a speculation. In so stating, we note that the Supreme Court did not dictate that the three enumerated factors are exhaustive. It only told us that *at least* three factors" are relevant. Perhaps such manipulation by the Executive might constitute an additional factor in some case in which it is in fact present. However, the notion that the United States deliberately confined the detainees in the theater of war rather than at, for example, Guantanamo, is not only unsupported by the evidence, it is not supported by reason. To have made such a deliberate decision to "turn off the Constitution" would have required the military commanders or other Executive officials making the situs determination to anticipate the complex litigation history set forth above and predict the *Boumediene* decision long before it came down.

Also supportive of our decision that the third factor weighs heavily in favor of the United States, as the district court recognized, is the fact that the detention is within the sovereign territory of another nation, which itself creates practical difficulties. Indeed, it was on this factor that the district court relied in dismissing the fourth petition, which was filed by an Afghan citizen detainee. While that factor certainly weighed more heavily with respect to an Afghan citizen, it is not without force with respect to detainees who are alien to both the United States and Afghanistan. The United States holds the detainees pursuant to a cooperative arrangement with Afghanistan on territory as to which Afghanistan is sovereign. While we cannot say that extending our constitutional protections to the detainees would be in any way disruptive of that relationship, neither can we say with certainty what the reaction of the Afghan government would be.

In sum, taken together, the second and especially the third factors compel us to hold that the petitions should have been dismissed. *** [T]he jurisdiction of the courts to afford the right to habeas relief and the protection of the Suspension Clause does not extend to aliens held in Executive detention in the Bagram detention facility in the Afghan theater of war. ***

Notes

1. Switching the Constitution On and Off. The District Court in *Maqaleh* held that habeas extends to the three non-Afghan detainees in this case. Applying *Boumediene's* multi-part test, the District Court stressed the lack of procedures provided to the detainees, that they had been transferred by the government from other places to Bagram (undercutting claims that habeas was impracticable there), the objective indicia of U.S. control over the base, as well as *Boumediene's* emphasis on the need to prevent the Executive from "switch[ing] the Constitution on or off at will." On appeal, one of the appellate judges inquired how he could or should consider the quite strong separation of powers pronouncements in *Boumediene*, when those concerns are not included in the explicit multi-part test the Court articulated. How could a lower court apply *Boumediene's* concern with the Executive switching the Constitution on and off whe that might extend, constitutional habeas to every case. Is there a fundamental tension (or lack of clarity) in *Boumediene's* focus on Guantanamo on the one hand and, on the other, the need not to let the Executive "switch the Constitution on or off at will"? Ultimately, how can that tension be resolved?

2. Global War. If in practical terms the war on terror is global in scope, to what extent should that fact inform the reach of habeas corpus? To what degree do you worry that the Executive will create places without law?

3. Long Term Detention. In its motion to dismiss in *Maqaleh*, the Government noted that "the United States would not detain enemy combatants on any long-term basis at a facility that it did not control." If this is the case, does *Boumediene* extend constitutional habeas to all long-term U.S. detention facilities? To U.S. embassies?

4. Citizenship. The District Court opinion in *Maqaleh* drew a line between the one Afghan and three non-Afghan detainees, finding constitutional habeas did not extend to the Afghani because to do so might create friction with the Afghan government. To what degree do you agree with the Court's assessment? Even after *Boumediene*, are you comfortable with a federal court, instead of the military or the State Department, making that sort of decision?

5. If Not Bagram, Where? Writing in THE NEW YORKER, Amy Davidson critiqued the Obama Administration's position on detention generally, asking: "So closing Guantánamo increases the need for a new Guantánamo, and barring the use of secret prisons just means that you need to find a new place to stash secret prisoners?" Do you agree with this critique? Why would the Obama Administration, which committed to closing Guantanamo, seek to keep the judiciary out of Bagram?

6. Administrative Changes. The day prior to the filing of briefs in the *Maqaleh* appeal, the Obama Administration announced new guidelines to provide Bagram detainees additional process beyond the UECRB the District Court had criticized. These procedures include appointment of a personal representative (a military official, not a lawyer) charged with collecting evidence and presenting[it to a military review board, which will assess each prisoner's detention every six months. As reported by THE NEW YORK TIMES, a Defense Department official explained the impetus of the new procedures in this way: "We want to be able to go into court and say we have good review procedures." How should new procedures impact judicial review? Will the courts in applying *Boumediene* have to answer Justice Roberts' call to squarely address what process detainees are constitutionally due?

7. What is a reasonable period of time? *Boumediene* held that the Executive must have a "reasonable amount of time" before the Suspension Clause applies, but did not indicate what such a reasonable time would be. While it is clear that "[t]he right to invoke the privilege of habeas corpus does not accrue from the day a petitioner is captured," when does it accrue? And should that timeline be informed by the practical considerations (or other factors) weighed by the Court in *Boumediene*?

8. Bagram Litigation Revived? After the Circuit Court issued its opinion, the detainees sought a rehearing. The court refused to rehear the case but stated that the detainees could seek to amend their petitions and plead additional facts which might change the outcome. At the time of this publication, the detainees have moved to amend their habeas petitions, and the district judge has issued an order permitting them to do so. Under both *Boumediene* and the circuit court's opinion, what facts do you believe they would need to plead for the writ to extend to them?

9. After Jurisdiction, How Much Deference? The Supreme Court, on the same day it released *Boumediene*, considered the habeas petitions of two U.S. citizens detained by the U.S. in Iraq. This decision received almost no treatment in the press, which was full of *Boumediene*. Consider, as you read this case, what it implies for habeas decisions in other foreign venues.

MUNAF v. GEREN
553 U.S. 674 (2008)

CHIEF JUSTICE ROBERTS delivered the opinion of the Court.

The Multinational Force-Iraq (MNF-I) is an international coalition force operating in Iraq composed of 26 different nations, including the United States. The force operates under the unified command of United States military officers, at the request of the Iraqi Government, and in accordance with United Nations (U.N.) Security Council Resolutions. Pursuant to the U.N. mandate, MNF-I forces detain individuals alleged to have committed hostile or warlike acts in Iraq, pending investigation and prosecution in Iraqi courts under Iraqi law.

These consolidated cases concern the availability of habeas corpus relief arising from the MNF-I's detention of American citizens who voluntarily traveled to Iraq and are alleged to have committed crimes there. We are confronted with two questions. *First,* do United States courts have jurisdiction over habeas corpus petitions filed on behalf of American citizens challenging their detention in Iraq by the MNF-I? *Second,* if such jurisdiction exists, may district courts exercise that jurisdiction to enjoin the MNF-I from transferring such individuals to Iraqi custody or allowing them to be tried before Iraqi courts? ***

Petitioner Shawqi Omar, an American-Jordanian citizen, voluntarily traveled to Iraq in 2002. In October 2004, Omar was captured and detained in Iraq by U.S. military forces operating as part of the MNF-I during a raid of his Baghdad home. Omar is believed to have provided aid to Abu Musab al-Zarqawi-the late leader of al Qaeda in Iraq-by facilitating his group's connection with other terrorist groups, bringing foreign fighters into Iraq, and planning and executing kidnappings in Iraq. *** The raid netted an Iraqi insurgent and four Jordanian fighters along with explosive devices and other weapons.*** Following Omar's arrest, a three-member MNF-I Tribunal composed of American military officers concluded that Omar posed a threat to the security of Iraq and designated him a "security internee." The tribunal also found that Omar had committed hostile and warlike acts, and that he was an enemy combatant in the war on terrorism. In accordance with Article 5 of the Geneva Convention, Omar was permitted to hear the basis for his detention, make a statement, and call immediately available witnesses.

In addition to the review of his detention by the MNF-I Tribunal, Omar received a hearing before the Combined Review and Release Board (CRRB)-a nine-member board composed of six representatives of the Iraqi Government and three MNF-I officers. The CRRB, like the MNF-I Tribunal, concluded that Omar's continued detention was necessary because he posed a threat to Iraqi security. At all times since his capture, Omar has remained in the custody of the United States military operating as part of the MNF-I.

Petitioner Munaf, a citizen of both Iraq and the United States, voluntarily traveled to Iraq with several Romanian journalists. He was to serve as the journalists' translator and guide. Shortly after arriving in Iraq, the group was kidnapped and held captive for two months. After the journalists were freed, MNF-I forces detained Munaf based on their belief that he had orchestrated the kidnappings.

A three-judge MNF-I Tribunal conducted a hearing to determine whether Munaf's detention was warranted. The MNF-I Tribunal reviewed the facts surrounding Munaf's capture, interviewed witnesses, and considered the available intelligence information. Munaf was present at the hearing and had an opportunity to hear the grounds for his detention, make a statement, and call immediately available witnesses. At the end of the hearing, the tribunal found that Munaf posed a serious threat to Iraqi security, designated him a "security internee," and referred his case to the CCCI for criminal investigation and prosecution.

During his CCCI trial, Munaf admitted on camera and in writing that he had facilitated the kidnapping of the Romanian journalists. He also appeared as a witness against his alleged co-conspirators. Later in the proceedings, Munaf recanted his confession, but the CCCI nonetheless found him guilty of kidnapping. On appeal, the Iraqi Court of Cassation vacated Munaf's conviction and remanded his case to the CCCI for further investigation. The Court of Cassation directed that Munaf was to "remain in custody pending the outcome" of further criminal proceedings.

The Solicitor General argues that the federal courts lack jurisdiction over the detainees' habeas petitions because the American forces holding Omar and Munaf operate as part of a multinational force. Brief for Federal Parties 17-36. The habeas statute provides that a federal district court may entertain a habeas application by a person held "in custody under or by color of the authority of the United States," or "in custody in violation of the Constitution or laws or treaties of the United States." (3). MNF-I forces, the argument goes, "are not operating solely under United States authority, but rather 'as the agent of' a multinational force." Omar and Munaf are thus held pursuant to international authority, not "the authority of the United States," and they are therefore not within the reach of the habeas statute.[2]

The United States acknowledges that Omar and Munaf are American citizens held overseas in the immediate " 'physical custody' " of American soldiers who answer only to an American chain of command. The MNF-I itself operates subject to a unified American command. "[A]s a practical matter," the Government concedes, it is "the President and the Pentagon, the Secretary of Defense, and the American commanders that control what ... American soldiers do," including the soldiers holding Munaf and Omar. In light of these admissions, it is unsurprising that the United States has never argued that it lacks the authority to release Munaf or Omar, or that it requires the consent of other countries to do so.

We think these concessions the end of the jurisdictional inquiry. The Government's argument-that the federal courts have no jurisdiction over American citizens held by American forces operating as multinational agents-is not easily reconciled with the text of § 2241(c)(1). That section applies to persons held "in custody under or by color of the authority of the United States." An individual is held "in custody" by the United States when the United States official charged with his detention has "the power to produce" him. The disjunctive "or" *** makes clear that actual custody by the United States suffices for jurisdiction, even if that custody could be viewed as "under ... color of" another authority, such as the MNF-I. ***

We now turn to the question whether United States district courts may exercise their habeas jurisdiction to enjoin our Armed Forces from transferring individuals detained within another sovereign's territory to that sovereign's government for criminal prosecution. The nature of that question requires us to proceed "with the circumspection appropriate when this Court is adjudicating issues inevitably entangled in the conduct of our international relations." Here there is the further consideration that those issues arise in the context of ongoing military operations conducted by American Forces overseas. We therefore approach these questions cognizant that "courts traditionally have been reluctant to intrude upon the authority of the Executive in military and national security affairs." ***

The habeas petitioners argue that the writ should be granted in their cases because they have "a legally enforceable right" not to be transferred to Iraqi authority for criminal proceedings under both the Due Process Clause and the Foreign Affairs Reform and Restructuring Act of 1998 (FARR Act), and because they are innocent civilians who have been unlawfully detained by the United States in violation of the Due Process Clause. With respect to the transfer claim, petitioners request an injunction prohibiting the United States from transferring them to Iraqi custody. With respect to the unlawful

---

[2] These cases concern only American citizens and only the statutory reach of the writ. Nothing herein addresses jurisdiction with respect to alien petitioners or with respect to the constitutional scope of the writ.

detention claim, petitioners seek "release"-but only to the extent that release would not result in "unlawful" transfer to Iraqi custody. Both of these requests would interfere with Iraq's sovereign right to "punish offenses against its laws committed within its borders." We accordingly hold that the detainees' claims do not state grounds upon which habeas relief may be granted, that the habeas petitions should have been promptly dismissed, and that no injunction should have been entered.

*** At the outset, the nature of the relief sought by the habeas petitioners suggests that habeas is not appropriate in these cases. Habeas is at its core a remedy for unlawful executive detention. The typical remedy for such detention is, of course, release. But here the last thing petitioners want is simple release; that would expose them to apprehension by Iraqi authorities for criminal prosecution-precisely what petitioners went to federal court to avoid. At the end of the day, what petitioners are really after is a court order requiring the United States to shelter them from the sovereign government seeking to have them answer for alleged crimes committed within that sovereign's borders.

The habeas petitioners do not dispute that they voluntarily traveled to Iraq, that they remain detained within the sovereign territory of Iraq today, or that they are alleged to have committed serious crimes in Iraq. Indeed, Omar and Munaf both concede that, if they were not in MNF-I custody, Iraq would be free to arrest and prosecute them under Iraqi law. There is, moreover, no question that Munaf is the subject of ongoing Iraqi criminal proceedings and that Omar would be but for the present injunction. Munaf was convicted by the CCCI, and while that conviction was overturned on appeal, his case was remanded to and is again pending before the CCCI. The MNF-I referred Omar to the CCCI for prosecution at which point he sought and obtained an injunction that prohibits his prosecution.

Given these facts, our cases make clear that Iraq has a sovereign right to prosecute Omar and Munaf for crimes committed on its soil. As Chief Justice Marshall explained nearly two centuries ago, "[t]he jurisdiction of the nation within its own territory is necessarily exclusive and absolute." *Schooner Exchange v. McFaddon,* 7 Cranch 116, (1812).

This is true with respect to American citizens who travel abroad and commit crimes in another nation whether or not the pertinent criminal process comes with all the rights guaranteed by our Constitution. "When an American citizen commits a crime in a foreign country he cannot complain if required to submit to such modes of trial and to such punishment as the laws of that country may prescribe for its own people." ***

The habeas petitioners nonetheless argue that the Due Process Clause includes a "[f]reedom from unlawful transfer" that is "protected *wherever* the government seizes a citizen." We disagree. Not only have we long recognized the principle that a nation state reigns sovereign within its own territory, we have twice applied that principle to reject claims that the Constitution precludes the Executive from transferring a prisoner to a foreign country for prosecution in an allegedly unconstitutional trial. *** In the present cases, the habeas petitioners concede that Iraq has the sovereign authority to prosecute them for alleged violations of its law, yet nonetheless request an injunction prohibiting the United States from transferring them to Iraqi custody. *** [H]abeas is not a means of compelling the United States to harbor fugitives from the criminal justice system of a sovereign with undoubted authority to prosecute them.

Petitioners' "release" claim adds nothing to their "transfer" claim. That claim fails for the same reasons the transfer claim fails, given that the release petitioners seek is release in a form that would avoid transfer. Such "release" would impermissibly interfere with Iraq's "exclusive jurisdiction to punish offenses against its laws committed within its borders," the "release" petitioners seek is nothing less than an order commanding our forces to smuggle them out of Iraq. ***

Moreover, because Omar and Munaf are being held by United States Armed Forces at the behest of the Iraqi Government pending their prosecution in Iraqi courts, release of *any* kind would interfere with the sovereign authority of Iraq "to punish offenses against its laws committed within its borders," This point becomes clear given that the MNF-I, pursuant to its U.N. mandate, is authorized to "take all necessary measures to contribute to the maintenance of security and stability in Iraq," and specifically to provide for the "internment [of individuals in Iraq] where this is necessary for imperative reasons of security,"

While the Iraqi Government is ultimately "responsible for [the] arrest, detention and imprisonment" of individuals who violate its laws, the MNF-I maintains physical custody of individuals like Munaf and Omar while their cases are being heard by the CCCI. Indeed, Munaf is currently held at Camp Cropper pursuant to the express order of the Iraqi Courts. As that court order makes clear, MNF-I detention is an integral part of the Iraqi system of criminal justice. MNF-I forces augment the Iraqi Government's peacekeeping efforts by functioning, in essence, as its jailor. Any requirement that the MNF-I release a detainee would, in effect, impose a release order on the Iraqi Government.

The habeas petitioners acknowledge that *some* interference with a foreign criminal system is too much. They concede that "it is axiomatic that an American court does not provide collateral review of proceedings in a foreign tribunal." We agree, but see no reason why habeas corpus should permit a prisoner detained within a foreign sovereign's territory to prevent a trial from going forward in the first place. *** Rather, "the same principles of comity and respect for foreign sovereigns that preclude judicial scrutiny of foreign convictions necessarily render invalid attempts to shield citizens from foreign prosecution in order to preempt such nonreviewable adjudications."

To allow United States courts to intervene in an ongoing foreign criminal proceeding and pass judgment on its legitimacy seems at least as great an intrusion as the plainly barred collateral review of foreign convictions. ***

There is of course even more at issue here: *** [T]he Constitution allows the Executive to transfer American citizens to foreign authorities for criminal prosecution. It would be passing strange to hold that the Executive lacks that same authority where, as here, the detainees were captured by our Armed Forces for engaging in serious hostile acts against an ally in what the Government refers to as "an active theater of combat."

Such a conclusion would implicate not only concerns about interfering with a sovereign's recognized prerogative to apply its criminal law to those alleged to have committed crimes within its borders, but also concerns about unwarranted judicial intrusion into the Executive's ability to conduct military operations abroad. ***

Petitioners contend that these general principles are trumped in their cases because their transfer to Iraqi custody is likely to result in torture. This allegation was raised in Munaf's petition for habeas, but not in Omar's. Such allegations are of course a matter of serious concern, but in the present context that concern is to be addressed by the political branches, not the judiciary. *** Even with respect to claims that detainees would be denied constitutional rights if transferred, we have recognized that it is for the political branches, not the judiciary, to assess practices in foreign countries and to determine national policy in light of those assessments. ***

The Executive Branch may, of course, decline to surrender a detainee for many reasons, including humanitarian ones. Petitioners here allege only the possibility of mistreatment in a prison facility; this is not a more extreme case in which the Executive has determined that a detainee is likely to be tortured but decides to transfer him anyway. Indeed, the Solicitor General states that it is the policy of the United States *not* to transfer an individual in circumstances where torture is likely to result. *** The Judiciary is not suited to second-guess such determinations-determinations that would require federal courts to pass judgment on foreign justice systems and undermine the Government's ability to speak with one voice in this area. ***

Petitioners briefly argue that their claims of potential torture may not be readily dismissed on the basis of these principles because the FARR Act prohibits transfer when torture may result. Neither petitioner asserted a FARR Act claim in his petition for habeas, and the Act was not raised in any of the certiorari filings before this Court. Even in their merits brief in this Court, the habeas petitioners hardly discuss the issue. The Government treats the issue in kind. Under such circumstances we will not consider the question.[6]

Finally, the habeas petitioners raise the additional argument that the United States may not transfer a detainee to Iraqi custody, not because it

---

[6] We hold that these habeas petitions raise no claim for relief under the FARR Act and express no opinion on whether Munaf and Omar may be permitted to amend their respective pleadings to raise such a claim on remand. Even if considered on the merits, several issues under the FARR Act claim would have to be addressed. First, the Act speaks to situations where a detainee is being "returned" to "a country." *** It is not settled that the Act addresses the transfer of an individual located in Iraq to the Government of Iraq; arguably such an individual is not being "returned" to "a country"-he is already there. Second, claims under the FARR Act may be limited to certain immigration proceedings.

would be unconstitutional to do so, but because the "[G]overnment may not transfer a citizen without legal authority." The United States, they claim, bears the burden of "identify[ing] a treaty or statute that permits it to transfer the[m] to Iraqi custody." ***

The habeas petitioners rely prominently on [a case] where we ruled that the Executive may not extradite a person held within the United States unless "legal authority" to do so "is given by act of Congress or by the terms of a treaty," But [this case] is readily distinguishable. It involved the extradition of an individual from the United States; this is not an extradition case, but one involving the transfer to a sovereign's authority of an individual captured and already detained in that sovereign's territory. In the extradition context, when a "fugitive criminal" is found within the United States, " 'there is no authority vested in any department of the government to seize [him] and surrender him to a foreign power,' " in the absence of a pertinent constitutional or legislative provision. But Omar and Munaf voluntarily traveled to Iraq and are being held there. They are therefore subject to the territorial jurisdiction of that sovereign, not of the United States. Moreover, as we have explained, the petitioners are being held by the United States, acting as part of MNF-I, at the request of and on behalf of the Iraqi Government. It would be more than odd if the Government had no authority to transfer them to the very sovereign on whose behalf, and within whose territory, they are being detained. ***

For all the reasons given above, petitioners state no claim in their habeas petitions for which relief can be granted, and those petitions should have been promptly dismissed. The judgments below and the injunction entered against the United States are vacated, and the cases are remanded for further proceedings consistent with this opinion.***

JUSTICE SOUTER with whom JUSTICE GINSBURG and JUSTICE BREYER join, concurring.

The Court holds that "[u]nder circumstances such as those presented here, ... habeas corpus provides petitioners with no relief." .The Court's opinion makes clear that those circumstances include the following: (1) Omar and Munaf "voluntarily traveled to Iraq." . They are being held (2) in the "territory" of (3) an "all[y]" of the United States, (4) by our troops, (5) "during ongoing hostilities" that (6) "involv[e] our troops." (7) The government of a foreign sovereign, Iraq, has decided to prosecute them "for crimes committed on its soil." And (8) "the State Department has determined that ... the department that would have authority over Munaf and Omar ... as well as its prison and detention facilities have generally met internationally accepted standards for basic prisoner needs." Because I consider these circumstances essential to the Court's holding, I join its opinion.

The Court accordingly reserves judgment on an "extreme case in which the Executive has determined that a detainee [in United States custody] is likely to be tortured but decides to transfer him anyway." I would add that nothing in today's opinion should be read as foreclosing relief for a citizen of the United States who resists transfer, say, from the American military to a foreign government for prosecution in a case of that sort, and I would extend the caveat to a case in which the probability of torture is well documented, even if the Executive fails to acknowledge it. Although the Court rightly points out that any likelihood of extreme mistreatment at the receiving Government's hands is a proper matter for the political branches to consider, if the political branches did favor transfer it would be in order to ask whether substantive due process bars the Government from consigning its own people to torture. And although the Court points out that habeas is aimed at securing release, not protective detention, habeas would not be the only avenue open to an objecting prisoner; "where federally protected rights [are threatened], it has been the rule from the beginning that courts will be alert to adjust their remedies so as to grant the necessary relief."

Notes

1. Policy. Do you think the Court correctly steps back from ordering transfer of the petitioners? List the factors on each side of the habeas relief ledger. Would the ledger be the same if the petitioners were held at Guantanamo?

2. Breadth. Does the concurrence challenge any aspect of the primary opinion in this case? If not, why was it written?

3. Ramifications. Does *Munaf* make *Boumediene* a hollow promise to most "war on terror" detainees? Does it help explain why very few transfers to Guantanamo were made during the Iraq war and subsequent insurgency? If President Obama had closed Guantanamo and moved the detainees to Bagram and other overseas prisons, would that have prevented the courts from ordering release of those moved?

4. Remember WWII Enemy Detention? What do you conclude would happen today if the United States detained enemy combatants in the territorial U.S., as it did during WWII? Would habeas petitions be heard by the courts? What likelihood would there have been in WWI that errors were made in detaining certain individuals? The following D.C. Circuit cases will give you further thoughts on answering these questions. First, however, a note of introduction.

C. GUANTANAMO II: IMPLEMENTING *BOUMEDIENE*

Chief Justice Roberts' dissent in *Boumediene* said "The Court's analysis leaves [the detainees] with only the prospect of further litigation to determine the content of their new habeas right, followed by further litigation to resolve their particular cases, followed by further litigation before the D.C. Circuit-where they could have started had they invoked the DTA procedure." Even more bluntly, Justice Scalia's dissent opined: "Henceforth, as today's opinion makes unnervingly clear, how to handle enemy prisoners in this war will ultimately lie with the branch that knows least about the national security concerns that the subject entails."

In short, Boumediene opened the door to a flood of Guantanamo habeas petitions. And the flood came: over 50 cases decided as of September 2010, with another hundred or so pending. Of the initial 53 petitions, 38 have been successful, an astonishing success rate of over 70%, as catalogued by an excellent student note by Nathaniel H Nesbitt, "Meeting Boumediene's Challenge: The Emergence of an Effective Habeas Jurisprudence and Obsolescence of New Detention Legislation," 95 Minn. L. Rev. 244 (2010). This note argues that, because the D.C. Circuit has resolved a number of the uncertainties foreseen by critics of *Boumediene*, there is no need for legislation to create the "rules of the road" for Guantanamo habeas proceedings. This is an issue you shuld ponder as you go through the cases. Meanwhile, the cases excerpted below are the lawyer's critical tools for handling habeas proceedings, at least until legislation or Supreme Court guidance is forthcoming.

These cases can be viewed as responding to two primary concerns: (1) Will habeas proceedings compromise national security? and (2) Will the detainees be given a fair shake in habeas proceedings? Judicial answers, typically for the law, are indirect, for the courts focus not on public policy but on legal process and remedies. After *Boumediene*, in anticipation of a flood of petitions, *In re Guantanamo Bay Detainee Litigation*, 567 F. Supp. 2d 83 (D.D.C. 2008) designated Judge Hogan to "coordinate and manage" the litigation. Judge Hogan in turn issued a Case Management Order (CMO), see 2008 WL 4858241 (D.D.C. Nov. 6, 2008), which addressed issues concerning discovery, burden of proof, and access to classified evidence. Somewhat schizophrenically, the burden was placed on the government to show it was "more likely than not" that the detainee should continue to be detained but judges were allowed to grant a "rebuttable presumption" to the Government's evidence.

As the district court litigation moved forward under the CMO procedures, different judges issued inconsistent opinions on (1) substantive detention standards, including the tension between the Government's habeas burden and its beneficial rebuttable presumption, (2) how and when to assess evidence concerning whether an individual was wrongly detained, and (3) the relief available to detainees receiving favorable decisions on their petitions. The D.C. Circuit has resolved the dissonance of the district court decisions in the following cases, which I have introduced with headings based on the preceding three categories.

1. DETENTION STANDARDS AND HABEAS BURDEN OF PROOF

AL-BIHANI v. OBAMA
590 F. 3d 866, reh'g en banc den 619 F. 3d 1 (D.C. Cir. 2010),
cert. den. 2011 WL 1225807

BROWN, Circuit Judge:

*** Al-Bihani's many arguments present this court with two overarching questions regarding the detainees at the Guantanamo Bay naval base. The first concerns whom the President can lawfully detain pursuant to statutes passed by Congress. {This part of the opinion is in Chapter IV]. The second asks what procedure is due to detainees challenging their detention in habeas corpus proceedings. ***

We now turn to Al-Bihani's procedural challenge. He claims the habeas process afforded him by the district court fell short of the requirements of the Suspension Clause and that his case should be remanded for rehearing in line with new, more protective procedures. *** Al-Bihani *** claims the district court erred by: (1) adopting a preponderance of the evidence standard of proof; (2) shifting the burden to him to prove the unlawfulness of his detention; (3) neglecting to hold a separate evidentiary hearing; (4) admitting hearsay evidence; (5) presuming the accuracy of the Government's evidence; (6) requiring him to explain why his discovery request would not unduly burden the government; and (7) denying all but one of his discovery requests. In support of these claims, Al-Bihani cites statutes prescribing habeas procedure for review of federal and state court convictions and analogizes to a number of cases concerning review of detentions related to criminal prosecutions. ***

Al-Bihani's argument clearly demonstrates error, but that error is his own. Habeas review for Guantanamo detainees need not match the procedures developed by Congress and the courts specifically for habeas challenges to criminal convictions. *Boumediene's* holding explicitly stated that habeas procedures for detainees "need not resemble a criminal trial." It instead invited "innovation" of habeas procedure by lower courts, granting leeway for "[c]ertain accommodations [to] be made to reduce the burden habeas corpus proceedings will place on the military." *Boumediene's* holding therefore places Al-Bihani's procedural argument on shaky ground. The Suspension Clause protects only the fundamental character of habeas proceedings, and any argument equating that fundamental character with all the accoutrements of habeas for domestic criminal defendants is highly suspect.

In considering Al-Bihani's argument, we recognize that the Great Writ is not a static institution and it did not begin its life looking like it does today. *** As the twentieth century progressed, the protections and rules of criminal habeas expanded further to account for a growing number of recognized constitutional and statutory rights and to manage the sheer number of petitions coursing through the federal courts. Rules governing habeas petitions apart from the criminal sphere-such as those challenging post-removal-period detention in the immigration context, and those filed pursuant to the Force Act of 1833, developed separately. This brief account of habeas' evolving nature serves to make clear that, in the shadow of *Boumediene*, courts are neither bound by the procedural limits created for other detention contexts nor obliged to use them as baselines from which any departures must be justified. Detention of aliens outside the sovereign territory of the United States during wartime is a different and peculiar circumstance, and the appropriate habeas procedures cannot be conceived of as mere extensions of an existing doctrine. Rather, those procedures are a whole new branch of the tree.

Al-Bihani, however, argues his case does not rest on that branch. He points to one of the seven concurring opinions in *Al-Marri v. Pucciarelli, 534 F.3d 213, 269 (4th Cir.2008)* (Traxler, J., concurring in the judgment), to support his contention that the Supreme Court did not authorize less demanding procedures for a case like his. Judge Traxler's opinion reasoned the *Hamdi* Court blessed lower procedural standards only upon a showing of undue hardship by the government, but such hardship was especially clear when a petitioner was seized on a foreign battlefield where the prospect of high evidentiary standards might interfere with military operations. Because the petitioner in *Al-Marri* was seized by federal law enforcement in Illinois, Judge Traxler concluded that as a general rule he was "entitled to the normal due process protections available to all within this country," absent a satisfactory showing by the government. We do not express an opinion on whether or when different habeas procedures are appropriate for petitioners seized domestically pursuant to the AUMF; those questions are for another case. It is enough for us to point out that Judge Traxler's opinion is of no help to Al-Bihani; he falls squarely in the category of petitioners that Judge Traxler and the Supreme Court in *Hamdi* deemed deserving of leaner procedures.

Unlike either Hamdi or Al-Marri, Al-Bihani is a non-citizen who was seized in a foreign country. Requiring highly protective procedures at the tail end of the detention process for detainees like Al-Bihani would have systemic effects on the military's entire approach to war. From the moment a shot is fired, to battlefield capture, up to a detainee's day in court, military operations would be compromised as the government strove to satisfy evidentiary standards in anticipation of habeas litigation. Al-Bihani suggests no such danger is posed in his case because the evidence presented in the Government's return consisted mainly of records of interrogations that took place at Guantanamo and not of evidence procured from the battlefield. Logically, however, had the district court imposed stringent standards of evidence in the first instance, the government may well have been obligated to go beyond Al-Bihani's interrogation records and into the battlefield to present a case that met its burden. That the district Court's tailored procedure prevented such a scenario cannot possibly make the procedure constitutionally infirm.

With Al-Bihani's limited procedural entitlement established as a general matter, we turn to the specific procedural claims warranting serious consideration. The question of what standard of proof is due in a habeas proceeding like Al-Bihani's has not been answered by the Supreme Court. Attempting to fill this void, Al-Bihani argues the prospect of indefinite detention in this unconventional war augurs for a reasonable doubt standard or, in the alternative, at least a clear and convincing standard. The government disagrees, arguing that *Hamdi's* plurality opinion indirectly endorsed a preponderance standard when it suggested due process requirements may have been satisfied by a military tribunal, the regulations of which adopt a preponderance standard.

We believe the Government's argument stands on more solid ground. In addition to the *Hamdi* plurality's approving treatment of military tribunal procedure, it also described as constitutionally adequate-even for the detention of U.S. citizens-a "burden-shifting scheme" in which the government need only present "credible evidence that the habeas petitioner meets the enemy-combatant criteria" before "the onus could shift to the petitioner to rebut that evidence with more persuasive evidence that he falls outside the criteria." That description mirrors a preponderance standard. We emphasize our opinion does not endeavor to identify what standard would represent the minimum required by the Constitution. Our narrow charge is to determine whether a preponderance standard is unconstitutional. Absent more specific and relevant guidance, we find no indication that it is.

As already discussed, traditional habeas review did not entail review of factual findings, particularly in the military context. Where factual review has been authorized, the burden in some domestic circumstances has been placed *on the petitioner* to prove his case under a clear and convincing standard. If it is constitutionally permissible to place that higher burden on a citizen petitioner in a routine case, it follows a priori that placing a lower burden on the government defending a wartime detention-where national security interests are at their zenith and the rights of the alien petitioner at their nadir-is also permissible.

We find Al-Bihani's hearsay challenges to be similarly unavailing. Al-Bihani claims that government reports of his interrogation answers-which made up the majority, if not all, of the evidence on which the district court relied-and other informational documents were hearsay improperly admitted absent an examination of reliability and necessity. He contends, in fact, that government reports of his interrogation answers were "*double* hearsay" because his answers were first translated by an interpreter and then written down by an interrogator. We first note that Al-Bihani's interrogation answers themselves were not hearsay; they were instead party-opponent admissions that would have been admitted in any U.S. court. That they were translated does not affect their status. *** Other information, such as a diagram of Al Qaeda's leadership structure, was also hearsay.

But that such evidence was hearsay does not automatically invalidate its admission-it only begins our inquiry. We observe Al-Bihani cannot make the traditional objection based on the Confrontation Clause of the Sixth Amendment. This is so because the Confrontation Clause applies only in criminal prosecutions, and is not directly relevant to the habeas setting. The Confrontation Clause seeks to ensure the reliability of evidence, but it also seeks to eliminate the ephemeral perception of unfairness associated with the use of hearsay evidence. Al-Bihani, however, does not enjoy a right to the psychic value of excluding hearsay and whatever right he has is not an independent procedural entitlement. Rather, it operates only to the extent that it provides the baseline level of evidentiary reliability necessary for the "meaningful" habeas proceeding *Boumediene* requires under the Suspension Clause.

Therefore, the question a habeas court must ask when presented with hearsay is not whether it is admissible-it is always admissible-but what probative weight to ascribe to whatever indicia of reliability it exhibits. This approach is evident in the relevant caselaw. *Boumediene* did not say exactly how a habeas court should treat hearsay, but it broadly required that a court be able to "assess the sufficiency of the Government's evidence." In *Hamdi,*the Supreme Court said hearsay "may need to be accepted as the most reliable available evidence" as long as the petitioner is given the opportunity to rebut that evidence. *** [A] panel of this court in the related context of DTA review did not reject hearsay evidence as inadmissible, but rather considered it and deemed it insufficient to support detention because the panel could not "assess the reliability" of its " bare assertions" in the absence of contextual information. *Parhat v. Gates,* 532 F.3d 834, 847 (D.C.Cir.2008).

A procedure that seeks to determine hearsay's reliability instead of its mere admissibility comports not only with the requirements of this novel circumstance, but also with the reality that district judges are experienced and sophisticated fact finders. Their eyes need not be protected from unreliable information in the manner the Federal Rules of Evidence aim to shield the eyes of impressionable juries. *** [I]n a detainee case, the judge acts as a neutral decisionmaker charged with seizing the actual truth of a simple, binary question: is detention lawful? This is why the one constant in the history of habeas has never been a certain set of procedures, but rather the independent power of a judge to assess the actions of the Executive. This primacy of independence over process is at the center of the *Boumediene* opinion, which eschews prescribing a detailed procedural regime in favor of issuing a spare but momentous guarantee that a "judicial officer must have adequate authority to make a determination in light of the relevant law and facts."

In Al-Bihani's case, the district court clearly reserved that authority in its process and assessed the hearsay evidence's reliability as required by the Supreme Court. First, the district court retained the authority to assess the weight of the evidence. Second, the district court had ample contextual information about evidence in the Government's factual return to determine what weight to give various pieces of evidence. Third, the district court afforded Al-Bihani the opportunity in a traverse to rebut the evidence and to attack its credibility. Further, Al-Bihani did not contest the truth of the majority of his admissions upon which the district court relied, enhancing the reliability of those reports. We therefore find that the district court did not improperly admit hearsay evidence.

The rest of Al-Bihani's procedural claims can be disposed of without extended discussion. His claim that the burden of proof was placed on him is based on a strained reading of the hearing transcript that twists and magnifies questions asked by the judge. This claim has no merit and we need not consider it further. Likewise, Al-Bihani's claim that an evidentiary hearing was denied to him in violation of his right to a hearing is groundless. First, while courts reviewing state or federal court decisions have the discretion to grant fact hearings upon a proper showing by a petitioner, Al-Bihani cites no authority that a petitioner in his position is entitled to such a hearing as of right. Second, it is clear from the CMO and the transcript of the full habeas hearing that the district court did hear the facts of Al-Bihani's case and provided ample opportunity in conference and in a hearing for the parties to air concerns over evidence. To the extent that Al-Bihani possesses any right to a hearing to develop facts or argue evidentiary issues, it was satisfied by the district Court's procedure.

Finally, regarding Al-Bihani's challenge to the discovery procedures adopted by the district court and to the denial of most of his discovery requests, we are inclined to find the procedures were permissible and the Court's denial was not an abuse of discretion. However, we need not reach these issues. Even assuming error, the errors were harmless because discovery would not have changed the outcome of the case. None of the discovery requests that were denied would have had any impact on the factual basis on which the district court found Al-Bihani to be properly detained. All of the discovery requests pertained to the disputed fact surrounding whether Al-Bihani attended Al Qaeda training camps. The district court assiduously avoided those facts in its decision.

Al-Bihani's detention is authorized by statute and there was no constitutional defect in the district Court's habeas procedure that would have affected the outcome of the proceeding. ***

BROWN, Circuit Judge, concurring:

The Supreme Court in *Boumediene* and *Hamdi* charged this court and others with the unprecedented task of developing rules to review the propriety of military actions during a time of war, relying on common law tools. We are fortunate this case does not require us to demarcate the law's full substantive and procedural dimensions. But as other more difficult cases arise, it is important to ask whether a court-driven process is best suited to protecting both the rights of petitioners and the safety of our nation. The common law process depends on incrementalism and eventual correction, and it is most effective where there are a significant number of cases brought before a large set of courts, which in turn enjoy the luxury of time to work the doctrine supple. None of those factors exist in the Guantanamo context. The number of Guantanamo detainees is limited and the circumstances of their confinement are unique. The petitions they file, as the *Boumediene* Court counseled, are funneled through one federal district court and one appellate court. And, in the midst of an ongoing war, time to entertain a process of literal trial and error is not a luxury we have.

While the common law process presents these difficulties, it is important to note that the Supreme Court has not foreclosed Congress from establishing new habeas standards in line with its *Boumediene* opinion. *** These cases present hard questions and hard choices, ones best faced directly. Judicial review, however, is just that: *re*-view, an indirect and necessarily backward looking process. And looking backward may not be enough in this new war. The saying that generals always fight the last war is familiar, but familiarity does not dull the maxim's sober warning. In identifying the shape of the law in response to the challenge of the current war, it is incumbent on the President, Congress, and the courts to realize that the saying's principle applies to us as well. Both the rule of law and the nation's safety will benefit from an honest assessment of the new challenges we face, one that will produce an appropriately calibrated response. *** In this case, I remain mindful that the conflict in which Al-Bihani was captured was only one phase of hostilities between the United States and Islamic extremists. The legal issues presented by our nation's fight with this enemy have been numerous, difficult, and to a large extent novel. What drives these issues is the unconventional nature of our enemy: they are neither soldiers nor mere criminals, claim no national affiliation, and adopt long-term strategies and asymmetric tactics that exploit the rules of open societies without respect or reciprocity.

War is a challenge to law, and the law must adjust. It must recognize that the old wineskins of international law, domestic criminal procedure, or other prior frameworks are ill-suited to the bitter wine of this new warfare. We can no longer afford diffidence. This war has placed us not just at, but already past the leading edge of a new and frightening paradigm, one that demands new rules be written. Falling back on the comfort of prior practices supplies only illusory comfort.

WILLIAMS, Senior Circuit Judge, concurring in part and concurring in the judgment:

I agree with the majority's decision to affirm the district Court's denial of Al Bihani's petition for a writ of habeas corpus. I take *** a significantly different view as to the necessity of reaching any of Al Bihani's procedural arguments. For purposes of both my analysis and the majority's, the petitioner has conceded facts that render his detention lawful-thereby obviating any need to discuss the constitutionality of the district Court's factfinding process. *** Because the petitioner's detention is lawful by virtue of facts that he has conceded-a conclusion that the majority seems not to dispute-the majority's analysis of the constitutionality of the *procedures* the district court used is unnecessary. Nothing in this case turns on the questions whether "preponderance of the evidence" is a constitutionally permissible standard of proof in Guantanamo detainees' habeas proceedings, whether the district Court's approach to the admission of hearsay evidence is consistent with the minimum requirements of the Suspension Clause as the Supreme Court construed it in *Boumediene,* 553 U.S. 723 or whether petitioners in Al Bihani's circumstance do or don't enjoy only a "limited procedural entitlement ... as a general matter." These matters are analytically irrelevant to the outcome of this appeal, since the facts that Al Bihani says are correct readily yield a ruling that his detention is legally permissible. ***

Notes

1. GITMO Lawyering Basics. The Protective Order sharply limits access for Guantanamo detainees' lawyers to both classified information and their clients. To meet with a detainee client, a lawyer must agree to comply with all of the terms of the Protective Order and acquire security clearance at the "Secret" level or higher. The Protective Order imposes sharp limits on what kind of information a lawyer may share with her client, or about her client to others. All meetings between a detainee and lawyer are visually monitored on closed-circuit television, or by military police sitting outside an open door. All notes a lawyer takes during client meetings are likewise maintained by the government. Additionally, the lawyer must provide all documents generated during a client meeting, including work product generated by the attorney, to a "privilege team," which may report the contents thereof to the Commander at Guantanamo Bay if that information "reasonably could be expected to result in immediate and substantial harm to the national security." All mail between the lawyer and detainee is likewise screened by the privilege team. The Protective Order also forbids a lawyer from bringing any material not previously reviewed and cleared by the government into a detainee meeting. Lawyers are not permitted to speak on the phone to detainee-clients. Nothing in the order precludes the Government's use of classified information for any purpose.A subsequent amendment created procedures for counsel to follow in order to disclose a petitioner's classified statements to that petitioner. Order *in re* Guantanamo Litigation, 2009 WL 2143732 (D.C. D. Ct., 2009).

2. Detainee Lawyer Perspectives. Detainee lawyers have bridled at these restrictions. In addition to the general unwieldiness of reaching and staying at Guantanamo Bay, one lawyer commented it took ten months after agreeing to represent a detainee to meet with him, and "procedures were established to make even the filing of routine documents as cumbersome as possible." H. Candace Gorman, "My Experiences Representing a Guantanamo Detainee." 35 LITIGATION 3. All documents, even extensions, changes of address, etc., must be cleared by a Court Security Officer ("CSO"), and filed by courier service rather than electronically. Government attorneys screen all filings prior to filing. Additionally, any filings drawing on classified material have to be prepared on government computers in a government office in Washington, and lawyers have complained that facilities such as copiers there were in poor repair. Furthermore, the Protective Order creates Catch-22 situations such as a detainee being "cleared for release" but his attorney can't tell anyone about it for five months. Andy Worthington, "Justice Department Pointlessly Gags Guantanamo

Attorney," The Public Record, *available at* http://pubrecord.org/law/6126/justice-department-pointlessly/.

3. The Laundry List. Review the list of seven procedural challenges al-Bihani made concerning the procedures for habeas in Guantanamo detainee cases. Was his case strengthened or weakened by the number of objections? If you, as his attorney, decided to focus on one or two reasons, which would you have chosen?

4. Criminal Trials or Criminal Habeas. The Supreme Court said in Boumediene that habeas procedures "need not resemble a criminal trial." Do criminal habeas procedures, to which the habeas petitioners sought to analogize, resemble criminal trials? Isn't the issue in a criminal habeas case, like that in the Guantanamo habeas cases, simply whether there was sufficient reason to release the petitioner? Why shouldn't immigration habeas cases "challenging post-removal-period detentions be a satisfactory analogy? Why would "leaner procedures" be suggested than in *al-Marri* (supra Chapter V)?

5. Standard of Proof. Why does the Court refuse to say "what standard [of proof] would represent the minimum required by the Constitution"? Is the "burden-shifting" approach approved by the court the same as a "predominance of the evidence" standard? What would be lower and higher standards than predominance? Would the court in a close case require a habeas petitioner to show by "clear and convincing evidence" that he should be released? Why is Guantanamo "wartime detention" and why does the court stress that the petitioner is an alien? Would a citizen detained at Guantanamo deserve more protection in a habeas proceeding than that accorded to al-Bihani?

6. Hearsay Evidence. The court holds it permissible to use hearsay evidence in habeas proceedings. Does this mean that the dispute over use of hearsay evidence in military commission trials of enemy combatants compared to the presumed exclusion of hearsay evidence in federal court trials is really insubstantial? What does this analysis forget? You will see more on this issue in Chapters VIII and IX.

7. Re-view. Judge Brown complains that judicial review and development of habeas procedures by the courts is a poor way to deal with habeas cases involving Guantanamo detainees. Do you agree? Would Congress be a better forum for developing habeas procedures?

8. Reaching Out. Do you agree with Judge Williams that none of the procedural issues in this case should have been addressed? Why do you think the court did so?

2. HOW AND WHEN TO CONSIDER EVIDENCE

AL-ADAHI v. OBAMA
2010 WL 2756551 (C.A.D.C. 2010)

RANDOLPH, Senior Circuit Judge:

In the summer of 2001, a thirty-nine year-old Yemeni security guard took a six-month leave of absence from his job to move to Afghanistan. Leaving his wife and his two children, he stayed at the Kandahar home of his brother-in-law, a close associate of Usama bin Laden. Twice he met personally with bin Laden. From Kandahar he moved into a guesthouse used as a staging area for al-Qaida recruits. He then attended al-Qaida's Al Farouq training camp, where many of the September 11th terrorists had trained. He traveled between Kabul, Khost, and Kandahar while American forces were launching attacks in Afghanistan. Among other explanations for his movements, he claimed that he had decided to take a vacation. After sustaining injuries requiring his hospitalization, he crossed the Pakistani border on a bus carrying wounded Arab and Pakistani fighters. This man, Mohammed Al-Adahi, who is now a detainee at Guantanamo Bay Naval Base, admits all of this but insists he was not a part of al-Qaida and never fought against the United States. Others identified him as a [redacted] ***

Pakistani authorities captured Al-Adahi in late 2001. In 2004, a Combatant Status Review Tribunal determined, by a preponderance of evidence, that he was part of al-Qaida. Al-Adahi filed his habeas corpus petition in 2005. In 2008 the Supreme Court ruled that despite statutes depriving the federal courts of jurisdiction to hear habeas petitions from Guantanamo detainees, the Suspension Clause of the Constitution at least preserved the writ as it existed in 1789.

Al-Adahi's habeas petition presented the question whether he was part of al-Qaida and therefore justifiably detained under the Authorization for Use of Military Force. The district court *** found "no reliable evidence in the record that Petitioner was a member of al-Qaida" and ruled that he should be released. ***

The Authorization for Use of Military Force empowers the President "to use all necessary and appropriate force against those nations, organizations, or persons he determines planned, authorized, committed, or aided the terrorist attacks that occurred on September 11, 2001, or harbored such organizations or persons, in order to prevent any future acts of international terrorism against the United States by such nations, organizations or persons." "[A]ll necessary and appropriate force" includes the power to capture and detain those described in the congressional authorization. The government may therefore hold at Guantanamo and elsewhere those individuals who are "part of" al-Qaida, the Taliban, or associated forces. *See Awad v. Obama,* No. 09-5351, slip op. at 18 (D.C.Cir. June 2, 2010); *Al-Bihani v. Obama,* 590 F.3d 866, 872, 874-75 (D.C.Cir.2010).

Whether Al-Adahi fit that description was and is the ultimate issue. The obvious preliminary question is what sort of factual showing does the government, or the detainee, have to make? In this court the question is open. *Al-Bihani* held that the government does not have to prove the legality of detention "beyond a reasonable doubt" or by "clear and convincing evidence." *Al-Bihani* also decided that the preponderance-of-the-evidence standard is constitutionally permissible. But we have yet to decide whether that standard is required.

The district judge in this case adopted the preponderance standard. Other district judges in our circuit have done the same. Their rationale is unstated. After *Boumediene*, the district judges met in executive session and decided to coordinate proceedings in Guantanamo habeas cases. On November 6, 2008, the coordinating judge issued a Case Management Order. *In re Guantanamo Bay Detainee Litig.*, Misc. No. 08-442, 2008 WL 4858241 (D.D.C. Nov.6, 2008). The Order stated, among other things, that the government should bear the burden of proving by a preponderance of the evidence that the petitioner's detention is lawful. In support, the Order cited *Boumediene*. But *Boumediene* held only that the "extent of the showing required of the Government in these cases is a matter to be determined."

Boumediene also held that in determining the scope of the writ, "the analysis may [must?] begin with precedents as of 1789, for the Court has said that 'at the absolute minimum' the Clause protects the writ as it existed when the Constitution was drafted and ratified." Yet we are aware of no precedents in which eighteenth century English courts adopted a preponderance standard. Even in later statutory habeas cases in this country, that standard was not the norm. For years, in habeas proceedings contesting orders of deportation, the government had to produce only "some evidence to support the order." In such cases courts did not otherwise "review factual determinations made by the Executive." In habeas petitions challenging selective service decisions, the government also had the minimal burden of providing "some evidence" to support the decision. Habeas petitions contesting courts martial required the government to show only that the military prisoner had received, in the military tribunal, "full and fair consideration" of the allegations in his habeas petition. And in response to habeas petitions brought after an individual's arrest, the government had to show only that it had probable cause for the arrest.

After oral argument, we ordered the parties to file supplemental briefs discussing "what factual showing" (if any) the government must make to justify detaining Al-Adahi. The supplemental briefs we received were not exactly illuminating. The government stated that "in the circumstances currently presented in this Guantanamo habeas litigation," a preponderance standard is "appropriate," although "a different and more deferential standard may be appropriate in other cases or contexts," Al-Adahi readily agreed with the government that the preponderance standard should govern his case. We are thus left with no adversary presentation on an important question affecting many pending cases in this court and in the district court. Although we doubt, for the reasons stated above, that the Suspension Clause requires the use of the preponderance standard, we will not decide the question in this case. As we did in *Al-Bihani*, we will assume *arguendo* that the government must show by a preponderance of the evidence that Al-Adahi was part of al-Qaida.

The district court divided the Government's evidence into five categories in rough chronological order: Al-Adahi's trip to Afghanistan; his meetings with bin Laden; his stay in an al-Qaida guesthouse; his military training at Al Farouq; and his other, later activities in Afghanistan. We will generally follow the Court's organization, but before we get to the specifics we need to mention an error that affects much of the district Court's evaluation of the evidence. The error stems from the Court's failure to appreciate conditional probability analysis.

"Many mundane mistakes in reasoning can be traced to a shaky grasp of the notion of conditional probability." JOHN ALLEN PAULOS, INNUMERACY: MATHEMATICAL ILLITERACY AND ITS CONSEQUENCES 63 (1988). The key consideration is that although some events are independent (coin flips, for example), other events are dependent: "the occurrence of one of them makes the occurrence of the other more or less likely ...." Dr. Paulos gives this example: "the probability that a person chosen at random from the phone book is over 250 pounds is quite small. However, if it's known that the person chosen is over six feet four inches tall, then the conditional probability that he or she also weighs more than 250 pounds is considerably higher."

Those who do not take into account conditional probability are prone to making mistakes in judging evidence. They may think that if a particular fact does not itself prove the ultimate proposition (*e.g.*, whether the detainee was part of al-Qaida), the fact may be tossed aside and the next fact may be evaluated as if the first did not exist. This is precisely how the district court proceeded in this case: Al-Adahi's ties to bin Laden "cannot prove" he was part of Al-Qaida and this evidence therefore "must not distract the Court." The fact that Al-Adahi stayed in an al-Qaida guesthouse "is not in itself sufficient to justify detention." Al-Adahi" attendance at an al-Qaida training camp "is not sufficient to carry the Government" burden of showing that he was a part" of al-Qaida. And so on. The government is right: the district court wrongly "required each piece of the Government's evidence to bear weight without regard to all (or indeed any) other evidence in the case. This was a fundamental mistake that infected the Court's entire analysis."

Having tossed aside the Government's evidence, one piece at a time, the court came to the manifestly incorrect-indeed startling-conclusion that "there is no reliable evidence in the record that Petitioner was a member of al-Qaida and/or the Taliban." When the evidence is properly considered, it becomes clear that Al-Adahi was-at the very least-more likely than not a part of al-Qaida. And that is all the government had to show in order to satisfy the preponderance standard.

Al-Adahi served in the Yemeni army for two years and was later employed as a security guard at the Yemeni state oil company. In July 2001 he took a six-month leave of absence from his job and left his wife and his two children to travel with his sister Amani to Afghanistan (by way of Pakistan). Amani had entered into an arranged marriage with Riyadh Abd Al-Aziz Almujahid, a Yemeni citizen then residing in Kandahar.

Riyadh was affiliated with al-Qaida. He arranged for Amani's and Al-Adahi's trip to Afghanistan. He helped them obtain passports from the passport agency in their hometown of Ta'iz. He then sent Al-Adahi to the Yemeni capital city of Sana'a. Al-Adahi was instructed to wear a red jacket and wait outside a specified building for a man he did not know. This man,

Ali Yayha, recognized Al-Adahi and gave him two plane tickets and travel money. Yayha also arranged for Al-Adahi and Amani to obtain visas. The government presented evidence that al-Qaida paid for Al-Adahi's and Amani's trip. Al-Adahi admitted that the sort of arrangements that Riyadh made for him and his sister were the same as those al-Qaida used for bringing jihadist recruits to Afghanistan. And he described how Riyadh had obtained Al-Adahi's travel funds from "the Saudi who handled the money" for al-Qaida in Kandahar. That Al-Adahi was an al-Qaida recruit is also supported by a witness's statement-not addressed by the district court-that Al-Adahi was a [redacted].

Riyadh was "from mujahidin"-that is, those who fought against the Russians and in the Afghan civil war. Many mujahidin frequented the guesthouse Riyadh operated in Kandahar. Al-Adahi stayed at Riyadh's house, located in the same compound. Al-Adahi told interrogators that Riyadh "had achieved a very high status" in al-Qaida. Like Al-Adahi, Riyadh was described to interrogators as a [redacted] And Al-Adahi admitted that Riyadh's compound was very close to the compound of Mullah Omar, the leader of the Taliban.

Bin Laden hosted the male-only celebration of Riyadh's marriage to Al-Adahi's sister. Bin Laden held the celebration at his compound, which Al-Adahi described as "surrounded by a concrete fence further secured by a large metal gate." Inside the compound, a group of armed guards "draped in munitions belts, grenades, and Kalashnikov rifles" welcomed the wedding guests. At the party, bin Laden gave a speech congratulating Riyadh. Al-Adahi and bin Laden were introduced and sat next to each other during the meal.

Several days later, bin Laden summoned Al-Adahi for another meeting. According to Al-Adahi, at his meeting bin Laden asked him about people he was connected with in Yemen-some of whom were involved in jihad. (The events following the meeting, including Al-Adahi's showing up at the al-Qaida training camp, suggest that more transpired in the meeting than what Al-Adahi related.) In the habeas proceedings, Al-Adahi tried to explain his personal audience with bin Laden on the basis that "meeting with Bin Laden was common for visitors to Kandahar." This is, as the government points out, utterly implausible. Al-Adahi's story was "contradicted by the undisputed evidence that in 2001 Usama bin Laden, who knew he was a military target of the United States, had gone into hiding under tight security...."

As to the latter point the district court said nothing, despite the well-settled principle that false exculpatory statements are evidence-often strong evidence-of guilt. The court characterized the rest of the evidence about Al-Adahi's meetings with bin Laden as "sensational and compelling" but not "actual, reliable evidence that would justify" detention. The Court's statements are incomprehensible. On what possible ground can the court say that the evidence on this subject was, on the one hand, "compelling," and yet say, on the other hand, that it was not "actual" and "reliable"? All that comes to mind is the idea that two personal meetings with bin Laden are not enough to prove that an individual is part of al-Qaida. If that is what the court intended, then it was once again engaging in the mistaken reasoning we mentioned in connection with conditional probability analysis. The court rounded off its discussion by characterizing the Government's presentation as merely indicating that Al-Adahi had "familial ties to Usama bin Laden," a statement incorrect as a factual matter (Al-Adahi's family ties were to a top aide of bin Laden's) and one that misses the strong thrust of the evidence. The evidence derived its power not only from Al-Adahi's family relationships, but also from his meetings with bin Laden. That close association made it far more likely that Al-Adahi was or became part of the organization.

Rather than grasping this essential point, the district court called the evidence regarding the meetings a distraction-something that should not divert "the Court from its essential focus-the nature of Al-Adahi's own conduct, upon which this case must turn." Here again the Court's remarks are perplexing. If Al-Adahi's meetings with bin Laden were not his "own conduct," whose conduct were they?

The next event in this narrative greatly strengthened the Government's case against Al-Adahi. Not long after his second meeting with bin Laden, Al-Adahi moved to the Al Nebras guesthouse. He said he wanted to go there because it was a gathering place for Muslims, as if that distinguished it from any other place he stayed during his time in Afghanistan. Al Nebras was not just another gathering place: it served as a staging area for al-Qaida recruits en route to the Al Farouq training camp. Al-Adahi was treated like a recruit. Staff at the guesthouse instructed him and the other recruits on how to pack and prepare for their training before taking a bus to Al Farouq. The district court seemed to think that Al-Adahi's stay at the guesthouse-one or two days-was evidence in his favor because it was so brief. But the court failed to take into account that Al Nebras functioned as a way station.

The district court dealt with this evidence in the following way: "the guesthouse evidence is not in itself sufficient to justify detention." Note the "not in itself." Again the court erred. Al-Adahi's voluntary decision to move to an al-Qaida guesthouse, a staging area for recruits heading for a military training camp, makes it more likely-indeed, very likely-that Al-Adahi was himself a recruit. There is no other sensible explanation for his actions. This is why we wrote in *Al-Bihani* that an individual's attendance at an al-Qaida guesthouse is powerful-indeed "overwhelming [ ]"-evidence that the individual was part of al-Qaida.

Al-Adahi left the guesthouse after a few days and, as expected, entered al-Qaida's Al Farouq training camp. By then it was August 2001. At least eight of the September 11th hijackers had trained at Al Farouq. While Al-Adahi was there, he received training in rocket-propelled grenades, other weapons, and basic physical fitness, as well as some classroom instruction. His statements to interrogators indicated that he had a deep knowledge of the operation of Al Farouq. He described camp leaders in a manner that showed he was familiar with them; he reported details of the camp's training regimen and layout; and he identified the types of weapons used for training. He also knew the training routines of other recruits.

The district court seemed to think it important to determine Al-Adahi's motive for attending the al-Qaida training camp. We do not understand why. Whatever his motive, the significant points are that al-Qaida was intent on attacking the United States and its allies, that bin Laden had issued a *fatwa* announcing that every Muslim had a duty to kill Americans, and that Al-Adahi voluntarily affiliated himself with al-Qaida.

According to Al-Adahi, he stayed at Al Farouq for seven to ten days, and then was expelled for smoking tobacco, a violation of a camp rule. The government introduced evidence casting doubt on Al-Adahi's explanation for leaving the camp. This evidence-which included Al-Adahi's own statements-showed that trainees expelled from Al Farouq were treated as spies and beaten. Al-Adahi left Al Farouq unharmed. His story was that the camp's instructors treated him gently because they were close to his brother-in-law Riyadh. The government offered another explanation. Al-Adahi did not spend a great deal of time in the camp because he needed little training. He was not a green, untested, recruit. He had served in the Yemeni army, and he had been working as a security guard in Yemen. As to his loyalty to the al-Qaida cause, his sister was married to one of bin Laden's most trusted associates.

The district court reached the following conclusions about Al-Adahi's attendance at Al Farouq: (1) this was "not affirmative evidence that Al-Adahi embraced al-Qaida, accepted its philosophy, and endorsed its terrorist activities"; and (2) his training at Al-Farouq did not show that he "occup[ied] some sort of structured role in the hierarchy of the enemy force" or could "be deemed a member of the enemy's armed forces."

The court appeared to rule that an individual must embrace every tenet of al-Qaida before United States forces may detain him. There is no such requirement. When the government shows that an individual received and executed orders from al-Qaida members in a training camp, that evidence is sufficient (but not necessary) to prove that the individual has affiliated himself with al-Qaida. *Gherebi v. Obama,* 609 F.Supp.2d 43, 69 (D.D.C.2009). Al-Adahi's statements confirm that he received and followed orders while he was at Al Farouq. His attendance at an al-Qaida military training camp is therefore-to put it mildly-strong evidence that he was part of al-Qaida. In *Al-Bihani,* we stated that if a person stays in an al-Qaida guesthouse or attends an al-Qaida training camp, this constitutes "overwhelming" evidence that the United States had authority to detain that person..

The district court ruled that Al-Adahi did not "receive and execute" orders because he violated the camp rule against smoking tobacco. This was error. Al-Adahi's violation of a rule or rules did not erase his compliance with other orders. One would not say that an Army trainee ceased to be part of the Army if he failed to shine his shoes or overslept one morning. Furthermore, there was no evidence that Al-Adahi ever affirmatively disassociated himself from al-Qaida, even though he "accepted his expulsion."

The district court ended its discussion of Al-Adahi's training at Al Farouq with the following statement: Al-Adahi's "admission that he trained at Al Farouq is not sufficient to carry the Government's burden of showing that he was a part, or substantial supporter, of enemy forces." We disagree that this evidence, standing alone, was insufficient. In any event, we are sure that the court erred in treating this evidence as if it stood alone.

The court gave similar treatment to the Government's proof that Al-Adahi wore the same model of Casio watch the military has linked to al-Qaida and terrorist activity. When Pakistani authorities picked up Al-Adahi they confiscated his watch. A witness reported seeing him wearing the Casio watch before his capture. The district court threw out these telling facts because, after all, "Casio watches are hardly unique items, even in Afghanistan."

It is true that not everyone in Afghanistan with a Casio watch could be identified with al-Qaida. But the evidence did not relate to every such person. It related to a particular individual wearing a Casio model favored by al-Qaida leaders, an individual who had met with bin Laden, had stayed in an al-Qaida guesthouse, and had trained in an al-Qaida camp.

The government also introduced other evidence of Al-Adahi's close connection to the al-Qaida leadership. Al-Adahi had detailed personal knowledge about a group of twelve men who worked for bin Laden. For example, he knew that one man was a trained sniper and could read, write, and speak English; he knew that another spoke Pashtu and Farsi and sent men to Al Farouq for training; and he knew that one "had fat thighs but was quick," owned a four-door pickup truck, fought in Chechnya and Bosnia, and had been with bin Laden in Sudan.

This evidence tended to show Al-Adahi's close relationship with these men and thus strengthened the probability that he was part of al-Qaida. Yet the district court declined to credit the evidence because it was possible that Al-Adahi could have learned the biographical information in some other way, particularly since some of the men were from his hometown in Yemen. In so ruling the court committed what a noted historian has called "the fallacy of the possible proof." "Valid empirical proof requires not merely the establishment of possibility, but an estimate of probability." Yet the court spoke only of a possible alternative explanation for Al-Adahi's knowledge of bin Laden's bodyguards. At no point did the court make any finding about whether this alternative was more likely than the Government's explanation. But such a "comparative judgment about the evidence" is at the heart of the preponderance standard of proof.

Al-Adahi was in Kabul when the September 11 attacks occurred. He said that he then decided to take a month long vacation and travel throughout the countryside. He said he went to Kabul because he was bored staying in Kandahar. When the United States began its military campaign in Afghanistan on October 7, 2001, Al-Adahi claimed he was still in Kabul. About a week and a half after the bombing began, he left for Khost, Afghanistan, where he stayed in a mosque for about two weeks. He said he then left Khost to return to Kandahar to search for his sister. He spent another two to three weeks in Kandahar, including two or three days in a hospital recuperating from injuries to his arm and side. Al-Adahi said he sustained his injuries in a motorcycle accident. He offered different versions of how the accident occurred: he hit a speed bump on his way to the market; he crashed into a cart as he was riding around Kandahar; he fell off his motorcycle while attempting to flee the United States bombing; he crashed trying to avoid a small car.

Al-Adahi left the hospital for Pakistan on a bus carrying wounded Arabs and Pakistanis. At one point in his interrogation, Al-Adahi described these fourteen men as Taliban soldiers; but he testified at the habeas proceeding that he learned this only from a newspaper article.

From Al-Adahi's movements in Afghanistan, his injuries, his shifting versions of his supposed motorcycle accident, and his capture on a bus loaded with wounded Taliban fighters, the government infers that Al-Adahi was complying with "bin Laden's order to persist in the jihad" after the American attacks. The district court, once again treating items of evidence in isolation, pronounced that "there is no evidence that [Al-Adahi] sought to join or was already part of a band of fighters fleeing the region." The court was wrong, and clearly so. Al-Adahi's capture on a bus carrying only himself and wounded Taliban fighters constituted such evidence, as did his injuries, his movements in the country, and the contradictions contained in his explanations. We do not say that any of these particular pieces of evidence are conclusive, but we do say that they add to the weight of the Government's case against Al-Adahi and that the district court clearly erred in tossing them aside.

One of the oddest things about this case is that despite an extensive record and numerous factual disputes, the district court never made any findings about whether Al-Adahi was generally a credible witness or whether his particular explanations for his actions were worthy of belief. The Court's omissions are particularly striking in light of the instructions in al-Qaida's training manuals for resisting interrogation. For those who belong to al-Qaida, "[c]onfronting the interrogator and defeating him is part of your jihad." To this end al-Qaida members are instructed to resist interrogation by developing a cover story, by refusing to answer questions, by recanting or changing answers already given, by giving as vague an answer as possible, and by claiming torture. Put bluntly, the instructions to detainees are to make up a story and lie. Despite this the district court displayed little skepticism about Al-Adahi's explanations for his actions. To the extent the court expressed any doubts, it addressed them to the Government's case and did so on the mistaken view that each item of the Government's evidence needed to prove the ultimate issue in the case.

We could go on, but what we have written thus far is enough to show that the district court clearly erred in its treatment of the evidence and in its view of the law. *Cf. Barhoumi v. Obama,* No. 09-5383, slip op. at 12-13 (D.C.Cir. June 11, 2010); *Awad,* slip op. at 17. The Court's conclusion was simply not a "permissible view [ ] of the evidence." And it reached this conclusion through a series of legal errors, as we have discussed. We have already mentioned the suggestion in *Al-Bihani* that attendance at either an al-Qaida training camp or an al-Qaida guesthouse "would seem to overwhelmingly, if not definitively, justify" detention. The evidence against Al-Adahi showed that he did both-stayed at an al-Qaida guesthouse and attended an al-Qaida training camp. And the evidence showed a good deal more, from his meetings with bin Laden, to his knowledge of those protecting bin Laden, to his wearing of a particular model of Casio watch, to his incredible explanations for his actions, to his capture on a bus carrying wounded Arabs and Pakistanis, and so on. One of the most damaging and powerful items of evidence against him is classified. In all there can be no doubt that Al-Adahi was more likely than not part of al-Qaida. We therefore reverse and remand with instructions to the district court to deny Al-Adahi's petition for a writ of habeas corpus.[6]

Notes

1. **Institutional Competence.** The district judge, who heard all the evidence, said there was "no reliable evidence" to believe Al-Adahi was "a member of al-Qaida." The D.C. Circuit reversed. Which court was in the better position to evaluate the evidence? Which court was in the better position to establish the lens through which evidence should be evaluated? Why was there a reversal with no remand?

2. **Standard for Detention.** What does this case add to *Al-Bihani* concerning the constitutionally required standard for military detention? If not, why did the court discuss historical materials concerning the history of deportation, selective service decisions, courts martial, and probable cause for arrest?

3. **Conditional Probability.** The court's presentation of this basic concept seems airtight as a matter of logic. Is it equally airtight as a method of deciding on the admissibility of evidence? In trials generally, isn't evidence admitted item by item? What is the standard for admissibility under the Federal Rules of Evidence? Returning to this case, is conditional probability really about admissibility of evidence?

---

[6] Al-Adahi filed a cross-appeal. He argues that the district court had no authority to admit hearsay bearing on his habeas petition. We rejected that argument in *Al-Bihani,* 590 F.3d at 879, and again in *Awad. Al-Bihani* also forecloses Al-Adahi's argument that admitting hearsay violated his Sixth Amendment right of confrontation. The district court did not abuse its discretion by not ruling separately on the reliability of each item of hearsay, despite Al-Adahi's claim that the case management order required it to do so. *Barhoumi,* slip op. at 9-10. His claim that statements he made outside the presence of counsel should be suppressed also fails: Al-Adahi cites no precedent extending the *Miranda v. Arizona,* 384 U.S. 436 (1966), line of cases beyond the criminal context. As we noted in *Al-Bihani,* these constitutional habeas proceedings are not subject to all the protections given to defendants in criminal prosecutions. Al-Adahi points to the Army Rules of Professional Responsibility as also requiring suppression of his ex parte statements, but he waived this argument by failing to raise it until his cross-appeal reply brief. Al-Adahi also claims his statements should be suppressed pursuant to the Third Geneva Convention. Even if the Convention had been incorporated into domestic U.S. law and even if it provided an exclusionary rule, Congress has provided explicitly that the Convention's provisions are not privately enforceable in habeas proceedings. *See* Military Commissions Act of 2006 § 5, *Noriega v. Pastrana,* 564 F.3d 1290, 1296-97 (11th Cir.2009)*; Boumediene v. Bush,* 476 F.3d 981, 988 n. 5 (D.C.Cir.2007).

4. Bizarre Bits. There are plenty of these in the case. My favorites are the "every tenet" ruling, the no smoking assessment, and the role of the Casio watch. What are some others?

3. RELIEF AVAILABLE TO SUCCESSFUL HABEAS PETITIONERS

The Uighurs, a Muslim ethnic minority from western China, have been at odds with the People's Republic of China for some time. A number of Uighur men left China for Afghanistan prior to the 9/11 attacks intending to train in Afghanistan. Their goal was to engage, if needed, in military (self-defense?) actions against China, whom they considered occupiers of their lands. There is little to no evidence that the Uighurs fought against allied forces in Afghanistan, and they had no agenda involving the use of force against the United States.

During initial military operations in Afghanistan, the ethnic Uighurs were easy targets for bounty hunters seeking $5000 from the United States for alleged al Qaeda operatives; and twenty-two of them were turned over to allied forces. As D.C. Circuit Judge Rogers said in a dissent from granting the government a stay pending an appeal from a habeas decision of the District Court to release the Uighurs: "[T]hese petitioners *** were abducted by bounty hunters, brought by force to Guantanamo, and imprisoned as enemy combatants, which the government has conceded the petitioners are not." 2008 WL 4898963 (C.A.D.C.). *Parhat*, which you read in Chapter V, demonstrated the weakness of the evidence for detaining the Uighurs as enemy combatants (or under the Obama Administration's "detention authority").

Five Uighurs, who had been determined no longer to be enemy combatants by a Combatant Status Review Board at Guantanamo, were moved from Guantanamo to Albania, which agreed to provide them political asylum. This transfer occurred on May 5, 2006, three days prior to a habeas hearing scheduled before the D.C. Circuit. Following the transfer to Albania, the court found the habeas petition to be moot. The transfer led to a prompt protest by the People's Republic of China, which demanded that the men be returned to China. With no Albanian language skills, integration of these Uighurs proved somewhat difficult. See Tim Golden, "Chinese Leave Guantanamo for Albanian Limbo," NEW YORK TIMES, June 10, 2007.

The remaining seventeen Uighurs at Guantanamo then sought release through habeas actions. Counsel for the Uighurs argued successfully to the DC District Court that, since the United States Government acknowledges the Uighers are not enemy combatants, they should be released into the United States. A Uighur support group pledged to seek to integrate them, find jobs, teach them English, etc. Appeals from the "release the Uighurs" decision were taken. The two decisions of the D.C. Circuit which follow discuss the legal issues surrounding these Uighurs.

KIYEMBA v. OBAMA
555 F. 3d 1022, reh. en banc den. ,561 F. 3d 509 D.C.C.A.,(2009)

RANDOLPH, Senior Circuit Judge:

Seventeen Chinese citizens currently held at Guantanamo Bay Naval Base, Cuba, brought petitions for writs of habeas corpus. Each petitioner is an ethnic Uighur, a Turkic Muslim minority whose members reside in the Xinjiang province of far-west China. The question is whether, as the district court ruled, petitioners are entitled to an order requiring the government to bring them to the United States and release them here.

Sometime before September 11, 2001, petitioners left China and traveled to the Tora Bora mountains in Afghanistan, where they settled in a camp with other Uighurs. Petitioners fled to Pakistan when U.S. aerial strikes destroyed the Tora Bora camp. Eventually they were turned over to the U.S. military, transferred to Guantanamo Bay and detained as "enemy combatants."

Evidence produced at hearings before Combatant Status Review Tribunals in Guantanamo indicated that at least some petitioners intended to fight the Chinese government, and that they had received firearms training at the camp for this purpose. The Tribunals determined that the petitioners could be detained as enemy combatants because the camp was run by the Eastern Turkistan Islamic Movement, a Uighur independence group the military believes to be associated with al Qaida or the Taliban, and which the State Department designated as a terrorist organization three years after the petitioners' capture.

In the *Parhat* case, the court ruled that the government had not presented sufficient evidence that the Eastern Turkistan Islamic Movement was associated with al Qaida or the Taliban, or had engaged in hostilities against the United States or its coalition partners. Parhat therefore could not be held as an enemy combatant. The government saw no material differences in its evidence against the other Uighurs, and therefore decided that none of the petitioners should be detained as enemy combatants.

Releasing petitioners to their country of origin poses a problem. Petitioners fear that if they are returned to China they will face arrest, torture or execution. United States policy is not to transfer individuals to countries where they will be subject to mistreatment. *** Diplomatic efforts to locate an appropriate third country in which to resettle them are continuing. In the meantime, petitioners are held under the least restrictive conditions possible in the Guantanamo military base.

As relief in their habeas cases, petitioners moved for an order compelling their release into the United States. Although the district court assumed that the government initially detained petitioners in compliance with the law, the court thought the government no longer had any legal authority to hold them. As to the appropriate relief, the court acknowledged that historically the authority to admit aliens into this country rested exclusively with the political branches. Nevertheless, the court held that the "exceptional" circumstances of this case and the need to safeguard "an individual's liberty from unbridled executive fiat," justified granting petitioners' motion.

Our analysis begins with several firmly established propositions ***. There is first the ancient principle that a nation-state has the inherent right to exclude or admit foreigners and to prescribe applicable terms and conditions for their exclusion or admission. This principle, dating from Roman times, received recognition during the Constitutional Convention and has continued to be an important postulate in the foreign relations of this country and other members of the international community.

For more than a century, the Supreme Court has recognized the power to exclude aliens as " 'inherent in sovereignty, necessary for maintaining normal international relations and defending the country against foreign encroachments and dangers-a power to be exercised exclusively by the political branches of government' " and not "granted away or restrained on behalf of any one." *** Justice Frankfurter summarized the law as it continues to this day: "Ever since national States have come into being, the right of the people to enjoy the hospitality of a State of which they are not citizens has been a matter of political determination by each State"-a matter "wholly outside the concern and competence of the Judiciary."

As a result, it "is not within the province of any court, unless expressly authorized by law, to review the determination of the political branch of the Government to exclude a given alien." With respect to these seventeen petitioners, the Executive Branch has determined not to allow them to enter the United States. The critical question is: what law "expressly authorized" the district court to set aside the decision of the Executive Branch and to order these aliens brought to the United States and released in Washington, D.C.?

The district court cited no statute or treaty authorizing its order, and we are aware of none. *** Decisions of the Supreme Court and of this court-decisions the district court did not acknowledge-hold that the due process clause does not apply to aliens without property or presence in the sovereign territory of the United States.[9] *** The district court also sought to support its order by invoking the idea embodied in the maxim *ubi jus, ibi remedium*-where there is a right, there is a remedy. We do not believe the maxim reflects federal statutory or constitutional law. Not every violation of a right yields a remedy, even when the right is constitutional. Application of the doctrine of sovereign immunity to defeat a remedy is one common example. ***

Much of what we have just written served as the foundation for the Supreme Court's opinion in *Shaughnessy v. United States ex rel. Mezei*, 345 U.S. 206 (1953), a case analogous to this one in several ways. The government held an alien at the border (Ellis Island, New York). He had been denied entry into the United States under the immigration laws. But no other country was willing to receive him. The Court ruled that the alien, who

---

[9] The Guantanamo Naval Base is not part of the sovereign territory of the United States. Congress so determined in the Detainee Treatment Act of 2005 § 1005(g). The Immigration and Nationality Act, also does not treat Guantanamo as part of the United States

petitioned for a writ of habeas corpus, had not been deprived of any constitutional rights. In so ruling the Court necessarily rejected the proposition that because no other country would take Mezei, the prospect of indefinite detention entitled him to a court order requiring the Attorney General to release him into the United States. As the Supreme Court saw it, the Judiciary could not question the Attorney General's judgment. ***

And so we ask again: what law authorized the district court to order the government to bring petitioners to the United States and release them here? It cannot be that because the court had habeas jurisdiction it could fashion the sort of remedy petitioners desired. The [Court] in *Mezei* also had habeas jurisdiction, yet *** the Supreme Court held that the decision whether to allow an alien to enter the country was for the political departments, not the Judiciary. Petitioners and the amici supporting them invoke the tradition of the Great Writ as a protection of liberty. As part of that tradition, they say, a court with habeas jurisdiction has always had the power to order the prisoner's release if he was being held unlawfully. But as in *Munaf v. Geren, -- U.S. ----*, 128 S.Ct. 2207, 2221 (2008), petitioners are not seeking "simple release." Far from it. They asked for, and received, a court order compelling the Executive to release them into the United States outside the framework of the immigration laws. Whatever may be the content of common law habeas corpus, we are certain that no habeas court since the time of Edward I ever ordered such an extraordinary remedy.

An undercurrent of petitioners' arguments is that they deserve to be released into this country after all they have endured at hands of the United States. But such sentiments, however high-minded, do not represent a legal basis for upsetting settled law and overriding the prerogatives of the political branches. We do not know whether all petitioners or any of them would qualify for entry or admission under the immigration laws.[14] We do know that there is insufficient evidence to classify them as enemy combatants-enemies, that is, of the United States. But that hardly qualifies petitioners for admission. Nor does their detention at Guantanamo for many years entitle them to enter the United States. Whatever the scope of habeas corpus, the writ has never been compensatory in nature. The government has represented that it is continuing diplomatic attempts to find an appropriate country willing to admit petitioners, and we have no reason to doubt that it is doing so. Nor do we have the power to require anything more. ***

We have the following response to Judge Rogers's separate opinion.

---

[14] The government asserts that petitioners would not qualify for admission under the immigration laws. They would need visas which they do not have, and a court could not order the Executive Branch to grant them visas. The government also suggests that petitioners are ineligible for another reason-even though the United States was not their target, they allegedly engaged in "terrorist activity" *** which would mandate their removal*** . Petitioners object that the evidence is insufficient to back up the government's claim. The dispute cannot be resolved at this stage. Petitioners have not applied for admission pursuant to the immigration laws; the immigration authorities therefore have made no formal determination of their immigration status. For the same reason, petitioners are not entitled to parole *** , a remedy that can be granted only to an applicant for admission and only in the exclusive discretion of the Secretary of Homeland Security.

1. Judge Rogers: "The power to grant the writ means the power to order release." *** The question here is not whether petitioners should be released, but where. That question was not presented in *Boumediene* and the Court never addressed it. *** [N]ever in the history of habeas corpus has any court thought it had the power to order an alien held overseas brought into the sovereign territory of a nation and released into the general population. ***

2. Judge Rogers: "[T]he district court erred by ordering release into the country without first ascertaining whether the immigration laws provided a valid basis for detention as the Executive alternatively suggested." *** [T]he government has never asserted, here or in the district court, that it is holding petitioners pursuant to the immigration laws. *** What then is Judge Rogers talking about when she insists on evaluating petitioners' eligibility for admission under the immigration laws? None of the petitioners has even applied for admission. Perhaps she thinks a court should decide which, if any, of the petitioners would have been admitted if they had applied. *** Aliens are not eligible for admission into the United States unless they have applied for admission. Numerical limits may render them ineligible, as may many other considerations. The Secretary has wide discretion with respect to several categories of applicants and the decisions of consular officers on visa applications are not subject to judicial review. ***

ROGERS, Circuit Judge, concurring in the judgment:

In *Boumediene v. Bush* (2008), the Supreme Court held that detainees in the military prison at Guantanamo Bay ("Guantanamo") are "entitled to the privilege of habeas corpus to challenge the legality of their detentions," and that a "habeas court must have the power to order the conditional release of an individual unlawfully detained." Today the court nevertheless appears to conclude that a habeas court lacks authority to order that a non-"enemy combatant" alien be released into the country (as distinct from be admitted under the immigration laws) when the Executive can point to no legal justification for detention and to no foreseeable path of release. I cannot join the Court's analysis because it is not faithful to *Boumediene* and would compromise both the Great Writ as a check on arbitrary detention and the balance of powers over exclusion and admission and release of aliens into the United States recognized by the Supreme Court to reside in the Congress, the Executive, and the habeas court. Furthermore, that conclusion is unnecessary because this court cannot yet know if detention is justified here. Due to the posture of this case, the district court has yet to hear from the Executive regarding the immigration laws, which the Executive had asserted may form an alternate basis for detention. The district court thus erred in granting release prematurely, and I therefore concur in the judgment. ***

The majority does not adopt outright the Executive's argument that detention here is justified under an extra-statutory Executive power, but instead seems to conclude that the habeas court lacks the power to order the release of non-"enemy combatant" Guantanamo detainees from indefinite detention, even where such detention is not justified by statute. The effect, however, is much the same. To reach this conclusion, the majority has recast the traditional inquiry of a habeas court from whether the Executive has shown that the detention of the petitioners is lawful to whether the petitioners can show that the habeas court is "expressly authorized" to order aliens brought into the United States. Along the way, the majority's analysis, tends to conflate the power of the Executive to classify an alien as "admitted" within the meaning of the immigration statutes, and the power of the habeas court to allow an alien physically into the country. ***

In sum, the majority aims to safeguard the separation of powers by ensuring that the judiciary does not encroach upon the province of the political branches. But just as the courts are limited to enumerated powers, so too is the Executive, and the habeas court exercises a core function under Article III of the Constitution when it orders the release of those held without lawful justification. Indeed habeas is not an encroachment, but "a time-tested device" that "maintain[s] the 'delicate balance of governance' that is itself the surest safeguard of liberty," The petitioners have the privilege of the writ including the right to invoke the Court's power to order release and *** a habeas court has the power to order the release into the United States of unadmitted aliens whom the Executive would prefer to detain indefinitely but as to whom the Executive has exercised no lawful detention authority. The petitioners seeking release into the United States are seventeen Uighurs who come to the court as unadmitted aliens who are not "enemy combatants" or otherwise shown by the Executive, when afforded the opportunity, to be dangerous or a threat to U.S. interests, and as to whom the Executive as yet has failed to show grounds for their detention, which appears indefinite. *** I would conclude, *** that, were the district court to ascertain thereafter that petitioners' detention is not lawful and has become effectively indefinite *** it would have the power to order them conditionally released into the country.

*****

Review of the decision en banc was sought in *Kiyemba*. Because the opinions concerning whether the case should be reviewed en banc sharply focused the issues, I have reproduced edited versions of these opinions below.

KIYEMBA v. OBAMA
561 F. 3d 509 (D.C.C.A., 2009)

Rehearing En banc Denied July 27, 2009

GINSBURG, Circuit Judge:

*** According to the Government's theory, because the right to challenge a transfer is "ancillary" to and not at the "core" of habeas corpus relief, § 2241(e)(1) still bars the district court from exercising jurisdiction over the instant claims. *** The Court in *Boumediene* did not draw (or even suggest the existence of) a line between "core" and "ancillary" habeas issues, neither of which terms appears in the opinion. Rather, the Court stated simply that § 2241(e)(1) "effects an unconstitutional suspension of the writ." Accordingly, we read *Boumediene* to invalidate § 2241(e)(1) with respect to all habeas claims brought by Guantanamo detainees, not simply with respect to so-called "core" habeas claims.

The Government next argues the second provision of MCA § 7 stripped the district court of jurisdiction. That provision eliminates court jurisdiction over "any other action against the United States or its agents relating to any aspect of the ... transfer" of a detainee. This case does not come within the reach of § 2241(e)(2), however. That provision applies by its terms to "any other action"-meaning other than a petition for a writ of habeas corpus, which is the subject of § 2241(e)(1). The detainees' claims are not in the nature of an action barred by § 2241(e)(2) because, based upon longstanding precedents, it is clear they allege a proper claim for habeas relief, specifically an order barring their transfer to or from a place of incarceration. ***

A court considering a request for preliminary relief must examine four factors: (1) the moving party's likelihood of success on the merits; (2) irreparable injury to the moving party if an injunction is denied; (3) substantial injury to the opposing party if an injunction is granted; and (4) the public interest. *** The detainees here seek to prevent their transfer to any country where they are likely to be subjected to further detention or to torture. Our analysis of their claims is controlled by the Supreme Court's recent decision in *Munaf*. *** *Munaf* precludes a court from issuing a writ of habeas corpus to prevent a transfer on the grounds asserted by the petitioners here; therefore the detainees cannot prevail on the merits of their present claim and the Government is entitled to reversal of the orders as a matter of law. *** [A]s the present record shows, the Government does everything in its power to determine whether a particular country is likely to torture a particular detainee. *** [T]he detainees are not liable to be cast abroad willy-nilly without regard to their likely treatment in any country that will take them. Under *Munaf,* however, the district court may not question the Government's determination that a potential recipient country is not likely to torture a detainee. In light of the Government's policy, a detainee cannot prevail on the merits of a claim seeking to bar his transfer based upon the likelihood of his being tortured in the recipient country. ***

To the extent the detainees seek to enjoin their transfer based upon the expectation that a recipient country will detain or prosecute them, *Munaf* again bars relief. After their release from the custody of the United States, any prosecution or detention the petitioners might face would be effected "by the foreign government pursuant to its own laws and not on behalf of the United States." *** Judicial inquiry into a recipient country's basis or procedures for prosecuting or detaining a transferee from Guantanamo would implicate not only norms of international comity but also the same separation of powers principles that preclude the courts from second-guessing the Executive's assessment of the likelihood a detainee will be tortured by a foreign sovereign. Furthermore, the requirement that the Government provide pre-transfer notice interferes with the Executive's ability to conduct the sensitive diplomatic negotiations required to arrange safe transfers for detainees.

In short, "habeas is not a means of compelling the United States to harbor fugitives from the criminal justice system of a sovereign with undoubted authority to prosecute them." Therefore, the district court may not issue a writ of habeas corpus to shield a detainee from prosecution or detention at the hands of another sovereign on its soil and under its authority. As a result, the petitioners cannot make the required showing of a likelihood of success on the merits necessary to obtain the preliminary relief they here seek. ***

KAVANAUGH, Circuit Judge, concurring:

I agree with and join the persuasive opinion of the Court. Under current law, the U.S. Government may transfer Guantanamo detainees to the custody of foreign nations without judicial intervention-at least so long as the Executive Branch declares, as it has for the Guantanamo detainees, that the United States will not transfer "an individual in circumstances where torture is likely to result." ***

First, our disposition does not preclude Congress from further regulating the Executive's transfer of wartime detainees to the custody of other nations. *** *Second,* in the absence of a meritorious statutory claim, the detainees argue that they have a constitutional due process right against "transfer to torture"-and, therefore, to judicial reassessment of the Executive's conclusion that transfer to a foreign nation's custody is unlikely to result in torture. But both *Munaf* and the deeply rooted "rule of non-inquiry" in extradition cases require that we defer to the Executive's considered judgment that transfer is unlikely to result in torture. Those precedents compel us to reject the detainees' argument that the court second-guess the Executive's conclusion in this case. *** Transfers are a traditional and lawful aspect of U.S. war efforts. When waging war, the United States captures and detains enemy combatants. *** And the "Judiciary is not suited to second-guess such determinations." ***

GRIFFITH, Circuit Judge, concurring in the judgment in part and dissenting in part:

*** I agree with the majority that the district court has subject matter jurisdiction to hear the detainees' challenges to their transfers. *** Statutory habeas may in fact exist for these detainees and cover claims against unlawful transfer, but for now this remains an open question, and the Constitution provides a more sure footing for jurisdiction. *** Transfer to continued detention on behalf of the United States in a place where the writ does not reach would be unlawful and may be enjoined. The question we must consider is what process courts must use to determine whether the Government's proposed transfers run afoul of that bar. The majority holds that the district court must defer to the Executive's sworn representations that transfer to the physical custody of a foreign government will not involve continued detention on behalf of the United States. ***

Fundamental to a prisoner's habeas rights is the Government's duty to appear in court to justify his detention. *** To vindicate the detainees' habeas rights, *Boumediene* requires the court to "conduct a meaningful review" of the Government's reasons for the detention, which includes, at the very least, the rudimentaries of an adversary proceeding. Calling the jailer to account must include some opportunity for the prisoner to challenge the jailer's account.

Here the nine detainees claim their transfers may result in continued detention on behalf of the United States in places where the writ does not extend, effectively denying them the habeas protections *Boumediene* declared are theirs. *** It is significant that the government has submitted sworn declarations assuring the court that any transfer will result in release from U.S. authority. If the Government's representations are accurate, each transfer will be lawful, for in habeas the only relevant judicial inquiry about a transfer is whether it will result in continued detention on behalf of the United States in a place where the writ does not run. *** When an individual entitled to habeas protections faces the prospect of continued detention-be it by the United States at Guantanamo Bay or on its behalf after transfer to a foreign nation-he must be afforded some opportunity to challenge the Government's case. *** Although the status of these detainees has been put to an adversarial process, whether their transfers will be lawful has not. I do not see how the court can safeguard the habeas rights *Boumediene* extended to these detainees without allowing them to challenge the Government's account.

Munaf is not to the contrary. The majority makes much of its language that courts may not "second-guess" the government" determinations, but it overlooks a significant difference between that case and ours: the *Munaf* petitioners knew in advance that the government intended to transfer them to Iraqi authorities and had the opportunity to demonstrate that such a transfer would be unlawful. There was no need for the *Munaf* Court to consider an issue at the center of this dispute: whether notice is required to prevent an unlawful transfer. *** Critical to *Munaf's* holding was the need to protect Iraq's right as a foreign sovereign to prosecute the petitioners. No such interest is implicated here. The Court also emphasized Iraq's status as an ally and the fact that the petitioners had voluntarily traveled to Iraq to commit crimes during ongoing hostilities. Again, nothing similar is involved in this case. Perhaps most important, the *Munaf* petitioners sought a unique type of relief, as the Court stressed:

> *** [W]hat petitioners are really after is a court order requiring the United States to shelter them from the sovereign government seeking to have them answer for alleged crimes committed within that sovereign's borders.

Given the significant differences between the circumstances of *Munaf* and this case, we are not required to hold that courts are foreclosed from exercising their habeas powers to enjoin a transfer without some opportunity for a detainee to challenge the Government's representation that his transfer will be lawful. *** The constitutional habeas protections extended to these petitioners by *Boumediene* will be greatly diminished, if not eliminated, without an opportunity to challenge the Government's assurances that their transfers will not result in continued detention on behalf of the United States. ***

Notes

1. Parsing the Opinions. What is the difference in the questions asked and answered by the majority and dissenters in *Kiyemba*? Which opinion do you think does the better job of explaining *Munaf*?

2. Judicial Impotence? Is habeas a hollow writ for those at Guantanamo? Did the judiciary wisely step back from issuing an order it could not enforce? Or did it demonstrate a lack of gumption in standing up to the Executive? Where was Congress during this showdown? Might that have had some effect on the outcome of *Kiyemba*?

3. Doctrine. Who has the better of the arguments concerning the meaning of the Supreme Court precedents?

4. Immigration and Terrorism. Chapter XI will deal with the intricate relationship between immigration and antiterrorism law in other contexts.

5. Followup to *Kiyemba*. The Obama Administration, in early 2009, sought assistance from other nations to take the remaining 17 Uighur detainees. It also sought to place some of the Uighurs in the United States, but that came to an end in June 2009 when Congress overwhelmingly passed a rider to an appropriations bill for the war in Afghanistan that banned resettling any Guantanamo detainees in the United States. Bermuda and Palau stepped forward, despite the fact that the Chinese government made clear to all who were tempted to make such a move that they would consider asylum to be a hostile act against China. The Uighurs became a cause célèbre in Bermuda, a colony of Britain, when it agreed to take some of the Uighurs. Britain took the position that its colony was not authorized to accept the Uighurs and in Bermuda, politicians were critical of the Prime Minister for granting asylum to persons the United States itself would not accept. Despite these problems, four Uighurs seem to be enjoying Bermuda and are on a track to citizenship there. See Eric Eckholm, "Out of Guantanamo, Uighurs Bask in Bermuda," NEW YORK TIMES, June 15, 2009. Palau offered to take the remaining 13 Uighurs.

6. Supreme Court Review? The Supreme Court denied review of a petition for certiorari in the following case which was not a counterterrorism case which shared several issues in common with the cases you have read in this section. Justices THOMAS and SCALIA dissented from the denial. As you read this dissent, consider whether the Court might take any of the cases from the DC Circuit in Section C of this chapter. Be prepared to argue this issue in class.

NORIEGA v. PASTRANA
130 S. Ct. 1002 (2010)

The petition for a writ of certiorari is denied.

Justice THOMAS, with whom Justice SCALIA joins, dissenting from denial of certiorari.

*** The questions presented are, in the Solicitor General's words: "1. Whether Section 5 of the Military Commissions Act of 2006, precludes petitioner from invoking the Geneva Convention Relative to the Treatment of Prisoners of War as a source of rights in a habeas corpus proceeding"; and "2.

Whether, assuming petitioner can assert a claim based on the Geneva Convention, his extradition to France would violate the Convention." Answering just the first of these questions would provide much-needed guidance on two important issues with which the political branches and federal courts have struggled since we decided *Boumediene.* The first is the extent, if any, to which provisions like Section 5 affect 28 U.S.C. § 2241 in a manner that implicates the constitutional guarantee of habeas corpus. The second is whether the Geneva Conventions are self-executing and judicially enforceable.

*** Noriega argued that his extradition to France would violate several provisions of the Third Convention and that the District Court erred in concluding otherwise. In response, the Government asserted that the court lacked jurisdiction over Noriega's claims because § 5(a) of the Military Commissions Act of 2006 (MCA) establishes that "[t]he Geneva Conventions are not self-executing" or judicially enforceable in habeas corpus actions. MCA § 5(a) provides:

> "No person may invoke the Geneva Conventions or any protocols thereto in any habeas corpus or other civil action or proceeding to which the United States, or a current or former officer, employee, member of the Armed Forces, or other agent of the United States is a party as a source of rights in any court of the United States or its States or territories."

*** [T]he threshold question in this case is whether MCA § 5(a) is valid. *** The Suspension Clause provides that "[t]he Privilege of the Writ of Habeas Corpus shall not be suspended, unless when in Cases of Rebellion or Invasion the public Safety may require it." U.S. Const., Art. I, § 9, cl. 2. Because the Clause addresses only the suspension-not the content or existence-of the "Privilege of the Writ," we have long recognized the "obligation" the first Congress "must have felt" to "provid[e] efficient means by which this great constitutional privilege should receive life and activity." But we have also steadfastly declined to adopt a date of reference by which the writ's constitutional content, if any, is to be judged, see *Boumediene,* and thus have left open the question whether statutory efforts to limit § 2241 implicate the Suspension Clause. This question, which has already divided the Court in other contexts, is clearly presented here. ***

Addressing Noriega's challenge to the Eleventh Circuit's decision would resolve the important statutory and constitutional questions here and would guide courts and the political branches in addressing the same and similar issues in other detainee cases. See, e.g., *Al-Bihani,* ("The Supreme Court has provided scant guidance on these questions, consciously leaving the contours of the substantive and procedural law of detention open for lower courts to shape in a common law fashion."). Recent court decisions, as well as recent Executive Branch court filings and policy determinations, specifically invoke the Geneva Conventions as part of the law that governs detainee treatment in the United States and abroad. For example, in September 2009, the U.S. District Court for the District of Columbia issued a redacted version of a classified memorandum opinion in which it granted habeas corpus relief in the oldest of the pending Guantanamo cases because the petitioner's indefinite detention was based "almost exclusively" on unreliable "confessions" obtained "using abusive techniques that violated the Army Field Manual and the 1949 Geneva Convention Relative to the Treatment of Prisoners of War." *Al Rabiah v. United States,* Civ. Action No. 02-828, Unclassified Mem. Op. (DC Sept. 17, 2009), pp. 1-2, 43.

Several recent D.C. Circuit decisions, one of which is now pending before us, similarly implicate the importance of the Geneva Convention and MCA § 5(a) questions in this case. In *Kiyemba v. Obama,* 555 F.3d 1022 (2009) (*Kiyemba I),* cert. granted, the petitioners, Guantanamo detainees who prevailed on their habeas corpus claims in federal court but cannot return to their home country, rely on the Geneva Conventions in claiming a right to be released in the territorial United States. Although the D.C. Circuit did not address MCA § 5(a) in rejecting this claim, the Government contends before this Court that MCA § 5(a) bars petitioners' reliance on the Conventions, and Judge Rogers' opinion concurring in the D.C. Circuit's judgment relies upon the same repatriation language in Article 118 of the Third Convention that Noriega raises here. In *Al-Bihani,* the D.C. Circuit directly invokes MCA § 5(a) in rejecting a Guantanamo detainee's claim that he was entitled to habeas corpus relief because his detention violated, *inter alia,* the Third Geneva Convention. Finally, the D.C. Circuit's decision in *Kiyemba v. Obama,* 561 F.3d 509 (2009) *(Kiyemba II),* implicates the issues here in holding, contrary to several recent district court decisions, that another MCA provision (MCA § 7(a)(2), does not deprive federal habeas corpus courts of jurisdiction to consider claims in which certain classes of detainees challenge their conditions of confinement under the Geneva Conventions.

The extent to which noncitizen detainees may rely on the Geneva Conventions as a source of rights against the United States has also been the subject of increasing debate in the political branches. *** Congress, in turn, is considering new legislation that would further clarify the extent to which detainees can enforce Geneva Convention obligations against the United States in federal courts, but progress on these proposals has been complicated by uncertainty over the statutory and constitutional questions in this case.

As noted, addressing these questions now, if only the statutory issues, would avoid years of litigation and uncertainty no matter what we conclude on the merits. A decision upholding MCA § 5(a) would obviate the need for detainees, the Government, and federal courts to struggle (as they did here) with Geneva Convention claims in habeas corpus proceedings. And, it would give the political branches a clearer sense of the constitutional limits to which new legislative or policy initiatives must adhere. The latter benefit would also follow if we were to invalidate MCA § 5(a). In addition, such a ruling could well allow us to reach the question we left open in *Hamdan-* whether the Geneva Conventions are self-executing and judicially enforceable-because this case is not governed by the Uniform Code of Military Justice provisions on which the *Hamdan* majority relied in holding Common Article III applicable to the proceedings in that case. Finally, if the Court were to conclude that the Conventions are self-executing and judicially enforceable in habeas corpus proceedings, this case would present two additional questions relevant to noncitizen detainee litigation: whether federal courts may classify such detainees as POWs under the Third Convention, and whether any of the Conventions requires the United States immediately to repatriate detainees entitled to release from U.S. custody. *** Accordingly, I would take the case and decide the questions presented in the Solicitor General's brief.

ESMAIL v. OBAMA

___ F. 3d ___, 2011 WL 1327701 (C.A.D.C. April 8, 2011)

PER CURIAM:

*** [T]he record contains sufficient facts *** to support the district court's conclusion that Esmail was "part of" al Qaeda at the time of his capture. *See Bensayah v. Obama,* 610 F.3d 718, 724–25 (D.C.Cir.2010) ("[T]he [Authorization for Use of Military Force] authorizes the Executive to detain, at the least, any individual who is functionally part of al Qaeda."); *see also Barhoumi v. Obama,* 609 F.3d 416, 423 (D.C.Cir.2010) (clarifying that in habeas appeals involving Guantanamo Bay detainees we review district court fact findings for clear error, and we review the ultimate issue of whether the detainee was "part of" al Qaeda *de novo*). ***

SILBERMAN, Senior Circuit Judge, concurring:

*** The government's evidence is easily sufficient to meet any evidentiary standard. *** I write separately for two reasons. First, *** even if petitioner could show he resolutely declined to "join" al Qaeda or the Taliban, *** so long as evidence showed he fought along side of al Qaeda, the Taliban, or with associated forces he would be covered by the Authorization for Use of Military Force.*** [21] My second point ***goes to the unusual incentives and disincentives that bear on judges *** charged with deciding these detainee habeas cases. In the typical criminal case, a good judge will vote to overturn a conviction if the prosecutor lacked sufficient evidence, even when the judge is virtually certain that the defendant committed the crime. *** When we are dealing with detainees, *** one can not help but be conscious of the infinitely greater downside risk to our country, and its people, of an order releasing a detainee who is likely to return to terrorism. *** [O]ur opinion in *Al - Adahi v. Obama,* 613 F.3d 1102 (D.C.Cir.2010), *** persuasively explains that in a habeas corpus proceeding the preponderance of evidence standard that the government assumes binds it, is unnecessary—and moreover, unrealistic. I doubt any of my colleagues will vote to grant a petition if he or she believes that it is somewhat likely that the petitioner is an al Qaeda adherent or an active supporter. Unless, of course, the Supreme Court were to adopt the preponderance of the evidence standard (which it is unlikely to do—taking a case might obligate it to assume direct responsibility for the consequences of

---

[21] Of course, "the purely independent conduct of a freelancer"—one who does not fight alongside of, or actively support, al Qaeda, the Taliban, or an associated force—"is not enough" to justify detention. *Bensayah v. Obama,* 610 F.3d 718, 725 (D.C.Cir.2010).

Boumediene v. Bush, 553 U.S. 723 (2008). But I, like my colleagues, certainly would release a petitioner against whom the government could not muster even "some evidence." [If] the executive branch does not release winning petitioners because no other country will accept them and they will not be released into the United States, *see Kiyemba v. Obama,* 605 F.3d 1046, 1048 (D.C.Cir.2010); *Kiyemba v. Obama,* 561 F.3d 509, 516 (D.C.Cir.2009), then the whole process leads to virtual advisory opinions. It becomes a charade prompted by the Supreme Court's defiant—if only theoretical—assertion of judicial supremacy *** by posturing on the part of the Justice Department, and providing litigation exercise for the detainee bar.

Review Problem

Senator Lindsey Graham introduced "The Terrorist Detention Review Act" on August 4, 2010 to provide consistency in developing the law of habeas corpus to deal with detainees after *Boumedienne.* Here are some components of the bill:It applies to "unprivileged enemy belligerents," including anyone who "was a member of, part of, or operated in a clandestine, covert, or military capacity on behalf of the Taliban, al Qaeda, or associated forces." §2256(a)(6)(C).

- It provides that in habeas actions "the government may provide notice [ex parte and under seal] to the District Court that it a particular organization is an "associated force of the Taliban or al Qaeda" and that the District Court "shall give utmost deference to inclusion of the organization in [such] notice." §2256(d).
- The bill states that the "burden shall be on the Government to prove by a preponderance of the evidence that the covered individual is an unprivileged enemy belligerent," that the District Court must consider the "totality of the circumstances and the evidence as a whole in determining whether the Government has carried its burden," and that the Government's evidence shall be entitled to a "rebuttable presumption that such evidence is authentic." §2256(e).
- Membership in al Qaeda, the Taliban, or associated forces is presumed for persons who "obtained military-style training" from such entities. Withdrawal of membership can only be rebutted by "clear and convincing evidence that the covered individual withdrew from the organization in question prior to capture." Id.
- Statements obtained from covered individuals, evidence obtained by "torture or cruel, inhuman, or degrading treatment" would be excluded in habeas proceedings, but "statements against interest" to CSRTs, ARBs or comparable review boards would be presumed reliable and admissible, as would statements given "as a result of treatment in compliance with the Army Field Manual." Id.
- Habeas petitions would be largely precluded for claims seeking (a) to collaterally attack military commission proceedings, and (b) to block transfers to third-party countries. §2256(f).

Discuss, using the cases you have read, the extent that the Graham Bill conforms to post-*Boumediene* habeas law on: (1) Identity of the enemy; (2) Scope of detention authority; (3) Bars to claims arguably protected by Suspension Clause; (4) Evidentiary presumptions; and (5) Voluntariness of statements

Who, Congress or the courts, is in the better position institutionally to develop habeas law dealing with detainees?

D. POLITICAL AVENUES OF RELEASE

The most important method of release remains beyond the reach of the courts—in negotiations between governments and decisions of executive officials. While diplomatic efforts are most often aimed at returning a detainee to his home country, some detainees have been transferred to third party countries. Repatriation raises a host of questions from the safety of detainees. Once repatriated will they face torture? What security threat do they pose after being freed? Will they return to violence against the United States?

As of January 2009, more than 525 of the approximately 770 detainees known to have been held at Guantanamo since 2002 had been repatriated. To date, detainees have been repatriated from Guantanamo without federal court intervention to a variety of countries, including Afghanistan, Albania, Australia, Bahrain, Bosnia, Egypt, France, Iran, Morocco, Jordan, Kuwait, Lybia, Pakistan, Spain, the Sudan, and the United Kingdom. Thousands more have been released from detention through executive action from U.S. facilities in Afghanistan and Iraq, and likely from CIA detention elsewhere. Secretary of Defense Robert Gates has testified that from Iraq alone, the military released 16,000 or 17,000 detainees in 2008 alone.

In the case of Guantanamo detainees, diplomacy is necessary for release even in the case of court ordered release. Indeed, even following a Court's ruling granting a detainee's habeas petition the Government facilitates the detainee's release through diplomacy.

A key question in these negotiations is whether the detainee will be free once repatriated and, if not, what restrictions will he face? Will the receiving government detain former U.S. prisoners or torture them? Does the receiving nation operate a full-fledged reintegration program or run a special detention facility for former detainees (and if not, should it)? And perhaps most importantly, does the receiving nation offer counseling, job training, or other re-integration programs that might help the newly-released detainees re-join social and economic life?

Like many former detainees of other conflicts (and, indeed, former criminal prisoners), former detainees held as terrorist suspects face social stigma, difficulty finding employment, and mental and physical health problems after release. These problems may bear on the choices and opportunities of former detainees to later engage in violence. Addressing these problems is a key, if complicated, question in ensuring successful counterterrorism policy.

The Saudi Arabian Reintegration Program. The most prominent reintegration program for those formerly detained by the United States as suspected terrorists is the program run by the Saudi Arabian government. The Saudi program reunites former detainees with their families, finds employment, helps with marriage and resettlement, and provides financial support. After visiting with their families, detainees are sent to a six-week program to attempt to change their ideas about jihad and non-Muslims through one-on-one discussions with religious scholars. Following this program they are moved to a half-way house where they receive vocational training, religious classes and counseling and are permitted family visits on holidays.

The program is heavily coordinated with the United States. The Saudis have briefed the CIA, FBI and Defense Department on the reintegration program, and U.S. officials have visited the reintegration facility in Riyadh. Indeed, if a detainee returns late from a holiday visit during his time in the program, American officials are notified. The former detainees are required to report regularly on their whereabouts, information that is passed on to Washington.

The Saudi program is the largest and longest running reintegration program and has become the model for similar programs in other countries. U.S. officials have praised the Saudi program and, according to a Saudi official, "The U.S. is more comfortable sending [Saudi detainees] back as they've seen the effectiveness of our program."

The Case of Yemen. Yemeni citizens make up by far the largest group of detainees remaining at the Guantanamo Bay detention facility. As of October, 2009, 117 Saudi citizens and 197 Afghans had left Guantanamo, while only 16 Yemenis had been transferred to Yemen.

Yemen, the poorest country in the Middle East, is an arid, unstable state plagued by a separatist insurgency and a growing al Qaeda presence. Yemen does not yet have a comprehensive reintegration program. The security implications of repatriating the remaining Yemeni detainees poses a daunting challenge to U.S. officials, and what to do with the Yemeni detainees remains one of the biggest obstacles to President Obama's express goal of closing the Guantanamo Bay detention facility by January, 2010.

Both U.S. and Yemeni authorities have said they want to repatriate as many Yemeni detainees as soon as possible—but negotiations over the details and funding of a Yemeni reintegration program have so far not been successful. In 2006, twenty-three al-Qaeda suspects escaped from Yemeni hands (digging a tunnel from their cell in the basement of the Yemen's main intelligence office to a local mosque, reportedly with the support of Yemeni officials), further shaking U.S. confidence in Yemen's counterterrorism capabilities.

The Yemeni detainees who have been returned have reportedly been further detained, and some allege tortured, by Yemeni security forces. The former detainees have reportedly received no counseling, job training, financial assistance, or other help reintegrating into Yemeni society.

Without a diplomatic solution, many Yemeni detainees who have been cleared by the U.S. for release remain at Guantanamo, and in 2009 several went on a protracted hunger strike to protest their prolonged detentions. U.S. officials have approached the Saudi and Yemeni governments to attempt to persuade them to move Yemeni detainees into the Saudi program, a proposal both governments have so far rejected, and the U.S. reportedly continues to work with Yemen to establish a reintegration program. Yemen is seeking funding for the program from the United States. See Human Rights Watch, No Direction Home: Returns from Guantanamo to Yemen (March, 2009). How the U.S. and Yemen resolve the fate of the remaining Guantanamo detainees is still uncertain.

The Challenge of Recidivism. One of the greatest challenges facing officials deciding whether to repatriate a detainee is the possibility that he will later, if repatriated, return to (or become engaged in) later terrorist violence against the United States.

As of April, 2009, the Defense Intelligence Agency reported that the overall rate of former Guantanamo detainees confirmed or suspected of reengaging in terrorist activity was 14%—with 27 confirmed and 47 suspected of engaging in terrorism. Secretary of Defense Gates testified before the Senate Armed Services committee in January of 2009 that "The recidivism numbers that I've been told until recently from Guantanamo have been on the order of about four or five percent, but there's been an uptick in that just over the last few months."

By contrast, according to the most current figures released by the U.S. Department of Justice Bureau of Justice Statistics: "Of the 272,111 persons released from prisons in 15 States in 1994, an estimated 67.5% were rearrested for a felony or serious misdemeanor within 3 years, 46.9% were reconvicted, and 25.4% resentenced to prison for a new crime." See http://www.ojp.usdoj.gov/bjs/crimoff.htm#recidivism.

Assuming these figures are roughly accurate, what do they say about terrorist recidivism or the effectiveness of reintegration programs? Do these figures indicate that the detainees are or are not the "worst of the worst" as U.S. officials have long asserted? Is terrorist recitivism more dangerous than crime by former criminals?

Closing Guantanamo Bay. On the second day after his inauguration, President Obama signed an executive order that calls for the closing of the Guantanamo Bay detention facility within one year's time. Upon issuing the order, the President said: "The message that we are sending the world is that the United States intends to prosecute the ongoing struggle against violence and terrorism and we are going to do so vigilantly and we are going to do so effectively and we are going to do so in a manner that is consistent with our values and our ideals."

Both politically and practically, closing Guantanamo presents a formidable challenge. It has proven difficult to transfer detainees to other countries, including their home nations. It is unclear how Guantanmo will be closed without the relocation of some prisoners to U.S.-based detention facilities. Critics, including many members of Congress, have staunchly opposed the transfer of detainees to U.S.-based facilities, arguing that they are too dangerous to be held in the United States.

On one side of the debate, Senate Majority Whip Dick Durbin and Senator Barbara Boxer of California argue that over three hundred convicted terrorists are already safely being held in U.S. prisons, demonstrating that dangerous detainees can be held in the U.S. without harming American national security. The chairman of the Joint Chiefs of Staff, Admiral Mike Mullen, agrees with this contention, saying "We have terrorists in jail right now...have had some for some time... They are in supermax prisons and they don't pose a threat."

By contrast, Senator Pat Roberts of Kansas, whose state lawmakers have considered as a possible location for Guantanamo detainees, said to Kansas reporters: "I've said it once. I'll say it many more times: Not in my back yard. Not in Kansas," Roberts said in a press conference with Kansas reporters. "I will shut down the Senate before I'll let that happen."

The political quagmire over closing Guantanamo—and the possibility that terrorist suspects might be transferred to U.S.-based facilities—was further highlighted in May of 2009, when the Senate rejected by a 90 to 6 vote the inclusion of funds in a spending bill that would be used to close Guantanamo.

At the same time, the military commissions process has ground to a stand-still, and many detainees are impossible to prosecute in federal court. What is to be done with the remaining Guantanamo Bay prisoners? Why would other nations accept prisoners U.S. lawmakers see as too dangerous to house in the United States, which boasts arguably the most secure criminal detention facilities in the world? Will the Obama Administration make its self-imposed deadline? What are the ultimate choices and tradeoffs that must be made in a decision to close or keep open the detention camp at Guantanamo?

The Congressional Research Service provides the following summary of the legal issues concerning the closing of Guantanamo:

> [T]he closure of the Guantanamo detention facility may raise complex legal issues, particularly if detainees are transferred to the United States. The nature and scope of constitutional protections owed to detainees within the United States may be different from the protections owed to those held elsewhere. The transfer of detainees into the country may also have immigration consequences. Criminal charges could also be brought against detainees in one of several forums— that is, federal civilian courts, the courts-martial system, or military commissions. The procedural protections afforded to the accused in each of these forums may differ, along with the types of offenses for which persons may be charged. This may affect the ability of U.S. authorities to pursue criminal charges against some detainees. Whether the military commissions established to try detainees for war crimes fulfill constitutional requirements concerning a defendant's right to a fair trial is likely to become a matter of debate, if not litigation. The issues raised by the proposed closure of the Guantanamo detention facility have broad implications.

Executive policies, legislative enactments, and judicial rulings concerning the rights and privileges owed to enemy belligerents may have long-term consequences for U.S. detention policy, both in the conflict with Al Qaeda and the Taliban and in future armed conflicts.

CRS, "Closing the Guantanamo Detention Center: Legal Issues," February 11, 2011

Guantanamo Review Task Force Final Report
January 22, 2010

*** On January 22, 2009, the President issued Executive Order 13492, calling for a prompt and comprehensive interagency review of the status of all individuals currently detained at the Guantanamo Bay Naval Base and requiring the closure of the detention facilities there. *** After evaluating all of the detainees, the review participants have decided on the proper disposition—transfer, prosecution, or continued detention—of all 240 detainees subject to the review.*** The decisions reached on the 240 detainees subject to the review are as follows:

- **126 detainees** were approved for transfer. To date, 44 of these detainees have been transferred from Guantanamo to countries outside the United States.
- **44 detainees** over the course of the review were referred for prosecution either in federal court or a military commission, and **36 of these detainees** remain the subject of active cases or investigations. The Attorney General has announced that the government will pursue prosecutions against six of these detainees in federal court and will pursue prosecutions against six others in military commissions.
- **48 detainees** were determined to be too dangerous to transfer but not feasible for prosecution. They will remain in detention pursuant to the Government's authority under the Authorization for Use of Military Force passed by Congress in response to the attacks of September 11, 2001. Detainees may challenge the legality of their detention in federal court and will periodically receive further review within the Executive Branch.
- **30 detainees** from Yemen were designated for "conditional" detention based on the current security environment in that country.***

*** By the end of 2002, 632 detainees had been brought to Guantanamo. *** Since 2002, a total of 779 individuals have been detained at Guantanamo *** Of the 779 *** approximately 530—almost 70 percent—were transferred or released from U.S. custody prior to 2009. The countries to which these detainees were transferred include Afghanistan, Albania, Algeria, Australia, Bahrain, Bangladesh, Belgium, Bosnia, Denmark, Egypt, France, Germany,

Iran, Iraq, Jordan, Kazakhstan, Kuwait, Libya, Maldives, Mauritania, Morocco, Pakistan, Qatar, Russia, Saudi Arabia, Somalia (Somaliland), Spain, Sudan, Sweden, Tajikistan, Tunisia, Turkey, Uganda, the United Arab Emirates, the United Kingdom, and Yemen.***

V. Detainee Review Guidelines. ***

A. Transfer Guidelines. *** **[A]** detainee should be deemed eligible for transfer if any threat he poses could be sufficiently mitigated through feasible and appropriate security measures.[5] *** [T]he Task Force was instructed to consider the totality of available information regarding the detainee, and to give careful consideration to the credibility and reliability of the available information. *** The second evaluation *** was an evaluation of potential destination (*i.e.,* receiving) countries. *** The third evaluation *** was a legal evaluation to ensure that any detainee falling outside the Government's lawful detention authority under the AUMF was recommended for transfer or release.

B. Prosecution Guidelines. *** [T]he Guidelines set forth standards used by federal prosecutors across the country to determine whether to charge a case, as set forth in the *United States Attorneys' Manual*. *** [A] case should be recommended for prosecution if the detainee's conduct constitutes a federal offense and the potentially available admissible evidence will probably be sufficient to obtain and sustain a conviction—unless prosecution should be declined because no substantial federal interest would be served by prosecution. Key factors *** include the nature and seriousness of the offense; the detainee's culpability in connection with the offense; the detainee's willingness to cooperate in the investigation or prosecution of others; and the probable sentence or other consequences if the detainee is convicted. *** For the evaluation of whether a detainee should be prosecuted in a military commission, Task Force prosecutors examined the potentially available admissible evidence and *** other factors were also significant in determining whether to recommend prosecution, including the need to protect classified information, such as intelligence sources and methods.

C. Detention Guidelines. *** [A] detainee should be considered eligible for continued detention under the AUMF only if (1) the detainee poses a national security threat that cannot be sufficiently mitigated through feasible and appropriate security measures; (2) prosecution of the detainee by the federal government is not feasible in any forum; and (3) continued detention without criminal charges is lawful. ***This legal evaluation addressed both the legal basis for holding the detainee under the AUMF and the Government's case

---

[5] The Guidelines further provided that a detainee should be deemed eligible for release if he does not pose an identifiable threat to the national security of the United States. Other than the 17 Chinese Uighur detainees, who were approved for "transfer or release," no detainees were approved for "release" during the course of the review.

for defending the detention in any habeas litigation. *** The scope of the AUMF's detention authority extends to those persons who "planned, authorized or committed or aided" the September 11 attacks, "harbored those responsible for those attacks," or "were part of, or substantially supported, Taliban or al Qaeda forces or associated forces that are engaged in hostilities against the United States or its coalition partners." Accordingly, only detainees who satisfied this standard could be designated for continued detention. ***

*Threat Characteristics.*** [T]he following groupings provide a rough overview of the recurring threat profiles seen in the population.

- *Leaders, operatives, and facilitators involved in terrorist plots against U.S. targets.* At the high end of the threat spectrum are leaders, planners, operatives, and facilitators within al-Qaida or associated groups who are directly implicated in terrorist plots against U.S. interests. Among the most notorious examples in this group are Khalid Sheikh Mohammed, the alleged mastermind of the September 11 attacks; Ramzi bin al-Shibh, the alleged principal coordinator of the September 11 attacks; Abd al-Rahim al-Nashiri, the alleged mastermind of the attack on the U.S.S. *Cole***. Roughly 10 percent of the detainees subject to the review appear to have played a direct role in plotting, executing, or facilitating such attacks.
- *Others with significant organizational roles within al-Qaida or associated terrorist organizations.* Other detainees played significant organizational roles within al-Qaida or associated terrorist organizations, even if they may not have been directly involved in terrorist plots against U.S. targets. This group includes, for example, individuals responsible for overseeing or providing logistical support to al-Qaida's training operations in Afghanistan; facilitators who helped move money and personnel for al-Qaida; a cadre of Usama bin Laden's bodyguards***. Roughly 20 percent of the detainees subject to the review fall within this category.
- *Taliban leaders and members of anti-Coalition militia groups.* The detainee population also includes a small number of Afghan detainees who occupied significant positions within the Taliban regime, and a small number of other Afghan detainees who were involved in local insurgent networks in Afghanistan implicated in attacks on Coalition forces. Less than 10 percent of the detainees subject to the review fall within this category.
- *Low-level foreign fighters.* A majority of the detainees reviewed appear to have been foreign fighters with varying degrees of connection to al-Qaida, the Taliban, or associated groups, but who lacked a significant leadership or other specialized role. These detainees were typically captured in combat zones during the early stages of U.S. military operations in Afghanistan ***. Many were relatively recent recruits to training camps in Afghanistan run by al-Qaida or other groups, where they received limited weapons training,

but do not appear to have been among those selected for more advanced training geared toward terrorist operations abroad.
• *Miscellaneous others.* The remaining detainees—roughly 5 percent—do not fit into any of the above categories. ***

Country of Origin. The Guantanamo detainees reviewed included individuals from a number of different countries, including Yemen, Afghanistan, China, Saudi Arabia, Algeria, Tunisia, Syria, Libya, Kuwait, and Pakistan. Approximately 40 percent—97 detainees—were Yemeni, while over 10 percent were Afghan. *** *Point of Capture.* The large majority of the detainees in the population reviewed—approximately 60 percent—were captured inside Afghanistan or in the Afghanistan-Pakistan border area. Approximately 30 percent of the detainees were captured inside Pakistan. The remaining 10 percent were captured in countries other than Afghanistan or Pakistan. *** *Arrival at Guantanamo.* Most of the detainees reviewed—approximately 80 percent—arrived at Guantanamo in 2002, having been captured during the early months of operations in Afghanistan. The remaining detainees arrived in small numbers over succeeding years. ***

VII. Transfer Decisions. *** 59 of the 240 detainees subject to review were approved for transfer or release by the prior administration *** 29 of the detainees subject to review were ordered released by a federal district court as the result of habeas litigation. Of these 29 detainees, 18 were ordered released after the government conceded the case. The remaining 11 detainees were ordered released after a court reached the merits of the case and ruled, based on a preponderance of the evidence, that the detainee was not lawfully held because he was not part of, or did not substantially support, al-Qaida, the Taliban, or associated forces.[13] *** Of the 29 detainees ordered released, 18 were among the 59 who had been approved by the prior administration for transfer or release. Thus, a total of 70 detainees subject to the review were either approved for transfer during the prior administration or ordered released by a federal court. *** [T]he 126 detainees unanimously approved for transfer include 44 who have been transferred to date—24 to their home countries,[14] 18 to third countries for resettlement,[15] and two to Italy for prosecution. Of the 82 detainees who remain at Guantanamo and who have been approved for transfer, 16 may be repatriated to their home countries

---

[13] A total of 14 detainees have won their habeas cases on the merits in district court. The government transferred three of these detainees in December 2008; thus, they were not subject to the review. Of the 11 remaining detainees who were reviewed under the Executive Order, seven have been transferred to date. Of the four who have not been transferred, the United States is appealing the district court's ruling in two of the cases, and is still within the time period to appeal the remaining two cases.

[14] The 24 detainees transferred to their home countries were repatriated to Afghanistan (5), Algeria (2), Chad (1), Iraq (1), Kuwait (2), Saudi Arabia (3), Somalia (Somaliland) (2), the United Kingdom (1), and Yemen (7).

[15] The 18 detainees transferred to third countries for resettlement were transferred to Belgium (1), Bermuda (4), France (2), Hungary (1), Ireland (2), Portugal (2), and Palau (6).

(other than Yemen) consistent with U.S. policies concerning humane treatment, 38 cannot be repatriated due to humane treatment or related concerns in their home countries (other than Yemen) and thus need to be resettled in a third country, and 29 are from Yemen. ***

There were considerable variations among the detainees approved for transfer. For a small handful of these detainees, there was scant evidence of any involvement with terrorist groups or hostilities against Coalition forces in Afghanistan. However, for most of the detainees approved for transfer, there were varying degrees of evidence indicating that they were low-level foreign fighters affiliated with al-Qaida or other groups operating in Afghanistan. Thousands of such individuals are believed to have passed through Afghanistan from the mid-1990s through 2001, recruited through networks in various countries in the Middle East, North Africa, and Europe. These individuals varied in their motivations, but they typically sought to obtain military training at one of the many camps operating in Afghanistan; many subsequently headed to the front lines to assist the Taliban in their fight against the Northern Alliance. For the most part, these individuals were uneducated and unskilled. At the camps, they typically received limited weapons training. While al-Qaida used its camps to vet individuals for more advanced training geared toward terrorist operations against civilian targets, only a small percentage of camp attendees were deemed suitable for such operations. The low-level fighters approved for transfer were typically assessed by the review participants not to have been selected for such training. Many were relatively recent recruits to the camps, arriving in Afghanistan in the summer of 2001. *** [A] decision to approve a detainee for transfer does not reflect a decision that the detainee poses no threat or no risk of recidivism. Rather, the decision reflects the best predictive judgment of senior government officials, based on the available information, that any threat posed by the detainee can be sufficiently mitigated through feasible and appropriate security measures in the receiving country. *** Some detainees were approved for transfer only to specific countries or under specific conditions, and a few were approved for transfer only to countries with pending prosecutions against the detainee (or an interest in pursuing a future prosecution). *** For certain detainees, the review participants considered the availability of rehabilitation programs and mental health treatment in the receiving country. *** [T]he Yemeni detainees posed a unique challenge: there were 97 Yemenis subject to the review *** Taking into account the current intelligence regarding conditions in Yemen, and the individual backgrounds of each detainee, the review participants unanimously approved 36 of the 97 Yemeni detainees for transfer subject to appropriate security measures. *** Under these transfer decisions, detainees would be returned to Yemen only at a time, and only under conditions, deemed appropriate from a security perspective. *** [O]nly seven of the 36 Yemeni detainees approved for transfer have been transferred to Yemen. *** The involvement of Al-Qaida in the Arabian Peninsula—the branch of al-Qaida based in Yemen—in the recent attempted bombing of an airplane headed to Detroit underscored the continued need for a deliberate approach toward any further effort to repatriate Yemeni detainees. *** These detainees may be considered for resettlement in third countries subject to appropriate security measures, if such options become available.

VIII. Prosecution Decisions. *** As the Task Force completed its prosecution reviews, it identified those cases that appeared feasible for prosecution in federal court, or at least potentially feasible, if certain investigative steps were pursued with success. ***For example, the Task Force determined that there were more than a thousand pieces of potentially relevant physical evidence (including electronic media) seized during raids in the aftermath of the September 11 attacks that had not yet been systematically catalogued and required further evaluation for forensic testing. There were potential cooperating witnesses who could testify against others at trial, and key fact witnesses who needed to be interviewed. Finally, certain foreign governments, which had been reluctant to cooperate with the military commissions, could be approached to determine whether they would provide cooperation in a federal prosecution. *** The Department of Justice and Department of Defense agreed upon a joint protocol to establish a process for determining whether prosecution of a referred case should be pursued in a federal court or before a military commission. Under the protocol—titled *Determination of Guantanamo Cases Referred for Prosecution*—there is a presumption that prosecution will be pursued in a federal court wherever feasible, unless other compelling factors make it more appropriate to pursue prosecution before a military commission. The evaluations called for under the protocol are conducted by teams of both federal and military prosecutors. Among the criteria they apply are: the nature of the offenses to be charged; the identity of the victims; the location of the crime; the context in which the defendant was apprehended; and the manner in which the case was investigated and by which investigative agency. The Attorney General, in consultation with the Secretary of Defense, makes the ultimate decision as to where a prosecution will be pursued.

*** [T]he Review Panel referred 44 cases to the Department of Justice for potential prosecution and a decision regarding the forum for any prosecution. *** On May 21, 2009, the Department of Justice announced that Ahmed Ghailani, who had previously been indicted in the United States District Court for the Southern District of New York for his alleged role in the 1998 bombings of the U.S. embassies in Kenya and Tanzania, would be prosecuted in federal court. *** On November 13, 2009, the Attorney General announced that the government would pursue prosecution in federal court in the Southern District of New York against the five detainees who had previously been charged before a military commission for their roles in the September 11 attacks. They are: Khalid Sheikh Mohammed, the alleged mastermind of the September 11 plot; Ramzi bin al-Shibh, the alleged coordinator of the September 11 plot who acted as intermediary between Khalid Sheikh Mohammed and the hijackers in the United States; Walid Muhammed Salih Mubarak Bin Attash (a.k.a. Khallad Bin Attash), an alleged early member of the September 11 plot who tested airline security on United Airlines flights between Bangkok and Hong Kong; Mustafa Ahmed al-Hawsawi, an alleged facilitator of hijackers and money to the United States from his base in Dubai; and Ali Abdul Aziz Ali (a.k.a. Ammar Baluchi), a second alleged facilitator of hijackers and money to the United States from his base in Dubai.

On the same day, the Attorney General also announced that the prosecution against Abd al-Rahim al-Nashiri, the alleged mastermind of the bombing of the U.S.S. *Cole*, would be pursued before a military commission. The Attorney General further decided that four other detainees whose cases were pending before military commissions when the Executive Order was issued would remain before the commissions: Ahmed al-Darbi, Noor Uthman, Omar Khadr, and Ibrahim al-Qosi. In January 2010, the Department of Justice announced that Obaidullah, whom OMC had charged but whose case had not yet been referred to a military commission, will remain in the military commission system.***

The Task Force concluded that for many detainees at Guantanamo, prosecution is not feasible in either federal court or a military commission. *** First, the vast majority of the detainees were captured in active zones of combat in Afghanistan or the Pakistani border regions. The focus at the time of their capture was the gathering of intelligence and their removal from the fight. They were not the subjects of formal criminal investigations, and evidence was neither gathered nor preserved with an eye toward prosecuting them. While the intelligence about them may be accurate and reliable, that intelligence, for various reasons, may not be admissible evidence or sufficient to satisfy a criminal burden of proof in either a military commission or federal court. One common problem is that, for many of the detainees, there are no witnesses who are available to testify in any proceeding against them.

Second, many of the detainees cannot be prosecuted because of jurisdictional limitations. In many cases, even though the Task Force found evidence that a detainee was lawfully detainable as part of al-Qaida—*e.g.*, based on information that he attended a training camp, or played some role in the hierarchy of the organization—the Task Force did not find evidence that the detainee participated in a specific terrorist plot. The lack of such evidence can pose obstacles to pursuing a prosecution in either federal court or a military commission. *** Notably, the principal obstacles to prosecution in the cases deemed infeasible by the Task Force typically did not stem from concerns over protecting sensitive sources or methods from disclosure, or concerns that the evidence against the detainee was tainted. ***

IX. Detention Decisions. ***With respect to any detainees who were not deemed appropriate for transfer, release, or prosecution, *** the review participants then considered whether the detainee's national security threat justified continued detention under the AUMF without criminal charges, and, if so, whether the detainee met the legal requirements for detention. *** 48 detainees were unanimously approved for continued detention under the

AUMF. Although each detainee presented unique issues, all of the detainees ultimately designated for continued detention satisfied three core criteria: First, the totality of available information—including credible information that might not be admissible in a criminal prosecution—indicated that the detainee poses a high level of threat that cannot be mitigated sufficiently except through continued detention; second, prosecution of the detainee in a federal criminal court or a military commission did not appear feasible; and third, notwithstanding the infeasibility of criminal prosecution, there is a lawful basis for the detainee's detention under the AUMF.

Broadly speaking, the detainees designated for continued detention were characterized by one or more of the following factors:

- Significant organizational role within al-Qaida, the Taliban, or associated forces. ***
- Advanced training or experience. ***
- Expressed recidivist intent. ***
- History of associations with extremist activity. ***

Detainees approved for continued detention under the AUMF will be subject to further reviews. First, in accordance with the Supreme Court's decision in *Boumediene v. Bush*, each detainee has the opportunity to seek judicial review of their detention by filing a petition for a writ of habeas corpus in federal court [and] each detainee approved for continued detention will be subject to periodic Executive Branch review.

X. Conditional Detention Decisions: Yemeni Detainees. ***30 detainees were approved for "conditional" detention, meaning that they may be transferred if one of the following conditions is satisfied: (1) the security situation improves in Yemen; (2) an appropriate rehabilitation program becomes available; or (3) an appropriate third-country resettlement option becomes available. ***

XI. Diplomatic Efforts. The *** Secretary of State created an office to lead the diplomatic efforts to transfer detainees and appointed an experienced career diplomat to serve as the Special Envoy for the Closure of the Guantanamo Bay Detention Facilities. *** To date, the diplomatic efforts taken under the Executive Order have led to the resettlement of 18 detainees in the following seven locations: Belgium, Bermuda, France, Hungary, Ireland, Palau, and Portugal. Resettlement negotiations are ongoing with a number of countries, *e.g.*, Spain, Switzerland, and Slovakia. In addition, Italy accepted two detainees for criminal prosecution on charges stemming from pre-9/11 activities. All efforts to resettle detainees include discussions with receiving governments about post-transfer security measures, as well as other issues such as the integration and humane treatment of resettled detainees. ***

E. COMPARATIVE PRACTICES

1. Israel. Israel has faced for many years the highest level of terrorism in the world, led by forces committed to destruction of the state. In the *Boumedienne* case before the Supreme Court, an amici curiae brief was filed by "Specialists in Israeli Military Law and Constitutional Law on behalf of petitioners (Boumedienne et. al.). After you read the following excerpt from the brief (at pp. 8-9), consider what weight you would give to it were you on the Court.

> "The Israeli experience demonstrates a democratic society's capacity to develop a practical, workable system of judicial review of detention orders, notwithstanding powerful countervailing interests of national security. Far from being anomalous, Israel's decision to extend substantive and procedural safeguards to detainees—including alleged enemy combatants—places Israel squarely within the customary practices of the democratic world.
>
> Under Israeli law, all detainees, regardless of nationality or the circumstances of their seizure, have a right of access to counsel and to independent courts empowered to review the basis for their detention and, when warranted, to order their release. In the words of the Ministry of Justice, "[A] detainee always has access to a court empowered to rule without delay on the lawfulness of his detention." If the Israeli court finds no basis for detention, or if it concludes that alternative means would suffice to meet the State's security needs, the Israeli court will order the detainee's immediate release.
>
> Israeli law establishes several distinct regimes regarding the treatment of administrative detainees. The regimes that govern within the State of Israel proper are distinct from those which apply in the occupied territories, as these areas (portions of the West Bank and, until recently, Gaza) are under military administration and are juridically distinct from Israel itself. In both cases, the rules applicable to criminal prosecution can differ from those applicable to administrative detention. In 2002, Israel also enacted a distinct framework for detention of "unlawful combatants," regardless of their place of seizure.
>
> As described below, each of these regimes—which govern detentions in the State of Israel, detentions in the occupied territories, and detentions of unlawful combatants—protects basic rights that theUnited States Government denies to Guantánamo detainees. Specifically, individuals detained by Israeli civilian or military authorities always have (1) the right to judicial review of the basis for their detention within no more than fourteen days of their seizure; (2) the right to have that review conducted by a judicial officer independent of the executive who is empowered, when the evidence warrants, to order their release; (3) the benefit of a standard that permits detention only when an individual poses a threat to State security and when no other means are available to neutralize that

threat; (4) the right to have the Government's evidence subjected to a searching examination by the court; (5) the right to judicial review without having coerced testimony used against them; (6) the right to have a judge independently evaluate any claim that classified information offered to support detention cannot be disclosed to them; (7) the right of access to counsel within no more than thirty-four days; and (8) the right to have the basis for their detention independently reviewed every six months at a fully adversarial hearing. Though the United States affords Guantánamo detainees none of these safeguards, Israel has proved through experience that each of them is workable and that each of them is essential to maintaining the rule of law."

2. Europe. Consider whether a non-US forum might be available for a treatment claim or habeas claim seeking release from Guantanamo. If there is such a claim, how would a remedy be fashioned? Boumediene filed an application in the European Court of Human Rights against Bosnia and Herzegovina for violating the European Convention on Human Rights, including freedom from torture, due process, right to personal liberty and security, freedom of religion and the right to life. His complaint is that he was illegally rendered by the Bosnian authorities to the United States and subsequently transported to Guantanamo. He alleged that he was detained in Bosnia based on unfounded U.S. allegations of planning to attack the U.S. and U.K. Embassies there and received a judicial order to prevent his rendition from the Bosnia and Herzegovina Human Rights Chamber before being sent to Guantanamo. Despite the U.S. Supreme Court ruling confirming his right to a federal court habeas hearing Boumediene remains at Guantanamo. *Boumediene* asked the ECHR to review Bosnia's continuing failure to satisfy its obligations under the Convention to ensure his safety, protect his rights, and seek his prompt return home to his family. If you were on the ECHR, how would you rule on this petition? How effective do you think any ruling in favor of Boumediene would be?

VIII

Civilian Trials of Alleged Terrorists

[T]here are some who say that law enforcement can't – or shouldn't – be used for counterterrorism. *** In my view*** it's not that law enforcement is *always* the right tool for combating terrorism. But it's also not the case that it's *never* the right tool. The reality, I think, is that it's *sometimes* the right tool. *** And that leads me to this question: as compared to the viable alternatives, what is the value of law enforcement in this war? *** I think law enforcement helps us win this war. *** When I say that law enforcement helps us win this war, I mean that it helps us disrupt, defeat, dismantle and destroy our adversaries (without destroying ourselves or our way of life in the process). In particular, law enforcement helps us in at least three ways – it can *disrupt* terrorist plots through arrests, *incapacitate* terrorists through incarceration resulting from prosecution, and gather *intelligence* from interrogation and recruitment of terrorists or their supporters via cooperation agreements.

> Assistant Attorney General David Kris, Speaking at the Brookings Institution, Washington, D.C. June 11, 2010

Alleged terrorists may be tried as criminals before civilian courts, military tribunals, or international courts. Most such trials occur in civilian courts, the subject of this chapter. The next chapter will cover trial by military commissions. International tribunals have seldom been used to try terrorists (see Chapter 1D), though one might argue that many persons tried by such tribunals have indeed engaged in acts of terrorism.

Section A of this chapter will provide an overview of civilian trials of terrorists in the United States.

The first hurdle in any terrorism case, covered in Section B, is whether the civilian court has jurisdiction over the defendant and the offense. Where the terrorism and the perpetrator are in the jurisdiction, this poses no problem. When the defendant and the crime are outside the jurisdiction which wishes to prosecute, there are issues of whether the statute allegedly violated allows extraterritorial application, and whether international law or treaties bar extraterritorial application of a criminal statute. In the United States, there may be a question whether the Constitution allows extraterritorial application of domestic law.

Second, there are specialized problems that apply to trials of alleged terrorists. Fairness requires that the defendant be able to present a full defense. This normally means access to witnesses and that the government disclose to the defense information relating to witnesses, documents, and other evidence, even if the information is adverse to the Government's case. The prosecution may face a dilemma: disclosure of information in a terrorism case may adversely affect national security, especially if the trial is open to the public and the media -- the norm for trials in civilian courts. This will be covered in Section C.

Finally, this chapter ends with a critique and defense of using domestic courts to try terrorism cases (Section D).

A. TERRORISM TRIALS IN THE UNITED STATES

Trials in notorious terrorism cases predate 9/11, with the Southern District of New York being the venue for many major trials, including those arising out of the 1993 World Trade Center Bombing and the 1998 bombings of the United States embassies in Kenya and Tanzania. The Department of Justice web site (last viewed September 30, 2010) tracks its progress in federal prosecution of terrorists using two categories of cases. Category I is "violations of federal statutes that are directly related to international terrorism," while Category II involves violations of other statutes "where the investigation involved an identified link to international terrorism." Neither category encompasses domestic terrorism cases such as Timothy McVeigh's bombing of the Murrah Federal Building in Oklahoma City.

The "unsealed convictions" total (a category that excludes sealed convictions and defendants charged but not convicted at trial or resolved by guilty pleas) from September 11, 2001 to March 18, 2010 exceeds 390 convictions, more than 150 in Category I and more than 240 in Category II. Prosecutors achieve convictions or plea agreements in more than 90 % of their cases, see Richard B. Zabel and James J. Benjamin, In pursuit of Justice: Prosecuting Cases in the Federal Courts (Human Rights First 2008), available at http://www.humanrightsfirst.info/pdf/080521-USLS-pursuit-justice.pdf. Many of the defendants have received lengthy terms of imprisonment.

Those convicted of international terrorism now serving sentences, mainly in the "Supermax" facility in Florence, Colorado, include Sheik Omar Abdel-Rahman, Ramzi Yousef, Ahmed Ressam, Wahid el-Hage, Richard Reid, Ahmed Omar Abu Ali, and Zacharias Moussaoui. Domestic terrorism inmates include Theodore Kaczynski and Terry Nichols. Timothy McVeigh was executed for his role in the 1995 Oklahoma City bombing. As the Department of Justice Notes in a June 30, 2009 press release, "More recent cases include those against individuals who provided material support to al-Qaeda and other terrorist groups, as well as against international arms trafficker Monzer al Kassar and the Somalian pirate charged in the hijacking of the *Maersk Alabama*." Examples are provided on the DoJ web site of both Category I and Category II convictions.

Here is a brief description of one terrorism trial by the Second Circuit Court of Appeals:

On May 29, 2001, a jury of the United States District Court for the Southern District of New York returned verdicts of guilt against defendants-appellants Mohamed Sadeek Odeh, Mohamed Rashed Daoud Al-'Owhali, and Wadih El-Hage as to numerous charges arising from their involvement in the August 7, 1998 bombings of the American Embassies in Nairobi, Kenya and Dar es Salaam, Tanzania (the "August 7 bombings").[1] The jury considered, but declined to impose, the death penalty on defendant-appellant Al-'Owhali. Between October 22 and October 24, 2001, the District Court (Leonard B. Sand, *Judge*) entered judgments of conviction against all three defendants and sentenced each of them to life imprisonment. Defendants are currently incarcerated and serving their sentences. All three now appeal their convictions, and El-Hage also appeals [his] sentence [and moves} for a new trial ***.This criminal case presents issues of great importance, many of which are complex and novel; consequently, this case has been in the federal courts for a decade. This case commenced in late 1998, when defendants were indicted for their participation in the August 7, 1998 bombings of American Embassies in Kenya and Tanzania-acts of terrorism that resulted in the deaths of over 200 people. Jury selection began in early 2001, and trial commenced in February of that year. The trial lasted nearly four months and concluded on May 29, 2001 when the jury reached unanimous verdicts of Defendants' guilt. In October 2001, the District Court imposed a sentence of life imprisonment on all defendants, judgment was entered, and defendants then filed timely appeals.[3] For the reasons described in greater detail below, as well as those set forth in *In re Terrorist Bombings of U.S. Embassies in East Africa (Fourth Amendment Challenges),* 552 F.3d 157 (2d Cir.2008), and *In re Terrorist Bombings of U.S. Embassies in East Africa (Fifth Amendment Challenges),* 552 F.3d 177 (2d Cir.2008), *** we conclude that none of the issues raised on appeal has merit, with the exception of El-Hage's challenge to his

---

[1] Also convicted was defendant Khalfan Khamis Mohamed, who initially appealed his conviction but later withdrew that appeal. Also indicted, but not tried, were Osama Bin Laden, Fazul Abdullah Mohammed, Muhammad Atef, Mustafa Mohamed Fadhil, Ahmed Khalfan Ghailani, Fahid Mohammed Msalam, Mamdouh Mahmud Salim, Ali Mohamed, Ayman al Zawahiri, Khaled al Fawwaz, Ibrahim Eidarous, Adel Abdel Bary, Saif al Adel, Abdullah Ahmed Abdullah, Muhsin Musa Matwalli Atwah, Anas al Liby, L'Houssiane Kherchtou, and Mohamed Suleiman al Nalfi.

[3] The case also involved lengthy pretrial and post-trial proceedings. Defendants filed extensive pretrial motions urging, *inter alia,* the severance of their trials, the dismissal of the indictments, the suppression of both physical evidence seized overseas and certain inculpatory statements, and release on bail. The District Court denied most of defendants' pretrial motions ***. In October 2003, the defendants moved, in the District Court, for a new trial. *** In November 2005, the District Court denied the motion for a new trial. *** [W]e heard this case on December 10, 2007.

sentence on the basis of the District Court's mandatory application of the United States Sentencing Guidelines based on then-binding Circuit precedent.***

In re Terrorist Bombings of U.S. Embassies in East Africa, 552 F. 3d 93 (2d Cir. 2008).

The materials in the remainder of this chapter are not designed to familiarize the reader with all aspects of such terrorism trials, but to hone in on some of the more important and recurring themes of such trials that are not the typical fare of other criminal trials.

B. JURISDICTION OF CIVILIAN COURTS.

Congress, in response to acts of terrorism overseas affecting United States property, United States nationals, or United States interests, has enacted a number of statutes with extraterritorial reach.   These include aircraft hijacking or sabotage (18 U.S.C. §§31-32), developing or possessing biological weapons (18 U.S.C §§175-178), and providing material support for terrorists (18 U.S.C. §§2339A-C).   Noting this development under 20 such statutes and the need for centralized coordination of such international matters, the U.S. Attorney's Manual provides that U.S. Attorneys must get authorization from the Assistant Attorney General for the Criminal Division before commencing such a prosecution.   The Manual Notes that "Overseas terrorist situations will undoubtedly entail coordination with one or more foreign governments and such coordination is best accomplished by and through the Department [of Justice] in consultation with the Department of State."

The following case explores how courts deal with statutes that do not explicitly create overseas jurisdiction over aliens.

UNITED STATES v. BIN LADEN
92 F. Supp. 2d 189 (S.D.N.Y., 2000)

SAND, District Judge.

[The Indictment] charges fifteen defendants with conspiracy to murder United States nationals, to use weapons of mass destruction against United States nationals, to destroy United States buildings and property, and to destroy United States defense utilities. The Indictment also charges defendants *** with numerous crimes in connection with the August 1998 bombings of the United States Embassies in Nairobi, Kenya, and Dar es Salaam, Tanzania, including 223 counts of murder. *** Odeh argues that [various] Counts must be dismissed because (a) they concern acts allegedly performed by Odeh and his co-defendants outside United States territory, yet (b) are based on statutes that were not intended by Congress to regulate conduct outside United States territory. More specifically, Odeh argues that "the following statutes that form the basis for the indictment fail clearly and unequivocally to regulate the conduct of foreign nationals for conduct outside the territorial boundaries of the United States." ***

*** Congress has the power to regulate conduct performed outside United States territory. It is equally well-established, however, that courts are to presume that Congress has not exercised this power-i.e., that statutes apply only to acts performed within United States territory-unless Congress manifests an intent to reach acts performed outside United States territory This "clear manifestation" requirement does not require that extraterritorial coverage should be found only if the statute itself explicitly provides for extraterritorial application. Rather, courts should consider "all available evidence about the meaning" of the statute, e.g., its text, structure, and legislative history.

Furthermore, the Supreme Court has established a limited exception to this standard approach for "criminal statutes which are, as a class, not logically dependent on their locality for the Government's jurisdiction, but are enacted because of the right of the Government to defend itself against obstruction, or fraud wherever perpetrated, especially if committed by its own citizens, officers, or agents." *United States v. Bowman*, 260 U.S. 94 (1922). As regards statutes of this type, courts may infer the requisite intent "from the nature of the offense" described in the statute, and thus need not examine its legislative history. The Court further observed that "to limit the [ ] locus [of such a statute] to the strictly territorial jurisdiction [of the United States] would be greatly to curtail the scope and usefulness of the statute and leave open a large immunity for frauds as easily committed by citizens on the high seas and in foreign countries as at home." ***

Odeh argues that *Bowman* is "not controlling precedent" because it "involved the application of [a] penal statute[ ] to United States citizens," i.e., not to foreign nationals such as himself. This argument is unavailing for three reasons. First, although *Bowman* "is expressly limited by its *facts* to prosecutions of United States citizens," its underlying rationale is not dependant on the nationality of the offender. Rather, *Bowman* rests on two factors: (1) the right of the United States to protect itself from harmful conduct-irrespective of the locus of this conduct, and (2) the presumption that Congress would not both (a) enact a statute designed to serve this protective function, and-where the statute proscribes acts that could just as readily be performed outside the United States as within it-(b) undermine this protective intention by limiting the statute's application to United States territory. Given that foreign nationals are in at least as good a position to perform extraterritorial conduct as are United States nationals, it would make little sense to restrict such statutes to United States nationals. *** Second, the Courts of Appeals-focusing on *Bowman* 's general rule rather than its peculiar facts-have applied this rule to reach conduct by foreign nationals on foreign soil. ***

Third, the irrelevance of the Defendant's nationality to the *Bowman* rule is reinforced by a consideration of the relationship between this rule and the principles of extraterritorial jurisdiction recognized by international law. Under international law, the primary basis of jurisdiction is the "subjective territorial principle," under which " a state has jurisdiction to prescribe law with respect to ... conduct that, wholly or in substantial part, takes place within its territory." International law recognizes five other principles of jurisdiction by which a state may reach conduct *outside* its territory: (1) the objective territorial principle; (2) the protective principle; (3) the nationality principle; (4) the passive personality principle; and (5) the universality principle. The objective territoriality principle provides that a state has jurisdiction to prescribe law with respect to "conduct outside its territory that has or is intended to have substantial effect within its territory." Restatement § 402(1)(c). The protective principle provides that a state has jurisdiction to prescribe law with respect to "certain conduct outside its territory by *persons not its nationals* that is directed against *the security of the state* or against a limited class of other state interests." The nationality principle provides that a state has jurisdiction to prescribe law with respect to "the activities, interests, status, or relations of its nationals outside as well as within its territory." The passive personality principle provides that "a state may apply law-particularly criminal law-to an act committed outside its territory by a person not its national where the victim of the act was its national." The universality principle provides that, "[a] state has jurisdiction to define and prescribe punishment for certain offenses recognized by the community of nations as of universal concern, such as piracy, slave trade, attacks on or hijacking of aircraft, genocide, war crimes, and perhaps *certain acts of terrorism*," regardless of the locus of their occurrence. Because Congress has the power to override international law if it so chooses, none of these five principles places ultimate limits on Congress's power to reach extraterritorial conduct. At the same time, however, "[i]n determining whether a statute applies extraterritorially, [courts] presume that Congress does not intend to violate principles of international law .... [and] in the absence of an explicit Congressional directive, courts do not give extraterritorial effect to any statute that violates principles of international law."

The *Bowman* rule would appear to be most directly related to the protective principle, which, as noted, explicitly authorizes a state's exercise of jurisdiction over "conduct outside its territory *by persons not its nationals*." Hence, an application of the *Bowman* rule that results in the extraterritorial application of a statute to the conduct of foreign nationals is consistent with international law. *** In light of the preceding general principles, we find that Congress intended each of the following statutory provisions to reach conduct by foreign nationals on foreign soil: *** Subsection 844(f)(1) provides:

> Whoever maliciously damages or destroys, or attempts to damage or destroy, by means of fire or an explosive, any building, vehicle, or other personal or real property in whole or in part owned or possessed by, or leased to, the United States, or any department or agency thereof, shall be imprisoned for not less than 5 years and not more than 20 years, fined under this title, or both.

Given (i) that this provision is explicitly intended to protect United States property, (ii) that a significant amount of United States property is located outside the United States, and (iii) that, accordingly, foreign nationals are in at least as good a position as are United States nationals to damage such property, we find, under *Bowman,* that Congress intended   [it] to apply extraterritorially-irrespective of the nationality of the perpetrator.

Subsection 844(f)(3) provides:

> Whoever engages in conduct prohibited by this subsection, and as a result of such conduct directly or proximately causes the death of any person, including any public safety officer performing duties, shall be subject to the death penalty, or imprisoned for not less than 20 years or for life, fined under this title, or both.

Given that this provision is dependent on Subsection 844(f)(1), our determination that Congress intended that Subsection to apply extraterritoriality-irrespective of the nationality of the offender, leads us to conclude that Congress likewise intended this Subsection to apply extra territorially-irrespective of the nationality of the offender.

Subsection 844(h) provides in relevant part:

> Whoever (1) uses fire or an explosive to commit any felony which may be prosecuted in a court of the United States, or (2) carries an explosive during the commission of any felony which may be prosecuted in a court of the United States, including a felony which provides for an enhanced punishment if committed by the use of a deadly or dangerous weapon or device shall, in addition to the punishment provided for such felony, be sentenced to imprisonment for 10 years.

The underlying substantive felony provision on which the Indictment predicates this ancillary provision is 18 U.S.C. § 2332(b). *** Because (i) Congress explicitly intended Section 2332(b) to apply extraterritorially, and (ii) foreign nationals are in at least as good a position as are United States national to engage in extraterritorial conspiracies to kill United States nationals, we find that Congress intended it to apply to foreign national offenders. ***

In contrast *** [statutes concerning] murders committed "[w]ithin the special maritime and territorial jurisdiction of the United States" [because they] specif[y] *locations* within which particular offenses may be committed. Hence, it simply makes no sense for a court to ask if it can be inferred, from " the nature of the offense" *** that Congress intended for the courts to have jurisdiction over instances of this offense committed "out side [sic] of the strict territorial jurisdiction" of the *United States.* *** This brings us to the Government's (apparent) attempt to apply the *Bowman* rule directly to *** the offense of murder. At first sight, it might be thought that this provision *** is susceptible to a *Bowman* analysis. It makes sense to ask whether congressional intent to apply a murder statute to murders committed beyond United States territory can be inferred from the nature of the offense of murder *** [because it has] its own jurisdictional element ***. [A] court must determine whether this murder was committed "[w]ithin the special maritime and territorial jurisdiction of the United States." *** [T]he legislative and interpretive history *** strongly supports Odeh's position that [this provision] does not concern lands outside the United States. *** [T]o say that the United States and another independent, sovereign nation, say, Kenya, have concurrent *territorial* jurisdiction over the United States Embassy premises in Nairobi is to say that these premises are "subject to the plenary authority of both the United States and Kenya" . Such a state of affairs is clearly inconsistent with the very idea of national sovereignty.

We hasten to emphasize that we are not contending that concurrent jurisdiction *per se* by two sovereign nations is inconsistent with international law. Under various circumstances, concurrent jurisdiction is permitted by international law. For example, if Nation A's jurisdiction over a particular offense is based on the subjective territorial principle, Nation B could have jurisdiction over the same offense based on one or more of the five jurisdictional principles on which extraterritorial jurisdiction may be based. *** Having concluded that an interpretation *** under which the United States has concurrent jurisdiction over United States embassy premises would violate international law, our work is not finished. It is well-established that Congress has the power to override international law. Courts are to presume, however, that Congress generally intends its statutes to be consistent with international law. This presumption can be overcome only by a clear statement of intent to override international law. No such expression of intent appears in either the text or the legislative history of Section 7(3).

In light of the foregoing considerations, we find that United States embassy premises in foreign countries are not "lands reserved or acquired for the use of the United States, and under the exclusive or concurrent jurisdiction thereof," and thus are not included within "the special territorial jurisdiction" of the United States. ***

Odeh argues that [various] Counts [concerning "[a] person who ... uses, threatens, or attempts or conspires to use, a weapon of mass destruction ... (1) against a national of the United States while such national is outside of the United States; ... or (3) against any property that is owned, leased or used by the United States ..., whether the property is within or outside of the United States, shall [be punished as further provided]" and "[w]hoever outside the United States ... engages in a conspiracy to kill[ ] a national of the United States shall [be punished as further provided],"] *** must be dismissed because these statutes are unconstitutional in that they exceed Congress's authority to legislate under the Constitution. *** Odeh suggests that there is but one constitutional grant of authority to legislate that could support these two statutory provisions: Article I, Section 8, Clause 10 *** grants Congress the authority "[t]o define and punish Piracies and Felonies committed on the high Seas, and Offenses against the Law of Nations." Odeh argues that, as "[t]he acts described in these two statutes ... are not widely regarded as offenses 'against the law of nations,' " these statutes exceed Congress's authority under Clause 10.

There are two problems with this argument. First, even assuming that the acts described *** are not *widely* regarded as violations of international law, it does not necessarily follow that these provisions exceed Congress's authority under Clause 10. Clause 10 does not merely give Congress the authority to punish offenses against the law of nations; it also gives Congress the power to "define" such offenses. Hence, provided that the acts in question are recognized by at least some members of the international community as being offenses against the law of nations, Congress arguably has the power to criminalize these acts pursuant to its power *to define* offenses against the law of nations. Second, and more important, it is not the case that Clause 10 provides the only basis [these crimes]. The Supreme Court has recognized that, with regard to foreign affairs legislation, "investment of the federal Government with the powers of external sovereignty did not depend upon the affirmative grants of the Constitution." *United States v. Curtiss-Wright Export Corp.,* 299 U.S. 304 (1936). Rather, Congress's authority to regulate foreign affairs "exist[s] as inherently inseparable from the conception of nationality." More specifically, this "concept of essential sovereignty of a free nation clearly requires the existence and recognition of an inherent power in the state to protect itself from destruction."

In penalizing extraterritorial conspiracies to kill nationals of the United States, *Section 2332(b)* is clearly designed to protect a vital United States interest. ***

Odeh argues that [reaching] "the deaths of Kenyan and Tanzanian citizens [as opposed to United States citizens] would be contrary to established principles of international law." More specifically, Odeh advances the following two arguments. First, given (i) that " *** the only arguable basis for jurisdiction over the deaths of foreign citizens is the principle of universality," (ii) that "[u]niversal jurisdiction results where there is *universal* condemnation of an offense, and a general interest in cooperating to suppress them, as reflected in *widely accepted* international agreements," and (ii) that "the universality principle does not encompass terrorist actions resulting in the deaths of individuals who are not diplomatic personnel," it follows that applying *Section 930(c)* to the deaths of "ordinary" foreign nationals on foreign soil would constitute a violation of international law.

There are two problems with this argument. First, because "universal jurisdiction is increasingly accepted for certain acts of terrorism, such as ... indiscriminate violent assaults on people at large," Restatement § 404, cmt. a, a plausible case could be made that extraterritorial application of Section 930(c) in this case *is* supported by the universality principle.

Second, it is not the case that the universality principle is the "only arguable basis for jurisdiction over the deaths of foreign citizens." *** [T]he protective principle is also an "arguable basis" for [its]extraterritorial application ***. Hence, the only question is whether a statute of general application-the extraterritorial application of which is acknowledged to be justified by the protective principle-is nevertheless restricted to victims who are citizens of the nation that enacted the statute. We are aware of no authority for this proposition. Nor is such a limitation consistent with the purposes the protective principle is designed to serve. Such a limitation could only weaken the protective function of a statute designed to protect United States interests. In providing for the death penalty where death results in the course of an attack on a Federal facility, *Section 930(c)* is clearly designed to deter attacks on Federal facilities. Given the likelihood that foreign nationals will be in or near Federal facilities located in foreign nations, this deterrent effect would be significantly diminished if Section 930(c) were limited to the deaths of United States nationals. To paraphrase *Bowman,* "to limit [the reach of Section 930(c) to the deaths of United States nationals] would be greatly to curtail the scope and usefulness of the statute and leave open a large immunity for [attacks against Federal facilities]." .

Odeh argues, second, that, even if the universality principle (or one of the four other principles) did authorize the application of Section 930(c) to the deaths of ordinary foreign nationals on foreign soil, such application would violate international law nevertheless, because (i) "[e]ven where one of the principles authorizes jurisdiction, a nation is nevertheless precluded from exercising jurisdiction where jurisdiction would be 'unreasonable,' " and (ii) application of Section 930(c) to the deaths of ordinary foreign nationals on foreign soil would be unreasonable.

According to the Restatement [§ 403(2)], the following factors are to be taken into account for the purpose of determining whether exercise of extraterritorial jurisdiction is reasonable:

> (a) the link of the activity to the territory of the regulating state, i.e., the extent to which the activity takes place within the territory, or has substantial, direct, and foreseeable effect upon or in the territory;

> (b) the connections, such as nationality, residence, or economic activity, between the regulating state and the person principally responsible for the activity to be regulated, or between that state and those whom the regulation is designed to protect;

> (c) the character of the activity to be regulated, the importance of regulation to the regulating state, the extent to which other states regulate such activities, and the degree to which the desirability of such regulation is generally accepted;

> (d) the existence of justified expectations that might be protected or hurt by the regulation;

> (e) the importance of the regulation to the international political, legal, or economic system;

> (f) the extent to which the regulation is consistent with the traditions of the international system;

> (g) the extent to which another state may have an interest in regulating the activity; and

(h) the likelihood of conflict with regulation by another state.

Given that factor (a) alludes to the subjective territorial principle and the objective territorial principle, it is not especially relevant to a statute, such as Section 930(c), based primarily on the protective principle. Much the same can be said of factor (b), as it alludes to the nationality principle, the subjective territorial principle, and the objective territorial principle. Factor (c), in contrast, is highly relevant to Section 930(c). It is important both to the United States and other nations to prevent the destruction of their facilities-regardless of their location; and such regulation is accordingly widely accepted among the nations of the world. As for factor (d), Section 930(c) protects the expectation of foreign nationals that they will be free of harm while on the premises of United States facilities. We can think of no "justified" expectation, however, that would be hurt by the extraterritorial application of Section 930(c). As for factor (e), in light of the prominent role played by the United States in "the international political, legal, and economic systems," the protection of United States facilities-regardless of their location-is highly important to the stability of these systems. Turning to factor (f), as indicated by the preceding discussion of factor (c), most, if not all, nations are concerned about protecting their facilities, both at home and abroad. Hence, Section 930(c) is highly consistent "with the traditions of the international system." As for (g), it must be acknowledged that when the United States facility is on foreign soil, and when the victims of the attack are nationals of the host nation, the host nation "has a keen interest in regulating and punishing [the] offenders." This is not to say, however, that the host nation has a greater interest than does the United States. Furthermore, even if it were the case that the host nation had a greater interest than the United States, this single factor would be insufficient to support the conclusion that application of Section 930(c) to the bombings of the two Embassies is unreasonable. Coming, finally, to factor (h), Odeh does not argue that application of Section 930(c) to the bombings would conflict with Kenyan and/or Tanzanian law, nor are we otherwise aware of such conflict. *** Factor (h) thus counts in favor of the reasonableness of applying Section 930(c) to the bombings.

Noting that "the Government has indicated that it will seek the death penalty" for his alleged crimes, Odeh argues that, " [b]ecause the imposition of the death penalty would be contrary to international law on the facts of this case, the Court should dismiss counts 7-239." Because "the Government has not determined against which defendants, if any, it will seek the death penalty," we agree with the Government's contention that this argument is premature. Therefore, we decline to consider it at this time. For the same reason, we grant Odeh's request for " an opportunity to revisit ... arguments [against the death penalty based on international law] should the Government ... seek the death penalty." ***

Notes

1. **The Basics.** Read over the portions of the opinion concerning the traditional bases of court jurisdiction. Do these bases work together as a consistent whole or is this simply an historical patchwork?

2. **Absentee Defendant?** Note the name of the defendant in the case title. Where is he? Can he be tried and convicted in absentia?

3. **Death Penalty.** If the death penalty is contrary to international law and the practice of most other "civilized nations," can a United States Court nevertheless impose that punishment? What of the maxim that "international law is part of United States law?" See *Roper v. Simmons*, 543 U.S. 551 (2005) (majority finds death penalty for juveniles under 18 unconstitutional, noting that "the United States is the only country in the world that continues to give official sanction to the juvenile death penalty"). The excerpts of Judge Brown's opinion in *al-Bihani* (both in the panel opinion and the en banc decision, supra Chapters V and VII) provide the most complete responses to these questions to date.

4. **Universality Principle.** Traditionally, a state's jurisdiction over particular international offenses is determined by the connection of the crime to the state in question. For example, if a crime happens within a state's territory or damages people or property connected to a state, that nation has the right, under international law, to prosecute the suspected offenders. Recently, however, courts have begun recognizing a "universal jurisdiction" that allows states that are in no way connected to or affected by a particular crime to prosecute suspects under international law. Such crimes are generally limited to *jus cogens* offenses, like torture, genocide, and war crimes; however, some courts have also applied the concept of universal jurisdiction to acts of terrorism not perpetrated by a nation or its leaders.

5. **Universality Policy.** On its face such jurisdiction seems beneficial because it allows any state to bring international criminals to justice when the suspects are beyond the reach of the nation directly affected by the crime In reality, universal jurisdiction has hidden negative consequences. Like other legal rights, the jurisdictional ability to prosecute crimes is negotiable. A particular nation that has jurisdiction may choose to exercise that jurisdiction, waive the right to prosecute, or even delegate its jurisdictional interest in the prosecution to another nation or international body. This allows nations to use their jurisdiction as a negotiating tool, trading the right to prosecute for concessions from the accused or from other nations, thus allowing the right to prosecute to flow to the highest-value user and for jurisdiction to be used to secure other legal and political goals. Universal jurisdiction destroys this ability. If every nation has the right to prosecute, such trades are impossible because jurisdiction is now a "public" and not a "private" resource. Negative effects flow from this limiting of prosecutorial options. For example, a suspect is arrested in Germany in connection with a terrorist bombing of a United States Embassy in Tanzania. Normally, under traditional international jurisdiction, the United States has jurisdiction to prosecute the suspect for the bombing and therefore the right to negotiate the prosecution in an attempt to locate the suspect's accomplices or other members of the terrorist network. Because the U.S. is the only country with the right to prosecute, the suspect may choose to cooperate for a lesser charge or even, if he is sufficiently innocent, for release. How would this change if, as under universal jurisdiction, any other country could prosecute him for the same crime?

Don't Germany and Tanzania have an interest in prosecution of the suspect? This being the case, would the suspect be more or less likely to cooperate? Similarly, how does universal jurisdiction limit negotiations with dictators in international efforts to convince them to step down from power? Is a dictator ever going to leave power peacefully if he can be prosecuted for war crimes by every country in the world? See generally, E. Kontorovich, *The Inefficiency of Universal Jurisdiction*, 2008 U. ILL. L. REV. 389 (2008).

C. FAIR TRIAL AND NATIONAL SECURITY

Terrorism trials in civilian courts often involve intense media scrutiny, beefed up security for the courthouse where the trial is held, and complex factual explanations of relationships among individuals alleged to be involved in conspiratorial enterprises. Media publicity may compromise the fairness of a trial before a jury made up of those who read newspapers or watch television. Courthouse security may increase the costs of such trials and, if the defendant is restrained, raise issues about whether the jury was prejudiced in its ability to uphold the presumption of innocence. Conspiracy trials, of terrorists or others, involve lawyers presenting complex exhibits, often introduced through expert witnesses.

The materials in this section, however, do not focus on these issues. Rather, they deal with the main lawyerly aspect of trying terrorism cases that differs from most other criminal trials--how civilian courts balance the openness of discovery involved in providing the defendant with a fair trial against national security interests that demand secrecy. The following cases cover (1) application of the Classified Information Procedures Act (CIPA) in terrorism trials and (2) use of the CIPA framework to handle witnesses.

1. THE CLASSIFIED INFORMATION PROCEDURES ACT (CIPA)

Here is a nutshell description of CIPA from *In re TERRORIST BOMBINGS OF U.S. EMBASSIES IN EAST AFRICA*, 552 F. 3d 93 (2d Cir. 2008):

> CIPA establishes rules for the management of criminal cases involving classified information.[20] Its animating purpose is "to harmonize a [criminal] Defendant's right to obtain and present exculpatory material," *United States v. Pappas*, 94 F.3d 795, 799 (2d Cir.1996) (internal quotation marks omitted), with the Government's need " 'to withhold information from discovery when disclosure would be inimical to national security,' " *United States v. Aref*, 533 F.3d 72, 79 (2d Cir.2008) (quoting *Zuckerbraun v. Gen. Dynamics Corp.*, 935 F.2d 544, 546 (2d Cir.1991)); *see also id.* at 78 (explaining

---

[20] "CIPA defines 'classified information' as 'information or material that has been determined by the United States Government pursuant to an Executive order, statute, or regulation, to require protection against unauthorized disclosure for reasons of national security.' " *United States v. Aref*, 533 F.3d 72, 78 n. 2 (2d Cir.2008) (quoting 18 U.S.C. app. 3 § 1(a)).

that the Government's ability to withhold classified information "most likely" derives from "the common-law privilege against disclosure of state secrets").

Section three of CIPA requires district courts to enter, "[u]pon motion of the United States," a protective order prohibiting "the disclosure of any classified information disclosed by the United States" to a criminal defendant. Section four provides that, if the discovery to be provided to the defense pursuant to the Federal Rules of Criminal Procedure includes classified information, the district court may, "upon a sufficient showing, ... authorize the United States to delete specified items of classified information[,] ... to substitute a summary of the information[,] ... or to substitute a statement admitting relevant facts that the classified information would tend to prove." Section five requires a defendant to give pretrial notice to the government and the court if he "reasonably expects to disclose or to cause the disclosure of classified information ... in connection with any trial or pretrial proceeding involving [his] criminal prosecution."

Section six requires district courts "to make all determinations concerning the use, relevance, or admissibility of classified information that would otherwise be made during the trial or pretrial proceeding" by means of a hearing that "shall be held in camera if the Attorney General certifies to the court in such petition that a public proceeding may result in the disclosure of classified information." Section six also provides that, before the district court holds such a hearing, the government must give the defendant "notice of the classified information that is at issue," as well as "such details as to the portion of the indictment or information at issue in the hearing as are needed to give the defendant fair notice to prepare for the hearing." If a district court authorizes "the disclosure of specific classified information," the government may move to substitute "for such classified information ... a statement admitting relevant facts that the specific classified information would tend to prove ... or a summary of the specific classified information." A district court must grant the Government's motion for a protective order "if it finds that the statement or summary will provide the defendant with substantially the same ability to make his defense as would disclosure of the specific classified information."

The following case provides an overview of the statute in operation with a number of constitutional challenges to that operation.

UNITED STATES v. LEE
90 F. Supp. 2d 1324 (D.N.M. 2000)

CONWAY, Chief Judge

THIS MATTER came on for consideration of the Motion of Dr. Wen Ho Lee for a Declaration that Sections 5 and 6 of the Classified Information Procedures Act (CIPA) are Unconstitutional as Applied. ***

The Classified Information Procedures Act (CIPA) provides for pretrial procedures to resolve questions of admissibility of classified information in advance of its use in open court. Under CIPA procedures, the defense must file a notice briefly describing any classified information that it "reasonably expects to disclose or to cause the disclosure of" at trial. Thereafter, the prosecution may request an *in camera* hearing for a determination of the "use, relevance and admissibility" of the proposed defense evidence. If the Court finds the evidence admissible, the government may move for, and the Court may authorize, the substitution of unclassified facts or a summary of the information in the form of an admission by the government. Such a motion may be granted if the Court finds that the statement or summary will provide the defendant with "substantially the same ability to make his defense as would disclosure of the specific classified information." If the Court does not authorize the substitution, the government can require that the defendant not disclose classified information. However, *** if the government prevents a defendant from disclosing classified information at trial, the court may: (A) dismiss the entire indictment or specific counts, (B) find against the prosecution on any issue to which the excluded information relates, or (C) strike or preclude the testimony of particular government witnesses. Finally, CIPA requires that the government provide the defendant with any evidence it will use to rebut the Defendant's revealed classified information evidence.

Defendant Lee contends that, as applied to him, the notice and hearing requirements of § 5 and § 6 of CIPA are unconstitutional. Specifically, Lee argues that § 5 and § 6 violate (1) his Fifth Amendment privilege against self-incrimination by requiring him to disclose his anticipated trial testimony to the government pretrial; (2) his Fifth Amendment right to remain silent unless and until he decides to testify; (3) his Fifth and Sixth Amendment rights to testify in his own defense; (4) his Fifth Amendment right to due process of law by requiring him to disclose significant aspects of his case without imposing a mandatory reciprocal duty on the prosecution and imposing vastly greater discovery burdens on the defense than on the government; and (5) his Sixth Amendment right to cross examine witnesses. Although I find Defendant's claims unjustified, I will nevertheless address them in turn.

*** Defendant argues that by forcing him to reveal portions of his potential testimony, CIPA unconstitutionally infringes upon his right to remain silent until and unless he decides to testify. Similarly, Defendant argues that if he chooses not to comply with the notice requirements, under the penalty of not being able to offer such testimony at trial, CIPA unconstitutionally denies him the right to testify on his own behalf. In either case, Defendant contends that CIPA forces him to pay a price in the form of a costly pretrial decision in order to preserve his constitutional rights at trial. ***

CIPA does not require that a defendant specify whether or not he will testify or what he will testify about. Instead, CIPA requires "merely a general disclosure as to what classified information the defense expects to use at trial, regardless of the witness or the document through which that information is to be revealed." Therefore, Defendant's argument that if he discloses the classified information his right to remain silent has been compromised (or in the alternative that if he refuses to disclose the classified information his right to testify has been compromised) is misplaced. Despite CIPA's requirements, Defendant still has the option of not testifying. Similarly, if the defense does not disclose classified information as required by CIPA, the defendant retains the option of testifying, albeit with the preclusion of any classified information.

In addition, the pretrial disclosure of certain aspects of a criminal defense is hardly a novel concept. *** Defendant [argues] that unlike the pretrial disclosures mandated by the Federal Rules of Criminal Procedure, CIPA requires that a defendant reveal " the contents of his own mind" by placing an additional burden on a defendant to reveal the " use, admissibility and relevance" of the proposed evidence. However, CIPA requires no more revelation of the Defendant's thoughts or plans than do the notice of alibi and similar rules of federal criminal procedure. Defendant is free to seek admission of evidence to support a number of different defenses, which he may adopt or abandon later. *** [T]he defendant in this case retains significant control over the presentation of his defense. CIPA merely provides a mechanism for determining the admissibility of classified information so that classified information is not inadvertently disclosed during open proceedings. Defendant still has the choice of presenting the evidence during trial or not, after it has been deemed admissible. "That the defendant faces ... a dilemma demanding a choice between complete silence and presenting a defense has never been thought an invasion of the privilege against compelled self-incrimination."

Defendant also argues that the burdens placed upon him by CIPA unconstitutionally violate his Fifth Amendment rights in that they do not advance any interests related to the fairness and accuracy of the criminal trial. However, Defendant's argument is unconvincing. CIPA is designed to "assure the fairness and reliability of the criminal trial" while permitting the government to "ascertain the potential damage to national security of proceeding with a given prosecution before trial." As the Supreme Court has noted, "it is obvious and unarguable that no governmental interest is more compelling than the security of the Nation." CIPA serves that interest "by providing a mechanism for protecting both the unnecessary disclosure of sensitive national security information and by helping to ensure that those with significant access to such information will not escape the sanctions of the law applicable to others by use of the greymail route." [5]   Accordingly, I find that CIPA does not violate Defendant's privilege against self-incrimination by infringing upon either his right to remain silent or his right to testify on his own behalf.

Defendant Lee next argues that § 5 and § 6 of CIPA violate his Sixth Amendment right to confront and cross-examine government witnesses by forcing him to notify the government pretrial (and explain the significance) of all the classified information he reasonably expects to elicit from prosecution witnesses on cross-examination and all such information that will be contained in defense counsel's questions to those witnesses.

Defendant contends that under CIPA, the "prosecution can shape its case-in-chief to blunt the force of the defense cross examination" and that the advance notice under CIPA "will impede effective defense cross-examination." However, the Confrontation Clause does not guarantee the right to undiminished surprise with respect to cross-examination of prosecutorial witnesses. Trial judges retain wide latitude insofar as the Confrontation Clause is concerned to impose reasonable limits on such cross-examination. Therefore, although the Confrontation Clause "guarantees the opportunity for effective cross-examination," it does not guarantee cross-examination "that is effective in whatever way, and to whatever extent, the defense may wish."

CIPA does not require that the defense reveal its plan of cross-examination to the government. CIPA also does not require that the defendant reveal what questions his counsel will ask, in which order, and to which witnesses. Likewise, the defendant need not attribute the information to any particular witness. CIPA merely requires that the defendant identify the classified information he reasonably intends to use. Because the only cited tactical disadvantage that may accrue, minimization of surprise, is slight, Defendant has failed to demonstrate that the requirements under CIPA render his opportunity for cross-examination ineffective.

Defendant's due process argument is based on the contention that CIPA's disclosure requirements violate the Due Process Clause by imposing a one-sided burden on the defense, without imposing a mandatory reciprocal duty on the prosecution. However, due process is only denied where the balance of discovery is tipped against the defendant and in favor of the government. *** Here, the CIPA burdens are not one-sided. First, the government has already agreed to allow Defendant and his counsel access to all classified files at issue in the indictment. Second, the government must produce all discoverable materials before the defense is required to file a § 5(a) notice. Third, before a § 6 hearing is conducted, the government must reveal details of its case so as to give the defense fair notice to prepare for the hearing. Specifically, the government must provide the defense with any portions of any material it may use to establish the "national defense" element of any charges against

---

[5] Greymail refers to a tactic employed by a defendant who threatens to disclose classified information with the hopes that the prosecution will choose not to prosecute in order to keep the information protected.

Lee. Fourth, under § 6(f), the government is required to provide notice of any evidence it will use to rebut classified information that the court permits the defense to use at trial. Finally, in addition to the discovery obligations under § 6 of CIPA, the government must also comply with the Federal Rules of Criminal Procedure and *Brady v. Maryland,* 373 U.S. 83 (1963).

Despite the fact that the Government's reciprocal duties under CIPA are not triggered until it decides to request a § 6 hearing, the overall balance of discovery is not tipped against Lee. On the contrary, modern pretrial practice in complex criminal cases contemplates extensive pretrial disclosures by both parties. Therefore, because the burdens of discovery under CIPA and the Federal Rules of Criminal Procedure are carefully balanced, Defendant's due process claim is without merit. ***

Notes

1. State Secrets and CIPA. CIPA, as Lee demonstrates, is a procedural mechanism. What is the source of the substantive interest protected by CIPA? This issue was explored as follows in *United States v. Aref,* 533 F. 3d 72 (2d Cir. 2008):

> *** CIPA section 4 *presupposes* a governmental privilege against disclosing classified information. It does not itself *create* a privilege. *** The most likely source for the protection of classified information lies in the common-law privilege against disclosure of state secrets. That venerable evidentiary privilege "allows the government to withhold information from discovery when disclosure would be inimical to national security." It would appear that classified information at issue in CIPA cases fits comfortably within the state-secrets privilege. *** [T]he House of Representatives Select Committee on Intelligence stated categorically in its report on CIPA that "the common law state secrets privilege is not applicable in the criminal arena." That statement simply sweeps too broadly.
>
> The Committee relied on three cases for this remarkable proposition. *** These cases *** do not hold that the Government cannot claim the state-secrets privilege in criminal cases. Instead, they recognize the privilege, but conclude that it must give way under some circumstances to a criminal Defendant's right to present a meaningful defense.
>
> Accordingly, we hold that the applicable privilege here is the state-secrets privilege. *See United States v. Klimavicius-Viloria,* 144 F.3d 1249, 1261 (9th Cir.1998) (holding that state-secrets privilege applies in CIPA cases). *** [But] the privilege can be overcome when the evidence at issue is material to the defense. This standard is consistent with *Roviaro v. United States,* 353 U.S. 53 (1957), where the Supreme Court held in a criminal case that the Government's privilege to withhold the identity of a confidential informant "must give way" when the information "is relevant and helpful to the defense of an accused, or is essential to a fair determination of a cause." Indeed, we have interpreted "relevant and helpful" under *Roviaro* to mean "material to the defense." We have also noted that the government-informant privilege at issue in *Roviaro* and

the state-secrets privilege are part of "the same doctrine."

Would it be fair to say that CIPA codifies the state secrets doctrine? Review the main points concerning the state secrets materials you studied earlier.

2. What is Classified? Does *Lee* make classified information wholly the prerogative of the executive branch, relegating the judiciary to a rubber stamp? If not, judging from the opinion, what role does the court play in determining the security status of government documents?

3. To Prosecute or Not to Prosecute? The Attorney General guidelines instruct prosecutors to weigh (1) likelihood of exposure of state secrets or classified information, (2) likely damage to national security, (3) likelihood of successful prosecution, and (4) the other interests promoted by prosecution. Hard choices may sometimes dictate not prosecuting. How does CIPA's interpretation in *Lee* affect the balance of prosecutorial decision making?

4. Disclose or Dismiss. As mentioned in footnote five of *Lee*, greymail is the threat by a defendant to disclose classified information during trial. CIPA was enacted to prevent the use of greymail by defendants with access to classified information by forcing defendants to disclose any intent to reveal such information before the trial begins and allows the government to seek protective orders for the information before trial. Is greymail an illegitimate defense threat? Might it sometimes be entirely proper? In *Lee* and the following cases, evaluate whether the greymail is legitimate. See Joshua L. Dratel, *Ethical Issues in Defending a Terrorism Case: How Secrecy and Security Impair the Defense of a Terrorism Case,* 2 CARDOZO PUB. L. POL'Y & ETHICS J. 81 (2003).

5. Defense Discovery and Prosecutorial Disclosure. *Brady v. Maryland,* 373 U.S. 83-87 (1963), the Jencks Act, 18 U.S.C. §§3500 (2000), and FR Crim. Proc. 16(a)(1) require the prosecution to turn information favorable to the defendant (if relevant to guilt or punishment), witness statements, and other evidence over to the defense. In terrorism and other prosecutions, this information may be classified. Sometimes, the prosecution may argue that it does not have such information—it is in the hands of the CIA. Will this strategy work? Not if the agency is "closely aligned" with the prosecution, though what that means is unclear. Would a 1996 law authorizing (but not requiring) intelligence agencies to turn over foreign and alien source materials to law enforcement agencies in the US make CIA documents discoverable if the CIA voluntarily gives information to the DoJ?

6. The Proper Balance? Consider how sections 4, 5, and 6 work in *Lee*. Is this fair to the defendant?

7. Disclosure of Prelitigation Information. Section 3 of CIPA protects "against the disclosure of any classified information disclosed by the United States to any defendant in any criminal case in a district court of the United States." What if the Defendant's counsel has classified information obtained before the criminal prosecution started? *United States v. Pappas,* 94 F.3d 795 (2d Cir.1996), held that CIPA was not meant to regulate such material:

> [T]he scope of CIPA prohibitions on a Defendant's disclosure of classified information may be summarized as follows: information conveyed by the Government to the defendant in the course of pretrial discovery or the presentation of the Government's case may be prohibited from disclosure, including public disclosure outside the courtroom, but information

acquired by the defendant prior to the criminal prosecution may be prohibited from disclosure only "in connection with the trial" and not outside the trial. Since [the defendant] acquired the information at issue before the trial, CIPA does not authorize the [d]istrict [c]ourt's order to the extent that the order prohibits public disclosure outside the court proceedings. Whatever protection the Government is entitled to obtain against such disclosure must be found in sources of law other than CIPA.

See also *United States v. Chalmers,* 2007 WL 591948 (S.D.N.Y. Feb. 27, 2007):

Pappas makes clear that § 3 of CIPA does not apply to public disclosure of classified information that [the defendant] may have obtained independently of this case. This ruling does not, however, release [the defendant] from any contractual or other legal obligations imposed when he first acquired such information. If any such obligations exist, [the defendant] is bound by them; this ruling does not release him from any such obligations or any other obligations imposed by law. *** [I]n accordance with *Pappas* and the intent of Congress ... [the defendant] must comply with CIPA, and this [c]ourt can, and will, regulate "what may be introduced in the trial context." The [c]ourt cannot, however, regulate [the Defendant's] handling of this information outside the context of this case.

Therefore, if the defendant is under any other legal or contractual obligations to ensure the confidentiality of the information at issue, those obligations still bind him.

8. The Dirty Bomber. Jose Padilla was first introduced to the public by Attorney General Ashcroft as an al Qaeda operative who intended to use nuclear materials in conjunction with traditional explosives. When he was later tried, the charges were much more modest, including conspiring to attack overseas targets and financially support terrorism. The United States was pilloried in the press for not pursuing its original case and was accused of having trumped up the dirty bomber allegations for political purposes. Does *Lee* give you any further ideas about what may have happened?

9. Veracity of Government Claims. A former CIA agent named Edwin P. Wilson was tried and convicted for illegally selling explosives to Libya, after the CIA submitted a falsified affidavit denying that Wilson was CIA. About 20 years later it came out that he was a CIA employee, and his conviction was vacated in *U.S. v. Wilson,* 289 F. Supp 2d 801 (S.D. Tex 2003).

***

The following case deals with the public interest in information concerning terrorism prosecutions when the government invokes CIPA. Consider, as you read it, how strong the people's interest is in knowing about what its government is doing versus the Government's need for secrecy in providing security to the people.

UNITED STATES v. AREF
533 F. 3d 72 (2d Cir. 2008), cert. den. 129 S.Ct.1583 (Mem.) (2009)

McLaughlin, Circuit Judge:

Both defendants were convicted on charges arising out of a sting operation. The jury found that they conspired to conceal the source of what a cooperator represented to be proceeds from the sale of a surface-to-air missile. According to the cooperator, the missile was to be used by terrorists against a target in New York City. Before trial, the Government sought, pursuant to the Classified Information Procedures Act ("CIPA"), two protective orders restricting discovery of certain classified information that, arguably, would have been otherwise discoverable. *** Based on an article in *The New York Times* (suggesting the defendants might have been subject to warrantless surveillance), Aref also moved to discover evidence resulting from any warrantless surveillance and to suppress any illegally obtained evidence or to dismiss the indictment. Both the Government's responses to the motion and the district Court's order denying the motion were sealed because they contained classified information. The district court also denied motions by the New York Civil Liberties Union (the "NYCLU") to intervene and to get public access to those sealed documents. ***

This Court has not yet established the standard by which we review a district Court's denial of a motion to intervene in a criminal case. Indeed, we have implied, but not squarely held, that such a motion is appropriate to assert the public's First Amendment right of access to criminal proceedings. We now hold that: (1) such a motion is proper, and (2) the applicable standard of review is abuse of discretion. *** Because "vindication of [the] right [of public access] requires some meaningful opportunity for protest by persons other than the initial litigants we now invoke this authority to hold that a motion to intervene to assert the public's First Amendment right of access to criminal proceedings is proper.

The NYCLU and *amici* argue that the district court erred by sealing in its entirety the March 10, 2006 Order and sealing nearly all of the March 10, 2006 Opposition. We disagree.

"[I]t is well established that the public and the press have a qualified First Amendment right to attend judicial proceedings and to access certain judicial documents." *** Documents to which the public has a qualified right of access may be sealed only if "specific, on the record findings are made demonstrating that closure is essential to preserve higher values and is narrowly tailored to serve that interest." The district court found that sealing the March 10, 2006 Opposition and Order met this standard because the Executive classified the documents for national-security purposes. The NYCLU and *amici* argue that the district Court's findings were insufficient because the court: (1) erroneously ruled that it lacked the power to review the Government's invocation of the security classifications; (2) failed to make specific findings on the record to support the conclusion that "higher values" justified sealing; and (3) improperly deferred to the Government's view of what could and could not be disclosed to the public.

First, we do not decide whether the district court erred in ruling that it lacked power to review security classifications because any such error was harmless. We have reviewed the sealed record and conclude that the Government established the classification levels employed (e.g., "Confidential," "Secret," and "Top Secret") were properly invoked pursuant to Executive Order.

Second, the NYCLU contends that the district Court *** failed to support sealing the documents with specific, on-the-record findings. However, we have held that while the findings must be made on the record for our review, "such findings may be entered under seal, if appropriate." The district court made sufficiently specific findings under seal that justified denying public access to the documents. Moreover, based on our own *in camera* review of the Government's submission to the district court, we conclude that the Government supported the need to keep the Opposition and Order sealed through a declaration or declarations from persons whose position and responsibility support an inference of personal knowledge; that the district court was made aware of particular facts and circumstances germane to the issues in this case; and that the Government made a sufficient showing that disclosure of the information sought would impair identified national interests in substantial ways. Therefore, the district Court's ruling as to higher values was supported by specific findings based on record evidence.

Third, while it is the responsibility of the district court to ensure that sealing documents to which the public has a First Amendment right is no broader than necessary, our independent review of the sealed documents satisfies us that closure here was narrowly tailored to protect national security. Thus, any error the district court might have committed in deferring to the Government as to whether more of the March 10, 2006 Opposition could be made public was harmless.

Although we affirm the district court in this case, we reinforce the requirement that district courts avoid sealing judicial documents in their entirety unless necessary. Transparency is pivotal to public perception of the judiciary's legitimacy and independence. "The political branches of government claim legitimacy by election, judges by reason. Any step that withdraws an element of the judicial process from public view makes the ensuing decision look more like fiat and requires rigorous justification." Because the Constitution grants the judiciary "neither force nor will, but merely judgment," The Federalist No. 78 (Alexander Hamilton), courts must impede scrutiny of the exercise of that judgment only in the rarest of circumstances. This is especially so when a judicial decision accedes to the requests of a coordinate branch, lest ignorance of the basis for the decision cause the public to doubt that "complete independence of the courts of justice [which] is peculiarly essential in a limited Constitution."

We recognize, however, that transparency must at times yield to more compelling interests. "It is obvious and unarguable that no governmental interest is more compelling than the security of the Nation." Given the legitimate national-security concerns at play here and the nature of the underlying documents at issue, we believe the district court acted appropriately in sealing the [documents]. ***

Notes

1. Procedure and Substance. The Court makes intervention very easy for the ACLU. In light of its resolution of the substantive question, how frequently do you think the ACLU or other watchdog organizations will seek to intervene?

2. CIPA in Habeas Cases? Does CIPA even apply in habeas proceedings? If so, how? The following two case excerpts explore this issue.

AL ODAH v. UNITED STATES
559 F. 3d 539 (D.C. Cir. 2009)

PER CURIAM:

*** The Department of Defense (DOD) ordered the detention at the U.S. Naval Base at Guantanamo Bay, Cuba of certain foreign nationals captured abroad after al Qaeda attacked the World Trade Center and the Pentagon on September 11, 2001. To determine whether Guantanamo Bay detainees are "enemy combatants," as defined by DOD, the Deputy Secretary of Defense established Combatant Status Review Tribunals (CSRTs). Each CSRT relied on an administrative record compiled by a military officer to support the Government's case for detention. Separate CSRTs concluded that the petitioners here were enemy combatants. To contest their detentions, they filed petitions for writs of habeas corpus in the United States District Court for the District of Columbia. ***

The district court directed disclosure to petitioners' counsel of the redacted classified information on the ground that it was "relevant to the merits of this litigation." In the context of criminal proceedings, however, this court has held that "classified information is not discoverable on a mere showing of theoretical relevance in the face of the Government's classified information privilege." Rather, "the threshold for discovery in this context further requires that ... [the] information ... is at least 'helpful to the defense of [the] accused.' " This standard applies with equal force to partially classified documents: "if some portion or aspect of a document is classified, a defendant is entitled to receive it only if it may be helpful to his defense." Hence, before the district court may compel the disclosure of classified information, it must determine that the information is both relevant *and* *material*-in the sense that it is at least helpful to the petitioner's habeas case. And because such disclosure is in the context of a habeas proceeding, the touchstone of which is the Court's "authority to conduct a meaningful review of both the cause for detention and the Executive's power to detain," *Boumediene,* 128 S.Ct. at 2269, the court must further conclude that access by petitioner's counsel (pursuant to a court-approved protective order) is necessary to facilitate such review.

Although both sides agree that materiality and not mere relevance is the threshold standard, they dispute whether the district court ordered disclosure based solely on relevance or whether it in fact made a materiality determination. The Court's order simply states that the classified information is "relevant." Although we acknowledge that the district court may well have considered materiality as an implicit part of the relevance analysis, the Order does not indicate whether that is the case. Absent such an indication and an explanation of the Court's reasoning, we cannot at this stage conclude that the redacted information is in fact material.

At the same time, we reject the Government's suggestion that its mere "certification"-that the information redacted from the version of the return provided to a detainee's counsel "do[es] not support a determination that the detainee is *not* an enemy combatant"-is sufficient to establish that the information is not material. That naked declaration simply cannot resolve the issue. *Cf. Parhat v. Gates,* 532 F.3d 834, 850 (D.C.Cir.2008) (rejecting "the Government's contention that it can prevail by submitting documents that read as if they were indictments or civil complaints, and that simply assert as facts the elements required to prove that a detainee falls within the definition of enemy combatant[, because] [t]o do otherwise would require the courts to rubber-stamp the Government's charges"). As the unredacted material was submitted to the court, it is the Court's responsibility to make the materiality determination itself.

Moreover, even if it is true that the redacted information in the return "does not support a determination that the detainee is *not* an enemy combatant"-i.e., that the information is not directly exculpatory-that is not the only ground upon which information may be material in the habeas context. The court must still assess whether the information is *actually* inculpatory, because the government submitted the full habeas return in support of its contention that the detainee *is* an enemy combatant.

Evaluation of that contention requires the court to assess the reliability of the sources upon which the return is based. Hence, indications of unreliability are themselves material. For example, the court may fear, or counsel may proffer evidence, that a source is biased or that his testimony was the product of coercion. Similarly, if a source asserts that he saw the petitioner at a particular place and time, evidence that the source was elsewhere at that time would discredit his claim.

Information that is not exculpatory on its face may also be material if it contains the names of witnesses who can provide helpful information. In this regard, the Government's further "certification," again on its own authority and without explanation, that the petitioner does not have a "need to know" "information pertaining to individuals other than the detainee" cannot end the inquiry. A list of individuals "other than the detainee" may be a list of witnesses useful to the detainee: for example, when the list names other detainees the government alleges trained at a certain al Qaeda training camp with the detainee, but who would testify to the contrary.

At oral argument, counsel for the government stated his "understanding that in the factual returns" that the government had been filing in more recent detainee habeas cases, "in most circumstances other detainee identities are not being withheld." In light of counsel's statement that "the government is using a somewhat different standard now," we asked the government to reconsider whether it wanted to continue withholding such material in the instant cases. Soon after oral argument, however, the Justice Department advised the court that the government continues to redact material pertaining to individuals other than the detainee at issue. "The rationale," the Department stated, is that a "list of individuals other than the petitioner ... do[es] not serve as affirmative evidence that the petitioner is an enemy combatant.".

The Government's rationale in this letter appears to be the inverse of the rationale it advanced in the declarations that originally accompanied the factual returns: the initial declarations stated that the redacted material does not tend to show that the detainee is *not* an enemy combatant (i.e., that it is not exculpatory), while this most recent letter states that the redacted material is not affirmative evidence that the detainee *is* an enemy combatant (i.e., that it is not inculpatory). But the fact that information does not serve as "affirmative evidence" against a detainee does not render it immaterial. Information that is exculpatory, that undermines the reliability of other purportedly inculpatory evidence, or that names potential witnesses capable of providing material evidence may all be material.

The Government's letter also belatedly offers to provide the district court with the Government's own "particularized assessment of whether the information is material." Such a proffer, combined with an explanation of why nondisclosure is warranted, is necessary for meaningful judicial decisionmaking, and the district court should not hesitate to require that it be filed contemporaneously with a government request for redactions

As the record now stands, without an explanation of the grounds for finding materiality by the district court and without support for the claim of immateriality from the government, we cannot resolve the issue of materiality on our own. A remand is therefore required.

As neither side disputes, the analogy to criminal proceedings also indicates that, before ordering disclosure of classified material to counsel, the court must determine that alternatives to disclosure would not effectively substitute for unredacted access. In criminal proceedings under the Classified Information Procedures Act (CIPA), for example, the government may move for alternatives to disclosing classified information, such as substituting "a statement admitting relevant facts that the specific classified information would tend to prove" or "a summary of the specific classified information." The district court must "grant such a motion ... if it finds that the statement or summary will provide the defendant with substantially the same ability to make his defense as would disclosure of the specific classified information."

These or other alternatives should also be available in habeas if the district court determines that a proposed admission or summary would suffice to provide the detainee with "a meaningful opportunity to demonstrate that he is being held pursuant to the erroneous application or interpretation of relevant law." We note, moreover, that although a finding of materiality is a prerequisite to ordering disclosure of classified information, it is not a prerequisite to ordering disclosure of an unclassified substitution. If the court determines that the assistance of petitioner's counsel would facilitate the making of a materiality determination, nothing bars it (assuming no other privilege is at issue) from compelling the government to produce an unclassified substitution that will enable counsel to assist the court.

As the record does not indicate whether the district court considered unclassified alternatives before ordering disclosure of classified information, this issue must be addressed on remand as well.

In *Boumediene*, the Supreme Court made clear that, although "[h]abeas corpus proceedings need not resemble a criminal trial," the "writ must be effective. The habeas court must have sufficient authority to conduct a meaningful review of both the cause for detention and the Executive's power to detain." Contrary to the Government's suggestion, this Court's opinion in *Bismullah* did not hold that the Government's submission of classified materials to the court for *in camera, ex parte* review ends that inquiry. *Bismullah* did indicate that, in DTA cases, "highly sensitive information, or information pertaining to a highly sensitive source or to anyone other than the detainee" should be presented first "to the court ex parte and in camera." And it further stated that, once such information is presented to the court, the "presumption" under the DTA that "counsel for a detainee has a 'need to know' all Government Information concerning his client" "is overcome." But *Bismullah* did not address how a district court should proceed once that *presumption* was overcome by an *ex parte, in camera* presentation. As indicated above, we now conclude that the habeas court should proceed by determining whether the classified information is material and counsel's access to it is necessary to facilitate meaningful review, and whether no alternatives to access would suffice to provide the detainee with the meaningful opportunity required by *Boumediene*.

On the current record, we are unable to determine whether the district court found that the redacted classified information was material to the detainees' cases and necessary to facilitate meaningful habeas review. Nor can we determine whether the court found that alternatives to disclosure were insufficient. Given the scope of the problems presented to the district court in the underlying proceedings, and the Court's prescience in anticipating the Supreme Court's conclusion in *Boumediene* regarding the availability of habeas, we do not make these observations by way of criticism. Nonetheless, they do require us to vacate the discovery order and to remand for further proceedings. Because we do so, we do not address additional issues that may become relevant if the threshold requirements for disclosure to counsel are met. As the Court said in *Boumediene*, "[w]e make no attempt to anticipate all of the evidentiary ... issues that will arise during the course of the detainees' habeas corpus proceedings," because "[t]hese and the other remaining questions are within the expertise and competence of the District Court to address in the first instance." Nor do we address "the content of the law that governs petitioners' detention," which is also a "matter yet to be determined." ***

In re GUANTANAMO BAY DETAINEE LITIGATION.
634 F. Supp. 2d 17 (D. D. C. 2009)

THOMAS F. HOGAN, District Judge.

*** *iii. If a court determines that a petitioner's classified statements are material, the government must provide the petitioner with the statements or a sufficient alternative*

Drawing from recent case law and relevant criminal statutes, the Court finds that a district court may order the disclosure of classified information over the Government's objection, if certain conditions are met. The district court would first determine if the information is material and would help facilitate meaningful habeas review. If the answer is affirmative to both questions, the court may order the disclosure of the classified information. If the government still objects to the disclosure of the classified information, it must provide a sufficient alternative to the information. If the government fails to provide such an alternative, the court may order an assortment of remedies.

The question of what determinations must be made before a court may order the government to disclose classified information to the petitioners in these habeas proceedings was not answered in *Boumediene* and is one of first impression in this Circuit. As the Supreme Court left any remaining questions to "the expertise and competence of the District Court," the Court will rely, by analogy, on the Classified Information Procedures Act ("CIPA"), which governs the procedures for handling classified information in criminal proceedings. The D.C. Circuit, in *Al Odah v. United States,* 559 F.3d 539, 544-47 (D.C.Cir.2009), similarly relied on CIPA "by analogy" in a case concerning procedures for ordering the disclosure of classified material to petitioners' counsel in these habeas proceedings.

In *Al Odah,* the government filed complete versions of the classified factual returns with the district court, but redacted some information in the copies provided to petitioners' counsel. The government redacted information pertaining to individuals other than the petitioner at issue or information that was "especially sensitive source-identifying information." Finding that the redacted material was relevant, the district court granted petitioners' counsel access to the unredacted classified factual returns. The D.C. Circuit, applying CIPA "by analogy," vacated the Court's order. Classified information is not discoverable, the Circuit stated, "on a mere showing of theoretical relevance in the face of the Government's classified information privilege." The Circuit ordered the government to provide the district court with an assessment of whether the redacted information was material and whether counsel's access to it was necessary for the court to conduct a meaningful review of the petitioner's detention. *See Al Odah,* 559 F.3d at 544-45. If the court determined that the information was material and necessary for meaningful review, and therefore discoverable, it must then determine whether "alternatives to access would suffice to provide the detainee with the meaningful opportunity [to challenge his detention as] required by *Boumediene.*"

The Court finds that the *Al Odah* framework, with its reliance on CIPA, is applicable here. *Al Odah* represents one of the few cases where the D.C. Circuit has discussed handling classified material for the Guantanamo Bay detainees. Moreover, the issue in that case is analogous to the issue here: the framework for ordering the dissemination of classified information over the Government's objection. If anything, the redactions at issue here are less tenable than the redactions in *Al Odah*. There, the government redacted information pertaining to other individuals, whereas here the government is denying petitioners' access to their own statements.

In applying *Al Odah,* the Court Notes that many statements from a given petitioner will be material. A petitioner's factual return, which forms the basis of the Government's detention decision, is based, in part, on that petitioner's statements. The Court questions whether the government can deny the materiality of statements that it has chosen to rely upon to justify a petitioner's detention. Nevertheless, such materiality determinations should be made by the Merits Judges on an individual basis.

As for alternatives, the government submits that it intends to declassify some of the petitioners' statements. For those statements that the government plans to declassify, declassification alone may not suffice. Timing is of the essence. As the Supreme Court admonished, "[w]hile some delay in fashioning new procedures is unavoidable, the costs of delay can no longer be borne by those who are held in custody." Petitioners, it continued, "are entitled to a prompt habeas corpus hearing." If the government cannot produce declassified statements in a timely manner, petitioners should not bear the "costs" in the form of delayed merits hearings. As for those statements that the government does not declassify, the Merits Judges would determine if alternatives to disclosure would effectively substitute for unredacted access to the statements. For example, under CIPA, the government may move to admit relevant facts that the specific classified information would tend to prove or provide a summary of the information. These or other alternatives are available in these habeas cases if the Merits Judges determine they "would suffice to provide the detainee with 'a meaningful opportunity to demonstrate that he is being held pursuant to the erroneous application or interpretation of relevant law.' " If the government fails to provide a sufficient alternative, and continues to object to the disclosure of a petitioner's material classified statements, then the Court may order an appropriate remedy.

Though *Al Odah* is silent on the consequences if the government fails to provide a sufficient alternative to material classified information, CIPA enumerates a number of remedies. Under CIPA, if the government objects to the disclosure of material classified information and fails to provide a sufficient alternative, the district court may dismiss counts in the indictment, make findings against the government on any issues as to which the excluded classified information relates, or preclude part of a witness's testimony. These remedies are likewise available to the Merits Judges in these proceedings. At a minimum, the government cannot rely on a petitioner's statement if it does not timely provide that petitioner with a sufficient alternative to that statement. ***

Notes

1. The Defendant's Own Statements. The court acknowledged that "providing a petitioner access to his own statements could alert him to the significance of details that he previously thought inconsequential. The Government's concern, however, appears to be the context, not the content, of the petitioner's words. Such concerns can be addressed by providing a petitioner with alternatives to the actual documents that contain the petitioner's statements." It also noted that "Counsel may not share information from classified documents containing a petitioner's statements besides the petitioner's words and the date the statements were made."

2. Coerced Statements. The Obama Administration has said it desires to try many Guantanamo detainees in civilian courts. How might a federal court likely deal with a Defendant's argument that, though he made the statement the government seeks to admit into evidence, the statement was obtained through harsh interrogation techniques? Would the statements be admissible in court if not obtained through torture?

2. USE OF THE CIPA FRAMEWORK FOR WITNESSES

CIPA deals with documents, not witnesses. However, in terrorism trials witnesses may pose similar issues to those posed by documents. If revealing witnesses would compromise intelligence sources, can the government deny defense counsel access to witnesses such as CIA field agents? Conversely, suppose the defense wants to obtain statements or testimony from witnesses held by the government for purposes of exoneration. Does the government have to allow access to such a potential witness? The following two cases explore these issues.

UNITED STATES v. MARZOOK
412 F. Supp. 2d 913 (N.D. Ill., 2006)

ST. EVE, District Judge.

*** Defendant Salah has filed a motion to suppress statements he allegedly made to Israeli authorities. Salah argues that he did not voluntarily make any statements that the government seeks to admit at trial. The United States has filed a motion to conduct certain portions of the suppression hearing in a closed courtroom, pursuant to the Classified Information Procedures Act. The United States has further asked the Court to approve certain procedures to ensure the safety of several witnesses, including allowing these witnesses to wear light disguise while they testify and to use non-public entrances to the courthouse and the courtroom. *** Each charge is premised upon and related to Salah's alleged support of the Hamas terrorist organization, both prior to and after the United States designated Hamas as a Specially Designated Terrorist Organization and a Foreign Terrorist Organization. *** Salah has submitted a sworn affidavit detailing the treatment he claims he received at the hands of his interrogators. Salah argues that he did not voluntarily give any of these statements. He contends that he involuntarily made such statements because Israeli authorities coerced and tortured him into making them. Given that Defendant Salah's affidavit makes a preliminary showing that a significant, disputed factual issue exists, the Court will hold an evidentiary hearing.

[At] [t]he suppression hearing *** the government intends to call approximately six or seven witnesses to testify. Two of these witnesses will be agents of the ISA. The ISA is an intelligence agency for the State of Israel that provides for Israel's internal security. The government has moved the Court to close the hearing to the public when these ISA agents testify. It argues that a closed hearing is mandated by the Classified Information Procedures Act, and warranted to protect the safety of the ISA agents and the sanctity of the ISA's intelligence gathering methods. *** At the suppression hearing, the Court will determine whether Defendant Salah's alleged statements are admissible at trial. The government has moved to have the testimony of the ISA agents at the hearing conducted *in camera* for the Court to resolve questions regarding the use and admissibility of Salah's statements. The government argues, and has provided supporting evidence, that the substance of the ISA agents' testimony is classified and thus cannot be disclosed to the public. The government does not seek to have Defendant Salah and his attorneys excluded from this testimony because the Israeli authorities have agreed to waive the classification designation as to the majority of this information as to Salah and his counsel ***. Instead, the government seeks to have these agents testify outside the presence of the public because Israel has not waived the classification designation generally. Thus, the primary issue presented to the Court is whether the public can have access to the testimonial information deemed classified at the suppression hearing.

The Classified Information Procedures Act ("CIPA"), "is essentially a procedural tool" for a court to address the relevance of classified information before it may be introduced. CIPA's "fundamental purpose is to 'protect [ ] and restrict[ ] the discovery of classified information in a way that does not impair the Defendant's right to a fair trial." CIPA is designed "to protect classified information from unnecessary disclosure at any stage of a criminal trial." It provides "pretrial procedures that will permit the trial judge to rule on questions of admissibility involving classified information before introduction of the evidence in open court." *** The government brings this motion pursuant to Sections 4 and 6 of CIPA. Section 4 provides:

> The court may permit the United States to make a written request for [an authorization to delete specified items in discoverable documents] in the form of a written statement to be inspected by the court alone. If the court enters an order granting relief following such an ex parte showing, the entire text of the statement of the United States shall be sealed and preserved in the records of the court to be made available to the appellate court in the event of an appeal.

Courts have held that this applies to testimony, as well as documents.

Section 6 of CIPA sets forth the "procedure for cases involving classified information." It provides that "the United States may request the court to conduct a hearing to make all determinations concerning the use, relevance, or admissibility of classified information that would otherwise be made during the trial or pretrial proceeding." Such a hearing *"shall be held in camera* if the Attorney General certifies to the court ... that a public proceeding may result in the disclosure of classified information."

A. The Substance of the Testimony. The ISA is a domestic intelligence agency for the State of Israel. By law, the ISA provides for the internal security of Israel. Israel is in a state of high risk given the terrorist operations working against Israel. Israel maintains the secrecy of the true identities of the ISA agents, as well as identifying characteristics. Given this secrecy and the ISA's safety concerns for its agents, Israel has never before permitted ISA agents to give live testimony in the United States. Although the Court cannot publicly disclose the substance of these agents' testimony in this case, generally speaking, these witnesses will testify regarding topics that are themselves classified, including the agents' work, work-related activities, procedures, interrogation techniques, investigative methods, and other counterintelligence and securities activities of the ISA. Defendant does not contradict the anticipated substance of the ISA agents' testimony. Based on the *in camera* submissions of the government, the Court finds that Israel has classified the substance of the testimony of these agents, as well as their true identities. As set forth below, the United States, in turn, treats this information as classified for purposes of CIPA.

B. The Anticipated Testimony Is Classified by Executive Order. Pursuant to Executive Order 12958, issued on April 17, 1995, as further amended by Executive Order 13292, issued on March 25, 2003, "information provided to the United States Government by a foreign government ... with the expectation that the information, the source of the information, or both, are to be held in confidence" or "information produced by the United States pursuant to or as a result of a joint arrangement with a foreign government ... requiring that the information, the arrangement, or both, are to be held in confidence" constitutes "foreign government information." Moreover, "the unauthorized disclosure of foreign government information is presumed to cause damage to the national security."

It is undisputed that Israel provided the substance of the testimony of the ISA agents to the United States with the expectation that it would be held in confidence. Given that Israel considers the true identities of the ISA agents and the substance of their testimony classified, American authorities have certified it as classified. *** Furthermore, Assistant Attorney General Alice Fischer has certified pursuant to Section 6(a) of CIPA that a public proceeding may result in the disclosure of classified information, and has requested an *in camera* proceeding. Accordingly, the Court grants the Government's request to close the hearing to the public when these agents testify ***. Defendant Salah and his counsel, as well as counsel for Co-Defendant Ashqar, may be present during this time. The Court will only permit those with the appropriate security clearance to remain in the courtroom during this testimony. ***

Defendant also challenges the designation of the agents' testimony as "classified" based on Section 1.8 of Executive Order 12958. Section 1.8 provides that "[i]n no case shall information be classified in order to: ... (2) prevent embarrassment to a person, organization, or agency." . Defendant argues, without any supporting evidence, that Israel has improperly designated the testimony at issue classified in order to prevent embarrassment and "to conceal Israel's use of harsh and illegal interrogation methods which violate international law as well as the law of Israel and the United States." Defendant therefore asks the Court to deem the testimony not classified.

At least one Circuit has held that a court cannot question the Executive's designation of material as classified. *See, e.g., United States v. Smith,* 750 F.2d 1215, 1217 (4th Cir.1984) ("[T]he government ... may determine what information is classified. A defendant cannot challenge this classification. A court cannot question it."). Although the Seventh Circuit has not addressed this precise issue in the context of CIPA, it has provided some guidance in the context of the Freedom of Information Act ("FOIA") where it has made clear that classification "decisions rest with the executive branch." *** It is a matter of conjecture whether the court performs any real judicial function when it reviews classified documents in camera. Without the illumination provided by adversarial challenge and with no expertness in the field of national security, the court has no basis on which to test the accuracy of the Government's claims. The court is limited to determining that the documents are the kinds of documents described in the Government's affidavit, that they have been classified in fact, and that there is a logical nexus between the information at issue and the claimed exemption. The court *** must defer to the agency's evaluation of the need to maintain the secrecy of the methods used to carry out such projects *** [but] the prospect of having to justify its classification decisions before a neutral arbiter causes a more thorough and objective presubmission review by the agency than would otherwise be the case. ***

[T]he Court need not resolve whether it can review the legitimacy of a classification designation in the context of CIPA where the statute does not provide for such review, because even if the Court had the authority to make such a determination, Defendant's challenge fails under the clear language of the Executive Order. *** The classification exception upon which Defendant relies provides that information should not be classified in order to "prevent embarrassment to a person, organization, or agency." Under a plain reading of the Executive Order, the State of Israel does not constitute a person, organization, or agency. *** Thus, even if Defendant's assertion is correct, the Executive Order does not preclude its classification ***[and] there is simply no evidence that these materials are classified merely to prevent embarrassment to Israel. ***

C. True Identities. The government also seeks to have the ISA agents' true names and identities remain undisclosed to the public, as well as

Defendant Salah. The government does not even know their true identities. Instead, the government seeks to have these agents testify using the pseudonyms under which the ISA agents conduct all of their ISA affairs. *** Under Israeli law, the true identities of these agents-including their names, identifying information, and physical characteristics-are classified. Their names are therefore classified under Executive Order 12958. The government thus has met its burden of proving that these identities constitute classified information. Accordingly, the Court orders that the ISA agents may testify using pseudonyms, and they do not have to disclose their true identities in court.

Allowing the ISA agents to testify using pseudonyms does not deprive Defendant of his Sixth Amendment right to confront these witnesses. *** Defendant will be able to physically face each of the ISA witnesses and to cross examine them. Although he will not know their true identities, they will identify themselves by their pseudonyms that they use in connection with their work. *** Defendant remains free to cross examine these witnesses on the basis of their direct testimony or any other proper basis. The use of pseudonyms is also appropriate for the security of these witnesses.

D. Review of Transcripts. Under Section 6 of CIPA, review of testimony differs from review of documents. Unlike a document which is static and which the Court can review in its entirety, live testimony is dynamic-neither the Court nor the parties can anticipate every question that counsel will ask these ISA witnesses nor every answer they will provide. As discussed above, the government has properly invoked CIPA based on the anticipated substance of the ISA agents' testimony, and Assistant Attorney General Fisher has certified that a public proceeding of the ISA agents' testimony may result in disclosure of classified information.

In order to ensure that all of the received testimony is in fact classified, however, the Court directs the United States to conduct a post-hearing review of the actual testimony of these ISA agents to confirm whether the government deems the entirety of each ISA agent's testimony classified. The Court directs the government to conduct this review within seven business days from the issuance of the final transcript. If the government deems the testimony not classified, the Court will promptly make it part of the public filing. This expedited review of the testimony will ensure that any information that is not classified will be made available to the public in a timely manner. If all of the testimony is classified, it will remain under seal.

Further, the Court directs the government to review any documents introduced into evidence during the testimony of these agents. To the extent these documents, or portions of them, are not classified, they will be available to the public no later than seven days from their admission into evidence.

E. The First and Sixth Amendments. Because the government seeks to apply the agents' testimony to the merits of the suppression hearing and thus practically, the CIPA hearing will coincide with a portion of the suppression hearing, the government must establish that courtroom closure squares with the Constitution, even though CIPA independently covers the agents' testimony. ***

The United States has rebutted the presumption of openness based on its showing that the anticipated testimony is classified and governed by CIPA as addressed above. The United States has an overriding interest in maintaining the agents' sensitive testimony-including testimony regarding intelligence gathering methods and counterintelligence measures-as classified in order to protect the national security of Israel and the relationship between Israel and the United States of sharing national security information. Public disclosure of this classified testimony would damage foreign relations and negatively impact national security. An open courtroom will defeat the overriding interest in maintaining the classification of this information because once it becomes public, the Court cannot reverse its disclosure. Thus, Defendant's "unconstitutional as applied" argument fails.

Even if the overriding need to protect the classified information at issue in this case did not support closure of the courtroom, the Court alternatively would seal the courtroom during the testimony of the ISA agents based on another overriding interest ***. [T]hese ISA agents face a serious, legitimate risk of grave danger if they were publicly identified. For example, various internet sites post descriptions and sketches of ISA agents so that the agents can be identified and targeted, and at least one internet site has offered a cash reward for information regarding the true identities of ISA agents. Closing the courtroom during their testimony is thus warranted.

The closure of the courtroom is narrowly tailored to address the CIPA interest and the security concerns. The courtroom will only be closed to the public during the testimony of the ISA agents. The remaining witnesses, including the Israeli police officers whom the government anticipates calling at the hearing, will testify in an open courtroom, and the attorneys' opening and closing statements will be public.

Defendant argues that the classification designation will apply to the testimony of the other witnesses in the case, including Salah's own testimony because he intends to testify about the information gathered by the ISA and the techniques used by them. Based upon the record before the Court, there is no indication that such testimony will be classified, nor has the government moved to have the courtroom closed during it. Second, the Government's post-hearing review of the testimony will ensure that non-classified information-to the extent there is any-is immediately made available to the public.

Finally, both Defendant and the Chicago Tribune make an alternative proposal to closing the courtroom for the ISA agents' testimony-namely, to bifurcate the ISA agents' testimony and have the ISA agents testify with the public present, and have the Court excuse the public from the courtroom when questions arise that will likely elicit classified information. *** Such a bifurcated procedure would be extremely disruptive, disjointed, and impractical. Compounding this is the fact that, pursuant to Section 9 of CIPA, the courtroom must be secured in advance of any classified testimony. Thus, each time the Court excused the public, the courtroom would have to be re-secured before a witness could provide any classified information. Such a timely procedure adds to the impracticability of this bifurcation proposal. ***

II. Other Security Measures   ***The government seeks permission to have the ISA agents testify in light disguise for "the protection of their identity, both for their ability to continue covert work as well as their safety and the safety of their families." *** The appearance of these agents presents legitimate security issues. Although light disguise would be appropriate in some circumstances, it is not necessary here where the courtroom will be closed to the public. The government contends that Defendant Salah and others in the courtroom will be able to publicly identify these agents if they do not wear light disguise. These are the same agents that previously questioned Defendant Salah. The government has not submitted any evidence or argument that these agents were in disguise at the time of such questioning, thus Salah presumably has already physically seen them at length. The only other individuals in the courtroom will be defense attorneys, court personnel who have security clearances, and federal agents. Without any evidence of why the extra precaution of light disguise is necessary in a closed courtroom, the Court denies the Government's request without prejudice. The Court orders that no one present in the courtroom can disclose or describe the physical identity of these ISA agents. *** The ISA agent witnesses may, however, use a private entrance to the courthouse and the courtroom. ***

Notes

1. CIPA and Witnesses. Does CIPA work as well for witnesses as it does for documents? What new factors are introduced here? Does use of CIPA with witnesses jeopardize the fairness of the trial?

2. Light Disguise. What is "light disguise" compared to disguise that is not light? Can you think of circumstances where light disguise of a witness would prejudice the ability of the defendant to have a fair trial?

3. Other Terrorism Trial Issues. Can the trial be closed if the defendant threatens to blurt out classified information? If the defendant insists on self-representation so he can, for example, publicly swear fealty to al Qaeda, is the court obligated to take measures to protect the defendant from himself? Should the court fear for the safety of the jurors or itself? What measures might the court take to cope with these concerns and will they prejudice the defendant? In publishing opinions with national security concerns, may the court make redactions? Keep the entire opinion secret?

***

Many of the issues in the note above were concerns at the trial of Zacharias Moussaoui, though the appellate decision below concerns a narrower issue --defense access to a witness in government custody.

UNITED STATES v. MOUSSAOUI
382 F. 3d 453 (C.A. 4, 2004)

WILKINS, Chief Judge.

The Government appeals a series of rulings by the district court granting Appellee Zacarias Moussaoui access to certain individuals ("the enemy combatant witnesses" or "the witnesses") for the purpose of deposing them ***; rejecting the Government's proposed substitutions for the depositions; and imposing sanctions for the Government's refusal to produce the witnesses. We are presented with questions of grave significance-questions that test the commitment of this nation to an independent judiciary, to the constitutional guarantee of a fair trial even to one accused of the most heinous of crimes, and to the protection of our citizens against additional terrorist attacks. ***

*** Moussaoui was arrested for an immigration violation in mid-August 2001 and, in December of that year, was indicted on several charges of conspiracy related to the September 11 attacks. In July 2002, the Government filed a superceding indictment charging Moussaoui with six offenses: conspiracy to commit acts of terrorism transcending national boundaries; conspiracy to commit aircraft piracy; conspiracy to destroy aircraft; conspiracy to use weapons of mass destruction; conspiracy to murder United States employees, and conspiracy to destroy property. The Government seeks the death penalty on the first four of these charges.

According to the allegations of the indictment, Moussaoui was present at an al Qaeda training camp in April 1998 *** arrived in the United States in late February 2001 and thereafter began flight lessons in Norman, Oklahoma. Other allegations in the indictment highlight similarities between Moussaoui's conduct and the conduct of the September 11 hijackers. Each of the four death-eligible counts of the indictment alleges that the actions of Moussaoui and his coconspirators "result[ed] in the deaths of thousands of persons on September 11, 2001." ***

Witness A was captured [Redacted]. Shortly thereafter, Moussaoui (who at that time was representing himself in the district court) moved for access to Witness A, asserting that the witness would be an important part of his defense. *** The district court concluded that Witness A could offer material testimony in Moussaoui's defense; in particular, the court determined that Witness A had extensive knowledge of the September 11 plot and that his testimony would support Moussaoui's claim that he was not involved in the attacks. At a minimum, the court observed, Witness A's testimony could support an argument that Moussaoui should not receive the death penalty if convicted. *** [It ruled] that the Government's national security interest must yield to Moussaoui's right to a fair trial. Accordingly, the court ordered that Witness A's testimony be preserved by *** deposition. In an attempt to minimize the effect of its order on national security, the district court ordered that certain precautions be taken. Specifically, the court directed that the deposition would be taken by remote video, with Witness A in an undisclosed location and Moussaoui, standby counsel, and counsel for the Government in the presence of the district court, [Redacted]

Noting that "[t]he unprecedented investment of both human and material resources in this case mandates the careful consideration of some sanction other than dismissal," the district court rejected the parties' claims that the indictment should be dismissed. Rather, the court dismissed the death notice, reasoning that Moussaoui had adequately demonstrated that the witnesses could provide testimony that, if believed, might preclude a jury from finding Moussaoui eligible for the death penalty. Further, because proof of Moussaoui's involvement in the September 11 attacks was not necessary to a conviction, and because the witnesses' testimony, if believed, could exonerate Moussaoui of involvement in those attacks, the district court prohibited the Government "from making any argument, or offering any evidence, suggesting that the defendant had any involvement in, or knowledge of, the September 11 attacks." In conjunction with this ruling, the district court denied the Government's motions to admit into evidence cockpit voice recordings made on September 11; video footage of the collapse of the World Trade Center towards; and photographs of the victims of the attacks. ***

With respect to the merits, the Government first argues that the district court erred in ordering the production of the enemy combatant witnesses for the purpose of deposing them. Within the context of this argument, the Government makes two related claims. First, the Government asserts that because the witnesses are noncitizens outside the territorial boundaries of the United States, there is no means by which the district court can compel their appearance on Moussaoui's behalf. Second, the Government maintains that even if the district court has the power to reach the witnesses, its exercise of that power is curtailed by the reality that the witnesses are in military custody in time of war, and thus requiring them to be produced would violate constitutional principles of separation of powers. *** The Government's argument rests primarily on the well established and undisputed principle that the process power of the district court does not extend to foreign nationals abroad. *** The Government's argument overlooks the critical fact that the enemy combatant witnesses are [Redacted] of the United States Government. Therefore, we are concerned not with the ability of the district court to issue a subpoena to the witnesses, but rather with its power to issue a writ of habeas corpus *ad testificandum* ("testimonial writ") to the witnesses' custodian. ***

The Government next argues that even if the district court would otherwise have the power to order the production of the witnesses, [its]orders are improper because they infringe on the Executive's warmaking authority, in violation of separation of powers principles.

A. *Immunity Cases*

We begin by examining the Government's reliance on cases concerning governmental refusal to grant immunity to potential defense witnesses. *** Nothing in the Fifth Amendment, or in any other constitutional provision, provides a means for overcoming this privilege once a potential witness has invoked it. However, through the Immunity of Witnesses Act, Congress has conferred upon the Attorney General statutory authority to grant use immunity to witnesses in order to obtain their testimony at trial. The Immunity Act grants the Attorney General or his designee exclusive authority and discretion to confer immunity.

The circuit courts, including the Fourth Circuit, have uniformly held that district courts do not have any authority to grant immunity, even when a grant of immunity would allow a defendant to present material, favorable testimony. *** These holdings have been based on the facts that no power to grant immunity is found in the Constitution and that Congress reserved the statutory immunity power to the Attorney General. Because a district court has no power to grant immunity to compel the testimony of a potential witness who has invoked the privilege against self-incrimination, a defendant has no Sixth Amendment right to such testimony.

The circuits are divided with respect to the question of whether a district court can ever compel the government, on pain of dismissal, to grant immunity to a potential defense witness. The Fourth Circuit, consistent with the majority rule, has held that a district court may compel the government to grant immunity upon a showing of prosecutorial misconduct and materiality.

Courts have noted that compelling the prosecution to grant immunity implicates the separation of powers. Decisions to grant or deny immunity are intimately tied to decisions regarding which perpetrators of crimes will be prosecuted, a core aspect of the Executive's duty to enforce the laws. *** The Government claims that these "immunity cases" stand for the proposition that, under certain circumstances, legitimate separation of powers concerns effectively insulate the Government from being compelled to produce evidence or witnesses. In fact, the majority rule and the law of this circuit stand for precisely the opposite proposition, namely, that courts *will* compel a grant of immunity, *despite the existence of separation of powers concerns,* when the defendant demonstrates that the Government's refusal to grant immunity to an essential defense witness constitutes an abuse of the discretion granted to the Government by the Immunity Act. A showing of misconduct is necessary because, as explained above, a defendant has no Sixth Amendment right to the testimony of a potential witness who has invoked the Fifth Amendment right against self-incrimination; therefore, the defendant has no Sixth Amendment right that could outweigh the Government's interest in using its immunity power sparingly. Governmental abuse of the immunity power, however, vitiates this interest because when the Government's misconduct threatens to impair the Defendant's right to a fair trial, it is proper for the district court to protect that right by compelling the Government to immunize the witness.

For these reasons, the analogy between this case and the immunity cases is inapt. The witnesses at issue here, unlike potential witnesses who have invoked their Fifth Amendment rights, are within the process power of the district court, and Moussaoui therefore has a Sixth Amendment right to their testimony. As discussed below, this right must be balanced against the

Government's legitimate interest in preventing disruption [Redacted] of the enemy combatant witnesses.

B. *Governing Principles*

*** This is not a case involving arrogation of the powers or duties of another branch. The district court orders requiring production of the enemy combatant witnesses involved the resolution of questions properly-indeed, exclusively-reserved to the judiciary. Therefore, if there is a separation of powers problem at all, it arises only from the burden the actions of the district court place on the Executive's performance of its duties. ***

C. *Balancing*

*** The Government alleges-and we accept as true-that [Redacted] the enemy combatant witnesses is critical to the ongoing effort to combat terrorism by al Qaeda. The witnesses are [Redacted] al Qaeda operatives who have extensive knowledge concerning not just the September 11 attacks, but also other past attacks, future operations, and the structure, personnel, and tactics of al Qaeda. Their value as intelligence sources can hardly be overstated. And, we must defer to the Government's assertion that interruption [Redacted] of these witnesses will have devastating effects on the ability to gather information from them. [Redacted] it is not unreasonable to suppose that interruption [Redacted] could result in the loss of information that might prevent future terrorist attacks.

The Government also asserts that production of the witnesses would burden the Executive's ability to conduct foreign relations. The Government claims that if the Executive's assurances of confidentiality can be abrogated by the judiciary, the vital ability to obtain the cooperation of other governments will be devastated.

The Government also reminds us of the bolstering effect production of the witnesses might have on our enemies. *** In summary, the burdens that would arise from production of the enemy combatant witnesses are substantial.

*** [I]n order to assess Moussaoui's interest, we must determine whether the enemy combatant witnesses could provide testimony material to Moussaoui's defense.

In the CIPA context, *** a defendant becomes entitled to disclosure of classified information upon a showing that the information "is relevant and helpful to the defense ... or is essential to a fair determination of a cause."

Because Moussaoui has not had-and will not receive-direct access to any of the witnesses, he cannot be required to show materiality with the degree of specificity that applies in the ordinary case. Rather, it is sufficient if Moussaoui can make a "plausible showing" of materiality. However, in determining whether Moussaoui has made a plausible showing, we must bear in mind that Moussaoui *does* have access to the [Redacted] summaries. ***

The district court did not err in concluding that Witness A could offer material evidence on Moussaoui's behalf. [Redacted] Several statements by

Witness A tend to exculpate Moussaoui. [Redacted] to undermine the theory (which the Government may or may not intend to advance at trial) that Moussaoui was to pilot a fifth plane into the White House. [Redacted] This statement is significant in light of other evidence [Redacted] This is consistent with Moussaoui's claim that he was to be part of a post-September 11 operation. ***Witness B could provide material evidence on behalf of Moussaoui. [Redacted] Witness B [Redacted] has indicated that Moussaoui's operational knowledge was limited, a fact that is clearly of exculpatory value as to both guilt and penalty. [Redacted] Thus, of all three witnesses, Witness B is of the greatest exculpatory value. *** We agree with the district court that a jury might reasonably infer, from Witness C [Redacted] that Moussaoui was not involved in September 11. We therefore conclude that Moussaoui has made a plausible showing that Witness C would, if available, be a favorable witness. ***

*** [T]he Government has stated that it will not produce the enemy combatant witnesses for depositions (or, we presume, for any other purpose related to this litigation). We are thus left in the following situation: the district court has the power to order production of the enemy combatant witnesses and has properly determined that they could offer material testimony on Moussaoui's behalf, but the Government has refused to produce the witnesses. Under such circumstances, dismissal of the indictment is the usual course. Like the district court, however, we believe that a more measured approach is required. Additionally, we emphasize that no punitive sanction is warranted here because the Government has rightfully exercised its prerogative to protect national security interests by refusing to produce the witnesses.

Although ***this is not a CIPA case, that act nevertheless provides useful guidance in determining the nature of the remedies that may be available. Under CIPA, dismissal of an indictment is authorized only if the government has failed to produce an adequate substitute for the classified information, and the interests of justice would not be served by imposition of a lesser sanction. CIPA thus enjoins district courts to seek a solution that neither disadvantages the defendant nor penalizes the government (and the public) for protecting classified information that may be vital to national security.

A similar approach is appropriate here. Under such an approach, the first question is whether there is any appropriate substitution for the witnesses' testimony. Because we conclude, for the reasons set forth below, that appropriate substitutions are available, we need not consider any other remedy.

A. *Standard*

CIPA provides that the government may avoid the disclosure of classified information by proposing a substitute for the information, which the district court must accept if it "will provide the defendant with substantially the same ability to make his defense as would disclosure of the specific classified information." We believe that the standard set forth in CIPA adequately conveys the fundamental purpose of a substitution; to place the defendant, as nearly as possible, in the position he would be in if the classified information (here, the depositions of the witnesses) were available to him. Thus, a substitution is an appropriate remedy when it will not materially disadvantage the defendant.

B. *Substitutions proposed by the Government*

The Government proposed substitutions for the witnesses' deposition testimony in the form of a series of statements derived from the [Redacted] summaries. The district court rejected all proposed substitutions as inadequate. The ruling of the district court was based on its conclusions regarding the inherent inadequacy of the substitutions and its findings regarding the specific failings of the Government's proposals. For the reasons set forth below, we reject the ruling of the district court that any substitution for the witnesses' testimony would be inadequate. We agree, however, with the assessment that the particular proposals submitted by the Government are inadequate in their current form.

First, the district court deemed the substitutions inherently inadequate because the [Redacted] reports, from which the substitutions were ultimately derived, were unreliable. This was so, the court reasoned, because the witnesses' [Redacted] The district court also complained that it cannot be determined whether the [Redacted] reports accurately reflect the witnesses' statements [Redacted] The court further commented that the lack of quotation marks in the [Redacted] reports made it impossible to determine whether a given statement is a verbatim recording or [Redacted].

The conclusion of the district court that the proposed substitutions are inherently inadequate is tantamount to a declaration that there could be no adequate substitution for the witnesses' deposition testimony. We reject this conclusion. The answer to the concerns of the district court regarding the accuracy of the [Redacted] reports is that those who are [Redacted] the witnesses have a profound interest in obtaining accurate information from the witnesses and in reporting that information accurately to those who can use it to prevent acts of terrorism and to capture other al Qaeda operatives. These considerations provide sufficient indicia of reliability to alleviate the concerns of the district court.

Next, the district court noted that the substitutions do not indicate that they are summaries of statements made over the course of several months. We agree with the district court that in order to adequately protect Moussaoui's right to a fair trial, the jury must be made aware of certain information concerning the substitutions. The particular content of any instruction to the jury regarding the substitutions lies within the discretion of the district court. However, at the very least the jury should be informed that the substitutions are derived from reports [Redacted] of the witnesses. The instructions must account for the fact that members of the prosecution team have provided information and suggested [Redacted] The jury should also be instructed that the statements were obtained under circumstances that support a conclusion that the statements are reliable.

We reject the suggestion of the district court that the Government acted improperly in attempting to organize the information presented in the substitutions. Counsel rarely, if ever, present information to the jury in the order they received it during pretrial investigations. Indeed, organizing and distilling voluminous information for comprehensible presentation to a jury is a hallmark of effective advocacy. In short, while there may be problems with the *manner* in which the Government organized the substitutions, the fact that the Government has attempted such organization is not a mark against it.

The district court identified particular problems with the proposed substitutions for Witness A's testimony. For example, the court noted that the proposed substitutions failed to include exculpatory information provided by Witness A and incorporated at least one incriminatory inference not supplied by Witness A's statements.[Redacted] Our own review of the proposed substitutions for the testimony of Witnesses B and C reveals similar problems.[Redacted] These problems, however, may be remedied as described below.

C. *Instructions for the District Court*

1. *Submission of Questions by Moussaoui* The Government's submissions in response to the Petition make clear that members of the prosecution team, [Redacted] have had some input [Redacted] the enemy combatant witnesses. Our review of the circumstances of this access indicates that the input by the prosecution team into the [Redacted] process has worked no unfairness on Moussaoui. Nevertheless, in order to provide Moussaoui with the fullest possible range of information from the witnesses, we direct the district court to provide Moussaoui with an opportunity to [Redacted] for [Redacted] discretionary use [Redacted] of the witnesses.

2. *Substitutions* For the reasons set forth above, we conclude that the district court erred in ruling that any substitution for the witnesses' testimony is inherently inadequate to the extent it is derived from the [Redacted] reports. To the contrary, we hold that the [Redacted] summaries (which, as the district court determined, accurately recapitulate the [Redacted] reports) provide an adequate basis for the creation of written statements that may be submitted to the jury in lieu of the witnesses' deposition testimony.

The compiling of substitutions is a task best suited to the district court, given its greater familiarity with the facts of the case and its authority to manage the presentation of evidence. Nevertheless, we think it is appropriate to provide some guidance to the court and the parties.

First, the circumstances of this case-most notably, the fact that the substitutions may very well support Moussaoui's defense-dictate that the compiling of substitutions be an interactive process among the parties and the district court. Second, we think that accuracy and fairness are best achieved by compiling substitutions that use the exact language of the [Redacted] summaries to the greatest extent possible. We believe that the best means of achieving both of these objectives is for defense counsel to identify particular portions of the [Redacted] summaries that Moussaoui may want to admit into evidence at trial. The Government may then offer any objections and argue that additional portions must be included in the interest of completeness, as discussed below. If the substitutions are to be admitted at all (we leave open the possibility that Moussaoui may decide not to use the substitutions in his defense), they may be admitted only by Moussaoui. Based on defense counsel's submissions and the Government's objections, the district court could then compile an appropriate set of substitutions. We leave to the discretion of the district court the question of whether to rule on the admissibility of a particular substitution (*e.g.*, whether a substitution is relevant) at trial or during pre-trial proceedings.

As previously indicated, the jury must be provided with certain information regarding the substitutions. While we leave the particulars of the instructions to the district court, the jury must be informed, at a minimum, that the substitutions are what the witnesses would say if called to testify; that the substitutions are derived from statements obtained under conditions that provide circumstantial guarantees of reliability; that the substitutions contain statements obtained over the course of weeks or months; that members of the prosecution team have contributed to [Redacted] the witnesses; and, if applicable, that Moussaoui has [Redacted] to the witnesses.

a. *Rule of Completeness*

Moussaoui asserts that allowing the Government to argue that additional portions of the summaries must be included in the substitutions will result in substitutions " larded with inculpatory information under the guise of ' completeness.' " Petition at 12, in violation of the Confrontation Clause, *see Crawford v. Washington,* 541 U.S. 36 (2004). And, indeed, the Government has indicated its view that the rule of completeness would allow it to designate an inculpatory portion of a witness' statement to counter an exculpatory statement by the same witness designated by Moussaoui.

The common law " rule of completeness" is partially codified in Federal Rule of Evidence 106, which provides, " When a writing or recorded statement or part thereof is introduced by a party, an adverse party may require the introduction at that time of any other part or any other writing or recorded statement which ought in fairness to be considered contemporaneously with it." The purpose of Rule 106 is "to prevent a party from misleading the jury by allowing into the record relevant portions of [a writing or recorded statement] which clarify or explain the part already received." *United States v. Wilkerson,* 84 F.3d 692, 696 (4th Cir.1996). "The rule is protective, merely. It goes only so far as is necessary to shield a party from adverse inferences, and only allows an explanation or rebuttal of the evidence received." *** In short, we wish to make clear that the rule of completeness is not to be used by the Government as a means of seeking the admission of inculpatory statements that neither explain nor clarify the statements designated by Moussaoui. On the other hand, the defense's ability to propose substitutions based on the language of the [Redacted] summaries is not a license to mislead the jury.

b. *CIPA*

On rehearing, both parties acknowledged our holding that CIPA does not apply here but indicated their belief that once the district court has approved substitutions for the witnesses' testimony, CIPA comes into play, with the result that the Government may object to the disclosure of the classified information in the substitutions and request that the district court adopt an alternative form of evidence. We disagree.

It must be remembered that the substitution process we here order is a *replacement* for the testimony of the enemy combatant witnesses. Because the Government will not allow Moussaoui to have contact with the witnesses, we must provide a remedy adequate to protect Moussaoui's constitutional rights. Here, that remedy is substitutions. Once Moussaoui has selected the portions of the [Redacted] summaries he wishes to submit to the jury and the Government has been given an opportunity to be heard, the district court will compile the substitutions, using such additional language as may be necessary to aid the understanding of the jury. Once this process is complete, the matter is at an end-there are to be no additional or supplementary proceedings under CIPA regarding the substitutions. ***

WILLIAMS, Circuit Judge, concurring.

*** Moussaoui has a Sixth Amendment right to compulsory process of these witnesses because (1) under *Rasul,* the district court has the power to grant a testimonial writ directed to [Redacted] of these witnesses, and (2) Moussaoui has made a sufficient showing that the witnesses would provide material and favorable testimony based on the charges in the indictment. The Government, however, has refused to provide access to the witnesses. Although I am troubled by the lack of interactivity in the process that generated the substitutions, that lack of interactivity is compelled by the substantial national security concerns surrounding these witnesses. I feel that in light of those concerns, the fact that the substitutions will not materially disadvantage the defendant-because he will be permitted to introduce every favorable statement from the witnesses while the Government will be precluded from introducing any inculpatory statements-adequately protects his Sixth Amendment rights. Accordingly, I concur in [this part] of Chief Judge Wilkins's opinion.

GREGORY, Circuit Judge, concurring in part and dissenting in part.

*** The remedy proposed by the majority does not begin to vindicate Moussaoui's rights. Thus, it is in formulating the remedy for the Government's refusal to comply with the district Court's order that I must part ways with the majority.

The majority directs that the district court itself compile substitutions for the witnesses' potential testimony, using portions of the [Redacted] summaries designated by Moussaoui, subject to objection by the Government. The majority further instructs that only Moussaoui may admit into evidence, or elect not to admit, the substitutions, subject, of course, to the district Court's ruling on admissibility. While I appreciate that the majority's solution to the difficult problem of ensuring Moussaoui's rights is an effort to put him as nearly as possible in the place where he would be if he were able to examine the witnesses, I respectfully suggest that this solution places the district court in a thoroughly untenable position. Moreover, this solution is contrary to CIPA's expectation that the Government shall provide proposed substitutions for classified information, and it essentially places the district court in the position of being an advocate in the proceedings.

Additionally, as the majority recognizes, because " many rulings on admissibility-particularly those relating to relevance-can only be decided in the context of a trial, most of the witnesses' statements cannot meaningfully be assessed for admissibility at this time." Asking the district court to pick and choose from among the summaries to compile substitutions for Moussaoui's use before the Government's evidence is forecast is a risky proposition at best. The [Redacted] summaries paint a complete, if disjointed, picture of the statements made by the witnesses to date; if the summaries are to be used as a substitution for the witnesses' testimony, they should be used in their entirety, subject to the district Court's trial rulings on admissibility of any given passage to which either party objects, whether on hearsay grounds, as cumulative, as unduly prejudicial, or upon any other evidentiary basis.

Additionally, I disagree with the majority's decision to vacate the district Court's order striking the Government's death notice at this juncture. *** [I]f a defendant is guilty of an offense, but played a small part in it, the jury (or, in a bench trial, the judge) could find that he was not sufficiently culpable to warrant the imposition of the death penalty.

Moussaoui argues that the witnesses could offer testimony that would show he did not participate in an act that directly resulted in death: they would testify, he contends, that he did not have an active role in the planned September 11 attack, nor did he know of the plan and fail to disclose that knowledge to investigators, who might have been able to use that knowledge to prevent the attack, when he was taken into custody and questioned prior to the attack. Moussaoui's theory of the case, as we understand it, is that even though he is a member of al Qaeda who has pledged his allegiance to Osama bin Laden, and even though he was willing to engage in terrorist acts, and was indeed training to participate in terrorist acts, he was not involved in the terrorist acts that occurred on September 11, 2001, nor did he know of the plans before the attack took place. Instead, his participation was to involve later attacks, attacks that may or may not have been planned to occur in the United States or against this country's interests abroad. We cannot know to any degree of certainty whether the witnesses at issue would absolve Moussaoui of any responsibility for any part of the September 11 operation, or knowledge of the planned attack, nor do we know if a jury would find credible any such testimony. However, because the Government has exercised its right to preclude Moussaoui from examining the witnesses, and based on the [Redacted] summaries in the present record, we must assume for present purposes that they would so testify.

Even if Moussaoui is permitted to admit substitutions derived from the [Redacted] summaries, those substitutions cannot be considered a functional equivalent of live (or deposition) testimony, nor are they adequate or sufficient to substitute for testimony. Because the summaries are not responses to the questions that Moussaoui would ask if given the opportunity to depose the witnesses, and because the jury will not be able to see the witnesses and judge their credibility, use of the summaries will necessarily place severe limits on the evidence Moussaoui can present in his defense, particularly during the penalty phase of a capital proceeding. The ultimate question that must be resolved to determine whether Moussaoui is eligible for the death penalty is this: Did he participate in the September 11 attack, or know of the attack in advance? If Moussaoui cannot ask this question of the witnesses who have direct knowledge, he is undeniably and irretrievably handicapped in his ability to defend himself from a sentence of death. The Government may argue that no one, other than Moussaoui himself, has stated he was not involved. Moussaoui has no access to those who could exonerate him from death eligibility, and the jury will not have any evidence upon which to base a finding in this regard except, possibly, for Moussaoui's own testimony, which he is not obligated to provide. Moussaoui will not be able to offer the most relevant evidence with which he might be able to avoid the death penalty. ***

I cannot disagree with the majority's statement that " [b]ecause the Government will not allow Moussaoui to have contact with the witnesses, this court must provide a remedy adequate to protect Moussaoui's constitutional rights." However, the majority's effort to craft such a remedy rings hollow. The majority boldly states that " input by the prosecution team into the [Redacted] process has worked no unfairness on Moussaoui," but directs that, " to provide Moussaoui with the fullest possible range of information from the witnesses," the district court must permit Moussaoui to [Redacted]. To say this is a "remedy" must be of cold comfort to Moussaoui. Although he may propose [Redacted]. The entire process is cloaked in secrecy, making it difficult, if not impossible, for the courts to ensure the provision of Moussaoui's rights. Although the prosecution is laboring under the same constraints [Redacted] Moussaoui has constitutional rights, not extended to the prosecution, that are implicated by this procedure. Because the majority decrees that this so-called "remedy" will fulfill this Court's obligation to protect Moussaoui's constitutional rights, today justice has taken a long stride backward.

To leave open the possibility of a sentence of death given these constraints on Moussaoui's ability to defend himself would, in my view, subvert the well-established rule that a defendant cannot be sentenced to death if the jury is precluded from considering mitigating evidence pertaining to the Defendant's role in the offense. A sentence of death requires " a greater degree of reliability" than any lesser sentence.

Here, the reliability of a death sentence would be significantly impaired by the limitations on the evidence available for Moussaoui's use in proving mitigating factors (if he is found guilty). Although it has been repeated often enough to have the ring of cliche, death is different. It is the ultimate penalty, and once carried out, it is irrevocable. A sentence of death cannot be imposed unless the defendant has been accorded the opportunity to defend himself fully; it cannot be imposed without the utmost certainty, the fundamental belief in the fairness of the result. Because Moussaoui will not have access to the witnesses who could answer the question of his involvement, he should not face the ultimate penalty of death. Accordingly, I would uphold the district Court's sanction to the extent that it struck the Government's death notice. On this basis, I must dissent.

Notes

1. **"The defendant from hell."** That is a description given to Moussaoui, who disrupted the courtroom, yelled at the judge, fired his lawyers, and ultimately pleaded guilty, swearing allegiance to al Qaeda in open court while denying intending to commit mass murder. His management of the case got him life imprisonment. After all this was over, Moussaoui tried to then argue that he was not provided information relevant to his defense under CIPA. The Fourth Circuit said that, having pled guilty, Moussaoui was too late to then revisit CIPA processes.

2. **CIPA and its Limits**. The Court finds CIPA inapplicable. Why isn't it? If CIPA is inapplicable, why does the court dwell on CIPA? Shouldn't the job of fixing the balance between trial fairness and national security when witnesses are involved be left to Congress rather than courts? Is this decision what Justice Scalia in *Hamdi* called the "Mr. Fix-it Mentality"?

3. **Military and Deportation Options**. If, contrary to all odds, Moussaoui had been found not guilty, what should be done with him? Could he be taken into military custody (see *Padilla v. Hanft* and *al-Marri*)? Tried by a military commission? Deported? What country would take him?

4. **Comparative Law.** After 9/11, when it was discovered that much of the planning for the attacks of the U.S. was conducted in Hamburg, the German government charged two men, Mounir El Motassadeq and Abdelghani Mzoudi, with conspiracy in connection with the attacks. Both men had lived with Mohammed Atta and other 9/11 pilots and had visited Afghanistan to meet with Al Qaida leaders. The lower court in Germany convicted both men. However, Germany's conspiracy laws require that witnesses available to support the defense's case be made available or that the prosecution have proven its case "beyond all doubt." Because the U.S. government refused to allow the testimony of Al Qaida operative Ramsi Benalshib, who in the defense had requested testify to prove the assertion that Motassadeq and Mzoudi were not involved in the 9/11 plot, and the prosecution could not prove its case "beyond all doubt" the two men's convictions were overturned on appeal. The men were later convicted of a lesser charge of "belonging to a terrorist organization." How does the German law differ from the U.S. law presented in Moussaoui? Which seems more just? See C.J.M. Safferling, *German Responses to 9/11*, 4 J. INT'L CRIM. JUST. 1152 (2006).

5. **Valuable Witnesses?** About the witnesses that the Government refused to produce in *Moussaoui*, the Court said "Their value as intelligence sources can hardly be overstated. And, we must defer to the Government's assertion that interruption [Redacted] of these witnesses will have devastating effects on the ability to gather information from them." If this true, why has the Government

had so much trouble obtaining convictions of enemy combatants in Guantanamo? Is it possible that these witnesses have provided information that has prevented attacks in the U.S. since 9/11?

D. CRITIQUE OF CRIMINAL JUSTICE FOR TERRORISTS

I have excerpted below an article that is critical of the criminal justice system as a tool for dealing with international terrorists and a speech by a high-ranking lawyer in the Department of Justice which, with qualifications, endorses the use of that system. Read both pieces and be prepared to state and defend your views on this issue.

We Need a National Security Court
By Andrew C. McCarthy and Alykhan Velshi
For AEI Publication

***The Folly of Criminal Prosecution *** [T]he leader of al Qaeda has actually been under indictment in this country for eight years – *i.e.*, throughout an unprecedented and undeterred spree of savage attacks from the embassy bombings, through the Cole, and finally through 9/11 and its aftermath. ***[I]n the eight years between the WTC bombing and 9/11, the international ranks of militant Islam swelled, and its operatives successfully attacked U.S. interests numerous times, with steadily increasing audacity and effectiveness. *** [D]uring the eight-year period under consideration, the virtually exclusive U.S. response was criminal prosecution. This proved dismally inadequate, particularly from the perspective of American national security. The period resulted in less than ten major terrorism prosecutions. Even with the highest conceivable conviction rate of 100 percent, *less than three dozen terrorists* were neutralized – at a cost that was staggering and that continues to be paid, as several of these cases remain in appellate or habeas litigation.[22] [E]qually alarming from the standpoint of what may reasonably be expected from criminal prosecutions, the system could not have

---

[22] The WTC bombing resulted in three related prosecutions: the 1993-94 trial of the four originally captured bombers, the 1995 seditious conspiracy case against Sheik Omar Abdel Rahman and eleven others, and a 1997 trial of Ramzi Yousef and another former fugitive. The Manila Air plot resulted in a 1996 trial of Ramzi Yousef and two others. Only six of the numerous defendants indicted in connection with the embassy bombings have appeared in the U.S. after arrest and/or extradition; of these, one pled guilty, four were convicted at trial, and one, Mamdouh Mahmud Salim (a/k/a Abu Hajer al Iraqi) – who was the most important terrorist charged given his high rank in al Qaeda – was severed after a barbaric escape attempt in 2000, during which he plunged several inches of a shiv through the eye of a prison guard, nearly killing him. He was later convicted of this attempted murder, but whether he will ever be tried for the embassy bombings is unknown. The Millennium plot resulted in the convictions of three terrorists. The attacks on the *Cole* and on Khobar Towers finally resulted in indictments – each many years after the fact (and the *Cole* long after 9/11) – but no American prosecutions. One defendant, Zacarias Moussaoui, was convicted in the U.S. for participation in the 9/11 plot. His trial and sentencing (to life imprisonment after the jury could not agree on the death penalty) took nearly five years to complete due to interminable delays over discovery issues (of the type we shall address shortly), and, in fact, might still be unresolved today but for the fact that he elected to plead guilty (and bray about his anti-American terrorism) rather than put the government to what promised to be a lengthy, complex trial.

tolerated many more terrorism cases.[23] ***

Essentially, we have shifted what are national-security (as opposed to police) functions from the ambit in which executive discretion to respond to threats is necessarily broad to the ambit in which executive action is heavily regulated and the federal courts, by performing their ordinary functions, actually empower our enemies. *** [G]overnment seeks to discipline an errant member of the body politic who has allegedly violated its rules. That member, who may be a citizen, an immigrant with lawful status, or even, in certain situations, an illegal alien, is vested with rights and protections under the U.S. constitution. Courts are imposed as a bulwark against suspect executive action; presumptions exist in favor of privacy and innocence; and defendants and other subjects of investigation enjoy the assistance of counsel, whose basic job is to put the government to maximum effort if it is to learn information and obtain convictions. The line drawn here is that it is preferable for the government to fail than for an innocent person to be wrongly convicted or otherwise deprived of his rights.

Not so in the realm of national security. There, government confronts a host of sovereign states and sub-national entities (particularly international terrorist organizations) claiming the right to use force. Here the executive is not enforcing American law against a suspected criminal but exercising national defense powers to protect the nation against external threats. Foreign hostile operatives acting from without and within are generally not vested with rights under the American constitution – and treating them as if they were can have disastrous consequences.[24] The galvanizing concern in the

---

[23] Most of the trials alluded to in the preceding note took many months to complete (*e.g.,* the blind sheik case took nine months, the embassy bombing and the first WTC trial took seven months), often at the conclusion of, literally, *years* of pretrial discovery and court proceedings. Typically, the appeals also take years to complete. (*E.g.,* the embassy bombing trial, completed over six years ago, is still on direct appeal, no doubt with years of habeas challenges ahead assuming the convictions are upheld.) Moreover, even assuming *arguendo,* and against all indications, that there were appreciably more than three dozen terrorists (a) who could practically have been captured and rendered to the U.S. for trial; (b) as to whom evidence existed that could have been used without irresponsibly compromising national security; and (c) as to whom such evidence would have been sufficient to satisfy the demanding proof hurdles for prosecution; there would of course remain the problem of securing courthouses, jail facilities, and trial participants throughout the United States.

[24] The discovery issues are addressed below. The problem of letting the guilty terrorist (as opposed to, say, the guilty tax cheat) go free because of insufficient evidence is obvious. One other example is noteworthy. In 2000, a superb district judge in New York, the Hon. Leonard B. Sand, came extremely close to suppressing the confession of Mohammed Daoud al-`Owhali, the bomber of the U.S. embassy in Nairobi responsible for well over 200 murders and untold other injuries and damage. In originally ordering the confession excluded, Judge Sand ruled that although al-`Owhali's admissions had been voluntary, federal agents had failed to give al-`Owhali *Miranda* warnings. In truth, al-`Owhali had no rights under the U.S. Constitution. He was a Saudi (pretending at the time to be a Yemeni) who was in the custody not of the U.S. but of Kenya (which does not follow *Miranda* or, for example, guarantee counsel at public expense during custodial interrogation), and whose only contact with the U.S. was to bomb our embassy. He had never set foot in this country or made application of any kind under the immigration laws. Even if one were, not unreasonably, to conclude that American agents minimally owe due process when they act overseas, this would mean only that they owed the process that is due under the circumstances that obtain. Moreover, it is clear that the American presence actually afforded al-`Ohwali *more* protections than he would have had if only the Kenyan authorities had

national security realm is to defeat the enemy, and ***"preserve the very foundation of all our civil liberties." The line drawn here is that government cannot be permitted to fail. ***

[P]rosecution in the justice system actually increases the threat because of what it conveys to our enemies. Nothing galvanizes an opposition, nothing spurs its recruiting, like the combination of successful attacks and a conceit that the adversary will react weakly. *** For militants willing to immolate themselves in suicide-bombing and hijacking operations, mere prosecution is a provocatively weak response. Put succinctly, where they are the sole or principal response to terrorism, trials in the criminal justice system inevitably cause more terrorism: they leave too many militants in place and they encourage the notion that the nation may be attacked with relative impunity.

*** Under discovery rules, the government is required to provide to accused persons, among many other things, any information in its possession that can be deemed "material to preparing the defense." Moreover, under current construction of the *Brady* doctrine, the prosecution must disclose any information that is even arguably material and exculpatory, and, in capital cases, any information that might induce the jury to vote against a death sentence, whether it is exculpatory or not (imagine, for example, the government is in possession of reports by vital, deep-cover informants explaining that a defendant committed a terrorist act but was a hapless pawn in the chain-of-command). The more broadly indictments are drawn, the more revelation of precious intelligence due process demands – and, for obvious reasons, terrorism indictments tend to be among the broadest.[25] The government must also disclose all prior statements made by witnesses it calls, and, often, statements of even witnesses it does not call. ***

It is freely conceded that this trove of government intelligence is routinely surrendered along with appropriate judicial warnings: defendants may use it only in preparing for trial, and may not disseminate it for other purposes. To the extent classified information is implicated, it is also

---

been interested in him. (Here, it is worth pausing to note that he killed many more Kenyans than Americans.) But Judge Sand initially concluded that al-'Owhali had a Fifth Amendment privilege against self-incrimination and thus *** that this privilege included a right to compliance with *Miranda*, which was utterly unrealistic in Kenya. The judge ultimately reversed himself and permitted the confession to be admitted – albeit in an opinion that dangerously assumes foreign alien combatants have rights under the Fifth Amendment. *** Without the confession, al-'Owhali would almost certainly have been acquitted.

[25] A terrorist who is acquitted due to insufficient evidence is not a person who will simply return to the commission of crimes; he is a danger to return to acts of war and indiscriminate mass homicide. The incentive for the Justice Department is thus to use every appropriate means to ensure conviction. One of the most appropriate is to present elaborate proof of the dangerousness of the terrorist enterprise of which the defendant is an operative. This approach has the dual benefit of placing acts in their chilling context while expanding the scope of evidentiary admissibility (particularly by resort to liberal rules for the admission of co-conspirator statements under Rule 801(d)(2)(E) and background evidence). While focus on the enterprise greatly enhances the prospects for conviction, however, it exponentially expands the universe of what may be discoverable.

theoretically subject to the constraints of the Classified Information Procedures Act. Nevertheless, and palpably, people who commit mass murder, who face the death penalty or life imprisonment, and who are devoted members of a movement whose animating purpose is to damage the United States, are certain to be relatively unconcerned about violating court orders (or, for that matter, about being hauled into court at all). Our congenial rules of access to attorneys, paralegals, investigators and visitors make it a very simple matter for accused terrorists to transmit what they learn in discovery to their confederates – and we know that they do so.[26] ***

As illustrated by the recent investigations conducted by Congress, the Silberman/Robb Commission, and the 9/11 Commission regarding pre-9/11 intelligence failures, the United States relies heavily on cooperation from foreign intelligence services, particularly in areas of the world from which threats to American interests are known to stem and where our own human intelligence resources have been inadequate. It is vital that we keep that pipeline flowing. Clearly, however, foreign intelligence services (understandably, much like our own CIA) will necessarily be reluctant to share information with our country if they have good reason to believe that information will be revealed under the generous discovery laws that apply in U.S. criminal proceedings.***

Islamic militants are significantly different both in make-up and goals from run-of-the-mill citizens and immigrants accused of crimes. They are not in it for the money; they desire neither to beat nor cheat the system, but rather to subvert and overthrow it; and they are not about getting an edge in the here and now – their aspirations, however grandiose they may seem to us, are universalist and eternal, such that the pursuit is, for the terrorist, more vital than living to see them attained. They are a formidable foe, and, as noted above, the national security imperatives they present are simply absent from the overwhelming run of criminal cases.

As a result, when we bring them into our criminal justice system, we have to cut corners – and hope that no one, least of all ourselves, will discern that with the corners we are cutting important principles. Innocence is not so readily presumed when juries, often having been screened for their attitudes about the death penalty, see intense courtroom security around palpably incarcerated defendants and other endangered trial participants. The legally required showing of cause for a search warrant is apt to be loosely construed

---

[26] A single example here is instructive. In 1995, just before trying the aforementioned seditious conspiracy case against the blind sheik and eleven others, one of the authors duly complied with Second Circuit discovery law by writing a letter to defense counsel listing 200 names of people and entities who might be alleged as unindicted co-conspirators – *i.e.*, people who were on the government's radar screen but whom there was insufficient evidence to charge. Six years later, that letter became evidence in the trial of those who had bombed our embassies in Africa. Within a short time of its being sent, the letter had found its way to Bin Laden in Sudan. It had been fetched for him by al-Qaeda operative Ali Mohammed who, upon obtaining it from one of his associates, forwarded it to al Qaeda operative Wadih El Hage in Kenya for subsequent transmission to bin Laden. Mohammed and El Hage were both convicted in the embassy bombing case. (*See* excerpts from Mohammed's guilty plea allocution made available by the State Department at http://usinfo.state.gov/is/Archive_Index/Ali_Mohamed.html.)

when agents, prosecutors, and judges know denial of the warrant may mean a massive bombing plot is allowed to proceed. For reasons already elaborated on, key government intelligence that is relevant and potentially helpful to the defense – the kind of probative information that would unquestionably be disclosed in a normal criminal case – may be redacted, diluted, or outright denied to a terrorist's counsel, for to disseminate it, especially in wartime, is to educate the enemy at the cost of civilian and military lives.

Since we obdurately declare we are according alleged terrorists the same quality of justice that we would give to the alleged tax cheat, we necessarily cannot carry all of this off without ratcheting down justice for the tax cheat – and everyone else accused of crime. Civilian justice is a contained, zero-sum arrangement. Principles and precedents we create in terrorism cases generally get applied across the board. This, ineluctably, effects a diminution in the rights and remedies of the vast majority of defendants – for the most part, American citizens who in our system are liberally afforded those benefits precisely because we presume them innocent. ***

Worse still, this state of affairs incongruously redounds to the benefit of the terrorist. Initially, this is because his central aim is to undermine our system, so in a very concrete way he succeeds whenever justice is diminished. Later, as government countermeasures come to appear more oppressive, it is because civil society comes increasingly to blame the government rather than the terrorists. In fact, the terrorists – the lightening rod for all of this – come perversely to be portrayed, and to some extent perceived, as symbols of embattled liberal principles, the very ones it is their utopian mission to eradicate. The ill-informed and sometimes malignant campaigns against the Patriot Act and the NSA's terrorist surveillance program are examples of this phenomenon.

In sum, trials in the criminal justice system don't work for terrorism. They work for terrorists.

Assistant Attorney General David Kris
Speaks at the Brookings Institution
Washington, D.C. ~ Friday, June 11, 2010

We often hear that before September 11, the United States took a "law enforcement approach" to counterterrorism. There is some truth in that, but I think it oversimplifies things. In fact, the 9/11 Commission found that before September 11, "the CIA was plainly the lead agency confronting al Qaeda"; law enforcement played a "secondary" role; and military and diplomatic efforts were "episodic." I was involved in national security before September 11, and that seems about right to me.

After September 11, of course, all of our national security agencies ramped up their counterterrorism activities: as our troops deployed to foreign battlefields and the Intelligence Community expanded its operations, the Department of Justice (DOJ) and the FBI also evolved. We began with an important legal change, tearing down the so-called "FISA wall," under which law enforcement and intelligence were largely separate enterprises and law enforcement was correspondingly limited as a counterterrorism tool. *** I think this legal change reflected, and also reinforced, the conclusion that law enforcement helps protect national security. Not that law enforcement is the only way to protect national security, or even that it's the best way. But I do think we came to a national consensus, in the years immediately after 9/11, that law enforcement is one important way of protecting national security.

This consensus led to significant structural changes at DOJ and the FBI. The Bureau integrated intelligence and law enforcement functions with respect to counterterrorism, and dramatically increased its resources and focus on intelligence collection and analysis. The FBI has long been the Intelligence Community element with primary responsibility for collecting and coordinating intelligence about terrorist threats in the United States, and since 9/11 it has made this mission its highest priority. It also led Congress to strengthen our counter-terrorism criminal laws and to create NSD, which combines terrorism and espionage prosecutors with intelligence lawyers and other intelligence professionals. *** [T]here are some who say that law enforcement can't – or shouldn't – be used for counterterrorism. They appear to believe that we should treat all terrorists exclusively as targets for other parts of the Intelligence Community or the Defense Department.

*** In my view*** it's not that law enforcement is *always* the right tool for combating terrorism. But it's also not the case that it's *never* the right tool. The reality, I think, is that it's *sometimes* the right tool. *** And that leads me to this question: as compared to the viable alternatives, what is the value of law enforcement in this war? Does it in fact help us win? Or is it categorically the wrong tool for the job – at best a distraction, and at worst an affirmative impediment?

I think law enforcement helps us win this war. And I want to make clear, for the limited purpose of today's remarks and in light of the nature of our current national debate, that this is not primarily a values-based argument. That is, I am not saying law enforcement helps us win in the sense that it is a shining city on a hill that captures hearts and minds around the world (although I do think our criminal justice system is widely respected). Values are critically important, both in themselves and in their effect on us, our allies, and our adversaries, but I am talking now about something more direct and concrete.

When I say that law enforcement helps us win this war, I mean that it helps us disrupt, defeat, dismantle and destroy our adversaries (without destroying ourselves or our way of life in the process). In particular, law enforcement helps us in at least three ways – it can *disrupt* terrorist plots through arrests, *incapacitate* terrorists through incarceration resulting from prosecution, and gather *intelligence* from interrogation and recruitment of terrorists or their supporters via cooperation agreements.

Here's some of the evidence for that argument. Between September 2001 and March 2010, DOJ convicted more than 400 defendants in terrorism-related cases. Some of these convictions involve per se terrorism offenses, while others do not – Al Capone was convicted of tax fraud rather than racketeering, but that doesn't make him any less of a gangster. Of course we have Najibullah Zazi and David Headley, both of whom have pleaded guilty and are awaiting sentencing, and now Faisal Shahzad, but there have been many others over the years, ranging from Ramzi Yousef (the first World Trade center bomber) to the East Africa Embassy bombers, to Richard Reid, to Ahmed Omar Abu Ali, all of whom are now serving life sentences in federal prison. Just in the past year, among others, Wesam al-Delaema was sentenced to 25 years for planting IEDs in Iraq, Syed Harris and Ehsanul Sadequee were sentenced to 13 and 17 years for providing material support to al Qaeda, and Oussama Kassir was sentenced to life in prison for attempting to establish a jihad training camp in the United States. Last year we also arrested two individuals in separate undercover operations after they allegedly tried to blow up buildings in Dallas, Texas and Springfield, Illinois. And there are many others.

Not all of these cases make the headlines and not all of the defendants we've convicted were hard-core terrorists or key terrorist operatives. As in organized crime or traditional intelligence investigations, aggressive and wide-ranging counter-terrorism efforts may net a lot of smaller fish along with the big fish. That may mean we are disrupting plots before they're consummated, and it may give us a chance to deter or recruit the smaller fish before they're fully radicalized.

We've also used the criminal justice system to collect valuable intelligence. *** The fact is that when the government has a strong prosecution case, the defendant knows he will spend a long time in prison, and this creates powerful incentives for him to cooperate with us.

There's a limit to what I can say publicly, of course, but I can say that terrorism suspects in the criminal justice system have provided information on all of the following:

- telephone numbers and e-mail addresses used by al Qaeda;
- al Qaeda recruiting techniques, finances, and geographical reach;
- terrorist tradecraft used to avoid detection in the West;
- their experiences at and the location of al Qaeda training camps;
- al Qaeda weapons programs and explosives training;
- the location of al Qaeda safehouses (including drawing maps);

- residential locations of senior al Qaeda figures;

- al Qaeda communications methods and security protocols;

- identification of operatives involved in past and planned attacks; and

- information about plots to attack U.S. targets.

The Intelligence Community, including the National Counterterrorism Center (NCTC), believes that the criminal justice system has provided useful information. ***

Having explained the basic affirmative case for law enforcement as a counter-terrorism tool, let me address some of the arguments on the other side. The first argument is that there's an inherent tension between national security and law enforcement. I think this argument confuses ends with means. The criminal justice system is a tool – one of several – for promoting national security, for protecting our country against terrorism. Sometimes it's the right tool; sometimes it's the wrong tool. That is no different than saying sometimes the best way to protect national security is through diplomacy, and sometimes it's through military action.

Another argument is that the criminal justice system is fundamentally incompatible with national security because it is focused on Defendants' rights. But this argument suffers from two basic flaws. First, the criminal justice system is not focused solely on Defendants' rights – it strikes a balance between Defendants' rights and the interests of government, victims, and society. And whatever the balance that has been struck, the empirical fact is that when we prosecute terrorists we convict them around 90% of the time. To be sure, the criminal justice system has its limits, and in part because of those limits it is not always the right tool for the job. But when the Executive Branch concludes that it is the right tool – as it has more than 400 times since September 11 – we in fact put steel on target almost every time.

The second flaw in the "undamental incompatibility" argument is equally significant. The criminal justice system is not alone in facing legal constraints; all of the U.S. Government's activities must operate under the rule of law. For example, the U.S. military operates under rules that require it to forego strikes against terrorists if they will inflict disproportionate harm on civilians. (It also has rules governing who may be detained, how detainees have to be treated, and how long they can be held.) These limits are real, and they are not trivial, but no one thinks they're a reason to abandon or forbid the use of military force against al Qaeda. (By the way, the point of this argument is not to equate the legal constraints in the two systems; they are in fact very different. The point is only to emphasize that all of our counterterrorism tools have legal limits – this is the price of living under the rule of law – and those limits inform judgments about which tool is best in any given case.)

Ultimately, the worth of the criminal justice system is a relative thing. In other words, its value as a counterterrorism tool must be compared to the value of other tools. Comparing the criminal justice system to the use of military force or diplomacy is difficult, because it shares so little in common with them. But as a tool for disrupting and incapacitating terrorists, and gathering intelligence, the criminal justice system is readily comparable with two others – detention under the law of war, and prosecution in a military commission. So I will turn to that comparison now.

Before I focus on the differences between these systems, however, I want to acknowledge the similarities of the two prosecution systems. Whether you're in civilian court or a military commission, there is the presumption of innocence; a requirement of proof beyond a reasonable doubt; the right to an impartial decision-maker; similar processes for selecting members of the jury or commission; the right to counsel and choice of counsel; the right to qualified self-representation; the right to be present during proceedings; the right against self-incrimination; the right to present evidence, cross-examine the Government's witnesses, and compel attendance of witnesses; the right to exclude prejudicial evidence; the right to exculpatory evidence; protections against double jeopardy; protections against ex post facto laws; and the right to an appeal. Both systems afford the basic rights most Americans associate with a fair trial.

As to the differences, an exhaustive comparison would require a longer discussion, but I have identified five relative advantages of our military authorities and five of the civilian system, viewed solely from the perspective of the government and their effectiveness in combating terrorism. I need to emphasize, however, that this is not nearly as detailed a comparison as you would need to make informed policy or operational judgments. The comparisons that really matter are far more granular and nuanced than anything that I can offer in this setting. Also, the extent and significance of the differences between the systems often turn on the facts of a particular case. There is no substitute for immersion in the details.

With those important caveats, here are five general advantages that using military authorities rather than civilian prosecution may offer to the government, depending on the facts:

1. Proof Requirements. In military commissions, the burden of proof is the same as in civilian court – beyond a reasonable doubt – but in non-capital cases only two-thirds of the jurors (rather than all of them) are needed for conviction. Under the law of war, if it's tested through a habeas corpus petition, the government need only persuade the judge by a preponderance of the evidence that the petitioner is part of al Qaeda or affiliated forces, though that is not always easy, as our track record in the Guantanamo cases has shown.

2. *Admissibility of Confessions.* In a military commission, unlike in federal court, *Miranda* warnings are not required to use the Defendant's custodial statements against him. While the voluntariness test generally applies in the commissions as it does in federal court, there's an exception in the commissions for statements taken at the point of capture on or near a battlefield. For law of war detention, the test is reliability, which may in practical effect be pretty similar to a basic voluntariness requirement.

3. *Closing the Courtroom.* While both federal trials and commission proceedings are generally open proceedings, compared to federal court, there may be some increased ability to close the courtroom in a military commission, and certain military commission trials have implemented a 45-second delay of the broadcast of statements to permit classified information to be blocked before it is aired in certain cases. There certainly is a greater ability to close the courtroom in a habeas corpus proceeding, and – unlike both military commission and civilian trials – the petitioner is not required to be present, which can help in dealing with classified information.

4. *Admissibility of Hearsay.* The hearsay rules are somewhat more relaxed in military commissions than in federal prosecutions, and they are significantly more relaxed in habeas proceedings. This can be good for the government in some cases, particularly in protecting sensitive sources, but it can also help the defendant/petitioner in some cases. In the *Hamdan* case, for example, Hamdan used the hearsay rules more than the government did.

5. *Classified Evidence.* The rules governing protection of classified information are very similar in the two prosecution forums – indeed, the military commission rules were modeled on the federal court rules. But the rules may be somewhat better in military commissions because they codify some of the federal case law and adopt lessons learned from litigating classified information issues in federal court. I would say the classified information rules in habeas proceedings over law of war detention are both more flexible and less certain.

Those are, in my view, the five main advantages that the government might enjoy in using military rather than civilian authorities. Now, here are the five main advantages of using federal courts rather than military commissions or law of war detention, subject to the same caveats as above:

1. *Certainty and Finality.* The rules governing civilian prosecutions are more certain and well-established than those in the other two systems. This can speed the process, reduce litigation risk, promote cooperation and guilty pleas, and result in reliable long-term incapacitation. This is a very significant factor for now, but it will hopefully recede over time as we gain more experience in the commissions.

2. *Scope.* The civilian criminal justice system is much broader than the other two – it has far more crimes (covering everything from terrorism to tax evasion), and applies to everyone. Military commissions are not available for U.S. citizens – folks like Anwar Awlaki and Faisal Shahzad – and neither commissions nor law of war detention apply to terrorists not related to al Qaeda or the Taliban: groups like Hamas, Hizbollah, or the FARC are out of bounds, as are lone wolf terrorists who may be inspired by al Qaeda but are not part of it (like the two individuals I mentioned who allegedly tried to blow up buildings in Illinois and Texas last year).

3.   Incentives for Cooperation. The criminal justice system has more reliable and more extensive mechanisms to encourage cooperation. While the military commissions have borrowed a plea and sentencing agreement mechanism from the courts-martial system which could be used for cooperation – Rule 705 – this system has not yet been tested in military commissions and its effectiveness is as yet unclear. In law of war detention, interrogators can offer detainees improvements in their conditions of confinement, but there is no "sentence" over which to negotiate, and no judge to enforce an agreement. Detainees may have little incentive to provide information in those circumstances. On the other hand, in some circumstances law of war detainees may lawfully be held in conditions that many believe are helpful to effective interrogation.

4. Sentencing. In federal court, judges impose sentences based in large part on tough sentencing guidelines, while sentencing in the military commissions is basically done by the jury without any guidelines. What little experience we have with the commissions suggests that sentencing in that forum is less predictable – two of the three commission defendants convicted thus far (including Osama bin Laden's driver) received sentences of 5-6 years, with credit for time served, and were released within months of sentencing. Under the law of war, of course, there is no sentence; if their detention is lawful, detainees may be held until the end of the conflict. But the Supreme Court has warned that if the circumstances of the current conflict "are entirely unlike those of the conflicts that informed the development of the law of war," the authority to detain "may unravel." As circumstances change, or if active combat operations are concluded, it is not clear how long the detention authority will endure.

Without going into too much detail, I should also say that there may be some advantages to bringing a capital case in federal court rather than in a military commission, in light of the different rules. The military commissions, for example, may not permit a capital sentence to be imposed following a guilty plea, at least for now.

5.   International Cooperation. Finally, the criminal justice system may help us obtain important cooperation from other countries. Unfortunately, some countries won't provide us with evidence we may need to hold suspected terrorists in law of war detention or prosecute them in military commissions. In some cases, they have agreed to extradite terrorist suspects to us only on the condition that they not be tried in military commissions. In such cases, use of federal courts may mean the difference between holding a terrorist and having him go free. This is not, of course, a plea to subject our counterterrorism efforts to some kind of global test of legitimacy; it is simply a hardheaded, pragmatic recognition that in some cases, where we need help from abroad, we will have to rely on law enforcement rather than military detention or prosecution.

To conclude, I think we cannot and should not immunize terrorists from prosecution any more than we should immunize them from the use of military strikes or our other counterterrorism tools. *** Having said that, we do need to educate ourselves about all of the tools in the President's national security toolbox. *** We also need to consider improving and sharpening our tools. *** We want to work with Congress to see if we can develop something that could help us, give us some more flexibility and clarity, in these narrow circumstances involving operational terrorists. The goal, always, is to promote and protect national security, and this may be one way to help do that.

IX

MILITARY COMMISSION TRIAL OF ALLEGED TERRORISTS

An important incident to the conduct of war is the adoption of measures by the military command not only to repel and defeat the enemy, but to seize and subject to disciplinary measures those enemies who in their attempt to thwart or impede our military effort have violated the law of war. It is unnecessary for present purposes to determine to what extent the President as Commander in Chief has constitutional power to create military commissions without the support of Congressional legislation. For here Congress has authorized trial of offenses against the law of war before such commissions. We are concerned only with the question whether it is within the constitutional power of the national government to place petitioners upon trial before a military commission for the offenses with which they are charged. We must therefore first inquire whether any of the acts charged is an offense against the law of war cognizable before a military tribunal, and if so whether the Constitution prohibits the trial.

CHIEF JUSTICE STONE, *Ex Parte Quirin*,
317 U.S. 1 (1942)

Trial by military commission is not new. In *Hamdan v. Rumsfeld*, infra, the Supreme Court noted that use of military commissions began "as such" in the United States in 1847 as a product of military necessity and limited jurisdiction of the court martial system, which was restricted "almost exclusively to members of the military force and to certain specific offences." More recently, such commissions were used in World War II.

Military commissions in the "War on Terror" have been controversial, for varying reasons. First, the conflict lacks some characteristics of earlier wars: it is not waged against a nation state, there has not been a formal declaration of war by Congress, and the war lacks a defined endpoint in the absence of an entity that could surrender. Second, some countries aligned with the United States in fighting in the conflicts in Iraq and Afghanistan do not use such commissions and some are opposed to them. Third, congressional authorization for commissions was shaky until recently. Fourth, the exigencies of field military commissions in earlier wars do not exist with respect to detainees held far from "thearers" of war. Fourth, the range of offenses that may be tried before commissions is broader than traditional war crimes. Fifth, only aliens are subject to military commission trials, while comparably-situated civilians are not. Sixth, evidence rules are relaxed in military commissions compared to civilian courts.

This chapter will examine in depth the legal foundations of military commissions (Part A), their jurisdiction (Part B), and their rules for operation (Part C). Part D will explore proposals for national security courts as a hybrid alternative to both civilian trials and military commissions.

A. LEGAL FOUNDATIONS

Shortly after the September 11, 2001 attacks on the World Trade Center and the Pentagon, President Bush said the United States was at "war." On September 18, 2001, Congress passed a Joint Resolution (the Authorization for Use of Military Force or AUMF) authorizing the President to use "all necessary and appropriate force against those nations, organizations, or persons he determines planned, authorized, committed, or aided the terrorist attacks" or "harbored such organizations or persons." Congress subsequently appropriated funds to conduct military actions in Afghanistan, to build a new detention facility at Guantanamo Bay, Cuba, and for other purposes. Other nations were enlisted to assist in tracking down terrorists, freezing their assets, and disrupting their plans. On November 13, 2001, President Bush issued the following military order, entitled "Detention, Treatment, and Trial of Certain Non-Citizens in the War Against Terrorism:"

> § 1 *** (e) To protect the United States and its citizens, and for the effective conduct of military operations and prevention of terrorist attacks, it is necessary for individuals subject to this order *** to be detained, and, when tried, to be tried for violations of the laws of war and other applicable laws by military tribunals. ***
>
> § 2 *** (a) The term "individual subject to this order" shall mean any individual who is not a United States citizen. ***
>
> § 4 *** (a) Any individual subject to this order shall, when tried, be tried by military commission for any and all offenses triable by military commission *** (c) [Such trials] shall at a minimum provide for *** (2) a full and fair trial, with the military commission sitting as the triers of both fact and law; (3) admission of such evidence as would *** have probative value to a reasonable person; *** (6) conviction only upon the concurrence of two-thirds of the members of the commission. ***
>
> § 7 *** (b) With respect to any individual subject to this order—(1) military tribunals shall have exclusive jurisdiction with respect to offenses by the individual ***

*****

President Bush's order was premised on a Civil War era Supreme Court decision and an order issued by President Roosevelt early in World War II authorizing military commission trial for eight German saboteurs, two of whom were American citizens. Excerpts from the Supreme Court decisions regarding both uses of military commissions follow.

Ex Parte MILLIGAN
71 U.S. 2 (1866)

*** On the 10th day of May, 1865, Lambdin P. Milligan presented a petition *** to be discharged from an alleged unlawful imprisonment. The case made by the petition is this: Milligan is a citizen of the United States; has lived for twenty years in Indiana; and, at the time of the grievances complained of, was not, and never had been in the military or naval service of the United States. On the 5th day of October, 1864, while at home, he was arrested by order of General Alvin P. Hovey, commanding the military district of Indiana; and has ever since been kept in close confinement. ***[H]e was brought before a military commission, convened at Indianapolis, by order of General Hovey, tried on certain charges and specifications; found guilty, and sentenced to be hanged ***.

Milligan insists that said military commission had no jurisdiction to try him *** because he was a citizen of the United States and the State of Indiana, and had not been, since the commencement of the late Rebellion, a resident of any of the States whose citizens were arrayed against the government, and that the right of trial by jury was guaranteed to him by the Constitution of the United States. *** During the late wicked Rebellion, the temper of the times did not allow that calmness in deliberation and discussion so necessary to a correct conclusion of a purely judicial question. Then, considerations of safety were mingled with the exercise of power; and feelings and interests prevailed which are happily terminated. Now that the public safety is assured, this question, as well as all others, can be discussed and decided without passion or the admixture of any element not required to form a legal judgment.

***The controlling question in the case is this: Upon the facts stated in Milligan's petition, and the exhibits filed, had the military commission mentioned in it jurisdiction, legally, to try and sentence him? *** No graver question was ever considered by this court, nor one which more nearly concerns the rights of the whole people; for it is the birthright of every American citizen when charged with crime, to be tried and punished according to law. *** By the protection of the law human rights are secured; withdraw that protection, and they are at the mercy of wicked rulers, or the clamor of an excited people. If there was law to justify this military trial, it is not our province to interfere; if there was not, it is our duty to declare the nullity of the whole proceedings. *** Have any of the rights guaranteed by the Constitution been violated in the case of Milligan? And if so, what are they?

Every trial involves the exercise of judicial power; and from what source did not military commission that tried him derive their authority? Certainly no part of judicial power of the country was conferred on them; because the Constitution expressly vests it 'in one supreme court and such inferior courts as the Congress may from time to time ordain and establish,' and it is not pretended that the commission was a court ordained and established by Congress. They cannot justify on the mandate of the President; because he is controlled by law, and has his appropriate sphere of duty, which is to execute, not to make, the laws; and there is 'no unwritten criminal code to which resort can be had as a source of jurisdiction.'

But it is said that the jurisdiction is complete under the 'laws and usages of war.' It can serve no useful purpose to inquire what those laws and usages are, whence they originated, where found, and on whom they operate; they can never be applied to citizens in states which have upheld the authority of the government, and where the courts are open and their process unobstructed. This court has judicial knowledge that in Indiana the Federal authority was always unopposed, and its courts always open to hear criminal accusations and redress grievances; and no usage of war could sanction a military trial there for any offence whatever of a citizen in civil life, in nowise connected with the military service. Congress could grant no such power; and to the honor of our national legislature be it said, it has never been provoked by the state of the country even to attempt its exercise. One of the plainest constitutional provisions was, therefore, infringed when Milligan was tried by a court not ordained and established by Congress, and not composed of judges appointed during good behavior.

Why was he not delivered to the Circuit Court of Indiana to be proceeded against according to law? No reason of necessity could be urged against it ***. The government had no right to conclude that Milligan, if guilty, would not receive in that court merited punishment; for its records disclose that it was constantly engaged in the trial of similar offences, and was never interrupted in its administration of criminal justice. If it was dangerous, in the distracted condition of affairs, to leave Milligan unrestrained of his liberty, because he 'conspired against the government, afforded aid and comfort to rebels, and incited the people to insurrection,' the law said arrest him, confine him closely, render him powerless to do further mischief; and then present his case to the grand jury of the district, with proofs of his guilt, and, if indicted, try him according to the course of the common law. If this had been done, the Constitution would have been vindicated, the law of 1863 enforced, and the securities for personal liberty preserved and defended.

***It is claimed that martial law covers with its broad mantle the proceedings of this military commission. The proposition is this: that in a time of war the commander of an armed force (if in his opinion the exigencies of the country demand it, and of which he is to judge), has the power, within the lines of his military district, to suspend all civil rights and their remedies, and subject citizens as well as soldiers to the rule of his will; and in the exercise of his lawful authority cannot be restrained, except by his superior officer or the President of the United States.

If this position is sound to the extent claimed, then when war exists, foreign or domestic, and the country is subdivided into military departments for mere convenience, the commander of one of them can, if he chooses, within his limits, on the plea of necessity, with the approval of the Executive, substitute military force for and to the exclusion of the laws, and punish all persons, as he thinks right and proper, without fixed or certain rules. *** Civil liberty and this kind of martial law cannot endure together; the antagonism is irreconcilable; and, in the conflict, one or the other must perish. *** It is essential to the safety of every government that, in a great crisis, like the one we have just passed through, there should be a power somewhere of suspending the writ of habeas corpus. *** Unquestionably, there is then an exigency which demands that the government, if it should see fit in the exercise of a proper discretion to make arrests, should not be required to produce the persons arrested in answer to a writ of habeas corpus. The Constitution goes no further. It does not say after a writ of habeas corpus is denied a citizen, that he shall be tried otherwise than by the course of the common law; if it had intended this result, it was easy by the use of direct words to have accomplished it. The illustrious men who framed that instrument *** limited the suspension to one great right, and left the rest to remain forever inviolable. But, it is insisted that the safety of the country in time of war demands that this broad claim for martial law shall be sustained. If this were true, it could be well said that a country, preserved at the sacrifice of all the cardinal principles of liberty, is not worth the cost of preservation. Happily, it is not so. *** It is difficult to see how the safety for the country required martial law in Indiana. If any of her citizens were plotting treason, the power of arrest could secure them, until the government was prepared for their trial, when the courts were open and ready to try them. It was as easy to protect witnesses before a civil as a military tribunal; and as there could be no wish to convict, except on sufficient legal evidence, surely an ordained and establish court was better able to judge of this than a military tribunal composed of gentlemen not trained to the profession of the law.

It follows, from what has been said on this subject, that there are occasions when martial rule can be properly applied. If, in foreign invasion or civil war, the courts are actually closed, and it is impossible to administer criminal justice according to law, then, on the theatre of active military operations, where war really prevails, there is a necessity to furnish a substitute for the civil authority, thus overthrown, to preserve the safety of the army and society; and as no power is left but the military, it is allowed to govern by martial rule until the laws can have their free course. As necessity creates the rule, so it limits its duration; for, if this government is continued after the courts are reinstated, it is a gross usurpation of power. Martial rule can never exist where the courts are open, and in the proper and unobstructed exercise of their jurisdiction. It is also confined to the locality of actual war. ***

*** If the military trial of Milligan was contrary to law, then he was entitled, on the facts stated in his petition, to be discharged from custody by the terms of the act of Congress of March 3d, 1863. *** But it is insisted that

Milligan was a prisoner of war, and, therefore, excluded from the privileges of the statute. It is not easy to see how he can be treated as a prisoner of war, when he lived in Indiana for the past twenty years, was arrested there, and had not been, during the late troubles, a resident of any of the states in rebellion. If in Indiana he conspired with bad men to assist the enemy, he is punishable for it in the courts of Indiana; but, when tried for the offence, he cannot plead the rights of war; for he was not engaged in legal acts of hostility against the government, and only such persons, when captured, are prisoners of war. If he cannot enjoy the immunities attaching to the character of a prisoner of war, how can he be subject to their pains and penalties? ***

The CHIEF JUSTICE delivered the following opinion.

Four members of the court, concurring ***, think it their duty to make a separate statement of their views of the whole case.

The act of Congress of March 3d, 1863, comprises all the legislation which seems to require consideration in this connection. *** The first section authorized the suspension, during the Rebellion, of the writ of habeas corpus throughout the United States by the President. The two next sections limited this authority in important respects. The second section required that lists of all persons, being citizens of states in which the administration of the laws had continued unimpaired in the Federal courts, who were then held or might thereafter be held as prisoners of the United States, under the authority of the President, otherwise than as prisoners of war, should be furnished to the judges of the Circuit and District Courts. *** And it was required, in cases where the grand jury in attendance upon any of these courts should terminate its session without proceeding by indictment or otherwise against any prisoner named in the list, that the judge of the court should forthwith make an order that such prisoner desiring a discharge, should be brought before him or the court to be discharged ***. The third section provided *** that any citizen, after the termination of a session of the grand jury without indictment or presentment, might, by petition alleging the facts and verified by oath, obtain the judge's order of discharge in favor of any person so imprisoned ***

The holding of the Circuit and District Courts of the United States in Indiana had been uninterrupted. The administration of the laws in the Federal courts had remained unimpaired. Milligan was imprisoned under the authority of the President, and was not a prisoner of war. *** His case was thus brought within the precise letter and intent of the act of Congress ***. It is clear upon this statement that the Circuit Court was bound to hear Milligan's petition for the writ of habeas corpus, called in the act an order to bring the prisoner before the judge or the court, and to issue the writ, or, in the language of the act, to make the order. The first question, therefore—Ought the writ to issue?—must be answered in the affirmative. And it is equally clear that he was entitled to the discharge prayed for. *** That the third question, namely: Had the military commission in Indiana, under the facts stated, jurisdiction to try and sentence Milligan? must be answered negatively is an unavoidable inference from affirmative answers to the other two. The military commission could not have jurisdiction to try and sentence

Milligan, if he could not be detained in prison under his original arrest or under sentence, after the close of a session of the grand jury without indictment or other proceeding against him.

Indeed, the act seems to have been framed on purpose to secure the trial of all offences of citizens by civil tribunals, in states where these tribunals were not interrupted in the regular exercise of their functions. *** These provisions obviously contemplate no other trial or sentence than that of a civil court, and we could not assert the legality of a trial and sentence by a military commission, under the circumstances specified in the act and described in the petition, without disregarding the plain directions of Congress.

But the opinion which has just been read goes further; and as we understand it, asserts not only that the military commission held in Indiana was not authorized by Congress, but that it was not in the power of Congress to authorize it *** We cannot agree to this. *** We think that Congress had power, though not exercised, to authorize the military commission which was held in Indiana. *** The Constitution itself provides for military government as well as for civil government. *** Congress has power to raise and support armies; to provide and maintain a navy; to make rules for the government and regulation of the land and naval forces; and to provide for governing such part of the militia as may be in the service of the United States. *** We think, therefore, that the power of Congress, in the government of the land and naval forces and of the militia, is not at all affected by the fifth or any other amendment. *** Congress is but the agent of the nation, and does not the security of individuals against the abuse of this, as of every other power, depend on the intelligence and virtue of the people, *** and upon the frequency of elections, rather than upon doubtful constructions of legislative powers? *** Congress has the power not only to raise and support and govern armies but to declare war. It has, therefore, the power to provide by law for carrying on war. This power necessarily extends to all legislation essential to the prosecution of war with vigor and success, except such as interferes with the command of the forces and the conduct of campaigns. That power and duty belong to the President as commander-in-chief. Both these powers are derived from the Constitution, but neither is defined by that instrument. Their extent must be determined by their nature, and by the principles of our institutions.

***We by no means assert that Congress can establish and apply the laws of war where no war has been declared or exists.

Where peace exists the laws of peace must prevail. What we do maintain is, that when the nation is involved in war, and some portions of the country are invaded, and all are exposed to invasion, it is within the power of Congress to determine in what states or district such great and imminent public danger exists as justifies the authorization of military tribunals for the trial of crimes and offences against the discipline or security of the army or against the public safety. *** We cannot doubt that, in such a time of public danger, Congress had power, under the Constitution, to provide for the organization of a military commission, and for trial by that commission of persons engaged in this conspiracy. The fact that the Federal courts were open was regarded by Congress as a sufficient reason for not exercising the power; but that fact could not deprive Congress of the right to exercise it. Those courts might be open and undisturbed in the execution of their functions, and yet wholly incompetent to avert threatened danger, or to punish, with adequate promptitude and certainty, the guilty conspirators. ***

Ex parte QUIRIN
317 U.S. 1 (1942)

Mr. CHIEF JUSTICE STONE delivered the opinion of the Court.

*** The question for decision is whether the detention of petitioners by respondent for trial by Military Commission, appointed by Order of the President of July 2, 1942, on charges preferred against them purporting to set out their violations of the law of war and of the Articles of War, is in conformity to the laws and Constitution of the United States. *** [W]e directed that petitioners' applications be set down for full oral argument at a special term of this Court, convened on July 29, 1942. *** On July 31, 1942, *** this Court *** denied petitioners' applications for leave to file petitions for habeas corpus. ***

All the petitioners were born in Germany; all have lived in the United States. All returned to Germany between 1933 and 1941. All except petitioner Haupt are admittedly citizens of the German Reich, with which the United States is at war. Haupt came to this country with his parents when he was five years old; it is contended that he became a citizen of the United States by virtue of the naturalization of his parents during his minority and that he has not since lost his citizenship. *** After the declaration of war between the United States and the German Reich, petitioners received training at a sabotage school near Berlin, Germany, where they were instructed in the use of explosives and in methods of secret writing. Thereafter petitioners *** boarded [two] German submarine[s] which proceeded across the Atlantic to Amagansett Beach on Long Island, New York [and Ponte Vedra Beach, Florida]. [They] landed on June 13 and June 17, 1942] in the hours of darkness *** carrying with them a supply of explosives, fuses and incendiary and timing devices. While landing they wore German Marine Infantry uniforms or parts of uniforms. Immediately after landing they buried their uniforms and the other articles mentioned and proceeded in civilian dress. *** All were taken into custody in New York or Chicago by agents of the Federal Bureau of Investigation. ***

The President, as President and Commander in Chief of the Army and Navy, by Order of July 2, 1942, appointed a Military Commission and directed it to try petitioners for offenses against the law of war and the Articles of War, and prescribed regulations for the procedure on the trial and for review of the record of the trial and of any judgment or sentence of the Commission. On the same day, by Proclamation, the President declared that 'all persons who are subjects, citizens or residents of any nation at war with the United States or who give obedience to or act under the direction of any such nation, and who during time of war enter or attempt to enter the United States *** through coastal or boundary defenses, and are charged with committing or attempting or preparing to commit sabotage, espionage, hostile or warlike acts, or violations of the law of war, shall be subject to the law of war and to the jurisdiction of military tribunals'. *** [A]ll such persons were denied access to the courts. ***

On July 3, 1942, the Judge Advocate General's Department of the Army prepared and lodged with the Commission [charges alleging violation of the law of war, violation of Article 81 of the Articles of War (corresponding with or giving intelligence to, the enemy), violation of Article 82 (spying), and conspiracy to commit these offenses]. The Commission met on July 8, 1942, and proceeded with the trial, which continued in progress while the causes were pending in this Court. On July 27th, *** all the evidence for the prosecution and the defense had been taken by the Commission and the case had been closed except for arguments of counsel. *** [T]the state and federal courts *** have been open and functioning normally. ***

Petitioners' main contention is that the President is without any statutory or constitutional authority to order the petitioners to be tried by military tribunal for offenses with which they are charged; that in consequence they are entitled to be tried in the civil courts with the safeguards, including trial by jury, which the Fifth and Sixth Amendments guarantee to all persons charged in such courts with criminal offenses [and that the President's Order conflicts with certain of the Articles of War]. The Government challenges each of these propositions *** [and] also insists that petitioners must be denied access to the courts, both because they are enemy aliens or have entered our territory as enemy belligerents, and because the President's Proclamation undertakes in terms to deny such access to the class of persons defined by the Proclamation ***. But *** neither the Proclamation nor the fact that they are enemy aliens forecloses consideration by the courts of petitioners' contentions that the Constitution and laws of the United States constitutionally enacted forbid their trial by military commission. As announced in our per curiam opinion we have resolved those questions by our conclusion that the Commission has jurisdiction to try the charge preferred against petitioners. ***

We are not here concerned with any question of the guilt or innocence of petitioners.[2] Constitutional safeguards for the protection of all who are charged with offenses are not to be disregarded in order to inflict merited punishment on some who are guilty. But the detention and trial of petitioners—ordered by the President in the declared exercise of his powers as Commander in Chief of the Army in time of war and of grave public

---

[2] As appears from the stipulation, a defense offered before the Military Commission was that petitioners had had no intention to obey the orders given them by the officer of the German High Command.

danger—are not to be set aside by the courts without the clear conviction that they are in conflict with the Constitution or laws of Congress constitutionally enacted.

Congress and the President, like the courts, possess no power not derived from the Constitution. But one of the objects of the Constitution, as declared by its preamble, is to 'provide for the common defence.' *** The Constitution thus invests the President as Commander in Chief with the power to wage war which Congress has declared, and to carry into effect all laws passed by Congress for the conduct of war and for the government and regulation of the Armed Forces, and all laws defining and punishing offences against the law of nations, including those which pertain to the conduct of war.

By the Articles of War, Congress has provided rules for the government of the Army. It has provided for the trial and punishment, by courts-martial, of violations of the Articles by members of the armed forces and by specified classes of persons associated or serving with the Army. But the Articles also recognize the 'military commission' appointed by military command as an appropriate tribunal for the trial and punishment of offenses against the law of war not ordinarily tried by court martial. Articles 38 and 46 authorize the President, with certain limitations, to prescribe the procedure for military commissions. Articles 81 and 82 authorize trial, either by court martial or military commission, of those charged with relieving, harboring or corresponding with the enemy and those charged with spying. And Article 15 declares that 'the provisions of these articles conferring jurisdiction upon courts-martial shall not be construed as depriving military commissions *** or other military tribunals of concurrent jurisdiction in respect of offenders or offenses that by statute or by the law of war may be triable by such military commissions *** or other military tribunals'. Article 2 includes among those persons subject to military law the personnel of our own military establishment. But this, as Article 12 provides, does not exclude from that class 'any other person who by the law of war is subject to trial by military tribunals' and who under Article 12 may be tried by court martial or under Article 15 by military commission.

Similarly the Espionage Act of 1917, which authorizes trial in the district courts of certain offenses that tend to interfere with the prosecution of war, provides that nothing contained in the act 'shall be deemed to limit the jurisdiction of the general courts-martial, military commissions, or naval courts-martial'.

From the very beginning of its history this Court has recognized and applied the law of war as including that part of the law of nations which prescribes, for the conduct of war, the status, rights and duties of enemy nations as well as of enemy individuals. By the Articles of War, and especially Article 15, Congress has explicitly provided, so far as it may constitutionally do so, that military tribunals shall have jurisdiction to try offenders or offenses against the law of war in appropriate cases. Congress, in addition to making rules for the government of our Armed Forces, has thus exercised its authority to define and punish offenses against the law of nations by sanctioning, within constitutional limitations, the jurisdiction of military commissions to try persons for offenses which, according to the rules and precepts of the law of nations, and more particularly the law of war, are cognizable by such tribunals. And the President, as Commander in Chief, by his Proclamation in time of war his invoked that law. By his Order creating the present Commission he has undertaken to exercise the authority conferred upon him by Congress, and also such authority as the Constitution itself gives the Commander in Chief, to direct the performance of those functions which may constitutionally be performed by the military arm of the nation in time of war.

An important incident to the conduct of war is the adoption of measures by the military command not only to repel and defeat the enemy, but to seize and subject to disciplinary measures those enemies who in their attempt to thwart or impede our military effort have violated the law of war. It is unnecessary for present purposes to determine to what extent the President as Commander in Chief has constitutional power to create military commissions without the support of Congressional legislation. For here Congress has authorized trial of offenses against the law of war before such commissions. We are concerned only with the question whether it is within the constitutional power of the national government to place petitioners upon trial before a military commission for the offenses with which they are charged. We must therefore first inquire whether any of the acts charged is an offense against the law of war cognizable before a military tribunal, and if so whether the Constitution prohibits the trial. We may assume that there are acts regarded in other countries, or by some writers on international law, as offenses against the law of war which would not be triable by military tribunal here, either because they are not recognized by our courts as violations of the law of war or because they are of that class of offenses constitutionally triable only by a jury. It was upon such grounds that the Court denied the right to proceed by military tribunal in *Ex parte Milligan.* But as we shall show, these petitioners were charged with an offense against the law of war which the Constitution does not require to be tried by jury. ***

But petitioners insist that even if the offenses with which they are charged are offenses against the law of war, their trial is subject to the requirement of the Fifth Amendment that no person shall be held to answer for a capital or otherwise infamous crime unless on a presentment or indictment of a grand jury, and that such trials by Article III, § 2, and the Sixth Amendment must be by jury in a civil court. *** Presentment by a grand jury and trial by a jury of the vicinage where the crime was committed were at the time of the adoption of the Constitution familiar parts of the machinery for criminal trials in the civil courts. But they were procedures unknown to military tribunals, which are not courts in the sense of the Judiciary Article, and which in the natural course of events are usually called upon to function under conditions precluding resort to such procedures. *** [W]e must conclude that § 2 of Article III and the Fifth and Sixth Amendments cannot be taken to have extended the right to demand a jury to trials by military commission, or to have required that offenses against the law of war not triable by jury at common law be tried only in the civil courts.

The fact that 'cases arising in the land or naval forces' are excepted from the operation of the Amendments does not militate against this conclusion. Such cases are expressly excepted from the Fifth Amendment, and are deemed excepted by implication from the Sixth. It is argued that the exception, which excludes from the Amendment cases arising in the armed forces, has also by implication extended its guaranty to all other cases; that since petitioners, not being members of the Armed Forces of the United States, are not within the exception, the Amendment operates to give to them the right to a jury trial. But we think this argument misconceives both the scope of the Amendment and the purpose of the exception.

We may assume, without deciding, that a trial prosecuted before a military commission created by military authority is not one 'arising in the land *** forces', when the accused is not a member of or associated with those forces. But even so, the exception cannot be taken to affect those trials before military commissions which are neither within the exception nor within the provisions of Article III, § 2, whose guaranty the Amendments did not enlarge. No exception is necessary to exclude from the operation of these provisions cases never deemed to be within their terms. An express exception from Article III, § 2, and from the Fifth and Sixth Amendments, of trials of petty offenses and of criminal contempts has not been found necessary in order to preserve the traditional practice of trying those offenses without a jury. It is no more so in order to continue the practice of trying, before military tribunals without a jury, offenses committed by enemy belligerents against the law of war. ***

We cannot say that Congress in preparing the Fifth and Sixth Amendments intended to extend trial by jury to the cases of alien or citizen offenders against the law of war otherwise triable by military commission, while withholding it from members of our own armed forces charged with infractions of the Articles of War punishable by death. *** We conclude that the Fifth and Sixth Amendments did not restrict whatever authority was conferred by the Constitution to try offenses against the law of war by military commission, and that petitioners, charged with such an offense not required to be tried by jury at common law, were lawfully placed on trial by the Commission without a jury. ***

We have no occasion now to define with meticulous care the ultimate boundaries of the jurisdiction of military tribunals to try persons according to the law of war. It is enough that petitioners here, upon the conceded facts, were plainly within those boundaries, and were held in good faith for trial by military commission, charged with being enemies who, with the purpose of destroying war materials and utilities, entered or after entry remained in our territory without uniform--an offense against the law of war. We hold only that those particular acts constitute an offense against the law of war which the Constitution authorizes to be tried by military commission. ***

Mr. JUSTICE MURPHY took no part in the consideration or decision of these cases.

Notes

1. **Questioning *Quirin*.** The Supreme Court heard argument two days after the military commission evidence was closed and before counsel's final arguments. The decision was issued two days later and the written opinion followed three months thereafter on October 29, 1942. Meanwhile, six of the defendants had been executed. Is anything wrong with this picture? *See* Louis Fisher, *Military Tribunals: The Quirin Precedent*, Congressional Research Service Report to Congress (March 26, 2002). Justices Scalia and Stevens in *Hamdi* suggested there was, describing the case as "not this Court's finest hour." *Hamdi*, 542 U.S. 507, 569 (2004).

2. **Distinguishing *Milligan*.** *Quirin* distinguished *Ex parte Milligan*, 71 U.S. 2 (1866). Was the Court correct to place no emphasis on the availability of civilian courts to try the *Quirin* defendants? How do you think *Ex Parte Milligan's* arguments about the openness of courts cut with regard to present detainees? How much did place of capture (both in the U.S. and in a peaceful state), lack of membership in an enemy army, citizenship, and confidence in the Indiana courts play in to the Court's decision in *Milligan*? How much should similar factors be weighed with regard to the military commission of allegedly terrorist detainees? And how do they cut? Consider a given case, e.g. of a detainee who is not a member of Al Qaeda, is not a U.S. citizen, and was captured on U.S. soil.

3. **The U.S. Citizen.** The Court Notes that Haupt "became a citizen of the United States by virtue of the naturalization of his parents during his minority and that he has not since lost his citizenship." Is the Court's decision with respect to Haupt inconsistent with *Milligan*? How important is citizenship to the analysis in either *Milligan* or *Quirin*?

4. **Habeas Corpus and Military Commissions.** Recall from Chapter VII that after WW.II, Eisentrager received a full military commission trial prior to the hearing of his habeas corpus petition and that the Supreme Court in *Boumediene* focused on the inadequacy of procedural protections afforded in the CSRTs in Guantanamo in order to hold both that the Suspension Clause reaches detainees held there and that CSRTs are not an adequate substitute for habeas. Holding all other factors constant, does trial by military commission act as an adequate substitute for habeas? What procedural protections might the Court find necessary to foreclose the reach of the Suspension Clause or act as an adequate substitute for constitutional habeas under *Boumediene*?

5. **Citizens and Others.** President Bush's order (unlike President Rosevelt's) applied only to non-citizens. Could the President have made it applicable to citizens working on behalf of (or communicating with) foreign-based terrorist organizations? Could an American citizen accused of terrorism be tried by a military commission *not* set up under the 2001 Executive Order? What is the relevance of 18 U.S.C. § 4001(a), which states "[N]o citizen shall be imprisoned or otherwise detained except pursuant to an Act of Congress." Is the AUMF such an "Act of Congress"? Consider this last question as you read the next case.

*****

The following Supreme Court decision struck down the military commissions established in the President's November 13, 2001 military order. The decision was later mooted by enactment of the Military Commissions Act of 2006.

HAMDAN v. RUMSFELD
548 U.S. 557 (2006)

JUSTICE STEVENS announced the judgment *** and delivered the opinion of the Court ***.

Petitioner Salim Ahmed Hamdan, a Yemeni national, is in custody at an American prison in Guantanamo Bay, Cuba. *** Hamdan was captured by militia forces and turned over to the U. S. military. *** [Later] the President deemed him eligible for trial by military commission *** [and] charged [him] with one count of conspiracy "to commit ... offenses triable by military commission." Hamdan *** concedes that a court-martial constituted in accordance with the Uniform Code of Military Justice (UCMJ), would have authority to try him. His objection is that the military commission the President has convened lacks such authority, for two principal reasons: First, neither congressional Act nor the common law of war supports trial by this commission for the crime of conspiracy—an offense that, Hamdan says, is not a violation of the law of war. Second, Hamdan contends, the procedures that the President has adopted to try him violate the most basic tenets of military and international law ***. [W]e conclude that the military commission convened to try Hamdan lacks power to proceed because its structure and procedures violate both the UCMJ and the Geneva Conventions. ***

The military commission, a tribunal neither mentioned in the Constitution nor created by statute, was born of military necessity. *** When the exigencies of war next gave rise to a need for use of military commissions, during the Civil War, *** a single tribunal often took jurisdiction over ordinary crimes, war crimes, and breaches of military orders alike. *** Generally, though, the need for military commissions during this period—as during the Mexican War—was driven largely by the then very limited jurisdiction of courts martial: "The *occasion* for the military commission arises principally from the fact that the jurisdiction of the court-martial proper, in our law, is restricted by statute almost exclusively to members of the military force and to certain specific offences defined in a written code."

Exigency alone, of course, will not justify the establishment and use of penal tribunals not contemplated by Article I, § 8 and Article III, § 1 of the Constitution unless some other part of that document authorizes a response to the felt need. See *Ex parte Milligan*, 4 Wall. 2, 121 (1866) ("Certainly no part of the judicial power of the country was conferred on [military commissions]"); *Ex parte Vallandigham,* 1 Wall. 243, 251 (1864); see also *Quirin*, 317 U. S., at 25 ("Congress and the President, like the courts, possess no power not derived from the Constitution"). And that authority, if it exists, can derive only from the powers granted jointly to the President and Congress in time of war. *In re Yamashita*, 327 U. S. 1, 11 (1946).

The Constitution makes the President the "Commander in Chief" of the Armed Forces, but vests in Congress the powers to "declare War ... and make Rules concerning Captures on Land and Water," to "raise and support Armies," to "define and punish ... Offences against the Law of Nations," and "To make Rules for the Government and Regulation of the land and naval Forces." The interplay between these powers was described by Chief Justice Chase in the seminal case of *Ex parte Milligan:*

> The power to make the necessary laws is in Congress; the power to execute in the President. *** Congress cannot direct the conduct of campaigns, nor can the President, or any commander under him, without the sanction of Congress, institute tribunals for the trial and punishment of offences, either of soldiers or civilians, unless in cases of a controlling necessity, which justifies what it compels, or at least insures acts of indemnity from the justice of the legislature.

Whether Chief Justice Chase was correct in suggesting that the President may constitutionally convene military commissions "without the sanction of Congress" in cases of "controlling necessity" is a question this Court has not answered definitively, and need not answer today. For we held in *Quirin* that Congress had, through Article of War 15, sanctioned the use of military commissions in such circumstances. Article 21 of the UCMJ, the language of which is substantially identical to the old Article 15 and was preserved by Congress after World War II, reads as follows:

> Jurisdiction of courts-martial not exclusive.

> The provisions of this code conferring jurisdiction upon courts-martial shall not be construed as depriving military commissions, provost courts, or other military tribunals of concurrent jurisdiction in respect of offenders or offenses that by statute or by the law of war may be tried by such military commissions, provost courts, or other military tribunals.

We have no occasion to revisit *Quirin*'s controversial characterization of Article of War 15 as congressional authorization for military commissions. Contrary to the Government's assertion, however, even *Quirin* did not view the authorization as a sweeping mandate for the President to "invoke military commissions when he deems them necessary." Rather, the *Quirin* Court recognized that Congress had simply preserved what power, under the Constitution and the common law of war, the President had had before 1916 to convene military commissions—with the express condition that the President and those under his command comply with the law of war.[23] ***

The Government would have us dispense with the inquiry that the *Quirin* Court undertook and find in either the AUMF or the DTA specific, overriding

---

[23] Whether or not the President has independent power, absent congressional authorization, to convene military commissions, he may not disregard limitations that Congress has, in proper exercise of its own war powers, placed on his powers. See *Youngstown Sheet & Tube Co.* v. *Sawyer,* 343 U. S. 579, 637 (1952) (Jackson, J., concurring). The Government does not argue otherwise.

authorization for the very commission that has been convened to try Hamdan. Neither of these congressional Acts, however, expands the President's authority to convene military commissions. First, while we assume that the AUMF activated the President's war powers, and that those powers include the authority to convene military commissions in appropriate circumstances, there is nothing in the text or legislative history of the AUMF even hinting that Congress intended to expand or alter the authorization set forth in Article 21 of the UCMJ.

Likewise, the DTA [Detainee Treatment Act of 2005] cannot be read to authorize this commission. Although the DTA, unlike either Article 21 or the AUMF, was enacted after the President had convened Hamdan's commission, it contains no language authorizing that tribunal or any other at Guantanamo Bay. *** Together, the UCMJ, the AUMF, and the DTA at most acknowledge a general Presidential authority to convene military commissions in circumstances where justified under the "Constitution and laws," including the law of war. Absent a more specific congressional authorization, the task of this Court is, as it was in *Quirin*, to decide whether Hamdan's military commission is so justified.

*** Commissions historically have been used in three situations. [The first two, concerning martial law and occupied territories, are not relevant]. *** The third type of commission, convened as an "incident to the conduct of war" when there is a need "to seize and subject to disciplinary measures those enemies who in their attempt to thwart or impede our military effort have violated the law of war," *Quirin*, has been described as "utterly different" from the other two.[27] Not only is its jurisdiction limited to offenses cognizable during time of war, but its role is primarily a factfinding one-to determine, typically on the battlefield itself, whether the defendant has violated the law of war. The last time the U. S. Armed Forces used the law-of-war military commission was during World War II. In *Quirin*, this Court sanctioned President Roosevelt's use of such a tribunal to try Nazi saboteurs captured on American soil during the War. And in *Yamashita*, we held that a military commission had jurisdiction to try a Japanese commander for failing to prevent troops under his command from committing atrocities in the Philippines. *** *Quirin* represents the high-water mark of military power to try enemy combatants for war crimes.

The classic treatise penned by Colonel William Winthrop *** describes at least four preconditions for exercise of jurisdiction by a tribunal of the type convened to try Hamdan. First, "[a] military commission, (except where otherwise authorized by statute), can legally assume jurisdiction only of offenses committed within the field of the command of the convening commander." The "field of command" in these circumstances means the "theatre of war." Second, the offense charged "must have been committed within the period of the war." No jurisdiction exists to try offenses "committed either before or after the war." Third, a military commission not

---

[27] *** [C]ommissions convened during time of war but under neither martial law nor military government may try only offenses against the law of war.

established pursuant to martial law or an occupation may try only "[i]ndividuals of the enemy's army who have been guilty of illegitimate warfare or other offences in violation of the laws of war" and members of one's own army "who, in time of war, become chargeable with crimes or offences not cognizable, or triable, by the criminal courts or under the Articles of war." Finally, a law-of-war commission has jurisdiction to try only two kinds of offense: "Violations of the laws and usages of war cognizable by military tribunals only," and "[b]reaches of military orders or regulations for which offenders are not legally triable by court-martial under the Articles of war." *** Hamdan's commission lacks jurisdiction to try him unless the charge "properly set[s] forth, not only the details of the act charged, but the circumstances conferring *jurisdiction*." *** [Materials concerning this aspect of the case are included infra in section B2]

We have assumed, as we must, that the allegations made in the Government's charge against Hamdan are true. We have assumed, moreover, the truth of the message implicit in that charge -- viz., that Hamdan is a dangerous individual whose beliefs, if acted upon, would cause great harm and even death to innocent civilians, and who would act upon those beliefs if given the opportunity. It bears emphasizing that Hamdan does not challenge, and we do not today address, the Government's power to detain him for the duration of active hostilities in order to prevent such harm. But in undertaking to try Hamdan and subject him to criminal punishment, the Executive is bound to comply with the Rule of Law that prevails in this jurisdiction.***

The CHIEF JUSTICE took no part in the consideration or decision of this case.

JUSTICE BREYER, with whom JUSTICE KENNEDY, JUSTICE SOUTER, and JUSTICE GINSBURG join, concurring.

*** The Court's conclusion ultimately rests upon a single ground: Congress has not issued the Executive a "blank check." Indeed, Congress has denied the President the legislative authority to create military commissions of the kind at issue here. Nothing prevents the President from returning to Congress to seek the authority he believes necessary. ***

JUSTICE KENNEDY *** concurring.

Military Commission Order No. 1, which governs the military commission established to try petitioner Salim Hamdan for war crimes, exceeds limits that certain statutes, duly enacted by Congress, have placed on the President's authority to convene military courts. This is not a case, then, where the Executive can assert some unilateral authority to fill a void left by congressional inaction. It is a case where Congress, in the proper exercise of its powers as an independent branch of government, and as part of a long tradition of legislative involvement in matters of military justice, has considered the subject of military tribunals and set limits on the President's authority. *** Trial by military commission raises separation-of-powers concerns of the highest order. Located within a single branch, these courts carry the risk that offenses will be defined, prosecuted, and adjudicated by executive officials without independent review. *** It is imperative, then, that when military tribunals are established, full and proper authority exists for the Presidential directive.

The proper framework for assessing whether Executive actions are authorized is the three-part scheme used by Justice Jackson in his opinion in *Youngstown*. *** "When the President acts pursuant to an express or implied authorization of Congress, his authority is at its maximum, for it includes all that he possesses in his own right plus all that Congress can delegate." "When the President acts in absence of either a congressional grant or denial of authority, he can only rely upon his own independent powers, but there is a zone of twilight in which he and Congress may have concurrent authority, or in which its distribution is uncertain." And "when the President takes measures incompatible with the expressed or implied will of Congress, his power is at its lowest ebb."

In this case, as the Court observes, the President has acted in a field with a history of congressional participation and regulation. In the Uniform Code of Military Justice (UCMJ) *** Congress has set forth governing principles for military courts. The UCMJ as a whole establishes an intricate system of military justice. It authorizes courts-martial in various forms; it regulates the organization and procedure of those courts; it defines offenses and rights for the accused; and it provides mechanisms for appellate review. As explained below, the statute further recognizes that special military commissions may be convened to try war crimes. While these laws provide authority for certain forms of military courts, they also impose limitations, at least two of which control this case. If the President has exceeded these limits, this becomes a case of conflict between Presidential and congressional action-a case within Justice Jackson's third category, not the second or first. ***

[T]he UCMJ *** allows the President to implement and build on the UCMJ's framework by adopting procedural regulations, subject to three requirements: (1) Procedures for military courts must conform to district-court rules insofar as the President "considers practicable"; (2) the procedures may not be contrary to or inconsistent with the provisions of the UCMJ; and (3) "insofar as practicable" all rules and regulations *** must be *** the same for military commissions as for courts-martial unless such uniformity is impracticable. *** Although we can assume the President's practicability judgments are entitled to some deference, *** military courts may depart from federal-court rules whenever the President "considers" conformity impracticable; but the statute requires procedural uniformity across different military courts "insofar as [uniformity is] practicable," not insofar as the President considers it to be so. *** Congress' chosen language, then, is best understood to allow the selection of procedures based on logistical constraints, the accommodation of witnesses, the security of the proceedings, and the like. Insofar as the "[p]retrial, trial, and post-trial procedures" for the military commissions at issue deviate from court-martial practice, the deviations must be explained by some such practical need. *** Absent more concrete statutory guidance, this historical and statutory background-which suggests that some practical need must justify deviations from the court-martial model-informs the understanding of which military courts are "regularly constituted" under United States law.

In addition, whether or not the possibility, contemplated by the regulations here, of midtrial procedural changes could by itself render a military commission impermissibly irregular, an acceptable degree of independence from the Executive is necessary to render a commission "regularly constituted" by the standards of our Nation's system of justice. And any suggestion of Executive power to interfere with an ongoing judicial process raises concerns about the proceedings' fairness. Again, however, courts-martial provide the relevant benchmark. Subject to constitutional limitations, see *Ex parte Milligan,* 4 Wall. 2 (1866), Congress has the power and responsibility to determine the necessity for military courts, and to provide the jurisdiction and procedures applicable to them. The guidance Congress has provided with respect to courts-martial indicates the level of independence and procedural rigor that Congress has deemed necessary, at least as a general matter, in the military context. ***

In assessing the validity of Hamdan's military commission, the precise circumstances of this case bear emphasis. The allegations against Hamdan are undoubtedly serious. *** Nevertheless, the circumstances of Hamdan's trial present no exigency requiring special speed or precluding careful consideration of evidence. For roughly four years, Hamdan has been detained at a permanent United States military base in Guantanamo Bay, Cuba. And regardless of the outcome of the criminal proceedings at issue, the Government claims authority to continue to detain him based on his status as an enemy combatant. *** [T]he structure and composition of the military commission deviate from conventional court-martial standards. Although these deviations raise questions about the fairness of the trial, no evident practical need explains them. *** These structural differences between the military commissions and courts-martial—the concentration of functions, including legal decisionmaking, in a single executive official; the less rigorous standards for composition of the tribunal; and the creation of special review procedures in place of institutions created and regulated by Congress-remove safeguards that are important to the fairness of the proceedings and the independence of the court. *** [M]oreover, the basic procedures for the commissions deviate from procedures for courts-martial, in violation of § 836(b). As the Court explains, the Military Commission Order abandons the detailed Military Rules of Evidence, which are modeled on the Federal Rules of Evidence. *** Instead, the order imposes just one evidentiary rule: "Evidence shall be admitted if ... the evidence would have probative value to a reasonable person." *** As the Court explains, the Government has made no demonstration of practical need for these special rules and procedures, either in this particular case or as to the military commissions in general; nor is any such need self-evident. For all the Government's regulations and submissions reveal, it would be feasible for most, if not all, of the conventional military evidence rules and procedures to be followed. *** In light of the conclusion that the military commission here is unauthorized under the UCMJ, I see no need to consider several further issues ***

JUSTICE THOMAS, with whom JUSTICE SCALIA joins, and with whom JUSTICE ALITO joins [in part] dissenting.

*** [I]n the very context that we address today, this Court has concluded that "the detention and trial of petitioners-ordered by the President in the declared exercise of his powers as Commander in Chief of the Army in time of war and of grave public danger-are not to be set aside by the courts without the clear conviction that they are in conflict with the Constitution or laws of Congress constitutionally enacted." *Ex parte Quirin.*

Under this framework, the President's decision to try Hamdan before a military commission for his involvement with al Qaeda is entitled to a heavy measure of deference. In the present conflict, Congress has authorized the President "to use all necessary and appropriate force***". As a plurality of the Court observed in *Hamdi*, the "capture, detention, and *trial* of unlawful combatants, by 'universal agreement and practice,' are 'important incident[s] of war,'" and are therefore "an exercise of the 'necessary and appropriate force' Congress has authorized the President to use." ***

[T]he Court determines the scope of this power based exclusively on Article 21 of the Uniform Code of Military Justice (UCMJ), 10 U.S.C. § 821, the successor to Article 15 of the Articles of War, which *Quirin* held "authorized trial of offenses against the law of war before [military] commissions." As I shall discuss below, Article 21 alone supports the use of commissions here. Nothing in the language of Article 21, however, suggests that it outlines the entire reach of congressional authorization of military commissions in all conflicts -- quite the contrary, the language of Article 21 presupposes the existence of military commissions under an independent basis of authorization. Indeed, consistent with *Hamdi*'s conclusion that the AUMF itself authorizes the trial of unlawful combatants, the original sanction for military commissions historically derived from congressional authorization of "the initiation of war" with its attendant authorization of "the employment of all necessary and proper agencies for its due prosecution." Accordingly, congressional authorization for military commissions pertaining to the instant conflict derives not only from Article 21 of the UCMJ, but also from the more recent, and broader, authorization contained in the AUMF.[2] ***

*** Here, as evidenced by Hamdan's charging document, the Executive has determined that the theater of the present conflict includes "Afghanistan, Pakistan and other countries" where al Qaeda has established training camps, and that the duration of that conflict dates back (at least) to Usama bin Laden's August 1996 *Declaration of Jihad Against the Americans*. *** The starting point of the present conflict (or indeed any conflict) is not determined by congressional enactment, but rather by the initiation of

---

[2] Although the President very well may have inherent authority to try unlawful combatants for violations of the law of war before military commissions, we need not decide that question because Congress has authorized the President to do so.

hostilities. Thus, Congress' enactment of the AUMF did not mark the beginning of this Nation's conflict with al Qaeda, but instead authorized the President to use force in the midst of an ongoing conflict. Moreover, while the President's "war powers" may not have been activated until the AUMF was passed, the date of such activation has never been used to determine the scope of a military commission's jurisdiction.[3] *** Hamdan is an unlawful combatant charged with joining and conspiring with a terrorist network dedicated to flouting the laws of war. ***

*** [T]he procedure of such commissions "has [not] been prescribed by statute," but "has been adapted in each instance to the need that called it forth." Indeed, this Court has concluded that "[i]n the absence of attempts by Congress to limit the President's power, it appears that, as Commander in Chief of the Army and Navy of the United States, he may, in time of war, establish and prescribe the jurisdiction and procedure of military commissions." This conclusion is consistent with this Court's understanding that military commissions are "our common-law war courts."[15] As such, "[s]hould the conduct of those who compose martial-law tribunals become [a] matter of judicial determination subsequently before the civil courts, those courts will give great weight to the opinions of the officers as to what the customs of war in any case justify and render necessary."

The Court nevertheless concludes that at least one provision of the UCMJ amounts to an attempt by Congress to limit the President's power. *** Article 36 of the UCMJ authorizes the President to establish procedures for military commissions ***. Far from constraining the President's authority, Article 36 recognizes the President's prerogative to depart from the procedures applicable in criminal cases whenever *he alone* does not deem such procedures "practicable." While the procedural regulations promulgated by the Executive must not be "contrary to" the UCMJ, only a few provisions of the UCMJ mention "military commissions," and there is no suggestion that

---

[3] Even if the formal declaration of war were generally the determinative act in ascertaining the temporal reach of the jurisdiction of a military commission, the AUMF itself is inconsistent with the plurality's suggestion that such a rule is appropriate in this case. The text of the AUMF is backward looking, authorizing the use of "all necessary and appropriate force against those nations, organizations, or persons he determines planned, authorized, committed, or aided the terrorist attacks that occurred on September 11, 2001." Thus, the President's decision to try Hamdan by military commission-a use of force authorized by the AUMF-for Hamdan's involvement with al Qaeda prior to September 11, 2001, fits comfortably within the framework of the AUMF. In fact, bringing the September 11 conspirators to justice is the *primary point* of the AUMF. By contrast, on the plurality's logic, the AUMF would not grant the President the authority to try Usama bin Laden himself for his involvement in the events of September 11, 2001.

[15] Though it does not constitute a basis for any holding of the Court, the Court maintains that, as a "general rule," "the procedures governing trials by military commission historically have been the same as those governing courts-martial." While it is undoubtedly true that military commissions have invariably employed most of the procedures employed by courts-martial, that is not a requirement. Moreover, such a requirement would conflict with the settled understanding of the flexible and responsive nature of military commissions and the President's wartime authority to employ such tribunals as he sees fit.

the procedures to be employed by Hamdan's commission implicate any of those provisions.

Notwithstanding the foregoing, the Court concludes that Article 36(b) of the UCMJ *** requires the President to employ the same rules and procedures in military commissions as are employed by courts-martial *"insofar as practicable."* The Court further concludes that Hamdan's commission is unlawful because the President has not explained why it is not practicable to apply the same rules and procedures to Hamdan's commission as would be applied in a trial by court martial.

This interpretation of § 836(b) is unconvincing. As an initial matter, the Court fails to account for our cases***. *** In *Yamashita*, this Court concluded that Article 15 of the Articles of War preserved the President's unfettered authority to prescribe military commission procedure. The Court explained, "[b]y thus recognizing military commissions in order to preserve their traditional jurisdiction over enemy combatants unimpaired by the Articles, Congress gave sanction ... to *any use* of the military commission contemplated by the common law of war."[16]; see also *Quirin; Madsen.* *** And this Court recognized that Article 15's preservation of military commissions as common-law war courts preserved the President's commander-in-chief authority to both "establish" military commissions and to "prescribe [their] procedure[s]." *Madsen* (explaining that Congress had "refrain[ed] from legislating" in the area of military commission procedures, in "contras[t] with its traditional readiness to ... prescrib[e], with particularity, the jurisdiction and procedure of United States courts-martial"). ***

Given these precedents, the Court's conclusion that Article 36(b) requires the President to apply the same rules and procedures to military commissions as are applicable to courts-martial is unsustainable. *** Moreover, the Court's conclusion is flatly contrary to its duty not to set aside Hamdan's commission "without the *clear* conviction that [it is] in conflict with the ... laws of Congress constitutionally enacted." *Quirin.*

Nothing in the text of Article 36(b) supports the Court's sweeping conclusion that it represents an unprecedented congressional effort to change the nature of military commissions from common-law war courts to tribunals that must presumptively function like courts-martial. And such an interpretation would be strange indeed. The vision of uniformity that motivated the adoption of the UCMJ, embodied specifically in Article 36(b), is nothing more than uniformity across the separate branches of the armed services. *** [C]onsistent with this Court's prior interpretations of Article 21

---

[16] The Court suggests that Congress' amendment to Article 2 of the UCMJ, providing that the UCMJ applies to "persons within an area leased by or otherwise reserved or acquired for the use of the United States," deprives *Yamashita*'s conclusion respecting the President's authority to promulgate military commission procedures of its "precedential value." But this merely begs the question of the scope and content of the remaining provisions of the UCMJ. Nothing in the additions to Article 2, or any other provision of the UCMJ, suggests that Congress has disturbed this Court's unequivocal interpretation of Article 21 as preserving the common-law status of military commissions and the corresponding authority of the President to set their procedures pursuant to his commander-in-chief powers. See *Quirin*, 317 U. S., at 28; *Yamashita*, 327 U. S., at 20; *Madsen v. Kinsella*, 343 U. S. 341, 355 (1952).

and over a century of historical practice, it cannot be understood to require the President to conform the procedures employed by military commissions to those employed by courts-martial.

Even if Article 36(b) could be construed to require procedural uniformity among the various tribunals contemplated by the UCMJ, Hamdan would not be entitled to relief. Under the Court's reading, the President is entitled to prescribe different rules for military commissions than for courts-martial when he determines that it is not "practicable" to prescribe uniform rules. The Court does not resolve the level of deference such determinations would be owed, however, because, in its view, "[t]he President has not . . . [determined] that it is impracticable to apply the rules for courts-martial." This is simply not the case. On the same day that the President issued Military Commission Order No. 1, the Secretary of Defense explained that "the president decided to establish military commissions because he wanted the option of a process that is different from those processes which we already have, namely the federal court system . . . and the military court system," and that "[t]he commissions are intended to be different . . . because the [P]resident recognized that there had to be differences to deal with the unusual situation we face and that a different approach was needed." The President reached this conclusion because "we're in the middle of a war, and . . . had to design a procedure that would allow us to pursue justice for these individuals while at the same time prosecuting the war most effectively. And that means setting rules that would allow us to preserve our intelligence secrets, develop more information about terrorist activities that might be planned for the future so that we can take action to prevent terrorist attacks against the United States. . . . [T]here was a constant balancing of the requirements of our war policy and the importance of providing justice for individuals . . . and *each* deviation from the standard kinds of rules that we have in our criminal courts was motivated by the desire to strike the balance between individual justice and the broader war policy."

The Court provides no explanation why the President's determination that employing court-martial procedures in the military commissions established pursuant to Military Commission Order No. 1 would hamper our war effort is in any way inadequate to satisfy its newly minted "practicability" requirement. On the contrary, this determination is precisely the kind for which the "Judiciary has neither aptitude, facilities nor responsibility and which has long been held to belong in the domain of political power not subject to judicial intrusion or inquiry.'" And, in the context of the present conflict, it is exactly the kind of determination Congress countenanced when it authorized the President to use all necessary and appropriate force against our enemies. Accordingly, the President's determination is sufficient to satisfy any practicability requirement imposed by Article 36(b).

The plurality further contends that Hamdan's commission is unlawful because it fails to provide him the right to be present at his trial ***. But § 839(c) applies to courts-martial, not military commissions. *** Section

839(c) simply does not address the procedural requirements of military commissions.

The Court contends that Hamdan's military commission is also unlawful because it violates Common Article 3 of the Geneva Conventions. ***

JUSTICE ALITO, dissenting [omitted]

Notes

1. **The Court's Interpretive Lens**. The majority and the dissenters differ on deferring to the President in wartime. Which side has the better argument and why?

2. **Judicial Process and War**. How intrusive—or necessary—is judicial process in wartime? Who should decide how much due process is appropriate? Historically, the Court has ruled against a president during an armed conflict only a handful of times and is ever reluctant to act when faced with a challenge to a president during wartime. Many commentators have argued that the Court, in *Hamdan* (as well as *Rasul* and later *Boumediene*) "stepped up" against the President. How much do you think *Hamdan* represents such a step?

3. **Responses to *Hamdan***. Could the President trump the Court's decision unilaterally by stating reasons for not using court-martial processes? Should he have gone to Congress for legislation (as he did) and if so, what should have been the content of the legislation?

4. **Presidential Popularity**. Numerous constitutional analysts have said that "the Court follows the election returns" or "pays attention to the polls." Some examples of decisions adverse to unpopular presidents that you have read include *Youngstown*, *US v. Nixon*, and *Clinton v. Jones*. Conversely, decisions favorable to popular presidents include *Ex Parte Quirin*, *Dames & Moore v. Regan*, *Korematsu v. United States*, and *Johnson v. Eisentrager*. At the time of the *Hamdan* decision, George W. Bush's approval rating was around 35%, down from over 90% shortly after the 9/11 terrorist attacks. Do you think this did or should affect the Court's decision?

5. **The Military Commissions Act of 2006.** The Military Commissions Act of 2006 (MCA) specifically authorized use of military commissions to try unlawful enemy combatants. It thus overturned *Hamdan's* holdings that trial of alleged terrorists by military commission was not authorized by Congress. The relevant provisions are set forth below:

"§ 948b. Military commissions generally

"(a) PURPOSE.—This chapter establishes procedures governing the use of military commissions to try alien unlawful enemy combatants engaged in hostilities against the United States for violations of the law of war and other offenses triable by military commission.

"(b) AUTHORITY FOR MILITARY COMMISSIONS UNDER THIS CHAPTER.—The President is authorized to establish military commissions under this chapter for offenses triable by military commission as provided in this chapter. ***

"(f) STATUS OF COMMISSIONS UNDER COMMON ARTICLE 3.—A military commission established under this chapter is a regularly constituted court, affording all the necessary 'judicial guarantees which are recognized as indispensable by civilized peoples' for purposes of common Article 3 of the Geneva Conventions.

"(g) GENEVA CONVENTIONS NOT ESTABLISHING SOURCE OF RIGHTS.—No alien unlawful enemy combatant subject to trial by military commission under this chapter may invoke the Geneva Conventions as a source of rights. ***

6. Geneva Conventions. Congress also provided that the military commissions it was establishing were "regularly constituted courts" in compliance with the Geneva Conventions. Would this determination be binding on the courts?

B. JURISDICTION OF MILITARY COMMISSIONS

The following sections concern some of the central components of the military commission system established by the MCA of 2006. Section 1 concerns jurisdiction over persons. Section 2 addresses the jurisdiction of civilian courts to review decisions of military tribunal processes. Section 3 deals with jurisdiction over offenses.

1. JURISDICTION OVER PERSONS

UNITED STATES v. OMAR AHMED KHADR
UNITED STATES COURT OF MILITARY COMMISSION REVIEW
Military Commission
September 24, 2007

ROLPH, Deputy Chief Judge:

In this appeal by the Government (hereinafter Appellant) we are called upon to interpret for the first time the jurisdictional provisions contained in *the Military Commissions Act of 2006* (hereinafter M.C.A.) as they relate to the trial by military commission of a Canadian citizen, Omar Ahmed Khadr, Appellee (hereinafter Mr. Khadr). Mr. Khadr was captured on the battlefield in Afghanistan in 2002, is currently detained in Guantanamo Bay, Cuba, and was pending trial upon charges that were referred for trial before a military commission. ***

Appellant charged Mr. Khadr with various offenses arising during the period from on or about June 2002 to on or about July 27, 2002. The allegations include murder of a U.S. Soldier in violation of the law of war; attempted murder of U.S. military or coalition forces by making and planting improvised explosive devices (IEDs) in violation of the law of war; conspiracy with Osama bin Laden, Ayman al Zawahiri and other members of al Qaeda, an international terrorist organization, to attack civilians, destroy property, and commit murder – all in violation of the law of war; providing material or resources in support of al Qaeda and international terrorism; and spying, ***. Each charge and specification alleged against Mr. Khadr asserts the jurisdictional claim that he is "a person subject to trial by military commission as an *alien unlawful enemy combatant*." *** On September 7, 2004, a three-member C.S.R.T. unanimously determined that Mr. Khadr was properly classified as an "enemy combatant" and an individual who was "a member of, or affiliated with al Qaeda," as defined by a memorandum issued by the Deputy Secretary of Defense on July 7, 2004. ***

The determination of whether an individual captured on the battlefield is a "lawful" or "unlawful" enemy combatant carries with it significant legal consequences (both international and domestic) relating to the treatment owed that individual upon capture and ultimate criminal liability for participating in war-related activities associated with the armed conflict. The Third Geneva Convention Relative to the Treatment of Prisoners of War (GPW III)—signed in 1949 and entered into force in 1950 following battlefield atrocities occurring during World War II—sought to carefully define "lawful combatant" for all signatory nations.

Article 4, GPW III makes it clear that lawful combatants will generally only include the regular armed forces of a party to the conflict, including "members of militias or volunteer corps forming part of such armed forces." Also included are members of other militia, volunteer corps, and organized resistance movements belonging to a State party to the conflict so long as they fulfill the following conditions:

1) They are under the command of an individual who is responsible for their subordinates;

2) They wear a fixed distinctive sign or symbol recognizable at a distance;

3) They carry their arms openly; and

4) They conduct their operations in accordance with the laws and customs of war.

This critical determination of "lawful" or "unlawful" combatant status is far more than simply a matter of semantics. Without any determination of lawful or unlawful status, classification as an "enemy combatant" is sufficient to justify a detaining power's continuing detention of an individual captured in battle or taken into custody in the course of ongoing hostilities. However, under the well recognized body of customary international law relating to armed conflict, and specific provisions of GPW III, lawful combatants enjoy "combatant immunity" for their pre-capture acts of warfare, including the targeting, wounding, or killing of other human beings, provided those actions were performed in the context of ongoing hostilities against lawful military targets, and were not in violation of the law of war. Lawful enemy combatants enjoy all the privileges afforded soldiers under the law of war, including combatant immunity and the protections of the Geneva Conventions if wounded or sick, and while being held as prisoners of war (POWs). Additionally, lawful enemy combatants facing judicial proceedings for any of their actions in warfare that violate the law of war, or for post-capture offenses committed while they are POWs, are entitled to be tried by the same courts, and in accordance with the same procedures, that the detaining power would utilize to try members of its own armed forces (i.e., by court-martial for lawful enemy combatants held by the United States). *** [T]echnical "crimes" committed by lawful combatants authorized to use force in the context of ongoing hostilities may not be prosecuted unless those offenses are unrelated to the conflict, or violate the law of war or international humanitarian law. At the conclusion of the armed conflict, lawful combatants who are held as POWs are entitled to be safely and expeditiously repatriated to their nation of origin.

Unlawful combatants, on the other hand, are not entitled to "combatant immunity" nor any of the protections generally afforded lawful combatants who become POWs. Unlawful combatants remain civilians and may properly be captured, detained by opposing military forces, and treated as criminals under the domestic law of the capturing nation for any and all unlawful combat actions. *** Unlawful combatants are likewise subject to capture and detention, but in addition they are subject to trial and punishment by military tribunals for acts which render their belligerency unlawful. *** Under the M.C.A., unlawful enemy combatants who engage in hostilities against the United States or its co-belligerents, or materially support such, are subject to trial by military commission for violations of the law of war and other offenses made triable by that statute. *See* §§ 948a(1)(A)(ii) and 948b(a). ***

Appellant's appeal requires us to address two important issues. First, whether the military judge erred in ruling that Mr. Khadr's September, 2004 C.S.R.T. classification as an "enemy combatant" was insufficient to satisfy the congressionally mandated requirement, established in the M.C.A., that military commission jurisdiction shall exist solely over offenses committed by "alien unlawful enemy combatants." Second, if we answer the first question negatively, we must determine whether the military judge erred in ruling that neither the military commission nor the military judge were empowered under the M.C.A. to receive evidence, and thereafter assess Mr. Khadr's status as an "alien unlawful enemy combatant" for purposes of determining the commission's criminal jurisdiction over him.***

Under M.C.A. § 948c, only an "alien unlawful enemy combatant is subject to trial by military commission." The M.C.A., in § 948a(1)(A), defines "unlawful enemy combatant" as follows:

> (i) a person who has engaged in hostilities or who has purposefully and materially supported hostilities against the United States or its co-belligerents who is not a lawful enemy combatant (including a person who is part of the Taliban, al Qaeda, or associated forces); or

> (ii) a person who, before, on, or after the date of the enactment of the Military Commissions Act of 2006, has been

determined to be an unlawful enemy combatant by a Combatant Status Review Tribunal or another competent tribunal established under the authority of the President or the Secretary of Defense.

Appellant contends Mr. Khadr's designation as an "enemy combatant" by his C.S.R.T. in 2004 was itself sufficient to establish the military commission's jurisdiction and that the military judge erred in ruling otherwise. *** [W]e are now asked to categorically equate the administration's prior pronouncements regarding members of the Taliban and al Qaeda, and use of the term "enemy combatant" throughout the C.S.R.T. process, with "unlawful enemy combatant" as defined in the M.C.A., and attribute that extrapolation to the "clear intent" of Congress. *** In light of the plain language of the M.C.A., and applying common logic and reasoning, we decline to accept the Appellant's position. We believe the Congress, well aware of the fact that "trial by military commission is an extraordinary measure raising important questions about the balance of powers in our constitutional structure," was abundantly clear in precisely establishing the jurisdictional prerequisites it intended to mandate prior to any criminal proceeding before such a commission could occur. *** It is unequivocally clear to us from the plain language of the M.C.A. that Congress intended trials by military commission to be utilized solely and exclusively to try only "alien unlawful enemy combatants." The M.C.A.'s jurisdictional provisions (§§ 948c and 948d) and definitions section (§ 948a(1)(A)(i)) make this intent perfectly clear. So also does the M.C.A.'s express admonition in § 948d(b) that military commissions "shall not have jurisdiction to try a lawful enemy combatant." Congress further stated that a C.S.R.T.'s (or other competent tribunal's) determination that a person is an "unlawful enemy combatant" would be dispositive for purposes of establishing jurisdiction for trial by military commission.[18] No such statement is made regarding a prior designation of a detainee as simply an "enemy combatant" and, in our opinion, such designation is not useful in resolving this ultimate issue of criminal jurisdiction under the M.C.A. *** Had Congress intended prior designations of detainees as mere "enemy combatants" to be sufficient to establish military commission jurisdiction, it was fully capable of saying this in the legislation. It did not. ***

*** It is reasonable to assume that Congress would seek to affirmatively declare the circumstances under which individual members of al Qaeda could become "unlawful enemy combatants" for purposes of exacting criminal liability under the M.C.A.. Limiting criminal responsibility solely to an individual (including a member of al Qaeda or the Taliban, or associated

---

[18] Though Congress intended to create a "safe harbor" for C.S.R.T. determinations made prior to and after the M.C.A.'s enactment, this provision cannot be used to transform an "enemy combatant" designation made for one purpose into a declaration of "unlawful enemy combatant" status for another. *** For purposes of resolving this Government appeal, we need not determine whether this "dispositive jurisdiction" provision deprives a military commission accused of a critical "judicial guarantee[ ] . . . recognized as indispensable by civilized people" under Common Article 3 of the Geneva Conventions (i.e., the right to affirmatively challenge the commission's *in personam* jurisdiction over him).

forces) who actually "engaged in hostilities or who has purposefully and materially supported hostilities against the United States or its co-belligerents" appears to be the clear intent of Congress, and requires more than mere membership in an organization for criminal responsibility to attach.[21] *** To accept Appellant's interpretation would allow criminal jurisdiction at a military commission to attach to members of the Taliban or al Qaeda who had never engaged in or supported hostilities. ***

The declared purpose of the C.S.R.T. process used to review the status of hundreds of foreign national detainees captured in Iraq and Afghanistan and currently held under Defense Department control at Guantanamo Bay Naval Base, Cuba—including Mr. Khadr—was solely to afford detainees "the opportunity to contest designation as an enemy combatant." *** Mr. Khadr's 2004 C.S.R.T. employed a less exacting standard than that contained in the M.C.A. for establishing "unlawful enemy combatant" status. A detainee could be classified as an "enemy combatant" under the C.S.R.T. definition simply by being a "part of" the Taliban or al Qaeda, without ever having engaged in or supported hostilities against the United States or its coalition partners. While such a classification would certainly be appropriate for authorizing continued detention during ongoing hostilities, it does not address in any way the "lawful" or "unlawful" nature of the detained combatant's belligerency under the M.C.A. Congress never stated that mere membership in or affiliation with the Taliban, al Qaeda, or associated forces was a sufficient basis for declaring someone to be an "unlawful enemy combatant" for purposes of exercising criminal jurisdiction over that person. *** As far as we can discern, the C.S.R.T.s were never tasked with making that determination. Instead, they conducted non-adversarial proceedings aimed at deciding, by a preponderance of the evidence, whether each detainee met the criteria for designation as an "enemy combatant" ***. In the M.C.A., military commission jurisdiction is limited solely to those who actually "*engaged* in hostilities or who . . . *purposefully and materially* supported hostilities. . . ." While Mr. Khadr's C.S.R.T. may have had more than sufficient evidence before it to properly classify him as an "alien unlawful enemy combatant," it was not charged with making that determination, and could not have applied the definition established by Congress, as it did not come into existence until October 2006—two years later. ***

We next examine the military judge's determination that "the military commission is not the proper authority, under the provisions of the M.C.A., to determine that Mr. Khadr is an unlawful enemy combatant in order to establish initial jurisdiction for this commission to try Mr. Khadr." *** We hold the military judge erred in two respects: first, in not affording Appellant

---

[21] Summary determinations of a group's unlawful combatant status would appear to violate the Supreme Court's ruling in *Hamdi v. Rumsfeld,* which recognized the fundamental right to notice and an opportunity to be heard on matters affecting a detainee's "enemy combatant" status determination. In *Hamdi,* Justice Souter suggested that U.S. Army regulations governing combatant status determinations, which were premised upon Article 5 of GPW III, would appear to preclude any "categorical pronouncement" regarding an individual's combatant status. Appellant appears to concede the necessity of individualized combatant status determinations.

the opportunity to present evidence in support of its position on the jurisdictional issue before the military commission; and second, in concluding that a C.S.R.T. (or another competent tribunal) determination of "unlawful enemy combatant" status was a prerequisite to referral of charges to a military commission, and that the military commission lacked the power to independently consider and decide this important jurisdictional matter under the M.C.A. *** Both the record of trial and the military judge's actions and rulings in this case demonstrate that the prosecution was not afforded the opportunity to present evidence to establish the military commission's *in personam* jurisdiction over Mr. Khadr. *** [W]e find the military judge abused his discretion in deciding this critical jurisdictional matter without first fully considering both the admissibility and merits of evidence Appellant offered to present on this issue.

We also conclude that the military judge erred in ruling he lacked authority under the M.C.A. to determine whether Mr. Khadr is an "unlawful enemy combatant" for purposes of establishing the military commission's initial jurisdiction to try him. The unambiguous language of the M.C.A., in conjunction with a clear and compelling line of federal precedent on the issue of establishing jurisdiction in federal courts, convince us the military judge possessed the independent authority to decide this critical jurisdictional prerequisite. "[A] federal court always has jurisdiction to determine its own jurisdiction." *United States v. Ruiz*, 536 U.S. 622, 627 (2002). A military commission is no different. *See* R.M.C. 201(b)(3)("A military commission always has jurisdiction to determine whether it has jurisdiction."). *** While we agree with the military judge's view that Congress contemplated an initial assessment of an accused's "unlawful enemy combatant" status prior to referral of charges to a military commission, we disagree with his conclusion that the only avenue for the assessment is that delineated in M.C.A. § 948a(1)A(ii). *** We find that *** facial compliance by the Government with all the pre-referral criteria contained in the Rules for Military Commissions, combined with an unambiguous allegation in the pleadings that Mr. Khadr is "a person subject to trial by military commission as an alien unlawful enemy combatant," entitled the military commission to initially and properly exercise *prima facie* personal jurisdiction over the accused until such time as that jurisdiction was challenged by a motion to dismiss for lack thereof, or proof of jurisdiction was lacking on the merits.

In our opinion, the M.C.A. is clear and deliberate in its creation of a bifurcated methodology for establishing an accused's "unlawful enemy combatant" status so as to permit that individual's trial before a military commission. These two methods are laid out in M.C.A. § 948a(1)A where an "unlawful enemy combatant" is defined as:

> (i) a person who has engaged in hostilities or who has purposefully and materially supported hostilities against the United States or its co-belligerents who is not a lawful enemy combatant (including a person who is part of the Taliban, al Qaeda, or associated forces); *or*
>
> (ii) a person who, before, on, or after the date of the enactment of the Military Commissions Act of 2006, has been determined to be an

unlawful enemy combatant by a Combatant Status Review Tribunal or another competent tribunal established under the authority of the President or the Secretary of Defense.

The disjunctive "or" between subsections (i) and (ii) clearly sets forth alternative approaches for establishing military commission jurisdiction. ***

Upon challenge, the first method by which the M.C.A. contemplates jurisdiction being established is by evidence being presented before the military judge factually establishing that an accused meets the definition of "unlawful enemy combatant" as contained in subsection (i). *In personam* criminal jurisdiction over a criminal accused is generally a question of law to be decided by the military judge, and is usually resolved only after presentation of evidence supporting jurisdiction and entry of corresponding findings of fact. There is a long and well-developed tradition in U.S. federal courts and, specifically, throughout military court-martial jurisprudence of military judges deciding matters of personal jurisdiction. Congress, clearly aware of historical court-martial practice, and desiring that military commissions mirror this firmly rooted practice to the maximum extent practicable, would not have deprived military commissions of the ability to independently decide personal jurisdiction absent an express statement of such intent. No such statement is contained anywhere in the M.C.A.

*** Although Congress assigned a jurisdictional "safe harbor" for prior C.S.R.T. (or other competent tribunal) determinations of "unlawful enemy combatant" status by statutorily deeming them "dispositive" of jurisdiction, it did not in any way preclude Appellant from proving jurisdiction before the military commission in the absence of such a determination. Indeed, the existence of a statutorily recognized path to achieve a "dispositive" determination of jurisdiction suggests that pretrial procedures and pleadings alleging jurisdiction should simply be viewed as "nondispositive." *** As Appellant Notes, [M.C.A. § 948a(1)(A)] (ii) makes it clear that the military judge is not at liberty to revisit a C.S.R.T.'s (or other competent tribunal's) finding of "unlawful enemy combatant" status *when there is such a finding*. However, nothing in the M.C.A. *requires* such a finding in order to establish military commission jurisdiction. *** Accordingly, we may properly find *** that Congress intended for military commissions to "apply the principles of law" and "the procedures for trial [routinely utilized] by general courts-martial . . . ." This would include the common procedures used before general courts-martial permitting military judges to hear evidence and decide factual and legal matters concerning the Court's own jurisdiction over the accused appearing before it.

This view is supported in the Rules for Military Commissions, which provide exactly such procedures. ***

The text, structure, and history of the M.C.A. demonstrate clearly that a military judge presiding over a military commission may determine both the factual issue of an accused's "unlawful enemy combatant status" and the corresponding legal issue of the military commission's *in personam* jurisdiction. A contrary interpretation would ignore the bifurcated structure of M.C.A. § 948(1)(A) and the long-standing history of military judges in general courts-martial finding jurisdictional facts by a preponderance of the evidence, and resolving pretrial motions to dismiss for lack of jurisdiction. The M.C.A. identifies two potential jurisdiction-establishing methodologies based upon an allegation of "unlawful enemy combatant" status. The first, reflected in § 948a(1)(A)(i), involves the clear delineation of the jurisdictional standard to be applied by a military commission in determining its own jurisdiction. The second, contained in § 948a(1)(A)(ii), involves a non-judicial related jurisdictional determination that is to be afforded "dispositive" deference by the military commission. Either method will allow the military commission's exercise of jurisdiction where "unlawful enemy combatant" status has been established by a preponderance of the evidence. This interpretation is consistent with the requirements of both the M.C.A. and with international law.[38]

Because we find the military judge had the power and authority under subsection (i) of § 948a(1)(A) of the M.C.A. to hear evidence concerning, and to ultimately decide, Mr. Khadr's "unlawful enemy combatant" status, we need not address whether or not a military commission is "another competent tribunal" under subsection (ii) to make that decision. ***

Judge FRANCIS and Judge HOLDEN concur.

Notes

1. **Appeal?** If you represented the detainee, Khadr, would you appeal this decision? If you were the government, would you perceive this decision to be a total win?

2. **Who is Khadr?** The youngest prisoner held at Guantanamo Bay, Khadr is often referred to as a child soldier. He was heavily wounded when captured as a fifteen year old by U.S. forces. He is also a Canadian citizen born in Toronto. Search him out on the internet. See if you can find pictures as well as text. What is his current situation? Does his story surprise you? Are there aspects of it that you think should inform the question of jurisdiction of a military commission?

2. APPELLATE JURISDICTION

KHADR v. UNITED STATES
529 F. 3d 1112 (D.C. Cir. 2008)

SENTELLE, Chief Judge:

Petitioner Omar Ahmed Khadr was captured on a battlefield in 2002, charged by the United States with war crimes, and referred to a military

---

[38] *See e.g.,* Article 45(2) of Protocol I to the Geneva Conventions. That Article suggests that a detained individual who is not being held as a POW has the right to assert an entitlement to POW status before a judicial tribunal, and that judicial adjudication of combatant status shall occur before trial for any alleged substantive offense. Following the M.C.A. procedures, as we interpret them here, would allow an accused to assert a claim of POW (i.e., lawful combatant) status at a pretrial motion session before the military judge. This pretrial determination of status would be fully in accord with Article 45(2) of Protocol I.

commission for trial. With this petition, Khadr seeks review of a preliminary procedural decision made in the course of the ongoing proceedings before the military commission. We dismiss the petition for lack of jurisdiction. The Military Commissions Act of 2006 limits our jurisdiction to review of "final judgment[s] rendered by a military commission" which have been "approved by the convening authority" and for which "all other appeals under [the Military Commissions Act] have been waived or exhausted." 10 U.S.C. § 950g(a)(1). The preliminary pretrial decision that Khadr contests is not such a "final judgment."

Omar Ahmed Khadr is a Canadian citizen who was taken into military custody in 2002 during the hostilities in Afghanistan. He was transported to the United States detention facility at Guantanamo Bay, Cuba, where he has since been detained. In 2004, a three-member Combatant Status Review Tribunal ("CSRT") determined that he was properly classified as an "enemy combatant" and as an individual who was "a member of, or affiliated with al Qaeda."

The United States charged Khadr under the Military Commissions Act of 2006 with murder in violation of the law of war, attempted murder in violation of the law of war, conspiracy, providing material support for terrorism, and spying. The charge alleges that Khadr murdered U.S. Army Sergeant First Class Christopher Speer on or about July 27, 2002 by throwing a hand grenade at U.S. forces; that Khadr attempted to murder U.S. or coalition troops between June 1 and July 27, 2002 by converting land mines into improvised explosive devices and planting them in the pathway of U.S. and coalition forces; that Khadr conspired with, and provided material support to, al Qaeda between June 1 and July 27, 2002 when he received training, conducted surveillance, and engaged in battle on al Qaeda's behalf; and that Khadr spied for al Qaeda by recording the travel patterns of U.S. forces. Each count charged that Khadr was "a person subject to trial by military commission as an alien unlawful enemy combatant." ***

The government asserts that this petition should be dismissed for lack of jurisdiction. *** As the party claiming subject matter jurisdiction, Khadr has the burden to demonstrate that it exists. He contends that jurisdiction is proper under the Military Commissions Act of 2006 and under the collateral order doctrine. We disagree.

The Military Commissions Act provides that "the United States Court of Appeals for the District of Columbia Circuit shall have exclusive jurisdiction to determine the validity of a final judgment rendered by a military commission (as approved by the convening authority) under this chapter," except that "[t]he Court of Appeals may not review the final judgment until all other appeals under this chapter have been waived or exhausted." Khadr contends that this jurisdictional provision has been satisfied because the military judge issued an order dismissing all charges and because all appeals of that order have been exhausted. We do not agree.

The military judge's order is not a "final judgment" as required***. It has long been well established that the reversal of a lower Court's decision sets aside that decision, leaves it "without any validity, force, or effect," and requires that it be treated thereafter as though it never existed. Once the military judge's order in this case was reversed by the CMCR, it lost all legal effect. An order that has become a legal nullity could not possibly constitute a "final judgment."[27]

Further, the "final judgment" must be "approved by the convening authority" to satisfy the statute. The military judge's order in this case has not been approved by the convening authority, nor could it be at this juncture. The Military Commissions Act defers convening authority review until after a military commission has found guilt and announced a sentence In this way, the statute clarifies that the "final judgment" contemplated by the statute is very "final." It is not a pretrial procedural decision like the one at issue here.

Khadr advances three main arguments in an attempt to evade the plain language requirements of 10 U.S.C. § 950g(a)(1)(A). None has merit. First, he argues that ***the Military Commissions Act *** allow[s] review of the military judge's order irrespective of the finality of the CMCR's decision *** Khadr next seeks support from jurisdictional procedures in the Uniform Code of Military Justice (UCMJ), but Congress expressly stated in the Military Commissions Act that the UCMJ does not apply to trials by military commission unless specifically indicated. *** Thus, the UCMJ provides no jurisdictional help to Khadr. Finally, Khadr argues that the Government has shown, through its conduct and regulations, that it agrees that an appeal is authorized in this case. Khadr points to notice he was given when he was served with the CMCR's decision "that Rules for Military Commission 908 and 1201 provide 'a right to petition the United States Court of Appeals for the District of Columbia Circuit' within 20 days of the date of this notification." Rules for Military Commission 908 and 1201, he argues, support the notice's statement because they speak in general terms of a right to appeal "the decision" of the CMCR on "any appeal." The problem with Khadr's argument is that "courts of appeals have only [the] jurisdiction [that] Congress has chosen to confer upon them" regardless of the actions of the parties, even when one of those parties is the Executive Branch. "Parties, of course, cannot confer jurisdiction; only Congress can do so." Thus, once Congress determined the limits of this Court's jurisdiction in the Military Commissions Act, no rule, regulation, or notice given by the Executive Branch could expand those limits. The statute requires a final judgment by a

---

[27] To the extent Khadr contends that the CMCR decision is a "final judgment" under the Military Commissions Act, he fares no better. Although Khadr asserts in his brief that the military judge's order is the appealable "final judgment," his petition to this court sought "review of the decisions of the [CMCR]," and the substance of his arguments on brief challenges the CMCR remand order rather than the military judge's order in his favor. But " '[a] remand order usually is not a final decision.' " Because the resolution of the jurisdictional issue does not leave "solely 'ministerial' proceedings," to be conducted by the military judge on remand, the CMCR's remand order is not final for purposes of appellate jurisdiction.

military commission, approved by the convening authority, for which all administrative review has been exhausted, and requires that Executive Branch rules and regulations "not be contrary to or inconsistent with" those statutory requirements. The regulations and notice given Khadr did not change the statutory preconditions to our jurisdiction. Because they have not yet been met in this case, the Military Commissions Act does not give us jurisdiction.

For the first time in its reply brief, the Government argued that the collateral order doctrine does not apply to proceedings under the Military Commissions Act. We generally refuse to entertain arguments raised for the first time in a party's reply brief. While we will not consider the Government's argument here, Khadr's argument fails even if the collateral order doctrine were to apply to proceedings under the Act.

The collateral order doctrine allows interlocutory review of a "small class" of decisions which "conclusively determine the disputed question, resolve an important issue completely separate from the merits of the action, and [are] effectively unreviewable on appeal from a final judgment." We hold that the order at issue here cannot satisfy the third requirement because it is reviewable on appeal from final judgment, and so will not consider the first two requirements of the doctrine. *** At issue here is a pretrial jurisdictional decision in a criminal case. ***Because jurisdictional decisions do not satisfy the doctrine's requirements, it necessarily follows that the decision in this case, which does not yet decide jurisdiction, does not warrant collateral order doctrine review. This procedural decision, as well as any subsequent jurisdictional decision, will be reviewable if necessary following a final judgment.

Khadr seeks special treatment for this procedural order because it involves a military commission. He contends that there is a public interest in ensuring the legality and legitimacy of military commissions and that the interest counsels in favor of reviewing procedural issues as they arise to make certain that military commissions are operating fairly and in conformity with the law. *** Thus, he argues, he satisfies the requirements of the doctrine as enunciated by the Supreme Court***: "it is not mere avoidance of a trial, but avoidance of a trial that would imperil a substantial public interest, that counts when asking whether an order is 'effectively' unreviewable if review is to be left until later."

There is no substantial public interest at stake in this case that distinguishes it from the multitude of criminal cases for which post-judgment review of procedural and jurisdictional decisions has been found effective. The Supreme Court *** clarified that the "substantial public interest" claimed by the petitioner cannot be solely his "right not to stand trial." There must also be "some particular value of a high order" that merits appealability prior to trial. *** There is no comparable significant public interest implicated here. Instead, Khadr has pointed solely to the interest that the public has in ensuring that all criminal proceedings are just. That interest does not warrant our interruption of this criminal proceeding just because it is a military commission. This Court will have opportunity to review this procedural decision post-judgment if necessary and can then determine whether the commission properly determined its jurisdiction and acted in conformity with the law. The collateral order doctrine does not authorize us to make those determinations now. *** [W]e dismiss the petition for lack of jurisdiction.

3. JURISDICTION OVER CRIMES

The following excerpts from *Hamdan v. Rumsfeld* offer an instructive look at what offenses were traditionally triable by military commission. Following these excerpts are materials concerning the offenses triable under the Military Commissions Act of 2006.

HAMDAN v. RUMSFELD
548 U.S. 557 (2006)

JUSTICE STEVENS

*** On July 3, 2003, the President announced his determination that Hamdan and five other detainees at Guantanamo Bay were subject to the November 13 Order and thus triable by military commission. *** Not until July 13, 2004, after Hamdan had commenced this action in the United States District Court for the Western District of Washington, did the Government finally charge him with the offense for which, a year earlier, he had been deemed eligible for trial by military commission.

The charging document, which is unsigned, contains 13 numbered paragraphs. *** Only the final two paragraphs, entitled "Charge: Conspiracy," contain allegations against Hamdan. Paragraph 12 charges that "from on or about February 1996 to on or about November 24, 2001," Hamdan "willfully and knowingly joined an enterprise of persons who shared a common criminal purpose and conspired and agreed with [named members of al Qaeda] to commit the following offenses triable by military commission: attacking civilians; attacking civilian objects; murder by an unprivileged belligerent; and terrorism." There is no allegation that Hamdan had any command responsibilities, played a leadership role, or participated in the planning of any activity.

Paragraph 13 lists four "overt acts" that Hamdan is alleged to have committed sometime between 1996 and November 2001 in furtherance of the "enterprise and conspiracy": (1) he acted as Osama bin Laden's "bodyguard and personal driver," "believ[ing]" all the while that bin Laden "and his associates were involved in" terrorist acts prior to and including the attacks of September 11, 2001; (2) he arranged for transportation of, and actually transported, weapons used by al Qaeda members and by bin Laden's bodyguards (Hamdan among them); (3) he "drove or accompanied [O]sama bin Laden to various al Qaida-sponsored training camps, press conferences, or lectures," at which bin Laden encouraged attacks against Americans; and (4) he received weapons training at al Qaeda-sponsored camps. ***

The charge against Hamdan *** alleges a conspiracy extending over a number of years, from 1996 to November 2001.[30] All but two months of that more than 5-year-long period preceded the attacks of September 11, 2001, and the enactment of the AUMF-the Act of Congress on which the Government relies for exercise of its war powers and thus for its authority to convene military commissions.[31] Neither the purported agreement with Osama bin Laden and others to commit war crimes, nor a single overt act, is alleged to have occurred in a theater of war or on any specified date after September 11, 2001. None of the overt acts that Hamdan is alleged to have committed violates the law of war. ***

There is no suggestion that Congress has, in exercise of its constitutional authority to "define and punish . . . Offences against the Law of Nations," U. S. Const., Art. I, § 8, cl. 10, positively identified "conspiracy" as a war crime. As we explained in *Quirin*, that is not necessarily fatal to the Government's claim of authority to try the alleged offense by military commission; Congress, through Article 21 of the UCMJ, has "incorporated by reference" the common law of war, which may render triable by military commission certain offenses not defined by statute. When, however, neither the elements of the offense nor the range of permissible punishments is defined by statute or treaty, the precedent must be plain and unambiguous. To demand any less would be to risk concentrating in military hands a degree of adjudicative and punitive power in excess of that contemplated either by statute or by the Constitution.[34] ***

This high standard was met in *Quirin;* the violation there alleged was, by "universal agreement and practice" both in this country and internationally, recognized as an offense against the law of war. Although the picture arguably was less clear in *Yamashita*, the disagreement between the majority and the dissenters in that case concerned whether the historic and textual evidence constituted clear precedent-not whether clear precedent was required to justify trial by law-of-war military commission.

At a minimum, the Government must make a substantial showing that the crime for which it seeks to try a defendant by military commission is

---

[30] The elements of this conspiracy charge have been defined not by Congress but by the President. See Military Commission Instruction No. 2, 32 CFR § 11.6 (2005).

[31] Justice Thomas would treat Osama bin Laden's 1996 declaration of jihad against Americans as the inception of the war. But even the Government does not go so far; although the United States had for some time prior to the attacks of September 11, 2001, been aggressively pursuing al Qaeda, neither in the charging document nor in submissions before this Court has the Government asserted that the President's *war powers* were activated prior to September 11, 2001. Justice Thomas' further argument that the AUMF is "backward looking" and therefore authorizes *trial by military commission* of crimes that occurred prior to the inception of war is insupportable. If nothing else, Article 21 of the UCMJ requires that the President comply with the law of war in his use of military commissions. As explained in the text, the law of war permits trial only of offenses "committed within the period of the war." ***

[34] While the common law necessarily is "evolutionary in nature," *** an act does not become a crime without its foundations having been firmly established in precedent. The caution that must be exercised in the incremental development of common-law crimes by the judiciary is *** all the more critical when reviewing developments that stem from military action.

acknowledged to be an offense against the law of war. That burden is far from satisfied here. The crime of "conspiracy" has rarely if ever been tried as such in this country by any law-of-war military commission not exercising some other form of jurisdiction,[35] and does not appear in either the Geneva Conventions or the Hague Conventions-the major treaties on the law of war. *** The Government cites *** sources that it says show otherwise. *** By any measure, they fail to satisfy the high standard of clarity required to justify the use of a military commission. *** If anything, *Quirin* supports Hamdan's argument that conspiracy is not a violation of the law of war. Not only did the Court pointedly omit any discussion of the conspiracy charge, but its analysis *** placed special emphasis on the *completion* of an offense; it took seriously the saboteurs' argument that there can be no violation of a law of war—at least not one triable by military commission—without the actual commission of or attempt to commit a "hostile and warlike act."

That limitation makes eminent sense when one considers the necessity from whence this kind of military commission grew: The need to dispense swift justice, often in the form of execution, to illegal belligerents captured on the battlefield. The same urgency would not have been felt vis-a-vis enemies who had done little more than agree to violate the laws of war. The *Quirin* Court acknowledged as much when it described the President's authority to use law-of-war military commissions as the power to "seize and subject to disciplinary measures those enemies *who in their attempt to thwart or impede our military effort* have violated the law of war." *** [N]one of the major treaties governing the law of war identifies conspiracy as a violation thereof. And the only "conspiracy" crimes that have been recognized by international war crimes tribunals (whose jurisdiction often extends beyond war crimes proper to crimes against humanity and crimes against the peace) are conspiracy to commit genocide and common plan to wage aggressive war, which is a crime against the peace and requires for its commission actual participation in a "concrete plan to wage war." *** [T]he Government has failed even to offer a "merely colorable" case for inclusion of conspiracy among those offenses cognizable by law-of-war military commission. Cf. *Quirin.* Because the charge does not support the commission's jurisdiction, the commission lacks authority to try Hamdan.

The charge's shortcomings are not merely formal, but are indicative of a broader inability on the Executive's part here to satisfy the most basic precondition—at least in the absence of specific congressional authorization—for establishment of military commissions: military necessity. Hamdan's tribunal was appointed not by a military commander in the field of battle, but by a retired major general stationed away from any active hostilities. Hamdan is charged not with an overt act for which he was caught redhanded

---

[35] The 19th-century trial of the "Lincoln conspirators," even if properly classified as a trial by law-of-war commission, is at best an equivocal exception. Although the charge against the defendants in that case accused them of "combining, confederating, and conspiring together" to murder the President, they were also charged *** with "maliciously, unlawfully, and traitorously murdering the said Abraham Lincoln." Moreover, the Attorney General who wrote the opinion defending the trial by military commission treated the charge as if it alleged the substantive offense of assassination.

in a theater of war and which military efficiency demands be tried expeditiously, but with an *agreement* the inception of which long predated the attacks of September 11, 2001 and the AUMF. That may well be a crime,[41] but it is not an offense that "by the law of war may be tried by military commission." None of the overt acts alleged to have been committed in furtherance of the agreement is itself a war crime, or even necessarily occurred during time of, or in a theater of, war. Any urgent need for imposition or execution of judgment is utterly belied by the record; Hamdan was arrested in November 2001 and he was not charged until mid-2004. These simply are not the circumstances in which, by any stretch of the historical evidence or this Court's precedents, a military commission established by Executive Order under the authority of Article 21 of the UCMJ may lawfully try a person and subject him to punishment.

JUSTICE THOMAS, ***dissenting:

*** The fourth consideration relevant to the jurisdiction of law-of-war military commissions relates to the nature of the offense charged. As relevant here, such commissions have jurisdiction to try "'violations of the laws and usages of war cognizable by military tribunals only'". In contrast to the preceding considerations, this Court's precedents establish that judicial review of "whether any of the acts charged is an offense against the law of war cognizable before a military tribunal" is appropriate. *Quirin*. However, "charges of violations of the law of war triable before a military tribunal need not be stated with the precision of a common law indictment." *Yamashita*. ***

In one key respect, the plurality departs from the proper framework for evaluating the adequacy of the charge against Hamdan under the laws of war. The plurality holds that where, as here, "neither the elements of the offense nor the range of permissible punishments is defined by statute or treaty, the precedent [establishing whether an offense is triable by military commission] must be plain and unambiguous." This is *** contrary to the presumption we acknowledged in *Quirin*, namely, that the actions of military commissions are "not to be set aside by the courts without the *clear conviction* that they are" unlawful. It is also contrary to *Yamashita*, which recognized the legitimacy of that military commission notwithstanding a substantial disagreement pertaining to whether Yamashita had been charged with a violation of the law of war. *** Hamdan has been charged with conduct constituting two distinct violations of the law of war cognizable before a military commission: membership in a war-criminal enterprise and conspiracy to commit war crimes. ***

Today a plurality of this Court would hold that conspiracy to massacre innocent civilians does not violate the laws of war. This determination is

---

[41] Justice Thomas' suggestion that our conclusion precludes the Government from bringing to justice those who conspire to commit acts of terrorism is therefore wide of the mark. That conspiracy is not a violation of the law of war triable by military commission does not mean the Government may not, for example, prosecute by court-martial or in federal court those caught "plotting terrorist atrocities like the bombing of the Khobar Towers."

unsustainable. The judgment of the political branches that Hamdan, and others like him, must be held accountable before military commissions for their involvement with and membership in an unlawful organization dedicated to inflicting massive civilian casualties is supported by virtually every relevant authority, including all of the authorities invoked by the plurality today. It is also supported by the nature of the present conflict. We are not engaged in a traditional battle with a nation-state, but with a worldwide, hydra-headed enemy, who lurks in the shadows conspiring to reproduce the atrocities of September 11, 2001, and who has boasted of sending suicide bombers into civilian gatherings, has proudly distributed videotapes of beheadings of civilian workers, and has tortured and dismembered captured American soldiers. But according to the plurality, when our Armed Forces capture those who are plotting terrorist atrocities like the bombing of the Khobar Towers, the bombing of the *U.S.S. Cole,* and the attacks of September 11—even if their plots are advanced to the very brink of fulfillment-our military cannot charge those criminals with any offense against the laws of war. Instead, our troops must catch the terrorists "redhanded," in the midst of *the attack itself,* in order to bring them to justice. Not only is this conclusion fundamentally inconsistent with the cardinal principal of the law of war, namely protecting non-combatants, but it would sorely hamper the President's ability to confront and defeat a new and deadly enemy. ***

*****

In the 2006 MCA, Congress responded to *Hamdan v. Rumsfeld* with respect to jurisdiction over offenses, specifically providing that conspiracy was an included offense. A complete list of the offenses covered by the 2006 MCA, designed to provide some flavor for its scope, is as follows: murder of protected persons; attacking civilians, civilian objects, or protected property; pillaging; denying quarter; taking hostages; employing poison or similar weapons; using protected persons or property as shields; torture, cruel or inhuman treatment; intentionally causing serious bodily injury; mutilating or maiming; murder in violation of the law of war; destruction of property in violation of the law of war; using treachery or perfidy; improperly using a flag of truce or distinctive emblem; intentionally mistreating a dead body; rape; sexual assault or abuse; hijacking or hazarding a vessel or aircraft; terrorism; providing material support for terrorism; wrongfully aiding the enemy; spying contempt; perjury and obstruction of justice. 10 U.S.C. § 950v. Conspiracy (§ 950v(b)(28)), attempts(§ 950t), and solicitation (§ 950u) to commit the defined acts are also punishable.

After reading the text of the conspiracy provision, consider the questions that follow.

(28) Conspiracy. Any person subject to this chapter who conspires to commit one or more substantive offenses triable by military commission under this chapter, and who knowingly does any overt act to effect the object of the conspiracy shall be punished, if death results to one or more of the victims, by death or such other punishment as a military commission under this chapter shall direct, and if death does not result to any of the victims, by such

punishment, other than death, as a military commission under this chapter may direct ***

Notes

1. **"Define and Punish."** Congress used its power to "define and punish" various offenses triable by military commission, overturning the lack of statutory basis rationale of *Hamdan*. Does this override traditional international law's lack of recognition of the offense of "conspiracy"? Consider the difference in the majoiryt and dissent view of conspiracy. The former talks of conspiracy in the abstract, the latter specific conspiracies. Does the MCA resolve this difference?

2. **Material Support.** Another provision of the MCA makes it unlawful to provide material support to terrorists (10 U.S.C. §950v(25)). May any alien who supplies or advises a foreign terrorist organization now be tried by military commission rather than a civilian criminal court? Is this provision constitutional, even as to a resident alien? See *al Marri* and *Humanitarian Law Project*, supra.

3. **Retroactivity.** While the 2006 MCA had an effective date (date of enactment), there was no provision saying that the crimes triable must have occurred to be triable by military commission. Was this a deliberate effort to vindicate such trials for 9/11 conspirators? Would this component of the MCA withstand scrutiny under the ex post facto clause of Article I ("No***ex post facto law shall be passed")?

4. **Ex Post Facto and Material Support.** The material support statutes would seem on their face to apply to Guantanamo Bay detainees trained by al Qaeda who materially supported al Qaeda and the Taliban against coalition forces. Sections 2339 A and B, however, applied until late 2001 only to conduct "in the United States," thus excluding those whose support outside the U.S. preceded the effective date of that change in the law. Military commissions have convicted two detainees, Salim Hamdan and Ali Hamza al-Bahlul, of material support based on a "joint criminal enterprise" theory of liability. Al-Bahlul appealed, arguing to the Court of Military Commission Review (CMCR) in March, 2011, that their material support for terrorism convictions are unconstitutional under the *Ex Post Facto* clause and a violation of the *nullum crimen sine lege* ("no crime without law") principle of international law.

First, they argue, material support was not a "plain and unambiguous" war crime prior to the MCA in 2006. The MCA, 10 U.S.C. § 950p, declares that it does not establish new crimes, but codifies existing crimes. They cite, among other authority, the 2009 testimony of Department of Defense General Counsel before the Senate Armed Services Committee that Congress should remove material support as an offense triable by military commission because appellate courts may find that 'material support for terrorism'…is not a traditional violation of the law of war." Testimony of Jeh Charles Johnson General Counsel, Department of Defense Hearing Before the Senate Armed Services Committee, "Military Commissions" Presented On July 8, 2009. Likewise, Asst. Atty. Gen. David Kris commented that, "there are serious questions as to whether material support for terrorism or terrorist groups is a traditional violation of the law of war." David Kris, statement to the Senate Subcommittee on Terrorism and Homeland

Security, July 7, 2009. Second, they argue that if material support is a recognized war crime now, it was not prior to the 2006 enactment of the MCA, and thus applying it to conduct that terminated in 2001 is a violation of the *Ex Post Facto* clause. Furthermore, they argue that the international law principle of *nullum crimen sine lege* ("no crime without law") requires that a criminal conviction can only based on law that existed at the time the defendant committed the acts or omissions, and that criminal liability was reasonably foreseeable. The analogy drawn by the government to joint criminal enterprise, they argue, is invalid because that is a theory of liability and not a standalone crime. Third, they argue that the elements of the crime of Material Support as stated in the MCA require no higher showing than is required to establish the court's personal jurisdiction over the defendant. All that is required for a conviction is a showing that someone has supported or is supporting Al Qaeda.

In its reply brief, the government argues that Congress in the Military Commissions Act of 2006 concluded that conspiracy to commit war crimes already constituted a violation of the laws of war. It finds support for this premise in the fact that international criminal courts have recognized Joint Criminal Enterprise liability, which, while not a standalone offense, has nearly identical proof requirements to Material Support. Second, the government argues Congress is owed deference when using its powers under the "define and punish" clause, citing *Hamdan,* to codify the existing common law of war. The government cites previous international tribunals' investigations of *ex post facto* issues (in international law terms, "principle of legality" issues), and found that starting with Nuremburg, the standard to determine whether a charge was ex post facto was whether it is foreseeable and accessible to the defendant that his conduct is criminal. Material Support, the government argues, is a form of conspiracy charge. Conspiracy is widely criminalized in both common law and civil jurisdictions, so it was foreseeable to a defendant in prior to the 2006 MCA that conspiratorial conduct was criminal. Third, the government cites the 1957 Army Field Manual, which listed conspiracy as a crime. The government claims the Field Manual is entitled to a great deal of deference, based on both the "define and punish" clause and war powers under *Youngstown*, because it is indicative of state practice.

However the CMCR decides these issues, it will not likely have the last word. The parties may appeal as of right to the D.C. Circuit, which will review legal issues de novo. *See* Steve Vladeck, "The Most Inexplicable One-Year Delay in Appellate History," available at: http://prawfsblawg.blogs.com/prawfsblawg/2011/01/the-most-preposterous-one-year-delay-in-appellate-history.html.

5. Aiding the Enemy and Duty of Allegiance. In addition to the material support issue, the CMCR asked al-Bahlul and the government for briefing on whether the offense of aiding the enemy is limited to those who have breached a duty of allegiance or loyalty to a sovereign state. Al-Bahlul said yes, citing a treatise that "what makes aiding the enemy criminal is not the support given, but the breach of fidelity it entails" and noting that in prior prosecutions for aiding the enemy in the Civil War and Philippines Insurrection, as well as later cases, the defendants owe the U.S. a duty of loyalty. The government replied that the duty is not so limited if the aid is either unlawfully engaging in war in the first place or is waging the war in an unlawful manner. It cited various prosecutions during wars with Indian tribes and prosecution of non-nationals in WWII, including *Quirin*. The government argues that Philippine Insurrection precedents are not on-point because "all persons in that conflict owed some duty of loyalty to the United States." The government also distinguishes non-prosecution of non-U.S. citizen Civil War blockade runners for aiding the enemy, because while they had no duty of loyalty to the US, they were aiding a recognized, lawful belligerent.

C. OPERATION OF MILITARY COMMISSIONS

Once again, the starting point for analysis of the procedures for operation of military commission trials is *Hamdan*. The following excerpt from Justice Stevens' opinion describes the procedures that the Court found to violate the UCMJ and the Geneva Conventions. Following these excerpts are materials concerning procedures under the Military Commissions Act of 2006.

HAMDAN v. RUMSFELD
126 S.Ct. 2749 (2006)

*** Whether or not the Government has charged Hamdan with an offense against the law of war cognizable by military commission, the commission lacks power to proceed. The UCMJ conditions the President's use of military commissions on compliance not only with the American common law of war, but also with the rest of the UCMJ itself, insofar as applicable, and with the "rules and precepts of the law of nations," *Quirin*, including, *inter alia*, the four Geneva Conventions signed in 1949. See *Yamashita*. The procedures that the Government has decreed will govern Hamdan's trial by commission violate these laws.

The commission's procedures are set forth in Commission Order No. 1, which was amended most recently on August 31, 2005 -- after Hamdan's trial had already begun. Every commission established pursuant to Commission Order No. 1 must have a presiding officer and at least three other members, all of whom must be commissioned officers. § 4(A)(1). The presiding officer's job is to rule on questions of law and other evidentiary and interlocutory issues; the other members make findings and, if applicable, sentencing decisions. § 4(A)(5). The accused is entitled to appointed military counsel and may hire civilian counsel at his own expense so long as such counsel is a U.S citizen with security clearance "at the level SECRET or higher." §§ 4(C)(2)-(3). The accused also is entitled to a copy of the charge(s) against him, both in English and his own language (if different), to a presumption of innocence, and to certain other rights typically afforded criminal defendants in civilian courts and courts-martial. See §§ 5(A)-(P). These rights are subject, however, to one glaring condition: The accused and his civilian counsel may be excluded from, and precluded from ever learning what evidence was presented during, any part of the proceeding that either the Appointing Authority or the presiding officer decides to "close." Grounds for such closure "include the protection of information classified or classifiable . . .;

information protected by law or rule from unauthorized disclosure; the physical safety of participants in Commission proceedings, including prospective witnesses; intelligence and law enforcement sources, methods, or activities; and other national security interests." § 6(B)(3). Appointed military defense counsel must be privy to these closed sessions, but may, at the presiding officer's discretion, be forbidden to reveal to his or her client what took place therein.

Another striking feature of the rules governing Hamdan's commission *** permit the admission of *any* evidence that, in the opinion of the presiding officer, "would have probative value to a reasonable person." Under this test, not only is testimonial hearsay and evidence obtained through coercion fully admissible, but neither live testimony nor witnesses' written statements need be sworn. Moreover, the accused and his civilian counsel may be denied access to evidence in the form of "protected information" (which includes classified information as well as "information protected by law or rule from unauthorized disclosure'"and "information concerning other national security interests," so long as the presiding officer concludes that the evidence is "probative" *** and that its admission without the accused's knowledge would not "result in the denial of a full and fair trial." Finally, a presiding officer's determination that evidence "would not have probative value to a reasonable person" may be overridden by a majority of the other commission members. ***

Hamdan raises both general and particular objections to the procedures set forth in Commission Order No. 1. His general objection is that the procedures' admitted deviation from those governing courts-martial itself renders the commission illegal. Chief among his particular objections are that he may, under the Commission Order, be convicted based on evidence he has not seen or heard, and that any evidence admitted against him need not comply with the admissibility or relevance rules typically applicable in criminal trials and court-martial proceedings. ***

*** The procedures and evidentiary rules used to try General Yamashita near the end of World War II deviated in significant respects from those then governing courts-martial. The force of that precedent, however, has been seriously undermined by post-World War II developments. *** The procedures and rules of evidence employed during Yamashita's trial departed so far from those used in courts-martial that they generated an unusually long and vociferous critique from two Members of this Court. *** At least partially in response to subsequent criticism of General Yamashita's trial, the UCMJ's codification of the Articles of War after World War II expanded the category of persons subject thereto to include defendants in Yamashita's (and Hamdan's) position, and the Third Geneva Convention of 1949 extended prisoner-of-war protections to individuals tried for crimes committed before their capture. *** [UCMJ] Article 36 places two restrictions on the President's power to promulgate rules of procedure for courts-martial and military commissions alike. First, no procedural rule he adopts may be "contrary to or inconsistent with" the UCMJ—however practical it may seem. Second, the rules adopted must be "uniform insofar as practicable." That is, the rules applied to military commissions must be the same as those applied to courts-martial unless such uniformity proves impracticable.

Hamdan *** maintains that the procedures described in the Commission Order are inconsistent with the UCMJ and that the Government has offered no explanation for their deviation from the procedures governing courts-martial *** Among the inconsistencies Hamdan identifies is that between § 6 of the Commission Order, which permits exclusion of the accused from proceedings and denial of his access to evidence in certain circumstances, and the UCMJ's requirement that "[a]ll ... proceedings" other than votes and deliberations by courts-martial "shall be made a part of the record and shall be in the presence of the accused." Hamdan also observes that the Commission Order dispenses with virtually all evidentiary rules applicable in courts-martial.***

Without reaching the question whether any provision of Commission Order No. 1 is strictly "contrary to or inconsistent with" other provisions of the UCMJ, we conclude that the "practicability" determination the President has made is insufficient to justify variances from the procedures governing courts-martial. Subsection (b) of Article 36 was added after World War II, and requires a different showing of impracticability from the one required by subsection (a). Subsection (a) requires that the rules the President promulgates for courts-martial, provost courts, and military commissions alike conform to those that govern procedures in *Article III courts*, "so far as *he considers* practicable." Subsection (b), by contrast, demands that the rules applied in courts-martial, provost courts, and military commissions-whether or not they conform with the Federal Rules of Evidence-be "uniform *insofar as practicable*." Under the latter provision, then, the rules set forth in the Manual for Courts-Martial must apply to military commissions unless impracticable.

The President here has determined *** that it is impracticable to apply the rules and principles of law that govern "the trial of criminal cases in the United States district courts," to Hamdan's commission. We assume that complete deference is owed that determination. The President has not, however, made a similar official determination that it is impracticable to apply the rules for courts-martial. And even if subsection (b)'s requirements may be satisfied without such an official determination, the requirements of that subsection are not satisfied here.

Nothing in the record before us demonstrates that it would be impracticable to apply court-martial rules in this case. There is no suggestion, for example, of any logistical difficulty in securing properly sworn and authenticated evidence or in applying the usual principles of relevance and admissibility. Assuming *arguendo* that the reasons articulated in the President's Article 36(a) determination ought to be considered in evaluating the impracticability of applying court-martial rules, the only reason offered in support of that determination is the danger posed by international terrorism. Without for one moment underestimating that danger, it is not evident to us why it should require, in the case of Hamdan's trial, any variance from the rules that govern courts-martial.

The absence of any showing of impracticability is particularly disturbing when considered in light of the clear and admitted failure to apply one of the most fundamental protections afforded not just by the Manual for Courts-Martial but also by the UCMJ itself: the right to be present. Whether or not that departure technically is "contrary to or inconsistent with" the terms of the UCMJ, the jettisoning of so basic a right cannot lightly be excused as "practicable." *** Article 36 *** not having been complied with here, the rules specified for Hamdan's trial are illegal. ***

The procedures adopted to try Hamdan also violate the Geneva Conventions. The Court of Appeals dismissed Hamdan's Geneva Convention challenge on three independent grounds: (1) the Geneva Conventions are not judicially enforceable; (2) Hamdan in any event is not entitled to their protections; and (3) even if he is entitled to their protections, *Councilman* abstention is appropriate. ***

The Court of Appeals relied on *Johnson v. Eisentrager,* 339 U.S. 763(1950), to hold that Hamdan could not invoke the Geneva Conventions to challenge the Government's plan to prosecute him in accordance with Commission Order No. 1. *** We may assume that "the obvious scheme" of the 1949 Conventions is identical in all relevant respects to that of the 1929 Convention, and even that that scheme would, absent some other provision of law, preclude Hamdan's invocation of the Convention's provisions as an independent source of law binding the Government's actions and furnishing petitioner with any enforceable right. For, regardless of the nature of the rights conferred on Hamdan, they are, as the Government does not dispute, part of the law of war. And compliance with the law of war is the condition upon which the authority set forth in *Article 21* is granted.

For the Court of Appeals, acknowledgment of that condition was no bar to Hamdan's trial by commission. As an alternative to its holding that Hamdan could not invoke the Geneva Conventions at all, the Court of Appeals concluded that the Conventions did not in any event apply to the armed conflict during which Hamdan was captured. The court accepted the Executive's assertions that Hamdan was captured in connection with the United States' war with al Qaeda and that that war is distinct from the war with the Taliban in Afghanistan. It further reasoned that the war with al Qaeda evades the reach of the Geneva Conventions. We, like Judge Williams, disagree with the latter conclusion.

The conflict with al Qaeda is not, according to the Government, a conflict to which the full protections afforded detainees under the 1949 Geneva Conventions apply because Article 2 of those Conventions (which appears in all four Conventions) renders the full protections applicable only to "all cases of declared war or of any other armed conflict which may arise between two or more of the High Contracting Parties." 6 U.S.T., at 3318. Since Hamdan was captured and detained incident to the conflict with al Qaeda and not the conflict with the Taliban, and since al Qaeda, unlike Afghanistan, is not a "High Contracting Party" -- *i.e.*, a signatory of the Conventions, the protections of those Conventions are not, it is argued, applicable to Hamdan.

We need not decide the merits of this argument because there is at least one provision of the Geneva Conventions that applies here even if the relevant conflict is not one between signatories. Article 3, often referred to as Common Article 3 because, like Article 2, it appears in all four Geneva Conventions, provides that in a "conflict not of an international character occurring in the territory of one of the High Contracting Parties, each Party n62 to the conflict shall be bound to apply, as a minimum," certain provisions protecting "persons taking no active part in the hostilities, including members of armed forces who have laid down their arms and those placed *hors de combat* by . . . detention." One such provision prohibits "the passing of sentences and the carrying out of executions without previous judgment pronounced by a regularly constituted court affording all the judicial guarantees which are recognized as indispensable by civilized peoples." *Ibid.*

The Court of Appeals thought, and the Government asserts, that Common Article 3 does not apply to Hamdan because the conflict with al Qaeda, being "'international in scope,'" does not qualify as a "'conflict not of an international character.'" That reasoning is erroneous. The term "conflict not of an international character" is used here in contradistinction to a conflict between nations. So much is demonstrated by the "fundamental logic [of] the Convention's provisions on its application." Common Article 2 provides that "the present Convention shall apply to all cases of declared war or of any other armed conflict which may arise between two or more of the High Contracting Parties." High Contracting Parties (signatories) also must abide by all terms of the Conventions vis-A-vis one another even if one party to the conflict is a nonsignatory "Power," and must so abide vis-A-vis the nonsignatory if "the latter accepts and applies" those terms. Common Article 3, by contrast, affords some minimal protection, falling short of full protection under the Conventions, to individuals associated with neither a signatory nor even a nonsignatory "Power" who are involved in a conflict "in the territory of" a signatory. The latter kind of conflict is distinguishable from the conflict described in Common Article 2 chiefly because it does not involve a clash between nations (whether signatories or not). In context, then, the phrase "not of an international character" bears its literal meaning.

Although the official commentaries accompanying Common Article 3 indicate that an important purpose of the provision was to furnish minimal protection to rebels involved in one kind of "conflict not of an international character," *i.e.*, a civil war, the commentaries also make clear "that the scope of the Article must be as wide as possible." In fact, limiting language that would have rendered Common Article 3 applicable "especially [to] cases of civil war, colonial conflicts, or wars of religion," was omitted from the final version of the Article, which coupled broader scope of application with a narrower range of rights than did earlier proposed iterations.

Common Article 3, then, is applicable here and, as indicated above, requires that Hamdan be tried by a "regularly constituted court affording all the judicial guarantees which are recognized as indispensable by civilized peoples." While the term "regularly constituted court" is not specifically defined in either Common Article 3 or its accompanying commentary, other sources disclose its core meaning. The commentary accompanying a provision of the Fourth Geneva Convention, for example, defines "'regularly constituted'" tribunals to include "ordinary military courts" and "definitely exclude all special tribunals." GCIV Commentary 340 (defining the term "properly constituted" in Article 66, which the commentary treats as identical to "regularly constituted"); see also *Yamashita*, 327 U.S., at 44 (Rutledge, J., dissenting) (describing military commission as a court "specially constituted for a particular trial"). And one of the Red Cross' own treatises defines "regularly constituted court" as used in Common Article 3 to mean "established and organized in accordance with the laws and procedures already in force in a country." ***

Inextricably intertwined with the question of regular constitution is the evaluation of the procedures governing the tribunal and whether they afford "all the judicial guarantees which are recognized as indispensable by civilized peoples." Like the phrase "regularly constituted court," this phrase is not defined in the text of the Geneva Conventions. But it must be understood to incorporate at least the barest of those trial protections that have been recognized by customary international law. Many of these are described in Article 75 of Protocol I to the Geneva Conventions of 1949, adopted in 1977 (Protocol I). Although the United States declined to ratify Protocol I, its objections were not to Article 75 thereof. Indeed, it appears that the Government "regards the provisions of Article 75 as an articulation of safeguards to which all persons in the hands of an enemy are entitled." Among the rights set forth in Article 75 is the "right to be tried in [one's] presence." Protocol I, Art. 75(4)(e). ***

Common Article 3 obviously tolerates a great degree of flexibility in trying individuals captured during armed conflict; its requirements are general ones, crafted to accommodate a wide variety of legal systems. But *requirements* they are nonetheless. The commission that the President has convened to try Hamdan does not meet those requirements.

Notes

1. *Hamdan* Overruled by MCA. The procedures specified by the 2006 MCA had Congress' stamp of approval. These procedures were also supplemented by the Rules for Military Commissions referred to in *al-Marri*. The MCA procedures were intended to satisfy Common Article 3 concerns.

2. Challenges to Military Commissions in Federal Courts. While a number of detainees have sought to challenge trial by military commissions in federal courts, no federal court has yet reached the merits of such a question, instead generally relying on the abstention doctrine to hold that challenges to commissions should be resolved on post conviction appeal. Below is an example of such a challenge in which the federal court abstained from intervening. Consider as you read whether the federal courts should abstain in this context—and why you think they did.

HAMDAN v. GATES

565 F. Supp. 2d 130 (D.D.C. 2008)

JAMES ROBERTSON, District Judge.

Salim Ahmed Hamdan seeks a preliminary injunction that would stop his trial by military commission pending federal court review of *** his claims that the trial will violate the Constitution and the Geneva Conventions. ***

[I]n October 2006, Congress enacted the Military Commissions Act. In Section 3(a)(1) of that Act, Congress gave military commissions jurisdiction to try "alien unlawful enemy combatant[s]." Under the Act, a military commission is made up of at least five officers, and is presided over by a military judge. Many of the procedures for an MCA commission parallel those that had been established by the President's order. Before and after passage of the MCA, the applicable rules have required that the defendant be represented by appointed military counsel and have the ability to retain private counsel (as Hamdan has), that he be informed of the charges against him, that he be presumed innocent until proven guilty beyond a reasonable doubt, that he receive (with important qualifications) the evidence that the prosecution intends to produce at trial and any known exculpatory evidence, that he not be required to testify at trial, and that he be allowed to present evidence and cross-examine witnesses.

The procedures codified by the MCA also include significant improvements. Previously, the accused could be excluded from the proceedings, and evidence admitted against him without his knowledge. The MCA repairs that problem by requiring the presence of the defendant unless, after being warned, he persists in conduct that justifies his exclusion in order to protect the safety of others or to avoid disrupting the proceedings. While the MCA adopts fairly permissive standards allowing for the use of hearsay and requires the party opposing admission to prove unreliability, whenever the government intends to use hearsay, it must notify the defendant "sufficiently in advance to provide the adverse party with a fair opportunity to meet the evidence" and must explain "the particulars of the evidence (including information on the general circumstances under which the evidence was obtained)."

The curtailment of confrontation rights through the broad allowance of hearsay is one of a number of ways in which MCA commissions depart from standards that would be applied in either U.S. criminal trials or courts-martial. Another departure, and a startling one, is that *** evidence obtained by "coercion" may be used against the defendant so long as the military judge decides that its admission is in the interest of justice and that it has "sufficient" probative value. *Compare Chambers v. Florida,* 309 U.S. 227 (1940) (reversing conviction and excluding evidence obtained through five days of coercive interrogation).

That said, one of the most substantial improvements under the MCA is in the structure for review of convictions. Before the MCA, the President himself, or the Secretary of Defense acting at his direction, was vested with final reviewing authority. There was no provision for independent review outside the military's chain of command. Under the MCA, defendants convicted by military commission are afforded three levels of appellate review. A defendant may first appeal his conviction to a Court of Military Commission Review (CMCR), comprised of at least three military judges or civilians with "comparable qualifications" appointed by the Secretary of Defense. After exhausting (or waiving) proceedings before the CMCR, the defendant has an appeal of right to the D.C. Circuit, which has "exclusive jurisdiction to determine the validity of a final judgment rendered by a military commission." The Court of Appeals has jurisdiction to review all "matters of law" in order to consider "whether the final decision was consistent with the standards and procedures specified" in the MCA and with "the Constitution and laws of the United States." Finally, *** the Supreme Court may review the final judgment of the Court of Appeals on a writ of *certiorari* ***

*** On April 5, 2007, the Convening Authority authorized two new charges against Hamdan, both of which had recently been "codified" under the MCA. Charge I was, and is, for conspiracy in violation of 10 U.S.C. § 950v(b)(28); Charge II is for providing material support for terrorism in violation of 10 U.S.C. § 950v(b)(25). *** [A]s a result of hearings held on December 5 and 6, 2007, the military judge issued an opinion finding Hamdan to be an unlawful enemy combatant. In that same opinion, issued on December 19, 2007, the judge also rejected a number of constitutional arguments-Hamdan's *ex post facto,* bill of attainder and equal protection challenges-relying on the D.C. Circuit's now-vacated opinion in *Boumediene v. Bush,* 476 F.3d 981 (D.C.Cir.2007), which had held that detainees at Guantanamo have no cognizable constitutional rights. *** Hamdan argues that the Commission lacks *** lacks subject matter jurisdiction over the crimes for which he has been charged. ***

As to subject matter jurisdiction, Hamdan argues that the Commission lacks power to proceed because the charges filed against him violate the Constitution's *ex post facto,* define and punish, and bill of attainder clauses. He also asserts that the MCA violates the equal protection component of Fifth Amendment due process by subjecting only aliens to trial by military commission, and that the Commission's potential allowance of certain kinds of hearsay evidence and evidence obtained through coercion will violate his Geneva Convention and due process rights.

The government argues that as a result of a provision in Section 3(a)(1) of the Military Commissions Act, *** this Court lacks jurisdiction to decide Hamdan's claims and that, even if jurisdiction does exist, "the comity-based abstention doctrine recognized in [*Schlesinger v. Councilman,* 420 U.S. 738 (1975)] ... require [s] this Court to stay its hand until the completion of the military commission process." Aside from any claims based on the Geneva Conventions, the government stresses that each claim that Hamdan has raised is "fully cognizable on direct review [by the D.C. Circuit] if he is convicted by military commission."[3] ***

Hamdan *** argues that, if and to the extent that § 950j(b) does strip this Court of jurisdiction, either to challenge the MCA tribunal's jurisdiction or to deal with his other constitutional claims about the Commission, it "violate[s] the Suspension Clause by precluding access to the Great Writ without providing an adequate, alternative remedy."

That argument presents important constitutional questions that I need not, and therefore will not, attempt to answer. "If there is one doctrine more deeply rooted than any other in the process of constitutional adjudication it is that we ought not to pass on questions of constitutionality . . . unless such adjudication is unavoidable." ***

First, the application of habeas corpus that Hamdan wishes to advance here is different from the one recognized in *Boumediene*. *Boumediene* dealt with a challenge to detention. Hamdan insists in his reply brief that he also challenges his detention, but the gist of the challenge presented in this motion for preliminary injunction is to the jurisdiction of the Military Commission, an issue farther removed from the "historical core" of the Writ than was the case in *Boumediene*.

Second, unlike the petitioners in *Boumediene*, Hamdan has had a CSRT *and* a two-day jurisdictional hearing before the Commission, at which he was represented by counsel, and will now have a fully adversarial trial that will provide a further test of the premise of his detention. As Justice Kennedy observed in *Boumediene*, "habeas corpus review may be more circumscribed if the underlying detention proceedings are more thorough than they were here. The *Boumediene* petitioners' right to immediate habeas hearings was tied to the fact that "there has been no trial by a military commission for violations of the laws of war" nor had there been "a rigorous adversarial process to test the legality of their detention."

Unlike the detainees in *Boumediene,* Hamdan has been informed of the charges against him and guaranteed the assistance of counsel. He has been afforded discovery. He will be able to call and cross-examine witnesses, to challenge the use of hearsay, and to introduce his own exculpatory evidence. He is entitled to the presumption of innocence. And, most importantly, if Hamdan is convicted, he will be able to raise each of his legal arguments before the D.C. Circuit, and, potentially, the Supreme Court.

The question of whether section § 950j(b) violates the Suspension Clause is both novel and complex. It is by no means controlled by the four corners of *Boumediene*. What must be considered is "whether there are suitable alternative processes in place to protect against the arbitrary exercise of government power." "What matters is the sum total of procedural protections afforded to the detainee at all stages, direct and collateral."

---

[3] The MCA purports to bar defendants from asserting defenses or invoking rights based on the Geneva Conventions. *See 10 U.S.C. § 948b(g)*. Should Hamdan be convicted, nothing in the MCA bars him from asserting on appeal, as he does in this motion, that § 948b(g) violates the Supremacy Clause and the separation of powers. *See United States v. Klein,* 80 U.S. 128 (1872)

As an example of the complexity of the question presented by Hamdan's Suspension Clause challenge, and the inadvisability of attempting to decide it now, consider that a traditional function of a habeas court is to "allow[ ] prisoners to introduce exculpatory evidence that was either unknown or previously unavailable to the prisoner" at the time that the Executive made the decision to detain. Because the MCA provides that the D.C. Circuit's jurisdiction on direct review is limited to "matters of law," it appears that the Court of Appeals would be barred from considering a claim of innocence based on previously unavailable evidence. Whether the constitution entitles Hamdan to raise such a claim collaterally, in habeas, is an entirely speculative question at this point, first, because such claims may not actually arise, and, second, because the question cannot be answered without accessing how much procedure Hamdan did, in fact, actually receive.

Hamdan's focus now is not on post-trial habeas, of course. What he seeks is pre-trial relief to avoid being subjected to a trial that, in his submission, will be unlawful. His claims of unlawfulness, however, are all claims that should or must be decided in the first instance by the Military Commission, and then raised before the D.C. Circuit, as necessary, on appeal. The Supreme Court's decision in *Councilman* requires federal courts to give "due respect to the autonomous military judicial system created by Congress." *Councilman* involved court-martial proceedings against a U.S. service member, to be sure, and not a military commission, but its central rationale is applicable here. *Councilman* requires the courts to respect the balance that Congress has struck in creating a military justice system, "a critical element of which is the Court of Military Appeals consisting of civilian judges completely removed from all military influence or persuasion." Considerations of comity were inapplicable when Hamdan's petition was first before me in 2004 because, as I said then, "whatever can be said about the Military Commission established under the President's Military Order, it is not autonomous, and it was not created by Congress." With the enactment of the MCA, that is no longer the case: "Hamdan is to face a military commission ... designed ... by a Congress that ... act[ed] according to guidelines laid down by the Supreme Court." Additionally, because the MCA gives Hamdan an appeal of right to an Article III court, direct review will be even more "removed from all military influence or persuasion" than in *Councilman.*

The long-standing exception to *Councilman* abstention is that defendants may raise, pre-trial, "substantial arguments that a military tribunal lacks personal jurisdiction over them," but I find no "substantial argument" about jurisdiction in this case. Hamdan urges that the military judge "made a finding of unlawful enemy combatancy in December 2007 based on a misapplication of *relevant law,*" by failing to address the merits of his constitutional arguments, by misapplying the Geneva Conventions, and by denying him the ability to call certain exculpatory witnesses. But Hamdan's summary assertion of these claims does not automatically make his jurisdictional challenge a substantial one. Hamdan does not explain how the applicable jurisdictional standards contained in 10 U.S.C. § 948a(1) were violated by the military judge's application of law to the facts adduced at the

December 2007 jurisdictional hearing. The absence of a full-scale habeas hearing as to Hamdan's classification as an unlawful enemy combatant does not, by itself, raise a substantial question about the Commission's jurisdiction to proceed. Moreover, under the D.C. Circuit's recent decision in *Khadr v. United States*, 529 F.3d 1112 (D.C.Cir. 2008), all of Hamdan's jurisdictional arguments can be addressed, if necessary, following final judgment in accordance with § 950g. Where both Congress and the President have expressly decided when Article III review is to occur, the courts should be wary of disturbing their judgment.

I find that Hamdan's chances of prevailing on the merits of his prayer for injunctive relief are uncertain; that he has shown no public interest reason for an injunction; that the disruption that would be caused by a last-minute delay of his trial would be significant; and that the irreparable injuries he asserts do not outweigh the other preliminary injunction factors.

The eyes of the world are on Guantanamo Bay. Justice must be done there, and must be seen to be done there, fairly and impartially. But Article III judges do not have a monopoly on justice, or on constitutional learning. A real judge is presiding over the pretrial proceedings in Hamdan's case and will preside over the trial. He will have difficult decisions to make, as judges do in nearly all trials. The questions of whether Hamdan is being tried *ex post facto* for new offenses, whether and for what purposes coerced testimony will be received in evidence, and whether and for what purpose hearsay evidence will be received, are of particular sensitivity. If the Military Commission judge gets it wrong, his error may be corrected by the CMCR. If the CMCR gets it wrong, it may be corrected by the D.C. Circuit. And if the D.C. Circuit gets it wrong, the Supreme Court may grant a writ of *certiorari*.

The motion for preliminary injunction is **denied.**

Notes

1. Bush Administration Military Commission Proceedings. During President George W. Bush's two terms in office, only three men were convicted through the Military Commissions process, with only two full-scale trials completed. The first conviction, in 2007, was of David Matthew Hicks of Australia, who was convicted of material support to terrorism under a plea agreement in 2007. While a military commission sentenced Hicks to seven years confinement, as part of the pretrial agreement, Hick's sentence was limited to not more than nine months confinement to be served in Australia as part of a transfer agreement with the United States. In 2008 after the first full-scale trial, Salim Hamdan was found guilty of one count of providing material support for terrorism and sentenced to five and a half years imprisonment, but credited with five years for time served, the remainder to be served in Yemen per a transfer agreement. Finally, Ali Hamza Ahmad Suliman al Bahlul of Yemen was sentenced to life imprisonment for multiple counts of conspiracy, solicitation to commit certain war crimes, and providing material support for terrorism in connection with his role as al Qaeda's "propaganda chief." During most of Mr. Bahlul's trial, he refused representation and boycotted most of the proceedings.

2. Why So Little Use of Military Commissions? Why were there so few convictions under the Bush Administration? While there are many possible explanations, one former military prosecutor filed a declaration in federal court stating that the system of handling evidence against detainees under the military commissions was so chaotic that it was impossible to prepare a successful prosecution. Peter Finn, *Evidence in Terror Cases Said to Be in Chaos*, WASH. POST., Jan. 14, 2009, at A08. In addition, the Bush Administration official in charge of determining whether to prosecute detainees before the military commission decided that because the treatment of at least one high value detainee, Mohammed al-Qahtani, who allegedly planned to participate in the 9/11 attacks, "met the legal definition of torture," she did not refer his case for prosecution. Bob Woodward, *Detainee Tortured, Says U.S. Official*, WASH. POST., Jan. 14, 2009, at A01.

3. President Obama Suspends Military Commissions. Upon taking office, President Obama on January 22, 2009 issued and Executive Order, E.O. 13492, entitled "Review and Disposition of Individuals Detained at the Guantanamo Bay Naval Base and Closure of Detention Facilities," 74 Federal Register 4897, January 22, 2009. The Order called for the closing of the Guantanamo Bay detention facility as well as the review of all detainees at Guantanamo to assess if they should be transferred, released, prosecuted on criminal charges, or continue to be detained by the U.S. The Order halted all proceedings before military commissions for 120 days during the pendancy of the review. In adhering to the order, the government has requested multiple continuances before various military commission courts. Hearings in the current cases continued, however, as they did not constitute a 'proceeding' for purposes of the President's Order.

4. Military Commission Suspension Ends. On May 15, 2009 President Obama announced that the commissions would resume under new procedures, alongside prosecutions in federal courts. Those new procedures would include (1) a ban on the use of evidence secured by cruel, inhuman, or degrading treatment; (2) a requirement that the party submitting hearsay evidence demonstrate its reliability; and (3) permitting detainees to choose military counse from among those normally available in the Office of Military Commissions. General Counsel, Department of Defense, Memorandum of May 13, 2009, *Changes to the Manual for Military Commissions*.

In July of 2009, Obama's Detention Policy Task Force issued its preliminary report, which reaffirmed that the Administration would pursue convictions before military commissions in cases involving suspected violations of the laws of war, though stating that federal criminal prosecutions were preferable. Memorandum from the Detention Policy Task Force to the Attorney General and the Secretary of Defense, July 20, 2009. In addition, the report laid out criteria to govern how the Administration would use in a given detainee's case. These included:

- The nature and gravity of offenses or underlying conduct; identity of victims; location of offense; location and context in which individual was apprehended; and the conduct of the investigation.

- Protection of intelligence source and methods; venue; number   of defendants; foreign policy concerns; legal or evidentiary problems; efficiency and resource concerns.

• The extent to which the forum and offenses that can be tried there permit a full presentation of the wrongful conduct, and the available sentence upon conviction.

The January deadline to close Guantanamo, set by the President's first Executive Order, passed with the facility still in operation. The Detention Policy Task Force finished its review, determining that about 50 detainees would continue to be held without trail, reportedly because they are too difficult to prosecute and too dangerous to release, approximately 40 would be prosecuted before either military commission or federal court, and the remaining 110 would be released once a suitable country had agreed to accept them. *Detainees Will Still Be Held, but Not Tried, Official Says*, NY TIMES, Jan. 22, 2010, at A14.

5. The Military Commissions Act of 2009. In October of 2009, Congress enacted the Military Commissions Act of 2009, an amendment to the earlier MCA. The new law granted suspected terrorists greater due process rights than its predecessor. For instance, the 2009 MCA flatly prohibits the introduction of detainee statements obtained through torture, coercion, or cruel, inhuman and degrading treatment, an expansion of the earlier prohibition. It further guarantees detainees a right to present evidence in his defense and access to outside counsel, either pro bono or at detainee expense, or military counsel at government expense. Detainees facing the death penalty are afforded two government funded lawyers, at least one of whom is to be learned in relevant cases. The Act provides more access for defense counsel to examine classified evidence, protects detainees from being forced to testify against their will, and permits detainees to attend all military commission proceedings, and allows detainees to cross examine government witnesses and introduce their own. The bill permits hearsay evidence but requires that the party submitting the evidence provide the other party with its intention to introduce it and the circumstances under which the evidence was obtained, and the court must deem such evidence probative and find that direct testimony is not available as a practical matter. Under the 2006 MCA, detainees were labeled "unlawful enemy combatants," while the 2009 law terms them "alien unprivileged enemy belligerents," which military prosecutors state is more in line with the Geneva Conventions.

6. New Manual for Military Commissions. In addition, the Department of Defense issued a new Manual for Military Commissions in 2010. It included several major changes: a right to self representation; that pleading guilty precludes a death sentence; that detention prior to the military commission may not be applied to the sentence to be served; and a privilege against self-incrimination.

7. Comparisons and Constitutionality. The 2009 MCA amendments have been hailed by many as an improvement to the prior military commissions system. At the same time, human rights groups argue that, even with these improvements, part of the 2009 MCA is unconstitutional. To review this issue in details, you might start with the chart contained in Jennifer K. Elsea, *Comparison of Rights in Military Commission Trials and Trials in Federal Criminal Court*, Jan. 26, 2010.

8. Post MCA 2009 Resumption of Military Commissions. In December 2009, Attorney General Eric Holder announced that five men accused of organizing the September 11th attacks would be tried in federal court. Five others would remain in military commissions, including Omar Khadr, a Canadian citizen captured as a teenager in Afghanistan; Abd al-Rahim al-Nashiri, whose charges relating to the bombing of the U.S.S. Cole were withdrawn; Ahmed Mohammed Ahmed Haza al Darbi, accused of conspiring to blow up oil tankers; and two other unnamed men. The Administration announced it would prosecute Khalid Sheikh Mohammed, the alleged 9/11 mastermind, before a federal court, but security, cost, and political concerns have led to a review of that decision.

9. Khadr: The Odd First Commission Trial. The first of these cases scheduled to trial was that of Omar Khadr, a "child soldier" who was 18 at the time he was captured. According to Mathew Waxman, the top detainee affairs official during the Bush Administration, "There is a great deal of international skepticism and hostility toward military commissions, and this is a very tough case with which to push back against that skepticism and hostility." Charlie Savage, *U.S. Wary of Example Set by Tribunal Case*, NY TIMES, Aug 27, 2010.

10. Loose Ends and End Game. In August of 2010, Ibrahim al-Qosi, a cook for al-Qaeda officials in Afghanistan, pled guilty to conspiracy and providing material support for terrorism. However, as of al-Qosi's conviction, the Administration had no plan as to how it would house detainees who had been convicted by the military commissions. Peter Finn, WASH. POST, *U.S. Lacks Policy on Housing Detainees Convicted in Military Commissions*, Aug. 12, 2010. The chief military prosecutor, Navy Capt. John Murphy, said in an interview, "Will there be a moment when the commissions have ended? Yes, but it could very well be years from now." Peter Finn, *Resumed Military Panels Face New Challenges*, WASH. POST Dec. 4, 2009.

D. A NATIONAL SECURITY COURT?

Most of the criticism of military commissions has been from civil liberties advocates who argue that military commissions violate basic principles of fairness, including principles embedded in the Bill of Rights. As Professor Jack Goldsmith has noted, military commissions "raise scores of unresolved legal issues like the proper rules of evidence and whether material support and conspiracy, usually the main charges, can be brought in a tribunal since they may not be law-of-war violations." Professor Stephen Vladeck says the Supreme Court has suggested that the limits to military commission jurisdiction over offenses they may come from Article I, which authorizes Congress to "define and punish . . .Offences against the Law of Nations." U.S. Const. art I, § 8, c. 10. Vladeck argues that as such, jurisdiction of military commissions may be constitutionally limited to violations of international law. At the same time, because *Quirin* held that military tribunals are excepted from the requirements of Article II, § 2 (trial by jury) and the Fifth and Sixth Amendments in trying "offenses committed by enemy belligerents against the laws of war," *Quirin*, 317 U.S. 1, 41 (1942), Article III and the Fifth and Sixth Amendments may place several provisions of the 2009 MCA in serious constitutional jeopardy. *See* Stephen Vladeck, *The Laws of War as a Constitutional Limit on Military Jurisdiction*, 4 NAT'L SEC. L. & POL'Y (2010). Do you agree with this argument? What other powers of Congress might support military commissions?

Another criticism of military commissions comes from a practical direction. It argues that military commissions have not worked in the "War on Terror" and unnecessarily irritates allies of the United States in that "war." The military commissions have not secured the numbers of convictions that their proponents expected—and potential defendants before the commissions have languished as the public and the Administration debate which forum is most appropriate for their trials.

Beginning in 2006, a variety of scholars and commentators proposed that instead of or in addition to trying courts in military commissions or federal courts, Congress should create a specialized National Security Court. Most of these proposals suggested such a court would use procedures less demanding than those of the federal courts and that the increased expertise would be brought to the trials of alleged terrorists. The following excerpt from Andrew McCarthy and Alykhan Velshi, was one of the first and most prominent of such proposals.

WE NEED A NATIONAL SECURITY COURT

By Andrew C. McCarthy and Alykhan Velshi
For AEI Publication

*** [T]he DTA and MCA ***are not, however, a comprehensive solution to the manifold difficulties in dealing with enemy combatants that the war on terror portends for the nation in the years ahead. *** [T]he military commissions system – although framed in language that is not geographically limited – was principally designed to address the problem of those already in custody in Guantanamo Bay. ***[T]hese detainees form only a portion of those currently in custody and, in light of the expectation that the war on terror may continue for many years, a fraction of those who will eventually be captured. The DTA and MCA, moreover, do not address the two central complaints about the processing of war-on-terror detainees through the military justice system rather than the criminal justice system: (a) the limited judicial role, and (b) the sclerosis of the military proceedings to date.

The first of these complaints has profound diplomatic resonance even if its legal validity is limited at best. Legally, the DTA and MCA should answer the dubious contention that unfairness inheres in any system in which the executive branch alone is prosecutor, judge, jury, jailer and, occasionally, executioner. The DTA and MCA provide for review by the federal judiciary of the military proceedings. That review is limited, as it should be. *** Still, the military commissions system does not address the objections other nations and some prominent former members of the U.S. foreign service have lodged against the military proceedings due to what they portray as the tribunals' lack of independence from the executive branch. *** [T]he United States needs, and will continue to need, the cooperation of other nations in order to capture terrorists, to glean intelligence from them, and to neutralize them by lengthy periods of incarceration. If the extent of judicial participation in U.S. combatant proceedings is objectionable to our allies, that cooperation could be jeopardized. ***If other nations, unwilling to prosecute and sufficiently punish terrorists themselves, become similarly unwilling to extradite them to the United States due to what they regard as a lack of fundamental fairness and independence in the prospective trial proceedings, it will be cold comfort indeed that those proceedings are perfectly adequate (even exemplary) under our Constitution and laws.

Finally, the poor performance of the executive branch, and its political fall-out, must be acknowledged. It is freely conceded that many delays – especially those related to appellate litigation – in the combatant status review and commission process have been beyond the military's control, and, surely, the executive branch cannot be faulted for failing to anticipate that the Supreme Court would depart from its precedents *** All that said, however, the long delay in charging any combatants – especially in the year following the 9/11 attacks, when opposition was muted – and the failure to complete even one commission after five years cannot be justified. The military commission procedures are comprehensive and exceedingly fair to combatants. Had they been carried out efficiently, we would by now have had completed commissions recognized by the U.S. courts and the international audience as models of integrity. The controversy in which we are currently embroiled, and the need for additional legislation, is in part traceable to the failure of the military courts to exhibit themselves as a viable alternative. It is a failure in execution, not in conception.

*** It is thus time for Congress to create a national security court for terrorism cases. Such a tribunal, under the stewardship of Article III judges but heavily regulated by Congress, would publicly reaffirm our national commitment to due process of law (and thus encourage other nations to cooperate with us in the apprehension and trial of terrorists) without materially harming our security or imperiling our armed forces. *** Congress should establish a special national security court (NSC) with jurisdiction over cases involving international terrorism and other national security issues, including judicial review of enemy combatant detentions, within limits that respect the prerogatives of the political branches. *** Like the FISA court, the NSC would have district and appellate court components, both drawn from the national pool of experienced federal judges. ***

The new NSC's appellate tribunal (not its district court) would have jurisdiction to review combatant status review tribunals – just as the D.C. Circuit, rather than a district court, currently has it under the MCA. The CSRT-review would be highly deferential to the executive branch (especially while war still ensues), there being no reason to believe it is not being performed in good faith by the military. Thus, one round of judicial review by an appellate court (empowered to remand the case back to the military for additional proceedings if necessary) is perfectly adequate – with the proviso that certiorari review may be sought in the Supreme Court.

The NSC would, in addition, be given concurrent original jurisdiction over offenses that by statute or under the laws of war may currently be tried by military commissions, as well as jurisdiction over other statutory offenses common to international terrorism cases. It would have jurisdiction over any alleged offenders, regardless of where in the world they have been apprehended (including inside the United States), if those offenders qualify as alien enemy combatants upon the determination of a CSRT.

Designed in this manner, the NSC would ensure development of judicial expertise in the complex legal issues peculiar to this realm, including among others: classified information procedures ***, the laws and customs of war, international humanitarian law, the limited entitlements of aliens under U.S. law, and the strict construction of discovery rights in national security cases. Not only would this expertise enable the judges sitting on the NSC to dispense justice fairly and more efficiently; it would also result in the affected executive branch agencies (primarily, the Justice Department, the Defense Department, and the components of the intelligence community) having to adapt to but a single body of jurisprudence. ***

3. _Governing law in general._ The NSC's jurisdiction over CSRT-reviews and trials would extend only to alien combatants captured during the war on terror. It would not extend to American citizens. *** [S]ome captured combatants (_e.g._, John Walker Lindh, Yaser Esam Hamdi and, for a time, Jose Padilla), and an even greater number of terrorism defendants charged in civilian courts, have been U.S. nationals. Still, the vast majority of operatives waging war on behalf of, and facilitating, al Qaeda and its affiliates have been aliens. Many of these have had no plausible claim on U.S. legal protections. Because Americans are vested with such protections, fashioning procedures that would suffice for them yet be consistent with the minimalist approach of the NSC would be extremely challenging, to say the least. *** By establishing the NSC and defining its jurisdiction to cover both violations of the laws of war and statutes relevant to civilian terrorism prosecutions, the NSC could handle any prosecution involving an alien enemy combatant in the war on terror, regardless of whether that combatant could be specifically tied to 9/11, and regardless of whether the prosecution was based on a traditional "war crime," an offense traditionally triable by a military commission, or one of the statutory offenses commonly used to prosecute terrorists in the civilian courts.

4. _Detention of enemy combatants._ The NSC would oversee a new process for monitoring and reviewing the detention of alien enemy combatants captured by our military (and allied forces) outside U.S. territory and detained wherever the military chooses to detain them (including within the United States). *** Within a reasonable time after capture, the Justice Department would report to the NSC the fact that an alleged unlawful combatant had been captured in a particular theater of combat and was being detained. Presumptively within one year of capture, the military would hold a CSRT pursuant to the procedures currently in place. Assuming the detainee is designated an alien enemy combatant, the appeal process would proceed, first in the military system and, ultimately, to the appellate tribunal of the NSC.*** [R]eview in the NSC would be limited to challenging compliance at the appellant's CSRT with the military's standards and procedures for CSRTs. To avoid the empirical problem of judicial activism, the Congress would make clear that the grounds it has set forth are the only available grounds for judicial review.

In connection with each certified combatant, the Justice Department would also certify to the NSC (at the district court level) that hostilities were ongoing in the war on terror, that hostilities were ongoing in the theater of combat relevant to the particular enemy combatant (which, of course, will not necessarily be the place where the combatant was captured), and that it was in the national security interest of the United States that the combatant continue to be held because of the likelihood that he would resume operations against the United States if released. The CSRT determination would be reviewed annually, as would DOJ's certification.

The Government's certification would be unreviewable as long as the executive branch represented that combat operations were still ongoing in the theater which was the predicate (or were the predicates) for finding the particular detainee an alien enemy combatant. Here, it is worth pausing to rehearse that, once prospects for useful intelligence have been exhausted, the sole justification for holding enemy combatants is to prevent them from rejoining the battle. While it is often observed that the global war on terror may go on indefinitely, this does not mean it will go on *throughout the world* indefinitely.

*** [O]nce the government could no longer certify that combat operations were ongoing in the relevant theater(s) for a particular combatant, it would be given six months either to release the combatant, charge him with crimes in the NSC, or show probable cause, to the satisfaction of an NSC judge, to believe the combatant, if released, would take up arms against the United States in another theater of combat.

The latter proceeding would be akin to a bail hearing in the federal courts. ***The proceeding could be held under seal to the extent necessary to protect national security (and especially information about combat operations), and the government could introduce classified information on the same basis as is now done in CSRTs.

If the NSC found in favor of the government, the determination would be reviewed annually, just as original CSRT determinations were reviewed annually. *** If the NSC ruled in favor of the combatant, the government would also be permitted, as of right, to appeal, during the pendency of which the combatant would continue to be detained*** This system, among other things, would serve to blunt the resonant criticism that detainees could be held interminably because the war on terror may last, as Justice O'Connor surmised in *Hamdi*, for several generations. *** The proceedings described above would provide an oversight role for the independent judiciary without interfering in the conduct of the war; set a reasonable hurdle for the government to surmount if it is deemed necessary to hold combatants after hostilities have ended in the theater where they were operating; and prescribe a finite end-point at which it would be time to charge or release.

5. *Trial of Enemy Combatants.* Trials before the NSC would combine features of military commissions, which give pride of place to national security, with the stewardship of Article III judges independent of the executive branch. ***[T]he overriding mission – into which the judicial function is being imported for very limited purposes – remains executive and military. *** NSC judges would be a check against arbitrariness but they would not have any general supervisory authority over the conduct of proceedings and they would not be at liberty to create new entitlements by analogizing to ordinary criminal proceedings.*** There would no longer be any colorable complaint that the authority advancing the allegations was the same authority determining the legal and factual validity of the allegations.

Essentially, NSC trials would add the Article III judges to the existing military commission format. *** With Article III judges performing a valuable but appropriately harnessed role, trials would otherwise go forward much like they do under the current commission procedures. Juries would generally be comprised of five military officers, properly qualified as fair and impartial.

The current rules for the commissions have come under harsh criticism from human rights and Defendants' advocacy groups. Most of these criticisms, however, stem from basic assumptions that are simply invalid – *e.g.*, that the patent security threat faced by the nation in wartime cannot justify the use of classified information which is not disclosed to the enemy combatant or the public (but is disclosed to the combatant's lawyer); or that there is no meaningful difference in American and international law between the entitlements of Americans and aliens, or between those of privileged and unprivileged combatants, and consequently that any trial procedure that provides less protection than an accused would receive under the Bill of Rights, the Federal Rules of Criminal Procedure, or the Uniform Code of Military Justice violates the Constitution and U.S. treaty obligations.

In fact, as we have seen, alien enemy combatants, who are unprivileged because they flout the laws of war, have no entitlements under the Constitution. That being the case, the current commission procedures are extraordinarily fair to the accused. To reiterate, they provide for [MCA, Sec. 949]:

- the presumption of innocence;
- burden of proof on the prosecution;
- the right to be presented with the charges in advance of trial;
- access to evidence the prosecution intends to introduce and to any exculpatory evidence known to the prosecution;
- the right to a trial presumptively open to the public (except for portions sealed for national defense or witness security purposes);

- the choice to testify or decline to do so, and the right against any negative inference from a refusal to testify;

- access to reasonably available evidence and witnesses; access to investigative resources as "necessary for a full and fair trial";

- the right to present evidence and to cross-examine witnesses;

- the right to interpreters if necessary;

- the right to be present at all stages of the proceedings except in connection with the presentation of information protected for national defense or witness security purposes (in which case at least military defense counsel and possibly civilian defense counsel may be present);

- access to sentencing evidence on the same basic terms as trial evidence; and

- the right to present evidence and address the court at sentencing.

These basic rights, moreover, have been supplemented by standard discovery procedures which require the prosecution to disclose, well in advance of trial:

- the names and contact information of all witnesses the prosecution intends to call at trial along with a synopsis of the witness's anticipated testimony;

- a curriculum vitae of any expert witness the prosecution intends to call as a witness, in addition to any expert reports or examinations relevant to the expert's opinion testimony, and a synopsis of that anticipated testimony;

- any statements of the accused in the Government's possession which the prosecution intends to offer at trial; any such statements if they were sworn to, written or signed, and any such statements in response to interrogation, whether or not the prosecution intends to offer them at trial;

- any prior statements by prospective prosecution witnesses that are relevant to the subject matter of the witness's anticipated testimony and that are in the possession of, or known to, the prosecution; and

- where an alternative to in-person trial testimony has been proposed, notice of the method, circumstances and persons present when the alternative was created, and an explanation for why the alternative should be permitted.

These rules bring the trial of alien enemy combatants so close to the standards for trials of American citizens in civilian courts that the complaints about them border on the frivolous. It is true, for example, that the standard for evidentiary admissibility – namely, whether, in the judgment of the court, "the evidence would have probative value to a reasonable person" – is slightly less rigorous than that which governs civilian trials and courts martial. As argued earlier, however, less rigor must be allowed for given the drastic differences between evidence collection in combat and domestic law enforcement spheres; and the commission standard would pass constitutional muster if applied to citizens, let alone to alien enemy combatants. Similarly, discovery is somewhat more limited in the commission context than in civilian trials and courts martial.* But, again, the marginal difference is eminently justifiable and comfortably within constitutional norms – notwithstanding that it is being applied to those who have no constitutional rights.

The existing procedures, with Article III judges presiding but under circumstances where Congress had made clear the limits on their authority and provided liberally for the executive branch to seek immediate review of judicial excesses, would be more than adequate to provide trials that were models of fairness and integrity. A few additional provisions would also be helpful. For example, the statute of limitations for terrorist crimes should be eliminated (as it is for murder in many jurisdictions) so that trials could be delayed as necessary to avoid holding them – and risking disclosures helpful to the enemy – during combat in the pertinent theater. It should also be made crystal clear that defendants are not permitted to represent themselves in NSC proceedings.

Finally, Congress should make clear that the *Brady* exculpatory evidence doctrine, in NSC cases, is intended to reflect the *Brady* doctrine as originally conceived rather than the elastic concept *Brady* has become in modern practice. As first promulgated, *Brady* was a due-process rule that required the government to reveal to the defense any material evidence in its possession that actually demonstrated the defendant was not guilty. In the ensuing decades, the doctrine has been enlarged to embrace much that is neither exculpatory, admissible, nor particularly germane but that might be thought helpful to the defense presentation. That may be a desirable development in the civilian system, but it has no place in matters of national security, and could, if not cabined, undermine the entire purpose of an NSC, which is to provide basic due process while contributing to the national security imperative of defeating the enemy. ***

Congressional action to create a National Security Court would strike a proper balance between the imperatives of public safety and military success, on the one hand, and our commitment to due process, on the other. It would provide an appropriate forum for fairly detaining and trying terrorists no matter how long the war on terror ensues, and would have the beneficial side-effect of removing from our criminal justice system cases for which it was not designed and the handling of which necessarily reduces the quality of justice afforded by the system. Finally, it would accomplish the admirable ends that the authorization of military commissions has been unable to achieve, while simultaneously providing a court system other nations would be far more likely to favor – dramatically increasing the likelihood that they would be willing to capture terrorists operating in their territories and extradite them to the United States. ***

*****

The proposals for a National Security Court have been met with much controversy. Below is a critique of National Security Courts by a group of academics and former federal judges, prosecutors, ambassadors, and government officials.

A CRITIQUE OF "NATIONAL SECURITY COURTS"

A Report By The Constitution Project's Liberty And Security Committee June 23, 2008

***Recently, some scholars and government officials have called for the creation of "national security courts"—specialized hybrid tribunals that would review the preventive detention of suspected terrorists (both within and outside of the territorial United States), conduct the detainees' criminal trials, or, in some cases, both. Advocates for these courts claim that they offer an attractive middle ground between adherence to traditional criminal processes and radical departures from those processes.

For the reasons that follow, we *** believe that the proposals to create these courts should be resisted. The proposals are surprisingly—indeed alarmingly—underdeveloped. More seriously, they neglect basic and fundamental principles of American constitutional law, and they assume incorrectly that the traditional processes have proven ineffective. The idea that there is a class of individuals for whom neither the normal civilian or military criminal justice systems suffice presupposes that such a class of individuals is readily identifiable—and in a manner that does not necessarily pre-judge their guilt. The idea that national security courts are a proper third way for dealing with such individuals presupposes that the purported defects in the current system are ones that cannot adequately be remedied within the confines of that system, and yet can be remedied in new tribunals without violating the Constitution.

We believe that the government can accomplish its legitimate goals using existing laws and legal procedures without resorting to such sweeping and radical departures from an American constitutional tradition that has served us effectively for over two centuries. ***

Advocates of national security courts that would try terrorism suspects claim that traditional Article III courts are unequipped to handle these cases. This claim has not been substantiated, and is made in the face of a significant — and growing — body of evidence to the contrary. A recent report released by Human Rights First persuasively demonstrates that our existing federal courts are competent to try these cases. The report examines more than 120 international terrorism cases brought in the federal courts over the past fifteen years. It finds that established federal courts were able to try these cases without sacrificing either national security or the Defendants' rights to a fair trial. The report documents how federal courts have successfully dealt with classified evidence under the Classified Information Procedures Act (CIPA) without creating any security breaches. It further concludes that courts have been able to enforce the Government's Brady obligations to share exculpatory evidence with the accused, deal with Miranda warning issues, and provide means for the government to establish a chain of custody for physical evidence, all without jeopardizing national security.

Of course, our traditional federal courts have not always done everything that the government would like them to do. They are, after all, constrained by well-established constitutional limits on prosecutorial power. For example, no federal court would permit the prosecution to present witnesses without protecting the Defendant's constitutional right to confront those witnesses against him or her. Nor would a federal court permit the prosecution to rely on a coerced confession in violation of a Defendant's Fifth Amendment right against self-incrimination. But creating a new set of courts would not repeal existing constitutional rights. Conversely, to the extent that the existing rules are not constitutionally compelled, ordinary federal courts (or Congress, where applicable) can modify them when it is shown that the modification is necessary to accommodate the Government's legitimate interests.

Most importantly, there is the intrinsic and inescapable problem of definition. Whereas the argument for specialized courts for tax and patent law is that expert judges are particularly necessary given the complex subject-matter, proposals for specialized courts for terrorism trials are based on the asserted need for relaxed procedural and evidentiary rules and are justified on the ground that terrorists do not deserve full constitutional protections. This creates two fundamental constitutional problems. First, justifying departures from constitutional protections on the basis that the trials are for terrorists undermines the presumption of innocence for these individuals. Second, if a conviction were obtained in a national security court using procedural and evidentiary rules that imposed a lesser burden on the government, then the defendant would be subjected to trial before a national security court based upon less of a showing than would be required in a traditional criminal proceeding. The result would be to apply less due process to the question of guilt or innocence, which, by definition, would increase the risk of error. And, if the government must make a preliminary showing that meets traditional rules of procedure and evidence in order to trigger the jurisdiction of a national security court, such a showing would also enable it to proceed via the traditional criminal process.

National security courts for criminal prosecutions are not just unnecessary; they are also dangerous. They run the risk of creating a separate and unequal criminal justice system for a particular class of suspects, who will be brought before such specialized courts based on the very allegations they are contesting. Such a system undermines the presumption of innocence for these defendants***. It was Justice Frankfurter who wrote that "It is a fair summary of history to say that the safeguards of liberty have frequently been forged in controversies involving not very nice people." Committee members strongly believe that the shadow of terrorism must not be the basis for abandoning these fundamental tenets of justice and fairness.

In addition, these proposals are alarmingly short on details with respect to the selection of judges for these national security courts. Although there is a history of creating specialized federal courts to handle particular substantive areas of the law (e.g., taxation; patents), unlike tax and patent law, there is simply no highly specialized expertise that would form relevant selection criteria for the judges. Establishing a specialized court solely for prosecutions of alleged terrorists might also create a highly politicized process for nominating and confirming the judges, focusing solely on whether the nominee had sufficient "tough on terrorism" credentials — hardly a criterion that lends itself to the appearance of fairness and impartiality.

None of the above is to deny that there is a class of individuals who may be tried in appropriate military tribunals. Persons captured by the U.S. military as part of an armed conflict have traditionally been subject to military jurisdiction under the laws of war. This principle is well-established, but it has long coexisted with the complementary principle that only individuals who are properly subject to military jurisdiction under the laws of war may be so tried. Military tribunals may not try offenders or offenses unless they are encompassed by traditional laws of war.

Just as there is no need to establish national security courts to replace traditional Article III courts, so too there is no need to create such tribunals to handle cases that would normally be tried by military courts. ***

1. Prosecutions for terrorism offenses can and should be handled by traditional Article III courts, except that combatants captured on the battlefield who would be subject to traditional military jurisdiction may be tried by military courts for offenses properly triable by such courts.***

2. We should not create specialized national security courts to oversee a system of preventive detention for terrorism suspects. Apart from detention under the laws of war, the United States government should only be permitted to detain an individual suspected of a terrorism offense if it can make a probable cause showing to a judge and it intends to prosecute that individual, or if appropriate, as part of immigration removal proceedings. ***

The idea that national security courts are a proper third way for dealing with such individuals presupposes that the purported defects in the current system are ones that cannot adequately be remedied within the confines of that system, and yet can be remedied in hybrid tribunals without violating the Constitution. We strongly disagree. Traditional Article III courts can meet the challenges posed by terrorism prosecutions, and proposals to create national security courts should be rejected as a grave threat to our constitutional rights.

Review Problem

Using exceptional hacking skills to exploit a loophole to obtain access to military and diplomatic documents, unemployed computer scientist Rex McNabb downloaded hundreds of thousands of classified documents onto a disc he labeled "Mastermind." McNabb provided these documents to WikiStuff, a website housed on rental servers wholly owned by the American entrapreneur Bill Zuckerberg, located in the United States. WikiStuff released these documents to various news outlets and, after minor editing, posted them. WikiStuff is financed through ad revenue, subscription services that allow fine-tuned topic searches, and support from contributors.

The WikiStuff editor, Thom Tweedy, is an Australian citizen who lived in Sweden for several years before receiving documents from McNabb. After Ecuador's President Rafael Corres, a left-leaning populist critical of U.S. foreign policy, heard that the United States was pressuring Sweden to bring Tweedy to the US, he offered to host Tweedy and WikiStuff from his nation. Tweedy, who feared Sweden might turn him over to the United States or prosecute him for rape of two Swedish women, sneaked off to Ecuador.

The documents posted on WikiStuff drew interest from many quarters. The media dwelled on salacious statements by US diplomats critical of foreign leaders and information concerning military operations in Iraq and Afghanistan. Other observers found substantial information on WikiStuff concerning various terrorist plots, their principals, and sources of information about these plots.

One such observer was Abdullah Oblongata (AO, as he is called), an American techie who lives in Yemen and assists with publication of *Inspire*, a glossy English-language publication for al Qaeda in the Arabian Peninsula (AQAP). AQAP, formed in January 2009 from a merger of al Qaeda's Yemeni and Saudi branches, has several hundred members and is loyal to Osama bin Laden. AO was asked by AQAP leaders to see whether its operations were compromised in the WikiStuff documents. In the course of his searches, AO came across a reference to a Yemeni blacksmith in a remote village who provided information to the CIA about an aborted AQAP plot to send explosives on UPS cargo planes to the United States in printer cartridges, blowing up the planes mid-flight. The severed head of the blacksmith was found the next morning in the town square atop a pole with an Arabic sign reading "Traitor to Allah."

1. For what crimes might McNabb be prosecuted, and in what forum(s)? Would your answers change if he was in the U.S. Army?

2. Assume Tweedy is prosecuted for providing "material support" to terrorist organizations. Assess the viability of his First Amendment defense.

3. Assume Zuckerberg is also prosecuted for providing "material support" to terrorist organizations. What defenses could he raise?

4. "Abu Maghrib," a Moroccan picked up in Afghanistan in 2002, is detained at Guantanamo Bay. Some of the WikiStuffs documents tend to support his claim that he was not a member of al-Qaeda but a fruit merchant specializing in Afghani pomegranates. Assess whether he may use the WikiStuff material as part of a habeas petition or in his defense before a military commission, and if his lawyers would face any personal liability for using the WikiStuff documents if they chose to do so without clearing that use with the government beforehand.

X

MILITARY FORCE AND TERRORISM

Rogue states and terrorists do not seek to attack us using conventional means. They know such attacks would fail. Instead, they rely on acts of terror and, potentially, the use of weapons of mass destruction—weapons that can be easily concealed, delivered covertly, and used without warning.*** The United States has long maintained the option of preemptive actions to counter a sufficient threat to our national security. The greater the threat, the greater is the risk of inaction— and the more compelling the case for taking anticipatory action to defend ourselves, even if uncertainty remains as to the time and place of the enemy's attack. To forestall or prevent such hostile acts by our adversaries, the United States will, if necessary, act preemptively. The United States will not use force in all cases to preempt emerging threats, nor should nations use preemption as a pretext for aggression. Yet in an age where the enemies of civilization openly and actively seek the world's most destructive technologies, the United States cannot remain idle while dangers gather.

National Security Strategy (2002)
(The Bush Doctrine)

[T]his judgment of ours does not make confronting terrorism any easier. That is the fate of democracy, in whose eyes not all means are permitted, and to whom not all the methods used by her enemies are open. At times democracy fights with one hand tied behind her back. Despite that, democracy has the upper hand, since preserving the rule of law and recognition of individual liberties constitute an important component of her security stance. At the end of the day, they strengthen her and her spirit, and allow her to overcome her difficulties.

A. BARAK, HCJ 5100/94 *The Public Committee against Torture in Israel v. The State of Israel,* 53(4) PD 817, 845

Both domestic and international law govern the use of military force. The Authorization for the Use of Military Force (AUMF) discussed in the preceding chapters broadly authorized a military response to the terrorist attacks of September 11. This section contains some domestic law materials, but much of the chapter deals with international law.

618

Section A introduces the law governing the use of military force in response to terrorist attacks. International law governs military force through two bodies of law: *jus ad bellum*, the law governing the resort to force, and *jus in bello*, the law governing the conduct of hostilities. The former forbids the use of force except (1) in self-defense in response to an armed attack and (2) in accordance with U.N. Security Council authorization under Chapter VII of the U.N. Charter. The cases below examine the parameters of the right to use force in self-defense. The second category of law is often referred to as international humanitarian law ("IHL") or the law of armed conflict. Codified in the four Geneva Conventions and their Additional Protocols, IHL seeks to minimize suffering in war by restricting the means and methods of warfare and protecting persons not participating in hostilities. To do so, IHL categorizes all persons as either combatants (soldiers and other members of state armed forces) or civilians and sets forth rights and protections for each category.

Section B considers the legitimacy of inflicting collective punishments in response to terrorist actions, specifically demolition of homes and mass deportation. Section C, Targeted Killing, illustrates the complexity of the legal arguments and practical choices involved in use of military force in responding to international terrorist organizations. Finally, Section D examines two very different approaches to judicial review of military actions—the approach of the United States and the approach of Israel.

A. MILITARY FORCE IN RESPONSE TO TERRORIST ATTACKS

The legitimate use of military force by nations, whether in response to terrorism or otherwise, has customarily been confined to self-defense. The classic statement of this principle came in an 1842 letter from U.S. Secretary of State Daniel Webster to his British counterpart, Lord Ashburton in connection with the Caroline Incident. Canadian troops crossed the Niagara River to the American side and attacked the steamer *Caroline*, which had been running arms and materiel to insurgents on the Canadian side, killing one American and setting fire to the *Caroline*. In response to a British claim of self defense, Webster wrote:

> [R]espect for the inviolable character of the territory of independent states is the most essential foundation of civilization. *** [I]t is just, that, while it is admitted that exceptions growing out of the great law of self-defense do exist, those exceptions should be confined to *cases in which the necessity of that self-defense is instant, overwhelming, and leaving no choice of means, and no moment for deliberation.* (emphasis added).

Webster also included a requirement of proportionality in an earlier communication with his British counterparts, stating that "It will be for [Her Majesty's Government] to show, also, that the local authorities of Canada, even supposing the necessity of the moment authorized them to enter the territories of The United States at all, did nothing unreasonable for excessive; since the act, justified by the necessity of self-defense, must be limited by that necessity, and kept clearly within it."

The United Nations Charter contains two provisions that bring the Webster formulation into the modern world.

> Article 2(4). All Members shall refrain in their international relations from the threat or use of force against the territorial integrity or political independence of any state, or in any other manner inconsistent with the Purposes of the United Nations.

> Article 51. Nothing in the present Charter shall impair the right of individual or collective self-defence if an armed attack occurs against a Member of the United Nations, until the Security Council has taken measures necessary to maintain international peace and security. Measures taken by Members in the exercise of the right of self-defence shall be immediately reported to the Security Council and shall not in any way affect the authority and responsibility of the Security Council under the present Charter to take at any time such action as it deems necessary in order to maintain or restore international peace and security.

The United Nations has, on various occasions, passed resolutions condemning the use of military force. For example, U.N. General Assembly Resolution No. 41/38 (1986), following a United States missile attack on Libya in response to the bombing of a West German discotheque that killed U.S. servicemen:

> *"The General Assembly,* ***1. Condemns the military attack perpetrated against the Socialist People's Libyan Arab Jamahiriya on 15 April 1986, which constitutes a violation of the Charter of the United Nations and of international law; 2. Calls upon the Government of the United States in this regard to refrain from the threat or use of force in the settlement of disputes and differences with the Libyan Arab Jamahiriya and to resort to peaceful means in accordance with the Charter of the United Nations;***"

Governments may or may not respond to such resolutions by changing their actions, and the United Nations may impose sanctions upon countries in response to noncompliance. In addition, nations accused of illegally using military force sometimes attempt to explain their actions to the rest of the world. For example, after it bombed a chemical plant in Sudan and an al-Qaeda camp in Afghanistan, in response to the 1998 Embassy bombings, the Clinton Administration explained:

> In accordance with Article 51 of the United Nations Charter*** the United States has exercised its right of self-defence in responding to a series of armed attacks against

United States Embassies and United States Nationals. *** In response to these terrorist attacks, and to prevent and deter their continuation, United States armed forces today struck at a series of camps and installations used by the Bin Laden organization to support terrorist actions against the United States and other countries. *** The targets struck, and the timing and method of attack used, were carefully designed to minimize risks of collateral damage to civilians and to comply with international law, including the rules of necessity and proportionality.

Similarly, Israel explained its 2006 attacks across its border into Lebanon as follows:

This morning, Hezbollah terrorists unleashed a barrage of heavy artillery and rockets into Israel, causing a number of deaths. In the midst of this horrific and unprovoked attack, the terrorists infiltrated Israel and kidnapped two Israeli soldiers, taking them into Lebanon. *** Israel thus reserves the right to act in accordance with Article 51 of the Charter of the United Nations and exercise its right of self-defence when an armed attack is launched against a Member of the United Nations. The State of Israel will take the appropriate actions to secure the release of the kidnapped soldiers and bring an end to the shelling that terrorizes our citizens. Identical Letters dated 12 July 2006 from the Permanent Representative of Israel to the United Nations addressed to the Secretary-General and the President of the Security Council, S/2006/515.

Following the al Qaeda attacks on the United States of September 11, 2001, the United Nations explicitly recognized that the use of military force by the United States in the territory of Afghanistan would be legitimate:

The Security Council,

***Recognizing the inherent right of individual or collective self-defence in accordance with the Charter,

1. *Unequivocally condemns* in the strongest terms the horrifying terrorist attacks which took place on 11 September 2001 in New York, Washington (D.C.) and Pennsylvania and *regards* such acts, like any act of international terrorism, as a threat to international peace and security;

2. *Expresses* its deepest sympathy and condolences to the victims and their families and to the People and Government of the United States of America;

3. *Calls* on all States to work together urgently to bring to justice the perpetrators, organizers and sponsors of these terrorist attacks and *stresses* that those responsible for

aiding, supporting or harbouring the perpetrators, organizers and sponsors of these acts will be held accountable;

4. *Calls also* on the international community to redouble their efforts to prevent and suppress terrorist acts including by increased cooperation and full implementation of the relevant international anti-terrorist conventions and Security Council resolutions, in particular resolution 1269 of 19 October 1999;

5. *Expresses* its readiness to take all necessary steps to respond to the terrorist attacks of 11 September 2001, and to combat all forms of terrorism, in accordance with its responsibilities under the Charter of the United Nations; ***U.N. Security Council Resolution 1368.

Collective and nation-state responses to terrorism have also been authorized. Article 5 of The Washington Treaty for NATO justifies collective use of force as follows:

The Parties agree that an armed attack against one or more of them in Europe or North America shall be considered an attack against them all and consequently they agree that, if such an armed attack occurs, each of them, in exercise of the right of individual or collective self-defence recognised by Article 51 of the Charter of the United Nations, will assist the Party or Parties so attacked by taking *** such action as it deems necessary, including the use of armed force, to restore and maintain the security of the North Atlantic area. *** [A]ll measures taken as a result thereof shall immediately be reported to the Security Council. Such measures shall be terminated when the Security Council has taken the measures necessary to restore and maintain international peace and security.

Shortly after the 9/11 attacks on the United States, NATO Secretary-General Lord Robertson stated:

[I]t has now been determined that the attack against the United States on 11 September was directed from abroad and shall therefore be regarded as an action covered by Article 5 of the Washington Treaty, which states that an armed attack on one or more of the Allies in Europe or North America shall be considered an attack against them all. *** [T]he United States of America can rely on the full support of its 18 NATO Allies in the campaign against terrorism.

The United States Congress, in response to these attacks, passed the Authorization to Use Military Force (AUMF) on September 18, 2001:

That the President is authorized to use all necessary and appropriate force against those nations, organizations, or persons he determines planned, authorized, committed, or aided the terrorist attacks that occurred on September 11,

2001, or harbored such organizations or persons, in order to prevent any future acts of international terrorism against the United States by such nations, organizations or persons.

Soon thereafter, the United States began military operations in Afghanistan against Al Qaeda and the Taliban. The international community has generally accepted the United States military action as self-defense in response to an armed attack.

In 2002, the White House issued a new National Security Strategy of the United States of America, in which the President set forth a new doctrine regarding the pre-emptive use of force by the United States. The parts of that document reproduced below quickly became known as "the Bush Doctrine."

National Security Strategy (2002)

*** [N]ew deadly challenges have emerged from rogue states and terrorists. None of these contemporary threats rival the sheer destructive power that was arrayed against us by the Soviet Union. However, the nature and motivations of these new adversaries, their determination to obtain destructive powers hitherto available only to the world's strongest states, and the greater likelihood that they will use weapons of mass destruction against us, make today's security environment more complex and dangerous. *** We must be prepared to stop rogue states and their terrorist clients before they are able to threaten or use weapons of mass destruction against the United States and our allies and friends.

*** It has taken almost a decade for us to comprehend the true nature of this new threat. Given the goals of rogue states and terrorists, the United States can no longer solely rely on a reactive posture as we have in the past. The inability to deter a potential attacker, the immediacy of today's threats, and the magnitude of potential harm that could be caused by our adversaries' choice of weapons, do not permit that option. We cannot let our enemies strike first.

*** For centuries, international law recognized that nations need not suffer an attack before they can lawfully take action to defend themselves against forces that present an imminent danger of attack. Legal scholars and international jurists often conditioned the legitimacy of preemption on the existence of an imminent threat—most often a visible mobilization of armies, navies, and air forces preparing to attack.

We must adapt the concept of imminent threat to the capabilities and objectives of today's adversaries. Rogue states and terrorists do not seek to attack us using conventional means. They know such attacks would fail. Instead, they rely on acts of terror and, potentially, the use of weapons of mass destruction—weapons that can be easily concealed, delivered covertly, and used without warning.

The targets of these attacks are our military forces and our civilian population, in direct violation of one of the principal norms of the law of warfare. As was demonstrated by the losses on September 11, 2001, mass civilian casualties is the specific objective of terrorists and these losses would be exponentially more severe if terrorists acquired and used weapons of mass destruction.

The United States has long maintained the option of preemptive actions to counter a sufficient threat to our national security. The greater the threat, the greater is the risk of inaction— and the more compelling the case for taking anticipatory action to defend ourselves, even if uncertainty remains as to the time and place of the enemy's attack. To forestall or prevent such hostile acts by our adversaries, the United States will, if necessary, act preemptively.

The United States will not use force in all cases to preempt emerging threats, nor should nations use preemption as a pretext for aggression. Yet in an age where the enemies of civilization openly and actively seek the world's most destructive technologies, the United States cannot remain idle while dangers gather.

*****

In March 2003, the United States, along with the United Kingdom and several other nations, invaded Iraq. In addition to its reliance on United Nations Security Council resolutions – and Iraq's continued breach of those resolutions – the United States argued that the invasion was justified as a pre-emptive use of force to dismantle the threat posed by an Iraq that possessed weapons of mass destruction and was potentially in cooperation with international terrorist organizations, namely al Qaeda.

In July 2006, Hezbollah conducted a cross border raid into Israel and killed eight Israeli soldiers and captured two others. In response, Israel began attacking targets throughout southern Lebanon in an attempt to win the release of the soldiers, root out Hezbollah and end Hezbollah's rocket attacks on northern Israel. United Nations Secretary General Kofi Annan condemned Hezbollah's attack and capture of the Israeli soldiers and recognized Israel's right to self-defense, while also condemning Israel's use of force as excessive and disproportionate. Hezbollah responded to Israel's bombardment with hundreds of rocket attacks a day on northern and central Israel and Israel continued its aerial barrage of southern Lebanon and began a ground campaign as well, designed to create a buffer zone along the Israeli-Lebanon border. After a month of fighting, the parties agreed to a United Nations-brokered ceasefire and a beefed-up international presence in southern Lebanon.

The cases that follow discuss the use of force in self-defense. In reading these cases, consider the following questions:

> 1. Does the Bush doctrine comply with international law regarding the use of force and the right of self-defense?

> 2. Was the invasion of Afghanistan an acceptable use of force under international law? How about the invasion of Iraq? If the United States thought (even if erroneously) that Iraq had secret WMDs? Ties to al Qaeda?

3.   Did Israel have a right to respond in self-defense to Hezbollah's cross-border raid and capture of Israeli soldiers? Was Israel's response lawful under international law?

4.   Should there be different standards for the use of force in response to terrorist attacks, or threatened terrorist attacks, than for the use of force in response to attacks or threatened attacks by another state? If so, why? How would those standards differ?

CASE CONCERNING MILITARY AND PARAMILITARY ACTIVITIES IN AND AGAINST NICARAGUA

(NICARAGUA v. UNITED STATES OF AMERICA)
International Court Of Justice
1986 I.C.J. 14

[In the 1980's, the "Contra" rebels in Nicaragua opposed the government. The United States provided aid to the Contras and to El Salvador as the conflict spread beyond Nicaragua's borders. Nicaragua brought the United States to the International Court of Justice, arguing that the United States had provided aid to the rebels by mining harbors and attacking ports and other facilities, in violation of international law. The United States responded by claiming that it was acting in collective self-defense on behalf of its allies. The Court did not address the question of pre-emptive self-defense, but focused on whether an armed attack had occurred and whether the measures allegedly taken in self-defense were legally appropriate. Excerpts of the Court's opinion appear below.]

195.   In the case of individual self-defence, the exercise of this right is subject to the State concerned having been the victim of an armed attack. Reliance on collective self-defence of course does not remove the need for this. There appears now to be general agreement on the nature of the acts which can be treated as constituting armed attacks. In particular, *** an armed attack must be understood as including not merely action by regular armed forces across an international border, but also "the sending by or on behalf of a State of armed bands, groups, irregulars or mercenaries, which carry out acts of armed force against another State of such gravity as to amount to" (inter alia) an actual armed attack conducted by regular forces, "or its substantial involvement therein". *** But the Court does not believe that the concept of "armed attack" includes not only acts by armed bands where such acts occur on a significant scale but also assistance to rebels in the form of the provision of weapons or logistical or other support. Such assistance may be regarded as a threat or use of force, or amount to intervention in the internal or external affairs of other States. ***

227. [Laying mines in Nicaraguan waters and certain attacks on Nicaraguan ports, oil installations and a naval base] constitute infringements of the principle of the prohibition of the use of force, ***unless they are justified by circumstances which exclude their unlawfulness, a question now to be examined. ***

228. *** [T]he Court finds that, subject to the question whether the action of the United States might be justified as an exercise of the right of self-defence, the United States has committed a prima facie violation of [the principle of the non-use of force] by its assistance to the *contras* in Nicaragua, by "organizing or encouraging the organization of irregular forces or armed bands *** for incursion into the territory of another State", and "participating in acts of civil strife *** in another State" ***.

229. *** For the Court to conclude that the United States was lawfully exercising its right of collective self-defence, it must first find that Nicaragua engaged in an armed attack against El Salvador, Honduras or Costa Rica.

230. *** Even assuming that the supply of arms to the opposition in El Salvador could be treated as imputable to the Government of Nicaragua, to justify invocation of the right of collective self-defence in customary international law, it would have to be equated with an armed attack by Nicaragua on El Salvador. ***[T]he Court is unable to consider that, in customary international law, the provision of arms to the opposition in another State constitutes an armed attack on that State. ***

[The Court noted that while El Salvador, Costa Rica and Honduras did announce at various times that they were victims of armed attacks and request United States assistance in collective self-defense, they did not do so in a timely manner "indicative of a belief by the State in question that it was the victim of an armed attack by Nicaragua, and of the making of a request by the victim State to the United States for help in the exercise of collective self-defence." (para. 232).]

237. Since the Court has found that the condition *sine qua non* required for the exercise of the right of collective self-defence by the United States is not fulfilled in this case, *** even if the United States activities in question had been carried on in strict compliance with the canons of necessity and proportionality, they would not thereby become lawful. If however they were not, this may constitute an additional ground of wrongfulness. [The Court found that United States measures did not meet the requirements of necessity.] First, these measures were only taken, and began to produce their effects, several months after the major offensive of the armed opposition against the Government of El Salvador had been completely repulsed (January 1981), and the actions of the opposition considerably reduced in consequence. Thus it was possible to eliminate the main danger to the Salvadorian Government without the United States embarking on activities in and against Nicaragua. Accordingly, it cannot be held that these activities were undertaken in the light of necessity. Whether or not the assistance to the *contras* might meet the criterion of proportionality, the Court cannot regard the United States activities *** relating to the mining of the Nicaraguan ports and the attacks on ports, oil installations, etc., as satisfying that criterion. Whatever uncertainty may exist as to the exact scale of the aid received by the Salvadorian armed opposition from Nicaragua, it is clear that these latter United States activities in question could not have been proportionate to that aid. ***

238. ***[T]he plea of collective self-defence against an alleged armed attack on El Salvador, Honduras or Costa Rica, advanced by the United States to justify its conduct toward Nicaragua, cannot be upheld ***

CASE CONCERNING OIL PLATFORMS
(ISLAMIC REPUBLIC OF IRAN v. UNITED STATES)
International Court Of Justice
2003 ICJ 161

[On October 19, 1987 and April 18, 1988, United States warships destroyed three Iranian offshore oil production complexes. Iran brought the United States to the International Court of Justice, claiming that the attacks constituted a fundamental breach of a United States-Iran treaty and international law. The United States claimed, both at the time of the attack and before the Court, that its attacks on the oil platforms were justified as necessary and appropriate acts of self-defense, in response to what it regarded as armed attacks by Iran.]

47. On 19 October 1987, four destroyers of the United States Navy, together with naval support craft and aircraft, approached the Reshadat R-7 platform. Iranian personnel was warned by the United States forces via radio of the imminent attack and abandoned the facility. The United States forces then opened fire on the platform; a unit later boarded and searched it, and placed and detonated explosive charges on the remaining structure. [The United States took similar action against the R-4 platform, which was not originally in the plan, but was seen as a "target of opportunity".] As a result of the attack, the R-7 platform was almost completely destroyed and the R-4 platform was severely damaged. ***

48. The nature of this attack, and its alleged justification, was presented by the United States to the United Nations Security Council in the following terms (letter from the United States Permanent Representative of 19 October 1987, S/19219):

> "In accordance with Article 51 of the Charter of the United Nations, I wish, on behalf of my Government, to report that United States forces have exercised the inherent right of self-defence under international law by taking defensive action in response to attacks by the Islamic Republic of Iran against United States vessels in the Persian Gulf.
>
> At approximately 11 p.m. Eastern Daylight Time on 16 October 1987, a Silkworm missile fired by Iranian forces from Iranian-occupied Iraqi territory struck the *Sea Isle City,* a United States flag vessel, in the territorial waters of Kuwait. This is the latest in a series of such missile attacks against United States flag and other non-belligerent vessels in Kuwaiti waters in pursuit of peaceful commerce. These actions are, moreover, only the latest in a series of unlawful armed attacks by Iranian forces against the United States,

including laying mines in international waters for the purpose of sinking or damaging United States flag ships, and firing on United States aircraft without provocation.

At approximately 7 a.m. Eastern Daylight Time on 19 October 1987, United States naval vessels destroyed the Iranian military ocean platform at Rashadat *[sic]* (also known as Rostam) in international waters of the Persian Gulf. The military forces stationed on this platform have engaged in a variety of actions directed against United States flag and other non-belligerent vessels and aircraft. They have monitored the movements of United States convoys by radar and other means; co-ordinated minelaying in the path of our convoys; assisted small-boat attacks against other non-belligerent shipping; and fired at United States military helicopters, as occurred on 8 October 1987. Prior warning was given to permit the evacuation of the platform."

51. *** Therefore, in order to establish that it was legally justified in attacking the Iranian platforms in exercise of the right of individual self-defence, the United States has to show that attacks had been made upon it for which Iran was responsible; and that those attacks were of such a nature as to be qualified as "armed attacks" within the meaning of that expression in Article 51 of the United Nations Charter, and as understood in customary law on the use of force. *** The United States must also show that its actions were necessary and proportional to the armed attack made on it, and that the platforms were a legitimate military target open to attack in the exercise of self-defence.

[The Court examined the evidence the United States presented and concluded that the evidence was not sufficient to demonstrate Iranian responsibility for the attack and that the United States did not meet the burden of proving an armed attack by Iran on the United States.]

76. *** [The Court then addressed the requirement of necessity, a key condition of the right to self-defence, finding that even if it accepted the contention that there was in fact an armed attack, the United States' response did not meet the condition of necessity.] In the case both of the attack on the *Sea Isle City* and the mining of the USS *Samuel B. Roberts,* the Court is not satisfied that the attacks on the platforms were necessary to respond to these incidents. ***[T]here is no evidence that the United States complained to Iran of the military activities of the platforms, in the same way as it complained repeatedly of minelaying and attacks on neutral shipping, which does not suggest that the targeting of the platforms was seen as a necessary act. The Court would also observe that in the case of the attack of 19 October 1987, the United States forces attacked the R-4 platform as a "target of opportunity", not one previously identified as an appropriate military target.

CASE CONCERNING ARMED ACTIVITIES ON THE TERRITORY OF THE CONGO

DEMOCRATIC REPUBLIC OF THE CONGO v. UGANDA
International Court Of Justice
2005 ICJ 168

[On 23 June 1999 the Democratic Republic of the Congo (DRC) instituted proceedings before the Court against Uganda for acts of aggression in 1998 and 1999. After Laurent Kabila overthrew the President of Zaire and took power in the renamed DRC in 1997, he granted Uganda substantial military influence in the eastern portions as a way to help maintain control. In 1998, he called for the withdrawal of foreign troops from Congolese territory. On August 2, 1998, there was an attempted coup and the DRC claims that Uganda began its military intervention in the DRC soon thereafter. Ugandan troops captured several towns and airports and began providing support to Congolese armed groups opposed to Kabila's government. Uganda claims that it was the victim of cross-border attacks from Congolese territory between 1994 and 1997 and that, "by August-September 1998, as the DRC and the Sudan prepared to attack Ugandan forces in eastern Congo, its security situation had become untenable. Uganda submits that 'in response to this grave threat, and in the lawful exercise of its sovereign right of self-defence', it made a decision on 11 September 1998 to augment its forces in eastern Congo and to gain control of the strategic airfields and river ports in northern and eastern Congo in order to stop the combined forces of the Congolese and Sudanese armies as well as the anti-Ugandan insurgent groups from reaching Uganda's borders." The Court examined the facts extensively and reached the following conclusions.]

141. In the light of this assessment of all the relevant evidence, the Court is now in a position to determine whether the use of force by Uganda within the territory of the DRC could be characterized as self-defence. ***

143. *** [Although Uganda claims that it did not use force in response to an anticipated attack], [t]he Court feels constrained, however, to observe that the wording of the Ugandan High Command document on the position regarding the presence of the UPDF in the DRC makes no reference whatever to armed attacks that have already occurred against Uganda at the hands of the DRC (or indeed by persons for whose action the DRC is claimed to be responsible). Rather, the position of the High Command is that [the military operation] is necessary "to secure Uganda's legitimate security interests". The specified security needs are essentially preventative -- to ensure that the political vacuum does not adversely affect Uganda, to prevent attacks from "genocidal elements", to be in a position to safeguard Uganda from irresponsible threats of invasion, to "deny the Sudan the opportunity to use the territory of the DRC to destabilize Uganda". Only one of the five listed objectives refers to a response to acts that had already taken place -- the neutralization of "Uganda dissident groups which have been receiving assistance from the Government of the DRC and the Sudan".

144. While relying heavily on this document, Uganda nonetheless insisted to the Court that after 11 September 1998 the UPDF was acting in self-defence in response to attacks that had occurred. ***

146. ***[W]hile Uganda claimed to have acted in self-defence, it did not ever claim that it had been subjected to an armed attack by the armed forces of the DRC. The "armed attacks" to which reference was made came rather from the [Allied Democratic Forces, a Congolese rebel group]. The Court has found above *** that there is no satisfactory proof of the involvement in these attacks, direct or indirect, of the Government of the DRC. The attacks did not emanate from armed bands or irregulars sent by the DRC or on behalf of the DRC . *** The Court is of the view that, on the evidence before it, even if this series of deplorable attacks could be regarded as cumulative in character, they still remained non-attributable to the DRC.

147. For all these reasons, the Court finds that the legal and factual circumstances for the exercise of a right of self-defence by Uganda against the DRC were not present. Accordingly, the Court has no need to respond to the contentions of the Parties as to whether and under what conditions contemporary international law provides for a right of self-defence against large-scale attacks by irregular forces. Equally, since the preconditions for the exercise of self-defence do not exist in the circumstances of the present case, the Court has no need to enquire whether such an entitlement to self-defence was in fact exercised in circumstances of necessity and in a manner that was proportionate. The Court cannot fail to observe, however, that the taking of airports and towns many hundreds of kilometres from Uganda's border would not seem proportionate to the series of transborder attacks it claimed had given rise to the right of self-defence, nor to be necessary to that end. ***

Separate Opinion of Judge SIMMA

[Judge Simma agrees with the Court's judgment, but wants the Court to address the use of force in self-defense against attacks by irregular forces, that is, whether Uganda could lawfully have repelled rebel attacks on Congolese territory if the rebel attacks met the threshold of an armed attack. Judge Simma criticized the Court for making statements in several cases that leave the law in this area unclear]

10. The most recent -- and most pertinent -- statement in this context is to be found in the (extremely succinct) discussion by the Court in its *Wall* Opinion of the Israeli argument that the separation barrier under construction was a measure wholly consistent with the right of States to self-defence enshrined in Article 51 of the Charter . *** [T]he Court replied that Article 51 recognizes *** an inherent right of self-defence in the case of an armed attack by one State against another. Since Israel did not claim that the attacks against it were imputable to a foreign State, however, Article 51 of the Charter had no relevance in the case of the wall ***

11. Such a restrictive reading of Article 51 might well have reflected the state, or rather the prevailing interpretation, of the international law on self-defence for a long time. However, in the light of more recent

developments not only in State practice but also with regard to accompanying *opinio juris,* it ought urgently to be reconsidered ***. As is well known, these developments were triggered by the terrorist attacks of September 11, in the wake of which claims that Article 51 also covers defensive measures against terrorist groups have been received far more favourably by the international community than other extensive re-readings of the relevant Charter provisions, particularly the "Bush doctrine" justifying the pre-emptive use of force. Security Council resolutions 1368 (2001) and 1373 (2001) cannot but be read as affirmations of the view that large-scale attacks by non-State actors can qualify as "armed attacks" within the meaning of Article 51.

12. *** [T]he almost complete absence of governmental authority in the whole or part of the territory of certain States has unfortunately become a phenomenon as familiar as international terrorism . *** [I]f armed attacks are carried out by irregular forces from such territory against a neighbouring State, these activities are still armed attacks even if they cannot be attributed to the territorial State, and, further, *** it "would be unreasonable to deny the attacked State the right to self-defence merely because there is no attacker State and the Charter does not so require so."

13. *** [T]he lawfulness of the conduct of the attacked State in the face of such an armed attack by a non-State group must be put to the same test as that applied in the case of a claim of self-defence against a State, namely, does the scale of the armed action by the irregulars amount to an armed attack and, if so, is the defensive action by the attacked State in conformity with the requirements of necessity and proportionality?

14. In applying this test to the military activities of Uganda on Congolese territory from August 1998 onwards, *** while the activities that Uganda conducted in August in an area contiguous to the border may still be regarded as keeping within these limits, the stepping up of Ugandan military operations starting with the occupation of the Kisangani airport and continuing thereafter, leading the Ugandan forces far into the interior of the DRC, assumed a magnitude and duration that could not possibly be justified any longer by reliance on any right of self-defence. ***

LEGAL CONSEQUENCES OF THE CONSTRUCTION OF A WALL IN THE OCCUPIED PALESTINIAN TERRITORY

ISRAELI SEPARATION BARRIER CASE
International Court of Justice
2004 I.C.J. 131

*** 83. According to the report of the Secretary-General, in its northernmost part, the wall as completed or under construction barely deviates from the Green Line. It nevertheless lies within occupied territories for most of its course. The works deviate more than 7.5 kilometres from the Green Line in certain places to encompass settlements, while encircling Palestinian population areas. *** Elsewhere, on the other hand, the planned route would deviate eastward by up to 22 kilometres. In the case of Jerusalem, the existing works and the planned route lie well beyond the

Green Line and even in some cases beyond the eastern municipal boundary of Jerusalem as fixed by Israel.

84. On the basis of that route, approximately 975 square kilometres (or 16.6 per cent of the West Bank) would, according to the report of the Secretary-General, lie between the Green Line and the wall. This area is stated to be home to 237,000 Palestinians. If the full wall were completed as planned, another 160,000 Palestinians would live in almost completely encircled communities, described as enclaves in the report. As a result of the planned route, nearly 320,000 Israeli settlers (of whom 178,000 in East Jerusalem) would be living in the area between the Green Line and the wall.

85. Lastly, it should be noted that the construction of the wall has been accompanied by the creation of a new administrative regime. Thus in October 2003 the Israeli Defence Forces issued Orders establishing the part of the West Bank lying between the Green Line and the wall as a "Closed Area". Residents of this area may no longer remain in it, nor may non-residents enter it, unless holding a permit or identity card issued by the Israeli authorities. According to the report of the Secretary-General, most residents have received permits for a limited period. Israeli citizens, Israeli permanent residents and those eligible to immigrate to Israel in accordance with the Law of Return may remain in, or move freely to, from and within the Closed Area without a permit. Access to and exit from the Closed Area can only be made through access gates, which are opened infrequently and for short periods.

86. The Court will now determine the rules and principles of international law which are relevant in assessing the legality of the measures taken by Israel. Such rules and principles can be found in the United Nations Charter and certain other treaties, in customary international law and in the relevant resolutions adopted pursuant to the Charter by the General Assembly and the Security Council. However, doubts have been expressed by Israel as to the applicability in the Occupied Palestinian Territory of certain rules of international humanitarian law and human rights instruments. The Court will now consider these various questions.

87. [The Court first refers to the principle of non-use of force in Article 2(4) of the United Nations Charter and then considered international conventions in addition to the United Nations Charter and found that the 4th Geneva Convention applies to the occupied territories.] ***

95. The Court notes that, according to the first paragraph of Article 2 of the Fourth Geneva Convention, that Convention is applicable when two conditions are fulfilled: that there exists an armed conflict (whether or not a state of war has been recognized); and that the conflict has arisen between two contracting parties. If those two conditions are satisfied, the Convention applies, in particular, in any territory occupied in the course of the conflict by one of the contracting parties. *** This interpretation reflects the intention of the drafters of the Fourth Geneva Convention to protect civilians who find themselves, in whatever way, in the hands of the occupying Power. ***

[The Court concluded that construction of the wall would (1) impede the liberty of movement of the inhabitants of the Occupied Palestinian Territory as guaranteed by the International Covenant on Civil and Political Rights; (2) impede the exercise of the right to work, health, education, and an adequate standard of living under the International Covenant on Economic, Social and Cultural Rights and the United Nations Convention on the Rights of the Child; and (3) would contravene the prohibition in the Fourth Geneva Convention against deporting or transferring the civilian population of an occupied territory.]

138. The Court has thus concluded that the construction of the wall constitutes action not in conformity with various international legal obligations incumbent upon Israel. However, *** [Israel argues] that "the fence is a measure wholly consistent with the right of States to self-defence enshrined in Article 51 of the Charter"; the Security Council resolutions referred to, he continued, "have clearly recognized the right of States to use force in self-defence against terrorist attacks", and therefore surely recognize the right to use non-forcible measures to that end ***.

139. *** Article 51 of the Charter thus recognizes the existence of an inherent right of self-defence in the case of armed attack by one State against another State. However, Israel does not claim that the attacks against it are imputable to a foreign State.

The Court also notes that Israel exercises control in the Occupied Palestinian Territory and that, as Israel itself states, the threat which it regards as justifying the construction of the wall originates within, and not outside, that territory. The situation is thus different from that contemplated by Security Council resolutions 1368 (2001) and 1373 (2001), and therefore Israel could not in any event invoke those resolutions in support of its claim to be exercising a right of self-defence.

Consequently, the Court concludes that Article 51 of the Charter has no relevance in this case.

140. The Court has, however, considered whether Israel could rely on a state of necessity which would preclude the wrongfulness of the construction of the wall. *** In the light of the material before it, the Court is not convinced that the construction of the wall along the route chosen was the only means to safeguard the interests of Israel against the peril which it has invoked as justification for that construction.

141. The fact remains that Israel has to face numerous indiscriminate and deadly acts of violence against its civilian population. It has the right, and indeed the duty, to respond in order to protect the life of its citizens. The measures taken are bound nonetheless to remain in conformity with applicable international law.

142. In conclusion, the Court considers that Israel cannot rely on a right of self-defence or on a state of necessity in order to preclude the wrongfulness of the construction of the wall resulting from the considerations mentioned in paragraphs 122 and 137 above. The Court accordingly finds

that the construction of the wall, and its associated regime, are contrary to international law. ***

[By a vote of 14-1, the Court concluded that Israel had a duty to cease construction of the barrier, dismantle the structure, and make reparations for all damage caused by the construction.]

Declaration of JUDGE BUERGENTHAL

[Judge Buergenthal dissented from the decision to hear the case, believing that the ICJ did not have jurisdiction to render the advisory opinion. He then offered the following comments on the merits.]

5.   Whether Israel's right of self-defence is in play in the instant case depends, in my opinion, on an examination of the nature and scope of the deadly terrorist attacks to which Israel proper is being subjected from across the Green Line and the extent to which the construction of the wall, in whole or in part, is a necessary and proportionate response to these attacks. As a matter of law, it is not inconceivable to me that some segments of the wall being constructed on Palestinian territory meet that test and that others do not. But to reach a conclusion either way, one has to examine the facts ***. Since these facts are not before the Court, it is compelled to adopt the to me legally dubious conclusion that the right of legitimate or inherent self-defence is not applicable in the present case. ***

6.   There are two principal problems with this conclusion. The first is that the United Nations Charter, in affirming the inherent right of self-defence, does not make its exercise dependent upon an armed attack by another State ***. Moreover, *** the Security Council has made it clear that "international terrorism constitutes a threat to international peace and security" while *reaffirming* the inherent right of individual or collective self-defence . . ." *** "In its resolution 1368 (2001), adopted only one day after the September 11, 2001 attacks ***, the Security Council invokes the right of self-defence in calling on the international community to combat terrorism. In neither of these resolutions did the Security Council limit their application to terrorist attacks by State actors only ***. In fact, the contrary appears to have been the case. *** In assessing the legitimacy of [Israel's claim that it has a right to defend itself against terrorist attacks from across the Green Line], it is irrelevant that Israel is alleged to exercise control in the Occupied Palestinian Territory – *** the territory from which the attacks originate is not part of Israel proper. Attacks on Israel coming from across that line must therefore permit Israel to exercise its right of self-defence against such attacks, provided the measures it takes are otherwise consistent with the legitimate exercise of that right. *** [T]o determine whether or not the construction of the wall *** by Israel meets that test, all relevant facts bearing on issues of necessity and proportionality must be analysed. ***

Notes

1. **Domestic Law.** The Israeli Supreme Court, under domestic law, generally upheld the building of the separation barrier in the West Bank. *See Beit Sourik*

Village Council v. The Government of Israel, HCJ 2056/04 (2004). The Court, noting that both parties agreed that the 4th Geneva Convention applied to the situation, found that the international law applicable to belligerent occupation permits the military commander to take possession of an individual's land to build the security fence, on the condition that it is necessitated by military needs. Therefore, the Court held that "[T]o the extent that construction of the fence is a military necessity, it is permitted, therefore, by international law." But the Court barred seizures of certain land because the seizures would impose disproportionate harm to local inhabitants.

B. COLLECTIVE PUNISHMENT

Article 33. No protected person may be punished for an offence he or she has not personally committed. Collective penalties and likewise all measures of intimidation or of terrorism are prohibited.*** Reprisals against protected persons and their property are prohibited. ***

Article 49. Individual or mass forcible transfers, as well as deportations of protected persons from occupied territory to the territory of the Occupying Power or to that of any other country, occupied or not, are prohibited, regardless of their motive.

Nevertheless, the Occupying Power may undertake total or partial evacuation of a given area if the security of the population or imperative military reasons so demand. Such evacuations may not involve the displacement of protected persons outside the bounds of the occupied territory except when for material reasons it is impossible to avoid such displacement. Persons thus evacuated shall be transferred back to their homes as soon as hostilities in the area in question have ceased.

The Occupying Power undertaking such transfers or evacuations shall ensure, to the greatest practicable extent, that proper accommodation is provided to receive the protected persons, that the removals are effected in satisfactory conditions of hygiene, health, safety and nutrition, and that members of the same family are not separated. Geneva Convention IV

1. DEMOLITION OF HOMES

ALMARIN v. IDF COMMANDER IN GAZA STRIP
Supreme Court of Israel Sitting As The High Court Of Justice
HCJ 2722/92 (1992)

JUSTICE G. BACH

1.   The petitioner lives, together with his family, in Nuzirath in the Gaza Strip, in a house registered in his name (hereafter — 'the building').

The building has two storeys, and it contains five rooms, a kitchen, a shower and a toilet on the first floor, and another room and chicken coops on the second floor. One of the sons of the petitioner who lives in the building is Fuad Alamarin (hereafter — 'Fuad'), who was arrested on 24 May 1992 on a suspicion of having committed the murder of a fifteen-year-old Israeli school pupil called Helena Rapp in Bat-Yam.

The petition is directed against the decision of the IDF Commander in the Gaza Strip (hereafter — 'the respondent') to order the confiscation of the land on which the building stands and the destruction of the building, by exercising his power under r. 119 of the Defence (Emergency) Regulations, 1945 (hereafter — 'the Regulations'). The decision of the respondent was made on account of the fact that the aforesaid Fuad was one of the persons living in the building.

[On May 24, 1992, Fuad left home, taking two knives from the kitchen. He went to Bat-Yam and saw three girls at the bus stop. He told the police later that he decided then to kill one of the girls. He stabbed one girl, ran away, was caught by the police, and confessed to the murder. The IDF Commander in the Gaza Strip notified Fuad's family of his intention to order the destruction of the building and ordered the house to be sealed. Petitioner submitted an objection, which was rejected, and then filed a petition with this court, at which time an interim order was made to stay the order for destruction pending the outcome of the case. Petitioner makes two arguments: 1) respondent's authority to order confiscation, sealing and destruction of a building is limited by regulation r. 119 to the Gaza Strip and therefore respondent cannot order destruction of a house in Gaza because of an act perpetrated in Israeli territory; and 2) respondent was only authorized to order the confiscation and destruction of Fuad's room in the house, rather than the whole building, where many people live who played no role in the murder.] ***

5.   The argument about the territoriality of the respondent's authority under r. 119 of the Regulations and about the consequent illegality of the aforesaid s. 5B of the Order does not seem to me *prima facie* to have any weight, particularly when we are speaking of exercising the authority on account of a terrorist act carried out in the territory of the State of Israel. The approach that regards a violent act committed in Israel as if it were an act carried out 'abroad' in relation to the Gaza Strip seems to me to be artificial with respect to the issue under discussion. *** [The Court then found that because Fuad had taken a knife with the intent to do harm from the house in Gaza, there was no territorial issue under r. 119.]

6.   We are left with the alternative argument, that Fuad lived in a separate unit within the building, and therefore the respondent is authorized to destroy at most the room of that Fuad.

In order to examine this argument, the exact text of the relevant legislation ought to be before us. The following are the parts of r. 119 of the Regulations that are relevant to this petition:

'119. (I) A Military Commander may by order direct the forfeiture to the Government of Palestine [read: the Government of Israel] ... of any house, structure or land situated in any area, town, village, quarter or street the inhabitants or some of the inhabitants of which he is satisfied have committed, or attempted to commit, or abetted the commission of, or been accessories after the fact to the commission of, any offence against these Regulations involving violence or intimidation or any Military Court offence; and when any house, structure or land is forfeited as aforesaid, the Military Commander may destroy the house or the structure or anything in or on the house, the structure or the land...'

In view of this wording, it is not possible to accept the narrow construction of counsel for the petitioner with regard to the respondent's authority, when it is expressly stated here that the military commander may destroy any house —

'... the inhabitants *or some of the inhabitants* of which he is satisfied have committed...' (emphasis added).

From this it can be clearly seen that the authority of the commander extends also to those parts of an apartment or house that are owned or used by the members of the family of the suspect or by others, with regard to whom it has not been proved that they took part in the criminal activity of the suspect or that they encouraged it or even that they were aware of it. ***

7.   Nonetheless, I would like to point out that the above does not mean that the military commanders, who have the authority, are not required to use reasonable discretion and a sense of proportion in each case, nor that this court is not able or bound to intervene in the decision of the military authority, whenever the latter intends to exercise its authority in a way and manner that are unthinkable. Thus, for example, it is inconceivable that the military commander should decide to destroy a complete multi-storey house, which contains many apartments belonging to different families, merely for the reason that a person suspected of a terrorist act lives in a room in one of the apartments, and if nonetheless he should want to do this, this court could have its say and intervene in the matter. ***

9.   ***I would include the following considerations among the relevant factors for the decision of the military commander:

a. What is the seriousness of the acts attributed to one or more of those living in the building concerned, with regard to whom there is definite evidence that they committed them? ***

b. To what extent can it be concluded that the other residents, or some of them, were aware of the activity of the suspect or the suspects, or that they had reason to suspect the commission of this activity? ***

c. Can the residential unit of the suspect be separated in practice from the other parts of the building? Does it, in fact, already constitute a separate unit?

d. Is it possible to destroy the residential unit of the suspect without harming the other parts of the building or adjoining buildings? If it is not possible, perhaps the possibility that sealing the relevant unit is sufficient should be considered.

e. What is the severity of the result arising from the planned destruction of the building for persons who have not been shown to have had any direct or indirect involvement in the terrorist activity. What is the number of such persons and how closely are they related to the resident who is the suspect?

10.   Let us turn from the aforesaid general principles to the specific case before us:

a. It is hard to imagine more serious circumstances that those relating to the act attributed to the aforesaid Fuad. ***

b. The building is admittedly a two-storey house, but almost all the living rooms and bedrooms in it are on the ground floor. Fuad's room is also on this floor. All the persons living in the building share utilities (the entrance to the house, kitchen, bath, toilet), and a living room for common use, and they are all related.

c. The murder suspect, Fuad, lives in the building, and nothing separates his room on the ground floor from the other parts of the house. ***

11.   In view of all the aforesaid facts, I am satisfied that the decision of the respondent which is the subject of this petition does not show that he overstepped his authority, and that there is no justifiable cause for us to intervene in it.

Therefore I would propose to my esteemed colleagues that the petition should be denied and the interim order issued in this case should be revoked, without making an order for costs. ***

JUSTICE M. CHESHIN

***4.   In a minority judgment that I wrote in *Hizran v. IDF Commander in Gaza Strip* [1], I said that in applying r. 119 of the Defence (Emergency) Regulations the army commander does not have the authority to inflict collective punishment, and if we agree that a residential unit belonging to one person should be destroyed, it is not proper to destroy residential units belonging to others as well. *** Where someone is suspected of an act as a result of which a destruction order is made with regard to his home, I did not agree then, nor do I agree now, that someone else's home may be destroyed merely because he lives next to that person.

5.   Were we dealing in this case with a five-storey building, and the persons suspected of the act of murder and his family lived on the ground floor, and on the four floors above it there lived families unrelated to the family of the murder suspect, we may surely assume that the military commander would not have ordered the demolition of the whole house, namely the destruction of the four storeys inhabited by families totally unrelated to the family of the murder suspect. This, I believe, would be the

law, were we dealing with a house with only two storeys, and on the second storey there lived a family unrelated to the family of the murder suspect. The difference between these two examples and our case is this, that in the building under discussion there live three related families. I do not know what difference there is between this case and those other cases, seeing that the other family members were not partners in the wicked deed, either directly or indirectly, and no-one even suggests that they were in any way involved in the terrible deed.

6.   *** I agree that in the language of the regulation — in its literal text, in the words of my colleague — there is no basis for the restrictive construction, the construction which is acceptable to me. Indeed, the military commander has the authority, according to the text of the regulation, to order a wide-scale destruction such as the destruction of that five-storey building in the example I gave, and even far more than this, as I said in *Hizran v. IDF Commander in Gaza Strip* [1]. But that 'spirit' of the regulation [enacted under the British Mandate] vanished and became as if it had never existed, when there arose a greater spirit, in 1948, when the State was founded. Legislation that originated during the British Mandate — including the Defence (Emergency) Regulations — was given one construction during the Mandate period and another construction after the State was founded, for the values of the State of Israel — a Jewish, free and democratic State — are utterly different from the fundamental values that the mandatory power imposed in Israel. Our fundamental values — even in our times — are the fundamental values of a State that is governed by law, is democratic and cherishes freedom and justice, and it is these values that provide the spirit in constructing this and other legislation. ***

9.   Were my opinion accepted, we would issue a show cause order in order to ascertain what part of the building should be destroyed, or sealed, and the destruction order would apply only to the home of the murder suspect. But since I find myself in the minority, the case will be decided in accordance with the opinion of my colleagues.

2. MASS DEPORTATION

ASSOCIATION FOR CIVIL RIGHTS IN ISRAEL v. MINISTER OF DEFENCE
Supreme Court of Israel Sitting As a High
Court Of Justice HCJ 5973/92 (1992)

4.(a) Against the background of increasing Hamas activity ***, the Government, on 16th December 1992, decided as follows:

"456. *Security matters. In the Ministerial Committee for National Security Matters, authority is given to make emergency regulations for the issue of immediate deportation orders for the expulsion of persons inciting acts of terror* and it is decided (by a majority, one abstention) as follows:

(a) In view of the existence of a state of emergency and in order to safeguard public security - to instruct the Prime Minister and the Minister of Defence to order and empower the military commanders of Judea, Samaria and the Gaza Strip to issue orders in accordance with vital, immediate security needs relating to the temporary deportation, without prior notice, for the purpose of deporting inciters, of those of the residents of the territory who are, by their action, endangering human life or inciting such action, for such period as determined by the military commanders, but not exceeding two years.

(b) Any person departed as aforesaid may, within 60 days, appeal against his deportation to a special committee through a member of this family or his advocate in accordance with rules to be laid down in the orders". ***

[Following the orders, the commanders issued a total of 415 deportation orders for periods of 18 to 24 months. The deportation began on December 16, 1992 and was temporarily stayed by interim orders of the court. The interim orders were set aside on December 17, 1992.] ***

6.(a) The central argument of the Petitioners is that the deportation orders are void for a dual reason, both because the empowering order (namely the Temporary Provisions Order) is void *ab initio* and because of various defects which occurred in the course of issuing the individual orders. [Petitioners argued that there was insufficient legal basis for denying the deportee the right of prior hearing.]

(b) The act of deportation is contrary to both public international law and to Israeli administrative law, jointly and severally:

(1) Article 49 of the Fourth Geneva Convention relate to the Protection of Civilian Persons in time of War prohibits expulsion generally and mass expulsion in particular.

(2) Israeli law grants the right to a hearing *before* deportation ***. This right, which is laid down in Israeli law, should not be denied by security legislation in occupied territory. ***

11.   (a) In the present case, the Respondents have sought to modify the legal infrastructure by enacting the orders regarding the temporary provisions which expressly permit immediate expulsion, and allowing the possibility of applying to the consultative committee *after* the deportation.

(b) We have explained in the past on more than one occasion that this Court will review the legality of an act of the military administration and the validity thereof in accordance with the principles of Israeli administrative law, in order to decide whether the norms binding an Israeli public officer have been observed. *** Israeli administrative law requires as aforesaid, the grant of a right of hearing, and we have already stated that the more serious and irrevocable the results of the Government decision, the more essential is it that the person affected be allowed to state his objections and give his answer to the allegations against him so as to try to refute them.

(c) Moreover, hearing arguments from an intermediary rather than from the person concerned is inherently deficient in value and practicality. Statements made by counsel lose some of their force when the person making the statements on behalf of another *cannot* first meet with the person concerned in order to obtain from him information, guidance and instructions, and continue consulting with him routinely in respect of the factual allegations raised against him which are the basis of the hearing, and in respect of which his reply is sought, as he alone knows his exact case. Personal appearance, before the committee of the person in respect of whom the deportation order is made, is the foundation and essence the right to a hearing. ***

12. (a) The Respondents have put forward the argument that, according to the principles of administrative law, *there are circumstances in which vital interests of state security prevail over the duty to hold a prior hearing,* before carrying out the deportation order. In other words, in balancing these competing values, namely the right of hearing versus security needs and when the security circumstances are *of special weight,* the right to hearing should not be exercised in advance of carrying out the deportation but only subsequently, and the need to exercise the power immediately then constitutes an incontestable constraint. *** [The Court cited examples of situations in which an exception to the rule of a prior hearing was reasonable, such as when the military commander sees an operational need for immediate action to remove an obstacle or overcome opposition, for example, so as not to delay a military operation, or when the government seizes bad meat or orders a person with an infectious disease removed to a hospital.] ***

(d) The Respondents sought this time to refer in advance to the legislative option, and made the orders which are, as they are ratified, enacted "temporary provisions" permitting temporary deportation immediately after the issue of the order, the right of appeal being ancuitable only after the order is carried out. In our view the temporary provisions in the present case neither add nor subtract anything, whichever way one looks at it. If there is an exception to the right of a prior hearing, action can be taken in accordance with that exception and there is *no* need for a temporary provision; and if there is no exception to the right of hearing, the temporary provision is in any event invalid. As regards the question whether exceptions exist to the rules relating to the right to a hearing in deportation proceedings, as we have already stated, case law is to the effect that such exceptions do exist, and they are the result of the balance between the needs of security and the right to a hearing.

We have not seen fit here to take a view on the question of whether an exception to the right of hearing existed in the circumstances herein, since we accept - according to the rule in the *Kawasme* case (per Justice Landau and Y. Kahan) - that if there was no prior hearing, a subsequent hearing should be held, serving the object of giving an opportunity to the person concerned to present his case in detail, and the absence of a prior hearing does not per se invalidate the individual deportation orders.

13.   Is amending legislation in the present form valid, or, in other words, can the security legislation of a military commander determine that there was no legal duty to observe the right to a hearing before the deportation order was implemented? ***

16.   We shall conclude by referring to what was said by Judge Olshan (as he then was) in the Karbutli case [7], at p. 15:

> "Whilst it is correct that the security of the State which necessitates a person's detention is no less important than the need to safeguard the citizen's right, where both objectives can be achieved together, neither one nor the other should be ignored".

*** We find that as regards the personal expulsion orders, the absence of the right of prior hearing does not invalidate them. We order that the right of hearing should now be given as detailed above.

C. TARGETED KILLING

Slaying without a trial, assassination, and outlawry are categorically condemned by three prominent authorities as follows:

> The law of war does not allow proclaiming either an individual belonging to the hostile army, or a citizen, or a subject of the hostile government an outlaw, who may be slain without trial by any captor, any more than the modern law of peace allows such international outlawry; on the contrary, it abhors such outrage. The Lieber Code, Section 148.

> No person employed by or acting on behalf of the United States Government shall engage in, or conspire to engage in, assassination. Executive Order 12333, § 2.1.

> It is especially forbidden * * * to kill or wound treacherously individuals belonging to the hostile nation or army. (*HR, art. 23, par.* (b)) This article is construed as prohibiting assassination, proscription, or outlawry of an enemy, or putting a price upon an enemy's head, as well as offering a reward for an enemy "dead or alive". It does not, however, preclude attacks on individual soldiers or officers of the

enemy whether in the zone of hostilities, occupied territory, or elsewhere. U.S. Army Field Manual, 27-10,

Despite the strong language above, it is the practice of the United States to engage in targeted killings of terrorists. President Clinton used a cruise missile to target Osama bin Laden at al Qaeda training camps after the East African embassy attacks and President Bush used targeted killings to strike at al Qaeda leaders after the 9/11 attacks. President Obama has increased the frequency, expanded the geographic scope, and enhanced the listed targets for such killings.

Are targeted killings legal under domestic and international law? To get a feel for the complexity of the inquiry, consider the following introduction provided by Judge Bates in *Al-Aulaki v. Obama*, 727 F. Supp. 2d 1 (2010):

> Stark, and perplexing, questions readily come to mind, including the following: How is it that judicial approval is required when the United States decides to target a U.S. citizen overseas for electronic surveillance, but that, according to defendants, judicial scrutiny is prohibited when the United States decides to target a U.S. citizen overseas for death? Can a U.S. citizen-himself or through another-use the U.S. judicial system to vindicate his constitutional rights while simultaneously evading U.S. law enforcement authorities, calling for "jihad against the West," and engaging in operational planning for an organization that has already carried out numerous terrorist attacks against the United States? Can the Executive order the assassination of a U.S. citizen without first affording him any form of judicial process whatsoever, based on the mere assertion that he is a dangerous member of a terrorist organization? How can the courts, as plaintiff proposes, make real-time assessments of the nature and severity of alleged threats to national security, determine the imminence of those threats, weigh the benefits and costs of possible diplomatic and military responses, and ultimately decide whether, and under what circumstances, the use of military force against such threats is justified? When would it ever make sense for the United States to disclose in advance to the "target" of contemplated military action the precise standards under which it will take that military action? And how does the evolving AQAP [al Qaeda in the Arabian Peninsula, a terrorist organization formed in 2009 which is loyal to Osama bin Laden and led by a former Guantanamo detainee] relate to core al Qaeda for purposes of assessing the legality of targeting AQAP (or its principals) under the September 18, 2001 Authorization for the Use of Military Force?

To think through Judge Bates' questions in a structured way, it helps to recognize that targeted killings lie at the intersection of two different frameworks or paradigms for dealing with terrorists: the criminal law paradigm and the law of war paradigm.

Under the criminal law paradigm, police can kill criminals only in self-defence or if "the officer has probable cause to believe that the suspect poses a threat of serious physical harm," *Tennessee v. Garner*, 471 U.S. 1 (1985), and even then must refrain from risking the safety of innocent bystanders. Some states allow the police to use deadly force when the police believe it necessary "to avoid a [greater] harm or evil to himself or another." See Model Penal Code § 3.02. This defense might, for example, justify the killing of one engaged in a terrorist plot to kill many others. International human rights law reflects these same concerns, but with a couple of twists that are even more constraining. First, some authority indicates that "[b]efore resorting to the use of deadly force, all measures to arrest a person suspected of committing acts of terror must be exhausted," and that preemption of such attacks, but not retribution or revenge are legitimate bases for lethal force. U.N. Human Rights Committee, Concluding Observations of the Human Rights Committee: Israel, ¶ 15, U.N. Doc. CCPR/CO/78/ISR (Aug. 21, 2003). Second, outside the United States, international norms protecting state sovereignty preclude states from entering the territory of other states to carry out targeted killings. A 1989 Army Judge Advocate memorandum indicates this rule is not absolute; targeted killings may be used in self-defence even in peacetime under Article 51 of the United Nations Charter, and killing terrorists by military strikes rather than expeditionary "capture or kill" forces is permissible in peacetime when the risk to United States personnel is "deemed too great." Memorandum from W. Hays Parks, to The Judge Advocate General of the Army, "Executive Order 12333 and Assassination" (Dec. 4, 1989), available at http://www.loc.gov/rr/frd/Military_Law/pdf/12-1989.pdf.

Under the military law paradigm, the Parks Memorandum argued that the prohibition on assassination only applied to covert killings for political reasons, such as those documented by the Church Committee in 1975, which included eight CIA efforts to assassinate Fidel Castro and other unsuccessful CIA assassination efforts on other leaders whose actions were deemed contrary to United States interests. The prohibition did not, the memo argued, preclude the targeted killing of enemy combatants in wartime or the use of such killings against those posing a direct threat to United States citizens or national security even outside a theater of war. In the context of targeted killings of terrorists, the 1989 memo did not contemplate calling terrorists "enemy combatants" under international norms concerning what constitutes armed conflict, nor did it assess what was a "direct threat."

The following materials reflect a state of the law that is still unsettled. Section 1 presents what little United States law exists on targeted killings to provide factual context for these killings and the tools used by Judge Bates to avoid the "stark" and "perplexing" legal issues raised by this practice. Section 2, through the lens of an Israeli decision that provides the most comprehensive effort by any court in this area, explores the deeper problem targeted killing provides to the law. As you read these materials, it is worth separating in your mind two issues: (1) what, in the abstract, should the law require when a state targets a terrorist to be killed and (2) what role should the courts play in administering that abstract law, if any?

1. UNITED STATES TARGETED KILLINGS

The first use of a targeted killing after the 9/11 attacks occurred as follows, according to a Report of the Special Rapporteur critical of the United States:

> 611. ***six men were allegedly killed while traveling in a car on 3 November 2002, in Yemen, by a missile launched from a United States-controlled Predator drone aircraft. One of the persons in the car was allegedly suspected to be a senior figure of the Al-Qaeda organization. The strike was reportedly carried out with the cooperation and approval of the Government of Yemen.

> 612. [The Government of Yemen] reported that these persons were being sought by the judicial authorities on charges of involvement in terrorist activities, including in connection with the bomb attack against the United States destroyer *USS Cole* in the Port of Aden in October 2000 and against the French oil tanker *Limburg* in October 2002. The group had allegedly planned new acts of terrorism against oil, economic and strategic installations that would have adversely affected the international standing of Yemen, as well as its political and economic interests and external relations with other States. The Government stated that it had made every effort to bring these accused persons to justice and had promised them that they would not be harmed if they had come forward voluntarily to stand trial. The group however refused to comply and persisted in its resistance to, and evasion of, justice and in planning new acts of terrorism. The security forces in Yemen had instituted cooperation with the United States of America with a view to tracking the movements and whereabouts of this alleged terrorist group had been pursued on numerous occasions in a bid to bring it to justice. The Government stated that the group had always managed to escape until the date of the final manhunt which resulted in its members being killed. The Government finally wanted to reaffirm that these measures were taken in implementation of Security Council resolution 1373 concerning the suppression of terrorism, and in the context of security

cooperation and coordination between Yemen and the United States. It concluded that by turning a blind eye to this group and allowing it to remain at large, the right to life of a large number of innocent people would have been violated, and national and international security and order would have been put at risk. The Government stated that the measure taken was the only option capable of stopping this group and preventing it from carrying out its terrorist plans.

The United States response to this report was threefold: (1)"The Government of the United States has no comment on the specific allegations and findings concerning a November 2002 incident in Yemen, or the accuracy thereof," (2) "The Government of the United States respectfully submits that inquires related to allegations stemming from any military operations conducted during the course of an armed conflict with Al Qaida do not fall within the mandate of the Special Rapporteur," and (3)"The conduct of a government in legitimate military operations, whether against Al Qaida operatives or any other legitimate military target, would be governed by the international law of armed conflict."

The Obama Administration has dramatically increased the use of targeted killings, conducting as many in its first year as the Bush Administration conducted in its last three years combined. The geographic reach of such actions has expanded to include at least Afghanistan, Pakistan, Yemen and Somalia. Afghanistan is still a war zone for allied forces including the United States, but there has been public criticism of the United States by the Karzai government for collateral damage done in strikes by predator drones. Pakistan has approved of such strikes in its territory, apparently on a case-by-case basis and with public denials of its approval. Yemen announced that it had conducted the strikes in its own territory with Predator drones purchased from the United States, but documents posted by WikiLeaks in December 2010 revealed that in fact the United States conducted these strikes. It is unclear, as of the date of this writing, what authorization Somalia has given to United States targeted killings in its territory. Finally, as the facts of the next case indicate, the characteristics of terrorists targeted may have expanded during the Obama Administration.

AL-AULAQI v. OBAMA
727 F.Supp.2d 1 (D.D.C. 2010)

BATES, J.

*** Plaintiff seeks an injunction prohibiting defendants from intentionally killing Anwar Al-Aulaqi "unless he presents a concrete, specific, and imminent threat to life or physical safety, and there are no means other than lethal force that could reasonably be employed to neutralize the threat." *** This is a unique and extraordinary case. *** Vital considerations of national security and of military and foreign affairs (and hence potentially of state secrets) are at play. *** This case arises from the United States's alleged policy of "authorizing, planning, and carrying out targeted killings, including of U.S. citizens, outside the context of armed conflict." Specifically, plaintiff, a Yemeni citizen, claims that the United States has authorized the targeted killing of plaintiff's son, Anwar Al-Aulaqi, in violation of the Constitution and international law.

Anwar Al-Aulaqi is a Muslim cleric with dual U.S.-Yemeni citizenship who is currently believed to be in hiding in Yemen. Anwar Al-Aulaqi was born in New Mexico in 1971, and spent much of his early life in the United States, attending college at Colorado State University and receiving his master's degree from San Diego State University before moving to Yemen in 2004. On July 16, 2010, the U.S. Treasury Department's Office of Foreign Assets Control ("OFAC") designated Anwar Al-Aulaqi as a Specially Designated Global Terrorist ("SDGT") in light of evidence that he was "acting for or on behalf of al-Qa'ida in the Arabian Peninsula (AQAP)" and "providing financial, material or technological support for, or other services to or in support of, acts of terrorism[.]" *Designation of ANWAR AL-AULAQI Pursuant to Executive Order 13224 and the Global Terrorism Sanctions Regulations, 31 C.F.R. Part 594, 75 Fed.Reg. 43233 (July 16, 2010)* (hereinafter, "OFAC Designation"). In its designation, OFAC explained that Anwar Al-Aulaqi had "taken on an increasingly operational role" in AQAP since late 2009, as he "facilitated training camps in Yemen in support of acts of terrorism" and provided "instructions" to Umar Farouk Abdulmutallab, the man accused of attempting to detonate a bomb aboard a Detroit-bound Northwest Airlines flight on Christmas Day 2009. Media sources have also reported ties between Anwar Al-Aulaqi and Nidal Malik Hasan, the U.S. Army Major suspected of killing 13 people in a November 2009 shooting at Fort Hood, Texas. According to a January 2010 LOS ANGELES TIMES article, unnamed "U.S. officials" have discovered that Anwar Al-Aulaqi and Hasan exchanged as many as eighteen e-mails prior to the Fort Hood shootings.

Recently, Anwar Al-Aulaqi has made numerous public statements calling for "jihad against the West," praising the actions of "his students" Abdulmutallab and Hasan, and asking others to "follow suit." Michael Leiter, Director of the National Counterterrorism Center, has explained that Anwar Al-Aulaqi's "familiarity with the West" is a key concern for the United States, and media sources have similarly cited Anwar Al-Aulaqi's ability to communicate with an English-speaking audience as a source of "particular concern" to U.S. officials. But despite the United States's expressed "concern" regarding Anwar Al-Aulaqi's "familiarity with the West" and his "role in AQAP," the United States has not yet publicly charged Anwar Al-Aulaqi with any crime. For his part, Anwar Al-Aulaqi has made clear that he has no intention of making himself available for criminal prosecution in U.S. courts, remarking in a May 2010 AQAP video interview that he "will never surrender" to the United States, and that "[i]f the Americans want me, [they can] come look for me." ***

Plaintiff does not deny his son's affiliation with AQAP or his designation as a SDGT. Rather, plaintiff challenges his son's alleged unlawful inclusion on so-called "kill lists" that he contends are maintained by the CIA and the Joint Special Operations Command ("JSOC"). In support of his claim that the United States has placed Anwar Al-Aulaqi on "kill lists," plaintiff cites a number of media reports, which attribute their information to anonymous U.S. military and intelligence sources. For example, in January 2010, THE WASHINGTON POST reported that, according to unnamed military officials, Anwar Al-Aulaqi was on "a shortlist of U.S. citizens" that JSOC was authorized to kill or capture. A few months later, THE WASHINGTON POST cited an anonymous U.S. official as stating that Anwar Al-Aulaqi had become "the first U.S. citizen added to a list of suspected terrorists the CIA is authorized to kill." And in July 2010, National Public Radio announced-on the basis of unidentified "[i]ntelligence sources"-that the United States had already ordered "almost a dozen" unsuccessful drone and air-strikes targeting Anwar Al-Aulaqi in Yemen.

Based on these news reports, plaintiff claims that the United States has placed Anwar Al-Aulaqi on the CIA and JSOC "kill lists" without "charge, trial, or conviction." Plaintiff alleges that individuals like his son are placed on "kill lists" after a "closed executive process" in which defendants and other executive officials determine that "secret criteria" have been satisfied. Plaintiff further avers "[u]pon information and belief" that once an individual is placed on a "kill list," he remains there for "months at a time." Consequently, plaintiff argues, Anwar Al-Aulaqi is "now subject to a standing order that permits the CIA and JSOC to kill him ... without regard to whether, at the time lethal force will be used, he presents a concrete, specific, and imminent threat to life, or whether there are reasonable means short of lethal force that could be used to address any such threat."

The United States has neither confirmed nor denied the allegation that it has issued a "standing order" authorizing the CIA and JSOC to kill plaintiff's son. Additionally, the United States has neither confirmed nor denied whether-if it has, in fact, authorized the use of lethal force against plaintiff's son-the authorization was made with regard to whether Anwar Al-Aulaqi presents a concrete, specific, and imminent threat to life, or whether there were reasonable means short of lethal force that could be used to address any such threat. The United States has, however, repeatedly stated that if Anwar Al-Aulaqi "were to surrender or otherwise present himself to the proper authorities in a peaceful and appropriate manner, legal principles with which the United States has traditionally and uniformly complied would prohibit using lethal force or other violence against him in such circumstances."

Nevertheless, plaintiff alleges that due to his son's inclusion on the CIA and JSOC "kill lists," Anwar Al-Aulaqi is in "hiding under threat of death and cannot access counsel or the courts to assert his constitutional rights without disclosing his whereabouts and exposing himself to possible attack by Defendants." Plaintiff therefore brings four claims-three constitutional, and one statutory-on his son's behalf. He asserts that the United States's alleged policy of authorizing the targeted killing of U.S. citizens, including plaintiff's son, outside of armed conflict, "in circumstances in which they do not present concrete, specific, and imminent threats to life or physical safety, and where there are means other than lethal force that could reasonably be employed to neutralize any such threat," violates (1) Anwar Al-Aulaqi's Fourth Amendment right to be free from unreasonable seizures and (2) his Fifth Amendment right not to be deprived of life without due process of law. Plaintiff further claims that (3) the United States's refusal to disclose the criteria by which it selects U.S. citizens like plaintiff's son for targeted killing independently violates the notice requirement of the Fifth Amendment Due Process Clause. Finally, plaintiff brings (4) a statutory claim under the Alien Tort Statute ("ATS"), alleging that the United States's "policy of targeted killings violates treaty and customary international law."

Plaintiff seeks both declaratory and injunctive relief. First, he requests a declaration that, outside of armed conflict, the Constitution prohibits defendants "from carrying out the targeted killing of U.S. citizens," including Anwar Al-Aulaqi, "except in circumstances in which they present a concrete, specific, and imminent threat to life or physical safety, and there are no means other than lethal force that could reasonably be employed to neutralize the threat." Second, plaintiff requests a declaration that, outside of armed conflict, "treaty and customary international law" prohibit the [extrajudicial killing] of all individuals-regardless of their citizenship-except in those same, limited circumstances. Third, plaintiff requests a preliminary injunction prohibiting defendants from intentionally killing Anwar Al-Aulaqi "unless he presents a concrete, specific, and imminent threat to life or physical safety, and there are no means other than lethal force that could reasonably be employed to neutralize the threat." Finally, plaintiff seeks an injunction ordering defendants to disclose the criteria that the United States uses to determine whether a U.S. citizen will be targeted for killing.

Presently before the Court is defendants' motion to dismiss plaintiff's complaint on five distinct grounds: (1) standing; (2) political question; (3) "equitable discretion"; (4) lack of a cause of action under the ATS; and (5) the state secrets privilege. ***

I. *Standing.* *** Plaintiff has failed to provide an adequate explanation for his son's inability to appear on his own behalf, which is fatal to plaintiff's attempt to establish "next friend" standing. In his complaint, plaintiff maintains that his son cannot bring suit on his own behalf because he is "in hiding under threat of death" and any attempt to access counsel or the courts would "expos[e] him[ ] to possible attack by Defendants." But while Anwar Al-Aulaqi may have chosen to "hide" from U.S. law enforcement authorities, there is nothing preventing him from peacefully presenting himself at the U.S. Embassy in Yemen and expressing a desire to vindicate his constitutional rights in U.S. courts. Defendants have made clear-and indeed, both international and domestic law would require-that if Anwar Al-Aulaqi were to present himself in that manner, the United States would be "prohibit[ed] [from] using lethal force or other violence against him in such circumstances."

Plaintiff argues that to accept defendants' position-that Anwar Al-Aulaqi can access the U.S. judicial system so long as he "surrenders"-"would require the Court to accept at the standing stage what is disputed on the merits," since the Court would then be acknowledging that Anwar Al-Aulaqi is, in fact, currently "a participant in an armed conflict against the United States." Not so. The Court's conclusion that Anwar Al-Aulaqi can access the U.S. judicial system by presenting himself in a peaceful manner implies no judgment as to Anwar Al-Aulaqi's status as a potential terrorist. *All* U.S. citizens may avail themselves of the U.S. judicial system if they present themselves peacefully, and *no* U.S. citizen may simultaneously avail himself of the U.S. judicial system and evade U.S. law enforcement authorities. Anwar Al-Aulaqi is thus faced with the same choice presented to all U.S. citizens.[4]

It is certainly possible that Anwar Al-Aulaqi could be arrested-and imprisoned-if he were to come out of hiding to seek judicial relief in U.S. courts. Without expressing an opinion as to the likelihood of Anwar Al-Aulaqi's future arrest or imprisonment, it is significant to note that an individual's incarceration does not render him unable to access the courts ***. Indeed, "prisoners can, and do, bring civil suits all the time." Given that an individual's actual incarceration is insufficient to show that he lacks access to the courts, the mere prospect of Anwar Al-Aulaqi's future incarceration fails to satisfy [the] "inaccessibility" requirement.

Plaintiff argues, however, that if his son were to seek judicial relief, he would not be detained as an ordinary federal prisoner, but instead would be subject to "indefinite detention without charge." It is true that courts have, in some instances, granted "next friend" standing to enemy combatants being held "incommunicado." For example, in *Padilla v. Rumsfeld,* 352 F.3d 695 (2d Cir.2003), *rev'd and remanded on other grounds,* 542 U.S. 426 (2004), the Second Circuit granted an attorney "next friend" standing to file a habeas petition on behalf of an American citizen who was being detained as an enemy combatant at a U.S. naval base in South Carolina. The court in *Padilla* had little difficulty concluding that the real party in interest was unable to "access the courts" under *Whitmore,* as he had been denied "any contact with his counsel, his family or any other non-military personnel" for eighteen months. Similarly, in *Hamdi v. Rumsfeld,* 296 F.3d 278 (4th Cir.2002), *vacated on other grounds,* 542 U.S. 507 (2004), the Fourth Circuit

---

[4] In fact, it is possible that Anwar Al-Aulaqi would not even need to emerge from "hiding" in order to seek judicial relief. The use of videoconferencing and other technology has made civil judicial proceedings possible even where the plaintiff himself cannot physically access the courtroom. For example, courts frequently entertain habeas corpus petitions from detainees at Guantanamo Bay despite the fact that those detainees are not present in the courtroom. There is no reason why-if Anwar Al-Aulaqi wanted to seek judicial relief but feared the consequences of emerging from hiding-he could not communicate with attorneys via the Internet from his current place of hiding.

permitted the father of a military detainee to petition the court on his son's behalf, as the son was being "held incommunicado and subjected to an infinite detention ... without access to a lawyer."

But unlike the detainees in *Padilla* and *Hamdi,* Anwar Al-Aulaqi is not in U.S. custody, nor is he being held incommunicado against his will. To the extent that Anwar Al-Aulaqi is currently incommunicado, that is the result of his own choice. Moreover, there is reason to doubt whether Anwar Al-Aulaqi is, in fact, incommunicado. Since his alleged period of hiding began in January 2010, Anwar Al-Aulaqi has communicated with the outside world on numerous occasions, participating in AQAP video interviews and publishing online articles in the AQAP magazine *Inspire.* Anwar Al-Aulaqi has continued to use his personal website to convey messages to readers worldwide, and a July 2010 online article written by Anwar Al-Aulaqi advises readers that they "may contact Shayk [Anwar] Al-Aulaqi through any of the emails listed on the contact page." Needless to say, Anwar Al-Aulaqi's access to e-mail renders the circumstances of his existing, self-made "confinement" far different than the confinement of the detainees in *Padilla* and *Hamdi.*

Even if Anwar Al-Aulaqi were to be captured and detained, the conditions of his confinement would still need to be akin to those in *Padilla* and *Hamdi* before his father could be accorded standing to proceed as Anwar Al-Aulaqi's "next friend." In cases brought by purported "next friends" on behalf of detainees at Guantanamo Bay, courts have not presumed that the detainees lack access to the U.S. judicial system, but have required the would-be "next friends" to make a *showing* of inaccessibility. ***

Not only has plaintiff failed to prove that Anwar Al-Aulaqi lacks access to the courts, but he has also failed to show that he is "truly dedicated" to Anwar Al-Aulaqi's "best interests." *** Here, plaintiff has presented no evidence that his son wants to vindicate his U.S. constitutional rights through the U.S. judicial system. *** Indeed, to the extent that Anwar Al-Aulaqi has made his personal preferences known, he has indicated precisely the opposite-i.e., that he believes it is *not* in his best interests to prosecute this case. According to plaintiff's complaint, the media first reported that Anwar Al-Aulaqi had been added to the JSOC "kill list" as early as January 2010. However, at no point has Anwar Al-Aulaqi sought to challenge his alleged inclusion on the CIA or JSOC "kill lists," nor has he communicated any desire to do so. Although plaintiff maintains that "Anwar Al-Aulaqi *cannot* communicate with his father or counsel without endangering his own life," this contention is belied by the numerous public statements that Anwar Al-Aulaqi has made since his alleged period of hiding began. Several times during the past ten months, Anwar Al-Aulaqi has publicly expressed his desire for "jihad against the West," and he has called upon Muslims to meet "American aggression" not with "pigeons and olive branches" but "with bullets and bombs." Given that Anwar Al-Aulaqi has been able to make such controversial statements with impunity, there is no reason to believe that he could not convey a desire to sue without somehow placing his life in danger. Under these circumstances, the fact that Anwar Al-Aulaqi has chosen not to communicate any such desire strongly supports the inference that he does not want to litigate in the U.S. courts.

This inference is further corroborated by the content of Anwar Al-Aulaqi's public statements, in which he has decried the U.S. legal system and suggested that Muslims are not bound by Western law. As recently as April 2010, Anwar Al-Aulaqi wrote an article for the AQAP publication *Inspire,* in which he asserted that Muslims "should not be forced to accept rulings of courts of law that are contrary to the law of Allah." According to Anwar Al-Aulaqi, Muslims need not adhere to the laws of the "civil state," since "the modern civil state of the West does not guarantee Islamic rights." In a July 2010 *Inspire* article, Anwar Al-Aulaqi again expressed his belief that because Western "government, political parties, the police, [and] the intelligence services ... are part of a system within which the defamation of Islam is ... promoted ... the attacking of any Western target [is] legal from an Islamic viewpoint." He went on to argue that a U.S. civilian who drew a cartoon depiction of Mohammed should be "a prime target of assassination" and that "[a]ssassinations, bombings, and acts of arson" constitute "legitimate forms of revenge against a system that relishes the sacrilege of Islam in the name of freedom."

Such statements-which reveal a complete lack of respect for U.S. law and governmental structures as well as a belief that it is "legal" and "legitimate" to violate U.S. law-do not reflect the views of an individual who would likely want to sue to vindicate his U.S. constitutional rights in U.S. courts. After all, the substantive rights that are being asserted in this case are only provided to Anwar Al-Aulaqi by the *U.S. Constitution* and *international law.* Yet he has made clear his belief that "international treaties" do not govern Muslims, and that Muslims are not bound by *any* law-U.S., international, or otherwise-that conflicts with the "law of Allah." There is, then, reason to doubt that Anwar Al-Aulaqi would even regard a ruling from this Court as binding-much less that he would want to litigate in order to obtain such a ruling. Anwar Al-Aulaqi's public statement that "[i]f the Americans want me, [they can] come look for me" provides further evidence that he has no intention of making himself the subject of litigation in U.S. courts. In light of such remarks, this Court cannot conclude that Anwar Al-Aulaqi believes "taking legal action to stop the United States from killing" him would be in his "best interests." While he may very well wish to avoid targeted killing by the United States, all available evidence indicates that he does not wish "to file [suit] as a vehicle for accomplishing this purpose." *** Because plaintiff cannot show that Anwar Al-Aulaqi lacks access to the courts and that he is acting in Anwar Al-Aulaqi's best interests, plaintiff lacks standing to bring constitutional claims as his son's "next friend." ***

The Alien Tort Statute. Plaintiff brings his fourth and final claim under the Alien Tort Statute ("ATS"), alleging that the United States's "policy of targeted killings violates treaty and customary international law." *** Plaintiff is an alien, but in order for his ATS claim to survive a motion to dismiss, he must also show that (1) an alien suffers a legally cognizable tort-which rises to the level of a "customary international law norm"-when his U.S. citizen son is threatened with a future extrajudicial killing and (2) the United States has waived sovereign immunity for that type of claim. Because plaintiff has failed to make either showing, his ATS claim must be dismissed.

*** Plaintiff maintains that his alleged tort-extrajudicial killing-meets the high bar of *Sosa,* since there is a customary international law norm against state-sponsored extrajudicial killings, which has been "consistently recognized by U.S. courts" and "indeed codified in domestic law under the Torture Victim Protection Act."[10] Plaintiff is correct insofar as many U.S. courts have recognized a customary international law norm against past state-sponsored extrajudicial killings as the basis for an ATS claim. Significantly, however, plaintiff cites no case in which a court has ever recognized a "customary international law norm" against a *threatened* future extrajudicial killing, nor does he cite a single case in which an alien has ever been permitted to recover under the ATS for the extrajudicial killing of his U.S. citizen child. These two features of plaintiff's ATS claim-that it is based on a threat of a future extrajudicial killing, not an actual extrajudicial killing, that is directed not to plaintiff or to his alien relative, but to his U.S. citizen son-render plaintiff's ATS claim fundamentally distinct from all extrajudicial killing claims that courts have previously held cognizable under the ATS. *** If this Court were to conclude that alleged government threats-no matter how plausible or severe they may be-constitute international torts committed in violation of the law of nations, federal courts could be flooded with ATS suits from persons across the globe who alleged that they were somehow placed in fear of danger as a result of contemplated government action. Surely, as interpreted in *Sosa,* the ATS was not intended to provide a federal forum for such speculative claims.

The precise relief that plaintiff seeks here-an injunction against the President, the Secretary of Defense, and the Director of the CIA preventing them from carrying out specific national security measures abroad-is, as defendants point out, both "novel" and "extraordinary." The Supreme Court in *Sosa* did not call upon the federal courts to recognize such novel, extraordinary claims under the ATS, but rather merely "opened the door a crack to the possible recognition of new causes of action under international law (such as, perhaps, torture) if they were firmly grounded on an international consensus." ***

---

[10] The Torture Victim Protection Act of 1991 ("TVPA") provides in relevant part that "[a]n individual who, under actual or apparent authority, or color of law, of any foreign nation ... subjects an individual to an extrajudicial killing shall, in a civil action, be liable for damages to the individual's legal representative, or to any person who may be a claimant in an action for wrongful death." The Seventh Circuit has held that the TVPA "occup[ies] the field" with respect to claims alleging extrajudicial killing, *see Enahoro v. Abubakar,* 408 F.3d 877, 884-85 (7th Cir.2005), but most courts have found that the TVPA does not preclude ATS claims for extrajudicial killing. These courts view the TVPA and its legislative history as providing strong evidence that there is, in fact, a customary international law norm against extrajudicial killing, upon which an ATS claim may be based.

Moreover, even if the mere threat of a future state-sponsored extrajudicial killing did constitute a violation of the present-day law of nations, plaintiff could not bring an ATS claim based on the alleged threat of an extrajudicial killing of his U.S. citizen son. Significantly, the ATS authorizes federal jurisdiction over "civil actions *by an alien* for a tort only, committed in violation of the law of nations." Although plaintiff is an alien, his son is a U.S. citizen, and as such, Anwar Al-Aulaqi is not authorized to sue under the ATS. Given that Anwar Al-Aulaqi could not maintain an ATS action, plaintiff cannot instead bring an ATS action as a "next friend" or third party on Anwar Al-Aulaqi's behalf. In other words, plaintiff can only sue under the ATS if he alleges that he himself has suffered a tort that rises to the level of a "customary international law norm." *** Plaintiff cannot have it both ways. He either is bringing an ATS claim on behalf of his U.S. citizen son, alleging violations of Anwar Al-Aulaqi's right to be free from an extrajudicial killing, or he is bringing an ATS claim based on violations of his own right to be free from the emotional harm that he would suffer if his son were to be unlawfully killed. But the former fails as a result of Anwar Al-Aulaqi's U.S. citizenship, and the latter fails because there is not even domestic consensus as to whether a parent can recover for emotional injuries stemming from the death of his adult child, much less universal agreement that such a tort is actionable. ***

Because plaintiff brings his ATS claim against the President, the Secretary of Defense, and the Director of the CIA in their official capacities, his suit is tantamount to a suit against the United States itself. *** Thus, assuming that plaintiff could allege a cognizable tort under the ATS, his ATS claim still must fail absent a valid waiver of sovereign immunity. *** Given that there is no clear waiver of sovereign immunity permitting such "extraordinary relief," and that "[t]he Alien Tort Statute has never been held to cover suits against the United States or United States Government officials," *see El-Shifa Pharm. Indus. Co. v. United States,* 607 F.3d 836, 858 (D.C.Cir.2010) *(en banc)* (Kavanaugh, J., concurring), this Court declines to exercise its equitable discretion to grant such relief here. ***

The Political Question Doctrine. Defendants argue that even if plaintiff has standing to bring his constitutional claims or states a cognizable claim under the ATS, his claims should still be dismissed because they raise non-justiciable political questions. *** Judicial resolution of the "particular questions" posed by plaintiff in this case would require this Court to decide: (1) the precise nature and extent of Anwar Al-Aulaqi's affiliation with AQAP; (2) whether AQAP and al Qaeda are so closely linked that the defendants' targeted killing of Anwar Al-Aulaqi in Yemen would come within the United States's current armed conflict with al Qaeda; (3) whether (assuming plaintiff's proffered legal standard applies) Anwar Al-Aulaqi's alleged terrorist activity renders him a "concrete, specific, and imminent threat to life or physical safety,"; and (4) whether there are "means short of lethal force" that the United States could "reasonably" employ to address any threat that Anwar Al-Aulaqi poses to U.S. national security interests. Such determinations, in turn, would require this Court, in defendants' view, to understand and assess "the capabilities of the [alleged] terrorist operative to carry out a threatened attack, what response would be sufficient to address that threat, possible diplomatic considerations that may bear on such responses, the vulnerability of potential targets that the [alleged] terrorist [ ] may strike, the availability of military and nonmilitary options, and the risks to military and nonmilitary personnel in attempting application of non-lethal force." Viewed through these prisms, it becomes clear that plaintiff's claims pose precisely the types of complex policy questions that the D.C. Circuit has historically held non-justiciable under the political question doctrine.

Most recently, in *El-Shifa v. United States* the D.C. Circuit examined whether the political question doctrine barred judicial resolution of claims by owners of a Sudanese pharmaceutical plant who brought suit seeking to recover damages after their plant was destroyed by an American cruise missile. President Clinton had ordered the missile strike in light of intelligence indicating that the plant was "'associated with the [Osama] bin Ladin network' and 'involved in the production of materials for chemical weapons.' " The plaintiffs maintained that the U.S. government had been negligent in determining that the plant was tied "to chemical weapons and Osama bin Laden," and therefore sought "a declaration that the government's failure to compensate them for the destruction of the plant violated customary international law, a declaration that statements government officials made about them were defamatory, and an injunction requiring the government to retract those statements." Dismissing the plaintiffs' claims as non-justiciable under the political question doctrine, the D.C. Circuit explained that "[i]n military matters ... the courts lack the competence to assess the strategic decision to employ force or to create standards to determine whether the use of force was justified or well-founded." Rather than endeavor to resolve questions beyond the Judiciary's institutional competence, the court held that "[i]f the political question doctrine means anything in the arena of national security and foreign relations, it means the courts cannot assess the merits of the President's decision to launch an attack on a foreign target."

Here, plaintiff asks this Court to do exactly what the D.C. Circuit forbid in *El-Shifa*-assess the merits of the President's (alleged) decision to launch an attack on a foreign target. Although the "foreign target" happens to be a U.S. citizen, the same reasons that counseled against judicial resolution of the plaintiffs' claims in *El-Shifa* apply with equal force here. Just as in *El-Shifa,* any judicial determination as to the propriety of a military attack on Anwar Al-Aulaqi would "'require this court to elucidate the ... standards that are to guide a President when he evaluates the veracity of military intelligence.' "Indeed, that is just what plaintiff has asked this Court to do. *See* Compl., Prayer for Relief (d) (requesting that the Court order the defendants to "disclose the criteria used in determining whether the government will carry out the targeted killing of a U.S. citizen"). But there are no judicially manageable standards by which courts can endeavor to assess the President's interpretation of military intelligence and his resulting decision-based on that intelligence-whether to use military force against a terrorist target overseas. Nor are there judicially manageable standards by which courts may determine the nature and magnitude of the national security threat posed by a particular individual. In fact, the D.C. Circuit has expressly held that the question whether an organization's alleged "terrorist activity" threatens "the national security of the United States" is "nonjusticiable." *People's Mohahedin Org. of Iran v. U.S. Dep't of State,* 182 F.3d 17, 23 (D.C.Cir.1999). Given that courts may not undertake to assess whether a particular organization's alleged terrorist activities threaten national security, it would seem axiomatic that courts must also decline to assess whether a particular individual's alleged terrorist activities threaten national security. But absent such a judicial determination as to the nature and extent of the alleged national security threat that Anwar Al-Aulaqi poses to the United States, this Court cannot possibly determine whether the government's alleged use of lethal force against Anwar Al-Aulaqi would be "justified or well-founded." Thus, the second *Baker* factor-a "lack of judicially discoverable and manageable standards" for resolving the dispute-strongly counsels against judicial review of plaintiff's claims.

The type of relief that plaintiff seeks only underscores the impropriety of judicial review here. Plaintiff requests both a declaration setting forth the standard under which the United States can select individuals for targeted killing as well as an injunction prohibiting defendants from intentionally killing Anwar Al-Aulaqi unless he meets that standard-i.e., unless he "presents a concrete, specific, and imminent threat to life or physical safety, and there are no means other than lethal force that could reasonably be employed to neutralize the threat." Yet plaintiff concedes that the "imminence' requirement" of his proffered legal standard would render any "real-time judicial review" of targeting decisions "infeasible," and he therefore urges this Court to issue his requested preliminary injunction and then enforce the injunction "through an after-the-fact contempt motion or an after-the-fact damages action." *** Such military determinations are textually committed to the political branches. Moreover, any post hoc judicial assessment as to the propriety of the Executive's decision to employ military force abroad "would be anathema to ... separation of powers" principles. The first, fourth, and sixth *Baker* factors thus all militate against judicial review of plaintiffs' claims, since there is a "textually demonstrable constitutional commitment" of the United States's decision to employ military force to coordinate political departments (Congress and the Executive), and any after-the-fact judicial review of the Executive's decision to employ military force abroad would reveal a "lack of respect due coordinate branches of government" and create "the potentiality of embarrassment of multifarious pronouncements by various departments on one question."

The mere fact that the "foreign target" of military action in this case is an individual-rather than alleged enemy property-does not distinguish plaintiff's claims from those raised in *El-Shifa* for purposes of the political question doctrine. *** Plaintiff's claim is distinguishable from those asserted in these cases in only one meaningful respect: Anwar Al-Aulaqi *** is a U.S. citizen. *** Nevertheless, there is inadequate reason to conclude that Anwar

Al-Aulaqi's U.S. citizenship-standing alone-renders the political question doctrine inapplicable to plaintiff's claims. Plaintiff cites two contexts in which courts have found claims asserting violations of U.S. citizens' constitutional rights to be justiciable despite the fact that those claims implicate grave national security and foreign policy concerns. Courts have been willing to entertain habeas petitions from U.S. citizens detained by the United States as enemy combatants, *see, e .g., Hamdi,* 542 U.S. at 509, and they have also heard claims from U .S. citizens alleging unconstitutional takings of their property by the U.S. military abroad, *see, e.g., Ramirez de Arellano,* 745 F.2d at 1511-12. But habeas petitions and takings claims are both much more amenable to judicial resolution than the claims raised by plaintiff in this case. ***

To be sure, this Court recognizes the somewhat unsettling nature of its conclusion-that there are circumstances in which the Executive's unilateral decision to kill a U.S. citizen overseas is "constitutionally committed to the political branches" and judicially unreviewable. But this case squarely presents such a circumstance. The political question doctrine requires courts to engage in a fact-specific analysis of the "particular question" posed by a specific case, and the doctrine does not contain any "carve-out" for cases involving the constitutional rights of U.S. citizens. *** Contrary to plaintiff's assertion, in holding that the political question doctrine bars plaintiff's claims, this Court does not hold that the Executive possesses "unreviewable authority to order the assassination of any American whom he labels an enemy of the state." Rather, the Court only concludes that it lacks the capacity to determine whether a specific individual in hiding overseas, whom the Director of National Intelligence has stated is an "operational" member of AQAP, presents such a threat to national security that the United States may authorize the use of lethal force against him. This Court readily acknowledges that it is a "drastic measure" for the United States to employ lethal force against one of its own citizens abroad, even if that citizen is currently playing an operational role in a "terrorist group that has claimed responsibility for numerous attacks against Saudi, Korean, Yemeni, and U.S. targets since January 2009." *** [W]hether "drastic measures should be taken in matters of foreign policy and national security is not the stuff of adjudication, but of policymaking." Because decision-making in the realm of military and foreign affairs is textually committed to the political branches, and because courts are functionally ill-equipped to make the types of complex policy judgments that would be required to adjudicate the merits of plaintiff's claims, the Court finds that the political question doctrine bars judicial resolution of this case.

The Military and State Secrets Privilege. Defendants invoke the military and state secrets privilege as the final basis for dismissal of plaintiff's complaint. The state secrets privilege is premised on the recognition that "in exceptional circumstances courts must act in the interest of the country's national security to prevent disclosure of state secrets, even to the point of dismissing a case entirely." As the Ninth Circuit has recently explained, "contemporary state secrets doctrine encompasses two applications of this principle. One completely bars adjudication of claims premised on state secrets (the '*Totten* bar'); the other is an evidentiary privilege ('the *Reynolds* privilege') that excludes privileged evidence from the case and *may* result in dismissal of the claims ." *Jeppesen Dataplan,* 614 F.3d at 1077 (emphasis in original). *** Here, defendants do not argue that the very subject matter of this case is itself a "state secret." Rather, they contend that this case is one in which the "*Reynolds* privilege converges with the *Totten* bar," because "specific categories of information properly protected against disclosure by the privilege would be necessary to litigate each of plaintiff's claims." Defendants correctly note that the privilege protects information from disclosure "where there is a reasonable danger that disclosure would 'expose military matters which, in the interests of national security, should not be divulged .' "They argue that "where 'the claims and possible defenses are so infused with state secrets that the risk of disclosing them is both apparent and inevitable,' dismissal is required." And here, according to defendants, that is most certainly the case because

> [i]n unclassified terms, [the disclosure harmful to national security] includes information needed to address whether or not, or under what circumstances, the United States may target a particular foreign terrorist organization and its senior leadership, the specific threat posed by al-Qaeda, AQAP, or Anwar al-Aulaqi, and other matters that plaintiff has put at issue, including any criteria governing the use of lethal force.

But defendants also correctly and forcefully observe that this Court need not, and should not, reach their claim of state secrets privilege because the case can be resolved on the other grounds they have presented. It is certainly true that the state secrets privilege should be "invoked no more often or extensively than necessary." *Jeppesen Dataplan,* 614 F.3d at 1080. Indeed, last year the Attorney General promulgated a policy confirming that the state secrets privilege will only be invoked in limited circumstances involving a significant risk of harm to national security and after detailed procedures are followed (including personal approval of the Attorney General). And here, defendants have confirmed that the privilege has been invoked only after that careful review and adherence to the mandated procedures under the Attorney General's policy. *** [G]iven both the extraordinary nature of this case and the other clear grounds for resolving it, the Court will not reach defendants' state secrets privilege claim. *** [T]he Court will grant defendants' motion to dismiss. ***

Notes

1. **Ducking the Case: Holding and Dictum.** Do you agree with Judge Bates on the standing issue? Could the case be revived if the son acceded to the father's desire to seek an injunction? Even if the son remained in hiding and conveyed his wishes for his father to represent him? Doesn't the Court say that the father

has no standing even on the ATS claim? Why would the Court proceed to discuss the nature of that claim and the sovereign immunity response to it?

2. **Dual Nationality.** One student commentator on the decision suggests there was an even more fundamental problem with the decision:

> Before assuming that al-Aulaqi should be afforded the rights granted to American citizens, the court should have followed customary international law by first determining al-Aulaqi's dominant and effective nationality. Essentially, if the court had made the threshold determination that al-Aulaqi is a dominant and effective Yemeni national, why should he even be entitled to U.S. Constitutional protections?" *Abe Kannof, Dueling Nationalities: Dual Citizenship, Dominent & Effective Nationality, and the Case of Anwar al-Aulaqi* (manuscript submitted for publication in the EMORY LAW JOURNAL).

Do you agree? Would your decision on this issue be affected by the difficulty of ferreting out the target's "dominant and effective nationality"?

3. **The Target.** Anwar Al-Aulaqi is an English-language purveyor of videos that inspire others to attempt suicide missions. In addition, evidence shows he had contact with individuals who carried through with such missions. Assuming he has no operational role in AQAP, under which paradigm- the criminal or the military- does Al Aulaqi's targeting best fit?

4. **The Place.** Does it matter whether the Yemeni government authorizes the strike? That the UN authorized coalition military operations in Afghanistan but not Yemen? That AQAP supports an insurgency against the government of Yemen? Assuming self-defense does not justify targeting (not immediate or can't target citizen), might Yemen and the U. S. be co-belligerents in a non-international war on AQAP? A*l-Bihani v. Obama,* 590 F. 3d 866, supra Chapter V, says co-belligerency "only applie[s] to nation-states" in international conflicts, but Bradley and Goldsmith, "Congressional Authorization and the War on Terrorism," 118 HARV. L. REV. 2047, 2112 (2005) and Farley, "Targeting Anwar al-Aulaqi: A Case Study in U.S. Use of Force Justifications" (unpublished manuscript) suggest otherwise.

5. **The Terrorist Organization.** AQAP did not exist at the time of the 9/11 attacks. Does this matter under the AUMF (check the language if you have forgotten it)? Does AQAP fit better if (a) it was the result of the merger of al Qaeda organizations that were around earlier, (b) its organizational leaders include fighters captured in the initial coalition response to the 9/11 attacks, and (3) that AQAP has professed loyalty to Osama bin Laden?

6. **Strategic Choices.** Rather than killing Al Aulaqi with a drone strike, the United States might have sent in a team of military operatives to try to capture or kill him. In fact, soon after 9/11, Defense Secretary Donald Rumsfeld planned for Special Operations "hunter killer teams" to kill rather than capturing certain terrorist suspects. What are the benefits and disadvantages of using "hunter killer teams" rather than drone strikes?

7. **State Secrets.** At the end of his opinion, Judge Bates says he need not

decide the state secrets issue. Given your knowledge of the application of that
doctrine elsewhere, how do you think that issue should be decided in the context
of a case having a plaintiff with standing? What would be the components of the
alleged secret? Would public disclosure of the target's name waive or alter the
state secrets defense?

8. **Process for Targeting.** Relatively little is known about the process by
which the CIA selects targets like al-Aulaqi. According to John Rizzo, former
acting general counsel for the CIA, the process for selecting an individual to be
killed begins at the CIA Counterterrorist Center, where agents prepare "dossiers"
of roughly five pages for review by a team of CIA lawyers. Those lawyers select
dossiers to end with the phrase "Therefore we request approval for targeting for
lethal operation" for the CIA general counsel's signature. Neither the president
nor a court reviews the names of individuals. Tara Mckelvey, "Inside the Killing
Machine,"   NEWSWEEK   (Feb.   13,   2011),   available   at
http://www.newsweek.com/2011/02/13/inside-the-killing-machine.html.[JH1]

9. **Mission Creep and Paradigm Shift?** The United States allegedly has a
"hit list" of Afghan war lords who were helping finance the Taliban. Craig
Whitlock, "Afghans Oppose U.S. Hit List of Drug Traffickers," WASH. POST, Oct.
24, 2009. Is this a permissible use of targeted killing? Compare and contrast
"the new Islamic terrorism" and "narco-terrorism" in terms of using targeted
killing as a response.

10. **EO 12333.** Since assassinations by the United States government are
prohibited under EO 12333, why did Al-Aulaqi's father not argue that the
targeting of his son violated EO 12333?

11. **Implications of Illegality.** If targeted killings are illegal, Presidents
Clinton, George W. Bush, and Obama are serial killers, perhaps even war
criminals.   Criminal accusations were filed against Secretary Rumsfeld by
German human rights lawyer Wolfgang Kaleck under a statute purporting to
provide for universal jurisdiction, but the German Federal Prosecutor General
declined to investigate international human rights violations associated with the
handling of prisoners at Abu Ghraib and Guantánamo. Additionally, those
authorizing targeted killings might be subjected to tort judgments anywhere in
the world by relatives of terrorists or innocent bystanders killed in a strike, were
it not for sovereign immunity. See *Matar v. Dichter*, 563 F. 3d 9 (2d Cir. 2009)
(dismissing lawsuit by Center for Constitutional Rights against the head of the
Israel Security Agency, who had ordered the targeted strike.

12. **Academic Assessment.**   Blum and Heymann, "Law and Policy of
Targeted Killing," HARVARD NATIONAL SECURITY JOURNAL, available at
http://harvardnsj.com/2010/06/law-and-policy-of-targeted -killing/ (Posted June 27,
2010), what they call "the contours of the use of targeted killing," contours fitting
both a "more constrained war paradigm" and a "more lax law enforcement
paradigm." Targeted killing of some but not all terrorists would be allowed. A
"good place to start," according to Blum and Heymann, would be the following
components of the Israeli Supreme Court approach: (1) no use if the host state is
willing and able to arrest or disable the target; (2) target only those "actively and
directly involved in terrorist activities;" (3) "ensure an accurate identification"

through "verified and verifiable intelligence data from different and independent sources" and abort missions "when in doubt"; (4) consider collateral damage and "those [so] injured should generally be compensated"; and (5) use only "in the most urgent and necessary of cases," after alternatives have been exhausted. They say "external judicial review" is unnecessary because judges do not have expertise to make such decisions and are "not well situated" to do so. If you were charged with overseeing targeted killings of terrorists for the Obama Administration, would you adopt these guidelines? If you adopted them, to what extent would these guidelines determine the outcome of your decisions in individual cases?

13. Could Al-Aulaqi be Convicted? What connection between al-Aulaqi's videos and violence committed by a viewer must there be for him (or others like him) to be convicted for incitement to terrorism? In *Brandenburg v. Ohio*, 395 U.S. 444 (1969), the Supreme Court held that where speech advocates criminal conduct, it may not be penalized unless it is both *intended and likely* to produce "imminent lawless action." After *Humanitarian Law Project v. Holder*, however, *Brandenburg* may not be good law. The *HLP* Court held that neither specific intent nor a "likely" nexus with "imminent lawless action" is required for speech that promotes lawful non-violent goals of designated terrorist organizations. If the Court were to accept a challenge to a prosecution involving videos like al-Aulaqi's, what standard do you think it should adopt and why? Regardless, under *HLP*, could al-Aulaqi successfully be prosecuted for material support?

2. ISRAELI TARGETED KILLINGS

While the United States has since EO 12333 abhorred assassination as a tool of national policy, Israel has assassinated various enemy targets, including the Black September members following the Munich Olympics massacre in 1972 and the Secretary General of Hezbollah in 1992. After the Second Infitada began in September 2000, Israel made targeted killings an overt policy in fighting terrorism. Here is a concise description of how Israel goes about engaging in targeted killings:

> The process for approving targeted killing operations in Israel involves an intelligence "incrimination" of the target, which identifies the target as a person actively involved in acts of terrorism; a plan for the time, place, and means of the attack (most commonly, an airstrike); consideration of the danger of collateral damage; and a review of potential political ramifications. The complete plan must receive the approval of a top-level political official. There is no external review process, judicial or otherwise.

Blum and Heymann, *supra*, note page 658. These authors note that, by March 2002, "339 Palestinians had been killed in targeted killing operations during the Second Intifada: 201 intended targets and 129 innocent bystanders."

The following decision of the Supreme Court of Israel, written by the most distinguished Israeli jurist of modern times, is especially weighty authority concerning the legality of such operations.

THE PUBLIC COMMITTEE AGAINST TORTURE IN ISRAEL v. GOVERNMENT OF ISRAEL
(TARGETED KILLINGS CASE)[2005]
SUPREME COURT OF ISRAEL SITTING AS THE HIGH COURT OF JUSTICE HCJ 769/02 DECEMBER 11, 2005

President (Emeritus) A. BARAK:

The Government of Israel employs a policy of preventative strikes which causes the death of terrorists in Judea, Samaria, or the Gaza Strip. It fatally strikes these terrorists, who plan, launch, or commit terrorist attacks in Israel and in the area of Judea, Samaria, and the Gaza Strip, against both civilians and soldiers. These strikes at times also harm innocent civilians. Does the State thus act illegally? ***

2. In its war against terrorism, the State of Israel employs various means. As part of the security activity intended to confront the terrorist attacks, the State employs what it calls "the policy of targeted frustration" of terrorism. Under this policy, the security forces act in order to kill members of terrorist organizations involved in the planning, launching, or execution of terrorist attacks against Israel. During the second intifada, such preventative strikes have been performed across Judea, Samaria, and the Gaza Strip. According to the data relayed by petitioners, since the commencement of these acts, and up until the end of 2005, close to three hundred members of terrorist organizations have been killed by them. More than thirty targeted killing attempts have failed. Approximately one hundred and fifty civilians who were proximate to the location of the targeted persons have been killed during those acts. Hundreds of others have been wounded. The policy of targeted killings is the focus of this petition. ***

18. The normative system which applies to the armed conflict between Israel and the terrorist organizations in the area is complex. In its center stands the international law regarding international armed conflict. Professor Cassese discussed the international character of an armed conflict between the occupying state in an area subject to belligerent occupation and the terrorists who come from the same area, including the armed conflict between Israel and the terrorist organizations in the area, stating:

> "An armed conflict which takes place between an Occupying Power and rebel or insurgent groups – whether or not they are terrorist in character – in an occupied territory, amounts to an international armed conflict."

This law includes the laws of belligerent occupation. *** Alongside the international law dealing with armed conflicts, fundamental principles of Israeli public law, which every Israeli soldier "carries in his pack" and which go along with him wherever he may turn, may apply ***.

21. *** Are terrorist organizations and their members combatants, in regards to their rights in the armed conflict? Are they civilians taking an active part in the armed conflict? Are they possibly neither combatants nor civilians? What, then, is the status of those terrorists? ***

25. The terrorists and their organizations, with which the State of Israel has an armed conflict of international character, do not fall into the category of combatants. They do not belong to the armed forces, and they do not belong to units to which international law grants status similar to that of combatants. Indeed, the terrorists and the organizations which send them to carry out attacks are unlawful combatants. They do not enjoy the status of prisoners of war. They can be tried for their participation in hostilities, judged, and punished. *** Are they seen as civilians under the law? ***

26. Customary international law regarding armed conflicts protects "civilians" from harm as a result of the hostilities. *** From that follows also the duty to do everything possible to minimize collateral damage to the civilian population during the attacks on "combatants" ***. The approach of customary international law is that "civilians" are those who are not "combatants" *** Does that mean that the unlawful combatants are entitled to the same protection to which civilians who are not unlawful combatants are entitled? The answer is, no. Customary international law regarding armed conflicts determines that a civilian taking a direct part in the hostilities does not, at such time, enjoy the protection granted to a civilian who is not taking a direct part in the hostilities (see §51(3) of The First Protocol). *** [H]e is a civilian who is not protected from attack as long as he is taking a direct part in the hostilities. Indeed, a person's status as unlawful combatant is not merely an issue of the internal state penal law. It is an issue for international law dealing with armed conflicts. *** [C]ivilians who are unlawful combatants are legitimate targets for attack, and thus surely do not enjoy the rights of civilians who are not unlawful combatants, provided that they are taking a direct part in the hostilities at such time. ***

27. ***[T]he State asked us to recognize a third category of persons, that of unlawful combatants. *** The State's position is that the terrorists who participate in the armed conflict between Israel and the terrorist organizations fall under this category of unlawful combatants.

28. The literature on this subject is comprehensive ***. In our opinion, as far as existing law goes, the data before us are not sufficient to recognize this third category. That is the case according to the current state of international law, both international treaty law and customary international law ***. However, new reality at times requires new interpretation. Rules developed against the background of a reality which has changed must take on a dynamic interpretation which adapts them, in the framework of accepted interpretational rules, to the new reality ***.

29. *** [C]ivilians are not to be harmed in an indiscriminate attack; in other words, in an attack which, inter alia, is not directed against a particular military objective ***. That protection is granted to all civilians, excepting those civilians taking a direct part in hostilities. Indeed, the protection from attack is not granted to unlawful combatants who are taking a direct part in the hostilities. ***

31. The basic approach is thus as follows: a civilian – that is, a person who does not fall into the category of combatant – must refrain from directly participating in hostilities. A civilian who violates that law and commits acts of combat does not lose his status as a civilian, but as long as he is taking a direct part in hostilities he does not enjoy – during that time – the protection granted to a civilian. He is subject to the risks of attack like those to which a combatant is subject, without enjoying the rights of a combatant, e.g. those granted to a prisoner of war ***.

33. Civilians lose the protection of customary international law dealing with hostilities of international character if they "take . . . part in hostilities." What is the meaning of that provision? The accepted view is that "hostilities" are acts which by nature and objective are intended to cause damage to the army. *** According to the accepted definition, a civilian is taking part in hostilities when using weapons in an armed conflict, while gathering intelligence, or while preparing himself for the hostilities. Regarding taking part in hostilities, there is no condition that the civilian use his weapon, nor is there a condition that he bear arms (openly or concealed). It is possible to take part in hostilities without using weapons at all. ***

34. *** It seems accepted in the international literature that an agreed upon definition of the term "direct" in the context under discussion does not exist ***. Indeed, a civilian bearing arms (openly or concealed) who is on his way to the place where he will use them against the army, at such place, or on his way back from it, is a civilian taking "an active part" in the hostilities ***. However, a civilian who generally supports the hostilities against the army is not taking a direct part in the hostilities ***. Similarly, a civilian who sells food or medicine to unlawful combatants is also taking an indirect part in the hostilities. ***

38. *** A civilian taking a part in hostilities loses the protection from attack "for such time" as he is taking part in those hostilities. If "such time" has passed – the protection granted to the civilian returns. ***

39. *** On the one hand, a civilian taking a direct part in hostilities one single time, or sporadically, who later detaches himself from that activity, is a civilian who, starting from the time he detached himself from that activity, is entitled to protection from attack. He is not to be attacked for the hostilities which he committed in the past. On the other hand, a civilian who has joined a terrorist organization which has become his "home", and in the framework of his role in that organization he commits a chain of hostilities, with short periods of rest between them, loses his immunity from

attack "for such time" as he is committing the chain of acts. Indeed, regarding such a civilian, the rest between hostilities is nothing other than preparation for the next hostility. ***

40. These examples point out the dilemma which the "for such time" requirement presents before us. On the one hand, a civilian who took a direct part in hostilities once, or sporadically, but detached himself from them (entirely, or for a long period) is not to be harmed. On the other hand, the "revolving door" phenomenon, by which each terrorist has "horns of the alter" (1 Kings 1:50) to grasp or a "city of refuge" (Numbers 35:11) to flee to, to which he turns in order to rest and prepare while they grant him immunity from attack, is to be avoided ***. In the wide area between those two possibilities, one finds the "gray" cases, about which customary international law has not yet crystallized. There is thus no escaping examination of each and every case. In that context, the following four things should be said: first, well based information is needed before categorizing a civilian as falling into one of the discussed categories. Innocent civilians are not to be harmed. Information which has been most thoroughly verified is needed regarding the identity and activity of the civilian who is allegedly taking part in the hostilities (see *Ergi v. Turkey*, 32 EHRR 388 (2001)). *** Second, a civilian taking a direct part in hostilities cannot be attacked at such time as he is doing so, if a less harmful means can be employed. In our domestic law, that rule is called for by the principle of proportionality. Indeed, among the military means, one must choose the means whose harm to the human rights of the harmed person is smallest. Thus, if a terrorist taking a direct part in hostilities can be arrested, interrogated, and tried, those are the means which should be employed (see Mohamed Ali v. Public Prosecutor [1969] 1 A.C. 430). Trial is preferable to use of force. A rule-of-law state employs, to the extent possible, procedures of law and not procedures of force. That question arose in McCann v. United Kingdom, 21 E.H.R.R. 97 (1995), hereinafter McCann. In that case, three terrorists from Northern Ireland who belonged to the IRA were shot to death. They were shot in the streets of Gibraltar, by English agents. The European Court of Human Rights determined that England had illegally impinged upon their right to life (§2 of the European Convention on Human Rights). *** Arrest, investigation, and trial are not means which can always be used. At times the possibility does not exist whatsoever; at times it involves a risk so great to the lives of the soldiers, that it is not required ***. However, it is a possibility which should always be considered. It might actually be particularly practical under the conditions of belligerent occupation, in which the army controls the area in which the operation takes place, and in which arrest, investigation, and trial are at times realizable possibilities (see §5 of The Fourth Geneva Convention). Of course, given the circumstances of a certain case, that possibility might not exist. At times, its harm to nearby innocent civilians might be greater than that caused by refraining from it. In that state of affairs, it should not be used. Third, after an attack on a civilian suspected of taking an active part, at such time, in hostilities, a thorough investigation regarding the precision of the identification of the target and the circumstances of the attack upon him is to be performed (retroactively). That investigation must be independent ***.

42. *** The rule is that the harm to innocent civilians caused by collateral damage during combat operations must be proportionate ***. Civilians might be harmed due to their presence inside of a military target, such as civilians working in an army base; civilians might be harmed when they live or work in, or pass by, military targets; at times, due to a mistake, civilians are harmed even if they are far from military targets; at times civilians are forced to serve as "human shields" from attack upon a military target, and they are harmed as a result. In all those situations, and in other similar ones, *** the harm to the innocent civilians must fulfill, inter alia, the requirements of the principle of proportionality. ***

45. The proportionality test determines that attack upon innocent civilians is not permitted if the collateral damage caused to them is not proportionate to the military advantage (in protecting combatants and civilians). In other words, attack is proportionate if the benefit stemming from the attainment of the proper military objective is proportionate to the damage caused to innocent civilians harmed by it. That is a values based test. ***

46. That aspect of proportionality is not required regarding harm to a combatant, or to a civilian taking a direct part in the hostilities at such time as the harm is caused. Indeed, a civilian taking part in hostilities is endangering his life, and he might – like a combatant – be the objective of a fatal attack. That killing is permitted. However, that proportionality is required in any case in which an innocent civilian is harmed. Thus, the requirements of proportionality stricto senso must be fulfilled in a case in which the harm to the terrorist carries with it collateral damage caused to nearby innocent civilians. The proportionality rule applies in regards to harm to those innocent civilians (see § 51(5)(b) of The First Protocol). The rule is that combatants and terrorists are not to be harmed if the damage expected to be caused to nearby innocent civilians is not proportionate to the military advantage in harming the combatants and terrorists ***. Performing that balance is difficult. Here as well, one must proceed case by case, while narrowing the area of disagreement. Take the usual case of a combatant, or of a terrorist sniper shooting at soldiers or civilians from his porch. Shooting at him is proportionate even if as a result, an innocent civilian neighbor or passerby is harmed. That is not the case if the building is bombed from the air and scores of its residents and passersby are harmed ***. The hard cases are those which are in the space between the extreme examples. There, a meticulous examination of every case is required; it is required that the military advantage be direct and anticipated (see §57(2)(iii) of The First Protocol). Indeed, in international law, as in internal law, the ends do not justify the means. The State's power is not unlimited. Not all of the means are permitted. ***

However, when hostilities occur, losses are caused. The State's duty to protect the lives of its soldiers and civilians must be balanced against its duty to protect the lives of innocent civilians harmed during attacks on terrorists. That balancing is difficult when it regards human life. It raises moral and ethical problems ***. Despite the difficulty of that balancing, there's no choice but to perform it. ***

56. The scope of judicial review of the decision of the military commander to perform a preventative strike causing the deaths of terrorists in the area, and at times of innocent civilians, varies according to the essence of the concrete question raised. *** The Court asks itself what the international law is and whether the understanding of the military commander is in line with that law.

57. *** [T]he decision, made on the basis of the knowledge of the military profession, to perform a preventative act which causes the deaths of terrorists in the area *** is the responsibility of the executive branch. It has the professional-security expertise to make that decision. The Court will ask itself if a reasonable military commander could have made the decision which was made. The question is whether the decision of the military commander falls within the zone of reasonable activity on the part of the military commander. If the answer is yes, the Court will not exchange the military commander's security discretion with the security discretion of the Court ***. True, "military discretion" and "state security" are not magic words which prevent judicial review. However, the question is not what I would decide in the given circumstances, rather whether the decision which the military commander made is a decision that a reasonable military commander was permitted to make. ***

58. Between these two ends of the spectrum, there are intermediate situations. Each of them requires a meticulous examination of the character of the decision. To the extent that it has a legal aspect, it approaches the one end of the spectrum. To the extent that it has a professional military aspect, it approaches the other end of the spectrum. ***

60. *** The examination of the "targeted killing" – and in our terms, the preventative strike causing the deaths of terrorists, and at times also of innocent civilians – has shown that the question of the legality of the preventative strike according to customary international law is complex. *** The result of that examination is not that such strikes are always permissible or that they are always forbidden. The approach of customary international law applying to armed conflicts of an international nature is that civilians are protected from attacks by the army. However, that protection does not exist regarding those civilians "for such time as they take a direct part in hostilities" (§51(3) of The First Protocol). Harming such civilians, even if the result is death, is permitted, on the condition that there is no other less harmful means, and on the condition that innocent civilians nearby are not harmed. Harm to the latter must be proportionate. That proportionality is determined according to a values based test, intended to balance between the military advantage and the civilian damage. As we have seen, we cannot determine that a preventative strike is always legal, just as we cannot determine that it is always illegal. All depends upon the question whether

the standards of customary international law regarding international armed conflict allow that preventative strike or not.

61. The State of Israel is fighting against severe terrorism, which plagues it from the area. The means at Israel's disposal are limited. The State determined that preventative strikes upon terrorists in the area which cause their deaths are a necessary means from the military standpoint. These strikes at times cause harm and even death to innocent civilians. These preventative strikes, with all the military importance they entail, must be made within the framework of the law. ***. Every struggle of the state – against terrorism or any other enemy – is conducted according to rules and law. There is always law which the state must comply with. There are no "black holes" ***. In this case, the law was determined by customary international law regarding conflicts of an international character. Indeed, the State's struggle against terrorism is not conducted "outside" of the law. It is conducted "inside" the law, with tools that the law places at the disposal of democratic states.

62. The State's fight against terrorism is the fight of the state against its enemies. It is also law's fight against those who rise up against it. *** Indeed, in the State's fight against international terrorism, it must act according to the rules of international law ***. These rules are based on balancing. They are not "all or nothing". *** Indeed, the struggle against terrorism has turned our democracy into a "defensive democracy" or a "militant democracy" ***. However, we cannot allow that struggle to deny our State its democratic character.

63. The question is not whether it is possible to defend ourselves against terrorism. Of course it is possible to do so, and at times it is even a duty to do so. The question is how we respond. On that issue, a balance is needed between security needs and individual rights. That balancing casts a heavy load upon those whose job is to provide security. Not every efficient means is also legal. The ends do not justify the means. The army must instruct itself according to the rules of the law. That balancing casts a heavy load upon the judges, who must determine – according to the existing law – what is permitted, and what forbidden. *** Indeed, decision of the petition before us is not easy ***

64. In one case we decided the question whether the State is permitted to order its interrogators to employ special methods of interrogation which involve the use of force against terrorists, in a "ticking bomb" situation. We answered that question in the negative. In my judgment, I described the difficult security situation in which Israel finds itself, and added:

> "We are aware that this judgment of ours does not make confronting that reality any easier. That is the fate of democracy, in whose eyes not all means are permitted, and to whom not all the methods used by her enemies are open. At times democracy fights with one hand tied behind her back.

Despite that, democracy has the upper hand, since preserving
the rule of law and recognition of individual liberties
constitute an important component of her security stance. At
the end of the day, they strengthen her and her spirit, and
allow her to overcome her difficulties" (HCJ 5100/94 *The
Public Committee against Torture in Israel v. The State of
Israel,* 53(4) PD 817, 845).

Let it be so.

Vice President E. RIVLIN

1. I concur *** The question is whether reality hasn't created, de facto,
an additional group, with a special legal status. Indeed, the scope of danger
posed to the State of Israel and the security of her civilians by the terrorist
organizations, and the fact that the means usually employed against
lawbreaking citizens are not suitable to meet the threats posed by terrorist
activity, make one uneasy when attempting to fit the traditional category of
"civilians" to those taking an active part in acts of terrorism. They are not
"combatants" as per the definition in international law. *** [They] are
"unprivileged belligerents" ***. However, the very characteristics of the
terrorist organizations and their members that exclude them from the
category of "combatants" – lack of fixed distinctive emblems recognizable at a
distance and noncompliance with the laws and customs of war – create
difficulty. Awarding a preferential status, even if only on certain issues, to
those who choose to become "unlawful combatants" and do not act according
to the rules of international law and the rules of morality and
humanitarianism might be undesirable.

The classification of members of terrorist organizations under the
category of "civilians" is not, therefore, an obvious one. ***. Those of the
opinion that the third category of unlawful combatants exists emphasize that
its members include those who wish to blur the boundaries between civilians
and combatants ***. The difficulty intensifies when we take into account that
those who differentiate themselves from legal combatants on the one hand,
and from innocent civilians on the other, are not homogenous. They include
groups which are not necessarily identical to each other in terms of the
willingness to abide by fundamental legal and human norms. It is especially
appropriate, in this context, to differentiate between unlawful combatants
fighting against an army and those who purposely act against civilians.

It thus appears that international law must adapt itself to the era in
which we are living. *** The interpretation proposed by my colleague
President Barak in fact creates a new group, and rightly so. It can be derived
from the combatant group ("unlawful combatants") and it can be derived from
the civilian group. My colleague President Barak takes the second path. If we
go his way, we should derive a group of international-law-breaking civilians,
whom I would call "uncivilized civilians". In any case, there is no difference

between the two paths in terms of the result ***It is a dynamic interpretation which overcomes the limitations of a black letter reading of the laws of war.

3. Against the background of the differences between "legal" combatants and "international-law-breaking combatants", an analogy can be made between the means of combat permitted in a conflict between two armies, and "targeted killing" of terrorists ***. The attitude behind the "targeted killing" policy is that the weapons should be directed exclusively toward those substantially involved in terrorist activity. Indeed, in conventional war combatants are marked and differentiated from the civilian population. Those combatants can be harmed (subject to the restrictions of international law). Civilians are not to be harmed. Similarly, in the context of the fight against terrorism, it is permissible to harm international-lawbreaking combatants, but harm to civilians should be avoided to the extent possible. The difficulty stems, of course, from the fact that the unlawful combatants, by definition, do not act according to the laws of war, often disguising themselves within the civilian population, in contradiction to the express provisions of The First Protocol of The Geneva Conventions. They do so in order to gain an advantage from the fact that their opponent wishes to honor the rules of international law ***. However, even under the difficult conditions of combating terrorism, the differentiation between unlawful combatants and civilians must be ensured. That, regarding the issue at hand, is the meaning of the "targeting" in "targeted killing". That is the meaning of the proportionality requirement with which my colleague President Barak deals with extensively.

4. Regarding the implementation of the proportionality requirement, the appropriate point of departure emphasizes the right of innocent civilians. The State of Israel has a duty to honor the lives of the civilians of the other side. She must protect the lives of her own citizens, while honoring the lives of the civilians who are not subject to her effective control. When the rights of the civilians are before our eyes, it becomes easier for us to recognize the importance of placing restrictions upon the conduct of hostilities. ***

5. *** The duty to honor the lives of innocent civilians is thus the point of departure. Stemming from it is the requirement that collateral damage to civilians not be exaggerated, and that it be proportional to the benefit which will result from the operation. This values based attitude produces restrictions on the attack upon the unlawful combatants. The restrictions may relate to the type of weapons used during the targeted killing. The restrictions might lead to a decision to employ a means which presents less danger to the lives of innocent civilians. The restrictions might relate to the level of caution required regarding identification of the target. All these are restrictions which strive to fulfill the duty to honor the lives of the innocent civilians, and will be interpreted accordingly.

The point of departure is, thus, the rights of the innocent civilians, but it is not the endpoint. It cannot negate the human dignity of the unlawful combatants themselves. Indeed, international law does not grant them rights equal to those granted to lawful combatants or to innocent civilians. However, human dignity is a principle which applies to every person, even during combat and conflict. It is not dependent upon reciprocity. One of the conclusions stemming from that – which the State does not dispute – is where it is possible to arrest a terrorist taking a direct part in hostilities and to put him on trial, he will not be targeted. To bring him to trial is a possibility which should always be considered. However, as my colleague President Barak notes, at times that possibility might be completely impractical, or put the soldiers at too high a risk. ***

7. *** I am of the opinion that one cannot determine in advance that targeted killing is always illegal, just as one cannot determine in advance that under any circumstances it is legal and permissible. In order to be legal, such an act must comply with the rules of law, including the proportionality requirement, as discussed above, in light of the view which grants central weight to the right of the State of Israel to defend itself and the lives of its citizens, and at the same time holds the principle regarding human dignity as a fundamental principle. ***

JUDGE D. BEINISCH:

***The conclusion reached by President Barak, with which I concur, is that it cannot be said that this policy is always prohibited, just as it cannot be said that it is permitted in all circumstances according to the discretion of the military commander. *** As it appears from the interpretation in the President's judgment, there are qualifications and limitations on the power of the state to carry out acts of "targeted killing". It appears, from those qualifications, that not all involvement in terrorist activity constitutes taking "a direct part in hostilities" pursuant to §51(3), which is limited to activity at the core of the hostilities themselves – activity which, on the one hand, is not limited merely to the physical attack itself, but on the other hand does not include indirect aid. I agree that the dilemmas that arise in light of the interpretation of the components of said §51(3) require specific examination in each single case. It must be remembered that the purpose of "targeted killing" is to prevent harm to human life as part of the State's duty to protect its soldiers and civilians. Since §51(3) is an exception to the duty to refrain from causing harm to innocent civilians, great caution must be employed when removing the law's protection of the lives of civilians in the appropriate circumstances. In the framework of that caution, the extent of information for categorization of a "civilian" as taking a direct part in hostilities must be examined. The information must be well based, strong, and convincing regarding the risk the terrorist poses to human life – risk including continuous activity which is not merely sporadic or one-time concrete activity. I should like to add that in appropriate circumstances, information about the activity of the terrorist in the past might be used for the purposes of examination of the danger he poses in the future. I further add that in the framework of estimating the risk, the level of probability of life threatening hostilities is to be taken into account. On that point, a minor possibility is insufficient; a significant level of probability of the existence of such risk is required. I of course accept the determination that a thorough and independent (retrospective) examination is required, regarding the precision of the identification of the target and the circumstances of the damage caused. Two additional requirements are to be added to all those: first, "targeted killing" is not to be carried out when it is possible to arrest a terrorist taking a direct part in hostilities, without significant risk to the lives of soldiers; and second, the proportionality principle accepted as customary international law, according to which collateral damage must not be disproportionate, is to be adhered to. When the damage to innocent civilians is not of proper proportion to the benefit from the military activity (the test of "proportionality stricto senso"), the "targeted killing" is disproportionate. *** Ultimately, when an act of "targeted killing" is carried out in accordance with the said qualifications and in the framework of the customary laws of international armed conflict as interpreted by this Court, it is not an arbitrary taking of life, rather a means intended to save human life.

Thus, I too am of the opinion that in Israel's difficult war on terrorism which is plaguing her, it should not be sweepingly said that the use of "targeted killing" as one of the means for war on terrorism is prohibited, and the State should not be denied that means which, according to the opinion of those responsible for security, constitutes a necessary means for protection of the lives of its inhabitants. However, in light of the extreme character of "targeted killing", it should not be employed beyond the limitations and qualifications which have been outlined in our judgment, according to the circumstances of the merits of each case.

Thus it is decided that it cannot be determined in advance that every targeted killing is prohibited according to customary international law, just as it cannot be determined in advance that every targeted killing is permissible according to customary international law. The law of targeted killing is determined in the customary international law, and the legality of each individual such act must be determined in light of it.

Notes

1. **The Starting Point.** Emeritus President Barak says: "The normative system which applies to the armed conflict between Israel and the terrorist organizations in the area is complex. In its center stands the international law regarding international armed conflict." Why does he start here rather than with Israeli law? Where does he find authority concerning this law? How does this body of law divide combatants, civilians and others? Describe the positions of the Court's various members in categorizing terrorists. Do these differences matter to the outcome of determinations of legality? How do you think the Israeli Supreme Court would have characterized Anwar Al-Aulaqi had he been the target?

2. **International Humanitarian Law and Terrorism.** Is international humanitarian law in need of updating to deal with "the new reality" of terrorism?

Does the Israel Supreme Court's categorization of terrorists as civilians (albeit "international law-breaking civilians") simplify the analysis or complicate it? If the law needs updating, should this be done by treaty or is state-by state practice a better approach? The Court assumes there is an international rather than a non-international armed conflict, triggering a higher level of legal regulation. Is there any difference between the Hamas and Israel conflict, on the one hand, and the conflict going on in Afghanistan for almost a decade? United States law has generally assumed that Afghanistan is a non-international conflict.

3. **Adjusting the Paradigm.** The Israeli Court's choice of the war paradigm has some conceptual difficulties: blame rather than status drives the decision to target an individual, it is difficult to identify the target, and the operation does not take place on a battlefield. How does the Court take these factors into account in making its decision? Does it look at the culpability of the individual targeted? Level of collateral damage to civilians? Procedures for the targeting? Does the Court leave open the possibility of judicial review of some incidents? Of the possibility of compensating innocent victims (collateral damage) of targeted killings. One article well summarizes the decision as follows:

> "[T]he Israeli Supreme Court sought a middle ground between a more aggressive law enforcement paradigm and a tamer wartime paradigm. It chose the latter as its point of departure, but then, in consideration of the unique nature of the war on terrorism, added limitations and constraints on the government's war powers so as to remain as loyal as possible to the basic principles and values of the Israeli legal system." Blum and Heymann, "Law and Policy of Targeted Killing," HARVARD NATIONAL SECURITY JOURNAL, available at: http://harvardnsj.com/2010/06/law-and-policy-of-targeted -killing/ (Posted June 27, 2010),. If the Palestinian-Israeli conflict became more traditional, as it did in 2008, should the constraints against targeted killings imposed by the Court be loosened?

3. **Judicial Role.** What role does the Israeli Supreme Court craft for the judiciary in connection with targeted killings? Would this role work in the United States? What factors would play a role in explaining the differences in the two primary cases in this section?

4. **European Law.** Article 2 of the European Convention on Human Rights states:

> 1. Everyone's right to life shall be protected by law. No one shall be deprived of his life intentionally save in the execution of a sentence of a court following his conviction of a crime for which this penalty is provided by law.

> 2. Deprivation of life shall not be regarded as inflicted in contravention of this Article when it results from the use of force which is no more than absolutely necessary: (a) in defense of any person from unlawful violence; (b) in order to effect a lawful arrest or to prevent the escape of a person lawfully detained; (c) in action lawfully taken for the purpose of quelling a riot or insurrection.

In *McCann and Others v. United Kingdom*, European Court of Human Rights, 21 E.H.R.R. 97 (1996) the court held that Article 2 (2) was violated when counterterrorism personnel killed three individuals who were thought to have assembled a car bomb rigged to explode in Gibraltar by use of a remote detonator, saying it was not "absolutely necessary in defence of persons from unlawful violence within the meaning of Article 2(2)(a) of the Convention" to shoot to kill rather than shooting to wound the suspects. Nine members of the court dissented, saying:

> [C]ircumstances included a genuine belief on their part that the suspects might be about to detonate a bomb by pressing a button. In that situation, to shoot merely to wound would have been a highly dangerous course: wounding alone might well not have immobilized a suspect and might have left him or her capable of pressing a button if determined to do so. *** [W]e are satisfied that no failings have been shown in the organization and control of the operation by the authorities which could justify a conclusion that force was used against the suspects disproportionately to the purpose of defending innocent persons from unlawful violence.

Does this case explain why there have been no targeted killings by European nations?

5. Consistency? As between the United States, the Europeans, and the Israelis, who has the preferable approach concerning targeted killings?

D. THE ROLE OF JUDICIAL REVIEW

In the United States, judicial review of military matters is extremely limited. The Constitution divides responsibility for war-making between the Congress and the President. Congress has the power to declare war, appropriate money for military actions, and establish rules for governance of the armed services. The President, as commander-in-chief, has operational oversight for execution of war. Often, one is tempted to say, the courts have no role whatsoever in reviewing military actions.

"No role" is perhaps too strong a statement. Former Chief Justice William Rehnquist, in his book ALL THE LAWS BUT ONE: CIVIL LIBERTIES IN WARTIME (Vintage Books 1998) summarized much experience over two centuries of governance under the Constitution by noting that "there is some truth to the *Inter armes silent leges*, at least in a descriptive sense." The laws are not literally silenced, of course, but, as Chief Justice Rehnquist notes, there is a "reluctance of courts to decide a case against the government on an issue of national security during war."

An important limitation on judicial review during not only a declared war but in the midst of military engagement without such a declaration is that judicial review, with hierarchical appeals through the federal or state systems, is very slow. As Francis Biddle said of President Roosevelt's internment of Japanese Americans during World War II, "The Constitution has not greatly bothered any wartime President. That was a question of law, which ultimately the Supreme Court must decide. And meanwhile—probably a long meanwhile—we must get on with the war."

The Supreme Court has numerous tools at its disposal that reinforce its inclination to stay out of the fray during war. There are the passive virtues of avoiding cases by finding that the plaintiff lacks standing or that the case is not ripe, has been mooted, or involves a political question. Several Vietnam-era cases brought by drafted civilians or activated reservists all ended with lower court decisions finding the claims nonjusticiable.

Judicial avoidance of decision is reinforced at the Supreme Court level by the Court's ability to deny certiorari to an awkward case. Despite inconsistent reasons for finding the Vietnam cases not appropriate for judicial review and the existence of a long and unpopular war, the Supreme Court never agreed to hear any of these cases.

Two quotes from the World War II internment cases are indicative of a judicial hands-off approach:

> We cannot say that the war-making branches of the Government did not have ground for believing that in a critical hour such persons could not readily be isolated and separately dealt with, and constituted a menace to the national defense and safety, which demanded that prompt and adequate measures be taken to guard against it. *Hirabiyashi v. United States*, 320 U.S. 81 (1943) at 99.

> Executive power over enemy aliens, undelayed and unhampered by litigation, has been deemed, throughout our history, essential to war-time security....The resident enemy alien is constitutionally subject to summary arrest, internment and deportation whenever a declared war exists. *Johnson v. Eisentrager*, 339 U.S. 763 (1950).

Only after military activities have ceased do the courts become more venturesome in reviewing violations of civil liberties, as in *Ex Parte Milligan*, 4 Wall 2 (1866) (military commission trial of a southern sympathizer improper because the civilian courts were open) after the Civil War and *Duncan v. Kahanamoku*, 327 U. S. at 337 (1946) (martial law in Hawaii not justification for military court trial of civilian shipfitter for assault on navy personnel).

In the War on Terror, similar patterns have developed. The Supreme Court initially interpreted statutory law to find that Congress had not supported limitations on availability of judicial review of Guantanamo detainees (*Rasul* and *Hamdan*). Then, seven years after 9/11, finally held that a statutory restriction on the availability of the writ of habeas corpus was unconstitutional (*Boumediene*).

Against this background, the following case from Israel, the country that has had the most experience of any nation in dealing with terrorism, will come as quite a contrast. Amos N. Guiora, in GLOBAL PERSPECTIVES ON COUNTERTERRORISM, Aspen Publishers (2007) discusses the next case as follows:

> With the advent of operation "Ebb and Flow,"[1] the IDF arrested thousands of Palestinians suspected of involvement in terrorism. This was a response to a terrorist act that resulted in the deaths of thirty Israelis, many of them elderly, who had come together to celebrate the Passover meal.[2] The military operation had not been planned thoroughly in advance and critical non-combat issues were literally resolved "on the fly." As a result, a wide variety of important issues had not been considered and were left to individual initiative.[3]
>
> One of the issues that had not properly been planned was where to detain the thousands of Palestinians arrested daily.[4] As the detention process developed, initial screening of detainees was conducted at brigade headquarters; a process which required a significant amount of time, sometimes in questionable conditions.
>
> According to Military Order 378, as amended in 1997, a Palestinian may be held for eight days before seeing a judge.[5] When the IDF realized that the number of detainees who needed to be processed would result in a violation of the order, the military commander signed Order 1500. As a result of this Order, detainees could be held up to eighteen days without seeing a military judge. A petition was filed against this Order by Iad Ashak Mahmud Marab, a detainee.

---

[1] After the Passover eve attack at the Park Hotel in Netanya (2001) the IDF undertook a massive operation into the West Bank in order to break up terrorist infrastructures. The operation which included mass calls up of reserve units (the response was reported as 100 percent) was the largest such IDF operation in years.

[2] Passover Suicide Bombing at Park Hotel in Netanya, Israel Ministry of Foreign Affairs, Mar. 27, 2002 ***.

[3] As an example, this writer was serving as the Commander of the IDF School of Military Law ("SML"); based on a number of hurried phone calls and at the initiative of a few commanders, the officers of the SML lectured literally around the clock to reserve and obligatory service units alike as they were being deployed into the West Bank on an eleven point code of conduct concerning their conduct vis-à-vis the Palestinian civilian population. This code, based on international law, Israeli law, and the IDF ethical code was later taught via an interactive video developed by the School's officers.

[4] This writer was appointed by the Judge Advocate General to be responsible for the JAG's lessons learned and to draft a report that would be the basis for significant internal changes, including the preparation of the "JAG in the box" approach developed by the U.S. Air Force JAG.

[5] In Israel, according to section 9.3.3 of the penal code a detainee must be brought before a judge with 24 hours. *** The West Bank and the Gaza Strip have never been annexed to the State of Israel which is why the government is a military government; in addition, the laws of the State do not apply to the two Areas. The legislation of the Areas is drafted by the officers of the Judge Advocate General Corps and signed into being by the Commander of the Central Command or by the Commander of the Southern Command (both are Major Generals; the equivalent to two-star generals).

[As you read the following excerpt from the case, consider the following issues and questions]:

1. What does the phrase "security considerations are not magic words" mean?

2. What is the significance of judicial intervention when the issue is presented in real time rather than deferring until the conflict ends?

3. Detention must not be allowed to be arbitrary; rather an evidentiary basis must be established indicating that a particular detainee either endangers or may endanger security. How is this possible during operational counterterrorism?

4. In a time of combat, when terrorists fight with both hands in front of them, is such judicial activism responsible and reasonable? [President and Chief Justice Aharon Barak of the Israeli Supreme Court has stated that "democracies fight terrorism with one arm tied behind their back.] Unlike the U.S. Supreme Court, which deliberated *Hamdi* three years after Guantanamo was established, the [Israeli Supreme Court] heard *Marab* while the IDF was continuing to detain Palestinian terrorists meaning that solutions needed to be developed and implemented while the Court heard arguments.

MARAB v. IDF COMMANDER IN THE WEST BANK
HCJ 3239/02
July 28, 2002

PRESIDENT A. BARAK

1. Since September 2002, Palestinians have carried out many terrorist attacks against Israelis, both in Judea and Samaria as well as in Israel. The defense forces have been fighting this terrorism. To destroy the terrorist infrastructure, the Israeli government decided to carry out an extensive operation, Operation Defensive Wall. As part of this operation, which was initiated at the end of March 2002, the IDF forces entered various areas of Judea and Samaria. Their intention was to detain wanted persons as well as members of several terrorist organizations. As of May 5, 2002, about 7000 persons had been detained in the context of this operation. Among those detained were persons who were not associated with terrorism; some of these persons were released after a short period of time. Initial screening was done in temporary facilities which were set up at brigade headquarters. Those who were not released after this screening were moved to the detention facility in Ofer Camp. The investigation continued and many more were released. A number of the detainees were then moved to the detention facility in Kziot. As of May 15, 2002, of the 7000 persons who had been detained since the start of Operation Defensive Wall, about 1600 remained in

detention.

2.   The detentions were initially carried out under the regular criminal detention laws of the area, under the Defense Regulations Order (Judea and Samaria) (Number 378)-1970 [hereinafter Order 378]. It soon became clear that Order 378 did not provide a suitable framework for screening thousands of persons detained within a number of days. Thus, on May 5, 2002, respondent no. 1 promulgated a special order: Detention in Time of Warfare (Temporary Order) (Judean and Samaria) (Number 1500)-2002 [hereinafter Order 1500].

3.   Order 1500 established a special framework regarding detention during warfare. The order applied to a "detainee," which was defined as follows:

> Detainee —one who has been detained, since March 29, 2002, in the context of military operations in the area and the circumstances of his detention raise the suspicion that he endangers or may be a danger to the security of the area, the IDF, or the public.

The principal innovation of Order 1500 may be found in section 2(a):

> Notwithstanding sections 78(a)-78(d) of the Defense Regulations Order (Judea and Samaria) (Number 378)-1970 [hereinafter the Defense Regulations Order], an officer will have the authority to order, in writing, that a detainee be held in detention, for up to 18 days [hereinafter the detention period].

Under this section, officers are authorized to order the detention of a detainee for a period of 18 days, and a judicial detention order is not required. In order to continue holding a detainee beyond 18 days, however, a judge must be approached. ***

6. To conclude this review of the relevant defense regulations, it should be noted that Order 1500 was to remain in effect for a period of two months. *See* Order 1500, § 5. As this expiration date approached, the order was extended by Order: Detention in Time of Warfare (Temporary Order) (Amendment Number 2) (Judean and Samaria) (Number 1505)-2002 [hereinafter Order 1505]. This subsequent order made a number of significant changes in Order 1500. First, the definition of "detainee" was modified. The new definition was set in section 2:

> Detainee—one who has been detained in the context of the war against terrorism in the area, while the circumstances of his detention raise the suspicion that he endangers or may endanger the security of the area, IDF security, or the public security.

Second, the period of detention without judicial review was shortened. The 18-day period set by Order 1500 was replaced with a 12-day detention period. ***

The Authority to Detain for the Purpose of Investigation ***

From these provisions, we find that under Order 1500 as well as Order 1505—and similarly under Orders 1512 and 1518—detention may only be carried out where there is a "cause for detention." The cause required is that the circumstances of the detention raise the suspicion that the detainee endangers or may be a danger to security. Thus, a person should not be detained merely because he has been detained during warfare; a person should not be detained merely because he is located in a house or village wherein other detainees are located. The circumstances of his detention must be such that they raise the suspicion that he—he individually and no one else—presents a danger to security. Such a suspicion may be raised because he was detained in an area of warfare while he was actively fighting or carrying out terrorist activities, or because he is suspect of being involved in warfare or terrorism.

Of course, the evidentiary basis for the establishment of this suspicion varies from one matter to another. When shots are fired at the defense forces from a house, any person located in the house with the ability to shoot may be suspect of endangering security. This basis may be established against a single person or a group of persons. However, this does not mean that Orders 1500, 1505, 1512 or 1518 allow for "mass detentions," just as detaining a group of demonstrators for the purpose of investigation, when one of the demonstrators has shot at police officers, does not constitute mass detention. The only detention authority set in these orders is the authority to detain where there exists an individual cause for detention against a specific detainee. It is insignificant whether that cause applies to an isolated individual or if it exists with regard to that individual as part of a large group. The size of the group has no bearing. Rather, what matters is the existence of circumstances which raise the suspicion that the individual detainee presents a danger to security. Thus, for example, petitioner 1 was detained, as there is information that he is active in the Popular Front for the Liberation of Palestine, a terrorist organization. He recruited people for the terrorist organization. Petitioner 2 was detained because he is active in the *Tanzim*. Petitioner 3 was detained because he is a member of the *Tanzim* military. Thus, an individual cause for detention existed with regard to each of the individual petitioners. ***

Detention Without Judicial Intervention ***

26. Judicial intervention with regard to detention orders is essential.

As Justice I. Zamir correctly noted:

> Judicial review is the line of defense for liberty, and it must
> be preserved beyond all else.

HCJ 2320/98 *El-Amla v. IDF Commander in Judea and Samaria*, at 350.

Judicial intervention stands before arbitrariness; it is essential to the principle of rule of law. It guarantees the preservation of the delicate balance between individual liberty and public safety, a balance which lies at the base of the laws of detention.

***

[The Court then examined both international law and Israeli criminal and military law regarding the length of detention without judicial review.]

30.　　Against this normative background, which demands prompt judicial review of detention orders, the question again arises whether the arrangement established in Order 1500—under which a person may be detained for a period of 18 days without having been brought before a judge— is legal.　Similarly, is the arrangement established in Order 1505 legal? This arrangement—which was unaffected by Order 1512 or Order 1518—provided that a person may be detained for a period of 12 days without having being brought before a judge.　In answering these questions, the special circumstances of the detention must be taken into account.　"Regular" police detention is not the same as detention carried out "during warfare in the area," Order 1500, or "during anti-terrorism operations" Order 1505.　It should not be demanded that the initial investigation be performed under conditions of warfare, nor should it be demanded that a judge accompany the fighting forces.　We accept that there is room to postpone the beginning of the investigation, and naturally also the judicial intervention.　These may be postponed until after detainees are taken out of the battlefield to a place where the initial investigation and judicial intervention can be carried out properly.　Thus, the issue at hand rests upon the question: where a detainee is in a detention facility which allows for carrying out the initial investigation, what is the timeframe available to investigators for carrying out the initial investigation without judicial intervention?

31.　　In this regard, the respondents claim before us that it was necessary to allow the investigating officials 18 days—and after Order 1505, 12 days—to carry out "initial screening activities, before the detainee's case is brought before the examination of a judge."　This was due to the large number of persons being investigated, and constraints on the number of professional investigators. In their response, the respondents emphasized that "during the warfare operations, thousands of people were apprehended by the IDF forces, under circumstances which raised the suspicion that they were involved in terrorist activities and warfare.　The object of Order 1500 was to allow the "screening" and identification of unlawful combatants who were involved in terrorist activities.

This activity was necessary due to the fact that the terrorists had been carrying out their activities in Palestinian populations centers, without bearing any symbols that would identify them as members of combating forces and distinguish them from the civilian population, in utter violation of the laws of warfare." *See* para. 51 of the response brief from May 15, 2002. The respondents added that it is pointless to bring detainees before a judge, when they have not yet been identified, and the investigative material against them has not yet undergone the necessary processing.　This initial investigation, performed prior to bringing the detainee before the judge, is difficult and often demands considerable time.　This is due, among other reasons, to "the lack of cooperation on the part of those being investigated and their attempts to hide their identities, their hostility towards the investigating authorities due to nationalistic and ideological views, the inability to predetermine the time and place of the detentions, the fact that most of the investigations are based on confidential intelligence information which cannot be revealed to the person being investigated, and the difficulty of reaching potential witnesses."

32.   The respondents thus claim that the investigating authorities must be allowed the time necessary for the completion of the initial investigation. This will, of course, not exceed a period of 18 days, under Order 1500, or 12 days, under Order 1505, as it was amended in Orders 1512 and 1518. In this timeframe, all those detainees against whom there is insufficient evidence will be released. Only those detainees, whose initial investigation has been completed, such that the investigation is ready for judicial examination, will remain in detention.

In our opinion, this approach is in conflict with the fundamentals of both international and Israeli law. This approach is not based on the presumption that investigating authorities should be provided with the minimal time necessary for the completion of the investigation, and that only when such time has passed is there room for judicial review. The accepted approach is that judicial review is an integral part of the detention process. Judicial review is not "external" to the detention. It is an inseparable part of the development of the detention itself. At the basis of this approach lies a constitutional perspective which considers judicial review of detention proceedings essential for the protection of individual liberty. Thus, the detainee need not "appeal" his detention before a judge. Appearing before a judge is an "internal" part of the detention process. The judge does not ask himself whether a reasonable police officer would have been permitted to carry out the detention. The judge asks himself whether, in his opinion, there are sufficient investigative materials to support the continuation of the detention.

Indeed, the laws regarding detention for investigative purposes focus mainly on judicial decisions. In a "natural" state of affairs, the initial detention is performed on the authority of a judicial order. Of course, this state of affairs does not apply to the circumstances at hand. It is natural that the initial detention not be carried out on the authority of a judicial order. It is natural that the beginning of the initial investigation in the facility be performed within the context of the amended Order 1500. Judicial review will naturally come later. Even so, everything possible should be done to ensure prompt judicial review.

Indeed, the laws of detention for investigative purposes are primarily laws which guide the judge as to under what circumstances he should allow the detention of a person and under what circumstances he should order the detainee's release. Judicial detention is the norm, while detention by one who is not a judge is the exception. This exception applies to the matter at hand, since naturally, the initial detention is done without a judicial order. Nevertheless, everything possible should be done to rapidly pass the investigation over to the regular track, placing the detention in the hands of a judge and not an investigator. Indeed, the authority to detain as set by

Order 1500, as well as the detention authority under Orders 1505, 1512, and 1518, is not unique. This detention authority is part of the regular policing authority, *see* ¶ 24. Otherwise it could not be conferred upon an authorized officer. This nature of the detention authority affects its implementation. Like every detention authority, it must be passed over to the regular track of judicial intervention as quickly as possible. ***

34.   With this in mind, we are of the opinion that detention periods of 18 days, under Order 1500, and 12 days, under Orders 1505, 1512 and 1518, exceed appropriate limits. This detention period was intended to allow for initial investigation. However, that is not its proper function. According to the normative framework, soon after the authorized officer carries out the initial detention, the case should be transferred to the track of judicial intervention. The case should not wait for the completion of the initial or other investigation before it is brought before a judge. The need to complete the initial investigation will be presented before the judge himself, and he will decide whether there exists reasonable suspicion of the detainee's involvement to justify the continuation of his detention. Thus, Order 1500, as well as Orders 1505, 1512, and 1518, unlawfully infringes upon the Judge's authority, thus infringing upon the detainee's liberty, which the international and Israeli legal frameworks are intended to protect.

35.   How can this problem be resolved? We doubt that it would be suitable to substitute the periods of detention without judicial intervention set in Order 1500 and the amended Order 1505 with a shorter predetermined detention period. As we have seen, everything rests upon the changing circumstances, which are not always foreseeable. It seems, that due to the unique circumstances before us, the approach adopted by international law, which avoids prescribing set periods and instead requires that a judge be approached promptly, is justified. In any case, this is a matter for the respondents and not for us. Of course, presumably, this means that it will be necessary to substantially enlarge the staff of judges who will deal with detention. It was not argued before us that there is a lack of such judges. In any case, even if the claim had been raised before us, we would have rejected it and quoted President Shamgar's words in *Sajadia*, at 821:

> What are the practical implications of what has been said? If there are a large number of detainees, it will be necessary to increase the number of judges. Difficulty in organizing such an arrangement, which will increase the number of judges who are called to service in order that a detainee's appeal be heard promptly and effectively, cannot justify the length of the period during which the detainee is held before his case has been judicially reviewed. The current emergency conditions undoubtedly demanded large-scale deployment of forces to deal with the riots occurring in Judea, Samaria and the Gaza Strip, and the matter at hand—the establishment of a special facility in Kziot—is an example of this deployment of forces. However, by the same standards, effort and resources must be invested into the protection of the detainees' rights,

and the scope of judicial review should be broadened. If the large number of appeals so demands, ten or more judges may be called upon to simultaneously review the cases, and not only the smaller number of judges who are currently treating these matters. Such is the case—aside from the differences which stem from the nature of the matter—with regard to prosecutors as well. The number of prosecutors may also be increased, due to the need to hasten the appeal proceedings and the preparations thus involved.

Notably, under international law, judicial intervention may be carried out by a judge or by any other public officer authorized by law to exercise judicial power. This public officer must be independent of the investigators and prosecutors. He must be free of any bias. He must be authorized to order the release of the detainee.

36. Thus, we hold the 18-day detention period without judicial oversight under Order 1500, and the 12-day detention period without judicial oversight under Orders 1505, 1512, and 1518, to be null and void. ***

Detention Without Investigation

47. Section 2(b) of Order 1500 provides:

> The detainee shall be given the opportunity to voice his claims within eight days of his detention.

This provision remains valid under Order 1505. Section 2 of Order 1518 shortens this period of detention without investigation to four days. The petitioners claim that the provision itself is illegal. They assert that it constitutes an excessive violation of the detainee's liberty. It undermines the right to liberty and denies due process. It may lead to mistaken or arbitrary detrainments. Conversely, the respondents claim that the significance of the provision is that it compels the investigators to question the detainee within eight days, in order to make an initial investigation of his identity and hear his account of his detention. This period cannot be shortened due to the large number of detainees, on the one hand, and the constraints limiting the number of professional investigators, on the other. It was noted before us that the investigating officials have limited capabilities, and they are not equipped to deal with such a large number of detainees in a more compact schedule.

48. We accept that investigations should not be performed during warfare or during military operations, nor can the detainee's account be heard during this time. The investigation can only begin when the detainee, against whom there stands an individual cause for detention, is brought to a detention facility which allows for investigation.

Moreover, we also accept that at a location which holds large number of detainees, some time may pass before it is possible to organize for initial investigations. This, of course, must be done promptly. It is especially important to begin the investigation rapidly at this initial stage, since simple facts such as age, circumstances of detention and identity, which may determine whether the detention should be continued, may become clear at this stage. Of course, often this initial investigation is insufficient, and the investigation must continue. All of this must be done promptly.

Respondents are of course aware of this. Their argument is simple: there is a lack of professional investigators. Unfortunately, this explanation is unsatisfactory. Security needs, on the one hand, and the liberty of the individual on the other, all lead to the need to increase the number of investigators. This is especially true during these difficult times in which we are plagued by terrorism, and even more so when it was expected that the number of detainees would rise due to Operation Defensive Wall. Regarding the considerations of individual liberty that justify such an increase, Justice Dorner has stated:

Fundamental rights essentially have a social price. The preservation of man's fundamental rights is not only the concern of the individual, but of all of society, and it shapes society's image. *Ganimat*, at 645.

In a similar spirit, Justice Zamir, in *Tzemach*, at 281, has noted:

> A society is measured, among other things, by the relative weight it attributes to personal liberty. This weight must express itself not only in pleasant remarks and legal literature, but also in the budget. The protection of human rights often has its price. Society must be ready to pay a price to protect human rights.

Such is the case in the matter at hand. A society which desires both security and individual liberty must pay the price. The mere lack of investigators cannot justify neglecting to investigate. Everything possible should be done to increase the number of investigators. This will guarantee both security and individual liberty. Furthermore, the beginning of the investigation is also affected by our holding that the arrangements according to which a detainee may be held for 18 days without being brought before a judge, under Order 1500, and for 12 days, under Order 1505, 1512, and 1518, to be illegal. ***

49.   We conclude, from this, that the provisions of section 2(b) of Order 1500 and section 2 of Order 1518 are invalid.

Notes

1.   **Companion Case to Marab**. In *Center for the Defense of the Individual v. IDF Commander in the West Bank*, HCJ 3278/02 [2002]. During the Israel Defense Force's March 2002 Operation Defensive Wall, thousands of Palestinians were arrested daily without adequate advance arrangements – the initial screening was done in temporary – and not suitably prepared – facilities at brigade headquarters. Criticizing the last minute arrangements, the Israeli Supreme Court stated that: "[T]he need for minimal detention conditions was a natural result of the operation. There was no surprise in the matter. There was the possibility of preparing appropriate divisions with suitable detention conditions. What was done a number of days after the beginning of the operation

should have been done several days before it began." (para 26). Can you think of something the United States Supreme Court might have done after 9/11 that would be comparable?

XI

TERRORISM, IMMIGRATION, AND BORDER SECURITY

The BIA found that Parlak was ineligible for withholding of removal because he assisted with PKK fundraising and transported weapons into Turkey for use by the PKK, thus assisting in the persecution of others. An individual who assists in the persecution of others is ineligible for withholding of removal. *** The BIA determined that the record supported a finding that Parlak assisted in the persecution of others by providing funding for the PKK and transporting weapons into Turkey for use by the PKK. *** This case does not require that we trace the tricky contours of "assist" and "persecution" for all circumstances; we need only look to the plain meaning of the words to decide that smuggling weapons across an international border to aid the PKK in committing violent acts against Turks and Turkish-aligned Kurds constitutes assistance in persecution.

Parlak v. Holder, 578 F. 3d 457 (C.A. 6, 2009)

This chapter covers the relation between terrorism and a vast immigration system that involves millions of legal visitors to the United States and millions of illegal immigrants within the country's borders. It is not my intention to duplicate or repeat the offerings of immigration law courses.

Following an introduction to immigration (Part A), the chapter covers terrorism-based exclusion of aliens (Part B), questioning and detention of immigrants after 9/11 (Part C), deportation proceedings involving alleged terrorism (Part D), and comparative approaches to immigration control (Part E). The chapter concludes with a short note on non-immigration aspects of border security (Part F).

A. INTRODUCTION TO IMMIGRATION

Immigration is the essential ingredient to America's melting pot of cultures, a vital furnace for creativity and productivity. Our nation of immigrants continues to draw scientific and other talent from around the globe, as witnessed by the fact that a third of America's Nobel Prize laureates have been first-generation immigrants and more than 50 of the world leaders joining the War on Terrorism studied in or were official visitors to the United States. At the same time, individuals from other parts of the world may pose terrorist threats or foist unwanted problems on America. The September 11 terrorists, mainly in this country under expired and unmonitored student visas, took advantage of America's lax immigration policy to destroy lives and property. Soon after 9/11, President Bush issued a directive that explicitly linked immigration and terrorism, and in March 2003 the U.S. Immigration and Naturalization Service (INS) was incorporated into the new Department of Homeland Security (DHS) as Immigration and Customs Enforcement (ICE).

The balance between openness to immigration and closure of our borders for security reasons has shifted over the course of American history. Indeed, major changes in that balance have recently occurred and others are anticipated. *** [Two fundamental premises of immigration law [are (1)] that] "In the exercise of its broad power over naturalization and immigration, Congress regularly makes rules that would be unacceptable if applied to citizens." (*Mathews v. Diaz* (426 U.S. 67 (1976)) [and (2) that] "any policy toward aliens is vitally and intricately interwoven with contemporaneous policies in regard to the conduct of foreign relations, the war power, and the maintenance of a republican form of government." *Harisiades v. Shaughnessy* (342 U.S. 580 (1952).

[a] ENTRY OF ALIENS INTO AMERICA

Legal immigrants into the United States in 2001 numbered approximately a million, and about 30 million noncitizens enter the United States each year, mainly as tourists, students, and business visitors. Additionally, an unknown number of illegal aliens, mostly from Mexico, enter the country each year, generally in search of better employment opportunities than they have at home. The 2000 census data suggests that there are currently about 8.7 million foreigners in the United States without proper authorization, a number that U.S. Immigration officials say may have grown by over half a million per year since then.

Under United States law, illegal immigrants may be summarily stopped at the nation's borders and returned to their country of origin. As the Supreme Court has held, no due process is owed such excluded aliens, *The Chinese Exclusion Case* (130 U.S. 581 (1889)), and such individuals may be detained indefinitely if they seek to enter the United States, *Shaughnessy v. United States ex. Rel. Mezei* (345 U.S. 206 (1953)), once aliens enter the country, the Due Process clause applies to them, *Zadvydas v. Davis* (533 U.S. 678 (2001). While the proper aims and methods of immigration policy are highly controversial, the main challenge to enforcement of these laws is one of resources. Beefed-up resources to the Border Patrol and the Coast Guard, provided by the USA PATRIOT Act and the Homeland Security Act, are a partial answer to this concern.

Legal immigrants, on the other hand, are dealt with under a complex set of visa categories, including a variety of student and work visas. Recently, the main effort has been to monitor those issued such visas and the organizations to which they are attached more carefully than in the past. For example, the new Student and Exchange Visitor Information System (SEVIS) program requires colleges and universities to engage in reporting with respect to foreign students enrolled at their institutions. Employers, under the Immigration Reform and Control Act of 1986 (IRCA), are held responsible for ensuring that their workers possess proof of citizenship or appropriate work authorization (usually a "green card"). Not surprisingly, the tightening up on visas has led to significant delays in granting of visas and in some instances has probably deterred prospective students or employees from coming to this country.

Under the National Security Entry-Exit Registration System (NSEERS) implemented after 9/11, entrants into the country from specific "high-risk" countries (e.g. Iran, Syria and Sudan) are fingerprinted and photographed upon entry into the U.S.. In addition, new high-tech systems for identifying entrants at border crossings and international airports are in progress. The purpose of these systems is to cross-check fingerprints or other biodata on the entrant against databases of those issued visas and those on terrorist watch lists. Challenges to such systems, on privacy or perhaps equal protection grounds, are anticipated.

One special group of immigrants consists of those who seek asylum in this country, often based on allegations of torture or likely political punishment in their native lands. Until very recently, asylum-seekers were permitted to be released, generally to the custody of relatives in the United States, pending a decision whether to accept their petitions (which were backlogged by many months). The standard used by immigration judges was whether the individual posed a risk of flight or a danger to the community. [In 2002] the Attorney General reversed an immigration Judge's decision to release an asylum-seeker from Haiti that used the traditional criteria. The reasons for the reversal given by the Attorney General were (1) to discourage the migration of vast numbers of Haitians to the United States and (2) that Haiti was a "staging area" for terrorists from Arab and Muslim nations. ***

[b] TRACKING OF ALIENS

As of January 2009, DHS estimated that more than 11 million illegal aliens live and work in the United States under the radar of law enforcement and immigration authorities. Indeed, it is estimated that approximately 300,000 noncitizens in the United States subject to final orders for their removal are hiding out avoiding deportation. These "absconders" have recently been prioritized and enforcement agencies have been working to find and deport those who are males from certain Arab and Muslim countries.

The Department of Homeland Security is attempting to create computerized databases on those in the country on temporary visas and it has tightened up on those who overstay their visas. Additionally, male noncitizens from specific (mainly Muslim and Middle Eastern) countries have been required to register with federal authorities. Of 82,000 who registered as required, some 13,000 as of June 2003 have been ordered to appear in immigration court for deportation hearings. Many of these have wives holding green cards and children born in the U.S. (who are therefore U.S. citizens).

Congress passed the "Real ID Act," which imposed prescriptive federal driver's license standards, in 2005. The states have thus far resisted implementation because of the standards' high cost, and as a result the Department of Homeland Security has thrice extended the compliance date, until the end of 2013. More than half the states have refused to enforce the act, and the act's fate remains unclear. Nevertheless, state drivers' licenses are becoming more standardized and access to information concerning such licenses is becoming more available to law enforcement officials nationally.

In times of crisis, aliens in the United States have sometimes been targeted for arrest or detention for criminal actions to which their primary or only connection was their ethnicity. For example, in the Palmer Raids of 1919, the government rounded up thousands of immigrants suspected loosely of being involved in a number of small bombings in the U.S. thought to be tied to radicalism and the Russian Revolution. During World War II, those viewed as "alien" because of Japanese origins were incarcerated in detention camps on the west coast. And Middle Eastern male aliens bore the brunt of the post-September 11 detentions. In such crisis moments, government authorities, who would "rather be safe than sorry," have sometimes not adhered to civil liberties norms that this country cherishes.

[c] REMOVAL OF ALIENS

The point at which the legal "rubber meets the road" is in the deportation or removal process. The Immigration and Nationality Act (INA), which has undergone numerous revisions, provides for a process of hearings before special Article II tribunals. The Immigration Judges [IJs] who decide these cases may be reversed upon order of the Attorney General. Indeed, until the Supreme Court ruled it unconstitutional on separation of powers grounds, the law once provided that Congress could exercise a "legislative veto" over the Attorney General's decisions. *INS v. Chadha* (462 U.S. 919 (1983).

The Fifth Amendment due process clause applies to deportation processes, and aliens held in detention may seek release using the writ or habeas corpus, 28 U.S.C. § 2241, even though provisions of the INA preclude direct judicial review over decisions of the Attorney General. But neither the Constitution's applicability nor the availability of habeas corpus review affords those involved the same rights afforded criminal defendants. Two recent Supreme Court decisions are instructive.

In *Zadvydas v. Davis supra* pg. 696, the Court construed INA § 1231 not to allow indefinite detention of an alien following a final order of removal. It held that detention for 90 days was presumptively lawful and that further detention for an additional period of time "reasonably necessary to secure the alien's removal" was permissible. This construction, far from obvious from the statutory language, avoided a serious constitutional question: Is indefinite detention a permissible deprivation of liberty under the due process clause of the Fifth Amendment?

Even more recently, the Court considered whether an alien could be detained during the period of his removal proceedings. *Demore v. Kim* (538 U.S. 510 (2003). The Court held that this was permissible, distinguishing *Zadvydas* on two grounds. First, while Zadvydas was an alien for whom removal was "no longer practically attainable," so that detention did not serve an immigration purpose, the detention of Kim served the purpose of preventing his flight prior to or during the proceedings. The Court noted that 20% to 25 % of those detained in circumstances like Kim's did not show up for their removal proceedings.   Second, while Zadvydas' detention was "indefinite," and "potentially permanent," Kim's detention had a definite termination point (decision of his case), a period of time generally less than the 90 days presumed reasonable in *Zadvydas*.   The Court noted that removal proceedings are completed in an average time of 47 days and a median time of 30 days. ***

[The preceding selection was adapted and updated from Shanor and Hogue, NATIONAL SECURITY AND MILITARY LAW IN A NUTSHELL (West 2003)]

B. TERRORISM-BASED EXCLUSION OF ALIENS

Congress has long excluded aliens believed to pose a danger to the United States government or American people. For example, the Anarchist Act of 1901 barred the admission of those believed to adhere to anarchism (the opposition of all forms of government). During and leading up to the Cold War, Congress passed a set of laws that included, among other things, strong bars to aliens based upon their threat as members of the Communist Party, including their promotion of certain political and social beliefs (termed "ideological exclusion"). In the course of passing these laws, Congress made extensive findings that the Communist Party was an international terrorist organization committed to the violent overthrow of the United States government. The lawsuits challenging the Communist-era laws serve as the precedents against which many current laws are litigated.

In 1990, Congress enacted the current terrorism grounds for exclusion. Under those provisions, an alien seeking to enter the country may be barred on the ground that he or she engages in terrorist activity or is a representative or member of a designated foreign terrorist organization. Following 9/11, those grounds were expanded to deny entry to representatives of groups that endorse terrorism, prominent individuals who endorse terrorism, and (in certain circumstances) the spouses and children of aliens who are removable on terrorism grounds.

In 2008, Congress again modified the terrorism-related grounds for inadmissibility to exempt certain groups from the definition of "terrorist organization" and expand the waiver authority of immigration officials. In particular, the law prevented the African National Congress (ANC), the South African political party that led the sometimes-violent opposition to apartheid and was once designated by the United States as a terrorist organization, from again being considered as such.   It also provided immigration authorities the ability to exempt most terrorism-related grounds for exclusion with respect to activities undertaken in opposition to apartheid.

The terms "terrorist activity," "engage in terrorist activity," and "terrorist organization"— are expressly defined by the INA. "Terrorist activity" refers to certain, specified acts of violence. "Engaging in terrorist activity" includes the commission of direct acts of terrorism and certain activities in support of them. "Terrorist organization" is defined to include two general categories of groups: (1) groups that have been designated as terrorist organizations by the United States (i.e. groups that appear on published lists); and (2) other groups that carry out terror-related activities, but have not been designated, called non-designated terrorist organizations.

"Terrorist activity" is defined to be an act that was unlawful in the place where it was committed (or unlawful under U.S. law if it would have occurred here) and involve:

- The hijacking or sabotage of an aircraft, vessel, or other vehicle;
- Seizing or detaining, and threatening to kill, injure, or continue to detain, another individual in order to compel a third person (including a governmental organization) to do or abstain from doing any act as an explicit or implicit condition for the release of the individual seized or detained;
- A violent attack upon an internationally protected person (e.g., Head of State, Foreign Minister, or ambassador);
- An assassination;
- The use of any biological agent, chemical agent, or nuclear weapon or device;
- The use of any explosive, firearm, or other weapon or dangerous device (other than for mere personal monetary gain), with intent to endanger, directly or indirectly, the safety of one or more individuals or to cause substantial damage to property; or
- A threat, attempt, or conspiracy to commit any of the foregoing.

"Terrorist organization" includes these groups:

- Any group designated by the Secretary of State as a terrorist organization because it threatens the security of U.S. nationals the United States;
- Any group designated as a terrorist organization by the Secretary of State, and published as such in the *Federal Register*, after finding that the organization engages in terrorist activity; or
- Any group of two or more individuals, whether organized or not, which engages in, or has a subgroup that engages in terrorist activity.

"Engage in terrorist activity" is defined as actions taken by an individual or an organization of which he or she is a part including:

- Commit or incite to commit, under circumstances indicating an intention to cause death or serious bodily injury, a terrorist activity;
- Prepare or plan a terrorist activity;
- Gather information on potential targets for terrorist activity;
- Solicit funds or other things of value for (1) terrorist activity, (2) a

designated terrorist organization, or (3) a nondesignated terrorist organization;

- Solicit another individual to (1) engage in terrorist activity, (2) join a designated terrorist organization, or (3) join a non-designated terrorist organization;

- Commit an act that the individual knows, or reasonably should know, provides material support to (1) the commission of a terrorist activity, (2) an individual or organization that the individual knows or should reasonably know has committed or plans to commit a terrorist activity, (3) a designated terrorist organization or member of such an organization, or (4) a non-designated terrorist organization or a member of such an organization

These last three bullets do not apply if the actor can demonstrate by clear and convincing evidence that he or she did not know, and should not reasonably have known, that the organization was a terrorist organization.

There are additional terrorism-related grounds for inadmissibility or deportation. These include:

- Has engaged in a terrorist activity;

- Is known or reasonably believed to be engaged in or likely to engage in terrorist activity upon entry into the United States;

- Has, under circumstances indicating an intention to cause death or serious bodily harm, incited terrorist activity;

- Is a representative of (1) a designated or non-designated terrorist organization; or (2) any political, social, or other group that endorses or espouses terrorist activity;

- Is a member of (1) any designated terrorist organization; or (2) any non-designated terrorist organization, unless the alien can demonstrate by clear and convincing evidence that the alien did not know, and should not reasonably have known, that the organization was a terrorist organization;

- Endorses or espouses terrorist activity or persuades others to endorse or espouse terrorist activity or support a terrorist organization;

- Is the spouse or child of an alien who is inadmissible on terror-related grounds, if the activity causing the alien to be found inadmissible occurred within the last five years;

- Has received military-type training, from or on behalf of any organization that, at the time the training was received, was a terrorist organization.

- An additional, a catch-all provision provides that association with terrorist organizations may also be grounds for inadmissibility.

As you can see, these terms are defined broadly and do not depend on context or whether the group or activity is supported by the United States. For example, a pro-democracy group engaged in armed conflict against an oppressive regime, such as that of Saddam Hussein, could potentially be considered a "terrorist organization," even if the group's activities were supported by the United States. As a result, a person affiliated with that group could be barred from entrance to the U.S. and ineligible for asylum.

ADAMS v. BAKER,
909 F. 2d 643 (C.A. 1, 1990)

TORRUELLA, Circuit Judge.

At issue before this court is ***the denial of a nonimmigrant visa to an alien, Gerry Adams. *** In March, 1988, Gerry Adams, a citizen and resident of the Republic of Ireland, sought entry into the United States for the purpose of conducting a speaking tour. He proposed to address a variety of groups on subjects including the state of civil and human rights in the six counties referred to as Northern Ireland, as well as other related issues. At that time, Adams was the president of Sinn Fein, an organization which the United States Department of State believed to be the political arm of the Provisional Irish Republican Army ("IRA"), an organization engaged in terrorist activities in Northern Ireland and elsewhere. He was also an elected member of the British Parliament.

On the basis of the exclusionary provisions of *** the Immigration and Nationality Act of 1952, United States consular officers in Belfast, Ireland, in consultation with the Deputy Secretary of State, determined that Adams was ineligible for admission into the United States because of alleged advocacy of and personal involvement with terrorist violence. His visa application was consequently denied. ***

*** Nonimmigrant visas, such as the one sought by Adams, may be granted to aliens seeking temporary admission into the United States for a variety of reasons. It is the alien, however, who bears the burden of establishing "that he is eligible to receive such a visa ... or is not subject to exclusion under any provision of [the Act]...." *** Adams' visa application was denied [as] "(F) Aliens who advocate or teach or who are members of or affiliated with any organization that advocates or teaches ... (ii) the duty, necessity, or propriety of the unlawful assaulting or killing of any officer or officers (either of specific individuals or of officers generally) of the Government of the United States or of any other organized government, because of his official character; or (iii) the unlawful damage, injury, or destruction of property; or (iv) sabotage[.]"

But the mere fact of an alien's inclusion under that subsection is not necessarily dispositive. *** [T]he[se] provisions *** may be waived if the conditions enumerated by the McGovern Amendment ("Amendment"), 22 U.S.C. § 2691, are satisfied.

The amendment provides standards for the Secretary of State's determination of whether to recommend a waiver***. It essentially requires the granting of a waiver, because such a waiver can only be avoided if the Secretary can certify to the Speaker of the House of Representatives that admission of the alien would be contrary to the *security interests* of the United States. The Amendment, however, is applicable only to those aliens whose sole basis for exclusion is membership in or affiliation with a proscribed organization. "Nothing in this section may be construed as authorizing or requiring the admission to the United States of any alien who is excludible for reasons other than membership in or affiliation with a proscribed organization." Since Adams was excluded because of his alleged involvement with terrorist violence, rather than because of affiliation with a particular group, the McGovern Amendment does not provide independent authorization for his admittance into this country.

*** Additional exceptions *** mandate that aliens not be denied visas or admission into the United States "because of any past, current, or expected beliefs, statements, or associations which, if engaged in by a United States citizen in the United States, would be protected under the Constitution of the United States." *** That section does not apply, however, to aliens who "a consular official ... knows or has reasonable ground to believe has engaged, in an individual capacity or as a member of an organization, in a terrorist activity...." Terrorist activity is defined by that section as "the organizing, abetting, or participating in a wanton or indiscriminate act of violence with extreme indifference to the risk of causing death or serious bodily harm to individuals not taking part in armed hostilities." It is this provision which we address today.

*** Even where, as here, challenges to immigration legislation and decisions are made based upon constitutional rights and interests of United States citizens, the Supreme Court has "rejected the suggestion that more searching judicial scrutiny is required." In *Kleindienst v. Mandel,* 408 U.S. 753, *** [t]he issue *** was whether certain provisions of the Immigration and Nationality Act relating to denial of visas to particular classes of aliens were unconstitutional because they deprived American citizens of various First Amendment rights.[3] The Court held that: when the Executive exercises this power [to admit an alien] negatively on the basis of a facially legitimate and bona fide reason, the courts will neither look behind the exercise of that discretion, nor test it by balancing its justification against the First Amendment interests of those who seek personal communication with the applicant. Thus, if the Department of State's determination that Adams was ineligible to receive a visa *** and its concomitant refusal to grant him a waiver *** was based on a "facially legitimate and bona fide reason," we will be constrained to uphold Adams' exclusion. ***

---

[3] ***Gerry Adams, an unadmitted and non-resident alien, has no right, constitutional or otherwise, to enter the United States. Nor does he have standing to seek either administrative or judicial review of the consular officer's decision to deny him a visa. Consequently, while it is permissible to join Adams as a symbolic plaintiff, it is important to recognize that the only issue which may be addressed by this court is the possibility of impairment of United States citizens' First Amendment rights through the exclusion of the alien.

The Department of State determined that Adams was ineligible for a visa *** because of his advocacy of and personal involvement with IRA terrorist violence. The government concluded that *** Adams was excluded for reasons other than membership in a proscribed organization. It also found that there would be adverse foreign policy consequences associated with his admission. *** While "the mere abstract teaching ... of the moral propriety or even moral necessity for a resort to force and violence, is not the same as preparing a group for violent action and steeling it to such action," and cannot form the basis for exclusion, Adams' actions clearly went beyond the abstract. On the strength of the evidence before it, the district court could have reasonably concluded that these actions formed a "facially legitimate and bona fide reason" for denial of a visa to Adams.[4]

The State Department had evidence of Adams' involvement with, and leadership in, the IRA. In the affidavit submitted to the district court, the Deputy Secretary of State declared that "[t]here is reason to believe that, as commander of the Belfast Brigade, Adams had overall policy control over, and granted approval for, major PIRA terrorist operations carried out within the greater Belfast area." Not only did the State Department have information identifying Adams as the commanding officer of one of the three battalions of the IRA Belfast Brigade, but it also had evidence that he was the commander of the entire IRA Belfast Brigade during 1971-1972. Moreover, the Secretary of State had evidence of Adams' participation in a series of "Bloody Friday" bombings in Belfast, where 9 persons were killed and 130 were injured, as well as many other bombings. Finally, the State Department had information that Adams was a member of the IRA's Army Council, the body primarily responsible for setting the policy and strategy of the IRA, and which grants approval for major IRA terrorist campaigns. It believed that Adams was Chief-of-Staff of the Council for some period of time, and that, during his tenure, terrorist activities were intensified.

The consular judgment regarding Adams' relationship to terrorist violence and the reliability of the information used by the consular officer in reaching that judgment is subject only to very narrow review. *** [T]hat review is limited to the determination of whether there was sufficient evidence to form a "reasonable ground to believe" that the alien had engaged in terrorist activity. ***

The decision to prohibit an alien from entering the United States under Section 901 *does* require that the government "know[ ] or ha[ve] reasonable ground to believe" that the alien has "engaged in a terrorist activity." But the Rules of Civil Procedure and Evidence are not applicable to the consular processing of visa applications. Instead, consular officers are permitted to consider all available information in making their determinations. The

---

[4] *** [A]s president of Sinn Fein, Adams made multiple statements which provided a facially legitimate basis for excluding Adams from entrance into the United States. For example, in his inaugural address of that organization, Adams stated that "armed struggle is a necessary and morally correct form of resistance against [the governmental authorities in Northern Ireland]." *** [T]he State Department had competent evidence upon which it could reasonably find that Adams participated in terrorist activities. ***

evidence so used need not have qualified for admission in a court of law. Thus, "reasonable belief" may be formed if the evidence linking the alien to terrorist violence is sufficient to justify a reasonable person in the belief that the alien falls within the proscribed category.

The question of whether the evidence is sufficient, however, to support a finding of "reasonable belief" is a question of law which courts must resolve. Upon review, we think that there is sufficient evidence to support such a finding, and hence that there was a "legitimate and bona fide reason" underlying the government's decision to exclude Adams from the United States. The fact that the information relied upon by the government came from printed sources does not render that belief intrinsically suspect, and the district court did not err in so concluding. The evidence of Adams' involvement in the violent activities of the IRA, both as a policy maker and as a field commander, provides a "facially legitimate and bona fide reason" for his exclusion. In making this determination, it is important to note that there need only have been a reasonable belief that Adams was involved in terrorist activity: it is not necessary to have proven his involvement in the activity beyond a reasonable doubt.

*** Adams was denied entry because of his personal involvement with terrorism, rather than because of his ideas or his association with a particular group. Hence, neither the McGovern Amendment nor Section 901 of Public Law 100-204 apply.

Notes

1.   **First Amendment.** Can aliens be excluded for making statements that would be protected by the First Amendment? What principled justification could be offered for such exclusion?

2.   **McGovern Amendment.** Note that this statute is mandatory where applicable, requiring admission of the alien. Why does the court find it inapplicable here?

3.   **Alien rights.** Footnote 3 says the alien has no constitutional rights. Who does in the Gerry Adams admission context?

4.   **Dangerousness.** Is Gerry Adams a threat to the security interests of the United States? If not, should he be denied admission? Why was Iran's President Amedinijad admitted to the United States in September 2007 and allowed to speak at Columbia University?

5. **Irony.** Gerry Adams was granted a visa after he made "conciliatory comments" about ending violence in Northern Ireland. NYT 1/30/1994, A1.

CHEEMA v. ASHCROFT

383 F. 3d 848 (C.A.9, 2004)

NOONAN, Circuit Judge.

*** Harpal Singh Cheema (Cheema) and his wife Rajwinder Kaur (Kaur) petition for review of an order of the Board of Immigration Appeals (the Board) denying them asylum and the withholding of deportation and holding them eligible for relief under the Convention Against Torture and Other Cruel, Inhuman or Degrading Treatment or Punishment (CAT) but granting them only deferral of removal. ***

Cheema is a Sikh, born in India in 1958. He is a lawyer and a member of the Sikh Lawyers Association. In 1987, he helped to organize an enormous rally to protest the government of India's decision to divert water from the Punjab. Shortly after this public event, Indian police arrested Cheema, beat him with a wooden stick, and stretched his legs apart until the muscles began to break. He was released ten days later without charges.

In the aftermath in 1987, Cheema gave food and shelter to Gurjeet Singh and Charanjit Singh Channi, whom he describes as leaders in the All India Sikh Student Federation, an organization he describes as nonviolent. The government in its brief characterizes these two men as "well-known terrorists," although its citations to the record showing them to be leaders do not support the characterization of them as terrorists. In January 1989, Cheema was arrested and questioned as to their whereabouts. When he was unable to say, he was taken into the jail yard, stripped, bound, stretched repeatedly on a pulley, and finally subjected to a solid steel roller being rolled over his thighs, breaking the muscles and causing him to lose consciousness. The next day he was again tortured on the pulley. Twenty days after his arrest he was released without charges. He was unable to walk and was hospitalized for a month.

In May or June of 1989, Cheema was again arrested and taken to Amritsar for interrogation. He was beaten and his right leg broken by his police interrogators. He was brought before a magistrate, who ordered him taken to a hospital where his broken leg was set, but on remand to police custody the police broke it again. After three months in a jail hospital, he was discharged from custody. Charges against him were withdrawn.

In August 1990, Cheema fled to Canada and, two months later, entered the United States. He joined the Sikh Youth of America, described by him as supporting the Sikh movement for an independent Khalistan and "very much against any kind of violence." He was elected general secretary of this organization in 1991. Later in 1991, he helped organize the Khalistan Affairs Center, a lobbying office in the United States for the Sikh cause of independence from India *** Between 1990 and 1992, Cheema raised money in the United States to be sent to individual families that had suffered in the Punjab and to individuals injured in crossfire while trying to cross the border between Pakistan and India. If someone wanted "to send money to Pakistan," Cheema told them to contact Bittu, and he gave such potential donors Bittu's telephone number. Cheema himself did not handle any money, and he assured potential donors that their money would not go toward militant activities.

In February 1992, Cheema learned that his wife, Rajwinder Kaur, still in India, was ill. He returned and was seized by the police on his arrival at Bombay airport and flown to Delhi. He was shackled, blindfolded and interrogated about his activities in the United States. The next day the police applied electric currents to his tongue, lips, nostrils, and temples. He was then racked again by pulley. Three weeks later he was handed over to the Punjab police, again tortured by electricity and subjected to a mock execution. His mother, when allowed to visit him, could not recognize him. Three months later he was released on bail.

Cheema remained in hiding in India until May 1993, when he flew to New York City with his wife. Prior to 1993, Cheema had never had any conversation with the head of the militant Khalistan Commando Force, Paramjit Singh Panjwar. In 1995, after two bomb blasts in the Punjab, Cheema called Panjwar to see if he was responsible. When he denied involvement, Cheema spread his denial through the media. Thereafter, approximately once a month until September 1997, Cheema talked by telephone to Panjwar. In 1995, Cheema aided the escape from India to Germany of Panjwar's wife, who was not a militant. In the same year, Cheema sent $5,000 to Panjwar's grandfather in India to pay for heart surgery.

In 1991 and in 1997, Cheema raised money for the Sikh Defense Fund, which offered legal assistance to Sikhs detained in North America [and] for the United Sikhs Defense Committee, a similar organization. He also sent money to Akal Academy, a Sikh temple in Kathmandu, and to a school for the blind in Delhi. He has helped support three Sikh activists for human rights.

Rajwinder Kaur testified that since coming to the United States in 1993 she has sent money to aid Sikh widows and orphans. According to her, she has never engaged in providing financial or other support for Sikh militants, and she is not aware of her husband doing so. The government did not present any evidence contradicting this testimony.

On arrival in the United States in May 1993, Cheema and his wife were paroled into the country, but not admitted. In November 1993, in the first of twenty-six hearings before Immigration Judge Dana Marks Keener, they applied for asylum and withholding of deportation under the statute and for relief under CAT. Part of the INS's evidence in opposition consisted of classified information and testimony by government employees; this classification prevented its disclosure to the petitioners. The immigration judge held this evidence to be admissible***. The judge ordered the government to present any exculpatory evidence it had. None was produced. *** the judge found both petitioners fully credible as to what happened to them in India. The judge described Cheema as "an impressive witness. He is intelligent, thoughtful, well-spoken and sincere." The judge stated that his wife "was also a convincing witness. Her testimony was detailed, consistent, and plausible."

The judge did not believe some of Cheema's testimony regarding his fund raising in the United States. *** [T]the judge found Rajwinder Kaur not to have engaged in terrorist activity and to be entitled to asylum, to withholding of deportation, and to full relief under CAT. The judge in the exercise of her discretion denied Cheema asylum because of his "lack of candor." The judge ruled that Cheema was entitled to withholding of deportation, a nondiscretionary form of relief, but was seemingly barred this relief as a danger to the security of the United States because he had engaged in terrorist activities. The judge, however, found that this bar was subject to discretionary waiver under the Immigration and Nationality Act ("INA") § 243(h)(3) as amended by the Anti-Terrorism and Effective Death Penalty Act of 1996 ("AEDPA") § 413(f).

The judge held the waiver to be applicable and that, "to ensure compliance with the 1967 United Nations Protocol Relating to the Status of Refugees," Cheema was entitled to withholding of deportation. The judge found that Cheema also qualified for relief under CAT, but not full relief as under CAT the bar raised by the finding as to terrorist activity could not be waived. Significantly, the judge found neither Cheema nor his wife to be a danger to the security of the United States.

On appeal, the Board [of Immigration Appeals] *** found that Cheema had been brutally tortured by Indian authorities and that he "is one of the few prominent pro-Khalistan leaders in the world who would be in danger if returned to India." *** The Board held that Cheema had engaged in terrorist activity "by soliciting funds for individuals and groups, i.e. Bittu and Panjwar, that he knew or reasonably should have known or at least had reason to believe had committed terrorist activity;" and that Cheema had given material support to Bittu and Panjwar by connecting calls to them from Sikh militants. The Board further found that his wife had engaged in terrorist activity "by sending money to various Sikh groups ... she knew or reasonably should have known or had reason to believe had committed or planned to commit terrorist activity."

Contrary to the conclusions of the immigration judge, the Board held that these findings barred withholding of deportation, because the acts of financial support for terrorist persons or groups in India and the facilitation of telephone calls from such persons in India were acts such as to "necessarily endanger the lives, property and welfare of United States citizens and compromise the defense of the United States." The Board also held that the petitioners could not be granted withholding of deportation under CAT but only deferral of removal.***

A. STATUTORY FRAMEWORK

1.   *Withholding of Deportation.* INA § 241(a)(4)(B) renders deportable "[a]ny alien who has engaged, is engaged, or at any time after entry engages in any terrorist activity (as defined in § 212(a)(3)(B)(iii))."

"Terrorist Activity" is defined in INA § 212(a)(3)(B)(iii) as: "[T]o commit an act that the actor knows, or reasonably should know, affords material support, *** for the commission of a terrorist activity" ***

Notwithstanding a determination of terrorist activity an alien may be eligible for withholding of deportation or asylum. INA § 243, 8 U.S.C. § 1253, reads:

> (h) (1) The Attorney General shall not deport or return any alien *** to a country if the Attorney General determines that such alien's life or freedom would be threatened in such country on account of race, religion, nationality, membership in a particular social group, or political opinion [unless]
>
> (2) *** the Attorney General determines that- ***
>
> (D) there are reasonable grounds for regarding the alien as a danger to the security of the United States. ***
>
> (3) Notwithstanding any other provision of law, paragraph (1) shall apply to any alien if the Attorney General determines, in the discretion of the Attorney General, that- ***
>
> (B) the application of paragraph (1) to such alien is necessary to ensure compliance with the 1967 United Nations Protocol Relating to the Status of Refugees.

The instruction issued by the INS implementing AEDPA states that § 241(h)(3) is intended:

> to permit the Attorney General to provide withholding of deportation to aliens who have engaged in "terrorist activities" but do not pose a danger to the security of the United States. Thus, it should be applied in the same way as the exception to the terrorist grounds for denying asylum. ***

2.   *Asylum.* As the asylum applications were filed before April 1, 1997, they are not governed by the Illegal Immigration Reform and Immigrant Responsibility Act of 1996. They are governed by INA § 208, as amended by AEDPA § 421. *** The statute imposes a two-part analysis: (1) whether an alien engaged in a terrorist activity, and (2) whether there are not reasonable grounds to believe that the alien is a danger to the security of the United States. Having determined that Cheema and his wife engaged in terrorist activity, the Board turned to the second question of whether there are reasonable grounds for regarding them to be "a danger to the security of the United States."

In construing the phrase "danger to the security of the United States," the Board looked to several different definitions of the phrase "national security" but chose not "to adopt any of these definitions wholesale." Instead, the Board created its own test: an alien poses a danger to the security of the United States where the alien acts "in a way which 1) endangers the lives, property, or welfare of United States citizens; 2) compromises the national defense of the United States; or 3) materially damages the foreign relations or economic interests of the United States." We accept for the purposes of this appeal the Board's interpretation of the sense of "national security."

3. *CAT. [Convention Against Torture]* CAT creates a mandatory denial of withholding of deportation *** if "the Attorney General decides that ... there are reasonable grounds to believe that the alien is a danger to the security of the United States." ***

B. SUBSTANTIAL EVIDENCE

1. *Withholding of deportation.* *** Aliens who have engaged in terrorist activity are considered a danger to the security of the United States subject to a discretionary waiver. We review whether substantial evidence supports both the finding of terrorist activity and the determination that the alien is a danger to the security of the United States. ***

Rajwinder Kaur's actions do not constitute terrorist activity under § 212(a)(3)(B)(iii), much less does substantial evidence demonstrate that she is a danger to the security of the United States. *** If Rajwinder Kaur's one or two donations to unspecified widows and orphaned children are, without more, a reasonable basis to conclude that she posed a danger to the security of the United States, no alien could ever come within the "danger to the United States" exception.***

The Board chose to construe some of Cheema's acts as terrorist activity ***. We are unable to say that we are compelled to reach contrary conclusions. The question remains whether substantial evidence supports the Board's conclusion that there are "reasonable grounds" for regarding Cheema as a danger to our national security.

The Board chose the first criterion of national security, that is, whether Cheema "endangers the lives, property, or welfare of United States citizens." The Board did not address the alternative criteria relating to national defense or foreign relations and economic interests. *** The Board stated only its conclusion: *** Substantial evidence is required to link the finding of terrorist activity affecting India with one of the criteria relating to our national security. *** Contrary to the government's assertion, it is by no means self-evident that a person engaged in extra-territorial or resistance activities-even militant activities-is necessarily a threat to the security of the United States. One country's terrorist can often be another country's freedom-fighter. *** Without further evidence, it does not follow that an organization that might be a danger to one nation is necessarily a danger to the security of the United States.

History, indeed, is to the contrary. At least since 1848, the year of democratic revolutions in Europe, the United States has been a hotbed of sympathy for revolution in other lands, often with emigres to this country organizing moral and material support for their countrymen oppressed by European empires such as those of Austria, Britain and Russia. In the twentieth century, active revolutionaries such as De Valera and Ben Gurion worked in the United States for the liberation of their homelands. More recently, foreign anti-Communists living in the United States were active in encouraging and aiding movements against Communist tyranny in the Soviet Union and China. Much of this revolutionary activity would fall under the definition of terrorist activity as the Board interprets the statute. None of it had consequences for the lives and property of American citizens or the national defense, and the slight strains occasionally put on our foreign relations were more than offset by the reputation earned by the United States as a continuing cradle for liberty in other parts of the world.

That terrorist activity affecting a country struggling with strife cannot be equated automatically with an impact on the security of the United States is dramatically illustrated by the case of Nelson Mandela. In 1961, Mandela organized a paramilitary branch of the African National Congress, Umkhonto we Sizwe (MK) or "Spear of the Nation," to conduct guerrilla warfare against the ruling white government. Anthony Sampson, Mandela: The Authorized Biography, Knopf (1999) at 150. He then went into hiding to carry out the MK's mission: "to make government impossible," and began arranging for key leaders and their volunteers to go abroad for training in guerrilla warfare. Mandela was convicted by the South African government of treason in 1964 and sentenced to life in prison. In 1986, Congress passed the Comprehensive Anti-Apartheid Act, stating that its goal was to pressure the South African government to release Nelson Mandela from prison. It would not be sensible to conclude that Congress, in aiding a man convicted of treason by his own government, endangered the security of the United States or that the alien supporters of Mandela in this country were all deportable as terrorists endangering our national security.

To be clear, aliens who engage in terrorist activity *may* indeed affect this nation's security, but we cannot conclude that they always do so. Evaluation of this issue requires evidence, not speculation. If the INS, with the impressive resources of the federal government at its disposal, had provided reasons, backed by evidence, for finding Cheema and Rajwinder Kaur to be a threat to the national security of the United States, we would have a different case. But the Board simply does not provide those reasons.

Because the Board erred in determining whether Cheema was a "danger to the security of the United States," we remand to the Board to make that determination using the correct inquiry.

2.   *Asylum*. Because we are compelled to conclude that there is no evidence that Kaur engaged in terrorist activity, the Board erred in determining that Kaur is barred from the relief of asylum. The determination as to Cheema is to be made by the Board in the exercise of the discretion the statute has conferred upon the Attorney General. The determination is a negative one: there are not reasonable grounds for finding Cheema to be a danger to our national security. *** We will not deny the Board the opportunity to make this judgment.

3.   *CAT*. We defer to the Board's holding that Cheema's acts within the United States could be qualified as terrorist activity and affirm the Board's determination that full relief under CAT is barred for him. We affirm the Board's holding that Cheema may not be deported to the country where he is likely to be tortured. We recognize that this respite from torture is limited if the consequence is that a petitioner is deliberately detained in custody in this country. To be offered indefinite imprisonment as an alternative to likely torture is to be offered a harsh choice.

We disagree with the Board's denial of Rajwinder Kaur's CAT claim because there is no evidence that she engaged in terrorist activities while in the United States. ***

RAWLINSON, Circuit Judge, dissenting:

I must respectfully dissent.

Our review of asylum rulings made by the BIA has been curtailed in recent years. We may now reverse BIA's factual findings made in the context of ruling on an asylum application only if a contrary finding is *compelled* by the evidence. We must also defer to the BIA's interpretation of immigration law.

Here is what the evidence in this case showed:

• The State Department has identified the Khalistan Commando Force (KCF), headed by Paramjit Singh Panjwar, and the Sikh Student Federation Faction (SSF) headed by Daljit Singh Bittu, as "terrorist Sikh organizations."

• These organizations have engaged in robbery, murder, bombings, kidnappings, threats and general mayhem.

• Bittu has variously been sought for the assassination of relatives of India's Vice-President, the assassination of an Indian Army General, and the largest bank robbery in India's history.

• Bittu distributed weapons to various terrorist organizations, after receiving money from a source in the United States.

• The KCF has taken responsibility for a massacre of bus passengers, who were machine-gunned after the bus was forced from the road, and for a series of car bombings that left 300 dead and 1,200 injured.

• Panjwar and Bittu are described by the Petitioner, Cheema, as close personal friends on whose behalf he has raised thousands of dollars in the United States.

• Cheema has acted as a communications link to Bittu and Panjwar by routing telephone calls through his home in the United States, and thereby avoid detection by Indian authorities.

• Cheema served as a communications link during the kidnapping of the Romanian ambassador by Sikh terrorists.

• Cheema provided food and shelter to terrorists while they were fugitives from the police.

• Cheema's wife functioned in his stead during his absence.

It is not difficult to connect the dots from Cheema and his wife to Panjwar to Bittu and back again. The BIA's finding that Cheema materially supported terrorist activity is bolstered by substantial evidence, including Cheema's own testimony.

A finding that Cheema provided material support to major international terrorists in turn substantiates the BIA's finding that Cheema and his wife threaten the security of this country. Car bombings, assassinations of government officials, massacres-world wars have begun with less impetus. *** Contrary to the majority's apparent view, our country should not become a haven for those who desire to foment international strife from our shores. I would deny the petition.

Notes

1. Cheema's Wife. Is it as clear as the majority states that Cheema's wife did not provide material support to terrorists? Can providing money to widows and orphans ever be material support for terrorism? See the definition of material support in 18 USC 2339A (providing "any property, tangile or intangible, or service, including currency or monetary instruments" "knowing or intending that they are to be used in preparation for or carrying out [various specific terrorist crimes]" may be imprisoned for up to 15 years.

2. Terrorism and United States Security. Is it possible that any terrorism assisted from the US could endanger US security? Does it matter whether US security is defined in terms of US lives and property in the country, outside the country, or broadly to encompass foreign and economic relations? Note that the appellate court reversed based on the narrower ground of "US lives and property" used by the district court. Would it have reversed if the district Court's decision had been based on "US foreign and economic relations"? Should it matter whether or not the target country is an ally?

3. Enemy Combatants? Did Cheema get to see all of the evidence against him? Why not? Is he subject to the same evidentiary restrictions as the detainees at Guantanamo?

NEGUSIE v. HOLDER
555 U.S. ___, 129 S.Ct 1159 (2009)

JUSTICE KENNEDY delivered the opinion of the Court.

An alien who fears persecution in his homeland and seeks refugee status in this country is barred from obtaining that relief if he has persecuted others.

"The term 'refugee' does not include any person who ordered, incited, assisted, or otherwise participated in the persecution of any person on account of race, religion, nationality, membership in a particular social group, or political opinion." Immigration and Nationality Act (INA), § 101, 66 Stat. 166, as added by Refugee Act of 1980, § 201(a), 94 Stat. 102-103, 8 U.S.C. § 1101(a)(42).

This so-called "persecutor bar" applies to those seeking asylum, § 1158(b)(2)(A)(i), or withholding of removal, § 1231(b)(3)(B)(i). It does not disqualify an alien from receiving a temporary deferral of removal under the Convention Against Torture and Other Cruel, Inhuman or Degrading Treatment or Punishment (CAT).

In this case the Board of Immigration Appeals (BIA) determined that the persecutor bar applies even if the alien's   assistance in persecution was coerced or otherwise the product of duress. *** We reverse and remand for the agency to interpret the statute ***.

Petitioner in this Court is Daniel Girmai Negusie, a dual national of Eritrea and Ethiopia, his father having been a national of the former and his mother of the latter. Born and educated in Ethiopia, he left there for Eritrea around the age of 18 to see his mother and find employment. The year was 1994. After a few months in Eritrea, state officials took custody of petitioner and others when they were attending a movie. He was forced to perform hard labor for a month and then was conscripted into the military for a time. War broke out between Ethiopia and Eritrea in 1998, and he was conscripted again.

When petitioner refused to fight against Ethiopia, his other homeland, the Eritrean Government incarcerated him. Prison guards punished petitioner by beating him with sticks and placing him in the hot sun. He was released after two years and forced to work as a prison guard, a duty he performed on a rotating basis for about four years. It is undisputed that the prisoners he guarded were being persecuted on account of a protected ground-*i.e.,* "race, religion, nationality, membership in a particular social group, or political opinion." Petitioner testified that he carried a gun, guarded the gate to prevent escape, and kept prisoners from taking showers and obtaining fresh air. He also guarded prisoners to make sure they stayed in the sun, which he knew was a form of punishment. He saw at least one man die after being in the sun for more than two hours. Petitioner testified that he had not shot at or directly punished any prisoner and that he helped prisoners on various occasions. Petitioner escaped from the prison and hid in a container, which was loaded on board a ship heading to the United States. Once here he applied for asylum and withholding of removal. ***

In a careful opinion the Immigration Judge *** found that petitioner's testimony, for the most part, was credible. *** The judge, however, granted deferral of removal under CAT because petitioner was likely to be tortured if returned to Eritrea. *** We conclude that the BIA misapplied our precedent in *Fedorenko* as mandating that an alien's   motivation and intent are irrelevant to the issue whether an alien assisted in persecution. The agency must confront the same question free of this mistaken legal premise. ***

JUSTICE STEVENS would have the Court provide a definite answer to the question presented and then remand for further proceedings. That approach, however, is in tension with the "ordinary 'remand' rule." *** [W]e find it appropriate to remand to the agency for its initial determination of the statutory interpretation question and its application to this case. The agency's interpretation of the statutory meaning of "persecution" may be explained by a more comprehensive definition, one designed to elaborate on the term in anticipation of a wide range of potential conduct; and that expanded definition in turn may be influenced by how practical, or impractical, the standard would be in terms of its application to specific cases. These matters may have relevance in determining whether its statutory interpretation is a permissible one.***

JUSTICE SCALIA, with whom JUSTICE ALITO joins, concurring.

I agree with the Court that "the statute has an ambiguity" *** And I agree that a remand is in order. *** But good reasons for the agency's current practice exist-reasons adequate to satisfy the requirement that an agency act reasonably in choosing among various possible constructions of an ambiguous statute. The statute does not mandate the rule precluding the duress defense but does not foreclose it either; the agency is free to retain that rule so long as the choice to do so is soundly reasoned ***.The primary contention to the contrary is, in short, that barring aliens who persecuted under duress would punish purely "nonculpable" conduct. That argument suffers from at least three unjustified leaps of logic.

First, it implicitly adopts a view of "culpability" that is neither the only view nor one necessarily applicable here. The culpability of one who harms another under coercion is, and has always been, a subject of intense debate, raising profound questions of moral philosophy and individual responsibility. (The so-called "Nuremberg defense" comes readily to mind.) At common law, duress was not an accepted defense to intentional killing,; and in modern times, some states do not allow it as a defense to lesser crimes. Notably, there is no historical support for the duress defense when a soldier follows a military order he knows to be unlawful. It is therefore far from clear that precluding a duress defense here would, as petitioner alleges, "disregard principles of blame ... 'universal and persistent' in American law." All of this suggests that those who are coerced to commit wrong are at least *sometimes* "culpable" enough to be treated as criminals.

More importantly, this is not a criminal matter. This Court has long understood that an "order of deportation is not a punishment for crime." Asylum is a benefit accorded by grace, not by entitlement, and withholding that benefit from all who have intentionally harmed others-whether under coercion or not-is not unreasonable.

Second, petitioner assumes that the persecutor bar must have been intended merely to punish wrongdoing. But in the context of immigration law, "culpability" as a relevant factor in determining admissibility is only one facet of a more general consideration: desirability. And there may well be reasons to think that those who persecuted others, even under duress, would be relatively undesirable as immigrants. If, for example, the asylum laws grant entry to those who suffered the persecution, might it not be imprudent to also grant entry to the coerced persecutor, who may end up living in the same community as one of his victims? The Nation has a legitimate interest in preventing the importation of ethnic strife from remote parts of the world, and the agency may resolve the statutory ambiguity in a way that safeguards that interest.

Finally, *even if* culpability is the only relevant factor, and *even if* a narrow, criminal-law based view of culpability is the authoritative one, a bright-line rule excluding all persecutors-whether acting under coercion or not-might *still* be the best way for the agency to effectuate the statutory scheme. Immigration judges already face the overwhelming task of attempting to recreate, by a limited number of witnesses speaking through (often poor-quality) translation, events that took place years ago in foreign, usually impoverished countries. Adding on top of that the burden of adjudicating claims of duress and coercion, which are extremely difficult to corroborate and necessarily pose questions of degree that require intensely fact-bound line-drawing, would increase the already inherently high risk of error. And the *cost* of error (viz., allowing *un*coerced persecutors to remain in the country permanently) might reasonably be viewed by the agency as significantly greater than the cost of overinclusion under a bright-line rule (viz., denial of asylum to some coerced persecutors-who might anyway be entitled to protection under the Convention Against Torture, which includes no analogous persecutor bar). *** [A]lthough the agency's "objective effects" approach to the statute would seem to sweep beyond the duress scenario to encompass even an alien who had no idea that his actions would "objectively" assist in persecution, there is no reason why the agency cannot consider questions of *knowledge* separate and apart from questions of *duress*. Both can be said to relate to the mental state of the persecutor, but they present different problems which can be grappled with separately. ***

JUSTICE STEVENS, with whom JUSTICE BREYER joins, concurring in part and dissenting in part.

The narrow question of statutory construction presented by this case is whether the so-called "persecutor bar" disqualifies from asylum or withholding of removal an alien whose conduct was coerced or otherwise the product of duress. If the answer to that threshold question is "no," courts should defer to the Attorney General's evaluation of particular circumstances that may or may not establish duress or coercion in individual cases. But the threshold question the Court addresses today is a "pure question of statutory construction for the courts to decide." For that reason, while I agree with the Court's cogent explanation of why its misguided decision in *Fedorenko v. United States,* 449 U.S. 490 (1981), does not govern our interpretation of the persecutor bar, I would provide a definite answer to the question presented and then remand for further proceedings. *** [T]he persecutor bar does not disqualify from asylum or withholding of removal an alien whose conduct was coerced or otherwise the product of duress. *** Without an exception for involuntary action, the Refugee Act's bar would *** treat entire classes of victims as persecutors. The Act does not support such a reading.***

Congress passed the Refugee Act to implement the United Nations Convention Relating to the Status of Refugees and the 1967 United Nations Protocol Relating to the Status of Refugees, These treaties place a mandatory obligation on signatory states not to "expel or return ('refouler') a refugee in any manner whatsoever to ... territories where his life or freedom would be threatened on account of his race, religion, nationality, membership of a particular social group or political opinion." *** The Convention excludes from the *nonrefoulement* obligation of Article 33 persons who have "committed a crime against peace, a war crime, or a crime against humanity." It is this exception that the persecutor bar reflects. See, *e.g.,* The language of the Convention's exception is critical: We do not normally convict individuals of *crimes* when their actions are coerced or otherwise involuntary. Indeed, the

United Nations Handbook, to which the Court has looked for guidance in the past, states that all relevant factors, including "mitigating circumstances," must be considered in determining whether an alien's acts are of a "criminal nature" as contemplated by Article 1(F). Other states parties to the Convention and Protocol likewise read the Convention's exception as limited to culpable conduct. When we interpret treaties, we consider the interpretations of the courts of other nations, and we should do the same when Congress asks us to interpret a statute in light of a treaty's language. Congress' effort to conform United States law to the standard set forth in the U.N. Convention and Protocol shows that it intended the persecutor bar to apply only to culpable, voluntary acts-and it underscores that Congress did not delegate the question presented by this case to the agency.

While I would hold that the persecutor bar does not automatically disqualify from asylum or withholding of removal an alien who acted involuntarily, I would leave for the Attorney General-and, through his own delegation, the BIA-the question how the voluntariness standard should be applied. The agency would retain the ability, for instance, to define duress and coercion; to determine whether or not a balancing test should be employed; and, of course, to decide whether any individual asylum-seeker's acts were covered by the persecutor bar. ***

JUSTICE THOMAS, dissenting.

*** Because the INA unambiguously precludes any inquiry into whether the persecutor acted voluntarily, *i.e.,* free from coercion or duress, I would affirm the judgment of the Court of Appeals. I respectfully dissent. *** In sum, the INA's persecutor bar does not require that assistance or participation in persecution be voluntary or uncoerced to fall within the statute's reach. It instead "mandates precisely" what it says: "[A]n individual's service as a [prison] camp armed guard-whether voluntary or involuntary-ma[kes] him ineligible for" asylum or withholding of removal if the guard's service involved assistance or participation in the persecution of another person on account of a protected ground. Here, it is undisputed that petitioner served at a prison camp where guards persecuted prisoners because of their religious beliefs [and] carried out the persecution by preventing prisoners from escaping and by standing guard while at least one prisoner died from sun exposure. Petitioner, therefore, "assisted, or otherwise participated" in persecution and thus is statutorily disqualified from receiving asylum or withholding of removal under the INA. ***

PARLAK v. HOLDER
578 F. 3d 457 (C.A. 6, 2009)

JULIA SMITH GIBBONS, Circuit Judge.

Petitioner Ibrahim Parlak seeks review of the Board of Immigration Appeals' ("BIA") decision affirming the decision of the immigration judge ("IJ") ordering Parlak's removal from the United States pursuant to various provisions of the Immigration and Naturalization Act ("INA"). Specifically, Parlak argues that the BIA erred by: (1) determining that Parlak was removable for fraud or willful misrepresentation*** ; (2) determining that

Parlak was removable for engaging in terrorist activity; (3) determining that Parlak's removal could not be withheld because he persecuted others and thus lacked refugee status*** , rendering him ineligible for withholding of removal***; (4) failing to address properly the IJ's reliance on allegedly torture-induced evidence; and (5) denying Parlak's application for a grant of deferral of removal under the Convention Against Torture ("CAT").

Parlak, a native and citizen of Turkey, entered the United States in 1991. He applied for asylum, alleging that Turkish officials persecuted him because of his leading role in the Kurdish freedom movement. In his application he indicated that he was a "leading member of ERNK, which had close ties to the PKK." ERNK refers to the National Liberation Front of Kurdistan, and PKK is the Kurdistan Workers Party. A narrative statement included with the application related political involvement since 1975 (when Parlak would have been thirteen years old) and periods of police custody associated with his political activities during which Parlak was beaten and tortured. The narrative continued with the following statements. Parlak fled to Germany in 1980, where he continued his political activities. When he sought extension of his passport, Turkish officials refused, telling him he was wanted by the Turkish police and should return to Turkey. He therefore used a false passport. In 1987 he went to Syria and then to Lebanon to join the PKK. He remained in a PKK camp in Lebanon for eight months. He then returned to Syria and attempted an illegal return to Turkey. His effort to cross the border on May 21, 1988, with a dozen friends was unsuccessful; he and his friends were met with gunfire and shot back. On July 1, 1988, Parlak and seven friends successfully crossed the border from Syria into Turkey. They conducted political activities promoting Kurdish freedom. Turkish soldiers attacked on more than one occasion; various friends disappeared or were killed or injured. On October 29, 1988, Parlak was arrested and tortured and given a death sentence. His family paid a bribe for his release. In 1991 a policeman told him that his file would be reopened and "they will be looking for [him]." He left the country with a false passport. Based on this application, Parlak was granted asylum in the United States.

In 1994 Parlak successfully applied for an adjustment of status to lawful permanent resident, and in 1998 he applied for naturalization. He did not mention the 1988 arrest and conviction referred to in his asylum application in either the 1994 or 1998 applications and checked "no" in response to questions asking whether he had ever been arrested, charged, or convicted for breaking any law. Parlak's naturalization application was denied, apparently due to an outstanding 1995 Turkish arrest warrant and the fact that the PKK had been designated a terrorist organization in 1997.

Parlak was then charged with being removable at the time of his adjustment of status due to false statements made on his application for adjustment of status, specifically, the denial of an arrest, charge, or conviction and the denial of lending support to terrorist activities. Additional charges were later added, which included allegations of terrorist activity between 1985 and 1988. The terrorist activities alleged included organizing ERNK events that collected money for the PKK, receiving firearms training from the PKK in Lebanon, and actions associated with the 1988 efforts to enter Turkey from Syria. Parlak was alleged to have exchanged gunfire in the May 21 incident, resulting in the death of two Turkish soldiers, and to have dropped a grenade on that same occasion. The charges referred to a March 2004 Turkish conviction at which the death of the two soldiers was imputed to Parlak. Parlak was also alleged to have transported firearms and explosives into Turkey about June 1, 1988. The IJ conducted a hearing and ruled against Parlak on all charges. The BIA affirmed most of the IJ's rulings but vacated the IJ's finding that Parlak is an alien convicted of an aggravated felony. Parlak petitioned for review of the BIA decision in this court.***

The BIA found that Parlak was ineligible for withholding of removal because he assisted with PKK fundraising and transported weapons into Turkey for use by the PKK, thus assisting in the persecution of others. An individual who assists in the persecution of others is ineligible for withholding of removal. Parlak challenges both the factual findings supporting this conclusion and the legal analysis underlying the conclusion that he assisted in persecution. *** The BIA determined that the record supported a finding that Parlak assisted in the persecution of others by providing funding for the PKK and transporting weapons into Turkey for use by the PKK. The record does contain such evidence, none of which is derived from the Turkish conviction documents. *** Without considering Parlak's statements from the Turkish conviction documents, we affirm the BIA's factual findings.

Parlak also challenges the BIA's legal analysis, arguing that the BIA failed to distinguish between genuine assistance in persecution and inconsequential association with persecutors in determining when an individual assists in persecution. The BIA simply articulated the test as whether an individual "furthers persecution in some way," citing a 1988 BIA decision.

In *Fedorenko*, the Supreme Court determined that a concentration camp guard who shot at escaping inmates based on orders had "assisted in the persecution of civilians." In a footnote, the court provided:

> [A]n individual who did no more than cut the hair of female inmates before they were executed cannot be found to have assisted in the persecution of civilians. On the other hand, there can be no question that a guard who was issued a uniform and armed with a rifle and a pistol, who was paid a stipend and was regularly allowed to leave the concentration camp to visit a nearby village, and who admitted to shooting at escaping inmates on orders from the commandant of the camp, fits within the statutory language about persons who assisted in the persecution of civilians. Other cases may present more difficult line-drawing problems but we need decide only this case.

As Parlak notes, courts have since looked to *Fedorenko* for guidance in determining what constitutes "assisting in persecution." *** [T]he Supreme Court recently held that we are not necessarily bound by *Fedorenko's* analysis because the INA has a different structure and purpose than the statute applied in *Fedorenko,* the Displaced Persons Act of 1948 ("DPA"). *Negusie v. Holder,* 555 U.S. ----, 129 S.Ct. 1159 (2009). Specifically, the Supreme Court found that *** voluntariness is not necessarily irrelevant in determining whether an alien has assisted in persecution for purposes of the INA persecution bar. The Supreme Court remanded the matter to be decided by the BIA in the first instance.

Negusie's holding, however, does not prevent all analogizing between *Fedorenko* and INA cases. Parlak, unlike Negusie, has not claimed that his actions were involuntary. Given that *Negusie* analyzed *Fedorenko*'s application only in the context of allegedly involuntary actions, we find that *Fedorenko*'s analysis of what constitutes persecution remains instructive where voluntariness is not at issue. Mindful of the differences between the DPA and the INA, we agree with the only circuits to have addressed this issue since *Negusie* and look to *Fedorenko* for guidance in defining what constitutes "assisting in persecution." As with the facts before the Ninth Circuit, "[s]ince there is no question here that [Parlak] acted voluntarily, there is no reason to remand in light of *Negusie,* and the question of whether [Parlak] participated in persecution can be decided based on existing circuit precedent." ***

First, we conclude that the BIA's analysis was consistent with *Fedorenko.* To be sure, the BIA's statement that "[a] person assists in persecution of others when he furthers the persecution in *some* way" was vague and unhelpful on its own. As *Fedorenko* line-drawing shows, the issue is not whether the person assists in *some* way; rather the analysis requires distinguishing between "genuine assistance in persecution and inconsequential association with persecutors." But the BIA decision proceeded to compare Parlak's provision of weapons for PKK fighters with the coordination of arms shipments for the Provisional Irish Republican Army, which was found to qualify as "assisting in persecution" *** This type of analogizing is entirely consistent with *Fedorenko* and its progeny. Moreover, the facts do support a conclusion of general assistance in persecution. *** Parlak voluntarily and knowingly provided money, which he knew could be used by the PKK for anything, and weapons, which directly supported the PKK's persecution of others. Parlak's level of assistance is an order of magnitude greater than the harshest assessment one could possibly make about Diaz-Zanatta, and we find that a nexus exists between Parlak's actions and the persecution of others and that Parlak acted knowingly.

Secondly, even if we were to find *Fedorenko*'s interpretation of "assisting in persecution," *** inapplicable to Parlak, providing money and weapons to PKK fighters satisfies the plain meaning of the phrase. The Merriam-Webster Dictionary defines "assist" as "to give usually supplementary support or aid to." The same dictionary defines "persecution" as "the act or practice of persecuting especially those who differ in origin, religion, or social outlook." Black's Law Dictionary similarly defines "persecution" as "[v]iolent, cruel, and oppressive treatment directed toward a person or group of persons because of their race, religion, sexual orientation, politics, or other beliefs." This case does not require that we trace the tricky contours of "assist" and "persecution" for all circumstances; we need only look to the plain meaning of the words to decide that smuggling weapons across an international border to aid the PKK in committing violent acts against Turks and Turkish-aligned Kurds constitutes assistance in persecution.

Because the BIA did not err in its legal analysis and because its determination that Parlak assisted in the persecution of others was supported by substantial evidence, we affirm its conclusion that Parlak was ineligible for withholding of removal.

Finally, we conclude that the BIA did not err in rejecting Parlak's application for a deferral of removal under the Convention Against Torture pursuant to 8 C.F.R. § 1208.18. An applicant seeking relief under the CAT has the burden of proving that it is more likely than not that he will be tortured if removed to the proposed country. Parlak claims that the BIA erred because in assessing whether Parlak met his burden, it did not explicitly discuss Parlak's evidence that he had previously been tortured by Turkish officials.

"In deciding whether torture is more likely than not to occur upon the applicant's return to the country, we 'consider the possibility of future torture, including any evidence of past torture inflicted upon the applicant....' " While the BIA is required to *consider* "evidence" of past torture, neither [caselaw] nor 8 C.F.R. § 208.16(c)(3)(i) require the BIA to make an explicit factual *finding* as to whether an applicant has previously been tortured. In addition, the BIA is also required to consider "[o]ther relevant information regarding conditions in the country of removal."

Here, the BIA acknowledged that "there is some evidence that the respondent may face a possibility of mistreatment in Turkey." Because this evidence almost certainly included Parlak's assertions of past torture, the BIA's acknowledgment suggests that it properly "considered" the evidence of past torture. However, as required by 8 C.F.R. § 208.16(c)(3)(iv), the BIA also looked to other relevant evidence, including (1) the absence of evidence that Parlak is currently sought for any reason by the Turkish government and (2) reports that Turkey has taken significant steps toward eliminating torture. Weighing all the evidence, the BIA concluded that should Parlak return to Turkey, he would not be "more likely than not" to encounter torture. We conclude that the BIA considered the appropriate evidence, and substantial evidence supports its determination that Parlak did not meet his burden under the CAT.***

BOYCE F. MARTIN, JR., dissenting.

This country offers its immigrants the chance for a new beginning, but retains the right to revoke the freedom it offers should it discover a past it dislikes, no matter how remote or ancient the offenses. I have no quarrel with that: for the nation's immigrants, past may always be prologue. I dissent, however, because this awesome power was used here to railroad a man out of our country.

The majority evidently approves of this mistreatment, and, in so doing, commits three significant errors. First, the standard used to conclude that Parlak made a "willful misrepresentation" was incorrect. Second, the majority effectively ignores recent Supreme Court and Circuit precedent when it finds that Parlak is ineligible for withholding of his removal. Third, the immigration judge improperly relied on evidence likely induced through torture by Turkish Security Courts, and the Board and now the majority both claim the supernatural ability to block from the mind's eye this evidence, which the IJ cited roughly eighty times. This record is replete with error, and unless fixed, we will simply never know if Parlak's deportation is just. I would therefore remand this case to a different immigration judge for a fair adjudication-justice demands no less.

Ibrahim Parlak, a Turkish native, was convicted of Kurdish separatism by the now defunct Turkish "Security Courts." His conviction stemmed from a 1988 incident in Turkey involving a gun fight between Kurdish separatists and Turkish soldiers where two Turkish soldiers were killed. Parlak was arrested. While there, officials tortured him to obtain admissions of involvement with the Kurdistan Workers Party, known as the PKK, along with admissions of specific terrorist acts. He stated that the Turkish *gendarma* shocked him with electrodes, beat his genitalia, hung him by the arms, blindfolded him while depriving him of sleep, food, water and clothing, and anally raped him with a truncheon. J.A. 874; 981-82. According to Parlak, after he refused to comply fully (despite this torture), the authorities brought in his seventy-year old father.

After being interned for seventeen months, Parlak was released, though it is unclear whether that was because of a bribe or his cooperation. He left Turkey in 1991 and came to the U.S. where he was granted asylum based on his "well-founded fear of persecution." In his asylum application, he admitted supporting the PKK and he disclosed his 1988 arrest in Turkey. He adjusted his status in 1994 to lawful permanent resident, and, since 1994, has resided in Harbert, Michigan, where he owns a restaurant and is where his daughter was born. In 1998 he applied for naturalization, which the government denied on November 28, 2001.

*** At his removal hearing, the immigration judge, Elizabeth Hacker, ruled against Parlak on every point. She was apparently so convinced of his guilt that her opinion consisted largely of a cut-and-pasted agglomeration of the government's *pre-trial* briefs. Her opinion relied heavily on evidence obtained via torture by the Turkish Security Courts; she cited those documents roughly eighty times. On review, the Board of Immigration Appeals professed to affirm all of the IJ's factual findings and credibility determinations without regard to the Security Court documents, though it did not explain in detail how the IJ's conclusions could be supported without that evidence. The Board vacated the IJ's entirely meritless conclusion that Parlak murdered two Turkish soldiers, based wholly upon these same Turkish Security Court documents. But the Board repeated the IJ's other legal errors, many of which the majority repeats today.

Assuming *arguendo* (and *dubitante*) that Parlak is removable, the majority nevertheless blunders by approving of an incorrect legal standard for finding an immigrant ineligible for withholding of removal. Its decision effectively guts controlling precedent of the Supreme Court, every other court of appeals to have addressed the issue, and this Court.

Some removable immigrants may avoid deportation because they qualify for "withholding." An immigrant is ineligible for withholding by the "persecutor bar," however, if he "ordered, incited, assisted, or otherwise participated in the persecution of any person on account of race, religion, nationality, membership in a particular social group, or political opinion." The Board did not apply this standard, however. Rather, it invented its own, and held that an immigrant is ineligible for withholding of removal whenever he "furthers persecution in some way."

This inadequate and overbroad statement lacks the well-defined and well-settled requirements that courts have delineated as necessary to satisfy the persecutor bar. Specifically, this Court requires the government to show: first, a "nexus between the alien's   actions and the persecution of others such that the alien can fairly be characterized as having actually assisted or otherwise participated in such persecution," and second, "if such a nexus is shown, the alien must have acted with scienter; the alien must have had some level of prior or contemporaneous knowledge that persecution was being conducted." Moreover, *** to find an alien ineligible for a withholding, the government must prove that "the alien ... had some level of prior or contemporaneous knowledge that the persecution was being conducted."

Instead of applying this precedent, the majority, though conceding (as it must) that the Board's "furthers persecution in some way standard" was utterly "vague and unhelpful," inexplicably affirms anyway. That is wrong. Among its notable infirmities, this obviously inadequate "furthers the persecution in some way" standard in no way captures the "knowledge" requirement. So the proper result here would be to remand this case so the proper standard could be applied. ***

Further, to buttress its de novo application of a standard that neither the IJ nor Board considered, the majority performs its own I-know-persecution-when-I-see-it review. Indeed, the majority does not really approve of the (universally accepted) legal hurdles *Diaz-Zanatta* requires, as it rather incredibly remarks that this standard could very well be "inapplicable to Parlak," which is nonsense because the case propounds the standard for *all persecutor bar cases*. This leads into its conclusory statement that "the plain meaning" of the persecutor bar means that "smuggling weapons across an international border to aid the PKK in committing violent acts against Turks and Turkish-aligned Kurds constitutes assistance in persecution." Let's unravel this. First, the evidentiary conclusion that Parlak "smuggled" weapons across the border is dubious-the idea that a handful of men carried a complete cache of weapons over mountains over the course of fourteen days is not supported by the evidence. In any event, there is no evidence in the record that Parlak did anything "to aid the PKK in committing violent acts." Apart from the Security Court documents, it will be recalled that the most Parlak admitted to was that at one time he was part of the ERNK, a group which he admits had ties to the PKK, and that some of his fundraising efforts "might" have found their way to PKK coffers. Even assuming this was somehow sufficient, there was never a finding that the weapons he supposedly smuggled and buried-the actual basis for his supposed persecution of others-made it to the PKK and were used in "violent acts against Turks or Turkish-aligned Kurds," nor was there a showing that he had knowledge that they would be used in such a way. *See Diaz-Zanatta,* 558 F.3d at 460 ("It is not enough that information collected by Diaz-Zanatta and relayed by her to the SIE was used to persecute individuals if Diaz-Zanatta had no prior or contemporaneous knowledge of that; neither is it enough that Diaz-Zanatta knew that persecutions were taking place, if information Diaz-Zanatta collected and relayed to the military *was not used* in those persecutions.") (emphasis added).

Thus, without additional factfinding, the record is insufficient to sustain the majority's unique and self-directed analysis which manages the Janus-esque feat of applying a standard for the first time on appeal-and improperly so-while simultaneously casting doubt upon that same standard's continued validity. Accordingly, at a minimum, a remand is necessary.

Apart from the majority's misapplication of the persecutor bar in contravention of established precedent, the factual basis underlying the IJ's and Board's conclusions was compiled by an immigration judge who repeatedly cited evidence induced by torture. Of course, the IJ made no finding about whether the evidence was the result of torture or not, a sin which the Board and majority treat as a virtue. Yet when has it ever been proper to *assume,* in the face of strong evidence and testimony to the contrary, that such evidence is untainted? To its credit, even the Board knew it could not (at least publicly) rely on such evidence.***

In rejecting Parlak's contention that the record supporting his deportation is tainted, the majority demeans his supposedly "creative effort to import American criminal procedure rules prohibiting use of compelled confessions and harmless error analysis into the immigration context." Maj. Op. at 466 n. 7. The pot calls the kettle black. Though professing not to reach the question, the majority, citing no case, statute, or treaty, "creatively" muses on the theoretical significance of torture-induced evidence. One footnote asserts that if torture-induced evidence was admitted then Parlak nevertheless waived the right to exclude it, *id.,* and another provides a list of guesses on the proper course of what a domestic court could do with torture evidence.

Although this Court has held that the U.N. Convention Against Torture is not self-executing, the United States is nevertheless a signatory and the treaty states that torture induced evidence "shall not be invoked in any proceedings, except against a person accused of torture ...," 23 U.L.M. 1027, 1031 (1984). Further, "[i]t is well established that the Fifth Amendment entitles aliens to due process of law in deportation proceedings," and so due process and federal policy mandates that the government must shoulder the minimal burden of explaining *why* a court-federal, state, or immigration-ought to apply an exception to the general international rule of exclusion of torture-induced evidence. Instead, all we get is the majority's ill-considered dictum that somehow Parlak might be violating this Court's notion of fairness by requesting that he not be sent packing based on evidence obtained by torture. ***

The IJ, the Board, and now the majority have committed significant legal errors in adjudicating Parlak's removal proceedings. As a result, he will be deported without a fair determination of his legal status-three flawed opinions do not equal one correct one. Thus, there is something unreal about the majority's attempt to characterize its decision as the most straightforward of applications of immigration law when the foregoing proceedings have been anything but ordinary. There is nothing ordinary about the majority's blanket approval of an admittedly "vague and unhelpful" legal standard. And there is nothing ordinary (or proper) about a proceeding infected from the start by extensive reliance on evidence likely induced by torture, particularly where the IJ could not be bothered to do more than copy and paste swaths of the government's briefs. Those errors cannot be wished away by imaginative reconstruction-immigrants deserve better. ***

Stepping back, the Court is left with the impression that the vigor with which [the authorities] ha[ve] given this case, and particularly the manner in which it is pursing Petitioner's detention, stems from the introduction of the moniker "terrorist." I remain hopeful, nevertheless, that this case is but a sad remnant of an era of paranoid, overzealous, error-riddled, and misguided anti-terrorism and immigration enforcement now gone by the wayside. It is just a shame that, even if my hope proves true, it is too late for Ibrahim Parlak.***

PARLAK v. HOLDER
589 F. 3d 818 (6th Cir 2009) (en banc hearing denied)
cert. denied 130 S.ct. 3445 (2010)

The court having received a petition for rehearing en banc, and the petition having been circulated not only to the original panel members but also to all other active judges of this court, and less than a majority of the judges having favored the suggestion, the petition for rehearing has been referred to the original panel. The panel has further reviewed the petition for rehearing and concludes that the issues raised in the petition were fully considered upon the original submission and decision of the case. Accordingly, the petition is denied. Judge Martin would grant rehearing for the reasons stated in his dissent.

BOYCE F. MARTIN, Jr., Circuit Judge, dissenting from denial of rehearing en banc.

From 1994 until the government initiated deportation proceedings, Ibrahim Parlak operated a restaurant and raised his family in a small town in Michigan. There is no indication that he ever caused any problems here in the States. Why our government would elect to expend the time and money to rid our population of someone like Mr. Parlak is beyond me. As I acknowledged in my dissent to the panel opinion, however, "for the nation's immigrants, past may always be prologue," and, in any event, it is the government's prerogative to fritter away our resources as it sees fit. But one would assume that, if the government is going to expel a beneficial member of society for the alleged sins of his distant past, the government would go about its chosen folly correctly, in an above-board and dignified manner, and without over-reaching. One would further assume that those of us in the position of deciding Mr. Parlak's case, in the agency and in the judiciary, would demand this high standard of the government.

One would be wrong. In the hearing before the Immigration Judge, the government relied heavily upon evidence that no one genuinely disagrees was obtained by torture twenty-one years ago in a Turkish prison. Then, in a heartwarming display of adjudicative neutrality, the Immigration Judge issued an opinion that did little more than cut and paste from the government's briefs, typographical errors and torture-induced admissions included. Adding insult to injury, the Immigration Judge demonstrated either unprecedented gumption or an unfortunate insensitivity to irony in determining that Mr. Parlak lacked credibility based on his demeanor on the stand while at the same time giving credence to evidence obtained by torture-it is worth mentioning again-in a Turkish prison. Given this rather inauspicious start to Mr. Parlak's journey through our immigration system, one would assume that things would be righted at the next stop.

One would, again, be wrong. Having lost before the Immigration Judge, Mr. Parlak's next stop was the Board of Immigration Appeals. To its credit, the Board did not repeat the Immigration Judge's error with regard to the torture-induced evidence. Indeed, the Board's decision purports to disregard those portions of the Immigration Judge's opinion that rely on this evidence, though I have my doubts about the Board's ability to do this in practice. But, while it tried to repair the damage caused by the Immigration Judge, the Board caused even more harm on its way to affirming the judgment of the Immigration Judge.

A major issue before the Board was whether Mr. Parlak was eligible for withholding from removal-meaning that he could not be deported-or whether he was ineligible for withholding-meaning that he could be deported-due to the so-called "persecutor bar." The "persecutor bar" renders an immigrant deportable if, in the past, the immigrant "ordered, incited, assisted, or otherwise participated in the persecution of any person on account of race, religion, nationality, membership in a particular social group, or political opinion." 8 U.S.C. §§ 1101(a)(42)(B), 1158(b)(2)(A)(i), 1231(b)(3)(B)(i). Both the plain language of the statute and settled precedent from the circuits recognize that operation of the "persecutor bar" requires a direct nexus between the immigrant's actions and the persecution of another as well as an intent to persecute or knowledge that persecution was occurring. However, instead of employing this relatively uncomplicated inquiry to determine whether the evidence against Mr. Parlak triggered the "persecutor bar," the Board employed its own misguided inquiry to determine whether Mr. Parlak's actions of long ago "further[ed] persecution in some way." Finding that Mr. Parlak's actions did, indeed, further persecution in some way, the Board found that he was ineligible for withholding from removal. My colleagues on the panel describe this inquiry as "vague and unhelpful." I would describe it as grossly over-inclusive and as having sprung, unwanted and uncontrollable, from the collective mind of the Board like Athena from the head of Zeus, except without Athena's wisdom and elegance. But semantics aside, we all agree that the Board's inquiry was incorrect. One would assume that, in the face of a fundamentally flawed proceeding in front of the Immigration Judge and an incorrect analysis by the Board, the next body to examine this case would send Mr. Parlak's case back to start afresh.

One would, for a third time, be wrong. Mr. Parlak appealed the Board's decision to our Court. I believe that my colleagues on the panel recognized that the case came before us suffering from numerous procedural infirmities, and the majority's opinion shows that they tried mightily to inject some semblance of reason into the decisions of the Immigration Judge and the Board. Although I applaud their effort, I disagree with many of their legal conclusions. ***

But my larger question, and the first of two main reasons I believe this case should have been reheard *en banc,* is why the majority felt compelled to undertake this effort at all. The Board indisputably used the wrong standard in analyzing Parlak's case. In this situation, the Supreme Court instructs us to remand the case so that it may be analyzed in the first instance under the correct law. *Negusie v. Holder,* 555 U.S. ----, 129 S.Ct. 1159, 1167, 173 L.Ed.2d 20 (2009). And, before this case, it was the settled practice of our Court to remand when the Board or Immigration Judge apply the incorrect law.

Remanding in situations such as this serves two basic functions, one practical and one pedagogical. Practically, we remand because our question on review is whether "substantial evidence" supports the Immigration Judge's or the Board's legal conclusions as to deportation. How can we tell if substantial evidence supports another adjudicator's legal conclusions if the adjudicator employed the wrong legal analysis? Pedagogically, we remand to remind all involved that the proceedings in front of the Immigration Judge and the Board are not mere formalities on the way to an ultimate decision by the courts of appeals, but instead must be carried out in accordance with the law. Instead of remanding, however, the majority undertook what should have been the work of the Immigration Judge and the Board on remand by conducting a de facto *de novo* review of Mr. Parlak's claims. This undertaking directly contradicts instructions from the Supreme Court, as well as the binding precedent and common practice of this Court. Thus, this case should have been reviewed en banc.

This leads into the second reason that I believe the *en banc* Court should have taken this case. As it stands, the majority's attempt to clear away the problems caused by the Immigration Judge and the Board is likely the final word on Mr. Parlak's removal. But the majority's opinion did not fix the problems; it compounded them. On behalf of our Court, the opinion offers a tip of the hat to the highly questionable result without so much as a wag of the finger at the unquestionably flawed process, leaving me to wonder why we even maintain the pretense of procedure.

As I stated a few years ago, our recent immigration practice has effectively changed Emma Lazarus's beautiful words at the base of the Statue of Liberty from a solicitation seeking the tired, poor, huddled masses of the world into the exhortation "don't let the door hit you on the way out". If this is what the law dictates, then we judges may not stand in the way. But our Court would have done well to convene to let it be known that, though we will not interfere with the deliberative execution of the immigration laws, we will not be accomplices in the government's unprincipled slamming of doors on those "tempest-tost" who, like Mr. Parlak, seek nothing more than to "breathe free." ***

Notes

1. **Majority and Dissent.** Which is more convincing and why?

2. **Administrative Process.** What is your opinion of deportation processes from this case?

3. **Judicial Review.** Which opinion is most faithful to the correct standard for factual review of the administrative process and why?

4. **Deportation for Terrorism.** What connection is required to justify deportation? Who has the Burden of proof? Is there a statute of limitations? Do you think Parlak was deportable for terrorism ties? What use would there be for a remand?

5. **Supreme Court Review**? What would you emphasize in a cert petition on Parlak's behalf?

6. **CAT**. Should Parlak win on the ground that he is likely to be tortured if returned to Turkey?

7. **Deportation vs. Admission:** In the Border Protection, Antiterrorism, and Illegal Immigration Control Act of 2005, Congress for the first time applied the terrorism-link standards developed for admission to the U.S. to deportation cases even though, from an individual rights perspective, removal and admission are very different. As one commentator points out, refusing to admit a foreign national into the U.S. "leads to a disappointed expectation" on the part of the applicant. However, deporting someone from the U.S. leads to "a deprivation of benefits already being enjoyed." David A. Martin, "Refining Imigration Law's Role in Counterterrorism," Brookings Institution, Jan. 2009. The stakes are particularly high when the government seeks to deport a lawful permanent resident, who has built a life in the U.S., may have a spouse or children who are American citizens, and may own a business. What roots did Parlak have in his community, and should the courts have taken those roots into account in determining whether to deport him? More generally, should the government consider the same links in the same way when determining whether to issue someone a visa to enter the U.S. and whether to deport somebody already lawfully admitted into the U.S.?

Denial and Delay: The Impact of the Immigration Law's "Terrorism Bars" on Asylum Seekers and Refugees in the United States

Human Rights First
November, 2009

Immigration Laws that target individuals who have engaged in or supported the commission of terrorist acts serve two very legitimate goals: to exclude from the United States people who threaten our national security, and to penalize people who have engaged in or supported acts of violence that are inherently wrongful and condemned under U.S. and international law. *** But over the past eight years, thousands of legitimate refugees who pose no threat to the United States have had their applications for asylum, permanent residence, and family reunification denied or delayed due to overly broad provisions of U.S. immigration law that were intended to protect the United States against terrorism. Changes to the immigration laws as part of the USA PATRIOT Act in 2001 and the REAL ID Act in 2005 greatly expanded provisions relating to "terrorism." The enactment of these new provisions also drew attention to the longstanding overbreadth of the immigration law's pre-existing definition of "terrorist activity."

Under these new and old laws, as they have been expansively interpreted by the federal agencies charged with enforcing them, refugees who were victimized by armed groups, including by groups the U.S. has officially designated as terrorist organizations, are being treated as "terrorists" themselves. Any refugee who ever fought against the military forces of an established government is being deemed a "terrorist." The fact that some of these refugees were actually fighting alongside U.S. forces shows how far removed the immigration law's "terrorist" labels have become from actual national security concerns. Refugees who voluntarily helped any group that used armed force are suffering the same fate—regardless of who or what the group's targets were and regardless of whether the assistance the refugee provided had any logical connection to violence.

Over 18,000 refugees and asylum seekers have been directly affected by these provisions to date. Currently, over 7,500 cases pending before the Department of Homeland Security are on indefinite hold based on some actual or perceived issue relating to the immigration law's "terrorism"-related provisions. The overwhelming majority of these cases are applications for permanent residence or family reunification filed by people who were granted asylum or refugee status several years ago and have been living and working in the United States since then. In fact, in order to keep a person's case on hold based on the immigration law's "terrorism bars," the Department of Homeland Security must believe that the person does *not* pose a danger to the United States—this is a requirement of the agency's "hold" policy.

In 2007, Congress attempted to address the impact of these provisions on a few groups of refugees through piecemeal statutory changes, and also broadened the discretionary authority of the Secretaries of State and Homeland Security to grant "waivers" to exempt individual refugees from the impact of these provisions. These changes were helpful to particular groups of refugees who benefited from the partial implementation of the government's expanded waiver authority.

But the failure to address the flawed definitions and legal interpretations at the root of this problem, and the reliance on a cumbersome and duplicative "waiver" process as the exclusive means of resolving their unintended effects, have left many refugees in limbo—labeled as "terrorists," threatened with deportation back to persecution, separated from their families, and in some cases detained for lengthy periods. The implementation of "waivers," whose positive impact has mainly benefited refugees overseas, has not kept pace with the growing backlog in the United States.

Human Rights First, which has continued to monitor the impact of the immigration law's "terrorism"-related provisions on asylum seekers and refugees, is regularly receiving new reports of asylum seekers and refugees who are being affected by these provisions. Some of these recent or ongoing examples include:

- A refugee from Burundi was detained for over 20 months in a succession of county jails because the U.S. Department of Homeland Security and the immigration judge who would otherwise have granted him asylum took the position that he had provided "material support" to a rebel group because armed rebels robbed him of four dollars and his lunch.

- A young girl kidnapped at age 12 by a rebel group in the Democratic Republic of the Congo, used as a child soldier, and later threatened for advocating against the use of children in armed conflict, has been unable to receive a grant of asylum, as her application has been on hold for over a year because she was forced to take part in armed conflict as a child.

- A man who fled political and religious persecution in Bangladesh has had his application for permanent residence placed on indefinite hold because he took part in his country's successful struggle for independence—in 1971.

- The minor children of members of the democratic opposition from Sudan who were granted asylum in the United States years ago have been prevented from becoming permanent residents because the peaceful political activities of their parents have been deemed to constitute "material support to a terrorist organization."

The Obama Administration inherited this situation nine months ago, and is reviewing the range of potential solutions. The Administration should avoid the temptation to continue to take a piecemeal approach to this problem. Unless the core problems with the law and its interpretation are addressed, many of the issues raised in this report will go unresolved. Refugees who seek asylum in this country will continue to risk delayed adjudications, prolonged separation from family, and deportation in violation of the Refugee Convention. Attempts to deal with the overbreadth of the "terrorism bars" through a waiver process will continue to swallow the time of senior officials at U.S. Citizenship & Immigration Services, Immigration &

Customs Enforcement, the DHS Offices of General Counsel and Policy, the Executive Office for Immigration Review and other components of the Department of Justice, the Department of State, and the National Security Council. And there will be no end to the jarring contradictions—with historical reality and other law—that our immigration system's understanding of "terrorism" continues to generate on a daily basis.

A more effective approach would be to fix the underlying statutory definitions and agency legal positions that have created this problem. Not only would such an approach allow the protection of the victims of persecution who seek refuge in this county, it would also help to ensure that the United States is no longer labeling medical professionals who treat the wounded, parents who pay ransom to their children's kidnappers, and refugees who engaged in or supported military action against regimes—from Saddam Hussein in Iraq to the oppressive military junta still in power in Burma—that had blocked peaceful avenues for political change, as "terrorists" or supporters of terrorism by virtue of those facts alone.

C. QUESTIONING AND DETENTION OF IMMIGRANTS AFTER 9/11

After the attacks of 9/11, the United States government questioned a large number of individual immigrants to find out what they knew about the events of 9/11. The following cases provide (1) a picture of what some of these roundups involved, (2) the conditions of detention for those held, if only temporarily, and (3) the extent to which these efforts to obtain information concerning past and planned terrorist activity were able to be kept secret.

CENTER FOR NAT. SECURITY STUDIES v. U.S. DEPARTMENT OF JUSTICE
331 F. 3d 918 (C.A.D.C. 2003)

SENTELLE, Circuit Judge:

Various "public interest" groups (plaintiffs) brought this Freedom of Information Act (FOIA) action against the Department of Justice (DOJ or government) seeking release of information concerning persons detained in the wake of the September 11 terrorist attacks, including: their names, their attorneys, dates of arrest and release, locations of arrest and detention, and reasons for detention. The government objected to release, and asserted numerous exceptions to FOIA requirements in order to justify withholding the information. ***

*** In the course of the post-September 11 investigation, the government interviewed over one thousand individuals about whom concern had arisen. The concerns related to some of these individuals were resolved by the interviews, and no further action was taken with respect to them. Other interviews resulted in the interviewees being detained. As relevant here, these detainees fall into three general categories.

The first category of detainees consists of individuals who were questioned in the course of the investigation and detained by the INS for violation of the immigration laws (INS detainees). INS detainees were initially questioned because there were "indications that they might have connections with, or possess information pertaining to, terrorist activity against the United States including particularly the September 11 attacks and/or the individuals or organizations who perpetrated them." Based on the initial questioning, each INS detainee was determined to have violated immigration law; some of the INS detainees were also determined to "have links to other facets of the investigation." Over 700 individuals were detained on INS charges. As of June 13, 2002, only seventy-four remained in custody. Many have been deported. INS detainees have had access to counsel, and the INS has provided detainees with lists of attorneys willing to represent them, as required by 8 U.S.C. § 1229(b)(2) (2000). INS detainees have had access to the courts to file *habeas corpus* petitions. They have also been free to disclose their names to the public.

The second category of detainees consists of individuals held on federal criminal charges (criminal detainees). The government asserts that none of these detainees can be eliminated as a source of probative information until after the investigation is completed. According to the most recent information released by the Department of Justice, 134 individuals have been detained on federal criminal charges in the post-September 11 investigation; 99 of these have been found guilty either through pleas or trials. While many of the crimes bear no direct connection to terrorism, several criminal detainees have been charged with terrorism-related crimes, and many others have been charged with visa or passport forgery, perjury, identification fraud, and illegal possession of weapons. Zacarias Moussaoui, presently on trial for participating in the September 11 attacks, is among those who were detained on criminal charges.

The third category consists of persons detained after a judge issued a material witness warrant to secure their testimony before a grand jury, pursuant to the material witness statute, 18 U.S.C. § 3144 (2000) (material witness detainees). Each material witness detainee was believed to have information material to the events of September 11. The district courts before which these material witnesses have appeared have issued sealing orders that prohibit the government from releasing any information about the proceedings. The government has not revealed how many individuals were detained on material witness warrants. At least two individuals initially held as material witnesses are now being held for alleged terrorist activity.

The criminal detainees and material witness detainees are free to retain counsel and have been provided court-appointed counsel if they cannot afford representation, as required by the Sixth Amendment to the Constitution. In sum, each of the detainees has had access to counsel, access to the courts, and freedom to contact the press or the public at large.

B. The Litigation

On October 29, 2001, plaintiffs submitted a FOIA request to the Department of Justice seeking the following information about each detainee:

1) name and citizenship status; 2) location of arrest and place of detention; 3) date of detention/arrest, date any charges were filed, and the date of release; 4) nature of charges or basis for detention, and the disposition of such charges or basis; 5) names and addresses of lawyers representing any detainees; 6) identities of any courts which have been requested to enter orders sealing any proceedings in connection with any detainees, copies of any such orders, and the legal authorities relied upon by the government in seeking the sealing orders; 7) all policy directives or guidance issued to officials about making public statements or disclosures about these individuals or about the sealing of judicial or immigration proceedings. To support its FOIA request, plaintiffs cited press reports about mistreatment of the detainees, which plaintiffs claimed raised serious questions about "deprivations of fundamental due process, including imprisonment without probable cause, interference with the right to counsel, and threats of serious bodily injury."

In response to plaintiffs' FOIA request, the government released some information, but withheld much of the information requested. As to INS detainees, the government withheld the detainees' names, locations of arrest and detention, the dates of release, and the names of lawyers. As to criminal detainees, the government withheld the dates and locations of arrest and detention, the dates of release, and the citizenship status of each detainee. The government withheld all requested information with respect to material witnesses. Although the government has refused to disclose a comprehensive list of detainees' names and other detention information sought by plaintiffs, the government has from time to time publicly revealed names and information of the type sought by plaintiffs regarding a few individual detainees, particularly those found to have some connection to terrorism.***

*** [T]he government contended that FOIA Exemptions 7(A), 7(C), and 7(F) allow the government to withhold the requested documents as to all three categories of detainees. These exemptions permit withholding information "compiled for law enforcement purposes" whenever disclosure: "(A) could reasonably be expected to interfere with enforcement proceedings, ... (C) could reasonably be expected to constitute an unwarranted invasion of personal privacy, ... or (F) could reasonably be expected to endanger the life or physical safety of any individual." ***

As to Exemption 7(A), the declarations state that release of the requested information could hamper the ongoing investigation by leading to the identification of detainees by terrorist groups, resulting in terrorists either intimidating or cutting off communication with the detainees; by revealing the progress and direction of the ongoing investigation, thus allowing terrorists to impede or evade the investigation; and by enabling terrorists to create false or misleading evidence. As to Exemption 7(C), the declarations assert that the detainees have a substantial privacy interest in their names and detention information because release of this information would associate detainees with the September 11 attacks, thus injuring detainees' reputations and possibly endangering detainees' personal safety. Finally, as to Exemption 7(F), the government's declarations contend that release of the information could endanger the public safety by making terrorist attacks more likely and could endanger the safety of individual detainees by making them more vulnerable to attack from terrorist organizations. For these same reasons, the counterterrorism officials state that the names of the detainees' lawyers should also be withheld. ***

II. The FOIA Claims

A. Names of Detainees

*** Exemption 7(A) allows an agency to withhold "records or information compiled for law enforcement purposes, but only to the extent that the production of such law enforcement records or information ***could reasonably be expected to interfere with enforcement proceedings.". *** Exemption 7(A) does not require a presently pending "enforcement proceeding." ***[I]t is sufficient that the government's ongoing September 11 terrorism investigation is likely to lead to such proceedings.

The threshold question here is whether the names of detainees were "compiled for law enforcement purposes." Because the DOJ is an agency "specializ[ing] in law enforcement," its claim of a law enforcement purpose is entitled to deference. To establish a law enforcement purpose, DOJ's declarations must establish (1) "a rational nexus between the investigation and one of the agency's law enforcement duties;" and (2) "a connection between an individual or incident and a possible security risk or violation of federal law." The government's proffer easily meets this standard. ***

Nonetheless, plaintiffs contend that detainees' names fall outside Exemption 7 because the names are contained in arrest warrants, INS charging documents, and jail records. Since these documents have traditionally been public, plaintiffs contend, Exemption 7 should not be construed to allow withholding of the names. We disagree. Plaintiffs are seeking a comprehensive listing of individuals detained during the post-September 11 investigation. The names have been compiled for the "law enforcement purpose" of successfully prosecuting the terrorism investigation. As compiled, they constitute a comprehensive diagram of the law enforcement investigation after September 11. Clearly this is information compiled for law enforcement purposes. ***

Next, plaintiffs urge that Exemption 7(A) does not apply because disclosure is not "reasonably likely to interfere with enforcement proceedings." We disagree. Under Exemption 7(A), the government has the burden of demonstrating a reasonable likelihood of interference with the terrorism investigation. The government's declarations, viewed in light of the appropriate deference to the executive on issues of national security, satisfy this burden. *** [T]he government's expectation that disclosure of the detainees' names would enable al Qaeda or other terrorist groups to map the course of the investigation and thus develop the means to impede it is reasonable. *** This information could allow terrorists to better evade the ongoing investigation and more easily formulate or revise counter-efforts. In short, the "records could reveal much about the focus and scope of the [agency's] investigation, and are thus precisely the sort of information exemption 7(A) allows an agency to keep secret." ***

For several reasons, plaintiffs contend that we should reject the government's predictive judgments of the harms that would result from disclosure. First, they argue that terrorist organizations likely already know which of their members have been detained. We have no way of assessing that likelihood. Moreover, even if terrorist organizations know about some of their members who were detained, a complete list of detainees could still have great value in confirming the status of their members. *** After disclosure, this detainee could be irreparably compromised as a source of information.

More importantly, some detainees may not be members of terrorist organizations, but may nonetheless have been detained on INS or material witness warrants as having information about terrorists. Terrorist organizations are less likely to be aware of such individuals' status as detainees. Such detainees could be acquaintances of the September 11 terrorists, or members of the same community groups or mosques. These detainees, fearing retribution or stigma, would be less likely to cooperate with the investigation if their names are disclosed. Moreover, tracking down the background and location of these detainees could give terrorists insights into the investigation they would otherwise be unlikely to have. After disclosure, terrorist organizations could attempt to intimidate these detainees or their families, or feed the detainees false or misleading information. It is important to remember that many of these detainees have been released at this time and are thus especially vulnerable to intimidation or coercion. While the detainees have been free to disclose their names to the press or public, it is telling that so few have come forward, perhaps for fear of this very intimidation.

We further note the impact disclosure could have on the government's investigation going forward. A potential witness or informant may be much less likely to come forward and cooperate with the investigation if he believes his name will be made public.

Plaintiffs next argue that the government's predictive judgment is undermined by the government's disclosure of some of the detainees' names. *** The disclosure of a few pieces of information in no way lessens the government's argument that complete disclosure would provide a composite picture of its investigation and have negative effects on the investigation. Furthermore, *** strategic disclosures can be important weapons in the government's arsenal during a law enforcement investigation. *** [T]he Third Circuit confronted a similar issue involving the INS detainees when it considered the constitutionality of closed deportation hearings in *North Jersey Media Group, Inc. v. Ashcroft,* 308 F.3d 198 (3d Cir.2002), *cert. denied,* 538 U.S. 1056 (2003). The court *** did not search for specific evidence that each of the INS detainees was involved in terrorism, nor did it embark on a probing analysis of whether the government's concerns were well-founded. *** [T]he concerns expressed in the government's declarations seem credible-and inasmuch as the declarations were made by counterterrorism experts with far greater knowledge than this Court-we hold that the disclosure of the names of the detainees could reasonably be expected to interfere with the ongoing investigation.***

B. Identity of Counsel

*** The government contends that a list of attorneys for the detainees would facilitate the easy compilation of a list of all detainees, and all of the dangers flowing therefrom. It is more than reasonable to assume that plaintiffs and *amici* press organizations would attempt to contact detainees' attorneys and compile a list of all detainees. As discussed above, if such a list fell into the hands of al Qaeda, the consequences could be disastrous. ***

C. Other Detention Information

Having held that the government properly withheld the names of the detainees pursuant to Exemption 7(A), we easily affirm the portion of the district Court's ruling that allowed withholding, under Exemption 7(A), of the more comprehensive detention information sought by plaintiffs. ***

III. Alternative Grounds

We turn now to plaintiffs' alternative grounds for seeking disclosure of the detainees' names and detention information. Although FOIA does not mandate disclosure, plaintiffs contend that disclosure is independently required by both the First Amendment and the common law right of access to government information. We address these contentions in turn, and conclude that neither is meritorious. ***

*** Plaintiffs characterize the information they seek as "arrest records," and contend that the public has a right of access to arrest records under the First Amendment, as interpreted in *Richmond Newspapers, Inc. v. Virginia*. We disagree. Plaintiffs seek not individual arrest records, but a comprehensive listing of the individuals detained in connection with a specified law enforcement investigation as well as investigatory information about where and when each individual was arrested, held, and released. The narrow First Amendment right of access to information recognized in *Richmond Newspapers* does not extend to non-judicial documents that are not part of a criminal trial, such as the investigatory documents at issue here. ***[A]s the Court explained in *Houchins*: "[t]he public's interest in knowing about its government is protected by the guarantee of a Free Press, but the protection is indirect. The Constitution itself is neither a Freedom of Information Act nor an Official Secrets Act." Rather, disclosure of government information generally is left to the "political forces" that govern a democratic republic. *** We will not convert the First Amendment right of access to criminal judicial proceedings into a requirement that the government disclose information compiled during the exercise of a quintessential executive power-the investigation and prevention of terrorism. The dangers which we have catalogued above of making such release in this case provide ample evidence of the need to follow this course. *** Plaintiffs have no First Amendment right to receive the identities of INS and material witness detainees, nor are they entitled to receive information about the dates and locations of arrest, detention, and release for each detainee.

We also reject plaintiffs' final claim that disclosure is required by the common law right of access to public records. *** Even if the common law right applies to executive records, the government contends, FOIA has displaced the common law right. [We agree.]***

TATTLE, Circuit Judge, dissenting:

*** While the government's reasons for withholding *some* of the information may well be legitimate, the Court's uncritical deference to the government's vague, poorly explained arguments for withholding broad categories of information about the detainees, as well as its willingness to fill in the factual and logical gaps in the government's case, eviscerates both FOIA itself and the principles of openness in government that FOIA embodies. *** Although I have no doubt that some of the requested information is exempt from FOIA's mandatory disclosure requirement, the court treats disclosure as an all-or-nothing proposition, repeatedly emphasizing the breadth of the plaintiffs' request-the fact that they seek the names and other information pertaining to "every single individual detained in the course of the government's terrorism investigation," -as a justification for accepting the government's own very broad, categorical refusal to release the bulk of the requested information. This all-or-nothing approach runs directly counter to well-established principles governing FOIA requests. Nothing in the statute requires requesters to seek only information not exempt from disclosure. To the contrary, the government bears the burden of reviewing the plaintiffs' request, identifying functional categories of information that are exempt from disclosure, and disclosing any reasonably segregable, non-exempt portion of the requested materials. The government fails to satisfy that burden in this case, for the range of circumstances included in the government's exemption request do not "characteristically support" an inference that the information would interfere with its terrorism investigation. ***

The government gives us no reason to think that releasing the names of these innocent detainees could interfere with its investigation. Indeed, the government never really asks us to believe that disclosure of the names of innocent persons having no knowledge of terrorist activity would in any way impede its ability to gather information from those who do have such knowledge. Instead, it asserts that "a detainee who knows his name will be made public may be deterred from cooperating now or in the future for fear of retaliation by terrorist organizations against him or his family and associates." Although the court accepts this argument, it is ultimately not an argument for withholding detainees' names, but rather for withholding the names of people who have information that might be helpful to law enforcement officials. These are two different categories of people ***. These two groups thus merit different treatment. In fact, several statutory provisions address precisely the problem the government identifies, but all of them are aimed at protecting the identities of those people who provide information, not people the government questions because it thinks they *might* have information but who turn out not to. FOIA Exemption 7(A) protects the identities of witnesses where disclosure might pose a risk of interference in the form of witness intimidation or coercion, FOIA Exemption 7(D) protects the identities of sources who choose to provide information to law enforcement agents on a confidential basis, and the National Security Act protects the identity of intelligence sources in order to prevent those sources from "clos[ing] up like a clam,". The government can and should rely on these provisions to protect the names of detainees who provide information to law enforcement agents or whom the government believes will be able to provide such information in the future. The government may not, however, preemptively withhold the identities of innocent detainees who do not now, and may never, have any information of use to the terrorism investigation.

The only argument that could conceivably support withholding innocent detainees' names is the assertion that disclosure of the names "*may* reveal details about the focus and scope of the investigation and thereby allow terrorists to counteract it." *** The government's failure to provide an adequate explanation is all the more glaring given that the detainees represent only a subset-and quite possibly a very small subset-of persons questioned in connection with this investigation. As a result, even if releasing detainee names were to provide some insight into the terrorism investigation, that insight would be limited. Releasing the names of the detainees, but not the names of those questioned in connection with the investigation, can paint only a partial-and possibly misleading-picture of the government's investigative strategy. For example, if the government detains two people in Detroit but questions a thousand in Chicago, wouldn't release of the detainee information wrongly lead terrorist organizations to believe that the government was focusing on Detroit, not Chicago?

The second failing in both the government's request and the Court's analysis is that they treat all detainee information the same, despite the fact that each item of information that plaintiffs seek about the detainees-names, attorneys' names, dates and locations of arrest, places of detention, and dates of release-is clearly of very different value to terrorists attempting to discern the scope and direction of the government's investigation. Although the Reynolds declaration tells us that "releasing the names of the detainees who may be associated with terrorism and their place and date of arrest would reveal the direction and progress of the investigations," it does not tell us, for example, whether releasing the detainees' names and dates of arrest, but not their places of arrest-or even releasing the dates of arrest alone-would involve the same danger. The Reynolds declaration, moreover, contains no justification at all for withholding dates of release. Indeed, the government has already disclosed the release dates of detainees who had been held on federal criminal charges. This information may seem unimportant, but from the FOIA requesters' point of view, it could be highly relevant to the question of how the government is treating the persons it has detained. Taken together, arrest and release dates can tell the public how long persons have been detained, raising concerns about possible constitutional violations.

The government's allegations of harm are also undercut by the fact that it has itself provided several other means by which this information can become public. Not only do detainees remain free to inform whomever they choose of their detention, but on numerous occasions since September 11, the government itself has disclosed precisely the kind of information it now refuses to provide under FOIA.

Because the court concludes that Exemption 7(A) applies to the government's entire request, it never addresses the government's alternative arguments under Exemptions 7(C), 7(F), and 3. In my view, none of these provisions supports the government's refusal to disclose the detainee information either. ***

Exemption 7(C) permits the government to withhold law enforcement records where their release "could reasonably be expected to constitute an unwarranted invasion of personal privacy." *** Because the statute refers not to invasions of privacy generally, but to "unwarranted" invasions of privacy, courts evaluating claims for 7(C) exemption must do more than simply identify a privacy interest that will be compromised by disclosure of information. Instead, they must "balance the public interest in disclosure against the interest Congress intended the Exemption to protect." *** To be sure, detainees may have a unique interest in avoiding association with the crimes of September 11. Even so, that interest is clearly outweighed by the public interest in knowing whether the government, in investigating those heinous crimes, is violating the rights of persons it has detained. *** Moreover, plaintiffs offer ample evidence of agency wrongdoing. The record includes hundreds of pages of newspaper articles, human rights reports, and congressional testimony reporting alleged governmental abuses such as holding detainees for long periods without allowing them to seek or communicate with counsel and without charging them. *** Finally, plaintiffs need the information they request to confirm or refute the compelling evidence of agency wrongdoing *** The government next invokes Exemption 7(F), which permits withholding law enforcement records where their release "could reasonably be expected to endanger the life or physical safety of any individual." Here again, the government's evidence fails to establish that the entire range of records encompassed in the plaintiffs' FOIA request "could reasonably be expected" to endanger the detainees. ***

Finally, the government invokes Exemption 3, which exempts from disclosure matters that are "specifically exempted from disclosure by statute ..., provided that such statute ... requires that the matters be withheld from the public in such a manner as to leave no discretion on the issue." According to the government, Exemption 3, which encompasses Federal Rule of Criminal Procedure 6(e)'s prohibition on the disclosure of "matters occurring before the grand jury," excuses it from disclosing the names of detainees held on material witness warrants, since "each of these warrants was issued to procure a witness's testimony before a grand jury." As such, the government contends that Exemption 3 provides a ground for nondisclosure independent of Exemption 7. *** Saying that the material witness detainees were held in order to secure their testimony is quite different from saying that their testimony is "likely to occur" before a grand jury. Indeed, the record indicates that at least seven material witnesses have been released without testifying before a grand jury, so in their cases, it seems more accurate to say that their testimony is quite *unlikely* to occur before a grand jury. ***

No part of the government's exemption request better illustrates its infirmities than its refusal to disclose the names of the detainees' attorneys. *** In the first place, attorneys' names are quite clearly not a proxy for the names of their clients. *** Even assuming that releasing attorneys' names will somehow facilitate identification of the detainees, the Court's all-or-nothing approach again impermissibly shifts the burden of identifying exempt information from the government to plaintiffs. The government's Exemption 7(A) argument for withholding lawyers' names thus fails for the same reason as its 7(A) argument for withholding the names of all detainees. How would releasing the names of attorneys representing innocent clients with no connection to terrorist activities interfere with the government's terrorism investigation? Neither the court nor the government provides an explanation.

The government's second argument fares no better. The notion that the government must withhold the attorneys' names for their own good is flatly inconsistent with lawyers' roles as advocates and officers of the court in our fundamentally open legal system. Having voluntarily assumed this public role, lawyers have little expectation of anonymity. ***

Although I think it unreasonable to infer that all of the information plaintiffs seek in their FOIA request qualifies for exemption, the government may be able to point to more narrowly defined categories of information that might justify the inference. For example, while nothing in the record supports the government's contention that releasing the names of innocent detainees would harm the investigation, perhaps the government could justify withholding the places of arrest on the ground that such information might provide terrorist organizations with some insight into the government's investigative methods and strategy. I would therefore remand to allow the government to describe, for each detainee or reasonably defined category of detainees, on what basis it may withhold their names and other information.

Notes

1. **Choose Sides.**   Who has the better of the argument, the majority or the dissent?

2. **Other Avenues for Info?**   How strong is the argument that, if detainees wanted their information known, they could publicize it?

3. **Mosaics and More.**   How real are the dangers of information exposure that convince the majority?

4. **Gadflies.**   What legitimate interest does the plaintiff have in the information sought? Kate Martin, Director of the CNSS, said after the decision that "people are arrested in secret, deported in secret, and two and a half years later, we still don't know the names." NYT 1/13/2004, A1. Do you agree with her summary of the decision?

KANDAMAR v. GONZALES
464 F.3d 65 (C.A.1,2006)

SARIS, District Judge [sitting by designation].

Petitioner Abdelaziz Kandamar, a native and citizen of Morocco, seeks review of an order of the Board of Immigration Appeals ("BIA") dismissing an appeal of a final order of removal. In its order, the BIA affirmed the decision of the Immigration Judge ("IJ") denying Petitioner's motion to suppress evidence taken by the Department of Homeland Security ("DHS") [1] at the special registration interview under the National Security Entry-Exit Registration System ("NSEERS"). Kandamar claims that NSEERS violated his equal protection and due process rights. In the alternative, Kandamar asserts that the IJ erred in denying the application for voluntary departure because during the special registration DHS had taken Kandamar's expired passport, which was allegedly necessary to obtain a valid travel document. *** Kandamar, a native and citizen of Morocco, entered the United States as a nonimmigrant B-2 visitor on April 28, 1999. He was authorized to remain in the country until May 23, 1999. Kandamar overstayed his visa. He has no criminal history.

On August 12, 2002, the Department of Justice issued an NSEERS notice for the registration of certain young male nonimmigrant aliens from designated countries. As of March 1, 2003, the Immigration and Naturalization Service was dissolved and its functions were transferred to DHS. This opinion will refer to both agencies as DHS. The NSEERS notice required these nonimmigrants to appear before, register with, answer questions from, and present documents, including a passport and an I-94 card, to DHS. The NSEERS notice also specified that DHS conduct the interview under oath and record answers.

On January 15, 2003, Kandamar reported to the John F. Kennedy Federal Building in Boston without counsel to comply with the special registration procedures under the newly-issued NSEERS notice. As instructed, he brought his passport, which had expired, and his I-94 departure record. DHS officers took these documents. At the conclusion of the interview, Kandamar was placed into removal proceedings and charged with removability *** for remaining longer than permitted following admission as a nonimmigrant visitor. He was issued a Notice To Appear. *** On July 29, 2003, Kandamar appeared at a hearing with counsel, and the IJ continued the case again at the request of counsel. On August 11, 2003, Kandamar filed a three-page motion to suppress the evidence obtained by DHS "by unlawful search and seizure," alleging that NSEERS constitutes racial profiling and discrimination based on national origin; violates substantive due process because its use "to entrap nationals of certain countries" is fundamentally unfair; and violates equal protection by treating legal and illegal entrants differently.

At the hearing on August 12, 2003, Kandamar denied removability.

---

[1] As of March 1, 2003, the Immigration and Naturalization Service was dissolved and its functions were transferred to DHS. This opinion will refer to both agencies as DHS.

Kandamar's counsel challenged the constitutionality of NSEERS and, alternatively, asked for voluntary departure. Stating that Kandamar's passport had expired, he explained: "However, the Government has [his] passport and the Moroccan Consulate won't give him a new passport without the old passport." After setting a date for a hearing on the merits of the motion to suppress, the IJ returned to the issue of voluntary departure: ***Kandamar's counsel did not ask for a return of the passport. *** [T]he IJ held that the court "is not able to rule on the constitutionality of the regulations," denied Kandamar's application for voluntary departure because he was not statutorily eligible for the relief due to the lack of any travel documents permitting entry to Morocco, and ordered that Kandamar be removed and deported to Morocco. *** [T]he IJ succinctly explained that the lack of a passport or any other travel document precluded voluntary departure. No greater hearing or rationale was necessary on the point.

Kandamar's primary protest is that the DHS improperly seized his passport at the special registration. The issue is poorly vetted in the record as the government does not cite any legal authority to support the seizure of the passport. *** While he alerted the IJ to the fact DHS seized the passport, he did not urge the IJ to order DHS to return it, although he knew a travel document would have to be produced at the merits hearing. Moreover, the bare-bones allegation that Morocco would not renew the passport without the presentation of the expired one does not demonstrate that diligent efforts were made before the removal hearing to secure one

Kandamar raises a multi-pronged attack on NSEERS, arguing that the evidence obtained from the NSEERS interview should be suppressed because NSEERS, both facially and as applied to him, is fundamentally unfair in violation of the Fourth and Fifth Amendments. *** In the immigration context, the Supreme Court *** has concluded that the cost of the exclusionary rule generally outweighs its benefits in the context of civil deportation hearings. The Court thus held that the exclusionary rule generally should not apply in that context, but may have left the door open in cases of "egregious violations of Fourth Amendment or other liberties that might transgress notions of fundamental fairness and undermine the probative value of the evidence obtained." *** We examine Kandamar's claims to determine whether there is evidence of an "egregious violation" of the Fourth Amendment or other liberties.***

Next, although the argument is not clear-cut, Kandamar argues that the NSEERS special registration was so coercive that a reasonable person would have believed that he was not free to leave. We have held that in some circumstances, statements by an arrested alien can be involuntary and coerced in violation of the Due Process Clause of the Fifth Amendment. Kandamar claims that DHS's restraint violated the regulation governing administrative detention *** because the inherent nature of special registration creates an atmosphere where a reasonable person would conclude he is not free to leave. Section 287.8(b) provides: "Interrogation is questioning designed to elicit specific information. An immigration officer, like any other person, has the right to ask questions of anyone as long as the immigration officer does not restrain the freedom of an individual, not under arrest, to walk away."

Kandamar did not squarely present this argument that his interview was so coercive as to be tantamount to detention to either the IJ or the BIA. A petitioner is generally required to exhaust administrative remedies with the BIA before raising an issue in a petition for review of a final order of removal.   *** When constitutional claims "involve procedural errors correctable by the BIA, applicants must raise such claims as part of their administrative appeal."   *** Kandamar failed to exhaust his administrative remedies to preserve his claim.

Kandamar also argues that the IJ should have granted him a hearing about what transpired at the special registration, an issue that was argued to the BIA. Kandamar did not proffer any specific evidence of any government misconduct by threats, coercion or physical abuse to the IJ or the BIA with regard to his NSEERS interview that would constitute egregious government conduct.   There is no evidence that Kandamar asked to leave, was told he could not leave, or was restrained from leaving during the interview.   *** Most importantly, immigration counsel did not request an evidentiary hearing before the IJ but rested on her brief, which did not raise this claim at all.

Kandamar's most interesting due process claim is the poorly developed argument made to the BIA that NSEERS is fundamentally unfair because it violates the equal protection principles embodied in the Fifth Amendment, contending that it only affects nationals of certain countries and thus constitutes blatant racial profiling. This is the type of fundamental constitutional claim the BIA is powerless to address. *** We have held that aliens are entitled to equal protection of the law under the Fifth Amendment. However, Congress may permissibly set immigration criteria based on an alien's nationality or place of origin.   The Supreme Court has long held that judicial review of line-drawing in the immigration context is deferential ***

The Supreme Court has not had occasion to address directly the level of scrutiny that pertains to an equal protection challenge based on national origin in the immigration context.   In *Nguyen v. INS*, 533 U.S. 53 (2001), the Supreme Court held that a statute that imposed different requirements for a child's acquisition of citizenship depending on the gender of the citizen parent did not violate the equal protection guarantee embodied in the Due Process Clause of the Fifth Amendment.   Finding that the statute's gender-based "classification serves 'important governmental objectives and that the discriminatory means employed' are 'substantially related to the achievement of those objectives,' " it declined to "decide whether some lesser degree of scrutiny pertains [in an equal protection challenge] because the statute implicates Congress' immigration and naturalization power."

Congress has given the Attorney General great latitude in setting special registration requirements. 8 U.S.C.§ 1305. Section 1305(b) provides:

The Attorney General may in his discretion, upon ten days notice, require the natives of any one or more foreign states, or any class or group thereof, who are within the United States and who are required to be registered under this title, to notify the Attorney General of their current addresses and furnish such additional information as the Attorney General may require.

The rationale for establishing NSEERS is set forth in the Federal Register as follows: "Recent terrorist incidents have underscored the need to broaden the special registration requirements for nonimmigrant aliens from certain designated countries, and other nonimmigrant aliens whose presence in the United States requires closer monitoring, to require that they provide specific information at regular intervals to ensure their compliance with the terms of their visas and admission, and to ensure that they depart the United States at the end of their authorized stay. ***" On November 22, 2002, "[i]n light of recent events, and based on intelligence information available to the Attorney General," the Attorney General designated that certain adult males who were nationals and citizens from Morocco and other countries were subject to NSEERS.

Petitioner argues in conclusory fashion that the classification based on national origin violates equal protection principles. Every court to address the issue has rejected a challenge to NSEERS registration on equal protection grounds. Possibly, the events of September 11, 2001, and terrorist activities around the world, inform the degree of scrutiny to be applied, but we in any event give deference to the Attorney General's requirement that young males from certain countries be subject to special registration. We hold that a special registration system serves legitimate government objectives of monitoring nationals from certain countries to prevent terrorism and is rationally related to achieving these monitoring objectives. *See Narenji v. Civiletti*, 617 F.2d 745, 747 (D.C.Cir.1979) (finding there was a rational basis for the special registration of Iranian students after the taking of hostages in the United States embassy in Iran).

It is worth emphasizing that the decision to remove Petitioner was based on the fact that he had overstayed his visa, not based on his national origin. To be sure, Moroccan nationals were required to register with DHS while a person in the same situation but not from one of the NSEERS countries would not have been placed in removal proceedings. However, a claim of selective enforcement based on national origin is virtually precluded by *Reno v. American-Arab Anti-Discrimination Committee,* 525 U.S. 471(1999) (involving Palestinians affiliated with a political group targeted for deportation for routine immigration violations). In *Reno,* the Supreme Court held that courts lack jurisdiction *** over most selective prosecution claims: "When an alien's continuing presence in this country is in violation of the immigration laws, the Government does not offend the Constitution by deporting him for the additional reason that it believes him to be a member of an organization that supports terrorist activity." The Supreme Court did, however, leave open "the possibility of a rare case in which the alleged basis of discrimination is so outrageous that the foregoing considerations can be overcome."   *** There is nothing in this record to demonstrate outrageous discrimination.

Finally, in a twist on an earlier contention, Petitioner asserts that the evidence derived from the examination, specifically from the passport, should be suppressed because the seizure was a violation of the Fourth Amendment and was fundamentally unfair.   While the seizure is troubling because the government has cited no legal authority for holding the passport, Kandamar has not demonstrated any prejudice resulting from the seizure that would warrant reversal of the removal order here.   In this case, Kandamar admitted his identity at each of the IJ hearings.   The government had a copy of Kandamar's I-94 departure record, which establishes Kandamar's temporary admission into the United States and his overstay, in its own files. Certainly, there can be little doubt about DHS's authority to inspect and photograph the passport and other documentation.   Therefore, in light of the availability of untainted government records and lack of egregious government misconduct, any error that occurred from a seizure would be harmless. ***

Notes

1. Gotcha. Kandamar voluntarily showed up in response to the NSEERS process. Then his passport was wrongly confiscated. The court holds he has no redress. Why? Was the FBI wrong to use minor immigration violations against people who might have a connection to terrorism?

2. Policy Problems? What do you think was the impact of the NSEERS program on immigrant communities in the US? Did it make them more or less likely to help in the identification of potential terrorists?

3. Equal Protection. Were you surprised that the court held that racial profiling did not violate the equal protection clause? Does the court apply traditional strict scrutiny analysis? What level scrutiny is involved?

4. Exclusionary Rule. What evidence does Kandamar seek to have excluded and why?

5. Constitutional Interpretation. Did the events of 9/11 change the standard for interpreting the Constitution? Did they change the rights of foreign nationals who were here legally before 9/11?

6. Liability of Officials for Wrongful Detention of Immigrants. Review Iqbal v. Hasty supra Chapter III. Recall from whom Iqbal was seeking damages and why the Supreme Court denied relief. Would monetary relief possibly be available from jailers of detainees after Iqbal an if so, on what theories? Is the remedial framework altered at all when the detainee is an immigrant as opposed to a material witness or military detainee?

7. Institutional Decisionmaking. Who should decide whether an individual with alleged terrorist ties should be segregated? Who should decide whether to impose "harsh conditions" during confinement? Do your answers change if the detainee is an immigrant subject to deportation?

8. **Mathews Factors.** Why was it acceptable to place Iqbal in the SHU without notice and a chance for rebuttal, but not acceptable to keep him there? Which one of the Mathews factors shifted in Iqbal's favor with the longer detention?

D. DEPORTATION OF ALLEGED TERRORISTS

Deportation proceedings are administrative rather than judicial proceedings, but in many respects follow standard models for adversary proceedings, with full involvement of counsel, pleadings and hearing processes before an Immigration Judge, appeals to a specialized Board of Immigration Appeals, and review by the federal courts. The cases which follow concern departures from normal administrative adjudicatory processes. The first concerns secret evidence in deportation cases involving alleged terrorists. The second concerns "special interest" cases closed to the public because of alleged terrorism-based national security concerns.

AMERICAN-ARAB ANTI-DISCRIMINATION COMMITTEE v. RENO
70 F. 3d 1045 (C.A. 9, 1995)

D.W. NELSON, Circuit Judge:

*** After initiating deportation proceedings, the INS arrested the eight named aliens in this case in January 1987. They were detained for several weeks in maximum security prisons and then released pending the outcome of deportation proceedings. The INS charged all but Mungai under various provisions of the McCarran-Walter Act of 1952 ("the 1952 Act") for membership in an organization, the Popular Front for the Liberation of Palestine ("PFLP"), that allegedly advocates the doctrines of world communism. *** In April 1987, the individual plaintiffs and several organizations initiated an action for damages, a declaration that the provisions of the 1952 Act under which the eight were charged are unconstitutional facially and as applied, and injunctive relief against the investigation, arrest, and deportation of aliens pursuant to the challenged provisions. *** Later, the INS added a charge *** alleging that Hamide and Shehadeh were associated with a group that advocates the unlawful assaulting or killing of government officers.

In April and May of 1987, former FBI director William Webster testified to Congress that "[a]ll of them were arrested because they are alleged to be members of a world-wide Communist organization which under the McCarran Act makes them eligible for deportation ... in this particular case if these individuals had been United States citizens, there would not have been a basis for their arrest." ***

On April 5, 1991, after the repeal of the 1952 Act, the INS instituted new proceedings against permanent resident aliens Hamide and Shehadeh under the "terrorist activity" provision of the Immigration Act of 1990 ("the IMMACT") (rendering deportable "[a]ny alien who has engaged, is engaged, or at any time after entry engages in terrorist activity ***." *** All eight aliens then filed suit in district court claiming that the INS had singled them out for selective enforcement of the immigration laws based on the impermissible motive of retaliation for constitutionally protected associational activity. *** Meanwhile, in June of 1987, Barakat and Sharif applied for legalization under the IRCA. In 1991, they received Notices of Intent to Deny because the INS, using undisclosed classified information, considered them excludable ["members of or affiliated with any organization that advocates or teaches ... (ii) the duty, necessity, or propriety of the unlawful assaulting or killing of any officer or officers (either of specific individuals or of officers generally) of the Government of the United States or of any other organized government, because of his or their official character"]. Barakat and Sharif filed suit in district court challenging the use of classified information on several grounds, including a due process claim. The district court found that it had jurisdiction, and it issued a preliminary injunction against the confidential use of classified information. Following an *in camera, ex parte* examination of materials provided by the INS, the court concluded that use of the undisclosed information against Barakat and Sharif would constitute a due process violation, and it granted a permanent injunction against its use on January 24, 1995.

*** The Government does not dispute that the Due Process Clause protects Barakat and Sharif, but it contends that reliance on undisclosed information to determine legalization satisfies the demands of due process.

b. Statutory and Regulatory Authority for Summary Process

*** At the time that Barakat and Sharif applied for legalization, the INS regulations required that all issues of statutory eligibility for immigration benefits, including legalization, be determined solely on the basis of information in the record disclosed to the applicant***. However, after a three-year delay, the INS finally issued Notices of Intent to Deny to Barakat and Sharif in March 1991, pursuant to amended regulations, effective upon publication as interim rules in January 1991, that extended the confidential use of classified information to statutory entitlement determinations. The INS claimed that the information's "protection from unauthorized disclosure is required in the interests of national security *** "

The Government cites section 235(c) of the Immigration and Nationality Act, 8 U.S.C. § 1225(c) (as amended), as authority for use of the undisclosed classified information in the legalization determination. That statute establishes the powers of INS officers to inspect aliens "seeking admission or readmission," to temporarily detain aliens who are not entitled to enter "at the port of arrival," and to exclude aliens on the particular finding by the Attorney General that confidential information supports that exclusion, 8 U.S.C. § 1225(c) (allowing summary process for exclusion). We do not, however, accept the proposition that denying a resident alien legalization is the same thing as "exclusion".

Use of summary process in settings other than exclusion raises troubling due process concerns. *** [E]ven reentering permanent resident aliens, who enjoy few rights because of the admitted power of Congress over entry into the country, are entitled to additional due process safeguards when subjected to the summary exclusion process. ***

This limitation of the classified information provision to the exclusion context comports with the requirement that administrative and judicial review of deportation orders be based on "reasonable, substantial, and probative evidence on the record considered as a whole." 8 U.S.C. § 1105a(a)(4); *see Whetstone v. INS,* 561 F.2d 1303, 1306 (9th Cir.1977) (finding that "[d]eportation on a charge not presented in the order to show cause, or at the hearing, would offend due process" because record evidence must establish the basis for deportation). Because legalization decisions are reviewable under the deportation review provisions, the statutory scheme does not support use of summary process which relies on secret information as an alternative to regular hearing requirements. ***

c. The Mathews Balancing Test

(1) The Private Interest Affected

Aliens who have resided for more than a decade in this country, even those whose status is now unlawful because of technical visa violations, have a strong liberty interest in remaining in their homes. Similarly, the denial of legalization impacts the opportunity of an alien to work, which also raises constitutional concerns. The statute provides an entitlement not subject to denial according to the discretion of the Attorney General, as long as the eligibility requirements are satisfied. Thus, the district court did not err in finding that the private interests affected are truly substantial.

(2) The Risk of Erroneous Deprivation and Value of Safeguards

There is no direct evidence in the record to show what percentage of decisions utilizing undisclosed classified information result in error; yet, as the district court below stated, "One would be hard pressed to design a procedure more likely to result in erroneous deprivations." Without any opportunity for confrontation, there is no adversarial check on the quality of the information on which the INS relies. *** [T]he very foundation of the adversary process assumes that use of undisclosed information will violate due process because of the risk of error. We conclude that the district court did not err in finding that there is an exceptionally high risk of erroneous deprivation when undisclosed information is used to determine the merits of the admissibility inquiry.

(3) The Governmental Interest

The Government seeks to use undisclosed information to achieve its desired outcome of prohibiting these individuals whom it perceives to be threats to national security from remaining in the United States while protecting its confidential sources involved in the investigation of terrorist organizations. Yet the Government has offered no evidence to demonstrate that these particular aliens threaten the national security of this country. In fact, the Government claims that it need not. It relies on general pronouncements in two State Department publications about the PFLP's involvement in global terrorism and on the President's recent broad

Executive Order prohibiting "any United States persons" from transacting business with the PFLP. *See* Exec.Order No. 12947 (January 23, 1995) (finding "that grave acts of violence committed by foreign terrorists that disrupt the Middle East peace process constitute an unusual and extraordinary threat to the national security, foreign policy, and economy of the United States"). We take judicial notice of these government documents on appeal for the limited purpose of assessing the strength of the Government's interest, yet we find these data insufficient to tip the *Mathews* scale towards the Government. These aliens have been free since the beginning of this litigation almost eight years ago, without criminal charges being brought against them for their activities. According to the district court, the government's *in camera* submission targets the PFLP: although it indicates that the PFLP advocates prohibited doctrines and that the aliens are members, it does not indicate that either alien has personally advocated those doctrines or has participated in terrorist activities.

If Barakat and Sharif engage in any deportable activities, the government is not precluded from contesting their legalization or from instituting deportation on the basis of non-secret information. If the Government chooses not to reveal its information in order to protect its sources, the only risk it faces is that attendant to tolerance of Barakat's and Sharif's presence so long as they do not engage in deportable activities. Thus, although the Government undoubtedly has a legitimate interest in protecting its confidential investigations, it has not demonstrated a strong interest in this case in accomplishing its goal of protecting its information while prohibiting these aliens' legalization.

The Government's attempt to bolster its interest by relying on permitted uses of undisclosed information is misguided. Although the courts have allowed the Government to keep certain information confidential, the exceptions to full disclosure are narrowly circumscribed. For example, a formal claim of a "state secrets privilege" may prevent discovery and shield the use of materials against the Government in tort litigation for damages. However, the failure to disclose information prevents its use in the adversary proceeding: the effect of upholding the privilege is "that the evidence is unavailable, as though a witness had died." Even in those rare cases when the privilege operates as a complete shield to the government and results in the dismissal of a plaintiff's suit, the information is simply unavailable and may not be used by either side. Here, the Government does not seek to shield state information from disclosure in the adjudication of a tort claim against it; instead, it seeks to use secret information as a sword against the aliens.

Because of the danger of injustice when decisions lack the procedural safeguards that form the core of constitutional due process, the *Mathews* balancing suggests that use of undisclosed information in adjudications should be presumptively unconstitutional. Only the most extraordinary circumstances could support one-sided process. We cannot in good conscience find that the President's broad generalization regarding a distant foreign policy concern and a related national security threat suffices to support a process that is inherently unfair because of the enormous risk of error and the substantial personal interests involved. *** [U]se of undisclosed classified information under these circumstances violates due process. *** [W]e affirm the Court's issuance of a permanent injunction against the use of undisclosed classified information in legalization proceedings pursuant to § 1255a.

Notes

1. **Statutory Authority.** Did Congress approve use of secret evidence in deportation cases? If there is statutory silence, what should guide the courts? Is suspension of deportation entirely in the AG's discretion? If so, does it mater whether the AG uses secret information?

2. **Secret Evidence and Accurate Decisions**. Isn't there a significant danger that secret evidence may be "malicious, untrue, unreliable, or inaccurately reported" and the defendant have no opportunity to reply to such falsehoods? See Jay v. Boyd, 351 U.S. 345 (1956) (majority unconcerned; dissenters worried). If the secret evidence is from foreign language sources, isn't there also a danger of mistranslation?

3. **Alternatives.** What might solve secret evidence problems short of disclosure to defendants themselves? Disclosure to their counsel? How about providing written summaries of the evidence to the defendants and/or their counsel? Should counsel be required to have security clearances? Could the immigration judge be given a more proactive role? Should the judge be security cleared?

4. **State Secrets.** The government may keep secret evidence in a case that it believes would compromise state security. What showing must the government make to prevail on exclusion of evidence that the defendant would like to have admitted (sometimes called "graymail")? Is the immigration judge competent to make such decisions? Should the level of showing be different in immigration cases than in other proceedings?

5. **Alien Terrorist Removal Court.** The Antiterrorism and Effective Death Penalty Act of 1996 (P.L. 104-132) created the Alien Terrorist Removal Court, consisting of five U.S. District Court judges. The Attorney General may bring petitions before the court for removal of aliens on the ground that they are terrorists. The court is modeled after the FISA courts and its decisions are appealable to the U.S. Court of Appeals for the District of Columbia.

*****

The following case challenges the security measures to be applied to in immigration court proceedings involving deportation of an alleged terrorist or a person who allegedly has ties to terrorists. In particular, it concerns the extent to which immigration hearings should be open to the public and to the media.

NORTH JERSEY MEDIA GROUP v. ASHCROFT
308 F.3d 198 (C.A. 3, 2002)

BECKER, Chief Judge.

This civil action was brought *** by a consortium of media groups seeking access to "special interest" deportation hearings involving persons whom the Attorney General has determined might have connections to or knowledge of the September 11, 2001 terrorist attacks. This category was created by a directive issued by Michael Creppy, the Chief United States Immigration Judge, outlining additional security measures to be applied in this class of cases, including closing hearings to the public and the press. *** The District *** held that the case was governed by the test developed in *Richmond Newspapers, Inc. v. Virginia,* 448 U.S. 555 (1980), a murder case in which the trial judge had ordered that the courtroom be cleared of all persons except witnesses. In striking down the closure order, the Supreme Court noted an "unbroken, uncontradicted history" of public access to criminal trials in Anglo American law running from "before the Norman Conquest" to the present. It emphasized that it had not found "a single instance of a criminal trial conducted in camera in any federal, state, or municipal court during the history of this country." The Supreme Court held that the right of the press and public to attend criminal trials "is implicit in the guarantees of the First Amendment." While the Court acknowledged the State's argument that the Constitution nowhere explicitly guarantees the public's right to attend criminal trials, it nonetheless held the right implicit due to the fact that the Framers drafted the Constitution against a backdrop of popular access.***

The only Circuit to deal with these issues has resolved them in favor of the media. *See Detroit Free Press v. Ashcroft,* 303 F.3d 681(6th Cir.2002). However, we find ourselves in disagreement with the Sixth Circuit. In our view the tradition of openness of deportation proceedings does not meet the standard required by *Richmond Newspaper,***. Deportation procedures have been codified for approximately 100 years but, despite their constant reenactment during that time, Congress has never explicitly guaranteed public access. Indeed, deportation cases involving abused alien children are mandatorily closed by statute, and hearings are often conducted in places generally inaccessible to the public. While INS regulations promulgated in 1964 create a *rebuttable* presumption of openness for most deportation cases, we conclude that a recently-created regulatory presumption of openness with significant statutory exceptions does not present the type of "unbroken, uncontradicted history" that *Richmond Newspapers* and its progeny require to establish a First Amendment right of access.

The most difficult case for the government is *FMC v. South Carolina State Ports Authority,* 535 U.S. 743 (2002). *** We recognize that, at least since the 1960s, formalized deportation proceedings have borne an undeniable procedural resemblance to civil trials, and that, read broadly, *Ports Authority*'s language might therefore suggest that the same First Amendment rights exist in each context. While we find the issue debatable, as we explain more extensively *infra,* we believe that *Ports Authority*'s approach was inextricably tied to its underlying premise that sovereign immunity shields nonconsenting states from complaints brought by private persons, regardless of where private persons bring those complaints. In contrast, we find that there has never been a fundamental right of access to all government proceedings. Even today, many are closed by statute, including such frequent and important matters as Social Security hearings. Without a fundamental right of access comparable to nonconsenting states' right to freedom from private claims, we decline to loose *Ports Authority* from its Eleventh Amendment moorings. ***

This case arises in the wake of September 11, 2001, a day on which American life changed drastically and dramatically. The era that dawned on September 11th, and the war against terrorism that has pervaded the sinews of our national life since that day, are reflected in thousands of ways in legislative and national policy, the habits of daily living, and our collective psyches. *** As we will now explain in detail, we find that the application of the *Richmond Newspapers* experience and logic tests does not compel us to declare the Creppy Directive unconstitutional. ***

A. The Creppy Directive

Shortly after the attacks of September 11, 2001, the President ordered a worldwide investigation into those atrocities and related terrorist threats to the United States. Over the course of this ongoing investigation, the government has become aware of numerous aliens who are subject to removal from the United States for violating immigration laws. The Immigration and Naturalization Service has detained and initiated removal proceedings against many of these individuals.

The Department of Justice, which oversees the INS, has identified some aliens whose situations are particularly sensitive and designated their hearings "special interest" cases. According to Dale L. Watson, the FBI's Executive Assistant Director for Counterterrorism and Counterintelligence, the designated aliens "might have connections with, or possess information pertaining to, terrorist activities against the United States." (Watson Dec.) For example, special interest cases include aliens who had close associations with the September 11 hijackers or who themselves have associated with al Qaeda or related terrorist groups.

The Department of Justice has reviewed these designations periodically and removed them in many cases that it determined were less sensitive than previously believed. For those cases that retain the "special interest" designation, however, Chief Immigration Judge Creppy issued a memorandum (the "Creppy Directive") implementing heightened security measures. The Directive requires immigration judges "to close the hearing[s] to the public, and to avoid discussing the case[s] or otherwise disclosing any information about the case[s] to anyone outside the Immigration Court." It further instructs that "[t]he courtroom must be closed for these cases-no visitors, no family, and no press," and explains that the restriction even "includes confirming or denying whether such a case is on the docket or scheduled for a hearing." In short, the Directive contemplates a complete information blackout along both substantive and procedural dimensions.

In closing special interest deportation hearings, the Government's stated purpose is to avoid disclosing potentially sensitive information to those who may pose an ongoing security threat to the United States and its interests. The Government represents that "if evidence is offered about a particular phone number link between a detainee and a number connected to a terrorist organization or member," the terrorists "will be on notice that the

United States is now aware of the link" and "may even be able to determine what sources and methods the United States used to become aware of that link." (Watson Declaration.) Equally important, however, is "information that might appear innocuous in isolation [but that] can be fit into a bigger picture by terrorist groups in order to thwart the Government's efforts to investigate and prevent terrorism." (*Id.*) For example, information about how and why special interest aliens were detained "would allow the terrorist organizations to discern patterns and methods of investigation"; information about how such aliens entered the country "would allow the terrorist organization to see patterns of entry, what works and what doesn't"; and information "about what evidence the United States has against members of a particular cell collectively" would reveal to the terrorist organization which of its cells have been significantly compromised. (*Id.*)

The Government offers a litany of harms that might flow from open hearings. Most obviously, terrorist organizations could alter future attack plans, or devise new, easier ways to enter the country through channels they learn are relatively unguarded by the Department of Justice. They might also obstruct or disrupt pending proceedings by destroying evidence, threatening potential witnesses, or targeting the hearings themselves. Finally, if the government cannot guarantee a closed hearing, aliens might be deterred from cooperating with the ongoing investigation. *** While we agree with the District Court's conclusion that *Richmond Newspapers* analysis is proper in the administrative context, we disagree with its application and hold that under that test, there is no First Amendment right to attend deportation proceedings.***

B. *Applicability of* Richmond Newspapers *to Administrative Proceedings*

The Government contends that while *Richmond Newspapers* properly applies to civil and criminal proceedings under Article III, the Constitution's text militates against extending First Amendment rights to non-Article III proceedings such as deportation. Its premise is one of *expressio unius est exclusio alterius:* Article III is silent on the question of public access to judicial trials, but the Sixth Amendment expressly incorporates the common law tradition of public trials, thus supporting the notion that the First Amendment likewise incorporates that tradition for Article III purposes. (Gov't Brief at 21-22.) Articles I and II, conversely, *do* address the question of access, and they *do not* provide for Executive or Legislative proceedings to be open to the public. To the Government, the absence of an explicit guarantee of access for Article I and II proceedings (as exists in Article III) gives rise to a distinction with a difference because, without an incorporating provision parallel to the Sixth Amendment, the Framers must have intended to deny the public access to political proceedings.

The Government's suggestion is ultimately that we should not apply *Richmond Newspapers* where the Constitution's structure dictates that no First Amendment right applies, and should instead let the political branches (here, the Executive, acting through the Justice Department) determine the proper degree of access to administrative proceedings.

Our own jurisprudence precludes this approach *** *Richmond Newspapers* requires that when a court assesses a claimed First Amendment right of access, it must "consider[ ] whether the place and process have historically been open to the press and general public ... [and] whether public access plays a significant positive role in the functioning of the particular process in question." This language seems to place the burden of proof on the party alleging a First Amendment right. While we acknowledge a current presumption of openness in most deportation proceedings, we find that this presumption has neither the pedigree nor uniformity necessary to satisfy *Richmond Newspapers*'s first prong. We also conclude that under a logic inquiry properly acknowledging both community benefits *and* potential harms, public access does not serve a "significant positive role" in deportation hearings. ***

*A. The "Experience" Test ***

2. Is the history of open deportation proceedings sufficient to satisfy the *Richmond Newspapers* "experience" prong?

For a First Amendment right of access to vest under *Richmond Newspapers,* we must consider whether "the place and process have historically been open to the press and general public," because such a "tradition of accessibility implies the favorable judgment of experience." Noting preliminarily that the question whether a proceeding has been "historically open" is only arguably an objective inquiry, we nonetheless find that based on both Supreme Court and Third Circuit precedents, the tradition of open deportation hearings is too recent and inconsistent to support a First Amendment right of access. ***

In *Richmond Newspapers* itself, the Court noted an "unbroken, uncontradicted history" of public access to criminal trials in Anglo American law running from "before the Norman Conquest" to the present, and it emphasized that it had not found "a single instance of a criminal trial conducted in camera in any federal, state, or municipal court during the history of this country." Likewise, in *Publicker,* 733 F.2d at 1059, we found that access to civil trials at common law was "beyond dispute."

The tradition of open deportation hearings is simply not comparable. While the *expressio unius* distinction between exclusion and deportation proceedings is a tempting road to travel, we are unwilling effectively to craft a constitutional right from mere Congressional silence, especially when faced with evidence that some deportation proceedings were, and are, explicitly closed to the public or conducted in places unlikely to allow general public access. Although the 1964 Department of Justice regulations did create a presumption of openness, a recent-and-rebuttable-regulatory presumption is hardly the stuff of which Constitutional rights are forged. ***

3. Relaxing the *Richmond Newspapers* experience requirement would lead to perverse consequences.

As we have explained in detail *supra,* there is no fundamental right of access to administrative proceedings. Any such access, therefore, must initially be granted as a matter of executive grace. The Government contends that by relaxing the need for a "1000-year tradition of public access," we would permanently constitutionalize a right of access whenever an executive agency does not consistently bar all public access to a particular proceeding. We do not adopt this reasoning in its entirety, for *** we have sometimes found a constitutional right of access to proceedings that did not exist at common law.

Nevertheless, we agree with the Government that a rigorous experience test is necessary to preserve the "basic tenet of administrative law that agencies should be free to fashion their own rules of procedure." Were we to adopt the Newspapers' view that we can recognize a First Amendment right based solely on the logic prong if there is no history of closure, we would effectively compel the Executive to close its proceedings to the public *ab initio* or risk creating a constitutional right of access that would preclude it from closing them in the future. Under such a system, reserved powers of closure would be meaningless. It seems possible that, ironically, such a system would result in less public access than one in which a constitutional right of access is more difficult to create.

At all events, we would find this outcome incredible in an area of traditional procedural flexibility, and we are unwilling to reach it when a reasonable alternative is present. By insisting on a strong tradition of public access in the *Richmond Newspapers* test, we preserve administrative flexibility and avoid constitutionalizing ambiguous, and potentially unconsidered, executive decisions. ***

In this case the Government presented substantial evidence that open deportation hearings would threaten national security. Although the District Court discussed these concerns as part of its strict scrutiny analysis, they are equally applicable to the question whether openness, on balance, serves a positive role in removal hearings. We find that upon factoring them into the logic equation, it is doubtful that openness promotes the public good in this context.

The Government's security evidence is contained in the declaration of Dale Watson, the FBI's Executive Assistant Director for Counterterrorism and Counterintelligence. Watson presents a range of potential dangers, the most pressing of which we describe here.

First, public hearings would necessarily reveal sources and methods of investigation. That is information which, "when assimilated with other information the United States may or may not have in hand, allows a terrorist organization to build a picture of the investigation." (Watson Dec. at 4.) Even minor pieces of evidence that might appear innocuous to us would provide valuable clues to a person within the terrorist network, clues that may allow them to thwart the government's efforts to investigate and prevent future acts of violence. *Id.*

Second, "information about how any given individual entered the country (from where, when, and how) may not divulge significant information that would reveal sources and methods of investigation. However, putting entry information into the public realm regarding all 'special interest cases' would allow the terrorist organization to see patterns of entry, what works and what doesn't." *Id.* That information would allow it to tailor future entries to exploit weaknesses in the United States immigration system.

Third, "[i]nformation about what evidence the United States has against members of a particular cell collectively will inform the terrorist organization as to what cells to use and which not to use for further plots and attacks." *Id.* A related concern is that open hearings would reveal what evidence the government lacks. For example, the United States may disclose in a public hearing certain evidence it possesses about a member of a terrorist organization. If that detainee is actually involved in planning an attack, opening the hearing might allow the organization to know that the United States is not yet aware of the attack based on the evidence it presents at the open hearing. *Id.*

Fourth, if a terrorist organization discovers that a particular member is detained, or that information about a plot is known, it may accelerate the timing of a planned attack, thus reducing the amount of time the government has to detect and prevent it. If acceleration is impossible, it may still be able to shift the planned activity to a yet-undiscovered cell. *Id.* at 7.

Fifth, a public hearing involving evidence about terrorist links could allow terrorist organizations to interfere with the pending proceedings by creating false or misleading evidence. Even more likely, a terrorist might destroy existing evidence or make it more difficult to obtain, such as by threatening or tampering with potential witnesses. Should potential informants not feel secure in coming forward, that would greatly impair the ongoing investigation. *Id.*

Sixth, INS detainees have a substantial privacy interest in having their possible connection to the ongoing investigation kept undisclosed. *Id.* at 8."Although some particular detainees may choose to identify themselves, it is important to note that as to all INS detainees whose cases have been placed in the special interest category concerns remain about their connection to terrorism, and specifically to the worst attack ever committed on United States soil. Although they may eventually be found to have no connection to terrorist activity, discussion of the causes of their apprehension in open court would forever connect them to the September 11 attacks." *Id.* While this stigma concern exists to some extent in many criminal prosecutions, it is noteworthy that deportation hearings are regulatory, not punitive, and there is often no evidence of any criminal wrongdoing.

Finally, Watson represents that "the government cannot proceed to close hearings on a case-by-case basis, as the identification of certain cases for closure, and the introduction of evidence to support that closure, could itself expose critical information about which activities and patterns of behavior merit such closure." (Watson Dec. at 8-9.) Moreover, he explains, given judges' relative lack of expertise regarding national security and their inability to see the mosaic, we should not entrust to them the decision whether an isolated fact is sensitive enough to warrant closure.

The Newspapers are undoubtedly correct that the representations of the Watson Declaration are to some degree speculative, at least insofar as there is no concrete evidence that closed deportation hearings have prevented, or will prevent, terrorist attacks. But the *Richmond Newspapers* logic prong is unavoidably speculative, for it is impossible to weigh objectively, for example, the community benefit of emotional catharsis against the security risk of disclosing the United States' methods of investigation and the extent of its knowledge. We are quite hesitant to conduct a judicial inquiry into the credibility of these security concerns, as national security is an area where courts have traditionally extended great deference to Executive expertise. *See, e.g., Zadvydas v. Davis,* (noting that "terrorism or other special circumstances" might warrant "heightened deference to the judgments of the political branches with respect to matters of national security"). The assessments before us have been made by senior government officials responsible for investigating the events of September 11th and for preventing future attacks. These officials believe that closure of special interest hearings is necessary to advance these goals, and their concerns, as expressed in the Watson Declaration, have gone unrebutted. To the extent that the Attorney General's national security concerns seem credible, we will not lightly second-guess them.[15]

We are keenly aware of the dangers presented by deference to the executive branch when constitutional liberties are at stake, especially in times of national crisis, when those liberties are likely in greatest jeopardy. On balance, however, we are unable to conclude that openness plays a positive role in special interest deportation hearings at a time when our nation is faced with threats of such profound and unknown dimension.

*** Deportation proceedings' history of openness is quite limited, and their presumption of openness quite weak. They plainly do not present the type of "unbroken, uncontradicted history" that *Richmond Newspapers* and its progeny require to establish a First Amendment right of access. We do not decide that there is no right to attend administrative proceedings, or even that there is no right to attend any immigration proceeding. Our judgment is confined to the extremely narrow class of deportation cases that are determined by the Attorney General to present significant national security concerns. In recognition his experience (and our lack of experience) in this field, we will defer to his judgment. We note that although there may be no judicial remedy for these closures, there is, as always, the powerful check of political accountability on Executive discretion. ***

---

[15] ***[W]e do not here defer to the Executive on the basis of its plenary power over immigration. We do not question that the "power to expel or exclude aliens" is "a fundamental sovereign attribute ... largely immune from judicial control," for indeed there is no dispute as to the government's substantive power to expel the special interest detainees. Rather, what is at stake is the *means* the government has chosen to exercise that plenary power. ***The issue at stake in the Newspapers' suit is not the Attorney General's power to expel aliens, but rather his power to exclude reporters from those proceedings. This is plainly a constitutional challenge to the means he has chosen to effect a permissible end, and under *Zadvydas* we owe no executive deference. We defer only to the executive insofar as it is expert in matters of national security, not constitutional liberties.

Others have been less impressed. Michael Kelly has written in the Washington Post: *"Democracies die behind closed doors".* So they do, sometimes. But far more democracies have succumbed to open assaults of one sort or another-invasions from without, military coups and totalitarian revolutions from within-than from the usurpation-by-in-camera-incrementalism that Judge Keith fears.

Democracy in America does at this moment face a serious threat. But it is not the threat the judge has in mind, at least not directly. It is true that last September's unprecedented mass-slaughter of American citizens on American soil inevitably forced the government to take security measures that infringed on some rights and privileges. But these do not in themselves represent any real threat to democracy. A real threat could arise, however, should the government fail in its mission to prevent another September 11. If that happens, the public will demand, and will get, immense restrictions on liberties.

Although Mr. Kelly ultimately sided with openness on a case-by-case basis, we find his quoted statements powerful. They certainly seem appropriate to the decision to close the deportation hearings of those who may have been affiliated with the persons responsible for the events of September 11th, all of the known perpetrators of which were aliens. And they are consonant with the reality that the persons most directly affected by the Creppy Directive are the media, not the aliens who may be deported. As always, these aliens are given a heavy measure of due process-the right to appeal the decision of the Immigration Judge (following the closed hearing) to the Board of Immigration Appeals (BIA) and the right to petition for review of the BIA decision to the Regional Court of Appeals. ***

SCIRICA, Circuit Judge, dissenting.

At issue is not whether some or all deportation hearings of special interest aliens should be closed, but who makes that determination. *** The Constitution is silent on the right to public access. But the Supreme Court has framed a qualified right of access that may be overcome by sound reasons. Because no reason is more compelling than national security, closure of special interest alien deportation hearings may well be warranted. *** I would find a qualified right of access to deportation hearings. Because I believe that Immigration Judges can make these determinations with substantial deference to national security, I would affirm the District Court's judgment. ***

Congress has provided for presumptively open deportation proceedings from the moment that it first enacted an immigration statutory framework. This century of unbroken openness, especially within the nascent tradition of the administrative state, "implies the favorable judgment of experience" under the *Richmond Newspapers* test. *** Public access to deportation hearings serves the same positive functions as does openness in criminal and civil trials. But the logic inquiry cannot consist merely of a recitation of the factors supporting open proceedings. *** I agree with the majority that the District Court erred in failing to consider the countervailing interest of national security.

The issue in this case is "whether the press and public have a First Amendment right to attend deportation hearings." The logic analysis set forth by the Supreme Court is directed at a particular structural type of proceeding-in this case, deportation hearings-not a subset based on specific designations such as terrorism. *** At this stage, we must consider the value of openness in deportation hearings generally, not its benefits and detriments in "special interest" deportation hearings in particular. If a qualified right of access is found to attach to deportation hearings generally, the analysis *then* turns to whether particular issues raised in individual cases override the general limited right of access.

Were the logic analysis focused only on special interest cases, I would agree that national security would likely trump the arguments in favor of access. Although paramount in certain deportation cases-like terrorism-national security is not generally implicated in the panoply of deportation hearings that occur throughout the United States. There are many grounds for deportation-marriage fraud, moral turpitude convictions, and aggravated felonies, to name a few-that do not ordinarily implicate national security.

Accordingly, the demands of national security under the logic prong of *Richmond Newspapers* do not provide sufficient justification for rejecting a qualified right of access to deportation hearings in general. To conclude otherwise would permit concerns relevant only to a discrete class of cases to determine there is no qualified right of access to *any* of the broad range of deportation proceedings, a departure from *Richmond Newspapers*. Whether national security interests justify closure of individual deportation hearings is a question properly addressed in the next step's more particularized inquiry.

Having found a qualified right of access to deportation hearings, the question remains whether the government has a sufficient justification to "override the qualified First Amendment right of access" by application of the Creppy Directive.

Where a qualified right of access has been found, courts ordinarily have required a substantial showing to deny access. *** The District Court found the Creppy Directive failed to pass muster under this test because, inter alia, it was "not persuaded that the more narrow method of *in camera* disclosure of sensitive evidence ... is not an acceptable means of avoiding a compromise of the government's investigation."

The government contends it is entitled to greater deference than is captured in this test because of two independent considerations. First, it contends it enjoys broad deference in the immigration area. And second, it argues the District Court erred in failing to afford it the special deference due the political branches in matters concerning national security.

The District Court undervalued the deference due the government in national security cases. Courts have consistently recognized the need for "heightened deference to the judgments of the political branches with respect to matters of national security" when "terrorism or other special circumstances" are at issue. *Zadvydas,* 533 U.S. at 696, 121 S.Ct. 2491. A "principle of judicial deference ... pervades the area of national security." *Franklin v. Massachusetts,* 505 U.S. 788, 818 (1992). Consequently, courts have not demanded that the government's action be the one the court itself deems most appropriate in "cases involving discrete categories of governmental action in which there are special reasons to defer to the judgment of the political branches."

On the other hand, deference is not a basis for abdicating our responsibilities under the First Amendment. At issue is whether the Creppy Directive constitutes an impermissible restriction on the press and public's right of access to deportation hearings. Moreover, there is no apparent reason to abandon the traditional framework for assessing the relative force of the government's interests as against the right of access, so long as deference is afforded the judgments of the Executive Branch in these matters.

In this case, the government's asserted interest-national security-is exceedingly compelling. Closure in some-or perhaps all-special interest cases may be necessary and appropriate. In fact, the Department of Justice regulations, enacted in 1964, expressly authorize an Immigration Judge to hold closed hearings to protect the public interest. But the question remains whether the Creppy Directive's blanket closure rule-which removes the decision to close the hearing from the Immigration Judge on a case-by-case basis-is reasonably necessary for the protection of national security.

The government contends that a case-by-case closure of removal proceedings would permit the release of sensitive information, potentially revealing sources, patterns and methods of investigation. But there is no reason that all of the information related to a particular detainee cannot be kept from public view. Even the initial determination to close a proceeding- and to seal the entire record-can be accomplished in camera and under seal. The government need only make the required showing of special interest, under seal to the Immigration Judge, subject to appellate review. In making their determinations, Immigration Judges should grant substantial deference to national security interests. A similar procedural framework has proven workable with criminal prosecutions.[15]

The government maintains that these protections would be ineffective given the complexities in combating terrorism. It contends that individual, seemingly innocuous pieces of information, including a special interest alien's name, could be harmful to national security when compiled by terrorists into a mosaic. This seems correct. Nevertheless, the government could make the same argument to an Immigration Judge, who could determine, with

---

[15] The Classified Information Procedures Act provides for pretrial conferences and motion hearings to determine limits on the use and disclosure of classified and national security related information in criminal prosecutions. These proceedings may be held in camera and, in certain circumstances, ex parte. Congress also has created the Foreign Intelligence Surveillance Court to hold closed reviews of search warrant requests on a case-by-case basis, rejecting a framework where the Department of Justice makes its own judgments on these matters in national security cases.

substantial deference, that the apparently innocuous information provides appropriate grounds for closure.

The Watson Declaration also expresses the fear that open deportation hearings could provide evidence to terrorists that certain border crossings offer a greater chance for illegal entry than others. At oral argument, government counsel offered an intriguing hypothetical where open hearings would reveal evidence that 0-of-30 terrorists had entered the United States successfully through Philadelphia, while the rate was 30-of-30 in New York City. Here too, however, the government could make this argument during a closed preliminary hearing at which the Immigration Judge, with appropriate deference to national security, could assess the government's concerns about publicizing patterns of information.

The Creppy Directive and the pre-existing Department of Justice regulations both accommodate the government's national security responsibilities. But a case-by-case approach would permit an Immigration Judge to independently assess the balance of these fundamental values. Because this is a reasonable alternative, the Creppy Directive's blanket closure rule is constitutionally infirm. *** Because I believe national security interests can be fully accommodated on a case-by-case basis, I would affirm that part of the District Court's judgment. ***

Notes

1. **Balancing Values.** The picture of values clashing—national security versus the First Amendment—is misleading. Isn't it possible to reconcile the two through a process by which the executive does not have the exclusive say as to when national security is implicated? Isn't that what happens with CIPA evidence?

2. **Cert Denied.** Many (myself included) were surprised when the split in circuits between the Third and Sixth Circuits on the important issues involved did not lead the Supreme Court to grant cert in this case. Would a cert grant today, after media revelations concerning prisoner abuse, the Terrorist Surveillance Program, and other matters be positioned any differently than at the time this case was rejected?

3. **Privacy and Secrecy.** In times of external crisis, two trends seem to develop: decreased government sensitivity to citizen privacy and increased government secrecy. Can you explain why these trends occur simultaneously? Can you think of specific instances in the War on Terror and how they might be defused?

E. COMPARATIVE APPROACHES TO IMMIGRATION CONTROL

Some countries in Europe have taken a harder line on immigration than the United States. For example, Italy has enacted strict immigration controls and a campaign to fingerprint all Gypsies in the country despite a Council of Europe that said the policies "lack human rights and humanitarian principles and may spur further xenophobia." (The Associated Press, European rights watchdog criticizes Italian immigration crackdown, INTERNATIONAL HERALD TRIBUNE, July 29, 2008). Muslims have been even less welcome. Across Europe, there has been a backlash against mosque construction. Switzerland planned a national referendum in 2008 to ban the construction of minarets on mosques while a province in southern Austria required mosques to blend in with their surroundings, effectively banning them altogether. (Mosques increasingly not welcome in Europe, USA Today, July 17, 2008).

SECRETARY OF STATE FOR THE HOME DEPARTMENT v. REHMAN
(Consolidated Appeals) [2001] UKHL 47, [2003] 1 AC 153
(House of Lords, 2001)

LORD SLYNN OF HADLEY:

1. My Lords, Mr Rehman, the appellant, is a Pakistani national, born in June 1971 in Pakistan. He was educated and subsequently, after obtaining a master's degree in Islamic studies, taught at Jamiah Salfiah in Islamabad until January 1993. On 17 January 1993 he was given an entry clearance to enable him to work as a minister of religion with the Jamait Ahle-e-Hadith in Oldham. His father is such a minister in Halifax and both his parents are British citizens. He arrived here on 9 February 1993 and was subsequently given leave to stay until 9 February 1997 to allow him to complete four years as a minister. He married and has two children born in the United Kingdom. In October 1997 he was given leave to stay until 7 January 1998 to enable him to take his family to Pakistan from which he returned on 4 December 1997. He applied for indefinite leave to remain in the United Kingdom but that was refused on 9 December 1998. In his letter of refusal the Secretary of State said:

"the Secretary of State is satisfied, on the basis of the information he has received from confidential sources, that you are involved with an Islamic terrorist organisation Markaz Dawa Al Irshad (MDI). He is satisfied that in the light of your association with the MDI it is undesirable to permit you to remain and that your continued presence in this country represents a danger to national security. In these circumstances, the Secretary of State has decided to refuse your application for indefinite leave to remain in accordance with paragraph 322(5) of the Immigration Rules (HC 395).

"By virtue of section 2(1)(b) of the Special Immigration Appeals Commission Act 1997 you are entitled to appeal against the Secretary of State's decision as he has personally certified that [sic] your departure from the United Kingdom to be conducive to the public good in the interests of national security."

The Secretary of State added that his deportation from the United Kingdom would be conducive to the public good "in the interests of national security because of your association with Islamic terrorist groups". Mr Rehman was told that he was entitled to appeal, which he did, to the Special Immigration Appeals Commission by virtue of section 2(1)(c) of the Special Immigration Appeals Commission Act 1997. The Special Immigration Appeals Commission (Procedure) Rules 1998 (SI 1998/1881) allowed the Secretary of State to make both an open statement and a closed statement, only the former being disclosed to Mr Rehman. The Secretary of State in his open statement said:

> "The Security Service assesses that while Ur Rehman and his United Kingdom-based followers are unlikely to carry out any acts of violence in this country, his activities directly support terrorism in the Indian subcontinent and are likely to continue unless he is deported. Ur Rehman has also been partly responsible for an increase in the number of Muslims in the United Kingdom who have undergone some form of militant training, including indoctrination into extremist beliefs and at least some basic weapons training. The Security Service is concerned that the presence of returned jihad trainees in the United Kingdom may encourage the radicalisation of the British Muslim community. His activities in the United Kingdom are intended to further the cause of a terrorist organisation abroad. For this reason, the Secretary of State considers both that Ur Rehman poses a threat to national security and that he should be deported from the United Kingdom on [the] grounds that his presence here is not conducive to the public good for reasons of national security."

2. The appeal was heard both in open and in closed sessions. The Commission in its decision of 20 August 1999 held:

> "That the expression 'national security' should be construed narrowly, rather than in the wider sense contended for by the Secretary of State and identified in the passages from Mr. Sales's written submissions cited above. We recognise that there is no statutory definition of the term or legal authority directly on the point. *** In the circumstances, and for the purposes of this case, we adopt the position that a person may be said to offend against national security if he engages in, promotes, or encourages violent activity which is targeted at the United Kingdom, its system of government or its people. This includes activities directed against the overthrow or destabilization of a foreign government if that foreign government is likely to take reprisals against the United Kingdom which affect the security of the United Kingdom or

of its nationals. National security extends also to situations where United Kingdom citizens are targeted, wherever they may be. This is the definition of national security which should be applied to the issues of fact raised by this appeal".

3. They then considered the allegations of fact and they said:

"we have asked ourselves whether the Secretary of State has satisfied us to a high civil balance of probabilities that the deportation of this appellant, a lawful resident of the United Kingdom, is made out on public good grounds because he has engaged in conduct that endangers the national security of the United Kingdom and, unless deported, is likely to continue to do so. In answering this question we have to consider the material, open, closed, and restricted, the oral evidence of witnesses called by the respondent, and the evidence of the appellant produced before us. We are satisfied that this material and evidence enables us properly to reach a decision in this appeal ***."

4. The Commission declined to set out in detail their analysis of the "open", "restricted" and "closed" evidence on the basis that this would be capable of creating a serious injustice and they confined themselves to stating their conclusions, namely:

"1. Recruitment. We are not satisfied that the appellant has been shown to have recruited British Muslims to undergo militant training as alleged.

"2. We are not satisfied that the appellant has been shown to have engaged in fund-raising for the LT [Lashkar Tayyaba] as alleged.

"3. We are not satisfied that the appellant has been shown to have knowingly sponsored individuals for militant training camps as alleged.

"4. We are not satisfied that the evidence demonstrates the existence in the United Kingdom of returnees, originally recruited by the appellant, who during the course of that training overseas have been indoctrinated with extremist beliefs or given weapons training, and who as a result allow them to create a threat to the United Kingdom's national security in the future"

They added:

"We have reached all these conclusions while recognising that it is not disputed that the appellant has provided sponsorship, information and advice to persons going to Pakistan for the forms of training which may have included militant or extremist training. Whether the appellant knew of the militant content of such training has not, in our opinion, been satisfactorily established to the required standard by the evidence. Nor have we overlooked the appellant's statement that he sympathised with the aims of LT in so far as that organization confronted what he regarded as illegal violence in Kashmir. But, in our opinion, these sentiments do not justify the conclusion contended for by the respondent. It follows, from these conclusions of fact, that the respondent has not established that the appellant was, is, and is likely to be a threat to national security. In our view, that would be the case whether the wider or narrower definition of that term, as identified above, is taken as the test. Accordingly we consider that the respondent's decisions in question were not in accordance with the law or the Immigration Rules (paragraph 364 of HC 395) and thus we allow these appeals".

6. The Secretary of State appealed. The Court of Appeal considered that the Commission had taken too narrow a view of what could constitute a threat to national security in so far as it required the conduct relied on by the Secretary of State to be targeted at this country or its citizens. The Court of Appeal also considered *** that the test was not whether it had been shown "to a high degree of probability" that the individual was a danger to national security but that a global approach should be adopted "taking into account the executive's policy with regard to national security". Accordingly they allowed the appeal and remitted the matter to the Commission for redetermination applying the approach indicated in their judgment. ***

8. The 1971 Act contemplates first a decision by the Secretary of State to make a deportation order under section 3(5) of that Act, in the present case in respect of a person who is not a British citizen "(b) if the Secretary of State deems his deportation to be conducive to the public good". There is no definition or limitation of what can be "conducive to the public good" and the matter is plainly in the first instance and primarily one for the discretion of the Secretary of State. The decision of the Secretary of State to make a deportation order is subject to appeal by section 15(1)(a) of the 1971 Act save that by virtue of section 15(3):

> "A person shall not be entitled to appeal against a decision to make a deportation order against him if the ground of the decision was that his deportation is conducive to the public good as being in the interests of national security or of the relations between the United Kingdom and any other country or for other reasons of a political nature."

9. Despite this prohibition there was set up an advisory procedure to promote a consideration of the Secretary of State's decision under that Act. This however was held by the European Court of Human Rights in Chahal v United Kingdom (1996) 23 EHRR 413 not to provide an effective remedy within section 13 of the European Convention for the Protection of Human Rights and Fundamental Freedoms (1953) (Cmnd 8969). Accordingly the Commission was set up by the 1997 Act and by section 2(1)I a person was given a right to appeal to the Commission against

"any matter in relation to which he would be entitled to appeal under subsection 1(a) of section 15 of [the 1971 Act] (appeal to an adjudicator or the Appeal Tribunal against a decision to make a deportation order), but for subsection (3) of that section (deportation conducive to public good) ..."

The exclusion of the right of appeal if the decision to deport was on the ground that deportation was conducive to the public good on the basis that it was in the interests of national security or of the relations between the United Kingdom and any other country or for any other reasons of a political nature was thus removed.

10. Section 4(1) of the 1997 Act provides that the Commission:

"(a) shall allow the appeal if it considers-(i) that the decision or action against which the appeal is brought was not in accordance with the law or with any immigration rules applicable to the case, or (ii) where the decision or action involved the exercise of a discretion by the Secretary of State or an officer, that the discretion should have been exercised differently, and (b) in any other case, shall dismiss the appeal."

11. It seems to me that on this language and in accordance with the purpose of the legislation to ensure an "effective remedy", within the meaning of article 13 of the European Convention, that the Commission was empowered to review the Secretary of State's decision on the law and also to review his findings of fact. It was also given the power to review the question whether the discretion should have been exercised differently. Whether the discretion should have been exercised differently will normally depend on whether on the facts found the steps taken by the Secretary of State were disproportionate to the need to protect national security.

12. From the Commission's decision there is a further appeal to the Court of Appeal on "any question of law material to" the Commission's determination: section 7(1).

13. The two main points of law which arose before the Court of Appeal are now for consideration by your Lordships' House. Mr Kadri has forcefully argued that the Court of Appeal was wrong on both points.

14. As to the meaning of "national security" he contends that the interests of national security do not include matters which have no direct bearing on the United Kingdom, its people or its system of government. "National security" has the same scope as "defence of the realm". ***
Moreover he says that since the Secretary of State based his decision on a recommendation of the Security Service it can only be on matters within their purview and that their function, by section 1(2) of the Security Service Act 1989, was:

"the protection of national security and, in particular, its protection against threats from espionage, terrorism and sabotage, from the activities of agents of foreign powers and from actions intended to overthrow or undermine parliamentary democracy by political, industrial or violent means."

He relies moreover on statements by groups of experts in international law, the Johannesburg Principles on National Security, Freedom of Expression and Access to Information, as approved on 1 October 1995 in Johannesburg which stressed as:

"Principle 2. Legitimate national security interests

"(a) A restriction sought to be justified on the ground of national security is not legitimate unless its genuine purpose and demonstrable effect is to protect a country's existence or its territorial integrity against the use or threat of force, or its capacity to respond to the use or threat of force, whether from an external source, such as a military threat, or an internal source, such as incitement to violent overthrow of the government.

"(b) In particular, a restriction sought to be justified on the ground of national security is not legitimate if its genuine purpose or demonstrable effect is to protect interests unrelated to national security, including, for example, to protect a government from embarrassment or exposure of wrongdoing, or to conceal information about the functioning of its public institutions, or to entrench a particular ideology, or to suppress industrial unrest."

15. It seems to me that the appellant is entitled to say that "the interests of national security" cannot be used to justify any reason the Secretary of State has for wishing to deport an individual from the United Kingdom. There must be some possibility of risk or danger to the security or well-being of the nation which the Secretary of State considers makes it desirable for the public good that the individual should be deported. But I do not accept that this risk has to be the result of "a direct threat" to the United Kingdom as Mr Kadri has argued. Nor do I accept that the interests of national security are limited to action by an individual which can be said to be "targeted at" the United Kingdom, its system of government or its people as the Commission considered. The Commission agreed that this limitation is not to be taken literally since they accepted that such targeting:

> "includes activities directed against the overthrow or destabilization of a foreign government if that foreign government is likely to take reprisals against the United Kingdom which affect the security of the United Kingdom or of its nationals."

16. I accept as far as it goes a statement by Professor Grahl-Madsen in The Status of Refugees in International Law (1966):

"A person may be said to offend against national security if he engages in activities directed at the overthrow by external or internal force or other illegal means of the government of the country concerned or in activities which are directed against a foreign government which as a result threaten the former government with intervention of a serious nature."

That was adopted by the Commission but I for my part do not accept that these are the only examples of action which makes it in the interests of national security to deport a person. It seems to me that, in contemporary world conditions, action against a foreign state may be capable indirectly of affecting the security of the United Kingdom. The means open to terrorists both in attacking another state and in attacking international or global activity by the community of nations, whatever the objectives of the terrorist, may well be capable of reflecting on the safety and well-being of the United Kingdom or its citizens. The sophistication of means available, the speed of movement of persons and goods, the speed of modern communication, are all factors which may have to be taken into account in deciding whether there is a real possibility that the national security of the United Kingdom may immediately or subsequently be put at risk by the actions of others. To require the matters in question to be capable of resulting "directly" in a threat to national security limits too tightly the discretion of the executive in deciding how the interests of the state, including not merely military defence but democracy, the legal and constitutional systems of the state, need to be protected. I accept that there must be a real possibility of an adverse affect on the United Kingdom for what is done by the individual under inquiry but I do not accept that it has to be direct or immediate. Whether there is such a real possibility is a matter which has to be weighed up by the Secretary of State and balanced against the possible injustice to that individual if a deportation order is made.

17. In his written case Mr Kadri appears to accept (contrary it seems to me to his argument in the Court of Appeal that they were mutually exclusive and to be read disjunctively) that the three matters referred to in section 15(3) of the 1971 Act, namely "national security", "the relations between the United Kingdom and any other country" or "for other reasons of a political nature" may overlap but only if action which falls in one or more categories amounts to a direct threat. I do not consider that these three categories are to be kept wholly distinct even if they are expressed as alternatives. As the Commission itself accepted, reprisals by a foreign state due to action by the United Kingdom may lead to a threat to national security even though this is action such as to affect "relations between the United Kingdom and any other country" or to be "of a political nature". The Secretary of State does not have to pin his colours to one mast and be bound by his choice. At the end of the day the question is whether the deportation

is conducive to the public good. I would accept the Secretary of State's submission that the reciprocal co-operation between the United Kingdom and other states in combating international terrorism is capable of promoting the United Kingdom's national security, and that such co-operation itself is capable of fostering such security "by, inter alia, the United Kingdom taking action against supporters within the United Kingdom of terrorism directed against other states". There is a very large element of policy in this which is, as I have said, primarily for the Secretary of State. This is an area where it seems to me particularly that the Secretary of State can claim that a preventative or precautionary action is justified. If an act is capable of creating indirectly a real possibility of harm to national security it is in principle wrong to say that the state must wait until action is taken which has a direct effect against the United Kingdom.

18. National security and defence of the realm may cover the same ground though I tend to think that the latter is capable of a wider meaning. But if they are the same then I would accept that defence of the realm may justify action to prevent indirect and subsequent threats to the safety of the realm.

19. The United Kingdom is not obliged to harbour a terrorist who is currently taking action against some other state (or even in relation to a contested area of land claimed by another state) if that other state could realistically be seen by the Secretary of State as likely to take action against the United Kingdom and its citizens.

20. I therefore agree with the Court of Appeal that the interests of national security are not to be confined in the way which the Commission accepted.

21. Mr Kadri's second main point is that the Court of Appeal were in error when rejecting the Commission's ruling that the Secretary of State had to satisfy them, "to a high civil balance of probabilities", that the deportation of this appellant, a lawful resident of the United Kingdom, was made out on public good grounds because he had engaged in conduct that endangered the national security of the United Kingdom and, unless deported, was likely to continue to do so. The Court of Appeal *** said:

> "However, in any national security case the Secretary of State is entitled to make a decision to deport not only on the basis that the individual has in fact endangered national security but that he is a danger to national security. When the case is being put in this way, it is necessary not to look only at the individual allegations and ask whether they have been proved. It is also necessary to examine the case as a whole against an individual and then ask whether on a global approach that individual is a danger to national security, taking into account the executive's policy with regard to national security. When this is done, the cumulative effect may establish that the individual is to be treated as a danger, although it cannot be proved to a high degree of probability

that he has performed any individual act which would justify
this conclusion."

22. Here the liberty of the person and the opportunity of his family to
remain in this country is at stake, and when specific acts which have already
occurred are relied on, fairness requires that they should be proved to the
civil standard of proof. But that is not the whole exercise. The Secretary of
State, in deciding whether it is conducive to the public good that a person
should be deported, is entitled to have regard to all the information in his
possession about the actual and potential activities and the connections of the
person concerned. He is entitled to have regard to precautionary and
preventative principles rather than to wait until directly harmful activities
have taken place, the individual in the meantime remaining in this country.
In doing so he is not merely finding facts but forming an executive judgment
or assessment. There must be material on which proportionately and
reasonably he can conclude that there is a real possibility of activities
harmful to national security but he does not have to be satisfied, nor on
appeal to show, that all the material before him is proved, and his conclusion
is justified, to a "high civil degree of probability". Establishing a degree of
probability does not seem relevant to the reaching of a conclusion on whether
there should be a deportation for the public good.

23. Contrary to Mr Kadri's argument this approach is not confusing
proof of facts with the exercise of discretion-specific acts must be proved, and
an assessment made of the whole picture and then the discretion exercised as
to whether there should be a decision to deport and a deportation order made.

24. If of course it is said that the decision to deport was not based on
grounds of national security and there is an issue as to that matter then "the
Government is under an obligation to produce evidence that the decision was
in fact based on grounds of national security": see Council of Civil Service
Unions v Minister for the Civil Service [1985] AC 374, 402. That however is
not the issue in the present case.

25. On the second point I am wholly in agreement with the decision
of the Court of Appeal.

26. In conclusion even though the Commission has powers of review
both of fact and of the exercise of the discretion, the Commission must give
due weight to the assessment and conclusions of the Secretary of State in the
light at any particular time of his responsibilities, or of Government policy
and the means at his disposal of being informed of and understanding the
problems involved. He is undoubtedly in the best position to judge what
national security requires even if his decision is open to review. The
assessment of what is needed in the light of changing circumstances is
primarily for him. On an appeal the Court of Appeal and your Lordships'
House no doubt will give due weight to the conclusions of the Commission,
constituted as it is of distinguished and experienced members, and knowing
as it did, and as usually the court will not know, of the contents of the
"closed" evidence and hearing. If any of the reasoning of the Commission
shows errors in its approach to the principles to be followed, then the courts
can intervene. In the present case I consider that the Court of Appeal was

right in its decision on both of the points which arose and in its decision to remit the matters to the Commission for redetermination in accordance with the principles which the Court of Appeal and now your Lordships have laid down. I would accordingly dismiss the appeals.

*****

Notes

1. **London Bombings**. On July 7, 2005, three bombs exploded within 50 seconds of each other in the London Underground. A fourth bomb exploded nearly an hour later on a London bus. The attacks claimed 52 commuters and the four suicide bombers and injured 700 more. It was the largest terrorist attack on London's transit system in its history.

In response to the bombings, in August, 2005 British Home Secretary Charles Clarke issued the following list of "unacceptable behaviour" which would be grounds for exclusion or deportation from the U.K.

EXCLUSION OR DEPORTATION FROM THE UK ON NON-CONDUCIVE GROUNDS: CONSULTATION DOCUMENT
www.homeoffice.gov.uk/documents/cons-deportation-050805

1. The Home Secretary has powers to exclude or deport non-UK citizens on the grounds that their presence in the UK is not conducive to the public good.

2. These powers apply both to those who are not yet in the UK (exclusions) and to those who have temporary or indefinite leave to remain in the UK (deportation).

3. The Home Secretary must and will act consistently, proportionately and reasonably in applying these powers, having regard to the importance of upholding UK values.

4. Where the Home Secretary is personally applying these powers to exclude, there is no statutory right of appeal although his decision can be challenged through judicial review. Where he is applying these powers to deport, or where other Home Office Ministers or Immigration or Entry Clearance Officers are applying them on his behalf to exclude or deport, there is a right of appeal. ***

6. The Home Secretary announced on 20 July that he would broaden the exercise of these powers to deal more fully and systematically with those who in effect, represent an indirect threat under the same categories, in particular those who foment terrorism or seek to provoke others to terrorist acts.

7. Because of the need to tread very carefully in areas which relate to free speech, the Home Secretary announced that he would consult on a list of unacceptable behaviours which demonstrate such an indirect threat. This list is indicative not exhaustive and is set out below.

List of Unacceptable Behaviours

The list of unacceptable behaviours covers any non-UK citizen whether in the UK or abroad who uses any means or medium including:-

Writing, producing, publishing or distributing material

Public speaking including preaching

Running a website

Using a position of responsibility such as teacher, community or youth leader

To express views which the Government considers:

  • Foment terrorism or seek to provoke others to terrorist acts

  • Justify or glorify terrorism

  • Foment other serious criminal activity or seek to provoke others to serious criminal acts

  • Foster hatred which may lead to intra community violence in the UK

  • Advocate violence in furtherance of particular beliefs and those who express what the Government considers to be extreme views that are in conflict with the UK's culture of tolerance

2. Limits on Deportation. As you read the article below, consider whether the law on this topic, which you explored in a non-immigration context earlier in this book, would be equally applicable in the United States.

3. U. K. Deportation. In 2008, the Court of Appeals blocked deportation of Abu Qatada, a radical cleric referred to as "Osama bin Laden's right-hand man in Europe," to Jordan. The Court of Appeal blocked Qatada's deportation despite a "no torture" guarantee by Jordan. Related cases featuring less prominent terror suspects forced the Home Office to abandon deportation cases against twelve Libyan suspects. The UK House of Lords reversed Abu Qatada's case in 2009, offering the following observations:

> The prohibition on receiving evidence obtained by torture is not primarily because such evidence is unreliable or because the reception of the evidence will make the trial unfair. Rather it is because "the state must stand firm against the conduct that has produced the evidence". That principle applies to the state in which an attempt is made to adduce such evidence. It does not require this state, the United Kingdom, to retain in this country to the detriment of national security a terrorist suspect unless it has a high degree of assurance that evidence obtained by torture will not be adduced against him in Jordan. *** There is in my opinion no authority for a rule that, in the context of the application of article 6 to a foreign trial, the risk of the use of evidence obtained by torture necessarily amounts to a flagrant denial of justice. *** The *** real risk that a statement has been obtained by torture is not enough to make it inadmissible in

> proceedings before SIAC [Special Immigration Appeals Commission]. The burden is upon the appellant to satisfy SIAC on a balance of probability that the statement was so obtained. *** In addition to the question of using evidence obtained by torture, Abu Qatada also submitted that his trial would be a flagrant denial of justice because it would take place before a military court, which was not *** an independent tribunal. SIAC found that although the judges were part of a military hierarchy and the court would therefore not have complied with article 6 in its application to a Member State, they would in fact act judicially and the trial would therefore not be a flagrant denial of justice. Omar Othman (aka Abu Qatada) v. Secretary of State for the Home Department, UKHL 10 (2009)

One of the Law Lords, agreeing with the decision, nevertheless noted that:

> The fact that it was thought necessary to obtain the assurances is itself a demonstration that, without them, there was a real risk that treatment contrary to article 3 would be resorted to. There was no question of obtaining a general undertaking that the states concerned would abandon such practices. What was sought were assurances specific to each individual. The context in which they were given was one in which it must be assumed that practices that are objectionable because they are in breach of norms that are agreed internationally are still commonplace. Can it ever be said that, in such circumstances, assurances that particular individuals will not be subjected to them may be accepted as reliable? Is it realistic to expect that the risk of their being subjected to it can be met by monitoring? What sanctions, if any, can be imposed in the event of it being discovered that the assurances have been breached?

In the same month as the Law Lords' decision, Qatada was awarded £2,500 by the European Court of Human Rights in a lawsuit he filed against the UK, after judges ruled that his detention without trial in the UK breached his human rights. Abu Qatada, still in Britain as this book went to press, appealed the House of Lords decision to the European Court of Human Rights in a last attempt to avoid being deported.

F. NON-IMMIGRATION BORDER SECURITY

Inbound and outbound foreign trade represents and enormous portion of the U.S. economy. In 2006 the United States exported over $1 trillion in goods and imported $1.8 trillion more. http://www.census.gov/compendia/statab/brief.html). In the growing global economy, the U.S. has become an ever-expanding hub for goods flowing in and out of the country. In 1996, U.S. ports processed 7.8 million containers for import and 7 million export containers. In 2007, those numbers grew to 7.8 million export containers and 18.5 million import containers. Los Angeles, the nation's busiest port, handled 1.3 million export containers and 4.3 million imports in 2007 (U.S. Department of Transportation Maritime Administration, available at http://www.marad.dot.gov/MARAD_statistics/). Finally, the customs and border patrol is responsible for almost 7,000 miles of border between the U.S. and Canada and the U.S. and Mexico, borders through which $2 trillion of goods passed in 2008 (U.S. Customs and Border Patrol, http://www.cbp.gov/xp/cgov/trade).

Export Controls. To enhance national security, the United States prevents certain defense and other technologies (e.g. encryption) from being exported in order to avoid those items from being used against it by a malevolent third party. In addition, the U.S. is a participant in the Wassenaar Arrangement, an alliance of 40 countries that cooperates to prevent the export of a mutually agreed list of defense and other dual-purpose technologies. Goods are assigned an Export Control Classification Number (ECCN), a specific alpha numeric code that identifies the level of export control for articles, technology and software.

For most goods, companies are allowed to self assign their ECCN. However, for items with encryption technology, the company must request a product classification ruling from the Bureau of Industry and Security (BIS), which is part of the U.S. Department of Congress. The exporter or U.S. Principal Party in Interest is held responsible for the correct classification of any export and is required to ensure that all applicable export controls requirement are met prior to making the export regardless of how many companies, foreign or domestic, have contributed to the manufacture or distribution of the technology.

Munitions list articles and technologies are regulated by the Department of State and are controlled under the International Traffic in Arms Regulation (ITAR). Further, the Office of Foreign Assets Control (OFAC) division of the Department of the Treasury maintains a list of countries subject to economic sanctions, which further restricts exports regardless of ECCN classification. Those countries include Somalia, Iran and Cuba. In June of 2008, some, but not all of the sanctions against North Korea were lifted to make it possible to import goods directly from there without notifying the U.S. government.

Port Safety. While the Customs and Border Patrol has historically controlled goods entering the country, the events of 9/11 seemed to place a new urgency on regulation, with fears rising that terrorists would be able to use the nation's ports to bring in nuclear material for a dirty bomb or disrupt shipping by exploding a container on a ship in a U.S. port. Just prior to adjourning for the 2006 elections, Congress passed the SAFE Port Act (Pub L. 109-347), which implemented several measures to tighten port security. For example, the Customs Trade Partnership Against Terrorism (C-TPAT) created by the Act is a voluntary initiative with the goal of building cooperative relationships between government and business. Examples of companies that are accepted into the C-TPAT program are importers, carriers, consolidators, licensed customs brokers, and manufacturers. By becoming a member of C-TPAT, a company will be recognized by the Customs and Border Patrol (CBP) and experience fewer inspections at the border and priority processing by CBP.

Another provision in the SAFE Port Act created the Container Security Initiative, in which the U.S. government works with foreign authorities to certify that overseas ports meet certain safety standards which allow the identification and inspection of high-risk cargo containers originating at those ports. As of March, 2008, there were 58 CSI ports worldwide, handling 86 percent of the container cargo destined for the U.S. Once identified, the high-risk containers are scanned by large-scale X-ray and gamma ray machines and radiation detection devices and are examined by U.S. and host country customs officials before loading on a vessel destined for the U.S. These containers do not then require an inspection once they arrive in the U.S.

In 2002, Congress passed the Maritime Transportation Security Act, which was a precursor to the SAFE Port Act. The MTSA required that personnel requiring unescorted access to secure port areas to carry a tamper-resistant identification card which would contain biometric information, such as a fingerprint. The Customs and Border Patrol estimates that over 1.2 million individuals will apply for the Transportation Workers Identification Card (TWIC), but as of 2008, the program was still being rolled out.

Dubai World Ports Controversy. In February 2006, a private company entered into an agreement to sell its interest in managing six major U.S. seaports to a company owned by the government of the United Arab Emirates (UAE). Once the possible sale became public, there was an outcry from some members of Congress and the media that such a sale would compromise port security.

Ironically, the management of the ports was already handled by a foreign company, the Peninsular and Oriental Steam Navigation Company (P&O) of Great Britain, which sold their business to Dubai Ports World. Furthermore, other U.S. ports are also run by foreign-owned companies and had been for some time. Security in all the ports was and would continue to be handled by the Customs and Border Patrol and the U.S. Coast Guard. However, the fact that Dubai Ports World was owned by an Arab government may have created the flashpoint. In addition, since President Bush had already approved the sale and urged Congress to do the same, his political opponents saw an opportunity to make political hay by introducing legislation to delay the sale. Ultimately, the controversy was resolved when Dubai Ports World decided to sell the U.S. port operations to an American company, but the incident was a black eye for the Bush administration in its relations with a friendly Arab government.

XII

TERRORISM AND COMPENSATION

> Civil litigation against Iran under the FSIA state sponsor of terrorism exception represents a failed policy. *** Beyond the lack of assets available for execution of judgments, *** these civil actions inevitably must confront deeply entrenched and fundamental understandings of foreign state sovereignty, conflicting multinational treaties and executive agreements, and the exercise of presidential executive power in an ever-changing and increasingly complex world of international affairs.
> *In re ISLAMIC REPUBLIC OF IRAN TERRORISM LITIGATION*, 659 F. Supp. 2d 31 (D.D.C. 2009)

Victims of terrorism and counterterrorism may have civil claims against those who have injured or assisted those who injured them, those who failed to take appropriate precautions to avoid the injury, or those who insured against the risk which caused injury.

We have seen some examples of civil actions in earlier chapters. Although the Alien Tort Statute (see Chapter II) could apply in suits where the underlying conduct occurs in the United States rather than abroad, ordinary tort law provides a more direct remedy. The ATS might be an indirect way in the United States for aliens to sue the United States for counterterrorism operations that allegedly involved the torture of the plaintiff. But this suit would be greeted with defenses covered elsewhere like sovereign immunity (Chapter III) or the state secrets doctrine (Chapter VI).

So this chapter explores civil compensation claims outside the contexts where such issues have previously arisen. Part A looks at possible defendants and defenses in connection with claims based on injuries from acts of terrorism. Part B concerns claims by victims of counterterrorism operations.

A. VICTIMS OF TERRORISM

The injured victim of a terrorist act must look circumspectly for potential sources of civil redress. Often the terrorist who caused the damage is dead or impecunious, so the plaintiff must seek those who supported the terrorist or enabled the acts of terrorism. If such an entity is a sovereign state, the pocket will be deep, but states and their agents have special defenses. These are the topics explored in section 1 below. Groups or individuals who support terrorists who cause injury may also be sued, as Part 2 explores. Part 3 looks at claims against governments and businesses that allegedly fail to take sufficient steps to avoid injuries from terrorists. Finally, Part 4 considers compensation fund and insurance claims by victims of terrorism.

1. SUITS AGAINST FOREIGN STATES AND THEIR AGENTS

Sovereign states are generally accorded immunity for tort claims in their own courts and the courts of other countries. However, there is an exception for such immunity when the state has supported or engaged in terrorism. In the United States, The National Defense Authorization Act for Fiscal Year 2008 modified the Anti-Terrorism and Effective Death Penalty Act of 1996 by broadening the exception to the immunity of a sovereign state:

28 U.S.C. §1605A

(a) In general.--

> **(1) No immunity.**--A foreign state shall not be immune from the jurisdiction of courts of the United States or of the States in any case not otherwise covered by this chapter in which money damages are sought against a foreign state for personal injury or death that was caused by an act of torture, extrajudicial killing, aircraft sabotage, hostage taking, or the provision of material support or resources for such an act if such act or provision of material support or resources is engaged in by an official, employee, or agent of such foreign state while acting within the scope of his or her office, employment, or agency.
>
> **(2) Claim heard.**--The court shall hear a claim under this section if--
>
> **(A)(i)(I)** the foreign state was designated as a state sponsor of terrorism at the time the act described in paragraph (1) occurred, or was so designated as a result of such act ***
>
> **(ii)** the claimant or the victim was, at the time the act described in paragraph (1) occurred--
>
> **(I)** a national of the United States;
>
> **(II)** a member of the armed forces; or
>
> **(III)** otherwise an employee of the Government of the United States, or of an individual performing a contract awarded by the United States Government, acting within the scope of the employee's employment; ***
>
> **(c) Private right of action.**--A foreign state that is or was a state sponsor of terrorism *** and any official, employee, or agent of that foreign state while acting within the scope of his or her office, employment, or agency, shall be liable *** for personal injury or death caused by acts described in subsection (a) (1) of that foreign state, or of an official, employee, or agent of that foreign state, for which the courts of the United States may maintain jurisdiction under this

section for money damages. In any such action, damages may include economic damages, solatium, pain and suffering, and punitive damages. In any such action, a foreign state shall be vicariously liable for the acts of its officials, employees, or agents.

The following description of an act of terrorism supported by a state gives a vivid picture of why courts sometimes award large damages to the survivors of victims of such acts:

GATES v. SYRIAN ARAB REPUBLIC
580 F. Supp. 2d 53 (D.D.C., 2008)

ROSEMARY M. COLLYER, District Judge.

It was a sunny day somewhere in Iraq and a light wind blew the long curtains into the room through the open door. A group of men clad in total black, faces covered, stood on a Persian rug facing a camera. Before them, a single man knelt. Dressed in an orange jumpsuit, hands bound behind his back, feet similarly bound, with eyes covered and mouth gagged, he rarely moved. One of the standing men began to read a proclamation in Arabic. It continued at length. Suddenly he stopped. The man in the orange jumpsuit tensed. Another of the men in black stepped forward and knocked the kneeling man over onto his side. Brandishing a knife, the man in black began to slice at the neck of the victim lying on the floor. The dying man audibly moaned and gurgled, as it took some time to cut all around his neck and through his bones before the head could be lifted in seeming triumph.

There is no doubt that al-Tawhid wal-Jihad ("al-Qaeda in Iraq") beheaded U.S. civilian contractors Jack Armstrong and Jack Hensley in the manner described, which it videotaped and played on the Internet for all the world, and ultimately this Court, to see. The question raised by this lawsuit is whether the Syrian Arab Republic can be held liable for money damages to the families of the two men pursuant to the Foreign Sovereign Immunities Act (the "FSIA").

*** [T]he mother and sister of Jack Armstrong and *** the widow and minor daughter of Jack Hensley *** allege that*** Syria provided material support and resources to the al-Tawhid wal-Jihad ("al-Qaeda in Iraq") and its leader, Abu Mus'ab al-Zarqawi ("Zarqawi"). *** None of the Defendants filed an answer or otherwise appeared. The Court proceeded to a default setting *** which requires a court to enter a default judgment against a non-responding foreign state only where "the claimant establishes his claim or right to relief by evidence satisfactory to the court." *** There has never been any dispute as to who killed Jack Armstrong or Jack Hensley or a competing claim of responsibility by another terrorist group. *** The execution videos of Mr. Armstrong and Mr. Hensley *** depict each American man blindfolded, gagged, and kneeling on the ground. *** The video footage records awful sounds: kicking and efforts to escape, muffled cries, and labored breathing by the man wielding the knife. Copious amounts of blood are shown. ***It would have would have taken several minutes before the victim lost consciousness due to the clumsy nature of the decapitation. *** The horrific sights and sounds of the videos have but one clear purpose-to glorify acts of terrorism, mayhem, and murder and to frighten the viewer. There is no doubt that Zarqawi and his organization, al-Qaeda in Iraq, killed Messrs. Armstrong and Hensley. Their remains were recovered after officials found them dumped in various locations in Baghdad.

*** Plaintiffs presented expert witness testimony and testimony from an Iraqi countryman concerning Syria's assistance to Zarqawi and al-Qaeda in Iraq. From this evidence, certain conclusions are clear. Syria was the critical geographic entry point for Zarqawi's fighters into Iraq, and served as a "logistical hub" for Zarqawi. Syria supported Zarqawi and his organization by: (1) facilitating the recruitment and training of Zarqawi's followers and their transportation into Iraq; (2) harboring and providing sanctuary to terrorists and their operational and logistical supply network; and (3) financing Zarqawi and his terrorist network in Iraq. Once Zarqawi beheaded civilian Nicholas Berg, the depth of his inhumanity was obvious but Syria did not withdraw its support. ***

The FSIA specifies that a court cannot enter a default judgment against a foreign state "unless the claimant establishes his claim or right to relief by evidence satisfactory to the court." Section 1608(e) provides protection to foreign States from unfounded default judgments rendered solely upon a procedural default. *** By its failure to appear and defend itself, Syria put itself at risk that the Plaintiffs' uncontroverted evidence would be satisfactory to prove its points. *** In this case, service upon all Defendants was perfected under 28 U.S.C. § 1608(a), which governs service on foreign states.[8] Obviously, Syria is a foreign state. Further, the law treats each of the other Defendants as the foreign state. Syrian Military Intelligence is considered to be the foreign state itself because its core functions are governmental, not commercial. Further, President Assad and General Shawkat are categorized as the foreign state itself because "an officer of an entity that is considered the foreign state itself under the core functions test should also be treated as the state itself for purposes of service of process under § 1608." While the Complaint asserts claims against Syria, Syrian Military Intelligence, President Assad, and General Shawkat, service was never completed against any individual Defendant. Because each Defendant is treated as the state itself under the FSIA and because Plaintiffs never served the individuals as such, Syria is the only Defendant in this case against whom damages can be sought.

The FSIA provides "the sole basis for obtaining jurisdiction over a foreign state in the courts of this country." Accordingly, this Court lacks jurisdiction over Syria unless one of the FSIA's enumerated exceptions applies. Here, the state-sponsored terrorism exception to sovereign immunity applies. Moreover, the FSIA was recently amended to provide a private cause of action by which a foreign state that sponsors terrorism can be held liable

---

[8] Service upon Defendants in this case was accomplished via 28 U.S.C. § 1608(a)(3) through delivery of the required documents (translated into Arabic) to an agent of Defendants via international courier service, evidenced by a signed return-receipt dated October 27, 2006.

for certain enumerated damages arising from terrorist activities: economic damages, solatium, pain and suffering, and punitive damages.

Section 1605A(a) provides that a foreign state shall not be immune from the jurisdiction of U.S. courts in cases where plaintiffs seek money damages for personal injury or death caused by hostage taking, torture, or extrajudicial killing, if the damages were caused by [the actions listed in the statute]. *** Plaintiffs originally brought this action under the FSIA's Flatow Amendment (published as a note to 28 U.S.C. § 1605), which provided a private right of action under the FSIA against individual officials, employees and agents of a foreign state, but did not provide a private right of action against the foreign state itself. *See Cicippio-Puleo,* 353 F.3d at 1027 (D.C. Cir. 2004).* On January 28, 2008, the President signed into law the Defense Authorization Act for Fiscal Year 2008 ("Defense Authorization Act"). Section 1083 of the Defense Authorization Act sets forth a new provision, 28 U.S.C. § 1605A, which waives sovereign immunity for states that sponsor terrorism and provides a private right of action against such states. The Court has permitted Plaintiffs to proceed in this suit under the new statutory provisions.

The new provision explicitly allows a private cause of action directly against a foreign state itself, a right of action which previously had been limited to suit against that government's leaders in their personal capacities. *** Under § 1605A(c), U.S. citizens who are victims of state-sponsored terrorism can sue a responsible foreign state directly. Significantly, state law no longer controls the nature of the liability and damages that may be sought when it is a foreign government that is sued: Congress has provided the "specific source of law" for recovery. By providing for a private right of action and by precisely enumerating the types of damages recoverable, Congress has eliminated the inconsistencies that arise in these cases when they are decided under state law.

Reading the new statute as it is written, the Court concludes that State-law claims for damages are not available against a foreign state that has engaged in state-sponsored terrorism. *** The only cause of action permissible against Syria is a federal cause of action under the FSIA. Thus, Plaintiffs' claims under state law will be dismissed.

Plaintiffs have presented evidence satisfactory to the Court in support of all elements of a claim under § 1605A. Syria was a state-sponsor of terrorism,[10] and the Plaintiffs are and decedents were U.S. Citizens. The critical issue in this case is whether Syria, and its officials acting within the

---

* (relocated fn.) *Flatow* came into disuse after the D.C. Circuit's opinion in *Cicippio-Puleo* that found no basis in the FSIA for a direct claim against a foreign state. However, with the amendment to the FSIA enacted by the Defense Authorization Act, specifying that solatium damages are available under federal law, opinions such as *Flatow* provide insight into the nature of such damages.

[10] *** Syria has been designated by the U.S. Department of State as a state sponsor of terrorism continuously since December 29, 1979, and its continued designation as such was noted in 2004, and again in 2005, *See also* Syria Accountability Act (Congress directed that "(2) the Government of Syria should ... (B) cease its support for 'volunteers' and terrorists who are traveling from and through Syria into Iraq to launch attacks .")

scope of their employment, provided material support and resources to Zarqawi and to al-Qaeda in Iraq.

Syria in fact did provide material support and resources to Zarqawi and al-Qaeda in Iraq which contributed to hostage taking, torture, and extrajudicial killings. Section 1605A(h)(3) defines "material support or resources" to have "the meaning given that term in section 2339A of title 18."Section 2339A provides:

> 'material support or resources' means any property, tangible or intangible, or service, including currency or monetary instruments or financial securities, financial services, lodging, training, expert advice or assistance, safehouses, false documentation or identification, communications equipment, facilities, weapons, lethal substances, explosives, personnel ... and transportation, except medicine or religious materials.

To determine whether a defendant country has provided material support to terrorism, courts consider first, whether a particular terrorist group committed the terrorist act and second, whether the defendant foreign state generally provided material support or resources to the terrorist organization which contributed to its ability to carry out the terrorist act. The types of support that have been identified as "material" have included, for example, financing and running camps that provided military and other training to terrorist operatives; allowing terrorist groups to use its banking institutions to launder money; and allowing terrorist groups to use its territory as a meeting place and safe haven, Such support has been found to have contributed to the actual terrorist act that resulted in a plaintiff's damages when experts testify that the terrorist acts could not have occurred without such support; or that a particular act exhibited a level of sophistication in planning and execution that was consistent with the advanced training that had been supplied by the defendant state; or when the support facilitated the terrorist group's development of the expertise, networks, military training, munitions, and financial resources necessary to plan and carry out the attack.

Plaintiffs proved, by evidence satisfactory to the Court, that Syria provided substantial assistance to Zarqawi and al-Qaeda in Iraq and that this led to the deaths by beheading of Jack Armstrong and Jack Hensley. Plaintiffs showed that Syria's provision of material support and resources was inevitably approved and overseen by President Assad and General Shawkat, acting within the scope of their official duties. Syria served as Zarqawi's organizational and logistical hub from 2002 to 2005. During this time, Syria supported Zarqawi by providing him a passport and by providing munitions, training, recruiting, and transportation to him and his followers ***

It was the Syrian government's foreign policy to support al-Qaeda in Iraq in order to topple the nascent Iraqi democratic government. In 2003, the foreign minister of Syria stated publicly that it was in Syria's interest to see the U.S. invasion of Iraq fail. The very brutality of Zarqawi's acts against American civilians-broadcast on the Internet for greatest impact-was intended to weaken U.S. resolve to succeed in Iraq. Syria's aid to Zarqawi, from at least 2002 to 2005, was no impetuous or unknowing act. Indeed, not only was it foreseeable that Zarqawi and his terrorist organization would engage in terrorist activities in Iraq to destabilize that country (in concert with Syrian foreign policy), but also Zarqawi had beheaded civilian Nicholas Berg and could be expected to attack civilians again. The murders of Jack Armstrong and Jack Hensley were a foreseeable consequence of Syria's aid and support to Zarqawi and al-Qaeda in Iraq.

In sum, jurisdiction over Syria is consistent with § 1605A(a), the state-sponsored terrorism exception to sovereign immunity, and Plaintiffs have provided evidence satisfactory to the Court in support of their private cause of action for damages under § 1605A(c).

Damages for a private action for proven acts of terrorism by foreign states under the FSIA may include economic damages, solatium, pain and suffering, and punitive damages. *** The cruel, calculated, and public manner in which the kidnappings and beheadings of Messrs. Armstrong and Hensley were broadcast added to the Plaintiffs' damages. The malice and political objectives that motivated the murders also increased these damages. *** The terrorists slaughtered Jack Armstrong and Jack Hensley as a propaganda act of terrorism. The brutality quotient was maximized to achieve the maximum amount of terror and horror, which was markedly felt by Fran Gates, Jack Armstrong's mother, who felt compelled to watch the Internet video showing her son's gruesome murder so she would know he was actually gone; the sight of it will never leave the inside of her eyelids. Jan Smith, on the other hand, fell into a deep and lengthy depression so that, to this day, she cannot speak of her brother without copious tears and cannot bear to think of the nature of his death, which she dare not watch for fear that her struggles with mental health stability will be upset. Pati Hensley remains afraid and so emotionally roiled that she cannot work. Sara Hensley grieves constantly and feels a huge hole in her life. *** The trier of fact has broad discretion in calculating damages for pain and suffering.

During their decapitations, each man suffered unimaginable mental and physical agony. There is no evidence that their senses were impaired or that there was any effort to anesthetize either man prior to his murder. *** These decapitations were so awful because, anatomically, it is almost impossible to decapitate someone quickly with the tool and technique used by Zarqawi's terrorists. *** The Court finds that the evidence is fully satisfactory to prove the pain and suffering experienced by Jack Armstrong and Jack Hensley while they remained conscious before they died. It awards compensatory damages for pain and suffering in the amount of $50,000,000.00 to the estate of each. ***

As amended, the FSIA now specifically allows an award of punitive damages for personal injury or death resulting from an act of state-sponsored terrorism. Several factors are considered in the analysis of whether to award punitive damages and how substantial an award should be. Those factors include the character of the defendant's acts; the nature and extent of harm to the Plaintiffs that the Defendant caused or intended to cause; the need for deterrence; and the wealth of the Defendant. The purpose of punitive damages is two-fold: to punish those who engage in outrageous conduct and to deter others from similar conduct in the future. ***

Al-Qaeda in Iraq wanted the world at large to know that Jack Armstrong and Jack Hensley died in conscious pain and terror. Syria was a willing and substantial supporter of Zarqawi and his terrorist organization and knew, full well, that they were capable of this kind of barbarism after the brutal and public acts of terrorism against Nicholas Berg. Through the Internet, Zarqawi and his fellow terrorists transformed heinous acts into infamous and indelible propaganda that served the Syrian political ends. The world at large must shout these actions down in infamy. *** In hopes that substantial awards will deter further Syrian sponsorship of terrorists, the Court will award to the estate of Jack Armstrong punitive damages in the amount of $150,000,000.00, and to the estate of Jack Hensley punitive damages in the amount of $150,000,000.00.

Notes

1. Where was Syria? Syria did not defend itself against this suit. Why not? By mid-2005, there were large default judgments in 32 cases involving the terrorism exception to the FSIA totaling almost $7 trillion. See Jennifer K. Elsea, Suits Against Terrorist States by Victims of Terrorism (Cong. Res. Serv. RL 31258). How could these amounts be collected?

2. Causation. Section 1605 provides an exception to sovereign immunity only when injury or death "was *caused by* an act of torture, extrajudicial killing, aircraft sabotage, hostage taking, or the provision of material support or resources ... for such an act." Does this require "but for" causation and if so, was Syria the "but for" cause of the gruesome deaths described in the opinion? In *Kilburn v. Socialist People's Libyan Arab Jamahiriya*, 376 F. 3d 1123 (D.C. Cir. 2004), the court adopted a "proximate cause standard which it applied as follows: "The complaint alleges that, after the United States bombed Tripoli, "Libyan agents in Lebanon made it known that they wanted to purchase an American hostage to murder in retaliation." It specifically asserts that Peter Kilburn "was purchased and killed by members of the Arab Revolutionary Cells," "whose acts were funded *and directed* by Libya". *** If proven, these allegations are more than sufficient to establish that the acts of the Libyan defendants were the proximate cause of Peter Kilburn's injury and death." Does Syria in *Gates* likewise satisfy the "proximate cause" standard?

3. Executive and Legislative Roles. In *Cucippio-Puleo*, the case overturned by the legislation discussed in *Gates*, the solicitor general's brief for the executive branch provided the argument the court accepted. Why did the President not want the plaintiffs to recover? Is compensation to victims consistent with effective counterterrorism policy towards particular state sponsors of terrorism? Would it matter whether the state was Syria or Iran or North Korea? Why would the two political branches see victim compensation against state sponsors of terrorism so differently?

4. Burdens of proof. *Price v. Socialist People's Libyan Arab Jamahiriya*, 389 F.3d 192 (D.C. Cir. 2004) discussed the burden of proof concerning sovereign immunity as follows:

> "Application of this exception entails the reconciliation of two rival propositions. On the one hand, because a foreign sovereign "has immunity from trial and the attendant burdens of litigation," its claim of immunity from suit should be resolved "as early in the litigation as possible," lest the purpose to be served by sovereign immunity be unduly compromised. On the other hand, a court is poorly equipped to resolve factual disputes at an early stage in litigation -- as reflected in the ordinary rules of procedure. *** Regardless of the procedures the court follows, however, the sovereign "defendant bears the burden of proving that the plaintiff's allegations do not bring its case within a statutory exception to immunity."

5. Sauce for the Gander? Other countries (like Iran) have passed legislation allowing their citizens to sue the United States for violations of human rights or interference in their countries' affairs. What, if anything, should this have to do with what US law is or should be?

6. Collecting Judgments against Foreign States. One can attach assets of private judgment debtors located in the U.S., and the commercial assets of state sponsors of terrorism can be reached. 18 U.S.C. §1610(b)(2). Many such assets are in practice blocked, frozen, or forfeited under various federal statutes (including, for example, assets of Iran and Cuba in the United States). Congress has passed legislation to make these assets available to satisfy judgments, but has usually allowed the President to avoid the operation of such statutes in "the national security interest" of the United States. The President has asserted that interest. Victims of terrorism can also use the 2000 Victims of Trafficking and Violence Protection Act to receive payment from the U.S. Treasury in exchange for the U.S. taking over victim interests after payment is made. The following case illustrates the difficulties of collection from sovereign states even after substantial amendments to the FSIA discussed in *Gates*.

7. Judgments against a sovereign and foreign policy concerns. The VTPA and TRIA created mechanisms for satisfying judgments in terrorism-related claims under the FSIA by attaching assets of foreign sovereigns. Given the diplomatically sensitive nature of this activity, Congress put restrictions on what assets could be attached. Does diplomatic and foreign policy strategy outweigh an individual's right to collect on a valid judgment? The following case addresses this question.

In re ISLAMIC REPUBLIC OF IRAN TERRORISM LITIGATION
659 F. Supp. 2d 31 (D.D.C. 2009)

ROYCE C. LAMBERTH, Chief Judge.

For more than a decade now, this Court has presided over what has been a twisting and turning course of litigation against the Islamic Republic of Iran under the state sponsor of terrorism exception of the Foreign

Sovereign Immunities Act (FSIA). *** The cases against Iran that will be addressed by the Court today involve more than one thousand individual plaintiffs [who] have demonstrated through competent evidence *** that Iran has provided material support to terrorist organizations, like Hezbollah and Hamas, that have orchestrated unconscionable acts of violence that have killed or injured hundreds of Americans. As a result of these civil actions, Iran faces more than nine billion dollars in liability in the form of court judgments for money damages. Despite plaintiffs' best efforts to execute these court judgments, virtually all have gone unsatisfied. *** The primary purpose of this opinion is to consider whether and to what extent [the 2008 amendments to the FSIA] apply retroactively to a number of civil actions against Iran that were filed, and, in many instances, litigated to a final judgment prior to the enactment of the 2008 NDAA. *** Today, the Court also reaches an even more fundamental conclusion: Civil litigation against Iran under the FSIA state sponsor of terrorism exception represents a failed policy. *** The truth is that the prospects for recovery upon judgments entered in these cases are extremely remote. The amount of Iranian assets currently known to exist with the United States is approximately 45 million dollars, which is infinitesimal in comparison to the 10 billion dollars in currently outstanding court judgments. Beyond the lack of assets available for execution of judgments, however, these civil actions inevitably must confront deeply entrenched and fundamental understandings of foreign state sovereignty, conflicting multinational treaties and executive agreements, and the exercise of presidential executive power in an ever-changing and increasingly complex world of international affairs.

Unfortunately, the enactment of *** the 2008 NDAA continues and expands the terrorism exception and its failed policy of civil litigation as the means of redress in these horrific cases. *** As a result of these latest reforms, the victims in these cases will now continue in their long struggle in pursuit of justice through costly and time-consuming civil litigation against Iran. *** To assist this Court in these matters going forward, the Court will invite the United States to participate in these actions by filing a brief in response to the many issues addressed in this opinion. ***

The Foreign Sovereign Immunities Act of 1976 (FSIA) is the sole basis of jurisdiction over foreign states in our courts. *** The state sponsor of terrorism exception *** was repealed last year by the 2008 NDAA and replaced with a new exception at § 1605A. ***. The issue is whether the plaintiffs in actions that were filed, at least initially, under the now-repealed § 1605(a)(7), can now avail themselves of the additional entitlements associated with the new exception, § 1605A. *** [T]errorism cases that were filed prior the enactment of the 2008 NDAA, and which do not qualify for retroactive treatment under the new exception, are governed by the prior statute, § 1605(a)(7).

The new terrorism exception clears away a number of legal obstacles, including adverse court rulings, that have stifled plaintiffs' efforts to obtain relief in civil actions against designated state sponsors of terrorism. *** Under the [terrorism] exception, foreign sovereign immunity is eliminated in two different categories of terrorism cases: (1) those in which the designated foreign state is alleged to have committed certain acts of terrorism, i.e., torture, extrajudicial killing, aircraft sabotage, or hostage taking; and (2) those in which the designated state is alleged to have provided "material support or resources" for such terrorist acts. ***

The statute is intended to protect American victims of state-sponsored terrorism, and therefore only United States citizens and nationals may rely on its grant of subject matter jurisdiction. *** Most of the actions in this Court against Iran have proceeded under that portion of the terrorism exception relating to "the provision of material support or resources" for terrorist acts. *** [T]here is no "but-for" causation requirement with respect to cases that rely on the material support component of the terrorism exception to foreign sovereign immunity; "[s]ponsorship of a terrorist group which causes personal injury or death of United States national alone is sufficient to invoke jurisdiction." Once the requirements for jurisdiction over a foreign state are satisfied under the FSIA, then that foreign state can be held liable in a civil action "in the same manner and to the same extent as a private individual under like circumstances." *** Prior to the enactment of last year's reforms in the 2008 NDAA, however, these exceptions to the general rule of immunity for foreign government property were limited almost exclusively to property relating to the commercial activities of the foreign sovereign within the United States. Given the lack of formal relations between the United States and Iran, these provisions have been of little utility to the judgment creditors of Iran in FSIA terrorism cases. Thus, the FSIA facilitated a somewhat ironic and perverse outcome because on the one hand, in § 1605(a)(7), it created an opportunity for terrorism victims to sue Iran for money damages, while on the other hand, in §§ 1609 and 1610, it denied these victims the legal means to enforce their court judgments.[13]

In addition to the immunity from attachment or execution that the FSIA has long provided to foreign property, assets held within United States Treasury accounts that might otherwise be attributed to Iran are the property of the United States and are therefore exempt from attachment or execution by virtue of the federal government's sovereign immunity. *** Because the federal government has assumed control over significant portions of what limited Iranian assets remain in the United States, plaintiffs' efforts to enforce judgments under the FSIA have often pitted victims of terrorism against the Executive Branch. *** In the case of Iran, *** very few blocked assets exist. In fact, according to OFAC's latest report, there are only 16.8 million dollars in blocked assets relating to Iran. This amount is inconsequential-a mere drop in the bucket-when compared to the staggering 9.6 billion dollars in outstanding judgments entered against Iran in terrorism cases as of August 2008***. The amount of Iranian non-blocked assets within the United States, as reported to OFAC, is similarly inconsequential in

---

[13] Another challenge for plaintiffs looking to collect on their judgments in this context is that many of the world's leading financial institutions are agencies or instrumentalities of foreign nations and are therefore immune from jurisdiction of the United States Courts under the FSIA. ***

comparison to Iran's liability under the FSIA terrorism exception. According to OFAC, the amount of non-blocked Iranian assets is merely 28 million dollars.[17] *** Congress has continued to fuel expectations in these actions by broadly subjecting Iran to suit for sponsorship of terrorism while simultaneously ignoring the fact that the prospects for recovery are virtually nonexistent. ***

In light of the significant setbacks that plaintiffs experienced *** Congress implemented a number of major reforms last year. *** § 1605A accomplishes four basic objectives. This new terrorism statute (1) furnishes a cause of action against state sponsors of terrorism; (2) makes punitive damages available in those actions; (3) authorizes compensation for special masters; and (4) implements new measures designed to facilitate the enforcement of judgments. *** [T]he new law now expressly provides that designated state sponsors of terrorism may be subject to a federal cause of action for money damages if those terrorist states cause or otherwise provide material support for an act of terrorism that results in the death or injury of a United States citizen or national. *** The new cause of action included with the new terrorism exception § 1605A has a new and expanded statute of limitations. *** The second key reform found in § 1605A is the availability of punitive damages. *** Only time will tell whether § 1610(g) will enable plaintiffs going forward with actions under § 1605A to experience greater success in executing civil judgments against Iranian assets. ***

Today the Court must determine whether the new terrorism exception should be applied retroactively to reach cases that were originally filed under § 1605(a)(7) prior to enactment of the new statute, § 1605A. *** [T]his Court construes § 1083(c)(2)(A) broadly, consistent with the remedial purposes of the new anti-terrorism enactment *** regardless of when those actions were filed [and] reads the requirement that the prior actions must be adversely impacted on the grounds that § 1605(a)(7) and the Flatow Amendment failed to establish a cause of action against a foreign state to include those instances in which plaintiffs failed to recover punitive damages, a critical component of these terrorism actions.

Section 1083(c)(3), the provision concerning "related actions" offers another method by which certain prior actions may be filed with the Court as new actions under § 1605A. *** [It] offers an avenue of relief in those cases that reached final judgment some years prior to the enactment of the 2008 NDAA and therefore are less likely to be "before the court[ ] in any form," as required for treatment on motion under § 1083(c)(2). [The new law also] allows plaintiffs in a prior action under § 1605(a)(7) to file an action under the new law, § 1605A, as a related case to any other pending action that was timely commenced under § 1605(a)(7) and based on the same terrorist act or incident. In other words, plaintiffs' right to proceed under the new section is

---

[17] In fairness, it is important to emphasize here that "there is no requirement for U.S. persons to report non-blocked assets to OFAC." Thus, arguably, there could be any number of undisclosed, non-blocked Iranian assets within the jurisdiction of the United States courts. In light of the lack of formal relations between Iran and the United States, however, the prospect of large sums of Iranian assets being located within the jurisdiction of the federal courts seems remote.

not tied exclusively to their prior action; plaintiffs may identify other cases that are pending under § 1605(a)(7) that are based on the same act or incident. *** Subsection § 1083(c)(2)(B), referred to as "Defenses Waived," purports to limit "[t]he defenses of res judicata, collateral estoppel, and limitation period" in any new action under § 1605A. *** In other words, prior judgments under the state sponsor terrorism exception to the FSIA are not to be given any preclusive effect in new actions brought under the current version of the terrorism exception. *** [T]here are both winners and losers in today's omnibus opinion. *** If counsel for plaintiffs in these action have in good faith misunderstood or misapplied § 1083(c) to their respective actions-and are time-barred from taking advantage of the new state sponsor of terrorism exception-then they may consider filing a motion for relief under Rule 60 ***

[Do] these particular legislative enactments abrogate final judgments in a manner that the Supreme Court has determined is "repugnant to the text, structure, and traditions of Article III[?]" *** [T]he Article III question presented in this case requires the consideration of two distinct but related issues. *** The first question is whether § 1083(c)(3) calls for the reopening of final judgments entered before its enactment and therefore contravenes Article III as construed by the Supreme Court in *Plaut.* The second question is assuming that § 1083(c)(3) does not direct the reopening of final judgments, does § 1083(c)(2)-the waiver of res judicata and collateral estoppel effect of any prior terrorism FSIA action-nonetheless offend Article III because Congress has directed the Courts to ignore fundamental and longstanding judicial doctrine. Both issues are constitutional questions of first impression.

*** § 1083(c) does not violate Article III of the United States Constitution. *** Section 1083(a) simply repeals § 1605(a)(7) entirely and replaces it with the new provision § 1605A. *** Rather than revisiting prior cases under the old "pass-through" system of § 1605(a)(7), § 1083 is geared instead toward bringing into existence a whole new statutory regime-one that has as its cornerstone a new federal cause of action against foreign states, for which punitive damages may be awarded. *** [T]he FSIA is a far-reaching, retrospective law-the statute reaches conduct by foreign powers that long predates its enactment and it directly addresses sensitive matters of foreign relations, which, as the Court emphasized, are inherently subject to "current political realities and relationships." It is beyond question that foreign relations matters are soundly committed to the political branches. And while neither the retrospective nature of the FSIA, nor the fact that it directly concerns our relationships with foreign nations, is enough to justify a usurpation of the federal courts' powers and responsibilities under Article III, there must be at least be some recognition *** that the political branches have greater authority and leeway with respect to decisions apportioning the liability of foreign nations. *** *See Dames & Moore v. Regan,* 453 U.S. 654 (1981); *see also Youngstown Sheet & Tube,* 343 U.S. at 637 (Jackson, J., concurring). *** While it is the Federal Judiciary that decides individual cases and controversies arising under federal law, it is our political branches that ultimately bear full responsibility for our relations with foreign powers.

Having decided that § 1083(c)(3) does not direct the reopening of final judgments in violation of Article III, this Court is of the view that the waiver of res judicata and collateral estoppel in § 1083(c)(2)(B) should also withstand Constitutional scrutiny under the narrow facts of these cases. *** [T]he Supreme Court has stated that the "[a]pplication of res judicata and collateral estoppel is central to the purpose for which civil courts have been established, the conclusive resolution of disputes within their jurisdictions." Thus, a statutory directive instructing courts to waive res judicata and collateral estoppel may raise separation of powers concerns under Article III. *** It seems to this Court that Congress has little business directing whether or when those judicial doctrines should be invoked any more than this Judge should play a role in directing federal appropriations. *** For Article III purposes, the question is not necessarily whether the preclusion doctrines of res judicata or collateral estoppel have been invoked by the Legislative Branch; it is simply whether Congress has in effect directed the reopening of final judgments for money damages. Here, that sort of Article III violation-albeit in the most technical sense-has not occurred.[29] Accordingly, this judge cannot say that the waiver of res judicata or collateral estoppel are offensive under the circumstances presented in this case.

Moreover, *** it strains credulity to assert that Iran has any reliance interests or settled expectations with respect to prior civil actions litigated against it under § 1605(a)(7). Indeed, the notion is almost laughable because that nation has never appeared in any of the terrorism actions that have been litigated against it in this Court.

Finally, applying any of the preclusion doctrines with respect to actions that were previously litigated to a final judgment under the former version of the state sponsor of terrorism exception, would completely undermine the purpose behind the most recent enactment § 1605A. ***   Technically speaking, it is an open question whether a foreign state is even entitled to Due Process under the Fifth Amendment because the Supreme Court expressly declined to consider the question in *Republic of Argentina v. Weltover, Inc.,* and has not revisited the issue since. 504 U.S. 607 (1992). *** [T]he issue of whether the statutory waiver of preclusion defenses like res judicata offends the Due Process Clause is not ripe for consideration at this time.

In contrast to the Article III question, which speaks to the power of this Court to decide cases independently, free from interference from the political branches, the Due Process issue (if there is any) speaks to the degree of fairness to which Iran may or may not be entitled as a party named in these FSIA terrorism cases. To the extent that there is an argument that the statutory waiver of res judicata or collateral estoppel amounts to a violation of Due Process with respect to the treatment of Iran as a civil defendant, that

---

[29] It might very well be a different case if Congress had directed that res judicata and collateral estoppel are waived [such as] if Congress had directed the Courts to reinstate, all the claims that this Court and others had previously dismissed under that very same provision. As Congress in this case has seen fit to create an entirely new cause of action under § 1605A, and has repealed § 1605(a)(7) outright, this Court need not reach that more difficult issue.

argument is best articulated in the first instance by Iran itself. *** [T]he Iranian Government has elected not to defend itself during the merits phases of these actions [but] Iran has appeared repeatedly before the federal courts during the postjudgment phases of these actions, and has successfully defeated efforts by plaintiffs to execute the default civil judgments entered against the Government of Iran. *See, e.g., Ministry of Defense and Support for the Armed Forces of the Islamic Republic of Iran v. Elahi,* --- U.S. ----(April 21, 2009) (demonstrating how Iran litigated an action from the district court all the way through to the Supreme Court and thereby prevented certain FSIA judgment creditors from attaching one of its assets here in the United States). In view of these facts, this Court sees no reason to sua sponte examine whether the waiver of preclusion doctrines in new actions under § 1605A might somehow compromise purported Due Process rights of that foreign sovereign. ***

The cases this Court will examine here break down into roughly three categories ***. The first category of cases are those in which counsel for plaintiffs have taken a "belt and suspenders" approach by invoking both § 1083(c)(2) and (c)(3). *** The second category of cases involves those actions in which plaintiffs' counsel rely only on § 1083(c)(3), and so the attorneys in these actions have simply filed new actions under § 1605A as related actions to their prior cases, or as related to other cases pending under § 1605(a)(7) based on the same act or incident. The third category of cases are those in which plaintiffs' counsel have failed to invoke either § 1083(c)(2) or (c)(3), and yet, strangely, the attorneys in this category of cases have nonetheless filed motions that presume the right to relief under § 1605A. Without saying as much, it appears that counsel in this last category of cases have operated under the flawed assumption that § 1605A is automatically retroactive to their cases. *** [C]ounsel for most plaintiffs in these actions had only 60 days from the enactment of § 1083 in which they had to elect to proceed under § 1605A. *** In view of the very real potential for injustice these statutory issues of first impression may work for plaintiffs, this Court hereby emphasizes that the denial of relief under § 1605A is without prejudice. Plaintiffs may want to consider whether this Court has authority under Rule 60(b) to grant relief under the circumstances presented by their respective cases. *** Whether counsel assert reasons of "mistake, inadvertence, surprise, or excusable neglect" under (b)(1) or "any other reason that justifies relief" under (b)(6), empty rhetoric or *post hoc* justifications will not suffice. *** Additionally, *** detailed analysis with respect to the merits of the underlying claims is necessary to ensure that any decision granting relief under Rule 60(b) "will not be an empty exercise of futile gesture." ***

The most difficult issues confronting this unique area of the law relate to how plaintiffs in these FSIA terrorism cases might enforce their court judgments against the Islamic Republic of Iran. *** Today, the overwhelming majority of successful FSIA plaintiffs with judgments against Iran still have not received the relief that our courts have determined they are entitled to under the law.[44] ***

The experience of this Court in presiding over these actions for over a decade now has revealed that the political compromise achieved through the FSIA terrorism exception and its related enactments is superficial, filled with contradictions, and utterly in denial of practical and political realities-to say nothing of separation-of-powers problems-that courts can do little to address. Moreover ***the most recent reforms *** may even make matters worse.

To be sure, the changes *** appear, on the surface at least, to be extraordinarily advantageous to plaintiffs. *** [W]hat the Court sees in § 1083 is not so much meaningful reform, but rather the continuation of a failed policy and an expansion of the empty promise that the FSIA terrorism exception has come to represent. Through the enactment of § 1083, the political branches have promoted or otherwise acquiesced in subjecting Iran to sweeping liability while simultaneously overlooking the proverbial elephant in the room-and that is the fact that these judgments are largely unenforceable due to the scarcity of Iranian assets within the jurisdiction of the United States courts. *** Even if one assumes, however, that there are sufficient Iranian assets within the jurisdiction United States courts to satisfy the billions of dollars in judgments entered in these civil suits, *** whatever non-blocked assets might be found may be held by certain large financial institutions that are in fact agencies of instrumentalities of other foreign nations, which are in and of themselves subject to sovereign immunity under the FSIA. *** [I]t is the sovereign immunity from jurisdiction afforded to the financial entities of other foreign states-and not of Iran-that frequently frustrates recovery.

Moreover, plaintiffs still have the burden of proving Iranian ownership-whether beneficial or otherwise-of the assets at issue, which can be extraordinary challenging in this context. *** Finally, United States sovereign immunity will remain an issue under § 1610(g), as nothing prevents the President from seizing Iranian assets and vesting title to them in the U.S. Treasury, as Presidents have often done in the interest of important foreign policy objectives. Accordingly, the language in § 1610(g)(2) *** does not abrogate United States sovereign immunity with respect to

---

[44] This Court's observations and comments in this part of the opinion and throughout relate only to civil actions against Iran under the FSIA terrorism exception. The Court therefore does not express any views with respect to the viability of actions against other state sponsors of terrorism. While it appears that similar issues as those that impact actions against Iran may also be present in civil actions against other state sponsors of terrorism under either *§ 1605(a)(7)* or *§ 1605A*, cases against Iran face a number of unique challenges, such as the Algiers Accords and the establishment of the Iran-United States Claims Tribunal, which make it particularly difficult for plaintiffs to recover in these actions. Finally, the vast majority of cases that have been filed in this Court under the FSIA terrorism exception, have been filed against Iran. Thus, this Court does not want to assume problems or issues in other FSIA terrorism cases in which it has much more limited experience. *** [T]he Court's opinion today concerns only the FSIA terrorism exception. This Court does not address the Antiterrorism Act; the Torture Victim Protection Act; the Alien Tort Claims Act; or any other civil statutes that may permit civil actions for personal injury or death caused by terrorist acts.

funds held in the United States treasury.[48]

In terms of real and tangible property that Iran owns in the United States, much of it was once used for diplomatic or consular purposes by Iran and is therefore subject to the Vienna Conventions on Diplomatic and Consular Relations. *** Beyond the scarcity of Iranian assets, however, there are a number of other fundamental problems that confront these actions against Iran under the FSIA terrorism exception. In terms of United States foreign policy and national security objectives, one of the perverse outcomes of Congress' legislative victories over the Executive Branch is that what limited resources might have served as a bargaining chip that the President could have used in dealings with Iran are now subject to depletion as a result of the TRIA. These frozen assets, once at the disposal of the President in his management of foreign policy crises under the IEEPA and other authorities, are now largely subject to the jurisdiction of the Article III courts to be divided up among what few plaintiffs first lay claim to them in satisfaction of judgments *** .

Finally, because of the potential for these lawsuits to interfere with the foreign policy prerogatives of the President, another fundamental problem is that these actions have often pitted victims of terrorism against the Executive Branch, engendering a tremendous amount of acrimony in these victims toward the Federal Government, and, at times, the President. *** The administration has consistently maintained that such a lawsuit is barred by the Algiers Accords. *** [S]uccessive presidential administrations have intervened to quash writs of attachment issued by judgment creditors of Iran against Iranian diplomatic properties ***. Thus, victims of Iran-sponsored terrorism have grown increasingly frustrated as the Department of Justice has repeatedly opposed them in this context and defeated them in litigation. This frustration has been exacerbated by the fact that many high-level Executive officials, to include the President at times, have expressed sympathy for these victims and have even made public pronouncements of support for their cause, thereby sending mixed, and even outright contradictory signals.

The Executive Branch, in its dealings with Congress and in litigation before this Court, often takes the position that these actions threaten to undermine United States foreign policy and national security interests, both with respect to Iran specifically, as well as with respect to our relations with other nations more broadly. *** In frustration and anger, the victims, their lawyers, and even some members of Congress, have unfairly accused the Administration of defending Iran and siding with terrorists. *** What the victims, their attorneys, and backers in Congress apparently fail to see, or perhaps conveniently overlook, is that these actions frequently run into direct conflict with other sources of law, including bilateral Executive agreements, multilateral treaty obligations, and numerous other statutory and regulatory

---

[48] This Court is not overlooking the possibility of execution of judgments through enforcement proceedings in foreign jurisdictions, as least one scholar has recently suggested as a still-viable means of recovery in these actions. *** [E]nforcement of these terrorism judgments in foreign jurisdictions is a difficult prospect in these actions ***

authorities relating to foreign policy and the President's powers to manage national security crises. ***

As Congress usually backs the victims in their desire to press forward with lawsuits against Iran in the courts, the FSIA terrorism exception has had another unfortunate consequence of turning these already extraordinary lawsuits against a foreign power into high stakes contests between the two political branches. *** Like the victims, this Court finds itself relegated to the role of a powerless and frustrated bystander at times because under Article III this Court has neither foreign affairs powers nor any of the plenary authorities that are rightly vested in the political branches under our Constitution. *** All these problems might be easy enough to ignore, if it were not for the real people involved. ***

[A]s a measure devised to achieve justice for victims, the FSIA terrorism exception has failed *** It has not deterred Iran. *** Now today, in 2009, and ten years after this Court first found itself in the disquieting predicament of having to quash the first efforts of victims to enforce judgments achieved in this Court under the original version of the FSIA terrorism exception, this Court finds itself committed to a new round of litigation under the terms of § 1083 of the 2008 NDAA and a new, and supposedly improved, FSIA terrorism exception, § 1605A. *** Quite simply, this is déjà vu all over again.

The new terrorism exception § 1605A-much like § 1605(a)(7) before it-is in many respects a lie. The truth is, as long as civil litigation is the means by which our political branches choose to redress the harms suffered as a result of terrorism sponsored by Iran, the victims in these cases will continue to be unwitting participants in a meaningless charade. *** What this Court hopes our political branches will realize and appreciate today is that it is extraordinarily difficult to tell these victims that the rights and remedies they believe they are entitled to under the FSIA terrorism exception either do not exist or cannot be enforced. *** How much longer should this meaningless kabuki dance continue? *** Numerous commentators in the legal community, among others, have called for the repeal of the terrorism exception [and] there have been some efforts at systemic reforms introduced in Congress in recent years in the form of proposals for alternative compensations scheme that shift away from the private litigation paradigm. Most of these proposals would have established what would in essence function as a government insurance program in which qualifying victims of terrorism and their loved ones could file claims with the government for compensation. To date, none of these proposals has gotten any traction on Capitol Hill. ***

Looking back on these matters now, the Court cannot help but see the wisdom in two of Justice Rehnquist's opinions, both of which formed part of this Court's analysis of issues addressed earlier in today's decision. *** [W]hat this Court sees as an essential take-away from *Dames & Moore* is the discussion of the history of the longstanding practice of Executive claims settlement as a means to redress claims of United States nationals against foreign sovereigns. As Justice Rehnquist's discussion points out, Executive settlement of claims is a practice that reaches far back to the time of President George Washington, and numerous other American Presidents have exercised this authority consistently throughout our history. Moreover, as the Court's opinion observes, Executive claims settlement is a practice that has been reinforced by Congress though statutes establishing claims settlement commissions, such as the Foreign Claims Settlement Commission under the International Claims Settlement Act of 1949. Historically speaking, claims settlement by the Executive has often proven to be the only effective means of redress of those claims that originate during a period of strained relations with another nation. *** [Congress and the President] should pull together to find meaningful, workable solutions, rather than finding new and creative ways to push these tragic claims back onto the Courts. The private litigation has not worked, and simply is not workable, in this highly sensitive context involving affairs with a hostile nation. *** It would indeed be naive and insulting to the victims to suggest that these difficult cases can be resolved through cash pay outs from our Federal Government. Nothing could be further from the truth. Justice requires accountably for Iran, and a claims authority that simply doles out compensation to victims will not achieve that end any more than actions before this Court will.

The accountability aspect of the justice these victims seek certainly does not admit of any easy answers ***. It seems to this Court, however, that [a commission might be established to] include administrative law judges within the Executive Branch who could adjudicate claims under the terrorism exception and the body of law around it, as modified for such administrative proceedings. Through that process, the Executive Branch could obtain a thorough record of these horrific cases with the active participation of the victims, and thus these matters could then be more easily presented to the policy makers within the Executive Branch who are in the best position to hold Iran accountable. To enhance the prospect of accountability in these matters, the record from hearings on these case could then be published in an annual report to both Congress and the President and made available publicly to the citizens at large in an effort to keep these matters in focus.

Another advantage of a claims commission process within the Executive Branch is that Executive departments, and particularly the Department of State, have superior access to data and information that can help verify these terrorist incidents, and determine more reliably to what extent Iran may have played a role in supporting a particular act of terrorism. *** Similarly, the Executive Branch through the Treasury Department, particularly OFAC, is in the best position to locate assets of Iran in the United States, including unblocked assets. Accordingly, if it is empowered to do so, such a commission would be most capable of tracking down these assets and could more effectively liquidate them in satisfaction of claims, which would provide real accountability and might also defray the costs of the commission. *** Finally, the commission might work on an ongoing basis to make recommendations on how best to structure a large settlement with Iran, and perhaps other state sponsors of terrorism as well, in the event of normalization. ***

There is an important dialogue occurring in our nation over how best to deal with terrorism, including state sponsors of terrorism like Iran, but neither tough rhetoric nor large, unenforceable court judgments will help to resolve these extraordinarily sensitive and complex matters. *** The White House may have declared the war on terrorism over, but the threat of terrorism remains very real, and Americans will continue to suffer casualties as a result of this insidious and murderous evil. These victims certainly deserve justice, but the private litigation approach to redress is unsustainable and works at cross purposes of the President's foreign policy initiatives other developments that may lead to lasting change and peace. *** Thus, today's decision is merely a roadmap for the long road ahead that awaits these victims in renewed litigation before this Court under the FSIA terrorism exception, a provision of law that so far has gotten the victims of terrorism no closer to the justice they seek. *** This meaningless charade under the FSIA has gone on far too long. ***

Notes

1. **The Basics.** After reading this opinion, you should be able to (a) chronicle the development of the terrorism exception to the FSIA, (2) comprehend both the retroactivity issue and why the court believes this part of the 2008 amendments is constitutional, and (3) understand the impediments that lie before the plaintiffs.

2. **Politics.** Congress been more receptive to victim claims against state sponsors of terrorism than the President. Why? Then why hasn't Congress fixed the problems in this area? Do you agree with the Court's suggested solution?

3. **Court Options.** Do you sympathize with the Court or think the judge is just whining? Given the Court's perception of the endemic problem with civil litigation as a way to deal with state sponsors of terrorism, wouldn't he have done better to hold the retroactivity provisions unconstitutional? If he had done so, what would have happened next? What will happen given this ruling?

4. **Where is Iran?** What alternative to defaulting did Iran have in this litigation? Outside litigation, what are Iran's options? Do the suits discussed here have any effect on diplomatic relations between the US and Iran? Do they have any effect on trade with Iran?

2. SUITS AGAINST PRIVATE TERRORIST SUPPORTERS

Any national of the United States injured in his or her person, property, or business by reason of an act of international terrorism, or his or her estate, survivors, or heirs, may sue therefore in any appropriate district court of the United States and shall recover threefold the damages he or she sustains and the cost of the suit, including attorney's fees. Anti-Terrorism Act, 18 U.S.C. 2333

BOIM v. HOLY LAND FOUNDATION FOR RELIEF AND DEVELOPMENT

549 F. 3d 685 (CA7, 2008) (en banc), cert den. Oct. 2009

POSNER, Circuit Judge.

In 1996 David Boim, a Jewish teenager who was both an Israeli citizen and an American citizen, living in Israel, was shot to death by two men at a bus stop near Jerusalem. His parents filed this suit four years later, alleging that his killers had been Hamas gunmen and naming as defendants Muhammad Salah plus three organizations: the Holy Land Foundation for Relief and Development, the American Muslim Society, and the Quranic Literacy Institute. *** The complaint accused the defendants of having provided financial support to Hamas before David Boim's death and by doing so of having violated 18 U.S.C. § 2333(a), which provides that "any national of the United States injured in his or her person, property, or business by reason of an act of international terrorism, or his or her estate, survivors, or heirs, may sue therefor in any appropriate district court of the United States and shall recover threefold the damages he or she sustains and the cost of the suit, including attorney's fees." ***

The first panel opinion rejected the argument that the statute does not impose liability on donors to groups that sponsor or engage in terrorism. *** Before deciding what a plaintiff must prove in order to recover from a donor under section 2333, we should decide whether the statute applies. Section 2333 does not say that someone who assists in an act of international terrorism is liable; that is, it does not mention "secondary" liability, the kind that 18 U.S.C. § 2 creates by imposing criminal liability on "whoever commits an offense against the United States or aids, abets, counsels, commands, induces or procures its commission," or "willfully causes an act to be done which if directly performed by him or another would be an offense against the United States." *** So statutory silence on the subject of secondary liability means there is none; and section 2333(a) authorizes awards of damages to private parties but does not mention aiders and abettors or other secondary actors. *** To read secondary liability into section 2333(a), moreover, would enlarge the federal courts' extraterritorial jurisdiction. The defendants are accused of promoting terrorist activities abroad. Congress has the power to impose liability for acts that occur abroad but have effects within the United States, but it must make the extraterritorial scope of a statute clear.

The first panel opinion discussed approvingly an alternative and more promising ground for bringing donors to terrorist organizations within the grasp of section 2333. The ground involves a chain of explicit statutory incorporations by reference. The first link in the chain is the statutory definition of "international terrorism" as "activities that ... involve violent acts or acts dangerous to human life that are a violation of the criminal laws of the United States," that "appear to be intended ... to intimidate or coerce a civilian population" or "affect the conduct of a government by ... assassination," and that "transcend national boundaries in terms of the means by which they are accomplished" or "the persons they appear intended to intimidate or coerce.". *** [Sections 2331 and 2333] are part of the same statutory scheme and are to be read together. *** Section 2331(1)'s definition of international terrorism (amended in 2001 by the PATRIOT Act, but in respects irrelevant to this case) includes not only violent acts but also "acts dangerous to human life that are a violation of the criminal laws of the United States." Giving money to Hamas, like giving a loaded gun to a child (which also is not a violent act), is an "act dangerous to human life." And it violates a federal criminal statute enacted in 1994 and thus before the murder of David Boim-18 U.S.C. § 2339A(a), which provides that "whoever provides material support or resources ..., knowing or intending that they are to be used in preparation for, or in carrying out, a violation of [18 U.S.C. § 2332]," shall be guilty of a federal crime. So we go to 18 U.S.C. § 2332 and discover that it criminalizes the killing (whether classified as homicide, voluntary manslaughter, or involuntary manslaughter), conspiring to kill, or inflicting bodily injury on, any American citizen outside the United States.

By this chain of incorporations by reference (section 2333(a) to section 2331(1) to section 2339A to section 2332), we see that a donation to a terrorist group that targets Americans outside the United States may violate section 2333. Which makes good sense as a counterterrorism measure. Damages are a less effective remedy against terrorists and their organizations than against their financial angels. Terrorist organizations have been sued under section 2333, but to *collect* a damages judgment against such an organization, let alone a judgment against the terrorists themselves (if they can even be identified and thus sued), is *** well-nigh impossible. These are foreign organizations and individuals, operating abroad and often covertly, and they are often impecunious as well. So difficult is it to obtain monetary relief against covert foreign organizations like these that Congress has taken to passing legislation authorizing the payment of judgments against them from U.S. Treasury funds. E.g., Victims of Trafficking and Violence Protection Act of 2000, But that can have no deterrent or incapacitative effect, whereas suits against financiers of terrorism can cut the terrorists' lifeline.

And whether it makes good sense or not, the imposition of civil liability through the chain of incorporations is compelled by the statutory texts-as the panel determined in its first opinion. But in addition the panel placed a common law aiding and abetting gloss on section 2333. The panel was worried about a timing problem: section 2339A was not passed until 1994, and the defendants' contributions to Hamas began earlier. But that is not a serious problem on the view we take of the standard for proving causation under section 2333; we shall see that the fact of contributing to a terrorist organization rather than the amount of the contribution is the keystone of liability. *** Few future cases will be affected by the timing issue ***.

In addition to providing material support after the effective date of section 2339A, a donor to terrorism, to be liable under section 2333, must have known that the money would be used in preparation for or in carrying out the killing or attempted killing of, conspiring to kill, or inflicting bodily injury on, an American citizen abroad. We know that Hamas kills Israeli

Jews; and Boim was an Israeli citizen, Jewish, living in Israel, and therefore a natural target for Hamas. But we must consider the knowledge that the donor to a terrorist organization must be shown to possess in order to be liable under section 2333 and the proof required to link the donor's act to the injury sustained by the victim. The parties have discussed both issues mainly under the rubrics of "conspiracy" and "aiding and abetting." Although those labels are significant primarily in criminal cases, they can be used to establish tort liability, and there is no impropriety in discussing them in reference to the liability of donors to terrorism under section 2333 just because that liability is primary. Primary liability in the form of material support to terrorism has the character of secondary liability. Through a chain of incorporations by reference, Congress has expressly imposed liability on a class of aiders and abettors.

When a federal tort statute does not create secondary liability, so that the only defendants are primary violators, the ordinary tort requirements relating to fault, state of mind, causation, and foreseeability must be satisfied for the plaintiff to obtain a judgment. But when the primary liability is that of someone who aids someone else, so that functionally the primary violator is an aider and abettor or other secondary actor, a different set of principles comes into play. Those principles are most fully developed in the criminal context, but we must be careful in borrowing from criminal law because the state-of-mind and causation requirements in criminal cases often differ from those in civil cases. For example, because the criminal law focuses on the dangerousness of a defendant's conduct, the requirement of proving that a criminal act caused an injury is often attenuated and sometimes dispensed with altogether, as in the statutes that impose criminal liability on providers of material support to terrorism (18 U.S.C. §§ 2339A, B, and C), which do not require proof that the material support resulted in an actual terrorist act, or that punish an attempt (e.g., 18 U.S.C. § 1113) that the intended victim may not even have noticed, so that there is no injury. The law of attempt has no counterpart in tort law, because there is no tort without an injury.

So prudence counsels us not to halt our analysis with aiding and abetting but to go on and analyze the tort liability of providers of material support to terrorism under general principles of tort law. We begin by noting that knowledge and intent have lesser roles in tort law than in criminal law. A volitional act that causes an injury gives rise to tort liability for negligence if the injurer failed to exercise due care, period. But more is required in the case of intentional torts, and we can assume that since section 2333 provides for an automatic trebling of damages it would require proof of intentional misconduct even if the plaintiffs in this case did not have to satisfy the state-of-mind requirements of sections 2339A and 2332 (but they do). *** To give money to an organization that commits terrorist acts is not intentional misconduct unless one either knows that the organization engages in such acts or is deliberately indifferent to whether it does or not, meaning that one knows there is a substantial probability that the organization engages in terrorism but one does not care. *** So it would not be enough to impose liability on a donor for violating section 2333, even if there were no state-of-mind requirements in sections 2339A and 2332, that the average person or a reasonable person would realize that the organization he was supporting was a terrorist organization, if the actual defendant did not realize it. That would just be negligence. *** To give a small child a loaded gun would be a case of *criminal* recklessness and therefore satisfy the state of mind requirement for liability under section 2333 and the statutes that it incorporates by reference. For the giver would know he was doing something extremely dangerous and without justification. *** That you did not desire the child to shoot anyone would thus be irrelevant, not only in a tort case, but in a criminal case.

A knowing donor to Hamas-that is, a donor who knew the aims and activities of the organization-would know that Hamas was gunning for Israelis ***, that Americans are frequent visitors to and sojourners in Israel, that many U.S. citizens live in Israel *** and that donations to Hamas, by augmenting Hamas's resources, would enable Hamas to kill or wound, or try to kill, or conspire to kill more people in Israel. And given such foreseeable consequences, such donations would "appear to be intended ... to intimidate or coerce a civilian population" or to "affect the conduct of a government by ... assassination," as required by section 2331(1) in order to distinguish terrorist acts from other violent crimes, though it is not a state-of-mind requirement; it is a matter of external appearance rather than subjective intent, which is internal to the intender.

It is true that "the word 'recklessness' in law covers a spectrum of meaning, ranging from gross negligence in an accident case to the conduct of a robber in shooting at a pursuing policeman without aiming carefully." *** But when, as in the passages we have quoted both from judicial opinions and from the *Restatement,* recklessness entails actual knowledge of the risk, the tort concept merges with the criminal concept, which likewise "generally permits a finding of recklessness only when a person disregards a risk of harm of which he is aware." *** Critically, the criminal (like the tort) concept of recklessness is more concerned with the nature and knowledge of the risk that the defendant creates than with its magnitude. *** Ordinarily, it is true, the risk *is* great in a probabilistic sense; for the greater it is, the more likely it is to materialize and so give rise to a lawsuit or a prosecution and thus be mentioned in a judicial opinion. The greater the risk, moreover, the more obvious it will be to the risk taker, enabling the trier of fact to infer the risk taker's knowledge of the risk with greater confidence, though *** subject to rebuttal..

But probability isn't everything. The risk that one of the workers on a project to build a bridge or a skyscraper will be killed may be greater than the risk that a driver will be killed by someone who flings rocks from an overpass at the cars traveling on the highway beneath. But only the second risk, though smaller, is deemed excessive and therefore reckless. *** [T]he risk must be "weighed against the lack of social utility of the activity" in adjudging its reasonableness. *** So if you give a person rocks who has told you he would like to kill drivers by dropping them on cars from an overpass, and he succeeds ***, you are guilty of providing material support to a murderer, or equivalently of aiding and abetting-for remember that when the primary violator of a statute is someone who provides assistance to another he is functionally an aider and abettor. The mental element required to fix liability on a donor to Hamas is therefore present if the donor knows the character of that organization. ***

That brings us to our next question-the standard of causation in a suit under section 2333. *** In all these cases the requirement of proving causation is relaxed because otherwise there would be a wrong and an injury but no remedy because the court would be unable to determine which wrongdoer inflicted the injury. If "each [defendant] bears a like relationship to the event" and "each seeks to escape liability for a reason that, if recognized, would likewise protect each other defendant in the group, thus leaving the plaintiff without a remedy," the attempt at escape fails; each is liable. *** The cases that we have discussed do not involve monetary contributions to a wrongdoer. But then criminals and other intentional tortfeasors do not usually solicit voluntary contributions. Terrorist organizations do. But this is just to say that terrorism is *sui generis*. So consider an organization solely involved in committing terrorist acts and a hundred people all of whom know the character of the organization and each of whom contributes $1,000 to it, for a total of $100,000. The organization has additional resources from other, unknown contributors of $200,000 and it uses its total resources of $300,000 to recruit, train, equip, and deploy terrorists who commit a variety of terrorist acts one of which kills an American citizen. His estate brings a suit under section 2333 against one of the knowing contributors of $1,000. The tort principles that we have reviewed would make the defendant jointly and severally liable with all those other contributors. The fact that the death could not be traced to any of the contributors *** and that some of them may have been ignorant of the mission of the organization (and therefore not liable under a statute requiring proof of intentional or reckless misconduct) would be irrelevant. The knowing contributors as a whole would have significantly enhanced the risk of terrorist acts and thus the probability that the plaintiff's decedent would be a victim, and this would be true even if Hamas had incurred a cost of more than $1,000 to kill the American, so that no defendant's contribution was a sufficient condition of his death.

This case is only a little more difficult because Hamas is (and was at the time of David Boim's death) engaged not only in terrorism but also in providing health, educational, and other social welfare services. The defendants other than Salah directed their support exclusively to those services. But if you give money to an organization that you know to be engaged in terrorism, the fact that you earmark it for the organization's nonterrorist activities does not get you off the liability hook. The reasons are twofold. The first is the fungibility of money. If Hamas budgets $2 million for terrorism and $2 million for social services and receives a donation of $100,000 for those services, there is nothing to prevent its using that money for them while at the same time taking $100,000 out of its social services "account" and depositing it in its terrorism "account."

Second, Hamas's social welfare activities reinforce its terrorist activities both directly by providing economic assistance to the families of killed, wounded, and captured Hamas fighters and making it more costly for them to defect (they would lose the material benefits that Hamas provides them), and indirectly by enhancing Hamas's popularity among the Palestinian population and providing funds for indoctrinating schoolchildren. Anyone who knowingly contributes to the nonviolent wing of an organization that he knows to engage in terrorism is knowingly contributing to the organization's terrorist activities. And that is the only knowledge that can reasonably be required as a premise for liability. To require proof that the donor *intended* that his contribution be used for terrorism-to make a benign intent a defense-would as a practical matter eliminate donor liability except in cases in which the donor was foolish enough to admit his true intent. It would also create a First Amendment Catch-22, as the only basis for inferring intent would in the usual case be a defendant's public declarations of support for the use of violence to achieve political ends.

Although liability under section 2333 is broad, to maintain perspective we note two cases that fall on the other side of the liability line. One is the easy case of a donation to an Islamic charity by an individual who does not know (and is not reckless, in the sense of strongly suspecting the truth but not caring about it) that the charity gives money to Hamas or some other terrorist organization. The other case is that of medical (or other innocent) assistance by nongovernmental organizations such as the Red Cross and Doctors Without Borders that provide such assistance without regard to the circumstances giving rise to the need for it. Suppose an Israeli retaliatory strike at Hamas causes so many casualties that the local medical services cannot treat all of them, and Doctors Without Borders offers to assist. And suppose that many of the casualties that the doctors treat are Hamas fighters, so that Doctors Without Borders might know in advance that it would be providing medical assistance to terrorists.

However, section 2339A(b)(1) excludes "medicine" from the definition of "material resources." And even if the word should be limited (an issue on which we take no position) to drugs and other medicines, an organization like Doctors Without Borders would not be in violation of section 2333. It would be helping not a terrorist group but individual patients, and, consistent with the Hippocratic Oath, with no questions asked about the patients' moral virtue. It would be like a doctor who treats a person with a gunshot wound whom he knows to be a criminal. If doctors refused to treat criminals, there would be less crime. But the doctor is not himself a criminal unless, besides treating the criminal, he conceals him from the police (like Dr. Samuel Mudd, sentenced to prison for trying to help John Wilkes Booth, Lincoln's assassin, elude capture) or violates a law requiring doctors to report wounded criminals. The same thing would be true if a hospital unaffiliated with Hamas but located in Gaza City solicited donations.

Nor would the rendering of medical assistance by the Red Cross or

Doctors Without Borders to individual terrorists "appear to be intended ... to intimidate or coerce a civilian population" or "affect the conduct of a government by ... assassination," and without such appearance there is no international terrorist act within the meaning of section 2331(1) and hence no violation of section 2333. Nor is this point limited to the rendering of *medical* assistance. For example, UNRWA (the United Nations Relief and Works Agency for Palestine Refugees in the Near East) renders aid to Palestinian refugees that is not limited to medical assistance to individual refugees. But so far as one can glean from its website, it does not give money to organizations, which might be affiliates of Hamas or other terrorist groups; it claims to be very careful not to employ members of Hamas or otherwise render any direct or indirect aid to it.

To the objection that the logic of our analysis would allow the imposition of liability on someone who with the requisite state of mind contributed to a terrorist organization in 1995 that killed an American abroad in 2045, we respond first that that is not this case-the interval here was at most two years (1994, when section 2339A was enacted, to 1996, when Boim was killed)-and second that the imposition of liability in the hypothetical case would not be as outlandish, given the character of terrorism, as one might think. (There would of course be no defense of statute of limitations, since the limitations period would not begin to run until the tort was committed, and that would not occur until the injury on which suit was based was inflicted.) Terrorism campaigns often last for many decades. Think of Ireland, Sri Lanka, the Philippines, Colombia, Kashmir-and Palestine, where Arab terrorism has been more or less continuous since 1920. Seed money for terrorism can sprout acts of violence long after the investment. In any event, whether considerations of temporal remoteness might at some point cut off liability is not an issue we need try to resolve in this case.

An issue to which the first panel opinion gave much attention (but which received little attention from the parties afterward), is brought into focus by our analysis of the elements of a section 2333 violation. That is whether the First Amendment insulates financiers of terrorism from liability if they do not intend to further the illegal goals of an organization like Hamas that engages in political advocacy as well as in violence. If the financier knew that the organization to which it was giving money engaged in terrorism, penalizing him would not violate the First Amendment. Otherwise someone who during World War II gave money to the government of Nazi Germany solely in order to support its anti-smoking campaign could not have been punished for supporting a foreign enemy.

But it is true that "an organization is not a terrorist organization just because one of its members commits an act of armed violence without direct or indirect authorization, even if his objective was to advance the organization's goals, though the organization might be held liable to the victim of his violent act." *** The defendants in the present case could not be held liable for acts of violence by members of Hamas that were not authorized by Hamas. Nor would persons be liable who gave moral rather than material support, short of incitement, to violent organizations that have political aims. As intimated earlier in this opinion, a person who gives a speech in praise of Hamas for firing rockets at Israel is exercising his freedom of speech, protected by the First Amendment. But as Hamas engages in violence as a declared goal of the organization, anyone who provides *material* support to it, knowing the organization's character, is punishable (provided he is enchained by the chain of statutory incorporations necessary to impose liability under section 2333) whether or not he approves of violence.

Enough about the liability standard. *** A principal basis for the district Court's finding that the Foundation had violated the statute was the Court's giving collateral estoppel effect to findings made in *Holy Land Foundation for Relief & Development v. Ashcroft*, 219 F.Supp.2d 57 (D.D.C.2002), affirmed, 333 F.3d 156 (D.C.Cir.2003). *** In 2001 the Secretary of the Treasury determined that the Foundation "acts for or on behalf of" Hamas, and an order freezing the Foundation's funds was issued. The Foundation sued in the District of Columbia. The district court there found that the Secretary's finding was not "arbitrary and capricious" (the standard of review) and upheld the blocking order. Although the court recited extensive evidence that the Foundation knew that Hamas was and had long been a terrorist organization, and it appears that most or perhaps all of the evidence related to its knowledge before 1996 when David Boim was killed, the validity of the blocking order did not depend on the Foundation's knowledge. If someone is giving money to an organization that the government knows to be a terrorist organization, any subsequent gift can be blocked whether or not the donor knows (or agrees with the government concerning) the nature of the recipient. *** So the judgment against the Foundation must be reversed and the case against it remanded for further proceedings to determine its liability. ***

Nor should donors to terrorism be able to escape liability because terrorists and their supporters launder donations through a chain of intermediate organizations. Donor *A* gives to innocent-appearing organization *B* which gives to innocent-appearing organization *C* which gives to Hamas. As long as *A* either knows or is reckless in failing to discover that donations to *B* end up with Hamas, *A* is liable. Equally important, however, if this knowledge requirement is not satisfied, the donor is not liable. And as the temporal chain lengthens, the likelihood that a donor has or should know of the donee's connection to terrorism shrinks. But to set the knowledge and causal requirement higher than we have done in this opinion would be to invite money laundering, the proliferation of affiliated organizations, and two-track terrorism (killing plus welfare). Donor liability would be eviscerated, and the statute would be a dead letter. ***

To show that the murder of David Boim was the work of Hamas, the Boims submitted the declaration of Dr. Ruven [*sic*] Paz, a former member of the Israeli security community who describes himself as an expert in terrorism and counter-terrorism, Islamic movements in the Arab and Islamic world, Palestinian Islamic groups, and Palestinian society and politics. Based on his review of various exhibits submitted in connection with this case, his independent research, and his knowledge of how Hamas and other Islamic terror organizations operate, Paz concluded that Hinawi and Al-Sharif had murdered David Boim, that Hinawi and Al-Sharif were members of Hamas at the time they killed Boim, and that Hamas itself had accepted responsibility for the murder. *** We accept the panel majority's description of the infirmities of the evidence on which Reuven Paz (formerly research director of Shin Bet, Israel's domestic security agency) based his expert opinion. But we do not agree that the district court abused its discretion in allowing the opinion into evidence. *** [A]n expert is not limited to relying on admissible evidence in forming his opinion. *** An expert on terrorism in the Arab world, fluent in Arabic, Paz explained that the websites of Islamic movements and Islamic terrorist organizations have long been accepted by security experts as valid, important, and indeed indispensable sources of information. Terrorist organizations rely on the web to deliver their messages to their adherents and the general public. The United States Institute for Peace, a nonpartisan federal institution created by Congress, published an extensive report, submitted to the district court along with Paz's declaration, on the use of the Internet by terrorists. And-critically-the defendants presented no evidence to contradict Paz: no evidence that the killing of Boim was *not* a Hamas hit. Had they thought Paz had mistranslated the Arabic judgment against Hinawi, they could have provided the district court with their own translation. Had they doubted that Paz can identify a Hamas website (he gave the web addresses of several of them), they could have presented testimony to that effect. Paz's 12-page declaration is detailed, concrete, and backed up by a host of exhibits. The district court did not abuse its discretion in admitting his evidence; and with it in the record and *nothing* on the other side the court had no choice but to enter summary judgment for the plaintiffs with respect to Hamas's responsibility for the Boim killing. ***

ROVNER, Circuit Judge, with whom WILLIAMS, Circuit Judge, joins, concurring in part and dissenting in part, [and with which Judge Wood joins in relevant respects].

At this late stage in the litigation, we are now turning to a fundamental question: Are we going to evaluate claims for terrorism-inflicted injuries using traditional legal standards, or are we going to re-write tort law on the ground that "terrorism is *sui generis* "? My colleagues in the majority have opted to "relax[ ]"-I would say eliminate-the basic tort requirement that causation be proven, believing that "otherwise there would be a wrong and an injury but no remedy because the court would be unable to determine which wrongdoer inflicted the injury." The choice is a false one. The panel took pains to identify a number of ways in which the plaintiffs might establish a causal link between the defendants' financial contributions to (and other support for) Hamas and the murder of David Boim. It is not the case that the plaintiffs were unable show causation, it is rather that they did not even make an attempt; and that was the purpose of the panel's decision to remand the case. But rather than requiring the plaintiffs to present evidence of causation and allowing the factfinder to determine whether causation has been shown, the majority simply deems it a given, declaring as a matter of law that any money knowingly given to a terrorist organization like Hamas is a cause of terrorist activity, period. This sweeping rule of liability leaves no role for the factfinder to distinguish between those individuals and organizations who directly and purposely finance terrorism from those who are many steps removed from terrorist activity and whose aid has, at most, an indirect, uncertain, and unintended effect on terrorist activity. The majority's approach treats all financial support provided to a terrorist organization and its affiliates as support for terrorism, regardless of whether the money is given to the terrorist organization itself, to a charitable entity controlled by that organization, or to an intermediary organization, and regardless of what the money is actually used to do.

The majority's opinion is remarkable in two additional respects. By treating all those who provide money and other aid to Hamas as primarily rather than secondarily liable-along with those who actually commit terrorist acts-the majority eliminates any need for proof that the aid was given with the intent to further Hamas's terrorist agenda. Besides eliminating yet another way for the factfinder to distinguish between those who deliberately aid terrorism from those who do so inadvertently, this poses a genuine threat to First Amendment freedoms. Finally, the majority sustains the entry of summary judgment on a basic factual question-Did Hamas kill David Boim?-based on an expert's affidavit that both relies upon and repeats multiple examples of hearsay. *** [T]he majority gives its blessing to circumventing the rules of evidence altogether.

*** *One point of clarification at the outset.* The majority's opinion reads as though the defendants were writing checks to Hamas, perhaps with a notation on the memo line that read "for humanitarian purposes." If indeed the defendants were directing money into a central Hamas fund out of which all Hamas expenses-whether for humanitarian or terrorist activities-were paid, it would be easy to see that the defendants were supporting Hamas's terrorism even if their contributions were earmarked for charity. In fact, the case is not as simple as that. For example, much of the money that defendant HLF provided to Hamas apparently was directed not to Hamas per se but to a variety of zakat committees and other charitable entities, including a hospital in Gaza, that were controlled by Hamas. *See Holy Land Found. for Relief & Dev. v. Ashcroft,* 219 F.Supp.2d 57, 70-71 (D.D.C.2002), *j. aff'd,* 333 F.3d 156 (D.C.Cir.2003). I gather that this is a distinction without a difference in the majority's view, and certainly I agree that if the zakat committees and other recipients of HLF's funding were mere fronts for Hamas or were used to launder donations targeted for Hamas generally, then those donations ought to be treated as if they were direct donations to Hamas itself. But to the extent that these Hamas subsidiary organizations actually were engaged solely in humanitarian work and HLF was sending its money to those subsidiaries to support that work, HLF is one or more significant steps removed from the direct financing of terrorism and the case for HLF's liability for terrorism is, in my view, a much less compelling one. Defendant AMS is yet another step removed, in that AMS is alleged to have contributed money not to Hamas but to HLF.

Moreover, the type of support that can give rise to civil liability is not limited to financial support. As the panel discussed in *Boim I,* civil liability under section 2333(a) can result from the provision of "material support or resources" to terrorism and to terrorist organizations as prohibited by 18 U.S.C. §§ 2339A and 2339B, and "material support or resources" is defined broadly to include not only weapons and money but "any property, tangible or intangible, or service," including such things as lodging, expert advice, training, and personnel. § 2339A(b)(1). Notably, the plaintiffs have sought to hold AMS liable, and the district court found it liable, not simply for the financial support it provided to HLF, but for various types of pro-Hamas advocacy, such as hosting Hamas speakers at its conferences, publishing sympathetic editorials in its newsletter, and the like. *** So the majority's rule has the potential to sweep within its reach not only those who write checks to Hamas and the organizations that it controls but also individuals and groups who support Hamas and its affiliates in myriad other ways, including those who advocate on Hamas' behalf. ***

The majority has chosen to evaluate the prospective liability of the defendants in this case through the lens of primary liability, reasoning that those who provide financial and other aid to terrorist organizations are themselves engaging in terrorism and thus may be held liable on the same basis as those who actually commit terrorist acts. *** I continue to believe that Congress when it enacted section 2333(a) subjected to civil liability not only those who engage in terrorism but also those who aid or abet terrorism. The government as an *amicus curiae* has expressed agreement with that view. The secondary liability framework is a much more natural fit for what the defendants here are alleged to have done and *** the elements of aiding and abetting serve a useful function in distinguishing between those who intend to aid terrorism and those who do not.

But even if I am wrong about the availability of secondary liability under section 2333(a), I have my doubts about the viability of the majority's theory of primary liability. For there are conceptual problems with this approach, particularly as it is applied in this case. *** It may be more plausible to say, as the majority does, that one who provides financial support to Hamas, even to its charitable subsidiaries, is "provid[ing] material support or resources" to Hamas's terrorist acts in violation of section 2339A(a) by increasing the heft of Hamas's purse. But that theory too has its problems. The language of section 2339A(a) requires that the material support or resources be given with the knowledge or intent that they "*are to be used* in preparation for, or in carrying out" one of a number of specified crimes, including as relevant here the killing of American citizens. In other words, the donor must at least know that the financial or other support he lends to Hamas *will be used* to commit terrorist acts. In *Boim I,* the panel agreed that giving money to Hamas with the purpose of financing its terrorism would both violate section 2339A(a) and give rise to civil liability under section 2333. But at that early stage of this litigation, the Boims had a straightforward and direct theory that Hamas's American contributors (including HLF) intended for their money be used to support terrorism, that the zakat committees and other humanitarian organizations to which these contributors were sending their money were mere fronts for Hamas, and that the money received by these front organizations was laundered and funneled into Hamas's coffers to fund terrorist activity, including the attack that took David Boim's life. That theory was consistent with the express terms of section 2339A(a). But that is no longer the Boims' theory (they have long since abandoned it in favor of aiding and abetting and conspiracy), nor is it the majority's. The majority posits that any money given to a Hamas affiliate, even if it is given with a benign intent and even if it is actually put to charitable use, furthers Hamas's terrorism in one way or another. Even if that is so, not all donors will know or intend that their contributions will be used to commit the sorts of criminal acts identified in section 2339A(a). And what the statute proscribes is the knowing or intentional support of specific terrorist acts, not the knowing support of a terrorist organization. If nothing else, the defendants' contributions to charitable organizations controlled by Hamas would present a factual question as to whether the defendants knew that they were supporting the murder of American citizens or any of the other crimes listed in section 2339A(a).

Causation, as the majority acknowledges, is a staple of tort law, and yet the majority relieves the plaintiffs of any obligation to demonstrate a causal link between whatever support the defendants provided to Hamas and Hamas's terrorist activities (let alone David Boim's murder in particular). Instead, the majority simply declares as a matter of law that any money given to an organization like Hamas that engages in both terrorism and legitimate, humanitarian activity, necessarily enables its terrorism, regardless of the purpose for which the money was given or the channel through which the organization received it. *** The majority offers no rationale for relieving the plaintiffs of the burden of showing causation, and there is none that I can discern. ***

The majority's decision to carve out an exception to its sweeping liability rule for non-governmental organizations like the Red Cross and Doctors Without Borders who provide humanitarian aid to individuals affiliated with Hamas lays bare the weakness of the rule's analytical underpinnings. Providing medical care on the battlefield to individuals that one knows are Hamas terrorists undoubtedly would have the effect of aiding Hamas's terrorism-patching up an injured terrorist enables him to strike again. I do not doubt that such aid could be given for noble and compassionate reasons, but neither do I doubt that from the standpoint of the Israelis whom Hamas targets, the knowing provision of medical care to individual terrorists could be and would be understood as aid to terrorism. One can also imagine scenarios in which medical aid could be provided for ignoble and devious reasons. *** My colleagues reason that there is a distinction between providing aid to an individual, even if he is terrorist, and aid to a terrorist organization. But to my mind, that is a distinction without a difference when one knows that the individual being aided is engaged in terrorism (or is recklessly indifferent to that possibility). *** The distinction between aiding an organization and aiding individual members of that organization does not hold up. *** If a plaintiff were required to establish a donor's intent to aid terrorism, along with a causal link between the aid provided and terrorist activity, then the factfinder would be able to draw reasoned, pragmatic distinctions (subject, of course, to appellate review) between those defendants who are truly enabling terrorism and those who are not. ***

The secondary liability framework that we outlined in *Boim I,* and on which the plaintiffs built their entire case against the defendants, provides a more grounded and effective way of identifying and distinguishing between the types of support and supporters that actually aid terrorism and those that do not. *** Proof of intent would serve two important functions. First, it would serve to single out the most culpable of Hamas's financiers and other supporters by focusing on those who actually mean to contribute to its terrorist program, as opposed to those who may unwittingly aid Hamas's terrorism by donating to its charitable arm. *** The intent requirement would also play a vital role in protecting the First Amendment rights of those accused of facilitating Hamas's terrorism. The possibility that a section 2333(a) suit might implicate First Amendment rights is not an abstract one. Even to the extent that such a suit is based on the money that a defendant has contributed to an organization that engages in terrorism, the defendant's First Amendment rights must be accounted for, given that donating money to an organization, though it is not speech in and of itself, is one way to express affinity with that organization and to help give voice to the viewpoints that organization espouses. *** Certainly, given the government's paramount interest in battling terrorism, the government may prospectively ban, and even criminalize, donations to an organization that it deems a terrorist organization. *** But when an organization engages in both legal and illegal activities and donations to that organization have not been prohibited, a donor may not be held civilly liable for the organization's illegal activity based solely on his contributions, for to do so would infringe upon the defendant's First Amendment freedoms. *** One need only look again at the conduct for which AMS was held liable ***: hosting Hamas speakers at its conferences, publishing pro-Hamas articles and editorials in his newsletters, rallying support for HLF when it was declared a terrorist organization, and so forth. All of that conduct involves pure speech. *** Moreover, should there be evidence that a defendant has made statements in support of the use of violence to achieve political ends, relying on such statements as proof that the defendant provided financial or other aid to a terrorist organization with the intent to support its terrorist activities would not, as the majority suggests, pose a First Amendment problem.

Finally, the majority treats Dr. Paz's affidavit as sufficient evidence that Hamas was responsible for David Boim's murder. Although the majority recognizes that Paz relied on a variety of unauthenticated electronic and documentary sources for his conclusion, it nonetheless deems his affidavit admissible and sufficient to sustain summary judgment for the plaintiffs on this point because an expert is free in forming his opinion to rely on evidence that would not be admissible in court. *** Paz's opinion is based exclusively on what these websites and documents say; he has no personal knowledge of who killed David Boim. So if these sources are not genuine or say something other than what he has represented, then his opinion is worthless. *** Terrorism is a scourge, but it is our responsibility to ask whether it presents so unique a threat as to justify the abandonment of such time-honored tort requirements as causation. Our own response to a threat can sometimes pose as much of a threat to our civil liberties and the rule of law as the threat itself. *** [I]n our zeal to bring justice to bereaved parents, we must not lose sight of the need to prove liability on the facts that are presented to the court. Assumptions and generalizations are no substitute for proof. Particularly because, unfortunately, this probably will not be the last case brought by a victim of international terrorism, it is crucial that we be as clear as we can in fleshing out the statutory requirements and that we do not rush to judgment. *** I am still of the view that this case needs to be remanded for further proceedings. ***

I believe that the following is a fair summary of the formal requirements that the *en banc* majority has announced for proving a case under § 2333:

1. Act requirement: the defendant must have provided material assistance, in the form of money or other acts, directly or indirectly, to an organization that commits terrorist acts.

2. State of mind requirement: the defendant must either know that the donee organization (or the ultimate recipient of the assistance) engages in such acts, or the defendant must be deliberately indifferent to whether or not it does so.

3. Causation: there is no requirement of showing classic "but-for" causation, nor, apparently, is there even a requirement of showing that the defendant's action would have been sufficient to support the primary actor's unlawful activities or any limitation on remoteness of liability. ***

*** I find it ill-advised to exempt plaintiffs suing under § 2333 on a "material assistance" theory from showing causation is that this approach also appears to eliminate the need to show what was classically called "proximate cause." *** At some point, the harm is simply too remote from the original tortious act to justify holding the actor responsible for it. It may be the case that the boundaries of liability are wider for intentional torts, but that does not mean that they are limitless. In part, this reflects the reality that as the temporal or factual chain between the tortious act and the harm becomes ever longer, the likelihood of intervening or superseding causes becomes greater. The *en banc* majority freely concedes that there are no limits at all to its rule, and that a donor who gave funds to an organization affiliated with Hamas in 1995 might still be liable under § 2333 half a century later, in 2045. I see no warrant for assuming that § 2333, unlike the rest of tort law, contains no scope-of-liability limitations. I note as well that such an open-ended rule would be in serious tension with the general four-year statute of limitations Congress has passed for civil actions based on statutes passed after 1990 (like this one).

The scope of the causation element is not my only concern about the *en banc* majority's opinion. My other problem is with its application of the principles that, at a high level of generality, state the law correctly. As I noted earlier, the plaintiffs must prove that the defendant provided material assistance to an organization that commits terrorist acts. But what does it take to qualify as such an organization? The Boims did not sue Hamas, nor does their case rely on the proposition that QLI or AMS sent money directly to Hamas. We must decide how far down the chain of affiliates, in this shadowy world, the statute was designed to reach, and how deeply Hamas must be embedded in the recipient organization. QLI and AMS argue strenuously that at worst they sent money to charitable organizations with some kind of link to Hamas. Some might have been analogous to wholly owned subsidiaries; some might have been analogous to joint ventures; some might have been independent entities that accepted funding from Hamas as well as other more reputable organizations. The record throws little light on these matters, because the district court thought them irrelevant. As I understand the *en banc* majority opinion, it is saying that even if an independent day care center receives $1 from organization H known to be affiliated with Hamas, not only the day care center but also anyone who gave to H is liable for all acts of terrorism by Hamas operatives from that time forward against any and all Americans who are outside the United States.

That is a proposition of frightening, and I believe unwise, breadth. The *en banc* majority has tried to carve out humanitarian non-governmental organizations like the American Red Cross and Doctors Without Borders, which (fortuitously) may also benefit from a "medical services" exemption in the statute. But I am not sure that it has succeeded. Those worthy organizations are not the only ones committed to nondiscriminatory treatment of all needy human beings. *** The *en banc* majority also slides over the statutory requirement (derived from its chain of statutory connections) that the entity providing material assistance must know that the donee plans to commit terrorist acts against U.S. citizens. All that is necessary, we are told, is that a donor [to Hamas-and presumably to another organization with an adequate link to Hamas, whatever that may be] who knew the aims and activities of the organization [only Hamas? or the affiliated recipient?]-would know that Hamas was gunning for Israelis, that Americans are frequent visitors to and sojourners in Israel, that some Israeli citizens have U.S. citizenship as well, and that donations to Hamas, by augmenting Hamas's resources, would enable Hamas to kill or wound, or try to kill, or conspire to kill more people in Israel.

This is awfully vague. Americans travel, and are known to travel, to every country on the face of the globe-they even go to places like Antarctica that are not even countries. If one could, it would be more realistic and sound as a legal matter simply to hold that it makes no difference whether or not the terrorist acts that the organization commits are directed toward

Americans. The only problem with such a holding-which otherwise would be a routine application of the doctrine of transferred intent-is that the statutory basis for a tort action under § 2333 depends upon a finding that the material support violated U.S. federal criminal law, and that here the crime in question is the killing of an American citizen outside the United States. In my view, given the language of the statutes that Congress has passed thus far, we are required to take a more restricted view of § 2333. A statute focusing on extraterritorial killings of Americans would still be a strong tool against terrorist activities and organizations that threaten vital U.S. interests. Al Qaeda, for example, trumpets its intent to target Americans whenever and wherever it can. If the plaintiffs could show both that Hamas has done the same thing and further that Hamas's intent should be attributed to the donee organization (recalling once again that neither QLI nor AMS gives money directly to Hamas), then a § 2333 claim may proceed; otherwise, it may not. Put differently, I find it difficult to read § 2333 as creating a claim against an organization that has, in effect, declared war on the entirety of civilization. ***

Notes

1. **Plaintiffs.** Why would Congress limit those who may sue under §2333 to "national[s] of the United States"? There is another statute, the Alien Tort Statute (ATS), 28 U.S.C. §1350 (2000) that provides for United States court jurisdiction over "any civil action by an alien for a tort only, committed in violation of the law of nations or a treaty of the United States." See the cases in Chapter 1 concerning the limits of the ATS.

2. **Breadth of Liability.** Terrorist perpetrators can clearly be sued, but often these actors would be dead (e.g. suicide bombers), unable to pay a judgment, or evasive (particularly if they are overseas). Congress meant others to be liable whose role was less direct, so tort as well as criminal liability for "material support" seems within the scope of the statute. The tort theory disputes in *Boim* are over (1) primary v. secondary liability, (2) causation and proximate cause, and (3) the intent needed. Which opinion, the majority or the dissent, seems to have the better of each of these arguments?

3. **First Amendment.** The Seventh Circuit's en banc decision preceded the Supreme Court's decision in *Holder v. Humanitarian Law Project*, which you read in Chapter II. Consider the majority and dissenting opinions in light of *HLP*.

4. **Doctors Without Borders.** Why is there such a gulf between the majority and dissent over the consequences of the decision for humanitarian aid organizations? Suppose a law school clinic were to provide advice about the requirements of international law to Hamas (or to an organization that supports Hamas. Would it potentially be liable in tort to plaintiffs like the Boims?

5. **Forum.** Since the act occurred overseas, why didn't this case get dismissed on *forum non conveniens* grounds even though the defendants were based in the United States? The ATA, in §2334, requires that the "foreign court is significantly more convenient and appropriate" and that the foreign court "offers a remedy which is substantially the same as the one available in the courts of the United States."

6. Proof Problems. How will the plaintiff obtain information about not only the defendant's relation to the terrorist act but also about its intent? Such information might be in the possession of uncooperative foreign officials or even sympathetic United States officials who will not release the information for state secrets reasons. Does this explain the role of Dr. Paz in this litigation? Do you agree with the majority or dissent concerning how the courts should evaluate such testimony?

7. Another Case, Other Theories. *Boim* is the leading case concerning tort liability of material supporters, but it is not the only case. In *Linde v. Arab Bank*, 384 F. Supp. 2d 571 (E.D.N.Y 2005.) the court used an "aiding and abetting" framework to hold that a bank headquartered in Jordan but with a New York branch potentially liable under section 2333. Here are the facts on which this ruling was principally premised:

> The complaints identify *** prominent terrorist organizations operating in Palestinian controlled territory. *** The complaints also identify several charities that plaintiffs allege operate as front organizations for HAMAS, assisting it in carrying out its terrorist activities ***. Several of the charities maintain bank accounts at Arab Bank through which the Bank provides them with financial services, such as receiving deposits and processing wire transfers. The complaints allege that the Bank knows that these organizations are fronts which support Hamas's terrorist activities, and that the Bank's continued provision of banking services to these groups facilitates their illegal activities. The complaints identify one Arab Bank account number that plaintiffs allege belongs to HAMAS itself, and which HAMAS uses to collect funds in support of violent activities. *** Plaintiffs allege that the Bank is the exclusive administrator of the death and dismemberment benefit plan [provided by the Saudi Committee In Support of the Intifada AL Quds ("Saudi Committee"), a private charity registered with the Kingdom of Saudi Arabia]. Once the Saudi Committee prepares a list of eligible martyrs, the list is provided to the Bank. Arab Bank, in consultation with the Saudi Committee and local representatives of HAMAS, finalizes the lists, maintains a database of persons eligible to receive benefits under the death and dismemberment plan, and opens a dollar account for each beneficiary. Families who choose to collect the benefit must present to the Bank an official certification from the Palestinian Authority that includes the individualized identification number of the martyr. *** Plaintiffs allege that these payments create an incentive to engage in terrorist acts by rewarding all Palestinian terrorists, regardless of their affiliation with a particular group.*** Plaintiffs' allegations are sufficient to establish secondary liability under each one of these theories. As to conspiracy, they adequately allege that Arab Bank knowingly and intentionally agreed to provide services to organizations it knew to be terrorist organizations and that they were injured by an overt act which was done in furtherance of the common scheme. It is not necessary that they allege that Arab Bank either planned, or

intended, or even knew about the particular act which injured a plaintiff. *** Administering the death and dismemberment benefit plan further supports not only the existence of an agreement but Arab Bank's knowing and intentional participation in the agreement's illegal goals. *** The same allegations support aiding and abetting liability. The complaints allege that the financial services provided by Arab Bank, and the administration of the death and dismemberment benefit plan, provided substantial assistance to international terrorism. They also allege that the Bank's administration of the benefit plan encouraged terrorists to act. These allegations are well within the mainstream of aiding and abetting liability. They describe the wrongful acts performed by the terrorists, the defendant's general awareness of its role as part of an overall illegal activity, and the defendant's knowing and substantial assistance to the principal violation.

8. Services as Support. Is providing assistance by doing the normal work of the bank (providing services for customers) indicative of intent to further criminal terrorist activities by the customer? On the other hand, what is the intent of a corporation, other than the acts it does as an entity? Would a forger who provided fake passports to all who were willing to pay the price be liable under the material support statute if a passport was obtained by an al Qaida member? Is here any further information needed to convict him?

9. Individual Donors. Do *Boim* and *Linde* make it dangerous to give money to any organization that might give funds to widows and orphans of deceased terrorists? If a person gives money to an organization that does much regular charitable work but also supports "martyr'" dependents, is the individual liable for tort claims? Again, see the section on "material support" of terrorist organizations in Chapter II.

10. Donor Advice. What would you advise an individual who is considering giving money to an Islamic charity? Is it surprising that gifts to Islamic charities have dropped dramatically in the past few years?

3. LIABILITY FOR FAILURE TO PROTECT AGAINST TERRORISM

a. Government Liability

MACHARIA v. UNITED STATES
334 F.3d 61 (D.C. Cir. 2003)

TATTEL, Circuit Judge

Appellants, a prospective class of more than 5,000 Kenyan citizens and businesses injured in the 1998 bombing of the United States Embassy in

Nairobi, Kenya, sued the United States under the Federal Tort Claims Act alleging that the government negligently failed to secure the Embassy and to warn of a potential terrorist attack. ***

At approximately 10:30 on the morning of August 7, 1998, an explosives-laden truck dispatched by the al Qaeda terrorist network approached the entrance to the rear parking lot of the United States Embassy in Nairobi, Kenya. An embassy guard, a Kenyan employed by UIIS, a security company working under contract with the State Department, refused to open the Embassy gate. Blocked from entering the compound, one of the two terrorists began shooting while the other threw a flash grenade at another guard. Unarmed and unable to notify the Embassy's detachment of United States Marines either by telephone or radio, the guards ran for cover. Although apparently still off-premises, the terrorists detonated their explosives, causing massive internal damage to the Embassy, killing 44 Embassy employees and approximately 200 Kenyan citizens, injuring some 4,000 individuals, and causing the collapse of an adjacent building. Approximately nine minutes later, another al Qaeda terrorist detonated an explosives-laden truck some thirty-five feet from the outer wall of the United States Embassy in Dar Es Salaam, Tanzania. That attack killed twelve people and injured eighty-five. ***

The FTCA authorizes district courts to hear suits for money damages against the United States "for injury or loss of property, or personal injury or death caused by the negligent or wrongful act or omission of any employee of the Government ... if a private person ... would be liable to the claimant in accordance with the law of the place where the act or omission occurred." The Act's waiver of sovereign immunity has various exceptions, however. We agree with the district court that three of those exceptions -- discretionary function, foreign country, and independent contractor -- bar appellants' claims under counts I and II.

Discretionary Function Exception

The FTCA's discretionary function exception bars claims "based upon the exercise or performance or the failure to exercise or perform a discretionary function or duty on the part of a federal agency or an employee of the Government, whether or not the discretion involved be abused." In *United States v. Gaubert*, 499 U.S. 315 (1991), the Supreme Court established a two-part test for determining whether the discretionary function exception applies in a particular case. First, because "the exception covers only acts that are discretionary in nature, acts that involve an element of judgment or choice," *Gaubert's* first step requires that we determine whether any "federal statute, regulation, or policy specifically prescribes a course of action for an employee to follow." If one does, "the employee has no rightful option but to adhere to the directive." Under *Gaubert's* second step, which applies when there is no "federal statute, regulation, or policy" and when the "challenged conduct involves an element of judgment," the court must decide "whether the judgment is of the kind that the discretionary function exception was designed to shield." "Because the purpose of the exception is to prevent judicial 'second-guessing' of legislative and administrative decisions grounded in social, economic, and political policy through the medium of an action in tort," the Supreme Court explained, "when properly construed, the exception protects only governmental actions and decisions based on considerations of public policy."

In this case, even after several months of discovery, appellants failed to establish, as *Gaubert*'s first step requires, the existence of a "federal statute, regulation, or policy" that applies to any of the government's allegedly negligent conduct, including the government's alleged failure to secure the Embassy and to warn of a potential attack. This failure is hardly surprising, for as the district court explained, "determinations about what security precautions to adopt at American embassies, and what security information to pass on, and to whom this information should be given, do not involve the mechanical application of set rules, but rather the constant exercise of judgment and discretion." *** In short, embassy security is vested in the discretion of State Department employees, from the Secretary to the foreign service officers at various embassies.

Conceding that they "did not rely on any documents" to demonstrate that a "federal statute, regulation, or policy" applied to the government's conduct, appellants contend that the discretionary function exception is nevertheless inapplicable because the government failed to follow an *unwritten* federal policy. *** Even assuming an unwritten practice can satisfy the statute's requirement, appellants have failed to establish that DS had a *mandatory* obligation to file a trip report. ***

Having failed to identify a relevant "federal statute, regulation, or policy" under *Gaubert*'s first step, appellants contend that the discretionary function exemption is inapplicable under the second step because the government's conduct was the product of simple negligence rather than social, political, or economic considerations. Specifically, appellants cite twenty-one instances of alleged government negligence, from its failure to fix a pin in the drop bar at the Embassy's rear parking lot to its failure to timely design a training program for vehicle bomb recognition and prevention that led to appellants' injuries. *** [A]s the government points out in its brief, "decisions about foreign embassies, especially their location and structure, require agency officials to account for policy objectives, and consult and negotiate with the host country-actions that, by their very nature, affect foreign relations." ***

Foreign Country and Independent Contractor Exceptions

Our conclusion regarding the discretionary function exception leaves only appellants' allegations of negligence by Embassy guards. According to appellants, the Kenyans UIIS hired as Embassy guards lacked adequate training and equipment, and negligently failed to identify and stop the terrorists from detonating the bomb. *** The FTCA's waiver of sovereign immunity applies only to tortious acts undertaken by "officers or employees of any federal agency ... and persons acting on behalf of a federal agency in an official capacity." *** A critical element in distinguishing an agency from a contractor," the Court explained, "is the power of the Federal Government 'to control the detailed physical performance of the contractor.'"

Appellants contend that DS designed the Embassy's contracts for employing local guards, handled all payments to UIIS, and regularly provided advice regarding the contracts. They also contend that the contract required UIIS to provide the State Department with the names of the local guards it employed, to submit the names of all personnel to the Department for approval, to ensure that guards wear uniforms approved by the Department, and to conduct inventories as directed by the Department. Far from demonstrating day-to-day State Department supervision of the contractor, however, these allegations establish only that "the contract set forth detailed guidelines and regulations that the contractor was required to conform with as it implemented its hiring, supervision and training of Embassy local guards." *** [T]o the extent that appellants allege negligent supervision of local guards by State Department employees located in the United States, those allegations are, for the reasons given above, barred by the discretionary function exception.***

A. v. UNITED KINGDOM AND IRELAND
8 E.H.R.R. CD49 (1986)
European Commission on Human Rights

The applicant's husband, a foreman and a part-time reserve constable in the RUC, was abducted and shot dead on 31 August 1980, whilst driving a milk lorry. (This was a regular run he did to help out in the family dairy business.) It appears that he resisted arrest by the IRA and was shot. His body was taken away and not given up by the IRA until 13 days later when his body was abandoned 20 yards from the County Monaghan border. This caused the applicant and the family great anxiety and suffering. The Provisional IRA claimed responsibility and first said that they were holding the applicant's husband for interrogation, and only after massive public protest and a direct appeal by the applicant on television was it admitted that he was dead and his body returned by being left at the roadside. The applicant still suffers from nerves and nightmares. ***

1.   The applicant complains of violations of the [European] Convention on behalf of herself in respect of the murder of her husband. She states that this murder does not itself ground a claim, because no Government can be expected to guarantee absolutely the life of any citizen, but that, rather, the claim is grounded in the totality of the circumstances in which she lives and in the legislative measures and practices of the respondent States, which have failed to take adequate and effective measures to counter terrorism and to protect the applicant and others like her. ***

2.   However, under Art. 25 of the Convention, an individual applicant can only complain to the Commission of alleged violations of his or her own Convention rights but not, by an *actio popularis*, of complaints concerning rights of third persons

3.   It follows that the Commission, in its examination of the present application, must limit its consideration to the applicant's own situation and to the murder of her husband.

4.   The Commission holds that the applicant, as the wife who was affected by the death of her husband, may in this respect claim to be a "victim", in the sense of Art. 25. ***

5.   The applicant submits that the murder of her husband by terrorists was made possible by the respondent State's failure to prevent terrorism; that no domestic remedy was available in respect of this failure; ***

15.   The Commission observes that the applicant's complaint concerning her present situation in Northern Ireland raises the question of State responsibility for the protection of the right to life in accordance with Art. 2 of the Convention. It follows that this complaint cannot be declared inadmissible, under Art. 27(2), as being incompatible with the Convention *ratione personae*, on the ground that it is directed against acts of private persons.

16.   Art. 2(1) of the Convention states that everyone's right to life "shall be protected by law". The applicant does not suggest that there are no laws in Northern Ireland protecting the right to life, or that they are not applied.

17.   It is the applicant's case that Art. 2(1) interpreted in the light of the phrase "The High Contracting Parties shall secure ... the rights and freedoms defined in Section I" in Art. 1 of the Convention, requires the United Kingdom, in the emergency situation prevailing in Northern Ireland, to protect the right to life not only by criminal prosecution of offenders but also by such preventive control, through deployment of its armed forces, as appears necessary to protect persons who are considered to be exposed to the threat of terrorist attacks.

18.   The Commission has already found (that Art. 2, which states that "the right of life shall be protected by law" , may, as other Convention Articles, indeed give rise to positive obligations on the part of the State. That, however, does not mean that a positive obligation to exclude any possible violence could be deduced from this Article.

19.   The Commission does not find that it can be its task, in its examination of the present applicant's complaint under Art. 2, to consider in detail, as she appears to suggest, the appropriateness and efficiency of the measures taken by the United Kingdom to combat terrorism in Northern Ireland.

20.   The Commission notes from the applicant's submissions that the army strength in Northern Ireland was raised from 4,000 to about 10,500 men and that, between August 1969 and December 1981, several hundred members of the armed and security forces lost their lives there combating terrorism.

21.   The Commission cannot find that the United Kingdom was required under the Convention to protect the applicant by measures going beyond those actually taken by the authorities in order to shield life and limb of the inhabitants of Northern Ireland against attacks from terrorists. The applicant's submissions concerning the breakout from Maze Prison and the attempt to block frontier crossings cannot in the Commission's view lead to the conclusion that the United Kingdom is in respect of the applicant in breach of Art. 2 of the Convention.

22.   The Commission concludes that the applicant's complaint under Art. 2 against the United Kingdom concerning her own situation in Northern Ireland is manifestly ill-founded within the meaning of Art. 27(2) of the Convention.

23.   In the light of its above considerations under Art. 2 the Commission finds no issues under the other Convention Articles invoked by the applicant in support of her complaint against the United Kingdom. *** Held, *** *complaints inadmissible.*

Notes

1. Consistency. Are *Macharia* and *A v. UK and Ireland* inconsistent? If not, which provides the better rule of law and why?

2. Total Bar? Are there any circumstances in which either the United States or European Union courts would find governments liable for negligently failing to protect a citizen from terrorism?

b. Business Liability

STANFORD v. KUWAIT AIRWAYS CORPORATION
89 F.3d 117 (2d Cir. 1996)

MCLAUGHLIN, Circuit Judge

Four terrorists boarded Middle Eastern Airlines ("MEA") flight 426 in Beirut, Lebanon. The flight ended in Dubai, United Arab Emirates where the four terrorists disembarked, and connected with Kuwait Airways flight KU221, bound for Karachi, Pakistan. Three American diplomats, William Stanford, Charles Hegna, and Charles Kapar were also on board KU221. Shortly after take-off from Dubai, the terrorists hijacked KU221, forcing the pilot to turn north. The plane landed in Tehran, Iran and sat on the airport tarmac for days while the terrorists tortured the three American diplomats, finally murdering Hegna and Stanford. Plaintiffs, Charles Kapar and the estates of the two deceased diplomats, brought this suit alleging that MEA's negligence was a proximate cause of the injuries and deaths occurring aboard KU221. *** Plaintiffs appeal, arguing that MEA owed them a duty to use due care to avoid the known risk of hijacking, MEA breached that duty by failing to screen passengers adequately in Beirut, and this breach was a proximate cause of their injuries. We reverse and remand for a new trial.

In May, 1983, the International Air Transport Association ("IATA") held its 21st Security Advisory Committee meeting in Montreal, Canada to discuss security measures among member airlines. *** The meeting discussed one particular method for terrorists to capitalize on the lax security at a "dirty" airport and board a plane bound for a more secure airport. Upon arrival at the more secure airport, the terrorists would transfer to a "target" airline and then hijack the target plane: "The would be terrorist may well have travelled on the original Carrier without any intention of committing a terrorist act against that Carrier, but with the object of a transfer to another target Carrier." *** IATA cautioned its members that "the only solution to this situation is to create circumstances where some degree of reliance can be placed on the security measures of other States." *** MEA, Kuwait Airways, and other members of IATA, participated in a program of "interline" ticketing, a reciprocal arrangement whereby a single ticket written by one airline for a flight on that airline will also accommodate the same passenger's flight on a second airline. *** Passengers need only one ticket and one baggage check to travel on both airlines.

An MEA official admitted that he knew, in December 1984, that the security measures at Beirut airport were minimal. Specifically, MEA knew that X-ray machines for checking passengers' luggage were not operating and that metal detectors were apparently functioning but "locked" and not in use. In addition, MEA was aware or, in the exercise of reasonable prudence, should have been aware that many airlines had ceased all operations out of Beirut because of the threats of violence coming from Islamic militants in Beirut.

MEA maintained, however, that it was helpless to offer additional security measures because airport security was under the sole control of the Lebanese army. An MEA official testified that the military conducted searches of passengers and luggage by hand, but did not employ any more sophisticated forms of security screening. He also testified that MEA never asked the Lebanese military to strengthen the security measures at the Beirut airport.

MEA's employees at the Beirut airport were responsible for selling and examining passengers' tickets, checking the information on the tickets against visas and passports, and receiving baggage from the passengers. These employees were the first line of defense between hijackers who slipped through the ludicrous security at Beirut Airport and innocent passengers aboard MEA and connecting flights. Nevertheless, they did not perform any other searches, known as "secondary screening," of passengers or their bags. ***

On December 2, 1984, ***, four Hezbollah hijackers purchased interline tickets for travel from Beirut to Bangkok, Thailand, via Dubai and Karachi. They began their journey by presenting their interline tickets to the MEA agents at the Beirut airport, where they boarded MEA flight 426 to Dubai.

The hijackers' tickets had a stench about them. They had been purchased on very short notice with cash, and the flight traced an outlandish route: the passengers were to fly on MEA from Beirut to Dubai, where they were then to connect with Kuwait Airways to Karachi, and from there continue on to Bangkok. This itinerary was bizarre because: (1) there were regularly scheduled direct flights between Beirut and Bangkok; (2) the four terrorists were the only passengers aboard MEA 426 to connect with a Kuwaiti airline--every other passenger aboard who happened to be travelling to Karachi connected in Dubai with a Pakistani International Airlines flight; and (3) there was another scheduled MEA flight from Beirut directly to

Karachi on December 4th, a day after the hijackers' actual departure. If the hijackers had waited for this next flight, they would have avoided (a) the stop at Dubai, and (b) an unnecessary twenty-hour layover in Karachi while waiting for the same December 4th plane that would eventually take them to Bangkok. Still another suspicious feature of the journey was that the men were travelling one-way, a very long distance, without any checked baggage. None of this apparently raised the eyebrow of any MEA employee.

Upon arrival in Dubai, the hijackers alighted MEA flight 426 and headed for their target: Kuwait Airways flight KU221. KU221 had originated in Kuwait City, bound for Karachi with a fateful stop in Dubai. It carried William Stanford, Charles Hegna and Charles Kapar. The three were employed by the United States Department of State, Agency for International Development, and were en route from Kuwait City to their base of operations in Karachi. KU221 stopped in Dubai to refuel and to pick up additional passengers heading for Karachi. Passengers connecting to KU221 from other flights were required to take a bus on the tarmac to KU221 and climb a set of stairs to enter the jet through the forward door of the plane.

A Kuwait Airlines official placed a table at the top of the stairs leading to the forward door of flight KU221, where he checked connecting passengers' carry-on luggage as they boarded. One witness, Neil Beeston, testified that he saw three of the four hijackers standing on the tarmac near the unguarded- and not in use-- rear stairs of the airplane during the boarding process. Other testimony established that the tarmac, in general, was poorly lit and not well guarded.

Once KU221 was airborne, and over the Gulf of Oman, two hijackers burst into the cockpit, pressed a grenade against the flight commander's neck and ordered him to fly the plane to Mehrabad Airport in Tehran. The flight crew complied, landing in Tehran ***. The four hijackers were armed with pistols, explosives, and other weapons. They released the women and children passengers, but singled out Hegna, Stanford, Kapar and a fourth American, John Costa, and forced them into the first-class cabin. Over the next six days the hijackers murdered Hegna and Stanford and beat and tortured Kapar and Costa, using them as pawns to gain the release of . . . prisoners in Kuwait. Iranian commandos raided the aircraft on December 9th, rescued the remaining passengers, and captured the hijackers.

No one knows how the hijackers got their weapons on board flight KU221. *** In addition, there was evidence that it was a common practice in the Middle East to allow one passenger to check in for a number of other passengers, thus allowing armed passengers to avoid contact with airline officials. *** The case against MEA went to trial but the jury was unable to reach a verdict. The court declared a mistrial. Later, MEA moved for judgment as a matter of law . . ., and the court granted the motion. *** The court reasoned that: (1) there was insufficient evidence for the jury to conclude that MEA owed plaintiffs a duty of care to avoid the risk of hijacking on another airline; (2) MEA's inaction was not a proximate cause of any of the injuries; and (3) the failure of (a) security at the Dubai airport and (b) Kuwait Airways's secondary screening measures were independent intervening acts breaking the causal chain that might have linked MEA's actions to the injury and deaths aboard flight KU221.

Plaintiffs appeal arguing that: (1) MEA had a duty to use due care to avoid the risk of hijacking within the interline system; (2) there was sufficient evidence for a jury to conclude that the failure of MEA to use due care was a proximate cause of the injuries; and (3) the foreseeable negligence of (a) the security officials at Dubai and (b) Kuwait Airways were not intervening acts breaking the causal link between MEA and the injuries and deaths. ***

It is elementary that to find a party liable in negligence, there must have been a duty -- a relationship between the two parties such that society imposes an obligation on one to protect the other from an unreasonable risk of harm. The question here is: did the circumstances in this case create a duty on the part of MEA to protect Kapar, Hegna, and Stanford? We think they did, and hold, as a matter of law, that MEA had a duty to protect the plaintiffs from unreasonable risk of foreseeable harm. *** In determining whether a duty exists, a court should examine: (1) the relationship between the parties; and (2) the reasonable foreseeability of harm to the person injured. ***

Although the plaintiffs were not passengers on an MEA flight, it is too late in the day to suggest that contractual privity is a prerequisite to the existence of a duty. *** Thus, even without contractual privity,

> whenever one person is by circumstances placed in such a position with regard to another that every one of ordinary sense who did think would at once recognize that if he did not use ordinary care and skill in his own conduct with regard to the circumstances he would cause danger of injury to the person or property of the other, a duty arises to use ordinary care and skill to avoid such danger.

Stagl v. Delta Airlines, Inc., 52 F.3d 463, 469 (2d Cir. 1995) ***

Plaintiffs demonstrated that MEA joined an enterprise with interline airlines, including Kuwait Airways, to facilitate travel among the cooperating carriers. MEA's participation in interline arrangements with other IATA airlines was a lucrative venture. It expanded the reach of their routes, and facilitated inter-airline travel. Interline carriers shared the profits resulting from this cooperative endeavor.

In addition, based on evidence produced at trial, a jury could properly find that: as early as May, 1983, the Security Advisory Committee of IATA issued a warning that terrorists would board airlines at airports with poor security, and transfer to target airlines at other airports with tighter security. *** While it is unclear from the record to whom IATA issued the warning, MEA, as a member of IATA, knew or, in the exercise of reasonable care should have known, of the warning. In addition, MEA was fully aware of the poor security measures at the Beirut airport. ***

IATA concluded that a critical way to protect passengers aboard target flights was to place increased reliance on security measures directed toward passengers upon their initial entry into the interline system. Thus, IATA implicitly recognized the principle that "duty is largely grounded in the natural responsibilities of societal living and human relations, such as have the recognition of reasonable men . . . ." ***

Accordingly, a jury could reasonably find that when MEA accepted interline passengers aboard its planes in Beirut, it knew or should have known that there was a danger that terrorists would try to board their airline only to transfer later to a vulnerable, interline target airplane. MEA operated out of Beirut airport, amidst heightened political tensions, an ongoing terrorist campaign that posed continuing threats against American and Kuwaiti citizens and establishments, and lax airport security. In addition, MEA was armed with information regarding unique terrorist hijacking tactics. Accepting interline passengers, while perhaps not normally a function implicating the safety of third parties, became such a function under the perilous circumstances existent at that time in Beirut.

The duty to protect third parties "arises under circumstances where the party is in a position so that 'anyone of ordinary sense who thinks will at once recognize that if he does not use ordinary care and skill in his own conduct with regard to those circumstances, he will cause danger of injury to . . . [another].'" *** If MEA, in the exercise of ordinary care, should have recognized that under these circumstances, knowing what it knew, there was an unreasonable risk of hijacking to passengers aboard its flight and other connecting flights, then the jury could find that MEA should have implemented secondary screening measures or warned other interline members of a possible threat of hijacking. ***

In determining the existence of a duty, a court may examine the reasonable foreseeability of harm to the party injured. *** There was evidence that MEA knew: (1) of the threatened attacks by Hezbollah terrorists; (2) that terrorists were boarding flights in dirty airports to infiltrate other airlines; (3) that the Beirut airport had extraordinarily poor security; and (4) that the four hijackers who boarded in Beirut had tickets which teemed with suspicion. A jury could reasonably find, under these circumstances, that if MEA did nothing, it would create a zone of risk that stretched at least as far as the innocent passengers aboard flights with which the four hijackers would eventually connect. It lay well within ordinary prudence for an airline to realize that persons at the dirty Beirut airport who purchased tickets on short notice with cash, checked no luggage for a flight from the Middle East to the Far East, and took a circuitous route aboard flights which (a) they did not have to take to reach their destination, (b) created inordinate delays and layovers, and (c) no other passenger aboard MEA flight 426 took, posed a hijacking threat. *** We conclude that MEA, as a first leg interline carrier, had a duty to protect passengers on other interline connecting flights from unreasonable risk of harm through the use of reasonable precautions in the face of reasonably foreseeable risks.

On the evidence presented a jury could reasonably find that MEA failed to take reasonable precautions in the face of foreseeable risks. This question should be left for the jury to decide on retrial.

[The Court concluded that the district court wrongly held that plaintiffs failed to establish proximate cause.] [T]his is a case where reasonable minds can differ. The plaintiffs presented testimony and circumstantial evidence from which a reasonable person could infer that MEA's failure to act proximately caused Kapar's injuries and the deaths of Stanford and Hegna. ***

[A] reasonable juror could conclude that the terrorists had the weapons in their possession at the very beginning of their journey in Beirut. One could reasonably conclude that the hijackers boarded the MEA flight armed (consistent with the modus operandi outlined in the IATA circular) and, once in Dubai, one "clean" hijacker checked in for the other three who attempted to bypass the Kuwait Airways official at the forward door by entering the rear stairwell. One could infer from the facts that (1) the cleaning crew discovered nothing, (2) no one left the plane, and (3) the plane's panels were not disturbed, that the weapons were not already aboard KU221 when it arrived in Dubai. *** While reasonable minds could differ on this evidence, there is not such a dearth of proof on the issue of causation as to justify taking the matter away from the jury.

Finally, the district court concluded that plaintiffs failed to establish a proximate link between MEA and the injuries and deaths aboard flight KU221, because the negligence of the security officials and of the Kuwait Airways employees in Dubai were independent intervening acts breaking the causative chain. *** Again, we must disagree. The causative link is not broken by the negligent conduct of a third person when such conduct is normal or foreseeable under the circumstances. ***

We recognize, as the district court did, that this is an "anguishingly distressing case." *** And we concede it is a close call. We conclude, however, that MEA was not so far removed from the actions aboard the ill-fated Kuwait Airways flight as to be entitled to judgment as a matter of law. MEA took on responsibilities in the clouded atmosphere of threatened terrorist attacks, with knowledge of terrorist hijacking tactics. With this awareness and knowledge it had a commensurate duty to protect those within a foreseeable scope of danger. Accordingly, we reverse the district Court's grant of MEA's Rule 50(b) motion, and remand the case for a new trial.

Notes

1. Steak and Sizzle. What are the atmospheric comments that the court presents to show that MEA and Kuwait Airlines were negligent? Would these items be relevant in ordinary tort litigation?

2.   Policy. What changes do you think will result from this judgment? Is this the right way to insure greater prevention steps? What other alternatives can you imagine?

3.   Precedent. Discuss the extent to which this case might have ramifications on American and United Air Lines in connection with the September 11 attacks. Try distinguishing the cases, then analogizing the cases. What does this exercise show you about the choices of victims in deciding whether to sue or seek relief from the Victim Compensation Fund? Would victims in the twin towers be similarly situated to passengers on the jets that struck the towers? The next case presents the landscape of that fund, private suits, and ground victims.

IN RE SEPTEMBER 11TH LITIGATION
280 F. Supp.2d 279 (S.D.N.Y. 2003)

ALVIN K. HELLERSTEIN, District Judge

The injured, and the representatives of the thousands who died from the terrorist-related aircraft crashes of September 11, 2001, are entitled to seek compensation. By act of Congress, they may seek compensation by filing claims with a Special Master established pursuant to the Air Transportation Safety and System Stabilization Act of 2001 (49 U.S.C. § 40101) ("the Act"). Or they may seek compensation in the traditional manner, by alleging and proving their claims in lawsuits, with the aggregate of their damages capped at the limits of defendants' liability insurance. If they choose the former alternative, their claims will be paid through a Victim Compensation Fund from money appropriated by Congress, within a relatively short period after filing. Claimants will not have to prove fault or show a duty to pay on the part of any defendant. The amount of their compensation, however, may be less than their possible recovery from lawsuits, for non-economic damages are limited to $ 250,000, economic damages are subject to formulas that are likely to be less generous than those often allowable in lawsuits, and punitive damages are unavailable. I have discussed, and upheld, certain portions of the Act and regulations related to the Fund in Colaio v. Feinberg, 262 F. Supp. 2d 273 (S.D.N.Y. 2003), appeal filed, June 6, 2003.

Approximately seventy of the injured and representatives of those who died, and ten entities which sustained property damage, have chosen to bring lawsuits against defendants whom they claim are legally responsible to compensate them: the airlines, the airport security companies, the airport operators, the airplane manufacturer, and the operators and owners of the World Trade Center. The motions before me challenge the legal sufficiency of these lawsuits, and ask me to dismiss the complaints because no duty to the plaintiffs existed and because the defendants could not reasonably have anticipated that terrorists would hijack several jumbo jet airplanes and crash them, killing passengers, crew, thousands on the ground, and themselves. I discuss in this opinion the legal duties owed by the air carriers, United and American Airlines, and other airlines and airport security companies affiliated with the air carriers to the plaintiffs who were killed and damaged on the ground in and around the Twin Towers and the Pentagon; by the Port Authority of New York and New Jersey ("Port Authority") and World Trade Center Properties LLC ("WTC Properties") to those killed and injured in and around the Twin Towers; and by the Boeing Company, the manufacturer of the "757" jets that were flown into the Pentagon and the field near Shanksville, Pennsylvania, to those killed and injured in the two crashes. I hold in this opinion that each of these defendants owed duties to the plaintiffs who sued them, and I reject as well defendants' alternative arguments for dismissal. ***

The Air Transportation Safety and System Stabilization Act of 2001 ("the Act"), passed in the weeks following the September 11 attacks, provides that those who bring suit "for damages arising out of the hijacking and subsequent crashes" must bring their suits in the United States District Court for the Southern District of New York. The Southern District has "original and exclusive jurisdiction" "over all actions brought for any claim (including any claim for loss of property, personal injury, or death) resulting from or relating to the terrorist-related aircraft crashes of September 11, 2001," with the exception of claims to recover collateral source obligations and claims against terrorists and their aiders, abettors and conspirators, The Act provides that the governing law shall be "derived from the law, including choice of law principles, of the State in which the crash occurred unless such law is inconsistent with or preempted by Federal law." Thus, all cases, whether arising out of the crashes in New York, Virginia, or Pennsylvania, must be brought in the Southern District of New York, to be decided in accordance with the law of the state where the crash occurred. ***

Plaintiffs' individual pleadings have been consolidated into five master complaints, one for the victims of each crash and one for the property damage plaintiffs. Plaintiffs allege that the airlines, airport security companies, and airport operators negligently failed to fulfill their security responsibilities, and in consequence, the terrorists were able to hijack the airplanes and crash them into the World Trade Center, the Pentagon, and the field in Shanksville, Pennsylvania, killing passengers, crew, and thousands in the World Trade Center and the Pentagon and causing extensive property damage. The complaints allege that the owners and operators of the World Trade Center, World Trade Center Properties LLC and the Port Authority of New York and New Jersey, negligently designed, constructed, maintained, and operated the buildings, failing to provide adequate and effective evacuation routes and plans. Plaintiffs who died in the crashes of American flight 77 and United flight 93 also sue Boeing, the manufacturer of the two "757" airplanes, for strict tort liability, negligent product design, and breach of warranty.

*** The Aviation Defendants concede that they owed a duty to the crew and passengers on the planes, but contend that they did not owe any duty to "ground victims." The Port Authority and WTC Properties argue that they did not owe a duty to protect occupants in the towers against injury from hijacked airplanes and, even if they did, the terrorists' actions broke the chain of proximate causation, excusing any negligence by the WTC Defendants. And Boeing argues that it did not owe a duty to ground victims or passengers, and that any negligence on its part was not the proximate cause for the harms suffered by the plaintiffs. ***

Plaintiffs allege that the Aviation Defendants negligently failed to carry out their duty to secure passenger aircraft against potential terrorists and weapons smuggled aboard, enabling the terrorists to hijack and crash four airplanes. Plaintiffs argue that the Aviation Defendants employed their security measures specifically to guard against hijackings, and knew or should have known that the hijacking of a jumbo jet would create substantial risks of damage to persons and property, not only to passengers and crew, but also to people and property on the ground. Plaintiffs assert also that terrorism was a substantial international concern, and that suicidal acts by terrorists seeking to cause death, injury and havoc to as many innocent people as possible had become a frequently used strategy. ***

Airlines typically recognize responsibility to victims on the ground. *** However, counsel did not concede duty in relation to those killed and injured on the ground in the September 11, 2001 aircraft crashes. The "potential for a limitless liability to an indeterminate class of plaintiffs," he argued, made the instant cases distinguishable. The distinction, in his opinion, is "not [a] difference in kind," but "the law of extraordinary consequences [which] can sometimes draw a distinction based on degree." He explained:

> We are in an area of policy and there are lines to be drawn that may occasionally seem arbitrary. But what really distinguishes our case from [the hypothetical example of an airplane crash into Shea Stadium while taking off from, or landing at, La Guardia airport] is the intentional intervening acts of the third party terrorists. ***

It is the Court's job to "fix the duty point by balancing factors," including the following:

> the reasonable expectations of parties and society generally, the proliferation of claims, the likelihood of unlimited or insurer-like liability, disproportionate risk and reparation allocation, and public policies affecting the expansion or limitation of new channels of liability.

*** [P]laintiffs are favored by the first of the factors set out above, for plaintiffs and society generally could have reasonably expected that the screening performed at airports by the Aviation Defendants would be for the protection of people on the ground as well as for those in airplanes. Ours is a complicated and specialized society. We depend on others charged with special duties to protect the quality of the water we drink and the air we breathe, to bring power to our neighborhoods, and to enable us to travel with a sense of security over bridges, through tunnels and via subways. We live in the vicinity of busy airports, and we work in tall office towers, depending on others to protect us from the willful desire of terrorists to do us harm. Some of those on whom we depend for protection are the police, fire and intelligence departments of local, state and national governments. Others are private companies, like the Aviation Defendants. They perform their screening duties, not only for those boarding airplanes, but also for society generally. It is both their expectation, and ours, that the duty of screening was performed for the benefit of passengers and those on the ground, including those present in the Twin Towers on the morning of September 11, 2001.

Nothing that I hold or say should be considered as any form of ruling on the reasonableness of the Aviation Defendants' conduct. Nor should it be construed as a finding on whether their conduct was the proximate cause of plaintiffs' damages, or whether that of the terrorists' constituted an intervening act breaking the chain of causation. I simply hold that the Aviation Defendants, and plaintiffs and society generally, could reasonably have expected that the screening methods at Logan, Newark, and Dulles airports were for the protection of people on the ground as well as for those on board the airplanes that the terrorists hijacked.

The second factor to consider is "the proliferation of claims." *532 Madison Ave.*, 750 N.E.2d at 1101. Proliferation, however, should not be mistaken for size of number. As long as the claimants are known and circumscribed by those "who have, as a result of these events, suffered personal injury or property damage," there is not an impermissible proliferation. *** Plaintiffs, the ground victims in the cases before me, complain of directly-caused physical injuries to their persons or property. Their number may be large, tragically large, and the potential liability may be substantial if negligence and cause is proven, but the class is not indefinite and claims at this point cannot proliferate. Furthermore, the defendants will be liable only if plaintiffs sustain their burden of proof, with the aggregate liability of the air carriers, aircraft manufacturers, airport sponsors, and persons with a property interest in the World Trade Center capped by federal statute to the limits of their liability insurance coverage. Thus, "the likelihood of unlimited or insurer-like liability," the third factor of 532 Madison Avenue, does not weigh heavily against a finding of duty.

The fourth factor of 532 Madison Avenue is "disproportionate risk and reparation allocation." This inquiry probes who was best able to protect against the risks at issue and weighs the costs and efficacy of imposing such a duty. The airlines, and the airport security companies, could best screen those boarding, and bringing objects onto, airplanes. *** [T]he Aviation Defendants could best control the boarding of airplanes, and were in the best position to provide reasonable protection against hijackings and the dangers they presented, not only to the crew and passengers, but also to ground victims. Imposing a duty on the Aviation Defendants best allocates the risks to ground victims posed by inadequate screening, given the Aviations Defendants' existing and admitted duty to screen passengers and items carried aboard.

Lastly, recognition of a duty on the part of the Aviation Defendants would not substantially expand or create "new channels of liability," the fifth and last factor of 532 Madison Avenue. New York courts have found on other occasions that aircraft owners and operators owe a duty to those on the ground who may be harmed or sustain property damage resulting from improper or negligent operation of an aircraft. Although these cases involved injuries resulting from negligent operation or maintenance of airplanes, rather than negligence in regulating the boarding of airplanes, there is no principled distinction between the modes of negligence. *** Accordingly, I hold on the pleadings that the Aviation Defendants owed a duty of care to the ground victim plaintiffs. ***

*** The Port Authority of New York and New Jersey and WTC Properties LLC move to dismiss all claims brought against them as owners and operators of the World Trade Center for loss of life, personal injury, and damage to nearby property and businesses resulting from the collapse of the Twin Towers. *** Plaintiffs allege that the WTC Defendants: 1) failed to design and construct the World Trade Center buildings according to safe engineering practices and to provide for safe escape routes and adequate sprinkler systems and fireproofing; 2) failed to inspect, discover, and repair unsafe and dangerous conditions, and to maintain fireproofing materials; 3) failed to develop adequate and safe evacuation and emergency management plans; 4) failed to apply, interpret and/or enforce applicable building and fire safety codes, regulations and practices; and 5) instructed Tower Two occupants to return to their offices and remain in the building even while the upper floors of Tower One were being consumed by uncontrolled fires following the airplane crash into Tower One. ***

The WTC Defendants argue that the complaints against them should be dismissed because they had no duty to anticipate and guard against deliberate and suicidal aircraft crashes into the Towers, and because any alleged negligence on their part was not a proximate cause of the plaintiffs' injuries. The Port Authority argues also that it is entitled to immunity because the complained-of conduct essentially consisted of governmental functions. *** Plaintiffs argue that defendants owed a duty, not to foresee the crimes, but to have designed, constructed, repaired and maintained the World Trade Center structures to withstand the effects and spread of fire, to avoid building collapses caused by fire and, in designing and effectuating fire safety and evacuation procedures, to provide for the escape of more people. *** The duty of landowners and lessors to adopt fire-safety precautions applies to fires caused by criminals. *** Likewise, the WTC Defendants owed a duty to the occupants to create and implement adequate fire safety measures, even in the case of a fire caused by criminals such as those who hijacked flights 11 and 175 on September 11, 2001.

The criteria for establishing the existence of duty, discussed previously in the context of the Aviation Defendants' duty to ground victims, applies as well to the duty of landowners to lessees and business occupants. First, the parties and society would reasonably expect that the WTC Defendants would have a duty to the occupants of the Twin Towers in designing, constructing, repairing and maintaining the structures, in conforming to appropriate building and fire safety codes, and in creating appropriate evacuation routes and procedures should an emergency occur. Second, although a large number of claims have been filed against the WTC Defendants, there is no danger that the number will proliferate beyond those who died in the collapse of the structures or were injured while trying to escape. Similarly, the WTC Defendants are not subject to unlimited or insurer-like liability, for they can be held liable only after a showing of fault and only to those who suffered death, personal injury, or property damage resulting from their alleged negligence. Furthermore, by specific provision of the Air Transportation Safety and System Stabilization Act, their liability is limited to their insurance coverage. Fourth, the defendants' relationship with the plaintiffs, as their landlord or the landlord of their employer, placed the WTC Defendants in the best position to protect against the risk of harm. And fifth, as discussed above, imposing a duty on the WTC Defendants in the situation at hand will not create new channels of liability, for the New York courts have held traditionally that landlords owe duties of safety and care to the occupants of leased premises and their invitees.

A finding of duty also requires a consideration of the nature of plaintiffs' injuries, and the likelihood of their occurrence from a particular condition. "Defining the nature and scope of the duty and to whom the duty is owed requires consideration of the likelihood of injury to another from a dangerous condition or instrumentality on the property; the severity of potential injuries; the burden on the landowner to avoid the risk; and the foreseeability of a potential plaintiff's presence on the property." The criteria are clearly satisfied, for the severity and likelihood of potential injuries of people unable to escape from a heavily occupied building before fires envelope evacuation routes is high. The more difficult question is whether the injuries arose from a reasonably foreseeable risk.

Plaintiffs argue that the WTC Defendants had a duty to exercise reasonable care in order to mitigate the effects of fires in the Twin Towers. They allege that defendants knew about the fire safety defects in the Twin Towers, as evident by the Allied litigation concerning inadequate fireproofing in the construction of the buildings; that defendants could have reasonably foreseen crashes of airplanes into the Towers, given the near miss in 1981 of an Aerolineas Argentinas Boeing 707 and the studies conducted during the Towers' construction reporting that the Towers would be able to withstand an aircraft crash; that defendants were aware of numerous fires and evacuations that had occurred at the World Trade Center since its creation, including arson fires in 1975 and the 1993 terrorist-caused explosion in the garage under Tower One; and that the World Trade Center continued to be a prime target of terrorists. A finding of duty does not require a defendant to have been aware of a specific hazard. It is enough to have foreseen the risk of serious fires within the buildings and the goal of terrorists to attack the building. ***

This is a very early point in the litigation. There has been no discovery, and defendants' motions to dismiss accept, as they must, all allegations of the complaints. I hold that the WTC Defendants owed a duty to the plaintiffs, and that plaintiffs should not be foreclosed from being able to prove that defendants failed to exercise reasonable care to provide a safe environment for its occupants and invitees with respect to reasonably foreseeable risks. ***

Some of those who were injured and the successors of those who died in the Pentagon, in American Airlines flight 77 which crashed into the Pentagon, and in United Air Lines flight 93 which crashed into the Shanksville, Pennsylvania field, claim the right to recover against Boeing, the manufacturer of the two "757" jets flown by United and American. Plaintiffs allege that Boeing manufactured inadequate and defective cockpit doors, and thus made it possible for the hijackers to invade the cockpits and take over the aircraft. Boeing moves to dismiss the lawsuits. *** [Two suits also] charge Boeing with strict tort liability and negligent design based on an unreasonably dangerous design of the cockpit doors. ***

Boeing moves to dismiss both the claims of negligent design and breach of warranty, arguing that it did not owe a duty to prevent the use of the plane as a weapon, and that the independent and supervening acts of the terrorists, not Boeing's acts, caused the injuries of the plaintiffs. *** Boeing argues that its design of the cockpit was not unreasonably dangerous in relation to reasonably foreseeable risks, and that the risk of death to passengers and ground victims caused by a terrorist hijacking was not reasonably foreseeable. The record at this point does not support Boeing's argument. There have been many efforts by terrorists to hijack airplanes, and too many have been successful. The practice of terrorists to blow themselves up in order to kill as many people as possible has also been prevalent. Although there have been no incidents before the ones of September 11, 2001 where terrorists combined both an airplane hijacking and a suicidal explosion, I am not able to say that the risk of crashes was not reasonably foreseeable to an airplane manufacturer. Plaintiffs have alleged that it was reasonably foreseeable that a failure to design a secure cockpit could contribute to a breaking and entering into, and a take-over of, a cockpit by hijackers or other unauthorized individuals, substantially increasing the risk of injury and death to people and damage to property. I hold that the allegation is sufficient to establish Boeing's duty.

Boeing also argues that the regulations of the Federal Aviation Administration ("FAA") relating to design of passenger airplanes did not require an impenetrable cockpit door, and thus its designs, which satisfied FAA requirements, could not be defective. However, the only support provided by Boeing for its argument is an after-the-fact FAA policy statement, issued to explain why the FAA, in 2002, was requiring airplane manufacturers to provide such doors even though the FAA previously had not done so.

> Flightcrew compartment doors on transport category airplanes have been designed principally to ensure privacy, so pilots could focus their entire attention to their normal and emergency flight duties. The doors have not been designed to provide an impenetrable barrier between the cabin and the flightcrew compartment. Doors have not been required to meet any significant security threat, such as small arms fire or shrapnel, or the exercise of brute force to enter the flightcrew compartment.

67 Fed. Reg. 12,820-12,824 (Mar. 19, 2002).

Boeing has not proffered the parameters that existed when it manufactured its "757" jumbo-jet airplanes that United and American flew on September 11, 2001. Boeing also has not shown the extent to which FAA regulations determined how passenger airplanes were to be constructed. Although a FAA promulgation of standards for the design and manufacture of passenger aircraft may be entitled to weight in deciding whether Boeing was negligent, statements by the FAA characterizing what its former regulations required does not dictate the totality of the duty owed by aircraft manufacturers. Boeing's argument is not sufficient to support its motion to dismiss the complaints against it.

Notes

1. **Entity Liability.** Why are courts seemingly more willing to find businesses liable for failure to protect against terrorist attacks than the state?

2. **September 11 Victim Compensation Fund of 2001 (49 U.S.C. § 40101).** This compensation fund allowed claimants to receive compensation from government in exchange for giving up right to sue anyone but hijackers and their accomplices. Eligibility was limited to "Individuals present at the World Trade Center, Pentagon or Shanksville, Pennsylvania site at the time of the crashes and who suffered physical harm ... as a direct result of the terrorist-related aircraft crashes;" (28 C.F.R. §104.2) The 9/11 fund was administered by Special Master charged with determining "the extent of the harm to the claimant, including any economic and non-economic losses" and the amount of compensation "based on the harm to the claimant, the facts of the claim, and the individual circumstances of the claimant." *Colaio v. Feinberg*, 262 F. Supp.2d 273 (S.D.N.Y. 2003) upheld the Special Master's discretion in determining the amount of awards and how to factor in the various types of considerations. Because the fund was based largely on tort principles, it looked to earnings of the victims in determining the economic losses. Non-economic damages were set at a standard amount based on the number of dependants of the victim. 97% of eligible families submitted claims. The size of the average award was $1.8 million, and the highest award paid was $6.9 million. After reading *Stanford v. Kuwait Airways* and *In Re September 11th Litigation*, what would your advice have been had a spouse of a victim asked you for your advice whether to opt in or out of the fund? What further factual inquiries would you have made of your client?

3. **Scope of Recovery.** The September 11th Victims' Compensation Fund left out many people who could have claimed physical harm arising from the attacks of that day (e.g. rescuers and others around the World Trade Center site who were exposed to the dust cloud created by the towers' collapse). What was Congress' motivation in limiting the group? Do these individuals have other recourse? Were relatives of the terrorist bombing of the Murrah Building in Oklahoma City justified in complaining that they were not entitled to compensation under any such fund?

4. **Insurance**. The 9/11 compensation fund did not preclude insurance recoveries by families of the victims, and substantial sums were paid out. Indeed, the owner of the World Trade Center received billions of dollars in insurance

payments, following extensive litigation over whether the damage done by the terrorists should be treated under the policy as one incident or two (both towers together or each tower separately). Insurance companies lobbied for and were successful in obtaining passage of legislation that would prevent terrorist acts from wiping out their assets. This statute, the Terrorist Risk Insurance Act of 2002, requires property insures to make coverage available that does not differ materially from coverage for non-terrorism events. When such coverage is provided, the Federal Government assumes most of the liability insurers might incur as a result of terrorism, reimbursing insurers for 90% of their losses above a moderate threshold. The government's liability is limited to $100 billion per year. This legislation was extended to 2014 in December, 2007 after significant opposition from those who said that the uncertainty of insuring against terrorist casualties was now much more predictable than in 2002. The extension changed some of the perameters of the insurance. The amount of property and casualty losses that trigger federal payments increased from $5 million to $50 million in 2006 and $100 million in 2007; the financial stake of insurers increased from $15 billion to $25 billion in 2006 and $27.5 billion in 2007 and thereafter.

5. Comparative Law: Israel Note. Compensation for death and injury in Israel is provided under the Victims of Hostile Action (Pensions) Law (1970). It provides compensation for bodily injuries suffered in terrorist attacks, as well as compensation to family members. Benefits are provided to those wounded in terrorist attacks and families of those killed in terrorist attacks. The amounts provided have been equated to benefits provided to injured soldiers and to the families of soldiers killed in action. The statute views civilian victims of terrorism as involuntary soldiers by making no distinction between civilians harmed by war and civilians harmed by terrorists. Israeli courts have generally taken a generous approach in determining whether an act qualifies as a "hostile act" under the law to meet the requirement for compensation. Interestingly. The Attorney General has ruled that Palestinian victims of Jewish terrorism deserve equal treatment. The compensation scheme covers Israeli citizens and residents, both in Israel and while abroad; foreign nationals harmed by a hostile act while in Israel or in the Territories administered by Israel, provided that they entered Israel legally; and overseas employees of the state of Israel or of an employer pre-approved for that purpose by the Minister of Labor. Injured victims receive a lengthy list of benefits, including medical care, a living stipend, disability compensation, additional monetary benefits, and professional rehabilitation. A separate Israeli law, the Property Tax and Compensation Fund Law (1961), provides compensation for property damage. The statute covers war damage (direct damage to property) and indirect damage. Under this statute, the courts have ruled that in order for the event in question to be considered a hostile act, a claimant must prove a motive of hostility to show that the hostility was against the State of Israel. That is, the claimant must prove that the Israeli identity or nexus was the justification or causing the damage to the property. **6. Policy.** Which approach, the tort, insurance, and fund approach of the United States, or the Israeli approach, is better for dealing with losses from terrorists' acts?

B. VICTIMS OF COUNTERTERRORISM

1. CLAIMS AGAINST THE GOVERNMENT UNDER U.S. LAW

Governmental immunity and qualified immunity of government agents are the two primary barriers to compensation for victims of counterterrorism operations. As we will see, these barriers are substantial, so few cases address whether particular counterterrorism operations would be compensable under standard tort principles of intentional torts or negligence. The two cases in this section consider, respectively, (1) the government's own liability and (2) liability of high ranking government officials. Issues concerning rank-and-file implementation of counterterrorism operations is outside the scope of this chapter, but is addressed in courses concerning governmental liability generally, including actions under 42 U.S.C. §1983.

EL-SHIFA PHARMACEUTICAL INDUSTRIES CO. v. U.S.
607 F.3d 836 (C.A.D.C., 2010) (en banc)

GRIFFITH, Circuit Judge:

The owners of a Sudanese pharmaceutical plant sued the United States for unjustifiably destroying the plant, failing to compensate them for its destruction, and defaming them by asserting they had ties to Osama bin Laden. *** The plaintiffs *** allege that striking the plant was a mistake, that it "was not a chemical weapons facility, was not connected to bin Laden or to terrorism, and was not otherwise a danger to public health and safety." *** "All of the justifications for the attack advanced by the United States were based on false factual premises and were offered with reckless disregard of the truth based upon grossly incomplete research and unreasonable analysis of inconclusive intelligence."

This lawsuit is only one of several actions the plaintiffs pursued to recoup their losses. They also sued the United States in the Court of Federal Claims, seeking $50 million as just compensation under the Takings Clause of the Constitution. The court dismissed the suit on the ground that "the enemy target of military force" has no right to compensation for "the destruction of property designated by the President as enemy war-making property." The United States Court of Appeals for the Federal Circuit affirmed, holding that the plaintiffs' takings claim raised a nonjusticiable political question. On the legislative front, one member of the House of Representatives introduced a bill to compensate those who suffered injuries or property damage in the missile strike, and a resolution directing the claims court to investigate the matter and issue a report to the House. Both the bill and the resolution died in committee.

*** The plaintiffs sought at least $50 million in damages under the Federal Tort Claims Act, claiming negligence in the government's investigation of the plant's ties to chemical weapons and Osama bin Laden and trespass in its destruction of the plant "without consent or justification." Their complaint also included a claim under the law of nations seeking a judicial declaration that the United States violated international law by failing to compensate them for the unjustified destruction of their property. Finally, the plaintiffs claimed that the President and other senior officials defamed them by publishing false statements linking *** the plant to bin Laden, international terrorism, or chemical weapons, knowing those statements were false or making them with reckless disregard for their veracity. The plaintiffs sought extraordinary relief: "[a] declaration that claims made by agents of the United States that Mr. Idris or El-Shifa are connected to Osama bin Laden, terrorist groups or the production of chemical weapons are false and defamatory" and "[a]n order requiring the United States to issue a retraction [of those claims] in the form of a press release."

The district court granted the government's motion to dismiss the complaint for lack of subject-matter jurisdiction, concluding that sovereign immunity barred all of the plaintiffs' claims. The court also noted that the complaint "likely present[ed] a nonjusticiable political question." *** The plaintiffs appealed, challenging only the dismissal of their claims alleging a violation of the law of nations and defamation. The plaintiffs have abandoned any request for monetary relief, but still seek a declaration that the government's failure to compensate them for the destruction of the plant violated customary international law, a declaration that statements government officials made about them were defamatory, and an injunction requiring the government to retract those statements. A divided panel of this court affirmed the district court, holding that these claims are barred by the political question doctrine. ***

*** In the seminal case of *Baker v. Carr,* the Supreme Court explained that a claim presents a political question if it involves:

> [1] a textually demonstrable constitutional commitment of the issue to a coordinate political department; or [2] a lack of judicially discoverable and manageable standards for resolving it; or [3] the impossibility of deciding without an initial policy determination of a kind clearly for nonjudicial discretion; or [4] the impossibility of a Court's undertaking independent resolution without expressing lack of the respect due coordinate branches of government; or [5] an unusual need for unquestioning adherence to a political decision

already made; or [6] the potentiality of embarrassment from multifarious pronouncements by various departments on one question. 369 U.S. at 217, 82 S.Ct. 691. ***

Disputes involving foreign relations, such as the one before us, are "quintessential sources of political questions." Because these cases raise issues that "frequently turn on standards that defy judicial application" or "involve the exercise of a discretion demonstrably committed to the executive or legislature "[m]atters intimately related to foreign policy and national security are rarely proper subjects for judicial intervention." *** [W]\we must conduct "a discriminating analysis of the particular question posed" in the "specific case" before the court to determine whether the political question doctrine prevents a claim from going forward. *** The political question doctrine bars our review of claims that, regardless of how they are styled, call into question the prudence of the political branches in matters of foreign policy or national security constitutionally committed to their discretion. A plaintiff may not, for instance, clear the political question bar simply by "recasting [such] foreign policy and national security questions in tort terms." *** For example, in reviewing the Secretary of State's designation of a group as a "foreign terrorist organization" under the Antiterrorism and Effective Death Penalty Act, 8 U.S.C. § 1189 (2006), we may decide whether the government has followed the proper procedures, whether the organization is foreign, and whether it has engaged in terrorist activity, but we may not determine whether "the terrorist activity of the organization threatens the security of United States nationals or the national security of the United States." *** The conclusion that the strategic choices directing the nation's foreign affairs are constitutionally committed to the political branches reflects the institutional limitations of the judiciary and the lack of manageable standards to channel any judicial inquiry into these matters. *** It is not the role of judges to second-guess, with the benefit of hindsight, another branch's determination that the interests of the United States call for military action.

The case at hand involves the decision to launch a military strike abroad. Conducting the "discriminating analysis of the particular question posed" by the claims the plaintiffs press on appeal, we conclude that both raise nonjusticiable political questions. The law-of-nations claim asks the court to decide whether the United States' attack on the plant was "mistaken and not justified." The defamation claim similarly requires us to determine the factual validity of the government's stated reasons for the strike. If the political question doctrine means anything in the arena of national security and foreign relations, it means the courts cannot assess the merits of the President's decision to launch an attack on a foreign target, and the plaintiffs ask us to do just that. ***

We begin our analysis with the rule we have already identified and upon which both parties agree: courts cannot reconsider the wisdom of discretionary foreign policy decisions. The plaintiffs' law-of-nations claim falls squarely within this prohibition because it would require us to declare that the bombing of the El-Shifa plant was "mistaken and not justified." Whether an attack on a foreign target is justified-that is whether it is warranted or well-grounded-is a quintessential "policy choice[ ] and value determination[ ] constitutionally committed for resolution to the halls of Congress or the confines of the Executive Branch." *** Whether the circumstances warrant a military attack on a foreign target is a "substantive political judgment[ ] entrusted expressly to the coordinate branches of government," and using a judicial forum to reconsider its wisdom would be anathema to the separation of powers. Undertaking a counterfactual inquiry into how the political branches would have exercised their discretion had they known the facts alleged in the plaintiffs' complaint would be to make a political judgment, not a legal one.

Moreover, *Baker*'s prudential considerations counsel judicial restraint as well. First, the court lacks judicially manageable standards to adjudicate whether the attack on the El-Shifa plant was "mistaken and not justified." We could not decide this question without first fashioning out of whole cloth some standard for when military action is justified. The judiciary lacks the capacity for such a task. *** In short, the decision to launch the military attack on the El-Shifa plant was constitutionally committed to the political branches, and this court is neither an effective nor appropriate forum for reweighing its merits. ***

Indeed, the law-of-nations claim suffers from flaws similar to those the Federal Circuit identified in the plaintiffs' previous claim that the bombing was a taking because it was mistaken. As the Federal Circuit explained, "In essence ... the [plaintiffs] are contending that the President failed to assure himself with a sufficient degree of certainty" of the factual basis for his decision to strike the plant. The plaintiffs would have the federal courts "provide them with an opportunity to test that contention, and in the process, require this court to elucidate the ... standards that are to guide a President when he evaluates the veracity of military intelligence." This we cannot do.

In refusing to declare the El-Shifa attack "mistaken and not justified," we do not mean to imply that the contrary is true. We simply decline to answer a question outside the scope of our authority. *** The plaintiffs also claim that anonymous government officials defamed them by making statements linking them to bin Laden and international terrorism. *** We begin by noting that the court cannot judge the veracity of the President's initial public explanations for the attack for the same reasons we cannot examine whether the attack was "mistaken and not justified." The President's statements justifying the attack are "inextricably intertwined" with a foreign policy decision constitutionally committed to the political branches, because determining whether the President's statements were true would require a determination "whether the alleged conduct *should* have occurred." A decision in favor of the plaintiffs would unavoidably involve a rejection of the Clinton Administration's stated justifications for launching the missile strike. A decision against the plaintiffs would affirm the wisdom of the Administration's decision to attack.

The plaintiffs maintain, however, that even if the political question doctrine bars review of the President's initial justifications for the attack, the court may nevertheless judge the veracity of the subsequent justifications, which, they allege, offer different explanations for the strike. These allegedly defamatory statements are reviewable, the plaintiffs contend, because they do not state "the *actual* justification for the decision to attack the plant." Rather, the plaintiffs allege that these statements are *"post hoc* pretext"- defamatory efforts at political damage control. Mr. Idris was, in fact, associated with terrorism." According to the plaintiffs, we can review these later justifications for the attack because they bear no relation to the President's initial justifications-that the plant was associated with bin Laden and involved in producing chemical weapons.

We disagree. The allegedly defamatory statements cannot be severed from the initial justifications for the attack. The court cannot adjudicate the truth of the government's later justifications because, despite the plaintiffs' arguments to the contrary, they are fundamentally the same as the initial justifications. *** On the day the United States destroyed the El-Shifa plant, President Clinton told the American people that he ordered the strike in part because the plant was "associated with the bin Laden network" and was a "chemical weapons-related facility." *** All of the allegedly defamatory statements essentially repeat the President's initial justification for the strike. Each describes a connection between bin Laden and the plant through its owner, Salah Idris. *** Contrary to the plaintiffs' contentions, these statements do not represent a break from the President's contemporaneous explanation of his reasons for launching the strike. At most, they elaborate upon the nature of the connection between the plant and bin Laden-a connection the President offered on the day of the attack as one reason for taking military action. ***

We conclude our political question analysis by addressing the plaintiffs' argument that they are asking nothing more than that we review the government's designation of them as supporters of the nation's enemies, something courts have done in other contexts. This argument fails.

The plaintiffs point first to cases permitting judicial review of the enemy status of persons detained after being seized by the U.S. military on the battlefield. *See, e.g., Boumediene v. Bush,* 553 U.S. 723 (2008); *Parhat v. Gates,* 532 F.3d 834 (D.C.Cir.2008). But the political question doctrine does not preclude judicial review of prolonged Executive detention predicated on an enemy combatant determination because the Constitution specifically contemplates a judicial role in this area. The plaintiffs can point to no comparable constitutional commitment to the courts for review of a military decision to launch a missile at a foreign target.

The plaintiffs also point to another line of cases in which courts have reviewed Executive Branch determinations that a certain asset is "enemy property" or belongs to a terrorist organization and therefore is eligible for seizure pursuant to statute. These cases are not helpful to the plaintiffs for the same reasons the detainee cases are not. None required the courts to scrutinize a decision constitutionally committed wholly to the political branches. Indeed, the Supreme Court has suggested that judicial review of enemy-property designations made to effect statutorily authorized asset seizures is constitutionally mandated. ("[C]laims based on the most fundamental liberty and property rights of this country's citizenry, such as the Takings and Due Process Clauses of the Fifth Amendment, are justiciable, even if they implicate foreign policy decisions.") No comparable constitutional commitment to the judiciary exists in this case. The plaintiffs do not ask whether the government's conduct was prohibited by the Constitution. Instead, they seek declarations that the President should not have launched a military strike that the plaintiffs deem unwise and ill founded, and an injunction requiring the government to retract its justifications for the attack. The Constitution denies the courts the ability to grant such extraordinary relief.

Our colleagues agree that the district court lacked jurisdiction but would affirm on a different ground. Their proposed alternative relies on the rule that federal courts lack jurisdiction to hear legally "insubstantial" claims. The Supreme Court and this court have applied this rule narrowly, setting a high bar for dismissal that plaintiffs' claims do not meet. *** Plaintiffs' claims are not so unsound as to warrant dismissal on this jurisdictional ground. There is "room for the inference that the question[s] sought to be raised can be the subject of controversy." Perhaps the district court would have dismissed plaintiffs' claims for failure to state a claim under Rule 12(b)(6) had the case proceeded to the merits. But whether a claim is so insubstantial as to deprive the federal courts of jurisdiction is a "separate question from whether a complaint is subject to dismissal under Federal Rule of Civil Procedure 12(b)(6) for failing to state a claim on which relief may be granted." The cases relied upon by the concurrence might "render [plaintiffs'] claims of doubtful or questionable merit," but they do not "foreclose the subject" and therefore "do not render them insubstantial." ***.

Our concurring colleagues charge the court with "*sub silentio* expand [ing] executive power." To the contrary, it is they who would work a *sub silentio* expansion. By asserting the authority to decide questions the Constitution reserves to Congress and the Executive, some would expand judicial power at the expense of the democratically elected branches. And by stretching beyond all precedent the limited category of claims so frivolous as not to involve a federal question, all would permit courts to decide the merits of disputes under the guise of a jurisdictional holding while sidestepping obstacles that are truly jurisdictional. ***

GINSBURG, Circuit Judge, with whom Circuit Judge ROGERS joins, concurring in the judgment:

*** I write separately [because] [t]he Court today expands the political *question* doctrine by reading into several of our recent cases something of a new political *decision* doctrine. On that approach, we are first to identify some "conduct" or "decision" (the opinion alternates) constitutionally committed to the Executive and then to ask whether the plaintiff's "claim[ ] ... call[s] into question," "require[s] the court to reassess," or is "inextricably intertwined with" that Executive conduct or decision. If so, then the claim is non-justiciable, regardless whether the court would actually have to decide a political question in order to resolve it.

The Court" approach departs sharply from that prescribed in *Baker v. Carr,* which calls for a "discriminating inquiry into the precise facts and posture of the particular case" in order to detect "a political question's presence," unless there is such a question and it is "inextricable from the case at bar," then we are to decide it, even if "our decision may have significant political overtones." The innovation adopted by the Court contravenes the Supreme Court's teaching that "[t]he doctrine of which we treat is one of political questions, not one of political cases."

If the Court today followed *Baker v. Carr,* then there would be no occasion to consider whether the application of the political question doctrine in a statutory case threatens the separation of powers by, as Judge Kavanaugh says, "systematically favor[ing] the Executive Branch over the Legislative Branch." Under *Baker v. Carr* a statutory case generally does not present a non-justiciable political question because "the interpretation of legislation is a recurring and accepted task for the federal courts." [There might be] rare exceptions in which a statute called for a decision constitutionally committed to the President and hence not subject to judicial review.

Under the Court's new political decision doctrine, however, even a straightforward statutory case, presenting a purely legal question, is non-justiciable if deciding it could merely reflect adversely upon a decision constitutionally committed to the President. *** The result of staying the judicial hand is to upset rather than to preserve the constitutional allocation of powers between the executive and the legislature.

KAVANAUGH, Circuit Judge, with whom Chief Judge SENTELLE joins, and with whom Circuit Judges GINSBURG and ROGERS join as to Part I, concurring in the judgment:

*** Federal courts lack subject matter jurisdiction over claims that are "so insubstantial, implausible, foreclosed by prior decisions of this Court, or otherwise completely devoid of merit as not to involve a federal controversy." Plaintiffs' two claims in this case fall into that category. *** First, to obtain relief for the allegedly false statements by Government officials that had linked plaintiffs to bin Laden, plaintiffs raised a federal defamation claim against the United States. The problem for plaintiffs is that there is no federal cause of action for defamation available against the United States. Second, plaintiffs claimed that the failure of the United States to compensate them for the allegedly mistaken bombing and destruction of their property violated a customary international law norm recognized under the Alien Tort Statute, 28 U.S.C. § 1350. But plaintiffs have cited no customary international law norm that would require compensation by the United States under the Alien Tort Statute for mistaken war-time bombings.

First, *** Congress has enacted a number of causes of action that can be brought against the United States or against Government officials for acts taken in their official capacities. But Congress has not created a defamation cause of action against the United States. Moreover, the Supreme Court has never recognized a federal common-law defamation cause of action against the United States. Indeed, the Court has not endorsed any federal common-law causes of action against the Government during the post-*Erie* period. And the Court several times has expressly declined to do so, noting that creation of new causes of action is a function typically best left to Congress. *** [P]laintiffs might also be alleging a purported *state* common-law cause of action against the United States, although their complaint never quite says as much. Even so, any such state-law cause of action may not be brought against the United States absent congressional authorization to that effect. ***

Plaintiffs also seek a declaration that the United States violated customary international law, as cognizable under the Alien Tort Statute, because the United States failed to compensate plaintiffs for the allegedly mistaken destruction of their property.*** The ATS may encompass other established customary international law norms so long as they do not have "less definite content and acceptance among civilized nations than the historical paradigms familiar when § 1350 was enacted" in 1789. *** But plaintiffs cite no authority suggesting that the mistaken destruction of property during extraterritorial war-related activities-or denial of an administrative claim seeking compensation for the same-violates an established norm of customary international law. ***

The straightforward approach outlined [above] would readily resolve this case. But the majority opinion instead relies on the notoriously "murky and unsettled" political question doctrine to dismiss the complaint. Because of the importance of the political question doctrine to the law of this Circuit, I believe it important to respond to the majority opinion and to explain my disagreement with its political question theory.

The key point for purposes of my political question analysis is this: Plaintiffs do not allege that the Executive Branch violated the Constitution. Rather, plaintiffs allege that the Executive Branch violated congressionally enacted statutes that purportedly constrain the Executive. The Supreme Court has never applied the political question doctrine in cases involving statutory claims of this kind. *** [T]he proper separation of powers question in this sort of statutory case is whether the statute as applied infringes on the President's exclusive, preclusive authority under Article II of the Constitution. That is a weighty question-and one that must be confronted directly through careful analysis of Article II, not resolved *sub silentio* in favor of the Executive through use of the political question doctrine.

The political question doctrine has occupied a more limited place in the Supreme Court's jurisprudence than is sometimes assumed. The Court has relied on the doctrine only twice in the last 50 years. *** Importantly, the Supreme Court has invoked the political question doctrine only in cases alleging violations of the Constitution. This is a statutory case. The Supreme Court has never applied the political question doctrine in a case involving alleged *statutory* violations. Never. ***

There is good reason the political question doctrine does not apply in cases alleging statutory violations. If a court refused to give effect to a statute that regulated Executive conduct, it necessarily would be holding that Congress is unable to constrain Executive conduct in the challenged sphere of action. As a result, the court would be ruling (at least implicitly) that the statute intrudes impermissibly on the Executive's prerogatives under Article II of the Constitution. In other words, the court would be establishing that the asserted Executive power is exclusive and preclusive, meaning that Congress cannot regulate or limit that power by creating a cause of action or otherwise.

Applying the political question doctrine in statutory cases thus would not reflect benign deference to the political branches. Rather, that approach would systematically favor the Executive Branch over the Legislative Branch-without the courts' acknowledging as much or grappling with the critical separation of powers and Article II issues. The fact that use of the political question doctrine in statutory cases loads the dice against the Legislative Branch presumably explains why there is no Supreme Court precedent applying the doctrine in statutory cases-and why the Executive Branch (sometimes wary, for a variety of reasons, of advancing a straight Article II argument) may want the courts to invoke the doctrine in statutory cases of this sort. *** It is particularly important to confront the question directly because of the significance of such questions to our constitutional separation of powers. As Justice Jackson rightly explained, any claim of exclusive, preclusive Executive authority-particularly in the national security arena-"must be scrutinized with caution, for what is at stake is the equilibrium established by our constitutional system." *Youngstown Sheet & Tube Co. v. Sawyer,* 343 U.S. 579, 638 (1952) (Jackson, J., concurring).

The approach suggested in this opinion is consistent with the results, if not all the reasoning, of this Court's recent cases declining to entertain certain tort suits in the national security arena. In those cases, as in this case, the plaintiffs asserted no cognizable cause of action. The Federal Tort Claims Act does not apply to suits for actions that occur in foreign countries or that encompass discretionary functions, among other exceptions. The Alien Tort Statute has never been held to cover suits against the United States or United States Government officials; the statute furnishes no waiver of sovereign immunity. And *** the Torture Victim Protection Act does not extend to suits against American officials except in the unusual case where such an official acts "under color of foreign law."

The absence of a cause of action covering the national security activities at issue in [prior cases] or this case is hardly surprising. The political branches, mindful of the need for Executive discretion and flexibility in national security and foreign affairs, are unlikely to unduly hamper the Executive's ability to protect the Nation's security and diplomatic objectives. Relatedly, it is well-established that courts must be cautious about interpreting an ambiguous statute to constrain or interfere with the Executive Branch's conduct of national security or foreign policy.[5] And apart from all that, if a statute were passed that clearly limited the kind of Executive national security or foreign policy activities at issue in these cases, such a statute as applied might well violate Article II. ***

To say that the courts must directly confront the critical separation of powers and Article II issues posed by this kind of statutory case is not to say that the Executive lacks any exclusive, preclusive Article II authority. The Executive plainly possesses a significant degree of exclusive, preclusive Article II power in both the domestic and national security arenas.

In the national security realm, although the topic is of course hotly debated, most acknowledge at least some areas of exclusive, preclusive Presidential power-where Congress cannot regulate and the Executive "wins" even in Justice Jackson's *Youngstown* Category Three. For example, courts have generally accepted that the President possesses exclusive, preclusive power under the Commander-in-Chief Clause of Article II to command troop movements during a congressionally authorized war.

This case involves President Clinton's unilateral decision to bomb suspected al Qaeda targets. In the wake of the August 1998 al Qaeda attacks on U.S. personnel and property in Tanzania and Kenya, President Clinton ordered these attacks "in exercise" of the United States' "inherent right of self-defense." As authority for the bombings, President Clinton cited his Commander-in-Chief power under Article II.

A statute regulating or creating a cause of action to challenge the President's short-term bombing of foreign targets in the Nation's self-defense (or contesting the Executive Branch's subsequent statements about it as defamatory) might well unconstitutionally encroach on the President's exclusive, preclusive Article II authority as Commander in Chief.

But we need not definitively answer the sensitive and weighty Article II question in this case. *** Congress has not created any cognizable cause of action that would apply to President Clinton's decision to bomb El-Shifa or

---

[5] In cases reviewing the Executive's designation of foreign terrorist organizations, we held that the statute left to the Executive Branch the determination whether a group threatened the security of the United States. *See People's Mojahedin v. Dep't of State,* 182 F.3d 17, 23-25 (D.C.Cir.1999). This seems a straightforward application of [the] principle of statutory interpretation, not any broad holding about the political question doctrine.

later Executive Branch statements about the bombing. Indeed, the only remotely relevant statute in this case is the War Powers Resolution, which seems to support the President's authority to conduct unilateral military operations for at least 62 days without specific congressional approval.

Given that no cause of action exists here, the political question and Article II issues in this case have an abstract and hypothetical air to them. In these circumstances, we *** should decline the opportunity to expound on the scope of the President's exclusive, preclusive Commander-in-Chief authority under Article II. ***

Notes

1. **Consequentialism.** Would potential after-the-fact tort liability keep the President from using military force? Would declaratory relief disarm the President from responding militarily to terrorism? Are there any real-world consequences to the theory differences between the majority and concurring opinions?

2. **Theory of the Political Question Doctrine.** The majority says this is a routine application of the doctrine, the concurring judges that it is unprecedented and dangerous. The majority says the doctrine takes the courts where they belong—on the sidelines. The concurring opinions say this view is anything but neutral in the balance of Executive and Legislative power. Who is correct?

3. **Constitution, Statute, Jurisdiction, Merits.** Generally, courts decide cases on statutory grounds where doing so would avoid a tough constitutional question. Is the majority guilty of violating this fundamental precept? It is also generally the rule that jurisdiction decisions come before merits inquiries; where there is no jurisdiction, reaching the merits is improper. Do the concurring judges forget this fundamental precept? Is there any principled way to decide which precept should govern in a case in which both are at work?

4. **Article II Power.** Review the materials in Chapter X if you have any doubts concerning whether the President had the authority to bomb the el-Shifa plant without United Nations approval. Did the President need Congress to approve before bombing? This issue is addressed in Chapter XIII.

2. CLAIMS AGAINST OTHER GOVERNMENTS

ISAYEVA v. RUSSIA
Application no. 57950/00
European Court of Human Rights
24 February 2005

1.   The case originated in an application against the Russian Federation lodged with the Court under Article 34 of the Convention for the Protection of

Human Rights and Fundamental Freedoms ("the Convention") by a Russian national, Ms Zara Adamovna Isayeva ("the applicant"), on 27 April 2000. ***

3.   The applicant alleged that she was a victim of indiscriminate bombing by the Russian military of her native village of Katyr-Yurt on 4 February 2000. As a result of the bombing, the applicant's son and three nieces were killed. She alleged a violation of Articles 2 and 13 of the Convention. ***

9.   The applicant was born in 1954 and is a resident of Katyr-Yurt, Achkhoy-Martan district, Chechnya. ***

12.   In autumn 1999 Russian federal military forces launched operations in Chechnya. In December 1999 rebel fighters ("*boyeviki*") were blocked by the advancing federal forces in Grozny, where fierce fighting took place.

13.   The applicant submits that at the end of January 2000 a special operation was planned and executed by the federal military commanders in order to entice the rebel forces from Grozny. Within that plan, the fighters were led to believe that a safe exit would be possible out of Grozny towards the mountains in the south of the republic. Money was paid by the fighters to the military for information about the exit and for the safe passage. Late at night on 29 January 2000 the fighters left the besieged city and moved south. They were allowed to leave the city. However, once they had left the city they were caught in minefields and the artillery and air force bombarded them along the route. ***

15.   A significant group of Chechen fighters – ranging from several hundred to four thousand persons entered the village of Katyr-Yurt early on the morning of 4 February 2000. According to the applicant, the arrival of the fighters in the village was totally unexpected and the villagers were not warned in advance of the ensuing fighting or about safe exit routes.

16.   The applicant submitted that the population of Katyr-Yurt at the relevant time was about 25,000 persons, including local residents and internally displaced persons (IDPs) from elsewhere in Chechnya. She also submitted that their village had been declared a "safe zone", which attracted people fleeing from fighting taking place in other districts of Chechnya.

17.   The applicant submitted that the bombing started suddenly in the early hours of 4 February 2000. The applicant and her family hid in the cellar of their house. When the shelling subsided at about 3 p.m. the applicant and her family went outside and saw that other residents of the village were packing their belongings and leaving, because the military had apparently granted safe passage to the village's residents. The applicant and her family, together with their neighbours, entered a Gazel minibus and drove along Ordzhonikidze road, heading out of the village. While they were on the road, the planes reappeared, descended and bombed cars on the road. This occurred at about 3.30 p.m.

18.   The applicant's son, Zelimkhan Isayev (aged 23) was hit by shrapnel and died within a few minutes. Three other persons in the vehicle were also wounded. During the same attack the applicant's three nieces were killed: Zarema Batayeva (aged 15), Kheda Batayeva (aged 13) and Marem (also

spelled Maryem) Batayeva (aged 6). The applicant also submitted that her nephew, Zaur Batayev, was wounded on that day and became handicapped as a result.

19.   The applicant submitted that the bombardment was indiscriminate and that the military used heavy and indiscriminate weapons, such as heavy aviation bombs and multiple rocket launchers. In total, the applicant submits that over 150 people were killed in the village during the bombing, many of whom were displaced persons from elsewhere in Chechnya. ***

23.   According to the Government, at the beginning of February 2000 a large group of Chechen fighters, headed by the field commander Gelayev and numbering over 1,000 persons forced their way south after leaving Grozny. On the night of 4 February 2000 they captured Katyr-Yurt. The fighters were well-trained and equipped with various large-calibre firearms, grenade- and mine-launchers, snipers' guns and armoured vehicles. Some of the population of Katyr-Yurt had already left by that time, whilst others were hiding in their houses. The fighters seized stone and brick houses in the village and converted them into fortified defence points. The fighters used the population of Katyr-Yurt as a human shield.

24.   Early in the morning of 4 February 2000 a detachment of special forces from the Ministry of the Interior was ordered to enter Katyr-Yurt because information had been received about the fighters' presence in the village. The detachment entered the village, but after passing the second line of houses they were attacked by the fighters, who offered fierce resistance using all kinds of weapons. The unit sustained casualties and had to return to its positions.

25.   The federal troops gave the fighters an opportunity to surrender, which they rejected. A safe passage was offered to the residents of Katyr-Yurt. In order to convey the information about safe exit routes, the military authorities informed the head of the village administration. They also used a mobile broadcasting station which entered the village and a Mi-8 helicopter equipped with loudspeakers. In order to ensure order amongst the civilians leaving the village, two roadblocks were established at the exits from the village. However, the fighters prevented many people from leaving the village.

26.   Once the residents had left, the federal forces called on the air force and the artillery to strike at the village. The designation of targets was based on incoming intelligence information. The military operation lasted until 6 February 2000. The Government submitted that some residents remained in Katyr-Yurt because the fighters did not allow them to leave. This led to significant civilian casualties - 46 civilians were killed, including Zelimkhan Isayeb, Zarema Batayeva, Kheda Batayeva and Marem Batayeva , and 53 were wounded. ***

162.   The applicant alleged that her right to life and the right to life of her son and other relatives was violated by the actions of the military. She also submitted that the authorities had failed to carry out an effective and

adequate investigation into the attack and to bring those responsible to justice. She relied on Article 2 of the Convention, which provides:

"1. Everyone's right to life shall be protected by law. No one shall be deprived of his life intentionally save in the execution of a sentence of a court following his conviction of a crime for which this penalty is provided by law.

2. Deprivation of life shall not be regarded as inflicted in contravention of this article when it results from the use of force which is no more than absolutely necessary:

(a) in defence of any person from unlawful violence;

(b) in order to effect a lawful arrest or to prevent the escape of a person lawfully detained;

(c) in action lawfully taken for the purpose of quelling a riot or insurrection."

172. Article 2, which safeguards the right to life and sets out the circumstances when deprivation of life may be justified, ranks as one of the most fundamental provisions in the Convention, from which in peacetime no derogation is permitted under Article 15. Together with Article 3, it also enshrines one of the basic values of the democratic societies making up the Council of Europe. The circumstances in which deprivation of life may be justified must therefore be strictly construed. The object and purpose of the Convention as an instrument for the protection of individual human beings also requires that Article 2 be interpreted and applied so as to make its safeguards practical and effective.

173. Article 2 covers not only intentional killing but also the situations in which it is permitted to "use force" which may result, as an unintended outcome, in the deprivation of life. However, the deliberate or intended use of lethal force is only one factor to be taken into account in assessing its necessity. Any use of force must be no more than "absolutely necessary" for the achievement of one or more of the purposes set out in sub-paragraphs (a) to (c). This term indicates that a stricter and more compelling test of necessity must be employed than that normally applicable when determining whether State action is "necessary in a democratic society" under paragraphs 2 of Articles 8 to 11 of the Convention. Consequently, the force used must be strictly proportionate to the achievement of the permitted aims.

174. In the light of the importance of the protection afforded by Article 2, the Court must subject deprivations of life to the most careful scrutiny, taking into consideration not only the actions of State agents but also all the surrounding circumstances.

175. In particular, it is necessary to examine whether the operation was planned and controlled by the authorities so as to minimise, to the greatest extent possible, recourse to lethal force. The authorities must take appropriate care to ensure that any risk to life is minimised. The Court must also examine whether the authorities were not negligent in their choice of action ***

176. Similarly, the State's responsibility is not confined to circumstances where there is significant evidence that misdirected fire from agents of the state has killed a civilian. It may also be engaged where they fail to take all feasible precautions in the choice of means and methods of a security operation mounted against an opposing group with a view to avoiding and, in any event, minimising, incidental loss of civilian life. ***

179. It is undisputed that the applicant and her relatives were attacked when trying to leave the village of Katyr-Yurt through what they had perceived as safe exit from heavy fighting. It is established that an aviation bomb dropped from a Russian military plane exploded near their minivan, as a result of which the applicant's son and three nieces were killed and the applicant and her other relatives were wounded. This brings the complaint within the ambit of Article 2. The Government suggested that the use of force was justified in the present case under paragraph 2 (a) of Article 2 of the Convention being absolutely necessary due to the situation in Katyr-Yurt at the time.

180. The Court accepts that the situation that existed in Chechnya at the relevant time called for exceptional measures by the State in order to regain control over the Republic and to suppress the illegal armed insurgency. Given the context of the conflict in Chechnya at the relevant time, those measures could presumably include the deployment of army units equipped with combat weapons, including military aviation and artillery. The presence of a very large group of armed fighters in Katyr-Yurt, and their active resistance to the law-enforcement bodies, which are not disputed by the parties, may have justified use of lethal force by the agents of the State, thus bringing the situation within paragraph 2 of Article 2.

181. Accepting that the use of force may have been justified in the present case, it goes without saying that a balance must be achieved between the aim pursued and the means employed to achieve it. The Court will now consider whether the actions in the present case were no more than absolutely necessary for achieving the declared purpose. In order to do so the Court will examine, on the basis of the information submitted by the parties and in view of the above enumerated principles (see §§ 172-178 above), whether the planning and conduct of the operation were consistent with Article 2 of the Convention. ***

184. The applicant submits that the military must have known in advance about the very real possibility of the arrival of a large group of fighters in Katyr-Yurt, and further submits that they even incited such an arrival. The Court notes a substantial amount of evidence which seems to suggest that the fighters' arrival was not so unexpected for the military that they had no time to take measures to protect the villagers from being caught up in the conflict. ***

186. In contrast, the applicant and other villagers questioned stated that they had felt safe from fighting due to the substantial military presence in the district, roadblocks around the village and the apparent proclamation of the village as a "safety zone". An OMON detachment was stationed directly in Katyr-Yurt. The villagers' statements describe the arrival of fighters and

the ensuing attack as something unexpected and not foreseen (see §§ 15, 59, 110 above).

187. The Court has been given no evidence to indicate that anything was done to ensure that information about these events was conveyed to the population before 4 February 2000, either directly or through the head of administration. However, the fact that the fighters could have reasonably been expected, or even incited, to enter Katyr-Yurt clearly exposed its population to all kinds of dangers. Given the availability of the above information, the relevant authorities should have foreseen these dangers and, if they could not have prevented the fighters' entry into the village, it was at least open to them to warn the residents in advance. ***

188. Taking into account the above elements and the reviewed documents, the Court concludes that the military operation in Katyr-Yurt was not spontaneous. The operation, aimed at either disarmament or destruction of the fighters, was planned some time in advance. ***

189. The Court regards it as evident that when the military considered the deployment of aviation equipped with heavy combat weapons within the boundaries of a populated area, they also should have considered the dangers that such methods invariably entail. There is however no evidence to conclude that such considerations played a significant place in the planning. In his statement Major-General Nedobitko mentioned that the operational plan, reviewed with Major-General Vladimir Shamanov in the evening on 3 February 2000, referred to the presence of refugees. This mere reference cannot substitute for comprehensive evaluation of the limits of and constraints on the use of indiscriminate weapons within a populated area. According to various estimates, the population of Katyr-Yurt at the material time constituted between 18,000 and 25,000 persons. There is no evidence that at the planning stage of the operation any serious calculations were made about the evacuation of civilians, such as ensuring that they were informed of the attack beforehand, how long such an evacuation would take, what routes evacuees were supposed to take, what kind of precautions were in place to ensure safety, what steps were to be taken to assist the vulnerable and infirm etc. ***

191. The Court considers that using [these heavy weapons] in a populated area, outside wartime and without prior evacuation of the civilians, is impossible to reconcile with the degree of caution expected from a law-enforcement body in a democratic society. No martial law and no state of emergency has been declared in Chechnya, and no derogation has been made under Article 15 of the Convention (see § 133). The operation in question therefore has to be judged against a normal legal background. Even when faced with a situation where, as the Government submit, the population of the village had been held hostage by a large group of well-equipped and well-trained fighters, the primary aim of the operation should be to protect lives from unlawful violence. The massive use of indiscriminate weapons stands in flagrant contrast with this aim and cannot be considered compatible with the standard of care prerequisite to an operation of this kind involving the use of lethal force by State agents.

192. During the investigation, the commanders of the operation submitted that a safe passage had been declared for the population of Katyr-Yurt; that the population has been properly informed of the exit through the head of administration and by means of a mobile broadcasting station and a helicopter equipped with loudspeakers; and that two roadblocks were opened in order to facilitate departure.

193. The documents reviewed by the Court confirm that a measure of information about a safe passage had indeed been conveyed to the villagers. ***

195. Once the information about the corridor had spread, the villagers started to leave, taking advantage of a lull in the bombardments. The presence of civilians and civilian cars on the road leading to Achkhoy-Martan in the afternoon of 4 February 2000 must have been fairly substantial. One of the witnesses submitted that many cars were lined up in Ordzhonikidze Street when they were leaving (see § 45 above). The applicant stated that their neighbours were leaving with them at the same time (see § 17 above). Colonel R. stated that on the first day of bombing the villagers left Katyr-Yurt *en masse* by the road to Achkhoy-Martan (see § 77 above). The soldiers manning the roadblock leading to Achkhoy-Martan must have seen people escaping from the fighting. This must have been known to the commanders of the operation and should have led them to ensure the safety of the passage.

196. However, no document or statement by the military refers to an order to stop the attack or to reduce its intensity. While there are numerous references in the servicemen's statements to the declaration of a humanitarian corridor, there is not a single statement which refers to the observance of any such corridor. The statements by the air-controllers and military pilots reviewed by the Court do not contain any reference to information about a humanitarian corridor or an obligation to respect it. Nor does it appear that they were at any moment alerted by the servicemen manning the roadblock leading to Achkhoy-Martan, or by the operation's commanders, to the presence of departing civilians in the streets. Their own evaluation of the targets seems to have been impaired by poor visibility and the pilots denied in their statements having seen any civilians or civilian vehicles. ***

200. To sum up, accepting that the operation in Katyr-Yurt on 4-7 February 2000 was pursuing a legitimate aim, the Court does not accept that it was planned and executed with the requisite care for the lives of the civilian population.

201. The Court finds that there has been a violation of Article 2 of the Convention in respect of the responding State's obligation to protect the right to life of the applicant, her son Zelimkhan Isayev and her three nieces, Zarema Batayeva, Kheda Batayeva and Marem Batayeva. ***

231. Article 41 of the Convention provides:

"If the Court finds that there has been a violation of the Convention or the Protocols thereto, and if the internal law of the High Contracting Party concerned allows only partial reparation to be made, the Court shall, if necessary, afford just satisfaction to the injured party."

[The Court unanimously found a violation of Article 2 and held that Russia is to pay the applicant]:

(i) EUR 18,710 (eighteen thousand seven hundred ten euros) in respect of pecuniary damage;

(ii) EUR 25,000 (twenty-five thousand euros) in respect of non-pecuniary damage;

(iii) EUR 10,926 (ten thousand nine hundred twenty-six euros) in respect of costs and expenses; ***

Notes

1. What Law? What law is the Court applying in this case? Would we see the same result if this Court or another entity were to apply international humanitarian law to the situation?

2. Result. Is the Court requiring too much of Russia here? Can any country mount an effective counterterrorism operation (leaving aside whether the conflict in Chechnya was a counterterrorism operation or an actual armed conflict) without running afoul of international humanitarian law or human rights law?

3. Moscow Theater Raid. In April 2004, a Moscow court awarded compensation to the family of Timur Khaziyev, a musician who was the primary breadwinner for his family; wife and daughter. The compensation set was a one-time payment and monthly stipend. In May 2004, the Russian Supreme Court rejected a claim for moral compensation for victims of the raid, including claims for a child's death. Assuming the theater raid operation was botched, is this decision consistent with *Isayeva*?

4. Damages. Are the damages awarded here consistent with damages claims in the United States? Should the level of damages affect the substantive law of liability?

5. *Yilmaz v. Turkey*, (2004) ECHR 35875/97 8 July 2004. The court considered the claim of a woman killed in the aftermath of clash between Turkish gendarmerie and PKK. The Court, unable to reach a determination regarding who killed her, held that there was no violation of the right to life under Article 2 of the Convention. However, the Court found that the Turkish failure to provide prompt and effective investigation constituted a violation of Article 2 through the failure to comply with the obligation, implicit in Article 2, to hold an effective official investigation when an individual has been killed by the use of force. The court also found a violation of Article 13 for failure to provide an effective remedy.

3. CLAIMS AGAINST PRIVATE PARTIES

HATFILL v. THE NEW YORK TIMES COMPANY
416 F.3d 320, en banc reh. den 427 F. 3d 253 (4th Cir. 2005)

SHEDD, Circuit Judge

Dr. Steven J. Hatfill sued The New York Times Company ("The Times") and columnist Nicholas Kristof, alleging claims under Virginia law for defamation and intentional infliction of emotional distress. ***

In the fall of 2001, shortly after the terrorist attacks on the World Trade Center and the Pentagon, someone mailed letters laced with anthrax to several news organizations and members of Congress. At least five people died as a result of contact with these letters, and the federal government launched an investigation to identify and capture the responsible party or parties. By May 2002, the Federal Bureau of Investigation ("FBI") had not made any arrests.

Kristof writes a regular column for the editorial page of The Times. During the spring and summer of 2002, Kristof wrote several columns criticizing the FBI's investigation. From May through July 2002, Kristof focused his attention on the FBI's handling of information related to a man he called "Mr. Z." According to Kristof, circumstantial evidence pointed to Mr. Z, who was widely suspected by other scientists of involvement in the anthrax mailings. In Kristof's opinion, the FBI had not moved aggressively enough against Mr. Z. In August 2002, Kristof identified Mr. Z as Dr. Steven J. Hatfill, a research scientist employed by the Department of Defense.

Kristof's columns expressed opinions about the progress of the FBI's investigation based on factual assertions concerning Hatfill. In a column published on May 24, 2002, Kristof urged his readers to "light a fire" under the FBI in its investigation of the anthrax mailings since "[e]xperts in the bioterror field are already buzzing about a handful of individuals who had the ability, access and motive to send the anthrax." According to Kristof, these experts suspected "one middle-aged American who has worked for the United States military biodefense program and had access to the labs at Fort Detrick, Md. His anthrax vaccinations are up to date, he unquestionably had the ability to make first-rate anthrax, and he was upset at the United States government in the period preceding the anthrax attack." According to Kristof, the FBI had been "painstakingly slow in its investigation" of this person and unnamed others.

Kristof repeated this theme in a column published on July 2, 2002, writing that "the bureau's lackadaisical ineptitude in pursuing the anthrax killer continues to threaten America's national security by permitting him to strike again or, more likely, to flee to Iran or North Korea." As to the identity of this killer, Kristof offered the following:

Some in the biodefense community think they know a likely culprit, whom I'll call Mr. Z. *** He denies any wrongdoing, and his friends are heartsick at suspicions directed against a man they regard as a patriot. Some of his polygraphs show evasion, I hear, although that may be because of his temperament. If Mr. Z were an Arab national, he would have been imprisoned long ago. But he is a true-blue American with close ties to the U.S. Defense Department, the C.I.A. and the American biodefense program. On the other hand, he was once caught with a girlfriend in a biohazard "hot suite" at Fort Detrick, surrounded only by blushing germs.

Kristof argued that the FBI's handling of this information reflected a casual approach to the investigation. *** Having called the FBI to account for the slow pace of its investigation, Kristof put a series of rhetorical questions to the FBI concerning Mr. Z particularly:

> *Do you know how many identities and passports Mr. Z has and are you monitoring his international travel?* I have found at least one alias for him, and he has continued to travel abroad on government assignments, even to Central Asia.

> *Why was his top security clearance suspended in August, less than a month before the anthrax attacks began?* This move left him infuriated. Are the C.I.A. and military intelligence agencies cooperating fully with the investigation?

> *Have you searched the isolated residence that he had access to last fall?* The F.B.I. has known about this building, and knows that Mr. Z gave Cipro to people who visited it. This property and many others are legally registered in the name of a friend of Mr. Z, but may be safe houses operated by American intelligence.

> *Have you examined whether Mr. Z has connections to the biggest anthrax outbreak among humans ever recorded, the one that sickened more than 10,000 black farmers in Zimbabwe in 1978-80?* There is evidence that the anthrax was released by the white Rhodesian Army fighting against black guerillas, and Mr. Z has claimed that he participated in the white army's much-feared Selous Scouts. Could rogue elements of the American military have backed the Rhodesian Army in anthrax and cholera attacks against blacks? Mr. Z's resume also claims involvement in the former South African Defense Force; all else aside, who knew that the U.S. Defense Department would pick an American who had served in the armed forces of two white-racist regimes to work in the American biodefense program with some of the world's deadliest germs?

In his July 12, 2002 column, Kristof suggested that Mr. Z might have been involved in a previous attack against B'nai B'rith offices in April 1997 *** Kristof also suggested that Mr. Z might have been involved with another set of "anthrax hoaxes" in February 1999: *** The next week Kristof wrote that Mr. Z had been interviewed by the FBI four times and that his home had been searched twice during the course of the investigation. Kristof noted that the Army had hired Mr. Z in 1997 to work with Ebola and Marburg viruses, even though he had previously worked with the armed forces of Rhodesia and apartheid South Africa.

Finally, on August 13, 2002, Kristof identified his Mr. Z as Dr. Steven J. Hatfill:

> It's time for me to come clean on "Mr. Z." *** I didn't name him. But over the weekend, Mr. Z named himself. He is Steven J. Hatfill, 48, a prominent germ warfare specialist who formerly worked in the Army labs at Fort Detrick, Md. Hatfill made a televised statement on Sunday, describing himself as "a loyal American" and attacking the authorities and the media for trying "to smear me and gratuitously make a wasteland of my life."
>
> The first thing to say is that the presumption of innocence has already been maimed since 9/11 for foreign Muslims, and it should not be similarly cheapened with respect to Dr. Hatfill. It must be a genuine assumption that he is an innocent man caught in a nightmare. There is not a shred of traditional physical evidence linking him to the attacks. Still, Dr. Hatfill is wrong to suggest that the F.B.I. has casually designated him the anthrax "fall guy." ***
>
> So far, the only physical evidence is obscure: smell. Specially trained bloodhounds were given scent packets preserved from the anthrax letters and were introduced to a variety of people and locations. This month, they responded strongly to Dr. Hatfill, to his apartment, to his girlfriend's apartment and even to his former girlfriend's apartment, as well as to restaurants that he had recently entered (he is under constant surveillance). The dogs did not respond to other people, apartments or restaurants.
>
> Putting aside the question of Dr. Hatfill and the anthrax, there are two larger issues. First is the F.B.I.'s initial slowness in carrying out the anthrax investigation. *** Second is the need for much greater care within the U.S. biodefense program. *** To its credit, in the last few months, the bureau has finally picked up its pace. *** People very close to Dr. Hatfill are now cooperating with the authorities, information has been presented to a grand jury, and there is reason to hope that the bureau may soon be able to end this unseemly limbo by either exculpating Dr. Hatfill or arresting him.

As this column illustrates, Kristof's argument about the progress of the FBI's investigation of the anthrax mailings had much to do with specific allegations concerning Hatfill. *** Hatfill filed this lawsuit on July 13, 2004, asserting claims for defamation and intentional infliction of emotional distress. *** Count One alleges that The Times' publication of Kristof's columns defamed Hatfill by implying that Hatfill was involved in the anthrax mailings. *** A defamatory charge may be made expressly or by "inference, implication or insinuation." *** Hatfill contends that Kristof's columns defamed him by imputing to him the commission of crimes of moral turpitude, namely, the murders of five people who were exposed to the anthrax letters. If the columns fairly can be read to make such a charge, then they are defamatory *per se*. *** Hatfill's complaint adequately alleges that Kristof's columns, taken together, are capable of defamatory meaning. *** [A] reasonable reader of Kristof's columns likely would conclude that Hatfill was responsible for the anthrax mailings in 2001.[5] *** Because Kristof's columns, taken together, are capable of defamatory meaning under Virginia law, the district court erred in dismissing Count One.[7]

Count Two alleges that each of eleven discrete factual assertions contained in Kristof's columns separately defamed Hatfill by incriminating him in the anthrax mailings. The district court dismissed this count on the grounds that *** none of the eleven statements is independently capable of defamatory meaning. *** Broadly grouped, Hatfill complains about five sets of factual assertions in Kristof's columns. First, Hatfill complains about Kristof's assertion that he had the ability, access, and motive to make and send the anthrax. Second, Hatfill complains about Kristof's statement that he had access to an "isolated residence" where he gave Cipro to visitors. Third, Hatfill complains about the allegation that he had up-to-date anthrax vaccinations himself. Fourth, Hatfill complains about Kristof's charge that he failed three polygraph examinations in 2002. Finally, Hatfill complains about the allegation that he "was once caught with a girlfriend in a biohazard 'hot suite' at Fort Detrick . . . surrounded only by blushing germs."

Taken in the context of the columns in which they appear, and considered in light of [various cases] all of these statements but one are capable of incriminating Hatfill in the anthrax mailings. With the exception of the final statement--that Hatfill had been caught with a girlfriend in a biohazard hot suite at Fort Detrick--these statements link Hatfill to anthrax generally and the investigation specifically and give rise to an inference that he was involved in the anthrax mailings. ***

Count Three alleges that the publication of Kristof's columns constituted intentional infliction of emotional distress. The Times argues, however, that the complaint fails to allege conduct that qualifies as

---

[5] At this stage of the litigation, there is no evidence to show whether or to what extent Kristof's columns were, as the district court stated, "accurate report[s] of [an] ongoing investigation." *** In describing all this evidence, Kristof's columns did not merely report others' suspicions of Hatfill; they actually *generated* suspicion by asserting facts that tend to implicate him in the anthrax murders.

[7] Contrary to the district Court's assertion, it is immaterial whether Kristof actually intended to defame Hatfill. We stated in *Chapin* that "a libel-by-implication plaintiff must make an especially rigorous showing *where the expressed facts are literally true*. The language must not only be reasonably read to impart the false innuendo, but it must also affirmatively suggest that the author intends or endorses the inference." In this case, Hatfill alleges *both* that the inference--that he was responsible for the anthrax mailings--is false *and* that the factual assertions from which that inference arises are false. Since the district court was required to accept Hatfill's assertion that the facts upon which Kristof based his defamatory charge were false, *Chapin* is inapposite.

"outrageous" under Virginia law and emotional distress so severe that Virginia law would permit recovery. *** Accepting Hatfill's allegations as true, The Times intentionally published false charges accusing him of being responsible for anthrax mailings that resulted in five deaths, without regard for the truth of those charges and without giving Hatfill an opportunity to respond. Given the notoriety of the case, the charge of murder, and the refusal to permit comment by Hatfill's counsel, we conclude that the alleged misconduct is extreme or outrageous under Virginia law.

The Times argues that Hatfill cannot use an intentional-infliction-of-emotional-distress claim to avoid constitutional limitations on defamation actions. We are confident, however, that the relevant constitutional limitations cannot be avoided as easily as The Times imagines. If Hatfill ultimately cannot prevail on his defamation claims because he is unable to satisfy constitutional requirements for recovery, then he likely will be unable to prove that The Times' misconduct was intentional or reckless or that such misconduct was sufficiently outrageous to warrant recovery. At this stage of litigation, our sole concern is whether Hatfill's allegations, taken as true, describe intentional and outrageous misconduct. We conclude that they do. ***

NEIMEYER, Circuit Judge, dissenting.

Dr. Steven Hatfill's defamation complaint alleges at bottom that four columns written by columnist Nicholas Kristof and published in the *New York Times* during the period from July to August 2002 accused Dr. Hatfill of being the anthrax murderer. The essential question therefore is whether these columns, taken together or individually, may fairly be read to accuse Dr. Hatfill of the murders. Because I can find nothing in the letter or spirit of the columns that amounts to such an accusation, I would affirm.

The columns, when read fairly, send the message:

(1) that the FBI's investigation of the anthrax murders was lackadaisical and unimaginative;

(2) that the FBI should have begun pursuing obvious leads that created suspicion about Dr. Hatfill and that, based on circumstantial evidence, Dr. Hatfill should have been the leading suspect; and

(3) that, while there was circumstantial evidence pointing to Dr. Hatfill, no "traditional physical evidence linking him to the attacks" existed and that there "must [have been] a genuine assumption that he [was] an innocent man caught in a nightmare.'"

These points were amplified by examples of suspicious circumstances, but nowhere does any column accuse Dr. Hatfill of committing the murders. The columns' purpose was to put into operation prosecutorial machinery that would determine whether Dr. Hatfill committed the crimes and "end this unseemly limbo by either exculpating Dr. Hatfill or arresting him." *** [W]hether Kristof's descriptions of the various items of circumstantial evidence were accurate is irrelevant because (1) inaccurately reporting the suspicious circumstances surrounding a suspect does not amount to inaccurately accusing--either expressly or impliedly--the suspect of actually committing the crime, and (2) historical circumstances recounted in the columns and not disputed by Dr. Hatfill were sufficient to support the columns' stated suspicion about him. Reporting suspicion of criminal conduct--even elaborately and sometimes inaccurately--does not amount to an accusation of criminal conduct as necessary to support Dr. Hatfill's claim. ***

[Wilkinson, Circuit Judge, dissenting from the denial of rehearing en banc.]

*** The panel viewed its inquiry as limited to consideration of whether plaintiff had "adequately pled the elements of his claims under Virginia law." *** [It] has read Virginia law aggressively to permit a wide array of defamation suits against news organizations. A court that reads state law so expansively when deciding a motion to dismiss creates a "threat . . . of pecuniary liability" that "may impair the unfettered exercise of . . . First Amendment freedoms." *** Viewed as a whole, the columns do not pin guilt on plaintiff, but instead urge the investigation of an undeniable public threat. *** The columns expressly avoid premature accusation by repeatedly reminding readers that the burden of the government's failure falls not only upon the public, who seek the safety of identifying the true culprit, but also upon plaintiff, who deserves an end to the "unseemly limbo" of being a suspect. *** In view of their overall purpose and in light of their repeated disclaimers, these columns cannot "naturally and presumably be understood . . . as charging a crime."

*** The third count of plaintiff's complaint states a cause of action for intentional infliction of emotional distress. *** I am quite at a loss to see how publication of these columns "go[es] beyond all possible bounds of decency." They report on a matter of unquestioned public interest with urgent national security implications. The First Amendment expressly specifies that the "civilized community" in which we live is one that encourages public commentary of this type. Even assuming the columns contain the asserted factual errors, their publication is neither "intolerable" nor "atrocious." ***

The consequences of this decision for the First Amendment run deep. If one purpose of public commentary is to assess the functioning of government, these columns were surely in that vein. *** The perils of inaction and of overzealous action on the part of law enforcement are alike proper subjects for a free press. *** These columns were hard-hitting, to be sure, but they did not forsake the essential balance that our law requires. ***[D]efendant was simply doing its job. It is a job that the Constitution protects, and I would not construe gray areas of Virginia law to punish it and deter others from performing it.

Judge MICHAEL and Judge KING join me in this dissent.

Notes

1. **Subsequent History of Hatfill and the N.Y. Times.** The NY Times' motion for summary judgment was granted, with the court finding that Hatfill was a limited purpose public figure and that the newspaper did not publish its

claims with actual malice. "Plaintiff should have foreseen that by providing interviews, delivering lectures, and publishing articles on the subject of the bioterrorism threat, a public interest in him would arise. Because Plaintiff engaged in a course of conduct that was likely to invite attention and scrutiny, Plaintiff cannot now claim that he was a private figure who was dragged into this controversy unwillingly." Hatfill v. New York Times Co., 488 F.Supp. 2d 522, 530 (E.D. Va., 2007)

2.   Hatfill and the Government. On June 27, 2008, the Justice Department announced that it would pay $4.6 million to settle a lawsuit filed by Dr. Hatfill. The lawsuit, filed five years earlier, accused the FBI and Justice Department officials of leaking information about him to the press in violation of the Privacy Act. The government admitted no liability but decided settlement was "in the best interest of the United States," according to a Justice Department spokesman. What are these interests and why would such a large payment be in these interests?

3.   The Real Culprit? One month after the FBI paid a $4.6 million settlement to Steven Hatfill in June 2008, Dr. Bruce Ivins, who worked for the U.S. Army's biodefense center, committed suicide, apparently as prosecutors were preparing to charge him with the anthrax attacks. A panel of psychiatrists which was provided extensive access to Dr. Ivins' medical records concluded, in a 298-page report released in March 2011, that "Dr. Ivins was psychologically disposed to undertake the mailings; his behavioral history demonstrated his potential for carrying them out; and he had the motivation and the means."

4. Defamation and Terrorism Investigations. Do the rules for defamation change because of the subject matter? Should a person become a public figure merely by virtue of their status as a target of an investigation of terrorism? In an atmosphere of heightened awareness of imminent danger, can one who does not fit the classic profile of a terrorist get caught up in suspicion? Might an atmosphere of fear cause us to lower our standards of protecting individuals in favor of protecting the public?

XIII

EXECUTIVE POWER TO COUNTER TERRORISM

Emergency does not create power. . . . While emergency does not create power, emergency may furnish the occasion for the exercise of power. . . . But even the war power does not remove constitutional limitations safeguarding essential liberties.

HOME BUILDING & LOAN ASS'N v. BLAISDELL,
290 U.S. 398 (1934)

This chapter concerns the institutional allocation of power in the United States for dealing with terrorism or, more specifically, the new Islamic fundamentalist brand of terrorism. It draws upon materials covered for their substance earlier in the book and so, despite its importance, has been saved for last.

Part A provides a brief introduction to the Constitutional framework for and historical examples of the exercise of presidential power. Part B presents the Supreme Court's frameworks for looking at presidential power. Part C reviews the assertion of the "unitary executive" theory of presidential power in the aftermath of the attacks of 9/11. Finally, Part D examines some materials concerning institutional design and political theory that bear on the question of authority to deal with terrorism.

A. INTRODUCTION

The Articles of Confederation, ratified in 1781, contained neither a federal executive branch nor a judicial branch of government. Each state explicitly retained its sovereignty (Article II) and the powers of the "confederacy" of states resided in "the United States in Congress assembled." (Article I) This body was empowered to exercise not only legislative powers but also executive powers and some judicial functions—all within boundaries drawn to preserve state sovereignty. Article X provided that a "Committee of the States, or any nine of them" could "execute, in the recess of Congress" "such of the powers of Congress" as the Congress or nine states "shall from time to time think expedient to vest with them."

The Articles' structural limits on executive power did not last long. On September 17, 1787, the Constitutional Convention submitted the Constitution of the United States of America to the states for ratification. Following pitched debates between those favoring the Constitution (Federalists) and those opposing it (Antifederalists), the Constitution was ratified in mid-1788. George Washington was inaugurated as the first President of the United States on April 30, 1789, and the Congress met in early 1789. One of the first acts of this Congress was adoption of a Bill of Rights to be sent the states for ratification.

Article II of the Constitution begins with these words: "The executive Power shall be vested in a President of the United States of America." Later parts of the remarkably brief Article II require that the President "take Care that the Laws be faithfully executed" and serve as the "Commander-in-Chief" of the Army and Navy as well as state militias when called into service of the United States. Article II provides the President the power to appoint (with the advice of the Senate for principal officers) the other members of the executive branch of the government. Art II, Section 2, clause 2, provides that the President shall "make treaties" with the consent of two-thirds of the Senate; Section 3 notes that he shall "receive Ambassadors and other public Ministers."

It is clear that the changes from a very weak executive to a much stronger executive was intended to more efficiently run the federal government and unify the states under a popular leader (George Washington). One commentator, about whom we shall see more in this chapter, has this to say:

> Hamilton and the other Federalists *** understood the executive to be functionally best matched in speech, unity, and decisiveness to the unpredictable high-stakes nature of foreign affairs. *** Rational action on behalf of the nation in a dangerous world would be best advanced by executive action. *** The Framers rejected the legislative supremacy of the revolutionary state governments in favor of a Presidency that would be independent of Congress, elected by the people, and possessed with speed, decision, and vigor to guide the nation through war and emergency. *** John Yoo, CRISIS AND COMMAND: A HISTORY OF EXECUTIVE POWER FROM GEORGE WASHINGTON TO GEORGE W. BUSH (Kaplan, 2010).

On the other hand, the Constitution also provides ample powers for Congress related to the exercise of armed force. Congress is given power in Article I, section 8:

> [10] To define and punish Piracies and Felonies committed on the high Seas, and Offenses against the Law of Nations;

> [11] To declare War, grant Letters of Marque and Reprisal, and make Rules concerning Captures on Land and Water;

> [12] To raise and support Armies, but no Appropriation of Money to that Use shall be for a longer Term than two Years;

> [13] To provide and maintain a Navy;

[14] To make Rules for the Government and Regulation of the land and naval Forces;

[15] To provide for calling forth the Militia to execute the Laws of the Union, suppress Insurrections and repel Invasions;

[16] To provide for organizing, arming, and disciplining, the Militia ***

[17] To exercise *** Authority over *** the Erection of Forts, Magazines, Arsenals, dockyards, and other needful Buildings ***

Congress may thus constrain the executive in fighting wars or dealing with emergencies by refusing to fund and by legislating rules for the conduct of such enterprises. Finally, Congress can refuse to confirm nominees of the President to significant military offices and may impeach the President for "high crimes and misdemeanors."

Presidents who have commanded military force have generally been both powerful and popular. To deal with extraordinary situations, they have sometimes cut constitutional corners. For example, President Roosevelt's military commission to deal with German saboteurs, hardly a model of fair process, was approved of by the Supreme Court in *Ex Parte Quirin*, 317 U.S. 1 (1942), supra Chapter IX. Even though the Supreme Court limited President Lincoln's use of a military commission in *Ex Parte Milligan*, 71 U.S. 2 (1866), supra Chapter V, Lincoln exercised extraordinary power during the Civil War.

While revered for saving the Union and freeing the slaves, Lincoln is less well known for unilaterally suspending the writ of habeas corpus and replacing usual law enforcement with martial law—including military detention without trial even though Article I of the Constitution, which enumerates Congressional powers, states that "The privilege of the Writ of Habeas Corpus shall not be suspended, unless when in Cases of Rebellion or Invasion the public Safety may require it." In *Ex Parte Merryman*, 17 F. Cas. 144 (1861), the judiciary addressed the constitutionality of this action and recognized that only Congress, not the President, could suspend the writ, saying "the people of the United States are no longer living under a government of laws." Lincoln ignored the ruling and responded in a message to Congress:

> These measures, whether strictly legal or not, were ventured upon under what appeared to be a popular demand, and a public necessity; trusting, then as now, that Congress would readily ratify them. *** Nevertheless, the legality and propriety of what has been done under it are questioned, and the attention of the country has been called to the proposition that one who is sworn to "take care that the laws be faithfully executed" should not himself violate them. *** To state the question more directly, Are all the laws but one to go unexecuted, and the Government itself go to pieces lest that

one be violated? Even in such a case, would not the official oath be broken if the Government should be overthrown when it was believed that disregarding the single law would tend to preserve it?

A month later, Congress declared all of Lincoln's actions "with regard to the army and navy" "valid" as if "they had been issued and done" by Congress and later expressly authorized the suspension of the writ in the Habeas Corpus Act of 1863. What does this history teach about extra-constitutional Presidential action? Was Lincoln right? Does the answer depend on whether he had—or continued to maintain—public support for his policies, regardless of the law or Constitution?

B. SUPREME COURT FRAMEWORKS

Few Supreme Court cases have dealt with "emergency" powers of the President. The Constitution does not generally mention emergencies, though it does contain provisions dealing with several dire contingencies. Congress may call forth the militia in a particular type of emergency, "to execute the Laws of the Union, suppress Insurrections and repel Invasions." Art. I, section 8, clause 15. Congress may suspend habeas corpus "when in Cases of Rebellion or Invasion the public Safety may require it." Art. I, section 9, clause 2. No presidential power is specifically mentioned to deal with emergencies, though "The United States shall guarantee to every State *** a Republican Form of Government, and shall protect each of them from Invasion" and in limited circumstances protect states "against domestic violence." Art. IV, section 4.

Some emergencies may justify states in doing what they would otherwise be barred by the Constitution from doing. For example, a state may lay imposts or duties when "absolutely necessary for executing its inspection Laws." Art. I, section 10, cl. 2. A state may also engage in war or war-related activities, including agreements or compacts with foreign countries when "actually invaded, or in such imminent Danger as will not admit of delay.

Civil liberties may also be infringed in emergencies by states, when otherwise they might not be. As the Supreme Court said in *Jacobson v. Massachussetts*, 197 U.S. 11 (1905),

> Upon the principle of self-defense, of paramount necessity, a community has the right to protect itself against an epidemic of disease which threatens the safety of its members. It is to be observed that when the regulation in question was adopted smallpox, according to the recitals in the regulation adopted by the board of health, was prevalent to some extent in the city of Cambridge, and the disease was increasing. *** There is, of course, a sphere within which the individual may assert the supremacy of his own will, and rightfully dispute the authority of any human government,-especially of any free

government existing under a written constitution, to interfere with the exercise of that will. But it is equally true that in every well-ordered society charged with the duty of conserving the safety of its members the rights of the individual in respect of his liberty may at times, under the pressure of great dangers, be subjected to such restraint, to be enforced by reasonable regulations, as the safety of the general public may demand. An American citizen arriving at an American port on a vessel in which, during the voyage, there had been cases of yellow fever or Asiatic cholera, he, although apparently free from disease himself, may yet, in some circumstances, be held in quarantine against his will on board of such vessel or in a quarantine station, until it be ascertained by inspection, conducted with due diligence, that the danger of the spread of the disease among the community at large has disappeared. The liberty secured by the 14th Amendment, this court has said, consists, in part, in the right of a person 'to live and work where he will'; and yet he may be compelled, by force if need be, against his will and without regard to his personal wishes or his pecuniary interests, or even his religious or political convictions, to take his place in the ranks of the army of his country, and risk the chance of being shot down in its defense. It is not, therefore, true that the power of the public to guard itself against imminent danger depends in every case involving the control of one's body upon his willingness to submit to reasonable regulations established by the constituted authorities, under the sanction of the state, for the purpose of protecting the public collectively against such danger.

Saying that Congress may suspend habeas corpus or that states may infringe liberties in emergencies is a far cry from saying that the President has emergency powers. One case that argues for a broad conception of executive authority (indeed one far broader than needed to resolve the case) is the decision that follows.

UNITED STATES v. CURTISS–WRIGHT
299 U.S. 304 (1936)

MR. JUSTICE SUTHERLAND delivered the opinion of the Court.

On January 27, 1936, an indictment was returned in the court below, the first count of which charges that appellees, *** conspired to sell in the United States certain arms of war, namely, fifteen machine guns, to Bolivia, a country then engaged in armed conflict in the Chaco, in violation of the Joint Resolution of Congress approved May 28, 1934, and the provisions of a proclamation issued on the same day by the President of the United States pursuant to authority conferred by section 1 of the resolution. ***

The whole aim of the resolution is to affect a situation entirely external to the United States, and falling within the category of foreign affairs. *** It will contribute to the elucidation of the question if we first consider the differences between the powers of the federal government in respect of foreign or external affairs and those in respect of domestic or internal affairs. That there are differences between them, and that these differences are fundamental, may not be doubted.

The two classes of powers are different, both in respect of their origin and their nature. The broad statement that the federal government can exercise no powers except those specifically enumerated in the Constitution, and such implied powers as are necessary and proper to carry into effect the enumerated powers, is categorically true only in respect of our internal affairs. In that field, the primary purpose of the Constitution was to carve from the general mass of legislative powers then possessed by the states such portions as it was thought desirable to vest in the federal government, leaving those not included in the enumeration still in the states. That this doctrine applies only to powers which the states had is self-evident. And since the states severally never possessed international powers, such powers could not have been carved from the mass of state powers but obviously were transmitted to the United States from some other source. ***

As a result of the separation from Great Britain by the colonies, acting as a unit, the powers of external sovereignty passed from the Crown not to the colonies severally, but to the colonies in their collective and corporate capacity as the United States of America. *** Rulers come and go; governments end and forms of government change; but sovereignty survives. A political society cannot endure without a supreme will somewhere. Sovereignty is never held in suspense. When, therefore, the external sovereignty of Great Britain in respect of the colonies ceased, it immediately passed to the Union. *** It results that the investment of the federal government with the powers of external sovereignty did not depend upon the affirmative grants of the Constitution. The powers to declare and wage war, to conclude peace, to make treaties, to maintain diplomatic relations with other sovereignties, if they had never been mentioned in the Constitution, would have vested in the federal government as necessary concomitants of nationality. *** In this vast external realm, with its important, complicated, delicate and manifold problems, the President alone has the power to speak or listen as a representative of the nation. He makes treaties with the advice and consent of the Senate; but he alone negotiates. Into the field of negotiation the Senate cannot intrude; and Congress itself is powerless to invade it. As Marshall said in his great argument of March 7, 1800, in the House of Representatives, "The President is the sole organ of the nation in its external relations, and its sole representative with foreign nations."

*** [W]e are here dealing not alone with an authority vested in the President by an exertion of legislative power, but with such an authority plus the very delicate, plenary and exclusive power of the President as the sole organ of the federal government in the field of international relations—a power which does not require as a basis for its exercise an act of Congress, but which, of course, like every other governmental power, must be exercised in subordination to the applicable provisions of the Constitution. It is quite apparent that if, in the maintenance of our international relations, embarrassment—perhaps serious embarrassment—is to be avoided and success for our aims achieved, congressional legislation which is to be made effective through negotiation and inquiry within the international field must often accord to the President a degree of discretion and freedom from statutory restriction which would not be admissible were domestic affairs alone involved. Moreover, he, not Congress, has the better opportunity of knowing the conditions which prevail in foreign countries, and especially is this true in time of war. He has his confidential sources of information. He has his agents in the form of diplomatic, consular and other officials. Secrecy in respect of information gathered by them may be highly necessary, and the premature disclosure of it productive of harmful results.***

Notes

1. **Implied Presidential Powers.** Could this case have been decided without reference to the Constitution? Were the broad pronouncements about Presidential power necessary to the decision? As an interesting aside, Justice Department lawyers representing the President have been known to refer to the case informally as "*Curtiss-Wright*, so I'm right."

2. **Preconstitutional Powers.** Why does the Court say the President is "the sole organ of the federal government in the field of international relations?" Is the text clear on this? Is historical practice clear? Are you comfortable with the Court's assessment of preconstitutional powers?

3. **Functionalism.** What preconceptions about the type of foreign policies the United States should have are implicit in the Court's analysis?

*****

Curtiss-Wright has not been overruled, but its methodology has not been replicated in later cases. Rather, the general framework for resolving issues of presidential power has stemmed from the next case and, in particular, from Justice Jackson's concurrence in the decision.

YOUNGSTOWN SHEET & TUBE CO. v. SAWYER
343 U.S. 579 (1952)

MR. JUSTICE BLACK delivered the opinion of the Court.

We are asked to decide whether the President was acting within his constitutional power when he issued an order directing the Secretary of Commerce to take possession of and operate most of the Nation's steel mills. The mill owners argue that the President's order amounts to lawmaking, a legislative function which the Constitution has expressly confided to the Congress and not to the President. The Government's position is that the order was made on findings of the President that his action was necessary to avert a national catastrophe which would inevitably result from a stoppage of steel production, and that in meeting this grave emergency the President was acting within the aggregate of his constitutional powers as the Nation's Chief Executive and the Commander in Chief of the Armed Forces of the United States. ***

The President's power, if any, to issue the order must stem either from an act of Congress or from the Constitution itself. There is no statute that expressly authorizes the President to take possession of property as he did here. Nor is there any act of Congress to which our attention has been directed from which such a power can fairly be implied. Indeed, we do not understand the Government to rely on statutory authorization for this seizure. There are two statutes which do authorize the President to take both personal and real property under certain conditions. However, the Government admits that these conditions were not met ***. The Government refers to the seizure provisions of one of these statutes (§ 201(b) of the Defense Production Act) as "much too cumbersome, involved, and time-consuming for the crisis which was at hand."

Moreover, the use of the seizure technique to solve labor disputes in order to prevent work stoppages was not only unauthorized by any congressional enactment; prior to this controversy, Congress had refused to adopt that method of settling labor disputes. When the Taft–Hartley Act was under consideration in 1947, Congress rejected an amendment which would have authorized such governmental seizures in cases of emergency. ***

It is clear that if the President had authority to issue the order he did, it must be found in some provisions of the Constitution. And it is not claimed that express constitutional language grants this power to the President. The contention is that presidential power should be implied from the aggregate of his powers under the Constitution. Particular reliance is placed on provisions in Article II which say that "the executive Power shall be vested in a President *** "; that "he shall take Care that the Laws be faithfully executed"; and that he "shall be Commander in Chief of the Army and Navy of the United States."

The order cannot properly be sustained as an exercise of the President's military power as Commander in Chief of the Armed Forces. *** Even though "theater of war" be an expanding concept, we cannot with faithfulness to our constitutional system hold that the Commander in Chief of the Armed Forces has the ultimate power as such to take possession of private property in order to keep labor disputes from stopping production. This is a job for the Nation's lawmakers, not for its military authorities.

Nor can the seizure order be sustained because of the several constitutional provisions that grant executive power to the President. In the framework of our Constitution, the President's power to see that the laws are faithfully executed refutes the idea that he is to be a lawmaker. The Constitution limits his functions in the lawmaking process to the recommending of laws he thinks wise and the vetoing of laws he thinks bad. And the Constitution is neither silent nor equivocal about who shall make laws which the President is to execute. *** The President's order does not direct that a congressional policy be executed in a manner prescribed by Congress—it directs that a presidential policy be executed in a manner prescribed by the President. *** The power of Congress to adopt such public policies as those proclaimed by the order is beyond question. It can authorize the taking of private property for public use. It can makes laws regulating the relationships between employers and employees, prescribing rules designed to settle labor disputes, and fixing wages and working conditions in certain fields of our economy. The Constitution did not subject this law-making power of Congress to presidential or military supervision or control. ***

MR. JUSTICE JACKSON, concurring in the judgment and opinion of the court.

*** A judge, like an executive adviser, may be surprised at the poverty of really useful and unambiguous authority applicable to concrete problems of executive power as they actually present themselves. *** The actual art of governing under our Constitution does not and cannot conform to judicial definitions of the power of any of its branches based on isolated clauses or even single Articles torn from context. While the Constitution diffuses power the better to secure liberty, it also contemplates that practice will integrate the dispersed powers into a workable government. It enjoins upon its branches separateness but interdependence, autonomy but reciprocity. Presidential powers are not fixed but fluctuate, depending upon their disjunction or conjunction with those of Congress. We may well begin by a somewhat over-simplified grouping of practical situations in which a President may doubt, or others may challenge, his powers, and by distinguishing roughly the legal consequences of this factor of relativity.

1. When the President acts pursuant to an express or implied authorization of Congress, his authority is at its maximum, for it includes all that he possesses in his own right plus all that Congress can delegate. In these circumstances, and in these only, may he be said (for what it may be worth), to personify the federal sovereignty. If his act is held unconstitutional under these circumstances, it usually means that the Federal Government as an undivided whole lacks power. A seizure executed by the President pursuant to an Act of Congress would be supported by the strongest of presumptions and the widest latitude of judicial interpretation, and the burden of persuasion would rest heavily upon any who might attack it.

2. When the President acts in absence of either a congressional grant or denial of authority, he can only rely upon his own independent powers, but there is a zone of twilight in which he and Congress may have concurrent authority, or in which its distribution is uncertain. Therefore, congressional inertia, indifference or quiescence may sometimes, at least as a practical matter, enable, if not invite, measures on independent presidential responsibility. In this area, any actual test of power is likely to depend on the imperatives of events and contemporary imponderables rather than on abstract theories of law.

3. When the President takes measures incompatible with the expressed or implied will of Congress, his power is at its lowest ebb, for then he can rely

only upon his own constitutional powers minus any constitutional powers of Congress over the matter. Courts can sustain exclusive Presidential control in such a case only by disabling the Congress from acting upon the subject. Presidential claim to a power at once so conclusive and preclusive must be scrutinized with caution, for what is at stake is the equilibrium established by our constitutional system.

Into which of these classifications does this executive seizure of the steel industry fit? It is eliminated from the first by admission, for it is conceded that no congressional authorization exists for this seizure. *** Can it then be defended under flexible tests available to the second category? It seems clearly eliminated from that class because Congress has not left seizure of private property an open field but has covered it by three statutory policies inconsistent with this seizure. *** This leaves the current seizure to be justified only by the severe tests under the third grouping, where it can be supported only by any remainder of executive power after subtraction of such powers as Congress may have over the subject. In short, we can sustain the President only by holding that seizure of such strike-bound industries is within his domain and beyond control by Congress. ***

The Solicitor General seeks the power of seizure in three clauses of the Executive Article, the first reading, "The executive Power shall be vested in a President of the United States of America." Lest I be thought to exaggerate, I quote the interpretation which his brief puts upon it: "In our view, this clause constitutes a grant of all the executive powers of which the Government is capable." If that be true, it is difficult to see why the forefathers bothered to add several specific items, including some trifling ones.

The example of such unlimited executive power that must have most impressed the forefathers was the prerogative exercised by George III, and the description of its evils in the Declaration of Independence leads me to doubt that they were creating their new Executive in his image. Continental European examples were no more appealing. And if we seek instruction from our own times, we can match it only from the executive powers in those governments we disparagingly describe as totalitarian. I cannot accept the view that this clause is a grant in bulk of all conceivable executive power but regard it as an allocation to the presidential office of the generic powers thereafter stated.

The clause on which the Government next relies is that "The President shall be Commander in Chief ***." But just what authority goes with the name has plagued Presidential advisers who would not waive or narrow it by nonassertion yet cannot say where it begins or ends. It undoubtedly puts the Nation's armed forces under Presidential command. Hence, this loose appellation is sometimes advanced as support for any Presidential action, internal or external, involving use of force, the idea being that it vests power to do anything, anywhere, that can be done with an army or navy.

That seems to be the logic of an argument tendered at our bar—that the President having, on his own responsibility, sent American troops abroad derives from that act "affirmative power" to seize the means of producing a supply of steel for them. ***

I cannot foresee all that it might entail if the Court should endorse this argument. Nothing in our Constitution is plainer than that declaration of a war is entrusted only to Congress. Of course, a state of war may in fact exist without a formal declaration. But no doctrine that the Court could promulgate would seem to me more sinister and alarming than that a President whose conduct of foreign affairs is so largely uncontrolled, and often even is unknown, can vastly enlarge his mastery over the internal affairs of the country by his own commitment of the Nation's armed forces to some foreign venture. ***

Assuming that we are in a war de facto, whether it is or is not a war de jure, does that empower the Commander-in-Chief to seize industries he thinks necessary to supply our army? The Constitution expressly places in Congress power "to raise and support Armies" and "to provide and maintain a Navy." This certainly lays upon Congress primary responsibility for supplying the armed forces. Congress alone controls the raising of revenues and their appropriation and may determine in what manner and by what means they shall be spent for military and naval procurement. ***

There are indications that the Constitution did not contemplate that the title Commander-in-Chief of the Army and Navy will constitute him also Commander-in-Chief of the country, its industries and its inhabitants. He has no monopoly of "war powers," whatever they are. ***

The third clause in which the Solicitor General finds seizure powers is that "he shall take Care that the Laws be faithfully executed ***." That authority must be matched against words of the Fifth Amendment that "No person shall be *** deprived of life, liberty, or property, without due process of law ***." One gives a governmental authority that reaches so far as there is law, the other gives a private right that authority shall go no farther. These signify about all there is of the principle that ours is a government of laws, not of men, and that we submit ourselves to rulers only if under rules.

The Solicitor General lastly grounds support of the seizure upon nebulous, inherent powers never expressly granted but said to have accrued to the office from the customs and claims of preceding administrations. The plea is for a resulting power to deal with a crisis or an emergency according to the necessities of the case, the unarticulated assumption being that necessity knows no law. ***

The vagueness and generality of the clauses that set forth presidential powers afford a plausible basis for pressures within and without an administration for presidential action beyond that supported by those whose responsibility it is to defend his actions in court. The claim of inherent and unrestricted presidential powers has long been a persuasive dialectical weapon in political controversy. ***

The appeal, however, that we declare the existence of inherent powers ex necessitate to meet an emergency asks us to do what many think would be wise, although it is something the forefathers omitted. They knew what emergencies were, knew the pressures they engender for authoritative action, knew, too, how they afford a ready pretext for usurpation. We may also suspect that they suspected that emergency powers would tend to kindle emergencies. Aside from suspension of the privilege of the writ of habeas corpus in time of rebellion or invasion, when the public safety may require it, they made no express provision for exercise of extraordinary authority because of a crisis. I do not think we rightfully may so amend their work, *** although many modern nations have forthrightly recognized that war and economic crises may upset the normal balance between liberty and authority. Their experience with emergency powers may not be irrelevant to the argument here that we should say that the Executive, of his own volition, can invest himself with undefined emergency powers. ***

In view of the ease, expedition and safety with which Congress can grant and has granted large emergency powers, certainly ample to embrace this crisis, I am quite unimpressed with the argument that we should affirm possession of them without statute. Such power either has no beginning or it has no end. If it exists, it need submit to no legal restraint. I am not alarmed that it would plunge us straightway into dictatorship, but it is at least a step in that wrong direction.

As to whether there is imperative necessity for such powers, it is relevant to note the gap that exists between the President's paper powers and his real powers. The Constitution does not disclose the measure of the actual controls wielded by the modern presidential office. That instrument must be understood as an Eighteenth–Century sketch of a government hoped for, not as a blueprint of the Government that is. Vast accretions of federal power, eroded from that reserved by the States, have magnified the scope of presidential activity. Subtle shifts take place in the centers of real power that do not show on the face of the Constitution.

Executive power has the advantage of concentration in a single head in whose choice the whole Nation has a part, making him the focus of public hopes and expectations. ***

The essence of our free Government is "leave to live by no man's leave, underneath the law"—to be governed by those impersonal forces which we call law. Our Government is fashioned to fulfill this concept so far as humanly possible. The Executive, except for recommendation and veto, has no legislative power. The executive action we have here originates in the individual will of the President *** We do not know today what powers over labor or property would be claimed to flow from Government possession if we should legalize it, what rights to compensation would be claimed or recognized, or on what contingency it would end. With all its defects, delays and inconveniences, men have discovered no technique for long preserving free government except that the Executive be under the law, and that the law be made by parliamentary deliberations.

Such institutions may be destined to pass away. But it is the duty of the Court to be last, not first, to give them up.

MR. JUSTICE DOUGLAS, concurring [omitted]

MR. JUSTICE FRANKFURTER, concurring.

*** It is absurd to see a dictator in a representative product of the sturdy democratic traditions of the Mississippi Valley. The accretion of dangerous power does not come in a day. It does come, however slowly, from the generative force of unchecked disregard of the restrictions that fence in even the most disinterested assertion of authority. *** The question before the Court comes in this setting. Congress has frequently—at least 16 times since 1916—specifically provided for executive seizure of production, transportation, communications, or storage facilities. In every case it has qualified this grant of power with limitations and safeguards. This body of enactments *** demonstrates that Congress deemed seizure so drastic a power as to require that it be carefully circumscribed whenever the President was vested with this extraordinary authority. ***In any event, nothing can be plainer than that Congress made a conscious choice of policy in a field full of perplexity and peculiarly within legislative responsibility for choice. In formulating legislation for dealing with industrial conflicts, Congress could not more clearly and emphatically have withheld authority than it did in [the Taft–Hartley Act of] 1947. ***It cannot be contended that the President would have had power to issue this order had Congress explicitly negated such authority in formal legislation. Congress has expressed its will to withhold this power from the President as though it had said so in so many words. ***

MR. CHIEF JUSTICE VINSON, with whom MR. JUSTICE REED and MR. JUSTICE MINTON join, dissenting.

The President of the United States directed the Secretary of Commerce to take temporary possession of the Nation's steel mills during the existing emergency because "a work stoppage would immediately jeopardize and imperil our national defense and the defense of those joined with us in resisting aggression, and would add to the continuing danger of our soldiers, sailors and airmen engaged in combat in the field." *** One is not here called upon even to consider the possibility of executive seizure of a farm, a corner grocery store or even a single industrial plant. Such considerations arise only when one ignores the central fact of this case—that the Nation's entire basic steel production would have shut down completely if there had been no Government seizure. Even ignoring for the moment whatever confidential information the President may possess as "the Nation's organ for foreign affairs," the uncontroverted affidavits in this record amply support the finding that "a work stoppage would immediately jeopardize and imperil our national defense."

*** [The] whole of the "executive Power" is vested in the President. *** This comprehensive grant of the executive power to a single person was bestowed soon after the country had thrown the yoke of monarchy. Only by instilling initiative and vigor in all of the three departments of Government, declared Madison, could tyranny in any form be avoided. Hamilton added: "Energy in the Executive is a leading character in the definition of good government. It is essential to the protection of the community against foreign attack; it is not less essential to the steady administration of the laws; to the protection of property against those irregular and highhanded combinations which sometimes interrupt the ordinary course of justice; to the security of liberty against the enterprises and assaults of ambition, of faction, and of anarchy." It is thus apparent that the Presidency was deliberately fashioned as an office of power and independence. Of course, the Framers created no autocrat capable of arrogating any power unto himself at any time. But neither did they create an automaton impotent to exercise the powers of Government at a time when the survival of the Republic itself may be at stake. ***

A review of executive action demonstrates that our Presidents have on many occasions exhibited the leadership contemplated by the Framers when they made the President Commander in Chief, and imposed upon him the trust to "take Care that the Laws be faithfully executed." With or without explicit statutory authorization, Presidents have at such times dealt with national emergencies by acting promptly and resolutely to enforce legislative programs, at least to save those programs until Congress could act. Congress and the courts have responded to such executive initiative with consistent approval.

*** The broad executive power granted by Article II to an officer on duty 365 days a year cannot, it is said, be invoked to avert disaster. Instead, the President must confine himself to sending a message to Congress recommending action. Under this messenger-boy concept of the Office, the President cannot even act to preserve legislative programs from destruction so that Congress will have something left to act upon. There is no judicial finding that the executive action was unwarranted because there was in fact no basis for the President's finding of the existence of an emergency for, under this view, the gravity of the emergency and the immediacy of the threatened disaster are considered irrelevant as a matter of law. *** Faced with the duty of executing the defense programs which Congress had enacted and the disastrous effects that any stoppage in steel production would have on those programs, the President acted to preserve those programs by seizing the steel mills. There is no question that the possession was other than temporary in character and subject to congressional direction—either approving, disapproving or regulating the manner in which the mills were to be administered and returned to the owners. The President immediately informed Congress of his action and clearly stated his intention to abide by the legislative will. No basis for claims of arbitrary action, unlimited powers or dictatorial usurpation of congressional power appears from the facts of this case. ***

Notes

1. **Constitutional Theory.** There is no majority rationale in *Youngstown*. Each of the opinions adopts a very different methodology for assessing the constitutionality of the seizure of the mills.

(a) Under JUSTICE BLACK's formalist approach, does the President's power depend at all on whether Congress has or has not acted? Does JUSTICE DOUGLAS solve this problem?

(b) Under JUSTICE JACKSON's functionalist approach, how does the Court decide which zone fits any particular action of the President?

(c) What do you think of JUSTICE FRANKFURTER'S use of history?

(d) Do you agree with the Court that, whatever the substantive outcome of the case, this is a proper decision for the Supreme Court to be making? Why or why not?

2. **Fluctuating Powers Approach.** JUSTICE JACKSON's concurrence breaks the actions of the President into three categories: (1) Where the President acts in accord with the express or implied authorization of Congress, (2) Where the President acts in the absence of any Congressional declaration on the matter, and (3) Where the President acts in direct contradiction to the express or implied will of Congress. The President's powers fluctuate with each category, being the greatest in the first category and the least in the third category. Although JUSTICE JACKSON wrote only for himself in his concurrence, his approach appears to be the one accepted by today's Court, *see Dames & Moore v. Regan*, infra. JUSTICE REHNQUIST, author of the Court's opinion in *Dames & Moore*, was JUSTICE JACKSON's clerk at the time *Youngstown* was decided.

*****

JUSTICE JACKSON'S approach became the law when a majority of the Court adopted it, albeit with one significant modification, in the following case:

DAMES & MOORE v. REGAN
453 U.S. 654 (1981)

JUSTICE REHNQUIST delivered the opinion of the Court.

*** On November 4, 1979, the American Embassy in Tehran was seized and our diplomatic personnel were captured and held hostage. In response to that crisis, President Carter, acting pursuant to the International Emergency Economic Powers Act (hereinafter IEEPA), declared a national emergency on November 14, 1979, and blocked the removal or transfer of "all property and interests in property of the Government of Iran, its instrumentalities and controlled entities and the Central Bank of Iran which are or become subject to the jurisdiction of the United States. *** " On November 15, 1979, the Treasury Department's Office of Foreign Assets Control issued a regulation providing that "[u]nless licensed or authorized *** any attachment, judgment, decree, lien, execution, garnishment, or other judicial process is null and void with respect to any property in which on or since [November 14, 1979,] there existed an interest of Iran." The regulations also made clear that any licenses or authorizations granted could be "amended, modified, or revoked at any time." ***

On December 19, 1979, petitioner Dames & Moore filed suit in the United States District Court for the Central District of California against the

Government of Iran, the Atomic Energy Organization of Iran, and a number of Iranian banks. In its complaint, petitioner alleged that *** it was owed $3,436,694.30 plus interest for services performed under the contract prior to the date of termination.***

On January 20, 1981, the Americans held hostage were released by Iran pursuant to an [Executive] Agreement entered into the day before ***. The Agreement stated that "[i]t is the purpose of [the United States and Iran] *** to terminate all litigation as between the Government of each party and the nationals of the other, and to bring about the settlement and termination of all such claims through binding arbitration." In furtherance of this goal, the Agreement called for the establishment of an Iran–United States Claims Tribunal which would arbitrate any claims not settled within six months. Awards of the Claims Tribunal are to be "final and binding" and "enforceable *** in the courts of any nation in accordance with its laws." Under the Agreement, the United States is obligated "to terminate all legal proceedings in United States courts involving claims of United States persons and institutions against Iran and its state enterprises, to nullify all attachments and judgments obtained therein, to prohibit all further litigation based on such claims, and to bring about the termination of such claims through binding arbitration." In addition, the United States must "act to bring about the transfer" by July 19, 1981, of all Iranian assets held in this country by American banks. ***

On January 19, 1981, President Carter issued a series of Executive Orders implementing the terms of the agreement. *** On February 24, 1981, President Reagan issued an Executive Order in which he "ratified" the January 19th Executive Orders. Moreover, he "suspended" all "claims which may be presented to the *** Tribunal" and provided that such claims "shall have no legal effect in any action now pending in any court of the United States." The suspension of any particular claim terminates if the Claims Tribunal determines that it has no jurisdiction over that claim; claims are discharged for all purposes when the Claims Tribunal either awards some recovery and that amount is paid, or determines that no recovery is due. ***

The parties and the lower courts, confronted with the instant questions, have all agreed that much relevant analysis is contained in *Youngstown Sheet & Tube Co. v. Sawyer*, 343 U.S. 579 (1952). *** Although we have in the past found and do today find Justice Jackson's classification of executive actions into three general categories analytically useful, we should be mindful of Justice Holmes' admonition *** that "[t]he great ordinances of the Constitution do not establish and divide fields of black and white." Justice Jackson himself recognized that his three categories represented "a somewhat over-simplified grouping," and it is doubtless the case that executive action in any particular instance falls, not neatly in one of three pigeonholes, but rather at some point along a spectrum running from explicit congressional authorization to explicit congressional prohibition. This is particularly true as respects cases such as the one before us, involving responses to international crises the nature of which Congress can hardly have been expected to anticipate in any detail.

*** The Government *** has principally relied on [this statutory language]:

*** [T]he President may, under such regulations as he may prescribe, by means of instructions, licenses, or otherwise, investigate, regulate, direct and compel, nullify, void, prevent or prohibit, any acquisition, holding, withholding, use, transfer, withdrawal, transportation, importation or exportation of, or dealing in, or exercising any right, power, or privilege with respect to, or transactions involving, any property in which any foreign country or a national thereof has any interest; by any person, or with respect to any property, subject to the jurisdiction of the United States.

The Government contends that the acts of "nullifying" the attachments and ordering the "transfer" of the frozen assets are specifically authorized by the plain language of the above statute. ***Because the President's action in nullifying the attachments and ordering the transfer of the assets was taken pursuant to specific congressional authorization, it is "supported by the strongest of presumptions and the widest latitude of judicial interpretation, and the burden of persuasion would rest heavily upon any who might attack it." *Youngstown*, 343 U.S., at 637 (Jackson, J., concurring). Under the circumstances of this case, we cannot say that petitioner has sustained that heavy burden. ***

Although we have concluded that the IEEPA constitutes specific congressional authorization to the President to nullify the attachments and order the transfer of Iranian assets, there remains the question of the President's authority to suspend claims pending in American courts. Such claims have, of course, an existence apart from the attachments which accompanied them. ***

[We conclude] that neither the IEEPA nor the Hostage Act constitutes specific authorization of the President's action suspending claims[.] [H]owever, [this] is not to say that these statutory provisions are entirely irrelevant to the question of the validity of the President's action. We think both statutes highly relevant in the looser sense of indicating congressional acceptance of a broad scope for executive action in circumstances such as those presented in this case. *** [T]he IEEPA delegates broad authority to the President to act in times of national emergency with respect to property of a foreign country. The Hostage Act similarly indicates congressional willingness that the President have broad discretion when responding to the hostile acts of foreign sovereigns.

*** [W]e cannot ignore the general tenor of Congress' legislation in this area in trying to determine whether the President is acting alone or at least with the acceptance of Congress. As we have noted, Congress cannot anticipate and legislate with regard to every possible action the President may find it necessary to take or every possible situation in which he might act. Such failure of Congress specifically to delegate authority does not, "especially *** in the areas of foreign policy and national security," imply "congressional disapproval" of action taken by the Executive. On the contrary, the enactment of legislation closely related to the question of the President's authority in a particular case which evinces legislative intent to accord the President broad discretion may be considered to "invite" "measures on independent presidential responsibility," *Youngstown*, 343 U.S., at 637 (Jackson, J., concurring). ***

In light of all of the foregoing—the inferences to be drawn from the character of the legislation Congress has enacted in the area, such as the IEEPA and the Hostage Act, and from the history of acquiescence in executive claims settlement—we conclude that the President was authorized to suspend pending claims. As Justice Frankfurter pointed out in *Youngstown*, 343 U.S., at 610–611, "a systematic, unbroken, executive practice, long pursued to the knowledge of the Congress and never before questioned *** may be treated as a gloss on 'Executive Power' vested in the President by s 1 of Art. II." Past practice does not, by itself, create power, but "long-continued practice, known to and acquiesced in by Congress, would raise a presumption that the [action] had been [taken] in pursuance of its consent. *** " Such practice is present here and such a presumption is also appropriate. In light of the fact that Congress may be considered to have consented to the President's action in suspending claims, we cannot say that action exceeded the President's powers.

Our conclusion is buttressed by the fact that the means chosen by the President to settle the claims of American nationals provided an alternative forum, the Claims Tribunal, which is capable of providing meaningful relief. *** Just as importantly, Congress has not disapproved of the action taken here. *** Quite the contrary, the relevant Senate Committee has stated that the establishment of the Tribunal is "of vital importance to the United States." We are thus clearly not confronted with a situation in which Congress has in some way resisted the exercise of Presidential authority.

Finally, we re-emphasize the narrowness of our decision. We do not decide that the President possesses plenary power to settle claims, even as against foreign governmental entities. *** But where, as here, the settlement of claims has been determined to be a necessary incident to the resolution of a major foreign policy dispute between our country and another, and where, as here, we can conclude that Congress acquiesced in the President's action, we are not prepared to say that the President lacks the power to settle such claims. ***

Notes

1. **Political Necessity.** The Court's decision has been criticized as pure politics (a "political decision politically made") and for its shoddy methodology ("crisis atmosphere *** Court should have demanded more specific legislative approval for the president's far-reaching measures"). Do you agree?

2. **Comparisons.** (a) Does *Dames & Moore* reject Justice Black's methodology in *Youngstown*? Is there anything in the Constitution's text that gives the President inherent foreign affairs (but not domestic affairs) powers?

(b) Do you agree that *Dames & Moore*, "[By] finding legislative 'approval' when Congress had given none, *** inverted the *Steel Seizure* holding—which construed statutory nonapproval of the president's act to mean legislative disapproval—[and] condoned legislative inactivity at a time that demanded interbranch dialogue and bipartisan consensus"? Harold Koh, The National Security Constitution: Sharing Power after the Iran–Contra Affair, 139–140 (1990).

(c) Why did the Court characterize President Truman's seizure of the steel mills as "domestic" and President Carter's Executive Agreement establishing the Iran–United States Claims Tribunal as "foreign affairs"? Is the line between the two capable of principled judicial delineation?

(d) How did President Carter manage to avoid going to the Senate for its "Advice and Consent" under Article II, § 2, cl. 2 concerning the Claims Tribunal Agreement?

*****

In light of the preceding three cases, consider the following notes and questions concerning Presidential and Congressional authority to respond to the 9/11 attacks and more generally to international Islamic terrorism.

1. Who has Responsibility? When the 9/11 attacks occurred, the President promptly ordered that all airline flights be suspended and placed fighter jets over New York and Washington, D.C. to patrol the airspace with directions to shoot down any unauthorized planes. Where did he obtain the power to take those actions? Was the President exercising "emergency" authority (see *Jacobsen*), the authority of the sovereign (*Curtiss-Wright),* or some aspect of the powers jointly constitutionally entrusted to Congress and the President (Youngstown)? If the latter, was presidential authority at its weakest since the Posse Comitatus Act prohibits using military force to undertake police actions within the United States? The provisions of this Act are in the Statutory Guide, infra.

2. National Emergencies Act. As it turns out, there is statutory authority for the President, rather than Congress, to engage in "emergency" actions in the United States. Congress authorized the President, in the National Emergencies Act of 1976 (NEA), to declare emergencies which, once declared, can be followed by extraordinary Executive actions. The Act requires the President to specifically state which statutory powers he is invoking and requires the President to periodically report the status of declared emergencies to Congress. It terminates declared emergency powers after one year, but permits annual renewals by the President, provided he notifies Congress. President Bush declared a national emergency pursuant to the Act on September 14, 2001. This emergency has been renewed annually, most recently by President Obama in September of 2010.

3. Purpose of the NEA. One of the central purposes of the NEA was to prevent open-ended and indefinite states of emergency. At the time of the Act's passage, there were four standing emergency declarations (of 1933, 1950, 1970, and 1971), each activating the entire range the statutorily delegated emergency powers, some 470 provisions of federal law. The Act terminated the grant of powers activated by those invocations, returning them to their dormant state and thereby requiring the President to re-invoke a specific emergency in order to use the powers granted by Congress. The Act provides that Congress may, through a joint resolution of the House and Senate, cancel a national emergency declaration by the President. To date, Congress has never exercised this statutory power to limit the President's authority to invoke emergency powers. Has the NEA proven to be a failure? Ten years on, do we have a permanent state of emergency as a result of the terrorist attacks of 9/11?

4. Asset Freezing. The International Emergency Economic Powers Act (IEEPA) authorizes the President to declare a national emergency with respect to "any unusual and extraordinary threat, which has its source in whole or in part outside the United States, to the national security, foreign policy, or economy of the United States." 50 U.S.C. § 1701(a). Under the Act, when the President has declared an emergency he may embargo any transactions involving "any interest of any foreign country or a national thereof." This statute is the basis, as discussed in Chapter III, for freezing of assets of organizations designated as Specially Designated Global Terrorists. In Executive Order 13224, 66 Fed. Reg 49079 (Sept 23, 2001), the President declared terrorism threats to be a national emergency, blocked certain assets immediately (such as those of al Qaeda and bin Laden), and established an executive process for the Treasury Secretary to block assets of further organizations and individuals. President Bush's order also provided for blocking assets of those "assist in, sponsor, or provide financial, material, or technological support for, or financial or other services to or in support of, such acts of terrorism" and provided for blocking assets of those "associated with" designated terrorist organizations. This final provision was later modified in response to a judicial decision to mean "(a) To own or control [an SDGT]; or (b) To attempt, or to conspire with one or more persons, to act for or on behalf of or to provide financial, material, or technological support, or financial or other services, to [an SDGT]." 31 C.F.R. § 594.316. See generally Chapter IIIE.

5. The AUMF. The broadest specific power for Presidential exercise of emergency power was the Authorization for Use of Military Force (AUMF) passed as a joint congressional resolution on September 18, 2001. The AUMF, which is still in force and has no termination date, authorizes the President to use all necessary and appropriate force against those nations, organizations, or persons he determines planned, authorized, committed, or aided the terrorist attacks that occurred on September 11, 2001, or harbored such organizations or persons, in order to prevent any future acts of international terrorism against the United States by such nations, organizations or persons." As you have seen in earlier chapters, this was said by the Supreme Court to permit the President to militarily detain "enemy combatants" (later those identified in the AUMF) at Guantanamo and elsewhere. *Hamdi v. Rumsfeld*, 542 U.S. 507 (2004). It was not viewed as an open-ended authorization to try "unlawful enemy combatants" by military commission. *Hamdan v. Rumsfeld*, 548 U.S. 557 (2006).

6. The USA PATRIOT Act. The Uniting and Strengthening America by Providing Appropriate Tools Required to Intercept and Obstruct Terrorism Act of 2001, or USA PATRIOT Act (October 2001) authorized detentions of immigrants, searches without the knowledge of the owner, expanded use of National Security Letters, broadened definitions of money laundering and currency crimes, additional funding for a variety of agencies and purposes (such as border patrol agents and FBI translators); and increased access of law enforcement agencies to a variety of types of records, including those of public libraries. It also amended FISA to permit searches gathering foreign intelligence information as its "significant" instead of "primary" purpose, removing "the wall" between intelligence gathering and criminal prosecution. Various provisions of this statute are discussed throughout this book.

7. The Homeland Security Act. The Homeland Security Act of 2002 was the largest reorganization of executive agencies in over fifty years. It created the Department of Homeland Security (DHS) as well as the cabinet position of Secretary of Homeland Security. The new DHS absorbed twenty-two existing federal agencies, including the Immigration and Naturalization Service, Customs Service, Secret Service, Coast Guard, Federal Emergency Management Administration and Border Patrol. DHS was tasked with the objectives of preventing and reducing the risk of terrorist attacks on the United States, but the FBI retained control of investigating attacks that might occur. The new goliath agency was also charged with continuing to carry out the functions of the agencies that it combined. The Act authorized the DHS Secretary to ensure exchange of information related to threats of terrorism, develop a national plan for responding to biological, chemical, nuclear, and other terrorist threats, determine vulnerabilities of critical U.S. infrastructure and evaluate the effectiveness of security of institutions, facilities, and infrastructure that might be targets of terrorist attacks. What institutional pressures does the Homeland Security Act, and various agencies' interests in acquiring budgetary funds and the larger powers that come with them place on executive power?

8. Inherent Presidential Power? Suppose there had been none of the statutes discussed in notes 2 through 7 above. Under *Youngstown*, there would be either a "twilight zone" of congressional silence or possibly even implied congressional opposition where the President is "at his weakest." That merely begs the question, however, because *Youngstown* concedes there is some area of Article II power even in opposition to Congress. The following excerpts cover three areas of assertions of Article II Executive powers made by the Bush Administration: (1) authority to ignore parts of laws the President thinks intrude on his powers, (2) authority to engage in interrogations of terrorist suspects without regard for international norms and treaties prohibiting torture, and (3) authority to engage in surveillance outside the framework of FISA. The materials below, while involving matters covered earlier in this book, focus on the allocation of constitutional authority as between the President and Congress.

9. *Curtiss-Wright* and *Boumediene*: two views of sovereignty? In *Boumediene*, the Court noted that:

Guantanamo Bay is not formally part of the United States. And under the terms of the lease between the United States and Cuba, Cuba retains 'ultimate sovereignty' over the territory while the United States exercises 'complete jurisdiction and control.' ***[I]t is not altogether uncommon for a territory to be under the *de jure* sovereignty of one nation, while under the plenary control, or practical sovereignty, of another. *** [W]e accept the Government's position that Cuba, and not the United States, retains *de jure* sovereignty over Guantanamo Bay. As we did in *Rasul*, however, we take notice of the obvious and uncontested fact that the United States, by virtue of its complete jurisdiction and control over the base, maintains *de facto* sovereignty over this territory."

In *Boumediene*, the Court—not the Executive—decided the scope of the dispositive form of sovereignty (de facto sovereignty). Is this in tension with the vision of sovereignty expressed in *Curtiss-Wright*? How does the Court's two conceptions of sovereignty compare?

10. The War Powers Resolution and Libya. In March 2011, President Obama ordered air strikes on Libya, pursuant to a United Nations resolution aimed at creating a no-fly zone. He did so without seeking Congressional authorization, though he did send Congressional leaders a letter stating that "I have directed these actions, which are in the national security and foreign policy interests of the United States, pursuant to my constitutional authority to conduct U.S. foreign relations and as Commander in Chief and Chief Executive." Since the Korean War, Presidents including Truman, Johnson, Nixon, and Clinton have engaged in military action without Congressional approval. In 1973, Congress passed the War Powers Resolution, which required Congressional authority in order to devote American troops except in an emergency, and even in an emergency required retroactive Congressional authorization after a set number of days. Is the War Powers Resolution constitutional? Did President Obama have the authority to decide to engage in combat regardless?

C. PRESIDENTIAL POWER AFTER 9/11

The executive power shall be vested in a President of the
United States of America.
-U.S. Constitution, Article II, clause 1

This Part provides materials from the front lines of the responses to 9/11, materials that center around a theory sometimes referred to as "the unitary executive." In the aftermath of 9/11, the executive branch embraced a set of emergency measures that have been criticized as beyond its powers. This section provides the first hand arguments in favor of those emergency powers, as well as responsive critiques. These include: The Power to Ignore Statutes, The Power to Interrogate, and The Power to Surveil.

Consider, as you read these materials, who has the stronger legal arguments and whether the executive's decisions were reasonable ones you might have recommended. These materials raise central themes that run throughout this book: who should decide how to respond to, and prevent, national security emergencies—Congress, the Courts, the Executive, or some combination thereof? What are the temporal or geographic limits on states of war or emergency? What institutional designs, incentives, and accountability mechanisms shape laws and policy choices in this arena, and what should they be? What is the ultimate source of authority and democratic legitimacy for responses to terrorism and what is the true meaning and scope of American sovereignty?

1. THE POWER TO IGNORE STATUTES

A signing statement is a written pronouncement added by the President upon the signing of a bill into law. The Constitution does not discuss signing statements, though Article 1, §7 does require that if the President decides to veto a bill that he inform Congress what his objections are, so that Congress can reconsider it or, by a two-thirds vote, override his veto. Presidents have used signing statements since nearly the time of the founding, including to signal their intentions to ignore or alter part of a bill, though the Administrations since the 1980s have made significantly greater use of them than previous Presidents.

Does the Executive Branch have the power to ignore or alter how laws are executed under the "Take Care" clause, requiring that he "shall take Care that the Laws be faithfully Executed?" Can the President refuse to enforce, in whole or in part, laws he believes are unconstitutional or interpret them in a way contrary to Congressional intent? What if he thinks the Supreme Court will agree with him? What constitutional status do Presidential signing statements have—and does it matter whether it relates to foreign policy or military action? Is the constitutionality of signing statements affected by the constitutional framework for Presidential vetoes? Why might a President write a signing statement, *e.g.* to mobilize public opinion, signal to Congress his intent, or simply to express his interpretation of the law? Does such a statement alter the law, or the constitutionality of the President's actions in taking care that it be executed? Are signing statements a good idea – or should the President instead veto a bill or try to persuade Congress to pass a different law if he thinks one is unconstitutional?

Think about these questions while considering the following signing statements attached to acts related to combating terrorism:

(a) The President added the following statement to an amendment to the United States Senate Department of Defense Appropriations Act of 2006, termed the Amendment on (1) the Army Field Manual and (2) Cruel, Inhumane, Degrading Treatment, known as the McCain Torture Amendment. This amendment altered the Detainee Treatment Act of 2005 [as Title X], to prohibit inhumane treatment of prisoners by confining interrogations to the techniques in the Army Field Manual.

The executive branch shall construe Title X ***, relating to detainees, in a manner consistent with the constitutional authority of the President to supervise the unitary executive branch and as Commander in Chief and consistent with the constitutional limitations on the judicial power, which will assist in achieving the shared objective of the Congress and the President, evidenced in Title X, of protecting the American people from further terrorist attacks. Further,*** noting that the text and structure of Title X do not create a private right of action to enforce Title X, the executive branch shall construe Title X not to create a private right of action.

(b) A statement added by the President to the USA Patriot Improvement and Reauthorization Act of 2006, which required regular and detailed reports about the use of its statutory powers, reads:

The executive branch shall construe the provisions of H.R. 3199 that call for furnishing information to entities outside the executive branch *** in a manner consistent with the President's constitutional authority to supervise the unitary executive branch and to withhold information the disclosure of which could impair foreign relations, national security, the deliberative processes of the Executive, or the performance of the Executive's constitutional duties.

2. THE POWER TO INTERROGATE

The divide between understandings of executive power has perhaps nowhere been more apparent than in the debate over the lawfulness of torture and enhanced interrogation techniques. Below is an excerpt of one memo on the question issued in 2002 by the Office of Legal Counsel, the branch of the Justice Department that provides authoritative legal advice to the President and all Executive branch agencies, as well as a critique by then Dean of Yale Law School, Harold Koh. The primary memoranda regarding such interrogation techniques that have been released were made public in April of 2009. Several of these memos have since been withdrawn by the Office of Legal Counsel—including the memo below.

Jay Bybee, Office of Legal Counsel
Memorandum for Alberto R. Gonzales, Counsel to the President
Re: Standards of Conduct for Interrogation
under 18 U.S.C. §§ 2340-2340A
August 1, 2002

You have asked for our Office's views regarding the standards of conduct under the Convention Against Torture and Other Cruel, Inhuman and Degrading Treatment or Punishment as implemented by Sections 2340-2340A of title 18 of the United States Code. As we understand it, this question has arisen in the context of the conduct of interrogations outside of the United States. ***

We conclude that for an act to constitute torture as defined in Section 2340, it must inflict pain that is difficult to endure. Physical pain amounting to torture must be equivalent in intensity to the pain accompanying serious physical injury, such as organ failure, impairment of bodily function, or even death. ***

Section 2340A makes it a criminal offense for any person "outside the United States [to] commit[] or attempt[] to commit torture." Section 2340 defines the act of torture as an:

> act committed by a person acting under the color of law specifically intended to inflict severe physical or mental pain or suffering (other than pain or suffering incidental to lawful sanctions) upon another person within his custody or physical control. ***

V. The President's Commander-in-Chief Power

Even if an interrogation method arguably were to violate Section 2340A, the statute would be unconstitutional if it impermissibly encroached on the President's constitutional power to conduct a military campaign. As Commander-in-Chief, the President has the constitutional authority to order interrogations of enemy combatants to gain intelligence information concerning the military plans of the enemy. The demands of the Commander-in-Chief power are especially pronounced in the middle of a war in which the nation has already suffered a direct attack. In such a case, the information gained from interrogations may prevent future attacks by foreign enemies. Any effort to apply Section 2340A in a manner that interferes with the President's direction of such core war matters as the detention and interrogation of enemy combatants thus would be unconstitutional.***

At the outset, we should make clear the nature of the threat presently posed to the nation. While your request for legal advice is not specifically limited to the current circumstances, we think it is useful to discuss this question in the context of the current war against the al Qaeda terrorist network. The situation in which these issues arise is unprecedented in recent American history. Four coordinated terrorist attacks, using hijacked commercial airliners as guided missiles, took place in rapid succession on the morning of September 11, 2001. These attacks were aimed at critical government buildings in the Nation's capital and landmark buildings in its financial center. *** [T]hese attacks were part of a violent campaign against the United States that is believed to include an unsuccessful attempt to destroy an airliner in December 2001l a suicide bombing attack in Yemben on the *U.S.S. Cole* in 2000; the bombings of the United States Embassies in Kenya and in Tanzania in 1998; an unsuccessful attempt to destroy the World Trade Center in 1993; and the ambush of U.S. servicemen in Somalia in 1993.***

In response, the Government has engaged in a broad effort at home and abroad to counter terrorism. *** Despite these efforts, numerous upper echelon leaders of al Qaeda and the Taliban, with access to active terrorist cells and other resources, remain at large. *** Al Qaeda continues to plan further attacks, such as destroying American civilian airliners and killing American troops, which have fortunately been prevented. It is clear that bin

Laden and his organization have conducted several violent attacks on the United States and its nationals, and that they seek to continue to do so. Thus, the capture and interrogation of such individuals is clearly imperative to our national security and defense. Interrogation of captured al Qaeda operatives may provide information concerning the nature of al Qaeda plans and the identities of its personnel, which may prove invaluable in preventing further direct attacks on the United States and its citizens.***

***[T]he President enjoys complete discretion in the exercise of his Commander-in-Chief authority and in conducting operations against hostile forces. Because both "[t]he executive power and the command of the military and naval forces is vested in the President," the Supreme Court has unanimously stated that it is *the President alone* [] who is constitutionally invested with the *entire charge of hostile operations.*" *Hamilton v. Dillin*, 88 U.S. (21 Wall.) 73, 87 (1874) (emphasis added). That authority is at its height in the middle of a war.

In light of the President's complete authority over the conduct of war, without a clear statement otherwise, we will not read a criminal statute as infringing on the President's ultimate authority in these areas. *** In order to respect the President's inherent constitutional authority to manage a military campaign against al Qaeda and its allies, Section 2340A must be construed as not applying to interrogations undertaken pursuant to his Commander-in-Chief authority. ***Congress lacks authority under Article I to set the terms and conditions under which the President may exercise his authority as Commander in Chief to control the conduct of operations during a war.*** [T]he President's power to detain and interrogate enemy combatants arises out of his constitutional authority as Commander in Chief.

Congress may no more regulate the President's ability to detain and interrogate enemy combatants then it may regulate his ability to direct troop movements on the battlefield. Accordingly, we would construe Section 2340A to avoid this constitutional difficulty, and conclude that it does not apply to the President's detention and interrogation of enemy combatants pursuant to his Commander-in-Chief authority. Likewise, we believe that, if executive officials were subject to prosecution for conducting interrogations when they were carrying out the President's Commander-in-Chief powers, "it would significantly burden and immeasurably impair the President's ability to fulfill his constitutional duties." These constitutional principles preclude an application of Section 2340A to punish officials for aiding the President in exercising his exclusive constitutional authorities.***

It could be argued that Congress enacted 18 U.S.C. § 2340A with full knowledge and consideration of the President's Commander-in-Chief power, and that Congress intended to restrict his discretion in the interrogation of enemy combatants. Even were we to accept this argument, however, we conclude that the Department of Justice could not enforce Section 2340A against federal officials acting pursuant to the President's constitutional authority to wage a military campaign.

Indeed, in a different context, we have concluded that both courts and prosecutors should reject prosecutions that apply federal criminal laws to activity that is authorized pursuant to one of the President's constitutional powers. *** Further we concluded that the Department of Justice could not bring a criminal prosecution against a defendant who had acted pursuant to an exercise of the President's constitutional power. "*** Nor could the Legislative Branch or the courts require or implement the prosecution of such an individual." Although Congress may define federal crimes that the President, through the Take Care Clause, should prosecute, Congress cannot compel the President to prosecute outcomes taken pursuant to the President's own constitutional authority. If Congress could do so, it could control the President's authority through the manipulation of federal criminal law.

The President's constitutional power to protect the security of the United States and the lives and safety of its people must be understood in light of the Founders' intention to create a federal government "clothed with all the powers requisite to the complete execution of its trust." *The Federalist* No. 23, at 147 (Alexander Hamilton) (Jacob E. Cooke ed. 1961). *** As Hamilton explained in arguing for the Constitution's adoption, because "the circumstances which may affect pubic safety" are not "reducible within certain determinate limits."

***The text, structure, and history of the Constitution establish that the Founders entrusted the President with the primary responsibility, and therefore the power, to ensure the security of the United States in situations of grave and unforeseen emergencies. The decisions to deploy military force in the defense of the United States interests is expressly placed under Presidential authority by the Vesting Clause and by the Commander-in-Chief Clause. This Office has long understood the Commander-in-Chief Clause in particular as an affirmative grant of authority to the President. The Framers understood the Clause as investing the President with the fullest range of power understood at the time of the ratification of the Constitution as belonging to the military commander. In addition, the structure of the Constitution demonstrates that any power traditionally understood as pertaining to the executive—which includes the conduct of warfare and the defense of the nation—unless expressly assigned in the Constitution to Congress, is vested in the President. Article II, Section 1 makes this clear by stating that the "executive Power shall be vested in a President of the United States of America." That sweeping grant vest in the President an unenumerated "executive power" and contrasts with the specific enumeration of the powers—those "herein"—granted to Congress in Article I. The implications of constitutional text and structure are confirmed by the practical consideration that national security decisions require the unity in purpose and energy in action that characterize the Presidency rather than Congress.[21]

---

[21] Judicial decisions since the beginning of the Republic confirm the President's constitutional power and duty to repel military action against the United States and to take measures to prevent the recurrence of an attack. As Justice Joseph Story said long ago, "[i]t may be fit and proper for the government, in the exercise of the high discretion confided to the executive, for great public purposes, to act on a sudden emergency, or to prevent an irreparable mischief, by summary measures, which are not found in the text of the laws." *The Apollon*, 22 U.S. (9 Wheat.) 362, 366-67 (1824).***

"The first of the enumerated powers of the President is that he shall be Commander-in-Chief. And, of course, the grant of war power includes all that is necessary and proper for carrying those powers into execution." *Johnson v. Eisentrager*, 339 U.S. 763, 788 (1950). In wartime, it is for the President alone to decide what methods to use to best prevail against the enemy. ***In the *Prize Cases*, 67 U.S. (2 Black) 635, 670 (1862), for example, the Court explained that whether the President "in fulfilling his duties as Commander in Chief" had appropriately responded to the rebellion of the southern states was a question "to be *decided by him*" and which the Court could not question but must leave to "the political department of the Government to which this power was entrusted."

One of the core functions of the Commander in Chief is that of capturing, detaining, and interrogating members of the enemy. It is well settled that the President may seize and detain enemy combatants, at least for the duration of the conflict, and the laws of war make clear that prisoners may be interrogated for information concerning the enemy, its strength, and its plans. Numerous Presidents have ordered the capture, detention, and questioning of enemy combatants during virtually every major conflict in the Nation's history, including recent conflicts such as the Gulf, Vietnam, and Korean wars. Recognizing this authority, Congress has never attempted to restrict or interfere with the President's authority on this score.

Any effort by Congress to regulation the interrogation of battlefield combatants would violate the Constitution's sole vesting of the Commander-in-Chief authority in the President. There can be little doubt that intelligence operations, such as the detention and interrogation of enemy combatants and leaders, are both necessary and proper for the effective conduct of a military campaign. Indeed, such operations may be of more importance in a war with an international terrorist organization that one with the conventional armed forces of a nation-state, due to the former's emphasis on secret operations and surprise attacks against civilians. Congress can no more interfere with the President's conduct of the interrogation of enemy combatants than it can dictate strategic or tactical decisions on the battle field. Just as statutes that order the President to conduct warfare in a certain manner or for specific goals would be unconstitutional, so too are laws that seek to prevent the President from gaining the intelligence he believes necessary to prevent attacks upon the United States.***

Professor Harold Hongju Koh
Dean, Yale Law School
Testimony before the U.S. Senate Committee on the Judiciary
regarding the Nomination of Alberto Gonzales as Attorney General
of the United States
January 7, 2005

*** I appear today solely to comment upon Mr. Gonzales' positions regarding three issues on which I have both legal expertise and government experience: the illegality of torture and cruel, inhuman and degrading treatment, the scope of the President's constitutional powers to authorize torture and cruel treatment by U.S. officials, and the applicability of the Geneva Conventions on the Laws of War to alleged combatants held in U.S. custody.

With respect to these three issues, my professional opinion is that United States law and policy have been clear and unambiguous. Torture and cruel, inhuman and degrading treatment are both illegal and totally abhorrent to our values and constitutional traditions. No constitutional authority licenses the President to authorize the torture and cruel treatment of prisoners, even when he acts as Commander-in-Chief. Finally, the U.S. has long recognized the broad applicability of the Geneva Conventions, which is a critical safeguard for our own troops now serving in more than 130 countries around the world. These legal standards apply to all alleged combatants held in U.S. custody. *** Mr. Gonzales' record and public statements could be read to suggest: first, that the extraordinary threats that we face in the war on terrorism somehow require that the President act above the law, and second, that those who are deemed "enemy combatants" or are held on Guantanamo live outside the protections of the Convention Against Torture and the Geneva Conventions as "rights-free persons" in "rights-free zones."

***[T]he August 1, 2002 OLC memorandum grossly overreads the inherent power of the President under the Commander-in-Chief power in Article II of the Constitution. The memorandum claims that criminal prohibitions against torture do "not appl[y] to interrogations undertaken pursuant to [the President's] Commander-in-Chief authority," id. at 35. Yet the Eighth Amendment does not say "nor [shall] cruel and unusual punishments [be] inflicted" except when the Commander-in-Chief orders, and the Fifth Amendment's Due Process Clause nowhere sanctions executive torture.

As remarkably, the August 1 memorandum declares that "[a]ny effort by Congress to regulate the interrogation of battlefield combatants would violate the Constitution's sole vesting of the Commander-in-Chief authority in the President." But if the President has the sole constitutional authority to sanction torture, and Congress has no power to interfere, it is unclear why the President should not also have unfettered authority to license genocide or other violations of fundamental human rights.[17] In a stunning failure of lawyerly craft, the August 1, 2002 OLC Memorandum nowhere mentions the landmark Supreme Court decision in *Youngstown Steel & Tube Co. v. Sawyer,* where Justice Jackson's concurrence spelled out clear limits on the President's constitutional powers.

Under these parts of the August 1, 2002 OLC memorandum (which unlike the narrow torture definition have not been formally replaced), the President would have constitutional power to ignore the criminal prohibition against torture in 18 U.S.C. § § 2340-40A, or to flout the recent Defense Authorization Act, which states that "[i]t is the policy of the United States

---

[17] If the U.S. President has authority, as Commander-in-Chief, to authorize torture in the name of war, it is hard to explain why Saddam Hussein could not similarly authorize torture under his parallel Commander in Chief power.

to— (1) ensure that no detainee shall be subject to torture or cruel, inhuman, or degrading treatment or punishment that is prohibited by the Constitution, laws, or treaties of the United States." Moreover, this reading of the President's Commander-in-Chief power would even allow him to order subordinates to trump Congress' power under Article I, section 8, clause 10 to "define and punish ... offences against the law of nations" such as torture.

This sweeping view of the President's powers to conduct the war on terror has not been confined to the area of torture. In a recently unearthed OLC memorandum to Mr. Gonzales' office, dated two weeks after September 11, then-Deputy Assistant Attorney General John C. Yoo asserted that "[t]he historical record demonstrates that the power to initiate military hostilities, particularly in response to the threat of an armed attack, rests exclusively with the President." This remarkably overbroad assertion not only ignores Congress' power "to declare war," Art. I, sec. 8, cl. 11, but also suggests that several centuries of congressional participation in initiating war—including the declarations of war in the War of 1812 and the two world wars, the authorizing statutes in the two Gulf Wars, the Korean War, the Indochina conflict, and after September 11—were all constitutionally unnecessary.

Mr. Gonzales' own brief statements have also urged a broad view of the president' constitutional powers to conduct the "war on terror." In claims that have now been largely rejected by the United States Supreme Court, he has asserted the President's broad power as Commander-in-Chief to label detainees as enemy combatants and to detain them indefinitely and incommunicado without judicial oversight or express congressional authorization.[22] In a speech before the American Bar Association's Standing Committee on Law and National Security, Mr. Gonzales suggested that when detaining so-called "enemy combatants," "there is no rigid process for making such determinations—and certainly no particular mechanism required by law. Rather, these are the steps that we have taken in our discretion." Later in the same address, he suggested that in such actions, the President was constrained less by the rule of law than "as a matter of prudence and policy."***

Notes

1. Emergency. Whose view of Executive power do you find more persuasive in the context of the debate over enhanced interrogation techniques? Regardless of the correct legal answer, do you think Jay Bybee's recommendation reasonable— or the right thing—given the threats the administration faced? To what degree does it matter whether Bybee might face criminal, civil, or professional penalties for making the wrong call about the threat or emergency? What if his memo had

---

[22] See *Rasul v. Bush*, 124 S.Ct. 2686 (2004) (ruling that alien "enemy combatants" on Guantanamo are entitled to raise their claims on writs of habeas corpus); *Hamdi v. Rumsfeld*, 124 S.Ct. 2633 (2004) (ruling 8-1 that U.S. citizens held as "enemy combatants" in military custody are constitutionally entitled to an opportunity to be heard before an independent tribunal).

remained secret—beyond the reach of democratic response or political repercussions?

2. Changing Political Tides. In a 2009 *Memorandum Regarding Status of Certain OLC Opinions Issued in the Aftermath of the Terrorist Attacks of September 11, 2001*, OLC "confirm[ed] that certain propositions stated in several opinions issued by the Office of Legal Counsel in 2001-2003 respecting the allocation of authorities between the President and Congress in matters of war and national security do not reflect the current views of this Office." It further stated:

> The federal prohibition on torture, 18 U.S.C. §§ 2340-2340A, is constitutional, and I believe it does apply as a general matter to the subject of detention and interrogation of detainees conducted pursuant to the President's Commander in Chief authority. The statement to the contrary from the August 1, 2002, memorandum *** has been withdrawn and superseded, along with the entirety of the memorandum, and in any event I do not find that statement persuasive. The President, like all officers of the Government, is not above the law. He has a sworn duty to preserve, protect, and defend the Constitution and to execute the laws of the United States faithfully, in accordance with the Constitution.

Does this imply that the previous memo was wrong—or instead that different Administrations, different political moments, or different perceived threats produce alternative views constitutional interpretations? Is the reasoning of the 2002 memo valid beyond the crisis of 9/11, in other future emergencies, or in times of relative peace?

3. The Role of Lawyers. No lawyer has faced criminal, civil, or professional repercussions for legal advice provided regarding interrogation techniques. Jay Bybee, author of the memo above, was elevated to the Ninth Circuit Court of Appeals and John Yoo, author of the 2002 memo published under Bybee's name, is a prominent legal academic at the University of California at Berkley. In 2009, the Department of Justice's Office of Professional Responsibility, following an extended investigation, concluded that Bybee and John Yoo had committed "intentional professional misconduct" when they "knowingly failed to provide a thorough, objective, and candid interpretation of the law" and recommended referral to the Bar for disciplinary action. However, Deputy Attorney General David Margolis, in 2010 reversed this decision. Margolis expressly disavowed "an endorsement of the legal work" which he found to be "flawed" and to "contain[] errors more than minor." However, he concluded that while Bybee and Yoo had exercised "poor judgment," there was no "professional misconduct" sufficient for the Justice Department to refer them for disciplinary action. As in house lawyers, are attorney advisors at the Office of Legal Counsel sufficiently well positioned to provide independent legal counsel? Institutionally, what sort of checks should exist for legal advice by government attorneys? Should they face individual criminal repercussions, bar sanctions, or civil suits? Or should checks be political upon the offices they hold—and the President they serve? Would frank legal advice to the President be destroyed by these mechanisms?

4. Impending Circuit Split? Jose Padilla sued John Yoo for abusive detention and interrogation. *Padilla v. Yoo*, 633 F.Supp.2d 1005 (N.D. Cal. 2009), held that a *Bivens* claim exists for Padilla and that Yoo was not entitled to qualified immunity. In contrast, *Estela Lebron v. Rumsfeld*, 2011 WL 554061 (D.S.C. 2011) (Estela Lebron is Padilla's mother) ruled no *Bivens* remedy existed for these alleged abuses and that the defendants were entitled to qualified immunity. It relied on the fact that legal opinions "had officially sanctioned the use of the techniques in question." Appeals in these cases are pending in the Fourth and Ninth Circuits. To what degree should legal advice sanction the actions of executive officials? What sort of liability, if any, do you believe should attach for legal advice to senior government policy makers, and why? How important is ensuring frank advice to the President, especially in times of crisis? How does liability affect executive function or democratic dialog on national security policy? Reconsider standing, state secrets, and immunity issues in cases like *Mohamed v. Jeppesen Dataplan*, *Arar v. Ashcroft*, *Al Kidd v. Ashcroft*, and *Ashcroft v. Iqbal* in this light. Do these doctrines influence the separation of powers calculus?

5. Institutional Roles. Senator Barak Obama argued that "[t]he president does not have power under the Constitution to unilaterally authorize a military attack in a situation that does not involve stopping an actual or imminent threat to the nation." Charlie Savage, *Barack Obama's Q&A*, BOSTON GLOBE (Dec. 20, 2007). After becoming President, he authorized military attacks on Libya forces without seeking Congressional authorization. Harold Koh, while Dean at Yale Law, opposed the President's use of torture, but after becoming Legal Adviser to the State Department, Koh defended the legality of targeted killing, Did Libya pose "an actual or imminent threat to the nation" or did the President's view change? Is Koh's argument that the President can kill but not torture consistent or did his position shift? To what degree do or should institutional roles influence interpretations of executive power?

3. THE POWER TO SURVEIL

Following 9/11, as discussed in Chapter IV, the President authorized the National Security Agency to monitor phone calls, emails, text messages, and web browsing of induals where the government "has a reasonable basis to conclude that one party to the communication is a member of al Qaeda, affiliated with al Qaeda, or a member of an organization affiliated with al Qaeda, or working in support of al Qaeda" and that one party to the conversation is "outside of the United States." The justification given for surveillance by the Department of Justice follows, along with a response by a group of legal academics.

U.S. Department of Justice
Legal Authorities Supporting the Activities of the National Security
Agency Described by the President
January 19, 2006

As the President has explained, since shortly after the attacks of September 11, 2001, he has authorized the National Security Agency ("NSA") to intercept international communications into and out of the United States of persons linked to al Qaeda or related terrorist organizations. The purpose of these intercepts is to establish an early warning system to detect and prevent another catastrophic terrorist attack on the United States. This paper addresses, in an unclassified form, the legal basis for the NSA activities described by the President ("NSA activities"). *** The NSA activities are an indispensable aspect of this defense of the Nation. By targeting the international communications into and out of the United States of persons reasonably believed to be linked to al Qaeda, these activities provide the United States with an early warning system to help avert the next attack. For the following reasons, the NSA activities are lawful and consistent with civil liberties.

The NSA activities are supported by the President's well-recognized inherent constitutional authority as Commander in Chief and sole organ for the Nation in foreign affairs to conduct warrantless surveillance of enemy forces for intelligence purposes to detect and disrupt armed attacks on the United States. The President has the chief responsibility under the Constitution to protect America from attack, and the Constitution gives the President the authority necessary to fulfill that solemn responsibility. The President has made clear that he will exercise all authority available to him, consistent with the Constitution, to protect the people of the United States.

In the specific context of the current armed conflict with al Qaeda and related terrorist organizations, Congress by statute has confirmed and supplemented the President's recognized authority under Article II of the Constitution to conduct such warrantless surveillance to prevent further catastrophic attacks on the homeland. In its first legislative response to the terrorist attacks of September 11th, Congress authorized the President to "use all necessary and appropriate force against those nations, organizations, or persons he determines planned, authorized, committed, or aided the terrorist attacks" of September 11th in order to prevent "any future acts of international terrorism against the United States." Authorization for Use of Military Force, Pub. L. No. 107-40, § 2(a). History conclusively demonstrates that warrantless communications intelligence targeted at the enemy in time of armed conflict is a traditional and fundamental incident of the use of military force authorized by the AUMF. The Supreme Court's interpretation of the AUMF in *Hamdi v. Rumsfeld*, 542 U.S. 507 (2004), confirms that Congress in the AUMF gave its express approval to the military conflict against al Qaeda and its allies and thereby to the President's use of all traditional and accepted incidents of force in this current military conflict— including warrantless electronic surveillance to intercept enemy communications both at home and abroad. This understanding of the AUMF demonstrates Congress's support for the President's authority to protect the Nation and, at the same time, adheres to Justice O'Connor's admonition that "a state of war is not a blank check for the President," *Hamdi*, 542 U.S. at 536 (plurality opinion), particularly in view of the narrow scope of the NSA activities.

The AUMF places the President at the zenith of his powers in authorizing the NSA activities. Under the tripartite framework set forth by Justice Jackson in *Youngstown Sheet & Tube Co. v. Sawyer*, 343 U.S. 579, 635-38 (1952) (Jackson, J., concurring), Presidential authority is analyzed to determine whether the President is acting in accordance with congressional authorization (category I), whether he acts in the absence of a grant or denial of authority by Congress (category II), or whether he uses his own authority under the Constitution to take actions incompatible with congressional measures (category III). Because of the broad authorization provided in the AUMF, the President's action here falls within category I of Justice Jackson's framework. Accordingly, the President's power in authorizing the NSA activities is at its height because he acted "pursuant to an express or implied authorization of Congress," and his power "includes all that he possesses in his own right plus all that Congress can delegate." ***

The NSA activities are consistent with the preexisting statutory framework generally applicable to the interception of communications in the United States—the Foreign Intelligence Surveillance Act ("FISA"), as amended *** and relevant related provisions. *** Although FISA generally requires judicial approval of electronic surveillance, FISA also contemplates that Congress may authorize such surveillance by a statute other than FISA. *See* 50 U.S.C. § 1809(a) (prohibiting any person from intentionally "engag[ing] . . . in electronic surveillance under color of law except as authorized by statute"). The AUMF, as construed by the Supreme Court in *Hamdi* and as confirmed by the history and tradition of armed conflict, is just such a statute. Accordingly, electronic surveillance conducted by the President pursuant to the AUMF, including the NSA activities, is fully consistent with FISA and falls within category I of Justice Jackson's framework.

Even if there were ambiguity about whether FISA, read together with the AUMF, permits the President to authorize the NSA activities, the canon of constitutional avoidance requires reading these statutes in harmony to overcome any restrictions in FISA and Title III, at least as they might otherwise apply to the congressionally authorized armed conflict with al Qaeda. Indeed, were FISA and Title III interpreted to impede the President's ability to use the traditional tool of electronic surveillance to detect and prevent future attacks by a declared enemy that has already struck at the homeland and is engaged in ongoing operations against the United States, the constitutionality of FISA, as applied to that situation, would be called into very serious doubt. In fact, if this difficult constitutional question had to be addressed, FISA would be unconstitutional as applied to this narrow context. Importantly, the FISA Court of Review itself recognized just three years ago that the President retains constitutional authority to conduct foreign surveillance apart from the FISA framework, and the President is certainly entitled, at a minimum, to rely on that judicial interpretation of the Constitution and FISA.***

As Congress expressly recognized in the AUMF, "the President has authority under the Constitution to take action to deter and prevent acts of international terrorism against the United States," especially in the context of the current conflict. Article II of the Constitution vests in the President all executive power of the United States, including the power to act as Commander in Chief of the Armed Forces, *see* U.S. Const. art. II, § 2, and authority over the conduct of the Nation's foreign affairs. As the Supreme Court has explained, "[t]he President is the sole organ of the nation in its external relations, and its sole representative with foreign nations." *United States v. Curtiss-Wright Export Corp.*, 299 U.S. 304, 319 (1936) (internal quotation marks and citations omitted). In this way, the Constitution grants the President inherent power to protect the Nation from foreign attack, *see, e.g., The Prize Cases*, 67 U.S. (2 Black) 635, 668 (1863), and to protect national security information, *see, e.g., Department of the Navy v. Egan*, 484 U.S. 518, 527 (1988).

To carry out these responsibilities, the President must have authority to gather information necessary for the execution of his office. The Founders, after all, intended the federal Government to be clothed with all authority necessary to protect the Nation. *See, e.g., The Federalist* *** No. 41, at 269 (James Madison) ("Security against foreign danger is one of the primitive objects of civil society . . . . The powers requisite for attaining it must be effectually confided to the federal councils."). Because of the structural advantages of the Executive Branch, the Founders also intended that the President would have the primary responsibility and necessary authority as Commander in Chief and Chief Executive to protect the Nation and to conduct the Nation's foreign affairs. Thus, it has been long recognized that the President has the authority to use secretive means to collect intelligence necessary for the conduct of foreign affairs and military campaigns. ***.

In reliance on these principles, a consistent understanding has developed that the President has inherent constitutional authority to conduct warrantless searches and surveillance within the United States for foreign intelligence purposes. Wiretaps for such purposes thus have been authorized by Presidents at least since the administration of Franklin Roosevelt in 1940. *** Indeed, while FISA was being debated during the Carter Administration, Attorney General Griffin Bell testified that "the current bill recognizes no inherent power of the President to conduct electronic surveillance, and I want to interpolate here to say that *this does not take away the power [of] the President under the Constitution*."

The courts uniformly have approved this longstanding Executive Branch practice. Indeed, every federal appellate court to rule on the question has concluded that, even in peacetime, the President has inherent constitutional authority, consistent with the Fourth Amendment, to conduct searches for foreign intelligence purposes without securing a judicial warrant. *See In re Sealed Case*, 310 F.3d 717, 742 (Foreign Intel. Surv. Ct. of Rev. 2002) ("[A]ll the other courts to have decided the issue [have] held that the President did have inherent authority to conduct warrantless searches to obtain foreign intelligence information . . . . *We take for granted that the President does have that authority and, assuming that is so, FISA could not encroach on the President's constitutional power*.") (emphasis added).

In *United States v. United States District Court*, 407 U.S. 297 (1972) (the *"Keith"* case), the Supreme Court concluded that the Fourth Amendment's warrant requirement applies to investigations of wholly *domestic* threats to security—such as domestic political violence and other crimes. *** After *Keith*, each of the three courts of appeals that have squarely considered the question have concluded—expressly taking the Supreme

Court's decision into account—that the President has inherent authority to conduct warrantless surveillance in the foreign intelligence context. *See, e.g., Truong Dinh Hung,* 629 F.2d at 913-14; *Butenko,* 494 F.2d at 603; *Brown,* 484 F.2d 425-26.

From a constitutional standpoint, foreign intelligence surveillance such as the NSA activities differs fundamentally from the domestic security surveillance at issue in *Keith.* As the Fourth Circuit observed, the President has uniquely strong constitutional powers in matters pertaining to foreign affairs and national security. "Perhaps most crucially, the executive branch not only has superior expertise in the area of foreign intelligence, it is also constitutionally designated as the pre-eminent authority in foreign affairs." *Truong,* 629 F.2d at 914***.[2]

The present circumstances that support recognition of the President's inherent constitutional authority to conduct the NSA activities are considerably stronger than were the circumstances at issue in the earlier courts of appeals cases that recognized this power. All of the cases described above addressed inherent executive authority under the foreign affairs power to conduct surveillance in a peacetime context. The courts in these cases therefore had no occasion even to consider the fundamental authority of the President, as Commander in Chief, to gather intelligence in the context of an ongoing armed conflict in which the United States already had suffered massive civilian casualties and in which the intelligence gathering efforts at issue were specifically designed to thwart further armed attacks. Indeed, intelligence gathering is particularly important in the current conflict, in which the enemy attacks largely through clandestine activities and which, as Congress recognized, "pose[s] an unusual and extraordinary threat," AUMF pmbl.

Among the President's most basic constitutional duties is the duty to protect the Nation from armed attack. *** As the Supreme Court emphasized in the *Prize Cases,* if the Nation is invaded, the President is "bound to resist force by force"; "[h]e must determine what degree of force the crisis demands" and need not await congressional sanction to do so. *The Prize Cases,* 67 U.S. at 670 ***. Indeed, "in virtue of his rank as head of the forces, [the President] has certain powers and duties with which Congress cannot interfere." In exercising his constitutional powers, the President has wide discretion, consistent with the Constitution, over the methods of gathering intelligence about the Nation's enemies in a time of armed conflict.***

---

[2] *Keith* made clear that one of the significant concerns driving the Court's conclusion in the domestic security context was the inevitable connection between perceived threats to domestic security and political dissent. As the Court explained: "Fourth Amendment protections become the more necessary when the targets of official surveillance may be those suspected of unorthodoxy in their political beliefs. The danger to political dissent is acute where the Government attempts to act under so vague a concept as the power to protect 'domestic security.'" *Keith,* 407 U.S. at 314; *see also id.* at 320. Surveillance of domestic groups raises a First Amendment concern that generally is not present when the subjects of the surveillance are foreign powers or their agents.

Letter of Law School Deans and Professors to House and Senate Leaders
January 9, 2006

Dear Members of Congress:

We are scholars of constitutional law and former government officials. We write in our individual capacities as citizens concerned by the Bush Administration's National Security Agency domestic spying program, as reported in the New York Times, and in particular to respond to the Justice Department's December 22, 2005 letter to the majority and minority leaders of the House and Senate Intelligence Committees setting forth the administration's defense of the program. Although the program's secrecy prevents us from being privy to all of its details, the Justice Department's defense of what it concedes was secret and warrantless electronic surveillance of persons within the United States fails to identify any plausible legal authority for such surveillance. Accordingly the program appears on its face to violate existing law.

The basic legal question here is not new. In 1978, after an extensive investigation of the privacy violations associated with foreign intelligence surveillance programs, Congress and the President enacted the Foreign Intelligence Surveillance Act (FISA). *** FISA comprehensively regulates electronic surveillance within the United States, striking a careful balance between protecting civil liberties and preserving the "vitally important government purpose" of obtaining valuable intelligence in order to safeguard national security. S. Rep. No. 95-604, pt. 1, at 9 (1977).

With minor exceptions, FISA authorizes electronic surveillance only upon certain specified showings, and only if approved by a court. The statute specifically allows for warrantless wartime domestic electronic surveillance— but only for the first fifteen days of a war. 50 U.S.C. § 1811. It makes criminal any electronic surveillance not authorized by statute, *id.* § 1809; and it expressly establishes FISA and specified provisions of the federal criminal code (which govern wiretaps for criminal investigation) as the "*exclusive* means by which electronic surveillance . . . may be conducted," 18 U.S.C. § 2511(2)(f) (emphasis added).

The Department of Justice concedes that the NSA program was not authorized by any of the above provisions. It maintains, however, that the program did not violate existing law because Congress implicitly authorized the NSA program when it enacted the Authorization for Use of Military Force (AUMF) against al Qaeda. *** But the AUMF cannot reasonably be construed to implicitly authorize warrantless electronic surveillance in the United States during wartime, where Congress has expressly and specifically addressed that precise question in FISA and limited any such warrantless surveillance to the first fifteen days of war.

The DOJ also invokes the President's inherent constitutional authority as Commander in Chief to collect "signals intelligence" targeted at the enemy, and maintains that construing FISA to prohibit the President's actions would raise constitutional questions. But even conceding that the

President in his role as Commander in Chief may generally collect signals intelligence on the enemy abroad, Congress indisputably has authority to regulate electronic surveillance within the United States, as it has done in FISA. Where Congress has so regulated, the President can act in contravention of statute only if his authority is exclusive, and not subject to the check of statutory regulation. The DOJ letter pointedly does not make that extraordinary claim.

Moreover, to construe the AUMF as the DOJ suggests would itself raise serious constitutional questions under the Fourth Amendment. The Supreme Court has never upheld warrantless wiretapping within the United States. Accordingly, the principle that statutes should be construed to avoid serious constitutional questions provides an additional reason for concluding that the AUMF does not authorize the President's actions here. ***

The DOJ concedes that the NSA program involves "electronic surveillance," which is defined in FISA to mean the interception of the contents of telephone, wire, or email communications that occur, at least in part, in the United States. *** NSA engages in such surveillance without judicial approval, and apparently without the substantive showings that FISA requires—e.g., that the subject is an "agent of a foreign power." *** The DOJ does not argue that FISA itself authorizes such electronic surveillance; and, as the DOJ letter acknowledges, 18 U.S.C. § 1809 makes criminal any electronic surveillance not authorized by statute.

The DOJ nevertheless contends that the surveillance is authorized by the AUMF, signed on September 18, 2001, which empowers the President to use "all necessary and appropriate force against" al Qaeda.*** This argument fails for four reasons.

First, and most importantly, the DOJ's argument rests on an unstated general "implication" from the AUMF that directly contradicts express and specific language in FISA. ***

As noted above, Congress has comprehensively regulated all electronic surveillance in the United States, and authorizes such surveillance only pursuant to specific statutes designated as the "exclusive means by which electronic surveillance . . . and the interception of domestic wire, oral, and electronic communications may be conducted." *** Moreover, FISA specifically addresses the question of domestic wiretapping during wartime.). Thus, even where Congress has declared war—a more formal step than an authorization such as the AUMF—the law limits warrantless wiretapping to the first fifteen days of the conflict. *** The DOJ letter remarkably does not even mention FISA's fifteen-day war provision, which directly refutes the President's asserted "implied" authority. ***

Second, the DOJ's argument would require the conclusion that Congress implicitly and *sub silentio* repealed 18 U.S.C. § 2511(2)(f), the provision that identifies FISA and specific criminal code provisions as "the exclusive means by which electronic surveillance . . . may be conducted." Repeals by implication are strongly disfavored; they can be established only by "overwhelming evidence." *** The AUMF and § 2511(2)(f) are not irreconcilable, and there is no evidence, let alone overwhelming evidence, that Congress intended to repeal § 2511(2)(f).

Third, Attorney General Alberto Gonzales has admitted that the administration did not seek to amend FISA to authorize the NSA spying program because it was advised that Congress would reject such an amendment. The administration cannot argue on the one hand that Congress authorized the NSA program in the AUMF, and at the same time that it did not ask Congress for such authorization because it feared Congress would say no.[5]

Finally, the DOJ's reliance upon *Hamdi v. Rumsfeld*, 542 U.S. 507 (2004), to support its reading of the AUMF is misplaced. A plurality of the Court in Hamdi held that the AUMF authorized military detention of enemy combatants captured on the battlefield abroad as a "fundamental incident of waging war." *** The plurality expressly limited this holding to individuals who were "part of or supporting forces hostile to the United States or coalition partners *in Afghanistan and who engaged in an armed conflict against the United States there.*" *** It is one thing, however, to say that foreign battlefield capture of enemy combatants is an incident of waging war that Congress intended to authorize. It is another matter entirely to treat unchecked warrantless domestic spying as included in that authorization, especially where an existing statute specifies that other laws are the "exclusive means" by which electronic surveillance may be conducted and provides that even a declaration of war authorizes such spying only for a fifteen-day emergency period. ***

Construing FISA and the AUMF according to their plain meanings raises no serious constitutional questions regarding the President's duties under Article II. Construing the AUMF to permit unchecked warrantless wiretapping without probable cause, however, would raise serious questions under the Fourth Amendment. ***

We do not dispute that, absent congressional action, the President might have inherent constitutional authority to collect "signals intelligence" about the enemy abroad. Nor do we dispute that, had Congress taken no action in this area, the President might well be constitutionally empowered to conduct domestic surveillance directly tied and narrowly confined to that goal—subject, of course, to Fourth Amendment limits. ***

But FISA specifically *** dictat[ed] that FISA and the criminal code are the "exclusive means" of conducting electronic surveillance. In doing so, Congress did not deny that the President has constitutional power to conduct electronic surveillance for national security purposes; rather, Congress properly concluded that "even if the President has the inherent authority in

---

[5] The administration had a convenient vehicle for seeking any such amendment in the USA PATRIOT Act of 2001, Pub. L. No. 107-56, 115 Stat. 272, enacted in October 2001. The Patriot Act amended FISA in several respects, including in sections 218 (allowing FISA wiretaps in criminal investigations) and 215 (popularly known as the "libraries provision"). Yet the administration did not ask Congress to amend FISA to authorize the warrantless electronic surveillance at issue here.

the absence of legislation to authorize warrantless electronic surveillance for foreign intelligence purposes, Congress has the power to regulate the conduct of such surveillance by legislating a reasonable procedure, which then becomes the exclusive means by which such surveillance may be conducted." H.R. Rep. No. 95-1283, pt. 1, at 24 (1978) (emphasis added). This analysis, Congress noted, was "supported by two successive Attorneys General." ***

To say that the President has inherent authority does not mean that his authority is exclusive, or that his conduct is not subject to statutory regulations enacted (as FISA was) pursuant to Congress's Article I powers. As Justice Jackson famously explained in his influential opinion in *Youngstown Sheet & Tube Co. v. Sawyer*, 343 U.S. at 635 (Jackson, J., concurring), the Constitution "enjoins upon its branches separateness but interdependence, autonomy but reciprocity. Presidential powers are not fixed but fluctuate, depending upon their disjunction or conjunction with those of Congress." For example, the President in his role as Commander in Chief directs military operations. But the Framers gave Congress the power to prescribe rules for the regulation of the armed and naval forces, Art. I, § 8, cl. 14, and if a duly enacted statute prohibits the military from engaging in torture or cruel, inhuman, and degrading treatment, the President must follow that dictate. As Justice Jackson wrote, when the President acts in defiance of "the expressed or implied will of Congress," his power is "at its lowest ebb." *** In this setting, Jackson wrote, "Presidential power [is] most vulnerable to attack and in the least favorable of possible constitutional postures." ***

Absent a serious question about FISA's constitutionality, there is no reason even to consider construing the AUMF to have implicitly overturned the carefully designed regulatory regime that FISA establishes.***

The principle that ambiguous statutes should be construed to avoid serious constitutional questions works against the administration, not in its favor. Interpreting the AUMF and FISA to permit unchecked domestic wiretapping for the duration of the conflict with al Qaeda would certainly raise serious constitutional questions. The Supreme Court has never upheld such a sweeping power to invade the privacy of Americans at home without individualized suspicion or judicial oversight.

The NSA surveillance program permits wiretapping within the United States without either of the safeguards presumptively required by the Fourth Amendment for electronic surveillance—individualized probable cause and a warrant or other order issued by a judge or magistrate. ***

In conclusion, the DOJ letter fails to offer a plausible legal defense of the NSA domestic spying program. If the Administration felt that FISA was insufficient, the proper course was to seek legislative amendment, as it did with other aspects of FISA in the Patriot Act, and as Congress expressly contemplated when it enacted the wartime wiretap provision in FISA. One of the crucial features of a constitutional democracy is that it is always open to the President—or anyone else—to seek to change the law. But it is also beyond dispute that, in such a democracy, the President cannot simply violate criminal laws behind closed doors because he deems them obsolete or impracticable. *****

Note

What is the source of legitimacy for actions taken in an emergency? A House report issued while FISA was under consideration noted that "the decision as to the standards governing when and how foreign intelligence electronic surveillance should be conducted is and should be a political decision, in the best sense of the term, because it involves the weighing of important public policy concerns—civil liberties and national security. Such a political decision is one properly made by the political branches of Government together, not adopted by one branch on its own and with no regard for the other. Under our Constitution legislation is the embodiment of just such political decisions." H. Rep. 95-1283, pt. I, at 21-22. Is Congress in fact more directly responsible to the electorate than the President? Does that matter when assessing actions undertaken in an emergency? If the President acts alone, from where does he ultimately derive his authority?

D. INSTITUIONAL DESIGN AND POLITICAL THEORY

The final section of this chapter provides additional theoretical materials through which you can consider the cases and materials presented in the course of this book. Some of these materials urge you to consider institutional design questions—from the broadest constitutional level to smaller details of funding structure and doctrines of judicial review. Others ask you to consider which branch of government is best suited to respond to a crisis. Some question the scope and contours of American sovereignty. And others press the question: From where do governmental actors gain their authority or legitimacy to act in a crisis?

1. THE UNITARY EXECUTIVE

The first of these debates revolves around the scope of executive power and the functional abilities of the branches of government. John Yoo, a prominent lawyer within the Bush Administration, has been a strong advocate for a robust understanding of executive powers. In his words:

> Hamilton and the other Federalists ***** understood the executive to be functionally best matched in speech, unity, and decisiveness to he unpredictable high-stakes nature of foreign affairs. ***** Rational action on behalf of the nation in a dangerous world would be best advanced by executive action. Edward Corwin observed that the executive's advantages in foreign affairs include "the unity of office, its capacity for secrecy and dispatch, and its superior sources of information, to which should be added the fact that it is always on hand and ready for action, whereas the houses of Congress are in adjournment much of the time." ***** [T]he Constitution creates a mass of executive power that can help Presidents rise to the challenges of the modern age. This

power does not ebb and flow with the political tides, but finds its origins in the very creation of the executive. The Framers rejected the legislative supremacy of the revolutionary state governments in favor of a Presidency that would be independent of Congress, elected by the people, and possessed with speed, decision, and vigor to guide the nation through war and emergency. They did not carefully define and limit the executive power, as they did the legislative, because they understood that they could not see the future."

CRISIS AND COMMAND: A HISTORY OF EXECUTIVE POWER FROM GEORGE WASHINGTON TO GEORGE W. BUSH (Kaplan, 2010).

Others have taken a different view. Deborah Pearlstein, for instance, has argued that, functionally speaking, modern thinkers must reconsider the superiority of executive rather than multi-branch action, even in times of national security crisis.

> [T]he new functionalists' attention to the structural *benefits* of flexibility, unity, and speed grossly discounts the *burdens* such organizational characteristics impose on the executive branch security structures tasked with carrying out counterterrorism operations. ***[O]ne can begin to identify why and how such burdens emerge day-to-day. Organization analysis can teach, for example, how competitive organizational structures inside today's complex executive branch (unitary in theory only) can make actors more likely to shirk core responsibilities. The focus on organizational incentives makes it possible to see, for example, why deferential review in some contexts may be worse than no review at all. *** In the end, the alternative approach to evaluating the branches' comparative institutional competences proposed here leads to a far more favorable view of multi-branch participation in programs geared to addressing the terrorist threat.

Deborah Pearlstein, *Form and Function in the National Security Constitution*, 41 CONN. L. REV. 1549 (2008).

Justice Kagan, herself formerly a key White House aide in the Clinton Administration, has argued that the executive has grown dramatically, and dramatically more unitary—and did so well before 9/11, even in the realm of domestic affairs:

> [P]residential control of administration, in critical respects, expanded dramatically during the Clinton years, making the regulatory activity of the executive branch agencies more and more an extension of the President's own policy and political agenda. Faced for most of his time in office with a hostile Congress but eager to show progress on domestic issues, Clinton and his White House staff turned to the bureaucracy to achieve, to the extent it could, the full panoply of his

domestic policy goals. Whether the subject was health care, welfare reform, tobacco, or guns, a self-conscious and central object of the White House was to devise, direct, and/or finally announce administrative actions—regulations, guidance, enforcement strategies, and reports—to showcase and advance presidential policies. In executing this strategy, the White House in large measure set the administrative agenda for key agencies, heavily influencing what they would (or would not) spend time on and what they would (or would not) generate as regulatory product.

Elena Kagan, *Presidential Administration*, 114 Harv. L. Rev. 2245, 2248 (2001).

Notes

1. Speed, Decision, and Vigor. Do you agree with Perlstein or Yoo? Does Yoo overstate the actual abilities of the executive branch to act swiftly or effectively in a time of crisis? Does Pearlstein minimize the difficulties of getting a wide range of executive branch officials, each with differing agendas, on the same page?

2. Crisis or the Welfare State? Are arguments for increased executive power necessarily a byproduct of national security threat? To what degree might they be a byproduct of the rise of the welfare state? Of the political incentives and challenges facing a President? Or of the institutional need of bureaucrats to perpetuate and expand their own powers?

2.   TWO THEORIES OF SOVEREIGNTY

Two major philosophical theories of sovereignty inform the debates above regarding executive power and the role of law, particularly in an emergency: those of Carl Schmitt and Hannah Arendt. Schmitt's theory is based upon the notion of the "exception." He argues that the "[s]overeign is he who decides on the exception" and that "the exception is to be understood to refer to a general concept in the theory of the state, and not merely to a construct applied to any emergency decree or state of siege." Carl Schmitt, POLITICAL THEOLOGY: FOUR CHAPTERS ON THE CONCEPT OF SOVEREIGNTY (MIT Press, 1988).

The "normal" legal order for Schmitt depends on the existence of the exception; of existential threat and the sovereign who decides upon the exception. Similarly, his understanding of politics is premised upon the distinction "between friend and enemy." Carl Schmitt, THE CONCEPT OF THE POLITICAL (2007). "An enemy exists only when at least potentially, one fighting collectivity of people confronts a similar collectivity." Politics, for Schmitt, is created by the ever present threat to group survival:

> The political is the most intense and extreme antagonism, and every concrete antagonism becomes that much more political the closer it approaches the most extreme point, that of the friend-enemy grouping. *** [A]s an ever present possibility [war] is the leading presupposition which determines in a characteristic way human action and thinking and thereby creates a specifically political behavior.

*** A world in which the possibility of war is utterly eliminated, a completely pacified globe, would be a world without the distinction between friend and enemy and hence a world without politics.

Authority need not come from law, indeed for Schmitt it lies outside of it, because continued existence of the power to decide (and of the state) in an emergency "is undoubted proof of its superiority over the validity of the legal norm. *** The state suspends the law in the exception on the basis of its right of self-preservation."

Hannah Arendt offers a contrasting understanding of sovereignty, politics, law, and legitimacy. For Arendt, politics is created by the internal bonds of a community, not a threat from the outside. She explains:

> The men of the American Revolution, on the contrary, understood by the very opposite of a pre-political natural violence. To them, power came into being when and where people would get together and bind themselves through promises, covenants, and mutual pledges; only such power, which rested on reciprocity and mutuality, was real power and legitimate***. Hannah Arendt, ON REVOLUTION (Penguin 2006).

For Arendt, "[p]olitics is based on the fact of human plurality." Hannah Arendt, THE PROMISE OF POLITICS (Jerome Kohn, Ed., 2005). For her, "[t]yrannies are doomed because they destroy the togetherness of men: by isolating men from one another they seek to destroy human plurality. They are based on the one fundamental experience which I am altogether alone, which is to be helpless *** unable to enlist the help of my fellow men."

Politics, then, is a coming together for joint decision and action. And law is constitutive of politics – because the "law produces the arena where politics occurs" and "defines the space in which men live with one another without using force." Law "is prepolitical, but in the sense that it is constitutive for all further political action and interaction. Just as the walls of a city, to which Heraclitus once compared the law, must first be built before there can be a city identifiable by its shape and borders, the law determines the character of its inhabitants." For Arendt, law is that which creates the space for democratic legitimacy and authority for mutual action.

Notes

1. **Applying philosophy to cases.** Do either Schmitt's or Arendt's theories resonate with the above arguments for and against executive powers? With arguments made in cases presented earlier in this book?

2. **Popular Sovereignty versus the Exception.** Are Arendt's and Schmitt's theories necessarily at odds? Or do they simply address different situations— Arendt's the mutually creative power of a political community during non-emergencies, and Schmitt the power of the state during exceptions? Which view of politics do you find more compelling—and which do you think is most helpful, or most descriptive, of executive action during our present moment?

3. Germany, France, and World War II. Carl Schmitt is one of the most controversial political philosophers of the twentieth century, due in large part to his participation in Hitler's Germany and efforts to develop a theory of sovereignty for the Third Reich. Comparatively, how did the pre-war German constitution structure the separation of powers? Peter Lindseth explains: "It was this prevalent notion of unlimited parliamentary power, in particular as it related to the permissible scope of legislative delegation to the executive, that distinguished the French and German interwar constitutional experiences from the American one.*** By the third and fourth decades of the twentieth century, the notion of parliamentary supremacy paradoxically provided the foundation, through its support for extreme delegations [of legislative power to the executive], for the degeneration of the parliamentary system into dictatorship. *** By 1933 and 1940 respectively, the practice of unchecked delegation in Germany and France led ultimately to the collapse of the parliamentary system into one in which all effective governmental power would, as a matter of constitutional doctrine, be fused in the person of the national leader." Peter L. Lindseth, *The Paradox of Parliamentary Supremacy: Delegation, Democracy, and Dictatorship in Germany and France, 1920s-1950s,* 113 YALE L. J. 1341 (2004). What practical constitutional structures might be considered Schmittian? In keeping with Arendt's theories?

4. *Perpetual State of Exception.* Giorgio Agamben, in his book THE STATE OF EXCEPTION, explores the relationship between the power of the State and the rights of individuals. Agamben argues that "modern totalitarianism can be defined as the establishment, by means of the state of exception, of a legal civil war that allows for the physical elimination not only of political adversaries but of entire categories of citizen who for some reason cannot be integrated into the political system." Giorgio Agamben, THE STATE OF EXCEPTION, 2 (U. Chi. Press 2005). Is the exception as dangerous as Agamben believes? Might the war on terror present a permanent state of the exception—and what would that mean for democratic (or executive) legitimacy? Does emergency diminish overtime, or does the populace just get used to it?

3.   LEGITIMACY AND AUTHORITY

From where does governmental action gain its legitimacy? Does the Constitution implicitly provide authority for extra-constitutional action? Must the Constitution directly support action—or should politics ultimately decide whether choices made in an emergency were legitimate, or the right call?

Bruce Ackerman argues that traumas such as 9/11 will recur, and that we must therefore rethink constitutional structures for allow for more flexibility in short term emergencies—in order to prevent a downward cycle of increasing repression of civil liberties.

> Terrorist attacks will be a recurring part of our future. ***
> [W]e urgently require new constitutional concepts to deal with
> the protection of civil liberties. Otherwise, a downward cycle
> threatens: After each successful attack, politicians will come up
> with repressive laws and promise greater security—only to find
> that a different terrorist band manages to strike a few years later.
> This disaster, in turn, will create a demand for even more

repressive laws, and on and on. *** It is tempting to respond to this grim prospect with an absolutist defense of traditional freedom: No matter how large the event, no matter how great the ensuing panic, we must insist on the strict protection of all rights all the time. I respect this view but do not share it. No democratic government can maintain popular support without acting effectively to calm panic and to prevent a second terrorist strike. *** To avoid a repeated cycle of repression, defenders of freedom must consider a more hard-headed doctrine—one that allows short-term emergency measures but draws the line against permanent restrictions.   Above all else, we must prevent politicians from exploiting momentary panic to impose long-lasting limitations on liberty. Designing a constitutional regime for a limited state of emergency is a tricky business.   Unless careful precautions are taken, emergency measures have a habit of continuing well beyond their time of necessity. Governments should not be permitted to run wild even during the emergency; many extreme measures should remain off limits. Nevertheless, the self-conscious design of an emergency regime may well be the best available defense against a panic-driven cycle of permanent destruction.   This is a challenge confronting all liberal democracies.*** September 11 and its successors will not pose such a grave existential threat, but major acts of terrorism can induce short-term panic. It should be the purpose of a newly fashioned emergency regime to reassure the public that the situation is under control, and that the state is taking effective short-term actions to prevent a second strike. This reassurance rationale *** requires something more: a reconsideration of the self-confident American belief that we are better off without an elaborate set of emergency provisions in our own Constitution, and that we should rely principally on judges to control our panic-driven responses to crises. ***[T]his common law prejudice *** will no longer serve us well under the conditions likely to prevail in the twenty-first century. *** What should a proper emergency constitution look like?   *** The first and most fundamental dimension focuses on an innovative system of political checks and balances, ***[including] constitutional mechanisms that enable effective   short-run   responses   without   allowing   states   of emergency   to become permanent fixtures. *** Given the formidable obstacle course presented by Article V of the U.S. Constitution, my proposal is a nonstarter as a formal amendment. Nevertheless much of the design could be introduced as a 'framework statute' within the terms of the existing Constitution. Congress took a first step in this direction in the 1970s when it passed the National Emergencies Act. But the experience under this Act demonstrates the need for radical revision. Bruce Ackerman, *The Emergency Constitution*, 113 YALE L.J. 1029 (2004).

Is Ackerman right to predict a downward spiral of infringements on civil liberties—and a failure of the courts and the constitution to adequately respond? Is he overly optimistic that Congress might pass an adequate framework statute for emergency measures or that the period of "emergency" could be sufficiently cabined?

In response, Laurence Tribe and Patrick Gudridge have argued that:

> The issue is whether constitutional law, as we experience it (make it, interpret it, teach it, deploy it) in all its ordinary complexity, should in important respects be set to the side and suspended during certain defined episodes that will punctuate our lives as we engage in the grave business of fighting terrorism. *** [Ackerman] relies almost entirely on the legislative process—rather than on substantive constitutional protections—as a check on extreme violations of civil liberties. Ackerman assumes that, in the United States at least, there will ordinarily be no effective judicial "backstopping," no second look and thus no second chance to acknowledge constitutional expectations, apropos legislative determinations to declare (or presumably continue) states of emergency. *** Sharply separating states of emergency from ordinary constitutional periods requires that the usual resources of constitutional law—Ackerman's "fog" and "legalisms"—be set to the side, rendered (or recognized as) unavailable for judicial use. One consequence is that rights that we ordinarily regard as well-established and richly elaborated appear, within the emergency context, as only awkwardly justifiable. *** As the experience following September 11 makes all too plain, building an imaginary wall around a state of emergency and proclaiming only a thin emergency constitution to be operative inside that wall offers no realistic hope of preventing the ripple effects of any given terrorist attack, and of the government responses to that attack, from breaking through cracks in that wall and bleeding into ordinary affairs—into the broad vistas of American life that bear no real connection to the attack, to the techniques it employed, or to the risks it represents. So any realistic assessment of what that constitutional bargain with the devil might be expected to yield had better not proceed on the wishful premise that whatever zone is covered by the emergency constitution even begins to define the ways in which our liberties are likely to be diluted as a result of what the latest attack will have wrought in the collective consciousness of the nation. And, lest anyone suppose that accepting an emergency constitution will do no harm in the realms that lie beyond its defined reach, it should be remembered that the sense of security that comes with the territory whenever we talk the talk of emergency measures with self-limiting sunset clauses—a sense of security without

which the bargain would never have seemed so tempting in the first place—is the very thing that threatens to lull us into being most forgiving of government encroachment in the interest of patriotism precisely when the lessons of history teach us we had best be most on guard. Laurence H. Tribe & Patrick O. Gudridge, *The Anti-Emergency Constitution*, 113 YALE L.J. 1801 (2004).

Are Tribe and Gudridge too absolutist in their stance? Is the Aniti-Emergency Constitution at best not politically feasible, or at worst a suicide pact? Can the constitution with its current structures and limitations respond adequately to the crisis of terrorism, and are courts up to the task of ensuring the respect for existing limitations?

Politics might perhaps offer a mechanism for checks on emergency powers. Jules Lobel argues that:

> [T]he undermining of liberal constitutional restraints on executive emergency power during the twentieth century has been caused less by legislative failure or by executive arrogance, than by the transformation of the eighteenth century world and the rise of American power in global affairs. *** Three frameworks have been proffered for resolving this tension between law and necessity. The absolutist perspective contends that the government has no emergency power to deal with crisis other than that specifically provided by the Constitution.*** [T]he second, relativist position argues that the Constitution is a flexible document that permits the President to take whatever measures are necessary in crisis situations. ***Liberal constitutionalism sought throughout the eighteenth and early nineteenth centuries to resolve the tension between law and necessity through a third approach, one that preserved the dichotomy between ordinary and emergency power by positing a boundary line separating and protecting the normal constitutional order from the dark world of crisis government. Emergency and normal times were counterposed, resulting in distinct legal regimes. Normalcy permitted a governmental structure based on separation of powers, respect for civil liberties and the rule of law, while emergencies required strong executive rule, premised not on law and respect for civil liberties, but rather on discretion to take a wide range of actions to preserve the government. *** Liberal thought premises constitutional democracy upon the tension between polar opposites: between law and politics, public and private, state and civil society, universal and particular, reason and desire, self and other.***
>
> The current crisis of liberalism reflects, in part, the transitional age in which we live—an era caught between the traditional   nation-state   system   and   the   increasing

interdependence of the international community. *** To the extent it is possible to look beyond the short-term solutions of the liberal model, a transformative vision must insist on two very different, but complementary changes from our present situation. The first would be the further development of the international system of governance, supplementing nation-states and simultaneously weakening the "us-versus-them" perspective that characterizes the present nation state system. The second change would involve reviving communalist politics, in which the citizenry, often acting through local communities, plays a more active role in determining our relations with peoples of other nations. *** [T]he changing global and domestic context presents a possibility for transforming the liberal model by providing international and communalist restraints on governmental power. Such a solution would attempt to overcome the fears that lead to the necessity for emergency power, instead of merely limiting emergency power by means of legal rules. Jules Lobel, *Emergency Power and the Decline of Liberalism*, 98 YALE L.J. 1385 (1989).

To what degree to you believe politics effectively function to cabin, or legitimize the actions of the executive in an emergency—particularly when elections come years apart? What other institutional structures, such as the secrecy of national security programs, mediate political accountability mechanisms? Is Lobel's hope for a new kind of politics utopian or necessary? Or are existing legal separation of powers and current forms of democratic engagement up to the task of this new form of national security crises?

STATUTORY GUIDE

DEFINING TERRORISM

10 U.S.C. § 950v(a)(24) TERRORISM.—Any person subject to this chapter who intentionally kills or inflicts great bodily harm on one or more protected persons, or intentionally engages in an act that evinces a wanton disregard for human life, in a manner calculated to influence or affect the conduct of government or civilian population by intimidation or coercion, or to retaliate against government conduct, shall be punished, if death results to one or more of the victims, by death or such other punishment as a military commission under this chapter may direct, punishment, other than death, as military commission under this chapter may direct.

18 U.S.C. § 2331(1):
(1) the term "international terrorism" means activities that--
(A) Involve violent acts of acts dangerous to human life that are a violation of the criminal laws of the United States or of any State, or that would be a criminal violation if committed within the jurisdiction of the United States or of any State;
(B) Appear to be intended-
    (i) to intimidate or coerce a civilian population;
    (ii) to influence the policy of a government by intimidation or coercion; or to affect the conduct of a government by mass destruction, assassination or kidnapping; and
(C) Occur primarily outside the territorial jurisdiction of the United States, or transcend national boundaries in terms of the means by which they are accomplished, the persons they appear intended to intimidate or coerce, or the locale in which their perpetrators operate or seek asylum.

18 U.S.C. § 2331(5):
(5) the term "domestic terrorism" means activities that--
    (A) involve acts dangerous to human life that are a violation of the criminal laws of the United States or of any State;
    (B) appear to be intended--
        (i) to intimidate or coerce a civilian population;
        (ii) to influence the policy of a government by intimidation or coercion; or
        (iii) to affect the conduct of a government by mass destruction, assassination, or kidnapping; and
    (C) occur primarily within the territorial jurisdiction of the United States

22 U.S.C. § 2656f(d)(2) the term "terrorism" means premeditated, politically motivated violence perpetrated against noncombatant targets by subnational groups or clandestine agents;

DESIGNATING TERRORIST ORGANIZATIONS

8 U.S.C. § 1189(a)

(1) In general

(2) The Secretary is authorized to designate an organization as a foreign terrorist organization in accordance with this subsection if the Secretary finds that—

(I) The hijacking or sabotage of any conveyance....

(II) The seizing or detaining, and threatening to kill, injure, or continue to detain, another individual in order to compel a third person including a governmental organization) to do or abstain from doing any act as an explicit or implicit condition for the release of the individual seized or detained.

(III) A violent attack upon an internationally protected person.

(IV) The use of any—

(a) biological agent, chemical agent, or nuclear weapon or device, or

(b) explosive, firearm, or other weapons or dangerous device (other than for mere personal monetary gain), with intent to endanger, directly or indirectly, the safety of one or more individuals or to cause substantial damage to property. ...

(VI) A threat, attempt, or conspiracy to do any of the foregoing.

PROVIDING MATERIAL SUPPORT FOR TERRORISM

18 U.S.C. § 2339A (2006). Providing Material Support to Terrorists.

(a) Offense.--Whoever provides material support or resources or conceals or disguises the nature, location, source, or ownership of material support or resources, knowing or intending that they are to be used in preparation for, or in carrying out, a violation of or [various offenses] or in preparation for, or in carrying out, the concealment of an escape from the commission of any such violation, or attempts or conspires to do such an act, shall be fined under this title, imprisoned not more than 15 years, or both, and, if the death of any person results, shall be imprisoned for any term of years or for life. A violation of this section may be prosecuted in any Federal judicial district in which the underlying offense was committed, or in any other Federal judicial district as provided by law.

(b) Definitions.--As used in this section--

(1) the term "material support or resources" means any property, tangible or intangible, or service, including currency or monetary instruments or financial securities, financial services, lodging, training, expert advice or assistance, safehouses, false documentation or identification, communications equipment, facilities, weapons, lethal substances, explosives, personnel (1 or more individuals who may be or include oneself), and transportation, except medicine or religious materials;

(2) the term "training" means instruction or teaching designed to impart a specific skill, as opposed to general knowledge; and

(3) the term "expert advice or assistance" means advice or assistance derived from scientific, technical or other specialized knowledge.

18 U.S.C. § 2339B. Providing Material Support or Resources to Designated Foreign Terrorist Organizations.

(a) Prohibited activities.--

    (1) Unlawful conduct.--Whoever knowingly provides material support or resources to a foreign terrorist organization, or attempts or conspires to do so, shall be fined under this title or imprisoned not more than 15 years, or both, and, if the death of any person results, shall be imprisoned for any term of years or for life. To violate this paragraph, a person must have knowledge that the organization is a designated terrorist organization (as defined in subsection (g)(6)), that the organization has engaged or engages in terrorist activity (as defined in section 212(a)(3)(B) of the Immigration and Nationality Act), or that the organization has engaged or engages in terrorism (as defined in section 140(d) (2) of the Foreign Relations Authorization Act, Fiscal Years 1988 and 1989). ***

    (2) Financial institutions.--Except as authorized by the Secretary, any financial institution that becomes aware that it has possession of, or control over, any funds in which a foreign terrorist organization, or its agent, has an interest, shall--

        (A) retain possession of, or maintain control over, such funds; and

        (B) report to the Secretary the existence of such funds in accordance with regulations issued by the Secretary. ***

(g) Definitions.--As used in this section-- ***

    (4) the term "material support or resources" has the same meaning given that term in section 2339A (including the definitions of "training" and "expert advice or assistance" in that section); ***

(h) Provision of personnel.--No person may be prosecuted under this section in connection with the term "personnel" unless that person has knowingly provided, attempted to provide, or conspired to provide a foreign terrorist organization with 1 or more individuals (who may be or include himself) to work under that terrorist organization's direction or control or to organize, manage, supervise, or otherwise direct the operation of that organization. Individuals who act entirely independently of the foreign terrorist organization to advance its goals or objectives shall not be considered to be working under the foreign terrorist organization's direction and control.

(i) Rule of construction.--Nothing in this section shall be construed or applied so as to abridge the exercise of rights guaranteed under the First Amendment to the Constitution of the United States.

(j) Exception.--No person may be prosecuted under this section in connection with the term "personnel", "training", or "expert advice or assistance" if the provision of that material support or resources to a foreign terrorist organization was approved by the Secretary of State with the concurrence of the Attorney General.

18 U.S.C. § 2339C – Collecting Funds for Terrorist Organizations

(a) Offenses.--

(1) In general.--Whoever, in a circumstance described in subsection (b), by any means, directly or indirectly, unlawfully and willfully provides or collects funds with the intention that such funds be used, or with the knowledge that such funds are to be used, in full or in part, in order to carry out--

(A) an act which constitutes an offense within the scope of a treaty specified in subsection (e)(7), as implemented by the United States, or
(B) any other act intended to cause death or serious bodily injury to a civilian, or to any other person not taking an active part in the hostilities in a situation of armed conflict, when the purpose of such act, by its nature or context, is to intimidate a population, or to compel a government or an international organization to do or to abstain from doing any act, shall be punished as prescribed in subsection (d)(1).

(2) Attempts and conspiracies.--Whoever attempts or conspires to commit an offense under paragraph (1) shall be punished as prescribed in subsection (d)(1).

(3) Relationship to predicate act.--For an act to constitute an offense set forth in this subsection, it shall not be necessary that the funds were actually used to carry out a predicate act.

(b) Jurisdiction.--There is jurisdiction over the offenses in subsection (a) in the following circumstances--

(1) the offense takes place in the United States ***

(c) Concealment.--Whoever--

(1)

(A) is in the United States; or
(B) is outside the United States and is a national of the United States or a legal entity organized under the laws of the United States (including any of its States, districts, commonwealths, territories, or possessions); and

(2) knowingly conceals or disguises the nature, location, source, ownership, or control of any material support or resources, or any funds or proceeds of such funds--

(A) knowing or intending that the support or resources are to be provided, or knowing that the support or resources
were provided, in violation of section 2339B of this title; or
(B) knowing or intending that any such funds are to be provided or collected, or knowing that the funds were provided or collected, in violation of subsection (a), shall be punished as prescribed in subsection (d)(2).

(e) Definitions. – In this section –

(1) the term "funds" means assets of every kind, whether tangible or intangible, movable or immovable, however acquired, and legal documents or instruments in any form, including electronic or digital, evidencing title to, or interest in, such assets, including coin, currency,

bank credits, travelers checks, bank checks, money orders, shares, securities, bonds, drafts, and letters of credit;

(2) the term "government facility" means any permanent or temporary facility or conveyance that is used or occupied by representatives of a state, members of a government, the legislature, or the judiciary, or by officials or employees of a state or any other public authority or entity or by employees or officials of an intergovernmental organization in connection with their official duties;

(3) the term "proceeds" means any funds derived from or obtained, directly or indirectly, through the commission of an offense set forth in subsection (a);

(4) the term "provides" includes giving, donating, and transmitting;

(5) the term "collects" includes raising and receiving;

(6) the term "predicate act" means any act referred to in subparagraph (A) or (B) of subsection (a)(1);

(7) the term "treaty" means—[9 treaties listed]

(8) the term "intergovernmental organization" includes international organizations;

(9) the term "international organization" has the same meaning as in section 1116(b)(5) of this title;

(10) the term "armed conflict" does not include internal disturbances and tensions, such as riots, isolated and

sporadic acts of violence, and other acts of a similar nature;

(11) the term "serious bodily injury" has the same meaning as in section 1365(g)(3) of this title;

(12) the term "national of the United States" has the meaning given that term in section 101(a)(22) of the Immigration and Nationality Act (8 U.S.C. 1101(a)(22));

(13) the term "material support or resources" has the same meaning given that term in section 2339B(g)(4) of this title; and

(14) the term "state" has the same meaning as that term has under international law, and includes all political subdivisions thereof.

(f) Civil penalty.--In addition to any other criminal, civil, or administrative liability or penalty, any legal entity located within the United States or organized under the laws of the United States, including any of the laws of its States, districts, commonwealths, territories, or possessions, shall be liable to the United States for the sum of at least $10,000, if a person responsible for the management or control of that legal entity has, in that capacity, committed an offense set forth in subsection (a).

18 U.S.C. § 2339D

(a) Offense.— Whoever knowingly receives military-type training from or on behalf of any organization designated at the time of the training by the Secretary of State under section 219(a)(1) of the Immigration and Nationality Act as a foreign terrorist organization shall be fined under this title or imprisoned for ten years, or both. To violate this subsection, a person must have knowledge that the organization is a designated terrorist organization (as defined in subsection (c)(4)), that the organization has engaged or engages in terrorist activity (as defined in section 212 of the Immigration and Nationality Act), or that the organization has engaged or engages in terrorism (as defined in section 140(d)(2) of the Foreign Relations Authorization Act, Fiscal Years 1988 and 1989).

(b) Extraterritorial Jurisdiction.— There is extraterritorial Federal jurisdiction over an offense under this section. ***

CIVIL LIABILITY FOR TERRORISM

28 U.S.C. § 1350 (Alien Tort Statute)

The district courts shall have original jurisdiction of any civil action by an alien for a tort only, committed in violation of the law of nations or a treaty of the United States.

ELECTRONIC SURVELLIANCE

18 U.S.C. § 2709 (Foreign Intelligence Surveillance Act § 215)

Counterintelligence access to telephone toll and transactional records

(a) Duty to provide.–A wire or electronic communication service provider shall comply with a request for subscriber information and toll billing records information, or electronic communication transactional records in its custody or possession made by the Director of the Federal Bureau of Investigation under subsection (b) of this section.

(b) Required certification.–The Director of the Federal Bureau of Investigation, or his designee in a position not lower than Deputy Assistant Director at Bureau headquarters or a Special Agent in Charge in a Bureau field office designated by the Director, may–

> (1) request the name, address, length of service, and local and long distance toll billing records of a person or entity if the Director (or his designee) certifies in writing to the wire or electronic communication service provider to which the request is made that the name, address, length of service, and toll billing records sought are relevant to an authorized investigation to protect against international terrorism or clandestine intelligence activities, provided that such an investigation of a United States person is not conducted solely on the basis of activities protected by the first amendment to the Constitution of the United States; and

> (2) request the name, address, and length of service of a person or entity if the Director (or his designee) certifies in writing to the wire or electronic communication service provider to which the request is made that the information sought is relevant to an authorized investigation to protect against international terrorism or clandestine intelligence activities, provided that such an investigation of a United States person is not conducted solely upon the basis of activities protected by the first amendment to the Constitution of the United States.

(c) Prohibition of certain disclosure –

(1) If the Director of the Federal Bureau of Investigation, or his designee in a position not lower than Deputy Assistant Director at Bureau headquarters or a Special Agent in Charge in a Bureau field office designated by the Director, certifies that otherwise there may result a danger to the national security of the United States, interference with a criminal, counterterrorism, or counterintelligence investigation, interference with diplomatic relations, or danger to the life or physical safety of any person, no wire or electronic communications service provider, or officer, employee, or agent thereof, shall disclose to any person (other than those to whom such disclosure is necessary to comply with the request or an attorney to obtain legal advice or legal assistance with respect to the request) that the Federal Bureau of Investigation has sought or obtained access to information or records under this section.

(2) The request shall notify the person or entity to whom the request is directed of the nondisclosure requirement under paragraph (1).

(3) Any recipient disclosing to those persons necessary to comply with the request or to an attorney to obtain legal advice or legal assistance with respect to the request shall inform such person of any applicable nondisclosure requirement. Any person who receives a disclosure under this subsection shall be subject to the same prohibitions on disclosure under paragraph (1).

(4) At the request of the Director of the Federal Bureau of Investigation or the designee of the Director, any person making or intending to make a disclosure under this section shall identify to the Director or such designee the person to whom such disclosure will be made or to whom such disclosure was made prior to the request, except that nothing in this section shall require a person to inform the Director or such designee of the identity of an attorney to whom disclosure was made or will be made to obtain legal advice or legal assistance with respect to the request under subsection (a).

18 U.S.C § 3511
Judicial review of requests for information

(a) The recipient of a request for records, a report, or other information under section 2709(b) of this title, section 626(a) or (b) or 627(a) of the Fair Credit Reporting Act, section 1114(a)(5)(A) of the Right to Financial Privacy Act, or section 802(a) of the National Security Act of 1947 may, in the United States district court for the district in which that person or entity does business or resides, petition for an order modifying or setting aside the request. The court may modify or set aside the request if compliance would be unreasonable, oppressive, or otherwise unlawful.

(b)

(1) The recipient of a request for records, a report, or other information under section 2709(b) of this title, section 626(a) or (b) or 627(a) of the Fair Credit Reporting Act, section 1114(a)(5)(A) of the Right to Financial Privacy Act, or section 802(a) of the National Security Act of 1947, may petition any court described in subsection (a) for an order modifying or

setting aside a nondisclosure requirement imposed in connection with such a request.

(2) If the petition is filed within one year of the request for records, *** the court may modify or set aside such a nondisclosure requirement if it finds that there is no reason to believe that disclosure may endanger the national security of the United States, interfere with a criminal, counterterrorism, or counterintelligence investigation, interfere with diplomatic relations, or endanger the life or physical safety of any person. If, at the time of the petition, the Attorney General *** or the Director of the Federal Bureau of Investigation, or in the case of a request by a department, agency, or instrumentality of the Federal Government other than the Department of Justice, the head or deputy head of such department, agency, or instrumentality, certifies that disclosure may endanger the national security of the United States or interfere with diplomatic relations, such certification shall be treated as conclusive unless the court finds that the certification was made in bad faith. ***

(c) In the case of a failure to comply with a request for records *** the Attorney General may invoke the aid of any district court of the United States within the jurisdiction in which the investigation is carried on or the person or entity resides, carries on business, or may be found, to compel compliance with the request. The court may issue an order requiring the person or entity to comply with the request. Any failure to obey the order of the court may be punished by the court as contempt thereof. Any process under this section may be served in any judicial district in which the person or entity may be found.

(d) In all proceedings under this section, subject to any right to an open hearing in a contempt proceeding, the court must close any hearing to the extent necessary to prevent an unauthorized disclosure of a request for records ***. Petitions, filings, records, orders, and subpoenas must also be kept under seal to the extent and as long as necessary to prevent the unauthorized disclosure of a request for records ***.

(e) In all proceedings under this section, the court shall, upon request of the government, review ex parte and in camera any government submission or portions thereof, which may include classified information.

50 U.S.C. § 1881a. Procedures for targeting certain persons outside the United States other than United States persons

(a) Authorization- Notwithstanding any other provision of law, *** the Attorney General and the Director of National Intelligence may authorize jointly, for a period of up to 1 year from the effective date of the authorization, the targeting of persons reasonably believed to be located outside the United States to acquire foreign intelligence information.

(b) Limitations ***

> (1) may not intentionally target any person known at the time of acquisition to be located in the United States;

> (2) may not intentionally target a person reasonably believed to be located outside the United States if the purpose of such acquisition is to target a particular, known person reasonably believed to be in the United

States;

(3) may not intentionally target a United States person reasonably believed to be located outside the United States;

(4) may not intentionally acquire any communication as to which the sender and all intended recipients are known at the time of the acquisition to be located in the United States; and

(5) shall be conducted in a manner consistent with the fourth amendment to the Constitution of the United States.

50 U.S.C. § 1805(h) No cause of action shall lie in any court against any electronic communication service provider for providing any information, facilities, or assistance in accordance with a directive under this section.

50 U.S.C. § 1881b. Certain Acquisitions Inside the United States Targeting United States Persons Outside the United States.

(a) Jurisdiction of the Foreign Intelligence Surveillance Court-

(1) IN GENERAL- The Foreign Intelligence Surveillance Court shall have jurisdiction to review an application and to enter an order approving the targeting of a United States person reasonably believed to be located outside the United States to acquire foreign intelligence information *** and such acquisition is conducted within the United States. ***

(b) Application-

(1) IN GENERAL- *** Each application *** shall include--

(A) the identity of the Federal officer making the application;

(B) the identity, *** or a description of the United States person who is the target ***;

(C) a statement of the facts and circumstances relied upon 888 [that]the target *** is--

(i) a person reasonably believed to be located outside the United States; and

(ii) a foreign power, an agent of a foreign power, or an officer or employee of a foreign power;

(D) a statement of proposed minimization procedures ***;

(E) a description of the nature of the information sought and the type of communications or activities to be subjected to acquisition;

(F) a certification made by the Attorney General *** that--

(i) the certifying official deems the information sought to be foreign intelligence information;

(ii) a significant purpose of the acquisition is to obtain foreign intelligence information;

(iii) such information cannot reasonably be obtained by normal investigative techniques;

(iv) designates the type of foreign intelligence information being sought according to the categories described in section 101(e); and

(v) includes a statement of the basis for the certification that--

(I) the information sought is the type of foreign intelligence information designated; and

(II) such information cannot reasonably be obtained by normal investigative techniques;

(G) a summary statement of the means by which the acquisition will be conducted and whether physical entry is required to effect the acquisition;

(H) the identity of any electronic communication service provider necessary to effect the acquisition ***

(I) a statement of the facts concerning any previous applications that have been made to any judge of the Foreign Intelligence Surveillance Court involving the United States person specified in the application and the action taken on each previous application; and

(J) a statement of the period of time for which the acquisition is required to be maintained, provided that such period of time shall not exceed 90 days per application. ***

50 U.S.C. § 1881(c). Other acquisitions targeting United States persons outside the United States

(3)(A) Limitations

If a United States person targeted under this subsection is reasonably believed to be located in the United States during the effective period of an order issued pursuant to subsection (c), an acquisition targeting such United States person under this section shall cease unless the targeted United States person is again reasonably believed to be located outside the United States during the effective period of such order.

50 U.S.C. § 1885b. Preemption.

(a) In General- No State shall have authority to--

(1) conduct an investigation into an electronic communication service provider's alleged assistance to an element of the intelligence community;

(2) require through regulation or any other means the disclosure of information about an electronic communication service provider's alleged assistance to an element of the intelligence community;

(3) impose any administrative sanction on an electronic communication service provider for assistance to an element of the intelligence community; or

(4) commence or maintain a civil action or other proceeding to enforce a requirement that an electronic communication service provider disclose information concerning alleged assistance to an element of the intelligence community.

(b) Suits by the United States- The United States may bring suit to enforce the provisions of this section.
***

(d) Application- This section shall apply to any investigation, action, or proceeding that is pending on or commenced after the date of the enactment of the FISA Amendments Act of 2008. ***

TREATMENT OF CLASSIFIED INFORMATION

18 U.S.C. App. III. Classified Information Procedures Act ("CIPA")
§ 1 – Definitions
(a) "Classified information", as used in this Act, means any information or material that has been determined by the United States Government pursuant to an Executive order, statute, or regulation, to require protection against unauthorized disclosure for reasons of national security ***

§ 2 – Pretrial Conference
At any time after the filing of the indictment or information, any party may move for a pretrial conference to consider matters relating to classified information that may arise in connection with the prosecution. Following such motion, or on its own motion, the court shall promptly hold a pretrial conference to establish the timing of requests for discovery, the provision of notice required by section 5 of this Act, and the initiation of the procedure established by section 6 of this Act. In addition, at the pretrial conference the court may consider any matters which relate to classified information or which may promote a fair and expeditious trial. No admission made by the defendant or by any attorney for the defendant at such a conference may be used against the defendant unless the admission is in writing and is signed by the defendant and by the attorney for the defendant.

§ 3 – Protective Orders
Upon motion of the United States, the court shall issue an order to protect against the disclosure of any classified information disclosed by the United States to any defendant in any criminal case ***

§ 4 – Discovery of Classified Information by Defendants
The court may permit the United States to make a written request for [an authorization to delete specified items in discoverable documents] in the form of a written statement to be inspected by the court alone. If the court enters an order granting relief following such an ex parte showing, the entire text of the statement of the United States shall be sealed and preserved in the records of the court to be made available to the appellate court in the event of an appeal.

§ 5 – Notice of Defendant's Intention to Disclose Classified Information
(a) Notice by Defendant.— If a defendant reasonably expects to disclose or to cause the disclosure of classified information in any manner in connection with any trial or pretrial proceeding involving the criminal prosecution of such defendant, the defendant shall, within the time specified by the court or, where no time is specified, within thirty days prior to trial, notify the attorney for the United States and the court in writing. Such notice shall include a brief description of the classified information. Whenever a defendant learns of additional classified information he reasonably expects to disclose at any such proceeding, he shall notify the attorney for the United States and the court in writing as soon as possible thereafter and shall include a brief description of the classified information. No defendant shall disclose any information known or believed to be classified in connection with

a trial or pretrial proceeding until notice has been given under this subsection and until the United States has been afforded a reasonable opportunity to seek a determination pursuant to the procedure set forth in section 6 of this Act, and until the time for the United States to appeal such determination under section 7 has expired or any appeal under section 7 by the United States is decided.

(b) Failure to Comply.— If the defendant fails to comply with the requirements of subsection (a) the court may preclude disclosure of any classified information not made the subject of notification and may prohibit the examination by the defendant of any witness with respect to any such information.

§ 6 – Procedures for Cases Involving Classified Information

(a) Motion for Hearing.— Within the time specified by the court for the filing of a motion under this section, the United States may request the court to conduct a hearing to make all determinations concerning the use, relevance, or admissibility of classified information *** Upon such a request, the court shall conduct such a hearing. Any hearing held pursuant to this subsection (or any portion of such hearing specified in the request of the Attorney General) shall be held in camera if the Attorney General certifies to the court in such petition that a public proceeding may result in the disclosure of classified information. As to each item of classified information, the court shall set forth in writing the basis for its determination. Where the United States' motion under this subsection is filed prior to the trial or pretrial proceeding, the court shall rule prior to the commencement of the relevant proceeding.

(b) Notice–

(1) Before any hearing is conducted pursuant to a request by the United States under subsection (a), the United States shall provide the defendant with notice of the classified information that is at issue. Such notice shall identify the specific classified information at issue whenever that information previously has been made available to the defendant by the United States. When the United States has not previously made the information available to the defendant in connection with the case, the information may be described by generic category *** rather than by identification of the specific information of concern to the United States.

(2) Whenever the United States requests a hearing under subsection (a), the court, upon request of the defendant, may order the United States to provide the defendant, prior to trial, such details as to the portion of the indictment or information at issue in the hearing as are needed to give the defendant fair notice to prepare for the hearing.

(c) Alternative Procedure for Disclosure of Classified Information.—

(1) Upon any determination by the court authorizing the disclosure of specific classified information under the procedures established by this section, the United States may move that, in lieu of the disclosure of such specific classified information, the court order—

(A) the substitution for such classified information of a statement admitting relevant facts that the specific classified information would tend to prove; or

(B) the substitution for such classified information of a summary of the specific classified information. The court shall grant such a motion of the United States if it finds that the statement or summary will provide the defendant with substantially the same ability to make his defense as would disclosure of the specific classified information. The court shall hold a hearing on any motion under this section. Any such hearing shall be held in camera at the request of the Attorney General.

(2) The United States may, in connection with a motion under paragraph (1), submit to the court an affidavit of the Attorney General certifying that disclosure of classified information would cause identifiable damage to the national security of the United States and explaining the basis for the classification of such information. If so requested by the United States, the court shall examine such affidavit in camera and ex parte.

(d) Sealing of Records of In Camera Hearings.— If at the close of an in camera hearing under this Act *** the court determines that the classified information at issue may not be disclosed or elicited at the trial or pretrial proceeding, the record of such in camera hearing shall be sealed and preserved by the court for use in the event of an appeal. The defendant may seek reconsideration of the court's determination prior to or during trial.

(e) Prohibition on Disclosure of Classified Information by Defendant, Relief for Defendant When United States Opposes Disclosure.—

(1) Whenever the court denies a motion by the United States that it issue an order under subsection (c) and the United States files with the court an affidavit of the Attorney General objecting to disclosure of the classified information at issue, the court shall order that the defendant not disclose or cause the disclosure of such information.

(2) Whenever a defendant is prevented by an order under paragraph (1) from disclosing or causing the disclosure of classified information, the court shall dismiss the indictment or information; except that, when the court determines that the interests of justice would not be served by dismissal of the indictment or information, the court shall order such other action, in lieu of dismissing the indictment or information, as the court determines is appropriate. Such action may include, but need not be limited to—

(A) dismissing specified counts of the indictment or information;

(B) finding against the United States on any issue as to which the excluded classified information relates; or

(C) striking or precluding all or part of the testimony of a witness. An order under this paragraph shall not take effect until the court has afforded the United States an opportunity to appeal such order under section 7, and thereafter to withdraw its objection to the disclosure of the classified information at issue.

(f) Reciprocity.— Whenever the court determines pursuant to subsection (a) that classified information may be disclosed in connection with a trial or pretrial proceeding, the court shall, unless the interests of fairness do not so require, order the United States to provide the defendant with the information it expects to use to rebut the classified information. The court may place the United States under a continuing duty to disclose such rebuttal information. If the United States fails to comply with its obligation under this subsection, the court may exclude any evidence not made the subject of a required disclosure and may prohibit the examination by the United States of any witness with respect to such information.

§ 9 – Security Procedures

(a) Within one hundred and twenty days of the date of the enactment of this Act, the Chief Justice of the United States, in consultation with the Attorney General, the Director of National Intelligence, and the Secretary of Defense, shall prescribe rules establishing procedures for the protection against unauthorized disclosure of any classified information in the custody of the United States district courts, courts of appeal, or Supreme Court. Such rules, and any changes in such rules, shall be submitted to the appropriate committees of Congress and shall become effective forty-five days after such submission. ***

50 U.S.C. 1806(f) In camera and ex parte review by district court

Whenever a court or other authority is notified pursuant to subsection (c) or (d) of this section, or whenever a motion is made pursuant to subsection (e) of this section, or whenever any motion or request is made by an aggrieved person pursuant to any other statute or rule of the United States or any State before any court or other authority of the United States or any State to discover or obtain applications or orders or other materials relating to electronic surveillance or to discover, obtain, or suppress evidence or information obtained or derived from electronic surveillance under this chapter, the United States district court or, where the motion is made before another authority, the United States district court in the same district as the authority, shall, notwithstanding any other law, if the Attorney General files an affidavit under oath that disclosure or an adversary hearing would harm the national security of the United States, review in camera and ex parte the application, order, and such other materials relating to the surveillance as may be necessary to determine whether the surveillance of the aggrieved person was lawfully authorized and conducted. In making this determination, the court may disclose to the aggrieved person, under appropriate security procedures and protective orders, portions of the application, order, or other materials relating to the surveillance only where such disclosure is necessary to make an accurate determination of the legality of the surveillance.

DATA MINING AND PRIVACY

U.S. Const. Amend. 4: The right of the people to be secure in their persons, houses, papers, and effects, against unreasonable searches and seizures, shall not be violated, and no Warrants shall issue, but upon probable cause, supported by Oath or affirmation, and particularly describing the place to be searched, and the persons or things to be seized.

5 U.S.C. §552a(e) Agency Requirements. – Each agency that maintains a system of records shall –

(1) maintain in its records only such information about an individual as is relevant and necessary to accomplish a purpose of the agency required to be accomplished by statute or by executive order of the President; ***

(7) maintain no record describing how any individual exercises rights guaranteed by the First Amendment unless expressly authorized by statute ***

Freedom of Information Act

5 U.S.C. § 552. Public information; agency rules, opinions, orders, records, and proceedings

(b) [exceptions] ***

(7) records or information compiled for law enforcement purposes, but only to the extent that the production of such law enforcement records or information

(A) could reasonably be expected to interfere with enforcement proceedings,

(B) would deprive a person of a right to a fair trial or an impartial adjudication,

(C) could reasonably be expected to constitute an unwarranted invasion of personal privacy,

(D) could reasonably be expected to disclose the identity of a confidential source, including a State, local, or foreign agency or authority or any private institution which furnished information on a confidential basis, and, in the case of a record or information compiled by a criminal law enforcement authority in the course of a criminal investigation or by an agency conducting a lawful national security intelligence investigation, information furnished by a confidential source,

(E) would disclose techniques and procedures for law enforcement investigations or prosecutions, or would disclose guidelines for law enforcement investigations or prosecutions if such disclosure could reasonably be expected to risk circumvention of the law, or

(F) could reasonably be expected to endanger the life or physical safety of any individual.

DETENTION, TREATMENT, AND RELEASE

U.S. Const., Art. 1 § 9: ***The Privilege of the Writ of Habeas Corpus shall not be suspended, unless when in Cases of Rebellion or Invasion the public Safety may require it.***

United Nations Convention against Torture
Article 3

1. No State Party shall expel, return ("refouler") or extradite a person to another State where there are substantial grounds for believing that he would be in danger of being subjected to torture.

2. For the purpose of determining whether there are such grounds, the competent authorities shall take into account all relevant considerations

including, where applicable, the existence in the State concerned of a consistent pattern of gross, flagrant or mass violations of human rights.

8 U.S.C. § 1231 note

UNITED STATES POLICY WITH RESPECT TO INVOLUNTARY RETURN OF PERSONS IN DANGER OF SUBJECTION TO TORTURE

(a) Policy. - It shall be the policy of the United States not to

expel, extradite, or otherwise effect the involuntary return of any person to a country in which there are substantial grounds for believing the person would be in danger of being subjected to torture, regardless of whether the person is physically present in the United States

18 U.S.C. § 3144. Release or detention of a material witness.

If it appears from an affidavit filed by a party that the testimony of a person is material in a criminal proceeding, and if it is shown that it may become impracticable to secure the presence of the person by subpoena, a judicial officer may order the arrest of the person ***

28 U.S.C. § 1350 note.

Pub. L. 102–256, Mar. 12, 1992, 106 Stat. 73, provided that:

"SECTION 1. SHORT TITLE.

"This Act may be cited as the 'Torture Victim Protection Act of 1991'.

"SEC. 2. ESTABLISHMENT OF CIVIL ACTION.

"(a) Liability.—An individual who, under actual or apparent authority, or color of law, of any foreign nation—

"(1) subjects an individual to torture shall, in a civil action, be liable for damages to that individual; or

"(2) subjects an individual to extrajudicial killing shall, in a civil action, be liable for damages to the individual's legal representative, or to any person who may be a claimant in an action for wrongful death. ***

10 U.S.C. § 950g. Review by United States Court of Appeals for the District of Columbia Circuit; writ of certiorari to Supreme Court

(a) Exclusive Appellate Jurisdiction.— Except as provided in subsection (b), the United States Court of Appeals for the District of Columbia Circuit shall have exclusive jurisdiction to determine the validity of a final judgment rendered by a military commission (as approved by the convening authority and, where applicable, the United States Court of Military Commission Review) under this chapter. ***

(d) Scope and Nature of Review.— The United States Court of Appeals for the District of Columbia Circuit may act under this section only with respect to the findings and sentence as approved by the convening authority and as affirmed or set aside as incorrect in law by the United States Court of Military Commission Review, and shall take action only with respect to matters of law, including the sufficiency of the evidence to support the verdict.

(e) Review by Supreme Court.— The Supreme Court may review by writ of certiorari pursuant to section 1254 of title 28 the final judgment of the

United States Court of Appeals for the District of Columbia Circuit under this section.

42 U.S.C. § 2000dd. Prohibition on cruel, inhuman, or degrading treatment or punishment of persons under custody or control of the United States Government
(a) In general
No individual in the custody or under the physical control of the United States Government, regardless of nationality or physical location, shall be subject to cruel, inhuman, or degrading treatment or punishment.
(b) Construction
Nothing in this section shall be construed to impose any geographical limitation on the applicability of the prohibition against cruel, inhuman, or degrading treatment or punishment under this section. ***
(d) Cruel, inhuman, or degrading treatment or punishment defined
In this section, the term "cruel, inhuman, or degrading treatment or punishment" means the cruel, unusual, and inhumane treatment or punishment prohibited by the Fifth, Eighth, and Fourteenth Amendments to the Constitution of the United States, as defined in the United States Reservations, Declarations and Understandings to the United Nations Convention Against Torture and Other Forms of Cruel, Inhuman or Degrading Treatment or Punishment done at New York, December 10, 1984.

Military Commissions Act of 2006
28 U.S.C. § 2241. Power to grant writ [of habeas corpus]
(a) Writs of habeas corpus may be granted by the Supreme Court, any justice thereof, the district courts and any circuit judge within their respective jurisdictions. The order of a circuit judge shall be entered in the records of the district court of the district wherein the restraint complained of is had.
(b) The Supreme Court, any justice thereof, and any circuit judge may decline to entertain an application for a writ of habeas corpus and may transfer the application for hearing and determination to the district court having jurisdiction to entertain it.
(c) The writ of habeas corpus shall not extend to a prisoner unless--
    (1) He is in custody under or by color of the authority of the United States or is committed for trial before some court thereof; or
    (2) He is in custody for an act done or omitted in pursuance of an Act of Congress, or an order, process, judgment or decree of a court or judge of the United States; or
    (3) He is in custody in violation of the Constitution or laws or treaties of the United States; or
    (4) He, being a citizen of a foreign state and domiciled therein is in custody for an act done or omitted under any alleged right, title, authority, privilege, protection, or exemption claimed under the commission, order or sanction of any foreign state, or under color thereof, the validity and effect of which depend upon the law of nations; or
    (5) It is necessary to bring him into court to testify or for trial. ***

(e) (1) No court, justice, or judge shall have jurisdiction to hear or consider an application for a writ of habeas corpus filed by or on behalf of an alien detained by the United States who has been determined by the United States to have been properly detained as an enemy combatant or is awaiting such determination.

(2) Except as provided in paragraphs (2) and (3) of section 1005(e) of the Detainee Treatment Act of 2005 (10 U.S.C. 801 note), no court, justice, or judge shall have jurisdiction to hear or consider any other action against the United States or its agents relating to any aspect of the detention, transfer, treatment, trial, or conditions of confinement of an alien who is or was detained by the United States and has been determined by the United States to have been properly detained as an enemy combatant or is awaiting such determination. ***

18 U.S.C. § 2441

(d) Common Article 3 Violations

(1) PROHIBITED CONDUCT.—In subsection (c)(3), the term 'grave breach of common Article 3' means ***:

(A) TORTURE.—The act of a person who commits, or conspires or attempts to commit, an act specifically intended to inflict severe physical or mental pain or suffering (other than pain or suffering incidental to lawful sanctions) upon another person within his custody or physical control for the purpose of obtaining information or a confession, punishment, intimidation, coercion, or any reason based on discrimination of any kind.

(B) CRUEL OR INHUMAN TREATMENT.—

The act of a person who commits, or conspires or attempts to commit, an act intended to inflict severe or serious physical or mental pain or suffering (other than pain or suffering incidental to lawful sanctions), including serious physical abuse, upon another within his custody or control.
***

(2) DEFINITIONS.—In the case of an offense under subsection (a) by reason of subsection (c)(3)— ***

(D) the term 'serious physical pain or suffering' shall be applied for purposes of paragraph (1)(B) as meaning bodily injury that involves—

(i) a substantial risk of death;

(ii) extreme physical pain;

(iii) a burn or physical disfigurement of a serious nature (other than cuts, abrasions, or bruises); or

(iv) significant loss or impairment of the function of a bodily member, organ, or mental faculty; and

(E) the term 'serious mental pain or suffering' shall be applied for purposes of paragraph (1)(B) in accordance with the meaning given the term 'severe mental pain or suffering' (as defined in section 2340(2) of this title), except that—

(i) the term 'serious' shall replace the term 'severe' where it appears; and

(ii) as to conduct occurring after the date of the enactment of the Military Commissions Act of 2006, the term 'serious and non-transitory mental harm (which need not be prolonged)' shall replace the term 'prolonged mental harm' where it appears. ***

(5) DEFINITION OF GRAVE BREACHES.—The definitions in this subsection are intended only to define the grave breaches of common Article 3 and not the full scope of United States obligations under that Article." ***

(c) ADDITIONAL PROHIBITION ON CRUEL, INHUMAN, OR DEGRADING TREATMENT OR PUNISHMENT.—

(1) IN GENERAL.—No individual in the custody or under the physical control of the United States Government, regardless of nationality or physical location, shall be subject to cruel, inhuman, or degrading treatment or punishment.

(2) CRUEL, INHUMAN, OR DEGRADING TREATMENT OR PUNISHMENT DEFINED.—In this sub section, the term "cruel, inhuman, or degrading treatment or punishment" means cruel, unusual and inhumane treatment or punishment prohibited by the Fifth, Eighth, and Fourteenth Amendments to the Constitution of the United States, as defined in the United States Reservations, Declarations and Understandings to the United Nations Convention Against Torture and Other Forms of Cruel, Inhuman or Degrading Treatment or Punishment done at New York, December 10, 1984.

(3) COMPLIANCE.—The President shall take action to ensure compliance with this subsection, including through the establishment of administrative rules and procedures.

18 U.S.C. § 2441 notes
Implementation of Treaty Obligations
Pub. L. 109–366, § 6(a), Oct. 17, 2006, 120 Stat. 2632, provided that:
(a) IMPLEMENTATION OF TREATY OBLIGATIONS.—

(1) IN GENERAL.—The acts enumerated in subsection (d) of section 2441 of title 18, United States Code, as added by subsection (b) of this section, and in subsection (c) of this section, constitute violations of common Article 3 of the Geneva Conventions prohibited by United States law.

(2) PROHIBITION ON GRAVE BREACHES.—The provisions of section 2441 of title 18, United States Code, as amended by this section, fully satisfy the obligation under Article 129 of the Third Geneva Convention for the United States to provide effective penal sanctions for grave breaches which are encompassed in common Article 3 in the context of an armed conflict not of an international character. No foreign or international source of law shall supply a basis for a rule of decision in the courts of the United States in interpreting the prohibitions enumerated in subsection (d) of such section 2441.

(3) INTERPRETATION BY THE PRESIDENT.—

(A) As provided by the Constitution and by this section, the President has the authority for the United States to interpret the meaning and application of the Geneva Conventions and to promulgate higher standards and administrative regulations for violations of treaty obligations which are not grave breaches of the Geneva Conventions. ***

28 U.S.C. § 2241 notes
Treaty Obligations Not Establishing Grounds for Certain Claims
Pub. L. 109–366, § 5, Oct. 17, 2006, 120 Stat. 2631, provided that:

(a) IN GENERAL.—No person may invoke the Geneva Conventions or any protocols thereto in any habeas corpus or other civil action or proceeding to which the United States, or a current or former officer, employee, member of the Armed Forces, or other agent of the United States is a party as a source of rights in any court of the United States or its States or territories. ***

10 U.S.C. § 948r. Compulsory self-incrimination prohibited; treatment of statements obtained by torture and other statements

(a) IN GENERAL.—No person shall be required to testify against himself at a proceeding of a military commission under this chapter.

(b) EXCLUSION OF STATEMENTS OBTAINED BY TORTURE.—A statement obtained by use of torture shall not be admissible in a military commission under this chapter, except against a person accused of torture as evidence that the statement was made.

(c) STATEMENTS OBTAINED BEFORE ENACTMENT OF DETAINEE TREATMENT ACT OF 2005.—A statement obtained before December 30, 2005 (the date of the enactment of the Defense Treatment Act of 2005) in which the degree of coercion is disputed may be admitted only if the military judge finds that—

(1) the totality of the circumstances renders the statement reliable and possessing sufficient probative value; and

(2) the interests of justice would best be served by admission of the statement into evidence.

(d) STATEMENTS OBTAINED AFTER ENACTMENT OF DETAINEE TREATMENT ACT OF 2005.—A statement obtained on or after December 30, 2005 (the date of the enactment of the Defense Treatment Act of 2005) in which the degree of coercion is disputed may be admitted only if the military judge finds that—

(1) the totality of the circumstances renders the statement reliable and possessing sufficient probative value;

(2) the interests of justice would best be served by admission of the statement into evidence; and

Restatement (Third) of Foreign Relations Law
Restatement § 402 – Bases of Extraterritorial Jurisdiction

(1) (a) conduct that, wholly or in substantial part, takes place within its territory;

(b) the status of persons, or interests in things, present within its territory;

(c) conduct outside its territory that has or is intended to have substantial effect within its territory;

(2) the activities, interests, status, or relations of its nationals outside as well as within its territory; and

(3) certain conduct outside its territory by persons not its nationals that is directed against the security of the state or against a limited class of other state interests.

Restatement § 403(2) –Reasonableness of Extraterritorial Jurisdiction

(a) the link of the activity to the territory of the regulating state, i.e., the extent to which the activity takes place within the territory, or has substantial, direct, and foreseeable effect upon or in the territory;

(b) the connections, such as nationality, residence, or economic activity, between the regulating state and the person principally responsible for the activity to be regulated, or between that state and those whom the regulation is designed to protect;

(c) the character of the activity to be regulated, the importance of regulation to the regulating state, the extent to which other states regulate such activities, and the degree to which the desirability of such regulation is generally accepted;

(d) the existence of justified expectations that might be protected or hurt by the regulation;

(e) the importance of the regulation to the international political, legal, or economic system;

(f) the extent to which the regulation is consistent with the traditions of the international system;

(g) the extent to which another state may have an interest in regulating the activity; and

(h) the likelihood of conflict with regulation by another state.

Restatement § 404 cmt. a

Expanding class of universal offenses. This section, and the corresponding section concerning jurisdiction to adjudicate, § 423, recognize that international law permits any state to apply its laws to punish certain offenses although the state has no links of territory with the offense, or of nationality with the offender (or even the victim). Universal jurisdiction over the specified offenses is a result of universal condemnation of those activities and general interest in cooperating to suppress them, as reflected in widely-accepted international agreements and resolutions of international organizations. These offenses are subject to universal jurisdiction as a matter of customary law. Universal jurisdiction for additional offenses is provided by international agreements, but it remains to be determined whether universal jurisdiction over a particular offense has become customary law for states not party to such an agreement. See § 102, Comment *f*. A universal offense is generally not subject to limitations of time. There has been wide condemnation of terrorism but international agreements to punish it have not, as of 1987, been widely adhered to, principally because of inability to agree on a definition of the offense. The United States and six states (all in Latin America) have adopted a Convention to Prevent and Punish the Acts of

Terrorism Taking the Form of Crimes against Persons and Related Extortion that are of International Significance, 27 U.S.T. 3949, T.I.A.S. No. 8413 (1976). Universal jurisdiction is increasingly accepted for certain acts of terrorism, such as assaults on the life or physical integrity of diplomatic personnel, kidnapping, and indiscriminate violent assaults on people at large. See also § 477, Reporters' Note 6.

8 U.S.C § 1481 – Expatriation of Immigrants

(a) A person who is a national of the United States *** shall lose his nationality by voluntarily performing any of the following acts with the intention of relinquishing United States nationality-

(1) obtaining naturalization in a foreign state upon his own application or upon an application filed by a duly authorized agent, after having attained the age of eighteen years; or

(2) taking an oath or making an affirmation or other formal declaration of allegiance to a foreign state or a political subdivision thereof, after having attained the age of eighteen years; or

(3) entering, or serving in, the armed forces of a foreign state if (A) such armed forces are engaged in hostilities against the United States, or (B) such persons serve as a commissioned or non-commissioned officer; or

(4) (A) accepting, serving in, or performing the duties of any office, post, or employment under the government of a foreign state or a political subdivision thereof, after attaining the age of eighteen years if he has or acquires the nationality of such foreign state ***

(5) making a formal renunciation of nationality before a diplomatic or consular officer of the United States in a foreign state **

(6) making in the United States a formal written renunciation of nationality ***

(7) committing any act of treason against, or attempting by force to overthrow, or bearing arms against, the United States ***

MILITARY FORCE AND TERRORISM

Authorization for Use of Military Force, September 18, 2001, Public Law 107-40 [S. J. RES. 23]

§ 2. AUTHORIZATION FOR USE OF UNITED STATES ARMED FORCES.

(a) IN GENERAL- That the President is authorized to use all necessary and appropriate force against those nations, organizations, or persons he determines planned, authorized, committed, or aided the terrorist attacks that occurred on September 11, 2001, or harbored such organizations or persons, in order to prevent any future acts of international terrorism against the United States by such nations, organizations or persons.

United Nations Charter

Article 2(4). All Members shall refrain in their international relations from the threat or use of force against the territorial integrity or political independence of any state, or in any other manner inconsistent with the Purposes of the United Nations.

Article 51. Nothing in the present Charter shall impair the right of individual or collective self-defence if an armed attack occurs against a Member of the United Nations, until the Security Council has taken measures necessary to maintain international peace and security. Measures taken by Members in the exercise of the right of self-defence shall be immediately reported to the Security Council and shall not in any way affect the authority and responsibility of the Security Council under the present Carter to take at any time such action as it deems necessary in order to maintain or restore international peace and security.

European Convention on Human Rights ("ECHR")
Article 2

1. Everyone's right to life shall be protected by law. No one shall be deprived of his life intentionally save in the execution of a sentence of a court following his conviction of a crime for which this penalty is provided by law.
2. Deprivation of life shall not be regarded as inflicted in contravention of this Article when it results from the use of force which is no more than absolutely necessary: (a) in defence of any person from unlawful violence; (b) in order to effect a lawful arrest or to prevent the escape of a person lawfully detained; (c) in action lawfully taken for the purpose of quelling a riot or insurrection.

First Protocol of the Geneva Conventions
Article 51 – Protection of the Civilian Population

1. The civilian population and individual civilians shall enjoy general protection against dangers arising from military operations. To give effect to this protection, the following rules, which are additional to other applicable rules of international law, shall be observed in all circumstances.
2. The civilian population as such, as well as individual civilians, shall not be the object of attack. Acts or threats of violence the primary purpose of which is to spread terror among the civilian population are prohibited.
3. Civilians shall enjoy the protection afforded by this Section, unless and for such time as they take a direct part in hostilities.
4. Indiscriminate attacks are prohibited. Indiscriminate attacks are:
   a. those which are not directed at a specific military objective;
   b. those which employ a method or means of combat which cannot be directed at a specific military objective; or
   c. those which employ a method or means of combat the effects of which cannot be limited as required by this Protocol; and consequently, in each such case, are of a nature to strike military objectives and civilians or civilian objects without distinction.
5. Among others, the following types of attacks are to be considered as indiscriminate:
   a. an attack by bombardment by any methods or means which treats as a single military objective a number of clearly separated and distinct military objectives located in a city, town, village or other area containing a similar concentration of civilians or civilian objects; and

b. an attack which may be expected to cause incidental loss of civilian life, injury to civilians, damage to civilian objects, or a combination thereof, which would be excessive in relation to the concrete and direct military advantage anticipated.

6. Attacks against the civilian population or civilians by way of reprisals are prohibited.

7. The presence or movements of the civilian population or individual civilians shall not be used to render certain points or areas immune from military operations, in particular in attempts to shield military objectives from attacks or to shield, favor or impede military operations. The Parties to the conflict shall not direct the movement of the civilian population or individual civilians in order to attempt to shield military objectives from attacks or to shield military operations.

8. Any violation of these prohibitions shall not release the Parties to the conflict from their legal obligations with respect to the civilian population and civilians, including the obligation to take the precautionary measures provided for in Article 57.

Article 57 – Precautions in Attack

1. In the conduct of military operations, constant care shall be taken to spare the civilian population, civilians and civilian objects.

2. With respect to attacks, the following precautions shall be taken:
   a. those who plan or decide upon an attack shall:
      i. do everything feasible to verify that the objectives to be attacked are neither civilians nor civilian objects and are not subject to special protection but are military objectives within the meaning of paragraph 2 of Article 52 and that it is not prohibited by the provisions of this Protocol to attack them;
      ii. take all feasible precautions in the choice of means and methods of attack with a view to avoiding, and in any event to minimizing, incidental loss of civilian life, injury to civilians and damage to civilian objects;
      iii. refrain from deciding to launch any attack which may be expected to cause incidental loss of civilian life, injury to civilians, damage to civilian objects, or a combination thereof, which would be excessive in relation to the concrete and direct military advantage anticipated;
   b. an attack shall be canceled or suspended if it becomes apparent that the objective is not a military one or is subject to special protection or that the attack may be expected to cause incidental loss of civilian life, injury to civilians, damage to civilian objects, or a combination thereof, which would be excessive in relation to the concrete and direct military advantage anticipated;
   c. effective advance warning shall be given of attacks which may affect the civilian population, unless circumstances do not permit.

3. When a choice is possible between several military objectives for obtaining a similar military advantage, the objective to be selected shall be that the attack on which may be expected to cause the least danger to civilian lives and to civilian objects.

4. In the conduct of military operations at sea or in the air, each Party to the conflict shall, in conformity with its rights and duties under the rules of international law applicable in armed conflict, take all reasonable precautions to avoid losses of civilian lives and damage to civilian objects

5. No provision of this article may be construed as authorizing any attacks against the civilian population, civilians or civilian objects.

Fourth Geneva Convention
Article 3
No protected person may be punished for an offence he or she has not personally committed. Collective penalties and likewise all measures of intimidation or of terrorism are prohibited.*** Reprisals against protected persons and their property are prohibited.

Article 5
Where in the territory of a Party to the conflict, the latter is satisfied that an individual protected person is definitely suspected of or engaged in activities hostile to the security of the State, such individual person shall not be entitled to claim such rights and privileges under the present Convention as would, if exercised in the favour of such individual person, be prejudicial to the security of such State.

Where in occupied territory an individual protected person is detained as a spy or saboteur, or as a person under definite suspicion of activity hostile to the security of the Occupying Power, such person shall, in those cases where absolute military security so requires, be regarded as having forfeited rights of communication under the present Convention.

In each case, such persons shall nevertheless be treated with humanity and, in case of trial, shall not be deprived of the rights of fair and regular trial prescribed by the present Convention. They shall also be granted the full rights and privileges of a protected person under the present Convention at the earliest date consistent with the security of the State or Occupying Power, as the case may be.

Article 49
Individual or mass forcible transfers, as well as deportations of protected persons from occupied territory to the territory of the Occupying Power or to that of any other country, occupied or not, are prohibited, regardless of their motive.

Defense (Emergency) Regulations of Israel
R. 119 – "Seizure of Property under Israeli Law of War"
(I) A Military Commander may by order direct the forfeiture to the Government of Palestine [read: the Government of Israel] ... of any house, structure or land situated in any area, town, village, quarter or street the inhabitants or some of the inhabitants of which he is satisfied have committed, or attempted to commit, or abetted the commission of, or been accessories after the fact to the commission of, any offence against these Regulations involving violence or intimidation or any Military Court offence; and when any house, structure or land is forfeited as aforesaid, the Military

Commander may destroy the house or the structure or anything in or on the house, the structure or the land...'

USE OF MILITARY FORCE FOR LAW ENFORCEMENT
Posse Comitatus Act
18 U.S.C. § 1365 – "Posse Comitatus Restriction"
Whoever, except in cases and under circumstances expressly authorized by the Constitution or Act of Congress, willfully uses any part of the Army or the Air force as a posse comitatus or otherwise to execute the laws shall be fined under this title or imprisoned not more than two years, or both.

10 U.S.C. § 371 – Use of Information Collected by the Military
(a) The Secretary of Defense may, in accordance with other applicable law, provide to Federal, State, or local civilian law enforcement officials any information collected during the normal course of military training or operations that may be relevant to a violation of any Federal or State law within the jurisdiction of such officials.
(b) The needs of civilian law enforcement officials for information shall, to the maximum extent practicable, be taken into account in the planning and execution of military training or operations.
(c) The Secretary of Defense shall ensure, to the extent consistent with national security, that intelligence information held by the Department of Defense and relevant to drug interdiction or other civilian law enforcement matters is provided promptly to appropriate civilian law enforcement officials.

10 U.S.C. § 372 – Use of Military Equipment or Facilities
(a) In general.--The Secretary of Defense may, in accordance with other applicable law, make available any equipment (including associated supplies or spare parts), base facility, or research facility of the Department of Defense to any Federal, State, or local civilian law enforcement official for law enforcement purposes. ***

10 U.S.C. § 373 – Training and Advising Civilian Law Enforcement
The Secretary of Defense may, in accordance with other applicable law, make Department of Defense personnel available--
> (1) to train Federal, State, and local civilian law enforcement officials in the operation and maintenance of equipment, including equipment made available under section 372 of this title; and
> (2) to provide such law enforcement officials with expert advice relevant to the purposes of this chapter.

10 U.S.C. § 374 – Maintenance and Operation of Equipment
(a) The Secretary of Defense may, in accordance with other applicable law, make Department of Defense personnel available for the maintenance of

equipment for Federal, State, and local civilian law enforcement officials, including equipment made available under section 372 of this title. ***

(4) In this subsection:

(A) The term "Federal law enforcement agency" means a Federal agency with jurisdiction to enforce any of the following: ***

(v) Any law, foreign or domestic, prohibiting terrorist activities.

(B) The term "land area of the United States" includes the land area of any territory, commonwealth, or possession of the United States.

(c) The Secretary of Defense may, in accordance with other applicable law, make Department of Defense personnel available to any Federal, State, or local civilian law enforcement agency to operate equipment for purposes other than described in subsection (b)(2) only to the extent that such support does not involve direct participation by such personnel in a civilian law enforcement operation unless such direct participation is otherwise authorized by law.

10 U.S.C. § 375 – Restriction on Direct Participation by Military Personnel

The Secretary of Defense shall prescribe such regulations as may be necessary to ensure that any activity (including the provision of any equipment or facility or the assignment or detail of any personnel) under this chapter does not include or permit direct participation by a member of the Army, Navy, Air Force, or Marine Corps in a search, seizure, arrest, or other similar activity unless participation in such activity by such member is otherwise authorized by law.

10 U.S.C. § 380 – Enhancement of Cooperation with Civilian Law Enforcement

(a) The Secretary of Defense, in cooperation with the Attorney General, shall conduct an annual briefing of law enforcement personnel of each State (including law enforcement personnel of the political subdivisions of each State) regarding information, training, technical support, and equipment and facilities available to civilian law enforcement personnel from the Department of Defense. ***

TERRORISM, IMMIGRATION, AND BORDER SECURITY

8 U.S.C. § 1158

(a) Authority to apply for asylum

(1) In general. - Any alien who is physically present in the United States or who arrives in the United States (whether or not at a designated port of arrival and including an alien who is brought to the United States after having been interdicted in international or United States waters), irrespective of such alien's status, may apply for asylum in accordance with this section or, where applicable, section 235(b).

(2) Exceptions.

(A) Safe third country. - Paragraph (1) shall not apply to an alien if the Attorney General determines that the alien may be removed, pursuant to a bilateral or multilateral agreement, to a country (other than the country of the alien's nationality or, in the case of an alien having no nationality, the country of the alien's last habitual residence) in which the alien's life or freedom would not be threatened on account of race, religion, nationality, membership in a particular social group, or political opinion, and where the alien would have access to a full and fair procedure for determining a claim to asylum or equivalent temporary protection, unless the Attorney General finds that it is in the public interest for the alien to receive asylum in the United States. ***

(E) APPLICABILITY- Subparagraphs (A) and (B) shall not apply to an unaccompanied alien child (as defined in section 462(g) of the Homeland Security Act of 2002 (6 U.S.C. 279(g))).

(3) Limitation on judicial review. No court shall have jurisdiction to review any determination of the Attorney General under paragraph (2).

(b) Conditions for Granting Asylum. –

(1) In general. –

(A) ELIGIBILITY- The Secretary of Homeland Security or the Attorney General may grant asylum to an alien who has applied for asylum in accordance with the requirements and procedures established by **4/** the Secretary of Homeland Security or the Attorney General under this section if the Secretary of Homeland Security or the Attorney General determines that such alien is a refugee within the meaning of section 101(a)(42)(A).

(B) BURDEN OF PROOF-

(i) IN GENERAL- The burden of proof is on the applicant to establish that the applicant is a refugee, within the meaning of section 101(a)(42)(A) . To establish that the applicant is a refugee within the meaning of such section, the applicant must establish that race, religion, nationality, membership in a particular social group, or political opinion was or will be at least one central reason for persecuting the applicant. ***

(2) Exceptions. –

(A) In general. - Paragraph (1) shall not apply to an alien if the Attorney General determines that

(i) the alien ordered, incited, assisted, or otherwise participated in the persecution of any person on account of race, religion, nationality, membership in a particular social group, or political opinion;

(ii) the alien, having been convicted by a final judgment of a particularly serious crime, constitutes a danger to the community of the United States;

(iii) there are serious reasons for believing that the alien has committed a serious nonpolitical crime outside the United States prior to the arrival of the alien in the United States;

(iv) there are reasonable grounds for regarding the alien as a danger to the security of the United States;

(v) the alien is described in subclause (I), (II), (III), (IV), or (VI) of section 212(a)(3)(B)(i) or section 237(a)(4)(B) (relating to terrorist activity), unless, in the case only of an alien described in subclause (IV) of section 212(a)(3)(B)(i) , the Attorney General determines, in the Attorney General's discretion, that there are not reasonable grounds for regarding the alien as a danger to the security of the United States; or

(vi) the alien was firmly resettled in another country prior to arriving in the United States. ***

(C) Additional limitations. - The Attorney General may by regulation establish additional limitations and conditions, consistent with this section, under which an alien shall be ineligible for asylum under paragraph (1).

(D) No judicial review. - There shall be no judicial review of a determination of the Attorney General under subparagraph (A)(v).

(c)(3) Removal when asylum is terminated. - An alien described in paragraph (2) is subject to any applicable grounds of inadmissibility or deportability under section 212(a) and 237(a) , and the alien's removal or return shall be directed by the Attorney General in accordance with sections 240 and 241 . ***

(5) Consideration of asylum applications. –

(A) Procedures. - The procedure established under paragraph (1) shall provide that –

(i) asylum cannot be granted until the identity of the applicant has been checked against all appropriate records or databases maintained by the Attorney General and by the Secretary of State, including the Automated Visa Lookout System, to determine any grounds on which the alien may be inadmissible to or deportable from the United States, or ineligible to apply for or be granted asylum;

(ii) in the absence of exceptional circumstances, the initial interview or hearing on the asylum application shall commence not later than 45 days after the date an application is filed; ***

(B) Additional regulatory conditions. - The Attorney General may provide by regulation for any other conditions or limitations on the consideration of an application for asylum not inconsistent with this Act.

8 U.S.C. § 1182(a)(3)(B) – Terrorist activities

Any alien who-

(I) has engaged in a terrorist activity,

(II) a consular officer, the Attorney General, or the Secretary of Homeland Security knows, or has reasonable ground to believe, is engaged in or is likely to engage after entry in any terrorist activity (as defined in clause (iv));

(III) has, under circumstances indicating an intention to cause death or serious bodily harm, incited terrorist activity;

(IV) is a representative (as defined in clause (v)) of—

(aa) a terrorist organization (as defined in clause (vi)); or (bb) a political, social, or other group that endorses or espouses terrorist activity;

(V) is a member of a terrorist organization described in subclause (I) or (II) of clause (vi);

(VI) is a member of a terrorist organization described in clause (vi)(III), unless the alien can demonstrate by clear and convincing evidence that the alien did not know, and should not reasonably have known, that the organization was a terrorist organization;

(VII) endorses or espouses terrorist activity or persuades others to endorse or espouse terrorist activity or support a terrorist organization;

(VIII) has received military-type training (as defined in section 2339D(c)(1) of title 18, United States Code) from or on behalf of any organization that, at the time the training was received, was a terrorist organization (as defined in clause (vi)); or

(IX) is the spouse or child of an alien who is inadmissible under this subparagraph, if the activity causing the alien to be found inadmissible occurred within the last 5 years, is inadmissible.

8 U.S.C. § 1231(a)(4)(B) – Withholding Deportation

Exception for removal of nonviolent offenders prior to completion of sentence of imprisonment.-The Attorney General is authorized to remove an alien in accordance with applicable procedures under this Act before the alien has completed a sentence of imprisonment-

(i) in the case of an alien in the custody of the Attorney General, if the Attorney General determines that (I) the alien is confined pursuant to a final conviction for a nonviolent offense (other than an offense related to smuggling or harboring of aliens or an offense described in section 101(a)(43)(B) , (C) , (E) , (I) , or (L) of this title and (II) the removal of the alien is appropriate and in the best interest of the United States; or

(ii) in the case of an alien in the custody of a State (or a political subdivision of a State), if the chief State official exercising authority with respect to the incarceration of the alien determines that (I) the alien is confined pursuant to a final conviction for a nonviolent offense (other than an offense described in section 101(a)(43)(C) or (E)), (II) the removal is appropriate and in the best interest of the State, and (III) submits a written request to the Attorney General that such alien be so removed.

8 U.S.C. § 1253(h)(1) [pre-1996] The Attorney General shall not deport or return any alien *** to a country if the Attorney General determines that such alien's life or freedom would be threatened in such country on account of race, religion, nationality, membership in a particular social group, or political opinion [unless]

(2) *** the Attorney General determines that- ***

(D) there are reasonable grounds for regarding the alien as a danger to the security of the United States. ***

(3) Notwithstanding any other provision of law, paragraph (1) shall apply to any alien if the Attorney General determines, in the discretion of the Attorney General, that- ***

(B) the application of paragraph (1) to such alien is necessary to ensure compliance with the 1967 United Nations Protocol Relating to the Status of Refugees.

8 U.S.C. § 1305(b) – "Special Registration Requirement"

The Attorney General may in his discretion, upon ten days notice, require the natives of any one or more foreign states, or any class or group thereof, who are within the United States and who are required to be registered under this title, to notify the Attorney General of their current addresses and furnish such additional information as the Attorney General may require.

8 U.S.C. § 1158(b)(2)(A)(v) – Asylum of Immigrants from Terrorist States

(b) Conditions for granting asylum

    (1) In general

        (A) Eligibility– The Secretary of Homeland Security or the Attorney General may grant asylum to an alien who has applied for asylum in accordance with the requirements and procedures established by the Secretary of Homeland Security or the Attorney General under this section if the Secretary of Homeland Security or the Attorney General determines that such alien is a refugee within the meaning of section 1101(a)(42)(A) of this title. ***

    (2) Exceptions

        (A) In general– Paragraph (1) shall not apply to an alien if the Attorney General determines that--

            (i) the alien ordered, incited, assisted, or otherwise participated in the persecution of any person on account of race, religion, nationality, membership in a particular social group, or political opinion;

            (ii) the alien, having been convicted by a final judgment of a particularly serious crime, constitutes a danger to the community of the United States;

            (iii) there are serious reasons for believing that the alien has committed a serious nonpolitical crime outside the United States prior to the arrival of the alien in the United States;

            (iv) there are reasonable grounds for regarding the alien as a danger to the security of the United States;

            (v) the alien is described in subclause (I), (II), (III), (IV), or (VI) of section 1182(a)(3)(B)(i) of this title or section 1227(a)(4)(B) of this title (relating to terrorist activity), unless, in the case only of an alien described in subclause (IV) of section 1182(a)(3)(B)(i) of this title, the Attorney General determines, in the Attorney General's discretion, that there are not reasonable grounds for regarding the alien as a danger to the security of the United States; or

            (vi) the alien was firmly resettled in another country prior to arriving in the United States.

    (B) Special rules

(i) Conviction of aggravated felony– For purposes of clause (ii) of subparagraph (A), an alien who has been convicted of an aggravated felony shall be considered to have been convicted of a particularly serious crime.

(ii) Offenses– The Attorney General may designate by regulation offenses that will be considered to be a crime described in clause (ii) or (iii) of subparagraph (A).

(C) Additional limitations– The Attorney General may by regulation establish additional limitations and conditions, consistent with this section, under which an alien shall be ineligible for asylum under paragraph (1).

(D) No judicial review– There shall be no judicial review of a determination of the Attorney General under subparagraph (A)(v).

Special Immigration Appeals Commission Act of 1997 (U.K.)
2(1)(b)

(1) A person may appeal to the Special Immigration Appeals Commission against— (b) "any matter in relation to which he would be entitled to appeal under subsection 1(a) of section 15 of [the 1971 Act] (appeal to an adjudicator or the Appeal Tribunal against a decision to make a deportation order), but for subsection (3) of that section (deportation conducive to public good) ..."

4(1)

"(a) shall allow the appeal if it considers-(i) that the decision or action against which the appeal is brought was not in accordance with the law or with any immigration rules applicable to the case, or (ii) where the decision or action involved the exercise of a discretion by the Secretary of State or an officer, that the discretion should have been exercised differently, and (b) in any other case, shall dismiss the appeal."

Security Service Act of 1989 (U.K.)
1(2)

"the protection of national security and, in particular, its protection against threats from espionage, terrorism and sabotage, from the activities of agents of foreign powers and from actions intended to overthrow or undermine parliamentary democracy by political, industrial or violent means."

COMPENSATION FOR VICTIMS OF TERRORISM AND COUNTERTERRORISM

28 U.S.C. § 1605A – Terrorism Exception to the Foreign Sovereign Immunity Act ("FSIA")

(a) In general.--

(1) No immunity.--A foreign state shall not be immune from the jurisdiction of courts of the United States or of the States in any case not otherwise covered by this chapter in which money damages are sought against a foreign state for personal injury or death that was caused by an act of torture, extrajudicial killing, aircraft sabotage, hostage taking, or

the provision of material support or resources for such an act if such act
or provision of material support or resources is engaged in by an official,
employee, or agent of such foreign state while acting within the scope of
his or her office, employment, or agency.
(2) Claim heard.--The court shall hear a claim under this section if--
  (A)(i)(I) the foreign state was designated as a state sponsor of
  terrorism at the time the act described in paragraph (1) occurred, or
  was so designated as a result of such act ***
  (ii) the claimant or the victim was, at the time the act described in
  paragraph (1) occurred--
    (I) a national of the United States;
    (II) a member of the armed forces; or
    (III) otherwise an employee of the Government of the United
    States, or of an individual performing a contract awarded by the
    United States Government, acting within the scope of the
    employee's employment; ***

28 U.S.C. § 1606 – Extent of Liability
As to any claim for relief with respect to which a foreign state is not entitled
to immunity under section 1605 or 1607 of this chapter, the foreign state
shall be liable in the same manner and to the same extent as a private
individual under like circumstances; but a foreign state except for an agency
or instrumentality thereof shall not be liable for punitive damages; if,
however, in any case wherein death was caused, the law of the place where
the action or omission occurred provides, or has been construed to provide, for
damages only punitive in nature, the foreign state shall be liable for actual or
compensatory damages measured by the pecuniary injuries resulting from
such death which were incurred by the persons for whose benefit the action
was brought.

28 U.S.C. § 1608 – Service under FSIA
(a) Service in the courts of the United States and of the States shall be made
upon a foreign state or political subdivision of a foreign state:
  (1) by delivery of a copy of the summons and complaint in accordance
  with any special arrangement for service between the plaintiff and the
  foreign state or political subdivision; or
  (2) if no special arrangement exists, by delivery of a copy of the summons
  and complaint in accordance with an applicable international convention
  on service of judicial documents; or
  (3) if service cannot be made under paragraphs (1) or (2), by sending a
  copy of the summons and complaint and a notice of suit, together with a
  translation of each into the official language of the foreign state, by any
  form of mail requiring a signed receipt, to be addressed and dispatched by
  the clerk of the court to the head of the ministry of foreign affairs of the
  foreign state concerned, or
  (4) if service cannot be made within 30 days under paragraph (3), by
  sending two copies of the summons and complaint and a notice of suit,
  together with a translation of each into the official language of the foreign

state, by any form of mail requiring a signed receipt, to be addressed and dispatched by the clerk of the court to the Secretary of State in Washington, District of Columbia, to the attention of the Director of Special Consular Services--and the Secretary shall transmit one copy of the papers through diplomatic channels to the foreign state and shall send to the clerk of the court a certified copy of the diplomatic note indicating when the papers were transmitted. As used in this subsection, a "notice of suit" shall mean a notice addressed to a foreign state and in a form prescribed by the Secretary of State by regulation.

(b) Service in the courts of the United States and of the States shall be made upon an agency or instrumentality of a foreign state:

(1) by delivery of a copy of the summons and complaint in accordance with any special arrangement for service between the plaintiff and the agency or instrumentality; or

(2) if no special arrangement exists, by delivery of a copy of the summons and complaint either to an officer, a managing or general agent, or to any other agent authorized by appointment or by law to receive service of process in the United States; or in accordance with an applicable international convention on service of judicial documents; or

(3) if service cannot be made under paragraphs (1) or (2), and if reasonably calculated to give actual notice, by delivery of a copy of the summons and complaint, together with a translation of each into the official language of the foreign state--

(A) as directed by an authority of the foreign state or political subdivision in response to a letter rogatory or request or

(B) by any form of mail requiring a signed receipt, to be addressed and dispatched by the clerk of the court

to the agency or instrumentality to be served, or

(C) as directed by order of the court consistent with the law of the place where service is to be made.

(c) Service shall be deemed to have been made--

(1) in the case of service under subsection (a)(4), as of the date of transmittal indicated in the certified copy of the diplomatic note; and

(2) in any other case under this section, as of the date of receipt indicated in the certification, signed and returned postal receipt, or other proof of service applicable to the method of service employed.

(d) In any action brought in a court of the United States or of a State, a foreign state, a political subdivision thereof, or an agency or instrumentality of a foreign state shall serve an answer or other responsive pleading to the complaint within sixty days after service has been made under this section.

(e) No judgment by default shall be entered by a court of the United States or of a State against a foreign state, a political subdivision thereof, or an agency or instrumentality of a foreign state, unless the claimant establishes his claim or right to relief by evidence satisfactory to the court. A copy of any such default judgment shall be sent to the foreign state or political subdivision in the manner prescribed for service in this section.

28 USC § 2680. Exceptions to the Federal Tort Claims Act

***

(j) Any claim arising out of the combatant activities of the military or naval forces, or the Coast Guard, during time of war.

(k) Any claim arising in a foreign country. ***

Convention for the Protection of Human Rights and Fundamental Freedoms

Article 2 – Right to Life

1. Everyone's right to life shall be protected by law. No one shall be deprived of his life intentionally save in the execution of a sentence of a court following his conviction of a crime for which this penalty is provided by law.

2. Deprivation of life shall not be regarded as inflicted in contravention of this article when it results from the use of force which is no more than absolutely necessary:

   a. in defence of any person from unlawful violence;

   b. in order to effect a lawful arrest or to prevent the escape of a person lawfully detained;

   c. in action lawfully taken for the purpose of quelling a riot or insurrection.

Article 8 – Right to Respect for Private and Family Life

1. Everyone has the right to respect for his private and family life, his home and his correspondence.

2. There shall be no interference by a public authority with the exercise of this right except such as is in accordance with the law and is necessary in a democratic society in the interests of national security, public safety or the economic well-being of the country, for the prevention of disorder or crime, for the protection of health or morals, or for the protection of the rights and freedoms of others.

Article 11 – Freedom of Assembly or Association

1. Everyone has the right to freedom of peaceful assembly and to freedom of association with others, including the right to form and to join trade unions for the protection of his interests.

2. No restrictions shall be placed on the exercise of these rights other than such as are prescribed by law and are necessary in a democratic society in the interests of national security or public safety, for the prevention of disorder or crime, for the protection of health or morals or for the protection of the rights and freedoms of others. This article shall not prevent the imposition of lawful restrictions on the exercise of these rights by members of the armed forces, of the police or of the administration of the State.

Article 13 – Right to an Effective Remedy

Everyone whose rights and freedoms as set forth in this Convention are violated shall have an effective remedy before a national authority notwithstanding that the violation has been committed by persons acting in an official capacity.

Article 34 – Individual Applications

The Court may receive applications from any person, non-governmental organisation or group of individuals claiming to be the victim of a violation by one of the High Contracting Parties of the rights set forth in the Convention or the protocols thereto. The High Contracting Parties undertake not to hinder in any way the effective exercise of this right.

EMERGENCY POWERS AND EXECUTIVE AUTHORITY IN THE WAR ON TERRORISM

10 U.S.C. § 334 – Presidential Warning Requirement

Whenever the President considers it necessary to use the militia or the armed forces under this chapter, he shall, by proclamation, immediately order the insurgents to disperse and retire peaceably to their abodes within a limited time.

National Emergencies Act
50 U.S.C. § 1601

(a) All powers and authorities possessed by the President, any other officer or employee of the Federal Government, or any executive agency, as defined in section 105 of Title 5, as a result of the existence of any declaration of national emergency in effect on September 14, 1976, are terminated two years from September 14, 1976. Such termination shall not affect--

(1) any action taken or proceeding pending not finally concluded or determined on such date;

(2) any action or proceeding based on any act committed prior to such date; or

(3) any rights or duties that matured or penalties that were incurred prior to such date.

(b) For the purpose of this section, the words "any national emergency in effect" means a general declaration of emergency made by the President.

50 U.S.C. § 1621

(a) With respect to Acts of Congress authorizing the exercise, during the period of a national emergency, of any special or extraordinary power, the President is authorized to declare such national emergency. Such proclamation shall immediately be transmitted to the Congress and published in the Federal Register.

(b) Any provisions of law conferring powers and authorities to be exercised during a national emergency shall be effective and remain in effect (1) only when the President (in accordance with subsection (a) of this section), specifically declares a national emergency, and (2) only in accordance with this chapter. ***

50 U.S.C. § 1622

(a) Termination methods–Any national emergency declared by the President in accordance with this subchapter shall terminate if--

    (1) there is enacted into law a joint resolution terminating the emergency; or

    (2) the President issues a proclamation terminating the emergency. ***

(b) Termination review of national emergencies by Congress Not later than six months after a national emergency is declared, and not later than the end of each six-month period thereafter that such emergency continues, each House of Congress shall meet to consider a vote on a joint resolution to determine whether that emergency shall be terminated.

(c) Joint resolution; referral to Congressional committees; conference committee in event of disagreement; filing of report; termination procedure deemed part of rules of House and Senate [expedited procedures provided]

(d) Automatic termination of national emergency; continuation notice from President to Congress; publication in Federal Register–Any national emergency declared by the President in accordance with this subchapter, and not otherwise previously terminated, shall terminate on the anniversary of the declaration of that emergency if, within the ninety day period prior to each anniversary date, the President does not publish in the Federal Register and transmit to the Congress a notice stating that such emergency is to continue in effect after such anniversary.

50 U.S.C. § 1631

When the President declares a national emergency, no powers or authorities made available by statute for use in the event of an emergency shall be exercised unless and until the President specifies the provisions of law under which he proposes that he, or other officers will act. Such specification may be made either in the declaration of a national emergency, or by one or more contemporaneous or subsequent Executive orders published in the Federal Register and transmitted to the Congress.

Index

References are to Pages

935